INTERNATIONAL ENCYCLOPEDIA OF LINGUISTICS

SECOND EDITION

INTERNATIONAL ENCYCLOPEDIA

OF

LINGUISTICS

SECOND EDITION

WILLIAM J. FRAWLEY

Editor in Chief

Volume 1
AAVE–Esperanto

OXFORD
UNIVERSITY PRESS

2003

OXFORD
UNIVERSITY PRESS

Oxford   New York

Auckland   Bangkok   Buenos Aires   Cape Town   Chennai

Dar es Salaam   Delhi   Hong Kong   Istanbul   Karachi   Kolkata

Kuala Lumpur   Madrid   Melbourne   Mexico City   Mumbai

Nairobi   São Paulo   Shanghai   Taipei   Tokyo   Toronto

Copyright © 2003 by Oxford University Press, Inc.

Published by Oxford University Press, Inc.

198 Madison Avenue, New York, New York, 10016

http://www.oup-usa.org

Oxford is a registered trademark of Oxford University Press

Biographies of linguists are reprinted from *The Concise Oxford Dictionary of
Linguistics* by P. H. Matthews (1997) by permission of Oxford University
Press. © Oxford University Press 1997.

Special acknowledgment is made to Stephen Austin and Sons, Ltd., for
providing characters used in tables of writing systems for Burmese, Georgian,
Kannada, Khmer, Malayalam, and Tibetan.

Library of Congress Cataloging-in-Publication Data
International encyclopedia of linguistics / William J. Frawley,
editor-in chief.—2nd ed.
v. cm.
"Comprising more than one million words in four volumes."
William Bright was editor-in-chief of the 1992 edition.
Includes bibliographical references and index.
ISBN 0-19-513977-1 (set : alk. paper)
1. Linguistics—Encyclopedias. I. Frawley, William, 1953- II. Bright,
William, 1928- International encyclopedia of linguistics.
P29 .I58 2003
410'.3—dc21
2003000430
ISBN 0-19-516783-X (volume 1)

Printing number: 9   8   7   6   5   4   3   2   1

Printed in the United States of America
on acid-free paper

EDITORIAL AND PRODUCTION STAFF

Acquiring Editor

Christopher Collins

Executive Editor

Stephen Wagley

Project Editor

Martin Coleman

Editorial Assistant

Ryan Sullivan

Copy Editors

Jane McGary   Marta Steele

Proofreaders

Patti Brecht   Sylvia Cannizzaro   Mary Flower   Carol Holmes   Laura Lawrie   John Sollami

Indexer

Jane McGary

Compositor

Binghamton Valley Composition, LLC

Manufacturing Controller

Chris Critelli

Designer

Joan Greenfield

EDP Director

John Sollami

Editorial Development Director

Timothy J. DeWerff

Publisher

Karen Day

CONTENTS

INTERNATIONAL ENCYCLOPEDIA OF LINGUISTICS

SENIOR INTERNATIONAL ADVISERS

WALLACE CHAFE
Department of Linguistics, University of California at Santa Barbara

BERNARD COMRIE
Department of Linguistics, Max Planck Institute for Evolutionary Anthropology, Leipzig, Germany

DAVID CRYSTAL
Holyhead, Anglesey, Wales

KENNETH HALE (DECEASED)
Department of Linguistics, Massachusetts Institute of Technology

MORRIS HALLE
Department of Linguistics, Massachusetts Institute of Technology

HENRY HOENIGSWALD
Department of Linguistics, University of Pennsylvania

KAZUKO INOUE
Graduate School of Language Sciences, Kanda University of International Studies, Chiba-shi, Japan

ROBERT B. KAPLAN
Port Angeles, Washington

BHADRIRAJU KRISHNAMURTI
Center for Advanced Study in the Behavioral Sciences, Stanford, California

PETER LADEFOGED
Department of Linguistics, University of California, Los Angeles

DAVID LIGHTFOOT
Georgetown University

LISE MENN
Department of Linguistics, University of Colorado

JACOB MEY
Department of Linguistics, Institute for Language and Communication, Odense University, Denmark

BARBARA PARTEE
Department of Linguistics, University of Massachusetts, Amherst

MASAYOSHI SHIBATANI
Faculty of Letters, Kobe University, Japan

WERNER WINTER
Preetz, Germany

ARNOLD ZWICKY
Center for the Study of Language and Information, Stanford University

INTRODUCTION TO THE SECOND EDITION

The best way to understand this introduction to the second edition of *International Encyclopedia of Linguistics (IEL)* is to read William Bright's introduction to the first edition. The approach to and structure of this new edition are much the same as those of the previous one. My goal was to cover the entire discipline through cogent articles written by experts in language accessible to everyone, with the entries organized to reflect the conceptual dependencies of the field, thoroughly cross-referenced, easily searched and user friendly, while vigilantly preserving theoretical balance and neutrality.

Knowing that in linguistics, no error or bad choice, however minor, goes unreviewed, I nonetheless signed on to the same impossible task as Bright. But my job was much easier because I had Bright's extensive, careful work as a base. Those of us who have toiled in the reference industry know how essential a solid first edition is to future versions of a reference work. I know that I speak for the whole field in acknowledging Bill Bright's important role as originator of *International Encyclopedia of Linguistics* and, more generally, as patient overseer of the discipline.

Because of the substantial overlap between editions in organization and motivation, this introduction can be most useful by charting the divergences between the organization of these new volumes and Bright's. How does this edition compare with the first?

Coverage. The second edition of *IEL* contains 957 articles and about half as many more headwords and subheadwords, given an increase in blind entries (placeholder entries that point to others for their content). All the articles from the first edition are updated in some way, with most ranging from 40 percent revision to complete rewriting. About 15 percent of the articles are new and about 3 percent of the first-edition entries were eliminated from the second. The extensive updating of a ten-year-old reference work slated to endure at least another decade led to the addition of some theories and subfields, the elimination of others, expanded treatment of some existing concepts because of their rising importance, and reduced treatment of others because of their increasingly limited role in the field. Decisions about these matters were made with every attempt to keep to the high ground and to follow two reasonable dictates: first, not only include the core of the field and ideas of current influence, but also try to anticipate what will be current in the years to come; second, try to avoid pet theories and personal exposés. The first edition was especially strong on languages of the world and social and anthropological approaches to language. The second edition has maintained these strengths and given attention to new directions in the field, such as Optimality Theory, the Minimalist Program, the widening influence of functional and typological linguistics, the spreading impact of discourse analysis on subfields outside discourse proper (applied linguistics, computational linguistics, semantics), increasing detail in findings in formal linguistics, marked changes in applied linguistics (perhaps the most extensively revised topic area), and advances in computational and mathematical linguistics.

In the decade since the first edition appeared, linguistics has moved closer and closer to psychological and neurobiological inquiry, and so this edition has coverage of the various cognitive and evolutionary approaches to language, including neurolinguistics and brain imaging, cognitive science, critical periods of acquisition, linguistic relativity, learnability, and language disorders. Many subfields and concepts have been "unpacked," with their constituent ideas given explicit treatment: for example, there is a separate composite entry on phonological processes, with full treatment of assimilation, dissimilation, and so on. There are also major additions to the coverage of languages, with new articles on Zulu, Wolof, Khoisan, American Sign Language, world Englishes, and artificial languages. In the end, the guiding idea for coverage in *IEL* was to maximize information ("less is bore!") while preserving readability.

Entries and organization. Choices about what entries to include and the structure of the Encyclopedia were guided by three main principles:

1. *Choose entries that are neither too general nor too specific.* Which of the following terms should be a headword in the Encyclopedia: *sound, phoneme,* or *delayed release*? The natural response is that *IEL* should include all of them, but if it does, the volumes immediately begin to grow in length exponentially, thus sacrificing usability for coverage. The second edition tries to reach a middle ground between concepts that are highly abstract and those that are narrow and often theory specific, no matter how important any of them might be: *phoneme* is included, but *sound* is too general and *delayed release* too specific. In most cases, narrow concepts are embedded in articles and so can be found through the index. But the user will not find entries for *language, structure, speech*, or *linguistics;* "Grammar" and "Meaning" are blind entries, that is, placeholders that point to other entries for exposition. There are no separate entries for *INFL, regime,* or *garden path,* for example, influential concepts to be sure, but concepts that can be found under entries in the subfields in which these concepts occur (in these cases, "Phrase Structure," "Optimality Theory," and "Parsing").

2. *Organize entries to reflect the conceptual structure of the field.* On the whole, the second edition is more complex in organization than the first edition. Much effort was put into renaming entries ("Natural Language Processing" has become "Computational Linguistics"), inserting new entries for balance ("Morpheme" requires "Phoneme"), and reorganizing entries to reflect the way the concepts in the field relate to and depend on one another ("Neurolinguistics" has changed from a blind entry to a composite entry; "Discourse Markers" is a separate entry because it is an influential concept in its own right; "Applied Linguistics" is significantly less complex than might be expected because its potential subentries are all independent notions). There is significantly more nesting (entry with subentry and subsubentry). For example, "Language Change" is a new composite entry

subsuming all the approaches thereto; "Pragmatics and Contextual Semantics" has been split, and split again, to give explicit treatment of *implicature, presupposition,* and related notions; "Semantics," "Philosophy of Language," "Institutional Linguistics," and "Linguistics and Literature" are highly complex entries, subsuming various approaches and concepts given independent treatment in the first edition. Overall, the goal with this "complexification" of the Encyclopedia was to promote one-stop shopping, so that a user might find not only what he or she is looking for at an entry, but more of what the field itself sees as related to the notion under search.

3. *Ensure that entry choice and organization promote ease of use.* Nothing makes a user of a reference work more frustrated than to have a term or concept in mind, but never to be able to locate that term in the reference work—or to have to struggle so much to locate the term or concept that it might be more advisable to abandon the search altogether rather than come away from the search successful, but dazed. How to avoid these pitfalls? The second edition applies a number of heuristics to meet this challenge. The first edition limited entries at *L* and *S*, concerned with what lexicographers affectionately think of as the *clumping problem*, clusters of entries at particular headwords. An encyclopedia of linguistics would seem to have clumping at *L* and *S*: *language, linguistics, speech,* and so on. The second edition allowed *L*- and *S*- entries, and without much consequence. There are many more *C*-, *P*-, and *S*- entries anyway, whatever the policy for *L* and *S*. What this means is that entries in the first edition that had been modified to avoid *L* or *S* now appear at those letters: "Language Attitudes," rather than "Attitudes to Language," "Speech Perception" rather than "Perception of Speech." "Language Acquisition" is a blind entry, pointing to "Acquisition of Language." This was a deliberate choice because it was thought that users would have both *language* and *acquisition* in mind when searching for information on language development.

One peculiarly technical issue arose in considerations of headword choice. There are many terms in linguistics that are ambiguous across subfields: *free* and *bound* are technical concepts in both morphology and the syntax and semantics of anaphora; *case* is a term in both formal syntax and semantics; *feature* has different meanings in phonology, syntax, and semantics; *local*, *locality*, and *localization* mean certain things in semantics or grammatical theory, and quite other things in neurolinguistics; *declarative* has one meaning in syntax and a different one in computational linguistics. Every attempt was made in the second edition to make these ambiguities explicit and to point the user to the appropriate entries for these different meanings.

Finally, the entry list includes a number of new symbols and abbreviations: "AAVE," "OT," "LF," "GPSG," and "TAG." Notation has a significant place in linguistics, and a user of the Encyclopedia would no doubt have occasion to search the volumes with these nonlexical and nonphrasal entries in mind.

Blind entries. There are many more blind entries in the second edition than in the first in order to capture what was thought to be the search procedures of an intelligent user. But this again raises a selection issue: how to decide which terms should be blind entries? The second edition contains three major kinds of blind entries:

1. *Truly empty terms whose content is found elsewhere.* An example of this kind of blind entry is "AAVE," which directs the reader to a full entry for "African American Vernacular English." Other examples are "Assessment" pointing to "Language Testing" and "Onomatopoeia" pointing to "Sound Symbolism."
2. *Mid-level concepts that evoke higher-order terms (their full and partial superordinates) but do not merit separate treatment as discrete entries.* These are by far the largest class and the most complicated to justify. An example is "Agent," a core concept within semantics and grammatical theory and one that is included as a blind entry pointing to "Case" and "Thematic Roles." The editorial concern here was whether such terms—for example, *isogloss, perlocutionary act,* and *usage*—ought to be free standing. In the end this was a judgment call and the rule of thumb was to include as blind entries concepts that might be independently searched for but that do not stand entirely on their own conceptually and that make better sense for exposition in the entries on their superordinates. Thus, "Tiers" is a blind entry because it has semi-independent status in the field but is understood principally through "Autosegmental Phonology." The term *tiers* contrasts with a term like *tableau*, which the *IEL* user is likely to search for already knowing that it is part of "Optimality Theory" and so intrinsically bound to its superordinate concept.

3. *Concepts that, for epistemological or socio-political reasons intrinsic to the field at the moment, are too complicated to include as separate entries, despite their importance and status as a likely target of independent search.* A classical example of this type is "Syntax," an entry that gives no particular definition but points the reader to subfields and theories, where fuller, independent treatments can be found. Other examples are "Clinical Linguistics," "Competence," "Modularity," and "Representation."

Blind entries are signaled by *See*, and perhaps the best way to appreciate the three major classes of them is to think about what *See* means for each of these types. Category 1 construes *See* as *equals*: "LF" equals "Logical Form." Category 2 construes *See* as *is a part of* or *is best located under the larger concept of*: "Perlocutionary Act" is best located under the larger concept of "Pragmatics and Contextual Semantics." Category 3 construes *See* as *is best understood in the convergence of the concepts aggregated under*: "Transformational Grammar" is best understood in the convergence of the concepts aggregated under "Formal Grammar," "Principles and Parameters," "Minimalist Program," and "Transformations."

Blind entries were one area of editorial decision that could not be settled beforehand, but had to be managed as the volumes unfolded. Many of these choices depended on what authors were saying about terms and concepts and could not be predetermined from some bird's eye view of the field. But generally, the strategy was to avoid idiosyncrasy: the pointers in a blind entry should point somewhere useful. There is nothing more alienating than, for example, to seek the definition of *hirsute* in a dictionary and find it as a blind entry pointing to *nonglabrous*. Now what?

Format. The second edition differs from the first in several substantial ways with respect to presentation of material. Latinate signals to cross-references (*q.v.*) were replaced by *See* (a direct instruction to the user to consult another term; *See also* sends the user to related or alternate technical material), and all cross-references were grouped and located at natural breaking points in entries. Cross-references among language lists are indicated by small capitals in the opening paragraphs. Descriptive headnotes to composite entries in the first edition ("This article is concerned with . . .") were trimmed markedly to schematic tables of contents. Italics, small capitals, boldface, and other typographical distinctions were simplified to reliance on italics only for citation and emphasis. These changes were made to promote ease of access and recognizability.

Personnel and procedures. All Topic Editors from the first edition were invited to oversee revision of their areas. Almost all agreed, and the reconstituted group was renamed Consulting Editors. All Editorial Advisers of the first edition were also invited to participate again, with most agreeing, and this reconstituted group was renamed Senior International Advisers. William Bright served as Senior Consulting Editor.

Consulting Editors were charged with determining a revision plan for their areas, which was discussed in detail via e-mail, telephone, and personal visits with the Editor in Chief. This plan had to estimate extent of revisions and recommend additions or deletions. Consulting Editors also contacted all authors and oversaw the submission of articles from contract to final editing. Articles by deceased authors had to be revised by new authors, and authors who had left the field had to be contacted to determine their role in the second edition. These personnel matters were labor intensive and time consuming, and the Consulting Editors rose admirably to the challenge.

Senior International Advisers offered commentary on the overall structure and coverage of the Encyclopedia. The Senior Consulting Editor planned the revision with the Editor in Chief in a series of meetings over several years and served as periodic troubleshooter throughout the emergence of the work.

Revision plans, procedures for revising articles or submitting new ones, and various notices about policies were posted on the Encyclopedia website, which was located on a server at the University of Delaware, the Editor in Chief's previous institution (http://www.udel.edu/billf/iel.html). The Internet proved invaluable in this project since it allowed not only rapid transmittal of large amounts of information in various formats, but also remote, asynchronous access to a variety of materials for all contributors.

Illustrative material. The Encyclopedia is a complicated work, with a wide range of material illustrating and exemplifying issues and arguments. All this material was extensively revised. New formal notation was added and maps were redrawn. The boundaries of polities have changed markedly since 1992, as have the locales of languages within and across those polities. It is December 2002 as this introduction is being written: imagine how Central Asia looked in 1992! Color images of brain functioning were added. Tree diagrams of both linguistic structure and language families were edited. Diagrams of theoretical models were emended, as were orthographies. Linguistics, it turns out, is a heavily visual discipline.

Languages. Articles on language families are followed by lists of languages. *IEL* has a range of articles on languages, from extensive treatments of particular languages ("Zulu") to long expositions on major language families ("Germanic Languages"). There are also paragraph-length articles on intermediate-level language families (for example, "East Fijian Languages"), which were written by Bernard Comrie from Barbara Grimes's data and are included only if they appear as nodes in the *Ethnologue* database. These lists were compiled by Barbara Grimes—not by authors of the articles—using the *Ethnologue* and databases of SIL International (formerly the Summer Institute of Linguistics). These lists also include updated information on the demographics of the speakers. There remain great controversies in the field over which languages belong to which families, and, indeed, some of the groupings in the lists are at odds with the positions of the authors of the articles. The goal of including the lists was not to resolve controversies—or promote them!—but to ensure that the user has maximum information.

Biographies. Many more short biographies of figures in the history of linguistics were added to the new edition for the sake of comprehensiveness. So biographical entries now appear for figures from Aristotle and Joseph Justus Scaliger to Lev Vygotsky and Ken Hale. The motivation behind expanding these biographies was to offer the user a kind of dramatis personae of the field and so make the Encyclopedia more like a handbook. Most of the biographies were adapted from *The Concise Oxford Dictionary of Linguistics,* edited by P. H. Matthews, and are reprinted here courtesy of Oxford University Press.

Backmatter. The glossary that appeared in the first edition was eliminated and replaced by a more detailed index, supplemented by careful attention to definition of key terms at points where these terms initially appear in articles. It was thought that an extensively revised glossary, coordinated with the text of the volumes, would lead to duplication. Backmatter also includes a new systematic outline and a directory of contributors.

Acknowledgments. I must thank Bill Bright and Oxford University Press for giving me the opportunity to oversee this work. I know I drove Oxford's editorial staff to exasperation with some of my worries and insistence, but I hope not to fatal lengths. Their patience and diligence, as well as Bill's, are models to us all. The Consulting Editors put up with my polite reminders and incessant hectoring. Stephanie Baker, my very capable research assistant, read almost the entire work to check for ease of exposition and to ensure definition of terms. Bill Idsardi often gave me excellent advice on technical matters.

As the Encyclopedia was coming to the final phase of production, I left the University of Delaware, where I had been for twenty-three years, to become Dean of Arts and Sciences at George Washington University. This change, of course, was equivalent to adding on six or seven more encyclopedias to be completed at the same time! I thank my colleagues and staff at UD for their help and my new staff at GWU for seeing me through these trying times.

As always my wife, Maria, my children, Christopher and Emma, and our array of cats (Chloe, Pierre, Jasper, Lionel, Zeke, and Maisie) provided unyielding comfort and stability. Eternal thanks to them.

WILLIAM FRAWLEY, *Editor in Chief*

INTRODUCTION TO THE FIRST EDITION

The intention of the *International Encyclopedia of Linguistics (IEL)* is to provide a comprehensive source of up-to-date information on all branches of linguistics, aimed primarily at an audience of students and professional scholars in linguistics and adjacent fields. The publisher, Oxford University Press, has given me the fullest support in my effort to produce a reference work oriented toward the broadest possible view of linguistics, toward the importance of interdisciplinary studies, and toward open-minded attitudes toward theoretical controversies.

This work is designed to embrace the full range of linguistics, including descriptive, historical, comparative, typological, functionalist, and formalist specialties. Special attention is given to interrelations within branches of linguistics—with articles on the interface of, e.g., syntax and semantics—and to relations of linguistics with other disciplines. Areas of intersection with the social and behavioral sciences (such as ethnolinguistics, sociolinguistics, and psycholinguistics) receive major coverage, as does interdiscplinary work in language and literature, language and philosophy, mathematical linguistics, computational linguistics, and applied linguistics, in particular as concerned with language education.

The work is alphabetically, rather than topically, ordered. We have nevertheless attempted to preserve topical cohesion through three devices: (a) extensive cross-references between related articles; (b) a detailed index, including topical labels, technical terms, personal names, and geographical names; and (c) the organization of some articles in terms of composite entries—e.g. entries with subentries, as in 'Acquisition of Language', which is discussed with reference to first-language development under the headings (a) 'Meanings and Forms' and (b) 'Phonology', and then with reference to (c) 'Second-language Acquisition'. Note that such subentries are or-

dered alphabetically except under 'History of Linguistics', where they are arranged chronologically.

The longer articles consist of signed essays of up to five thousand words in length, surveying large fields of study—e.g. phonetics, formal grammar, or anthropological linguistics. Shorter essays (also signed) deal with more specific topics within those fields; or with particular languages and language families which have been topics of extensive linguistic research; or with important scholars in the history of linguistics. A category of unsigned articles provides information on less-studied language families. Appended to both types of article on language families are 'language lists', which as a group give specific information on all the living languages of the world. The work concludes with a glossary and an extensive index.

The primary audience is seen as academic and professional, but interdisciplinary; thus articles are designed to be intelligible and useful to people in related disciplines, including teachers and advanced students in computer science, mathematics, philosophy, the social and behavioral sciences, and literary studies. It is hoped that readers will find the *IEL* to be unique in its comprehensive and authoritative coverage of all significant topics and viewpoints in linguistics, with attention both to 'accumulated wisdom' and to current research findings, at the professional academic level.

Some articles in this encyclopedia contain new research findings, not yet published elsewhere in comparable form. Most of them, however, are intended as research tools, serving to bring together timely information on the diverse subject matter and interdisciplinary connections which characterize the study of human language and languages. Because of the rapid development of linguistics, few individuals can control the current scholarly literature in all branches of the field; the goal of the *IEL,* then, is to give summaries of research, with detailed cross-references and bibliographies, to provide convenient access to the broadest possible spectrum of specialties.

Details on various aspects of the *IEL*'s background, policies, and practices are given in the following paragraphs.

Models and motivations. In many ways, a model for the present work was provided by the *International Encyclopedia of the Social Sciences* (ed. by David L. Sills, 1968). That work featured important coverage of linguistic topics, in particular as related to cultural anthropology. I was a contributor to it, and I have frequently consulted it for my research in anthropological linguistics and sociolinguistics. Some twenty years later, it seemed to me that linguistics had arrived at a stage of maturity and complexity to justify an encyclopedic reference work of its own, incorporating many features of the *IESS.*

Another factor in the planning of this encyclopedia has been my personal experience as an editor in the linguistic field. From 1966 to 1988, I served as editor of *Language,* the journal of the Linguistic Society of America; before and during that period, I also edited several books. In my editorial capacity, I dealt with scholars from all over the world, working in every subfield and school of linguistics, and I exercised the responsibility of holding their work to high standards of validity, originality, and clarity. As an officer of a major international scholarly organization, I also took pains to avoid partisanship, and I strove to give full consideration to quality research of all theoretical orientations. Finally, as a linguist having strong links with the social and behavioral sciences, I maintained a broad interdisciplinary outlook as to what could properly be considered as 'linguistics'. With this background, my goals for the *IEL* have been to maintain the same academic standards and interdisciplinary breadth, while nevertheless focusing the work toward the needs of reference users.

Until recently, no publication of encyclopedic scope has existed for the field of linguistics. However, such works clearly constitute 'an idea whose time has come'. During the period that the *IEL* has been in preparation, two such publications have appeared—and the scholars responsible for both are, in fact, also valued contributors to the *IEL!* One is *The Cambridge Encyclopedia of Language,* a one-volume work written by a single author (David Crystal, 1987) and aimed at a general audience; the other is *Linguistics: The Cambridge Survey* (ed. by F. J. Newmeyer, 1987), a four-volume collection of 'state

of the art' papers, written for professionals and emphasizing formal approaches to language. Still other publications have been announced: another one-volume, topically arranged work (but aimed at a more specialized audience than Crystal's); a work focusing primarily on language teaching; and a very ambitious, multivolume compendium on an advanced scholarly level.

It is clear that a rich choice will be available to the reading public. Nevertheless, I believe that the *IEL* makes a contribution not duplicated by any other work. Shorter encyclopedias are less expensive, and are easy to handle, but are limited not only in their subject coverage but in their diversity of viewpoint. Larger works overcome those defects; however, apart from their bulk and expense, the greater period required for their preparation increases the risk that their contents will become outdated during that time—especially in a field which changes as rapidly as modern linguistics. A work which is organized topically, rather than alphabetically, can give a more unified view of individual subfields; nevertheless, the *IEL*'s use of composite entries and extensive cross-references allows readers to integrate subfields, and at the same time preserves the convenience of alphabetical reference. More specialized works of reference will serve specialist audiences; however, I believe that the distinctive qualities of the *IEL* will meet the needs of a large core of students and scholars, in linguistics and adjacent disciplines, who are interested in the diversity of subfields and approaches which characterize the present-day study of language.

Goals. The aim of the *IEL,* and of individual articles within it, is not to say everything about any topic, but rather to give readers an appropriate orientation. For this reason, cross-references are used extensively, to avoid excessive repetition between articles. In addition, authors were asked to provide key bibliographical references for their articles, which will enable readers to pursue topics of interest as far as they desire.

It has been considered important that articles should be open to alternative viewpoints, and that they should avoid dogmatism. We have thought it especially desirable to maintain an even-handed approach in the *IEL*—considering the diverse intended readership, and considering too how rapidly orthodoxies can change in linguistics. Authors and topic editors (and indeed, the editor in chief) all have very definite opinions on particular matters of theory and methodology; but we have taken seriously our responsibility to let readers know what major viewpoints exist, and what the values of each may be. When topics involve a history of dispute, our desideratum has been that the relevant articles should reflect current consensus or its lack, whichever the case may be. We have felt that an encyclopedia is a place to explain unresolved issues, not to debate them.

How well have the *IEL*'s goals been achieved? What might have been done differently? As we go to press, I feel satisfied that we have met the goals of being wide-ranging, of representing a fair diversity of opinions, and of being as up-to-date as publication schedules will allow. My main autocriticism is that, although our articles on particular languages or language families contain abundant examples, I wish I had asked the authors of the other articles to put more emphasis on concrete exemplification. But reviewers and readers will have their own opinions; I hope they will let me know about them, in as much detail as possible.

Personnel and procedures. The board of editorial advisers, broad-based and international in scope, has provided top-level counsel both to the publisher and to myself as editor in chief. Its members have worked closely with me to determine the contents of the *IEL,* and to determine what individuals should serve as topic editors and as authors of articles. A number of these scholars have also agreed to serve as topic editors.

The topic editors, twenty-five in number, were appointed by me; each one has taken responsibility for a major subject area. I consulted them in order to determine the articles to be commissioned, the projected length of each, and the scholars who should be requested to write them. The topic editors then provided editorial supervision of the articles as they were written, and approved the manuscripts before sending them to me for final coordination and copyediting; I also continued to rely on their advice with regard to problems which arose during copyediting and proofreading. In some cases, topic editors nominated themselves to write specific articles in their areas of responsibility.

The authors, over four hundred in number, were chosen from around the world, on the basis of their reputation and expertise as known both to the topic editors and to me. Efforts were made to recruit authors who were not only recognized authorities on their subjects but who could also be relied on for clarity and definitiveness of statement.

After all bibliographical references were checked, copyediting of the articles was carried out by me and my assistants. Clarifications were sought, as necessary, through correspondence with authors—during the copyediting process, into the stage of reading galley proofs, and in some cases even beyond, to the stage of revised proofs.

Entry terms. Keeping in mind that the *IEL* will be consulted by readers who have some sophistication in linguistics but who nevertheless come from varying backgrounds, we have made an effort to choose entry terms (article titles) based on specific but relatively established concepts, and the articles themselves are organized with consideration for those concepts. We avoid entry terms beginning with the word 'Language' or 'Linguistics'; rather, we use terms such as 'Law and Language' (instead of 'Language of the Law'). Access to topics not chosen as entry terms is, of course, made possible through the index.

Spelling and alphabets. For consistency, American standard spellings have been used (e.g. *color, recognize*). Phonetic transcriptions follow either the International Phonetic Alphabet or conventional 'American usage', following authors' preference (see Pullum & Ladusaw 1986). Material from languages written in non-Latin alphabets is, in general, transliterated in the systems most used by international scholars of those languages; e.g., Cyrillic is transcribed with *š ž č j*, rather than *sh zh ch y.* Greek is also transliterated. Mandarin Chinese is written in pinyin spellings with tone marks.

Illustrative material. Care has been taken to make the content of articles as useful as possible through the inclusion of two types of illustrative material. One type consists of linguistic examples: words, phrases, and sentences in a wide range of natural languages. We follow the general practice of scholarly literature in linguistics by setting these off from the main text, for improved readability, and by numbering them for cross-reference. In complex examples, we give interlinear glosses for each morpheme or word, in addition to a freer translation.

The second type of illustrative material consists of graphic aids of several kinds, including hierarchical outlines, paradigmatic tables, graphs, sound spectrograms, and charts of writing systems, as well as maps to show the geographical distributions of dialects, languages, or language families. In complex illustrations, especially in the maps, the basic material was provided by authors in the form of informal sketches; these have then been reworked by professional graphic artists and cartographers, and checked by the authors and editors.

Biographies. Short biographical articles are included for a limited number of major linguists now deceased. The scholars for whom such articles have been written are ones who made contributions 'across the board' in linguistics, e.g. Edward Sapir and Roman Jakobson. Information on the work of other scholars, past and present, can be found in entries relating to their specialties or their schools of thought; e.g., contributions made to the field by J. R. Firth and by Noam Chomsky, respectively, are discussed under 'History of Linguistics' (in the article on 'The London School') and under 'Generative Grammar'.

Bibliography. Since an encyclopedia article cannot possibly say everything that is relevant about a topic, an important function of each essay is to direct readers to sources. All essays therefore end with a bibliographical listing of works cited, alphabetically arranged; typically, these include not only citations relevant to particular points but also works useful for general reference on a topic. Preference is given (other things being equal) to books rather than articles; to works in western European languages, especially English, rather than others; and to easily available rather than hard-to-find works such as unpublished dissertations. It is realized that linguistic research has progressed so rapidly in recent years that authors must often make reference to work which was not scheduled for publication at the time the articles were written; in such cases, however, acknowledgment is made by in-text reference, rather than by bibliographical citation of unpublished research.

In cases where publications are more accessible in reprinted form, we give information on the original publication first, because of its historical relevance, and then data on later and more available versions.

Language lists. Appended to the articles on language families are 'language lists' which represent an attempt to provide geographical, statistical, nomenclatural, and sociolinguistic information, to the extent that data are available for all living languages of the world, as well as for a selection of extinct languages. (Language names not used as headwords in these lists can be accessed through the index.) These lists have been prepared by Joseph and Barbara Grimes, based on the computerized files of the Summer Institute of Linguistics, with the permission of that organization (see also Grimes 1988). Additional information and corrections have been obtained from the authors of articles and from other reference sources, but the final form of the lists is my own responsibility. Readers should appreciate that the nomen-

clature and classification of languages are often controversial, and that data from different sources vary greatly in reliability; suggestions for further improvements will be welcome.

Glossary. A list of technical linguistic terms, prepared by David Crystal, is found at the end of this work. It is based both on definitions of technical terms given by *IEL* authors, in their respective articles, and on the files prepared by Crystal for his 1985 *Dictionary of Linguistics and Phonetics.*

Acknowledgments. Thanks for essential help of many kinds go to the Department of Linguistics at the University of California, Los Angeles; to the Department of Linguistics and the Institute of Cognitive Science at the University of Colorado, Boulder; to Professor Akio Kamio and the Department of English, Dokkyo University, Soka City, Japan, who provided me with an academic home during two periods in that country; to the members of the editorial board; to the topic editors; to all the authors; to Lise Menn, for constant supportiveness as both wife and colleague; to Claude Conyers and Jeffrey Edelstein at Oxford University Press, New York, who saw the project through to the end; to my indispensable editorial associate, Jane McGary; and to Gale Arce, David Attwooll, Melissa Axelrod, Kathleen M. Fenton, Daniel Hack, Philomena Mariani, William Mitchell, Susan Remkus, and Kenneth Wright.

WILLIAM BRIGHT, Editor in Chief

BIBLIOGRAPHY

Crystal, David. 1985. *A dictionary of linguistics and phonetics.* 2nd edition. Oxford: Blackwell.

Crystal, David. 1987. *The Cambridge encyclopedia of language.* Cambridge and New York: Cambridge University Press.

Grimes, Barbara (ed.) 1988. *Ethnologue: Languages of the world.* 11th edition. Dallas: Summer Institute of Linguistics.

Newmeyer, Frederick J. (ed.) 1987. *Linguistics: The Cambridge survey.* 4 vols. Cambridge and New York: Cambridge University Press.

Pullum, Geoffrey K., and William A. Ladusaw. 1986. *Phonetic symbol guide.* Chicago: University of Chicago Press.

Sills, David L. (ed.) 1968. *International encyclopedia of the social sciences.* 17 vols. New York: Macmillan and Free Press.

ABBREVIATIONS AND SYMBOLS

A adjective; agent; argument

A any syntactic category (in A-binding, A-over-A Principle)

AA Afroasiatic; Austro-Asiatic

abbr. abbreviation

abl. ablative

abs. absolutive

acc. accusative

ACH Association for Computers and the Humanities

ACL Association for Computational Linguistics

act. active; actor

AD Alzheimer's dementia

adess. adessive

adj. adjective

ADJP adjective phrase

adv. adverb(ial)

ADVP adverbial phrase

AE Achaemenid Elamite

AGR agreement

agt. agent(ive)

AI Artificial Intelligence

ALLC Association for Literary and Linguistic Computing

AM Ancient Mongolian

AMR Allomorphic Morphological Rule

AN Austronesian

an. animate

aor. aorist

AP adjective phrase

APG Arc Pair Grammar

API Association Phonétique Internationale

A-position argument position

AR Arumanian

Ar. Arabic

Arm. Armenian

ART article

ASL American Sign Language

ASP aspect

ASR Automatic Speech Recognition

ATN Augmented Transition Network

ATR advanced tongue root

AUX auxiliary

Av. Avestan

BCE Before Common Era (= B.C.)

BEAM Brain Electrical Activity Mapping

BI Bahasa Indonesia

BM Bahasa Melayu; Bokmål

BP bound pronoun; Brazilian Portuguese

B.P. Before Present

BS Balto-Slavic

BVC bound verb complement

C complement; complementizer; consonant

c. century

CA Classical Arabic; Componential Analysis; Contrastive Analysis; Conversational Analysis

ca. *circa*, approximately

CAP Control Agreement Principle

CAT Computerized Axial Tomography

caus. causative

c-command constituent command

CD Communicative Dynamism; Conceptual Dependency

CE Common Era (= A.D.)

CED Condition on Extraction Domain

CF Context-Free

CFG Context-Free Grammar

CFL Context-Free Language

chap. chapter

Ch.Sl. Church Slavic

CHO chômeur (in Relational Grammar)

CL Classical Latin; compensatory lengthening

clf. classifier

col. column

COMP complementizer

comp. comparative; complement

conj. conjunction; conjunctive

cont. continuative

cop. copula

CP Complementizer Phrase; Cooperative Principle

CR Comparative Reconstruction

CS Context-Sensitive

CSR Contemporary Standard Russian

c-structure constituent structure

CV cardinal vowel; consonant-vowel (syllable structure)

D dative; derivational; determiner; diacritic feature; dictionary

d. died

Da. Danish

DA Discourse Analysis

DAF delayed auditory feedback

dat. dative

dat.-acc. dative-accusative

DCG Definite-Clause Grammar

DD developmental dysphasia

decl. declension

def. definite

dem. demonstrative

deriv. derivative

desid. desiderative

DET determiner

dim. diminutive

dir. direction(al)

DM discourse marker

DO direct object

DP Determiner Phrase

DR Daco-Rumanian; discourse representation

DRS Discourse Representation Structure

DS marking Different Subject marking

D-structure an alternative conception to 'deep structure'

DTC Derivational Theory of Complexity

DTW Dynamic Time Warping

du. dual
DV dynamic verb
e empty category
E externalized
EA Eskimo-Aleut
ECP Empty Category Principle
emph. emphatic
encl. enclitic
Eng. English
ENHG Early New High German
EP European Portuguese
EQUI Equi-NP Deletion
erg. ergative
EST Extended Standard Theory
etc. et cetera
ex. example
exx. examples
F fall; formant
f. feminine; and following
F-R fall-rise
f-structure functional structure
F$_0$ fundamental frequency
Fa. Faliscan
fact. factive
FCR Feature Cooccurrence Restriction
fem. feminine
ff. and following (plural)
fig. figure
fl. *floruit,* flourished, lived
FLRP Fixed Language Recognition Problem
FN first name
foc. focus
Fr. French
FSD Feature Specification Default
FSP Functional Sentence Perspective
fut. future
G gender; glide
Gael. Gaelic
GB Government/Binding
G/D genitive/dative
gen. genitive
Ger. German
ger. gerund
Gk. Greek
Gmc. Germanic
Go. Gothic
GPC grapheme-phoneme conversion
GPSG Generalized Phrase Structure Grammar
GR Grammatical Relation
GS Generative Semantics
Guj. Gujarati
H hearer; high; hold (ASL)
habit. habitual
Hitt. Hittite
HM Hmong-Mien
hon. honorific

HPSG Head Driven Phrase Structure Grammar
HR high rise
Hz Hertz (cycles per second)
I inflection; internalized
IA Indo-Aryan; Item-and-Arrangement
IC Immediate Constituent; Inherent Complement
ICA Initial Consonant Alternation
ICM Idealized Cognitive Model
ID Immediate Dominance
IE Indo-European
iff if and only if
IG intonation group
II Indo-Iranian
IL Intensional Logic
ill. illative
imper. imperative
impers. impersonal
impf. imperfect(ive)
inan. inanimate
incl. including, inclusive
ind. independent
indef. indefinite
indic. indicative
inf. infinitive
INFL inflection
inst. instrumental
interj. interjection
intrans. intransitive
invol. involuntary
IO indirect object
IP Inflection Phrase; Item-and-Process
IPA International Phonetic Association or Alphabet
IR Internal Reconstruction
Ir. Iranian
irreg. irregular
IS Interactional Sociolinguistics
Ital. Italian
KA Krama Andhap (= Middle Javanese)
KI Krama Inggil (= High Javanese)
km kilometer(s)
L language; location (ASL); low
L1 first language
L2 second language
LA Latin America; linguistic area
La. Latin; Latvian
LAD Language Acquisition Device
LBH Late Biblical Hebrew
LF Lexical Function; Logical Form
LFG Lexical-Functional Grammar
LGA Local Government Area
LH left hemisphere
Lh. Lhasa
Li. Lithuanian
LIC lower incisor cavity

LIPOC language-independent preferred order of constituents
lit. literally
Lith. Lithuanian
LM Literary Mongolian
l-marking marking a lexical category
LN last name
loc. locative
LP Language Planning; Linear Precedence
LPC Linear Prediction Coefficient
LR low rise
LSA Linguistic Society of America
LSP Language for Specific Purposes
LU lexical unit
Lyc. Lycian
M mid; movement (in ASL); modal; mot (in Metrical Phonology)
m. masculine
MA Meso-American
masc. masculine
m-command maximal command
MCS Mildly Context-Sensitive
MDP Minimal Distance Principle
ME Middle English
MG Montague Grammar
MH Middle/Mishnaic Hebrew
MHG Middle High German
MIA Middle Indo-Aryan
mid. middle
MIT Massachusetts Institute of Technology
MK Mon-Khmer
MLU mean length of utterance
MM Middle Mongolian
Mod. modern
Mod.E. Modern English
MOP Maximal Onset Principle
MP Malayo-Polynesian; Middle Persian
MPR Mongolian People's Republic; morphophonological rule
ms millisecond
ms. manuscript
MSA Modern Standard Arabic
MSC Morpheme Structure Constraint
MSK Modern Standard Khmer
mss. manuscripts
MST Modern Standard Telugu
MT Machine Translation
N noun; number
n. note
NA North America; Northern Athabaskan
N/A nominative/accusative
NC Niger-Congo
NCC North Central Caucasian
n.d. no date

NE New English (= Modern English)
neg. negative
neut. neuter
Ng. Ngoko (= colloquial Javanese)
NGP Natural Generative Phonology
NHG New High German
NIA New Indo-Aryan
NL natural language
NLI Natural Language Interface
NLP Natural Language Processing
NM Natural Morphology
NN Nynorsk
No. Norwegian
nom. nominative
NOM nominal(ization)
nonfin. non-finite
NP New Persian; noun phrase
NS Nilo-Saharan
n.s. new series
NWC Northwest Caucasian
O object
obj. object
obl. oblique
obs. obsolete
OCS Old Church Slavic
OE Old English
OG Old Georgian
OHG Old High German
OI Old Iranian
OIA Old Indo-Aryan
OK Old Khmer
OM object marker
ON Old Norse
OP Old Persian; Old Portuguese; Old Prussian
OP null operator
OPer. Old Persian
opt. optative
ORuss. Old Russian
Os. Oscan
o.s. old series
OT Optimality Theory
P person; patient; phrase; predicator; preposition; position (in ASL)
PA Proto-Australian
PAE Proto-Athabaskan-Eyak
PAN Proto-Austronesian
PAn. Proto-Anatolian
PAS Preferred Argument Structure
pass. passive
pat. patient
PC pronominal clitic
PCA Pacific Coast Athabaskan
PCF Phonetically Consistent Form
pcl. particle
pcpl. participle
PCU Preferred Clause Unit
PD Proto-Dravidian

PDP Parallel Distributed Processing
Per. Persian
perf. perfect(ive)
pers. person
PET Positron Emission Tomography
PF Phonetic Form
pf. perfect(ive)
PGmc. Proto-Germanic
Phryg. Phrygian
PIE Proto-Indo-European
Pkt. Prakrit
pl. plural
PLD Primary Linguistic Data
PLu. Proto-Luvian
plupf. pluperfect
PM phrase-marker; Proto-Mayan
PN predicate nominal
PNC Proto-Niger-Congo
PNI Proto-Northern Iroquoian
POc. Proto-Oceanic
Pol. Polish
pol. polite
poss. possessive
postpos. postposition
PP prepositional phrase
PR Phonological Representation; Phonological Rule
PRED predicate
pref. prefix
prep. preposition
pres. present
prev. preverb
PRO pronoun, pronominal
prog. progressive
pron. pronoun
prt. particle
P-rule phonological rule
PS Phrase Structure; Preference Semantics
PSG Phrase Structure Grammar
PST Proto-Sino-Tibetan
PT patient-trigger; Proto-Tai
PTB Proto-Tibeto-Burman
Q quantifier; question
QH Qumranic Hebrew
q.v. *quod vide,* which see
qq.v. *quae vide,* which see (plural)
R root
RC relative clause
RE Recursively Enumerable
real. realis
redup. reduplication
refl. reflexive
rel. relative
rem. remote
repr. reprinted
REST Revised Extended Standard Theory

rev. revised
R-expression referring expression
RG Relational Grammar
RH right hemisphere
RN Relational Network
RP Recognition Problem; Received Pronunciation; referential pronoun
RR Readjustment Rule
R-rule Redundancy Rule
RT reading tradition
RTN Recursive Transition Network
Ru. Russian
S sentence; speaker; subject
SA stem augment
SAAD simple active affirmative declarative (sentence)
SBH Standard Biblical Hebrew
SC small clause; South Caucasian; Structural Change
Sc. Scandinavian
SCC Strict Cycle Condition
SD South Dravidian; Structural Description
SEA Southeast Asia(n)
sec. secondary; section
ser. series
SFH Semantic Feature Hypothesis
SG Stratificational Grammar; Standard Gujarati
sg. singular
SGML Standard Generalized Markup Language
SH Standard Hausa
SHWNG South Halmahera-West New Guinea
Skt. Sanskrit
Sl. Slavic
SM series marker
soc. sociative
SP Semantic Parsing; subject pronoun
Sp. Spanish
SPE *The Sound Pattern of English*
SS marking Same Subject marking
S-structure shallow structure
ST Sino-Tibetan
stat. stative
sub. subordinator
SUBCAT subcategorization
subj. subject
subjunc. subjunctive
subord. subordinate, subordinative
subst. substantive
superess. superessive
SUR Speech Understanding Research
SV stative verb
Sw. Swedish
SWITCH switch reference
syn. synonym, synonymous

Syr. Syriac

t trace

T title; *tu* (familiar address)

TAP tense-aspect pronoun (Hausa)

TB Tibeto-Burman

TBU Tone-Bearing Unit

TG Transformational Grammar; Tupí-Guaraní

Tib. Tibetan

TK Tai-Kadai

Toch. Tocharian

TOP topic

tr. transitive

trans. transitive

trig. trigger

T-rule transformational rule

TV transitive verb

U utterance

UA Uto-Aztecan

UC ultimate constituent

UG Universal Grammar

Ukr. Ukrainian

Um. Umbrian

URP Universal Recognition Problem

V verb; vowel; *vous* (polite address)

Ved. Vedic (Sanskrit)

ver. version

VH vowel harmony

VL Vulgar Latin

voc. vocative

vol. volume

VOT voice-onset time

VP verb phrase

W word

WFR Word-Formation Rule

WH Western Hausa

WH-word question-word (*what*, etc.)

W* language non-configurational language

WMP Western Malayo-Polynesian

WP Word-and-Paradigm

WT Western Tibetan

X any syntactic category (in X-Bar Theory)

Ø zero (covert element)

1 first person; subject (Relational Grammar)

2 second person; direct object (Relational Grammar)

3 third person; indirect object (Relational Grammar)

* non-attested form (hypothetical or reconstructed); Kleene star

< comes from

> becomes

→ is rewritten as (phrase structure rule)

⇒ is transformed into

α alpha, a variable

Δ delta, a dummy element in syntax

μ theta, thematic (role)

σ sentence; syllable

Σ sentence; stress

INTERNATIONAL ENCYCLOPEDIA OF LINGUISTICS

SECOND EDITION

A

AAVE. *Abbreviation for* African American Vernacular English.

ABBREVIATION. As a morphological process (also called "shortening" or "clipping"), distinct from coding (*ORD*, the airline symbol for Chicago's O'Hare airport), orthographic punning (*K9* 'canine'), and purely orthographic abbreviations (*ft.* 'foot, feet') with no distinct pronunciations. Some spoken abbreviations are based on orthography: initialisms like *TV* or *teevee,* acronyms like *scuba,* and clipped forms like *prof.* Others are based on pronunciation: *natch* from *naturally.* (For general reference, see Marchand 1969:391–395, 441–454; Adams 1973:135–160; Algeo 1975, 1977, 1978, 1980; Kreidler 1979; Bauer 1983:230–240; Cannon 1987:99–155; Oxford 1998; Hughes 2000:349–355; Stockwell and Minkova 2001:6–10.)

A word may be clipped to one of its morphemes, which then assumes the semantic range of the original word, as *parachute* is clipped in *paradoctor, paraglider,* and *paratrooper.* Similarly, a compound may be clipped to one of its words, which then becomes semantically equivalent to the original compound, e.g. *jet* from *jet plane.*

Shortening by the omission of a supposed derivational affix, as in *burgle* from *burglar,* is back formation. This process may also reanalyze the constituent structure of existing morphemes, as *typewrite* was formed from *typewriter,* historically *type + writer,* but understood as *typewrite + -er.*

Blends are either syntagmatic or paradigmatic. Syntagmatic parts of a compound may be combined by back-clipping, e.g. *sitcom* from *situation comedy*; or by contraction (combined back- and fore-clipping), e.g. *motel* from *motor hotel.* Paradigmatic blends may derive from synonyms, as *bonk* from *bong + conk,* or from words otherwise associated, as *workaholic* from *work + alco-holic.* Some forms involve both syntagmatic and paradigmatic blending; thus the computer term *bit* is from *binary digit,* but the word *bit* 'small piece' doubtless influenced its making.

BIBLIOGRAPHY

Adams, Valerie. 1973. *An introduction to Modern English word-formation.* London: Longman.

Algeo, John. 1975. The acronym and its congeners. In *The First LACUS Forum, 1974,* edited by Adam Makkai and Valerie B. Makkai, pp. 217–234. Columbia, S.C.: Hornbeam.

Algeo, John. 1977. Blends: A structural and systemic view. *American Speech* 52.47–64.

Algeo, John. 1978. The taxonomy of word making. *Word* 29.122–131.

Algeo, John. 1980. Where do all the new words come from? *American Speech* 55.264–277.

Bauer, Laurie. 1983. *English word-formation.* Cambridge and New York: Cambridge University Press.

Cannon, Garland. 1987. *Historical change and English word-formation: Recent vocabulary.* New York: Peter Lang.

Hughes, Geoffrey. 2000. *A History of English words.* Oxford: Blackwell.

Kreidler, Charles W. 1979. Creating new words by shortening. *Journal of English Linguistics* 13.24–36.

Marchand, Hans. 1969. *The categories and types of present-day English word-formation: A synchronic-diachronic approach.* 2d ed. Munich: Beck.

Oxford. 1998. *The Oxford dictionary of abbreviations.* Oxford: Oxford University Press.

Stockwell, Robert, and Donka Minkova. 2001. *English words: History and structure.* Cambridge: Cambridge University Press.

JOHN ALGEO

ABKHAZ-ADYGHE LANGUAGES. Also called Northwest Caucasian or West Caucasian languages. They

1

FIGURE 1. *Subgrouping of Abkhaz-Adyghe Languages*

Abkhaz-Abaza
  Abaza, Abkhaz
Circassian
  Adyghe, Kabardian
Ubykh

are spoken primarily in the northwestern Caucasus, though there are also sizable emigrant communities in Turkey and the Middle East.

LANGUAGE LIST

Abaza: also called Abazin, Abazintsy, Ashuwa. 44,900 speakers in European Russia, Asian Turkey, Germany, and USA. In European Russia: 34,800 speakers in Karachay-Cherkess Republic. Dialects are Tapanta, Ashkaraua, Bezshagh. Some dialects are partially intelligible with Abkhaz. 69.5% are fluent in Russian. More vigorous language use in Russia than in Turkey. Has literary status. Modified Cyrillic script. In Asian Turkey: 10,000 speakers. Dialects are Tapanta, Ashkaraua, Bezshagh. Bilingualism in Turkish. Roman script used in Turkey. In Germany: Ethnic population: 150.

Abkhaz: also called Abxazo. 105,000 speakers in Georgia, Ukraine, and Turkey. In Georgia: 101,000 speakers. Abkhaz Republic within Georgia, Black Sea coast. Dialects are Bzyb, Abzhui, Samurzakan. In Turkey: Coruh in northeastern Turkey, and some in northwest, mainly villages in Bolu and Sakarya Provinces. Dialects are Bzyb, Abzhui, Samurzakan. 96% bilingualism in Turkish.

Adyghe: also called Circassian, Lower Circassian, Kiakh, Kjax, West Circassian, Adygei, Adygey. 300,000 speakers in European Russia, Asian Turkey, Jordan, Syria, Iraq, Israel, Australia, Egypt, France, Germany, Macedonia, Netherlands, and USA. In European Russia: 125,000 speakers. Adygea Republic. Maikop is the capital. Dialects are Shapsug (Sapsug), Xakuchi, Bezhedukh (Bzedux, Bzhedug, Bezhehux-Temirgoi, Temirgoj, Chemgui), Abadzex (Abadekh, Abadzeg), Natuzaj (Natukhai). Some literature. Cyrillic script used. In Asian Turkey: 71,000 speakers. Ethnic population: 130,000 as of 1965. Villages in Kayseri, Tokat, Karaman Maras, and many other provinces in central and western Anatolia. 94% bilingualism in Turkish. Roman script. In Jordan: 44,280 speakers. In Syria: 25,000 speakers. In Iraq: 19,000 speakers. In Israel: Kafr Kama and Rehaniya, small border villages. Very slight dialect differences between the two villages. They understand radio programs in Adyghe from Jordan. Closest to Kabardian. Bilingualism in South Levantine Arabic.

Kabardian: also called Beslenei, Upper Circassian, East Circassian, Kabardino-Cherkes, Kabardo-Cherkes. 647,000 speakers in European Russia, Asian Turkey, Saudi Arabia, and USA. In European Russia: 443,000 speakers. Kabardino-Balkaria and Karachai-Cherkessia. Naltshik is the capital. Dialects are Greater Kabardian, Baksan, Lesser Kabardian, Malka, Mozdok, Kuban, Cherkes, Beslenei (Beslenej). Cyrillic alphabet. In Asian Turkey: 202,000 speakers. Most around Kayseri. 1,000 villages of Kabardian and Adyghe in Turkey. Close to Adygey, but a separate language.

Ubykh: also called Ubyx, Pekhi, Oubykh. Formerly spoken in European Turkey. Haci Osman village, near the Sea of Marmara, near Istanbul. The last fully competent speaker, Tevfik Esen, of Haci Osman, died in Istanbul in October 1992. A century ago there were 50,000 speakers in the Caucasus valleys east of the Black Sea. Most migrated to Turkey in 1894. The ethnic group now speaks a distinct dialect of Adyghe.   B. GRIMES

ABSOLUTE. *See* Case; Grammatical Relations; *and* Transitivity and Voice.

ACCENT. *See* Tone.

ACCUSATIVE. *See* Case; Grammatical Relations; *and* Transitivity and Voice.

ACHE-CHAMIC LANGUAGES. A branch of WESTERN MALAYO-POLYNESIAN. They are spoken in Sumatra, Indonesia, Vietnam, Cambodia, Thailand, and China.

LANGUAGE LIST

Aceh: also called Atjeh, Atjehnese, Achinese, Achehnese. 3,000,000 speakers in Sumatra, Indonesia, northern Aceh Province, northern and southern coasts around the tip of Sumatra. Dialects are Banda Aceh, Baruh, Bueng, Daja, Pase, Pidie (Pedir, Timu), Tunong. Bilingualism in Indonesian.

Cham, Eastern: also called Tjam, Chiem, Chiem Thành, Bhamam. 35,000 speakers in Vietnam and USA. In Vietnam: Thuan Hai, An Giang, Thành phó Hò Chi Minh, Nghia Bình, and Phú Khánh Provinces.

Cham, Western: also called Cambodian Cham, Tjam, Cham, New Cham. 253,100 speakers in Cambodia, Vietnam, Thailand, USA, Australia, France, Indonesia, Libya, Malaysia, Saudi Arabia, and Yemen. In Cambodia: 220,000 speakers. Near the major cities and along the Mekong River. The language differs somewhat from Eastern Cham of central Vietnam. Devanagari-based script. Roman script under discussion in USA and elsewhere. In Vietnam: 25,000 speakers near Chau Doc and Tay Ninh and 4,000 in Saigon Cholon.

FIGURE 1. *Subgrouping of Ache-Chamic Languages*

Ache
  Aceh
Chamic
  North Chamic
    Tsat
  South Chamic
    Coastal South Chamic
      Cham-Chru
        Eastern Cham, Western Cham, Chru
      Roglai
        Cacgia Roglai, Northern Roglai, Southern Roglai
    Plateau South Chamic
      Haroi, Jarai, Rade

In Thailand: Ban Khrue, Bangkok, and possibly in refugee camps. The language differs somewhat from Eastern Cham of central Vietnam. Recognized fairly recently as Cham. Speakers are thought to be remnants of the Cham ethnic group who fought in the Thai army about two hundred years ago. There are conflicting reports about whether the people in Thailand still speak Cham or have shifted to Central Thai. Old Devanagari-based script used. Roman script being discussed in USA and elsewhere.

Chru: also called Churu, Choru, Chu Ru, Chu, Cru, Kru, Chrau Hma, Cadoe Loang, Seyu. 11,000 speakers in Vietnam, France, and USA. 2 other countries. In Vietnam: Lam Dong and Thuan Hai Provinces. Dialects are Rai, Noang (La-Dang). Closely related to Cham. Bilingualism in Vietnamese.

Haroi: also called Hrway, Hroi, Hroy, Hoi, Aroi, Bahnar Cham. 35,000 speakers in Vietnam. Binh Dinh and Phu Yen Provinces.

Jarai: also called Djarai, Gia-Rai, Jorai, Cho-Rai, Chor, Mthur, Chrai, Gio-Rai. Around 257,000 speakers in Vietnam, Cambodia, USA. In Vietnam: 242,000 speakers. Gia Lai-Cong Tum Province. Dialects are Puan, Hodrung (Hdrung), Jhue, Aráp, Habau (Ho-Bau), To-Buan, Sesan, Chuty, Pleikly, Golar. In Cambodia: 15,000 speakers. Ratankiri Province, principally the districts of Bokeo, Andons, Meas, O Yadou, along northeastern border near Vietnam. Dialects are Puan, Hodrung (Hdrung), Jhue, Aráp, Habau (Ho-Bau), To-Buan, Sesan, Chuty, Pleikly, Golar. Possibly largely Puan (To-Buan) dialect.

Rade: also called Rhade, Raday, Rde, E-De, Edeh, De. 195,000 speakers in Vietnam and USA. In Vietnam: Dac Lac and part of Phú Khánh Provinces, centered around Banmethuot. Possibly also Cambodia. Dialects are Bih, Ndhur (Mdhur), Adham (A-Dham), Blo, Kodrao (Kdrao), Krung 1, Rde Kpa (Kpa). Bih (1,000 speakers) may be a separate language. The Krung 1 dialect is different from the Bahnaric language Krung 2, in Cambodia.

Roglai, Cacgia: also called Ra-Glai. 2,000 speakers in Viet-

nam. Thuan Hai Province, on the coast northeast of Phan Rang. It is considerably different from other Roglai varieties.

Roglai, Northern: also called Radlai, Adlai, Rayglay, Ra-Glai, Rang Glai, Noang, La-Oang. 25,000 speakers in Vietnam. Thuan Hai and Phú Khánh Provinces, in the mountains west and south of Nhatrang, and some near Dalat.

Roglai, Southern: also called Rai. 20,000 speakers in Vietnam. Thuan Hai Province, southern Vietnam. Closely related to Chru and Northern Roglai.

Tsat: also called Utsat, Utset, Huihui, Hui, Hainan Cham. 3,800 speakers in China. Ethnic population: 5,000 as of 2000. Southern Hainan, villages of Huixin and Huihui in the Yanglan suburban district of Sanya City. About 10% are monolingual. Others speak Chinese as second language. Perhaps 1% to 2% can also speak Li or Japanese. All ages. All domains. Oral use in local administration, business, religion, subject of instruction and supplemental aid in secondary schools, oral traditional literature. Vigorous language use. Parents transmit it to children. Speakers are positive about Tsat.   B. GRIMES

ACOUSTIC PHONETICS. Sound waves form the physical link between speaker and hearer. Central to the field of acoustic phonetics are the concepts and techniques of acoustic physics; but acoustic phonetic research also integrates knowledge about how speech signals are produced by a speaker, how they are perceived by a hearer, and how they are structured by the phonology of languages. From the linguist's point of view, acoustic phonetics provides quantitative information on the realization of the sound system of a language, supplementing the data available from auditory phonetics.

Acoustic phonetics is a relative newcomer to the discipline of phonetics. Developments in the 19th century in the field of acoustics laid its theoretical foundations; but it was given its real impetus in the 20th century, by techniques for recording sound and analyzing it electronically. The availability of computers for digital processing of signals gave it further momentum. Acoustic phonetics has become arguably the most successful branch of phonetics. Its primary data are easy to obtain (unlike, e.g., data on muscle activity in speech production); and advances in acoustic phonetics are often stimulated by the prospect of practical applications in such areas as telecommunications and human/computer interaction through speech.

This article will offer an introduction to some background concepts in acoustic phonetics, a summary of the acoustic properties of major classes of speech sounds, and a review of some of the roles of acoustic phonetics.

FIGURE 1. *Changes in Air Pressure through Time Associated with a Pure Tone.* The form is that of a sine wave.

FIGURE 1. *Changes in Air Pressure through Time Associated with a Pure Tone.* The form is that of a sine wave.

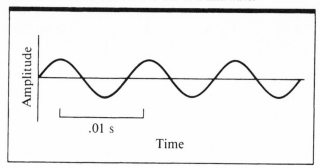

For more extensive introductions, see Ladefoged 1996 and Fry 1979. The seminal work in modern acoustic phonetics is Fant 1960, and wide-ranging, authoritative coverage of the field is to be found in Stevens 1998.

1. Background concepts. Sound consists of vibrations to which the ear is sensitive. Usually the ear is responding to tiny, fast oscillations of air molecules, which originate at a sound source. A tuning fork provides a familiar illustration: as an arm of the fork swings in one direction, it shunts adjacent molecules nearer to subsequent ones, causing a brief local increase in air pressure. The shunting effect spreads outward through further molecules; a wave of high pressure is radiating from the arm. Meanwhile, the arm swings back to, and overshoots, its rest position—as do the adjacent molecules. Their momentary increased separation from subsequent molecules means a reduction in pressure ("rarefaction"). A wave of low pressure now radiates in the wake of the wave of high pressure. As the oscillation of the fork continues, a regular succession of pressure highs and lows spreads outward.

At a point in the path of the radiating pressure changes, we could plot pressure against time as they sweep by. Figure 1 does this for a tone produced by an "ideal" tuning fork. Notice three properties of this waveform. First, the peaks and troughs have a particular *amplitude*; increasing the amplitude would cause the tone to sound louder. Second, the cycle of pressure variation takes a given time to repeat itself; this is the *period* of the wave. The shorter the period, the more repetitions or cycles of the wave there will be per second: i.e., its *frequency* will be higher. The wave shown has a period of .01 s (second); its frequency is 1/.01 = 100 Hz (Hertz, meaning cycles per second). Increasing the tone's frequency would cause it to sound higher in pitch. Third, the particular wave in Figure 1 shows a simple pattern of rising and falling pressure, called a *sine wave*.

The wave at the top of Figure 2 is more complex. Crucially, however, a complex wave can be analyzed as being made up of a number of sine waves of different frequencies—for this wave, three, as shown below it. If we add together the amplitudes of the component sine waves, or *harmonics*, at each point in time, we can recreate the complex wave. Such analysis of a complex wave is known as *Fourier analysis*.

The graph at the right in Figure 2 is another way of showing the essential information from this type of analysis. It plots each harmonic at its frequency by a line which shows the harmonic's relative amplitude. This kind of representation, called an *amplitude spectrum*, is of central importance in acoustic phonetics, as is the information it contains about the distribution of acoustic energy at different frequencies.

The harmonics in Figure 2 are at 100, 300, and 400 Hz. The highest common factor of these values is 100 Hz; this is the frequency of repetition of the complex wave, which is called its *fundamental frequency*, and which determines our perception of the pitch of this sound.

A repetitive or *periodic* wave will thus have energy in discrete harmonics at some (but not necessarily all) of the frequencies which are whole-number multiples of its fundamental frequency. In many occurring waves, however, it is not possible to discern a repeating cycle. In such *aperiodic* waves, there is no fundamental frequency; energy is present throughout the frequency range, rather than being banded into discrete harmonics.

2. Acoustics of speech. Figure 3 shows brief extracts from the waveforms of two rather different sounds taken from the word *speech*: the vowel [i] above, and the consonant [s] below. The vowel's waveform is roughly periodic, though more complex than that in Figure 2. The second waveform, from [s], consists of aperiodic noise. In general, voiced speech sounds (for which the vocal cords are vibrating) will have periodic waveforms. The rate of repetition of the wave, i.e. its fundamental frequency, directly reflects the rate of vibration of the vocal cords, and it cues the hearer's perception of pitch.

The schematic amplitude spectrum of the magnified fragment of [i] shows that it is rich in harmonics. Their amplitude is greater at certain frequencies, and this "shaping" of the spectrum determines the perception of a particular sound. The spectrum for the aperiodic [s] shows energy that is not banded into harmonics, but is present continuously over a range of frequencies. Again, the shape of the spectrum characterizes the sound.

Figure 4 illustrates the production of two different

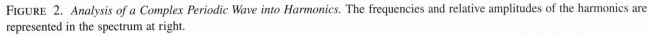

FIGURE 2. *Analysis of a Complex Periodic Wave into Harmonics.* The frequencies and relative amplitudes of the harmonics are represented in the spectrum at right.

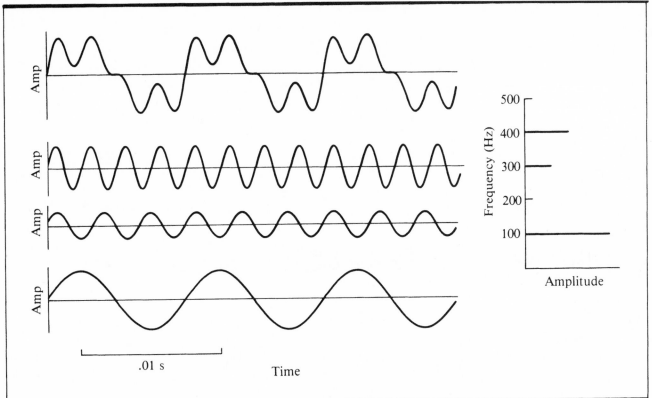

vowels, [ɑ] as in *palm* and [i] as in *heed.* At the bottom of the figure is the spectrum of the waveform produced by the vibrating larynx. This laryngeal *source* wave would sound like a buzz, if we could isolate it from the vocal tract. Its spectrum is rich in harmonics, whose amplitude gradually decreases with increasing frequency.

Above that can be seen alternative vocal tract shapes: on the left, that for [ɑ], and on the right that for [i]. The vocal tract is, in effect, a tube; and like any tube, e.g. a wind instrument, it has a number of *resonant frequencies,* at which the air in the tube is especially liable to vibrate in sympathy with another sound. The spectrum next to each vocal tract in Figure 4 shows how well the tract resonates at any frequency: in each case, three resonance peaks, or *formants,* can be seen. In practice, further formants exist at higher frequencies; but the first three are most important in determining vowel quality. Note that [ɑ] has a relatively high first formant (F_1) and a low second formant (F_2); for [i], F_1 is low and F_2 is high. The frequency of the formants is dependent on the shape of the vocal tract, and hence on the positioning of the tongue and lips.

The vocal tract acts on the laryngeal source as a *filter,* which enhances some harmonics relative to others. Thus, in the spectrum of the speech waveform as it emerges at the lips, each harmonic of the laryngeal source has an amplitude which is modified according to how near it is in frequency to a formant—as shown schematically in the two spectra at the top of Figure 4. Some details have been omitted for simplicity; however, this general conception of vowel production as the combination of a sound source at the larynx and the spectral shaping function of the vocal tract, known as the *source-filter model,* has been highly influential in acoustic phonetics.

Vowels have been discussed so far as though they were characterized by a steady-state vocal tract posture and corresponding spectrum. In fact, speech sounds rarely involve steady states: the vocal tract is in almost constant motion, and hence the spectrum of the speech wave is constantly changing. It would be possible to represent this as a series of spectra, and this is sometimes done; but another kind of display is more common in acoustic phonetics. This is illustrated schematically at the top of Figure 4. Assume that the vocal tract is moving contin-

FIGURE 3. *Waveforms of* [i] *and* [s]. Waveforms from (top) the vowel [i] and (bottom) the voiceless fricative [s], together with their schematic spectra.

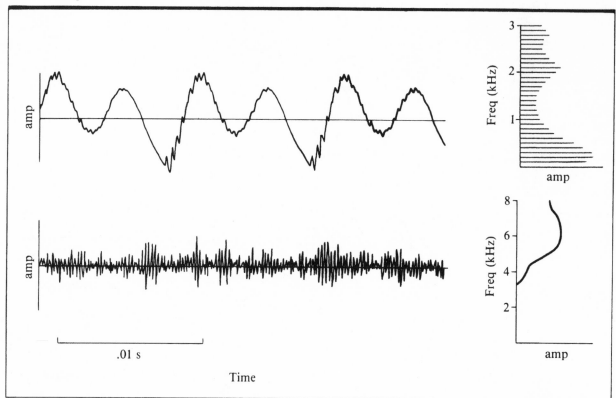

uously from the [ɑ] configuration to the [i] configuration. This would produce a diphthong sounding something like the word *eye*. In the new display, time runs from left to right; frequency, as before, is shown on the vertical axis. In effect, there is a third dimension: high-amplitude parts of the spectrum are shown as black. Thus it is possible to trace the changing formant frequencies as movements in the black bands. Note how, at the start and end of the diphthong, the bands coincide with the peaks in the spectra of the individual words.

This general kind of display is called a *spectrogram*. Real, as opposed to schematic, spectrograms have a range of shades of gray which indicate increasing amplitude; they allow much of the detail of the spectrum at a particular point to be inferred. From the 1940s onward, use was made of the *sound spectrograph*, a machine that uses analog electronics to produce spectrograms and other spectral displays; since the 1970s, digital computers have taken over this function.

Figure 5 shows a real spectrogram of the rhyming phrases "a bye," "a dye," "a guy." The movement of the first two formants in each word is similar to that shown

in Figure 4; like *eye,* these words have a diphthong that moves from an open vowel something like [ɑ] toward a close front vowel something like [i]. The consonants appear as almost blank on the spectrogram, because little sound radiates from the vocal tract when it is closed. Adjacent to them, the detailed trajectory of the formants, particularly F_2 and F_3, differs according to the consonant; thus, for the velar [g], these two formants appear rather close together. Such differing *formant transitions* are vital cues to our perception of consonants. They occur because, as the vocal tract closes for a consonant and as it opens again, its resonances change (as always when a tube changes shape). The way in which they change depends on where, along its length, the tract is closing— i.e. on the *place of articulation* of the consonant.

Part of the acoustic character of a consonant, then, seems to be explicable like that of a vowel: as changes in the resonances of the vocal tract tube. But consonants are considerably more complex acoustically than vowels. Many consonants have a source of acoustic energy other than the vibrating larynx; e.g. in an [s] (see Figure 3), aperiodic noise is produced when air is forced through a

FIGURE 4. *The Source-Filter Model of Speech Production.* The two vowel spectra (top) reflect the spectrum of the laryngeal source-wave, modified by the resonances (formants) of the vocal tract for [ɑ] (left) and [i] (right). At the top it is assumed that the vocal tract is moving between the two vowels, and the schematic spectrogram shows the changes through time of the first three spectral peaks.

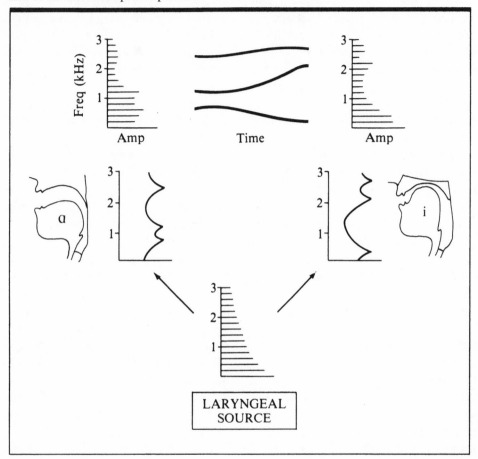

FIGURE 5. *Spectrogram of "a bye," "a dye," "a guy."* The frequencies of the first three formants at the start of the transitions from the stops are indicated in the stop portions.

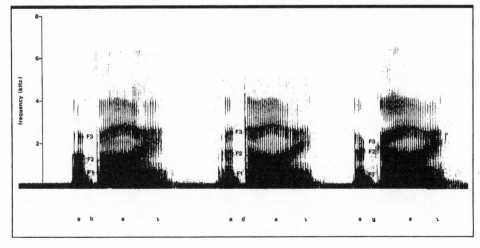

narrow gap at the alveolar ridge, and the flow becomes turbulent.

All fricatives involve the production of such noise at some point in the vocal tract. Voiceless fricatives like [s] have only this kind of source of acoustic energy; in voiced fricatives, like [z], noise is superimposed on energy from the vibrating vocal cords. The spectrum of the noise depends on the kind of turbulence which produces it, and on the way in which it is shaped by the resonances of the vocal tract. An [h] will have a formant structure rather like that of a vowel, because the aperiodic noise source (like the periodic voicing of a vowel) is at the end of the vocal tract. An [s], by contrast, will have a spectral shaping quite unlike that of a vowel.

Figure 6 is a spectrogram of "hazy sunshine." The [h] has a formant pattern somewhat like that of the vowel following it. The [z] shows two cues to the voicing which differentiates it from [s]: low-frequency energy at the bottom of the pattern, and a continuity of the vertical striations (each of which, as in vowels, indicates a cycle of vocal-cord vibration). By contrast, [s] and [z] share a similar high-frequency noise spectrum, because they are both alveolars; the spectrum of the post-alveolar [š] is rather different.

While fricatives result from turbulence in a steady airflow, the release of a stop brings a short burst of aperiodic acoustic energy at the moment when the air pressure, built up behind the closure, is released. The spectral distribution of energy in the burst varies according to the place of articulation of the stop; this supplements the formant transition cues discussed above.

Nasals are like vowels in that energy produced at the larynx is spectrally shaped by the resonance of a tube; here, however, the tube extends from the larynx through the nasal cavities. The acoustic complexity is increased because there is interaction with the resonances of the mouth cavity behind the oral closure. Nasalized vowels, as in French [ɔ̃] *on,* are similar to oral vowels, except that their spectrum is made more complex by the interaction of the resonances of the nasal cavity.

The acoustic dimensions that underlie suprasegmental properties are well established. Fundamental frequency correlates closely with perceived pitch, intensity with perceived loudness, and the duration of different acoustic events with length—although, in each case, the perceptual attribute may be influenced by other factors. More complex is the way in which all these acoustic dimensions combine to cue linguistic contrasts. For instance, stress or accent is cued by contributions from fundamental frequency, duration, and intensity, but the precise con-

stellation of cues varies according to language and according to the intonational context. Nor is there a sharp dividing line between dimensions supporting segmental and suprasegmental contrasts: for instance, in many languages vowel quality contributes to stress contrasts, with unstressed vowels being mid-centralized. Nonetheless, as in the case of segmental phonetics, quantitative analysis of the relevant dimensions leads to a much fuller understanding of the linguistic contrasts.

This treatment of the acoustics of speech has been far from complete. Not all types of segments have been considered, and only a little has been said about the prosodic or suprasegmental properties of speech. More generally, it has not explored the quantitative mathematical models which underlie the analysis of speech. It is this quantitative *Acoustic theory of speech* which gives acoustic phonetics the power to manipulate and replicate speech signals, and which opens the way to many of the applications discussed below.

3. The roles of acoustic phonetics. As an adjunct to phonology, acoustic phonetics can supplement the information on phonetic realization which is provided by auditory phonetics. The exact nature of a fine auditory distinction often is not clear from skilled listening alone; acoustic analysis can show objectively the contribution of spectral, durational, and other acoustic dimensions to the realization of a phonological contrast. Beyond this, acoustic phonetics can suggest appropriate phonological features for descriptive use. For example, there is little motivation in articulatory terms for the sound change by which the Germanic velar fricative at the end of the word *laugh* became labio-dental in modern English; but acoustic analysis suggests a similarity in terms of spectral shape. Both fricatives have a weighting of their energy toward the lower end of the spectrum; in terms of phonological features, they share the value [+grave].

Acoustic phonetics has an important role in the branch of cognitive psychology which deals with the perception of speech. In particular, the analyses of acoustic phonetics provide techniques for manipulating real speech signals, and for creating speech signals artificially by speech synthesis. Thus experimental stimuli can be created whose acoustic properties are precisely known, and which can be varied in controlled ways. It is then possible to discover exactly which properties of a sound are crucial for its perception by a hearer. For instance, it can be shown that, in identifying an English stop as voiceless rather than voiced (e.g. as a realization of /p/ rather than /b/), hearers are mainly sensitive to the delay in the onset of voicing after the release of the stop; but they also

FIGURE 6. *Spectrogram of "hazy sunshine"*

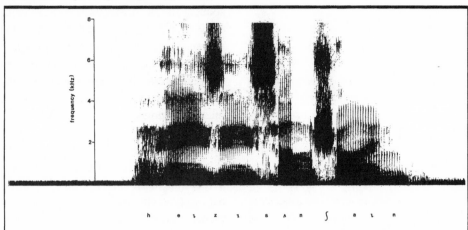

integrate information such as the strength of the stop burst and the trajectory of F_1 at the start of the vowel.

The study of how humans produce speech, too, benefits from a well worked-out acoustic theory of speech. It is now possible to implement mathematically explicit models of how certain aspects of the speech signal are created in the vocal tract. Perhaps the most advanced are analogs of the vocal tract tube as it acts as a filter on the glottal source. Given such a model, it is possible to predict formant values for any variation in the shape of the tube. Working back from the observed acoustic pattern of a speech sound, the articulatory events underlying the sound can be inferred. Quantitative models also exist for the creation of acoustic energy in the vocal tract, either by a purely aerodynamic process (as with fricative energy), or—in the case of the vocal cords—a process involving complex interactions of aerodynamics and properties of the vocal-cord tissues. To the extent that such models yield realistic acoustic signals, they confirm progress in understanding speech production.

Acoustic phonetic knowledge is crucial in speech technology, including automatic speech recognition, and speech output by computers. Much work in this area is motivated by the goal of allowing humans to interact with machines by using natural language. Part of the challenge is to find explicit and computationally tractable ways to represent existing acoustic phonetic knowledge. One particularly successful technique is linear prediction, which in some ways can be seen as an approximation to the source-filter model; it is applicable in speech synthesis and recognition. However, there are areas where existing knowledge is itself incomplete; this is particularly so in connection with the acoustic variation in a sound which occurs because of differences among individuals' vocal

tracts, and which causes difficulties in designing systems of speech recognition that can cope with a variety of speakers. Further progress in understanding speaker-to-speaker variation will also contribute to techniques for speaker recognition, to which acoustic phonetics is central.

Acoustic phonetics is not an isolated discipline with sharply defined borders. Its central object of study is the acoustic speech signal; but a purely physics-based study of the signal—ignoring how the signal is produced and perceived, and how it is structured linguistically—would contribute relatively little to our understanding of spoken communication. Acoustic phonetics thus proceeds in symbiosis with the study of speech production, speech perception, and linguistics generally.

[*See also* Articulatory Phonetics; Phonological Features; Speech Perception; *and* Speech Synthesis.]

BIBLIOGRAPHY

Fant, Gunnar. 1960. *Acoustic theory of speech production*. The Hague: Mouton.

Fry, Dennis B. 1979. *The physics of speech*. Cambridge and New York: Cambridge University Press.

Ladefoged, Peter. 1996. *Elements of acoustic phonetics*. 2d ed. Chicago: University of Chicago Press.

Stevens, Kenneth N. 1998. *Acoustic phonetics*. Cambridge, Mass.: MIT Press.

FRANCIS NOLAN

ACQUISITION OF LANGUAGE. [*This entry includes the following subentries:*

Phonology

Syntax

Phonology

The acquisition of the phonology of one's native language(s) includes mastery of the phonetic targets, phonemic contrasts, and morphophonemic alternations for the processing of language in both recognition and production (see Vihman 1996 and Jusczyk 1997 for reviews). A significant biological basis of this learning process is acknowledged even by those who reject nativist ideas about acquisition, and has been supported by cross-linguistic studies of the first two years of life. Most studies deal with Indo-European languages, notably Dutch, English, French, Swedish, and Welsh; Finnish, Chinese, Japanese, Thai, and Quiché (K'iche') Mayan are also represented.

1. Precursors of phonology: Pre-speech perception. Infants demonstrate preferential attention to the prosodic patterns of their own language from the first days of life. The fetus gains linguistic experience in the womb through hearing the sound of the mother's voice both "internally" and from the outside, filtered through the amniotic fluid. The prosodic information present in the lower frequency bands of the signal can reach fetal ears by the final trimester of pregnancy, when the auditory system is completely formed; segmental information, much of which is carried by higher frequencies, cannot. Prosody provides the initial entry into language, not only from establishment as an acoustic signal before birth but also from the intrinsic affective links between particular prosodic patterns and communicative meanings (Fernald 1992); these provide a foundation for the later-learned arbitrary (linguistic) form-meaning relations.

Young infants discriminate virtually all the segmental contrasts on which the phonological systems of the world's languages are based, and they do so whether or not a particular contrast occurs in the ambient language. For instance, American infants discriminate nasal from oral vowels, though these sounds do not contrast in English. Infant categorical response to consonantal contrasts was initially taken as evidence of innate "speech detectors," but later research revealing a similar response in other animal species suggests that the structure of the mammalian auditory system itself may shape the response, and indeed that speech may have evolved to fit

that system. (Categorical perception of non-speech sounds has been demonstrated as well; Jusczyk 1997.) Very young infants associate the visual appearance of degree of mouth opening with the corresponding vowel sound. Although this specific cross-modal link can be seen as "hard-wired" into the brain, an alternative interpretation assumes an intuitive or automatic infant production response—with or without overt imitation—to a within-repertoire phonetic gesture (arguably supported by "mirror neurons"; Stamenov and Gallese, 2002).

In the 1990s, experimental work on infant speech perception increasingly turned from studying discrimination (detection of changes) to probing longer-term representation for speech. These studies have revealed a clear developmental trend: for the first six months, it is primarily prosodic patterns that underlie a "familiarity response" to speech. Evidence of a holistic response to segmental patterns as early as four months is limited to stimuli that can be assumed to be imbued with strong affect for infants, such as the infant's own name. Aside from these exceptional words, preferential attention to a trained segmental pattern is not reported until seven months. Thereafter, steady gains in attention to native-language segmental patterning can be seen, along with a narrowing of attention to consonantal contrasts from broadly "universal" to native-language only by ten–twelve months. Cross-linguistic studies show infant preferential response to words familiar from everyday experience over unknown words by eleven months. Changes to the onset consonant of the unaccented syllable (initial in iambic French words [weak-strong], final in English trochaic words [strong-weak]) do not affect this preference, while changes to the accented syllable eliminate it. This suggests that, at this pre-speech-production stage, the accented syllable is more fully specified than other syllables in the child's representations for familiar words.

2. Precursors of phonology: Early vocal production. Infant non-crying vocal production develops steadily from a first period of reflexive sounds, through social comfort sounds (cooing and laughter, ca. two–five months), to phonatory expansion involving a range of prosodic effects—growling, yelling, and whispering. This increase in range of vocal production options accompanies anatomical changes in the infant vocal tract as it begins to assume the shape characteristic of adult humans, with lengthened pharynx and a right-angle bend. The major vocal landmark of the first year, readily recognized by an infant's caregivers, is the emergence of rhythmically produced "canonical syllables" with adult-like timing, often as a string of reduplicated babbling (six–eight months). Non-reduplicated or variegated babbling increases and differentiates gradually thereafter, culminating early in the second year, for some infants, in "expressive jargon," lengthy babbled sequences that reproduce aspects of the ambient language intonation pattern, producing a striking impression of "conversation without words."

The emergence of easily recognized babbled syllables in the middle of the first year appears to be maturationally based and fits into a broader framework of rhythmic motoric advances that occur around that age. One interpretation of the developmental match between the shift in the apparent basis for infant speech representation from prosody to segments (as outlined above) and the onset of CV production is the "articulatory filter" hypothesis. On this account, the experience of frequently producing CV syllables sensitizes infants to similar patterns in the input speech stream. (Deaf infants fail to persevere in CV syllable production at the typical age; compare the earlier production response to the sight and sound of vowels, noted above.)

The repertoire of sounds used in babbling is rather small, representing the core of sounds used in most languages. Within the limits of that core repertoire, babbling tends to reflect the phonetic profile of the ambient language (e.g. as regards vowel space). It also shows some tendency for consonant-vowel interactions: alveolar ("front") consonants are more likely to be followed by front vowels, labials by central vowels, and velar (back) consonants by back vowels. Whereas the CV associations can be taken to reflect simple jaw oscillation, the statistical matching of ambient-language vowel space suggests pure (implicit) distributional learning, an effect that has been empirically demonstrated in both adults and children (Saffran et al. 1996).

The period of non-reduplicated babbling generally overlaps considerably with the production of the first recognizable words, and the repertoire of word forms preferred by a given child generally is closely related to the most frequent elements in that child's babbling repertoire (for late talkers, this may not be true). Contrary to the predictions of many theoretical approaches, many early words tend to be more accurate than slightly later ones, probably because of selection on phonological grounds. Analyses of later word forms indicate that a child's first well-practiced, consistent supraglottal production patterns provide the basis for the later development of "canonical forms" (Menn 1983) or "word templates" (Vihman and Velleman 2000). These word templates abstract from and extend the piecemeal learning evidenced by the selection patterns of first words. The apparent paradox of such early word selection—how do children know which words not to attempt, or which sounds they cannot yet produce?—does not arise if we assume that the first words result from infants' matching of their own vocal patterns to the input speech signal.

3. Emergence of phonology in early speech. A child's earliest meaningful forms may lack adult models, or they may be phonetically less controlled. Their semantic properties may also be somewhat anomalous: they may be social or action-accompanying rather than referential. For these reasons, terms such as "proto-word," "phonetically consistent form," "vocable," and "context-limited word" have been used instead of "word" for the first recognizably recurrent meaningful units.

3.1. *Characteristics of proto-words and early words.* In contrast, some "earliest" words are accurate renditions of their adult models; if a few of them are conspicuously better approximations to the adult word than the rest of the child's output, these are termed "progressive phonological idioms." Such early forms are likely to be produced before the child's own word-form production begins to cohere into a system. Typically, each child then develops a more or less systematic way of rendering adult words within the constraints of his/her limited output repertoire of sound-sequences by the time she is producing 50 words or so. The inaccuracies in these renditions appear to be due (with a few exceptions) to motor programming or representation problems, rather than to misperceptions of the adult sound pattern; children can usually discriminate between two words that they render identically, except for a few auditorily confusable phones like [f] and [θ].

3.2. *Rules and processes.* Once the child's output becomes systematic, mapping from the adult model to the child's form may be regular enough to be captured by writing phonological rules. This is not true for all children; some map entire multiword phrases onto loosely articulated sequences (e.g. *I don't want it* rendered [aoa:]); others reorder the sounds of adult words to fit their own restricted output templates. Output templates for words may include patterns like "second vowel higher than first vowel," "medial consonant-glottal stop," "first consonant labial, second alveolar," and so on.

The shapes of such word templates are influenced by the particular language the child is learning. For example, initial consonants may be omitted in Finnish, French, or

Welsh word templates, but this pattern is rare in English. The difference is probably in the rhythmic structure: French and Welsh tend to have very long final syllables, while Finnish commonly has medial long consonants. These perceptually salient features of the input lead some children to disregard initial consonants, especially if they are not yet within the child's repertoire (e.g. initial fricatives or liquids).

More systematic mapping patterns, when found, include a number of natural processes such as devoicing of final stops ([bip] for *bib*), substitution of stops for fricatives ([ti] for *see*), reduction of consonant clusters to singletons ([pat], less commonly [fat], for *spot*), deletion of initial [h], and deletion of unstressed syllables ([næ]. ['nænæ] for *banana*). However, since a child may fail to use such processes on her earliest words and then start to use them somewhat later, many researchers regard these processes as natural failure modes rather than as innate rules that must be unlearned by the child. Other common processes for English-acquiring children that are not prominent (sometimes not attested) in adult language include voicing of initial stop consonants and various assimilations at a distance that ensure whole-word consonant harmonies, especially place assimilation and nasal assimilation. For several languages, including Catalan, English, Estonian, and French, it has been observed that an unstressed syllable may be replaced by a "dummy syllable" (either a stereotyped near-constant shape or a copy of the stressed syllable) instead of being deleted. Cluster simplification, usually accomplished by preservation of the most obstruent element, may instead be achieved by combining features from the several segments (e.g./s+nasal/ rendered as voiceless nasal;/sk/ rendered as [x]), even when the adult language does not possess the resulting feature combination. Constraint-based approaches such as Optimality Theory (Kager et al., to appear) can provide a formal description of such mappings.

In ascribing rules or processes to a child, the investigator must take into account the surface forms of the words the child hears, including dialect variants and the reduced forms of rapid casual speech. Ambient dialect forms are targets, not "errors," for the child, regardless of their social valuation; so are the normal assimilations and reductions of fluent speech (e.g., Eng. [hæftə] for *have to*. They cannot be analyzed as outputs of phonological processes for the child who is too young to be aware of the underlying forms.

4. Strategy variations. Initial avoidance of adult words outside a child's pre-speech production repertoire can be accounted for by positing that the child has a better capacity for representing practiced than unpracticed sound sequences, although some sounds produced in babble apparently cannot be used in early speech. Individual children vary in the extent to which they prefer to avoid adult words that they cannot yet render accurately. Experimental work concurs with diary studies in showing that such avoidance is especially likely in children who have produced fewer than about 75 different adult words. As a system develops, some children continue to avoid out-of-repertoire words; others freely adapt such words to fit within their templates.

5. Linguistic perception vs. production: Development after the onset of speech. Investigating the relation of perception to production during the period of acquisition of the sound system has required devising experimental techniques appropriate to the rapidly changing cognitive and motor abilities of the infant and young child. Although infants have phonetic perceptual and categorization abilities similar to, or indeed better than, those of adults, children as old as two often confuse minimal pairs and have a heavy bias to respond to the less familiar member of such a pair of stimulus words as though it were the more familiar one (e.g., pointing to a coat instead of a goat after the word *goat* has been especially taught for the purpose of testing the *k/g* discrimination). Clearly, different mechanisms are involved in discriminating repeated meaningless syllables as opposed to words; for example, differential response to words invokes long-term memory for the sound-meaning correspondence (even if the experimental paradigm does not require this), while the discrimination paradigms used with infants do not require such representations.

Children are not always aware of the degree of accuracy of their attempts. Numerous studies have reported interchanges of this kind: a child of two or three mispronounces a word (e.g. [fis] for *fish*), an adult requests the child to say [fiʃ] (emphasizing the final [ʃ]), and the child responds *I did say* [fis] (with similar emphasis). Since very young infants can, in general, make such discriminations, a possible explanation for such responses is that the toddler is listening "through" the surface form of the word to access the meaning rather than attending to the phonetic details. Experimental studies show such a shift in attention, from auditory discrimination of novel speech forms to sound-meaning mappings with discrimination of holistically dissimilar forms only, between eight and fourteen months (Stager and Werker 1997). After the child becomes aware of the difference between the target and her production, she may still be unable to manage any change in production (and may be able to comment on this). Later, correction can be approximated in imitation but not maintained in spontaneous speech; still later, a more correct form and the earlier form appear variably in production; and, finally, the more correct form is maintained. Progress through these phases may be rapid or slow, and a child may be at an advanced stage with respect to an early-acquired sound or sound-sequence while at a beginning stage with respect to a more difficult target.

6. Order of acquisition of phones and contrasts. The order of mastery of phones and phonemic contrasts and the age of mastery are variable across children. Phones that are dependent on precise relative timing of glottal and supra-laryngeal events (e.g. aspirated or glottalized stops) are generally acquired later than those that are not so dependent, other things being equal; also, phones that seem to require more precise positioning without tactile feedback (fricatives and liquids as opposed to stops) are acquired relatively late. The order of contrast acquisition proposed by Jakobson 1968 on the basis of general markedness is a good fit probabilistically, but many exceptions have been published, so his description in terms of "laws of irreversible solidarity" can no longer be considered appropriate.

Phonotactic constraints (evidenced by canonical forms and word templates) play a critical role in acquisition; as a result, the "order of acquisition" question is often unanswerable, even for an individual child. A particular phoneme might, for example, be generally correct for its intervocalic allophone, fully correct word-initially, absent in particular clusters, and rendered incorrectly in word-final position—all this apart from the possible interference of consonant assimilation in particular words. Although new consonant phones often are first mastered as initial singletons (at least in English), there is much individual variation; for English-speaking children, it is not uncommon that some or all of the fricatives first appear word-finally, while stops first appear word-initially. No general theory is yet able to account both for the degree of observed variation and the degree of observed commonality of acquisition of phones and phonemic contrasts across children.

7. Later phonological development. Well before children finish mastering the phonetic details of the ambient language, they have begun to acquire its morphology and morphophonemics. Phonological rules with a heavy natural component (e.g. voicing assimilation) appear to be acquired early, with the correct output form always present. Frequency and other factors interact in the acquisition of rules that apply to particular classes of morphemes (MacWhinney 1978), including the transparency and reliability of any semantic and/or phonological conditioning factors. Forms in which an ending happens to be very similar to a final stem syllable or consonant (e.g. the Eng. [-Iz] plural allomorph) tend to be acquired late. Rote application of a rule to a few frequent words precedes general application of the rule. Overgeneralization of a rule to cases where it should not apply is taken to be the hallmark of actual rule learning, and this interacts with the learning of subregularities conditioned by phonological factors or by membership in gender classes and conjugational or declensional classes.

Some nonproductive but well-evidenced morphophonological rules—such as the stem-final palatalizations in the Romance stratum of English (*correct/correction*; *invade/invasion*)—are apparently not learned until mid or late adolescence. Morphophonemic development in languages with complex morphology has not been well studied. Little is known about the acquisition of segmental or of tonal sandhi rules that apply across word boundaries, or of rules that apply in rapid speech, in spite of their evident productivity. The ability to understand and produce many aspects of English stress and intonation patterns develops gradually during the elementary-school years. English-speaking school-aged children may produce over-long vowels in lieu of the reduced vowel of unstressed syllables; such hypercorrection suggests awareness of reduction.

[*See also* Formal Grammar; Learnability; Phoneme; Phonological Processes; Phonology, Overview; Psycholinguistics; *and* Speech Perception]

BIBLIOGRAPHY

Fernald, Anne. 1992. Human maternal vocalizations to infants as biologically relevant signals. In *The adapted mind*, edited by Jerome H. Barkow et al. pp. 391–428. Oxford: Oxford University Press.

Jakobson, Roman. 1968. *Child language, aphasia, and phonological universals*. The Hague: Mouton.

Jusczyk, Peter W. 1997. *The discovery of spoken language*. Cambridge, Mass.: MIT Press.

Kager, René, Joe Pater, and Wim Zonneveld, eds. To appear. *Fixing priorities: Constraints in phonological acquisition*. Cambridge: Cambridge University Press.

MacWhinney, Brian. 1978. *The acquisition of morphophonology*. (Monographs of the Society for Research on Child Development, 43:1/2). Chicago: University of Chicago Press.

Menn, Lise. 1983. Development of articulatory, phonetic, and phonological capabilities. In *Language production*, vol. 2, edited by Brian Butterworth, pp. 3–49. London: Academic Press.

Saffran, Jenny R., Elissa L. Newport, and Richard N. Aslin. 1996. Word segmentation: The role of distributional cues. *Journal of Memory and Language* 35.606–621.

Stamenov, Maxim, and Victor Gallese. 2002. *Mirror neurons and the evolution of brain and language.* Amsterdam: Benjamins.

Stager, Christine L., and Janet F. Werker. 1997. Infants listen for more phonetic detail in speech perception than in word-learning tasks. *Nature* 388.381–382.

Vihman, Marilyn M. 1996. *Phonological development: The origins of language in the child.* Oxford: Basil Blackwell.

Vihman, Marilyn M., and Shelley L. Velleman. 2000. Phonetics and the origins of phonology. In *Phonological knowledge: Conceptual and empirical issues,* edited by Noel Burton-Roberts et al. pp. 305–339. Oxford: Oxford University Press.

Werker, Janet F., and Christine L. Stager. 2000. Developmental changes in infant speech perception and early word learning: Is there a link? In *Papers in laboratory phonology V: Acquisition and the lexicon*, edited by Michael B. Broe and Janet B. Pierrehumbert pp. 181–193. Cambridge: Cambridge University Press.

LISE MENN AND MARILYN MAY VIHMAN

Syntax

In learning a language, a child cracks a code constructed of arbitrary symbols (words) combined in patterns (syntax) that convey information about each word's role. To accomplish this, children must collect samples of the code, analyze them, and work out how the code's structure maps onto messages. Based on sentences they encounter, children form an idea of the structure of their language that is abstract enough that they can then produce and understand entirely new sentences, and detailed enough that they can retain information about the quirks of particular lexical items.

Productive language begins at about one year of age. Single-word utterances are typical at the start, and early productive vocabularies are dominated by nouns. Word combinations begin to appear at about 1.5 to 2.5 years. At first very short, typically only two or three words long, combinations gradually lengthen. Early sentences are often called "telegraphic" because they lack function morphology (*Throw ball* rather than *I'm throwing the ball*). Even these early sentences have structure, however, often exhibiting the correct word order for the language being learned. By age five, children's language is essentially adult-like, with sentences like *I bet you don't know how to play this* routine accomplishments. These familiar patterns are based partly on the growth of syntactic and lexical knowledge, and partly on the development of an efficient system for language production. Language comprehension typically shows earlier competence: 18-month-olds speak mostly in one-word utterances yet understand the significance of word order in longer sentences.

We generally assume that this feat of learning depends on species-specific capacities, since no other species learn our languages, and that it *is* a feat of learning, since children acquire the language used around them. The nature of learning mechanisms for syntax acquisition is controversial. Many theories propose that some constraints on acquisition are specific to language, constituting a universal grammar (UG) that permits children to create a highly structured system based on noisy and incomplete data. Other theories assume that syntax acquisition depends only on domain-general learning mechanisms and constraints. Regardless of its stance on this question, any theory of syntax acquisition must specify what elements the child can identify in the input before learning a grammar, and what learning mechanisms the child uses to construct a grammar based on those elements. These mechanisms must be constrained enough to explain the ways in which all human languages are alike, yet flexible enough to permit observed variation across languages.

1. The "bootstrapping problem." Syntactic regularities involve dependencies among classes of words. A child learning English learns that determiners precede their nouns; and that transitive verbs are followed by their objects. Learning syntactic dependencies requires identifying the categories over which they are defined— nouns and verbs, determiners and tense markers; but these categories, in turn, are defined by their positions in phrase structure. Nouns and verbs cannot be identified based on sound or meaning; ultimately, these categories are defined by the roles they play in a grammar. This reveals the fundamental circularity of syntax acquisition: the child needs phrase structure to create grammatical categories, yet needs grammatical categories to learn phrase structure. The question of how the child breaks into this circle is the "bootstrapping problem" of language acquisition (from the expression "Pull yourself up by your own bootstraps").

Research in this area explores what relevant cues children can detect in the linguistic environment, and how they might use these cues to create grammatical categories. Three kinds of cues are distributional patterns, phonological cues, and semantic information.

2. Distributional learning. Because grammatical categories are distributionally defined, children could begin by grouping words based on their occurrence in similar environments. Nouns and verbs occur with different function morphemes (*the*, *a*, *-s* vs. *is*, *can*, *-ing*) and in different sentence positions. Children could use intercorrelations among these contexts to create grammatical categories (Maratsos 1982). Formal analysis along these lines is assumed in all theories of syntax acquisition, and it has the last word in syntactic decisions even in theories that give semantics a starring role in early identification of syntactic categories. One example that makes clear the need for distributional analysis is that of gender categories of nouns. The distinction between masculine and feminine nouns, in languages that have it, is notorious for its lack of semantic basis, yet children learn it as they do other grammatical categories.

This procedure has its problems, of course. The contingencies so useful in differentiating grammatical categories are relationships between open-class categories like nouns and verbs, and the closed-class or function morphemes that co-occur with them. Without already knowing that contexts like *the* and *a* and affixed *-s* are important, children would have to look for these helpful correlations among an extremely large set of unhelpful ones. The computational intractability of this problem has prompted researchers to seek sources of constraint on the detection of distributional patterns. These include phonological and semantic cues to grammatical structure, as well as the architecture of learning mechanisms for distributional analysis.

Function morphemes, central to identifying grammatical categories, appear late in children's speech, but they influence children's comprehension much earlier. Even one-word speakers understand familiar nouns better when they are preceded by the determiner *the* rather than a misplaced function word (Gerken and McIntosh 1993). Computational analyses of speech to children suggest that distributional similarity can be used to sort words into major grammatical categories (Cartwright and Brent 1997, Mintz et al. 1995).

There have been some notable attempts to study the learning mechanisms involved in distributional analysis in toddlers or infants, and to explore the constraints on these mechanisms. Slobin 1985 proposes perceptual operating principles that bias children's hypotheses, including a bias to attend to the ends of words or utterances. Some studies focus on infants' ability to detect structure in small artificial languages (Gomez and Gerken 1999, Saffran et al. 1996). These artificial language-learning experiments are not presumed to approach the complexity of distributional analysis required to learn natural-language syntax; however, their findings establish that infants readily pick up distributional patterns in materials that have not yet been assigned any meaning.

3. Phonological cues. Sentences have prosodic or intonational structure as well as syntactic structure; prosody defines domains within which phonological processes operate. Major prosodic boundaries in speech tend to align with syntactic boundaries, so that syllables that end major constituents are often lengthened, undergo more pitch change, and are followed by longer pauses relative to syllables within phrases. The view known as "prosodic bootstrapping" suggests that acoustic cues associated with large-scale prosodic boundaries in speech constrain the child's syntactic hypotheses (Morgan and Demuth 1995). Considerable evidence suggests that prosody structures speech perception and memory for infants as well as adults.

Sound also participates in grammatical categorization via probabilistic phonological similarity within grammatical categories. One of the best examples is the enormous difference in duration, pitch accent, inventory of consonants, and token frequency between open-class words and closed-class or function words. A first-pass distinction between open- and closed-class words could be made based on this perceptible difference and could constrain distributional analysis. Grammatical categories like noun and verb also tend to share within-class phonological similarity. For example, English nouns and verbs differ in their distributions of syllable numbers (nouns tend to be longer) and in their stress patterns; gender classes of nouns share stable and useful phonological similarity.

4. Semantic cues. Another fundamental source of information for syntax acquisition is meaning. The value of semantics in grammatical categorization and phrase structure acquisition follows from the intimate relationship between form and meaning in language. Children have strong expectations about mappings between meaning and form. First, they assume that different forms have different meanings (Clark 1987); this applies both to individual words and to phrase-structure patterns. This simple assumption permits children to use within-class similarity in meaning to help sort words into grammatical categories and to draw semantic conclusions from distributional evidence for category membership. Second, there are more substantive correspondences between syntax and semantics. Across languages, nouns refer to objects or more abstract entities, while verbs and other terms have relational or predicative semantics. Such abstract links between form and meaning, to the extent that they are universal, could be part of the child's endowment for language acquisition: given knowledge of meaning, the child could draw syntactic inferences; given syntactic information, she could draw semantic conclusions.

One account based on this hypothesis is "semantic bootstrapping" (Pinker 1987), which proposes a detailed set of innate semantic triggers that link words with the elements of UG. On this view, object meanings trigger an internal category noun, linking particular object names with the role that nouns play in grammars. Certain predicate meanings trigger an internal category verb, spatial meanings trigger the category 'preposition' (or 'postposition'), and so on, for every grammatical category and phrase-structure configuration. On this theory, meaning constitutes a privileged source of information. Other views on the syntax-semantics interface suppose less detailed built-in links between meaning and syntax, to permit variation across languages. Not all languages have the same set of grammatical categories; thus, a set of semantic triggers that specifies all the grammatical categories needed for English is probably too specific.

5. The central role of verb learning. Learning large-scale syntactic categories like 'noun' and 'verb' is only part of the problem. The syntax of a clause depends on smaller subcategories within these abstract categories. In particular, the verb in a clause determines what other phrases can occur in the sentence, and what their roles in the sentence will be. To some degree, this is predictable from verb meaning. Across languages, verbs that describe action on an object tend to be transitive, with actor subjects; those that describe object motion along a path are often intransitive, with the moving theme as subject. Cross-linguistically, robust patterns in how verbs' arguments are linked with syntactic functions are reflected in various proposals for systematic linking of thematic roles (like agent and theme) and syntactic functions (like subject and object). Such links have played a major role in theories of syntax acquisition (Bloom 1991, Gleitman and Gleitman 1997, Pinker 1987).

The traditional approach to the role of verb learning in syntax acquisition has been essentially the semantic boot-strapping approach: if we assume that children can sometimes retrieve the semantics of sentences from extralinguistic context before learning the grammar, they could then use built-in links between semantics and syntax to impose syntactic structure on linguistic input. Knowing that a verb has an agent role in its semantic argument structure, for example, the child will conclude that the noun naming the agent is the subject of the sentence. By assuming that meaning is independently accessible and

that linguistic forms are semantically predictable, many acquisition theories make meaning the primary "boot-strap" into syntax.

The syntactic bootstrapping theory also relies on tight links between verb syntax and semantics to drive language acquisition, but it questions the primacy of semantic information. Lexical-semantic organization varies across languages; therefore, semantic representations are language-particular and cannot be assumed to be directly predictable from observations of events. Some words, in practice, are easy to grasp from context—when we hear the word *dog,* dogs are likely to be relevant. Verb and sentence meanings are more problematic. Even adults are poor at guessing what verb a parent is saying to a child from observation of the context alone, though they are much better at guessing the nouns, given the same kind of evidence (Gleitman and Gleitman 1997). The child's growing knowledge of syntax is proposed to fill this informational gap. Children assign different meanings to verbs presented in different syntactic contexts (Naigles 1990, Fisher 1996), even though they are used to describe the same scene. Simple aspects of sentence structure (the number of familiar nouns in the sentence, and their order) may provide some very early constraint on verb and sentence interpretation.

6. Integrating the cues. Which of the three classes of cues (distributional, phonological, semantic) is the primary source of data from which children create syntactic categories and structures? None is without difficulties. Distributional patterns are the sine qua non of syntax, and they are generally given the status of final arbiter in theories of syntax learning, but strings of morphemes are full of ambiguity. The English present-tense -*s* occurs with verbs (*she walks*), but the plural -*s* occurs with nouns (*two shoes*). Distributional analysis must be a protracted process of sorting out context-sensitive distributional patterns, heavily influenced by progress in morpheme segmentation and constrained by additional sources of information. Sound cues to grammatical phrase boundaries and categories are weak cues: prosodic boundaries are related to syntactic boundaries in complex ways, and the tendency for words within a grammatical category to have similar sound patterns is also limited. Meaning seems like a reliable cue, but gender categories of nouns must be acquired despite their lack of semantic predictability, and languages vary in how they map meanings onto grammatical categories. The picture that emerges from this is of a process of constrained distributional analysis over a multi-dimensional data set in which no single source of information can be relied on absolutely, and none can be ignored.

Commentators disagree on just how protracted this analysis process is. Many theories hold that abstraction is an early and robust property of children's linguistic analyses (Gomez and Gerken 1999, Pinker 1987), while others point out that children's skill at learning distributional facts about particular words makes it difficult to tell what level of knowledge underlies early word combinations (Pine et al. 1998, Tomasello 2000).

The process of learning which verbs occur with which sentence structures, like the acquisition of broader grammatical categories, shows the influence of multiple cues. Distributional analysis is important: observations of particular verbs in sentences provide information about their syntactic structures. Children also use semantic cues to predict that verbs whose meanings they know can occur in unattested sentence structures. These innovations are sometimes ungrammatical because they violate subcategorization facts for the verb, but they are semantically reasonable nonetheless. Even phonological information plays a role. For example, verbs that accept the dative alternation (*Mary gave a book to John*; *Mary gave John a book*) share semantic similarity, but they also tend to share the phonological property of having at most one metrical foot. This includes monosyllabic verbs like *give* and stress-initial bisyllabic verbs like *offer*, but not stress-final bisyllabic verbs like *explain*. These multiple sources of information, some obviously probabilistic and none clearly having the upper hand, give language acquisition its opportunistic, "bootstrapping" feel.

7. The contribution of the learner. The most striking evidence for the contribution of the learner to syntax acquisition comes from situations in which children receive impoverished linguistic input yet invent a syntax more systematic than the input should support. Children do not simply duplicate the input they receive. Instead, they regularize, imposing new structure on noisy data, or they invent from scratch communicative systems that exhibit properties of conventional languages.

Children whose profound hearing loss makes learning a spoken language impossible, and who are exposed to no sign-language model, invent "Home Sign" systems (Goldin-Meadow and Mylander 1998). Home signers create gestures that they combine into sentences. These sentences show signs of structure as found in established languages: signs glossed as verbs occur with predictable sets of noun-like arguments (*eat* has two arguments, *sleep* only one), and arguments appear in consistent positions.

The parents' gestures do not exhibit the same structure. Apparently, children need not learn that there exists a fundamental distinction between nouns (argument terms) and verbs (predicate terms)—for example, that a verb meaning 'eat' presupposes an eater and a thing eaten—or that the logical arguments of a verb can be specified by nouns in sentences. Such basic aspects of linguistic structure may follow from the structure of human knowledge and the pressures of human communication (Goldin-Meadow et al. 1996, Haiman 1985).

Children are also better syntax learners than adults. Adult learners of a first or second language honor morphological and syntactic regularities only probabilistically, but children who learn their native language from parents with a non-native command of it repair or "creolize" it, rather than accurately reproducing all the idiomatic irregularities of the input. One study examined the progress of a deaf child, Simon, whose only exposure to American Sign Language (ASL) was the inconsistent usage of his parents, late learners of ASL (Singleton and Newport, to appear). Simon regularized his parents' language, achieving a system that was more native-like than the input. Children and adults do not learn language in the same way: in failing to learn all the quirks in the input (though they certainly learn some), children create the analytic, regular syntactic, and morphological systems of human languages. The resilience of linguistic structure, despite variation in the input, tells us that fundamental aspects of syntax follow directly from the biases and constraints children bring to the task of learning and of communication.

[*See also* Psycholinguistics *and* Formal Grammar.]

BIBLIOGRAPHY

Bloom, Lois. 1991. *Language development from two to three.* New York: Cambridge University Press.

Cartwright, Timothy A., and Michael R. Brent. 1997. Syntactic categorization in early language acquisition: Formalizing the role of distributional analysis. *Cognition* 63.121–170.

Clark, Eve V. 1987. The principle of contrast: A constraint on language acquisition. In *Mechanisms of language acquisition*, edited by B. MacWhinney, pp. 1–33. Hillsdale, N.J.: Erlbaum.

Fisher, Cynthia. 1996. Structural limits on verb mapping: The role of analogy in children's interpretations of sentences. *Cognitive Psychology* 31.41–81.

Gerken, LouAnn, and Bonnie J. McIntosh. 1993. Interplay of function morphemes and prosody in early language. *Developmental Psychology* 29.448–457.

Gleitman, Lila R., and Henry Gleitman. 1997. What is language made out of? *Lingua* 100.29–55.

Goldin-Meadow, Susan, and Carolyn Mylander. 1998. Spontaneous sign systems created by deaf children in two cultures. *Nature* 291.279–281.

Goldin-Meadow, Susan, David McNeill, and Jenny Singleton. 1996. Silence is liberating: Removing the handcuffs on grammatical expression in the manual modality. *Psychological Review* 103.34–55.

Gomez, Rebecca, and LouAnn Gerken. 1999. Artificial grammar learning by 1-year-olds leads to specific and abstract knowledge. *Cognition* 70.109–135.

Haiman, John. 1985. *Iconicity in syntax.* Amsterdam: Benjamins.

Maratsos, Michael. 1982. The child's construction of grammatical categories. In *Language acquisition: The state of the art,* edited by E. Wanner and L. R. Gleitman, pp. 240–266. New York: Cambridge University Press.

Mintz, Toben H., Elissa L. Newport, and Thomas G. Bever. 1995. Distributional regularities of form class in speech to young children. In *Proceedings of NELS 25.* Amherst, Mass.: GLSA.

Morgan, James L., and Catherine Demuth. 1995. *Signal to syntax.* Hillsdale, N.J.: Erlbaum.

Naigles, Letitia. 1990. Children use syntax to learn verb meanings. *Journal of Child Language* 17.357–374.

Pine, Julian, Elena Lieven, and Caroline Rowland. 1998. Comparing different models of the development of the English verb category. *Linguistics* 36.807–830.

Pinker, Steven. 1987. The bootstrapping problem in language acquisition. In *Mechanisms of language acquisition,* edited by B. MacWhinney, pp. 399–441. Hillsdale, N.J.: Erlbaum.

Saffran, Jenny R., Richard N. Aslin, and Elissa L. Newport. 1996. Statistical learning by 8-month-old infants. *Science* 274.1926–1928.

Singleton, Jenny L., and Elissa L. Newport. To appear. When learners surpass their models: The acquisition of American Sign Language from inconsistent input. *Cognitive Psychology.*

Slobin, Daniel I. 1985. Crosslinguistic evidence for the language-making capacity. In *The crosslinguistic study of language acquisition,* edited by D. I. Slobin, vol. 1, pp. 1157–1256. Hillsdale, N.J.: Erlbaum.

Tomasello, Michael. 2000. Do young children have adult syntactic competence? *Cognition* 74.209–253.

CYNTHIA FISHER

Communicative Competence

The term "communicative competence" was coined by Dell Hymes in 1966 in a proposal to broaden the scope of knowledge and skills embodied in Noam Chomsky's definition of "linguistic competence" (Chomsky 1965). Hymes argued that speakers who were able to produce all the grammatical sentences of a language would be institutionalized if they went about trying to do so without consideration of appropriate contexts of use, and of the socially and culturally determined norms for production and interpretation. He augmented Chomsky's criterion of *systematic potential* (whether or not an utterance is a possible grammatical structure in a language) with knowledge of appropriateness (whether and to what extent a potential communicative form is suitable), occurrence (whether it is really enacted), and feasibility (whether it is possible under particular circumstances) (1974, 1987). Hymes's proposal was quickly adopted both by sociolinguists and by applied linguists in the field of foreign/second-language instruction: the requisite knowledge of speakers which must be accounted for includes not only rules for communication (both linguistic and sociolinguistic) and shared rules for interaction, but also the cultural roles and knowledge that are the basis for the context and content of communicative events and interaction processes. Communicative competence extends to both knowledge and expectation of who may or may not speak in certain settings, when to speak, how one may talk to persons of different statuses and rules, what nonverbal behaviors are appropriate in various contexts, what the routines for turn-taking are in conversation, how to ask for and give information, how to request, how to offer or decline assistance or cooperation, how to exercise power, and the like. For reference, see Gumperz 1984, Saville-Troike 1989.

Both the communicative knowledge and skills which may be attributed to a speech community and the communicative competence of individual speakers are highly variable constructs. First, as a collectivity, a speech community includes a range of language varieties and registers (and frequently even different languages), and it is very unlikely in a complex community that any single individual would be able to produce the full range of its available linguistic repertoire. Second, any one speaker has a variety of codes, styles, and registers from which to choose, and is not infrequently a member of more than one speech community—often to different degrees. For individuals who are members of multiple speech communities, which ones they orient themselves to at any given moment—which set of social and communicative rules they use—is part of the strategy of communication. Accounting for the nature of communicative competence thus "requires going beyond a concern with Language (capital L) or a language. It requires a focus on the ways in which communities, and persons, make use of a repertoire of languages (a focus pioneered by Charles

Ferguson). It requires a focus on the ways in which people do use language [. . .]" (Hymes 1993:13). Multilingual speakers' communicative competence includes knowledge of rules for the appropriate choice of language and for switching between languages, given a particular social context and communicative intent. Central to the concept is the notion that language is a social and cultural practice (Kramsch 1997). An extension has been made to "intercultural communicative competence," which requires an additional level of metacompetence involving explicit awareness of differential usages and ability to adapt communicative strategies to a variety of cultural situations (Kim 1991).

Among the most productive areas for application of this perspective has been the study of child language development, where it includes "discovery of how cultures themselves shape acquisition" (Hymes 1987:224; cf. Heath 1983, Ochs and Schieffelin 1995). In the field of foreign/second-language teaching, the concept has been applied to the development of "communicative approaches" to language teaching and testing (e.g. Savignon 1983); these have been widely accepted in most parts of the world.

[*See also* Discourse; Functional Linguistics; Psycholinguistics; *and* Sociolinguistics.]

BIBLIOGRAPHY

Chomsky, Noam. 1965. *Aspects of the theory of syntax*. Cambridge, Mass.: MIT Press.

Gumperz, John J. 1984. Communicative competence revisited. In *Meaning, form, and use in context: Linguistic applications* (Georgetown University Round Table on Languages and Linguistics, 1984), edited by Deborah Schiffrin, pp. 278–289. Washington, D.C.: Georgetown University Press.

Heath, Shirley Brice. 1983. *Ways with words: Language, life, and work in communities and classrooms*. Cambridge and New York: Cambridge University Press.

Hymes, Dell. 1974. *Foundations in sociolinguistics: An ethnographic approach*. Philadelphia: University of Pennsylvania Press.

Hymes, Dell. 1987. Communicative competence. In *Sociolinguistics: An international handbook of the science of language and society*, edited by Ulrich Ammon et al., pp. 219–229. Berlin: Mouton de Gruyter.

Hymes, Dell. 1993. Anthropological linguistics: A retrospective. *Anthropological Linguistics* 35.9–14.

Kim, Young Yun. 1991. Intercultural communicative competence: A systems-theoretic view. In *Cross-cultural interpersonal communication*, edited by Stella Ting-Toomey and Felipe Korzenny, pp. 259–275. Newbury Park, Calif.: Sage.

Kramsch, Claire. 1997. The privilege of the nonnative speaker. *PMLA* 112(3).359–369.

Ochs, Elinor, and Bambi B. Schieffelin. 1995. The impact of language socialization on grammatical development. In *The Handbook of Child Language*, edited by Paul Fletcher and Brian MacWhinney, pp. 73–94. Oxford: Blackwell.

Savignon, Sandra. 1983. *Communicative competence: Theory and classroom practice*. Reading, Mass.: Addison-Wesley.

Saville-Troike, Muriel. 1989. *The ethnography of communication*. 2d ed. (Language in society, 3.) Oxford: Blackwell.

MURIEL SAVILLE-TROIKE

Meanings and Forms

Language in children first emerges at around one year of age, when they begin to understand and produce their first words. At this point, they often express a range of meanings for which they have no words. They rely on gestures (pointing, reaching, miming actions) and combine these with vocalizations to indicate what they want or are interested in. As they come to segment the speech stream and identify word- and phrase-sized units, they begin to make use of some linguistic forms themselves, but their meanings for words and phrases, like their early pronunciations, often diverge from those of adults. Working out which meanings go with which forms is a lengthy task; the acquisition of meaning is intimately linked to the acquisition of morphological and syntactic forms as well. The major problem children face is how to assign to each form the meaning it conventionally carries in the speech community. They have to make inferences in context, relying on joint attention, physical co-presence, and conversational co-presence, to assign a preliminary meaning. They then test their hypotheses about meanings and revise them when necessary. Research has focused on the cognitive and social sources of children's hypotheses about meanings, and on the stages they go through as they learn more about the adult meanings.

The meanings children adopt are offered by adults in child-directed speech. Parents and caregivers offer words (*This is an owl*, *Look at the otter*) and relations between words (*An otter is a kind of animal*, *Ducks are birds*). They also offer children different perspectives on the same objects or events (*the spaniel* vs. *the dog* vs. *your pet*; *Give Jay the ball* vs. *Let Jay have the ball* vs. *Now Jay wants the ball*). Children take up these adult offers that license specific inferences in context about possible meanings. With joint attention, physical co-presence, and conversational co-presence as general guides, children can assign initial meanings that they can refine with subsequent exposures to adult usage. Along the way, however, they may make errors that reveal which inferences they have made so far, and how close their meanings are to the adult ones. Children also make errors in the forms of their first language. They over-regularize inflectional and derivational endings; they over-extend syntactic patterns; and they impose regularity in the shape of paradigms, where the language around them is irregular. Here research has focused on two problems: first, how children master conventional but irregular forms of the language, and second, how children get rid of regularized forms which they themselves have constructed. The first problem has received more attention than the second, and the kinds of over-regularization that children come up with are well-documented for a variety of languages. Less is known about how and why children get rid of early regularizations and other errors.

In acquisition, meaning and form must be taken together; one cannot be acquired without the other. But researchers have sometimes focused on a single aspect, without considering the necessary coordination between the two. Data from a variety of languages (Slobin 1995) suggest that all children start their acquisition of meaning and form in much the same way. Whether they continue on the same route, as they learn more complex meanings and forms, depends on how similar languages are—and on how many possible routes children may find, as they move toward an adult-like mastery of a language.

1. Lexical meanings. Children's earliest lexical meanings emerge with their first words, and often diverge from adult meanings for the same words (Clark, 2002). Children may over-extend a word beyond its adult meaning, e.g. using *dog* for horses and sheep as well as dogs; or they may under-extend a word, e.g. using *shoe* only for laced shoes being worn on the feet, but not for shoes of other types or in other places. They may use a word so that its meaning overlaps with, but does not coincide with, the adult's meaning—as when *horse* is used for riding horses and is extended to donkeys and zebras, but is not used for cart-horses. Finally, children's earliest meanings may be complete mismatches and fail to overlap at all with adult meanings.

However, production does not necessarily match comprehension. Children who produce *dog* for four-legged mammals other than dogs typically understand that *dog,* when heard from others, denotes only dogs and not other kinds of animals. Over-extensions in production, therefore, probably reflect a communicative strategy for talking about things, prior to mastery of the relevant labels. As children learn to produce their first hundred words, they may over-extend up to 40% of them. Under-

extensions and overlaps are harder to document; however, they may be even more pervasive in children's meanings, during a longer period, than over-extensions. The latter become rare by the age of 2;0 (i.e. 2 years, 0 months) to 2;6. Most observations about early meanings have come from diary studies of language production; however, researchers have also examined some sources of children's hypotheses about word-meanings by looking systematically at how children understand words, as well as when they produce them.

The stages in children's acquisition of word-meanings, in specific semantic domains, have been studied in some detail. Children's earliest hypotheses about word-meanings are often based on general conceptual knowledge about relevant domains. Thus, in the acquisition of locative terms, children appear to rely on two general (non-linguistic) strategies for coping with instructions using words like *in, on,* and *under.* The first, "Put X inside," applies to any locations that are containers; the second, "Put X on top," to places that are not containers. Children's attention to containers and supporting surfaces, in other words, provides their first hypotheses about the locative relations that words encode. Later, these interpretations become more specific, as they work out the contrasts in meaning offered by the words they hear in context: *in* and *on,* or *on* and *above* or *under.*

The coping strategies children rely on in the earliest stages of assigning meanings to unfamiliar words have been traced for a variety of locative terms (e.g. *in, on, up, down, under*), kinship terms (*mother, uncle, cousin, grandfather, daughter*), verbs of possession (*give, take, trade, buy, sell*), verbs of speaking (*ask, tell*), verbs of motion, and deictic terms (*I, here, that, go, bring*). As children add to their initial meanings, the errors they make change until their usage parallels that of adults. There has also been some research on how children build up taxonomies of terms in a hierarchy, for such domains as animals (e.g. *animal, dog, collie*); here we find little consistency in whether a superordinate like *animal* appears before or after a subordinate like *collie,* although terms at the generic or basic level (e.g. *dog*) typically enter first. Otherwise, the level of the earliest terms acquired appears to depend on their immediate usefulness to the young child. For instance, the lower-level *apple* and *orange* will be more useful than *fruit;* but higher-level *bug* will be more useful than *stag-beetle* or *aphid,* and *tree* more useful than *oak* or *elm.*

2. Word combinations. In their earliest word combinations, children talk about roles (e.g. agent, location, recipient) and actions in events. However, these early constructions appear to be lexically specific: they produce definite articles only with certain nouns; they combine certain verbs and nouns, but use only a small set of such combinations for several weeks or months. They take time to realize that one verb can occur with a large range of different nouns to denote objects-affected, that an article can precede almost every noun, or that an auxiliary verb can occur with many main verbs. They appear to build up constructions very slowly, word by word, as they hear more instances in child-directed speech.

Children just beginning to combine words show little evidence of marking such grammatical relations as "subject of" or "direct object of." The two-word combinations observable in children acquiring different languages appear similar in meaning; however, not all children try the same kinds of combinations prior to acquisition of morphological marking or of word order to signal grammatical relations (Brown 1973). A number of studies suggest that the earliest uses of word order in production are actually to signal new information, as opposed to information already given in the conversation or the nonlinguistic context. Only later, in languages where word order has a grammatical function, do children learn that too. Meanings attributable to structures emerge in production somewhat later than those attached to individual words in noun phrases, verb phrases, or prepositional phrases.

As their word combinations become longer, children fill out more of their phrases—adding articles, quantifiers, adjectives, prepositions, and other indicators of grammatical functions. They also begin to produce relative clauses, adverbial phrases and clauses, and complements; all these may require use of both word order and grammatical morphemes to mark structural relations among linguistic units (Clark, 2002, Maratsos 1983, Wanner and Gleitman 1982).

3. Grammatical morphemes. The affixes or free morphemes that mark grammatical relations among words begin to emerge during the first year of speech. In English, the first grammatical morphemes produced by children include aspectual *-ing*, plural *-s*, and past tense *-ed*. Later acquisitions are the articles *a* and *the*, the copula verb *be*, prepositions, and complementizers (e.g. *to, for, that*). In general, regular systems with few exceptions are mastered faster than systems with numerous small paradigms (cf. Turkish and Russian), or several genders marked by different affixes (cf. German and English). It also takes time to master the affixes for agreement in gender and number for noun and article, noun and adjective, or noun and verb combinations.

When children acquire inflections—whether for case, number, gender, person, tense, or aspect—they regularize the system. They typically choose the paradigm with the largest number of members (types, not tokens) and use it as a model for other nouns or verbs. In English, children regularize the past tense of irregular verbs like *see, buy, go* to produce *seed, buyed, goed*. In French, they regularize irregular verbs in *-ir* or *-re* to the *-er* paradigm, as in the past participles *couré* (for *couru* 'ran' < *courir* 'to run'), *metté* (for *mis* < *mettre* 'to put'), or *mordé* (for *mordu* < *mordre* 'to bite'). Where children have to choose among different affixes that, for instance, all mark the same case but are used with nouns of different gender, they often choose a single form for that meaning. Thus, in Russian, children at this stage produce *-om* for the instrumental on all nouns—masculine, feminine, and neuter.

The overall pattern of acquisition for grammatical morphemes falls into four stages. After an initial period of no use, one finds sporadic use of irregular forms, followed by early uses of regular forms; then comes a flood of regularizations that are gradually replaced by appropriate irregular forms. A major theoretical question here is how children come to replace *bringed*, say, by *brought*, or *foots* by *feet*. The same question applies to children's over-regularizations of syntactic patterns, as in such forms as *Don't say me that* (for *Don't say that to me*), or *Can I fill some salt into the bear?* (for *fill the bear with salt*) (MacWhinney 1987).

4. Word formation. The same question arises in the domain of word formation. Here too, children regularize irregular forms to fit their paradigms. They construct nouns for agents (e.g. *cooker* for *a cook*), for instruments (*driller* for *a drill*) and for states (*longness* for *length*). They often construct compound nouns; but in the early stage, they fail to do so appropriately (*open-man, open-door*, or *opener-door*, all for *door-opener*). And they also coin verbs—from nouns (e.g *to broom* for *to sweep*), from adjectives (*to dark* for *to darken*), and from prepositions (*to up* for *to raise*). In each case, some formations are pre-empted by existing words, and children have to learn that those meanings are conventionally expressed by other established forms.

5. Social meaning. Meaning in language derives from the senses associated with specific words and the constructions in which those words appear. Further meaning is added by the uses to which speakers put words and constructions—the conventions associated with particular forms within a social group. In most languages, speakers mark differences in status, power, and sex in their choices of address terms, words, and constructions. English-speaking children by age four or five know some of these conventions and differentiate among addressees by using imperatives (*Give me that ball*) or direct demands (*I want that ball*) for lower status, but hints (*It is fun to play with balls, isn't it?*) for higher status (Andersen 1990). Children may take several years to acquire the words and constructions involved and to know when to use which form, and to whom.

6. Meaning and form. Children make inferences about possible meanings and then build on these, adding or deleting details as they test their initial hypotheses by using words with the meanings they have assigned. When their uses match adult ones, their hypotheses are supported; when they do not, children must refine or change their hypotheses. One way to track these developments in meaning acquisition is to examine consistent errors, which provide clues to the meanings children have assigned to specific forms; changes in their errors mark the path being followed in development. Consistency in these errors also helps to identify general strategies of acquisition, whether for analyzing units of meaning and form in comprehension or for combining such elements in production. Similarities in children's initial coping strategies and in their uptake of pragmatic inferences about meanings (licensed by adult usage) help to identify the general learning mechanisms children bring to language. Tracking children's errors, along with what they tend to get right, is critical in finding what is universal across languages and in modeling the process of acquisition (Elman et al. 1996, MacWhinney 1999).

Research on the general process of acquisition—on what is general, and what is shaped by the structure of specific languages—contributes essential information to the puzzle of what to count as universal across languages. The study of language acquisition offers insight into the learning of complex systems and raises new questions about the kinds of models that will account adequately for both what and how children learn as they acquire a first language.

[*See also* Functional Linguistics; Learnability; Lexicon; Psycholinguistics; *and* Semantics.]

BIBLIOGRAPHY

Andersen, Elaine S. 1990. *Speaking with style.* London: Routledge.

Brown, Roger. 1973. *A first language: The early stages.* Cambridge, Mass.: Harvard University Press.

Clark, Eve V. 2002. *First language acquisition.* Cambridge: Cambridge University Press.

Elman, Jeffrey L., et al. 1996. *Rethinking innateness.* Cambridge, Mass.: MIT Press.

MacWhinney, Brian, ed. 1987. *Mechanisms of language acquisition.* Hillsdale, N.J.: Erlbaum.

MacWhinney, Brian, ed. 1999. *The emergence of language.* Mahwah, N.J.: Erlbaum.

Maratsos, Michael. 1983. Some current issues in the study of the acquisition of grammar. In *Handbook of child psychology,* vol. 3, *Cognitive development,* edited by John H. Flavell and Ellen M. Markman, pp. 707–786. New York: Wiley.

Slobin, Dan I., ed. 1995. *The cross-linguistic study of language acquisition.* 2 vols. 3rd ed. Hillsdale, N.J.: Erlbaum.

Wanner, Eric, and Lila R. Gleitman, eds. 1982. *Language acquisition: The state of the art.* Cambridge and New York: Cambridge University Press.

EVE V. CLARK

Critical Periods

In many domains and species, evolutionarily significant behaviors—for example, the acquisition of the species-typical mating song in finches and sparrows—develop partly through innate predispositions and are partly shaped by experience. In many of these systems, the effects of experience are limited to a *critical* or *sensitive period.*

A critical or sensitive period for learning is present when there is a relationship between the age (more technically, the developmental state of the organism) at which the crucial experience is presented to the organism and the amount of learning that results. In most such cases, the privileged time for learning is during early development, but this is not necessary (bonding in sheep occurs immediately surrounding parturition). The important feature is that there is a peak period of *plasticity,* occurring at some maturationally defined time in development, followed by reduced plasticity later in life. This contrasts with the presence in other systems of plasticity uniformly throughout life (open-ended learning), or an increase with age as experience or higher-level cognitive skills increase. The term "critical period" is sometimes used when there is an abrupt decline in plasticity and no residual plasticity after this period is over, whereas the term "sensitive period" is used when there is a more gradual decline, with some reduced plasticity remaining throughout life. However, most critical periods show more gradual offsets and more complex interactions between maturation and experiential factors than was implied by the original concept of a critical period, so the two terms are often used interchangeably.

1. Evidence of a critical or sensitive period for language. Lenneberg 1967 suggested that there is a critical period for human language acquisition, extending from birth to puberty. Within this period, language acquisition occurs as a result of ordinary exposure to a linguistic community; after this period, Lenneberg suggested, it occurs only with difficulty, and perhaps through different mechanisms than those used early in life. His evidence included the better speech outcome for deaf children with early hearing, and the improved recovery from aphasia when brain damage occurs during childhood. He also proposed a mechanism for this age effect that involves the maturation of lateralization. Since then, some of his evidence and his hypothesized mechanism have been questioned, but an extensive behavioral and neurobiological literature has suggested that there is indeed a change in language learning over age for both first- and second-language acquisition.

Case studies of feral or abused children who were isolated from exposure to their first language until after puberty (Curtiss 1977) show that they have extreme deficits in phonology, morphology, and syntax; however, the physical and cognitive status of such children may be a concern. Studies of populations of normal individuals permit one systematically to examine proficiency in relation to age of language exposure without concern for the physical status of the learning brain. These studies also show a strong relationship between the age of exposure to a language and the ultimate proficiency achieved in that language (Johnson and Newport 1989, Krashen et al. 1982, Long 1990, Newport 1990), though adult learners exhibit much less extreme deficits than do isolated children. Adult language-learners have an advantage in learning during the first months or year of exposure, but long-term outcome is clearly better for those who start learning during childhood. Peak proficiency, in control over the sound system and of grammatical structure, is displayed by those whose exposure to the language began in infancy or very early childhood. Increasing age of exposure results in a decline in average proficiency, beginning as early as ages four to six and continuing until proficiency reaches a plateau for adult learners (Johnson and Newport 1989, Newport 1990). However, individual variation also increases with age (Johnson and Newport 1989), and some late-learning individuals may approach the proficiency of early learners (Birdsong 1992).

These effects have been shown for both first and second languages, for both spoken and signed languages, and for measures of proficiency including degree of accent, production and comprehension of morphology and syntax, grammaticality judgments for morphology and syntax, and syntactic processing speed and accuracy. For example, Johnson and Newport 1989 have shown that Chinese or Korean immigrants who move to the United States and become exposed to English as a second language show strong effects of their age of exposure to the language on their ability to judge its grammatical structure many years later, even when the subjects are matched in the number of years of exposure. These effects are not due merely to interference from the first language: deaf adults who acquired American Sign Language as their primary language show effects of age of exposure on their grammatical skills in ASL as much as fifty years later, even though they may not control any other language with great proficiency (Newport 1990).

Age of exposure does not affect all aspects of language learning equally: acquisition of vocabulary and semantic processing occurs relatively normally in late learners. Critical-period effects thus appear to focus on the formal properties of language. Even among these, however, late learners acquire the basic word order of a language relatively well, while more complex aspects of grammar show stronger effects of late acquisition (Johnson and Newport 1989, Newport 1990). Further research is needed to characterize the structures most affected by age of learning.

Age of exposure also affects how language is represented in the brain, with similarities between the behavioral and neural results. PET, fMRI, and ERP studies all indicate strong left hemisphere activation for the first language in bilinguals; however, when second languages have been learned late (after seven years), the regions and patterns of activation are partially or completely non-overlapping with those for the first language. Neural organization for late-learned languages tends to be less lateralized and, like proficiency, varies considerably across individuals. The few available studies of early bilinguals or highly proficient late bilinguals report congruent results for first and second languages (Kim et al. 1997, Perani et al. 1996, 1998). As in behavior, age of acquisition has more pronounced effects on grammatical processing and its representation in the brain than on semantic processing (Weber-Fox and Neville 1996).

Taken together, these results provide fairly strong evidence for a critical or sensitive period in acquiring the phonological and grammatical patterns of the language and in organizing the neural mechanisms for handling these structures efficiently.

2. Age effects arise from a critical period? Do these age effects represent the outcome of a critical or sensitive period, or do they arise from variables correlated with age but not with maturation (Birdsong 1999)? Some investigators have argued that, to support a critical period hypothesis, age effects must coincide with puberty (though neural maturation continues through the late teens and does not cease at age twelve to thirteen). Others have suggested that, if there were a critical or sensitive period, no adult learners should achieve native proficiency (though sensitive periods in other species do show individual variation in adult plasticity). Finally, investigators have noted that it is difficult to distinguish a critical period from an interference effect (similar points have been made in discussions of interference in imprinting).

However, these strong or absolute characteristics are not true of critical or sensitive periods in other behavioral domains, most of which involve gradual declines in learning, with mature organisms retaining some (reduced, but not absent) ability to learn. If such complex phenomena are found within critical periods in other domains, they should also be expected for language learning.

[*See also* Evolution and Language; Formal Grammar; Learnability; Neurolinguistics; *and* Psycholinguistics.]

BIBLIOGRAPHY

Birdsong, David, ed. 1999. *Second language acquisition and the critical period hypothesis.* Mahwah, N.J.: Lawrence Erlbaum.

Curtiss, Susan. 1977. *Genie: A psycholinguistic study of a modern-day "wild child."* New York: Academic Press.

Johnson, Jacqueline S., and Elissa L. Newport. 1989. Critical period effects in second language learning: The influence of maturational state on the acquisition of English as a second language. *Cognitive Psychology* 21.60–99.

Kim, K. H. S., N. R. Relkin, K.-M. Lee, and J. Hirsch. 1997. Distinct cortical areas associated with native and second languages. *Nature* 388.171–174.

Krashen, S. D., Michael H. Long, and R. C. Scarcella. 1982. Age, rate, and eventual attainment in second language acquisition. In *Child–adult differences in second language acquisition*, edited by S. D. Krashen et al., pp. 161–172. Rowley, Mass.: Newbury House.

Lenneberg, Eric H. 1967. *Biological foundations of language.* New York: Wiley.

Long, Michael H. 1990. Maturational constraints on language development. *Studies in Second Language Acquisition* 12.251–285.

Newport, Elissa L. 1990. Maturational constraints on language learning. *Cognitive Science* 14.11–28.

Perani, D., S. Dehaene, F. Grassi, L. Cohen, S. F. Cappa, E. Dupoux, F. Fazio, and Jacques Mehler. 1996. Brain processing of native and foreign languages. *Neuroreport* 7.2439–2444.

Perani, D., E. Paulesu, N. S. Galles, E. Dupoux, S. Dehaene, V. Bettinardi, S. F. Cappa, F. Fazio, and Jacques Mehler.

1998. The bilingual brain: Proficiency and age of acquisition of the second language. *Brain* 121.1841–1852.

Weber-Fox, Christine, and Helen J. Neville. 1996. Maturational constraints on functional specializations for language processing: ERP and behavioral evidence in bilingual speakers. *Journal of Cognitive Neuroscience* 8.231–256.

ELISSA L. NEWPORT

Second-Language Acquisition

The study of S[econd-]L[anguage] A[cquisition] is a broad, interdisciplinary field of inquiry which aims to describe and explain the development and non-development of languages and language varieties beyond the first language. SLA researchers study children and adults learning naturalistically or with the aid of formal instruction, as individuals or in groups, and in foreign, second-language, and lingua franca settings. The research draws upon and contributes to knowledge and procedures in a variety of disciplines, including theoretical linguistics, neurolinguistics, psycholinguistics, sociolinguistics, historical linguistics, pidgin/creole studies, applied linguistics, psychology, sociology, anthropology, and education. SLA research findings are used to test hypotheses and build theories in those areas, as well as for a variety of practical purposes such as the improvement of language teaching, language testing, teacher education, and the design of instructional programs delivered through the medium of a second language or dialect (Larsen-Freeman and Long 1990).

The conditions producing SLA are diverse. It can result, for example, from simultaneous or sequential bilingual or multilingual exposure in infancy—as in the case of children born to parents with different first languages (L1s) who use them in the home and who may also live in a country where a third language is spoken. It is sometimes the product of either forced or voluntary educational experience, including submersion, immersion, bilingual education, foreign-language teaching, and other school, university, or vocational programs in which a second language (L2) is the medium or object of instruction. It can follow informal exposure to languages later in life, as with millions of migrant workers, refugees, and tourists. Finally, it is a routine experience for a substantial part of the world's population who live in multilingual societies.

While the SLA phenomenon is widespread, many aspects of the process itself remain something of a mystery. Only severely subnormal children fail to develop a high degree of proficiency in their native language; but relatively few people, however intelligent and motivated, reach such high standards in a second or third language, especially if they are first exposed to the additional language as adults. Is it that unsuccessful older learners simply do not learn as much as cognitively less developed children? Or is it that they cannot learn as much, or in the same way? Part of their *interlanguage* often appears to stabilize, or cease to develop, far short of a communicatively adequate and/or socially acceptable level. Sometimes, it is claimed, the stabilization is permanent, in which case it is referred to as *fossilization*, but the evidence for fossilization is sparse (Long, 2003).

Various explanations have been proposed for the heterogeneous achievement of SL learners, for both success and failure. Some researchers believe that development of both L1 and L2 is maturationally constrained, and that biological (usually neurophysiological) changes progressively diminish the older learner's capacity to learn—i.e., that there are one or more sensitive periods for SLA (Hyltenstam and Abrahamsson, 2003; Scovel 1988). Others hold that psychological and social factors, such as attitude, motivation, and social distance—or, collectively, the degree to which someone acculturates to the target language group—determine success and failure (Schumann 1978, Andersen 1983, Robinson 2001). Still others claim that learning depends on the degree of access to universal grammar (White, 2003), to innate general cognitive mechanisms (O'Grady, 2003), or to input and/or conversational opportunities, particularly access to comprehensible L2 samples from which the grammatical rules of the L2 can be induced (Hatch 1983, Krashen 1985). While all these variables may be relevant in some cases, counter-evidence exists to each as a single-factor explanation, and no one theory enjoys wide acceptance.

While unresolved issues abound, a good deal has been discovered about SLA through a relatively recent but steady empirical tradition (Spolsky 1989). To begin with, learner language is quite variable. Part of the variability is systematic, i.e. rule-governed, such that a learner may use alternate forms according to linguistic environment, situation, task, degree of planning, attention to speech, etc. For example, reflecting variation in linguistic context, learners initially tend to use the English regular past tense marker *-ed* and plural *-s* only on certain verbs and nouns, and to omit the forms elsewhere. They do so in a fairly predictable manner. However, part of the variability is non-systematic, or free. Thus learners may temporarily alternate between two verb forms or two negators (e.g. *No have* and *Don't have*) in an apparently arbitrary fashion, before gradually assigning different functions to the two items; at that point the variability begins to become systematic (Ellis 1994, Huebner 1983).

As in other kinds of language change, variation in interlanguage (IL) at one point in time often reflects developmental change over time (Preston 1996). This is one reason why the documented variability of ILs is not inconsistent with another of their well established qualities, namely systematicity. Some of the early research demonstrating this was inspired by work on L1 development. Thus, in longitudinal and cross-sectional studies, L1 researchers in the early 1970s discovered a common order of appearance for a set of grammatical morphemes 90 percent accurately supplied, in the speech of children learning English as L1, in obligatory contexts (linguistic environments where omission of the morphemes would result in ungrammaticality). The finding was quickly replicated for *E[nglish as a] S[econd] L[anguage]*—where, although not invariant, a common accuracy order (slightly different from the L1 order) was established for the elicited and spontaneous speech of children and adults, with or without formal instruction, and most interestingly, from a variety of L1 backgrounds. The following nine items, for example, were repeatedly found to reach 80 or 90 percent accurate suppliance in ESL in approximately this order: *-ing,* plural, copula, auxiliary, article, irregular past, regular past, 3sg. *-s,* and possessive *-'s.* Small but clear effects were observed for L1 differences, such as the later development of accuracy in articles by Japanese learners (with no articles in their L1); however, these were too rare to alter the sequence to any statistically significant degree.

Explanations for the L1 and L2 orders were elusive. Researchers found no consistent relationship to the syntactic and/or semantic complexity of the grammatical items concerned, their markedness, their perceptual saliency or, in the L2 case, their position in an instructional sequence. A combination of factors was probably at work. Accuracy orders did often correlate significantly with input frequency; however, input alone clearly could not account for the data—given that, among other problems, articles were always the most frequent item in English input, but reached criterion (in the sense of accurate suppliance) relatively late in the learner output.

While the morpheme studies were criticized methodologically, and the orders themselves remain in need of explanation, both L1 and L2 findings were usually ac-

TABLE 1. *Emergence of Negation*

Stage	Sample	Utterances
(1)	*No* + X	*No is cheap.*
		No you give him.
(2)	*no/not/don't* + V	*He not living here.*
		They don't have.
(3)	AUX + NEG	*I can't sing.*
		You mustn't go.
(4)	analyzed *don't*	*I didn't tell him.*
		She doesn't play.

cepted as demonstrating a role for powerful internal factors in the acquisition process—or, as was sometimes said, of an internal learner syllabus. This was an interpretation consistent with nativist theories in linguistics. Noam Chomsky's claims about acquisition, for example, would predict that an order would exist, although not the specific orders observed. As critics pointed out, the L1 and L2 findings pertained to a theoretically unmotivated miscellany of linguistically unrelated items, which, because language-specific, also revealed little about SLA in general.

While the accuracy orders were perhaps marginal with respect to nativist claims, providing only language-specific evidence, they certainly posed problems for neo-behaviorist models of language learning, and in SLA also for the *C[ontrastive] A[nalysis] H[ypothesis]*. This had claimed that differences between L1 and L2 led to difficulty in SLA, and governed the course of acquisition. Coupled with neo-behaviorist learning theory, the CAH had motivated the audio-lingual method of language teaching and its many variants, whose practitioners set out to eradicate L1 language "habits" and to inculcate new ones in learners through intensive drill work in areas of contrast between the L1 and the L2.

Strong independent evidence against the CAH, for systematicity in IL, and for a major learner contribution to SLA, was provided by work on so-called *developmental sequences* in IL, such as those for ESL negation and interrogatives, ESL and Swedish SL relative clauses, and German word order. Developmental sequences are fixed series of overlapping stages, each identified by the relative frequency and/or order of emergence of an interim IL structure, which learners must traverse in the acquisition of a target construction or rule system. Numerous studies have shown, for example, that ESL negation has a four-stage sequence, as shown in Table 1.

If only, say, Spanish speakers (whose L1 has pre-verbal

negation) produced pre-verbally negated constructions at stages (1) and (2), then L1 transfer could explain that aspect of the sequence. But in fact, all SL learners, whether naturalistic or instructed, initially produce pre-verbal negation—including Japanese speakers, whose L1 system is post-verbal. Turkish speakers begin Swedish SL negation that way, too, even though both L1 and L2 are post-verbal.

Why developmental sequences look the way they do is still unclear. It is difficult to untangle the effects of several forces which often converge on the same construction (Johnston 1997). In the early stages of many sequences, when the learner's linguistic resources in the L2 are limited, processing constraints are presumably at least partially responsible (Clahsen et al. 1982, Pienemann 1998). The need to reduce redundancy and discontinuity for ease of production and comprehension favors one simple, fixed word order, rather than more complex, variable orders (e.g. with the verb phrase interrupted by the negator). Language universals and typological markedness also seem to be at work (Rutherford 1984), since pre-verbal position is the most preferred (least marked) for negators in natural languages—including early child language, pidgins, creoles, ungrammatical foreigner talk (*No drink water!*), and highly conventionalized formulas (*No can do, Long time no see*).

There is clearly a danger of circularity in attempting to explain developmental IL constructions and sequences by appeals to universals and markedness, while simultaneously using the IL data to establish the universals and markedness relationships. Further, cognitive factors like processing constraints may themselves be causal where universals are concerned, in that some linguistic universals may be a function of universal processing constraints. However, the fact that several studies have found six stages in the development of Swedish SL and ESL relative clauses, corresponding to those predictable from Keenan and Comrie's 1977 noun phrase accessibility hierarchy, suggests that ILs tend to develop in ways consistent with typological universals, whatever gives rise to the universals in the first place (Eckman 1996). Some studies even find learners accepting and producing pronominal copies on grammaticality judgment and elicited production tasks (e.g. *Number seven is the woman who she is holding the child*), when neither their L1 nor the L2 (e.g. Italian and English) permit copies in any kind of relative clause. Results like these not only support the idea that ILs are responsive to language universals, but also that they are to some degree autonomous linguistic systems, not simply relexified versions of the L1 or poor approximations to the L2 (Davies et al. 1984).

Despite the striking commonality of the stages in developmental sequences, as with morpheme accuracy orders, local effects for L1 can be seen (Gass and Selinker 1992, Kellerman and Sharwood Smith 1986). Studies show that, while the order of basic stages in sequences appears to be immutable, L1 differences sometimes result in additional sub-stages, and also in swifter or slower passage through stages. L1 influence seems most likely at points in a sequence when an IL form is similar to an L1 structure. German learners of ESL, for example, sometimes follow their L1 pattern in producing utterances with the negator after the main verb (*David plays not soccer very good*), when they correctly begin to place it after the auxiliary. Likewise, speakers of languages like Spanish with pre-verbal negation in their L1 are slower to relinquish this as an IL strategy than speakers of languages like Japanese which do not have pre-verbal systems—presumably they perceive a similarity between their L1 systems and the pre-verbal negation of IL stages (1) and (2).

As indicated by these findings, the role of the L1 in SLA is far more complex than originally believed. To begin with, not just differences but also similarities between languages can cause learners difficulty. However, structural identity between L1 and L2 idioms, lexis, and syntax (but probably not phonology) does not necessarily result in transfer, as shown for example by adult Dutch learners' reluctance to transfer correct Dutch uses of the verb *break* into English (e.g. *His voice broke* and *She broke the world record*) if their L1 usages seem to them to be too idiomatic to be likely to occur in the L2. When the structure of the L1 does influence SLA, it generally operates in harmony with what appear to be natural developmental processes—as revealed by the findings on developmental sequences, which show them to be modified but not fundamentally altered by transfer. L1 influences also appear to be constrained by various kinds of linguistic markedness. In general, typologically unmarked L1 forms are more likely to be transferred than marked ones, unless the corresponding L2 form is also marked; however, beginners seem more willing to transfer both marked and unmarked forms. There is some evidence that learning difficulty arises only from L1/L2 differences involving greater L2 markedness, with degree of difficulty reflecting degree of markedness.

Many of the findings described briefly here suggest a more important role for classroom language learners than they have traditionally been accorded (Hyltenstam and Pienemann 1985, Chaudron 1988). Errors are largely beyond the teacher's control; they are inevitable and often a sign of progress, indicating formation of interim IL rules. They also show, if evidence were still needed, that SLA is not simply a process of habit formation. Acquisition sequences do not reflect instructional sequences; learning difficulty is a function of several factors, not just L1/L2 differences, some of them as yet rather poorly understood by researchers and teachers. Finally, learners do not pass from zero to full knowledge of a target construction in one step, although many syllabuses, textbooks, and teachers (and some SLA researchers) implicitly assume that they do—presenting one native-speaker structure at a time and practicing it, followed by another, in building-block fashion.

Formal instruction is still very valuable, however. Other SLA research is beginning to show that, while developmental sequences are unaffected, at least a periodic focus on language as object, or form, does have important benefits (Doughty and Williams 1998, Norris and Ortega 2000). It increases the rate of development. It appears to sensitize learners to communicatively redundant language forms—as evidenced by instructed learners' initial overuse of certain grammatical morphology, compared with naturalistic acquirers' greater tendency to delete those items. Finally, it may also raise the level of ultimate attainment where marked, low-frequency, or perceptually non-salient L2 structures are concerned. These are three of the areas otherwise particularly susceptible to premature stabilization.

[*See also* Bilingualism and Multilingualism; Interlanguage; Neurolinguistics; Psycholinguistics; *and* Sociolinguistics.]

BIBLIOGRAPHY

Andersen, Roger W., ed. 1983. *Pidginization and creolization as language acquisition*. Rowley, Mass.: Newbury House.

Chaudron, Craig. 1988. *Second language classrooms: Research on teaching and learning*. Cambridge and New York: Cambridge University Press.

Clahsen, Harald, Jürgen M. Meisel, and Manfred Pienemann. 1982. *Deutsch als Zweitsprache: Der Spracherwerb ausländischer Arbeiter*. Tübingen: Narr.

Davies, Alan, et al., eds. 1984. *Interlanguage*. Edinburgh: Edinburgh University Press.

Doughty, Catherine J., and Jessica Williams, eds. 1998. *Focus on form in classroom second language acquisition*. Cambridge: Cambridge University Press.

Eckman, Fred. 1996. A functional typological approach to second language acquisition in theory. In *Handbook of second language acquisition*, edited by William C. Ritchie and Tej K. Bhatia, pp. 195–211. San Diego, Calif.: Academic Press.

Ellis, Rod. 1994. *The study of second language acquisition.* Oxford and New York: Oxford University Press.

Gass, Susan, and Larry Selinker, eds. 1992. *Language transfer in language learning.* 2d ed. Amsterdam and Philadelphia: Benjamins.

Hatch, Evelyn Marcussen. 1983. *Psycholinguistics: A second language perspective.* Rowley, Mass.: Newbury House.

Huebner, Thom. 1983. *A longitudinal analysis of the acquisition of English.* Ann Arbor: Karoma.

Hyltenstam, Kenneth, and Nicolas Abrahamsson. 2003. Maturational constraints in second language acquisition. In *Handbook of second language acquisition*, edited by Catherine J. Doughty and Michael H. Long. Oxford: Blackwell.

Hyltenstam, Kenneth, and Manfred Pienemann, eds. 1985. *Modelling and assessing second language acquisition.* Clevedon, Avon, England: Multilingual Matters. San Diego, Calif.: College-Hill.

Johnston, M. 1997. *Development and variation in learner language.* Canberra: Australian National University dissertation.

Keenan, Edward L., and Bernard Comrie. 1977. Noun phrase accessibility and universal grammar. *Linguistic Inquiry* 8.63–99.

Kellerman, Eric, and Michael Sharwood Smith, eds. 1986. *Crosslinguistic influence in second language acquisition.* Oxford: Pergamon.

Krashen, Stephen D. 1985. *The input hypothesis.* London: Longman.

Larsen-Freeman, Diane, and Michael H. Long. 1990. *An introduction to second language acquisition research.* London: Longman.

Long, Michael H. 2003. Stabilization and fossilization in interlanguage development. In *Handbook of second language acquisition*, edited by Catherine J. Doughty and Michael H. Long. Oxford: Blackwell.

Norris, John, and Lourdes Ortega. 2000. Effectiveness in L2 instruction: A research synthesis and quantitative meta-analysis. *Language Learning* 50.417–528.

O'Grady, William. 2003. The radical middle: Nativism without Universal Grammar. In *Handbook of second language acquisition*, edited by Catherine J. Doughty and Michael H. Long. Oxford: Blackwell.

Pienemann, Manfred. 1998. *Processability theory.* Amsterdam and Philadelphia: Benjamins.

Preston, Dennis. 1996. Variationist linguistics and second language acquisition. In *Handbook of second language acquisition*, edited by William C. Ritchie and Tej K. Bhatia, pp. 229–265. San Diego, Calif.: Academic Press.

Robinson, Peter, ed. 2001. *Cognition and second language instruction.* Cambridge: Cambridge University Press.

Rutherford, William E., ed. 1984. *Language universals and second language acquisition.* (Typological studies in language, 5.) Amsterdam: Benjamins.

Schumann, John H. 1978. *The pidginization process: A model for second language acquisition.* Rowley, Mass.: Newbury House.

Scovel, Thomas. 1988. *A time to speak: A psycholinguistic inquiry into the critical period for human speech.* New York: Newbury House.

Spolsky, Bernard. 1989. *Conditions for second language learning.* Oxford: Oxford University Press.

White, Lydia. 2003. On the nature of interlanguage representation: Universal Grammar in the second language. In *Handbook of second language acquisition*, edited by Catherine J. Doughty and Michael H. Long. Oxford: Blackwell.

MICHAEL H. LONG

ACTIVE. *See* Case *and* Transitivity and Voice.

ADAMAWA LANGUAGES. Spoken in eastern Nigeria, northern Cameroon, and southern Chad, with some extension into the Central African Republic. They form one of the branches of ADAMAWA-UBANGI.

LANGUAGE LIST

Awak: also called Awok, Yebu. 6,000 speakers in Nigeria, state of Gombe, Kaltungo LGA.

Bali: also called Bibaali, Maya, Abaali, Ibaali. 2,000 speakers in Nigeria, state of Adamawa, Numan LGA, at Bali, 30 km from Numan on the road to Jalingo. Closely related to Kpasam. Speakers speak Hausa as second language, and some Bacama or Fulfulde.

Bangwinji: also called Bangunji, Bangjinge. 6,000 speakers in Nigeria, state of Bauchi, Balanga, Billiri, and Kaltungo LGAs. Dialects are Kaalo, Naaban. Noun class system is similar to Waja and Tula.

Bena: also called Ebina, Binna, Gbinna, Ebuna, Buna, Yongor, Yungur, Yangeru, Purra. "Lala" is a derogatory name sometimes used. 95,000 speakers in Nigeria, state of Adamawa, Guyuk, Gombi, and Song LGA, new settlements along the road from Song to Yola. Bilingualism in Fulfulde, Dera, Hausa.

Besme: also called Huner, Hounar, 'Unar, Beseme, Besemme, Bodor. 1,228 speakers in southwestern Chad, Tandjilé prefecture, Kélo and Lai subprefectures, in Besmé, Bodor, and three other villages along the Logone River northwest of Lai. Some bilingualism in Nancere and Chadian Arabic, but not universal nor at a high level.

Bolgo: 1,800 speakers in Chad. South central, Guéra prefecture,

FIGURE 1. *Subgrouping of Adamawa Languages*

Fali North Fali, South Fali Gey Kam Kwa La'bi **Leko-Nimbari** **Duru** **Dii** Dii, Duupa, Pape, Saa Duli **Voko-Dowayo** Peere **Vere-Dowayo** Doyayo **Vere-Gimme** **Gimme** Gimme, Gimnime **Vere** Koma, Mom Jango Longto **Leko** Kolbila, Nyong, Samba Leko, Wom **Mumuye-Yandang** **Mummuye** Gengle, Kumba, Mumuye, Pangseng, Rang, Teme, Waka **Yandang** Bali, Kpasam, Kugama, Yendang Nimbari **Mbum-Day** **Bua** Bolgo, Bon Gula, Bua, Fania, Gula Iro, Koke, Niellim, Noy, Tunia, Zan Gula Day **Kim** Besme, Goundo, Kim	**Mbum-Day** (continued) **Mbum** **Central Mbum** **Karang** Karang, Kare, Nzakambay, Pana Kuo **Northern Mbum** **Dama-Galke** Dama, Mono, Ndai **Tupuri-Mambai** Mambai, Mundang, Tupuri **Southern Mbum** Mbum **Unclassified Mbum** Dek, Laka, Pam, To **Waja-Jen** **Jen** Burak, Dza, Kyak, Leelau, Loo, Mághdì, Mak, Mingang Doso, Moo, Tha Longuda **Waja** **Awak** Awak, Kamo **Cham-Mona** Dijim-Bwilim, Tso Dadiya **Tula** Bangwinji, Tula, Waja **Yungur** Kaan Mboi **Yungur-Roba** Bena, Lala-Roba, Voro **Unclassified Adamawa** Oblo

Melfi subprefecture, east of the Barain, southeast of Melfi. Dialects are Bolgo Dugag (Small Bolgo), Bolgo Kubar (Big Bolgo). Most use Chadian Arabic as second language. Vigorous language use.

Bua: also called Boa, Boua, Bwa, 'Ba. 7,708 speakers in southern Chad, Moyen-Chari prefecture, Sarh subprefecture, around and to the northeast of Korbol; Guéra prefecture, Melfi subprefecture. A separate language from Niellim, Fania, Tounia, and Day. "Mana" or "Kobe" may be an alternate name or dialect. Bilingualism in Arabic is limited.

Burak: also called Buurak. 4,000 speakers in Nigeria. State of Bauchi, Billiri and Kaltungo LGAs, Burak town.

Dadiya: also called Dadia, Daadiya, Loodiya. 30,000 speakers in Nigeria, state of Bauchi, Balanga LGA; state of Taraba, Karim Lamido LGA; state of Adamawa, Numan LGA,

between Dadiya and Bambam. Dialects are Tunga (Boleri), Loofiyo, Kookwila, Loofaa. The dialect names are also names of settlements.

Dama: spoken in Cameroon. Small group in Rey-Bouba subdivision, Benoue division, North Province. May be a dialect of Mono.

Day: also called Dai. 49,916 speakers in southwestern Chad, Moyen-Chari prefecture, Sarh and Moïssala subprefectures, southwest of Sarh. Dialects are Bouna, Bangoul, Ngalo, Takawa-Béngoro. The dialects are inherently intelligible to each other's speakers.

Dek: spoken in Cameroon, North Province. It may be intelligible with Kari or Mbum.

Dii: also called Duru, Dourou, Durru, Nyag Dii, Yag Dii, Zaa. 47,000 speakers in Cameroon. Tchollire subdivision of

Mayo-Rey division, North Province; north and east of Ngaoundere, Ngaoundere subdivision, Vina division, Adamawa Province. Dialects are Mambe', Mamna'a, Goom, Boow, Ngbang, Sagzee (Saadje, Saakye), Vaazin, Home, Nyok. Goom may be a separate, related language instead of a dialect.

Dijim-Bwilim: 25,000 speakers in Nigeria, state of Bauchi, Balanga LGA; state of Gongola, Numan LGA. Dialects are Dijim (Cham, Cam), Bwilim (Mwano, Mwona, Mwomo, Mona, Mwana, Fitilai). Related to Lotsu-Piri.

Doyayo: also called Doohyaayo, Dowayayo, Doyaayo, Doyau, Donyayo, Donyanyo, Doayo, Dooyayo, Dooyaayo, Dowayo, Doowaayo, Tunga, Tuuno, Tungbo, Nomai. "Namshi", "Namchi", "Namci" are derogatory names sometimes used. 18,000 speakers in Cameroon. Northern Poli subdivision and around Poli, Benoue division, North Province. Dialects are Marke, Teere (Poli), Sewe. Perhaps 20% of the men are fairly bilingual in Bilkire Fulani for trading and everyday conversation. Perhaps 5% are bilingual in French.

Duli: also called Dui. Formerly spoken in Cameroon. Near Pitoa, Benoue division, North Province. Might have been the same as Gey, according to some scholars.

Duupa: also called Nduupa, Doupa, Dupa. 5,000 speakers in Cameroon. East of Poli, Faro and Benoue divisions, North Province. Related to Pape.

Dza: also called Janjo, Jenjo, Jen. 6,100 speakers in Nigeria state of Taraba, Karim Lamido LGA, and state of Adamawa, Numan LGA, Jen town, east of Karim-Lamido town, south of Bambuka town, by the Benue River bank. Dialects are Kaigama, Laredo (Ardido), Jaule (Joole).

Fali, North: 16,000 speakers in Cameroon. Around Dourbeye and Mayo-Oulo, Mayo-Oulo subdivision, Mayo-Louti division, North Province. Dialects are Dourbeye (Fali-Dourbeye), Bossoum (Fali-Bossoum, Bonum), Bveri (Fali Du Peske-Bori, Peske, Bori). Speakers are rapidly shifting to Adamawa Fulfulde.

Fali, South: 20,000 speakers in Cameroon. Around Hossere Bapara, Tsolaram, Hossere Toro, and Ndoudja; south of Dembo, Pitoa subdivision northeast of Garoua, Benoue division, North Province. Dialects are Fali-Tinguelin (Ndoudja, Mango, Ram, Toro), Kangou (Kaang, Kangu, Fali Kangou), Bele (Ngoutchoumi, Fali-Bele, Fali du Bele-Fere).

Fania: also called Fagnia, Fanya, Fanyan, Fana, Fanian, Mana, Kobe. 1,100 speakers in southeastern Chad, Guéra prefecture, Melfi subprefecture, west of Lake Iro, and north of Sarh, around Mouraye, Sengué, Malakonjo, Rim, Sisi, Karo villages. Dialects are Northern Fania, Southern Fania. A separate language from Bua. Most use Chadian Arabic as second language. Vigorous language use.

Gengle: also called Wegele, Momu, Yagele. Spoken in Nigeria. State of Adamawa, Mayo Belwa and Fufore LGAs. Bilingualism in Hausa.

Gey: also called Gueve, Gewe. Formerly spoken in Cameroon. Ethnic population: 1,900 as of 1982. East of Pitoa, Benoue division, North Province. The people are ethnically still somewhat distinct, but the language is extinct. They now speak Fulfulde.

Gimme: also called Kompara, Kompana, Koma Kompana, Panbe, Gimma. 3,000 speakers in Cameroon. West of Poli along the Nigerian border in the Alantika Mountains, on Saptou plain, Faro division, North Province. Fulfulde is used as second language. French proficiency is low. Church activities in Fulfulde.

Gimnime: also called Kadam, Komlama, Gimbe, Koma Kadam, Laame, Yotubo. 3,000 speakers in Cameroon. Northwest of Poli along Nigerian border, around Wangay in the Atlantika Mountains, Faro division, North Province. Close to Gimme.

Goundo: 30 speakers in Chad. Tanjilé prefecture, Laï and Kélo subprefectures, Goundo-Bengli, Goundo-Nangom, and Goundo-Yila villages. Bilingualism in Kabalay, Nancere. Speakers are over 40 years old. Younger people have shifted to Kabalay and Nancere.

Gula, Bon: also called Taataal, Poun, Bon, Bun, Gula Guera, Bon Goula. 1,200 speakers in Chad. Southeast, Guéra prefecture, Melfi subprefecture. North of Lake Iro, northeast of Zan. Bon and Ibir villages. The majority use Chadian Arabic as second language. Vigorous language use.

Gula, Zan: also called Gula Guera, Goula, Moriil. 4,000 speakers in southeastern Chad, Guéra prefecture, Melfi subprefecture, north of Lake Iro, around and to the northwest of Zan. Dialects are Zan, Chinguil. The majority use Chadian Arabic as second language.

Gula Iro: also called Goula Iro, Goula d'Iro, Kulaal. 3,500 speakers in Chad. Dialects are Pongaal (Ponaal), Tiaala, Tiitaal, Patool, Korintal. Not intelligible with Bon Gula or Zan Gula. Bilingualism in Arabic is limited, and there is almost none in Sar.

Kaan: also called Libo, Libbo, Kan. 10,000 speakers in Nigeria, state of Adamawa, Shellen, Song, and Numan LGAs. Most adults speak Hausa, Fulfulde, Mbula—Bwaza, Bwaza, or Dera as second language.

Kam: also called Yimwom, Nyiwom, Nyingwom. 5,000 speakers in Nigeria. State of Taraba Bali LGA, eighteen villages between Mayo Kam and Garba Chede. Bilingualism in Hausa, Fulfulde.

Kamo: also called Kamu, Nubama, Nyima, Ma. 20,000 speakers in Nigeria, state of Gombe, Billiri, Kaltungo, and Akko LGAs. Typologically close to Awak (no singular/plural noun suffixes).

Karang: also called Kareng, Mbum, Mbum-East, Laka, Lakka. 17,000 speakers in Cameroon and Chad. In Cameroon: In Padjama and from Tcholliere to Touboro, Mayo-Rey division, North Province. Dialects are Sakpu (Pandama, Tu'boro), Karang, Ngomi, Mbere. Related to Sakpu and

Pana. In Chad: 1,000 speakers. Dialects are Karang, Sakpu, Ngomi, Mbere. Closely related to Nzakambay and Kuo.

Kare: also called Karré, Kari, Kali. 93,000 speakers in Central African Republic and Cameroon. In Central African Republic: Boxoum and Bocaranga subprefectures. Dialects are Tale (Tali), Kari. Intelligible with Nzakambay. In Cameroon: Around Belel, Vina division, Adamawa Province, and Mayo-Rey division, North Province.

Kim: 15,354 speakers in southwestern Chad, Mayo-Kebbi prefecture, Bongor subprefecture, Logone River area, southeast of Bangor. Dialects are Garap (Éré), Gerep (Djouman, Jumam), Kolop (Kilop, Kolobo), Kosop (Kwasap, Kim). Dialects listed may be closely related languages. Formerly classified as Chadic.

Koke: also called Khoke. 600 speakers in southeastern Chad. Guéra prefecture, Melfi subprefecture, southeast of Melfi; around Daguéla, Sengué, and Djourab villages. The majority may be bilingual in Chadian Arabic or Fania.

Kolbila: also called Kolbilari, Kolbilla, Kolena, Kolbili, Zoono. 2,500 speakers in Cameroon. Related to Chamba Leko. Bilingualism in French.

Koma: also called Kuma. 35,000 speakers in Nigeria and Cameroon. In Nigeria: 32,000 speakers. State of Adamawa, Ganye and Fufore LGAs, Koma Vomni, Alantika Mountains. Dialects are Gomme (Damti, Koma Kampana, Panbe), Gomnome (Mbeya, Gimbe, Koma Kadam, Laame, Youtubo), Ndera (Vomni, Doome, Doobe). A language cluster. Three subdialects: Koma Vomni, Koma Beiya, and Koma Damti. Ndera and Gomnome speakers barely understand each other, but both understand Gomme. Some speakers understand Hausa, especially those on the plains, but the majority speak only Koma. In Cameroon: 3,000 speakers. Northwest of Tchamba in Atlantika Mountains along Nigerian border, Faro division, North Province. Dialects are Koma Ndera, Koma Damti, Leelu, Bangru, Zanu, Liu, Yeru. Related to Mom Jango.

Kpasam: also called Passam, Kpasham, Nyisam, 'Balo. 15,000 speakers in Nigeria, state of Adamawa, Numan LGA, Kpasham town, on the Numan-Jalingo road. Bilingualism in Hausa, Fulfulde, Bacama.

Kugama: also called Kugamma, Wegam, Yamale, Yamalo. 5,000 speakers in Nigeria, state of Adamawa, Fufore LGA. Bilingualism in Hausa, Gengle, Yendang, Kumba, Kona, Poli.

Kumba: also called Sate, Yofo, Isaro. Spoken in Nigeria. State of Adamawa, Mayo Belwa and Fufore LGAs. Bilingualism in Fulfulde, Hausa.

Kuo: also called Ko, Koh. 15,000 speakers in Chad and Cameroon. In Chad: Closely related to Karang and Nzakambay. In Cameroon: Between Sorombeo and Chad border, and around Garoua, North Province. Closely related to Karang.

Kwa: also called Kwah, Baa. 7,000 speakers in Nigeria. State

of Adamawa, Numan LGA, Gyakan and Kwa towns, near Munga. Dialects are Gyakan, Kwa. Bilingualism in Bacama.

Kyak: also called Bambuka, Nyakyak. 5,000 speakers in Nigeria, state of Taraba, Karim Lamido LGA.

La'bi: spoken in Cameroon. Touboro subdivision, Mayo-Rey division, North Province.

Laka: also called Lakka, Lau, Lao Habe, Godogodo. 5,000 speakers in Nigeria. State of Taraba, Karim Lamido LGA; state of Adamawa, Yola LGA. Related to Karang.

Lala-Roba: also called Gworam. 46,000 speakers in Nigeria. state of Adamawa, Gombi LGA, and state of Borno. Dialects are Lala (Lalla), Roba (Robba), Ebode. Bilingualism in Fulfulde, Ga'anda, Hausa.

Leelau: also called Lelau, Lelo, Munga Lelau, Munga. 5,000 speakers in Nigeria, state of Taraba, Karim Lamido LGA, between Bambuka and Karim-Lamido town, near Lake Mungah.

Longto: also called Voko, Woko, Boko, Lonto, Longbo, Longa, Gobeyo. 2,400 speakers in Cameroon. Around Voko, southwest of Poli to Faro Reserve, Faro division, North Province. Possibly in Nigeria.

Longuda: also called Nunguda, Nunguraba, Nungura, Languda, Longura. 32,000 speakers in Nigeria, state of Adamawa, Guyuk LGA; state of Bauchi, Balanga LGA. Dialects are Nya Ceriya (Banjiram, Cirimba), Nya Gwanda (Nyuwar, Gwandaba), Nya Guyuwa (Guyuk, Plain, Turuba), Nya Dele (Jessu), Nya Tariya (Taraba). Bilingualism in Hausa, Fulfulde, Dera, Waja, English.

Loo: also called Lo, Loh, Shunhu, Shungo. 8,000 speakers in Nigeria, state of Gombe, Kaltungo LGA; state of Taraba, Karim Lamido LGA, northeast of Karim Lamido town, off the Bambuka to Karim-Lamido road.

Mághdì: also called Tala, Widala. 2,000 speakers in Nigeria, state of Taraba, Karim Lamido LGA, a section of the Widala.

Mak: also called Panyam, Panya, Leemak, Lemak, Zo. Spoken in Nigeria, state of Taraba, Karim Lamido LGA, northeast of Karim Lamido town, off the Banbuka to Karim-Lamido road. Dialects are Panya, Zo.

Mambai: also called Mangbai, Mangbei, Manbai, Mambay, Mamgbay, Mamgbei, Mongbay. 2,500 speakers in Cameroon and Chad. In Cameroon: Along Mayo-Kebi River near the Chad border in extreme northern Bibemi subdivision, Benoue division, North Province. Speakers are reported to be bilingual in Mundang. In Chad: 2,067 speakers. Southwest, Mayo-Kebbi prefecture, Lere subprefecture, Cameroon border west of Lere. Speakers are reported to understand Mundang.

Mboi: also called Mboire, Mboyi, Gena. 19,000 speakers in Nigeria, state of Adamawa, Song, Fufore, and Gombi LGAs. Dialects are Banga, Mboi, Handa. Dialect cluster. Bilingualism in Hausa, Fulfulde, Bena, Gudu, Ga'anda.

Mbum: also called Mboum, Mboumtiba, Wuna, Buna. 51,000 speakers in Cameroon and Central African Republic. In

Cameroon: 38,600 speakers. Dialects are Mboum (West Mbum, Bum), Gbete (Kepere, Kpere, Pere, Ripere, Byrre, Pono, Vana). Speakers are rapidly becoming bilingual in Fulani. In Central African Republic: 12,500 speakers. Bocaranga subprefecture, along the Cameroon border.

Mingang Doso: also called Munga Doso, Ngwai Mungn, Doso. 3,000 speakers in Nigeria, state of Taraba, Karim Lamido LGA, 15 km east of Karim Lamido town. One village and associated hamlets.

Mom Jango: also called Vere, Verre, Were, Kobo. 88,000 speakers in Nigeria and Cameroon. In Nigeria: 84,000 speakers. State of Adamawa, Yola and Fufore LGAs, Verre hills. Dialects are Mom Jango, Momi (Ziri). Mom Jango and Momi are probably separate languages. 90% use Fulfulde as second language. In Cameroon: North of Tchamba on Nigerian border, Beka subdivision, Faro division, North Province.

Mono: also called Mon-Non. 1,100 speakers in Cameroon. North of Rey-Bouba around Kongrong along the Mayo-Godi River, Mayo-Rey division, North Province. Related to Dama.

Moo: also called Gwomu, Gwomo, Gwom, Gomu, NgwaaMóò, Yá á Mòò. 5,000 speakers in Nigeria, state of Taraba, Karim Lamido LGA, northeast of Karim Lamido town, off the Bambuka to Karim-Lamido road, close to Gomu Mountain.

Mumuye: also called Yoro. 400,000 speakers in Nigeria and Cameroon. In Nigeria: State of Taraba, Jalingo, Zing, Karim Lamido, Yorro, Bali LGAs; state of Adamawa, Ganye, Fufore, Yola, Numan, and Mayo Belwa LGAs. Dialects are Zinna, Dong, Yoro, Lankaviri, Gola (Bajama), Gongla, Kasaa, Saawa, Jalingo, Nyaaja, Jeng, Gnoore, Yaa, Sagbee, Shaari, Kugong, Mang, Kwaji, Meeka, Yakoko. Lankaviri dialect is sufficiently different from Zing to need separate literature. In Cameroon: Benoue division, North Province, if spoken at all in that country.

Mundang: also called Moundan, Moundang, Kaele, Nda. 205,000 speakers in Chad and Cameroon. In Chad: 160,880 speakers. Dialects are Kabi, Zasing (Yasing). A subdialect of Kabi is Kiziere, of Zasing is Torrock-Kaélé. In Cameroon: 44,700 speakers. Dialects are Kiziere, Imbana (Bana, Mbana, Imbara), Zasing (Yassing, Djasing, Yasing, Jasing, Zazing), Gelama.

Ndai: also called Galke, Pormi. Spoken in Cameroon. Tchollire, Mayo-Rey division, North Province.

Niellim: also called Mjillem, Nyilem, Nielim, Lua. 5,157 speakers in Chad. Dialects are Niellim, Tchini (Cuni, Cini), Niou. Tchini dialect is extinct.

Nimbari: also called Nyamnyam, Niamniam, Bari, Nimbari-Kebi, Nyam-Nyam du Mayo-Kebi. Spoken in Cameroon. Near Pitoa, Benoue and Mayo-Louti divisions, North Province. Not spoken in Chad or Nigeria.

Noy: also called Loo. 36 speakers in southern Chad, Moyen-Chari prefecture, Sarh and Koumra subprefectures, in the area between Sarh, Djoli, Bédaya, Koumra, and Koumogo villages. As of 1989, speakers were found to be shifting to Saa. Language name is Sar.

Nyong: also called Daganyonga, Daganonga, Nyongnepa, Mumbake, Mubako, Ndagam, Samba Bali. 17,000 speakers in Cameroon and Nigeria. In Cameroon: Near the Ndop plain in Balikuumbat, Baligansin, and Baligashu villages in Ngo-Ketunjia division, Baligham in Mezam division. They consider themselves to be the same ethnically as speakers of Samba Leko, but there is significant difficulty in inherent intelligibility. Speakers use Cameroons Pidgin (generally spoken and understood) or Standard English (by those educated beyond primary level) as second languages. In Nigeria: State of Adamawa, Mayo Belwa LGA, six villages. Bilingualism in Hausa, Fulfulde, Samba, Yendang, Kumba, Mumuye.

Nzakambay: also called Nzakmbay, Nzak Mbai, Nzaka Mbay, Mbum, Mboum, Njakambai, Mbum Nzakambay. 25,000 speakers in Chad and Cameroon. In southwestern Chad: 15,000 speakers, Logone Oriental prefecture, Baïbokoum subprefecture, Cameroon border, near Baïbokoum. Zoli is in the Monts de Lam area. Dialects are Nzakambay, Zoli. Closely related to Karang and Kuo. In Cameroon: 10,000 speakers. Around Touboro, Touboro subdivision, Mayo-Rey division, North Province.

Oblo: spoken in Cameroon. Near Tchollire, Mayo-Rey division, North Province.

Pam: spoken in Cameroon. Near Tchollire, Mayo-Rey division, North Province.

Pana: also called Pani. 83,000 speakers in Central African Republic, Chad, Nigeria, and Cameroon. In Central African Republic: 82,000 speakers. Bocaranga subprefecture. Dialects are Pana, Pondo, Gonge. In Chad: The Pana dialect is in Makele village, and the Gonge dialect in Giriwon and Diahoke villages. Dialects are Pana, Gonge. In Nigeria: Urban areas of Nigeria. In Cameroon: Touboro subdivision, Mayo-Rey division, North Province. Some are in urban areas.

Pangseng: spoken in Nigeria. State of Taraba, Karim Lamido LGA. Dialects are Pangseng, Komo, Jega.

Pape: also called Panon, Pa'non, Dugun, Pani. 7,000 speakers in Cameroon. Southeast of Poli, Poli subdivision, Faro division, North Province. Dialects are Saan, Naan. Close to Duupa and Saa.

Peere: also called Pere, Peer, Kutin, Koutin, Koutine, Kutine, Kutinn, Kotopo, Kotofo, Kotpojo, Potopo, Potopore, Patapori. 20,000 speakers in Cameroon and Nigeria. In Cameroon: 15,000 speakers. Dialects are Peer Muure, Zongbi (Djonbi), Dan Muure (Potopo, Kotopo, Kpotopo, Kotofo). There is a primer in Peere. In Nigeria: 5,000 speakers. State of Adamawa, Ganye LGA. Bilingualism in Fulfulde.

Rang: spoken in Nigeria, state of Taraba, Zing LGA. Close to Mumuye.

Saa: also called Sari, Saapa, Yinga. 3,500 speakers in Cameroon. In the middle of a massif with difficult access, southeast of Poli, Yinga canton, Faro division, North Province. Related to Pape.

Samba Leko: also called Chamba Leeko, Samba. 50,000 speakers in Cameroon and Nigeria. In Cameroon: Dialects are Samba Leko (Ndii, Lekon, Lego, Leko, Laeko, Suntai), Deenu (Koola), Bangla, Samba de Wangai, Sampara. Closely related to Kolbila. In Nigeria: State of Adamawa, Ganye, Fufore, Wukari, and Takum LGAs. Those in Donga now speak Jukun.

Teme: also called Tema. 4,000 speakers in Nigeria, state of Adamawa, Mayo Belwa LGA, along the banks of the Mayo Belwa River. Speakers use Hausa or Fulfulde as second language. Some can speak Kumba, Yendang, or Gengle.

Tha: also called Joole Manga, Kapawa. 1,000 speakers in Nigeria, state of Taraba, near Lau.

To: spoken in Cameroon and Central African Republic. In Cameroon: Touboro subdivision, Mayo-Rey division, North Province.

Tso: also called Lotsu-Piri, Cibbo, Tsóbó, Cuyi Tsó, Pire, Piri, Kitta. 16,000 speakers in Nigeria, state of Adamawa, Numan LGA; state of Bauchi, Kaltungo LGA. Dialects are Berbou, Gusubou, Swabou.

Tula: also called Kotule, Kutule. 30,000 speakers in Nigeria, state of Gombe, Kaltungo LGA, 30 km east of Billiri. Dialects are Kutule, Baule, Yili.

Tunia: also called Tounia, Tunya, Tun. 2,255 speakers in southern Chad, Moyen-Chari prefecture, Sarh subprefecture, in Sarh and about three small villages north of Sarh. Dialects are Tunya, Perim. Not intelligible with other Bua languages. 25% are bilingual in Niellim, others in Sar (the majority, but with low proficiency), Chadian Arabic, or French. Perim dialect is extinct.

Tupuri: also called Toupouri, Tuburi, Toubouri, Ndore, Ndoore, Wina, Tongoyna, Honya, Dema, Mata. 216,000 speakers in Cameroon and Chad. In Cameroon: 125,000 speakers. Southeastern Moulvouday plain east of Kaele, Kaele division; Kar-Hay subdivision, Mayo-Danay division, Far North Province. In southwestern Chad: 90,785 speakers, Mayo-Kebbi prefecture, Fianga subprefecture, around Fianga. Dialects are Bang-Ling, Bang-Were, Faale-Piyew, Podokge, Bang-Go, Kaele, Mata. The first four dialects listed are spoken in Chad, the last two in Cameroon.

Voro: also called Ebina, Ebuna, Buna, Bena, Woro, Yungur. Spoken in Nigeria, state of Adamawa, Guyuk and Song LGAs, south of the Dumne road, Waltande and associated hamlets.

Waja: also called Wiyaa, Wuya, Nyan Wiyau. 60,000 speakers in Nigeria, state of Gombe, Balanga, Akko, Yamaltu Deba LGAs; state of Adamawa, northern Michika LGA; state of Borno, Gwoza LGA; state of Taraba, Bali LGA. Dialects are Deruwo (Wajan Dutse), Waja (Wajan Kasa). Only small dialectal differences. Bilingualism in Fulfulde.

Waka: 5,000 speakers in Nigeria, state of Taraba, Karim Lamido LGA.

Wom: also called Pere, Perema, Pereba. 5,000 speakers in Nigeria. State of Adamawa, Fufore LGA. Closely related to Samba Leko.

Yendang: also called Yendam, Yandang, Nyandang, Yundum. 62,640 speakers in Nigeria, state of Adamawa, Mayo Belwa and Numan LGAs; state of Taraba, Yoro, Jalingo, Zing, and Karim Lamido LGAs. Dialects are Kuseki, Yofo, Poli (Akule, Yakule), Yoti. Bilingualism in Hausa, Fulfulde, Mumuye, English.

B. GRIMES

ADAMAWA-UBANGI LANGUAGES.

Formerly known as Adamawa-Eastern. They form one of the major branches of the NIGER-CONGO family. Adamawa-Ubangi languages are spoken in an area from eastern Nigeria through eastern Cameroon, southern Chad, the Central African Republic, and northern Democratic Republic of Congo, and into southwestern Sudan. The family falls into two subgroups, Adamawa and Ubangi.

[*For detailed lists of* Adamawa-Ubangi Languages, *see* Adamawa Languages, Ubangi Languages.]

B. GRIMES

ADDRESS.

Forms of address are one of the linguistic means by which speakers mark their psycho-social orientation to their addressees. Forms such as pronouns, names, and terms of endearment encode both status and solidarity relationships between speaker and addressee. (For reference, see R. Brown and Gilman 1960, R. Brown and Ford 1961, Ervin-Tripp 1969, P. Brown and Levinson 1987.)

It appears to be a worldwide phenomenon that *plural* pronouns can be used to *singular* addressees to show respect. In languages where this occurs, speakers have the choice of two forms when addressing someone: they choose between a singular, *familiar* form and a plural, *polite* form. These forms are conventionally referred to as T AND V forms; cf. French *tu* and *vous,* from Latin *tū* and *vōs.* (In some languages—e.g. modern German, Italian, and Spanish—third person forms are also used for politeness.)

When people interact, three patterns of pronoun usage are possible: mutual T, mutual V, and asymmetrical usage. Mutual T indicates that the interactants consider themselves to be socially *intimate* (intimacy is defined in terms of both shared values—kinship, sex, nationality, occupation, etc.—and frequency of contact). Mutual V, conversely, signals that the interactants do not consider themselves to be socially intimate. In symmetrical encounters, then, T forms are seen as encoding *intimacy* and social *closeness*, and V forms as encoding *respect* and social *distance.*

Asymmetrical T/V usage is found in interactions where there is a power imbalance: the more powerful speaker has the right to say T and to receive V. In different societies and at different times, the following relationships have been viewed as unequal, and have accordingly been characterized by asymmetrical pronoun usage: master/servant, parent/child, husband/wife, officer/soldier, employer/employee, customer/waiter.

The use of names mirrors the use of pronouns. Speakers can choose between symmetrical or asymmetrical naming, and symmetrical naming can mark intimacy or distance. In American and British English, for example, the three-way opposition consists of mutual F[irst] N[ame] *(Jane),* mutual T[itle+] L[ast] N[ame] *(Mrs. Jones),* or asymmetrical naming.

Asymmetrical usage encodes relationships of *power* or *status,* while symmetrical usage encodes *solidarity.* The co-existence of these two dimensions means that T forms and FN express both *condescension* and intimacy, while V forms and TLN express both *deference* and distance.

It has been argued that the use of particular address forms to encode deference is one aspect of Negative Politeness; i.e., by using V or TLN, or by saying *Sir/ Madam,* the speaker respects the hearer's "negative face." Conversely, the reciprocal use of T forms or FN, or of endearments and terms like *mate* and *buddy,* signals in-group solidarity, and is thus an aspect of Positive Politeness (the speaker pays attention to the hearer's "positive face"; see P. Brown and Levinson 1987).

Terms of endearment (e.g. *dear, honey*) are unmarked when used symmetrically between people who perceive their relationship as intimate. But these terms are also used asymmetrically in service encounters, where the relationship between server and customer is not one of intimacy. Age and gender seem to be salient categories here: younger customers can be called *dear* by older service personnel, and female customers by male personnel (Wolfson and Manes 1980). Such asymmetrical usage signals condescension; it is interesting to note that the only other context in which asymmetrical use of intimate forms is found is in the family, between parents and children. More generally, the asymmetrical use of address forms is a significant feature of linguistic sexism (Pauwels 1998).

Historically, there has been a shift from the *status* semantic to the *solidarity* semantic. This has been well documented for pronouns of address in European languages; symmetrical pronoun usage has become the norm in more and more contexts, and the use of mutual T is slowly growing. The same is true of other address forms: reciprocal FN is expanding at the expense of both reciprocal TLN and asymmetrical naming. It has been claimed that this shift reflects the development of more egalitarian societies. But it could also be seen, more cynically, as a cosmetic shift, involving the elimination of the overt marking of power asymmetries. The tendency to eliminate overt power markers is strongly associated with the growing *informalization* of the public domain, with the boundaries between public and private becoming increasingly blurred (Fairclough 1992).

[*See also* Discourse; Power and Language; Pragmatics and Contextual Semantics; *and* Register and Style.]

BIBLIOGRAPHY

Brown, Penelope, and Stephen Levinson. 1987. *Politeness: Some universals in language usage.* (Studies in interactional sociolinguistics, 4.) Cambridge and New York: Cambridge University Press.

Brown, Roger, and Marguerite Ford. 1961. Address in American English. *Journal of Abnormal and Social Psychology* 62.375–385.

Brown, Roger, and Albert Gilman. 1960. The pronouns of power and solidarity. In *Style in language,* edited by Thomas A. Sebeok, pp. 253–276. Cambridge, Mass.: MIT Press.

Ervin-Tripp, Susan M. 1969. Sociolinguistics. In *Advances in experimental social psychology,* edited by Leonard Berkowitz, vol. 4, pp. 93–107. New York: Academic Press.

Fairclough, Norman. 1992. *Discourse and social change.* Cambridge: Polity Press.

Pauwels, Anne. 1998. *Women changing language.* London: Longman.

Wolfson, Nessa, and Joan Manes. 1980. Don't 'dear' me! In *Women and language in literature and society,* edited by Sally McConnell-Ginet et al., pp. 79–92. New York: Praeger.

JENNIFER COATES

ADELUNG, JOHANN CHRISTOPH (1732–1806).

Author of important grammatical descriptions of German. Adelung had an important role in the history of general linguistics because of his last project, *Mithridates* (1806–1817), which compiled information, including versions of the Lord's Prayer, on all languages then known to European scholarship. The work was completed after Adelung's death by J. S. Vater.

[*See also* History of Linguistics, *article on* Seventeenth- and Eighteenth-Century Europe.]

ANNA MORPURGO DAVIES

ADJACENCY. Word-internal conditioning, of whatever kind, is commonly observed to be *local* rather than *remote*. In rules of derivation and compounding which are conditional on word-class categorizations, it tends to be the category of the immediate base, rather than of forms from which the base may itself be derived, which prohibits or encourages the rules' application. In the case of allomorphy and similar adjustments (such as additions, eliminations, or rearrangements of formatives), alternations likewise tend to be conditioned by neighboring rather than distant elements. (For general reference, see Harris 1942, Siegel 1978, Williams 1981, Plank 1985, and Carstairs 1987.)

The notion of distance admits of two interpretations: operational and linear. What seems to count in rules of word formation is the preceding category-determining operation, regardless of the location of its exponent. For example, the derivation of English patient nouns in *-ee* is subject to a categorial restriction to verbs; thus it makes no difference whether these verbal bases are formed by suffixation (e.g. $[[magnet]_N\text{-}ize]_V\text{-}ee$) or prefixation (e.g. $[de\text{-}[throne]_N]_V\text{-}ee$). The *-ee* is not syntagmatically contiguous with the verb-forming prefix *de-*, the exponent of the operation upon which the application of *-ee* suffixation is conditional. By contrast, in inflectional morphology, there is generally less reason to assign hierarchical constituent structure, corresponding to sequences of operations, to complex words; thus distance is perhaps more appropriately defined linearly, over strings of formatives.

Observations of instances of local word-internal conditioning, in English and elsewhere, have inspired the postulate of a general Adjacency Constraint. Its several versions, accommodated in various theoretical frameworks, differ somewhat in formulation and substance. Their restrictive force is difficult to gauge as long as no principled constraints are imposed on the passing-on of morphological properties throughout subsequent derivational stages or along strings of neighboring formatives, enabling these "inherited" properties to make their influence felt at a distance.

[*See also* Generative Morphology; Heads; Inheritance; *and* Morphology.]

BIBLIOGRAPHY

Carstairs, Andrew. 1987. *Allomorphy in inflexion.* London: Croom Helm.

Harris, Zellig S. 1942. Morpheme alternants in linguistic analysis. *Language* 18.169–180.

Plank, Frans. 1985. How disgrace-ful. *Acta Linguistica Hafniensia* 19:2.64–80.

Siegel, Dorothy. 1978. The Adjacency Constraint and the theory of morphology. *Northeastern Linguistic Society* 8.189–197. Amherst: University of Massachusetts.

Williams, Edwin. 1981. On the notions 'lexically related' and 'head of a word'. *Linguistic Inquiry* 12.245–274.

FRANS PLANK

ADJECTIVES. Although the word class of adjectives is now considered a major part of speech, it was long held to be a special type of noun ("noun adjective") and did not achieve autonomous word-class status until the late 17th century. The distinguishing feature of the adjective is the fact that it modifies a noun. Accordingly, adjectives function syntactically as pre- or post-modifiers of nouns, or as complements of nouns or nominal clauses. In many languages, adjectives are inflected in agreement with their nominal heads.

Another distinctive feature of adjectives is their ability to suggest characterizing qualities. Indeed, some linguists do not award full adjectival status to those premodifiers that have purely restrictive functions (e.g. *tidal* in *tidal wave*, or *previous* in *the previous chapter*), or to complements that simply denote states (e.g. *be asleep*).

Characterizing and state-denoting adjectives frequently refer to features that are perceived as variable in degree. If so, the adjective becomes "gradable." A gradable adjective can be modified by adverbs of degree, and it can occur in comparative (*sweeter*) and superlative (*sweetest*) forms.

Adjectives may also be modified by prefixes (e.g. *unkind*, *hyperactive*), by nouns (*grass-green*), and by other adjectives (*red-hot*). In the latter two cases, they normally form "compound adjectives." By means of derivational suffixes, including so-called zero-suffixation, adjectives can be converted into nouns, verbs, and almost regularly into adverbs. In many languages, it is also possible to use adjectives as heads of noun phrases without the addition of an affix (*the poor and the rich*).

[*See also* Derivational Morphology; Generative Morphology; Gradation; *and* Heads.]

BIBLIOGRAPHY

Aarts, Jan M. G., and Joseph P. Calbert. 1979. *Metaphor and non-metaphor: The semantics of adjective-noun combinations.* Tübingen: Niemeyer.

Bartning, Inge. 1980. *Remarques sur la syntaxe et la semantique de pseudo-adjectifs dénominaux en français.* 2d ed. Stockholm: Almqvist and Wiksell.

Beard, Robert. 1981. *The Indo-European lexicon: A full synchronic theory.* Amsterdam: North-Holland.

Dixon, Robert M. W. 1982. *Where have all the adjectives gone? And other essays in semantics and syntax.* Berlin: Mouton.

Fellbaum, C. D. Gross, and K. Miller. 1990. Adjectives in WordNet. *International Journal of Lexicography* 3.235–244.

Levi, Judith N. 1978. *The syntax and semantics of complex nominals*. New York: Academic Press.

Ljung, Magnus. 1970. *English denominal adjectives*. Göteborg: Acta Universitatis Gothoburgensis.

Meys, W. J. 1975. *Compound adjectives in English and the ideal speaker-listener: A study of compounds in a transformational-generative framework*. Amsterdam: North-Holland.

Paradis, Carita. 1997. *Degree modifiers of adjectives in spoken British English*. Lund: Lund University Press.

Riegel, Martin. 1985. *L'adjectif attribut*. Paris: Presses Universitaires de France.

Rusiecki, Jan. 1985. *Adjectives and comparison in English: A semantic study*. London: Longman.

Taylor, John. 1992. Old problems: Adjectives in cognitive grammar. *Cognitive Linguistics* 3.1–35.

Tucker, Gordon. 1998. *The lexicogrammar of adjectives: A systemic functional approach to lexis*. London and New York: Cassell.

Warren, Beatrice. 1984. *Classifying adjectives*. Göteborg: Acta Universitatis Gothoburgensis.

Wierzbicka, Anna. 1986. What's in a noun (or how do nouns differ from adjectives?). *Studies in Language* 10.353–389.

BEATRICE WARREN

ADJUNCT. *See* Adjunction; Phrase Structure; *and* Clause, *article on* Complementation.

ADJUNCTION. In the theory of generative grammar, transformations are said to map phrase markers into other phrase markers. Transformational operations are composed of elementary operations of permutation, deletion, copying, etc. (cf. Chomsky 1955:339–340). Transformations of permutation, or movement, are of two types: adjunction and substitution.

Substitution transformations (formally defined in Chomsky 1955:350) replace one terminal element with another without effecting any change in the structure produced by the phrase structure rules. The moved category is thus placed in a structural position which is generated independently of the transformational operation. An example is Raising to Subject (**e** is the identity element):

(1a)   **e** *appears* [$_s$*Harry to like music*].

(1b)   *Harry appears* [$_s$*to like music*].

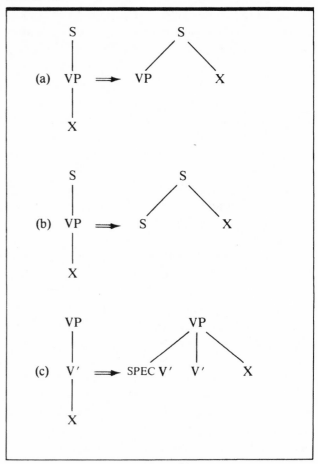

FIGURE 1. *Types of Adjunction.* (a) Sister adjunction of X to VP; (b) Chomsky adjunction of X to S; (c) Daughter adjunction of X to VP.

Raising to Subject is a substitution operation which replaces **e** in the matrix subject position of ex. (1a) with the moved N[oun] P[hrase] *Harry,* deriving (1b).

Adjunction transformations differ from substitution transformations in that further structure is created at the *landing site* of movement (Baltin 1978). Three kinds of adjunction have been discussed in the generative literature—*sister adjunction, Chomsky adjunction*, and *daughter adjunction*. These operations are illustrated schematically in Figures 1a–c. All types of adjunction can place material to the right or to the left of the node adjoined to; here the various types of adjunction to the right are illustrated.

These operations can be exemplified with rules proposed by Ross 1967. That work formulates *extraposition* as a rule which sister-adjoins a S[entence] to either a containing V[erb] P[hrase] or a containing S (Ross, p. 110). The operation of the rule is shown in Figure 2.

FIGURE 2. *Extraposition*

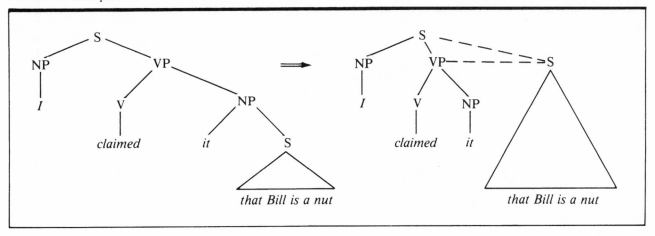

FIGURE 3. *Relative Clause Formation*

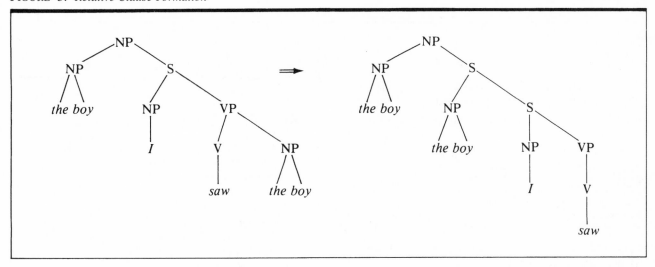

Here S is sister-adjoined either to VP or to S (Ross does not take a position on which possibility is correct). A later rule deletes *it*—resulting in an instance of 'vacuous extraposition', as no reordering takes place.

Relative Clause Formation is formulated as a Chomsky adjunction (Ross, p. 113). The operation of this rule is illustrated in Figure 3. The second occurrence of *the boy* is here Chomsky-adjoined to the S which contains it. A later rule presumably changes the second occurrence of *the boy* into a relative pronoun.

It-Replacement, a precursor of the rule of raising in ex. 1, is illustrated by Figures 4a–b (Ross, p. 158; cf. also Rosenbaum 1967). The subject of the S contained in the subject NP of Fig. 4a is substituted for *it* (this is an alternative formulation of the substitution operation dis-

cussed above); the remnant of that S, *for to like music,* is daughter-adjoined to the matrix VP. In this way, Figure 4b is derived from Figure 4a. *For* is deleted by a later rule, giving the correct surface structure.

An emphasis on restricting the power of transformations, characteristic of later versions of generative grammar, led to the proposal that only Chomsky adjunction was possible. This operation, unlike the other two, preserves intact the internal structure of the category adjoined to (cf. Chomsky 1981:141, fn. 39; and Riemsdijk's Principle of External Adjunction, 1978:284). May 1985 and Chomsky 1986 develop a rich theory of adjunction which has given rise to much discussion.

[*See also* History of Linguistics, *article on* Generative Grammar; Phrase Structure *and* Transformations.]

FIGURE 4. It-*Replacement*

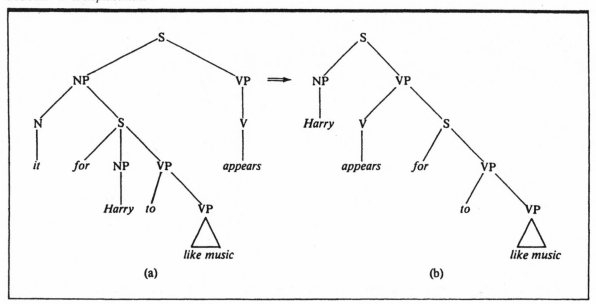

(a)   (b)

BIBLIOGRAPHY

Baltin, Mark R. 1978. Toward a theory of movement rules. Cambridge, Mass.: MIT dissertation. Published, New York: Garland, 1985.

Chomsky, Noam. 1955. *The logical structure of linguistic theory.* Published, New York: Plenum, 1975. Reprinted, Chicago: University of Chicago Press, 1985.

Chomsky, Noam. 1981. *Lectures on government and binding.* (Studies in generative grammar, 9.) Dordrecht: Foris.

Chomsky, Noam. 1986. *Barriers.* (Linguistic Inquiry monographs, 13.) Cambridge, Mass.: MIT Press.

May, Robert. 1985. *Logical Form: Its structure and derivation.* (Linguistic Inquiry monographs, 12.) Cambridge, Mass.: MIT Press.

Riemsdijk, Henk C. van. 1978. *A case study in syntactic markedness: The binding nature of prepositional phrases.* Lisse, Netherlands: de Ridder.

Rosenbaum, Peter S. 1967. *The grammar of English predicate complement constructions.* Cambridge, Mass.: MIT Press.

Ross, John Robert. 1967. *Constraints on variables in syntax.* MIT dissertation. Published as *Infinite syntax.* Norwood, N.J.: Ablex, 1986.

IAN G. ROBERTS

ADMIRALTY ISLANDS LANGUAGES. Spoken in Papua New Guinea, on the Admiralty Islands; they constitute a top-level component of the OCEANIC LANGUAGES.

FIGURE 1. *Subgrouping of Admiralty Islands Languages*

Eastern Admiralty Islands

> **Manus**
>> **East Manus**
>>> Andra-Hus, Elu, Ere, Kele, Koro, Kurti, Leipon, Lele, Nali, Papitalai, Ponam, Titan
>>
>> **Mokoreng-Loniu**
>>> Loniu, Mokerang
>>
>> Pak-Tong
>>
>> **West Manus**
>>> Bipi, Bohuai, Hermit, Khehek, Likum, Mondropolon, Nyindrou, Sori-Harengan
>
> **Southeast Islands**
>> Baluan-Pam, Lenkau, Lou, Nauna, Penchal

Western Admiralty Islands
> Kaniet, Seimat, Wuvulu-Aua

LANGUAGE LIST

Andra-Hus: also called Ahus, Ha'us. 810 speakers in Andra and Hus Islands.

Baluan-Pam: 1,000 speakers on Baluan and Pam Islands. Dialects are Baluan, Pam, close to each other. Baluan is more widely spoken. Speakers are moderately bilingual in Lou or Titan. "Baluan is more widely spoken" is unclear as to whether or not it means it is spoken by people from other ethnic group, which is not meant. Baluan has more speakers than Pam is what is meant.

Bipi: also called Sisi-Bipi. 1,200 speakers on west coast: Maso, Matahei, and Salapai villages, Bipi and Sisi Islands.

Bohuai: also called Pahavai, Pelipowai, Bowai, Pohuai,

Bohuai-Tulu, Tulu-Bohuai. 1,400 speakers in Bohuai, Peli Island, Pelipowai. Dialects are Keli, Bohuai, Tulu (Tulun, Tjudun). Close to Khehek. Bilingualism in Kurti, Titan, Ere.

Elu: 215 speakers on north coast of Manus Island. Most speakers are bilingual in Kurti.

Ere: also called Nane, E. 1,030 speakers on south coast: Drabitou, Lohe, Londru, Metawari, Pau, Piterait, Taui-Undrau, Hatwara, and Loi villages. Speakers are highly bilingual in Kele.

Hermit: also called Agomes, Luf, Maron. Formerly spoken in western Papua New Guinea and Luf and Maron Islands in Hermit Islands.

Kaniet: formerly spoken on Anchorite and western Kaniet Islands. Extinct since 1950.

Kele: also called Gele. 600 speakers on south coast inland: Buyang, Droia, Kawaliap, Koruniat, Tingau. Bilingualism in Kurti, Ere.

Khehek: also called Levei-Drehet, Levei-Ndrehet. 1,600 speakers in Soparibeu district: Ndrehet, Levei, and Bucho villages; Ndrehet is the center. Dialects are Levei (Lebei, Lebej), Drehet (Khehek, Chehek, Chechek), Bucho. Those in the Levei area speak a dialect closely related to that of Bucho.

Koro: 400 speakers. Close to, and possibly intelligible with, Papitalai. All ages. All or most domains. Nearly all the ethnic groups speak Koro.

Kurti: also called Kuruti, Kuruti-Pare, Ndrugul. 2,600 speakers on north central coast. None are monolingual. 95% use Tok Pisin, 30% use English as second language, 30% can use Kele or Mondropolon. All ages. All domains. Oral use in first three grades of school, singing and preaching in church, personal letters. Vigorous language use. Parents transmit it to children. Speakers have a positive attitude toward Kurti.

Leipon: also called Pitilu, Pityilu. 650 speakers in Lolo village, Hauwai, Ndrilo, and Pityilu Islands. Speakers are very bilingual in Lele.

Lele: also called Lele Hai, Hai, Usiai, Moanus, Manus, Elu-Kara. 1,300 speakers pn Manus Island.

Lenkau: 250 speakers on southwestern Rambutyo Island. One village only. Ethnic population: 250. Bilingualism in Titan, Penchal. All ages. Some or most roles retained for Lenkau. All or most of the ethnic group speak Lenkau.

Likum: 80 speakers. Bilingualism in Lindrou.

Loniu: also called Lonio, Ndroku. 460 speakers in Lolak and Loniu villages, south coast of Los Negros Island. Close to Bipi. Moderate bilingualism in Lele and Papitalai. All ages. Loniu used for all or most domains. 70% to 100% of the ethnic group speak Loniu.

Lou: 1,000 speakers on Lou Island. Three very similar dialects. Rei is dominant. Bilingualism in Baluan-Pam, Titan.

Mokerang: also called Mokareng, Mokoreng. 200 speakers on northern Los Negros Island and Ndrilo Island. All ages.

Mondropolon: 300 speakers on north central coast, Manus Island. Most speakers are bilingual in Kurti. All ages. Speakers are strongly supportive of Mondropolon.

Nali: also called Yiru. 1,800 speakers on southeastern Manus Island, and also its southwestern coast, northwest of Titan. Okro (200) and Nali (1,800) were said to be separate languages (in a year 2000 study). Speakers are moderately bilingual in Lele. Okro: 60% to 100% of children speak Okro. Most key domains are reserved for Okro. 40% to 100% of the ethnic group speak Okro. Okro speakers are strongly supportive of Okro.

Nauna: also called Naune. 100 speakers on Nauna Island. One village. Bilingualism in Titan.

Nyindrou: also called Lindrou, Lindau, Salien, Nyada. 4,200 speakers in ten villages around the west coast of Manus Island. The Babon dialect is spoken in three southern villages. Bilingual level estimates are Bipi: 0 73%, 1 8%, 2 19%, 3–5 0%; Harengam: 0 84%, 1 9%, 2 7%, 3–5 0%; Sori: 0 89%, 1 6%, 2 5%, 3–5 0%; Levei: 0 94%, 1 2%, 2 4%, 3–5 0%. Fewer than 5% are monolingual. All ages. All domains. Used in first three grades in school. Oral and written use in church. Oral use in local business. Vigorous language use. Parents transmit it to children. Speakers have a very positive attitude toward Nyindrou as part of their cultural heritage.

Pak-Tong: also called Tong-Pak. 970 speakers on Pak and Tong Islands. Dialects are Pak, Tong, nearly identical; Pak has more speakers.

Papitalai: 520 speakers in Naringel and Papitalai, Los Negros Island. Three dialects. Close to Koro. Speakers are moderately bilingual in Loniu.

Penchal: 550 speakers on Rambutyo Island. Three nearly identical dialects. Speakers are moderately bilingual in Titan languages.

Ponam: 420 speakers on Ponam Island. Close to Andra-Hus. Moderate bilingualalism in Kurti.

Seimat: also called Ninigo. 1,000 speakers on the Ninigo Islands and Anchorite Islands.

Sori-Harengan: 570 speakers in Manus Province. Sori is spoken on the northwestern coast of Manus Island and on the Sori and Harengan Islands off the coast. Dialects are Sori, Harengan, nearly identical. Speakers are moderately bilingual in Nyindrou.

Titan: also called Manus, Moanus, Tito, M'bunai. 3,850 speakers on M'buke, Mouk, and Rambutyo Islands. Two dialects.

Wuvulu-Aua: also called Aua-Viwulu, Viwulu-Aua. 1,000 speakers on Aua, Durour, Maty, and Wuvulu Islands. Dialects are Aua, Wuvulu (Wuu), nearly identical.

B. GRIMES

ADPOSITIONS. Members of this class of function words typically express various concrete relations of noun phrases with predicates, such as location, instrument, accompaniment, beneficiary, and cause. Adpositions are more commonly called "prepositions" or "postpositions," depending on their order with respect to their complement. Some typical examples of adpositions appear in (1):

(1)   a. English (prepositions)
          in, at, on, under, behind, above, after, with, for
       b. Basque (postpositions)
          lagun-ik gabe 'without friend'
          filma-ren gainean 'about the films'
          etxe atzean 'behind the house'

From a semantic point of view, we may distinguish between *grammatical adpositions* (e.g. *of* and *to* in English), which express very abstract syntactic relationships, and *concrete adpositions* (*before, behind, despite*). In some languages, grammatical adpositions are even used to mark the subject (e.g. Japanese *ga*) or the object (Spanish *a*). From a formal point of view, we may distinguish between *simple adpositions* like those in (1a) and *complex adpositions* (e.g. *in spite of, because of, in front of*). Complex adpositions are always concrete, and grammatical adpositions are always short and simple.

Languages with rich morphology often show person marking on their adpositions, e.g. Hungarian *mellett-em* 'beside me', *mellett-ed* 'beside you'. (Bakker, to appear). These markers often express agreement between the adposition and the complement in person and number.

Adpositions are more prominent in European languages like English or Russian than in languages in many other parts of the world, and it is perhaps for this reason that some linguists have regarded them as one of the four major word classes (along with noun, verb, and adjective). However, in contrast to nouns, which are always an open class, and verbs and adjectives, often an open class, adpositions are always a closed class in the sense that new adpositions do not normally come into a language by word formation or by borrowing. Moreover, this class is typically much smaller than it is in English or Russian, where grammarians have counted scores of adpositions.

To express relations that are coded with prepositions in European languages, many languages (especially in northern Asia, South Asia, and Australia) have rich case systems. For example, Even (a Tungusic languages of eastern Siberia) has cases not only for grammatical relations (accusative, dative), but also ablative (e.g. *jasal-duk* 'from the eye'), directive (*jasal-tiki* 'toward the eye'), instrumental (*jasal-ac* 'with the eye'), equative (*jasal-*

gacin 'like an eye'), and several others. Languages with more limited case systems tend to have only grammatical cases (e.g. accusative, ergative, genitive, dative), and thus no grammatical adpositions.

Where European languages have concrete prepositions, many languages have *relational nouns* such as 'back' (for 'behind'), 'face' (for 'in front of'), 'top' (for 'on'), or 'similarity' (for 'like'). These are linked to the complement in an ordinary possessive construction, and to the predicate by a simple preposition or a case-marker. For instance, Hausa (a Chadic language of Nigeria and Niger) has expressions like those in (2):

(2)   *à kâ-n teebùr* 'on the table' (lit. at top-of table)
       à bàaki-n hanyàa 'next to the road' (lit. at edge-of road)
       à madàdi-n Audù 'instead of Audu' (lit. 'at representative-of Audu')

Semantically, these correspond to English prepositions, but grammatically, they are not really different from an ordinary noun phrase preceded by a preposition.

Thus, languages may use cases instead of grammatical adpositions, and relational nouns instead of concrete adpositions. As a result, there are many languages that lack adpositions completely; most languages of Australia seem to be of this type. However, there is probably always a tendency for relational nouns to develop formal peculiarities corresponding to their special meanings, thus turning into real adpositions through the process of grammaticalization. For instance, most English compound prepositions derive from relational nouns, as is clear also from the fact that they often govern an *of* phrase as a complement (e.g. *in spite of, in front of, instead of, because of*); however, they have undergone various changes (e.g. *by cause of > because of, in my front > in front of me*, cf. older English *in my stead*).

Relational nouns are the most common diachronic sources for new adpositions, but adpositions may also come from adverbs (e.g. Modern Greek *píso apó to spiti* 'behind the house', from Classical Greek *opísoo* 'behind, in back'). This is a typical source of adpositions in European languages, so adpositions still often do double duty as adverbs (e.g. English *in, out, off, above, below*). It has been proposed that such adverbs should be regarded as "intransitive" (non-complement-taking) adpositions, but again, this analysis works better for European languages than for most non-European languages.

Adpositions may also come from verbs: in Chinese and other Southeast Asian languages, as well as in many West African languages, verbs function as adpositions do elsewhere and seem to be gradually turning into adpositions. Such verbs are called "coverbs" (e.g. Chinese *gei* 'give, for', as in *Wo gei ta mai xiangyan* 'I buy cigarettes for him', lit. 'I give him buy cigarettes'). Deverbal adpositions are also found in European languages (e.g. English *during*, French *pendant* 'during', Russian *nesmotrja* 'despite', lit. 'not looking').

Besides prepositions and postpositions, we occasionally find *circumpositions*, which consist of two elements bracketing the complement (e.g. *for X's sake*); *ambipositions*, which may occur on either side of the complement, e.g. Classical Greek *héneka* 'because of'; and *inpositions*, which occur between the constituents of a multiword complement (see Dryer, to appear).

[*See also* Case; Functional Linguistics; Grammaticalization; Parts of Speech; Semantics *and* Typology and Universals.]

BIBLIOGRAPHY

Bakker, Dik. To appear. Person marking on adpositions. In Dryer et al.

Dryer, Matthew S. To appear. Order of adposition and noun phrase. In Dryer et al.

Dryer, Matthew, Martin Haspelmath, David Gil, and Bernard Comrie. To appear. *World atlas of language structures.* Oxford: Oxford University Press.

Haspelmath, Martin. 1997. *From space to time: Temporal adverbials in the world's languages.* (Lincom Studies in Theoretical Linguistics, 3.) Munich and Newcastle: Lincom Europa.

Heine, Bernd. 1989. Adpositions in African languages. *Linguistique Africaine* 2.77–127.

Kortmann, Bernd, and Ekkehard König. 1992. Categorial reanalysis: The case of deverbal prepositions. *Linguistics* 30.671–697.

Svorou, Soteria. 1994. *The grammar of space.* Amsterdam: Benjamins.

Martin Haspelmath

ADVERBS. *See* Grammaticalization; Parts of Speech; *and* Typology and Universals.

AFFIXATION. The term "affixation" denotes the technique of concatenating affixes—morphological (not lexical) elements which are non-words—either directly to roots or stems, or to affixes in the case of affix cumulation, e.g. *conven-tion-al-iz-ation.* This "concatenative morphology" is generally more common than other techniques (conversion, ablaut, umlaut—or subtraction, as in dialectal German *hond* 'dog', *hon* 'dog-s').

Affixes which follow roots are called "suffixes," e.g. *dark-en(-ed)*; affixes which precede roots are called "prefixes," e.g. *(re-)en-list.* Suffixes are in general more common than prefixes (Cutler et al. 1985), and both are more common than other types of affix. The combination of a prefix and a suffix (e.g. *en-light-en*) is classified by some as a "circumfix" or "ambifix," but only when the prefix and suffix parts are not themselves autonomous (cf. *en-* and *-en* in *en-light-en,* cf. *en-list, dark-en*), but rather are divided parts of an autonomous affix (cf. Hall 2000).

An "infix" is an affix which divides the root by being inserted into it, e.g. the Latin *n-* infix in *vi/n/c-ō* 'I win' vs. *vīc-ī* 'I won' (cf. Moravcsik 2000). An "interfix" is a meaningless affix inserted between words (e.g. Spanish *-i-* in *pel-i-rrojo* 'red-haired' from *pelo* 'hair' and *rojo* 'red'), or between root and suffix (e.g. Spanish *-eg-* in *pedr-eg-oso* 'rocky', adjective from *piedra* 'rock', similar to *pel-oso* 'hairy' from *pelo*; cf. Dressler and Merlini 1990). The existence of "transfixes" (infixed circumfixes, Broselow 2000) is dubious; see Kilani-Schoch and Dressler 1984.

[*See also* Morphology; Generative Morphology; *and* Stem and Root.]

BIBLIOGRAPHY

Broselow, E. 2000. Transfixation. In *Morphologie/Morphology I*, edited by G. Booij et al., pp. 552–557. Berlin: de Gruyter.

Cutler, Anne, John A. Hawkins, and Gary Gilligan. 1985. The suffixing preference: A processing explanation. *Linguistics* 23.723–758.

Dressler, Wolfgang U., and Lavinia Merlini. 1986. How to fix interfixes? *Acta Linguistica Hungarica,* 36.53–67.

Hall, C. J. 2000. Prefixation, suffixation and circumfixation. In *Morphologie/Morphology I*, edited by G. Booij et al., pp. 535–545. Berlin: de Gruyter.

Kilani-Schoch, Marianne, and Wolfgang U. Dressler. 1984. Natural morphology and classical vs. Tunisian Arabic. *Wiener Linguistische Gazette* 33/34.51–68. Also in *Studia Gramatyczne* 7.27–47, 1985.

Moravcsik, Edith A. 2000. Infixation. In *Morphologie/Morphology I*, edited by G. Booij et al., pp. 545–552. Berlin: de Gruyter.

Wolfgang U. Dressler

AFRICAN AMERICAN VERNACULAR ENGLISH (AAVE). Since the mid-1960s, no single variety of American English has been the focus of as much scholarly research and publication, nor of as much public commentary and controversy, as African American Vernacular English (AAVE). What to call it has itself been an issue. Changes in the ethnic identifier, from "Negro" to "Black" to "African American," are relatively simple reflections of evolution in the preferred designations for its primary speakers. However, "Vernacular" replaced "Non-Standard" in the early 1970s as a less negative way of signaling that not every variety of English spoken by African Americans is included, that not all African Americans speak it, and that those who speak it do not do so all of the time. Finally, alternatives like "Ebonics" and "African American Language"—popularly equated with AAVE in recent public discussions, but with roots in the early 1970s—are potentially quite different in denotation and connotation. Ebonics, for one thing, theoretically includes linguistic and paralinguistic features from Caribbean and West African varieties as well as those of the United States, although in practice it does not. Moreover, both terms emphasize African ancestral roots and to some extent oppose classification of this variety as a "dialect" of English (see Williams 1975:vi; Rickford 1999:xxi–xxiii).

AAVE has attracted significant scholarly and popular interest because of its distinctiveness and vigor, its ubiquity in African American literature, music, life and culture, its connection with educational crises facing African American students, and the descriptive challenges and historical puzzles it poses for sociolinguists and variationists. For instance, variable rules were first introduced (in 1968) to handle the variable contraction and deletion of the AAVE copula ('he *is*/'*s*/Ø tall'), and the relative influence of African, English, and Creole sources in the development of AAVE is a subject of perennial interest.

Especially in its popular designation as Ebonics, AAVE is frequently associated with the current slang of black teenagers and young adults; however, slang words (like *phat* 'excellent' and *bustin out* 'looking good') tend to be relatively short-lived. Moreover, they are often regionally restricted and cross over into usage by young Americans more generally, regardless of their ethnicity. More distinctive, and in some ways more intriguing for what they reveal about interactional barriers between races, are old, geographically widespread lexical usages like *ashy* for the appearance of black skin in winter, and *kitchen* for the especially kinky hair at the nape of one's neck. These are familiar to African Americans of all ages but are virtually unknown to white Americans and other ethnic groups. African Americans are usually surprised

to discover that other Americans don't recognize or employ these lexical items, at least not in the "black" sense.

Of greater interest to linguists are AAVE's phonological and grammatical features. Many of the phonological features, like the simplification of same-voice clusters ([han] 'hand', [pas] 'past') or the realization of Standard English interdental fricatives as stops ([tin] 'thin', [den] 'then'), are shared with other metropolitan English dialects. However, their frequencies are often higher in AAVE than in other American dialects, and AAVE sometimes extends the processes to environments in which other American dialects do not (e.g. *r*-deletion between vowels, as in *Carol* > *Ca'ol*). Some of AAVE's characteristic phonology—e.g. the monophthongization of *ai* ([ra:d] 'ride') or the neutralization of [ɪ] and [ɛ] before nasals ([pɪn] 'pin' or 'pen') is shared by Southern white dialects too, a reflection of the fact that, until 1900, 90% of the African American population was concentrated in the South. (Who got what from whom is still an open question.)

AAVE does, however, have phonological features that are more distinctive. One is the rule deleting initial voiced stops in several tense-aspect auxiliaries (e.g. the unique use of *ain't* for 'didn't', or the realization of 'I don't know' as [a õ no] and 'I'm going to do it' as [ã mə du ɪt]). This is rare in English dialects except for Gullah and the Caribbean English creoles (e.g., *ben>en, go>o, da>a*), a fact with potential diachronic significance. Another distinctive feature is the pronunciation of the vowels in words like *pay* and *no* as monophthongs, without the offglides ([ey], [ow]) found in other varieties of American English. This is commonest among older African Americans (born before World War I), and is, interestingly, also characteristic of Caribbean English creoles.

Grammatically, the features that are most distinctive of AAVE, and the ones that have been most engaging to linguists, are in the verb phrase. They include the absence of present tense forms of the copula (*is*, *are*, but not *am*), and the use of a wide range of preverbal tense-aspectual markers, like invariant habitual *be* (*he be late* 'he is usually late'), stressed *BIN* to situate the initiation of a state in the remote past (*She BIN married* 'She has been married for a long time, and still is'), and *be done* for future or habitual resultant states (*he be done ate* 'he will have eaten' or 'he has usually already eaten').

Other AAVE grammatical features include multiple negation (*He ain't goin nowhere nohow*); the inversion of negative auxiliaries with indefinite pronoun subjects in declarative sentences (*Didn' nobody leave*); the use of *say* in serial verb-like constructions to introduce the complement of verbs like *tell* (*She told me say she would win*); existential *it* and *dey got* (*it's some chicken in the icebox, dey got some fine people here*); and the absence of possessive *-s* (*Mary∅ boychild*) and of third singular present tense *-s* (*he walk∅ a lot*). As with the phonological features, several of these grammatical features are also found in other English varieties, especially in the US South.

Quantitative studies of sociolinguistic variation in the US have often focused on African American communities, covering Harlem, Detroit, Washington, D.C., Wilmington (Delaware), Philadelphia, Hyde County (North Carolina), College Station (Texas), and Oakland, East Palo Alto, and Los Angeles in California. From these we have a rich picture of how AAVE use varies according to socioeconomic class, age, network, and style, making AAVE a prime exemplar of the orderly heterogeneity that is fundamental to sociolinguistics. For instance, studies of social-class variation from the 1960s (Harlem, Detroit) indicated that grammatical features like copula absence, multiple negation, and the absence of present tense *-s* were sharply stratified, with African American working-class and underclass speakers using them 50% to 75% of the time while middle-class speakers used them only 10% of the time or less. More recent studies of class variation in AAVE are rare, but from informal evidence and one or two systematic studies, it is clear that class stratification is as strong as ever. This explains in part why middle- and upper-class black luminaries like US Congressman Kweisi Mfume and entertainer Bill Cosby were so vocal in their critiques of the Oakland (California) school board's 1996 proposal to take Ebonics into account in teaching Standard English and Language Arts.

Use of AAVE is also more frequent among adolescents and young adults than among older speakers, except for receding features like the deletion of unstressed initial and medial syllables (e.g. *[a]bout, sec[re]t[ar]y*). It is more frequent, too, in informal conversation among African Americans who are friends or peer-group members, than in individual interactions between African Americans and whites, particularly when they are strangers. For several core AAVE features, especially ones—like invariant habitual *be* and preterit *had*—that appear to have undergone recent grammatical change, urban (rather than rural) youth appear to be the primary users. With respect to gender, early indications that males were much heavier users of AAVE features than were females have been challenged by recent fieldwork conducted by female researchers, and traditional claims that AAVE is relatively uniform across the US are increasingly being questioned. The need for more systematic investigation of regional variation is clear.

Urban African American youth—among the most vigorous speakers of AAVE—are often considerably behind grade level in reading, writing, and other subjects. Relatedly, they tend to have some of the highest drop-out, unemployment, and underemployment rates, and to be disproportionately targeted by the criminal justice system. Many of the contributing factors lie outside linguistics, including limited school facilities and trained teachers in urban ghettoes, low expectations, and institutional racism; but for more than thirty years, linguists have recognized that there are some linguistic elements to the problem, and have explored possible solutions (see Baratz and Shuy 1969, Adger et al. 1999). In fact, the earliest community studies of AAVE were funded by educational agencies who saw the potential relevance of linguistics.

Linguists working in this area often note the regular differences between the students' vernacular and the standard or mainstream English required by schools. IQ and other achievement tests can directly disadvantage AAVE speakers if these differences are not taken into account, and teachers who mistakenly interpret such differences as evidence of intellectual deficit or laziness can have stultifying effects on their students' performance. Linguists have proposed and led dialect-awareness workshops to counter teachers' negative attitudes and practices with respect to non-mainstream features and discourse patterns, and they have also advocated specific strategies for improving the teaching of curriculum-central subjects like reading and writing. These include systematic comparisons between the vernacular and standard varieties (contrastive analysis), exercises to increase students' bidialectal competence in speech and writing, and the use of dialect readers and other transitional strategies to improve the teaching of reading. Linguists were extensively involved in attempts to clear up public misunderstanding of the Oakland school board's "Ebonics" proposals to build on the vernacular's systematicity and expressiveness, and in the "King" case nearly two decades earlier, in which an Ann Arbor (Michigan) school was sued for failing to overcome the barriers to equal education posed by its teachers' negative attitudes to students' AAVE (see Baugh 2000, Rickford and Rickford 2000, Smitherman 2000). The most recent and geographically extensive intervention project is the Urban Minorities Reading Project, which analyzes the phonemic decoding errors of African American, Latino, and white students and uses an individualized reading manual to improve literacy scores. (Visit: www.ling.upenn.edu/~labov/UMRP/UMRP.html)

Finally, questions about the history and development of AAVE continue to stimulate research and controversy among linguists. They cluster around two issues: (i) To what extent did African, British English, and Creole sources contribute to the early development and subsequent history of AAVE? More specifically, was AAVE itself once a creole, like Jamaican and other English-based creoles in the Caribbean, or did the African indentured servants and slaves who came to the US from the 17th to the 19th century acquire the English dialects of British indentured servants and settlers here, without the extensive simplification and restructuring characteristic of pidginization and creolization? (ii) Has AAVE been diverging from white American vernaculars (and Standard English) in the 20th century, and is divergence rather than convergence its current trajectory? Although theoretically independent of (i), some linguists take the position that AAVE was primarily influenced by and convergent with white English vernaculars from the 17th century to the mid-19th, and that the most distinctive AAVE features emerged only in the 20th century, as blacks moved out of the South and faced sharp segregation in urban ghettoes.

Although there is no consensus on either issue, some of the parameters have shifted, and new kinds of data are being used. The early position of William Stewart and Joe Dillard that there was a widespread US plantation creole, comparable to Gullah on the South Carolina and Georgia Sea Islands, no longer meets with wide support. Creolists today tend to speak more of relative influences from creole sources, either through early slave importations from the Caribbean or through local developments in (Southern) American colonies where the demographic conditions for creolization were most favorable. In recent years, relevant data have come less from literary and other texts from earlier centuries, and more from recordings made with ex-slaves in the early 20th century, or with the descendants of African American emigrés to Liberia, Samaná in the Dominican Republic, and Nova Scotia, Canada ("diaspora" data). There has been more emphasis on detailed quantitative and linguistic analysis of specific variables, like copula absence and past-tense marking, and on detailed consideration of demographic and sociohistorical factors (see Mufwene et al. 1998, Poplack 2000, Wolfram and Bailey 2000).

[*See also* Bilingualism and Multilingualism; Diglossia; English; Pidgins and Creoles; Social Variation; *and* Sociolinguistics.]

BIBLIOGRAPHY

Adger, Carolyn Temple, Donna Christian, and Orlando Taylor, eds. 1999. *Making the connection: Language and academic achievement among African American students.* McHenry, Ill.: Delta Systems and Center for Applied Linguistics.

Baugh, John. 2001. *Beyond Ebonics.* Oxford: Oxford University Press.

Green, Lisa. 2002. *African American English: A linguistic introduction.* Cambridge: Cambridge University Press.

Labov, William. 1972. *Language in the inner city.* Philadelphia: University of Pennsylvania Press.

Lanehart, Sonja, ed. 2001. *Sociocultural and historical contexts of African American Vernacular English.* Amsterdam and Philadelphia: Benjamins.

Mufwene, Salikoko S., John R. Rickford, Guy Bailey, and John Baugh. 1999. *African American Vernacular English.* London: Routledge.

Poplack, Shana, ed. 2000. *The English history of African American Vernacular English.* Oxford: Blackwell.

Rickford, John R. 1999. *African American Vernacular English.* Oxford: Blackwell.

Rickford, John R., and Russell J. Rickford. 2000. *Spoken Soul: The story of black English.* New York: John Wiley.

Smitherman, Geneva. 2001. *Talkin that talk.* London: Routledge.

Williams, Robert L., ed. *Ebonics: The true language of black folks.* St. Louis, Missouri: Robert L. Williams.

Wolfram, Walt, and Erik Thomas. 2002. *The development of African American English.* Oxford: Blackwell.

JOHN R. RICKFORD

AFRICAN LANGUAGES. The African continent forms one of the most complex linguistic areas of the world; estimates of the number of languages spoken there range from seven hundred to three thousand. Barely more than one hundred have developed into standard languages. The majority of the languages are still unrecorded; for many, little but the name is known. Although early descriptions of African languages date back to the 17th century, African linguistics as a research field developed only during the 19th century.

1. Genetic classification. Until the 1950s, work on the linguistic classification of African languages was dominated by a threefold division into "Hamitic," "Sudanic," and "Bantu" languages (Meinhof 1936, Westermann

MAP 1. *Distribution of African Language Families*

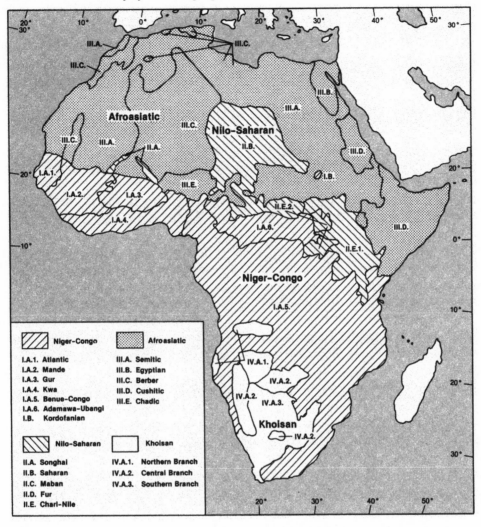

1935). This classification was based on a mixture of genetic/diachronic and typological/synchronic criteria; it was also used to develop a theory of the typological evolution of languages from an isolating structure (Sudanic) via an agglutinating stage (Bantu) to an inflectional (Hamitic) type.

The work of Greenberg 1955 marks a milestone in the history of language classification in Africa. It proposed a genetic classification of African languages into sixteen families; Greenberg 1963 presented a revised classification which reduced the number to four—Niger-Congo, Afroasiatic, Khoisan, and Nilo-Saharan (see Map 1). This work differs from that of various European scholars mainly in that it relies entirely on material relevant to genetic classification, as opposed to typological, areal, or other kinds of organization. Greenberg's methodological

principles are: (i) the sole relevance of forms; (ii) mass comparison, as against isolated comparisons between pairs of languages; and (iii) the exclusive use of linguistic evidence (Greenberg 1963:1). The last principle might seem redundant, but the history of language classification in Africa provides a number of cases where non-linguistic data have been adduced in order to define linguistic relationships.

The *Niger-Congo* family, in its current revision, contains by far the largest number of languages. It includes Kordofanian, a group of languages spoken in the western part of the Republic of the Sudan, as well as most of the languages of western, central, and southern Africa, belonging to such groups as Atlantic, Mande, Gur, Kwa, Benue-Congo, and Adamawa-Ubangi. The Benue-Congo branch includes more than 300 Bantu languages, which in earlier classifications had been treated as a separate family. Some of the most important African languages belong to Niger-Congo, e.g. Swahili, Zulu, Kikongo, Yoruba, Igbo, Twi, Manding (Bambara, Malinke, Dyula), Fula, and Wolof.

The *Afroasiatic* family, also called "Erythraic" or "Hamito-Semitic," is distributed throughout northern and eastern Africa. It includes the following subfamilies: Semitic, Berber, Cushitic, Chadic, and extinct Egyptian. With the exception of Semitic, all Afroasiatic languages are spoken exclusively on the African continent. While a number of Semitic languages are now spoken in Africa, they all originated in the Arabian peninsula. The Afroasiatic family includes such major African languages as Arabic, Hausa, Amharic, Oromo (Galla), and Somali.

Most of the *Nilo-Saharan* languages are found in the area of the Congo-Nile divide. This family includes the following branches: Songhai, Saharan, Maban, Fur, Chari-Nile, and Komuz. With the exception of Saharan and Chari-Nile, these branches consist essentially of one language each. Among the better known Nilo-Saharan languages are Nubian and Maasai (both of the Chari-Nile branch), and Kanuri, a Saharan language spoken to the west of Lake Chad.

Khoisan, referred to in Greenberg's earlier writings as the "Click family," includes the languages of the San ("Bushmen") and Khoekhoe ("Hottentots") of southern and southwestern Africa—as well as two East African "click languages," Sandawe and Hadza, both spoken in central Tanzania.

The overall framework of genetic classification proposed by Greenberg 1963 has remained largely unchanged since that date. However, a number of revisions have been proposed, and some have been accepted by the majority of Africanists. One issue concerns the relationship between two of the four language families. According to Gregersen 1972, Niger-Kordofanian and Nilo-Saharan belong to a single macro-family, which he proposes to call "Kongo-Saharan." Another topic of research has been the position of the Mande languages; Greenberg placed them in Niger-Congo, but other authors claim that they are not even part of Niger-Kordofanian (Mukarovsky 1966, Köhler 1975:240–245).

Khoisan, as a genetic unit, is accepted by the majority of scholars, with one exception: Hadza, the language of a few hundred traditional hunter-gatherers in the Lake Eyasi basin of northern Tanzania, shows relationships with Cushitic. The implications for the relationship between Khoisan and Afroasiatic, which includes Cushitic, remain to be investigated.

Although Greenberg's work represents considerable progress over that of previous writers, it leaves a number of questions open. His approach is largely inadequate for the *proof* of genetic relationship; it can do little more than offer initial hypotheses, to be substantiated by more reliable techniques like the comparative method. In a number of instances, languages or language groups have been placed in a given family solely on the basis of a handful of "look-alikes," i.e. morphemes of similar sound shape and meaning. The Nilo-Saharan family, in particular, must be regarded as a tentative grouping, the genetic unity of which remains to be established.

Observations like these have led some scholars to reject macro-level classifications and to concentrate on small-scale comparisons which involve only a limited number of closely related languages. This was the policy adopted by the International African Institute in its monograph series "Handbook of African Languages," published between 1948 and 1967. Other scholars have proposed "practical," referential classifications, based on arbitrary criteria; these provide convenient reference systems, but are of limited scientific use. The best known of these classifications is that of Guthrie 1948 for Bantu; another has been proposed by Dalby 1970 for the entire continent.

2. Typological and areal characteristics. Language comparison in Africa has overwhelmingly been confined to diachronic studies, especially to the reconstruction of patterns of genetic relationship. Interest in other kinds of linguistic classification has been limited. Until the 1950s, studies on the typology of African languages were based largely on a framework going back to Schlegel (cf. Doke 1950). However, the work of Houis 1970, 1971 marks a departure from 19th century typology. He correlates phonological and morphological features with word order, and distinguishes two main types in Africa. The first type has head + attribute word order, with noun + adjective and preposition + noun constructions—as well as both closed and open syllables, complex word structure, and rich morphology; this type lacks a phonemic contrast between oral and nasal vowels. Examples include West Atlantic languages like Fula, Temne, Diola, and Wolof as well as Hausa, the Bantu languages, and Nilotic languages like Acholi or Kalenjin. The second type has *rectum-regens* order (e.g. noun + postposition), open syllables only, simple word structure, and limited morphology; but there is a productive pattern of nominal compounding as well as distinct nasal vowels. Examples are the languages of the Voltaic, Mande, and Kwa groups of the Niger-Congo family.

Based on work on the order of meaningful elements

(Greenberg 1966), a word-order typology of more than 300 African languages has been presented by Heine 1975, 1976, and by Heine and Vossen (1981:422–436). Their taxonomy distinguishes eight discrete types, based on word order and on the presence vs. absence of a noun class system, of nominal case inflection, and of derivative verbal extension.

Like typology, areal linguistics is still a greatly under-developed field in Africa, although areal considerations have usually played a role in works on language classi-fication. For instance, ten of the fourteen criteria listed by Westermann 1935 in defining the "Sudanic" family—a grouping of several hundred languages, spoken in a broad belt from the extreme west to the extreme east of Africa—are suggestive of an areal relationship. Although system-atic research is still lacking, it seems that the structures of African languages can be correlated with combinations of genetic and areal factors. The Ethiopian Highlands can be defined as a kind of *Sprachbund* or *language area*. Of the six branches of the Afroasiatic family found there, three—Cushitic, Omotic, and Ethiopian Semitic—show a number of features which are virtually absent from Afroasiatic languages outside the area, but which are shared by non-Afroasiatic languages within it, e.g. the presence of ejective consonants and of Subject-Object-Verb syntax.

3. Features characteristic of African languages. None of the attempts made in the past has succeeded in proving that the African languages form a historical and/or typological unit. However, there are some features which are found only in Africa, or which are widespread there. Thus, click consonants occur in three of the four African language families; but while they are found throughout the Khoisan family, they occur in only one Afroasiatic lan-guage, Dahalo; and of the Niger-Congo languages, they are found only in those spoken in the vicinity of Khoisan, i.e. the Bantu languages of southern Africa.

Other noteworthy phonological characteristics of Af-rican languages include the widespread occurrence of complex tone systems, of vowel harmony, and of implo-sive or labiovelar consonants (*kp, gb*). African consonant systems have rightly been described as "simple" (Green-berg 1959:23); however, the language with the largest number of consonants in the world is thought to be !Xóõ (/Hua-Owani), a Khoisan language of Botswana and Namibia, which has 117 consonant phonemes (Traill 1985).

The majority of African languages have a system of noun classes, or genders. For one language, Zande, a Niger-Congo language of the Adamawa-Ubangi branch,

the origin of a gender system has been described in detail (Claudi 1985). By contrast, there is a conspicuous lack of ergative languages in Africa. So far, only two have been reported: Loma, a Mande language, and Anuak, a Western Nilotic language of the Nilo-Saharan family.

Semantic features which are characteristic of many African languages include the following: comparison is expressed by means of the verb 'defeat' ('X is big, defeats Y' = 'X is bigger than Y'); feeling and understanding by the verb 'see' or 'hear' ('I don't see/hear you' = 'I don't understand you'); conquering or having sexual inter-course, by the verb 'eat'; and smoking by the verb 'drink' ('Do you drink cigarettes?' = 'Do you smoke?').

The expression of spatial organization in terms of body parts is very common, with typical metaphorical equa-tions such as these (Heine 1986:4):

(1)   'head'   'above, upon, in front'
       'eye'   'before, in front'
       'face'   'in front'
       'back'   'behind'
       'buttock'   'under, behind'
       'belly'   'inside'
       'heart'   'in the middle'
       'foot/leg' 'under, below'

In many African languages, though not all, spatial orientation is structured differently than in European languages (cf. Hill 1974). In English, for instance, objects which do not have an inherent front-back orientation, like mountains or trees, are conceived as facing the speaker or deictic center. Thus *The tree is in front of the mountain* means that the tree is located between the mountain and the speaker, since the mountain is assumed to face the speaker. In many African languages, by contrast, such objects are conceived as facing in the *same* direction as the speaker or deictic center. Thus, in the example, the mountain is 'looking' in the same direction as the speaker, and therefore turns its 'back' to him/her. A tree between mountain and speaker is 'behind' rather than 'in front of' the mountain.

4. Lingua francas. The majority of African nations use European languages for official purposes—in most cases, English or French (in Cameroon, both of these). A few African languages have been recognized as na-tional official media, e.g. Swahili in Tanzania, Amharic in Ethiopia, and Somali in Somalia. National and inter-national communication in Africa is determined to some extent by the distribution of indigenous lingua francas, i.e., languages which are used habitually between people

MAP 2. *Lingua Francas of Africa*

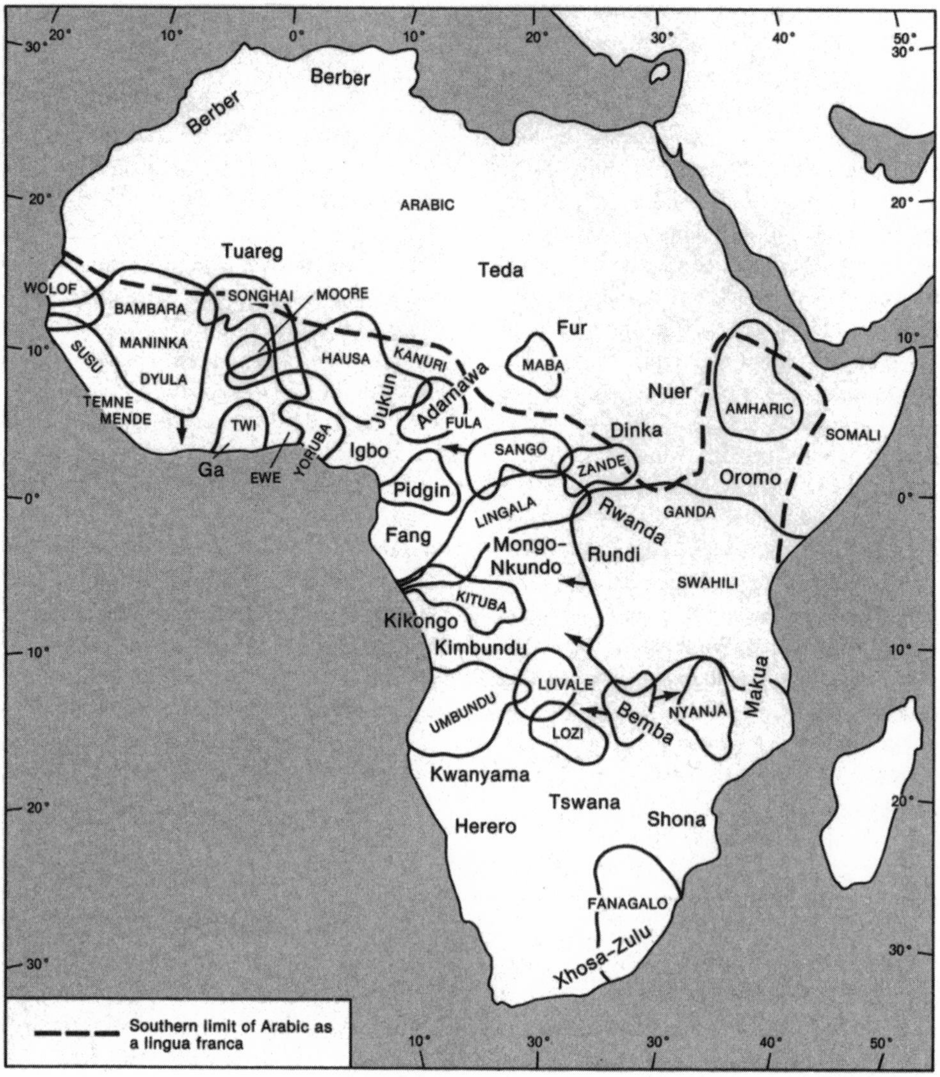

whose mother tongues are different (see Map 2). Some of these, like Swahili in East Africa or Maninka in West Africa, have spread over areas almost as large as Europe (see Heine 1970). Some have assumed the role of de facto national languages, e.g. Swahili in Kenya, Sango in Central Africa, Bambara (a variety of Maninka) in Mali, and Wolof in Senegal.

[*See also* Adamawa-Ubangi Languages; Afroasiatic Languages; Amharic; Arabic; Atlantic Languages; Benue-Congo Languages; Central Sudanic Languages; Edoid Languages; Ekoid Languages; Fula; Gur Languages; Hausa; Khoisan Languages; Kwa Languages; Mande Languages; Niger-Congo Languages; Nilo-Saharan Languages; Somali; Songhai Languages; Swahili; Yoruba; *and* Zulu.]

BIBLIOGRAPHY

Claudi, Ulrike. 1985. *Zur Entstehung von Genussystemen: Überlegungen zu einigen theoretischen Aspekten, verbunden mit einer Fallstudie des Zande.* Hamburg: Buske.

Dalby, David. 1970. Reflections on the classification of African languages, with special reference to the work of Sigismund Wilhelm Koelle and Malcolm Guthrie. *African Language Studies* 11.147–171.

Doke, Clement M. 1950. Bantu languages, inflexional with a tendency towards agglutination. *African Studies* 9.1–19.

Greenberg, Joseph H. 1955. *Studies in African linguistic classification.* New Haven, Conn.: Compass.

Greenberg, Joseph H. 1959. Africa as a linguistic area. In *Continuity and change in African cultures,* edited by William R. Bascom and Melville J. Herskovits, pp. 15–27. Chicago: University of Chicago Press.

Greenberg, Joseph H. 1963. *The languages of Africa.* (Indiana University Research Center in Anthropology, Folklore, and Linguistics, Publication 25; *International Journal of American Linguistics*, 29:1, part 2.) Bloomington.

Greenberg, Joseph H. 1966. Some universals of grammar with particular reference to the order of meaningful elements. In *Universals of language,* 2d ed., edited by Joseph H. Greenberg, pp. 73–113. Cambridge, Mass.: MIT Press.

Gregersen, Edgar A. 1972. Kongo-Saharan. *Journal of African Languages* 11.69–89.

Guthrie, Malcolm. 1948. *The classification of Bantu languages.* London and New York: Oxford University Press.

Heine, Bernd. 1970. *Status and use of African lingua francas.* (Afrika-Studien, 49.) Munich: Weltforum.

Heine, Bernd. 1975. Language typology and convergence areas in Africa. *Linguistics* 144.27–47.

Heine, Bernd. 1976. *A typology of African languages, based on the order of meaningful elements.* (Kölner Beiträge zur Afrikanistik, 4.) Berlin: Reimer.

Heine, Bernd. 1986. *The rise of grammatical categories: Cognition and language change in Africa.* (Sixteenth Annual Hans Wolff Memorial Lecture.) Bloomington: African Studies Program, Indiana University.

Heine, Bernd, and Rainer Vossen. 1981. Sprachtypologie. In *Die Sprachen Afrikas,* edited by Bernd Heine et al., pp. 407–444. Hamburg: Buske.

Heine, Bernd, and Derek Nurse, eds. 2000. *African languages: An introduction.* Cambridge: Cambridge University Press.

Hill, Clifford Alden. 1974. Spatial perception and linguistic encoding: A case study in Hausa and English. *Studies in African Linguistics,* Suppl. 5, pp. 135–148. Los Angeles: UCLA.

Houis, Maurice. 1970. Réflexion sur une double corrélation typologique. *Journal of West African Linguistics* 7:2.59–68.

Houis, Maurice. 1971. *Anthropologie linguistique de l'Afrique Noire.* (Le linguiste, 11.) Paris: Presses Universitaires de France.

Köhler, Oswin. 1975. Geschichte und Probleme der Gliederung der Sprachen Afrikas. In *Die Völker Afrikas und ihre traditionellen Kulturen,* vol. 1, *Allgemeiner Teil und südliches Afrika* (Studien zur Kulturkunde, 34), edited by Hermann Baumann, pp. 141–373. Wiesbaden: Steiner.

Meinhof, Carl. 1936. *Die Entstehung flektierender Sprachen.* Berlin: Reimer.

Mukarovsky, Hans. 1976–77. *A study of Western Nigritic.* 2 vols. (Beiträge zur Afrikanistik, 1–2.) Vienna: Institut für Ägyptologie und Afrikanistik der Universität Wien.

Traill, Anthony. 1985. *Phonetic and phonological studies of !Xóõ Bushman.* (Quellen zur Khoisan-Forschung, 1.) Hamburg: Buske.

Westermann, Diedrich. 1935. Charakter und Einteilung der Sudansprachen. *Africa* 8.129–149.

BERND HEINE

AFROASIATIC LANGUAGES. The Afroasiatic (or Afro-Asiatic) family includes the Semitic, Berber, Cushitic, Egyptian, and Chadic branches. Altogether, about 250 members of the family are known, most of them belonging to Chadic (130–150 languages) and Cushitic (about 50). A[fro-]A[siatic] languages today dominate the Middle East and North and Northeast Africa, and they also occur in West Africa. (For a survey, see Zaborski 1998; Takács 1999, vol. 1, 9–34; Diakonoff 1988; and D. Cohen 1988.)

Since around 1960, scholars have rejected a twofold division into Semitic and "Hamitic"; the latter was formerly conceived as comprising Berber, Cushitic, Egyptian, and part of Chadic, and sometimes other languages of Africa (now considered non-AA) that have masculine/feminine gender opposition. The term "Hamitic" is no longer used, though the whole family is still sometimes referred to as "Hamito-Semitic" (or rarely, "Semito-Hamitic"). New names for the whole family, such as "Erythraic" and "Lisramic," have gained little acceptance, but contracted "Afrasian" is used by some scholars. A hypothesis based mainly on negative evidence, claiming that the Omotic languages of southwestern Ethiopia may constitute another major AA branch, appears incorrect; these languages are better classified as West Cushitic, the most innovating section of Cushitic. Also unacceptable is an attempt to classify North Cushitic Beja, spoken mainly in Sudan, as another major independent branch of AA. The Berber branch is sometimes called "Libyco-Berber" or "Berber-Libyan," but this usage does not appear justified, primarily because the little-known language of the "Libyan" inscriptions (actually found mostly in today's Tunisia) does not show any special divergences in comparison with other Berber dialects. The extinct Guanche of the Canary Islands shows at least partial connections with Berber.

There is a broad consensus that the five major branches of AA are parallel and equal, but it is probable that the Semitic branch is closer to Berber owing to several verbal isomorphs, and that both Semitic and Berber are further related to somewhat more distant Cushitic. The resulting group is, in turn, close to Egyptian. Chadic, which has so far been explored only in part, can be provisionally considered the most distant branch of AA.

There is as yet no comparative grammar of AA, or even of Berber, Cushitic, or Chadic. The most important general sketch is Diakonoff 1988. The first comparative dictionary, apart from the pioneering work of M. Cohen 1947, has been compiled by Diakonoff and his collabo-

TABLE 1. *Selected Afroasiatic Pronominal Elements*

	'I'	'we'	'your' (masc.)	'your' (fem.)
Akkadian	ʾan-ā-ku	nînu (<*naḥnu)	-ka	-ki
Arabic	ʾan-ā	naḥnu	-ka	-ki
Berber	n-əkk	nəkkun	-k	
Beja	án-e	henén	(-ho)-ka	(-ho)-ki
Egyptian (Coptic)	ʾan-ak	ʾanan	-k	č (<*ki)
Hausa	ni	mu	-ka	-ki

rators (1993). It must be used with care, but it is better than the dictionary of Orel and Stolbova 1995; Ehret 1995 is the most controversial. Takács's 1999– etymological dictionary concentrates on Egyptian but is important for the whole AA family.

It now appears that the Old Semitic languages, especially Akkadian and Classical Arabic, are the most archaic, the closest to the Proto-AA stage, which was represented by a dialect cluster with partially overlapping and partially contradictory isoglosses. Within Berber, Tuareg is considered most archaic; and within Cushitic, Beja, Afar-Saho, and Rendille. Egyptian has many archaisms, but its verbal system has been radically restructured (though this interpretation is not universally accepted). The Chadic languages that we know at present seem to be quite innovative.

The main morphological elements common to AA are the personal pronouns: the independent forms; the suffixed forms, used for direct object or as possessives; and the verbal formant forms, prefixed and suffixed. Since about 1850 these pronouns, which are remarkably uniform, have been considered proof of the existence of the AA family; see Table 1.

The feminine suffix -*at*, also used for abstracts and singulatives, is also Proto-AA. Shared case morphemes include at least -*u* nominative, -*i* genitive, and -*a* absolute. Other common nominal elements are plural -V*w*/-*ū*, -*ān*, -*āt*, nominal prefix *m*V- and an adjectival suffix -*î*/-V*y*. Some patterns of "internal" plural—plural forms with ablaut (e.g. with -*a*-)—are also Proto-AA. The verbal systems of Semitic and Berber, and probably also of Chadic, have a basic morphological opposition between the so-called suffixal conjugations (with suffixed pronominal morphemes)—which are mainly stative but also "perfect," and, with possessive pronouns, "gerund"—and the prefixal conjugations, which are used with different ablaut patterns and/or vocalic endings to mark various tense/aspect/mode functions. Thus, in the suffixal conju-

gation, we have 1sg. Akkadian -*āku*, Berber -V*ġ*, Egyptian -*k-w-y*; in the prefixal conjugation, Proto-AA 1sg. *ʾa-*, 2sg. *t*V- (with -*i* for feminine), 3sg. masc. *y*V-, 3sg. fem. *t*V-, 1pl. *n*V-, 2pl. *t*V-, 3pl. *y*V-, with plural and feminine suffixes in the 2nd and 3rd plural. With different ablaut patterns, we have, e.g., Akkadian *i-prus* 'he split', *i-parras* 'he splits'; Touareg *i-krās* 'he bound', *i-kârrās* 'he binds'; Beja *i-hé* 'he is', *î-hi* 'he was'; Somali *ya-qaan* 'he knows', *yi-qiin* 'he knew'. The verbal derivational affixes of Proto-AA include causative *s*(V), reflexive and medial *t*(V)/-*t*-, and passive *n/m*, all of which probably go back to original auxiliaries. There is gemination, usually of the second radical consonant or its variant, long -*ā*- (before the second radical consonant), for intensive/durative/causative.

From a typological point of view, an extremely widespread use of internal inflection (ablaut) is the most characteristic trait of all the archaic and middle-stage AA languages, along with mainly consonantal (usually tri- or biconsonantal) roots. Attempts to reduce all Proto-AA roots to two consonants are mistaken. On the phonological level, a typical feature is the set of so-called emphatic consonants (realized phonetically as pharyngealized, velarized, or glottalized-ejective), as well as the occurrence of several laryngeal and pharyngeal phonemes. The vowel system was probably limited to three vowel phonemes *i a u*, with distinctive length.

Attempts to prove a relationship between AA and other languages or language families, such as Nubian or the mysterious Meroitic, have been unsuccessful. The only current hypotheses of broader relationship that merit attention are that of association with "Nostratic," and that of possible genetic links with some Saharan languages (e.g. the group of Teda/Tubu, Kanuri, Zaghawa, etc.).

[*See also* African Languages; Akkadian; Arabic; Berber Languages; Chadic Languages; Cushitic Languages; Egyptian; *and* Semitic Languages.]

BIBLIOGRAPHY

Cohen, David, ed. 1988. *Les langues chamito-sémitiques.* (Les langues dans le monde, 2.) Paris: CNRS.

Cohen, Marcel. 1947. *Essai comparatif sur le vocabulaire et la phonétique du chamito-sémitique.* Paris: Champion.

Diakonoff, Igor M. 1988. *The Afrasian languages.* Moscow: Nauka.

Diakonoff, Igor M., A. G. Belova, A. S. Chetverukhin, A. Yu. Militarev, V. Ya. Porkhomovsky, and O. V. Stolbova. 1993–. *Historical comparative vocabulary of Afrasian. St. Petersburg Journal of African Studies*, 2–.

Ehret, Christopher. 1995. *Reconstructing Proto-Afroasiatic (Proto-Afrasian): Vowels, tone, consonants and vocabulary.* Berkeley: University of California Press.

Orel, Vladimir E., and Olga V. Stolbova. 1995. *Hamito-Semitic etymological dictionary.* Leiden: E. J. Brill.

Takács, Gabor. 1999–. *Etymological dictionary of Egyptian.* Vol. 1–. Leiden: E. J. Brill.

Zaborski, Andrzej. 1998. La linguistique chamito-sémitique cinquante années après l'Essai Comparatif de Marcel Cohen. In *Actes du 1er Congrès Chamito-Sémitique de Fès*, edited by Mohammed El Medlaouï et al. pp. 23–35. Fez: Université Sidi Mohamed Ben Abdellah.

ANDRZEJ ZABORSKI

LANGUAGE LIST

The following language is unclassified within Afroasiatic.

Birale: also called Ongota, Birelle, Ifa'ongota. "Shanqilla" is a derogatory name sometimes used. 19 speakers remain in Ethiopia. Ethnic population: 89 as of 2000. One village on the west bank of the Weyt'o River, southeastern Omo region. Members of the ethnic group who do not speak Birale conduct their affairs in Tsamai. All speakers are old. Birale is not expected to last.   B. GRIMES

AGENT. *See* Case; Semantics; *and* Grammatical Relations.

AGGLUTINATING LANGUAGES. *See* Functional Linguistics *and* Polysynthesis.

AGRAMMATISM. The term "agrammatism" classically refers to a pathological verbal behavior sometimes observed in Broca's aphasia following a left prerolandic cerebral lesion. Generally occurring after a period of evolution such behavior is basically characterized, at the surface level, by the production of lacunary, "telegraphic" syntactic structures which prototypically lack grammatical morphemes:

(1)   *Ah yes! Strikes, uh, strikes, uh, red flags. Uh, uh, bludgeons, finally bludgeons, universities. Uh, ah yes! Ten per cent, uh, wages. Uh, oof! That's all.* (Lecours et al. 1983: 52)

(2)   *My uh mother died . . . uh . . . me . . . uh fi'teen. Uh, oh, I guess six month . . . my mother pass away. An'uh . . . an'en . . . uh . . . ah . . . seventeen . . . seventeen . . . go . . . uh high school. An uh . . . Christmas . . . well, uh, I uh . . . Pitt'burgh.* (Goodglass 1976:239)

According to Pitres 1898, J. P. F. J. Deleuze was the first clinician (in 1819) to report on an aphasic patient whose verbal output was deprived of pronouns, and was made up of infinitive verbs. The term "agrammatism" was introduced to the aphasiological literature by Kussmaul 1877.

The more specific surface manifestations of such a syndrome are easily identified in clinical terms:

(a) The rate of speech is slowed.

(b) Grammatical morphemes are deleted in most, if not all, tasks of sentence and discourse production.

(c) Verbal inflections are lost, with preferential use of the infinitive (e.g. in French) or the gerund (e.g. in English) instead of finite verb forms.

(d) The number and complexity of syntactic structures are reduced.

(e) The patient produces shortened ("telegraphic") utterances which show a preference for juxtaposition over embedding of sentence constituents (Goodglass 1976, Lecours et al. 1983).

Such symptoms are often accompanied by a comprehension deficit, which disrupts processing of the same grammatical constituents and structures which are affected in production (Zurif et al. 1972). However, there are counter-examples to such a "parallelistic" account of agrammatism; in these, "pure agrammatism of speech" is presented in the absence of any comprehension disorder (Miceli et al. 1983, Nespoulous et al. 1988).

Neuropsychologists, linguists, and psycholinguists have proposed many interpretative models of agrammatism; all attempt to link the pathological surface manifestations of the deficit with underlying, functional causes. They aim at determining whether the underlying deficit is an amo-dal structural deficit which affects one or several sub-components of the grammar of a natural language in all production and comprehension tasks—or a processing deficit, which disrupts the computations responsible for the active, dynamic, "on-line" processing of linguistic structures in production and/or comprehension. The frequent observation of cross-modal (or across-task) variability, in agrammatic patients as well as in other clinical types of aphasics, seems to support the latter hypothesis; however, the question is open to debate.

On the basis of the parallel presence of similar impairments in both production and comprehension, Zurif et al. 1972 thus claim that agrammatism is indeed a central grammatical deficit, crucially affecting syntax. However, Miceli et al. 1983 and Nespoulous et al. 1988, lacking such a parallel in their patients' symptomatology, conclude that agrammatism can disrupt the (syntactic?) processes necessary for sentence production without affecting language comprehension.

Psycholinguistic models of speech production all require, in order to process information from meaning to sound, the existence of different levels of linguistic representation, and of processes transcoding each representation into the next. Neurolinguists employ these models in attempts to determine the levels at which the causal deficit of agrammatic symptoms is located. Whether they state so explicitly or not, most consider the deficit to be a syntactic one, which thus disrupts both the building up and the parsing of syntactic structures. Other researchers report clearcut cases of pathological dissociation between morphological and syntactic processes (Tissot et al. 1973, Miceli et al. 1983, Nespoulous et al. 1988). For still others, the deficit is phonological: it leads to the deletion of grammatical markers in both production and comprehension, because these items are "clitic," unstressed morphemes, rather than "phonological words" (Kean 1979). Finally, some believe that agrammatism is the outcome of a specific processing deficit which reduces the availability of "closed-class" morphemes.

Neurolinguists more involved in the interpretation of "agrammatic comprehension" have put forward different strategies that are supposedly used by agrammatics to compensate for their syntactic parsing deficit. Thus they identify "heuristic" procedures which rely on semantic plausibility, animacy, or the linear order of nouns. Agrammatic patients are said to resort to these strategies in an attempt to overcome the impaired "algorithmic" syntactic processes that normally assign thematic roles to sentence constituents. Others, over the last decade of the 20th century (see Rigalleau et al. 1997 for a review), have laid particular emphasis on the specific role that agrammatism might play in "asyntactic comprehension," a limitation either of "working memory" capacity (Miyake et al. 1994, Caplan and Waters 1995) or, more generally, of "cognitive resources" available to the patients (Haarman and Kolk 1991, Frazier and Friederici 1991, Hagoort 1990).

In aphasic symptomatology in general, and in agrammatic symptomatology in particular, many researchers identify more than the mere negative manifestation of some underlying deficit. This dictates that, together with the direct effects of the impairment resulting from a cerebral lesion, its indirect effects—arising from potential adaptive strategies—must be carefully appraised (Kolk and van Grunsven 1985, Nespoulous et al. 1988).

Aphasia, and thus agrammatism, are almost never "all-or-none" phenomena; thus variability in performance must be accounted for, and its causal factors must be apprehended, be they temporal, mnestic, or attentional (Kolk and van Grunsven 1985).

Classical teaching on aphasia tended to distinguish agrammatism, characterized mainly by omissions of grammatical morphemes, from paragrammatism, characterized by replacements of items. Late 20th century neurolinguists have become uncomfortable with such a dichotomy (Heeschen 1985), especially considering the following facts:

(i) Both omissions and substitutions may be observed in a single agrammatic patient, and may systematically involve the same grammatical morphemes.
(ii) Language-specific structural constraints sometimes force the patient to produce substitutions rather than omissions, e.g. in Hebrew.

The study of agrammatism, at the end of the 20th century, is a prototypical example of multidisciplinary interaction among linguists, psycholinguists, and neuropsychologists; it clearly stresses the need for future research "to combine principled linguistic descriptions and careful on-line examinations" of actual linguistic behaviors following brain lesions (Grodzinsky et al. 1985).

[*See also* Aphasia; Neurolinguistics; Paragrammatism; *and* Psycholinguistics.]

BIBLIOGRAPHY

Caplan, David, and Gloria Waters. 1995. Aphasic disorders of syntactic comprehension and working memory capacity. *Cognitive Neuropsychology* 12:6.637–649.

Frazier, Lynn, and Angela Friederici. 1991. On deriving the properties of agrammatic comprehension. *Brain and Language* 49.224–309.

Goodglass, Harold. 1976. Agrammatism. In *Studies in neurolinguistics,* vol. 1, edited by Haiganoosh Whitaker and Harry A. Whitaker, pp. 237–260. New York: Academic Press.

Grodzinsky, Yosef, et al. 1985. Agrammatism: Structural deficits and antecedent processing disruptions. In Kean 1985, pp. 65–81.

Haarman, Henk, and Herman Kolk. 1991. A computer model of the temporal course of agrammatic sentence understanding: The effects of variation in severity and sentence complexity. *Cognitive Science* 15.49–87.

Hagoort, Peter. 1990. *Tracking the time course of language understanding in aphasia.* Zuptfen: Koninklijke Wörhrmann.

Heeschen, Claus. 1985. Agrammatism versus paragrammatism: A fictitious opposition. In Kean 1985, pp. 207–248.

Kean, Mary-Louise. 1979. Agrammatism: A phonological deficit? *Cognition* 7.69–83.

Kean, Mary-Louise, ed. 1985. *Agrammatism.* Orlando, Fla.: Academic Press.

Kolk, Herman H. J., and Marianne J. F. van Grunsven. 1985. Agrammatism as a variable phenomenon. *Cognitive Neuropsychology* 2.347–384.

Kussmaul, Adolf. 1877. *Die Störungen der Sprache.* Leipzig: Vogel. 5th ed., 1885.

Lecours, André Roch, et al. 1983. *Aphasiology.* London: Baillière/Tindall.

Miceli, Gabriele, et al. 1983. Contrasting cases of Italian agrammatic aphasia without comprehension disorder. *Brain and Language* 19.65–97.

Miyake, Akira, Patricia Carpenter, and Marcel Just. 1994. A capacity approach to syntactic comprehension disorders: Making normal adults perform like aphasic patients. *Cognitive Neuropsychology* 11:6.671–717.

Nespoulous, Jean-Luc, et al. 1988. Agrammatism in sentence production without comprehension deficits: Reduced availability of syntactic structures and/or of grammatical morphemes? *Brain and Language* 33.273–295.

Pitres, A. 1898. *L'aphasie amnésique et ses variétés cliniques.* Paris: Aljean.

Rigalleau, Francois, Jean-Luc Nespoulous, and Daniel Gaonac'h. 1997. La compréhension asyntaxique dans tous ses états des représentations linguistiques aux ressources cognitives. *L'Année Psychologique* 97.449–494.

Tissot, René, et al. 1973. *L'agrammatisme: Études neuropsycholinguistiques.* Brussels: Dessart.

Zurif, Edgar B., et al. 1972. Grammatical judgments of agrammatic aphasics. *Neuropsychologia* 10.405–418.

JEAN-LUC NESPOULOUS

AGRAPHIA. *See* Alexia and Agraphia.

AGREEMENT. [*This entry includes the following subentries:*
Overview
Noun Classification]

Overview

Agreement is a widespread and varied phenomenon in the world's languages. It has been investigated from different viewpoints, yet it remains deeply puzzling. Consider these Russian examples:

(1) *Tanja sidel-a   u okna*
Tanya sat-SG.FEM by window
'Tanya was sitting by the window'

(2) *Djadja Vanja sidel   u okna*
Uncle Vanya sat.SG.MASC by window
'Uncle Vanya was sitting by the window'

The form of the verb varies according to the subject noun phrase. This matching is the essential element of agreement. A working definition is provided by Steele: "The term *agreement* commonly refers to some systematic covariance between a semantic or formal property of one element and a formal property of another" (1978:610). In our examples, the form of the verb covaries systematically according to a semantic property, namely whether the subject noun phrase denotes a female or a male. This agreement in gender can equally apply to a formal property:

(3) *kniga ležal-a   na stole*
book lay-SG.FEM on table
'the book was lying on the table'

(4) *žurnal   ležal   na stole*
magazine lay.SG.MASC on table
'the magazine was lying on the table'

In (3), *kniga* 'book' controls feminine agreement; it belongs to the feminine gender because of its morphology, not for any semantic reason. Conversely, in (4), *žurnal* 'magazine' is masculine. The surprising thing is that we have information about the noun phrase expressed elsewhere—on the verb, in this case—and that this information is redundant.

Agreement is an area in which terms require care. For instance, some writers treat "agreement" and "concord" as synonymous; for others, the two are distinct (whether "agreement" is treated as the superordinate term or the subordinate term, or with some other distinction between the two). "Concord" appears to be dropping out of use, and since there is no distinction that is drawn consistently, this loss is to be welcomed.

Connected to the problem of terms is that of the scope of agreement. Suppose our first example continues with a clause having the subject *on-a* 'she' (example [2] would correspondingly continue with *on* 'he'). Would this systematic covariance count as agreement? For linguists interested specifically in agreement, typically it would: they say that personal pronouns agree as do verbs and adjectives, for example. Others, however, treat agreement as a type of local dependency, excluding covariance that goes beyond the clause. Barlow 1992:134–152 discusses this issue and concludes that there are no good grounds for distinguishing between agreement and antecedent–anaphor relations. Whatever one's view, it is important to realize that "agreement" is a larger or smaller phenomenon for different linguists.

Within agreement, we call the element that determines the agreement (say, the subject noun phrase) the *controller*. The element whose form is determined by agreement is the *target*. The syntactic environment in which agreement occurs is the *domain* of agreement. When we indicate in what respect there is agreement, we are referring to agreement *features*. Thus, number is an agreement feature, and it has the values singular, dual, plural, and so on. This is diagrammed in Figure 1.

Each of these elements shows a range of possibilities, which will need elucidation before we achieve a full typology. The controller is typically a noun phrase, but there are various complications involving quantified expressions and conjoined noun phrases. We are used to adjectives and verbs being potential targets, and pronouns too; but we also find articles, demonstratives, numerals, possessives, adverbs, and adpositions as targets (see Lehmann 1982:207–215 and Corbett 1991:106–112 for examples). Given a list of controllers and one of targets, why would we also need the notion of domain? This is needed because targets may behave differently in different syntactic environments; for instance, German adjectives agree when in attributive position but not when in the predicate. Specifying the possible domains cross-linguistically is a major task of current research. The prototypical agreement features are gender, number, and person, with honorificity as a rare possibility. The interesting feature effects in conjoined constructions have been investigated by Givón 1970 and Corbett 1991:261–

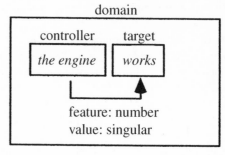

FIGURE 1. *Framework of Terms*

306. There is a fifth area of differentiation between languages, that of *conditions*; a particular agreement may be made possible or impossible by conditioning factors that are not themselves agreement features in the language in question. The conditions most often encountered are animacy, precedence, and definiteness.

Although in many instances only one agreement form is possible, there are also many cases in which agreement choices may be made, as discussed by Comrie 1975 and Corbett 2000:187–218. Investigation into the origin and development of agreement systems was given a flying start by Givón 1976, but that research has not been followed up as fully as might have been hoped (see Corbett 1995 for discussion).

The prospects for research into agreement include careful description of some of the richer systems (for instance, those of the languages of Daghestan, as in Polinsky and Comrie 1999), a fuller account of the rise of agreement systems, a more adequate general typology, and collaborative work with psycholinguists. Interest in the topic among psycholinguists has generally been limited so far to the more transparent kinds of agreement.

There is a considerable literature on agreement. For a list of monographs and collections, see the introduction to Corbett 1999. Important overviews include Moravcsik 1978 and Lehmann 1982. Formal approaches can be found in Pollard and Sag 1994:60–99 and Bresnan 2001:144–179.

[*See also* Adjectives; Case; Morphology; Syntactic Features; Verbs; *and* Word Orders.]

BIBLIOGRAPHY

Barlow, Michael. 1992. *A situated theory of agreement.* New York: Garland.

Bresnan, Joan. 2001. *Lexical-functional syntax.* Oxford: Blackwell.

Comrie, Bernard. 1975. Polite plurals and predicate agreement. *Language* 51.406–418.

Corbett, Greville G. 1991. *Gender.* Cambridge: Cambridge University Press.

Corbett, Greville G. 1995. Agreement (research into syntactic change). In *Syntax: An international handbook of contemporary research,* edited by Joachim Jacobs et al., vol. 2, pp. 1235–1244. Berlin: Walter de Gruyter.

Corbett, Greville G., ed. 1999. *Agreement.* (Special issue of *Folia Linguistica* 33.2.)

Corbett, Greville G. 2000. *Number.* Cambridge: Cambridge University Press.

Givón, Talmy. 1970. The resolution of gender conflicts in Bantu conjunction: When syntax and semantics clash. In *Chicago Linguistic Society* pp. 250–261.

Givón, Talmy. 1976. Topic, pronoun and grammatical agreement. In *Subject and topic,* edited by Charles N. Li, pp. 149–188. New York: Academic Press.

Lehmann, Christian. 1982. Universal and typological aspects of agreement. In *Apprehension: Das sprachliche Erfassen von Gegenständen: II: Die Techniken und ihre zusammenhang in Einzelsprachen,* edited by Hansjakob Seiler and Franz J. Stachowiak, pp. 201–267. Tübingen: Narr.

Moravcsik, Edith A. 1978. Agreement. In *Universals of human language, IV: Syntax,* edited by Joseph H. Greenberg et al., pp. 331–374. Stanford, Calif.: Stanford University Press.

Polinsky, Maria, and Bernard Comrie. 1999. Agreement in Tsez. *Folia Linguistica* 33:109–130.

Pollard, Carl, and Ivan A. Sag. 1994. *Head-driven phrase structure grammar.* Chicago: University of Chicago Press.

Steele, Susan. 1978. Word order variation: A typological study. In *Universals of human language, IV: Syntax,* edited by Joseph H. Greenberg et al., pp. 585–623. Stanford, Calif.: Stanford University Press.

GREVILLE G. CORBETT

Noun Classification

Widespread among the languages of the world is a partly or fully grammaticalized division of the noun lexicon into distinct classes. Several types of noun classification are traditionally distinguished (Allan 1977, Dixon 1982); the most distinctive are noun classes, numeral classifiers, classificatory verbs, and classificatory noun incorporation. Typical examples of classificatory noun incorporation are provided by Iroquoian languages (e.g. Cayuga): a taxonomically superordinate (generic) noun, for example, 'vehicle', is syntactically incorporated into the verb, and cross-classifies a specific noun ('truck,' 'bus') which is syntactically governed by the verb (Mithun 1986). Athabaskan languages (e.g. Navajo) have classificatory verbs, whose roots provide a semantically transparent classification of the intransitive subject or transitive object (Young and Morgan 1987).

Such classification provides information about the ref-

erent, for example, animacy, shape, texture, and grouping, in a way quite reminiscent of the distinctions made by the numeral classifiers found in Sino-Tibetan and other East Asian languages (Erbaugh 1986), and in the Mayan languages of Central America (Craig 1986a), among others. A numeral classifier system is an open set of classificatory particles which are syntactically associated with numerals (in some languages, morphologically bound to them); they may also be associated with demonstratives, adjectives, or the noun itself. Typically, the particle appears once in the N[oun] P[hrase]; however, agreement across elements of an NP does occur (e.g. in Thai or Kilivila). Particles may occur anaphorically in pragmatically focused (e.g. contrastive) discourse contexts. Although classifiers and nouns have distinctive syntactic positions in the NP, there is a lexical continuum from classifiers to full nouns: at least some classifiers in a system may be phonologically related (or identical) to nouns in the language. Numeral classifiers typically provide information about physical properties (e.g. animacy, shape, consistency, or arrangement), functional properties (tool, foodstuff, etc.), or the social status of the referent of the head noun—but not about sex (Denny 1976).

In contrast with numeral classifiers, noun class systems are characterized by agreement with constituents outside the NP (e.g. with verbs, predicate adjectives, locative deictics, or pronouns); by a higher degree of grammaticalization, evident in a closed system of a small number of classes; and by a lesser degree of semantic transparency. In discourse, the agreement marking on verbs and pronouns typically fulfils the unmarked anaphoric function of maintaining referential continuity. Noun class systems are especially evident in I[ndo-]E[uropean], Semitic, African (all families), and Caucasian languages. In many of these systems, the salient semantic basis of classification is the distinction between male and female sex; hence they are called "gender systems." The Niger-Congo languages of Africa (Heine 1982), particularly the Benue-Congo family (Hyman 1980), provide examples of noun class systems which are not based on sex, but are otherwise quite similar to gender systems in having low semanticity, closed classes, and agreement.

The study of gender goes back to the Greek philosophical roots of linguistics, with a continuous tradition of research and commentary up to the present (see Claudi 1985); scholars have focused on the issue of whether the membership of individual classes is conceptually motivated or arbitrary. Grimm 1890 championed the "Romantic" claim that IE gender categorization, both in its origins and its current state, is based on an extension of human sex-associated characteristics onto the inanimate world. Brugmann 1889 presented the Neogrammarian position: gender categories originated as an accident of the morphological and phonological shape of nouns, much of which has since been diachronically eroded; and the categorization has no semantic basis, beyond the distinction of sex for humans. The Brugmannian position has gained general acceptance in modern linguistics; noun class systems, and gender in particular, are often cited as paradigmatic instances of arbitrariness in language structure.

Recent research on semantic motivation, particularly that making use of new theoretical models of categorization (Lakoff 1987), has given new support to a generalized form of Grimm's position. Denny and Creider 1976, in a comparative reconstruction of Bantu noun classes, suggest that the original system had classes with clear semantic content, specifically reminiscent of numeral classifier systems. Dixon 1982 uncovers the underlying semantic structuring of noun classes in Dyirbal (Australia), in which mythic association plays a dominant role; for example, the sun is wife of the moon, and birds are the spirits of human females. Recent work has shown extensive semantic clustering within each of the three gender classes of German, based on folk taxonomic and prototype-theoretic principles. Taxonomically superordinate nouns tend to be neuter; those at basic levels have masculine, feminine, or neuter gender based on local clustering principles; and subordinates follow the gender of the basic-level term that dominates them (Zubin and Köpcke 1986).

Recent research on other language families and areas—for example, in the Amazon Basin, Australia, and New Guinea—brings into question the traditional typology of discrete types, particularly with increasing evidence for mixed types. A more general typological framework (Seiler 1986) is based on a scale of grammaticalization which ranges from highly grammaticalized, closed-class systems at one end to less grammaticalized, open-class systems at the other. Grammatical and semantic properties which covary along this continuum include the following:

(a) The number of classes and/or the openness of the system
(b) Agreement outside the NP
(c) The extent to which class membership is based on phonological and/or morphological (e.g. derivational) properties of the noun
(d) The degree of semantic motivation
(e) The breadth of polysemy in individual classes
(f) Freedom of class-switching in order to predicate information about the noun's referent
(g) The degree of lexicalization, that is, stable and exclusive membership of lexical items in particular classes

In this framework, the nominal classification system of a given language will tend to have dominant properties which are predicted by its position on the continuum. Thus German is fairly low on the continuum; Bantu systems are somewhat higher; and systems with numeral classifiers, classificatory verbs, and classificatory noun incorporation are still higher.

The main historical source of nominal classification systems is the nominal lexicon. This is well documented for numeral classifier and noun incorporation types, but not for more highly grammaticalized systems. However, Dixon 1982 suggests a nominal origin for at least one of the Dyirbal noun class markers; and Denny and Creider 1976 argue that Bantu classes originated in a classifier system, which would in turn have been derived from the nominal lexicon. It is generally argued that, as noun classification systems evolve, they move downward on the theoretical continuum sketched above; thus class membership becomes rigid, classes lose their semantic transparency, and morphophonological factors take over. A factor which operates against this overall trend is semantic remotivation—a process in which a combination of morphological, semantic, and gender-class shifts constitutes new semantic clustering within noun classes; this has been documented by Zubin and Köpcke 1984 for the affect lexicon in German.

[*See also* Case; Grammaticalization; Inflection; Morphology; *and* Semantics, *article on* Prototype Semantics.]

BIBLIOGRAPHY

Allan, Keith. 1977. Classifiers. *Language* 53.285–311.

Brugmann, Karl. 1889. Zur Frage der Entstehung des grammatischen Geschlechts. *Internationale Zeitschrift für Allgemeine Sprachwissenschaft* 9.100–109.

Claudi, Ulrike. 1985. *Zur Entstehung von Genussystemen: Überlegungen zu einigen theoretischen Aspekten, verbunden mit einer Fallstudie des Zande.* Hamburg: Buske.

Craig, Colette. 1986a. Jacaltec noun classifiers: A study in language and culture. In Craig 1986b, pp. 263–293.

Craig, Colette, ed. 1986b. *Noun classes and categorization.* (Typological studies in language, 7.) Amsterdam: Benjamins.

Denny, J. Peter. 1976. What are noun classifiers good for? *Chicago Linguistic Society* 12.122–132.

Denny, J. Peter, and Chet A. Creider. 1976. The semantics of noun classes in Proto-Bantu. *Studies in African Linguistics* 7.1–30. Reprinted in Craig 1986b, pp. 217–239.

Dixon, Robert M. W. 1982. Nominal classification. In Robert M. W. Dixon, *Where have all the adjectives gone?*, pp. 159–183. The Hague: Mouton.

Erbaugh, Mary S. 1986. Taking stock: The development of Chinese noun classifiers historically and in young children. In Craig 1986b, pp. 399–436.

Grimm, Jacob. 1890. *Deutsche Grammatik*, vol. 3. Gütersloh: Bertelsmann.

Heine, Bernd. 1982. African noun class systems. In *Apprehension: Das sprachliche Erfassen von Gegenständen*, vol. 1, *Bereich und Ordnung der Phänomene* (Language universals series, 1), edited by Hansjakob Seiler and Christian Lehmann, pp. 189–216. Tübingen: Narr.

Hyman, Larry, ed. 1980. *Noun classes in the Grassfields Bantu borderland.* (Southern California occasional papers in linguistics, 8.) Los Angeles: Department of Linguistics, University of Southern California.

Lakoff, George. 1987. *Women, fire, and dangerous things: What categories reveal about the mind.* Chicago: University of Chicago Press.

Mithun, Marianne. 1986. The convergence of noun classification systems. In Craig 1986b, pp. 379–397.

Seiler, Hansjakob. 1986. *Apprehension: Language, object, and order,* vol. 3, *The universal dimension of apprehension.* Tübingen: Narr.

Young, Robert W., and William Morgan. 1987. *The Navajo language: A grammar and colloquial dictionary.* 2d ed. Albuquerque: University of New Mexico Press.

Zubin, David A., and Klaus-Michael Köpcke. 1984. Affect classification in the German gender system. *Lingua* 63.41–96.

Zubin, David A., and Klaus-Michael Köpcke. 1986. Gender and folk taxonomy. In Craig 1986b, pp. 139–181.

DAVID A. ZUBIN

AINU. *See* Siberian Languages; Altaic Languages; *and* Languages of the World.

AKKADIAN. This Semitic language was spoken from the early 3rd to the middle of the 1st millennium BCE, in the area corresponding to modern Iraq and Syria and some neighboring regions. The term subsumes two major dialects, *Babylonian* and *Assyrian*. These underwent three broad stages of development, labeled Old (ca. 2000–1500 BCE), Middle (1500–1000), and Neo- (1000–500); their forerunner is known as Old Akkadian (2500–2000 BCE).

Some scholars consider Eblaite as a form of Old Akkadian, with which it is contemporary.

1. History. Old Babylonian is generally viewed as the classical stage of the language, because of a convergence of cultural and diachronic factors: it is the earliest stage of the language for which we have a large, differentiated, and culturally significant body of written documents. That Old Babylonian had a certain normative value is suggested by the fact that later cultural manifestations of the language were consciously modeled on it—especially Standard Babylonian, a literary "dialect" used in the mid-1st millennium BCE, when Akkadian as a spoken language had begun to disappear.

During the second half of the 2nd millennium, Akkadian came to be used as a lingua franca over all of southwestern Asia. Through its use as a shared medium of expression by speakers of different languages, it developed into a scribal lingo rather divorced from the natural linguistic development which it underwent separately in the core area of Babylonia and Assyria.

External influences are important in the study of Akkadian. Because of its cultural primacy, Sumerian seems clearly to have played a significant role in shaping linguistic development. Apart from its strong influence on the lexicon, characteristics that are frequently adduced are the fact that the configuration of Akkadian phonology is typologically highly advanced vis-à-vis later Semitic languages; and the Subject Object Verb character of its syntax. Other significant lexical influences came from Hurrian and Aramaic.

2. Sources. For sources on Akkadian, see Soden 1952, Gelb 1961, Hecker 1968, Groneberg 1987, and Huehnergard 1988. For historical connections, see Castellino 1962, Gelb 1969; for the writing system, Soden and Röllig 1967; and for dictionaries, Gelb et al. 1956, Soden 1965–1981. Linguistically oriented grammars are Reiner 1966, Buccellati 1996, and Huehnergard 1997.

The nature of the available sources places some significant limits on our understanding of Akkadian as a linguistic reality. First, there is the obvious fact that Akkadian is an extinct language. Exactly when it died is not apparent from the record: it is conceivable that, by the end of the Assyrian empire (7th c. BCE), Aramaic had already replaced Akkadian as the common spoken language in Mesopotamia.

Second, the textual evidence on which our knowledge of the language is based—while massive in size, and relatively varied in the nature and range of its repertoire—does not provide a transparent record of the spoken language. Except for letters, the bulk of the evidence comes to us through a pervasive scribal filter. Especially noticeable in formulaic, technical texts (whether pertaining to administration, law, cult, or scholarly practice), standardization is also to be reckoned with in the literary tradition, from myths and epics to hymns and wisdom texts. Finally, the extant evidence pertains primarily to urban elites; Amorite can be understood as the rural counterpart of urban Akkadian/Eblaite (though this is not the usual interpretation of Amorite).

3. Writing system. Graphemic analysis is of particular importance for a proper linguistic understanding of Akkadian—not only because our documentation is exclusively written, but also because of the complexities of the writing system. The philological tradition of Assyriology was intuitively responsive to the needs of graphemic analysis long before the concept was articulated theoretically; witness the modern repertories of both syllabic and logographic values, which are based on rigorous applications of a coherently perceived system of graphemic rules. The signs of the *cuneiform* script number in the hundreds, and corresponding values in the thousands (allowing for multiple values for each sign, or "polyphony"); however, it appears that the operative sign inventory within any given text genre ranges between two hundred and three hundred, and that multiple values are restricted in usage by rules of correlation. The incidence and significance of graphemics is such that independent linguistic work on the textual data must be based on knowledge of their graphemic embodiment. The fact that the writing system includes full vocalic notation (in contrast to the writing systems used for other Semitic languages) is deceptively simple in this respect.

We can claim only an approximate knowledge of phonetic realizations, gathered mostly from the comparative evidence of living Semitic languages; however, Akkadian phonemics is well understood. Uncertainties that still remain pertain primarily to distributional arrangements rather than to specific inventory items. Among the latter is the possibility of an extra sibilant in Old Akkadian; among the former, the questions of (i) whether vowels were allowed in word-initial position (alternatively, glottal stop would be required), and of (ii) the nature and position of stress.

Diachronically, Akkadian phonology is much more innovative than that of much later Semitic languages, as shown by the loss (already in Old Akkadian) of most laryngeals and pharyngeals, only partly offset by a vocalic change of *a* to *e*. An interesting phenomenon is Old Assyrian vowel harmony, whereby short unstressed vowels in pre-final position are assimilated in quality to the vowel that follows.

4. Morphology. Two major systems are operative, as in other Semitic languages. One, "internal" inflection, is built on the obligatory and exclusive interrelationship of two morphemes, called "root" and "pattern"; the other, "external" inflection, is based on the cumulative clustering of affixes before or after the nucleus—which in turn may or may not be derived through internal inflection. (In standard Akkadian grammars, internal inflection is understood as a process of word formation.) In contrast with other Semitic languages, where internal inflection is freely superimposed on loanwords, Akkadian avoids such new formations; this means that, since all verbal forms are based on internal inflection, the language has no clear examples of borrowed verbs. This is all the more striking in light of the heavy dependence of Akkadian on Sumerian in its nominal lexicon.

The nominal system makes full use of case endings. Three major cases are operative in the singular, roughly correlated with specific syntactic functions: the nominative (in *-um*) identifies the subject; the accusative (in *-am*), the object; and the genitive (in *-im*), the second component of a nominalized construct (e.g. *bīt awīlim* 'house of the man'). In the plural, a single oblique case (in *-ī*) subsumes the functions of both accusative and genitive, and *-ū* marks the case of the nominative. Partly retained in the script, case endings seem to have been lost by the early 1st millennium BCE.

An important characteristic of the verbal system is the absence of an aspect category. Instead, there are two other fundamental dimensions of verbal inflection. First, there are true tenses which locate the process in a temporal relationship to the speaker; besides the "present" (*iparras*, for present/future) and the preterit (*iprus*), traditional grammar recognizes a "perfect" (*iptaras*)—which has, however, been recently reinterpreted not as a tense but as a stem expressing the semantic category of "distance" (Buccellati 1996), or as a form admitting multiple relative values (Streck 1995). Second, inflection denotes either action or condition; the former is expressed by finite forms (the tenses and the imperative), and the latter by a form peculiar to Akkadian, the "permansive." This is traditionally viewed as a separate component of the verbal paradigm; however, it is structurally more appropriate to view it as an inflectional variation of the noun, including adjectives which can be derived from verbal roots (Buccellati 1996).

Important morphophonemic rules have been identified in Akkadian, with alternations conditioned by both internal and external inflection. A characteristic rule states that a sequence which contains (i) three syllables, of which the last two are short, and (ii) a certain type of morpheme boundary, is realized as two syllables; e.g., morphemic {damiq-um} is realized phonemically as /damqum/.

An interesting diachronic change is represented by the trend to abandon inflectional in favor of periphrastic forms. Thus for instance the separative form of the verb (with infixed *t,* e.g. *ittalak* 'he went away from, he left') or the allative (with suffixed *-am,* etc., e.g. *illikam* 'he went to, he came') may be understood (in the early periods) as synthetically referential to adjuncts of motion, even when such an adjunct is absent from the discourse; in later dialects, the referential value of the affixed forms is at best vestigial, and an analytical adjunct is required.

5. Syntax and semantics. These fields have been generally neglected, even though there has been a burgeoning interest in lexical matters. For semantics, this has meant that words have been studied for their denotational value in regard to specific realia; for syntax, phrases and sentences have been studied with attention to morphemic keywords.

Several syntactic traits are distinctive of Akkadian among Semitic languages. The following may be mentioned:

(a) The use of "virtual subordination" (where sentences are conjoined by the enclitic *-ma*) all but replaces normal subordination, in spite of the existence of a rich but underutilized inventory of conjunctions.

(b) Restrictive relative clauses occur without the use of a relative pronoun; instead, the noun occurs in a shortened form (the "construct state")—e.g. *awīl illiku* 'the man who came', vs. a non-restrictive clause with the relative pronoun, *awīlum ša illiku* 'the man, who came . . .'.

(c) Three nominal forms which are morphologically part of the inflectional structure of the verbal system (infinitive, verbal adjective, and participle) may govern the accusative, e.g. *bītam ina amārim* 'in seeing the house'.

[See also Aramaic; Cuneiform; Decipherment; Hurrian and Urartian; Semitic Languages; *and* Sumerian.]

BIBLIOGRAPHY

Buccellati, Giorgio. 1996. *A Structural grammar of Babylonian.* Wiesbaden: Harrassowitz.

Castellino, Giorgio R. 1962. *The Akkadian personal pronouns and verbal system in the light of Semitic and Hamitic.* Leiden: Brill.

Gelb, Ignace J. 1961. *Old Akkadian writing and grammar.* (Materials for the Assyrian dictionary, 2.) 2d ed. Chicago: University of Chicago Press.

Gelb, Ignace J. 1969. *Sequential reconstruction of Proto-Akkadian.* (Assyrological studies, 18.) Chicago: University of Chicago Press.

Gelb, Ignace J., et al. 1956–. *The Assyrian dictionary of the Oriental Institute of the University of Chicago.* 16 vols. Glückstadt, Germany: Augustin.

Groneberg, Brigitte R. M. 1987. *Syntax, Morphologie und Stil der jungbabylonischen "hymnischen" Literatur:* Teil 1, *Grammatik;* Teil 2, *Belegsammlung und Textkatalog.* (Freiburger altorientalische Studien, 14.) Wiesbaden: Steiner.

Hecker, Karl. 1968. *Grammatik der Kültepe-Texte.* (Analecta orientalia, 44.) Rome: Pontificium Institutum Biblicum.

Huehnergard, John. 1988. *The Akkadian of Ugarit.* (Harvard Semitic studies, 34.) Cambridge, Mass.: Harvard University Press.

Huehnergard, John. 1997. *A grammar of Akkadian.* (Harvard Semitic Studies, 45.) Atlanta: Scholars Press.

Reiner, Erica. 1966. *A linguistic analysis of Akkadian.* (Janua linguarum, Series practica, 21.) The Hague: Mouton.

Soden, Wolfram von. 1952. *Grundriss der akkadischen Grammatik.* (Analecta orientalia, 33.) Rome: Pontificium Institutum Biblicum.

Soden, Wolfram von. 1965–81. *Akkadisches Handwörterbuch.* 3 vols. Wiesbaden: Harrassowitz.

Soden, Wolfram von, and Wolfgang Röllig. 1967. *Das akkadische Syllabar.* (Analecta orientalia, 42.) 2d ed. Rome: Pontificium Institutum Biblicum.

Streck, Michael P. 1995. *Zahl und Zeit: Grammatik der Numeralia und des Verbalsystems in Spätbabylonischen.* (Cuneiform Monographs, 5) Gröningen: Styx.

GIORGIO BUCCELLATI

ALACALUFAN LANGUAGES. An isolated group native to southernmost Chile and the adjacent part of Argentina.

LANGUAGE LIST

Kakauhua: also called Kaukaue, Cacahue. Formerly spoken in Chile.

Qawasqar: also called Kaweskar, Kawesqar, Alacalufe, Alacaluf, Halakwulup. 20 speakers remain in Chile. Reports are that speakers are not bilingual in Spanish; 20% are monolingual in Qawasqar. The youngest speakers were from 3 to 20 years old in 1996. Speakers have positive attitude toward Qawasqar.   B. GRIMES

ALBANIAN. A branch of the Indo-European family, spoken predominantly in Albania, the Kosovo region of Serbia, and western Macedonia. The two main varieties are Tosk (the basis of the standard language) and Gheg. Arvanitika is the name given to the variety of Tosk spoken in Greece, Arbëreshë to that spoken in Italy.

LANGUAGE LIST

Albanian, Arbëreshë: 80,000 speakers in Italy. Ethnic population: 260,000 as of 1976. Southern; Calabria, Apulia, Basilicata, Molise, Sicily. Related to Tosk. Dialects are Sicilian Albanian, Calabrian Albanian, Central Mountain Albanian, Campo Marino Albanian. Speakers say the four Italian dialects are not inherently intelligible with each other. Speakers are bilingual in Italian and regional Italian varieties in varying degrees; one report says they are highly bilingual. Albanian is the language of the home. Strong position in some districts. Not used in schools. No official status.

Albanian, Arvanitika: also called Arvanitika, Arvanitic, Arberichte. 50,000 speakers in Greece. Attica (Attiki), Bocotia (Viotia), southern Euboea (Evia), and the island of Salamis (Salamina); Epyrus region and Athens. Related to Tosk. Mainly rural. Dialects are Thracean Arvanitika, Northwestern Arvanitika, South Central Arvanitika. Arvanitika is partially intelligible to speakers of Tosk. Dialects are perceived as unintelligible to speakers of other dialects. Bilingualism in Greek. Speakers are older people. Young people are migrating to Athens and assimilating as Greeks. Some cultural revival since the 1980s. Greek or Roman script.

Albanian, Gheg: also called Geg, Shgip. 2,000,000 speakers in Yugoslavia, Albania, Macedonia, Bulgaria, Romania, Slovenia, and USA. In Yugoslavia: 1,372,750 speakers. Ethnic population: 2,000,000 as of 1998. Kosova. Books are published in Gheg in Yugoslavia. Restrictions on Albanian at Kosovo's university since 1990. Not endangered. Official language. In Albania: 300,000 speakers. Northern Albania. Dialects are Mandrica, Ship (Kosove), Scutari, Elbasan—Tirana. Speakers may be bilingual in Standard Albanian. In Macedonia: 242,250 speakers. In Bulgaria: Not intelligible with Tosk Albanian.

Albanian, Tosk: also called Tosk, Arnaut, Shkip, Shqip, Skchip, Shquipepë, Zhgabe. 3,000,000 speakers in Albania, Turkey, USA, Belgium, Canada, Egypt, Germany, Sweden, and Ukraine. In Albania: 2,900,000 speakers. Mainly south-

ern Albania to the Shkumbi River. Dialects are Arbanasi (Zadar), Srem (Syrmia), Camerija, Korca. Reported to be inherently unintelligible with Gheg Albanian and partially intelligible with Arvanitika Albanian of Greece. Not intelligible with Arbëreshë of Italy. Tosk has been the basis of the official language for Standard Albanian since 1952. It is used in schools. National language. In western Turkey: Scattered. 96% of speakers can use Turkish as second language. In USA: Mostly Boston, New York, Philadelphia, Detroit, Chicago.   B. GRIMES

ALEXANDRIAN GRAMMARIANS. A group of scholars associated with the Library at Alexandria in Egypt from its foundation in the 3rd century BCE to around the 5th century CE. They were interested in establishing the correct text of ancient Greek authors and in giving a description of Greek grammar. Dionysius Thrax (2nd c. BCE), the author of the most famous Greek grammar, was a pupil of Aristarchus, the sixth head of the Library, and eventually founded his own school at Rhodes.

[*See also* History of Linguistics, *article on* Ancient Greece and Rome.]

ANNA MORPURGO DAVIES

ALEXIA AND AGRAPHIA. The disorder of alexia (sometimes called "acquired dyslexia") is the disturbance of reading subsequent to brain injury in a previously literate adult. Deficits may take the form of difficulty in reading comprehension and/or in oral reading. *Agraphia* refers to an acquired impairment of writing and/or spelling. Both alexia and agraphia are common following left-hemisphere brain damage.

The characterization of alexic and agraphic disorders centers on specific symptoms that are said to reflect disturbances in different cognitive components of the reading and spelling processes. Attention is focused on the types of *paralexias*, or reading errors (and *paragraphias*, or writing errors) that are produced, and on the properties of words that affect word reading and spelling.

1. Types of paralexias and word properties affecting reading in alexia. There are five main types of paralexias: *semantic, derivational, orthographic, regularization*, and *functor substitution*. Semantic paralexias are related to the target word semantically, but not orthographically (e.g. *forest* → 'trees'). They may be synonyms of the target word, or they may be antonyms, subordinates, superordinates, coordinates, or associates. Derivational paralexias are derived from the target word by adding, deleting, or substituting an affix (*building* → 'builder'). An orthographic paralexia shares at least 50% of its letters with the target word (*sleep* → 'step'). These errors are sometimes called "visual paralexias"; however, often they do not share even such gross visual features as overall shape or length (*appraise* → 'arise'). Regularizations are paralexias that appear to result from attempts to decode words phonologically (*bear* → 'beer'). Functor substitutions are paralexias in which one functor is substituted for another, seeming unrelated, functor (*him* → 'as'). Paragraphias are characterized in the same way as paralexias.

Several properties of words have been shown to affect reading (and spelling) ability in alexic and agraphic patients. Some patients have particular trouble with long words. Some are sensitive to form class and have particular difficulty with function words. The degree of abstractness of a word may affect patients' reading or spelling performance. Some patients have particular trouble with pseudowords like *jup*; others read (or write) pseudowords quite well, but get stuck on orthographically irregular words like *yacht*. The tendency of some of these alexic (and agraphic) symptoms to occur together, but dissociated from other symptoms, has led to the description of the major varieties of alexia and agraphia discussed below.

2. Central alexias and agraphias.

2.1. *Pure alexia,* also called "letter-by-letter reading," is characterized by an effect of word length on reading ability. Words with more letters are read more slowly and less accurately than words of fewer letters. Words spelled aloud to the patient can be identified; writing remains intact; and speech and language are normal, with the exception of occasional mild anomia, particularly for colors. Reading often appears to be accomplished in a left-to-right, letter-by-letter fashion. There is no analogous agraphia.

Anatomically, pure alexia is thought to reflect a "disconnection" of visual input from left-hemisphere language centers, caused by lesions in the left primary visual cortex and the splenium of the corpus callosum. Three functional explanations have been put forth. One postulates damage to the mechanism that recognizes "visual word forms." A second proposes that the mechanism that analyzes "letter forms" is disconnected from the visual

word form system. A third explanation sees the problem as a deficit of automatic identification of visual input, which includes, but is not limited to, the letter/form analysis system.

2.2. *Surface alexia* is characterized by difficulty in reading "irregular" words, as compared with regular words. (An irregular word is one whose pronunciation does not conform to the spelling-to-sound correspondence rules of the language, such as *pint*; a regular word is completely predictable on the basis of such rules, such as *mint*.) These patients may produce regularization errors (e.g. *come* → 'comb'), or errors that appear to be the result of a misapplication of spelling-to-sound correspondence rules (e.g. *note* → 'not'). Patients with surface alexia read pseudowords well. When they read real words, their comprehension is based on the pronunciation they give to the word. For example, if the word *come* were read as 'comb', the meaning attached to the word would be related to grooming hair, not to the act of moving toward something.

The spelling analogue of surface alexia is known as *surface agraphia* or *lexical agraphia*. Patients with lexical agraphia appear to rely on phonology to spell words, and they may produce regularization paragraphias (e.g., spelling *rhyme* as 'r-i-m-e'). Words with predictable spellings (*run*) are spelled better than words with irregular (*pint*) or unpredictable (*brain* {brane?}) spellings.

2.3. *Phonological alexia* characterizes a group of patients whose primary deficit is a relative inability to read pseudowords, as compared with real words. Some short pseudowords may be read correctly, and even long pseudowords typically are read with the correct initial phoneme. Real words may be read incorrectly, and words with more syllables may be more difficult than words with fewer syllables. In addition, these patients may also experience difficulty reading functors and words with affixes. The analogous deficit in spelling is known as *phonological agraphia*. In this syndrome, pseudowords are spelled poorly relative to real words. Mispelled words tend not to be phonologically plausible, and paragraphias tend to be of the orthographic variety.

2.4. *Deep alexia* applies to a particular subgroup of patients who have difficulty in reading pseudowords; the distinguishing feature of these patients is that they produce semantic paralexias during oral reading. In addition, their success in reading real words is affected by the part of speech and by the concreteness of the word. They also produce derivational and orthographic paralexias, and functor substitutions. They tend to have large lesions that include the left frontal lobe, with extension posteriorly to the central sulcus. Patients with *deep agraphia* cannot read pseudowords, produce semantic (e.g. writing 'butter' for *bread*) and derivational (*speaker* → 'speaking') paragraphias, and show part-of-speech and concreteness effects when attempting to spell. Deep agraphia typically accompanies deep alexia.

3. Visual alexias. Two types of alexic disorders reflect difficulties at a more peripheral stage of written word processing. *Attentional alexia* appears to be part of a general problem with selective attention. Patients have difficulty reading text; letters from adjacent words impinge on the word being read, resulting in orthographic paralexias. In *neglect alexia*, one side of a word or of a page of text is not read or is misread. This typically occurs within the context of a more general neglect of hemispace, but isolated neglect alexia has been reported as well.

[*See also* Aphasia *and* Neurolinguistics.]

BIBLIOGRAPHY

Coltheart, Max. 1981. Disorders of reading and their implications for models of normal reading. *Visible Language* 15.245–286.

Coltheart, Max, et al., eds. 1987. *Deep dyslexia*. 2d ed. London: Routledge and Kegan Paul.

Friedman, Rhonda B. 1988. Acquired alexia. In *Handbook of neuropsychology*, edited by François Boller and Jordan Grafman, pp. 377–391. Amsterdam: Elsevier.

Friedman, Rhonda B., and Martin L. Albert. 1985. Alexia. In *Clinical neuropsychology*, 2d ed., edited by Kenneth M. Heilman and Edward Valenstein, pp. 49–73. Oxford and New York: Oxford University Press.

Friedman, Rhonda B., and G. Glosser. 1998. Aphasia, alexia, and agraphia. In *Encyclopedia of mental health*, edited by H. Friedman, pp. 137–148. San Diego, Calif.: Academic Press.

Hinshelwood, James. 1900. *Letter-, word-, and mind-blindness*. London: H. K. Lewis.

Newcombe, Freda, and John C. Marshall. 1981. On psycholinguistic classifications of the acquired dyslexias. *Bulletin of the Orton Society* 31.29–46.

Patterson, Karalyn E. 1981. Neuropsychological approaches to the study of reading. *British Journal of Psychology* 72.151–174.

Patterson, Karalyn E., et al., eds. 1985. *Surface dyslexia: Neuropsychological and cognitive studies of phonological meaning*. London: Erlbaum.

Roeltgen, D. P., and S. Z. Rapsak. 1993. Acquired disorders of writing and spelling. In *Linguistic disorders and pathologies*, edited by G. Blanken et al. New York: Walter de Gruyter.

RHONDA FRIEDMAN

ALGIC LANGUAGES. A family of North America, comprising the ALGONQUIAN LANGUAGES as well as two languages of northwestern California, Wiyot and Yurok. The name *Ritwan* is used as a cover term for Wiyot and Yurok.

LANGUAGE LIST

Wiyot: formerly spoken in USA by 450 to 800 speakers in northwestern California. Last speaker died in 1962.

Yurok: 10 speakers in USA. Ethnic population: 3,000 to 4,500 possibly. Northwestern California. Bilingualism in English. Few if any full bloods younger than 20 years old.

B. GRIMES

ALGONQUIAN LANGUAGES. The Algonquian (less commonly, Algonkian) family comprises 30 or more languages, spoken around 1600 in northeastern and central North America—and, by the late 1980s, in parts of its original territory and at additional locations to the west and south. Proto-Algonquian has been reconstructed in considerable detail, and the internal history of the family is generally well understood. Algonquian is related to Wiyot and Yurok, two neighboring though quite dissimilar languages of northern California, which some specialists group together as the Ritwan family; the larger grouping is referred to as Algonquian-Wiyot-Yurok, Algonquian-Ritwan, or Algic. Proposed more distant relationships are extremely controversial. Useful references on the family include the descriptive and historical-comparative study of Bloomfield 1946; the grammars of Bloomfield 1962, Voorhis 1974, and Wolfart and Carroll 1981; the descriptive papers of Dahlstrom 1987 and 1995 and Goddard 1990; the historical survey of Goddard 1994; and the bibliography of Pentland and Wolfart 1982.

The Algonquian languages are conventionally divided into three geographical groupings: Eastern, Central, and Plains (see Map 1). The Eastern languages were, from north to south, Micmac and Maliseet-Passamaquoddy in the Maritime provinces and eastern Maine; Eastern Abenaki and Western Abenaki in the rest of northern New England; a diverse continuum of dialects and languages in southern New England and on eastern Long Island,

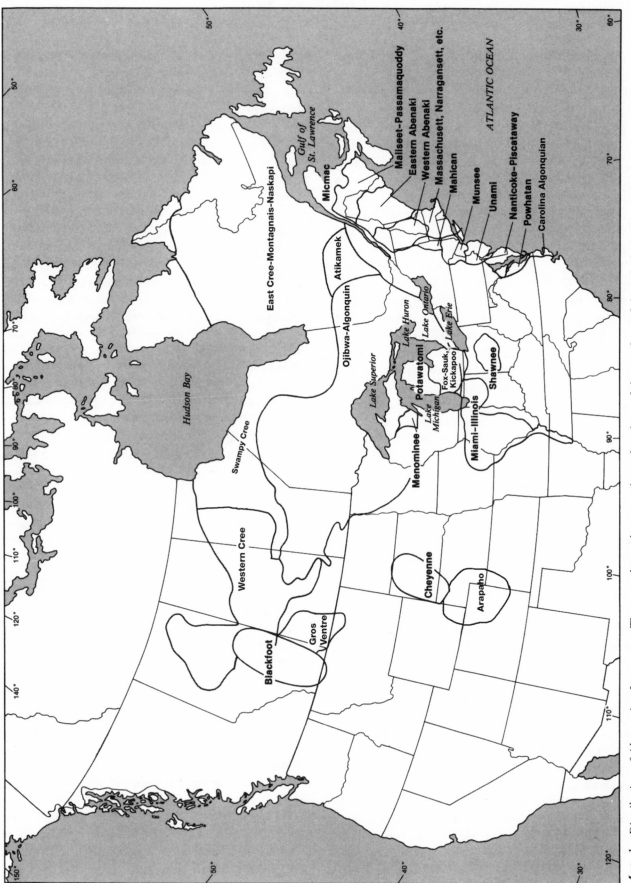

MAP 1. *Distribution of Algonquian Languages.* The map shows the approximate locations of the speakers of the principal Algonquian languages at the times of their earliest documentation, ranging from 1584 (Carolina Algonquian) to 1805 (Arapaho and Cheyenne).

including Massachusett and Narragansett; Mahican on the upper Hudson River; the Delaware languages Munsee and Unami in the lower Hudson valley, the Delaware River valley, and the area between; and the poorly known languages of the coastal plain south to northeastern North Carolina—those with some documentation are Nanticoke, Piscataway (Conoy), Powhatan or Virginia Algonquian, and Carolina Algonquian. In 2000 there were Micmac and Maliseet-Passamaquoddy speech communities in their original territories, and a few speakers each of Western Abenaki and Munsee; all the other Eastern languages were extinct.

The Central languages are those of the Cree-Montagnais continuum (Western Cree, Swampy Cree, Atikamek, East Cree, Montagnais, Naskapi), spoken from the lower north shore of the Gulf of St. Lawrence to the Rocky Mountains; Ojibwa-Algonquin, a less diverse and less extensive dialect continuum centering on the upper Great Lakes; Menominee, in Wisconsin; and several languages whose speakers have moved south and west from the upper Great Lakes in the historical period, namely Potawatomi, Fox-Sauk, Kickapoo, Shawnee, and Miami-Illinois. The Plains languages are Blackfoot, in Alberta and Montana; Arapaho, in Wyoming and Oklahoma; Gros Ventre (Atsina) in Montana; and Cheyenne, in Montana and Oklahoma. In 2000, all the Central and Plains languages except Miami-Illinois were still spoken, but Gros Ventre and Sauk were moribund.

The Eastern languages form a genetic subgroup, though a diverse one. The similarities of the Central languages are considered to be the result of some diffusion and, in general, of the conservatism of these languages. The Plains languages are the most divergent; all have undergone radical sound changes, and Blackfoot has many features that are poorly understood historically and that probably indicate that it constitutes a separate, archaic branch of the family.

The Ałgonquian languages generally have small phoneme inventories and simple phonologies; they have extensive head-marking inflectional morphology, and complex derivational morphology. Their syntax is predominantly non-configurational: grammatical functions are expressed morphologically, and discourse features are encoded by word order and sentence particles. Discontinuous syntactic constituents are common.

Proto-Algonquian had a single series of stops */p t č k/ and fricatives */s š h/, two phonetically indeterminate continuants */l/ (probably [r]) and */θ/ (probably [θ]), the nasals */m n/, and the semivowels */w y/. There were four short and four long vowels, */i e a o/ and */i: e: a: o:/. Clusters, with a limited number of first members, occurred only medially; there were no vowel sequences. The modern languages all lose some contrasts among the clusters and obstruents; they have from three to twelve vowels. Some have developed two series of stops and fricatives, and several have developed contrastive stress or pitch accent. Cheyenne has developed four contrastive tones from the interaction of length and tonal contrasts. In several languages, rhythmically determined vowel weakening and strengthening have given rise to divergent surface alternates for many morphemes.

Nouns are of animate or inanimate gender; many names for non-animate entities are grammatically animate. Nouns are inflected for number, possessor, and locative. Verbs appear in derivationally related pairs: intransitives are differentiated for the gender of the subject, and transitives for that of the object. Verbs are inflected for subject and (primary) object, and in some languages for secondary object; they may also bear a lexically specified valence for any of several oblique categories (location, oblique goal, manner, extent, etc.). Typically, there are many modes, divided into formally distinct orders; and most languages mark negation on the verb. The inflections for possessor, subject, and object function pronominally—or, with a coreferential noun phrase, as agreement. Pronominal inflection for possessor, and for some verbal arguments in the independent order, uses a set of prefixes; initial change, a modification in the first stem vowel, marks certain modes of the conjunct order; and all other inflection is by suffixes. Several patterns of stem-initial reduplication are found. Animate nouns and some pronominal inflections on verbs may mark a secondary 3rd person, the obviative, in the context of a primary animate 3rd person. The languages differ in the details, but basically the use of the obviative differentiates 3rd person animate arguments and tracks coreference or non-coreference. In addition, the assignment and shifting of obviative status can indicate focus, point of view, etc.

Stems normally are internally complex, except for some primary nouns and intransitive verbs. The verb-stem template includes an initial, an optional medial, and a final; each of the three components may be internally complex or derived from a stem. Primary initials ("roots") generally denote manner, state, condition, relation, or configuration, either inherent or resulting from an action; medials are incorporated nominals, sometimes functioning locatively or as classifiers; finals determine the category of the verb. Concrete finals denote the basic verbal notion—including, for transitives, the instrumentality of causation. A typical verb form is Fox *ka: hkihkinameške:-nawote* 'if an arrow scratches him on the skin': a stem consisting of initial *ka:hkihk-* 'scratched' + medial *-inameške:-* 'skin' + final *-(e)naw* 'hit (animate) by missile (causing . . .)', inflected with *-et* (3rd person passive, conjunct order, > *-ot* after *w*) + *-e* (subjunctive mode of conjunct order). Secondary derivation makes, e.g., (from nouns) verbs of being and possession, and (from verbs) agent, instrument, and abstract nouns—as well as transitivized and detransitivized verbs of several types, including reciprocals, middle reflexives, and derived passives.

BIBLIOGRAPHY

Bloomfield, Leonard. 1946. Algonquian. In *Linguistic structures of Native America* (Viking Fund publications in anthropology, 6), by Harry Hoijer et al., pp. 85–129. New York.

Bloomfield, Leonard. 1962. *The Menomini language.* Edited by Charles F. Hockett. New Haven, Conn.: Yale University Press.

Dahlstrom, Amy. 1987. Discontinuous constituents in Fox. In *Native American languages and grammatical typology,* edited by Paul D. Kroeber and Robert E. Moore, pp. 53–73. Bloomington: Indiana University Linguistics Club.

Dahlstrom, Amy. 1995. *Topic, focus and other word order problems in Algonquian.* Winnipeg: Voices of Rupert's Land.

Goddard, Ives. 1990. Aspects of the topic structure of Fox narratives: Proximate shifts and the use of overt and inflectional NPs. *International Journal of American Linguistics* 56.317–340.

Goddard, Ives. 1994. The west-to-east cline in Algonquian dialectology. In *Actes du Vingt-Cinquième Congrès des Algonquinistes,* edited by William Cowan, pp. 187–211. Ottawa: Carleton University.

Pentland, David H., and H. Christoph Wolfart. 1982. *A bibliography of Algonquian linguistics.* Winnipeg: University of Manitoba Press.

Voorhis, Paul H. 1974. *Introduction to the Kickapoo language.* (Language science monographs, 13.) Bloomington: Indiana University Research Center for the Language Sciences.

Wolfart, H. Christoph, and Janet F. Carroll. 1981. *Meet Cree: A guide to the Cree language.* 2d ed. Edmonton: University of Alberta Press.

IVES GODDARD

LANGUAGE LIST

Abnaki, Eastern: formerly spoken in USA. Ethnic population: 1,800 in the ethnic group including Western Abnaki in Canada. Near Bangor, Maine, one village spoke the dialect Penobscot. The last speaker of Penobscot died in the 1990s. Other dialects also extinct.

Abnaki, Western: also called Abenaki, Abenaqui, St. Francis. Spoken in Canada: Quebec on St. Lawrence River between Montreal and Quebec City. Bilingualism in French. All elderly.

Algonquin: also called Algonkin. 2,275 speakers in Canada. Ethnic population: 5,000. Southwestern Quebec, northwest of Ottawa, and in adjacent areas of Ontario (Golden Lake and Maniwaki). Several dialects. The southern (Miniwaki) and numerous northern varieties are very different. In the east Algonquin is the principal means of communication, and spoken by the majority of all ages. In the west most adults speak Algonquin, young adults may prefer the national languages, and children prefer the national languages, although some may speak Algonquin.

Arapaho: also called Arrapahoe. Spoken in USA. Ethnic population: 5,000. Wind River Reservation, Wyoming, and associated with the Cheyenne in western Oklahoma. Bilingualism in English. Most or all speakers are middle-aged or older.

Atikamekw: also called Tête De Boule, Attimewk, Attikamek, Atihkamekw, Atikamek. 3,995 speakers in Canada. Very different from Montagnais and Naskapi in the nearby area. Language complex or dialect continuum within Cree-Montagnais-Naskapi. Nonpalatalized r-dialect. Bilingualism in French. Vigorous language use. Roman orthography, based on French.

Blackfoot: also called Pikanii, Blackfeet. 5,800 speakers in Canada and USA. In Canada: 4,745 speakers. Ethnic population: 7,000 to 10,000. Blackfoot, Piegan, and Blood Reserves in southern Alberta. Dialects are Piegan, Blood. In some places Blackfoot is the principal language for older adults. Children and young adults tend to prefer English. In USA: Ethnic population: 5,000 to 8,000. Blackfeet Reservation, Montana. Dialects are Piegan, Blood. Bilingualism in English. In USA most or all speakers are elderly.

Carolina Algonquian: formerly spoken in northeastern North Carolina, USA.

Cheyenne: 1,721 speakers in USA. Ethnic population: 5,000. Northern Cheyenne Reservation, southeastern Montana; associated with Arapaho in western Oklahoma. In Montana most of the speakers are adults (parents and the elderly, 1998), but many of their children prefer English. In Oklahoma most speakers are middle-aged or older. As of 1998, the Northern Cheyenne in Montana had a summer camp for children, where five fluent speakers teach the language.

Chippewa: also called Southwestern Ojibwa, Ojibwe, Ojibway. Spoken in USA. Ethnic population: 103,826 as of 1990. Upper Michigan westward to North Dakota, and unconfirmed groups in Montana. Dialects are Upper Michigan-Wisconsin Chippewa, Central Minnesota Chippewa, Red

Lake Chippewa, Minnesota Border Chippewa. Turtle Mountain, North Dakota, Chippewa shares features with Central Minnesotan Chippewa. Red Lake Chippewa includes Northwest Angle on shore of Lake of the Woods. Nett Lake Chippewa, spoken on the Minnesota border, is closely related to Lac la Croix Chippewa (Rainy River Ojibwa of Northwestern Ojibwa) in Ontario. Most or all speakers are middle-aged or older. Concerted effort via language teaching in public schools and other efforts to reverse decline.

Cree, Moose: also called York Cree, West Shore Cree, West Main Cree. 4,500 speakers in Canada. Ethnic population: 5,000. Language complex or dialect continuum within Cree-Montagnais-Naskapi. Nonpalatalized l-dialect. Bilingualism in English. Vigorous language use. Cree syllabary, eastern finals.

Cree, Plains: also called Western Cree. 35,000 speakers in Canada and USA. In Canada: 34,000 speakers. North central Manitoba westward across Saskatchewan and central Alberta to the foot of the Rocky Mountains. Dialects are Plains Cree, Western York Cree. Language complex or dialect continuum within Cree-Montagnais-Naskapi. Nonpalatalized y-dialect. Bilingualism in English. All ages. Vigorous language use. Cree syllabary, western finals. In USA:1,000 speakers. North central Montana, Rocky Boy Reservation. Language complex or dialect continuum within Cree-Montagnais-Naskapi. Nonpalatalized y-dialect. Bilingualism in English. Most or all speakers in the USA are middle-aged or older. Cree syllabary.

Cree, Swampy: also called York Cree, West Shore Cree, Western Main Cree. 4,500 speakers in Canada. Ontario, along the coast of Hudson Bay and northwestern coast of James Bay, and inland. Dialects are Eastern Swampy Cree, Western Swampy Cree. Language complex or dialect continuum within Cree-Montagnais-Naskapi. Nonpalatalized n-dialect. Bilingualism in English. Vigorous language use. Cree syllabary, western finals.

Cree, Woods: 35,000 speakers in Canada. Ethnic population: 53,000 or more. Extreme north of Manitoba and Saskatchewan, almost to the border with Northwest Territories. Language complex or dialect continuum within Cree-Montagnais-Naskapi. Nonpalatalized th-dialect. Bilingualism in English. All ages. Vigorous language use. Cree syllabary, western finals.

East Cree, Northern: also called James Bay Cree. 5,308 speakers in Canada. West central Quebec, east coast of lower Hudson Bay and James Bay, communities of Whapmagoostui, Chisasibi, Wemindji, and most people in Eastmain. Language complex or dialect continuum within Cree-Montagnais-Naskapi. Sometimes classified as Montagnais. Palatalized y-dialect. Bilingualism in English. Vigorous language use. Cree syllabary, eastern finals.

East Cree, Southern: also called James Bay Cree. 7,306 speakers in Canada. Dialects are Inland East Cree (Mistis-

sini), Coastal East Cree. Language complex or dialect continuum within Cree-Montagnais-Naskapi. Sometimes classified as Montagnais. Palatalized y-dialect. Bilingualism in English. Vigorous language use. Cree syllabary, eastern finals.

Gros Ventre: also called Gros Ventres, Atsina, White Clay People, Ahahnelin, Ahe, Fall Indians, A' Ananin. Spoken in USA. Ethnic population: 1,200. Fort Belknap Reservation, Milk River, north central Montana. Bilingualism in English.

Kickapoo: also called Kikapoo, Kikap. Around 850 speakers in USA and Mexico. In USA: 539 speakers. Possibly intelligible with Sac and Fox (Mesquakie). In Oklahoma some younger people prefer English, and in Kansas most or all speakers are middle-aged or over. In Mexico: 300 speakers in Coahuila: Nacimiento de Kikap, 25 miles northeast of Muzquiz. Vigorous language use in Mexico.

Lumbee: also called Croatan. Formerly spoken in USA. Ethnic population: 30,000. Southern North Carolina and into South Carolina and Maryland.

Mahican: formerly spoken in the upper Hudson River valley and later in Wisconsin, USA.

Malecite-Passamaquoddy: also called Maliseet-Passamaquoddy. Approximately 1,500 speakers in Canada and USA. In Canada: 655 speakers. Ethnic population: 3,000 to 4,000. New Brunswick, villages along the Saint John River. Malecite mainly in Canada, Passamaquoddy in Maine, USA. Dialects are Malecite (Maliseet), Passamaquoddy. English is preferred by most younger speakers. Most speakers are older, but in some communities younger people may speak it. Interest in the language is increasing in some places. In USA:1,000 speakers. Ethnic population: 2,500 to 3,000. Maine, New Brunswick border area. Malecite mainly in Canada, Passamaquoddy mainly in Maine. Dialects are Malecite (Maliseet), Passamaquoddy. Bilingualism in English. As of 1998, most speakers of Passamaquoddy were elderly with younger speakers in a few areas. English is preferred by most younger speakers.

Menomini: also called Menominee. 39 speakers in Northeastern Wisconsin, on what was formerly the Menomini Reservation, USA. Ethnic population: 3,500. Bilingualism in English. Only elderly first-language speakers are left.

Mesquakie: also called Meskwakie, Sac and Fox, Sauk-Fox. 200 speakers in USA. Ethnic population: 1,200 as of 2000. Dialects are Fox, Sac, Mesquakie. Mesquakie at Tama, Iowa; Sac and Fox at Sac and Fox Reservation on eastern Kansas-Nebraska border and in central Oklahoma. Kansas and Oklahoma groups are closely related to Kickapoo of Oklahoma and Mexico. Bilingualism in English. In Iowa it is spoken by parents and the elderly (1998). Outside Iowa most or all speakers are middle-aged or older.

Miami: also called Miami-Illinois, Miami-Myaamia. Formerly spoken in USA. Dialects are Miami, Peoria. Ethnic population: 2,000 as of 1977. Dialects are Miami, Peoria. Miami in north central Indiana, Miami and Peoria in northeastern Oklahoma. Some still know a few words and phrases. A revitalization program is in progress.

Micmac: also called Mi'gmaq, Miigmag, Mi'kmaq, Restigouche. 8,500 speakers in Canada and USA. In Canada: 7,310 speakers. Ethnic population: 14,200 as of 1998. Among this latter group, 1,500 are in mainland Nova Scotia, 4,000 on Cape Breton Island, Nova Scotia, 800 on Prince Edward Island and Lennox Island, 4,550 on the east coast of New Brunswick, 3,150 on the Gaspé Peninsula, Quebec, 200 in Newfoundland. Dialects are Northern Micmac, Southern Micmac. Some speakers of Mi'gmaw, the Quebec dialect, have some difficulty understanding other dialects. There are no monolinguals. Most are bilingual in English, some in Quebec are bilingual in French. English used in religious services. Most Micmac speakers are adults, but many adults below 35 do not speak it. Younger speakers may prefer English. Most children learn English first, but there is an effort in many communities to teach children Micmac. In some communities usage is more vigorous. The number of speakers is decreasing. Three major writing systems used in teaching and writing. In USA: 1,200 speakers. Northern Maine near Fort Fairfield, Boston, Massachusetts, and small scattered places elsewhere in the USA.

Mohegan-Montauk-Narragansett: formerly spoken in USA. Ethnic population: 1,400. Connecticut, Rhode Island, Long Island, New York, Wisconsin. Dialects were Pequot-Mohegan, Narrangansett, Montauk (Shinnecock-Poosepatuck), Stockbridge.

Montagnais: also called Innu Aimun, Innu. 8,483 speakers in Canada. Ethnic population: 10,000. Dialects are Western Montagnais, Eastern Montagnais. Closely related to Naskapi. There are two or possibly three dialects based on the shifting of Proto-Algonquian /l/ (Southern Montagnais) to /n/ (Eastern Montagnais). Language complex or dialect continuum within Cree-Montagnais-Naskapi. The Mashteuiatsh are nearly all French-speaking. Most speakers are fluent in Quebec English (Sheshatshiu) or French (other communities). All ages. Women speakers of all ages and male speakers over 55 are mainly not fluent in Quebec English or French—a total of 3,000 people in this category. Vigorous language use in all but two communities. Rapid shift occurring in communities close to cities where the majority speak Quebec English or French. Large population of speakers in lower northern shore communities and Schefferville. Standardized Roman orthography, based on French.

Munsee: also called Delaware, Ontario Delaware. 7 speakers in Canada. Ethnic population: 400. Formerly spoken in southern Ontario, Moraviantown Reserve. Close to Unami in USA, but a separate language. Bilingualism in English. Only elderly speakers left.

Nanticoke: formerly spoken in USA. Ethnic population: 400 as of 1977. Southern Delaware and eastern Maryland.

Naskapi: also called Innu Aimuun. 1,177 speakers in Canada. Ethnic population: 1,177 as of 1996. Dialects are Western Naskapi, Eastern Naskapi (Innu). Language complex or dialect continuum within Cree-Montagnais-Naskapi. Closely related to Montagnais, but distinct. Palatalized y- (Western Naskapi) or n- (Eastern Naskapi). Bilingualism in English. Vigorous language use in both dialects. Slow shift occurring. Western Naskapi: modified Cree syllabary, Eastern Naskapi: Roman orthography based on French.

Ojibwa, Central: also called Central Ojibwe, Ojibway, Ojibwe. Spoken in Canada. Central Ontario from Lake Nipigon in the west to Lake Nipissing in the east. An area of transitional dialects.

Ojibwa, Eastern: also called Ojibwe, Ojibway. Spoken in Canada. Probably all speakers are bilingual in English, some in other Ojibwa varieties. Dying out in many areas. Concerted effort via language teaching in public schools and other efforts to reverse the decline.

Ojibwa, Northwestern: also called Northern Ojibwa, Ojibway, Ojibwe. 20,000 speakers in Canada. Southern northwest Ontario into Manitoba. Dialects are Berens River Ojibwa (Saulteaux), Lac Seul Ojibwa, Albany River Ojibwa, Lake of the Woods Ojibwa, Rainy River Ojibwa. Concerted effort via language teaching in public schools and other efforts to reverse decline in use.

Ojibwa, Severn: also called Northern Ojibwa, Ojibway, Ojibwe, Ojicree, Oji-Cree, Cree. 8,000 speakers in Canada. Ethnic population: 8,000 or fewer, possibly including some Northwestern Ojibwa. Northern northwest Ontario into Manitoba. Dialects are Winisk River Ojibwa, Severn River Ojibwa. Speakers are ages 50 and older. Vigorous language use. Concerted effort via language teaching in public schools and other efforts to reverse decline in use.

Ojibwa, Western: also called Saulteaux, Plains Ojibway, Ojibway, Ojibwe. 20,000 speakers in Canada. Ethnic population: 60,000. Westward from Lake Winnipeg into Saskatchewan with outlying groups as far west as British Columbia. All ages in most areas. Vigorous language use in most areas. In some areas young people and children may prefer English.

Ottawa: also called Odawa, Ojibwe, Ojibway. 5,395 speakers in Canada and USA. In Canada: Probably all speakers are bilingual in English, some in other Ojibwa varieties. Most adults and some younger speakers in a large population on Manitoulin Island. Vigorous language use on Manitoulin Island. Dying out in many other areas. Concerted effort via language teaching in public schools and other efforts to reverse the decline. In USA: Ethnic population: 20,000 (Ottawa and Chippewa). Lower Michigan and upper Michigan near Sault Ste. Marie. Probably all speakers are bilingual in English, some in other Ojibwa varieties. Ottawa is dying out in many US areas. Concerted effort via language teaching in public schools and other efforts to reverse the decline.

Piscataway: also called Conoy. Formerly spoken in Maryland, USA.

Nawathinehena: formerly spoken in USA among the Arapaho.

Powhatan: also called Virginia Algonquian. Formerly spoken in USA. Scattered in eastern Virginia and Powhatan Renape Nation, Rankokus Indian Reservation, Rancocas, New Jersey.

Potawatomi: also called Pottawotomi. 50 speakers in USA and Canada. In USA: Ethnic population: 25,000. Formerly spoken in southwestern and northern Michigan, northern Wisconsin, and northeastern Kansas. Bilingualism in English. In Canada: southern Ontario. Bilingualism in English.

Shawnee: 200 speakers in USA. Ethnic population: 2,000 as of 1977. Central and northeastern Oklahoma. Bilingualism in English. Most or all speakers are middle-aged or older.

Unami: also called Delaware, Lenni-Lenape, Lenape, Tla Wilano. Ethnic population: 13,500. Formerly spoken in USA in northeastern and west central Oklahoma, northern New Jersey and lower Delaware Valley. Related to Munsee in Ontario. Bilingualism in English.

Wampanoag: also called Massachusett, Massachusetts, Natick. Formerly spoken in USA southeastern Massachusetts. Ethnic population: 1,200. Bilingualism in English.   B. GRIMES

ALPHABET. *See* Writing and Written Language; Language Planning; Text; *and* Literacy.

ALTAIC LANGUAGES. This group of language families occupies large areas of Central and East Asia. From the 19th century on, this term has been used to refer to a phylum of language families thought to be genetically related, although the 20th century witnessed a still ongoing debate on the validity of this claim. Consequently, for some specialists, the term "Altaic" designates a linguistic convergence area without genetic connections, or one in which these are still undetermined. Conventionally, the Turkic, Mongolian, and Tungusic languages are united under this name ("Micro-Altaic"), but Korean and Japanese-Ryukyuan are increasingly viewed as members either of the putative genetic stock ("Macro-Altaic"), or of the Altaic *Sprachbund*. Theories advocating the inclusion of other languages of East Asia, such as Ainu, as well as the once popular connection of Altaic and Uralic, are now mostly dismissed, as far as the genetic hypothesis is concerned. Altaic languages are routinely incorporated in some hypotheses of deeper genetic relationship, or macro-phyla, such as Nostratic or Eurasiatic.

1. Classification. The *Mongolian* languages are spoken in the ("Outer") Mongolian Republic, as well as in

TABLE 1. *Time-depth of Selected (Micro-)Altaic Languages*

Family	Language	Earliest independent attestation (all dates CE)
Turkic	Old Turkic	ca. 720
Mongolian (?)	Kitan	ca. 1150
Tungusic	Jurchen	1185
Mongolian	Written Mongolian	1227
Turkic	Volga Bolgarian	13th c.
Tungusic	Written Manchu	1599
Mongolian	Written Oirat	1648

adjacent regions of the People's Republic of China and the Russian Federation. Mongolian proper forms a dialect continuum with two written prestige varieties: Khalkha in Outer Mongolia, and the official language of the Inner Mongolian Autonomous Region of China, based mainly on the Chakhar dialect. Other written languages of the family are Kalmyk, on the lower Volga, and Buryat, east of Lake Baikal in Russia. Dagur (in Manchuria and Xinjiang), Santa (Dongxiang), Monguor, Bao'an, Shira Yugur (in Gansu and Qinghai, China) are all virtually unwritten languages; Roman-based alphabets have been introduced for some of them only recently. The language of the Moghol in Afghanistan is now probably extinct.

Mongolian proper has been a written language since at least the 13th century (see Table 1 for the earliest attestations of Altaic languages). It was first written in a variety of scripts; the Uyghur-Mongolian script, adopted from Turkic Uyghur in the early 13th century, continues to be used today mainly in China, whereas in Outer Mongolia the literary standard of Khalkha uses the Cyrillic alphabet, as do Kalmyk and Buryat. The predecessor of present-day Kalmyk, Written Oirat, from 1648 on used another modification of the Uyghur script. The extinct language of the Kitan (Qidan, Liao) dynasty in northern China (907–1125), which was written in a script as yet only partly deciphered, may have been another language of the Mongolian family.

Tungusic languages are widespread in Siberia, the Russian Far East, and northeastern China. They are traditionally subdivided into Northern and Southern subgroups, though the details of this subclassification continue to be debated. The greatest density of different languages is found in the Lower Amur region (Map 1), where closely related Southern Tungusic Oroch and Udi(he), Nanai (called Hezhen in China), Ul'cha, Kili, and Orok (on Sakhalin Island) are spoken. Negidal, also spoken here, belongs to the Northern Tungusic group.

MAP 1. *Distribution of Tungusic Languages in the Amur Region*

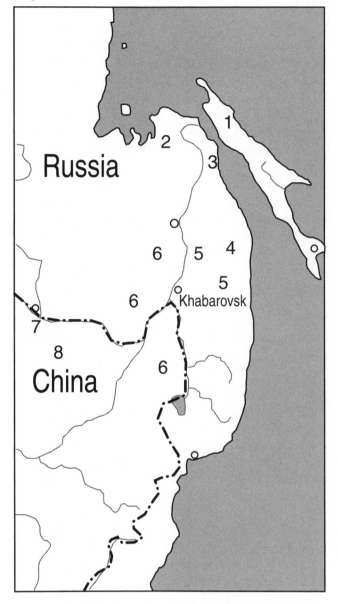

1. Orok	5. Udi(he)
2. Negidal	6. Nanai
3. Ul'cha	7. Manchu (of Aigun)
4. Oroch	8. Solon (=Ewenki)

The other Northern Tungusic languages occupy vast regions of Northern Siberia: Ewenki is found from the Yenisey River in the west to the Lena in the east, as well as in northeastern China, where its varieties are called Oroqen (Elunchun) and Ewenke (Solon) respectively. Ewen (Lamut) is spoken from the Lena to the Sea of Okhotsk and the Kamchatkan Peninsula in the east.

Only Manchu, still spoken by few people in Manchuria and by members of the Sibe (Xibo) nationality in Xinjiang, has a considerable literary tradition. It was the official language, written in an adaptation of the Uyghur-Mongol script, of the Qing (Manchu) dynasty, which ruled imperial China from 1644 to 1912 and produced a highly original and diverse literature. The earliest documents in a Tungusic language are a few texts in the language of the Jurchen, rulers of the Jin dynasty (1115–1234), both from the time of the dynasty itself and from Ming times, written in an autochthonous script. Jurchen is generally viewed as close to but taxonomically distinct from Manchu, although some researchers claim that it is its direct linguistic predecessor.

2. Typology. The Altaic languages show a very uniform overall typological makeup, including predominantly agglutinative morphology, mostly rigid SOV word order (with all the typical implications associated with this feature), converbs and nominalized verb forms as the main technique for coordination and subordination of clauses, and a variety of vowel harmony systems. These and other features shared by most Altaic languages (and by other languages of Eurasia, notably the Uralic languages) were instrumental in the formation of the Altaic Hypothesis (and its predecessor, the Ural-Altaic Hypothesis), which views these languages as genetically related and tries to reconstruct a common ancestor, Proto-Altaic. Classic statements of this theory are Ramstedt 1952, Poppe 1960 (Micro-Altaic plus Korean), and, including Japanese, Miller 1971 and Starostin 1991. The dissenting view, which tries to explain the typological and material commonalities of these languages as indicative of areal interaction and large-scale borrowing, has been developed by Németh 1912, Clauson 1956, Doerfer 1963, and Ščerbak 1997.

Although it is generally agreed that the Altaic languages share many lexical items, and, to a lesser degree, morphological markers, scholarly debate continues on the historical status of these elements and their validity as evidence of genetic relationship. Critics of the Altaic Hypothesis point to a scarcity of shared items of "basic vocabulary," lacunae in the proposed systems of regular sound correspondences among the individual families, and improper reconstructions of Proto-Turkic, Proto-Mongolian, and other forms, which then serve as input to comparisons on the Altaic level; they believe that a large number of words common to Mongolian and Turkic show signs of being loans from a specific subbranch of the latter (Bolgar-Chuvash). Given the still imperfect state of Mongolian, Tungusic, and related comparative (and, to a degree, even descriptive) linguistics, the discussion still focuses on philological and low-level linguistic issues, such as attestation, proper internal morphological analysis, semantics, and the historical status of most lexical and other items proposed as evidence of the ultimate genetic relationship of the Altaic languages.

[See also Mongolic Languages; Tungusic Languages; Turkic Languages; and Turkish]

BIBLIOGRAPHY

Clauson, Gerard. 1956. The case against the Altaic theory. *Central Asiatic Journal* 2.181–187.

Doerfer, Gerhard. 1963. *Türkische und mongolische Elemente im Neupersischen*, vol. 1, *Mongolische Elemente im Neupersischen*. (Akademie der Wissenschaften und der Literatur, Veröffentlichungen der Orientalischen Kommission, 16.) Wiesbaden: Franz Steiner.

Georg, Stefan, et al. 1999. Telling general linguists about Altaic. *Journal of Linguistics* 35.65–98.

Georg, Stefan. 2000. Haupt und Glieder der Altaischen Hypothese: Die Körperteilbezeichnungen im Türkischen, Mongolischen und Tungusischen. *Ural-Altaische Jahrbücher, Neue Folge* 16.1–40.

Miller, Roy Andrew. 1971. *Japanese and the other Altaic languages*. Chicago: University of Chicago Press.

Németh, Gyula. 1912. Die türkisch-mongolische Hypothese. *Zeitschrift der Deutschen Morgenländischen Gesellschaft* 66.549–76.

Ramstedt, Gustaf John. 1952–66. *Einführung in die Altaische Sprachwissenschaft. (I. Lautlehre 1957; II. Formenlehre 1952; III. Register 1966.)* Helsinki: Suomalais-Ugrilainen Seura.

Ščerbak, Aleksandr Michajlovič. 1997. *Rannie tjurksko-mongol'skie jazykovye svjazi (VIII–XIV vv.)*. Saint Petersburg: ILI RAN.

Starostin, Sergej Anatolevič. 1991. *Altajskaja problema i proischoĭdenie japonskogo jazyka*. Moscow: Nauka.

STEFAN GEORG

AMBIGUITY. *See* Semantics.

AMERICAN INDIAN LANGUAGES. *See* Meso-American Languages; North American Languages; South American Languages; *and* Anthropological Linguistics.

AMERICAN SIGN LANGUAGE. American sign Language (ASL) is a natural language, one of the world's signed languages. An estimated 100,000–500,000 people in the United States and Canada use ASL in their face-to-face communication. Among deaf people, ASL is learned either as a first language or as a second but preferred language. The deaf community is a multilingual one: its members use ASL as their primary language, but most are also fluent in the spoken and written language of the hearing community.

1. History. ASL is most closely related to French Sign Language (LSF). The historical contact between ASL and LSF came about in the 19th century, when the American Thomas Hopkins Gallaudet traveled to France to learn about methods for educating deaf children. The founder of the Paris Institute, the abbé de l'Epée, had developed a system called "methodical signing," which used the lexical stock of signs from LSF, highly modified to represent written French. Gallaudet and Laurent Clerc, a deaf teacher at the Institute, brought this system to Hartford, Connecticut, where in 1817 they established the first school for the deaf in America. The LSF-based methodical signs merged with the existing signed language dialects used in the deaf community at the time to produce ASL.

2. Linguistic structure. Modern linguistic analysis of ASL began with the pioneering work of William C. Stokoe. Stokoe 1960 offered the first linguistic analysis of ASL, demonstrating that it exhibits duality of patterning.

2.1. *Phonology.* Stokoe analyzed signs into three major phonological classes: handshape (the configuration that the hand assumes when producing the sign), location (the place where the sign is produced), and movement (the motion made in producing the sign). Linguists later added a fourth major class, orientation (the direction in which the palm faces when producing the sign). Linguists describe the phonology of ASL using a variety of theoretical models, including segmental, autosegmental, prosodic, and moraic.

2.2. *Morphology.* ASL is a highly synthetic language with tendencies toward polysynthesis, a typological characteristic that it shares with most other signed languages. ASL has complex verb morphology. Although tense is marked lexically, ASL exhibits extensive morphology for representing iterative, habitual, continuative, inceptive, and other verb aspects. Aspect is indicated by changes to the temporal profile of the root's lexical movement. This and other features of ASL morphology exhibit extensive iconicity (Wilcox 2002).

ASL relies on facial markers to signal intonation and

prosody; to mark interrogatives, imperatives, and other utterance types; and to indicate certain adverbial information, such as intensity of action. Facial markers also commonly signal speaker subjectivity.

2.3. Syntax. ASL is a S[ubject] V[erb] O[bject] language; however, because of its rich morphology, word order often is not required to signal grammatical relations. Spatial location and hand orientation are used, for example, to distinguish 'She looks at me' from 'I look at her.'

ASL discourse is characterized by a prevalence of topic-comment structure. Topics are marked grammatically, with the topic phrase accompanied by raised eyebrows, a slightly backward head tilt, and a pause between the topic and comment phrases. Topic-comment structure has been described as a kind of ASL sentence type, along with questions, imperatives, assertions, and others (Baker and Cokely 1980).

ASL distinguishes two types of interrogatives: *wh*-questions and yes-no questions. Yes-no questions are typically statements with the addition of facial markers, including raised eyebrows and head tilted forward. *Wh*-questions are indicated with a question word and facial markers, including brow furrow, eye squint, and head tilted backward or to one side (Cokely and Baker 1980). Imperatives are indicated by means of facial markers, including a brow furrow and maintaining eye contact with the person to whom the command is directed.

2.4. Pragmatics. Assertions in ASL generally take two forms: topic-comment structures, and sentences with a grammatical subject. Strength of assertion is marked in ASL predominantly by facial markers, such as head nod, brow furrow, and tight lips (Liddell 1980).

The ASL forms 'can' and 'future' may be used to signal strongly asserted information, particularly when they occur in clause-final or sentence-final position and with the facial markers just described. For example (from Janzen, Shaffer, and Wilcox 2000):

(1)   JOHN CAN PASS ENGLISH
     'John can pass English.'

(2)   [JOHN PASS ENGLISH]-topic [CAN]-brow-furrow/
     head-nod
     'I have no doubts that John can pass English.'

Topic-comment structure in ASL often serves to express indirect questions:

(3)   [TED BUY NEW CAR]-topic, CURIOUS
     'I wonder if Ted bought a new car.'

Indirect requests may be expressed in ASL with declarative forms, or with an explicit lexical marker of indirect request combined with yes-no question facial markers.

2.5. Grammaticization. Grammaticization operates in signed languages as it does in spoken languages. Deontic and epistemic modals in ASL developed out of lexical forms with concrete, embodied meanings. For example, the ASL modal auxiliary used to indicate ability and epistemic possibility developed historically from an ASL lexical form meaning 'possessing physical strength' (Wilcox and Wilcox 1995).

Grammaticization may be extended in the case of signed languages to account for the development of lexical and grammatical material, both manual and facial, from gestural sources. It has been proposed that ASL deontic and epistemic modal forms have developed from gestural sources (Wilcox and Wilcox 1995); that the ASL future marker developed from a lexical form meaning 'to leave,' which had its source in a pan-Mediterranean gesture signaling departure (Janzen and Shaffer 2002); and that the ASL negative ability marker 'cannot' can be traced to the deontic modal 'must' and ultimately to a gesture indicating financial obligation (Shaffer 2002). Topic marking has a communicative questioning gesture as its ultimate source, which grammaticized into yes-no question marking; this yes-no facial marker has grammaticized to mark topics (Janzen 1999).

3. Fingerspelling. Fingerspelling is a system of manually representing written letters. Both one-handed and two-handed fingerspelling systems exist; ASL uses a one-handed system. Fingerspelling is often used for proper names or technical terms and is a source of loanwords in signed languages; for example, 'of', 'all', 'sure', and several other English words have been borrowed into ASL through fingerspelling (Battison 1978). Rapid fingerspelling in discourse is characterized by extensive coarticulation.

[*See also* Grammaticalization *and* Sign Language.]

BIBLIOGRAPHY

Baker, Charlotte, and Dennis Cokely. 1980. *American Sign Language: A teacher's resource text on grammar and culture.* Silver Spring, Md.: T. J. Publishers.

Battison, Robbin. 1978. *Lexical borrowing in American Sign Language.* Silver Spring, Md.: Linstok Press.

Janzen, Terry. 1999. The grammaticization of topics in American Sign Language. *Studies in Language* 23.271–306.

Janzen, Terry, and Barbara Shaffer. 2002. Gesture as the substrate in the process of ASL grammaticization. In *Modality and structure in signed and spoken languages*, edited by Richard Meier, et al., pp. 199–223. Cambridge: Cambridge University Press.

Janzen, Terry, Barbara Shaffer, and Sherman Wilcox. 2000. Signed language pragmatics. In *Handbook of pragmatics*, edited by Jef Verschueren et al., pp. 1–20. Amsterdam: Benjamins.

Liddell, Scott. 1980. *American Sign Language syntax.* The Hague: Mouton.

Shaffer, Barbara. 2002. CAN'T: The negation of modal notions in ASL. *Sign Language Studies* 3(1).34–53.

Stokoe, William C. 1960. *Sign language structure.* Silver Spring, Md.: Linstok Press.

Wilcox, Phyllis, and Sherman Wilcox. 1995. The gestural expression of modality in American Sign Language. In *Modality in grammar and discourse*, edited by Joan Bybee and Suzanne Fleischman, pp. 135–162. Amsterdam: Benjamins.

Wilcox, Sherman. 1992. *The phonetics of fingerspelling.* Amsterdam: Benjamins.

Wilcox, Sherman. 2002. The iconic mapping of space and time in signed languages. In *Unfolding perceptual continua*, edited by Liliana Albertazzi, pp. 255–281. Amsterdam: Benjamins.

SHERMAN WILCOX

AMHARIC. The most prominent language of Ethiopia, Amharic was the official language under the constitution adopted in 1987 but was downgraded in 1997 to the status of a "working language" by the Tigré People's Liberation Front government, which took power in 1991. There is now no official language, but Amharic remains the main language of education and other official functions. The 1984 census of Addis Ababa, the capital and dominant urban center, showed that about half its 1,412,000 people claimed Amharic as their first language (population in 2000 about 2,300,000, but no figure on Amharic speakers is available). Addis Ababa is now one of two cities and nine ethnic "regional states" into which the country was divided in 1998. Total population is estimated at 2000 as 64,000,000. The second largest regional state is Amhara, with its capital at Bahir Dar on Lake T'ana, having a population of 13,834,297. Given the success of the Amharicization policy aggressively pursued by Haile Sillasé and his predecessor Minīlik, Amharic became the first or second language of most urban areas, of the educated elite, and of many others, so that it seems safe to assume that at least one-third of the total population (i.e. more than 21,000,000) speak Amharic. There are several hundred thousand Amharic speakers outside Ethiopia, especially in the United States, Israel, Sudan, and Kenya. Thus, in number of speakers, Amharic is second only to Arabic among living Semitic languages, and behind only Swahili and Hausa among indigenous African languages.

The most thorough survey of Ethiopian languages, though dating rapidly now, remains Bender et al. 1976; in addition to sociolinguistics and language in education, the volume includes a general overview, descriptions of Ethio-Semitic, the Ethiopian language area, Amharic (including regional variation), Tigrinya, Gi'iz, the Ethiopian writing system, and descriptions of other languages. For Amharic and the Amhara people, see Messing 1985. Among grammars of Amharic, Cohen 1936 is the classic. Hudson 1997 and Leslau 1995 are more recent and excellent reference sources. Appleyard 1995 is an outstanding pedagogical grammar and has accompanying tapes. Leslau 1973 is a sizable English-Amharic dictionary with illustrative sentences for each entry (there is also a concise version published in 1976), while Kane 1997 filled a long-standing gap with an excellent Amharic-English dictionary. For classification, see Hetzron 1972. Leslau 1965 is indispensable for literature on Ethio-Semitic up to 1965.

1. Classification. Amharic belongs to a branch of the Semitic family which also includes the extinct Epigraphic South Arabian and the Modern South Arabian languages. The Ethio-Semitic languages are divided into two branches: Northern, which consists of the extinct liturgical Gi'iz [giʕɨz] plus modern Tigré and Tigrinya; and Southern, a much larger and more complex group consisting of Amharic, Argobba, Gafat (extinct), Harari, and a geographical cluster of about fifteen "Gurage" languages. Ethio-Semitic is surrounded and interpenetrated by two distantly related Afroasiatic families, Cushitic and Omotic; it has little direct contact with scattered languages of the Nilo-Saharan phylum along the northern, western, and southwestern periphery of Ethiopia. Other than Amharic, the most important languages of Ethiopia and the adjoining "African horn" area are Tigrinya to the north, Oromo (formerly known as "Galla," a pejorative term) mainly to the south, and Somali to the east.

The major linguistic influence on Amharic and other Ethio-Semitic languages has been from Cushitic, especially the Agew (Central Cushitic) and H[ighland] E[ast] C[ushitic] branches (Sidamo and relatives).

2. Lexicon. The basic lexicon of Amharic is about 75% Semitic, including such items as *dʌm* 'blood', *ɨsat* 'fire', *ras* 'head', *motʌ* 'die', *bʌlla* 'eat', *hullu* 'all', and *nʌccʼ* 'white'. It also has such intrusions as *wɨšša* 'dog' (< HEC, cf. Sem. *kʌlb*); *sɨga* 'meat' (< Agew; cf. Sem. *bsr*); and *wɨha* 'water' (< Agew or HEC, cf. Sem. *may*).

Classical Giʻiz is a source of religious terms, and more recently of technical terminology. Greek also contributed religious terms, starting with the origins of Ethiopian Orthodox Christianity in the 4th century. Other languages have also had their periods and domains of influence, including Arabic, Portuguese, Italian, French, and English: e.g. *bunna* 'coffee' (Ar.); *fabrika* 'factory' (It.); *bosta* 'post (office)', *bolis* 'police' (Fr.); and *tayp* 'typewriter' (Eng.) There is little evidence that the word-coinage efforts of the Mengistu government in the 1970s and 1980s had much permanent effect, since the social context has departed from the pseudo-Marxist propaganda of the time.

3. Variation. Part of the reason for the dearth of systematic studies of Amharic dialectology may be the relative uniformity of the language over its core area. Phonologically, the present and former dominant urban centers of Addis Ababa and Gonder (the latter up to the end of the 18th century) form one group; but syntactically, Addis Ababa groups with Shewa and Wello provinces.

There are lexical differences between town and countryside, some phonological and semantic shifts, and some genuine lexical doublets—e.g., 'knife' is *billawa* in Addis Ababa, *karra* in some other areas. There are interesting secret languages or argots, especially those reported on by Leslau 1964; they include varieties used by merchants, minstrels, and persons 'possessed by a *zar* spirit'. In Addis Ababa around 1980, the basic formula of one variety transposed *gɨn* 'but' into *gaynʌn*, and *bunna bet* 'coffee house, bar' into *bwaynʌn baytʌt* (cf. Teshome and Bender 1983).

4. History. The self-name of Amharic is *am(h)arɨñña*, in which *-ñña* denotes 'language of' (similarly Tigrinya, Orominya, etc.). The term "Amhara" is folk-etymologized as being from a root *amr* 'be beautiful, peaceful, lovable, seductive'. Certainly there was an ancient region named Amhara on the northern side of the Blue Nile near the Bashilo confluence, in what is today Begemidir and Wello provinces; from there the language presumably spread over the past eight centuries. Early Amharic documents are relatively scarce; Giʻiz was used for most literary purposes.

Hetzron 1972 argues that Giʻiz was not the ancestor of the present-day Ethio-Semitic languages, but was instead a sister to Tigré and Tigrinya in the Northern group. Even

before the fall of the early Christian Ethiopian state at Aksum in the late 10th century, we find the beginnings of Amhara in a region whose autochthons were probably Agews. It is quite possible that the recruitment of military forces from diverse ethnicities in and around Amhara may have resulted in a triglossic situation—with the rulers speaking a Giʻiz-like language, the soldiers speaking a Giʻiz-based creole in addition to their own tongues, and the peasantry using both the creole and Agew. As with the Romance languages, the modern language is a descendant not of the literary standard, but of a vernacular—in this case, creolized. (For sources on Old Amharic, see Strelcyn 1964.)

Attempts at standardizing Amharic are mainly 20th-century developments. The establishment of an Ethiopian Language Academy began with an imperial proclamation of 1943; an Amharic Language Academy was implemented in 1972, and expansion to multilingual status occurred under the provisional military government in 1976. Among the tasks of the new Academy were the preparation of an Amharic dictionary, the coining of terms in technical areas such as physics and biology, and the preparation of dictionaries and literacy programs in several languages.

5. Phonology. Compared to "classical" Semitic languages, Amharic can be characterized as having ejective ("glottalized") consonants instead of pharyngealized ("emphatic") ones; a near lack of laryngeals and pharyngeals; a new palatal series; and an unusually rich vowel inventory of seven qualities, making up for loss of vowel length.

The consonantal phonemes are shown in Table 1 (cf. Cohen 1936:30); those which do not occur in all dialects, or are marginal where they occur, are enclosed in parentheses.

Articulation of consonants is not subject to much variation. Note the following:

(a) Labials: *b* → [β] between vowels, e.g. *addis abʌba* → [addis aβʌβa] → [addis aββa]. Labial *p pʼ* are rare (an Ethiopian and Middle Eastern areal characteristic): *p* is mainly in French loans (e.g. *posta*, usually pronounced *bosta* by the unsophisticated).

(b) Alveolars: Ejective *sʼ* (sometimes pronounced [tsʼ]) yields to *tʼ* in Shewa Province (e.g. *sʼʌhay* 'sun' > *tʼʌhay*).

(c) Palatals: *j* > *ž*, e.g. *jɨb* > *žɨb* 'hyena'. Even though palatals historically arose from apicals or velars, the process is not automatic today; e.g., in verbs, the fem. sg. imperative shows palatalization (*hid-i* 'go!'

TABLE 1. *Amharic Consonant Phonemes*

	Labial	Apical	Palatal	Velar	Labio-velar	Laryngeal
Occlusives						
Plain	(p)	t	c	k	(kʷ)	(ʔ)
Voiced	b	d	j	g	(gʷ)	
Ejective	(p')	t'	c'	k'	(k'ʷ)	
Fricatives						
Plain	f	s	š		(hʷ)	(h)
Voiced		z	ž			
Ejective		(s')				
Nasals	m	n	ñ			
Lateral		l				
Vibrant		r				
Semivowels	w		y			

→ *hij-i, hij*), but cf. *bet-e* 'my house', *anat'i* 'carpenter'.

(d) Velars and labiovelars: a common change is illustrated by *gondʌr* (a placename) > *gwʌndʌr*. Labials may also be rounded to [bʷ mʷ fʷ]. Contrasts like *gʌddʌlʌ* 'kill' vs. *gwʌddʌlʌ* 'lack' are rare. In Shewa, medial *k'* varies with *ʔ*, e.g. *bʌk'lo* 'mule' > *bʌʔlo*.

(e) Laryngeals: *h* is retained in common words like *wɨha* 'water', *c'ohʌ* 'shout'; but elsewhere, *h~k~Ø*, e.g. *(h)amsa~kamsa* 'fifty', *(h)agʌr* 'country', *am(h)ara* 'Amhara'. The glottal stop is often lost in words like *sʌʔat* 'hour, watch' and *sɨʔɨl* 'picture'.

The vowel phonemes consist of *i u e o a* plus higher central *ɨ* and lower centralized *ʌ* (sometimes transcribed *ä* or *ɛ*). The quality of the latter ranges from more fronted to lower and more back. It is the most frequent vowel in the language; e.g., it is the usual vowel in basic verb forms such as *sʌbbʌrʌ* 'he broke'.

The higher central *ɨ* corresponds to the neutral shwa (usually indicated by *ə*) elsewhere in Semitic. Although *ɨ* is largely predictable from phonotactics, it is distinctive—as seen by pairs like *sɨm* 'name' vs. *sʌm* 'wax', *gɨm* 'putrid' vs. *gum* 'fog', *t'ɨm* 'thirst' vs. *t'im* 'beard'.

Dialectally, *e* often has a palatal on-glide, e.g. [bʸet] 'house'. In words which once had laryngeals or pharyngeals, *ʌ* is often replaced by *a*. Vowels in sequence obey a hierarchy of strength; *a* absorbs others at one end, while *ɨ* is absorbed by others at the other end, and identical vowels generally coalesce. In some cases, however, glides are inserted (*o+o* → [oʷo], *i+a* → [iʸa]).

There are no long vowels, but geminate consonants abound, both lexically and morphologically. Initial clusters must have *l r* as a second member; finals are less restricted; and medials of more than two are broken up by epenthesis of *ɨ*.

6. Writing system. Amharic has an "alpha-syllabic" script; i.e., basic characters for consonants are obligatory, modified for seven "orders" of vowels, as shown in Table 2. The sixth order corresponds to both *ɨ* and zero, because of the often epenthetic nature of *ɨ*.

The script is a continuation of the one found in northern Ethiopia and coastal Arabia, used in ancient times for Epigraphic South Arabian languages and for Gi'iz. It is related to the other consonantal scripts of Middle Eastern antiquity. The innovation of a modification for vowels, beginning about 350 CE, may be a result of stimulus diffusion from India. Complications are introduced by the retention of two (consonantal!) symbols for *a* (representing ancient *ʔ ʕ*), three symbols for *h* (ancient *h ḥ x*), and two for *s'*. The system does not mark gemination; the sixth order is ambiguous; several distinctions are today only etymological; and there is a fair degree of irregularity. For these reasons, a revised, governmentally approved system was announced in the 1980s and may have accelerated the trend of doing away with the less common characters representing *h* and *s'*, as well as the labialized ones (see Table 2).

In Table 2, note the set of special symbols for labialized consonants, the punctuation marks, and the numeration symbols (some said to be derived from Greek letters). The latter are almost never used, except in dates, since their lack of zero makes arithmetic difficult.

7. Grammar. All modern Ethio-Semitic languages belong to a Northeast African convergence area, which also includes Cushitic, Omotic, and Nilo-Saharan languages. The basis of this convergence is S[ubject] O[bject] V[erb] syntax in the normal independent clause

TABLE 2. *The Amharic Script.* (From Bender et al. 1976:121–122.)

Basic Character	Order							Labialized					
	1st ʌ	2nd u	3rd i	4th a	5th e	6th ɨ	7th o	-wʌ	-wi	-wa	-we	-wɨ	-ya
h	ሀ	ሁ	ሂ	ሃ	ሄ	ህ	ሆ						
l	ለ	ሉ	ሊ	ላ	ሌ	ል	ሎ			ሏ			
h	ሐ	ሑ	ሒ	ሓ	ሔ	ሕ	ሖ			ሗ			
m	መ	ሙ	ሚ	ማ	ሜ	ም	ሞ			ሟ			
s	ሠ	ሡ	ሢ	ሣ	ሤ	ሥ	ሦ			ሧ			
r	ረ	ሩ	ሪ	ራ	ሬ	ር	ሮ			ሯ			ፘ
s	ሰ	ሱ	ሲ	ሳ	ሴ	ስ	ሶ			ሷ			
š	ሸ	ሹ	ሺ	ሻ	ሼ	ሽ	ሾ			ሿ			
k'	ቀ	ቁ	ቂ	ቃ	ቄ	ቅ	ቆ	ቈ	ቊ	ቋ	ቌ	ቍ	
b	በ	ቡ	ቢ	ባ	ቤ	ብ	ቦ			ቧ			
t	ተ	ቱ	ቲ	ታ	ቴ	ት	ቶ			ቷ			
c	ቸ	ቹ	ቺ	ቻ	ቼ	ች	ቾ			ቿ			
h	ኀ	ኁ	ኂ	ኃ	ኄ	ኅ	ኆ	ኈ	ኊ	ኋ	ኌ	ኍ	
n	ነ	ኑ	ኒ	ና	ኔ	ን	ኖ			ኗ			
ñ	ኘ	ኙ	ኚ	ኛ	ኜ	ኝ	ኞ			ኟ			
(a)	አ	ኡ	ኢ	ኣ	ኤ	እ	ኦ						
k	ከ	ኩ	ኪ	ካ	ኬ	ክ	ኮ	ኰ	ኲ	ኳ	ኴ	ኵ	
h	ኸ	ኹ	ኺ	ኻ	ኼ	ኽ	ኾ			ዃ			
w	ወ	ዉ	ዊ	ዋ	ዌ	ው	ዎ						
(a)	ዐ	ዑ	ዒ	ዓ	ዔ	ዕ	ዖ						
z	ዘ	ዙ	ዚ	ዛ	ዜ	ዝ	ዞ			ዟ			
ž	ዠ	ዡ	ዢ	ዣ	ዤ	ዥ	ዦ			ዧ			
y	የ	ዩ	ዪ	ያ	ዬ	ይ	ዮ						
d	ደ	ዱ	ዲ	ዳ	ዴ	ድ	ዶ			ዷ			
j	ጀ	ጁ	ጂ	ጃ	ጄ	ጅ	ጆ			ጇ			
g	ገ	ጉ	ጊ	ጋ	ጌ	ግ	ጎ	ጐ	ጒ	ጓ	ጔ	ጕ	
t'	ጠ	ጡ	ጢ	ጣ	ጤ	ጥ	ጦ			ጧ			
c'	ጨ	ጩ	ጪ	ጫ	ጬ	ጭ	ጮ			ጯ			
p'	ጰ	ጱ	ጲ	ጳ	ጴ	ጵ	ጶ						
s'	ጸ	ጹ	ጺ	ጻ	ጼ	ጽ	ጾ			ጿ			
s'	ፀ	ፁ	ፂ	ፃ	ፄ	ፅ	ፆ						
f	ፈ	ፉ	ፊ	ፋ	ፌ	ፍ	ፎ			ፏ			
p	ፐ	ፑ	ፒ	ፓ	ፔ	ፕ	ፖ						

order. Semitic probably had VSO order in ancient times; Gi'iz shows VSO with much variation—perhaps an effect of written transmission by non-native speakers.

Amharic marks number and gender in nouns, pronouns, and verbs, but the Semitic dual is absent. With nouns, number is often unmarked (e.g. *wʌmbʌr amt'a* 'bring a chair (or chairs)!' When necessary, *-o(c)c* (related to general Semitic *-at*) is used, e.g. *wʌndɨmmoc* 'brothers'. A few examples of archaic Semitic plural formations are preserved; and 'brother' and 'sister' have reciprocal plu-

rals, *wʌndɨmmamac* 'brothers (to each other)' and *ɨhɨtɨmmamac* 'sisters (to each other)'.

Gender distinctions consist of masculine (unmarked) and feminine (marked by suffix *-t* or concord in verb form). The latter is used for female beings, in diminutives, and for endearment or solidarity; thus a small boy or girl may be addressed as feminine, and *ayt'* 'mouse' is usually feminine.

N[oun] P[hrase]s are marked as definite by use of a demonstrative, possessive, or definite article (masc. *-u*, fem. *-wa*, *-itu*, *-itwa*). Definite NPs as objects are marked

TABLE 3. *Amharic Subject Pronouns*

	Singular		Plural
1sg.	Ø	1pl.	*n*
2sg.masc.	*t* or *k > h*	2pl.	*t* + pl. *-u*
2sg.fem.	*t, š*		
3sg.masc.	*y,* Ø	3pl.	*y* + pl. *-u*
3sg.fem.	*t, c*		

as accusative by *-n.* Nominative is unmarked; other case-marking is by prepositions and postpositions. Possessed nouns take two forms, e.g. *bet-e* 'house-my' or *yʌ-ne bet* 'of-me house'.

Pronouns mark gender in the 2/3sg.; deference is expressed by the use of variants of plural forms for 2nd and 3rd persons. The persons of verb subjects follow the Semitic pattern, with some idiosyncrasies, as shown in Table 3.

Amharic maintains the Semitic characteristic of consonantal skeletons carrying semantic values, with vocalic inserts for tense, aspect, etc. Verbs fall into two main lexical classes: (i) those with geminated medial consonant in the Imperfective (e.g. *yɨ-fʌʌllɨg-al* 'he wants'); and (ii) those without (*yɨ-sʌbr-al* 'he breaks'). The Semitic gemination for transitives, with non-gemination for intransitives, seems to have been transferred into aspects (on the contrary; i.e., gemination for Imperfect occurs in North Ethio-Semitic).

Verbs show the Semitic major division into Perfective (complete) vs. Imperfective (incomplete) action; the former has pronominal suffixes, while the latter has both prefixes and suffixes. There are five tenses:

(1)	Non-past:	*yɨ-sʌbr-al(l)*	'he breaks, is breaking, will break'
	Past:	*sʌbbʌr-ʌ*	'he broke'
	Past Continuous:	*yɨsʌbɨr nʌbbʌr*	'he was breaking'
	Perfect:	*sʌbro-al(l)*	'he has broken'
	Past Perfect:	*sʌbro nʌbbʌr*	'he had broken'

The past and perfect fall together in the negative. In subordinate clauses, normally only Non-past and Past are distinguished.

Morphological derivation is very active in Amharic. Most verbs have an intransitive (passive) *tʌ-* form (e.g. *tʌ-bʌlla* 'it was eaten'); many have forms with transitive (causative) *a-* or factitive (indirect causative) *as-* (*a-*

mʌtt'a 'he brought', *as-bʌlla* 'he caused someone to eat'). Other derivative verbs include the reciprocal, repetitive, and conative. Nouns and other form classes are also derived; e.g.,

(2) | *s'af-i* 'writer' < *s'af-ʌ* 'he wrote' |
| *s'ɨt'ota* 'gift' < *s'ʌtt'-ʌ* 'he gave' |

Amharic is not a "rigid" SOV language. It has some features which can be seen as transitional from the older Semitic VSO type. Thus Amharic retains Semitic prepositions like *lʌ-* 'for', *bʌ-* 'by', but it also has postpositions like *-wɨst'* 'in(side)', *-lay* 'on'. More common are "parapositions" having both components:

(3) | *ɨ-bet-wɨst'* 'at-house-in' |
| *kʌ-bet-hwala* 'from-house-back' |

Among typical SOV features are the preposing of subordinate clauses (e.g. *yʌ-hedʌ sʌw* 'of-went person', i.e. 'a person who went'), and the extensive use of a subordinate form known as the "converb" (less accurately, gerund):

(4) | *dabbo bʌl-t-ʌn wʌtʌt t'ʌtt'-ɨt-ʌn t'ʌgb-ʌn tʌgwaznʌ.* |
| bread eaten milk drunk satisfied we.set.out |
| 'Having eaten bread and drunk milk, we set out satisfied.' |

An interesting Ethiopian areal feature is the use of the verb 'say' as an auxiliary, both in many idiomatic expressions (5) and in subordinate constructions (6):

(5) | *zɨmm bʌl* 'say *zɨmm*', i.e. 'be quiet!' |
| *k'ucc' bʌl* 'say *k'ucc*'', i.e. 'sit!' |
(6) | *gʌrʌdwa yʌne nʌw bila wʌssʌdʌcciw.* |
| "The maid took it, saying, "It is mine" ', |
| i.e. ' . . . thinking it was hers'. |

There are two basic conjugated copular forms, both also used as verbal auxiliaries: (3sg. masc.) *nʌw* 'be', *allʌ* 'exist'. These are used only in the present; their shared past is *nʌbbʌr*. For the future, etc., *honʌ* 'become' and *norʌ* 'dwell', respectively, are used. Negatives are *aydʌllʌm* and *yʌllʌm*, respectively.

[*See also* African Languages *and* Semitic Languages.]

BIBLIOGRAPHY

Appleyard, David. 2000. *Colloquial Amharic*. London: Routledge.

Bender, Marvin Lionel, et al., eds. 1976. *Language in Ethiopia*. London and New York: Oxford University Press.

Cohen, Marcel. 1936. *Traité de langue amharique (Abyssinie)*. Paris: Institut d'Ethnologie. Reprinted, New York: Altai Press, 1970.

Demissie, Teshome, and Marvin Lionel Bender. 1983. An argot of Addis Ababa unattached girls. *Language in Society* 12.339–347.

Hetzron, Robert. 1972. *Ethiopian Semitic: Studies in classification*. (*Journal of Semitic Studies*, Monograph 2.) Manchester, U.K.: Manchester University Press.

Hudson, Grover. 1997. Amharic and Argobba. In *The Semitic languages*, edited by Robert Hetzron, pp. 457–85 London: Routledge.

Kane, Thomas L. 1990. *Amharic-English dictionary*. 2 vols. Wiesbaden: Harrassowitz.

Leslau, Wolf. 1964. *Ethiopian argots*. (Janua linguarum, Series practica, 17.) The Hague: Mouton.

Leslau, Wolf. 1965. *An annotated bibliography of the Semitic languages of Ethiopia*. The Hague: Mouton.

Leslau, Wolf. 1973. *English-Amharic context dictionary*. Wiesbaden: Harrassowitz. Concise edition, 1976.

Leslau, Wolf. 1995. *Reference grammar of Amharic*. Wiesbaden: Harrassowitz.

Messing, Simon D. 1985. *The Highland Plateau Amhara of Ethiopia*. Edited by M. Lionel Bender. New Haven, Conn.: Human Relations Area Files.

Strelcyn, Stefan. 1964. Materiaux pour l'étude de l'ancien Amharique. *Journal of Semitic Studies* 9.257–64.

M. LIONEL BENDER

A-MORPHOUS MORPHOLOGY. *See* Generative Morphology.

AMTO-MUSAN LANGUAGES. A family comprising the two languages Amto and Musan, spoken to the south of the Upper Sepik River in Papua New Guinea, not far from the border with the Indonesian province of Papua.

LANGUAGE LIST

Amto: also called Ki, Siwai, Siawi, Siafli. 200 speakers. Dialects are Amto, Siawi.

Musan: also called Musian, Musa. 70 speakers in Sandaun Province, village east of Amto.   B. GRIMES

AMUZGOAN LANGUAGES. A branch of the OTO-MANGUEAN family. They are spoken near the Pacific coast of Guerrero and Oaxaca states, Mexico.

LANGUAGE LIST

Amuzgo, Guerrero: also called Nomndaa. 23,000 speakers in southeastern Guerrero, community of Xochistlahuaca, Zacoalpan, Cochoapa, Huehuetonoc, Tlacoachistlahuaca, Guadalupe Victoria, Cozoyoapan. 67% intelligibility of San Pedro Amuzgos Amuzgo. Some bilingualism in Spanish. About 14,000 to 15,000 are monolingual. All ages. All domains. Oral use in local administration, business. Used as a teaching medium in school in grades 1–6. Oral and written use in religion. Vigorous language use. Parents transmit it to children. Spanish, Náhuatl, and Mixteco speakers living among them learn to speak it. Positive attitude.

Amuzgo, Ipalapa: also called Santa María Ipalapa Amuzgo. 2,000 speakers, according to a 1992 estimate, in Oaxaca, Putla district, about 8 to 10 miles northeast of San Pedro Amuzgos; five locations around Santa María Ipalapa. Just off the highway from Tlaxiaco to the coast. Not intelligible with other Amuzgo. Some bilingualism in Spanish. All ages.

Amuzgo, San Pedro Amuzgos: also called Amuzgo, Oaxaca, Amuzgo de San Pedro Amuzgos. 4,000 speakers in southwestern Oaxaca, Putla district, San Pedro Amuzgos. One town with outlying settlements. 76% intelligibility of Guerrero Amuzgo. Some bilingualism in Spanish.   B. GRIMES

ANALOGY. Analogical change, or simply analogy, is a historical process which projects a generalization from one set of expressions to another. The term "analogy" has been used also in reference to the acquisition of grammatical regularities by child or adult learners, and to the use (production or comprehension) of novel utterances. The latter was traditionally attributed wholly to analogy; today, analogy is sometimes postulated as a supplementary mechanism of derivative generation accounting for the use of utterances that are not directly generatable by the grammar.

Since the Neogrammarians, analogy has been ranked with regular phonological change and borrowing as one of the three basic kinds of linguistic change. It is the most heterogeneous and problematic of them; indeed, we are still not sure what the various processes considered "analogical" have in common, what causes them, or how they are constrained.

1. The traditional view distinguishes two types of analogy, *proportional* and *non-proportional*. Proportional analogy is represented as the solving of equations of the form A:B = C:X, where the terms are related by "associative links," for example, *nose* : *noses* = *eye* : X, where X = *eyes* (replacing the older plural *eyne*). But many putatively proportional changes cannot be represented as proportions, and many proportions do not correspond to plausible analogical changes; moreover, the "associative links" are ill-defined, and in any case insufficient (Morpurgo Davies 1978, 1998:255). Non-proportional analogy, for its part, subsumes an assortment of phenomena without unified analysis or principled relationship to proportional analogy. (The "Connectionist" morphology of Rumelhart and McClelland 1986 is similarly unconstrained; see Pinker and Prince 1988.)

Kuryłowicz 1964, 1977 sought to resolve the problems with proportional analogy by two means, as follows. First, Kuryłowicz proposed to enrich proportions, letting their terms be made more abstract by (i) stripping words of "redundant" morphemes, (ii) undoing the effects of automatic phonological rules, and (iii) allowing terms to be categories instead of particular words. Related proposals are that proportions can operate on distinctive feature representations (Garey 1959), and that several proportions can operate simultaneously in a single analogical change (Leed 1970).

Two examples can be cited from Kuryłowicz. First, Latin -*a* stems replace gen. sg. -*ās* with -*ī* from -*o* stems: fem. *bonās* > *bonaī* (> *bonae*), after masc. *bonī*. The proportion '*bonus* : *bonī* = *bona* : X' fails. Stripping the 'redundant' masc. nom. sg. -*us* gives the correct *bon-* : *bon*+*ī* = *bona* : *bonaī*. Second, in Classical Greek, -*nū*-stem verbs acquired subjunctives with long -*ō*-/-*ē*- by analogy with the subjunctives of the thematic verbs, for example, 3sg. middle subjunc. *rhēgnuétai* from indic. *rhégnutai*, after subjunc. *lúetai* from indic. *lúetai*. The proportion '*lúetai* : *lūétai* = *rhégnutai* : X' yields only *rhēgnútai*. If we suppose that thematic subjunctives were reanalyzed as containing the theme vowel *e*, contracted with a subjunctive morpheme *ē* (i.e. *lūétai* = /lū+e+é+tai/), then we get *rhēgnuétai* by building the proportion from the underlying forms: *lú*+*e*+*tai* : *lū*+*e*+*é*+*tai* = *rhég*+*nu*+*tai* : *rhēg*+*nu*+*é*+*tai*.

Second, Kuryłowicz proposed to constrain proportions by six "Laws of Analogy." The second of these says: "Analogy proceeds from basic forms to subordinated forms." The basic form, predicted to spread by analogy, is defined as one of the following:

(a) The most widely distributed form—that is, unmarked morphological categories such as 3rd person, singular, present, indicative, nominative, masculine (see Watkins 1962, Lahiri and Dresher 1983, 1984)

(b) The structurally most differentiated form, from which the others are most simply predictable (the basic allomorph of a morpheme)

These principles eliminate the worst weakness of proportions: their reversibility. For example, '*bona* : *bonās* = *bonus* : X' is impossible because masculine gender is unmarked.

Kuryłowicz's theory explicitly relates analogy to grammatical structure, replacing the "associative links" of the Neogrammarians by the morphological categories and relations of the language, and by the morphological analysis of the terms of proportions. This is important because, as in our Greek example, analogical proportions may presuppose a covert *reanalysis*, which may be syntagmatic or paradigmatic. All such reanalyses determine the possible course of analogy. (See Harris and Campbell 1995, Joseph 1998, and Lahiri 2000 for different perspectives on reanalysis.)

Syntagmatic reanalysis, or resegmentation, may reassign segments or features of a stem to its affixes, or vice versa. It may reduce allomorphy, spawn new affixes ("secretion"), relocate a contrast ("paradigmatic displacement"), or amalgamate affixes. An example is English -*ist*+*ic*, in words like *cannibalistic*; here -*ist* is itself an amalgam in Greek of -*iz* (English -*ize*) with the agent suffix -*tēs*, and both of these are in turn composites. Affix merger is often triggered by loss or semantic isolation of the intermediate stem (Kuryłowicz 1977:19).

Paradigmatic reanalysis includes several types. First, in *morphologization,* phonological variants become morphologically conditioned, typically when the rules relating them become opaque. Second, in lexicalization, phrases coalesce into compound words, and derived words into simple words. Third, in grammaticalization, morphemes lose some or all of their lexical content and acquire a grammatical function (Heine et al. 1991, Hopper and Traugott 1993). Thus lexical categories such as nouns, verbs, adjectives, and adverbs become non-lexical categories: auxiliaries, complementizers, pronouns, articles, pre- and post-positions, and other clitics (Givón 1971, Anderson 1980, 1988, Bybee 1985, Disterheft 1987). Similarly, heads of compounds and clitics become affixes; for example, Latin *cantāre habeō,* lit. 'to-sing I-have', becomes French *chanterai* 'I will sing'. Semantic case becomes grammatical case, and derivation becomes inflection. The reverse direction of change occurs, but is rare. Finally, in *recategorization*, a stem is assigned to a different morphological category. Thus deverbal analysis of originally denominal words like English *doubtful, hateful* led to unambiguously deverbal *resentful, forgetful*.

2. Analogy as optimization. Going a step further, we can eliminate the proportions altogether, and treat analogy as a process of optimization of grammatical structure. We can take the acquisition process as the causal mechanism: if learners' successive grammars increase in coverage and complexity, then analogical change is "imperfect learning," occurring when rules of intermediate grammars (or forms generated by them) are retained and become part of the linguistic norm. This approach has several advantages, as listed below.

The discontinuity of language transmission explains the possibility of radical reanalysis. Since learners try to match the speech of the community without having access to others' internalized grammars, they may construct very different grammars—as long as these generate nearly the same language. Even unique patterns may come to be apprehended as linguistic regularities, and may spread by analogy. For example, the suffix *-ess* is ultimately from the unique Greek *basílissa* 'queen'. Again, in Old English (Anglian), the suppletive paradigm of 'to be'—1sg. *eam*, 2sg. *earþ*, 3sg. *is*, pl. *sind*—gave rise to a unique 1sg. suffix *-m*, which was generalized first to the synonymous verb *bēon* (1sg. *bīo* > *bīo+m*), and from there to other "contracted" verbs, for example, 1sg. *flēo* > *flēo+m* 'I flee' (Hogg 1980).

The optimization approach predicts that analogical change can be channeled by the structure of the language as a whole (Kiparsky 1998, 2000). For example, obeying the rule of English that all prefixes are derivational, analogy has "secreted" new inflectional suffixes, such as the plural *-en* in *ox+en*—or the *-n* of predicative possessive pronouns, dialectally extended from *my, mine* to *your, yourn*, and *his, hisn*. But it has produced no inflectional prefixes. Thus the pattern *I, my* is not analyzed as prefixation of a genitive *m-*; analogical *you, *myou* or *it, *mit* are unthinkable. This analysis would also violate the English-specific constraint that prefixes are syllabic.

The optimization approach also brings many "non-proportional" analogical changes out of their theoretical limbo, as with the following processes.

First, *adaptation*—"a type of linguistic change which resembles analogic change, but goes on without model sets" (Bloomfield 1933:420)—arises from the composition of grammatical regularities. Thus the English coinages *sclerosed, cirrhosed* combine regular suffixation of *-ed* (cf. *jaundic+ed*) with regular "truncation" of suffixal *-is* (cf. *synthes+ize*).

Second, *contamination* and *blending* are illuminated by prosodic morphology (McCarthy and Prince 1995). Thus a productive derivational pattern in English is superimposition of the phonemic melody of one word upon the first foot of another, on the universal "Procrustean" principle that long melodies are chopped off *(choco-holic, tele-thon)*, while short melodies are extended to fit the template *(worka-holic, walka-thon)*.

Third, *leveling*, which is "non-proportional" because it does not require a non-alternating model paradigm, is the loss of listed allomorphs, or the simplification of the structural change of a rule. This includes partial leveling, which is especially recalcitrant to proportional treatment: in Sanskrit, the weak grade of laryngeal roots in *-am* changed from *-ā* to *-ām* (past pple. **krā+ta* > *krān+ta*); the rule "Lengthen *a* and delete *n*" was simplified to "Lengthen *a*."

Fourth, *phonological analogy*, the generalization of purely phonotactic distributional regularities (with no associative links or morphological relationships on which to build a proportion) is the generalization of phonological rules. For example, the voiceless aspirated palatal /ch/ of Sanskrit happened to occur, when medial, mostly as a geminate [cch]; the few simple occurrences were later geminated, generalizing the rule "Aspirated palatals, when medial, are geminated."

The optimization approach explains the above-mentioned properties of proportions. Why is it that proportions (i) relate basic and subordinate forms, (ii) can interact, (iii) are applicable to feature representations, and (iv) presuppose a morphological analysis of words? It is because grammatical rules do these things. 'Basic forms' win out (Kuryłowicz's second law) because they correspond to the "elsewhere" forms which appear wherever they are not pre-empted by other forms or rules—the least specified (maximally "unmarked") morpheme of a paradigmatic set, the least contextually restricted allomorph of a morpheme, or the underlying form among phonologically conditioned alternants. When the least specified form is indeterminate, so is the direction of leveling. For example, the allomorphy of the Sanskrit gerund, *-tvā* after simple roots and *-(t)ya* after compounds, is leveled in both directions in Middle Indic. (On bidirectional leveling, see Tiersma 1978, Hock 1986, and Dresher 2000, who argues that it occurs when no coherent rule can be discovered by learners.)

Moreover, *back-formation*—which requires "backward" proportions such as *relation : relate = emotion :* X (where X = *emote*), and is against Kuryłowicz's second law—is explainable as actualization of a latent base form, eliminating the obligatory subcategorization of the base.

Optimization theories differ on the criteria that they assume. For early generative theory, the grammar attained by learners (under the idealizations of instantaneous acquisition and homogeneous data) was the simplest grammar for the primary linguistic data on which it was based, given a canonical descriptive format. From this perspective, optimization is just grammar *simplification.* This is attractive because it is precisely defined, and because much of analogical change clearly does eliminate arbitrary complexity from the grammar—for example, loss or simplification of rules, or of grammatical formatives. But it is too unconstrained, and fails to account for some systematic structural preferences.

One approach envisages a set of structural *parameters,* each with a fixed number of settings, one of which is unmarked. The learner determines the values of those parameters, choosing the unmarked settings unless there is evidence to the contrary. Acquisition depends only on positive evidence, with linguistic data serving as a "triggering experience" rather than as a basis for hypothesis formation. Analogy should then tend towards unmarked parameter settings, and marked parameter settings should result from other processes of change.

Formal optimization fails for analogy because it precludes non-structural factors like function and frequency, as well as local optimization—word-by-word rule generalization or parameter unmarking, which need not simplify the grammar until completed. There have been attempts to sustain the view of analogy as simplification by requiring more "concrete" grammars, for example, the Alternation Condition (Kiparsky 1973) and Natural Generative Grammar (Vennemann 1974, Hooper 1976): if the lexical entry of a morpheme lists all its allomorphs, even when these are fully predictable from general rules, then sporadic leveling will count as simplification because it reduces the lexicon. This approach proved inadequate for both synchrony and change, and has been largely abandoned.

"Naturalness" theories attempt to capture features of both synchrony and change by "substantive" conditions which designate certain structures as preferred—for example, unmarked feature specifications (Chomsky and Halle 1968, chap. 9); unmarked rule order (Kiparsky 1968); natural processes (characterized by "metarules" in Chen 1973 and Ralph 1975); transparent rules (Kipar-

sky 1971, 1973); or paradigmatic uniformity and distinctness (Kiparsky 1972).

In Natural Morphology, such preference conditions are not just supplements to formal simplicity; they are supposed to do the entire job. This theory posits five parameters of optimization, weighted as follows:

(a) System congruity: words should conform to the organizing principles of the language's morphology
(b) Uniformity of inflection classes
(c) Uniformity of encoding: allomorphy should be avoided
(d) Transparency: morphology should be compositional and unambiguous
(e) Constructional iconicity (diagrammaticity): formal marking (e.g. by an affix) should coincide with morphological markedness

Parameters (a–b) are defined on the grammatical system of each language; the others are grammar-independent semiotic criteria. Thus Natural Morphology builds "functional" considerations directly into the definition of optimality; and it allows local checking of each condition, so that gradual changes driven by them optimize the system at each step. For details, see Mayerthaler 1981—where (e) is ranked above (c–d)—as well as Vennemann 1983; Wurzel 1984, 1985, 1987, 2000; Wurzel et al. 1994; Mayerthaler 1987; and Dressler 1987a.

Points (c–d) together constitute the "one-form/one-meaning" principle, alias "Humboldt's Universal" (Vennemann 1972) or "unifunctionality" (Slobin 1973, 1985). Avoidance of polysemy and blocking effects are also related (Aronoff 1976, Kiparsky 1983, Anderson 1988, Clark 1987, Andrews 2000, Gregerich 2001).

3. Interactionist theories. A problem for all optimization theories is that no single ranking is possible, because different kinds of "optimality" conflict. Thus parameter (c) of Natural Morphology, that allomorphy tends to be minimized, contradicts Kuryłowicz's first law, by which allomorphy tends to spread. This reflects conflicting functional pressures: allomorphy complicates the speaker's and learner's tasks; but it facilitates the hearer's, by increasing redundancy (see Shapiro 1974, Anttila 1975, Robinson 1980, Werner 1987). In addition, the role of frequency and saliency in determining the course of change remains unexplained, since they have no general structural correlate (although frequency for morphological categories partly corresponds to unmarked status).

Interactionist theories instead attempt to derive functional and frequency effects from the real-time acquisition and use of language, interacting with linguistic competence (Bever and Langendoen 1972, Vincent 1974, Kiparsky 1978, Zager 1981, Barr 1994). They see the constraints on analogical change as jointly determined by the source of innovated forms (imperfect learning, and perhaps lapses), and by their selective adoption into the linguistic system, the latter accounting for local analogy.

Specifically, we can assume that the likelihood of an innovation being adopted at a given point of the system is locally proportional to its functional value, and to the productivity (frequency and compositionality) of the process that derives it—but inversely proportional to its saliency, as measured by its distance from the old form, and to the old form's entrenchment, measured primarily by frequency. Hence the first innovations may penetrate, on the one hand, in productive morphological categories, and on the other hand, in infrequent lexemes (or uses of lexemes). The same factors appear to account also for selective actuation of other kinds of change (Naro 1981, Guy 1990).

As an illustration, consider phenomena of lexical split. An example of preferential regularization in productive categories is English *elder* > *older* in the comparative; the old form is retained as an extraparadigmatic derivative, with the specialized meaning 'senior'. An example of preferential regularization in less entrenched uses of a lexeme is *wove* > *weaved* in the specialized meaning 'moved irregularly': here there is a single morphological category, which is regularized in a specialized meaning of the lexeme. Thus, in lexical split, the 'secondary function' is sometimes reserved for the old form *(elder)*, and sometimes for the new *(weaved)*—a fact for which structural optimization theories offer no account. One proposal is that, in the *elder* type, the functional distinction arises after the regularization; but in the *wove* type, it predates it (Hock 1986:226, following Kuryłowicz's fourth law of analogy: "When a form is differentiated after a morphological change, the new form corresponds to its primary function, and the old form is restricted to its secondary function"). But this is stipulative, and in any case contradicts the actual chronology. In fact, in the *elder* type, the rise of the secondary meaning typically predates the regularization; the secondary meanings of *elder*, *tithe*, and *straight* are attested well before the appearance of regularized *older*, *tenth*, and *stretched*. In the *weaved* type, the meaning shift need not predate the regularization; for example, the motion-verb use of *weave* is attested long after its first weak forms. Another proposal is that *elder* is first lexicalized in a specialized function, escaping the morphological regularization

which affects its non-lexicalized homonym; but in *weaved/wove*, the semantic shift yields a new lexeme unburdened with the morphological irregularity of its source (Kiparsky 1974, Anderson 1988:359). This motivates the distinction between the two types, and fits the chronology; but the assumption of lexicalization is unwarranted. It is preferable to recognize degrees of productivity, with lexicalization as only the limiting case of unproductivity (see Barr 1994 for explicit development of this idea).

Interactionist theories thus see analogy as driven mainly by the acquisition of language, but shaped mainly by its use. This reconciles the apparent conflict between the system-governed, global properties of analogy, explained by optimization theories, and its piecemeal spread through the system, in patterns explainable through the real-time production and comprehension of speech.

[*See also* Borrowing; Grammaticalization; Historical Linguistics; Language Change; Morphology; Natural Morphology; *and* Phonological Processes.]

BIBLIOGRAPHY

Anderson, John M., and Charles Jones, eds. 1974. *Historical linguistics: Proceedings of the First International Conference on Historical Linguistics,* vol. 2, *Theory and description in phonology.* Amsterdam: North-Holland.

Anderson, Stephen R. 1980. On the development of morphology from syntax. In *Historical morphology* (Trends in linguistics, Studies and monographs, 17), edited by Jacek Fisiak, pp. 51–69. The Hague: Mouton.

Anderson, Stephen R. 1988. Morphological change. In *Linguistics: The Cambridge survey,* vol. 1, *Linguistic theory: Foundations,* edited by Frederick J. Newmeyer, pp. 324–362. Cambridge and New York: Cambridge University Press.

Andrews, Avery. 1990. Unification and morphological blocking. *Natural Language and Linguistic Theory* 8.507–558.

Anttila, Raimo. 1975. *The indexical element in morphology.* (Innsbrucker Beiträge zur Sprachwissenschaft, 12.) Innsbruck: Institut für Sprachwissenschaft der Universität.

Aronoff, Mark. 1976. *Word formation in generative grammar.* (*Linguistic Inquiry* monographs, 1.) Cambridge, Mass.: MIT Press.

Barr, Robin. 1994. *A lexical model of morphological change.* Ph.D. Dissertation, Harvard University.

Bever, Thomas G., and D. Terence Langendoen. 1972. The interaction of speech perception and grammatical structure in the evolution of language. In *Linguistic change and generative theory,* edited by Robert P. Stockwell and Ronald K. S. Macaulay, pp. 32–95. Bloomington: Indiana University Press.

Bloomfield, Leonard. 1933. *Language.* New York: Holt.

Bybee, Joan L. 1985. *Morphology: A study of the relation between meaning and form.* (Typological studies in language, 9.) Amsterdam: Benjamins.

Chen, Matthew. 1973. On the formal expression of natural rules in phonology. *Journal of Linguistics* 9.223–249.

Chomsky, Noam, and Morris Halle. 1968. *The sound pattern of English.* New York: Harper and Row.

Clark, Eve V. 1987. The principle of contrast. In *Mechanisms of language acquisition,* edited by Brian MacWhinney, pp. 2–10. Hillsdale, N.J.: Erlbaum.

Disterheft, Dorothy. 1987. The diachronic relationship of morphology and syntax. In Ramat et al. 1987, pp. 211–220.

Dresher, B. Elan. 2000. Analogical levelling of vowel length in Germanic. In Lahiri 2000a, pp. 47–70.

Dressler, Wolfgang U. 1987a. Word formation as part of natural morphology. In Dressler 1987b, pp. 99–126.

Dressler, Wolfgang U., ed. 1987b. *Leitmotifs in Natural Morphology.* (*Studies in Language,* Companion series, 10.) Amsterdam: Benjamins.

Garey, Howard. 1959. *Verte, grande* and *longue*: Three types of analogy in Old French. *Language* 35.605–611.

Giegerich, Heinz. 2001. Synonymy blocking and the Elsewhere Condition: Lexical morphology and the speaker. *Transactions of the Philosophical Society* 99.2.

Givón, Talmy. 1971. Historical syntax and synchronic morphology: An archaeologist's field trip. *Chicago Linguistic Society* 7.394–415.

Guy, Gregory. 1990. Saliency and the direction of syntactic change. To appear in *Language.*

Harris, Alice C., and Lyle Campbell. 1995. *Historical syntax in cross-linguistic perspective.* Cambridge: Cambridge University Press.

Heine, Bernd, Ulrike Claudi, and Friederike Hünnemeyer. 1991. *Grammaticalization: A conceptual framework.* Chicago: University of Chicago Press.

Hock, Hans Henrich. 1986. *Principles of historical linguistics.* (Trends in linguistics, studies and monographs, 34.) Berlin: Mouton de Gruyter.

Hogg, Richard M. 1980. Analogy as a source of morphological complexity. *Folia Linguistica Historica* 1:2.277–284.

Hooper, Joan B. 1976. *An introduction to natural generative phonology.* New York: Academic Press.

Hopper, Paul J., and Elizabeth Closs Traugott. 1993. *Grammaticalization.* Cambridge: Cambridge University Press.

Joseph, Brian. 1998. Diachronic morphology. In *The handbook of morphology,* edited by Andrew Spencer and Arnold M. Zwicky, pp. 351–373. Oxford: Blackwell.

Kiparsky, Paul. 1968. Linguistic universals and linguistic change. In *Universals in linguistic theory,* edited by Emmon Bach and Robert T. Harms, pp. 171–204. New York: Holt, Rinehart, and Winston.

Kiparsky, Paul. 1971. Historical linguistics. In *A survey of linguistic science,* edited by William O. Dingwall, pp. 577–642. College Park: University of Maryland Linguistics Program.

Kiparsky, Paul. 1972. Explanation in phonology. In *Goals of linguistic theory,* edited by Stanley Peters, pp. 189–227. New York: Prentice-Hall.

Kiparsky, Paul. 1973. Phonological representations. In *Three dimensions of linguistic theory,* edited by Osamu Fujimura, pp. 1–136. Tokyo: TEC.

Kiparsky, Paul. 1974. Remarks on analogical change. In Anderson and Jones 1974, pp. 257–275.

Kiparsky, Paul. 1978. Analogical change as a problem for linguistic theory. In *Linguistics in the seventies: Directions and prospects* (Studies in the linguistic sciences, 8), edited by Braj B. Kachru, pp. 79–96. Urbana: University of Illinois.

Kiparsky, Paul. 1983. Word-formation and the lexicon. In *1982 Mid-America Linguistics Conference papers,* edited by Frances Ingemann, pp. 3–29. Lawrence: Department of Linguistics, University of Kansas.

Kiparsky, Paul. 1998. Covert generalization. In *Proceedings of the First Mediterranean Conference of Morphology,* edited by Geert Booij et al., pp. 65–76.

Kiparsky, Paul. 2000. Analogy as optimization: "Exceptions" to Sievers' law in Gothic. In Lahiri 2000a, pp. 15–46.

Kuryłowicz, Jerzy. 1964. *The inflectional categories of Indo-European.* Heidelberg: Winter.

Kuryłowicz, Jerzy. 1977. Problèmes morphologiques généraux. In Jerzy Kuryłowicz, *Problèmes de linguistique indo-européenne,* pp. 7–52. Warsaw: Wydawnictwo Polskiej Akademii Nauk.

Lahiri, Aditi, ed. 2000a. *Analogy, levelling, markedness.* Berlin and New York: Mouton de Gruyter.

Lahiri, Aditi. 2000b. Verbal morphology in Bengali and Germanic. In Lahiri 2000a, pp. 71–124.

Lahiri, Aditi, and B. Elan Dresher, 1983/84. Diachronic and synchronic implications of declension shifts. *Linguistic Review* 3.141–163.

Leed, Richard L. 1970. Distinctive features and analogy. *Lingua* 26.1–24.

Mayerthaler, Willi. 1981. *Morphologische Natürlichkeit.* (Linguistische Forschungen, 28.) Wiesbaden: Athenaion.

Mayerthaler, Willi. 1987. System-independent morphological naturalness. In Dressler 1987b, pp. 25–58.

McCarthy, John, and Alan Prince. 1995. Prosodic morphology. In *The handbook of phonological theory,* edited by John A. Goldsmith, pp. 318–366. Cambridge, Mass., and Oxford: Blackwell.

Morpurgo Davies, Anna. 1978. Analogy, segmentation and the early Neogrammarians. *Transactions of the Philological Society* (London) 1978:36–60.

Morpurgo Davies, Anna. 1998. Nineteenth-century linguistics. In *History of linguistics,* edited by Giulio Lepschy, vol. 4.

Naro, Anthony. 1981. The social and structural dimensions of a syntactic change. *Language* 57.62–98.

Pinker, Steven, and Alan Prince. 1988. On language and connectionism: Analysis of a parallel distributed processing model of language acquisition. *Cognition* 28.73–194.

Ralph, Bo. 1975. *Phonological differentiation: Studies in Nordic language history.* Göteborg: Acta Universitatis Gothoburgiensis.

Ramat, Anna Giacolone, et al., eds. 1987. *Papers from the Seventh International Conference on Historical Linguistics.* (Current issues in linguistic theory, 48.) Amsterdam: Benjamins.

Robinson, Orrin Warner. 1980. An exception to Old High German umlaut. In *American Indian and Indo-European studies: Papers in honor of Madison S. Beeler* (Trends in linguistics, Studies and monographs, 16), edited by Kathryn Klar et al., pp. 449–460. The Hague: Mouton.

Rumelhart, David E., and James L. McClelland. 1986. On learning the past tenses of English verbs. In *Parallel distributed processing: Explorations in the microstructure of cognition,* vol. 2, *Psychological and biological models,* edited by David E. Rumelhart et al., pp. 216–271. Cambridge, Mass.: MIT Press.

Shapiro, Michael. 1974. Morphophonemics as semiotic. *Anthropological Linguistics* 15.29–49.

Slobin, Dan I. 1973. Cognitive prerequisites for the development of grammar. In *Studies of child language development,* edited by Charles A. Ferguson and Dan I. Slobin, pp. 175–211. New York: Holt, Rinehart, and Winston.

Slobin, Dan I. 1985. Crosslinguistic evidence for the language-making capacity. In *The crosslinguistic study of language acquisition,* vol. 2, *Theoretical issues,* edited by Dan I. Slobin, pp. 1157–1256. Hillsdale, N.J.: Erlbaum.

Tiersma, Peter. 1978. Bidirectional leveling as evidence for relational rules. *Lingua* 45.65–77.

Vennemann, Theo. 1972. Phonetic analogy and conceptual analogy. In *Schuchardt, the Neogrammarians, and the transformational theory of phonological change,* edited by Theo Vennemann and Terence H. Wilbur, pp. 181–204. Frankfurt: Athenäum.

Vennemann, Theo. 1974. Restructuring. *Lingua* 33.137–156.

Vennemann, Theo. 1983. Causality in language change: Theories of linguistic preferences as a basis for linguistic explanations. *Folia Linguistica Historica* 4.5–26.

Vincent, Nigel. 1974. Analogy reconsidered. In Anderson and Jones 1974, pp. 427–445.

Watkins, Calvert. 1962. *Indo-European origins of the Celtic verb.* Dublin: Dublin Institute of Advanced Studies.

Werner, Otmar. 1987. The aim of morphological change is a good mixture—not a uniform language type. In Ramat et al. 1987, pp. 591–606.

Wurzel, Wolfgang U. 1984. On morphological naturalness. *Nordic Journal of Linguistics* 7.165–183.

Wurzel, Wolfgang U. 1985. Morphologische Natürlichkeit und morphologischer Wandel: Zur Vorhersagbarkeit von Sprachveränderungen. In *Papers from the Sixth International Conference on Historical Linguistics,* edited by Jacek Fisiak, pp. 587–599. Amsterdam: Benjamins.

Wurzel, Wolfgang U. 1987. System-dependent morphological naturalness in inflection. In Dressler 1987b, pp. 59–96.

Wurzel, Wolfgang U. 2000. Inflectional systems and markedness. In Lahiri 2000a, pp. 193–214.

Wurzel, Wolfgang U., A. Bittner, and D. Bittner. 1994. *Grammatisch initierter Wandel.* Bochum: Brockmeyer.

Zager, D. 1981. *A real-time process model of morphology and change.* Dissertation, State University of New York at Buffalo.

PAUL KIPARSKY

ANALYTIC LANGUAGES. *See* Functional Linguistics.

ANAPHORA. [*This entry includes the following subentries:*
Formal Grammar
Logical Semantics]

Formal Grammar

Nominal expressions may be divided into three basic categories: (i) *anaphors,* such as reciprocals and reflexives; (ii) *pronominals,* such as *he, she;* and (iii) R[eferential]-expressions, such as names. In the Government and Binding (GB) framework outlined by Chomsky 1981, 1982, it is assumed that these nominal expressions may be either *overt* or *non-overt.* A non-overt anaphor is the empty element coindexed with a noun phrase, and is called NP-trace. An example of a non-overt pronominal is PRO, the phonetically unrealized counterpart of a pronoun. A non-overt R-expression is the empty element coindexed with a *wh*-element, called *wh*-trace or variable. For each type of nominal expression, a *binding requirement* specifies the domain in which a nominal expression may or may not have an antecedent. These requirements are referred to as the *binding principles* or the Binding theory.

A crucial distinction relevant to the understanding of the Binding theory is the one made between *A[rgument]-positions* and non-argument positions (A'-positions). Positions that receive grammatical functions (e.g. subject-of . . . object-of . . .) are A-positions; those that do not receive such functions are A'-positions. For instance, the *specifier* of COMP position is an A'-position. The Binding theory, as formulated by Chomsky 1981, is a theory of A-binding; it refers solely to antecedents that are in A-positions. This theory requires anaphors to be A-Bound—that is, to have a c-commanding antecedent in an A-position, in a certain domain. It requires pronominals to be A-free (not to have a c-commanding A-antecedent) in a certain domain; and, finally, it requires R-expressions to be A-free everywhere. A domain in which the anaphor must be bound and the pronominal must be free is referred to by Chomsky as the governing category (Chomsky 1981) or as the complete functional complex (1986). Thus, in (1a) below, the anaphoric reciprocal must be A-bound in the embedded clause; the antecedent of this reciprocal is *the students*. In (1b), the pronominal element must be A-free in the embedded clause; it has to be disjoint in reference from *Peter*. In (1c), the name *Mary* must be free throughout:

(1a)   *The teachers think the students help each other.*

(1b)   *Paul expects Peter to criticize him.*

(1c)   *She believes the girl caught Mary.*

In Chomsky 1986 and 1995, the binding requirement concerning anaphors is reduced to movement under the assumption that anaphors—in particular, reflexives—are subject to a covert extraction process that places them close to their antecedent. Chomsky's proposal raises the possibility that at least the binding requirements sensitive to locality—that is, those constraining anaphors and pronominals—are not independent requirements. Rather, they are to be subsumed under the theory of movement. This approach is developed within the Minimalist framework in Hornstein 2000 and Kayne 2001, which analyze the relation between the antecedent and the anaphor or the pronoun as an A-movement relation.

Given that movement is not restricted to A-movement, it is also expected that "binding" effects occur between a nominal expression and an antecedent in a A'-position. Cases of A'-disjointness effects applying to pronominals are discussed in Borer 1984, McCloskey 1990, Aoun and Li 1990 and Aoun and Choueiri 2000, among others. Furthermore, Shlonsky 1992 and Aoun, Choueiri, and Hornstein 2000 show that various disjointness requirements applying to resumptive pronominals are to be accounted for in terms of movement, thus incorporating the insights of the Generalized Binding theory (see Aoun 1985, 1986), which argued that the original Binding theory should be generalized from a theory of A-binding to a theory of A- as well as A'-binding.

[*See also* Control; Formal Grammar; C-Command; *and* Pronouns.]

BIBLIOGRAPHY

Aoun, Joseph. 1985. *A grammar of anaphora.* (Linguistic Inquiry monographs, 11.) Cambridge, Mass.: MIT Press.

Aoun, Joseph. 1986. *Generalized Binding: The syntax and Logical Form interpretation of WH-interrogatives.* (Studies in generative grammar, 26.) Dordrecht: Foris.

Aoun, Joseph, and Yen-Hui Audrey Li. 1990. Minimal disjointness. *Journal of Linguistics* 28.189–203.

Aoun, Joseph, and Lina Choueiri. 2000. Epithets. *Natural Language and Linguistic Theory* 18.1–39.

Aoun, Joseph, Lina Choueiri, and Norbert Hornstein. 2001. Resumption, movement and derivational economy. *Linguistic Inquiry* 32.371–403.

Borer, Hagit. 1984. Restrictive relatives in Modern Hebrew. *Natural Language and Linguistic Theory* 2.219–260.

Chomsky, Noam. 1981. *Lectures on government and binding.* (Studies in generative grammar, 9.) Dordrecht: Foris.

Chomsky, Noam. 1982. *Some concepts and consequences of the theory of government and binding.* (Linguistic Inquiry monographs, 6.) Cambridge, Mass.: MIT Press.

Chomsky, Noam. 1986. *Knowledge of language: Its nature, origins, and use.* New York: Praeger.

Chomsky, Noam. 1995. *The Minimalist program.* Cambridge, Mass.: MIT Press.

Hornstein, Norbert. 2000. *Move! A Minimalist theory of construal.* Oxford: Blackwell.

Kayne, Richard S. 2001. Pronouns and their antecedents. Ms., New York University.

McCloskey, James. 1990. Resumptive Pronouns, A-bar binding, and levels of representation in Irish. In *Syntax and Semantics 23: The syntax of the modern Celtic languages,* edited by R. Hendrick, pp. 199–256. San Diego, Calif.: Academic Press.

Shlonsky, Ur. 1992. Resumptive pronouns as a last resort. *Linguistic Inquiry* 23.443–468.

JOSEPH AOUN

Logical Semantics

Anaphoric pronouns present a variety of puzzles that have attracted the attention of linguists and philosophers alike. Linguists have been concerned mainly with questions about the syntactic constraints on antecedent/anaphor relations; by contrast, philosophers and logicians have traditionally been concerned with questions about the semantic content of anaphoric pronouns.

From a semantic perspective, anaphoric pronouns seem

to fall into three main categories: (i) those that function as devices of coreference; (ii) those that appear to function like the bound variables of logic; and (iii) those that resist direct incorporation into either of these categories, but which nonetheless appear to constitute a uniform semantic category.

1. Referential versus non-referential anaphors. Consider the following examples:

(1)   JOHN *respects students who argue with* HIM.

(2)   JOHN *likes* HIS *brothers.*

(Small capitals indicate some sort of intentional anaphoric connection.) Since the antecedents of the pronouns in these examples are referential expressions, it is natural to view the pronouns as referring to whatever their antecedents refer to (see Lasnik 1976, Evans 1977, 1980). We might therefore call these pronouns *referential anaphors.*

Pronouns with quantified antecedents cannot be treated as referential anaphors. Consider the following:

(3)   EVERY PROFESSOR *respects students who argue with* HIM.

(4)   NO MAN *likes* HIS *brothers.*

As Geach 1962 has argued, it makes no sense to inquire into the referents of the pronouns in examples like these. Furthermore, the pronouns in (3–4) are clearly not "pronouns of laziness" that stand for repeated occurrences of 'every professor' or 'no man'.

Typically, philosophers and logicians have treated pronouns in such examples as the natural-language counterparts of the bound variables of quantification theory. We now turn to this idea.

2. Quantification and bound anaphora. The logical forms of quantified sentences of the form *All Fs are Gs* and *Some Fs are Gs* can, of course, be represented with the aid of the standard unary quantifiers ∀ and ∃ of first-order logic. But *all* and *some* are not the only determiners that may introduce quantification; an adequate semantics must also handle sentences of the forms *No Fs are Gs, The F is G, Exactly one F is G, Few Fs are Gs, Most Fs are Gs,* and so on. This leads to two problems:

(a) With the aid of the equality sign $=$ and the negation sign $\neg$, it is possible to use ∃ and ∀ to represent sentences containing phrases of the form *no F, the F, exactly one F, exactly two Fs,* etc.; but the resulting formulas obscure the relationship between the syntactic structure of a sentence and its logical form. For example, if we agree with Russell that *The F is G* is true if and only if all Fs

are Gs and there is exactly one F, then the most perspicuous rendering of the logical form of this sentence is:

(5) $(\exists x)(Fx \,\&\, (\forall y)(Fy \supset y=x) \,\&\, Gx))$.

(b) A more serious problem is that there are sentences which provably cannot be represented within first-order logic, e.g. those of the form *Most Fs are Gs.*

Both these problems can be avoided by viewing natural-language quantification as *restricted.* The basic idea here is that determiners themselves are not actually quantifiers; rather, they are expressions that combine with their complements to form restricted quantifiers. Thus *every, some, most, the,* etc. combine with simple nouns like *donkey* (or *donkeys*), *man* (or *men*), etc. (or with complex nouns like *man who owns a donkey*), to form restricted quantifiers like *some man, most men, every man who owns a donkey,* etc. We can represent a quantifier *every man* as '[Every x: man x]'. This quantifier may combine with a predicate phrase like *is mortal*—which we can represent as '(x is mortal)'—to form the sentence *Every man is mortal*; this can be represented as:

(6)   [Every x: man x] (x is mortal).

Now consider sentences (3–4) again. If we treat the anaphoric pronouns in these examples as bound variables, their logical forms will be:

(3')   [Every x: professor x] x respects students who argue with x.

(4')   [No x: man x] (x likes x's brothers).

Evans 1977 has shown convincingly that not all pronouns which are anaphoric on quantifiers can be treated as bound variables. Consider the following examples:

(7)   *John bought some donkeys and Harry vaccinated them.*

(8)   *Just one man drank rum and he was ill afterwards.*

If the occurrence of *them* in (7) is treated as a bound variable, the logical form of the sentence will be:

(7')   [Some x: donkeys x] (John bought x & Harry vaccinated x).

But this is incorrect. (7') can be true even if Harry did not vaccinate *all* the donkeys John bought; but (7) cannot be. (If John bought ten donkeys, and Harry vaccinated only two of them, then (7') would be true, but (7) would not.) And if the pronoun *he* in (8) is treated as a bound variable, the logical form of the sentence will be:

(8')   [Just one *x*: man *x*] (*x* drank rum and *x* was ill afterwards).

This is also incorrect: suppose two men drank rum, and only one was ill afterwards; although (8) is false in such a scenario, (8') is true.

Evans pointed to a plausible *syntactic* explanation of these facts. In both (7) and (8), the pronoun is located outside the smallest sentence containing the quantifiers upon which it is anaphoric; hence it lies outside its *scope*, according to the most promising syntactic characterization of this notion. The scope of a natural-language quantifier appears to be everything that it "c-commands." (A node α c-commands a node β just in case the first branching node dominating α also dominates β, and neither α nor β dominates the other.) The sort of cross-sentential binding that would be needed to treat the pronouns in (7–8) as bound variables thus conflicts with a plausible syntactic constraint on semantic interpretation. The upshot of all this is that some anaphoric pronouns are neither bound nor genuinely referential.

3. Quantification and unbound anaphora. How are unbound pronouns to be understood when they are anaphoric on quantifiers? A plausible paraphrase of (7) is (9):

(9)   *John bought* SOME DONKEYS, *and Harry vaccinated* THE DONKEYS JOHN BOUGHT.

With this in mind, Evans 1977 suggested that the pronoun *them* in (7) is interpreted via the plural description *the donkeys John bought,* as what he calls an "E-type pronoun." Such a pronoun does not actually *stand* for a description; rather, it has its reference *fixed* by description (in the sense of Kripke 1972), and is therefore a "rigid designator." For example, in (7), the pronoun *them* is taken to refer to those objects denoted by *the donkeys John bought.*

A similar explanation obtains where the antecedent is singular. A plausible paraphrase of (10) is (11):

(10)   *John bought* A DONKEY, *and Harry vaccinated* IT.
(11)   *John bought* A DONKEY, *and Harry vaccinated* THE DONKEY JOHN BOUGHT.

On Evans's account, the pronoun *it* in (10) refers to the unique object denoted by the singular definite description *the donkey John bought.*

For Evans, this idea formed the basis of a quite general account of the semantic content of unbound anaphors. Consider the following examples:

(12)   JUST ONE MAN *drank rum, and* HE *was ill afterwards.*
(13)   SEVERAL POLICEMEN *came.* THEY *seemed to enjoy themselves.*

In (12), *he* has its reference fixed by *the man who drank rum;* in (13), *they* has its reference fixed by *the policemen who came.* In general, an unbound anaphoric pronoun refers to "those objects which *verify* (or that object which *verifies*) the sentence containing the antecedent quantifier" (Evans 1977:111). This means that, if *P* is an unbound pronoun which is anaphoric on a quantified N[oun] P[hrase] that we can render as "[Determiner *x*: F*x*]," occurring in a sentence we can render as "[Determiner *x*: F*x*](G*x*)," then the referent of *P* is fixed by the description that we can render as "[The *x*: F*x* & G*x*]."

Study of more complex examples has exposed several weaknesses in Evans's theory (see below), and the problems uncovered have tended to push semanticists in one of two directions. First, there have been attempts to modify and refine the general Evansian framework (e.g. Davies 1981, Neale 1990). Second, there have been attempts to replace the entire framework with a uniform, discourse-based approach (e.g. Kamp 1981, Heim 1982). We shall look at these in turn.

4. Descriptive anaphora. Evans's theory needs at least to be modified if it is to achieve anything like full generality. Evans rejected the view that unbound anaphors "go proxy" for descriptions; he favored the view that they have their referents fixed by description—on the grounds that such pronouns, unlike overt descriptions, do not interact "scopally" with other operators. But consider the following:

(14)   A MAN *murdered Smith, but John doesn't believe* HE *did.*
(15)   A MAN *murdered Smith. The police have reason to think* HE *injured himself in the process.*

If *he* goes proxy for *the man who murdered Smith,* there will be two readings for each of the anaphor clauses in these examples—the so-called de re and de dicto readings—depending on whether the description for which the pronoun goes proxy is given wide or narrow scope.

On this account, the anaphor clause of (14) is ambiguous between the following:

(14') [The x: man x & x murdered Smith] (John doesn't believe: x murdered Smith)

(14") John doesn't believe: [The x: man x & x murdered Smith] (x murdered Smith)

It is natural to interpret (14) as attributing to John a non-contradictory belief concerning the murderer, to the effect that he is *not* the murderer. On the proxy view, this is captured by the de re reading of the second conjunct. The de dicto reading is technically available to the proxy theorist, but it is obviously not the preferred interpretation. However, as Davies 1981 has pointed out, the de dicto reading of the second sentence in (15) is actually the more natural; yet Evans's theory explicitly precludes this reading.

Further support for the proxy theory comes from examples containing modal expressions:

(16) *Mary wants to marry* A RICH MAN. HE *must be a banker.*

The first sentence in (16) may be read either de re or de dicto. Further, the pronoun *he* can be anaphoric on *a rich man* on either reading. But as Karttunen 1976 has pointed out, the modal expression has to be there for the anaphora to work, if the antecedent sentence is to be interpreted de dicto. Consider the following:

(17) *Mary wants to marry* A RICH MAN. HE *is a banker.*

Here a de dicto reading is not possible for the antecedent clause if *he* is anaphoric on *a rich man.* This contrast between (16) and (17) is explicable on the assumption that the anaphoric pronoun in (16) goes proxy for the description *the man Mary marries,* which may take wide or narrow scope with respect to the modal expression. On the de dicto reading of the antecedent clause, the de re reading of the anaphor clause is infelicitous, because an implication of existence results from giving the description wide scope. But the de dicto reading of the anaphor clause is fine, because on such a reading the description is within the scope of the modal expression. In (17), however, there is no modal operator that can take wide scope over the pronoun; thus the sentence has no felicitous reading if the antecedent clause is read de dicto.

Within a theory that distinguishes bound and unbound anaphora, we can also account for the difference between restrictive and non-restrictive relative clauses. Following Quine 1960 and Evans 1977, it is customary to think of relative pronouns (as they occur in restrictive relative clauses) as devices of predicate abstraction, rather than as variables. On such an account, (18) and (19) are interpreted as (18') and (19'), respectively:

(18) *The man who loves Mary is happy.*
(18') [The x: man x & $[\lambda z](z$ loves Mary$)x$](x is happy).
(19) *The man whom Mary loves is happy.*
(19') [The x: man x & $[\lambda z]($Mary loves $z)x$](x is happy).

However, for simplicity, the relative pronouns in (18–19) are often thought of as variables bound by determiners, since (18') and (19') are equivalent to (18") and (19"):

(18") [The x: man x & x loves Mary](x is happy).
(19") [The x: man x & Mary loves x](x is happy).

Consider the following:

(20) *John bought some donkeys which were vaccinated by Harry.*
(21) *John bought some donkeys, which were vaccinated by Harry.*

In (20), the relative pronoun *which* is part of the NP *some donkeys which were vaccinated by Harry.* Since *which* is c-commanded by *some,* it is interpreted as a variable bound by the determiner. Thus the logical form of (20) is captured by:

(20') [Some x: donkeys x & Harry vaccinated x] (John bought x).

The truth of this is perfectly consistent with John's buying some donkeys that Harry does not vaccinate. The truth of (21), however, requires that Harry vaccinated *all* the donkeys that John bought. If the pronoun *which* in (21) is treated as an unbound anaphor that goes proxy for *the donkeys John bought,* this result follows. This suggests strongly that *which* is not c-commanded by *some* in (21).

5. Discourse referents. The discussion so far has presupposed a reasonably clear distinction between bound (i.e. c-command) and unbound anaphora: a pronoun anaphoric on a quantifier that c-commands it is treated as a bound variable; otherwise, it is interpreted as a description recoverable from the antecedent clause. However, alternative approaches that seek to treat all anaphoric pronouns in a unitary fashion have been developed by Kamp 1981 and Heim 1982. The initial motivation for this approach comes from so-called donkey sentences like (22–23), originally discussed by Geach 1962:

(22)   *If* A MAN *buys* A DONKEY, HE *vaccinates* IT.
(23)   *Every man who buys* A DONKEY *vaccinates* IT.

Both Evans's theory and the simple proxy theory fail here. For example, if the pronoun *it* in (23) is analyzed in terms of the singular description *the donkey he buys* (with *he* bound by *every man who buys a donkey*), the sentence will be true just in case every man who buys a donkey vaccinates the unique donkey he buys. Consequently, it will be false if any man buys more than one donkey. But this is wrong; the truth of (23) is quite compatible with some men buying more than one donkey, as long as every man who buys a donkey vaccinates *every* donkey he buys. It would appear, then, that the indefinite description *a donkey*—which can normally be treated as an existentially quantified phrase—has the force of a *universally* quantified phrase in (23). And in (22), both *a man* and *a donkey* appear to have universal force.

Kamp 1981 has proposed a common explanation of the "universalization" of the indefinite descriptions in such examples. The idea (very roughly) is that noun phrases supply "discourse referents" to *D[iscourse] R[epresentations]*; and that common nouns and predicates supply "conditions" on these. Typically, a discourse referent functions like a variable bound by an existential quantifier that takes scope over the entire discourse. On this account, an indefinite description is not inherently quantificational; rather, it introduces a discourse referent with conditions on it. These are imposed by, among other things, the predicative material that the indefinite contains. The DR for (22) might be represented as:

(24)   [man(x) & donkey(y) & buys(x,y)] IFTHEN [vaccinates(x,y)].

On the general assumption that a conditional of the form *If α then β* is true if and only if every way in which α can be true constitutes a way of β's being true, Kamp proposes that (24) is true if and only if every assignment of values to x and y that makes the antecedent true also makes the consequent true. Since this yields the correct

truth conditions for (22), the apparent universalization of the indefinite descriptions *a man* and *a donkey* is explained as a consequence of the general analysis of conditionals.

In light of the equivalence of (22–23), Kamp suggests that, although (23) is not actually a conditional (because the subject quantifier in (23) is a universal), we get a DR in which the indefinite *a donkey* has universal force. That is, the DR for (23) is given by:

(25)   [man(x) & donkey(y) & buys(x,y)] EVERY [vaccinates(x,y)].

This DR, like (24), is true if and only if every assignment of values to x and y that makes [man(x) & donkey(y) & buys(x,y)] true, also makes [vaccinates(x,y)] true.

One drawback of this proposal is that it does not seem to explain why indefinite descriptions also "universalize" when they are embedded in other quantifiers. Consider the following:

(26)   *Most men who buy a donkey vaccinate it.*

By analogy with (24–25), the DR for (26) will be:

(27)   [man(x) & donkey(y) & buys(x,y)] MOST [vaccinates(x,y)].

This DR is true just in case *most* assignments of values to x and y that make [man(x) & donkey(y) & buys(x,y)] true, also make [vaccinates(x,y)] true. But on its most natural interpretation, the truth of (26) requires that most men who buy a donkey vaccinate *every* donkey they buy—whereas (27) can be true as long as most of the donkeys that are bought by men are vaccinated by their respective buyers. Suppose Alan buys five donkeys, Bill buys one donkey, Clive buys one donkey, and no other man buys any donkeys. Then (27) will come out true if Alan vaccinates at least four of his donkeys, even if Bill and Clive do not vaccinate their respective donkeys; but in such a situation, (26) would be false. (It has been suggested that there is another reading of (26), which requires that most men who buy at least one donkey vaccinate most of the donkeys they buy; but (27) does not capture this alleged reading either.)

It is clear from this overview that both the simple descriptive theory and the simple DR theory must be refined if they are to do justice to the full range of antecedent/anaphor relations that exist between quantifiers and pronouns. More sophisticated versions of both theories are currently being developed.

[*See also* C-Command; Phrase Structure; Pronouns; *and* Semantics, *article on* Formal Semantics.]

BIBLIOGRAPHY

Davies, Martin. 1981. *Meaning, quantification, necessity: Themes in philosophical logic.* London: Routledge and Kegan Paul.

Evans, Gareth. 1977. Pronouns, quantifiers, and relative clauses (I). *Canadian Journal of Philosophy* 7.467–536. Reprinted in Evans 1985, pp. 76–152.

Evans, Gareth. 1980. Pronouns. *Linguistic Inquiry* 11.337–362. Reprinted in Evans 1985, pp. 214–248.

Evans, Gareth. 1985. *Collected papers.* Oxford: Clarendon Press. New York: Oxford University Press.

Geach, Peter. 1962. *Reference and generality: An examination of some medieval and modern theories.* Ithaca, N.Y.: Cornell University Press.

Heim, Irene. 1982. *Towards a unified semantics of definite and indefinite noun phrases.* Amherst: University of Massachusetts dissertation. Published, New York: Garland, 1988.

Kamp, Hans. 1981. A theory of truth and semantic interpretation. In *Formal methods in the study of natural language,* vol. 1, edited by Jeroen A. G. Groenendijk et al., pp. 277–322. Amsterdam: Mathematisch Centrum.

Karttunen, Lauri. 1976. Discourse referents. In *Notes from the linguistic underground* (Syntax and semantics, 7), edited by James McCawley, pp. 363–385. New York: Academic Press.

Kripke, Saul A. 1972. Naming and necessity. In *Semantics of natural language,* 2d ed., edited by Donald Davidson and Gilbert Harman, pp. 253–355. Dordrecht: Reidel. Revised as *Naming and necessity* (Oxford: Blackwell; Cambridge, Mass.: Harvard University Press, 1980).

Lasnik, Howard. 1976. Remarks on coreference. *Linguistic Analysis* 2.1–22.

Neale, Stephen. 1990. *Descriptions.* Cambridge, Mass.: MIT Press.

Quine, Willard van Orman. 1960. *Word and object.* Cambridge, Mass.: MIT Press.

STEPHEN NEALE

ANDAMANESE LANGUAGES. A family which comprises the family of indigenous languages of the Andaman Islands of India.

LANGUAGE LIST

Aka-Bea: also called Bea, Beada, Biada, Aka-Beada, Bojigniji, Bogijiab, Bojigyab. No longer spoken.

FIGURE 1. *Subgrouping of Andamanese Languages*

Great Andamanese
  Central Andamanese
    Aka-Bea, Aka-Kede, Aka-Kol, Akar-Bale, A-Pucikwar, Oko-Juwoi
Northern Andamanese
    Aka-Bo, Aka-Cari, Aka-Jeru, Aka-Kora
South Andamanese
  Jarawa, Önge, Sentinel

Aka-Bo: also called Bo, Ba. Formerly spoken on eastern central coast of North Andaman Island, and North Reef Island.

Aka-Cari: also called Cari, Chariar. Formerly spoken on northern coast of North Andaman Island, Landfall Island, and other nearby small islands.

Aka-Jeru: also called Jeru, Yerawa. Formerly spoken on interior and southern North Andaman Island, and Sound Island.

Aka-Kede: also called Kede. No longer spoken. Formerly spoken on central and north central Middle Andaman Island.

Aka-Kol: also called Kol. Formerly spoken on southeastern Middle Andaman Island.

Aka-Kora: also called Kora. Formerly spoken on northeastern and northern central coasts of North Andaman Island, and Smith Island.

Akar-Bale: also called Bale, Balwa. Formerly spoken on Ritchie's Archipelago, Havelock Island, Neill Island.

A-Pucikwar: also called Pucikwar, Puchikwar. 36 speakers. Formerly spoken on Boratang Island, southern coast of Middle Andaman Island, northeastern coast of South Andaman Island. Bilingualism in Hindi. Language shift to Hindi taking place. The Central Institute of Indian Languages (CIIL) is working to revive A-Pucikwar.

Jarawa: 200 speakers. Ethnic population: 300 as of 1999. Interior and southern central Rutland Island, central interior and southern interior South Andaman Island, 70 square km reserve. Different from Önge and Sentinel. Completely monolingual.

Oko-Juwoi: also called Oku-Juwoi, Juwoi, Junoi. Formerly spoken on western central and southwest interior Middle Andaman Island.

Önge: also called Ong. 96 speakers. Ethnic population: 110 as of 1999. Southern Andaman Islands, Dugong Creek and South Bay Islands. Speakers are mainly monolingual. Unfriendly toward outsiders.

Sentinel: also called Sentinelese. 50 speakers on southeastern Andaman Islands, Sentinel Island. Similar to Önge.

B. GRIMES

ANGAN LANGUAGES. Spoken in southeastern Papua New Guinea. They form a branch of the Central and Western Main Section of the proposed TRANS-NEW GUINEA LANGUAGES. Angaatiha and Susuami each constitute a separate sub-branch of the family; the other languages belong to the Angan Proper sub-branch.

LANGUAGE LIST

Akoye: also called Akoinkake, Lohiki, Obi, Mai-Hea-Ri, Maih-iri, Angoya, Akoyi. 800 speakers. Similar to Tainae.

Ampeeli-Wojokeso: also called Ampale, Ampele, Ambari, Safeyoka. 2,390 speakers in Morobe Province, Kaiapit, Lae-Wamba, and Menyamya districts. Dialects are Aiewomba, Wajakes (Wojokeso). Bilingualism in Tok Pisin, Yabem.

Angaatiha: also called Langimar, Angataha, Angaatiya, Angaataha. 1,200 speakers in Morobe Province, Menyamya district.

Ankave: also called Angave. 1,600 speakers in Gulf Province, Kerema district, in the valleys of the Mbwei and Swanson Rivers. Dialects are Sawuve, Wiyagwa, Wunavai, Miyatnu, Ankai, Bu'u.

Baruya: also called Barua, Yipma. 6,600 speakers in eastern Highlands Province, Marawaka district. Dialects are Wantakia, Baruya, Gulicha, Usirampia.

Hamtai: also called Hamday, Kapau, Kamea, Watut. "Kuku-kuku" is a derogatory name sometimes used. 45,000 speakers. Dialects are Wenta, Howi, Pmasa'a, Hamtai, Kaintiba.

Kamasa: 6 speakers remain. Formerly spoken in Morobe Province, in part of the Katsiong census unit. No children speak Kamasa. Second language used for most or all of the key domains except perhaps family. 30% or less of the ethnic group speak Kamasa.

Kawacha: also called Kawatsa. 12 speakers remain. Formerly spoken in Morobe Province, east of Ampale, in part of the Katsiong census unit. Bilingualism in Yagwoia. No children speak Kawacha. Kawacha not used except perhaps in family. 30% or less of the ethnic group speak Kawacha.

Menya: also called Menye, Menyama. 20,000 speakers in Morobe Province, Menyamya district, from the Papua border north along the Tauri River and its tributaries.

Simbari: also called Chimbari. 3,036 speakers in eastern Highlands Province, Marawaka district. A government school teaches children in English and Tok Pisin.

Susuami: 10 speakers remain. Formerly spoken in Morobe Province, Upper Watut Valley outside Bulolo. Most closely related to Kamasa. Bilingualism in Angaatiha. No children speak Susuami. Susuami not used except perhaps in family. Under 10% of the ethnic group speak Susuami.

Tainae: also called Ivori. 1,000 speakers in Gulf Province, Ivori-Swanson district. The main villages are Pio, Famba, and Paiguna. Close to Angoya.

Yagwoia: also called Kokwaiyakwa, Yeghuye. 9,000 speakers. Related to Menya, Simbari, Hamtai, Baruya. They speak Tok Pisin with routine proficiency to outsiders. Yagwoia spoken with other Yagwoia. B. GRIMES

ANIMAL COMMUNICATION. *See* Evolution and Language.

ANOMIA. The term "anomia" refers to mild or severe impairments of naming or word-finding following focal brain damage. Testing for anomia typically includes asking the individual to name pictures of objects, or requesting the correct response to a verbal description. Except when they also suffer obvious object agnosia, aphasic patients usually have little trouble recognizing the objects they cannot name; they can typically mime the object's use, select it from among others when its name is spoken, or give the correct name when they are supplied with its initial sound.

Within the generality that common names are easier to retrieve than rare ones (Newcombe et al. 1971), anomia can be modality-specific (tactile, visual, or auditory); there are also reports of category-specific anomias, such as color anomia—that is, an inability to name colors in the absence of known impairment in visual color-sensitivity. Especially intriguing are occasional reports of naming deficits limited to specific semantic categories, such as anomias for proper names (Semenza 1997), or a greater impairment in naming natural (living) versus nonliving (human-made) objects (Hillis and Caramazza 1991).

Anomic errors can take the form of semantic or phonological paraphasias. Semantic (verbal) paraphasias are incorrect responses that are related in meaning or in category to the desired name, for example, producing the word *soldier* for 'policeman'. This could reflect either (i) a looseness in category specification, or (ii) parallel activation of related responses, without inhibition of those which are not the best fit. Phonological (literal) paraphasias are responses in which phonemic elements are absent, distorted, or misplaced within an otherwise recognizable word. Such paraphasias can appear as complete neologisms.

While some degree of anomia is common in all forms of aphasia, anomia can appear as the primary form of language deficit. This is called "anomic aphasia" (also "nominal" or "amnesic" aphasia). Its clinical picture is that of a patient whose speech output is fluent and grammatical, but lacks essential content words. In the place of the substantive nouns and verbs, for example, the patient might produce numerous empty circumlocutions, using *that* and *do* in a variety of noun and verb positions, as in this example from Goodglass (1980:647), in which an anomic aphasic describes his son's career:

(1)   *Well he was two years away, away down for nothing. He didn't do it and got out and said I want to go over there and . . . how to do things, what he's doing now.*

As distinct from Wernicke's aphasia, anomic aphasics show relatively good auditory comprehension.

Although often associated with temporal-parietal injury, anomia has proven difficult to localize, since it can follow damage to a variety of cortical areas. Attempts to distinguish naming deficits by qualitative analyses of patients' errors (e.g. the relative proportion of semantic vs. phonological paraphasias) has met with only mixed success. (See Goodglass et al. 1997 for an illustration of how such error analyses can be conducted.)

Normal aging is often accompanied by a slowing in word-finding and an increase in "tip-of-the-tongue" experiences—the annoying inaccessibility of names of persons or objects that are well known to the individual (Burke et al. 1991). Anomia of a much more serious degree can appear as an early symptom of Alzheimer's dementia and is often observable earlier than other language deficits in that disorder (Nicholas et al. 1997).

[*See also* Aphasia; Neurolinguistics; *and* Dementia and Language.]

BIBLIOGRAPHY

Burke, Deborah M., Donald G. MacKay, J. S. Worthley, and E. Wade. 1991. On the tip of the tongue: What causes word finding failures in young and older adults? *Journal of Memory and Language* 30.542–579.

Goodglass, Harold. 1980. Disorders of naming following brain injury. *American Scientist* 68.647–655.

Goodglass, Harold, Arthur Wingfield, Mary R. Hyde, Jean B. Gleason, Nancy L. Bowles, and Roberta E. Gallagher. 1997. The importance of word-initial phonology: Error patterns in prolonged naming efforts by aphasic patients. *Journal of the International Neuropsychological Society* 3.128–138.

Hillis, Argye E., and Alfonso Caramazza. 1991. Category-specific naming and comprehension impairment: A double dissociation. *Brain* 114.2081–2094.

Newcombe, Freda, et al. 1971. Recognition and naming of object drawings by men with focal brain wounds. *Journal of Neurology, Neurosurgery and Psychiatry* 34.329–340.

Nicholas, Marjorie, Christine Barth, Loraine K. Obler, Rhoda Au, and Martin L. Albert. 1997. Naming in normal aging and dementia of the Alzheimer's type. In *Anomia: Neuroanatomical and cognitive correlates*, edited by Harold Goodglass and Arthur Wingfield, pp. 166–188. San Diego, Calif.: Academic Press.

Semenza, Carlo. 1997. Proper-name-specific aphasias. In *Anomia: Neuroanatomical and cognitive correlates*, edited by Harold Goodglass and Arthur Wingfield, pp. 115–134. San Diego, Calif.: Academic Press.

ARTHUR WINGFIELD

ANTHROPOLOGICAL LINGUISTICS. [*This entry includes the following subentries:*
Overview
Early History in North America
Social and Cultural Approaches to Language]

Overview

The field of anthropological linguistics—or, as some prefer, "linguistic anthropology"—has been dominated since the 1980s by North American scholars; they are heirs to a tradition of the "four-field" study of human beings, including physical anthropology, archaeology, socio-cultural anthropology, and linguistic anthropology. Many senior linguistic anthropologists trained with students of Edward Sapir; and linguistic anthropologists usually claim Sapir's teacher Franz Boas, Sapir himself, and his student Benjamin Whorf as the founders of their discipline. Yet the intellectual ancestry of this diverse field is complex, with roots in Prague School functionalism, "Neo-Bloomfieldian" American structuralism, dialectology, and social psychology (see Murray 1994). Outside the United States and Canada, recent attention in British social anthropology to the place of language in society claims descent from Malinowski's work on the functions of "primitive" languages (cf. Ardener 1971); Parkin 1982 labels this development "semantic anthropology." Other influential British work includes that of Bloch 1975 on political oratory in traditional societies, and Goody's cross-cultural studies of the impact of literacy (e.g. 1977). In France, the work of Claude Lévi-Strauss on the structural analysis of myth is especially significant; also to be noted are the studies of language among the Dogon of West Africa by Calame-Griaule 1965, and the cognitive anthropology of Sperber 1985.

In addition, French scholarship in general social theory has influenced linguistic anthropology internationally—e.g. Pierre Bourdieu's proposal that the forms of language can constitute a type of "symbolic capital," or Michel Foucault's concept of limits on expression constituted through a historical formation called the 'order of discourse'.

In North America, the term "anthropological linguistics" denotes a tradition of the description of non-Western languages, especially those of the Americas. Among those who might be called anthropological linguists, many are not academics (especially those affiliated with missionary organizations such as the Summer Institute of Linguistics); however, this designation was especially appropriate when linguistics was housed mainly within language departments. Thus students of non-Western languages, especially those not associated with Orientalist scholarship, were likely to affiliate with departments of anthropology. This association weakened with the founding of many independent departments of linguistics between 1950 and 1980—and with an increasing tendency for linguists who were not anthropologists to see the structure of language as a cognitive, rather than social, phenomenon. However, anthropological linguistics continues as a strong empiricist strand in linguistics. In addition to work on the structure of individual languages, recent scholarship in the field has emphasized areal studies and language contact phenomena. The study of language typology and universals, following especially on seminal proposals by Joseph Greenberg, has also been important.

In the past forty years, a new "linguistic anthropology," which explores the place of language in the life of human communities, has developed within anthropology, alongside "anthropological linguistics." The two subspecialties have a combined influence out of proportion to the small number of their scholars. This influence is partly a product of the honor accorded to the Boasian "four-field" tradition in American anthropology; in the 1984 reorganization of the American Anthropological Association, a permanent position on the governing board of the Association was reserved for the president of the Society for Linguistic Anthropology, regardless of the size of that body's membership. But it also arises from the centrality of the intellectual concerns of linguistic anthropology for the larger field, as well as from a tradition of theoretical influence from linguistics on anthropology. The latter is apparent in Lévi-Strauss's use of Jakobson's concept of "opposition" in structural anthropology; in the borrowing by Ward Goodenough, from the structuralist definition of grammar (especially from George Trager, cf. Murray 1994), of the idea that a culture consists of a set of rules which generate appropriate behavior; and in the continuing importance of the distinction of two types of ethnographic analysis, "emic" (insiders' categories) vs. "etic" (outsiders' categories), borrowed from the work of Kenneth Pike.

The recognition that human beings are biologically far more closely related to the great apes than had been imagined, and the identification of "protocultural" phenomena such as tool-making among chimpanzees, has given new importance to the study of language, both verbal and gestural, in the traditional anthropological task of defining human nature. Elsewhere, the methods of historical linguistics are important for the study of prehistory in archaeology. However, linguistic anthropology in the 2000s is most closely linked to the many subspecialties of socio-cultural anthropology—especially to those which explore the realm of symbols, ideas, and knowledge.

Cognitive anthropology, which studies the organization of the kinds of knowledge possessed by human beings as members of specific cultures and communities, is a modern development of an important strand of the Boasian tradition: the proposal that the patterns of language may reveal the structure of what Boas called "the fundamental ethnic ideas." One form of this proposal is the Sapir-Whorf Hypothesis. Ethnosemanticists such as Ward Goodenough, Floyd Lounsbury, and Charles Frake argued that ethnography could be given a rigorous methodological foundation through the structural analysis of carefully defined domains of language patterning, such as kinship and disease terminologies, using a distinctive-feature approach ("componential analysis"). Such analysis would provide evidence for the "rules of culture," i.e. the abstract knowledge that underlay cultural behavior. While some current cognitive anthropology deals with non-linguistic phenomena, most scholars in the field find their fundamental material in language observed in natural contexts, in relatively unstructured interviews, and in experimentation. Their concern is what "ways of speaking," thus observed, can reveal about the representation of cultural knowledge in a wide variety of domains: how such representations are organized, how they are deployed and reproduced, and what might be the limits on their diversity. Perhaps the most important contribution to the last question is the work on color terminology universals initiated by Brent Berlin and Paul Kay. The idea of the structure of knowledge as a checklist of distinctive features has been largely replaced by new conceptualizations, such as prototype theory and fuzzy logic; and by theories of radial and metaphorical categories, developed in cognitive linguistics (cf. Lakoff 1987). Sophisticated quantitative methods, such as factor analysis and multidimensional scaling, are used in the cognitive-anthropological analysis of language data; Dougherty 1985 and Holland and Quinn 1987 are good introductions to this field. A range of contemporary approaches from anthropology and linguistics is summarized in Gumperz and Levinson 1996.

A second important strand in linguistic anthropology is the *ethnography of speaking*, pioneered by Dell Hymes, John Gumperz, and their students. It develops the Prague School insight that language need not have the same functions in every social group; Hymes 1974, Bauman and Sherzer 1974, and Tedlock and Mannheim 1995 are good introductions to this field. The ethnography of speaking views speech (and other forms of communication, such as writing or sign languages) as social institutions, of which the "structure" of phonology, morphology, and syntax is only one component. These institutions can be investigated with ethnographic techniques, especially by participant observation of naturally occurring discourse in its cultural context. Ethnographers of speaking emphasize language use—since they see the skills manifested in use ("communicative competence"), rather than abstract knowledge of grammar, as most important in the construction of the social order through language. Usage is organized through higher-level patterning of a system of "speech events," i.e. communicative exchanges made meaningful by culturally specific structures of participants, codes and genres, affective tones, and other context-constructing elements.

The repertoire of communicative events and their organization differ among speech communities. These are not defined and differentiated by their dominant codes, e.g. "English," since many speech communities are multilingual. Instead, ethnographers of speaking endorse the view of Joshua Fishman that multilingualism is just one type of a more general phenomenon of code variation, which includes the register and dialect differentiation observed in relatively "monolingual" communities. Speech communities are differentiated by characteristic "discourse strategies" (Gumperz 1982), and by "metapragmatics," understandings about the purposes of communicative events.

Mismatches in speech-event structures, and differences in discourse strategies and metapragmatic norms, complicate communication across cultural boundaries, even where codes are shared. In complex pluralistic societies, they may cause "miscommunication," i.e. misunderstandings that result from differences in ways of using language, and may lead to negative evaluations of speakers. These, in turn, influence the unequal distribution of resources in society. Thus the distribution of discourse strategies in communities is an important focus for linguistic anthropologists; they share with variationist sociolinguists (e.g. Labov 1972) an interest in the social stratification of language variation, and in the organization of communicative networks.

The importance of discourse strategies in access to resources has led to increasing emphasis on the analysis of certain types of speech events which may be critical to such access. Thus linguistic anthropologists, sociologists, and others have taken techniques developed in the analysis of such events as greetings and curing rituals in traditional societies, and turned them to the investigation of communicative events in complex societies. The latter include political meetings, courtroom procedures, classroom discourse, and medical interviews, analyzed in order to understand how the allocation of power and resources is organized and reproduced through speaking; an example is the work of Philips 1983, who explores the communicative roots of educational failure among American Indian children.

Interest in the reproduction of social order through language use has also led to work on "language socialization," i.e. the development in children of characteristic patterns of usage (cf. Schieffelin and Ochs 1986). The conceptual apparatus for the analysis of speech events has been considerably refined; examples are the work of Philips 1972 on participant structures, Irvine 1979 on formality, and Brenneis 1987 on indirection. Such work also reveals an interest in cross-cultural regularities in the relationship between language form and language function—in the last work mentioned, common patterns in the use of indirection during the constitution of political arenas in "embedded egalitarian" speech communities.

Linguistic anthropologists emphasize language use. Thus the concept of "speech act," as used in pragmatics, has drawn their close attention, since it seems to offer a basic unit for the analysis of speaking. But problems in applying the concept cross-culturally to natural discourse have also led to empirical critiques of theories of speech acts and inference in pragmatics; these included a challenge to the universality of Grice's conversational postulates (Ochs Keenan 1976), and a critique of speech act theory (Rosaldo 1982).

The work of Silverstein (cf. 1976, 1979), influenced by the semiotics of Charles Peirce, is an important anthropological critique of pragmatics. Silverstein sees the patterning of goals and purposes in language use—"metapragmatics"—as variable across cultures. Metapragmatic patterning is expressed not only in usage, but also in "linguistic ideologies." These are beliefs about language structure and use which derive their supposedly self-evident nature from the important "indexical" function of language. Silverstein argues that the Western semantic and pragmatic tradition (including the work of Austin, Searle, and Grice), which emphasizes the referential functions of language and neglects indexicality, is an example of such a "linguistic ideology." Friedrich 1986 has also criticized the exclusive attention to referential function; his work emphasizes poetic imagination as an important source of patterning in language.

The findings of linguistic anthropology have yielded an important critique of field method. The linguistic-anthropological emphasis on observation of naturally occurring discourse derives partly from a suspicion that social-science interviewing and the techniques of linguistic elicitation may be metapragmatically biased (Briggs 1986). Hence linguistic anthropology continues to rely on "texts," i.e. recordings of discourse which is situated as naturally as possible. This has led to important developments in the analysis of patterning in texts across cultures. Linguistic anthropologists have also criticized the use of spoken words as "raw data" by other cultural anthropologists; they see discourse not as a transparent window through which norms and knowledge may be viewed, but as the very threads from which these are woven.

Linguistic anthropologists increasingly emphasize that language is locally constituted action and practice, rather than a manifestation of underlying "structure" (Duranti 1988). This is a natural theoretical development, given the emphasis on language use; but it also derives from *conversation analysis*, as carried out by ethnomethodologists in sociology, and from the increasing emphasis on action and practice in socio-cultural anthropology. Thus linguistic anthropologists tend to find grammatical theories such as those of Noam Chomsky—who sees the structure of language as entirely autonomous of its communicative use—to be somewhat irrelevant to their concerns. While linguistic anthropologists acknowledge the probability that there are biological constraints on the forms of language, many are critical of "biologism" as the privileged theoretical account of language universals; they argue that the search for explanations of language universals must include attention to cross-culturally variable processes of interaction.

Linguistic anthropology is a diverse and eclectic field, and not all scholars who have connections with it would necessarily endorse all the positions noted above. Linguistic anthropologists are, however, united by common emphases on the study of naturally occurring talk, and on recognition of the importance of cross-cultural diversity in the functions of language. They are also united by an insistence that language is closely embedded in human culture and society, and to a great degree constitutive of them. Thus they see the study of language structure and use as a logical project for anthropology.

[*See also* Discourse, *article on* Conversation Analysis; Ethnography of Speaking; Ethnosemantics; Fieldwork; North American Languages; Historical Linguistics, *article on* Culture History and Historical Linguistics; Sapir, Edward; Semiotics; Sociolinguistics; Ethnopoetics; Linguistic Relativity; *and* Whorf, Benjamin Lee.]

BIBLIOGRAPHY

Ardener, Edwin, ed. 1971. *Social anthropology and language.* London: Tavistock.

Bauman, Richard, and Joel Sherzer, eds. 1974. *Explorations in the ethnography of speaking.* London and New York: Cambridge University Press.

Bloch, Maurice, ed. 1975. *Political language and oratory in traditional society.* New York: Academic Press.

Brenneis, Donald. 1987. Talk and transformation. *Man* 22.499–510.

Briggs, Charles L. 1986. *Learning how to ask.* Cambridge and New York: Cambridge University Press.

Calame-Griaule, Geneviève. 1965. *Ethnologie et langage.* Paris: Gallimard.

Dougherty, Janet W. D., ed. 1985. *New directions in cognitive anthropology.* Urbana: University of Illinois Press.

Duranti, Alessandro. 1988. Ethnography of speaking: Towards a linguistics of the praxis. In *Linguistics: The Cambridge survey,* vol. 4, *Language: The socio-cultural context,* edited by Frederick J. Newmeyer, pp. 210–228. Cambridge and New York: Cambridge University Press.

Friedrich, Paul. 1986. *The language parallax: Linguistic parallelism and poetic indeterminacy.* Austin: University of Texas Press.

Goody, Jack. 1977. *The domestication of the savage mind.* Cambridge and New York: Cambridge University Press.

Gumperz, John J. 1982. *Discourse strategies.* (Studies in interactional sociolinguistics, 1.) Cambridge and New York: Cambridge University Press.

Gumperz, John, and Stephen Levinson, eds. 1996. *Rethinking linguistic relativity.* Cambridge: Cambridge University Press.

Holland, Dorothy, and Naomi Quinn, eds. 1987. *Cultural models in language and thought.* Cambridge and New York: Cambridge University Press.

Hymes, Dell. 1974. *Foundations in sociolinguistics: An ethnographic approach.* Philadelphia: University of Pennsylvania Press.

Irvine, Judith T. 1979. Formality and informality in communicative events. *American Anthropologist* 81.773–790.

Labov, William. 1972. *Language in the inner city: Studies in the Black English vernacular.* Philadelphia: University of Pennsylvania Press.

Lakoff, George. 1987. *Women, fire, and dangerous things: What categories reveal about the mind.* Chicago: University of Chicago Press.

Murray, Stephen O. 1994. *Theory groups and the study of language in North America.* Amsterdam and Philadelphia: Benjamins.

Ochs Keenan, Elinor. 1976. On the universality of conversational postulates. *Language in Society* 5.67–80.

Parkin, David, ed. 1982. *Semantic anthropology.* London: Academic Press.

Philips, Susan U. 1972. Participant structures and communicative competence: Warm Springs children in community and classroom. In *Functions of language in the classroom,* edited by Courtney B. Cazden et al., pp. 370–394. New York: Teacher's College Press.

Philips, Susan U. 1983. *The invisible culture: Communication in classroom and community on the Warm Springs Indian Reservation.* New York: Longman.

Rosaldo, Michelle Z. 1982. The things we do with words: Ilongot speech acts and speech act theory in philosophy. *Language in Society* 11.203–237.

Schieffelin, Bambi B., and Elinor Ochs, eds. 1986. *Language socialization across cultures.* (Studies in the social and cultural foundations of language, 3.) Cambridge and New York: Cambridge University Press.

Silverstein, Michael. 1976. Shifters, linguistic categories, and cultural description. In *Meaning in anthropology,* edited by Keith H. Basso and Henry A. Selby, pp. 11–55. Albuquerque: University of New Mexico Press.

Silverstein, Michael. 1979. Language structure and linguistic ideology. In *The elements: A parasession on linguistic units and levels,* edited by Paul R. Clyne et al., pp. 191–247. Chicago: Chicago Linguistic Society.

Sperber, Dan. 1985. *On anthropological knowledge.* (Cambridge studies in social anthropology, 54.) Cambridge and New York: Cambridge University Press.

Tedlock, Dennis, and Bruce Mannheim, eds. 1995. *The dialogic emergence of culture.* Urbana: University of Illinois Press.

JANE H. HILL

Early History in North America

The history of anthropological linguistics in North America parallels the history of the description and classification of native American languages, and is also closely related to the development and institutionalization of American anthropology. Hallowell 1960:23 notes: "Perhaps the underlying unity implied in the study of the inhabitants of a single great continent, despite their great diversity in many respects, accounts, in part, for the traditional emphasis later given in the United States to anthropology as the unified study of man." Language was the most effective means of categorizing the diverse Indian cultures.

The earliest students were amateurs in contact with native peoples. Cleric John Eliot (1604–1690) translated the Bible into an Algonkian language. His 1666 work, *The Indian grammar begun: An essay to bring the Indian language into rules,* assumed that all Indian languages were essentially the same, as did Roger Williams's *Key into the language of America* in 1643.

European philosophers eagerly incorporated such initial descriptions into their picture of human history. The discovery by William Jones that Sanskrit was related to Greek and Latin precipitated interest in collecting vocabularies from all of the world's languages. Catherine the Great of Russia collected masses of data in the late 18th century; Benjamin Franklin and George Washington were consulted for the second edition of her work, revised by J. S. Pallas. This project culminated in *Mithridates,* edited by J. C. Adelung and J. S. Vater between 1806 and 1817; over eight hundred pages were devoted to New World languages (Hallowell 1960:23–24).

Many American intellectuals and statesmen studied Indian languages as an avocation. This interest centered in the American Philosophical Society, founded in Philadelphia by Benjamin Franklin in 1769. Early members included Benjamin Smith Barton (1766–1815), Peter Stephen Duponceau (1760–1844), John Pickering (1777–1846), Jonathan Edwards (1745–1801), David Zeisberger (1721–1808), John Heckewelder (1743–1823), Thomas

Jefferson (1743–1826), Albert Gallatin (1761–1849), Henry Rowe Schoolcraft (1793–1864), and later John Wesley Powell (1834–1902), founder of the Bureau of American Ethnology.

The most distinguished amateur linguist was Thomas Jefferson, who collected Indian vocabularies in the years before his presidency. His *Notes on the State of Virginia,* not published until 1861, proposed collecting universal words for basic objects, to permit comparison with languages of the Old World; he believed that preservation of such materials was crucial, to allow study for all time. He also recognized the value of grammar in categorizing "the affinities of nations" (Hallowell 1960:25, 31–32). His plan to compare more than fifty Indian languages was sidetracked by the loss of his linguistic manuscripts in 1809, and by his political responsibilities. Jefferson's intellectual prestige did much to ensure that American scholars would take seriously their responsibility to describe and classify Indian languages.

During Jefferson's presidency, the Louisiana Purchase of 1803 led to the Lewis and Clark Expedition of 1804. Jefferson wrote a scientific questionnaire for the expedition; this was broadly ethnological, and vocabulary collection was emphasized. However, complete descriptions were not obtained for any tribe. The Literary and Historical Committee of the American Philosophical Society, which Jefferson headed until 1815, produced a late 18th century circular on the scope of ethnology, giving considerable attention to linguistics (Hallowell 1960:26).

Benjamin S. Barton, a professor of natural history and botany at the University of Pennsylvania, collected comparative vocabularies, mostly American Indian, and hoped to link North American languages to those of Asia. His work was dedicated to Jefferson.

John Pickering, a classical scholar and the first president of the American Oriental Society, edited the works of Williams and Eliot, making them more widely available, and collaborated on the *Mithridates* project. His 1820 "Essay on a uniform orthography for the Indian languages of North America" was widely used by missionaries to introduce an element of standardization and to permit comparison of diverse Indian languages.

Stephen Duponceau translated the works of Zeisberger and Heckewelder for the American Philosophical Society, identified Osage as a Siouan language, and attempted to link American and Siberian languages. His essay on American grammatical systems, then still seen as essentially uniform, received a prestigious prize in France in 1838. Duponceau coined the term "polysynthetic," first

used in print in 1819, to refer to the peculiar grammatical structure of American languages (Hallowell 1960:28).

Henry Rowe Schoolcraft married an Ojibwa woman and learned that language. He coined the terms "inclusive" and "exclusive" in 1834, to refer to the first person plural distinction in Amerindian languages. Schoolcraft was also influential in collecting Indian narratives and folklore (Murray 1994:32).

Albert Gallatin, Jefferson's Secretary of the Treasury and later ambassador to France and England, persuaded the Secretary of War (under whose jurisdiction Indian affairs fell), to circulate an extensive questionnaire. The results appeared in 1836 in Gallatin's *Synopsis of the Indians within the United States east of the Rocky Mountains and in the British and Russian possessions in North America.* This massive work included a map of tribal and linguistic groups.

Gallatin was the first president of the American Ethnological Society, founded in 1842, whose founders attempted to classify the Indians of the continent linguistically (Murray 1994:32–35). Gallatin established the comparative method in Amerindian linguistics, and set the boundaries of many linguistic families. His summary, recognizing 32 distinct families, was published by the Society in 1848 as an introduction to Horatio Hale's *Indians of North West America.*

The trend toward systematization of Indian linguistic and cultural boundaries continued through the work of George Gibbs for the Smithsonian Institution, founded in 1846. Gibbs's 1863 *Instructions for research relative to the ethnology and philology of America* adapted Pickering's phonetic alphabet, and proposed a 211-word vocabulary based primarily on Gallatin. This questionnaire was widely circulated; its results added substantially to the Smithsonian archives.

Joseph Henry (1797–1878), Secretary of the Smithsonian, considered anthropology crucial to reconstructing the past history of mankind. He encouraged John Wesley Powell, head of the Geological Survey of the Rocky Mountain Region, to concentrate on fieldwork, to distinguish his survey from the other three existing at the time. Powell's fieldwork with the Ute and Shoshone in the Southwest emphasized language, although he had no formal linguistic training.

In 1876, Powell received permission to use the 670 vocabularies then in the possession of the Smithsonian. A year later, he revised the Gibbs questionnaire in his *Introduction to the study of Indian languages* (issued in 1880 with slight revisions). Powell's linguistic questionnaire was used by many investigators, contributing further data to Smithsonian collections.

In 1879, Powell became head of the Bureau of (American) Ethnology, under the auspices of the Smithsonian—the first professional institution for anthropology in North America. Linguistics was crucial to Powell's mandate of mapping the diversity of native cultures. With a small permanent staff, and many amateur collaborators in direct contact with Indians, Powell produced in 1891 the first complete classification of American Indian languages into fifty-five independent stocks, later revised to fifty-eight (Darnell 1998:51–68). Minimal attention was paid to grammar, because Powell believed that American Indian grammars reflected stages of cultural evolution of the Indians, rather than historical diversity among them. Moreover, little systematic information about grammar was available to Powell and his staff. The taxonomic portion of the classification was largely the work of William Henshaw, a biologist. Albert Gatschet (the only staff member with any training in Indo-European linguistics) and John Owen Dorsey, a former missionary to the Sioux, were most directly responsible for the fieldwork; this was intended to fill gaps in basic knowledge, rather than to provide full descriptions of particular languages.

The classification was based—necessarily, given the skills of the Bureau staff—on surface inspection of vocabularies for cognates, rather than on the comparative method used in Indo-European studies. Powell was, in any case, more interested in grouping closely related tribes for practical purposes than in larger groupings which might reflect the culture history of the continent. Much of his linguistic classificatory work was supported by the United States Census, and was intended to aid in settling compatible groups together on reservations. The Bureau was supported by Congressional appropriation, and had to show practical relevance as well as scientific quality.

Powell presented no evidence for the connections he recognized; but he discussed each family, and indicated connections that might justify further study. In spite of his experience with Ute and Shoshone, Powell failed to accept the validity of the Uto-Aztecan stock, which links these languages to Nahuatl, the language of the Aztecs.

An alternative classification was proposed, also in 1891, by Daniel Garrison Brinton (1837–1899), a medical doctor associated with the American Philosophical Society (Darnell 1988). Brinton lacked the resources of Powell's Bureau for fieldwork and manuscript access; in fact, he declined to consult Smithsonian manuscripts, wanting to maintain the independence of his classification. Brinton proposed thirteen linguistic families for the continent; many of his categories are geographical units, unsupported by specific linguistic evidence. He presented very limited evidence for his classification, which was included in a larger ethnological study of the American Indian. He relied more extensively on grammar than did Powell, and correctly recognized the Uto-Aztecan stock. His effort was entirely eclipsed by the much more systematic efforts of Powell and his staff, which reflected the professionalization of American linguistics and anthropology, and left Brinton an anachronism in his own lifetime.

Brinton is best remembered for his *Library of Aboriginal American literature*—eight volumes published privately between 1882 and 1890, and largely devoted to his own library-based work with Mexican languages. Brinton's presentation of consecutive texts was an important (although largely unacknowledged) precedent for the next, professional, generation of linguists and anthropologists.

Powell was explicit that his classification was a preliminary one, intended to provide a baseline for further work by the Bureau and others. But the prestige and funding of the Bureau declined after Powell's death in 1902. In practice, moreover, the classification was perceived by American Indian linguists and anthropologists as an integrated unit. It remains the conservative baseline for Amerindian linguistics; however, the fieldwork of the next generation of anthropologists, largely trained by Franz Boas at Columbia University, resulted in a very different kind of classification of only six "super-stocks" by Edward Sapir (1888–1939), published in 1921 and revised slightly in 1929 (see Darnell 1998:199–242). Sapir's classification was directed toward reconstructing culture history, and explicitly applied the historical/comparative methods of Indo-European philology. It dominated American linguistics until the 1960s, when a more conservative standard for evidence of genetic relationship became widely held. Sapir's work on language varieties (according to, e.g., gender or social context) foreshadowed today's emphasis on these themes.

Powell encouraged description of particular Indian languages. The Bureau, along with the British Association for the Advancement of Science, supported the Northwest Coast fieldwork of Franz Boas (1858–1942) in the late

1880s and 1890s. Boas was appointed Honorary Philologist of the Bureau, and was assigned the task of preparing a *Handbook of North American Indian languages.* Three volumes of grammatical sketches appeared in 1911, 1922, and 1938. Boas depended not on the self-trained staff of the Bureau, but on his own first generation of students (Stocking 1974). The focus of American linguistics had shifted, largely due to Boas's efforts, toward detailed study of specific language based on first-hand fieldwork as a prelude to serious classificatory effort.

Americanist linguistic fieldwork sponsored by museums before World War I and by philanthropic foundations in the interwar period developed a characteristic conjunction of linguistic and anthropological methods and preoccupations (Darnell 2001:12–20). Culture was defined as a symbolic system carried in people's minds and embodied in the categories of their languages and the expressive character of their cultural texts. Boas argued that texts in Native American languages revealed "the native point of view" even after the disappearance of related cultural practices. Text collection was an urgent priority because of rapid culture change. Native speakers were enlisted as collaborators, and linguists worked with single individuals or communities over long periods. Many current efforts in language revitalization depend on the results of those textual collaborations.

[*See also* Boas, Franz; Endangered Languages; Fieldwork; History of Linguistics; North American Languages; *and* Sapir, Edward.]

BIBLIOGRAPHY

Darnell, Regna. 1988. *Daniel Garrison Brinton: The 'fearless critic' of Philadelphia.* Philadelphia: Department of Anthropology, University of Pennsylvania.

Darnell, Regna. 1998. *And along came Boas: Continuity and revolution in Americanist anthropology.* Amsterdam and Philadelphia: Benjamins.

Darnell, Regna. 2001. *Invisible genealogies: A history of Americanist anthropology.* Lincoln: University of Nebraska Press.

Hallowell, A. Irving. 1960. The beginnings of anthropology in America. In *Selected papers from The American Anthropologist, 1888–1920,* edited by Frederica de Laguna, pp. 1–90. New York: Harper and Row.

Murray, Stephen O. 1994. *Theory groups and the study of language in North America.* Amsterdam and Philadelphia: Benjamins.

Stocking, George W., Jr. 1974. The Boas plan for the study of American Indian languages. In *Studies in the history of linguistics: Traditions and paradigms,* edited by Dell Hymes, pp. 454–484. Bloomington: Indiana University Press.

REGNA DARNELL

Social and Cultural Approaches to Language

Since the early 1960s, linguists, anthropologists, sociologists, and other scholars have increasingly focused on the articulation of language and social life (see Gumperz and Hymes 1972, Goffman 1974). Spurred by questions about language variation, early studies applied dialectological methods to patterns of socially rather than regionally based variation. Such social dialectology was often framed in terms of the responsiveness of linguistic features to external determining variables, such as class, sex, and ethnicity. Labov's research (1972) on the social stratification of English in New York City exemplifies this approach, although it goes far beyond traditional dialectology in documenting the skill and artfulness of speakers.

From its beginning, such research has challenged assumptions central to both linguistic theory and traditional social analysis. Critical in its challenge to conventional contemporary theory in linguistics is the definition of the subject of linguistic inquiry itself: With what phenomena should scholars be concerned? How delimitable and autonomous is "language," and how might the analytical division between linguistic and extralinguistic phenomena be drawn most productively? Much contemporary linguistic analysis draws on a set of related premises: that a central promise of such research is the light it can shed on cognitive structures and processes; that the rigorous analysis of intralinguistic structures provides a powerful entry point for such investigations; and that the apparently extralinguistic dimensions of communicative behavior—"context"—are inconsequential for such investigations.

With its focus on socially patterned variation in linguistic performance and, increasingly, on the sophisticated analysis of variation within individual speakers' practices from situation to situation, such sociolinguistic research directly challenges the assumption that language can be treated as an autonomous system, independent of social context and of its speakers. At the least, this work expands the range of variables that shape linguistic behavior, and the variety of elements that figure in communicative practice. It also has clear methodological implications, posing basic questions about what can and must be taken into empirical account. Even the definition of a "language," a critical but often unexamined category in linguistic inquiry, is made problematic. The scholarly characterization of linguistic varieties as "standard" and "nonstandard," for example, represents social rather than linguistic judgments, reflecting the sociological characteristics of speakers rather than their cognitive or linguistic capabilities (Macaulay 1973).

Though challenging assumptions underlying linguistic theory, this early research still accepted traditional sociological categories—such as ethnic group, class, gender, or profession—as self-evident and relatively fixed. Among those whose research helped define this approach were Labov 1972, Macaulay 1977, Trudgill 1974, and Wolfram 1969. Language was seen as reflecting social variation; the dimensions along which social variation ranged were taken as given.

Other early research focused on interactional contexts, and the patterns of speakers' choice among various optional forms. Thus Brown and Gilman 1960 explored alternations between French *tu/vous,* German *du/Sie,* Russian *ty/vy* and their counterparts in various European languages, arguing that the choice of pronoun form was motivated by the dual dimensions of power and solidarity.

Concern for interactional events and speakers' options informs a range of disciplinary perspectives, in addition to that of social psychology as exemplified by Brown and Gilman's work. Ethnographic studies of language use— as seen in early writings like those in Gumperz and Hymes 1972 and Bauman and Sherzer 1974—addressed directly such questions as community values concerning language, speakers' repertoires and options, and the rhetorical strategies which might underlie patterns of language use. Thus Ervin-Tripp 1972 provided an important formal model of factors considered in selecting particular terms of address in American English. The choice of nickname, first name, title plus last name, or *Hey, you* was taken to reflect a speaker's well-calculated intentions; specific situation, relative status, and desired outcome were all taken into account.

While social dialectology stressed group membership as a determinant of broad-gauged dialectal competence, the interactional and ethnographic perspective highlighted social dimensions of particular communicative events as both constraints and incentives for more subtle choices. Both approaches, initially at least, assumed that "society" was unproblematic; yet some sociologists disagreed. Students of conversation analysis, as well as more broad-ranging theorists such as Erving Goffman, argued that social relations existed only in interaction, especially in the particulars of verbal exchange. They understood such variables as 'status' not as antecedent givens, but rather as animated in specific interactions. "Social structure" was itself an abstraction from ongoing practices; only in the organization of talk was the organization of social relationships created.

From these approaches emerged new questions. A first critical tension has to do with how large-scale or 'macro' social and economic features of groups, as studied in social dialectology, can be linked to micro phenomena such as conversations and other communicative events, as investigated by ethnographers of speaking. What kinds of information and interpretive models are necessary to fill in the gap between interactional and societal levels?

A second tension is between theories that see language use as reflecting social relationships (as in social dialectology) vs. those that consider that language plays an active *constitutive* role in creating and sustaining the social structure. The latter derives from the conversation-analysis tradition, from the emphasis on choice and creativity in the ethnography of speaking, and from anthropological interests in comparative rhetoric.

In a number of relatively egalitarian Pacific Island societies, for example, "society" above the level of the coresident family takes shape only through shared participation in various speech events (Myers and Brenneis 1984, Brenneis 1987). An understanding of what could be called 'local social organization' demands the analysis of verbal performance and of the assumptions—linguistic, rhetorical, aesthetic, and social—which underlie it. Schwartzman 1987:290 has similarly argued that, in the large-scale mental health bureaucracy that she has studied, "meetings may be *the* form that generates and maintains the organization as an entity." It is critical to note that the political dimension of these studies lies not so much in conscious, decision-oriented strategic language use as in the political events which particular shared ways of speaking make possible.

All these views emphasize a language's potential for social creativity and power; language use not only reflects social life, but also affords a means of changing it.

A third tension is that between unconscious linguistic practice and intentional choice. What do speakers take for granted about language, and what social understandings do those unrecognized premises entail? Thus, in recent studies of the rhetorical and literary underpinnings of writing in the social sciences (Nelson et al. 1987), scholarly opinion varies from those who see language as almost entirely the realm of unconscious constraint (a position strongly influenced by the work of Michel Foucault), to those who view it as primarily an arena for conscious choice.

A final tension is that between *universalist* and more *particularist* explanations. For example, Brown and Levinson 1978 posit sociolinguistic universals of politeness, expressed in a highly economical model of pan-human behavior. A restricted range of social dimensions and concerns is taken to underlie politeness practices worldwide. While the specifics of local behavior may vary considerably, such differences are seen much as surface phenomena—i.e. relatively inconsequential variations on deeper general patterns. Such theories, proposed primarily by linguists and sociologists, oppose the ethnographic emphasis on the complex particulars of individual speech communities.

Recent research has been most marked by a move from the examination of face-to-face interaction to a consideration of broader questions of political economy, colonialism, and state systems, informed throughout by a deep investment in historical analysis. Numerous works tackle the relationship between political economy and language. Hill and Hill's 1986 study of Mexicano (Nahuatl) speakers combines synchronic linguistic analysis with a detailed examination of the linguistic and social history of central Mexico. The work addresses questions of language syncretism and change, as well as of the role of linguistic practice in defining class and ethnic affiliation. Similarly, research on code-switching—such as that of Gal 1987, Heller 1989, and Woolard 1989—stresses the intimate relationship of economic and class position to decisions on language choice by bilinguals. These works effectively combine the detailed consideration of specific cases with a strong historical component.

A particularly rich area had to do with the study of linguistic ideology, the values associated with particular ways of speaking and writing. This work develops the sociolinguistic tradition of concern with prestige and stigmatization in language. Strongly influenced by such social theorists as Pierre Bourdieu, studies of linguistic ideology often conceptualize linguistic codes as symbolic capital: a real resource for social positioning and manipulation.

Research in this area, as represented in Schieffelin, Woolard, and Kroskrity 1998 and Kroskrity 2000, has provided provocative and empirically rich examinations of the intersection of politics, history, and language, both in kinds of situation that have long constituted the usual raw material of linguistic anthropological analysis, and in the premises underlying scholars' own practices of research and interpretation. Of special interest is what is not consciously ideological, but is instead taken for granted—more specifically, assumed as "fact." Such facts may derive their existence from the ways they are encoded in our largely unconscious knowledge of language, especially in "dominant discourses": the prevailing ways

of speaking which imply certain forms of social relations. Particularly important here are the works of Michel Foucault and of Mikhail Bakhtin, which suggest new ways of viewing multiple discourses and linguistically embodied resistance to dominant voices.

[*See also* Bilingualism and Multilingualism; Critical Linguistics; Discourse; Ethnography of Speaking; Linguistic Relativity; Social Variation; *and* Sociolinguistics, *article on* Sociology of Language.]

BIBLIOGRAPHY

Bauman, Richard, and Joel Sherzer, eds. 1974. *Explorations in the ethnography of speaking.* London and New York: Cambridge University Press.

Brenneis, Donald. 1987. Performing passions: Aesthetics and politics in an occasionally egalitarian community. *American Ethnologist* 14.236–250.

Brown, Penelope, and Steven C. Levinson. 1978. Universals in language usage: Politeness phenomena. In *Questions and politeness,* edited by Esther N. Goody, pp. 56–289. Cambridge and New York: Cambridge University Press. Revised as *Politeness: Some universals in language usage* Cambridge and New York: Cambridge University Press, 1987.

Brown, Roger, and Albert Gilman. 1960. The pronouns of power and solidarity. In *Style in language,* edited by Thomas A. Sebeok, pp. 253–276. Cambridge, Mass.: MIT Press.

Ervin-Tripp, Susan. 1972. On sociolinguistic rules: Alternation and co-occurrence. In Gumperz and Hymes 1972, pp. 213–250.

Gal, Susan. 1987. Codeswitching and consciousness in the European periphery. *American Ethnologist* 14.637–653.

Goffman, Erving. 1974. *Frame analysis: An essay in the organization of experience.* New York: Harper and Row.

Gumperz, John J., and Dell Hymes, eds. 1972. *Directions in sociolinguistics: The ethnography of communication.* New York: Holt, Rinehart, and Winston.

Heller, Monica, ed. 1989. *Codeswitching: Linguistic and anthropological perspectives.* The Hague: Mouton.

Hill, Jane H., and Kenneth C. Hill. 1986. *Speaking Mexicano: Dynamics of syncretic language in central Mexico.* Tucson: University of Arizona Press.

Kroskrity, Paul V., ed. 2000. *Regimes of language: Ideologies, polities, and identities.* Santa Fe, N.M.: School of American Research.

Labov, William. 1972. *Sociolinguistic patterns.* Philadelphia: University of Pennsylvania Press.

Macaulay, Ronald. 1973. Double standards. *American Anthropologist* 75.1324–1337.

Macaulay, Ronald. 1977. *Language, social class and education: A Glasgow study.* Edinburgh: Edinburgh University Press.

Myers, Fred R., and Donald Brenneis. 1984. Introduction: Language and politics in the Pacific. In *Dangerous words: Language and politics in the Pacific,* edited by Donald

Brenneis and Fred R. Myers, pp. 1–29. New York: New York University Press.

Nelson, John S., et al., eds. 1987. *The rhetoric of the human sciences: Language and argument in scholarship and public affairs.* Madison: University of Wisconsin Press.

Schieffelin, Bambi B., Kathryn A. Woolard, and Paul V. Kroskrity, eds. 1998. *Language ideologies: Practice and theory.* New York: Oxford University Press.

Schwartzman, Helen B. 1987. The significance of meetings in an American mental health center. *American Ethnologist* 14.271–294.

Trudgill, Peter. 1974. *Sociolinguistics: An introduction.* Harmondsworth, UK: Penguin.

Wolfram, Walter A. 1969. *A sociolinguistic description of Detroit Negro speech.* Washington, D.C.: Center for Applied Linguistics.

Woolard, Kathryn A. 1989. *Double talk: Bilingualism and the politics of ethnicity in Catalonia.* Stanford, Calif.: Stanford University Press.

DONALD BRENNEIS

ANTIPASSIVE. *See* Transitivity and Voice.

ANTONYMY. *See* Semantics.

APHASIA. [*This entry includes the following subentries*:
Overview
Psycholinguistic Approaches
Comparative Aphasiology]

Overview

Aphasia is a language impairment caused by focal damage to the brain of a previously normal language user. Disruptions in speech, auditory comprehension, and reading and writing processes may occur to varying degrees. A wide range of severity exists: one person with aphasia may experience only mild word-finding problems, while another loses nearly all ability to use or comprehend language.

Language functions are asymmetrically represented in the brain. Virtually all right-handed persons and a majority of left-handers are believed to have morphosyntactic, semantic, and phonological aspects of language lateralized to the left cerebral hemisphere. Rhythmic aspects of language—prosody and intonation—are typically lateralized to the right hemisphere.

1. The classical neuroanatomical model. In 1861, Pierre Paul Broca, a French surgeon, published a paper in which he described a patient with a severe speech deficit that prevented him from producing anything but the single syllable *tan*. Though he could not produce other words, he could change the intonation of this single utterance; his comprehension of spoken language was well preserved. When this patient died, Broca examined the brain and discovered a lesion involving the inferior frontal gyrus of the left hemisphere. From this and studies of similar patients, Broca suggested that the inferior frontal gyrus was responsible for the articulation of speech. This suggestion marked the first time that a cognitive function was related to a cortical area.

The set of symptoms that came to be called "Broca's aphasia" is characterized by slow, labored articulation of agrammatic speech. Comprehension of simple grammatical structures is generally spared, relative to the severity of the production deficit. The lesion site responsible for this pattern of symptoms was originally thought to be in the left inferior frontal lobe ("Broca's area"), adjacent to the area of the motor cortex that controls the movement of the tongue, lips, jaw, and vocal folds.

The classical neuroanatomical model of language was further developed by Carl Wernicke, a young German neurologist who in 1874 published a paper in which he described a type of aphasic language disturbance—and a related neuroanatomical site of damage—entirely different from those of Broca's patients. The type subsequently called "Wernicke's aphasia" is characterized by well-articulated, fluent speech that lacks appropriate content. Such speech is marked by *paraphasias*, the incorrect selection or execution of words. Wernicke noted that patients with these kinds of production difficulties also suffered from a disruption in the ability to comprehend speech. The lesion responsible for this set of symptoms was thought to be situated in a section of the posterior superior temporal lobe ("Wernicke's area"), immediately adjacent to the primary auditory cortex, which is not affected.

Wernicke argued that damage to different brain regions caused different patterns of aphasic disturbance; this implied that complex language functions, such as "comprehension," could be strictly localized to particular neural tissue. Perhaps more important, Wernicke's descriptions were accompanied by the outline of a formal model of the neuroanatomical organization of language. This model not only defined specific brain "centers" as responsible for the execution of basic language functions, but also specified that aphasias could result from lesions to the connections *between* these centers. This "connectionist" model forms the basis of the classical neuroanatomical approach that still guides theories of language-brain relationships today.

In 1965, the American neurologist Norman Geschwind elaborated on Wernicke's model to account for a variety of disturbances to higher cortical functions in addition to language. His approach enhanced Wernicke's by specifying several anatomical regions and the fiber tracts that connect them. Lesions to these tracts would result in specialized *disconnection* syndromes with their own unique sets of symptoms.

The best-known example of a neuroanatomical connection between language centers within the Wernicke-Geschwind model is the *arcuate fasciculus*, a bundle of fibers connecting the centers for the auditory analysis of speech (Wernicke's area) to the center for motor speech programming (Broca's area). According to the model, when these connections are damaged, the resulting pattern of symptoms is one in which speech is fluent (Broca's area intact), and comprehension is normal (Wernicke's area intact), but patients have difficulty repeating words that are spoken to them. This pattern of symptoms was called *conduction aphasia* to express the view that it represents a failure of transmission, or "conduction," from Wernicke's area, where incoming speech sounds are interpreted, to Broca's area, where the motor programs required for production are prepared.

2. Modern neuroanatomical approaches. Using modern developments in technology, scientists have begun to test this classical model. By analyzing the lesions of aphasic patients using structural neuroimaging and incorporating electrocortical stimulation and functional neuroimaging data into the model, we now accept that language involves many more cortical regions than just Wernicke's and Broca's areas. We also know that these newfound areas are extensively networked, and that the simple serial connectionist model is no longer sufficient to explain language comprehension and generation. Researchers have moved away from the modular approach, which held that language functions independently within the brain. Instead, we see that memory, attention, perception, and other nonlinguistic cognitive skills play a vital role in the language system.

Our understanding of speech production disorders has changed as a result of modern studies of cortical regions outside of Broca's area. For example, the insula, a small piece of neocortex hidden beneath the intersection of the frontal, parietal, and temporal lobes, has been linked to the ability to plan and coordinate the movements necessary for the articulation of speech (Dronkers 1996). Recent neuroimaging studies have also shown activation in the insula when patients do tasks requiring the articulation of single words, such as repetition, reading aloud, naming pictures, and word generation.

Studies have also confirmed the involvement of other cortical regions in speech production. The supplementary motor area plays a role in the initiation of sequential speech movements; the basal ganglia and the cerebellum help to modify pitch, loudness, and rate; and the primary motor face cortex and pre-motor cortex are involved in the execution of articulatory movements. Just as speech production involves more cortex than Broca's area alone, comprehension of the lexical and semantic aspects of language requires more than just Wernicke's area in the left temporal lobe. Sentence comprehension, for example, appears to utilize the anterior superior temporal gyrus, and echoic memory relies on the posterior superior temporal gyrus.

We now also accept that language extends beyond the left hemisphere. The melody of language—intonation and prosody—relies on the right hemisphere cortex for processing, as do other pragmatic aspects of language, such as the ability to infer humor or to engage appropriately in conversation. Patients with right hemisphere lesions may be unable properly to sequence their thoughts verbally. They are frequently hyperloquacious (too talkative) and may have difficulty staying on topic. With the advent of modern technology and the sophistication of linguistic analysis, the classic neuroanatomic model for language has been refined and revised to include much more cortex, within both the left and right hemispheres.

3. Linguistic and psycholinguistic approaches to aphasia. Historically, neurologists have used structure-function relationships represented by aphasia disorders to address basic neurological questions, similarly, linguists and psycholinguists have attempted to use performance data from aphasic patients to assess theories of language representation and processing. Much of this work has been carried out since the middle of the 20th century, perhaps stimulated by the assertion of Jakobson 1956 that linguistics was the proper discipline in which to study aphasia, since it is, after all, a disorder of language.

Subsequent linguistically oriented investigations of

aphasia were motivated by the belief that the forms that aphasia can take are constrained by the functional organization of the normal language system. Thus, the various patterns of language impairment that occur in aphasia should be explainable within the framework of existing linguistic theories. For example, patients with Broca's aphasia appear to have difficulty with sentence structures (perhaps implicating syntactic processing), whereas those with Wernicke's aphasia may have difficulty, even at the single-word level, with word meaning (semantics) or sound structure (phonology). A corollary to this notion was later made explicit in the form of an argument that the development of linguistic theories and psycholinguistic processing models could themselves be informed and constrained by the existence of particular forms of aphasic disorders (see the chapters on lexical, phonological and sentence processing in Sarno 1998).

Linguistic and psycholinguistic investigations of aphasia since Jakobson's day have focused on the apparently contrasting language disorders represented by Broca's and Wernicke's aphasias. Two major and related influences have shaped these investigations. The first is methodological: studies of aphasia, which historically were dominated by the case-study methods of neurology, have increasingly adopted the experimental approach of the emerging field of psycholinguistics. In contrast to the purely descriptive study of the types of language impairments that can occur, special tests have been designed as explicit assessments of the integrity of different language functions. Testing is carried out on groups of patients thought to be homogeneous (e.g. Broca's or Wernicke's aphasics), and results are subjected to statistical analysis. These methods, pioneered by Harold Goodglass and his colleagues at the Boston University Aphasia Research Center, have dominated the field of aphasia research in the United States and in much of Europe for decades (see Goodglass 1993).

The second major influence on linguistic and psycholinguistic investigations of aphasia was the development and specification of the theory of generative transformational grammar (Chomsky 1957). Although there had been a few earlier attempts to explain particular aphasic deficits by reference to specific aspects of theory, the influence of Chomsky's theory on aphasia research has been more general. Examinations of aphasic deficits have been motivated by the view that language is organized as a set of mental processes that can be investigated experimentally. The approach adopted was that language involves a set of independent components (e.g. phonology,

semantics, and syntax) that interact in the performance of language tasks such as comprehending and producing sentences. The field of psycholinguistics generally has been dominated by attempts to test these notions, and psycholinguistic investigations of aphasia have been similarly influenced.

Several avenues of aphasia research continue to be influenced by theoretical linguistics, such as the invocation of Trace Deletion hypothesis in accounting for the comprehension pattern found among some Broca's aphasic patients. Others are motivated by theories of processing limitations, such as decreased processing speed, or a limited capacity for handling multiple linguistic manipulations (see chapters in Stemmer and Whitaker 1998). The study of aphasia has intrigued linguists to this day because it provides a means by which language theory can be studied and tested.

4. The syndrome approach. The connectionist model led to the development of seven major aphasia syndromes, which are traditionally defined by impairments in certain language skills: fluency, auditory comprehension, repetition, and naming. The mildest form of aphasia, *anomia*, is characterized by word-finding problems, while the most severe syndrome, *global aphasia*, results in profound deficits in all aspects of language. It is marked by severe nonfluent output, near-total disruption in auditory comprehension, and an inability to repeat spoken words.

Individuals with *Wernicke's aphasia* experience difficulty matching words they hear to their meanings. They may understand very little, as even auditory comprehension of single words may be impaired. Although their speech is fluent and maintains appropriate prosody and intonation, it often lacks the content words that are necessary to convey ideas to a listener. They may use *semantic paraphasias*, substituting a related word for a target word (e.g. *table* for *chair*). *Neologisms*, or nonsense words, may also occur. The empty speech and disturbed comprehension of Wernicke's aphasia have been attributed to a specific disorder of the semantic component of the language system. The speech characteristics that support this analysis are illustrated by relatively sparse content and incorrect word usage in the following transcription of a Wernicke's aphasic patient telling the story of Cinderella:

(1)   *The girl the ladies wh the girl and two little girls hand they have on the hair and all that jazz uh she two the two girls she said uh she dressing their hair dress their*

*hair I think and dress your hair and beautiful dress
. . . nose and big mouth not you know but she is very
pretty.* (Time: 110 seconds.)

Some individuals with Wernicke's aphasia also produce
phonemic paraphasic errors, substituting or transposing
sounds in words, (e.g. *fetter* for *letter*). Experimental
study of the disordered productions of these patients has
suggested that they have a deficit at the level of selecting
phonemic sequences for output, rather than in achieving
a correct phonetic execution.

In contrast to Wernicke's aphasia, individuals with
Broca's aphasia typically have slow, effortful speech that
may lack grammatical markers. The words they choose,
however, may be enough to convey meaning to a listener.
Broca's aphasic patients experience deficits in articulatory agility, word-finding, and repetition. Motor speech
impairments such as dysarthria and apraxia frequently
coexist with Broca's aphasia. Patients can participate in
conversation through their understanding of single words
and short phrases, but they are sometimes impaired in
the comprehension of complex grammatical structures.
Observations of difficulty in production and comprehension of syntactic elements led to the hypothesis that the
symptoms found in Broca's aphasia represent a disruption
of syntactic aspects of language, but more recent work
has shown that there are many exceptions that undermine
this viewpoint.

Severe forms of Broca's aphasia may result in such
profound language production deficits that speech is
limited to recurring utterances—for example, a single
word or phrase repeated again and again. More often,
however, the major content of the patient's speech may
be apparent, but the syntactic elements that provide
sentence structure (the grammatical morphemes) are
missing, as in the following transcription of a Broca's
aphasic patient telling the Cinderella story:

(2)   *One time . . . (8 sec) the girl . . . (13 sec) workin' workin'
      . . . (20 sec) two two two three two . . . (4 sec) two
      mother and two sister . . . (6 sec) ok . . . (21 sec) the
      man uh the prince prince.* (Time: 136 seconds.)

Conduction aphasia, another major aphasia syndrome,
is characterized by fluent speech and a striking deficit in
the ability to repeat phrases and sentences. Comprehension is relatively intact, though not entirely spared, and
phonemic paraphasias are common. The syndrome of
transcortical motor aphasia is generally characterized by
nonfluent speech similar to that of a Broca's patient.

Patients often have difficulty initiating conversation and,
in acute cases, may be mute. The remarkable feature of
this aphasia type is the preserved ability accurately to
repeat phrases and sentences, despite severely restricted
spontaneous output. In contrast to transcortical motor
aphasia, individuals with *transcortical sensory aphasia*
typically have fluent speech but suffer from impaired
comprehension, similar to that seen in Wernicke's aphasia. Patients converse in a well-articulated, sometimes
overly fluent manner, with frequent paraphasias. They
have difficulty with confrontation naming tasks, but they
have an uncanny ability to repeat not just single words
but long, complex sentences. They may even make grammatical corrections to sentences they do not understand.

5. Criticisms of the "syndrome approach." The syndrome approach has not been without problems. First, it
is not always possible to assign an aphasic patient to one
of the classical syndromes; by some estimates, only about
half of all aphasic patients can be classified. Furthermore,
different assessment tools classify patients differently.
For example, the definition of "fluency" varies between
aphasia tests, so that an aphasic patient may fall into
different classifications depending on which test was
given. More important, the symptoms that make up
aphasia syndromes are not unique to a single syndrome.
A patient with lexical-semantic deficits might have Wernicke's, Broca's, global, or any other type of aphasia,
depending on the accompanying symptoms. Careful
study of individual patients has revealed that the specific
symptoms may occur in many different types of aphasia.

By focusing on syndromes, we often overlook important individual variations within aphasia types. Different
patients diagnosed with the same type of aphasia may
present with somewhat different symptoms. For example,
one patient with Broca's aphasia may be able to produce
single words, but another may be restricted to single
recurring words or syllables. For this reason, moreover,
use of the syndrome approach has not been helpful in
refining and building neuroanatomical models of language. Past attempts to localize the aphasias have failed,
partly because aphasia syndromes are collections of many
individual deficits that occur in language breakdown. A
more successful approach has been to study and localize
symptoms, rather than syndromes that occur in many
different aphasia types.

Furthermore, many unusual language deficits (e.g. optic
aphasia or category-specific naming deficits) cannot be
addressed using the traditional syndrome approach, yet
studies of these rare disorders, using single-case-study
methods, have been tremendously productive in helping

to understand the organization of language in the brain. For example, Elizabeth Warrington and her colleagues at the National Hospital in London have published a series of case reports documenting the occurrence of remarkably selective disruption or loss of semantic information (e.g. Warrington and Shallice 1984). Individual patients have been described in whom brain damage has very selectively affected the ability to comprehend or produce words from specific semantic categories, suggesting that distinctions such as "concrete vs. abstract" or "animate vs. inanimate" are honored in the cerebral organization of semantic function.

6. Therapeutic approaches to aphasia. During the 25 years or so that these linguistically and psycholinguistically motivated investigations of aphasia have been carried out, the development of therapies directed at improving language functions in aphasic patients has proceeded largely independently. Approaches to treatment have not usually adopted a componential view of language, and psycholinguistic researchers have not, in general, considered the rich source of information provided by patients' responses to particular interventions.

Speech and language pathologists, neurologists, and psychologists first began to offer aphasia rehabilitation to the many head-injured soldiers returning from the battlefields of World War II. Long-standing traditional methods of treating aphasia, still used by speech and language therapists today, are based largely on the theoretical view that aphasia is caused by impairments to a unitary language system. This view, put forth most compellingly by Schuell et al. 1965, holds that in persons with aphasia, all language modalities are affected, though to varying degrees. The "stimulation" approach to aphasia therapy, engendered by this view, involves stimulating impaired language functions—auditory comprehension, speech, and so on—as a means of recovering skills that are not lost but rather *interrupted* by brain injury.

The basic premise of the theory behind Schuell's approach—that language is an undifferentiated system—is in direct contrast to the componential view assumed by proponents of the psycholinguistic approach. This essential difference of opinion about the nature of language, and hence about the nature of aphasia, is probably responsible for the fact that aphasia research motivated by linguistic and psycholinguistic considerations has, until recently, had little impact on the development of aphasia therapies, and vice versa.

This situation has changed in recent years with the development of language-oriented therapies, which treat deficits to specific language components such as syntax.

Moreover, researchers interested in aphasia and related disorders have begun systematically testing hypotheses about the nature of patients' deficits by introducing training focused on carefully circumscribed functions. This trend has been most evident among "cognitive neuropsychologists" in Great Britain, who rely on detailed models of cognitive/linguistic function to provide a basis for clinical diagnosis and treatment. This model-oriented approach serves a dual purpose: the components of the model provide a basis for predicting the response to a specific intervention; and the response to intervention yields empirical evidence regarding the functional role of the target component in the model. This methodology is an emerging technique that can be used to relate the behavior of aphasic patients in more detail to models of normal language processing.

[*See also* Agrammatism; Alexia and Agraphia; Anomia; Apraxia; Neurolinguistics; Paragrammatism; Psycholinguistics; *and* Evolutional Language.]

BIBLIOGRAPHY

Broca, Pierre Paul. 1861. Remarques sur le siège de la faculté du langage articulé, suivies d'une observation d'aphémie (perte de la parole). *Bulletins de la Société d'anatomie (Paris)*, ser. 2, 6. 330–357.

Chomsky, Noam. 1957. *Syntactic structures*. The Hague: Mouton.

Dronkers, Nina F. 1996. A new brain region for coordinating speech articulation. *Nature* 384.159–161.

Geschwind, Norman. 1965. Disconnexion syndromes in animals and man. *Brain* 88.237–294.

Goodglass, Harold. 1993. *Understanding aphasia*. San Diego, Calif.: Academic Press.

Jakobson, Roman 1956. Two types of language and two types of aphasic disturbance. In *Fundamentals of language*, edited by Roman Jakobson and Morris Halle. The Hague: Mouton.

Sarno, M. T., ed. 1998. *Acquired aphasia*. 3rd ed. San Diego, Calif.: Academic Press.

Schuell, H., J. J. Jenkins, and E. Jimenez-Pabon. 1965. *Aphasia in adults*. New York: Harper and Row.

Stemmer, B., and H. A. Whitaker, eds. 1998. *Handbook of neurolinguistics*. San Diego, Calif.: Academic Press.

Warrington, E. K., and T. Shallice. 1984. Category specific semantic impairments. *Brain* 102.43–63.

Wernicke, C. 1874. *Der aphasische Symptomencomplex*. Breslau: Kohn and Weigert.

NINA DRONKERS AND RITA SLOAN BERNDT

Psycholinguistic Approaches

The primary goal of the field of neurolinguistics is to understand and explicate the neurological bases of lan-

TABLE 1. *Various Psycholinguistic Approaches to the Study of Aphasia*

Research Paper	Paradigm Used	Issue Investigated
Baker et al. 1981	Auditory discrimination; auditory/visual cross-modal matching	Relation between phonological and semantic factors in word recognition
Blumstein et al. 1980	Reading of words and acoustic analysis	Acoustic patterns of production of stop consonants
Caplan et al. 1985	Manipulation of objects, given auditorily presented sentences	Comprehension of syntactic structures of various types and complexity
Caplan and Waters 1999	Dual-task paradigm: auditory sentence processing with simultaneous cursor tracking	Resource allocation and the role of working memory in language comprehension
Caramazza and Zurif 1976	Picture pointing, given auditorily presented sentences	Syntactic and semantic factors influencing sentence comprehension
Linebarger et al. 1983	Grammaticality judgments to auditorily presented sentences	Exploration of patients' awareness of grammaticality across different types of morphological/syntactic violations
Milberg and Blumstein 1981	Lexical decision to visually presented words	Exploration of semantic structure of the lexicon
Saffran et al. 1989	Quantitative production analysis of narrative production	Syntactic properties of agrammatism in production
Swinney et al. 1989	Cross-modal lexical decision	Investigation of semantic context effects on lexical access
Tyler 1985	Auditory word monitoring	Investigation of syntactic and pragmatic factors influencing on-line sentence processing
Zurif et al. 1993	Cross-modal lexical decision	On-line syntactic parsing (gap-filling)

guage and speech, and to characterize the mechanisms and processes involved in language use. The study of neurolinguistics is broad-based; it includes language and speech impairments in the adult aphasias and in children, as well as reading disabilities and the lateralization of function as it relates to language and speech processing.

Psycholinguistic approaches to neurolinguistics provide a theoretical, as well as methodological, basis for the study of language and the brain. The field of psycholinguistics uses behavioral measures of normal adults and children to infer the nature of the processes and mechanisms used in language and speech. Applied to neurolinguistics, it provides a method of exploring how language and speech may change consequent to neurological damage. Exploring the differential patterns of breakdown in the language system provides a "window" into the organizational principles and processes involved in normal language, as well as insight into the neurological instantiation of language and speech (cf. Caplan 1987).

The area of study within neurolinguistics that has been investigated most extensively using psycholinguistic techniques is that of the adult aphasias. The language deficits of adult patients reflect the impairment of language and cognitive systems that were normal before injury or disease occurred. As a consequence, it is possible to explore how organic brain disease affects the functioning of a normally developed system. Many dif-

ferent research methodologies have been used to investigate the speech and language deficits of aphasic patients; Table 1 gives some examples of the research paradigms employed, and the particular questions explored.

Psycholinguistic investigations of aphasia, like psycholinguistic research generally, have been guided by consideration of the structural levels of the linguistic grammar—phonetics, phonology, syntax, semantics, and pragmatics or discourse. It has been the aim of this research to determine whether aphasic deficits reflect impairments at a particular level of representation—and within a particular level, whether structural linguistic principles can explain the language pattern—or whether language deficits reflect impairments in the processes involved in accessing or utlizing linguistic representations. In the former case, the structure of the linguistic representation itself is affected. In the latter, processing deficits affect access to the components of the grammar, or within individual components of the grammar; however, the linguistic representations themselves remain intact. Recent years have witnessed a growing consensus supporting processing deficit accounts of aphasia.

1. Phonetic/phonological deficits in aphasia. Nearly all aphasics, regardless of their clinical type, manifest some phonological deficits in speech output. These impairments may emerge, to varying degrees, in their spontaneous speech, in repetition, in reading, and even in naming objects. Patterns in phonological errors are consistent with the view that the underlying phonological system of the patient is still governed by structural principles intrinsic to the phonology of language, as well as to the phonology of the particular language (Sarno 1998). Universal principles related to distinctive feature theory, and to metrical phonology, govern the patterns of errors produced by patients. At the same time, the phonotactics of the patient's language is maintained. The stability of these patterns is evidenced by their occurrence in many different languages, including English, Turkish, French, German, Russian, and Finnish.

Although most aphasics display a phonological output disorder, there exists a select group of patients for whom production deficits are also phonetic in nature. These patients include, but are not limited to, Broca's aphasics, or patients with anterior brain damage (cf. Ryalls 1987). Acoustic analyses of the speech production of these patients, as well as physiological studies, reveal that the patients display difficulties in the timing of articulatory movements—especially in the timing of two independent articulators, e.g., the release of a closure and the onset of vocal cord vibration for the production of voiced and voiceless stop consonants. The basis of the phonetic disorder seems to reflect an inability to implement particular types of articulatory gestures or articulatory parameters, rather than a failure to instantiate particular phonetic features. Recent evidence suggests that these individuals have impairments in other aspects of temporal control that affect speech timing at the level of syllables, words, and sentences as well.

The perception of speech is also affected in aphasic patients. Most research has focused on the extent to which deficits in speech perception underlie, or contribute to, those in auditory comprehension. Patients have difficulty in labeling the sounds of speech, and in discriminating phonetically similar sound segments; but they seem to be able to perceive the acoustic dimensions relating to the phonetic categories of speech. Impairments in speech perception manifest themselves most clearly when the categories of speech are used in relation to higher-order language processing, especially as speech relates to lexical processing (cf. Sarno 1998). For instance, Blumstein et al. 1994 demonstrated that Wernicke's aphasic patients did not exhibit normal patterns of lexical status effects on phonetic identification, suggesting that they were unable to recruit lexical information to assist in processing ambiguous speech input. In contrast, Broca's aphasic patients seemed to rely to a greater extent than normal on lexical information in speech perception.

2. Lexical deficits in aphasia. Aphasic patients often have difficulties in naming objects and actions, and also display impairments in their comprehension. What is the nature of such deficits—and do they have a common basis? Two explanatory bases have been suggested. One is that the patients have an impairment at the level of lexical representation, and this affects the lexical or semantic structure of lexical entries. Evidence in support of this view is that aphasic patients, in particular Wernicke's aphasics, have difficulty in classifying words on the basis of their semantic relationships, or in determining whether two semantically related words "go together." More recent experimental paradigms have reduced support for this representational deficit perspective, as we will see.

The alternate view is that patients display a processing deficit, which affects access to lexical representations which are themselves intact. Evidence for this view comes from studies that investigate the on-line processing of words. Subjects may be asked to respond to lexical items, either by making a lexical decision about a word by naming aloud a visually presented target, or by monitoring for a target in an auditorily presented utterance. The time-course and pattern of response is used to infer whether the structure of the lexicon, or access to it, is affected. A commonly used methodology explores lexical "priming," or the influence of a word (or a series of words) on another. The relationship between the prime and target (whether formal or semantic) is systematically manipulated to assess links among the lexical items and the preservation of processing routines for lexical access. Controlling other task variables—such as the interval between prime and target, or the proportion of related trials—can provide insights into the impairment or sparing of the processing routines that contribute to word recognition.

In terms of lexical production, paradigms include picture and object naming tasks, with and without phonological and/or semantic cueing, as well as analysis of spontaneous production errors. The latter types of analyses may provide insights into the nature of lexical competition and the internal organization of the lexicon (e.g., in terms of phonological or orthographic neighbors, semantic categories, or syntactic categories).

A substantial amount of research has supported the view that lexical form and lexical semantics are stored and accessed independently, and thus may be selectively impaired. Investigations using on-line processing paradigms such as priming, and comparisons to off-line tasks such as comprehension or category judgments, have indicated that lexical representations and their organization are relatively intact. What seem to be impaired are the various processes involved in lexical access and retrieval or in the integration of lexical information into higher-order units.

3. Syntactic deficits in aphasia are common in both production and comprehension by aphasic patients. Many Broca's aphasics display productive agrammatism; in this deficit, grammatical markers and grammatical words, e.g. *is* or *have*, are selectively affected. Grammatical markers tend to be replaced; this usually reflects a reduction of the markedness of the particular inflectional ending. Grammatical markers are also often omitted. These substitutions and omissions, however, seem to obey certain constraints, since the patient consistently produces words allowable in the language. In addition, the full range of syntactic structures is severely restricted: embedded sentences, complementizers, and relative clauses rarely occur. In the most severe cases, subjects are restricted to the production of simple noun phrases or simple verb phrases. The failure of patients to produce correct syntactic structures does not seem to reflect a loss of the conceptual basis of these structures; patients often use alternative strategies to produce similar meanings, e.g. 'very happy' → *happy, happy*. Recently, careful methods have been developed for the analysis of language samples to determine the specific syntactic and morphological constructions used by aphasic patients in spontaneous speech or narrative discourse (e.g. Rochon et al. 2000). Although the analyses were originally designed for English, the principles may be applied cross-linguistically.

Interestingly, similar underlying agrammatic patterns have been shown to emerge across different languages, although the surface manifestations of agrammatic language profiles differ depending on how the language in question implements grammatical relations. In particular, we can see striking differences in the nature of the language output, depending on whether the typology of the language is analytic (as in Chinese, where grammar is realized by individual words with the use of few syntactic markings on words to convey meaning) or agglutinative (such as Turkish, where the grammar uses syntactic endings and infixes attached to word stems to convey meanings). Perhaps the single most influential factor affecting output is the amount of information conveyed by the particular grammatical structure or the grammatical ending in that language. Nonetheless, despite these differences across languages, there is a set of common features that patients with agrammatism share. Thus, it appears that the grammatical structure of human language is served by similar neural substrates, despite differences in the surface instantiations of such structure.

Research results indicate that agrammatic aphasics often display, in addition, comprehension deficits that are syntactic in nature. Patients display impairments in processing grammatical markers and function words—that is, closed-class words. In addition, they show impairments in the comprehension of syntactic structures such as embedded subject and object relatives, object cleft sentences, and reversible passive sentences.

There is debate in the literature concerning the underlying bases of such impairments. One view is that the difficulty is a central one, reflecting an impairment at a particular linguistic level of representation. However, there is little agreement about whether the level of representation affected is primarily phonological, lexical, or syntactic. Another view is that agrammatism reflects an impairment in processing, rather than in structure. Evidence in support of this view is that deficits emerge in some experimental paradigms, and not in others. For instance, whereas patients may exhibit asyntactic comprehension in picture identification or object manipulation tasks, they may be capable of rendering grammaticality judgments (Linebarger et al. 1983) and may (or may not) be sensitive to ungrammaticality and variations in syntactic structure in on-line sentence processing tasks, as indicated by reaction time (RT) measures (e.g. Baum 1988, Blumstein et al. 1998, Zurif et al. 1993). This suggests that the routines for accessing or processing structures are impaired, rather than the structures themselves.

In fact, various versions of processing resource limitation accounts of aphasia have been proposed in recent years (e.g. McNeil et al. 1991; see also references under "Agrammatism"). Such accounts have hypothesized constraints on the availability of computational space and/or speed, or impairments in the allocation of resources as underlying explanations of aphasic sentence processing deficits. An additional issue that remains unresolved is the extent to which such processing resources form part of a shared pool associated with language or broader cognitive domains, or are tied to specific linguistic components. In an effort to answer these questions, investigators have begun to utilize dual-task paradigms with aphasic patients (wherein two tasks are performed simultaneously, presumably competing for resources).

Grammatical deficits are also found in other aphasic patients. Wernicke's aphasics show paragrammatism, i.e., the juxtaposition of inappropriate grammatical markers (*I saw him to the boy*), as well as a restricted use of complex grammatical structures. In addition, they show syntactic deficits in comprehension. These patterns of impairment are often similar to those found in Broca's aphasics. However, it remains unclear whether these patterns reflect similar deficits in the two groups.

4. Discourse deficits in aphasia. Impairments in the production and comprehension of discourse have only recently been investigated in aphasic patients; more research on discourse processing has been conducted with other neurologically impaired populations, such as individuals with right hemisphere damage (RHD) or dementia of the Alzheimer type (DAT). Discourse production has been analyzed at both the macro-structure and micro-structure levels. Investigations have focused on the number and types of information units communicated, as well as the presence (or absence) of cohesive devices such as pronouns and anaphors (e.g. Bloom et al. 1995). Aphasic patients have been found to exhibit a reduction in the quantity of information communicated, as well as its informativeness. In contrast, principles of conversational interaction, including topic maintenance, seem to be preserved. Deficits in the *comprehension* of discourse have also been reported, particularly in the processing of anaphoric reference (e.g. Joanette and Brownell 1990; see also Leonard et al. 1997 for on-line studies with RHD patients).

5. Summary. Psycholinguistic investigations of aphasic patients suggest that language is independent of cognition, and that it is organized into quasi-autonomous subsystems of kinds similar to the components of a linguistic grammar. Aphasic impairments affect all levels of linguistic function, to a greater or lesser extent; within each component of the grammar, similar hierarchies of breakdown emerge across all aphasic patients. It is yet to be determined whether these impairments reflect deficits to similar or different underlying mechanisms and what specific mechanisms may be impaired in processing linguistic representations. Combining behavioral psycholinguistic approaches with passive and active neuroimaging

and activation techniques holds great promise for increasing our understanding of language-brain relationships.

[*See also* Neurolinguistics *and* Psycholinguistics.]

BIBLIOGRAPHY

Baker, Errol, et al. 1981. Interaction between phonological and semantic factors in auditory comprehension. *Neuropsychologia* 19.1–15.

Baum, Shari R. 1988. Syntactic processing in agrammatism: Evidence from lexical decision and grammaticality judgement tasks. *Aphasiology* 2.117–136.

Bloom, Ronald, et al. 1995. An examination of coherence and cohesion in aphasia. *Brain and Language* 51.206–209.

Blumstein, Sheila E., et al. 1980. Production deficits in aphasia: A voice-onset time analysis. *Brain and Language* 9.153–170.

Blumstein, Sheila E., et al. 1994. The role of lexical status on the phonetic categorization of speech in aphasia. *Brain and Language* 46.181–197.

Blumstein, Sheila E., et al. 1998. On-line processing of filler-gap constructions in aphasia. *Brain and Language* 61.149–168.

Caplan, David. 1987. *Neurolinguistics and linguistic aphasiology: An introduction.* Cambridge and New York: Cambridge University Press.

Caplan, David, et al. 1985. Syntactic determinants of sentence comprehension in aphasia. *Cognition* 21.117–175.

Caplan, David, and Gloria S. Waters. 1999. Verbal working memory and sentence comprehension. *Behavioral and Brain Sciences* 22.77–126.

Caramazza, Alfonso, and Edgar B. Zurif. 1976. Dissociation of algorithmic and heuristic processes in language comprehension: Evidence from aphasia. *Brain and Language* 3.572–582.

Joanette, Yves, and Hiram Brownell. 1990. *Discourse ability and brain damage: Theoretical and empirical perspectives.* New York: Springer.

Leonard, Carol, et al. 1997. The use of contextual information related to general world knowledge by right brain-damaged individuals in pronoun resolution. *Brain and Language* 57.343–359.

Linebarger, Marcia C., et al. 1983. Sensitivity to grammatical structure in so-called agrammatic aphasics. *Cognition* 13.361–392.

McNeil, Malcolm, et al. 1991. Toward the integration of resource allocation into a general theory of aphasia. In *Clinical aphasiology*, pp. 21–39, vol. 20, edited by T. E. Prescott. Austin, Tex.: Pro-Ed.

Milberg, William, and Sheila E. Blumstein. 1981. Lexical decision and aphasia: Evidence for semantic processing. *Brain and Language* 14.371–385.

Rochon, Elizabeth, et al. 2000. Quantitative analysis of aphasic sentence production: Further development and new data. *Brain and Language* 72.193–218.

Ryalls, John H., ed. 1987. *Phonetic approaches to speech production in aphasia and related disorders*. Boston: Little, Brown.

Saffran, Eleanor, et al. 1989. The quantitative analysis of agrammatic production: Procedure and data. *Brain and Language* 37.440–479.

Sarno, Martha Taylor, ed. 1998. *Acquired aphasia*. 3d ed. New York: Academic Press.

Swinney, David, et al. 1989. The effects of focal brain damage on sentence processing: An examination of the neurological organization of a mental module. *Journal of Cognitive Neuroscience* 1.25–37.

Tyler, Loraine K. 1985. Real-time comprehension processes in agrammatism: A case study. *Brain and Language* 26.259–275.

Waters, Gloria S., and David Caplan. 1996. The capacity theory of sentence comprehension: Critique of Just and Carpenter (1992). *Psychological Review* 103.761–772.

Zurif, Edgar B., et al. 1972. Grammatical judgments of agrammatic aphasics. *Neuropsychologia* 10.405–418.

Zurif, Edgar B., et al. 1993. An on-line analysis of syntactic processing in Broca's and Wernicke's aphasia. *Brain and Language* 45.448–464.

SHARI R. BAUM AND SHEILA E. BLUMSTEIN

Comparative Aphasiology

This article highlights some understandings of aphasic symptoms that depend critically on cross-linguistic comparison. Comparative aphasiology assumes that the best description of a symptom is one that generalizes across languages. The consequences of this assumption are illustrated by the following shift in a classical description. A symptom of agrammatic Broca's aphasia, based on French, English, and German, used to be described as "the omission of function words and inflectional endings." Theoretical accounts therefore attempted to unify these two types of grammatical morphemes—for example, by saying that less informative morphemes were omitted to reduce articulatory effort, or because they were stem-external parts of the phonological word. However, it is now known that endings are not omitted in languages where "unmarked" content word forms bear inflections (e.g. Finnish, Icelandic, or Italian). Agrammatic speakers of these languages instead tend to substitute frequent forms of a word, such as the infinitive or 3rd person present singular of a verb, or the nominative singular of a noun. The description of agrammatic Broca's aphasia has therefore been revised as involving "the omission of functors, and the substitution of more frequent inflected forms of a word for less frequent ones." (In languages where the most frequent forms are uninflected, this substitution *appears* to be omission of endings.) Theories that unified the treatment of functors and grammatical endings as "omissions," such as the least-effort theory, had to be discarded in favor of ones that describe these speakers as making errors in selecting forms from an inflectional paradigm (Menn and Obler 1990).

1. Persistence of language-particular patterns in aphasia. A widely used comprehension task requires subjects to manipulate small objects to act out word strings consisting of two concrete nouns (plus definite articles, if the language uses them) with an action verb. The nouns and the verb are given in all orders (e.g., *The cow the pencils kick; The pencils kick the cow*). Preferences in interpreting these strings, which are often ungrammatical or bizarre, differ across languages; people with aphasia have the same preferences for interpreting them as non-language-impaired speakers of the same language. Their grammar, though impaired, is not wiped out.

In grammaticality judgment, Italian subjects with Broca's aphasia are relatively more sensitive to errors of morphology and English-speaking aphasics to errors of word order, reflecting the relative importance of those components of morphosyntax in their languages. The statistical syntactic patterns of a language also persist in production. For example, non-language-impaired Italian speakers use relative clauses more frequently than their German-speaking counterparts do; aphasic Italian speakers use them more than aphasic German speakers. Reduced incidence of certain constructions in aphasic speech may be due to strategic avoidance. In agrammatic Dutch narratives, speakers use structures like *melk drinken* 'milk drink (infinitive)' = 'drinking milk' instead of SVO 'he drinks milk', avoiding verb agreement. Such non-finite structures support the "strategy" theory because they cannot be created simply by omitting parts of an indicative phrase (Kolk et al. 1990).

Is aphasia a deficit of language processing, or of mental representation of grammar? Exploiting the relatively free word order and rich morphology of Serbo-Croatian, Lukatela et al. 1995 showed that agrammatic speakers are able to distinguish between sentences with subject gaps

('The lady is kissing the man who is holding an umbrella') vs. object gaps ('The lady is kissing the man that the umbrella is covering') that were constructed with content words in the same order. These patients could comprehend but not produce such sentences, implicating processing rather than representation.

Non-canonical word order is difficult for aphasics. Even where word order is relatively free, aphasic speakers overuse canonical word order (or, rarely, another fixed word order). Within the noun phrase, a comparison of Swedish, French, Polish, German, and English (which differ in whether adjectives of various types precede or follow the noun) shows that modifiers that precede the adjective are more difficult than those that follow it, regardless of the semantic type of the modifier (Ahlsén et al. 1996).

2. Errors in bound grammatical morphemes. Semantically appropriate case marking may appear even when verbs and functors are omitted, but errors in inflection are extremely common. The rate of omission of definite/indefinite articles is a function of the semantic load carried by their gender and number markings. German articles are produced most often, then Italian, and then English; however, the substitution error rate is greatest in German (Bates et al. 1991). The larger the array of inflected forms of a word, the higher the frequency of substitution errors: German has more forms of articles than Italian, and aphasic speakers make many more substitution errors in German than in Italian. Japanese has no person or number agreement, and aphasic Japanese speakers can produce simple narratives without making verb errors, unlike aphasic speakers of most other languages.

Morphological substitutions are rarely more than one "morpho-semantic" feature away from the target, but the direction of the substitution varies. Dressler 1991 studied two Breton speakers with Wernicke's aphasia; in naming pictures of single objects that are likely to be found in multiples (e.g. leaf, tooth, finger) the subjects tended to give a plural response—and they produced dual responses for single 'ear', 'hand', and 'eye'.

3. Functor omissions. Functors are likely to be omitted, but those that are more informative are likely to be preserved; for example, there is virtually no omission of negative morphemes. Discourse-governed functors also seem less vulnerable, such as sentence-initial conjunctions ('and', 'and then') and Japanese sentence-final particles; however, Yiu and Worrall 1996 found disruption of utterance-final particles in a study of aphasic Chinese speakers. More work is needed in this area.

4. Phonology and tone. Are lexical (phonemic) tones under left hemisphere control like other phonemic phenomena, or under right hemisphere control, like emotional prosody? Based on perception and production studies of Chinese, Thai, and East Norwegian (e.g. Gandour 1987), phonemic tone seems to be controlled by the left hemisphere.

5. Conclusion. The contribution of the comparative approach in the 1980s and 1990s has been substantial: theories that seemed plausible on the basis of data from a single language have proven untenable, while the surviving approaches have been made more explicit. Cross-linguistic study shows that patterns of the native language are made "noisy," but not eradicated in aphasia. Adding new languages to comparative aphasiology still faces obstacles, including lack of native-speaker scholars who can produce appropriate grammatical analyses, lack of neurological expertise and diagnostic equipment in the areas of the world concerned, and limited access to affected populations.

[*See also* Neurology *and* Psycholinguistics.]

BIBLIOGRAPHY

Ahlsén, E., J. L. Nespoulous, M. Dordain, J. Stark, G. Jarema, D. Kadzielawa, L. K. Obler, and P. M. Fitzpatrick. 1996. Noun phrase production by agrammatic patients: A cross-linguistic approach. *Aphasiology* 10.543–560.

Bates, E., A. Friederici, and B. Wulfeck. 1987. Comprehension in aphasia: A cross-linguistic study. *Brain and Language* 32. 19–67.

Bates, E., B. Wulfeck, and B. MacWhinney. 1991. Cross-linguistic research in aphasia: An overview. *Brain and Language* 41.123–148.

Dressler, W. U. 1991. The sociolinguistic and patholinguistic attrition of Breton phonology, morphology, and morphonology. In *First language attrition,* edited by H. W. Seliger and R. M. Vago, pp. 99–112. Cambridge: Cambridge University Press.

Gandour, J. 1987. Tone production in aphasia. In *Phonetic approaches to speech production in aphasia and related disorders*, edited by J. H. Ryalls, pp. 45–57. Boston: College Hill Press.

Kolk, H., M. van Grunsven, and A. Keyser. 1990. Agrammatism in Dutch: Two case studies. In *Agrammatic aphasia*, edited by L. Menn and L. K. Obler, pp. 179–280. Amsterdam: Benjamins.

Lukatela, K., D. Shankweiler, and S. Crain 1995. Syntactic processing in agrammatic aphasia by speakers of a Slavic language. *Brain and Language* 49.50–76.

Menn, I., and L. K. Obler. 1990. Conclusion: Cross-language data and theories of agrammatism. In their *Agrammatic aphasia*, pp. 1369–1389. Amsterdam: Benjamins.

LISE MENN

APO DUAT LANGUAGES. Spoken in the northeastern part of the island of Borneo. They form a top-level constituent of the BORNEO subgroup of WESTERN MALAYO-POLYNESIAN.

LANGUAGE LIST

Kelabit: also called Kalabit, Kerabit. 1,650 speakers in Sarawak, Malaysia, and Kalimantan, Indonesia. In Sarawak, Malaysia: Northern Sarawak, in the remotest and highest of Borneo mountains. Dialects are Brung, Libbung, Lepu Potong, Bario, Lon Bangag. Long Napir, Long Seridan, Pa'Dalih, Long Leilang, Bruang may also be dialects. In Kalimantan, Indonesia: Remote mountains, on Sarawak border, northwest of Longkemuat. Mainly in Sarawak.

Lengilu: 3 speakers remain in Kalimantan, Indonesia. Formerly spoken in the northeast, between Sa'ban and Lundayeh.

Lundayeh: also called Southern Murut, Lun Daye, Lun Dayah, Lun Daya, Lun Dayoh, Lundaya. 38,100 speakers in Kalimantan, Indonesia, Sarawak, Malaysia, and Brunei. In Kalimantan, Indonesia: 25,000 speakers. Dialects are Lun Daye, Papadi, Lun Bawang (Long Bawan, Sarawak Murut). In Sarawak, Malaysia: 12,800 speakers on the southwestern border of Sabah and Sarawak. Dialects are Lun Bawang (Sarawak Murut), Lun Dayah, Adang, Balait (Tabun, Treng), Kolur, Padas, Trusan (Lawas, Limbang), Lepu Potong. In Brunei: Seven villages in Temburong district.

Putoh: 6,000 speakers in Kalimantan, Indonesia, in the northeast, east of Lundayeh and Sa'ban, Mentarang River, around Longberang, Mensalong, and Bangalan. Dialects are Pa Kembaloh, Abai.

Sa'ban: 1,000 speakers in Kalimantan, Indonesia, and Sarawak, Malaysia. In Kalimantan, Indonesia: Northeast on Sarawak border, south of Lundayeh. In Sarawak, Malaysia: Northeast on the Kalimantan border, northeast of Ramudu, Upper Baram, 4th division, including Long Banga'.

Tring: spoken in Sarawak, Malaysia, Long Terawan village, lower Tutoh River.

B. GRIMES

APOLLONIUS DYSCOLUS. Greek grammarian, working in Alexandria in the 2nd century CE. His work on syntax was very influential.

[*See also* History of Linguistics, *article on* Ancient Greece and Rome.]

ANNA MORPURGO DAVIES

APPLIED LINGUISTICS. [*This entry includes the following subentries:*
History
Concerns and Related Disciplines]

The subdiscipline of applied linguistics [AL] is an inquiry into the relevance of linguistic expertise to actual language experience. Whenever such expertise is drawn on to resolve a basic language-related problem, one may say that AL is being practiced. In this sense, AL is a technology that makes abstract ideas and research findings accessible and relevant to the real world; it mediates between theory and practice. The quest for knowledge characteristic of established academic disciplines is vitally important because all increase in our understanding of our world is worthwhile in itself, but it is also crucial that the understanding gained in the quest for "pure" knowledge be related somehow to everyday human experience. Scholarship has obligations to the nonscholarly world, and it is this need that AL intends to meet. Its starting point lies in the language-related problems of practical life, and it adduces insights from disciplinary areas of language study to the extent that such insights are relevant to their clarification and solution. But since aspects of human life other than language are generally implicated in such problems, AL is also drawn into a consideration of other fields of inquiry. The essential principle is that of relevance. (For general reference, see Halliday et al. 1964, Lado 1964, Corder 1973, Stern 1983, Widdowson 1979, 1984, Grabe and Kaplan 1992, Kaplan 2001.)

History

Applied linguistics is a field that has emerged relatively recently. In the years following World War II, scholars asked what lessons might be learned from the wartime experience for the future improvement of foreign language teaching. Between 1939 and 1945, specialists in linguistics were engaged in many countries, notably by the military in the United States and Britain, in order quickly to produce many personnel having competence in one or more foreign languages, including many languages previously regarded as "exotic" (for example, Arabic, Burmese, and Japanese).

From 1956 on, the idea that linguists could contribute usefully to the principled study of language learning and teaching gave rise to two pioneering institutions with the term "applied linguistics" in their title: the School of

Applied Linguistics (SAL) at Edinburgh University, and the Center for Applied Linguistics (CAL) in Washington, D.C. The Edinburgh SAL was initially funded by the British Council, a quasi-governmental body whose mandate includes the promotion of the English language abroad. It was set up as a department of the university providing courses for experienced teachers and teacher trainers from Britain and from overseas countries. Under its first director, J. C. Catford, and his successor, S. Pit Corder, SAL became a seminal force in spreading concepts of applied linguistics worldwide, both through its hundreds of students and through the *Edinburgh Course in Applied Linguistics* (Allen and Corder 1973–1977, 4 vols.).

CAL was established in 1959 by the Ford Foundation, whose concern to assist the rapid expansion of education in developing countries had led it to propose a series of language surveys in former British or French colonies in Africa that were approaching political independence. It was envisaged that large-scale projects would be set up to devise curricula for teaching English, together with new teaching materials and teacher-training programs. (The hoped-for development did not invariably occur, but the surveys provided the groundwork for much subsequent language planning activity.) The first director of CAL was Charles Ferguson, under whose leadership CAL achieved international renown as the base for many other projects in applied linguistics.

SAL and CAL reflected certain philosophical tenets concerning the educational and sociopolitical needs of developing countries:

(a) Such societies require rapid access by a substantial part of their population to a language of wider communication like English.
(b) The change from colonial status to independence must lead to a rapid change in the provision of access to English, from schooling limited to a small elite toward universal education.
(c) Conventional language teaching methods cannot provide what is needed quickly enough.
(d) A broad AL approach is more likely to succeed.

This optimism has been vindicated to some extent; virtually all schemes for the extension and improvement of national language teaching systems today use applied linguistics at some stage.

In France, the campaign to revitalize the teaching of the French language led to two government-backed AL projects. First, research into vocabulary frequency in spoken French was aimed at producing *Le français fondamental*, a definitive list of the 1,200 most frequent words, to be used as the basis of coursebooks for foreign learners of French. Second, the use of audiovisual technology in language teaching led to the structuro-global method and the pioneering audiovisual course *Voix et images de France*, in which a coursebook closely controlled in its vocabulary and grammar was integrated with slide projection, tape recordings, language laboratory work, and a strong oral classroom style. Many of France's leading linguists were involved in these early AL projects.

The Council of Europe, backed by the ministries of education of all western European countries (and influenced by SAL, CAL, and the French work), set up a Languages Project under the leadership of John L. Trim. Trim's group, which included scholars from most European countries, set out to establish the practical language needs, in work and leisure, of particular groups of language learners within Europe, and how those needs might be met. They were required to provide designers of language-teaching courses with basic information about what each category of learners would need to do in a foreign language, and about how to express such communicative activity in each language. They pioneered techniques for needs analysis and language description in the domain of communication, invoking David Wilkins's concept of "notions" (of time, place, motion, quantity, intellectual and emotional attitudes, etc.) and "functions" (describing, narrating, apologizing, questioning, etc.). For each language of Europe, they postulated an equivalent language learning/teaching load to reach a given minimum standard of achievement, or "threshold." The work took more than a decade to complete and resulted in the publication of threshold levels for many European languages. The first, *Threshold Level English* (Van Ek 1975), incorporates both Wilkins's work on notions and functions and an appendix by Louis Alexander on methodological implications of the threshold concepts. Threshold levels are not themselves coursebooks but were intended to be used widely as sources for the design of curricula and courses.

These projects are typical of early applied linguistics in that they applied the principles of rigorous linguistic study to provide the intellectual basis for the development and improvement of foreign language teaching. This tradition goes back at least to Comenius in the 17th century, Bernard Miège in the 18th, and François Gouin in the 19th. Since about 1900, this development has been associated increasingly with the linguistic sciences (see

Halliday et al. 1964): first with phonetics (Henry Sweet and Paul Passy), and eventually with a more general conception of linguistics in the work of such scholars as Otto Jespersen, Harold E. Palmer, C. C. Fries, Kenneth Pike, and Robert Lado (for an overview, see Howatt 1984).

The first international conference on applied linguistics was held in Nancy, France, in 1964. The participants were representative of most schools of thought in linguistics at the time. From it emerged the Association Internationale de Linguistiques Appliquée (AILA), an association of national AL associations, which publishes the *International Review of Applied Linguistics*. (For a review of the history of the American Association for Applied Linguistics and the British Association of Applied Linguistics, and of the journals *Applied Linguistics* and the *Annual Review of Applied Linguistics*, see Kaplan and Grabe 2000.)

AL has taken various paths because of differing theoretical perspectives, and several paradigms in linguistics have contributed to its evolution. From Bloomfieldian linguistics came three important early ideas:

(a) The concept of contrastive analysis, in which comparison of the learner's language with the target was believed to enable teachers to anticipate areas of learning difficulty.

(b) A belief that Bloomfield's linguistic theory, allied to B. F. Skinner's operant-conditioning psychological theory, should determine the content and method of language teaching.

(c) The elaboration of discrete-item techniques for testing, based on the same set of assumptions.

With the rise of Chomsky's cognitive view of language and learning, a gradual shift in the linguistic paradigm took place.

BIBLIOGRAPHY

Allen, J. P. B., and S. Pit Corder. 1973–1977. *The Edinburgh course in applied linguistics*, vol. 1; vol. 2, *Papers in applied linguistics*; vol. 3, *Techniques in applied linguistics*; vol. 4, *Testing and experimental methods* (edited by J. P. B. Allen and A. Davies). London: Oxford University Press.

Corder, S. Pit. 1973. *Introducing applied linguistics*. Harmondsworth: Penguin.

Grabe, William, and Robert B. Kaplan, eds. 1992. *Introduction to applied linguistics*. Reading, Mass.: Addison-Wesley.

Halliday, Michael A. K., Angus McIntosh, and Peter Strevens. 1964. *The linguistic sciences and language teaching*. London: Longman.

Howatt, A. P. R. 1984. *A history of English language teaching*. Oxford: Oxford University Press.

Kaplan, Robert B. 2001. *Oxford handbook of applied linguistics*. New York: Oxford University Press.

Kaplan, Robert B., and William Grabe. 2000. Applied linguistics and ARAL. *Annual Review of Applied Linguistics* 20:3–17.

Lado, Robert. 1964. *Language teaching*. New York: McGraw-Hill.

Stern, H. H. 1983. *Fundamental concepts of language teaching*. Oxford: Oxford University Press.

Van Ek, J. A. 1975. *Threshold level English in a European unit/credit system for modern language learning by adults*. Oxford: Pergamon; 2d ed., 1980.

Widdowson, Henry G. 1979, 1984. *Explorations in applied linguistics*. 2 vols. Oxford: Oxford University Press.

PETER STREVENS

Concerns and Related Disciplines

If we accept a definition of applied linguistics along the lines proposed at the start of this article, two questions follow from it. First, what kind of real-world problems does AL typically address? Second, which areas of theoretical inquiry have provided relevant insights?

Language can be problematic for people in many different ways. Significant issues include the following:

(a) Difficulties, physiologically or psychologically induced, may arise with the medium through which language is expressed, as in the case of speech disorders such as deafness and the difficulties of individuals who have received cochlear implants), The treatment of such disorders is the concern of the AL area of speech therapy.

(b) Language is used for communication and social control at individual and institutional levels of interaction within particular communities. This raises problems of the legitimate exercise of influence, or of power and language: the use of language to assert authority and to constrain conformity to institutional norms of use; and the uses of language to exercise ideological influence, to cajole, and to persuade.

(c) At a more macro level, there are problems concerning which languages should serve the general transactional and interactional needs of particular communities, and what decisions have to be taken in language policy and planning to ensure that the languages are made effective for this purpose.

(d) Language figures crucially in education, and problems arise over which language or variety is appropriate, and the lack of correspondence between the variety approved for schooling and that of upbringing and social interaction. Issues here concern bilingualism, multilingualism, bidialectalism, multiculturalism, translation, and interpretation.

(e) For many people, the most obvious problem with language arises when they are required to learn a second language as a school subject. It is this area of foreign or second language learning and teaching that has received most attention in AL.

Each of the five major problem areas described above requires reference to different aspects of language study, in combination with considerations proper to other disciplinary domains. This recognition that the problems that people experience with language are compounded with other, nonlinguistic factors distinguishes AL from what has been called "Linguistics Applied" (Widdowson 2000b). Although linguistic theory and description are clearly crucial, AL has also to be alert to insights deriving from other areas of inquiry, such as anthropology, sociology, psychology, political science, and—since it is concerned with cost-effectiveness in the practical world—economics. Kaplan 1980 takes the view that AL is the stage on which all of the human (social) sciences coalesce in the solution of human problems in which language is implicated. AL's mediating role requires it to be alert not only to what insights different disciplinary domains may offer, but also to the perceptions and preoccupations of the nonexpert people who experience the problems that AL seeks to address on their behalf. We now look at the five main problem areas outlined above to identify what kinds of linguistic or other inquiry might be relevant to them.

Speech therapy. Microlinguistic investigations in phonetics and in syntax assist in the diagnosis of pathological language disorders. Treatment then needs to consider various psycholinguistic and sociolinguistic factors, the attitudes of the patient, and the views of the larger society with reference to the condition and the patient. With speech therapy, it is particularly clear that problems cannot be dealt with simply by applying linguistics like a poultice, without regard for the way these problems are actually perceived and experienced.

Communication and social control. As linguistics in general has extended its scope during recent years to the way language functions in social context, AL has also addressed the particular problems that arise in various domains of use. Careful investigations have been undertaken of interactions between people in various social roles: physicians and patients, teachers and students, interactions in courts of law, and uses of language by advertisers, politicians, and government agencies. These studies go well beyond the textual description of the specialist terminology and syntactic structures that characterize the language of these interactions. They seek to account for the interaction strategies that are used—how participants position themselves in relation to each other, and how control is managed, particularly in encounters between parties of unequal power. Such studies refer to discourse analysis and pragmatics, to the description of the rhetorical regularities that characterize various types of use, to genre analysis, and to the notion of schema in artificial intelligence studies (which attempt to design computer programs to simulate the process of language use). What motivates these inquiries, from an AL point of view, is that once the essential nature of these interactions is made explicit by analysis, then people can be made aware of different conventions of communicative behavior, and of the extent to which language can be used or abused for the management and manipulation of social relations. This area of AL has become particularly associated with critical linguistics, an approach to description that is committed to the exposure and correction of social inequality in the use of language. AL work of this kind can be seen as the development of conventional textual study in rhetoric and literary criticism. It makes reference, however, to a wider range of disciplinary inquiry, and it focuses on the language of everyday life and its role in the exercise of power and maintenance of civil liberties.

Language planning and language policy. Another complex set of concerns stems from the reality of bilingualism and multilingualism in the 20th century. Political events have caused vast dislocations of populations during this century; great redistributions of population, particularly in urban centers, have thrown together speakers of different languages and varieties. This, coupled with the emergence of new political states out of former colonial empires, has created a need for language planning and language policy. Planning has essentially separated into two major subcategories: corpus planning and status planning. Corpus planning deals with norm selection and codification; that is, when a government chooses a previously unwritten variety as a national or an official language, it is necessary to identify an orthography for the new language, to describe its grammar and lexicon, to develop means by which that language may be taught to the citizens of the new polity who do not know it, to provide literacy programs in that language, and so on. Corpus planning results in the writing of dictionaries and grammars, in the standardization of spelling and pronunciation, and in the preparation of literacy materials. Status planning, in contrast, is concerned with the initial choice of language and with interaction among varieties in a sociocultural setting. It studies attitudes toward particular languages, functions of particular varieties within a society, and the social and political implications of various language choices. The issue of modernization is necessarily subsumed; as new nations emerge, they have concerns for the economic capacity of the polity to provide for its citizens. Modernization implies the availability of scientific and technical information and a concern with appropriate technology and its transfer, which in turn brings in education. Because English has become a world language of commerce, science, and technology and dominates electronic communication, a polity that has chosen an indigenous language as a national language for purposes of unity and identity still needs a language of wider communication, often English, in order to develop contacts beyond its own borders and to move toward modernization. This raises the question of whether the status of the domestic indigenous language, or even its survival, can be sustained in the face of this powerful intruder, sometimes seen as an instrument of imperialistic power. Again, the problems that AL confronts are compounded by many issues outside the domain of linguistics proper. In this case, we are concerned not only with matters like language change and standardization but also with economic, ethical, and political questions—with geolinguistics and glottopolitics (see Kaplan and Baldauf 1997).

Language in education. Centrally concerned with the institutional role of language, this field of AL considers the relationship between the languages and varieties used for secondary socialization through formal instruction, and those of primary socialization in the home and other contexts of social interaction (religion, recreation, and commerce). These matters bear both on general educational policy concerning the language or variety officially designated for schooling and on the attitudes and practices of everyone concerned with the educational process. They raise fundamental questions about the imposition of approved norms of language behavior and respect for different social and linguistic identities and about the

appropriate definition of competence and the means for assessing proficiency in language. There are matters of principle here that need to be referred to sociology of education and language, and to the sociological nature of knowledge. There is also a need to refer to microlinguistics and discourse analysis in order to describe the formal and functional differences among language varieties in grammar, lexis, and pragmatic features. A larger issue is translation and interpretation, which implicates education but extends into political action. The question of how competence can be evaluated brings in the area of language assessment.

Second language teaching and learning. Because AL has been associated closely with second or foreign language teaching, this is the area of its most extensive development. Language teachers have looked to disciplinary domains to provide them with principled guidance for the definition of their subject in respect to two basic questions: How should "language" be defined so that we can determine what to teach? And how may language learning itself be characterized to determine what processes of classroom instruction are likely to be effective?

Developments in language teaching may be divided historically into a series of phases characterized in terms of the relationship between these two questions. In the early twentieth century, language teaching focused on the definition of what was to be taught, without regard to the actual process of learning. It was based on a grammar/translation approach modeled on the teaching of classical languages, particularly Latin, where the available corpus was closed and limited largely to literary texts. Since there were no living native speakers of these languages, the ways in which native speakers acquired and used the languages could not be adduced as relevant to the pedagogic process. Teaching, therefore, was concerned exclusively with transmitting the formal properties of language defined in reference to classical categories, and learning was seen as the reflex of teaching. The purpose of the approach was to get learners to internalize these properties as a way of gaining access to meaning expressed through written language.

Ideas about language teaching changed with the advent of structuralism in linguistics and the coincident development of behaviorist psychology. Under structuralism, the formal properties of language were independently described in internal distributional terms, not in reference to external classical categories. This approach defined units for teaching structures or sentence patterns as specific to particular languages. Behaviorist psychology provided a model of learning as stimulus/response habit formation. Both linguistics and psychology insisted on the primacy of spoken language. Pedagogy now had authority from linguistics for a description of units to be taught, and from psychology for a definition of the learning process. Answers to the two questions converged on an approach that provided repetitive practice of structures, with emphasis on oral performance, so that the forms of language would become habitual.

This convergence of influences from the two disciplines was disturbed by the proposals of Noam Chomsky. On one hand, he challenged the behaviorist account of learning; on the other, he proposed a theory of language structure that was more abstract than the surface forms. Chomsky's cognitive theory of language essentially denies the primacy of overt behavior and the grammatical structures that correspond to it, characterizing them as superficial symptoms of deep-seated cognitive causes that are a function of an innate preprogrammed language faculty, or Language Acquisition Device. For Chomsky, the nature of language is necessarily bound up with the nature of language acquisition. This led language pedagogy to focus on the second question, that of the process of language learning; in AL, extensive inquiries were undertaken concerned with second language acquisition. The starting point of these inquiries was the redefinition of nonconformist "deviant" learner utterances as evidence not of error or failure to learn, but of underlying cognitive and creative processes intrinsic to the learning process and informed by its own developmental logic. Overt behavior is simply superficial evidence that something more cognitively significant is going on deeper in the mind.

Research on second language acquisition had the general effect of shifting the emphasis in pedagogy from teaching to learning. It was recognized that forcing learners into conformity could inhibit acquisition, that teacher input was not the same as learner intake, and that "errors" called not for summary correction but for appraisal as positive signs of achievement. Most of this research, however, concentrated on the acquisition of syntax as the psychological activity of the disembodied mind. More recently, AL, inspired by the work of Vygotsky, has turned its attention to sociocultural factors that affect the language learning process (see Lantolf 2000).

Parallel with developments in SLA, proposals were put forward about how the content of the language subject was to be defined, inspired by ideas from sociolinguistics and philosophy. Particularly influential were Dell Hymes's notion of communicative competence, speech act theory as expounded by the philosophers John L. Austin and John Searle, and the Firthian tradition of contextual linguistics as exemplified by the work of Michael Halliday. Pedagogy derived from these influences a definition of the language to be taught in terms of the pragmatics of its communicative use, rather than the semantics encoded in its forms. This resulted in the design of syllabuses based on notions and functions rather than on grammatical structures, most notably in the threshold level specifications of the Council of Europe. Subsequently, it became plain from work in discourse analysis, contrastive rhetoric, and pragmatics that communication cannot be characterized statically in terms of fixed correspondences between linguistic forms and communicative functions; rather, it is a dynamic process of realizing meaning in action. If what was to be taught was communicative competence, this could not be brought about by mere syllabus specification, but only by devising classroom activities that engaged learners in the purposeful negotiation of meaning by problem-solving. Thus, the issues of what was to be taught and how it was to be learned appeared to converge: learners acquire the ability to communicate in a language by using the language to communicate.

The question arises, however, of how far the learner's communicative use of language in the classroom should correspond with what is attested as authentic in actual native-speaker contexts of use. This question has become particularly prominent over recent years with developments in corpus linguistics. Very large amounts of textual data can now be processed by computer to reveal frequencies and patterns of occurrence that are inaccessible to intuition. This major development in linguistic description inevitably has repercussions on pedagogic thinking (see Wichmann et al. 1997). It has been argued that since we now have detailed profiles of how a particular language is really used, these should define the content of the language subject: teachers are in a position to teach the "real" language for the first time. It has been objected that for language to be meaningful in the classroom context, it has to engage with the learner's reality, and the authentic language of actual use is not the same as the appropriate language for learning. Moreover, the normal circumstances of use do not meet the necessary conditions for learning in that they do not focus explicit attention on the specific encoding devices of a language that need to be noticed to be acquired effectively (see Schmidt 1990).

Goals. We have seen the kinds of real-world problems with language that AL confronts by drawing on insights of potential relevance from various disciplinary domains. What distinguishes AL from the disciplines it draws on is that it reverses the idealization process that all disciplines to some degree depend on, and it reconstitutes the actuality from which it is abstracted. It seeks to reformulate language problems in ways that make them amenable to solution by realigning various disciplinary perspectives and relating them to the perceptions of the people who experience the problems in the first place, and who naturally tend to see these problems in very different terms than do linguists. In this sense, AL is a mediating process, involving both interpretation of theory and intervention in practice. It is wide-ranging and indeterminate, and this creates new problems. Almost any area of theory and description concerned with language can be said to have a *potential* bearing on the problems that people experience with language, so almost any area can be considered as falling within the scope of AL, whether this potential is specifically demonstrated or not. This, in effect, denies that there is anything distinctive about AL; rather, it is a convenient name given to a whole range of diverse psycholinguistic and sociolinguistic studies of the acquisition and use of language. Conversely, AL may be made too determinate, as when theoretical or descriptive findings are imposed on a problematic situation by disciplinary fiat without a critical inquiry into other relevant factors. This can occur when the findings of controlled experimental studies of learning are used to determine classroom procedures, or when it is assumed that linguistic descriptions of language, whether based on the abstract knowledge or the actual behavior of users, must necessarily determine what is appropriate for learning (see Widdowson 2000a). One reaction to the tendency to defer too readily to disciplinary authority is to deny the legitimacy of that authority; in some quarters, this has led to the belief that not only is AL not "linguistics applied," but that it has no particular relationship with linguistics at all and should rather be seen as the name given to any concern with language in the real world, whether informed by disciplinary inquiry or not. It should instead be informed, it is argued, by a critical attitude to established authority and a political commitment to the cause of social justice.

The problems outlined here concerning the goals and principles of AL have given rise to much debate (see Rampton 1995, 1997; Brumfit 1997; Widdowson 1998, 2000b; Davies 1999). This can be taken as an expression of uncertainty about the distinctive status of AL as an independent field of inquiry. It can also be seen more positively, however, as evidence of a continuing and critical evaluation of the defining principle of relevance in AL.

[*See also* Acquisition of Language; Bilingualism and Multilingualism; Critical Linguistics; Discourse; Institutional Linguistics; Language Planning; Power and Language; Diglossia; *and* Text.]

BIBLIOGRAPHY

Brumfit, C. J. 1997. Theoretical practice: Applied linguistics as pure and practical science. In *AILA Review 12: Applied linguistics across disciplines*, pp. 18–30.
Davies, Alan. 1999. *An introduction to applied linguistics.* Edinburgh: Edinburgh University Press.
Kaplan, Robert B. 1980. *On the scope of applied linguistics.* Rowley, Mass.: Newbury House.
Kaplan, Robert B., and Richard B. Baldauf, Jr. 1997. *Language planning from practice to theory.* Clevedon: Multilingual Matters.
Lantolf, James P., ed. 2000. *Sociocultural theory and second language learning.* Oxford: Oxford University Press.
Rampton, Ben. 1995. Politics and change in research in applied linguistics. *Applied Linguistics* 16.223–256.
Rampton, Ben. 1997. Returning in applied linguistics. *International Journal of Applied Linguistics.* 7.3–25.
Schmidt, Richard. 1990. The role of consciousness in second language learning. *Applied Linguistics* 11.17–46.
Wichmann, A., S. Fligelstone, S. McEmery, and T. G. Knowles, eds. 1997. *Teaching and language corpora.* London: Longman.
Widdowson, Henry G. 1998. Returning, calling the tune, and paying the piper: A reaction to Rampton. *International Journal of Applied Linguistics* 8.131–140.
Widdowson, Henry G. 2000a. Object language and language subject: On the mediating role of applied linguistics. *Annual Review of Applied Linguistics* 20.21–33.
Widdowson, Henry G. 2000b. On the limitations of linguistics applied. *Applied Linguistics* 21.3–25.

HENRY G. WIDDOWSON AND ROBERT B. KAPLAN

APRAXIA. In the neurological literature, the term "apraxia" defines the inability shown by some patients with left-brain damage to carry out correctly purposeful actions, although there are no elementary motor, sensory, or coordination deficits. In the majority of cases, the impairment is not contingent on the type of movement—

symbolic, expressive, describing the use of objects, etc.—or on the way it is elicited, e.g. by verbal command or imitation. What appears to be critical is the artificial condition in which the movement is produced: it is not prompted by environmental cues or internal urges, but by an examiner's request. Thus the patient may fail to wave goodbye on command, but does so when he leaves the room. (For reference, see Roy 1985, Miller 1989.)

Since apraxia is predominantly associated with left-hemisphere disease, the great majority of apraxic patients also have *aphasia*. Therefore it is important to make sure that patients' failure to execute the examiner's command does not result from a deficit of verbal comprehension. In some cases, the resemblance of the executed movement to the correct action (e.g., they put the palm of their hand on their forehead, when requested to salute) provides evidence that the message has been decoded. If doubt remains, one can test the imitation of movements made by the examiner, or one can present objects for the patient to demonstrate their use.

Different forms of apraxia have been distinguished, with reference to the stage at which the action program is disrupted and to the body part involved. In *ideational* apraxia, it is the idea of the movement that patients cannot evoke (De Renzi and Lucchelli 1988). Requested to demonstrate the use of objects, they hesitate, or use them in a wrong way, in wrong places, or in the wrong order. In *ideomotor* apraxia, the difficulty affects not the conceptual stage of the motor program, but its transfer to the executive areas, where it must be translated in appropriate commands to the muscles. Consequently, patients also fail when they are simply required to imitate movements, whether meaningful or meaningless, carried out by the examiner. They know what to do, but cannot select the appropriate innervation pattern.

Apraxia affects mainly the musculature of the limbs and mouth. The finding that limb and oral apraxia may occur independently suggests that they are related to discrete anatomical/functional structure. The planning of limb movements is organized by the left parietal lobe, which monitors the activity of motor areas through ipsilateral connections with the left premotor cortex, and through trans-callosal connections with the right premotor cortex. Accordingly, a left parietal lesion results in apraxia of both limbs, while a callosal lesion is associated with left-limb apraxia alone. Oral movements are organized more anteriorly in the left frontal premotor area, concerned with facial muscles. It apparently does not need the cooperation of the corresponding right cortical region to guide the activity of the brain-stem motor centers for cranial nerves. Oral apraxia has been implicated in the mechanism underlying the distorted speech of Broca's aphasics. The patient is unable to carry out on command, or to imitate, non-linguistic movements with the muscles of the mouth, lips, tongue, and throat (e.g. to whistle, to kiss, or to stick out the tongue). However, the same actions are performed correctly when carried out spontaneously. Some authors have endorsed the view that the lack of motor control on non-verbal movements, exhibited by Broca's aphasics, is also responsible for their laborious, effortful articulation and their distorted phonetic production. The term *apraxia of speech* has become popular to indicate the motor, rather than linguistic, nature of this speech disorder. It is not altogether clear, however, whether oral apraxia and apraxia of speech express disruption of the same mechanism. The finding that a few patients show oral apraxia without phonological articulatory impairment, and that the severity of the two disorders is not closely correlated, warns against their complete assimilation.

[*See also* Aphasia.]

BIBLIOGRAPHY

De Renzi, Ennio, and P. Faglioni. 1999. Apraxia. In *Handbook of clinical and experimental neuropsychology*, edited by G. Denes and L. Pizzamiglio, pp. 421–440. Hove: Psychology Press.

Miller, Niklas. 1989. *Dyspraxia and its management.* London: Croom Helm. Rockville, Md.: Aspen.

Roy, Eric A., ed. 1985. *Neuropsychological studies of apraxia and related disorders.* Amsterdam: North-Holland.

Ennio De Renzi

ARABIC. Before the Arab expansion as a result of the Muslim conquests in the 7th and 8th centuries CE, Arabic was the language of the nomadic tribes of northwestern and central Arabia; thus it is sometimes called "North Arabian," in contrast to Ancient or Epigraphic South Arabian, once spoken in Yemen and Hadhramaut. Along with Ancient South Arabian, Modern South Arabian, and the Semitic languages of Ethiopia, Arabic is often classified as South Semitic; it shares with these languages its very conservative phonology and the trait of "broken plurals" (see below). A new classification of the Semitic languages, proposed by Hetzron 1974, attaches more importance to features which Arabic shares with Canaanite (Ugaritic, Phoenician, and Hebrew), such as the 1st/

2nd person markers in the perfect (*-t-,* against *-k-* in South Arabian and Ethiopian), the internal passive, and the definite article *ha-* (with gemination of the following consonant, Arabic **ha-, *han- > ?al-*). Arabic is thus linked to Canaanite and Aramaic within the central branch of West Semitic.

The most detailed grammar of C[lassical] A[rabic] is Wright 1896. For a modern discussion of morphological and syntactic structures, see Fleisch 1968; for a dictionary, see Wehr 1979.

1. History. Arabic is first attested in epigraphic material found in central and northwestern Arabia, possibly dating back to between the 5th century BCE and the 3rd century CE. These Ancient North Arabian inscriptions are written in an alphabet derived from the South Arabian script, but the language is clearly different from Epigraphic South Arabian. Dialectal features and geographical distribution make it possible to distinguish Thamudic, Lihyanite, Safaitic, and Hasaitic (see Fischer 1982:17–29).

CA occurs in some inscriptions from the 2nd century CE onward. In its fully developed form, however, it appears first in pre-Islamic poetry, and then in the Qur'ān, during the first half of the 7th century (see Fück 1955, Fischer 1982:30–49). After the expansion of Islam, CA became the literary language of Islamic civilization, used by all educated people, whatever their native tongue. The commonly accepted form of CA was described by Arab grammarians during the 8th and 9th centuries. They standardized it at the same time; even so, they transmitted some information on dialectal variation. As a language of poetry and literature, CA has survived to the present. In the 19th and 20th centuries, it went through a process of revival, and developed into a linguistic medium appropriate for all areas of modern life. M[odern] S[tandard] A[rabic] is the official language of all Arab countries—and, alongside Hebrew, of Israel. MSA differs from CA only in vocabulary and stylistic features; the morphology and the basic syntactic norms have remained unchanged (see Beeston 1970, Stetkevych 1970).

Arabic was also adopted as a literary language by non-Muslims. When writing Arabic, the non-Muslims (and even some Muslims) did not always observe the norms laid down by the grammarians; thus they wrote Arabic with interference from their vernaculars. As a result, special sociolects, called Middle Arabic, arose—most important, Christian and Jewish Arabic. From the linguistic point of view, the texts of Middle Arabic give information about the dialects of their time; they prove

that diglossia, typical of the Arabic-speaking world today, emerged during the expansion of Islam, and perhaps even earlier (see Blau 1965, 1988).

As the language of Islamic education, Arabic deeply influenced the languages of all peoples who embraced Islam: first Persian, and then other Iranian languages, Turkish languages, Urdu, Bengali, Malay, etc., as well as African languages like Hausa and Swahili. Speakers of these languages adopted an enormous number of Arabic loanwords and expressions, especially in the field of Islamic religion and civilization. Muslims made use of the Arabic script to write their own native languages; some, like Persian and Urdu, are still written in Arabic letters. Just as Latin and Greek supply the European language community with scientific terms and an educated vocabulary, Arabic performs that function within the Islamic world; thus lexical items like *jāmiʕ* 'mosque', *madrasa* 'school', *qāʕida* 'rule' exist in nearly all languages of Muslim peoples.

Loanwords from Arabic entered European languages through language contact, mostly in Spain and Sicily, but also during the Crusades in Syria and Palestine. Words of Arabic origin, e.g. *algebra, alcohol* (both with the definite article *?al-*) *cotton, gazelle,* and *tariff,* are found in all European languages. The names of stars, e.g. *Algol, Altair, Fomalhaut,* and *Rigel,* owe their existence to scholarly language contacts at the end of the Middle Ages.

Arabic as a spoken language is widespread over an area from West Africa to the Persian Gulf; it is also spoken by more or less important minorities in non-Arab countries, including Nigeria, Chad, Turkey, and Iran. Small Arabic-speaking communities are found in Central Asia and Afghanistan; their dialects are greatly influenced by Iranian languages. In the Sudan, between Nigeria and Uganda, a pidginized variety of Arabic is used for communication among speakers of different African languages.

The Modern Arabic or Neo-Arabic colloquial language is structurally different from CA, and splits into numerous dialects (see Fischer and Jastrow 1980). In countries where MSA is the official language—used in writing, education, literature, and formal settings—a situation of diglossia exists. Native speakers acquire a Neo-Arabic dialect first, then learn MSA as a second language, according to the level of their education. Dialects of regions which are separated by great distances are not mutually intelligible, or only barely so; and speakers of such dialects communicate in a prestige dialect, such as

TABLE 1. *Arabic Consonants*

	Labial	Interdental	Alveolar	Palatal	Velar	Uvular	Pharyngeal	Glottal
Occlusives								
Voiceless								
Plain			t		k	q		ʔ
Emphatic			ṭ					
Voiced								
Plain	b		d	j	g			
Emphatic			ḍ					
Fricatives								
Voiceless								
Plain	f	θ	s	š	x		ḥ	h
Emphatic		θ̣	ṣ					
Voiced								
Plain		ð	z		γ		ʕ	
Emphatic		ð̣	(ẓ)					
Nasals	m		n					
Lateral			l					
Vibrant			r					
Semivowels	w			y				

the colloquial Arabic of Cairo, which has gained a high degree of acceptance because of its use in films. A spoken variety of MSA, commonly called Intermediate Arabic, lacks case markers and other specific features of CA, and shows interference from the dialects; it is increasingly used by educated people when they have to speak extemporaneously in interviews, debates, and similar semiformal settings.

Neo-Arabic dialects sometimes occur in a written standardized variety, e.g. in private letters, stage-plays, and songs; however, only Maltese Arabic has reached the status of an independent literary language. Maltese is mixed with numerous elements from Sicilian and Italian, especially in its lexicon, but also in syntactic structures. It is the native tongue of the Christian population of Malta, and is written in Latin characters.

Linguistic minorities live in great numbers in the Arab countries; the most important are the Berber-speaking populations in North Africa; the Kurdish-speaking tribes and the Neo-Aramaic-speaking groups in Syria and Iraq; and the speakers of Modern South Arabian languages in southern Yemen and Dhofar (Oman). The majority of people who belong to these minorities are bilingual. Another kind of bilingualism exists in Morocco, Algeria, and Tunisia, where educated people are generally familiar with French.

2. Phonology. The vowel inventory of CA consists of *a i u*, short and long. The consonants are shown in Table 1. The phoneme inventory of CA has preserved that of

Proto-Semitic (PS) almost completely, with a few exceptions: PS **p* > CA *f*, PS **g* > CA *j*, PS **ś* (perhaps a lateral) > CA *š*; by contrast, PS **š* > CA *s*. Hence CA has lost only one phoneme, PS **ś*.

This description of the phonemes reflects the standard of the Qur'ān readers, but regional allophonic variations exist. The glottal stop *ʔ* has phonemic status in every position: *ʔamara* 'he ordered', *yaʔmuru* 'he orders'; *saʔala* 'he asked', *yasʔalu* 'he asks'. The so-called "emphatics" are now pronounced as velarized, or sometimes as pharyngealized consonants. All consonants may be geminated; they are then pronounced as long consonants: *ra[ḥ]ala* 'he departed', *ra[ḥ:]ala* 'he transferred'.

Word stress is not distinctive, but is bound to syllabic structure: it falls upon the heavy syllable (CVC or CV̄) nearest the end of the word, except for the last syllable. However, it does not move beyond the third syllable from the end: *yastáʕmilu* 'he employs', *kitábun* 'a book', but *madrásatun* 'a school', *kátabat* 'she wrote'.

Vowels cannot be combined; however, there are combinations vowel + semivowel, e.g. *aw, ay*. One may also interpret *ī* as *iy*, and *ū* as *uw*. The combinations **iw *uy* produced by derivational rules become *iy uw*, respectively: **raʔā* + masc. pl. *ū* → *raʔaw* 'they saw', **miwlādun* 'birthday' (root morpheme *w-l-d*) → *mīlādun*, **buydun* 'white' (pl.) (root morpheme *b-y-ḍ*) → *bīḍun*.

Three-consonant clusters and syllables of the form CV̄C are not permitted. Where they would otherwise occur, an auxiliary vowel (usually *i*, seldom *u*) prevents their realization, or V̄C is shortened to VC. These rules influence the morphology: word forms beginning with CC must add an initial ʔV when they come at the beginning of an utterance, but not when internal: *šrab* 'drink!' → #ʔišrab, *ktub* 'write!' → #ʔuktub, but #ʔuktub θumma *šrab* 'Write, then drink!' The ʔa of the definite article ʔal- is also omitted within an utterance, and after a consonant it is replaced by an auxiliary vowel: *lam* ʔaktub 'I did not write' + ʔal-kitāba 'the book' → *lam* ʔaktub-i l-kitāba.

Shortening of V̄C takes place in the last syllable of the inflectional base: *qūmū* 'stand up! (masc. pl.)', but *qumna* 'stand up! (fem. pl.)'; ʔal-qāḍī 'the judge', but *qāḍī-n* → *qāḍin* 'a judge'.

Before a pause, one or more of the final segments of the word are dropped. Readers of the Qurʔān observe the following rules: long vowels are shortened; short vowels are dropped; *-n* is dropped if it is the marker of the indefinite, except that *-a-n* 'indefinite accusative' becomes *-ā*; and feminine nouns ending in *-at-u(n)*, *-at-i(n)*, *-at-a(n)* have the pausal form *-ah*. Examples are *rabbī* 'my lord' → *rabbi#* and even *rabb#*; *yuʕīdu* 'he brings back' → *yuʕīd#*; *ḥakīmun* 'wise' → *ḥakīm#*; *ʕajaban* 'a wonder' → *ʕajabā#*; *raqabatin, raqabatun, raqabatan* 'a neck' → *raqabah#*.

3. Writing system.

Arabic was first written in the Aramaic alphabet of the Nabateans. Around 500 CE, the Nabatean characters became the Arabic script. The Aramaic alphabet consisted of twenty-two graphemes, some of which had assumed the same shape; these graphemes had to be differentiated by diacritical dots above or below the letters in order to provide one grapheme for each of the twenty-eight consonantal phonemes of Arabic (see Fischer 1982:165–197). The present-day system is shown in Table 2. The graphemes represent consonantal phonemes. Gemination is indicated not by doubling the grapheme, but by the optional use of the sign ˝ (*tašdīd*).

The graphemes ʔalif, wāw, yāʔ are ambiguous; in addition to their consonantal values, they indicate the long vowels: ʔalif = ā, wāw = ū, yāʔ = ī; and in connection with the supplementary sign ع (*hamza*) they represent the glottal stop. The ʔalif indicates ʔ only in word-initial position, or when followed by *a*. In other cases, wāw, yāʔ, or Ø is written in positions where ʔ is to be read. Therefore *hamza* has been invented as a supplementary grapheme. The reason for this orthographic feature is that the writing system was originally established for the Hejaz dialect of CA, in which ʔ was

preserved only in initial position, and otherwise was replaced by *y, w,* or Ø.

Special signs have been introduced to mark the short vowels: ˊ (*fatḥa*) = a, ˏ (*kasra*) = i, ˀ (*ḍamma*) = u. The sign ˚ (*sukūn*) indicates that a consonant is not followed by a vowel. However, these signs are used only rarely, e.g. in the Qurʔān and in poetry, or sometimes to avoid misinterpretation.

The writing system does not represent speech in its textual phonemic form, since every unit is spelled as if spoken in isolation; i.e., every word appears in its pausal form. Initial auxiliary vowels are represented by ʔ, and the feminine endings *-at-u(n), -at-i(n), -at-a(n)* are written with *hāʔ* (with two additional dots indicating the reading *t*). Thus the phrase ʔinnī štaraytu baytan qabla sanatin '(Verily) I bought a house one year ago' is written ⟨ʔinnī ʔištarayt baytā qabl sanah⟩. As a result of this and other orthographic rules, a written Arabic text is not a direct representation of its phonemic equivalent.

4. Derivational morphology.

Like other Semitic languages, Arabic has root morphemes which consist solely of consonants. More than 90% of these have three consonants, and the rest have four or five. In addition to derivational prefixes and suffixes, discontinuous base morphemes combine with the roots. Thus the perfect base of the verb *katab-* 'wrote' contains the root morpheme *ktb* and the base morpheme $C_1aC_2aC_3$-. Combinations of morphemes establish nominal and verbal patterns, which are often related to a certain semantic class; the following are examples:

(a) $C_1\bar{a}C_2iC_3$- to the active participle, e.g. *kātibun* 'writing' to *ktb*

(b) $C_1aCC_2\bar{a}C_3$- to nouns denoting habitual occupations, e.g. *ṣarrāfun* 'cashier' to *ṣrf*, *xabbāzun* 'baker' to *xbz*

(c) $C_1uC_2ayC_3$- to diminutives, e.g. *kulaybun* 'little dog' to *klb*

(d) ʔa-$C_1C_2aC_3$- to nouns denoting colors or defects, e.g. ʔabyaḍu 'white' to *byḍ*, ʔaṭrašu 'deaf' to *ṭrš*

(e) ma-$C_1C_2aC_3$- to nouns of place, e.g. *mašrabun* 'drinking place' to *šrb*

Root morphemes with a semivowel are called "weak" roots; the instability of the semivowel in most patterns results in a long vowel, as in *qām-* 'stood up' = $C_1aC_2aC_3$-from *qwm*.

5. Noun inflection.

The morphologically marked categories are gender (masculine and feminine), number (singular, dual, and plural), case (nominative, genitive,

TABLE 2. *The Arabic Script*

Phonemic Value	Final	Medial	Initial	Alone	Numerical Value	Name
ʔ	ا			ا	1	ʔalif
b	ـب	ـبـ	بـ	ب	2	bāʔ
t	ـت	ـتـ	تـ	ت	400	tāʔ
θ	ـث	ـثـ	ثـ	ث	500	θāʔ
j	ـج	ـجـ	جـ	ج	3	jīm
ḥ	ـح	ـحـ	حـ	ح	8	ḥāʔ
x	ـخ	ـخـ	خـ	خ	600	xāʔ
d	ـد			د	4	dāl
ð	ـذ			ذ	700	ðāl
r	ـر			ر	200	rāʔ
z	ـز			ز	7	zāy
s	ـس	ـسـ	سـ	س	60	sīn
š	ـش	ـشـ	شـ	ش	300	šīn
ṣ	ـص	ـصـ	صـ	ص	90	ṣād
ḍ	ـض	ـضـ	ضـ	ض	800	ḍād
ṭ	ـط	ـطـ	طـ	ط	9	ṭāʔ
ð̣	ـظ	ـظـ	ظـ	ظ	900	ð̣āʔ
ʕ	ـع	ـعـ	عـ	ع	70	ʕayn
ɣ	ـغ	ـغـ	غـ	غ	1000	ɣayn
f	ـف	ـفـ	فـ	ف	80	fāʔ
q	ـق	ـقـ	قـ	ق	100	qāf
k	ـك	ـكـ	كـ	ك	20	kāf
l	ـل	ـلـ	لـ	ل	30	lām
m	ـم	ـمـ	مـ	م	40	mīm
n	ـن	ـنـ	نـ	ن	50	nūn
h	ـه	ـهـ	هـ	ه	5	hāʔ
w	ـو			و	6	wāw
y	ـى	ـيـ	يـ	ى	10	yāʔ

and accusative), and definiteness/indefiniteness. The masculine is unmarked. The feminine markers are -*at, -ā, -āʔ*; however, some feminine nouns lack the feminine marker, especially (but not exclusively) those which denote female beings, e.g. *ḥāmilun* 'a pregnant (woman)', *rijlun* 'foot'. However, when nouns marked with -*at* denote male beings, they are masculine, e.g. *xalīf-at-un* 'caliph'. The case-markers of the singular are nom. -*u*, gen. -*i*, acc. -*a*; the plural has a single marker for genitive and accusative. Definiteness is marked by the article ʔ*al*- (with assimilation to the following consonant, if interdental, alveolar, or *š*). Indefiniteness is marked by -*n* in the singular and in the feminine plural. Sample paradigms are shown in Table 3.

The genitive attribute follows its head noun immediately. Indefiniteness vs. definiteness is then indicated only on the second entity, the genitive:

(1) *muʕallimu madrasati-n* 'a teacher of a school'
      muʕallimu l-madrasati 'the teacher of the school'

Plural forms marked by suffixes, the so-called sound plurals, seldom occur. Most nouns take "broken" plurals, i.e. lexically fixed plurals in a variety of patterns. The plural pattern relating to a given singular is not predictable, as the following examples suggest:

(2) $C_1iC_2\bar{a}C_3$-*un*: *rajulun* 'man', pl. *rijālun*.
(3) $C_1uC_2uC_3$-*un*: *kitābun* 'book', pl. *kutubun*; *safīnatun* 'ship', pl. *sufunun*.
(4) ʔ*a*$C_1C_2\bar{a}C_3$-*un*: *qalamun* 'pencil', pl. ʔ*aqlāmun*.
(5) $C_1aC_2\bar{a}C_3iC_4$-*u*: *madrasatun* 'school', pl. *madārisu*.

All these plural forms are inflected like singular nouns.

6. Personal pronouns. There are two sets of personal pronouns: independent ones, and bound forms suffixed

TABLE 3. *Arabic Noun Paradigms*

	Indefinite	Definite
Masculine		
Singular		
Nom.	*muʕallimun* 'a teacher'	*ʔal-muʕallimu* 'the teacher'
Gen.	*muʕallimin*	*ʔal-muʕallimi*
Acc.	*muʕalliman*	*ʔal-muʕallima*
Dual		
Nom.	*muʕallimāni*	*ʔal-muʕallimāni*
Gen.-Acc.	*muʕallimayni*	*ʔal-muʕallimayni*
Plural		
Nom.	*muʕallimūna*	*ʔal-muʕallimūna*
Gen.-Acc.	*muʕallimīna*	*ʔal-muʕallimīna*
Feminine		
Singular		
Nom.	*muʕallimatun* 'a female teacher'	*ʔal-muʕallimatu* 'the female teacher'
Gen.	*muʕallimatin*	*ʔal-muʕallimati*
Acc.	*muʕallimatan*	*ʔal-muʕallimata*
Dual		
Nom.	*muʕallimatāni*	*ʔal-muʕallimatāni*
Gen.-Acc.	*muʕallimatayni*	*ʔal-muʕallimatayni*
Plural		
Nom.	*muʕallimātun*	*ʔal-muʕallimātu*
Gen.-Acc.	*muʕallimātin*	*ʔal-muʕallimāti*

TABLE 4. *Arabic Pronominal Forms*

	Independent Forms	Suffixal Forms
1sg.	*ʔanā*	*-ī/-nī*
1pl.	*naḥnu*	*-nā*
2sg.		
m.	*ʔanta*	*-ka*
f.	*ʔanti*	*-ki*
2du.	*ʔantumā*	*-kumā*
2pl.		
m.	*ʔantum*	*-kum*
f.	*ʔantunna*	*-kunna*
3sg.		
m.	*huwa*	*-hŭ/-hĭ*
f.	*hiya*	*-hā*
3du.	*humā*	*-humā/-himā*
3pl.		
m.	*hum(ū)*	*-hum/-him*
f.	*hunna*	*-hunna/-hinna*

TABLE 5. *Arabic Verb Paradigms*

	Perfect	Imperfect
1sg.	*katab-tu*	*ʔa-ktub-u*
1pl.	*katab-nā*	*na-ktub-u*
2sg.		
m.	*katab-ta*	*ta-ktub-u*
f.	*katab-ti*	*ta-ktub-ī-na*
2du.	*katab-tumā*	*ta-ktub-ā-ni*
2pl.		
m.	*katab-tum*	*ta-ktub-u-na*
f.	*katab-tunna*	*ta-ktub-na*
3sg.		
m.	*katab-a*	*ya-ktub-u*
f.	*katab-at*	*ta-ktub-u*
3du.		
m.	*katab-ā*	*ya-ktub-ā-ni*
f.	*katab-at-ā*	*ta-ktub-ā-ni*
3pl.		
m.	*katab-ū*	*ya-ktub-ū-na*
f.	*katab-na*	*ya-ktub-na*

to nouns, particles, and verbs. The suffixed pronouns, shown in Table 4 (except *-nī* 1sg.), have a possessive function when combined with nouns.

7. Verb inflection. The verb is given in dictionaries in the 3sg. masc. form of the perfect. Each verb yields two inflectional bases: one for conjugation with suffixed person markers, i.e. the perfect; and one for conjugation with prefixed person markers, i.e. the imperfect, subjunctive, and jussive (or "apocopate"). In most cases, these bases are differentiated by ablaut, e.g. suffixal *katab-*, prefixal *-ktub* 'write', as shown in Table 5.

The prefixal conjugation contains three moods: the imperfect indicative, marked by *-u* and *-na/-ni* in plural and dual forms, as well as in the 2sg. fem; the subjunctive, marked by *-a* and the absence of *-na/-ni* (*yaktub-a, yaktub-ū, yaktub-ā*); and the jussive or "apocopate" (shortened form), marked by Ø and absence of *-na/-ni* (*yaktub, yaktub-ū, yaktub-ā*). The suffixal conjugation refers to the perfective aspect and past time; the imperfect, to the imperfect aspect and to present/future time. However, the CA system of aspect and tense is very complex in its textual realization. The subjunctive and apocopate forms appear in specific syntactic environments: the apocopate is jussive, and is a reflex of the Proto-Semitic past tense. In CA, it is restricted to negative (*lam yaktub* 'he did not write') and conditional clauses. The imperative has no prefix: sg. masc. *ktub* (→ *ʔuktub*), *ktubī* (→ *ʔuktubī*), pl. masc. *ktubū* (→ *ʔuktubū*), fem. *ktubna* (→ *ʔuktubna*), du. *ktubā* (→ *ʔuktubā*).

The bulk of the verbs can be classified into ten patterns or stems. To demonstrate the verbal patterns, we use here the method of the Arab grammarians, who take *fˁl* from the verb *faˁala* 'to act'; see Table 6. The nominal pattern of Stem IX is reserved for colors and physical defects.

Besides these stems, an internal passive is marked by the perfect morpheme *CuCiC*-and the imperfect morpheme *C(a)CaC*, in combination with *u* as vowel of the person-markers:

(6)   *qatala* 'he killed', *qutila* 'he was killed'

(7)   *yaqtulu* 'he kills', *yuqtalu* 'he is killed'

(8)   *ʔistaˁmala* (*yastaˁmilu*) 'he employed (employs)', *ʔustuˁmila* (*yustaˁmalu*) 'he was (is) employed'

8. Syntax. The attribute follows its head noun. It agrees in gender, number, case, and definiteness with the nouns it qualifies:

(9)   *ʔumm-u-n qaliq-at-u-n* 'an uneasy mother'

(10) *fī bayt-i-hī l-qadīm-i* 'in his old house' (the personal pronoun makes the noun definite)

(11) *ʔal-rajul-āni l-ṣāliḥ-āni* 'the two good men'

In plurals, the adjective agrees with nouns denoting human beings only. In other cases, it takes the feminine singular:

(12) *jijāl-u-n ṣāliḥ-ūna* 'good men'

(13) *ban-āt-u-n ṣāliḥ-āt-u-n* 'good girls'
      but *ʔaˁmāl-u-n ṣāliḥ-at-u-n* 'good actions'

TABLE 6. *Arabic Verb Stems*

		Perfect	Imperfect
Basic	I.	*faˁala*	*yafˁalu*
		faˁila	*yafˁilu*
		faˁula	*yafˁulu*
Transitive/Causative	II.	*faˁˁala*	*yufaˁˁilu*
(a:i)	III.	*fāˁala*	*yufāˁilu*
	IV.	*ʔafˁala*	*yufˁilu*
Intransitive/Reflexive	V.	*tafaˁˁala*	*tafaˁˁala*
(no ablaut)	VI.	*tafāˁala*	*yatafāˁalu*
Passive	VII.	*ʔinfaˁala*	*yanfaˁilu*
Reflexive	VIII.	*ʔiftaˁala*	*yaftaˁilu*
Nominal	IX.	*ʔifˁalla*	*yafˁallu*
Causative + Reflexive	X.	*ʔistafˁala*	*yastafˁilu*

Demonstratives precede the noun, which takes the definite article:

(14) *hāðā l-bayt-u* 'this house'
      hāʔulāʔi l-rijāl-u 'these men'

The construction of the numerals is very complex. The cardinal numerals from three to ten have forms with and without the feminine marker *-at*; the quantified noun follows in the genitive plural. The numerals are marked with *-at* if the quantified noun is masculine, but are not marked in connection with feminine nouns. Compare the following:

(15) *θalāθ-at-u muˁallim-īna* 'three teachers'
      θalāθ-u muˁallim-āt-i-n 'three female teachers'

With numerals from eleven to nineteen and with the tens, the quantified noun appears in the accusative singular:

(16) *θalāθūna muˁallim-a-n* 'thirty teachers'

After the hundreds and thousands, the noun comes in the genitive singular:

(17) *θalāθ-u miʔ-at-i muˁallim-i-n* 'three hundred teachers'

The accusative is the case of the object, but it assumes other (mainly adverbial) functions:

(18) *ˁamaltu ˁamal-an ṣāliḥ-an* 'I did a good doing.'

(19) *ɣādartu l-bayta mašy-an* 'I left the house by walking.'

Thus the accusative ending -a(n) has become a marker for adverbial lexical units:

(20)   γād-an 'tomorrow'
         al-batt-at-a 'definitely (not)'

The nominal sentence has no copula. Word order is subject + predicate:

(21)   ʔal-ʔumm-u qaliq-at-u-n 'The mother is uneasy.'
(22)   bayt-u-hū qadīm-u-n 'His house is old.'

In the verbal sentence, the verb precedes the subject and agrees with it in gender, but not in number:

(23)   jāʔ-a l-muʕallim-ūna 'The teachers came.'
(24)   jāʔ-at i-l-muʕallim-āt-u 'The female teachers came.'

However, if the verb refers to a noun subject mentioned before, it must agree fully:

(25)   hāʔulāʔi muʕallim-ūna jāʔ-ū ʔamsi.
         'These are teachers (who) came yesterday.'

A nominal sentence may be transferred to the past by the verb kāna 'he was'. It then becomes a verbal sentence, and the predicate must be put in the accusative:

(26)   kānat i-l-ʔumm-u qaliq-at-a-n.
         'The mother was uneasy.'

There is a special type of clause expressing coincidence. It is coordinated by wa- 'and', and its word order is subject-predicate:

(27)   jāʔa l-muʕallimu wa-huwa yabtasimu/mubtasimun.
         'The teacher came, and he is smiling', i.e. 'The teacher came smiling.'

9. Modern dialects. MSA differs from CA in its loss of case endings, as well as of the markers of indicative and subjunctive. (On the whole, the CA pausal forms continue in modern dialects.) However, this loss of inflection had consequences for the linguistic structure. Neo-Arabic dialects have developed new markers for the genitive relationship, e.g. Egyptian Arabic il-bēt bitāʕ-ī 'the house of mine', with bitāʕ as an independent genitive morpheme. In many dialects, the system of personal pronouns has lost the contrast between masculine and feminine in the plural. In the verbal morphology, new markers of the indicative imperfect have developed, like Egyptian Arabic bi-yiktib 'he is writing' vs. yiktib (subjunctive). In all dialects except some in Yemen, the CA phonemes ḍ and ḏ̣ have merged to ḏ̣. Moreover, the interdental fricatives ð ð̣ θ have become alveolar stops (d ḍ t) in most urban dialects; there too, CA q is usually pronounced as [ʔ]. These and many other phonological and morphological changes give each dialect its specific characteristics.

[See also Semitic Languages.]

BIBLIOGRAPHY

Beeston, Alfred F. L. 1970. *The Arabic language today.* London: Hutchinson.

Blau, Joshua. 1965. *The emergence and linguistic background of Judaeo-Arabic: A study of the origins of Middle Arabic.* (Scripta judaica, 5.) Oxford: Oxford University Press. 2d ed., Jerusalem: Ben-Zvi Institute, 1981.

Blau, Joshua. 1988. *Studies in Middle Arabic and its Judaeo-Arabic variety.* Jerusalem.

Fischer, Wolfdietrich, ed. 1982. *Grundriss der arabischen Philologie,* vol. 1, *Sprachwissenschaft.* Wiesbaden: Reichert.

Fischer, Wolfdietrich, and Otto Jastrow, eds. 1980. *Handbuch der Arabischen Dialekte.* (Porta linguarum orientalium, n.s., 16.) Wiesbaden: Harrassowitz.

Fleisch, Henri. 1968. *L'Arabe classique: Esquisse d'une structure linguistique.* 2d ed. Beirut: Dar el-Machreq.

Fück, Johann. 1955. *Arabiya: Recherches sur l'histoire de la langue et du style arabe.* Paris: Didier.

Hetzron, Robert. 1974. La division des langues sémitiques. *Actes du Premier Congrès International de Linguistique Sémitique et Chamito-Sémitique* (Janua linguarum, Series practica, 159), edited by André Caquet and David Cohen, pp. 181–194. The Hague: Mouton.

Holes, Clive. 1995. *Modern Arabic: Structures, functions and varieties.* London and New York: Longman.

Stetkevych, Jaroslav. 1970. *The modern Arabic literary language: Lexical and stylistic developments.* Chicago: University of Chicago Press.

Wehr, Hans. 1979. *A dictionary of Modern Written Arabic.* Edited by J. Milton Cowan. 4th ed. Wiesbaden: Harrassowitz.

Wright, William, ed. 1896. *A grammar of the Arabic language.* 3d ed. 2 vols. Cambridge: Cambridge University Press. Reprinted, 1951.

WOLFDIETRICH FISCHER

ARAMAIC. The Aramaic branch of the Semitic language family comprises languages of inscriptions and documents dating from the 10th century BCE onward, several literary languages, and diverse dialects spoken to this day. It was a medium of international communication

MAP 1. *Sites of Early Aramaic Inscriptions*

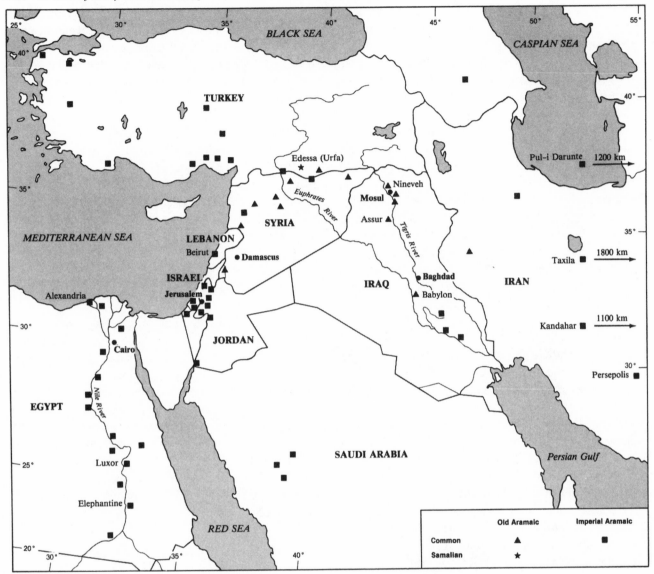

in the Near East for well over a thousand years, and is the language of important Christian and Jewish literatures; now, however, it has only about 200,000 speakers. The usual classification divides Aramaic languages into five periods: Old, Imperial, Middle, Late, and Modern. Geographical variation is evident in all these periods.

Old Aramaic is attested in inscriptions from the 10th to the 7th centuries BCE, found in Syria and Turkey. Of the two attested dialects, Samalian (sometimes referred to as Yaudic) disappeared early, and only Common Old Aramaic is closely related to later varieties of the language. For locations, see Map 1.

Imperial (or Official) Aramaic was widely used in the Assyrian, Babylonian, and Persian empires from about

700 to 200 BCE. It is attested in inscriptions and documents from Egypt to Pakistan, and in the biblical books of Daniel and Ezra. An important reason for the widespread official adoption of Aramaic, besides the movement of Arameans into Mesopotamia, may have been the simplicity of the Aramaic alphabet, as compared with the cuneiform syllabic/logographic writing system of Akkadian. Many pan-Aramaic phonological features emerged only after the Old Aramaic period and probably spread as characteristics of Imperial Aramaic. These include the shift of the Proto-Semitic interdentals to stops; the shift of the Proto-Semitic emphatic lateral consonant to ʕ; the reduction of unstressed short vowels in open syllables; and spirantization (see below).

Middle Aramaic comprises a diverse set of forms written from about 200 BCE to about 200 CE. All were approximations to Imperial Aramaic at a time when the spoken languages were more like Late Aramaic. Some of the Dead Sea Scrolls are written in Middle Aramaic, and a spoken form of the language was the native tongue of Jesus.

Late Aramaic includes six literary languages, the only surviving records of a dialect continuum which stretched from Palestine through Mesopotamia. In the west were Jewish, Samaritan, and Christian Palestinian Aramaic. In the east were Mandaic and Jewish Babylonian Aramaic; the latter is the language of the Babylonian Talmud, the core of traditional Jewish education to this day. Syriac, the literary and liturgical language of Christians throughout the Middle East, is geographically and linguistically intermediate between the Palestinian and Babylonian varieties. Aramaic gradually receded in most areas after the spread of Islam and Arabic, beginning in the 7th century.

Modern Aramaic includes four languages spoken today: (i) the Maʿlūla group, in Syria; (ii) Ṭūrōyo and Mlaḥsô, in southeastern Turkey; (iii) Northeastern Aramaic, in a region straddling northern Iraq and adjacent parts of Iran and Turkey; and (iv) modern Mandaic, in Khuzistan, Iran. For locations, see Map 2. The great majority of modern Aramaic speakers speak Northeastern Aramaic; they are the Christian and Jewish minorities of a region in which the Muslim majority speaks Kurdish and Azerbaijani Turkish. Northeastern Aramaic exhibits an astonishing amount of dialect variation; however, the ethnic self-designations "Assyrian" and "Chaldean" correlate mainly with Christian denomination, not with dialect; the term "Modern Syriac" is justified only by the script used by Christian speakers.

Throughout its history, Aramaic has both influenced and been influenced by many neighboring languages in vocabulary and in grammatical structure. The most important were Akkadian, Persian, Greek, and Hebrew—in varying degrees, according to time, place, and religious/cultural affiliation. Modern Aramaic has much vocabulary from Arabic, Kurdish, and Turkish as well as grammatical features. Yet even in the modern language, the great majority of the vocabulary can be traced to the native Aramaic lexicon.

Classical Syriac is the most extensively and precisely documented Aramaic language; its consonantal phonemes are shown in Table 1.

Labial, dental, and velar fricatives are phonemic at the surface level; but at a more abstract level, $\bar{p}$ $\underline{b}$ t $\underline{d}$ k $\bar{g}$ are variants of the corresponding stops p b t d k g. In an earlier stage of the language, the stops other than t and q, when postvocalic and not geminate, became fricatives by a rule of spirantization. However, in attested Syriac, this rule had become much less transparent—partly through the deletion of vowels after spirantization had applied, and partly through the creation of morphological and lexical exceptions.

We can reconstruct the following vowels for early Syriac: long $\bar{\imath}$ $\bar{e}$ $\bar{e}$ $\bar{a}$ $\bar{o}$ $\bar{u}$, short e a u ($\bar{e}$, higher than $\bar{e}$, is relatively rare). Short vowels are generally elided (not merely reduced) in open syllables. There is no known significant accent in Syriac, although both earlier and later Aramaic (Biblical and Modern) have phonemic stress.

Syriac was written from right to left in three related scripts, as shown in Tables 2a–b. Distinctive vowel qualities were indicated by optional diacritics, as in Hebrew and Arabic script.

Syriac has typical Semitic morphology, with prefixes and suffixes as well as discontinuous consonantal roots and vocalic stem morphemes. Nominal and verbal derivation involves both affixes and discontinuous morphology, as does verbal inflection; but nominal inflection is almost entirely affixal. As a consequence, borrowed nouns may retain their original vowels and syllabic shapes, but borrowed verbs are restructured to fit into Syriac canonical patterns.

The inflectional categories of the Syriac noun are gender (masculine/feminine), number (singular/plural), and "state." The last includes the categories Determinate, which is semantically unmarked; Absolute, found chiefly in predicate adjectives and in quantified nouns; and Construct, bound to a following possessor or specifying noun. (In earlier Aramaic, the unmarked state was the Absolute; while the Determinate state, formed with the suffix -$\bar{a}$, was semantically similar to English *the*. In Syriac, the form with -$\bar{a}$ may be semantically definite or indefinite.) An attributive adjective agrees with its noun in gender, number, and state.

Verbal derivation has three basic canonical patterns: an unmarked pattern; an "intensive" pattern, marked by the gemination of the middle root consonant; and a causative pattern with the prefix a-. For each of the three, a corresponding passive/reflexive is formed with the prefix *et(t)*- and a change of the stem vowels.

A Syriac verb has the following inflectional forms: Perfect (a past tense), Imperfect (future and modal), Active Participle (serving as the present tense), Passive Participle (perfect), Imperative, and Infinitive. The Per-

MAP 2. *Locations Where Aramaic Is Spoken*

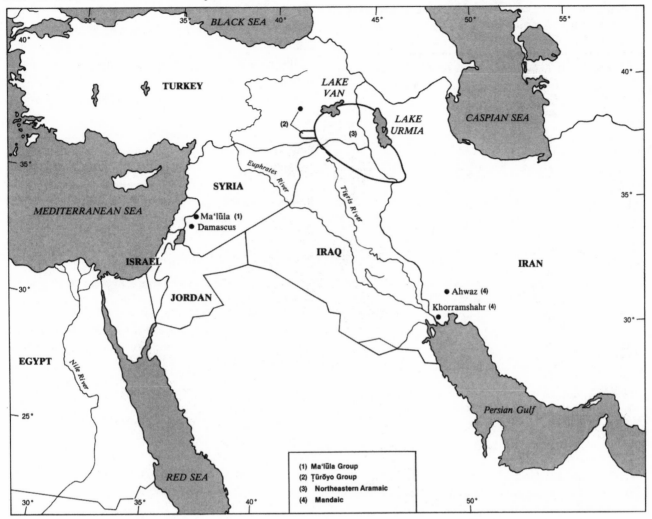

TABLE 1. *Syriac Consonants*

	Labial	Dental	Alveolar	Palato-alveolar	Velar	Uvular	Pharyngeal	Glottal
Stops								
Voiced	b	d			g			
Voiceless	p	t			k			(ʔ)
Emphatic		ṭ				q		
Fricatives								
Voiced	ḇ	ḏ	z		ḡ		ʕ	
Voiceless	p̄	ṯ	s	š	k̲		ḥ	
Emphatic			ṣ					
Nasals	m	n						
Vibrant		r						
Lateral		l						
Glide	w			y				h

TABLE 2a. *Traditional Order of Consonants in Syriac Scripts.* Variant forms used at the ends of words appear to the left in the table. Some of the sounds occur only in certain periods or dialects.

Serto	Estrangelo	Nestorian	Transcription
			ʔ, zero
			b, b̲
			g, g̲
			d, d̲
			h
			w
			z
			ḥ
			ṭ
			y
			k, k̲
			l
			m
			n
			s
			ʕ
			p, p̲
			ṣ
			q
			r
			š
			t, t̲

TABLE 2b. *Syriac Vowel Diacritics.* Jacobite symbols are written either above or below consonants; placement of Nestorian symbols is shown by the dash.

Jacobite (Western)		Nestorian (Eastern)	
	i		ī
	e		ē
	a		e
	o (< ā)		a
	u		ā
			o, ō
			u, ū

fect and Imperfect are inflected for the gender, number, and person of the subject; the Participles and Imperative are marked for gender and number only. The Passive Participle appears frequently in a syntactically active construction with present perfect meaning; the agent (the syntactic subject) is then marked with the preposition *l-,* which otherwise marks direct or indirect objects or pos-sessors, but not agents of passives. In this construction, the so-called Passive Participle can be formed even from intransitive verbs: *šmiʕ l-ī* 'I have heard', *azīl l-ī* 'I have gone'.

The order of verb, subject, and object in a sentence varies freely, but other features of word order follow Verb + Object typology; thus adjectives follow nouns, and prepositions precede their objects. Syriac sentences meaning 'A is B' contain no verb; instead, they have either (i) an enclitic pronoun agreeing with the subject, but following the first word of the predicate, or (ii) the particle *ʔīt̲* 'there is', with a pronominal suffix representing the subject.

[*See also* Semitic Languages.]

BIBLIOGRAPHY

Beyer, Klaus. 1986. *The Aramaic language: Its distribution and subdivisions.* Göttingen: Vandenhoeck and Ruprecht.

Fitzmyer, Joseph A. 1979. The phases of the Aramaic language. In Joseph A. Fitzmyer, *A wandering Aramean: Collected Aramaic essays* (Society of Biblical Literature, Monograph series, 25), pp. 57–84. Chico, Calif.: Scholars Press.

Fitzmyer, Joseph A., and Stephen A. Kaufman. 1992. *An Aramaic bibliography.* Baltimore Md.: Johns Hopkins University Press.

Greenspahn, Frederick E. 1998. *An introduction to Aramaic.* Atlanta: Scholars Press.

Jastrow, Otto. 1997. The Neo-Aramaic languages. In *The Semitic languages,* edited by Robert Hetzron, pp. 334–377. London and New York: Routledge.

Kaufman, Stephen A. 1974. *The Akkadian influences on Aramaic.* (Assyriological studies, 19.) Chicago: University of Chicago Press.

Kaufman, Stephen A. 1997. Aramaic. In *The Semitic languages,* edited by Robert Hetzron, pp. 114–130. London and New York: Routledge.

Krotkoff, Georg. 1982. *A Neo-Aramaic dialect of Kurdistan: Texts, grammar, and vocabulary.* (American Oriental series, 64.) New Haven: American Oriental Society.

Kutscher, Eduard Yechezkel. 1970. Aramaic. In *Current trends in linguistics,* edited by Thomas A. Sebeok, vol. 6, *Linguistics in South West Asia and North Africa,* pp. 347–412. The Hague: Mouton. Reprinted in E. Y. Kutscher, *Hebrew and Aramaic studies* (Jerusalem: Magnes, 1977), pp. 90–155.

Kutscher, Eduard Yechezkel. 1971. Aramaic. *Encyclopaedia Judaica* 3.259–287. Jerusalem: Keter.

Marcus, David. 1981. *A manual of Babylonian Jewish Aramaic.* Washington, D.C.: University Press of America.

Nöldeke, Theodor. 1904. *Compendious Syriac grammar.* London: Williams and Norgate. Reprinted with additions, Winona Lake, Ind.: Eisenbrauns, 2001.

Rosenthal, Franz. 1961. *A grammar of Biblical Aramaic.* (Porta linguarum Orientalium, n.s., 5.) Wiesbaden: Harrassowitz.

Rosenthal, Franz, ed. 1967. *An Aramaic handbook.* (Porta linguarum Orientalium, n.s., 10.) Wiesbaden: Harrassowitz.

Segert, Stanislav. 1975. *Altaramäische Grammatik mit Bibliographie, Chrestomathie und Glossar.* Leipzig: VEB Verlag Enzyklopädie.

Sokoloff, Michael. 1990. *A dictionary of Jewish Palestinian Aramaic of the Byzantine Period.* Ramat-Gan, Israel: Bar Ilan University Press.

Thackston, Wheeler M. 1999. *Introduction to Syriac: An elementary grammar with readings from Syriac literature.* Bethesda, Md.: IBEX.

ROBERT D. HOBERMAN

ARANDIC LANGUAGES.

ARANDIC LANGUAGES. A group spoken in the Northern Territory and Queensland, Australia; they form a branch of the PAMA-NYUNGAN family of AUSTRALIAN LANGUAGES.

LANGUAGE LIST

Alyawarr: also called Alyawarra, Alyawarre, Aljawara, Iliaura, Yowera. 1,500 speakers in Sandover and Tennant Creek areas, Northern Territory, and Queensland. Related to Arrernte, Arrernte Akerre, Anmatyerre, and Kaytetye. Speakers are somewhat bilingual in English. Roman alphabet.

Andegerebinha: 10 speakers remain in Northern Territory: Formerly spoken at Hay River, Pituri Creek area, east of Alyawarra.

Anmatyerre: also called Anmatjirra. 800 speakers in Mt. Allen, Northwest Alice Springs region. Dialects are Eastern Anmatyerre, Western Anmatyerre (Kalenthelkwe, Kelenthwelkere, Kelentheyewelrere).

Eastern Arrernte: also called Eastern Aranda, Arunta. 1,500 speakers in Northern Territory, Alice Springs area, Santa Teresa, Hats Range. Related to Mparntwe Arrernte, Alyawarr, Arrernte Akarre, Anmatyerre, Kaytetye, Western Arrarnta. English bilingual program in operation at a school at Santa Teresa. Western Arrartna and Eastern Arrernte are considered by some to be separate languages.

Kaytetye: also called Kaiditj, Kaititj, Gaididj. 200 speakers remain north of Alice Springs, Northern Territory. Related to Alyawarr. People generally speak Kriol.

Western Arrarnta: also called Aranda, Arunta. 1,000 speakers in Northern Territory, Alice Springs area, Hermannsburg. Dialects are Western Aranda, Akerre (Akara), Southern Aranda. Closely related to Alyawarr and Gaididj. Western Arrartna and Eastern Arrernte are considered by some to be separate languages. Southern Aranda is nearly extinct.

B. GRIMES

ARAUAN LANGUAGES. A family spoken in Amazonas, Brazil, with some overspill into Acre, Brazil, and Peru.

LANGUAGE LIST

Arua: also called Arawá. Formerly spoken in Brazil. Became extinct in 1877.

Banawá: also called Kitiya, Banavá, Banauá, Jafí. 70 speakers in Brazil. Not as close to Jamamadí linguistically as previously thought. Some bilingualism in Jamamadí, and a little in Portuguese. They prefer their own language.

Culina: also called Kulína, Kulyna, Corina, Madija, Madihá. 1,800 speakers in Brazil and Peru. In Brazil: 1,500 speakers. Amazonas, Acre. Minor changes from Peruvian dialect. In Peru: 300 speakers. Ethnic population: 300 to 400. Southeast, near Brazilian border, upper Purus and Santa Rosa Rivers. Some bilingualism in Spanish. Parents transmit Culina to their children. Linguists have been unsure about whether or not the Arauan languages are a subbranch of the Arawakan languages.

Dení: also called Dani. 600 speakers in Amazonas.

Jamamadí: also called Yamamadí, Kanamanti, Canamanti. 195 speakers in Amazonas, scattered over 200,000 square miles. Dialects are Bom Futuro, Jurua, Pauini, Mamoria (Mamori), Cuchudua (Maima), Tukurina. Other groups are called "Jamamadí" who are closer to Culina or Dení. Tukurina may be a separate language. Dialects or related languages: Araua, Pama, Sewacu, Sipo, Yuberi.

Jaruára: also called Jarawara, Yarawara. 155 speakers in Amazonas, near the Jamamadí, seven villages. Formerly considered a dialect of Jamamadí. All Jamamadí speakers also speak some Portuguese. All ages. Parents pass Jaruára to children. Vigorous language use. Spoken use of Jaruára in school, religious services, letters.

Paumarí: also called Purupurá. 700 speakers in Amazonas, in three villages mainly on the Purus River. Dialects are Paumarm (Pammari), Kurukuru (Curucuru), Uaiai, inherently intelligible. Speakers are fairly bilingual. As of 1984, half the speakers were under 12 years of age.

Suruahá: also called Suruwahá, Zuruahá, Mndios Do Coxodoá. 130 speakers in Amazonas.

B. GRIMES

ARAUCANIAN LANGUAGES. Spoken in southern Chile and in adjacent areas of Argentina. The surviving languages are listed below.

LANGUAGE LIST

Huilliche: also called Veliche, Huiliche. 2,000 speakers in Chile as of 1982. South of the Mapuche, Tenth Region, from Valdivia to Chiloé. Related to Mapudungun, but barely intelligible with it. Most of the ethnic group speaks Spanish as first language. Only elderly speakers. Used mainly among friends and for ceremonial purposes.

Mapudungun: also called Mapudungu, Mapuche. "Araucano" is a derogatory name sometimes used. 440,000 speakers in Chile and Argentina. In Chile: 400,000 speakers. Ethnic population: 928,000 as of 1992. Between the Itata and Tolten Rivers. Dialects are Moluche (Ngoluche, Manzanero), Picunche, Pehuenche. Easy intelligibility among all dialects. Pehuenche and Moluche are very close. Some bilingualism in Spanish. All ages. In Argentina: 40,000 speakers in provinces of Neuquen, Rio Negro, Chubut, Buenos Aires, La Pampa. One or more dialects.   B. GRIMES

ARAWAKAN LANGUAGES. The Arawakan family has the greatest geographical spread of any language family in Central and South America, extending south from Belize to Paraguay, and east from the Andes to the mouth of the Amazon. Voegelin and Voegelin 1977 list 119 languages in the family, showing 16 as extinct. Grimes 2000, a more reliable and up-to-date source, identifies fewer than 50 extant Arawakan languages. According to her estimates, the total number of Arawakan speakers could be as high as 645,000, of whom 87% belong to three groups: Wayuu (305,000), Garífuna (190,000), and Campa (67,000). "Campa" is a derogatory name for Asháninca and the five Ashéninca subgroups (Apurucayali, Pajonal, Perené, Pichis, Ucayali-Yurúa) and is also used for a group of closely related languages, including those just named and also Caquinte, Machiguenga, and Nomatsiguenga. For reference, see Noble 1965, Matteson et al. 1972, Derbyshire and Pullum 1986, Aikhenvald 1999.

Figure 1 shows an internal classification of Maipuran, which has long been recognized as the core of the Arawakan family; see Map 1. It is based on Payne 1990: 489, which uses a larger and more accurate set of data than any earlier classification. Aikhenvald (1999:67–71, with discussion on pp. 73–75) gives a slightly different internal classification and includes extinct languages for which descriptive materials are available. Voegelin and Voegelin depended on those earlier studies, and included a number of other languages in the Arawakan family, most of which belong to subgroups postulated as coordinate with Maipuran. At the present stage of research, it is impossible to say whether all, or any, of these (or other) languages will eventually be established as having a relationship with Maipuran that is close enough for them to be regarded as Arawakan. Figure 2 (from Payne

FIGURE 1. *Subgrouping of Maipuran (Core of the Arawakan Family)*

Central
  Mehinácu, Parecís, Waurá, Yawalapití
Eastern (Palikúr)
Northern
  Caribbean
    Garífuna, Wayuu, Island Carib, Lokono (Arawak), Paraujano, Taino
  Inland
    Achagua, Baniwa, Baré, Cabiyarí, Curripaco, Guarequena, Piapoco, Resígaro, Tariano, Yavitero, Yucuna
  Wapishana
Southern
  Bolivia-Paraná
    Baure, Guana, Ignaciano, Terêna, Trinitario
  Campa
    Asháninca, Ashéninca group, Caquinte, Machiguenga, Nomatsiguenga
  Purus
    Apurinã, Yine
Western
  Yanesha, Chamicuro

1990:365) tentatively suggests the languages that may possibly belong to such a larger Arawakan family.

With regard to the still higher level relationship of Arawakan to other families and stocks, the best known (though disputed) classification is that of Greenberg 1987, who sees Arawakan as most closely related to the Katembri, Otomaco, and Tinigua families in the Macro-Arawakan division of the Equatorial section of the Andean-Equatorial phylum (as well as to Guahibo, which here is included in Figure 2). He also places Tupian in the Equatorial section; but Rodrigues 1974:56, on the basis of more detailed comparative studies, affirms that Tupian is much more closely related to Cariban (shown by Greenberg in the Gê-Pano-Carib phylum) than it is to Arawakan.

The basic core of segmental phonological units in Maipuran languages consists of occlusives p t $t\!f$ k, fricatives s h, nasals m n, liquids l r, semivowels w y, high vowels i $ɨ$ u, and non-high vowels e a o. Phonemic length of consonants and vowels is common. Most languages have five vowels, though Yanesha has only three, and Wayuu has six. Some languages have modifications such as vowel nasalization, voicing of plosives and fricatives, and consonantal pre-aspiration, pre-nasalization, labialization, palatalization, or glottalization. The basic syllable pattern throughout the family is CV (and V

MAP 1. *Distribution of Maipuran Language Groups*

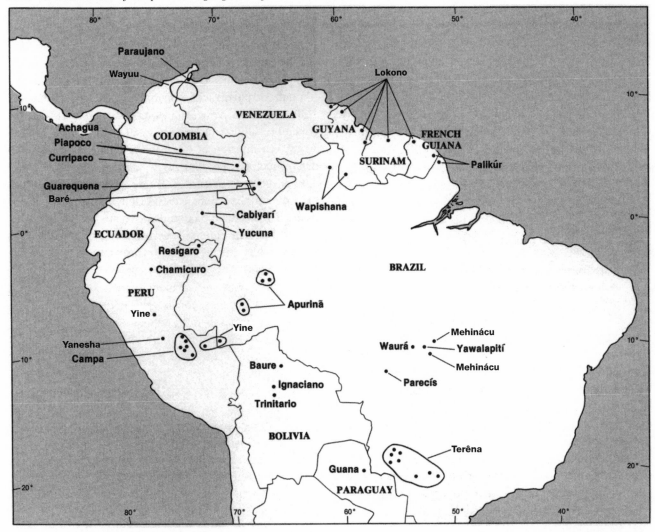

FIGURE 2. *Tentative Proto-Arawakan Proposal*

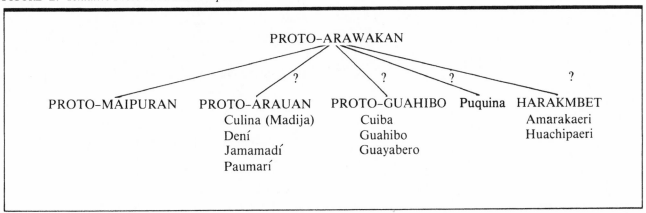

word-initially); sequences of two vowels occur in many languages, but syllable-final consonants are uncommon. The most frequently occurring morphophonemic processes are vowel loss and vowel harmony. Contrastive lexical tone is reported for only one language, Resígaro. This is almost certainly a borrowing from Huitotoan languages. Pitch-accent systems occur in at least two Southern languages, Nomatsiguenga and Terêna.

Morphologically, Maipuran languages are polysynthetic, mainly agglutinative. The verbal morphology is relatively complex. Verb roots do not normally occur as free forms. The following categories of derivational and inflectional morphemes regularly occur (the specific forms in parentheses, or their variants, occur in several languages):

(a) Subject person-marking prefixes (1st person nV- and, in some Caribbean languages, *ta-/da-*; 2nd person pV-).

(b) Object person-marking suffixes (3rd person *-r*V).

(c) Number, either as part of the person marker or as a separate affix.

(d) Incorporated noun classifiers—see (o) below.

(e) Category-changing and valence-changing affixes, including transitivizers, detransitivizers, e.g. reflexives, reciprocals, and passives (*-oa* and *-kV*), causatives (*ka-* or *-ka*), and verbalizers (*ka-* 'attributive', *ma-* 'privative', *-ta* 'general verbalizer').

(f) Locational, positional, directional (*-Vp* 'arriving, approaching'), and other suffixes of semantically adverbial type.

(g) Negation (*ma*).

(h) Verification/evidential markers which express the speaker's perspective or degree of responsibility concerning the utterance.

(i) Aspectual distinctions: perfective, completive, progressive, durative, and habitual. Sometimes a component of tense is included in the aspect marker; but tense, as a distinct category, is notably absent from most Arawakan languages.

(j) Root-final affix, empty of semantic content, of the form (V)*t(a)*.

(k) Subordinating and nominalizing suffixes (*-n*V, *-r*V, *-t*V).

(l) Copulas and auxiliary verbs (*ni*).

(m) Nominal inflection for possession, with person-marking possessor prefix—the same forms as the subject-marking verb prefixes of (a) above—and possession suffix (*-r*V).

(n) Gender agreement systems (lacking in Yanesha and Terêna, and minor in a few other southern languages). Nouns themselves are often not marked, but have inherent gender, usually masculine or feminine (occasionally a third distinction is made for non-human or inanimate). The system governs formal marking with free and bound pronouns—and often also with demonstratives, nominalizing suffixes, adjectives, and (less often) with certain verbal categories.

(o) Noun classifier systems (not reported for some northern languages); classifier affixes, based on shape and other characteristics of their associated nouns, are attached to constituents of noun phrases or are incorporated into the verb.

Much of what would be sentence syntax in other languages is expressed in the verb in Maipuran languages. This accounts for one major syntactic characteristic: most sentences in natural discourse do not have more than two constituents. S[ubject] and O[bject] noun phrases are especially infrequent; their referents often are signaled only by person, number, and gender markers in the verb. Basic order varies, when S and O noun phrases do occur: SVO is most representative for the family, but is frequently accompanied by VS for non-active intransitive verbs. VSO occurs in Yanesha, the "Campa" languages, and possibly Garífuna; VOS in Baure and Terêna; OSV (probably) in Apurinã; and SOV in Yine. At an earlier historical stage, SOV was probably the basic order in the family. This is supported by the predominance in today's languages of the phrasal orders noun + postposition and genitive + noun—patterns which tend to correlate with OV order in the clause. The structure of subordinate clauses differs little from that of main clauses, except for the addition of subordinating affixes or particles. Relative clauses often occur without an overt head noun (when there is one, they usually follow it), and the relativizing suffixes function more like nominalizers. Coordination of phrases and clauses is mainly by juxtaposition, although most languages have a few forms which can have a conjoining function. Passive constructions are mostly of the non-agentive, medio-passive type. See Aikhenvald 1999 for a more detailed description of the phonological and grammatical characteristics of Arawakan languages.

[*See also* South American Languages.]

BIBLIOGRAPHY

Aikhenvald, Alexandra Y. 1999. The Arawak language family. In *The Amazonian languages*, edited by R. M. W. Dixon and

Alexandra Y. Aikhenvald, pp. 65–106. Cambridge: Cambridge University Press.

Derbyshire, Desmond C., and Geoffrey K. Pullum, eds. 1986. *Handbook of Amazonian languages,* vol. 1. Berlin: Mouton de Gruyter.

Greenberg, Joseph H. 1987. *Language in the Americas.* Stanford, Calif.: Stanford University Press.

Grimes, Barbara F., ed. 2000. *Ethnologue: Languages of the world.* 14th ed. Dallas, Tex.: Summer Institute of Linguistics.

Matteson, Esther, et al., eds. 1972. *Comparative studies in Amerindian languages.* (Janua linguarum, Series practica, 127.) The Hague: Mouton.

Noble, G. Kingsley. 1965. *Proto-Arawakan and its descendants.* (Indiana University Research Center in Anthropology, Folklore, and Linguistics, Publication 38; *International Journal of American Linguistics,* 31:3, part 2.) Bloomington.

Payne, David L. 1990. A classification of Maipuran (Arawakan) languages based on shared lexical retentions. In *Handbook of Amazonian languages,* vol. 3, edited by Desmond C. Derbyshire and Geoffrey K. Pullum, pp. 355–499. Berlin: Mouton de Gruyter.

Rodrigues, Aryon Dall'Igna. 1974. Linguistic groups of Amazonia. In *Native South Americans: Ethnology of the least known continent,* edited by Patricia J. Lyon, pp. 51–58. Boston: Little Brown.

Voegelin, Charles F., and Florence M. Voegelin. 1977. *Classification and index of the world's languages.* New York: Elsevier.

DESMOND C. DERBYSHIRE

LANGUAGE LIST

Achagua: also called Ajagua, Xagua. 231 speakers in Colombia on Rio Meta near Puerto Gaitan. Close to Piapoco. Speakers are trilingual in Achagua, Spanish, and Piapoco. They speak Achagua in the home.

Ajyíninka Apurucayali: also called Ashéninca Apurucayali, Apurucayali Campa, Ajyéninka, Campa. 25,000 speakers in Peru. Apurucayali tributary of the Pachitea River. Not intelligible with other Campa languages.

Apurinã: also called Ipurinãn, Kangite, Popengare. 2,000 speakers in Brazil. Amazonas, Acre; scattered over one thousand miles of the Purus River from Rio Branco to Manaus.

Arawak: also called Lokono, Arowak. 2,400 speakers in Suriname, Guyana, French Guiana, and Venezuela. In Suriname: 700 speakers. Ethnic population: 2,051 in Suriname as of 1980. Scattered locations across the north of Suriname. Reported to be used only by the elderly in Suriname and Guyana. The young people use Sranan. In Guyana: 1,500 speakers. Ethnic population: 15,000. West coast and northeast along the Corantyne River. Others in the ethnic group are bilingual. Reported to be used primarily by the elderly in Guyana and Suriname. In French Guiana: 150 speakers. Coastal areas. Reported to be used only by the elderly. In Venezuela: Coastal area near Guyana, Delta Amacuro.

Asháninka: also called Ashéninca. "Campa" is a derogatory name sometimes used. 23,750 speakers in Peru. Ethnic population: 25,000 to 30,000. Apurimac, Ene, Perene, Tambo Rivers and tributaries. Closely related to Ashéninka, Caquinte, and Machiguenga. Vigorous language use.

Ashéninka Pajonal: also called Ashéninca, Atsiri, Pajonal. "Campa" is a derogatory name sometimes used. 7,000 speakers in Peru. Dialects are Pajonal Ashéninka (Ashéninka del Gran Pajonal), South Ucayali Ashéninka. Ethnic population: 14,000 to 20,000, including half in each dialect. Central Gran Pajonal area and western headwaters of the Ucayali River. Some bilingualism in Spanish. All but a handful in Pajonal Ashéninka and 1,000 in South Ucayali Ashéninka speak the language.

Ashéninca Perené: also called Perené, Campa. 9,000 speakers in Peru. Perené tributary of the Pachitea River. Not intelligible with other Campa languages.

Ashéninca Pichis: also called Pichis, Ashéninca. 3,000 speakers in Peru. Pichis and Sheshea tributaries of the Pachitea River. Not intelligible with other Campa languages. Some bilingualism in Spanish.

Ashéninca Ucayali-Yurúa: also called Yurúa-Ucayali Ashéninca. 7,235 speakers in Peru and Brazil. In Peru: 7,000 speakers. Tributaries of the Ucayali River. Not intelligible with other Campa varieties. In Brazil: 235 speakers in state of Acre.

Atorada: also called Atorad, Atorti, Atorai, Dauri. Spoken in Guyana and Brazil. In Guyana: Southwestern Guyana, near the Wapishana. Bilingualism in Wapishana. As of 2000, all speakers were over 50 years old. In Brazil: Spoken in Roraima. Bilingualism in Portuguese. All speakers are over 50 years old.

Baniva: also called Avani, Ayane, Abane. Formerly spoken in Venezuela, Colombian border area. Dialects are Baniva, Quirruba.

Baniwa: also called Baniua Do Içana, Maniba, Baniva, Baniba, Issana, Dakenei. Around 5,900 speakers in Brazil and Venezuela. In Brazil: 5,460 speakers. Middle Içana River, Amazonas. They go to Colombia or Venezuela mainly to work or trade. Dialects are Hohodené (Hohodena, Kadaupuritana), Siusy-Tapuya (Seuci, Siuci, Siusi). Related to Carútana and Curripaco. Several groups on the middle Içana and Ayarí Rivers who speak Baniwa: Hohodené, Kadaupuritana, Sucuriyu-Tapuya, Siusy-Tapuya, Irá-Tapuya, Kawá-Tapuya, Waliperedakenai. In Venezuela: 407 speakers. Amazonas, between the Curipaco and the Guarequena, along the Colombian border. Related to Carútana and Curripaco.

Baré: also called Barawana, Barauna, Barauana, Ihini, Arihini, Maldavaca, Cunipusana, Yavita, Mitua. Formerly spoken in Venezuela. Colombian border in extreme southwest, Amazonas, along the upper Rio Negro from Brazil-Venezuela border to the Casiquiare Canal, Maroa. Replaced by Spanish or Nhengatu.

Baure: 13 speakers remain in Bolivia. Ethnic population: 631. Formerly spoken in Beni department, northwest of Magdalena. Bilingualism in Spanish. Children and most adults were not using Baure 20 years ago.

Cabiyarí: also called Cabiuarí, Cauyare, Kauyarí, Cuyare, Kawillary. 50 speakers in Colombia. Cananarí River (tributary of the Apaporis and Vaupés).

Caquinte: also called Caquinte Campa, Aquenquetsatsare, Poyenisati. "Cachomashiri" is a derogatory name sometimes used. 300 speakers in Peru. Ethnic population: 300. Closest to Ashéninca Campa. Some bilingualism in Machiguenga. Almost none can converse at all in Spanish. Some use Ashéninca as second language. Some are borrowing words from Ashéninca or Machiguenga. All ages. All domains, oral and written use in church, written in letters between speakers. Caquinte is transmitted from parents to children. They have positive attitudes toward Caquinte. The Caquinte do not like to be called "Campa."

Carútana: also called Karutana, Arara Do Amazonas. 250 speakers in Brazil. Northwestern Amazonas, near Curripaco. Dialects are Adaru, Arara, Dzaui (Dzawi), Jauarete (Yawarete Tapuya), Jurupari (Yurupari Tapuya), Mapache, Uadzoli (Wadzoli), Urubu. Close to Curripaco and Baniwa. Arara may be distinct.

Chamicuro: also called Chamicura, Chamicolo. 2 speakers remain in Peru. Ethnic population: 10 to 20. Formerly spoken in Pampa Hermosa on a tributary of Huallaga. Bilingualism in Spanish. No children speakers.

Chané: formerly spoken in Salta, Argentina. Some have equated this name with "Guana" (Kaskiha) of Paraguay of Mascoian affiliation, or Terêna of Brazil of Arawakan affiliation, but these three languages are distinct. Chané has not been spoken for 300 years. Descendents are called "Izoceño" and now speak a variety of Chiriguano (Eastern Bolivian Guaraní).

Cumeral: formerly spoken in Colombia.

Curripaco: also called Curipaco, Kuripaco, Kurripaco, Koripako. 3,020 speakers in Colombia, Brazil, and Venezuela. In Colombia: 2,000 speakers. Guainia, Isana, and Inirida Rivers. Close to Baniwa and Carutana. In Brazil: 810 speakers in northwestern Amazonas. Dialects are Korripako (Karupaka), Unhun (Cadauapuritana, Enhen). Close to Baniwa and Carutana. In Venezuela: 210 speakers in Amazonas.

Garifuna: also called Caribe, Central American Carib, Black Carib, "moreno." Around 190,000 speakers in Honduras, Nicaragua, Guatemala, Belize, and USA. In Honduras: 98,000 speakers. Dialects are Eastern Garifuna, Western Garifuna. Eastern Garifuna is in Honduras and Nicaragua (leaves out /r/ and tends to shorten words), Western Garifuna in Guatemala and Belize. Related to Island Carib, with Spanish, English, and French borrowings. Fewer than 100 monolingual speakers. Others are bilingual in Spanish, and 5% trilingual with English. Family, friends, local administration, some church services, other. In some villages in Honduras, Spanish is replacing Garifuna. In about half of the villages, the people are proud of Garifuna. English-oriented orthography used for Belize, Spanish-oriented in Guatemala. The Western dialect is used as the written standard, and the orthography is being standardized. In USA: 65,000 speakers. New York City, Miami, New Orleans, Los Angeles. In Guatemala: 16,700 speakers. Izabal Department, two villages on the northeast coast: Livingston and Puerto Barrios. Related to Island Carib with Spanish, English, and French borrowings. Speakers are bilingual in Spanish. Spanish-oriented orthography used. In Belize: 12,274 speakers. Dangriga, Stann Creek, and Toledo along the coast, six villages. Bilingualism in Belize Creole. In Nicaragua: Ethnic population: 1,500 in Nicaragua. Regiòn Atlántica Autónoma del Sur, Orinoco village, far from speakers in other countries. Speakers are bilingual in Creole. Only elderly speakers left in Nicaragua.

Guana: also called Kinikinao, Chuala, Chana, East Paraná, Kinihinao, Equinao. Formerly spoken in Brazil, in Mato Grosso do Sul, near the Terêna. Related to Terêna, Irántxe.

Guarequena: also called Guarekena, Arequena, Urequema, Uerequema, Warekena. 705 speakers in Venezuela and Brazil, possibly some in Colombia. In Venezuela: 367 speakers. Village of Guzmán Blanco, half an hour below Maroa. San Miguel River, Amazonas. Bilingualism in Spanish. Only older people speak the language in Venezuela. In Brazil: 338 speakers. Amazonas, Rio Chié (Xié) and Içana near Venezuelan border. Many speak Nhengatu in Brazil. Those in centers are more bilingual. Spoken in remote areas. Most use Guarequena by preference.

Ignaciano: also called Moxo, Moxos, Mojos, Mojo. 4,500 speakers in Bolivia. Ethnic population: 20,805 with Trinitario. South central Beni. Limited intelligibility with Trinitario, similar to Spanish and Portuguese, with vowel reduction. Some bilingualism in Spanish, which is the language of instruction in schools. By the 1980s, fewer than 100 monolinguals, all older than 30. Most women can converse in Spanish. Much Spanish influence. Perhaps half of the children learn Ignaciano, others do not. Ignaciano used in town meetings unless outsiders present. Many use Ignaciano in daily life. Ignaciano a required subject in the lower school grades, one session per week. Speakers are encouraged to maintain ethnicity by the popularity of their many church-related pageants, to claim their lands according to timber rights, and various other improvements.

Iñapari: also called Inamari. 4 speakers remain in Peru. Formerly spoken on Piedras River, at the mouth of Sabaluyo, near Puerto Maldonado. Extinct in Bolivia. All are reported to be bilingual in Spanish. No children speakers.

Ipeka-Tapuia: also called Pato-Tapuya, Pato Tapuia, Cumata, Ipeca, Pacu, Paku-Tapuya, Payuliene, Payualiene, Palioariene. 135 speakers in Brazil. Içana, Amazonas. Some linguists treat it as a dialect of Siuci, itself a dialect of Baniwa.

Irántxe: also called Iranxe, Iranche, Münkü. 191 speakers in Brazil. Mato Grosso, headwaters of the Rio Cravari, tributary of the Rio Sangue, which is a tributary of the Rio Juruena. Dialects are Münkü (Mynky, Menku, Kenkü, Myy), Irántxe. Most are bilingual in Portuguese.

Island Carib: formerly spoken in Dominica and St. Vincent and the Grenadines. In Dominica: Formerly also in Lesser Antilles, excluding Trinidad. Was not intelligible with Garifuna (Black Carib). Vincentian on St. Vincent may have been closer to Garifuna (Black Carib) than to Island Carib. Became extinct in Dominica about 1920. Used a special language of Cariban origin to address men. In St. Vincent and the Grenadines: Not inherently intelligible with Garifuna in more than a limited way. Became extinct in Dominica and St. Vincent about 1920.

Machiguenga: also called Matsiganga, Matsigenka, Mañaries. 6,000 speakers in Peru. Urubamba, Camisea, Picha, Manu, Timpia, Tigompinia, Kompiroshiato, and Mishagua Rivers. Closest to Nomatsiguenga. There are minor differences among the dialects. Some bilingualism in Spanish. All ages.

Machinere: also called Manchinere, Manchineri, Manitenerí, Manitenére, Maxinéri. 400 speakers in Acre, Brazil. Distinct enough from Yine (Piro) in Peru to need separate literature. Manitenére may be different from Machinere.

Mandahuaca: also called Mandauaca, Mandawaka, Ihini, Arihini, Maldavaca, Cunipusana, Yavita, Mitua. 3,000 speakers in Venezuela and Brazil. In Venezuela: Colombian border in extreme southwest, Amazonas, east of the Baré on the Baria River and Casiquiare Canal. Related to Adzaneni, Yabâana, Masaca. In Brazil: Amazonas, upper Cauaboris, tributary of the Rio Negro, Colombian border. Related to Adzaneni, Yabâana, Masaca.

Mapidian: also called Mawayana, Maopityan. 64 speakers remain in Guyana and Brazil. In Guyana: Southwest Guyana, coexistence with speakers of Waiwai. 40 Mapidian are intermarried with Waiwai speakers and speak fluent Waiwai. In Brazil: 50 speakers. Roraima, with the Waiwai. People are fluent in Waiwai.

Mashco Piro: also called Cujareno, Cujareño. "Mashco" is a derogatory name sometimes used. 20 speakers remain in Peru. Formerly spoken in Manu Park, department of Madre de Dios. Cujar, Purus, Tahuamanu, Mishagua, and Piedras Rivers. Extinct in Bolivia. About 60% inherent intelligibility with Piro. "Mashco" is a derogatory name. All speakers are completely monolingual.

Mehináku: also called Mehinaco, Mahinaku, Minaco. 121 speakers remain in Brazil. Xingú Park, Mato Grosso. Somewhat intelligible with Waurá, but probably needs adapted literature. Bilingualism is limited.

Nanti: also called Cogapacori, Kogapakori. 300 speakers in Peru. Near the speakers of Machiguenga. Close to the Machiguenga language.

Nomatsiguenga: also called Nomatsiguenga Campa, Atiri. 4,500 speakers in Peru. South central Junín region. Closely related to other Campa languages and Machiguenga. Some bilingualism in Spanish and Áshaninca Campa. All ages.

Omejes: formerly spoken in Colombia.

Palikúr: also called Palikour, Palicur, Palijur. 1,400 speakers in Brazil and French Guiana. In Brazil: 800 speakers. Northern coastal tip along rivers, Amapá. Somewhat bilingual. In French Guiana: 600 speakers. Eastern border area.

Parecís: also called Paressí, Paresí, Haliti. 1,200 speakers in Brazil. Mato Grosso, 6,000 square km. Fifteen to twenty villages. Somewhat bilingual.

Paraujano: also called Parahujano. 20 speakers remain in Venezuela. Ethnic population: 4,306. Formerly spoken in area of Lake Maracaibo, near Guajiro, state of Zulia. Dialects are Alile, Toa. All are bilingual. Most speakers are women.

Piapoco: 4,652 speakers in Colombia and Venezuela. In Colombia: 4,542 speakers. Tributaries and lower Vichada River region, and Meta and Guaviare Rivers. Some bilingualism in Spanish. In Venezuela: 110 speakers in the area of San Fernando de Atapapo, Amazonas along the Orinoco.

Ponares: formerly spoken in Colombia.

Resígaro: also called Resígero. 11 speakers remain in Peru. Formerly spoken in northeastern Peru, Loreto department, in Bora and Ocaina villages. Bilingualism in Ocaina, Bora, Murui Huitoto, Spanish.

Salumã: also called Enawené-Nawé, Eneuene-Mare. 165 speakers in Brazil. Mato Grosso within northeastern Nambiquara reserve. Related to Parecis.

Saraveca: formerly spoken in Bolivia. Eastern jungle.

Taino: formerly spoken in Bahamas. Members of the ethnic group are also now in the USA, in Florida and New Jersey, in Puerto Rico, Santo Domingo, and Cuba. They are bilingual in Spanish or English. The ethnic group now speak Spanish, or a Spanish-Taino mixed language, not understood by Spanish speakers. They estimate their present language to be 55% Taino and 45% Spanish.

Tariano: also called Tarîna, Taliáseri. 100 speakers remain in Brazil and vestiges in Colombia. In Brazil: Ethnic population: 1,500. Middle Vaupés River, Santa Rosa (Juquira), Iauarete, Periquitos, and Ji-Ponta, Amazonas. All speakers are elderly in Brazil. No one has been located who speaks Tariano in Colombia, but the tribal identity is still maintained. The first language of most of the ethnic group is Tucano or Nhengatu. In Colombia: Ethnic population: 332 in Lower Papurí, Vaupés region. All speak Tucano.

Terêna: also called Tereno, Etelena. 15,000 speakers in Brazil. Mato Grosso do Sul, in twenty villages and two cities. Many speak limited Portuguese.

Tomedes: also called Tamudes. Formerly spoken in Colombia.

Trinitario: also called Moxos, Mojos. 5,500 speakers in Bolivia. Ethnic population: 20,805 with Ignaciano. South central Beni. Dialects are Loreto (Loretano), Javierano.

Tubarão: also called Aikan, Wari, Uari, Corumbiara, Kolumbiara. 90 speakers in Brazil. Rondônia, west of Vilhena, near the Cuiabá-Porto Velho Highway.

Wapishana: also called Wapichana, Wapichan, Wapitxana, Wapishiana, Wapisiana, Wapisana, Vapidiana, Wapixana. 7,500 speakers in Guyana and Brazil. In Guyana: 6,000 speakers. Southwest Guyana, south of the Kanuku Mountains, northwest of the Waiwai; a few villages. English is taught in school. Aruma may be extinct. In Brazil: 1,500 speakers. Roraima. People are somewhat bilingual in Portuguese.

Waurá: also called Uaura, Aura. 240 speakers in Brazil. Xingú Park, Mato Grosso. Partially intelligible with Mehinácu.

Wayuu: also called Guajiro, Goajiro, Guajira. 305,000 speakers in Colombia and Venezuela. In Colombia: 135,000 speakers. Guajira Peninsula on the Caribbean coast. In Venezuela: 170,000 speakers. State of Zulia, western Guajira Peninsula.

Xiriâna: spoken in Brazil. Tributaries of Demeni and Rio Negro, Amazonas, near Venezuela border.

Yabaâna: also called Jabaana, Yabarana. Formerly spoken in Brazil. Ethnic population: 90. Amazonas, headwaters of the Marauia and Cauaboris, tributaries of the left bank of Rio Negro.

Yanesha': also called Amuesha, Amuese, Amueixa, Amoishe, Amagues, Amage, Omage, Amajo, Lorenzo, Amuetamo, Amaje. 9,000 speakers in Peru. Ethnic population: 10,000. Central and eastern Pasco region and Junín, western jungle, headwaters of the Pachitea and Perene Rivers. Some bilingualism in Spanish.

Yavitero: also called Paraene. Formerly spoken in Venezuela. The last known speaker died in 1984.

Yawalapití: also called Jaulapiti, Yaulapiti. 140 speakers in Brazil. Xingú Park, Mato Grosso. Related to but not intelligible with Waurá and Mehinaku. Many understand another language of the Xingú because they have lived in other villages.

Yine: also called Piro, Pirro, Pira, Simirinche, Simiranch, Contaquiro. 4,000 speakers in Peru. Ethnic population: 4,000. Machinere in Brazil is different enough to need separate literature. Probably not more than 30% are fluent in Spanish. Nearly all are able to trade in Spanish. Those in the downriver area are more bilingual in Spanish than upriver Yine. Some can speak limited Machiguenga, Ashéninca, Nomatsiguenga, and Quechua. All ages. All domains. Oral and written Yine used in religious services. Parents pass Yine on to children. Yine in the upriver areas are determined to preserve the language. They are proud of their language and culture. Roman alphabet.

Yucuna: also called Matapi, Yukuna. 1,800 speakers in Colombia. Miriti-Parana (tributary Caquetá), Amazonas region. Some have moved to La Pedrera on the lower Caquetá, Araracuara, some to Leticia. In some traditional ceremonies they use a ritual language which is mostly unintelligible even to those who have learned it. 10 to 20 of the oldest speakers and many preschool children are monolingual in Yucuna. 1,500 have varying proficiency in Spanish. Nearly all formal education is in Spanish. Spanish used with outsiders. Some who have married Tanimuka speakers also speak Tanimuka. All domains. Oral and written Yucuna is sometimes used in church services, and oral Yucuna in the traditional religion. Yucuna is used for letter writing. Vigorous language use. Parents transmit Yucuna to their children and have a positive attitude toward Yucuna.   B. GRIMES

AREAL LINGUISTICS.

AREAL LINGUISTICS. [*This entry includes the following subentries:*
Overview
Geographical Distribution of Linguistic Features]

Overview

This field is the study of resemblances among languages based on geographic rather than genetic relationships. It may refer particularly to the study of linguistic areas—or, more broadly, to the study of the geographic distributions of linguistic phenomena generally, and often also to the history of those distributions.

For the synchronic study of distributions, "linguistic geography" would be a convenient term; but that has come in many quarters to mean "dialect geography," the detailed mapping of (mainly phonetic and lexical) variables within a single language community. The study of linguistic areas is concerned rather with phenomena that straddle language boundaries, and especially genetic boundaries. Note Emeneau's widely quoted definition of a "linguistic area" (1980:124) as "an area which includes languages belonging to more than one family but showing traits in common which are found not to belong to the other members of (at least) one of the families."

Emeneau would have liked to use the term "areal linguistics" for such studies; but he felt he could not, because the term had been pre-empted by the "Neolinguistic" school—then of considerable influence in Romance linguistics—in a peculiar sense. As an equivalent of the Italian *linguistica spaziale,* it referred to a determinedly anti-structural kind of study of the distribution and history of individual words—pursued, to be sure, across language boundaries ("Every word has its own history, and its own area")—which set its face against both phonemic theory and the principle of the regularity of *phonological change*, and saw itself as applying Crocean idealism to the understanding of linguistic phenomena. However, after two or three decades, this was no longer a major consideration; geographical, structural, and historical linguistics had meanwhile reached an understanding of sorts, and "areal linguistics" was freely used in other senses. Particularly in European linguistic circles, it has been used mainly in a broader sense, to cover both dialect geography and linguistic area studies, and much more as well. Although terminology is still not completely standardized, a sample of prevalent definitions follows.

Goossens 1973:319 defines the German term *Areallinguistik* as "that subdiscipline in which the agreements and differences among spatially contrastive linguistic systems or among geographically differentiated linguistic subsystems, and the distribution of these agreements, are interpreted with the help of cartographic representations." He divides it into three varieties:

(a) The *subsystemic* type studies geographic differences in usage within a single "language," e.g. standard English or standard German.

(b) The *diasystemic* type is concerned with "dialect geography" proper, and studies the distribution of features that differentiate the systems (dialects) constitutive of a geographically differentiated system-complex called "language" in another sense—a complex loosely definable as one in which the similarities remain more fundamental than the differences.

(c) The *intersystemic* type studies agreements that cross language boundaries.

Goossens notes that type (b) is the "most developed," having the great European linguistic atlases to its credit; and that the boundary between the first type and the second is not always clear. Here it might be remarked that dialect geography is not identical with dialectology. As Weinreich 1954 pointed out, it is possible to have a purely "structural" dialectology, comparing systems as such, without reference to geography, history, or culture. It is also possible, as Goossens notes, for the interpretation of dialect-geographical data to be informed by structural, i.e. intrasystemic considerations, as well as by extra-linguistic considerations.

In Russian linguistics, where there has been considerable interest in cross-linguistic comparisons, Desnitskaja 1977 nevertheless sees such studies as only one aspect of areal linguistics (*areal'naja lingvistika*). She proposes the following definition of the subject matter of the latter: (i) the processes of diffusion and integration of dialectal phenomena within a language; (ii) the results of language contact of both related and unrelated languages under conditions of geographic contiguity; (iii) the reflection of old contact situations in contemporary languages and toponymy ("areal reconstruction"); and (iv) the formation of new linguistic areas under the broadened conditions of linguistic and cultural contact in the present-day world, and the socio-historic typology of such areas.

Noting that "the factor of space is always connected with the factor of time," she would include the process of differentiation of a language family in its areal aspects—with the proviso that, the further removed from ascertainable contemporary areal distributions, the more hypothetical and uncertain the results become. Extra-linguistic factors (sociocultural, economic) are still of great interest in the interpretation of all these distributional facts. Desnitskaja rejects the proposal of Èdel'man 1968:3 to restrict the meaning of "areal linguistics" to the reconstruction of ancient areas, and to redefine "linguistic geography" as the study of contemporary distributions.

It should be clear from the foregoing that "areal linguistics" is too widely used in a broader sense to be restrictable to the study of "linguistic areas" as Emeneau defined them. For that subfield, the term "contact linguistics" is sometimes used. However, that is not quite the same thing, since it takes as its focus the dynamics of what happens when two languages are in contact—whether in a geographically definable area or otherwise, e.g. a colonial or an immigrant situation—rather than the integrated results in terms of mappability.

A suitable term is still needed. Goossens noted a key difference between his sub- and dia-systemic areal linguistics, on the one hand, and his intersystemic areal linguistics on the other: the first two are concerned with features that differentiate a single underlying system, but the third is concerned with features which unite systems that are basically separate. Genetic linguistics in general may be described as concerned with divergence from a common source, and with reconstructing that source from the areally scattered products of that divergence; however, the study of linguistic areas is concerned with the convergence of originally disparate elements on a geographical basis. The two subdisciplines address opposite ends of the process of linguistic change: where languages are coming from vs. where they are going. Thus "convergence linguistics" might be an appropriate term for that sub-field of areal linguistics concerned with linguistic areas.

Even this does not quite do justice to the complexity of the phenomenon of the linguistic area. In addition to the convergence (mutual influence) of viable neighboring languages in contact, termed *adstrata*, the formation of such an area may also involve the action of common *substrata* or *superstrata*, which introduce further complications. This should be distinguished from the situation where such a substratum or superstratum uniquely affects a single language—contributing to its differentiation from its genetic kin, but not forging a hidden link between it and other languages. To oversimplify slightly, a substratum is the subordinated language of a conquered or otherwise oppressed population, while a superstratum is the superimposed language of a conquering or otherwise dominating group. The eventual disappearance of such "strata," leaving effects on the surviving language of an area—sometimes via the route of pidginization and creolization—is part of their definition, according to some authorities. (For others, a subordinated living language affecting the dominant language of an area is also a substratum.) An example of a substratum is Gaulish in France; of a superstratum, Norman French in England. However, a superstratum should be distinguished from a *superimposed* language—i.e. a colonial, administrative, or "national" language, which exerts influence but does not disappear, such as Russian in the non-Russian parts of the former Soviet Union, or English (and Hindi) in India. It differs also from an *archistratum*, a Kultursprache from which peoples in a certain civilization draw their abstract and cultured vocabulary, such as Arabic in the Islamic world or Sanskrit in India. Such situations may change, of course—cf. the earlier position of Greek in the Balkans, or of Persian in India. This leads to a range of intermediate situations and questions; e.g., is a formerly superimposed language a "superstratum"?

Although it is now widely used, the term "linguistic area" itself has certain drawbacks, as Emeneau himself recognized. It was intended as an equivalent for the German *Sprachbund*; but (like "areal linguistics"), it is susceptible of a wider interpretation, and its literal equivalents in other languages in fact often have such meanings. Weinreich 1954:378–379 suggested "convergence area,"

pointing out that "Sprachbund" is unsatisfactory because "it implies a unit, as if a language either were or were not a member of a given Sprachbund." Moreover, the term has not always been used with care, especially outside of its original Praguean ambiance. Becker 1948, amid much valuable discussion (praised by Weinreich), appears to confuse it at times with the spheres of influence of the great archistratal languages of civilization: Latin, Arabic, Sanskrit, and Chinese. The last three of these have only a superficial lexical basis, i.e. no structural basis.

Emeneau's definition also needs some modification, mainly with regard to the proviso that the languages involved must belong to different families. This requirement happens to fit the South Asian area with which Emeneau was mainly concerned; but it does not fit the classic case of the Balkans or that of Western Europe, where all the languages (or those primarily involved) are Indo-European, albeit of different branches. This is no doubt what Emeneau meant, and we may replace "different families" with "different genetic stocks." He perhaps wished to avoid confusion with the problems of dialect distribution, language differentiation, and mutual influence within the same genetic stock that so complicate the notion of "areal linguistics" in Europe and that are also present in the Indian subcontinent.

The languages involved in an areal convergence may or may not ultimately be genetically related in some way; but the point is that the similarities in question, for which European scholars prefer the term "affinities," are independent of any such relationships. For example, German and Hungarian, which are quite unrelated genetically, both have separable verbal prefixes, a feature not found in the Uralic relatives of Hungarian. Similarly, Czech and most Central and Western Slovak dialects share with neighboring Hungarian an initial word stress, a pattern alien to other Slavic languages (Alexander 1983). Equally "areal," however, are a number of affinities between French and German, on opposite sides of the Romano-Germanic line but both Indo-European: front rounded vowels, the uvular *r*, colloquial substitution of the perfect for the preterit, the impersonal pronoun *on/man*, etc.

Despite efforts to define some constraints, it has been shown (see Thomason and Kaufman 1988, chap. 2) that languages in contact can affect one another at every level—phonetic, phonological, syntactic, semantic, idiomatic, and even morphological. The established "areas" afford many examples of all of these. The agency for this process is a population of bilinguals, significant either in proportionate numbers or in prestige and influence.

The real locus of language "contact" is the mind of the bilingual individual. One theory holds that, depending on the frequency and other conditions of use and consequent pressures, the bilingual's mind may try to adjust to the demands placed upon it by constructing what is in effect a supergrammar, in which economies are effected by bringing the rules of languages concerned more closely into alignment with one another. Less speculatively, bilinguals may simply carry over some of the habits of their first language; or they may try to accommodate non-native interlocutors by adjusting their own speech in the direction of the others' imperfect version of their language—and then carry some of these habits back into their normal speech. In either situation, the resultant altered language may be imitated further by non-bilinguals.

A major attempt to address this problem on a global scale and with reference to a hypothesis concerning the initial pattern of human settlement of the world (as well as another concerning the "stability" of various typological features) is found in Nichols 1992. In this complex work, Nichols outlines a typology of linguistic areas, distinguishing between *spread zones* (characterized by little genetic or structural diversity, language extinctions, and hence a partially unrecoverable history) and *residual zones* (characterized by great genetic and structural diversity, language preservation, and hence containing the best clues to deep prehistory) (1992:253)—a distinction crucial to her hypotheses.

In extreme cases, even of "borrowing," all that remains to identify the languages concerned are some of their words; their underlying phonology, syntax, grammatical categories, etc. become identical. More frequently, perhaps, only contiguous dialects in close contact are affected to such a degree; and only certain features spread from these to the larger speech communities beyond. Sometimes a single trait appears to characterize a wide area, without other features necessarily being affected.

When an attempt is made to map the features alleged to characterize an area, the resulting isoglosses will be found, as in dialect geography, not to coincide, but (if the area is real) to "bundle" sufficiently to outline roughly the boundaries of the area—which may turn out to be different than previously assumed. In the periphery, languages will turn out to be included by one isogloss and excluded by another. (Recall Weinreich's stricture against the Sprachbund concept above.) Some isoglosses will turn out not to define the area in question at all, but rather to link it (or parts of it) with other areas (see Masica

2001). In regions with a complex history of contacts in different directions, such overlap of areal affinity patterns is to be expected. Rumanian, for example, is in most respects—syntactic, semantic, and morphological—a "Balkan" language; but at the same time it is a peripheral participant in the "Eurasian" phonological area of Jakobson 1938.

Such mapping of features, tracing their actual distributions to their limits in surrounding languages, is essential—not only in defining the boundaries of a convergence area, but in determining whether the features are areal at all or due to random coincidence. Hook 1987 added an important tool to this line of inquiry by experimentally establishing that, when certain typological alternatives are traced on the ground, using native speakers at a series of points, they line up in a statistical progression correlated with distance, thus ruling out chance.

Not every feature characterizing an area will show such a distribution, however—or can even be plotted with isoglosses at all. In particular, the effects of substrata and superstrata may well not. They may instead show up merely as non-random distributions, e.g. as significant clustering or densities; but other techniques need to be developed to supplement the cartographic data (cf. Masica 1976, Appendix B.) It is not strictly necessary that languages sharing features be actually contiguous, but only that they be in "proximity": recent intrusions (e.g. Turkish in Asia Minor) may have interrupted their contiguity, although its effects remain. Certain very "broken" distributions may be the relics of former linguistic areas.

Much more work, employing more refined techniques of dialect geography—and going beyond them, since dialect geographers have rarely dealt with syntax—needs to be done on linguistic areas. Much previous research has consisted of identifying instances of convergence without pursuing distributions. A major area such as South Asia or the Balkans is likely to show complex patterns consonant with multiple origins, rather than a simple pattern of diffusion from a single center.

A precondition of the study of areal convergence is the clear identification, through sound correspondences, of the genetic relationships of the languages involved. In its absence, typological similarities among areally convergent languages have often been allowed to confuse the genetic picture, as shortcut indicators of genetic relationship. (Against taking them as such is the fact, brought to light in both areal and creole studies, that languages can drastically change their type.) Such questions have plagued the Amerindian and "Ural-Altaic" fields in particular. Trubetzkoy 1928 attempted to sort out the two types of "relationship": he proposed that *Sprachbünde* consist of languages which show great similarity in syntax and morphological structure, a good number of common culture-words, and sometimes also an "external" similarity in phonology—but without any systematic sound-correspondences, or agreement in phonetic content of morphological elements, or common basic words—and which are or have been in areal contact. Languages which share a common stock of basic words, agreements in the phonetic expression of morphological categories, and "above all" regular sound correspondences, constitute *Sprachfamilien*.

Areal factors may complicate the picture, even when genetic relationships are known—especially when closely related languages remain in contact and continue to influence one another, even while diverging from their common parent. This is the case in parts of Europe, and is particularly true of the Indo-Aryan group, where mutual borrowing and the spread of innovations across language boundaries has been so extensive as to make it difficult in some instances to identify the inherited regular element. It should be noted that linguistic areas may be characterized by common preservations, as well as by diffusion of innovations.

General typology is another subdiscipline which must be sorted out from areal linguistics. A number of features such as word order and associated features of syntax, commonly studied from this viewpoint, have very skewed distributions geographically; moreover, the features that are typologically associated, from a universal statistical standpoint, may be dissociated in non-random patterns when viewed areally. By virtue of these facts, they also become grist for the areal mill, and demand explanation even though none is obvious.

[*See also* Balkan Languages; Bilingualism and Multilingualism; Borrowing; Dialectology; Historical Linguistics, *article on* Typology and Universals; Language Change; Meso-American Languages; Phonological Processes; Pidgins and Creoles; South Asian Languages; *and* Southeast Asian Languages.]

BIBLIOGRAPHY

Alexander, Ronelle. 1983. On the definition of Sprachbund boundaries: The place of Balkan Slavic. In *Ziele und Wege der Balkanlinguistik* (Balkanologische Öffentlichungen, 5), edited by Norbert Reiter, pp. 13–26. Wiesbaden: Harrassowitz.

Becker, Henrik. 1948. *Der Sprachbund.* Leipzig: Humboldt.

Desnitskaja, Agnija Vasil'evna. 1977. K voprosu o predmete i metodax areal'noj lingvistiki. In *Areal'nye issledovanie v jazykoznanii i etnografii,* edited by M. A. Borodina, pp. 22–29. Leningrad: Nauka.

Èdel'man, Džoj Josifovna. 1968. *Osnovnye voprosy lingvističeskoi geografii.* Moscow: Nauka.

Emeneau, Murray B. 1980. *Language and linguistic area.* Stanford, Calif.: Stanford University Press.

Goossens, Jan. 1973. Areallinguistik. In *Lexikon der germanistischen Linguistik,* edited by Hans Peter Althaus et al., pp. 445–453. Tübingen: Niemeyer.

Hook, Peter E. 1987. Linguistic areas: Getting at the grain of history. In *Festschrift for Henry M. Hoenigswald on the occasion of his seventieth birthday* (Ars linguistica, 15), edited by George Cardona and Norman H. Zide, pp. 155–168. Tübingen: Narr.

Jakobson, Roman. 1938. Sur la théorie des affinités phonologiques entre les langues. In *Actes du Quatrième Congrès International de Linguistes,* pp. 48–59. Copenhagen: Munksgaard. Reprinted, with revisions, as Appendix IV to *Principes de phonologie,* by Nikolai S. Trubetzkoy, Paris: Klincksieck, 1949, pp. 351–365; and in *Selected writings,* vol. 1, *Phonological studies,* by Roman Jakobson (The Hague: Mouton, 1962), pp. 234–246.

Masica, Colin P. 1976. *Defining a linguistic area: South Asia.* Chicago: University of Chicago Press.

Masica, Colin P. 2001. The definition and significance of linguistic areas: Methods, pitfalls, and possibilities. In *Yearbook of South Asian languages and linguistics, 2001,* edited by Rajendra Singh. Delhi: Sage.

Matras, Yaron. 1998. Convergent development, grammaticalization, and the problem of "mutual isomorphism." In *Sprache in Raum und Zeit: In memoriam Johannes Bechert,* vol. 2, *Beiträge zu empirischen Sprachwissenschaft,* pp. 89–103. Tübingen: Gunter Narr.

Nichols, Johanna. 1992. *Linguistic diversity in space and time.* Chicago: University of Chicago Press.

Rosencvejg, V. Ju. 1976. *Linguistic interference and convergent change.* The Hague: Mouton.

Thomason, Sarah Grey, and Terrence Kaufman. 1988. *Language contact, creolization, and genetic linguistics.* Berkeley: University of California Press.

Trubetzkoy, Nikolai S. 1928. Proposition 16. *Acts of the First International Congress of Linguists, Leiden,* pp. 17–18.

Weinreich, Uriel. 1954. Is a structural dialectology possible? *Word* 10.388–400.

COLIN P. MASICA

Geographical Distribution of Linguistic Features

It is well known that some types of language structures are very unevenly distributed worldwide: clicks, for instance, are found as ordinary linguistic phonemes only in sub-Saharan Africa. An important finding of cross-linguistic work is that very few grammatical or phonological features have an even distribution worldwide; even when areal groups of continental or larger size are compared, the frequencies of structural features are usually quite different among them (see Dryer 1989, Nichols 1992, Cysouw 2002).

Worldwide comparison of grammatical structures requires rigorous definitions of the structural features, a basis for sampling the world's 6,800 languages (usually this basis is the genealogical family at some fairly consistent time depth), and enough comprehensive, reliable descriptive grammars that any given structural feature can be tracked through an entire sample. Advances in morphosyntactic analysis and steady progress in language description and comparison have made bird's-eye views of worldwide grammatical distributions a real possibility.

1. The geography of linguistic diversity. The term *stock* is used here for the oldest level of language family that can be both demonstrated and reconstructed using standard comparative-historical rigor. Examples are Indo-European, Uralic, Austronesian, Algic, Semitic, and Chadic—but not Indo-Uralic, which emerges as plausible but not firm in standard method, and not Afroasiatic, which is firmly demonstrable but not reconstructible. There are, at most, about 300 stocks worldwide. The stock, sampled from the bottom up (e.g. Dryer 1989) or from the top down (e.g. Nichols 1992), is the basis for most cross-linguistic grammatical surveys. Genealogical diversity is then defined as the ratio of stocks to land area, and sheer genealogical diversity is very unevenly distributed worldwide (see Map 1).

The ultimate determinant of stock diversity is political economy or social complexity (Austerlitz 1980): stocks are few in areas that have a long history of state and empire and therefore contain large and complex societies (such as parts of Africa and Eurasia), and they are more numerous in areas where societies are smaller and simpler (such as New Guinea or much of the Americas). Hyslop 1993 shows that, for purposes of sample design, the number of speakers of a language makes a good proxy for social complexity. Two geographical considerations are strongly correlated with economic scope (Nichols 1990, 1992): higher diversity is favored by coastline (compare western with interior North America; Jacobsen 1989), and by mild and non-arid climates (compare monsoonal northern with desert interior Australia). Hence, stock diversity is very low at high latitudes and

very high near tropical and subtropical coasts. At the hemispheric level, the notable genealogical diversity of the Americas is the result of their pre-contact political economy (Austerlitz 1980), much of which can be predicted from their ecology and geography (Diamond 1997, Nichols 1990). If individual languages rather than families are counted, the effect of geography is much the same, though absolute numbers are higher at all levels of density (Mace and Pagel 1995, Nettle 1999).

These principles hold equally well in the ancient human homeland, Africa, in early colonized Australia and New Guinea, and in the more recently colonized Americas. Unlike the situation in human genetics, Africa cannot be identified as the original homeland of human language by sheer linguistic diversity, either structural or genealogical, or by any other known linguistic evidence. Other principles are sometimes advanced to explain regional distributions as "secondary pile-ups": thus, the equatorial density in Africa has sometimes been attributed to retreat of populations before the advancing Sahara, or northern Australian density to retreat before the postglacial sea-level rise. However, the general principles mentioned above already account for these cases, and, given the mobility of societies and languages, it seems implausible that a secondary pile-up could last for ten thousand years or more.

Structural diversity can be measured as the number of different types that are well represented in an area and/ or as the ratio of that figure to area. For example, a continent in which all six logically possible word order types are frequent is more diverse than one in which all six occur but only two are frequent, and of course more diverse than one in which fewer types occur (Nichols 1992:237ff.). Unsurprisingly, in large areas structural diversity correlates strongly and positively with genealogical diversity. It is also generally higher in a set of languages drawn from around the world than in a set of equal size and equal genealogical diversity drawn from a single continent (Nichols 1992:246ff.), as is consistent with large-scale geographical bias and skewing.

Against this background of large-areal skewing in nearly every grammatical feature, it is difficult to identify universals in the sense of universally favored tendencies or correlations; universally present structural features would be easy to identify, but they are essentially nonexistent among concrete morphosyntactic properties, and nonexistent by definition among multi-valued typological features such as word order or alignment. Dryer 1989 identifies universal preferences by counting the number of large areas in which the frequency of the given feature or correlation exceeds expectation, and then determining whether the number of areas with the frequency is significant on a binomial test. Maslova 2000 shows that the frequencies of grammatical properties in today's languages almost certainly cannot be attributed to retention from a skewed primordial language population. (In any case, an inheritance fidelity of nearly 99% per 5,000 years would be required to retain a primordial grammatical property at more than 50% frequency in today's languages.)

In a number of continental interiors, especially at mid to high latitudes, a kind of language area forms that is called a *spread zone* by Nichols (1992:13ff.). Spread zones are characterized by long-standing patterns of repeated language spreads, low genealogical and structural diversity, and extinction of most or all prior languages in the area with every new spread (typically, the extinction results from language shift). Examples include the central Eurasian steppe and desert, North Africa, central Australia, interior North America, and probably southern Africa south of the rain forest zone. In the clearest case, central Eurasia, the past six millennia have seen repeated cycles of spreading of a language across the steppe and then into the adjacent desert, its subsequent diversification into shallow families, and another spread erasing even that modest level of diversity. Because most of the families have spread from the same general area, approximately southern Siberia, they bear strong areal resemblances to start with, and as a result even the substratal effects arising from language shift during a spread are mild. The net result, after several millennia, is a large stretch of territory with low stock diversity and strong structural resemblances.

A very different kind of area is the *accretion zone* (called "residual zone" in Nichols 1992), in which there are few large-scale spreads, immigrant languages tend to take root and contribute to the growing genealogical diversity, and diversity is very high. Examples are the Caucasus, the Ethiopian plateau, New Guinea, and western California. Where an accretion zone borders on a spread zone, spreading languages and survivors from previous spreads feed into the diversity, as in the Caucasus and Ethiopia. Language communities in a spread zone are often small, and there is much multilingualism. The frequencies of grammatical properties across the languages in a spread zone reflect their host continents to some extent, but in some respects they depart from their host continents and come to resemble one another,

suggesting that the combination of high diversity and high contact favors a kind of typological regression to a universal norm.

2. Some notable macro areas. A number of structural features have striking concentrations that converge to identify some very large language areas—in one case, a single but non-contiguous area. The entire Western Hemisphere, for instance, shows a very high frequency of the head-marking type, which is also found with moderate frequency in New Guinea but is very rare otherwise (see Nichols and Bickel, to appear c). Formal oppositions in possessive marking of the types often called "alienable" and "inalienable" possession are also very frequent in the Americas, as are obligatorily possessed "inalienable" nouns such as kin terms or body parts. Verb-initial word order, which is infrequent worldwide, is disproportionately common in the western Americas (Dryer 1989). Because the Americas were settled more recently than any other large area and had only one entry point (Beringia, today's eastern Siberia and western Alaska), and since in general there is no massive Western Hemisphere-wide areality, it is reasonable to ascribe these pan-American near-singularities to founder effects in some portion of the settling population. Most of the frequencies are statistically significant, so ascribing them to plain chance is not a good option, and certainly not a first option.

The great central Eurasian spread zone has produced a large but compact cluster of unusual features, such as strict head-final order including adjective-noun (Dryer 1989, 1992) and personal pronouns with *m* in the first person and *t* or the like in the second person (Nichols and Peterson 1996, to appear).

Western Eurasia, primarily its far western edge, and northern Africa show several unusual commonalities (Gensler 1993). Gensler cautiously refrains from identifying a causal mechanism. Vennemann (2001a, 2001b, to appear, and references therein) traces some of these sharings to prehistoric contacts of coastal Europeans with Phoenician seafarers and their cultural antecedents.

The Pacific Rim, from New Guinea and Melanesia north along the Asian Pacific coast and south down the American Pacific coast, exhibits several shared features that are uncommon or virtually nonexistent elsewhere. Numeral classifiers are perhaps the clearest example (see Map 2, and Nichols and Peterson 1996, Map 13). They are found all around the Pacific Rim, with a slight inland extension to the Himalayas and a discontinuity in the far

MAP 1. *Language Family Diversity*

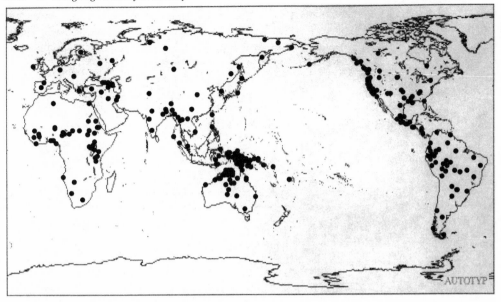

Dots are languages in the Autotyp sample (N = 288) (http://socrates.berkeley.edu/autotyp).
The sample seeks one language per major branch of each old and deep stock, one language
per young stock. Every language isolate is a separate stock and is in the sample.

north. (Gil, to appear, finds a token or two in Africa, but otherwise a Pacific Rim distribution.) Similar distributions are echoed, more sparsely, by multiple possessive classes (Nichols and Bickel, to appear a,b) and lack of overt noun plurals. A subtype of Pacific Rim distribution appears in features well attested in the western Americas and in Australia–New Guinea but not in mainland Asia; examples include the head-marking type (Nichols and Bickel, to appear c), reduplicated plurals (Map 3), and personal pronouns with *n* in the first person and *m* in the second (Nichols and Peterson 1996, to appear). In the Americas, the Pacific Rim features are a relatively recent overlay on an older linguistic population that stretches from coast to coast, a distribution that points to a relatively recent, though still ancient, colonization wave that entered coastally and spread coastally southward after the entire hemisphere had been settled by descendants of earlier immigrants (Nichols 2000, 2002). In Australasia, their predominance in New Guinea (and chiefly northern, near-coastal New Guinea) and Melanesia and their frequent absence from Australia suggest an eastward spread after the postglacial sea-level rise had separated Australia from New Guinea (Nichols 1997, 2000). The Pacific Rim discontinuity in the far north is part of a larger circum-Beringian language area that began to take shape very

early, probably in Siberia, but was brought to Chukotka and Alaska relatively recently, perhaps not much earlier than the time frames of the Eskimo-Aleut and Chukchi-Kamchatkan language family spreads (Fortescue 1998).

Nichols 1996 includes a proximity analysis based on frequencies of fifteen structural properties and proposes an abstract global geography. Africa, Europe, and southern Australia cluster in the far west; Asia, interior New Guinea, and coastal Australia form an Asian cluster; and the Americas plus New Guinea are an eastern cluster, with Central America at the far east. This schematic map shows that longitude (not always literal) is a strong geographical predictor of type frequencies. The placement of parts of Australia in Eurasia and of New Guinea partly in Asia and partly in the Americas seems to reflect a history in which early colonization was by a southern Asian linguistic population with affinities to the west, followed by many millennia of repeated colonization from a population of increasingly eastern cast. The eastern population, midway in its history, also spread north and colonized the Americas. Resemblances between New Guinea and the Americas, as well as the Pacific Rim distribution, reflect a colonization impetus from somewhere in Southeast Asia that sent people and their languages southeastward into the Pacific and (separately and

MAP 2. *Languages with Numeral Classifiers*

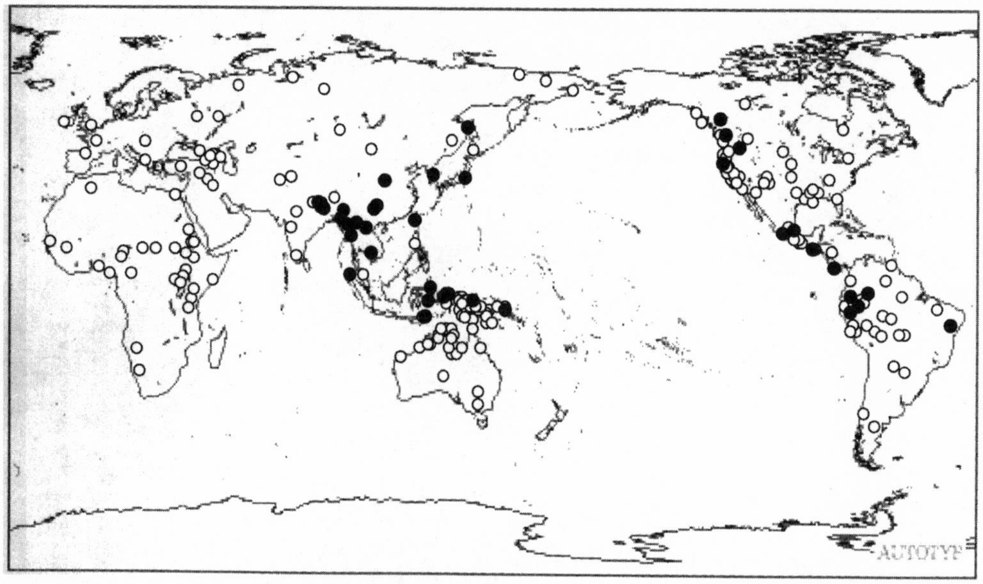

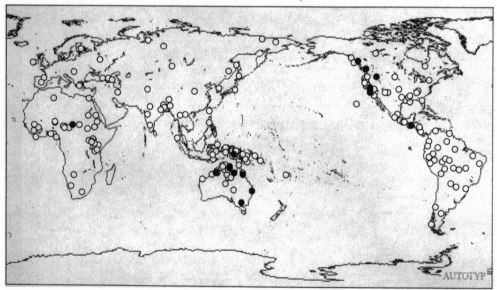

Filled circles = languages with numeral classifiers; empty circles = languages without numeral classifiers. N = 236. Languages are from the same sample as on Map 1.

MAP 3. *Languages Using Reduplication to Mark Plural of Nouns*

Filled circles = languages with reduplicated plurals; empty circles = languages without reduplicated plurals. True plurals only (not collectives, distributives, etc.). N = 220. Languages are from the same sample as on Map 1.

simultaneously) northward and eventually to the Americas.

3. Summary. Many aspects of the geographical distribution of linguistic structures can be interpreted as supporting what is known from human genetics and archaeology about human origins and the settlement of the globe. Independent of other disciplines, linguistic evidence alone argues for certain points in a global human prehistory: initial colonization of Australasia by a southern Eurasian population; subsequent increasing East or Northeast Asian influence; early colonization of the Americas; ultimate origin of the American linguistic population in the same pool as the ancestors of the coastal Australasian population; a later, but still early prehistoric, entry of the Pacific Rim population into the Americas from coastal Siberia and also (separately, from Southeast Asia) into northern Australasia; and some kind of shared history between Africa and pre-Indo-European Europe.

The linguistic evidence bears this analysis; it does not necessarily demand it, however, and both the history of ancient migrations and the linguistic evidence and sample breakdowns are sufficiently varied that interpreting prehistory is partly a matter of selecting supporting evidence. Much more work is needed to amass a large enough body of evidence that a best prehistory will emerge rather clearly. An enduring puzzle is how it might be (or whether it can be) that simple structural features can last long enough in large areal populations to point to their distant origins at time ranges like 50,000 years ago (the beginning of Pacific colonization), when they can change rapidly enough that known genealogical stocks, rarely over about 6,000 years in age, exhibit diversity in those same features. Transmission in families involves mostly inheritance (vs. non-inheritance), while transmission in areas involves a combination of diffusion and inheritance, and it must be that the combination of diffusion and inheritance makes for greater durability than inheritance alone. Much more work remains to be done before we will be in a position to explain—in terms of implicational correlations and the relative propensity of structural properties to diffuse, to be inherited, and to be generated—why a given set of properties is endemic in a given continent.

[*See also* Functional Linguistics; Grammaticalization; Historical Linguistics; Language Change; *and* Typology and Universals.]

BIBLIOGRAPHY

Austerlitz, Robert. 1980. Language-family density in North America and Eurasia. *Ural-Altaische Jahrbücher* 51.1–10.

Cysouw, Michael. 2002. Interpreting typological clusters. *Linguistic Typology* 6.69–93.

Diamond, Jared. 1997. *Guns, germs, and steel: The fates of human societies.* New York: Norton.

Dryer, Matthew. 1989. Large linguistic areas and language sampling. *Studies in Language* 13.257–292.

Dryer, Matthew. 1992. The Greenbergian word-order correlations. *Language* 68.81–138.

Dryer, Matthew, Bernard Comrie, David Gil, and Martin Haspelmath, eds. To appear. *World atlas of language structures.* Oxford: Oxford University Press.

Fortescue, Michael. 1998. *Language relations across Bering Strait.* London and New York: Cassell.

Gensler, Orin D. 1993. *A typological evaluation of Celtic/Hamito-Semitic syntactic parallels.* Berkeley: University of California, Berkeley, dissertation.

Gil, David. To appear. Numeral classifiers. In Dryer et al.

Hyslop, Catriona. 1993. *Towards a typology of spatial deixis.* Australian National University, Canberra. B. A. Honours thesis.

Jacobsen, W. H., Jr. 1989. *The Pacific orientation of western North American languages.* Paper presented at First Circum-Pacific Prehistory Conference, Seattle.

Mace, Ruth, and M. Pagel. 1995. A latitudinal gradient in the density of human languages in North America. *Proceedings of the Royal Society of London, B* 261.117–121.

Maslova, Elena. 2000. A dynamic approach to the verification of distributional universals. *Linguistic Typology* 4.307–333.

Nettle, Daniel. 1999. *Linguistic diversity.* Oxford: Oxford University Press.

Nichols, Johanna. 1990. Linguistic diversity and the first settlement of the New World. *Language* 66.475–521.

Nichols, Johanna. 1992. *Linguistic diversity in space and time.* Chicago: University of Chicago Press.

Nichols, Johanna. 1996. The geography of language origins. In *Proceedings of the Twenty-Second Annual Meeting, Berkeley Linguistics Society,* 267–78. Berkeley, Calif.

Nichols, Johanna. 1997. Modeling ancient population structures and movement in linguistics. *Annual Review of Anthropology* 26.359–384.

Nichols, Johanna. 2000. Estimating dates of early American colonization events. In *Time depth in historical linguistics,* vol. 2, edited by Colin Renfrew et al., pp. 643–663. Cambridge, UK: McDonald Institute for Archaeological Research.

Nichols, Johanna. 2002. The first American languages. *Memoirs of the California Academy of Sciences* 27.273–293.

Nichols, Johanna, and Balthasar Bickel. To appear a. Obligatorily and prohibited possessive inflection. In Dryer et al.

Nichols, Johanna, and Balthasar Bickel. To appear b. Possessive classification. Dryer et al.

Nichols, Johanna, and Balthasar Bickel. To appear c. Locus of marking. In Dryer et al.

Nichols, Johanna, and David A. Peterson. 1996. The Amerind personal pronouns. *Language* 72.336–371.

Nichols, Johanna, and David A. Peterson. To appear. Personal pronouns with *m* and/or *n*. In Dryer et al.

Vennemann, Theo. 2001. Atlantis Semitica: Structural contact features in Celtic and English. In *Historical Linguistics 1999*, edited by L. J. Brinton, pp. 351–369. Amsterdam and Philadelphia: Benjamins.

Vennemann, Theo. 2001. Germania Semitica: +*athal-* (OE *æ•el*, G *Adel*) 'nobility': With an appendix on Gk. *atlas*. *Sprachwissenschaft* 26.189–204.

Vennemann, Theo. To appear. Germania Semitica: Pre-Gmc. +*-at-* in E *maiden*, G *Magd/Mädchen*, Goth. *magaths*. *Amsterdamer Beitraege zur aelteren Germanistik* 56.

JOHANNA NICHOLS

ARGUMENT. *See* Case; Semantics; Formal Grammar; Subcategorization and Selection; *and* Grammatical Relations.

ARISTOTLE (384–322 BCE). Greek philosopher important in the early history of Western linguistics both for his general contributions to logic, rhetoric, and poetics and for a specific classification of speech units.

ANNA MORPURGO DAVIES

ARMENIAN. A language known from texts written after 405 CE, Armenian is an independent branch of the I[ndo]-E[uropean] family; but it is closest to Greek, Iranian (by diffusion), and perhaps Phrygian. There is one good bilingual dictionary for the classical language (Bedrossian 1875–1879); for the modern Western dialect, one may consult Kouyoumdjian 1950, 1961. A partial etymological dictionary exists in Hübschmann 1897, but the multivolume work of H. Adjarian, in Armenian (1926–1935), is surely the most complete ever prepared for any language. A modern etymological dictionary to the IE components is now appearing in fascicles (Greppin 1983).

A primer to the classical language was prepared by Thomson 1975, and a primer to the modern Western dialect by Bardakjian and Thomson 1977. Minassian 1980 is a grammar of the Eastern dialect, and Bardakjian and Vaux 1999 have prepared a primer for Modern Eastern Armenian.

Armenian is distinct from the other IE languages in some notable phonological characteristics; among the most significant is a shift which resembles Grimm's Law (IE **t *d *dh* > Arm. *t' t d*), yet has satem characteristics—thus IE **k̂ *ĝ *ĝh* > Arm. *s c* ([ts]) *j* ([dz]). Further, Armenian maintains reflexes of the laryngeals in initial position—though it now appears that only one color of the initial laryngeal, *a-*, can be supported (Olsen 1999). Armenian seems to offer no significant evidence for an IE voiceless aspirate series, and it lacks any threefold reflex of the interconsonantal laryngeal (see Hamp 1970). For the alphabet, see Table 1.

In morphology, Armenian provides limited testimony of original IE structures: with the movement of the accent to the penultimate position, Proto-Armenian lost its word-final syllables, and thus much of the nominal and verbal patterns of inflection. The aorist has the vestige of an *e*-augment, which finds parallels in Greek, Indo-Iranian, and Phrygian; however, this appears only with monosyllabic stems—cf. Arm. *edi* 'I put', Skt. *ádhām*; Arm. *elik'* 'he left', Gk. *élipe*. The present active indicative reflects the IE patterns fairly closely, but the root aorist is less faithful; see Table 2.

The present active infinitive in *-l* (*berel*) corresponds to the Slavic *-l* preterit, actually an old participle (Russ. *ja byl* 'I was'), and to the Tocharian gerundive (*kenäl* 'calling'). The IE infix **-sk̂e-*, of obscure lexical value, appears as *-c'-* in the Armenian subjunctive (*berec'im* 'may I bear'), as well as in the *s*-aorist (*gorc-eac'* 'he worked' < IE **worĝ-is-ā-sk̂-*). Full discussions of the phonology and morphology are found in Meillet 1936 and Schmitt 1981.

Armenian retains all seven IE noun cases—nominative, accusative, genitive, dative, locative, ablative, and instrumental. It has a unique plural in *-k'*, the same as used in verb patterns; numerous etymologies for this have been suggested, none persuasively.

Only a minority of the lexical items of Armenian descend directly from IE; a great many actively used roots are Iranian loans. At the earliest level, these were taken from Parthian (Arm. *bžišk* < Avestan *baešaza-* 'remedy'); but the traffic continued, and loans from the Islamic period are also abundant (Arm. *dirt* 'dregs' < Mod. Persian *durd*). Words came too from Greek and Syriac; but these, on the whole, were literary or religious terms, and infrequently part of the vernacular language

TABLE 1. *The Armenian Alphabet*

Upper Case	Lower Case	Transliteration	Numerical Value
Ա	ա	a	1
Բ	բ	b	2
Գ	գ	g	3
Դ	դ	d	4
Ե	ե	e	5
Զ	զ	z	6
Է	է	ē	7
Ը	ը	ə	8
Թ	թ	t'	9
Ժ	ժ	ž	10
Ի	ի	i	20
Լ	լ	l	30
Խ	խ	x	40
Ծ	ծ	c	50
Կ	կ	k	60
Հ	հ	h	70
Ձ	ձ	j	80
Ղ	ղ	ł	90
Ճ	ճ	č	100
Մ	մ	m	200
Յ	յ	y	300
Ն	ն	n	400
Շ	շ	š	500
Ո	ո	o	600
Չ	չ	č'	700
Պ	պ	p	800
Ջ	ջ	ǰ	900
Ռ	ռ	ř	1000
Ս	ս	s	2000
Վ	վ	v	3000
Տ	տ	t	4000
Ր	ր	r	5000
Ց	ց	c'	6000
Ւ	ւ	w	7000
Փ	փ	p'	8000
Ք	ք	k'	9000
Օ	օ	ō	——
Ֆ	ֆ	f	——

TABLE 2. *Armenian Verb Forms*

	Singular	Plural
Present Tense		
1.	*berem* 'I bear'	*beremk'*
2.	*beres*	*berēk'* (< **ber-e-y*, < **ber-e-tV-*, + *-k'* plural)
3.	*berē* (< **ber-e-y* < **ber-e-ti*)	*beren*
Aorist Tense		
1.	*beri* 'I bore'	*berak'*
2.	*berer*	*berik'*
3.	*eber*	*berin*

arméniennes and the *Annual of Armenian Linguistics* have published many of the more recent contributions.

More controversial is the existence of ancient Anatolian vocabulary in Armenian. Hittite (probably actually Luwian), as well as non-IE Hurrian and Urartian, have been designated. For the former, one notes Hitt. *purut-* 'clay', Arm. *brut* 'potter'; Luwian *apparanti-* 'future', Arm. *apaṙni* 'id.' (Greppin 1982, and see Puhvel 1998). From non-IE Anatolian, a few dozen examples are cited by Diakonoff 1971, e.g. Hurrian *hinzuri* 'apple', Arm. *xnjor*, and Urartian *ult'u* 'camel', Arm. *ułt*.

By the 10th century, there was abundant literary evidence for two major Armenian dialects (Karst 1901). One, which continued Classical phonology, is Eastern Armenian, and is now spoken largely in Iran and the former Soviet Union. The other is the Western dialect; it is currently spoken in Istanbul (though formerly in most of Turkey) and in the Levant, and is the most common dialect of emigrant Armenians. The situation is actually more complicated than this. Adjarian 1909 suggested that three separate dialect groups could be distinguished on the basis of morphology, rather than phonology, depending on how they formed their present tense: *sirum em* 'I love' (which essentially corresponds to the morphology of the Eastern dialects) vs. *kè sirem* and *sirel em* (in the morphology of the Western dialects). During World War II, and especially in the years following, A. S. Gharibian proposed a fourfold classification more dependent on phonology; this eventually grew to seven groups. It is well summarized by Pisowicz 1976. Finally, a more sensitive system, based on a multi-featured diagnosis which included 100 phonological and morphological features, has been proposed by G. B. Djahukian; this system divides the Armenian dialects into 11 separate

(Arm. *xarb* 'sword' < Syr. *xarbā*; Arm. *selin* 'seat' < Gk. *sellíon*). From the 9th century, Arabic loans became common; but it often is difficult to tell which of them came directly from Arabic, and which secondarily through Persian (Arm. *mambar* 'pulpit', Ar. *minbar*, Per. *mimbar*). These various levels of borrowing are best described by Hübschmann 1897; the *Revue des études*

groups (a summary is found in Greppin and Khachaturian 1986). Vaux 1998 is an extended study of dialect phonology.

[*See also* Indo-European Languages.]

BIBLIOGRAPHY

Adjarian, Hratchia. 1909. *Classification des dialectes arméniens.* Paris: Champion.

Bardakjian, Kevork B., and Robert W. Thomson. 1977. *A textbook of Modern Western Armenian.* Delmar, N.Y.: Caravan.

Bardakjian, Kevork B., and Bert Vaux. 1999. *Eastern Armenian: A text book.* Delmar, N.Y.: Caravan.

Bedrossian, Matthias. 1875–79. *New dictionary, Armenian-English.* Venice: St. Lazarus Armenian Academy. Reprinted, Beirut: Librairie du Liban, 1974.

Diakonoff, Igor M. 1971. *Hurrisch und Urartäisch.* (Münchener Studien zur Sprachwissenschaft, Beiheft, n.F., 6.) Munich: Kitzinger.

Gharibian, Ararat S. 1944. *Kratkij kurs armjanskogo jazyka.* Yerevan: Izdatel'stvo Lujs.

Greppin, John A. C. 1982. The Anatolian substrata in Armenian: An interim report. *Annual of Armenian Linguistics* 3.65–72.

Greppin, John A. C. 1991. Some effects of the Hurro-Urartian people and their languages upon the earliest Armenians. *Journal of the American Oriental Society* 111.720–730.

Greppin, John A. C., and Amalya A. Khachaturian. 1986. *A handbook of Armenian dialectology.* Delmar, N.Y.: Caravan.

Hamp, Eric P. 1970. Sanskrit *duhitā́,* Armenian *dustr,* and IE internal schwa. *Journal of the American Oriental Society* 90.228–231.

Hübschmann, Heinrich. 1897. *Armenische Grammatik,* vol. 1, *Armenische Etymologie.* (Bibliothek indogermanischen Grammatiken, 6.) Leipzig: Breitkopf and Härtel. Reprinted, Hildesheim: Olms, 1962.

Karst, Josef. 1901. *Historische Grammatik des Kilikisch-Armenischen.* Strassburg: Trübner.

Kouyoumdjian, Mesrob G. 1950. *A comprehensive dictionary, Armenian-English.* Cairo: Sahag-Mesrob.

Kouyoumdjian, Mesrob G. 1961. *A comprehensive dictionary, English-Armenian.* Cairo: Sahag-Mesrob.

Meillet, Antoine. 1936. *Esquisse d'une grammaire comparée de l'arménien classique.* 2d ed. Vienna: Imprimerie des PP. Mékhitharistes.

Minassian, Martiros. 1980. *Grammaire d'arménien oriental.* Delmar, N.Y.: Caravan.

Olsen, Birgit A. 1999. *The noun in biblical Armenian: Origin and word-formation.* Berlin: Mouton de Gruyter.

Pisowicz, Andrzej. 1976. *Le développement du consonantisme arménien.* Kraków: Polska Akademia Nauk.

Puhvel, Jaan. 1998. Remarks on the Anatolian sources of Armenian *laxur. Annual of Armenian Linguistics* 19.33–36.

Schmitt, Rudiger. 1981. *Grammatik des Klassisch-Armenischen, mit sprachvergleichenden Erläuterungen.* (Innsbrucker Beiträge zur Sprachwissenschaft, 32.) Innsbruck: Institut für Sprachwissenschaft der Universität Innsbruck.

Thomson, Robert W. 1975. *An introduction to Classical Armenian.* Delmar, N.Y.: Caravan.

Vaux, Bert. 1998. *The phonology of Armenian.* Oxford: Oxford University Press.

JOHN A. C. GREPPIN

ARTICLES. *See* Parts of Speech; Phrase Structure; *and* Typology and Universals.

ARTICULATORY PHONETICS. Linguists describe the sounds of the world's languages in terms of the postures and movements of the various physiological structures (the *organs of speech*) involved in the production of these sounds. A necessary tool for this description is a notation system for sound classification. The International Phonetic Alphabet is most commonly used, and will be employed here. (For general reference, see Ladefoged 2001, Ladefoged and Maddieson 1996, Laver 1994.)

On the basis of their different functions in speech production, the organs of speech may be grouped into three main physiological systems (see Figure 1): the *respiratory system* contains the lungs (enclosed by the rib cage) and the trachea or "windpipe"; the *larynx* or "voice-box" consists of interconnecting cartilages that enclose the twin muscular flaps of the vocal cords or vocal folds; and the *supralaryngeal* or *articulatory system* comprises movable organs in the mouth, such as the tongue, lips, lower jaw (or mandible), and soft palate (or velum), as well as relatively fixed structures such as the teeth and hard palate. (For general reference, see Zemlin 1981, Hardcastle 1976, Perkins and Kent 1986, Seikel, King, and Drumright 1997, Kent 1997.)

Each of these three physiological systems has a unique role to play in the speech process. The respiratory system produces an out-going flow of air under relatively constant pressure, which is modulated by the other two systems to produce the sounds of speech. The larynx (the anterior part of which is the "Adam's apple") is situated at the top of the trachea; it contains the vocal folds,

FIGURE 1. *Physiological Systems for Speech Production*

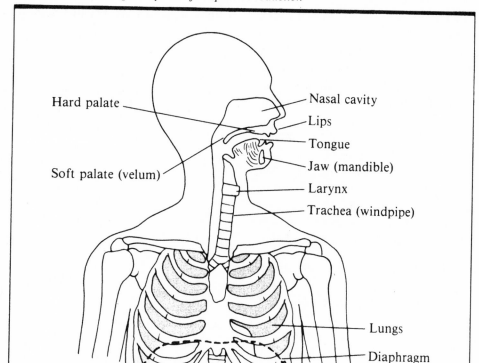

which function like an adjustable biological valve to modify the airstream from the lungs. Special muscles within the larynx alter the tension and length of the folds and the space between them (the glottis); these changes determine the pitch of the voice, whether the sound produced is voiced (folds close together and vibrating) or voiceless (folds wide apart), and the mode of vibration—whether, for example, breathy voiced (folds held somewhat apart) or creaky or laryngealized (folds somewhat forced together).

The various structures in the supralaryngeal system can change the shape of the airways within the mouth and nose cavities, and thus alter the resonances which characterize different speech sounds. They include the soft palate, which is a fleshy extension of the hard palate (or roof of the mouth); it acts like a valve to determine how much air can enter the nose cavity. When the valve is opened (as in [m] or [n] sounds), air can pass into the nose and resonate in this extra air chamber. Other mov-

able organs (articulators) are the tongue, lips, and lower jaw. The tongue is a relatively large organ, filling most of the mouth cavity. It is connected by muscles to external structures such as the lower jaw, the skull, and (indirectly) the larynx; and it is capable of achieving a wide range of different positions and shapes. For descriptive purposes, the surface of the tongue may be divided into (from front to back) the tip, blade, front, back, and root. Most of these articulatory organs in the supralaryngeal system are interconnected, so that movements of one organ can affect movements of another. During speech, these movements are also synchronized precisely with activities in the laryngeal and respiratory systems. Theories of coarticulation describe how these organs are coordinated during speech (see, e.g., Hardcastle and Hewlett 1999).

During speech, the articulators tend to alternate between relatively open and relatively constricted (or totally closed) configurations of the vocal tract. The open states are *vowels*; the closed or relatively closed states are *consonants*; and both forms are termed *segments*. The above outline describes the possibilities for consonant and vowel production in the world's languages. However, some sound characteristics are present at the level of entire syllables, or larger stretches of speech: these "suprasegmental" events are described in terms of *stress*, *tone*, and *intonation*.

1. Consonants. Within traditional articulatory phonetics, consonants are classified in terms of three main attributes: *place* of articulation, *manner* of articulation, and *voicing*.

1.1. *Place of articulation* refers to the location of the point of maximum constriction in the vocal tract. The following is a summary of the main places of articulation:

(a) Bilabial: made with the two lips (e.g. Eng. [p] in *apple*).
(b) Labiodental: lower lip with upper incisors (e.g. Eng. [f] in *fat*).
(c) Dental: tongue tip or blade with upper incisors (e.g. Eng. [θ] as in [θɪk] *thick*). (Sounds made with the tongue tip are called APICAL, and sounds made with the tongue blade are called LAMINAL.)
(d) Alveolar: tongue tip or blade with the alveolar ridge (the anterior part of the hard palate) (e.g. Eng. [t] as in *pat*).
(e) Retroflex: tongue tip with the back of the alveolar ridge (e.g. Malayalam [ʈ] as in [muʈʈu] 'knee').
(f) Postalveolar (or palato-alveolar): tongue blade with the back of the alveolar ridge (e.g. [ʃ] as in *she*).
(g) Palatal: front of the tongue with the hard palate (e.g. German [ç] as in *ich*).
(h) Velar: back of the tongue with the soft palate (e.g. Eng. [k] as in [tɪk] *tick*).
(i) Uvular: back of the tongue with the back of the soft palate (e.g. French [ʁ] in [ʁoz] *rose*).
(j) Pharyngeal: root of the tongue with the pharynx wall (e.g. Arabic [ʕ] in [ʕamm] 'uncle').

Some sounds involve the simultaneous use of two places of articulation. For example, Eng. [w] as in *wet* involves simultaneous constrictions at the lips and the velum. Some West African languages have labiovelar stops and nasals (e.g. [gb] in Yoruba).

1.2. *Manner of articulation* refers to the degree of constriction of the vocal tract, and to the way in which the constriction is made. A main subdivision distinguishes *obstruents*, in which the vocal tract is sufficiently constricted to interfere with free air flow, from *approxi-*

mants, which involve a lesser constriction more similar to that of vowels. Within the class of obstruents, four main variants can be distinguished:

(a) Fricatives involve sufficient constriction to produce frictional effects resulting in turbulent air flow—e.g. the hissing sound [s] in English *see*. They can be made at all the different places of articulation.
(b) Stops involve complete closure of the oral tract at some point.
(c) Nasals are a subdivision of stops; they involve complete oral tract closure, but an opening of the pathway between the soft palate and the pharynx wall—the pathway normally used for breathing through the nose.
(d) Affricates consist of a stop followed by a homorganic (same place of articulation) fricative (as in [tʃ], a voiceless postalveolar affricate bounding English *church*.

Lateral sounds are those in which the airstream is obstructed in the medial region of the vocal tract, with incomplete closure of one or both sides of the tongue. Laterals are most commonly approximants (e.g. Eng. [l] in *leaf),* but they can also be fricatives (e.g. Welsh [ɬan] 'church'). In addition, stops can be released laterally. Two minor variants in manner of articulation are *trills* and *flaps*. In trills, the articulators being constricted are set into vibration at a rate of about 30 Hertz (e.g. the Spanish alveolar trill in *perro* 'dog'). Trills can be made at a number of places of articulation. In flaps, an articulator strikes another a glancing blow with a very short (30–40 ms) contact duration (e.g. American Eng. [ɾ] in [læɾɾ] *ladder*). Most flaps involve the tongue tip.

1.3. *Voicing* refers to the extent of vocal fold vibration during a consonant. Most consonants are either voiced or voiceless during the entire period of maximal constriction. Voiceless stop consonants are additionally distinguished in terms of the time lag between the release of the articulation and the onset of voicing (the voice onset time, or VOT). If this lag is short (less than about 40 ms), stops are described as "voiceless unaspirated." If the lag is longer, the open glottis during the lag period gives rise to an interval of *h*-like noise called *aspiration*; consequently, these stops are described as "voiceless aspirated" stops. Three varieties—voiced, voiceless unaspirated, and voiceless aspirated stops—are distinctive in many languages (e.g. Thai).

1.4. *Additional airstream mechanisms.* Although all complete utterances in all languages are produced on a pulmonic egressive airstream, there are two additional ways in which the airstream can be actively manipulated within the vocal tract during the production of individual obstruents. In both cases, air is temporarily impounded within the tract by making an occlusion posterior to the place of articulation of an obstruent, either by closing the glottis (as in *ejectives* and *implosives*, produced with a glottalic airstream mechanism), or in the case of click sounds (in some South African languages) by the back of the tongue against the velum (velaric airstream mechanism).

2. Vowels. Traditionally vowels are classified in terms of the position of the highest point of the tongue, in a hypothetical two-dimensional space within the mouth. The two dimensions are the *front-back* position and the *high-low* or *open-close* dimension. The latter dimension is usually strongly related to another variable, the close-open continuum of the lower jaw or mandible. A third parameter is *lip rounding*, which also usually involves lip protrusion. The two-dimensional space for tongue position is hypothetical in the sense that it is usually inferred from auditory qualities of vowels, rather than directly observed.

The precise classification of a vowel phoneme in a particular language is often difficult to establish; the auditory quality of vowels varies with consonantal context, and to some extent with the idiolects of individual speakers. The most straightforward classification procedure is either to describe vowels in relation to a standard set (auditory reference points such as the Cardinal Vowels of Daniel Jones) or, to describe particular vowels of one language in relation to another language for which there is some agreement as to vowel quality. The Cardinal Vowel descriptive framework and the International Phonetic Alphabet include categories for four levels of vowel height: close, half close (or close-mid), half open (or open-mid), and open. It also includes three categories in the front-back axis: front, central, and back. Most rounded vowels in the world's languages are back vowels, since rounded back vowels have more auditory contrast with neighboring vowels than do rounded front vowels. Like consonants, most vowels are produced by a movement of the articulators toward a single point in the vocal tract; the time taken for the movements toward and away from this point tends to be similar, if averaged across contexts. These vowels are called *monophthongs*; they give rise to a single perceived auditory quality. Other vowels depart from this more or less symmetrical movement pattern, and may thus give rise to a changing auditory impression; these are called *diphthongs*. In some cases, they give rise to a distinctly double auditory impression, as their name implies.

Other less common properties of vowels should also be noted. In *nasalized* vowels, the soft palate is lowered as in nasal consonants (for example, French [mɛ̃] *main* 'hand'). In *rhotacized* vowels (e.g. [ɚ] as in Eng. *bird*), the tongue is elevated in the palatal region and retracted in the lower pharyngeal region; this causes a particular acoustic effect, specifically lowering of the third formant frequency.

A *secondary articulation* is a vowel-like articulation with a lesser degree of closure, which occurs concurrently with a (primary) consonantal articulation. There are four types of these. *Palatalization*, which is common in Slavic languages, is the addition of a high front tongue position (e.g. Russian [bratʲ] 'to take'). *Velarization* involves raising the back of the tongue (e.g. Eng. syllable-final [ɫ] as in [fɛɫ] *fell*). *Pharyngealization* is a narrowing of the pharynx, and is found in some Arabic "emphatic" consonants. *Labialization* is the addition of lip rounding; it can be combined with any of the other three secondary articulations.

[*See also* International Phonetic Alphabet; Intonation; Phonetics, *article on* Phonetic Transcription; Phonological Features; Phonology; Segments; *and* Tone.]

BIBLIOGRAPHY

Hardcastle, W. J. 1976. *Physiology of speech production: An introduction for speech scientists.* London: Academic Press.

Hardcastle, W. J., and N. Hewlett, eds. 1989. *Coarticulation: Theory, data and techniques.* Cambridge: Cambridge University Press.

Kent, Raymond D. 1997. *The speech sciences.* San Diego, Calif.: Singular.

Ladefoged, Peter. 2001. *A course in phonetics.* 4th ed. Orlando, Fla.: Harcourt College.

Ladefoged, Peter, and Ian Maddieson. 1996. *Sounds of the world's languages.* Oxford: Blackwell.

Laver, John. 1996. *Principles of phonetics.* Cambridge: Cambridge University Press.

Seikel, J. A.; D. W. King; and D. G. Drumright. 1997. *Anatomy and physiology for speech, language and hearing.* San Diego, Calif.: Singular.

Zemlin, Willard R. 1981. *Speech and hearing science: Anatomy and physiology.* 2d ed. Englewood Cliffs, N.J.: Prentice-Hall.

WILLIAM J. HARDCASTLE

ARTIFICIAL INTELLIGENCE. *See* Computational Linguistics *and* Cognitive Science.

ARTIFICIAL LANGUAGES. Also known as *planned* or *constructed languages,* particularly among enthusiasts. Languages, potential or actualized, intended for communicative use between humans, and brought into being through purposeful, intellectual agency. They are distinct from "natural" languages, which evolve out of other natural languages as far back as historical linguistics can determine; pidgins and creoles, which arise out of immediate communicative need rather than intellectual consideration; and formal languages as used in computer science, logic, mathematics, and formal semantics, which are not intended for ordinary human communication. The distinction between artificial and other languages is subtle; the human agency underlying them, for instance, marks only the endpoint of a continuum of language planning affecting all standardized languages. Likewise, there is only a contingent distinction between artificial languages and pidgins, or revived languages like Hebrew and Cornish; in many ways, such languages are quite similar.

Artificial languages display varying degrees of dependence on pre-existing natural languages. Those derived from existing languages, particularly in their lexicon, are termed *a posteriori;* these constitute the bulk of artificial languages. Those invented from whole cloth are termed *a priori.* Among a posteriori languages, there is a distinction between languages following natural models closely, particularly in morphology (*naturalistic*), and languages imposing greater regularity in their grammars (*schematic*). For example, while the lexicon of both Esperanto and Occidental is based on Western European languages, Esperanto is agglutinative (a trait uncharacteristic of its base languages), whereas Occidental attempts an ingenious emulation of Romance fusional derivational morphology. In the extreme case, a language can be an artificial subset of a single natural language, as with Basic English (introduced by Charles Kay Ogden in 1930).

Artificial languages fall into various classes according to their proclaimed purpose; different ideological choices can mean a language belongs to more than one class. The largest category is that of *auxiliary languages,* intended as (relatively) culturally neutral or simple languages for use between native speakers of different languages. There is a long history of such languages in Europe, but they have become particularly widespread since the 19th century. Although Solresol (Jean François Sudre 1866), an a priori language using only musical notes, gained early popularity, the most important contributions to the field have been Volapük (introduced by Johann Martin Schleyer in 1880), Esperanto (Ludwik Lejzer Zamenhof, 1887), Ido (Louis Couturat and Louis de Beaufront, 1907), Occidental (Edgar de Wahl, 1922), Novial (Otto Jespersen, 1928–1937), and Interlingua (International Auxiliary Language Association 1951). Of these, the latter are more naturalistic than the former, and the overall trend in auxiliary languages has been to stay close to a prototype Romance.

The idea of a universal auxiliary language may look increasingly utopian, given the current dominance of global English. Proposals for auxiliary languages are still undertaken, however; and the ideological/cultural niche filled by Esperanto in particular ensures it will survive for some time.

There are three other major classes of artificial language. *Logical* or *engineered languages* are created out of philosophical or logical concerns; they seek to reduce the ambiguity or vagueness inherent in natural languages, using more formal linguistic schemata. Such languages are related to the formal languages of logic and mathematics, although they typically reflect amateur rather than professional interest. Many artificial languages devised in the 17th and 18th century had this orientation (pioneering research in semantics), and often employed ideograms rather than alphabetic scripts; these were known as *pasigraphies,* and John Wilkins's Real Character (1668) is only the best known such attempt. Lojban (Logical Language Group 1988), based largely on predicate logic, is the best known modern logical language.

Fictional or *artistic languages* are devised either for literary purposes, or out of a hobbyist interest in creating languages for their own sake. This includes two instances notoriously prominent in 20th century popular culture: the languages invented by J. R. R. Tolkien, particularly Quenya, and Klingon (Marc Okrand, 1985), a language derived from the *Star Trek* television series. Both were invented by professional linguists, and have produced much secondary scholarship. Linguistic erudition is also employed to devise linguistic 'what-if' experiments, such as Brithenig (Andrew Smith, 1996), a thought experiment of a modern Celtic-tinged Romance language spoken in Britain, and Láadan (Suzette Haden Elgin, 1982), a language designed to express women's perspectives that natural languages are deemed structurally unable to. The hobbyist interest in constructing languages has been termed *conlanging,* and the artifacts *model languages.* The Internet has allowed such efforts to be widely disseminated, whereas previously they remained largely unpublished.

Secrecy languages are intended to conceal communication from outsiders. Unlike other artificial languages, there is typically less linguistic eclecticism and scholarship employed in their creation: they tend not to be "bookish" in origin. This class includes argots, cants, and "pig Latin"-type languages, which are usually trivial modifications of a natural language. It also includes *private languages* such as are occasionally reported to arise among children. Traditional, ritual languages, such as the various Australian "mother-in-law" languages, and in particular the phonologically eccentric Damin language formerly spoken by initiates of the Lardil people in Mornington Island, Australia, are also presumably artificial in origin.

Typologically, auxiliary languages tend to be unexceptional. Other types of artificial language often deliberately introduce oddities, as with Damin, or ignore naturalness, as with logical languages. Klingon also contains a number of typological jokes.

Artificial languages do not creolize as pidgins do: very few have an active speech community, let alone the opportunity to be passed on as a first language. Esperanto has by far the largest user community—estimates vary between fifty thousand and two million, and it is known to have over a thousand first-language speakers. (This typically arises when Esperanto is the home language of parents from different language backgrounds who met through knowledge of the language.) But these native speakers are too few in number, relative to the overall community, to have had a significant effect on the development of Esperanto.

Artificial language communities are often fissiparous: when a non-trivial number of adepts becomes involved, disputes about language design can lead to schism. When such schisms are overcome, the language community tends to become prescriptivist. Esperanto exemplifies this, although the community has made some allowance for both conscious experimentation and lexical drift. Unlike most natural language communities, prominent individuals (particularly lexicographers and authors) have a disproportionate influence on language development. Artificial language communities also place great value on literary production in the language, as proof of its validity.

[*See also* Languages of the World *and* Language Planning.]

BIBLIOGRAPHY

Eco, Umberto. 1995. *The search for the perfect language.* Oxford: Oxford University Press.

Forster, Peter G. 1982. *The Esperanto movement.* The Hague: Mouton.

Large, Andrew. 1985. *The artificial language movement.* Oxford: Blackwell.

Schubert, Klaus. 1989. *Interlinguistics: Aspects of the science of planned languages.* Berlin: Mouton de Gruyter.

Tolkien, John Roland Reuel. 1984. A secret vice. In *The monsters and the critics, and other essays,* edited by Christopher Tolkien, pp. 198–223. London: Allen and Unwin.

NICK NICHOLAS

ARU LANGUAGES. A branch of CENTRAL MALAYO-POLYNESIAN. They are spoken on the Aru Islands in the southeast of the Indonesian province of Maluku. A Nuclear Aru group is constituted by all the Aru languages except Ujir and West Tarangan.

LANGUAGE LIST

Barakai: also called Workai. 4,300 speakers. Dialects are Barakai, Mesiang. Closely related to Karey. Vigorous language use.

Batuley: also called Watulai, Gwataley. 3,840 speakers in seven villages in Aru on small islands off the east coast of Wokam Island, southern Maluku. Fairly closely related to Kompane to the north and Lola to the south, slightly more distant from Dobel. Vigorous language use. Batuley speakers consider Mariri to be a separate language.

Dobel: also called Sersifar Tannin, Doibel Lardi, Lardakobro'or, Kobroor, Doibel. 8,000 speakers. Dialects are Straits Dobel, Southeast Dobel, Northern Dobel, and possibly others. Related to Lola and Lorang. Dobo Malay, a dialect of Ambonese Malay, is used with outsiders and in the classroom. Only some pre-school children do not know Dobo Malay. Dobo Malay-influenced Indonesian used for speaking to non-Maluku people, opening and closing local political meetings, school classrooms, church services, and formal religious activities. Stable bilingualism with Dobo Malay and Indonesian used for certain domains, Dobel for others. Only a very few can speak Standard Indonesian. Some also speak Manombai. All ages speak Dobel. All domains, family, social interaction, local activities, conversations with local Chinese, traditional and political village meetings. Children play and interact in Dobel, some use in church services. Some letters written in it. Some speakers have written stories. Oral literature. Vigorous language use. Transmitted from parents to children. All Lorang speakers use Dobel as second language. Some Chinese merchants, who are speakers of Hokkien, learn Dobel. Speakers are proud of Dobel.

Karey: also called Kerei, Krei. 950 speakers. Village of Karey, east coast of Tarangan Island, southern Aru Islands. Vigorous language use.

Koba: 600 speakers. Intelligibility of Dobel is limited.

Kola: also called Warilau, Kulaha, Marlasi. 7,700 speakers in northern Aru Islands, all around the coast of Kola Island and adjacent islands. Twenty-two villages. Intelligibility testing showed Marlasi is intelligible to Kompane speakers, but with some possible adaptation of literature needed. Vigorous language use. Outsiders want to learn it.

Kompane: also called Komfana, Kongampani. 330 speakers in northeastern Aru in Kompane village on the east coast of Kongan Island, south of Kola and north of Wokam Islands. Closely related to Kola, linguistically between Kola and Batuley. Intelligibility of Kola is good, but some adaptation of literature may be needed. Vigorous language use.

Lola: 830 speakers in three villages of Lola, Warabal, and Jambuair on three islands east of Kobroor and Baun Islands, Aru Islands. Dialects are Lola, Warabal. Linguistically between Batuley and Dobel; close to Koba. In Lola some young people use Ambonese Malay among themselves. In Jambuair there are many non-Aru people, so Ambonese Malay is in common use. Most vigorous language use in Warabal.

Lorang: 325 speakers in the village of Lorang, center of Aru, on Koba Island. Closely related to Koba, and to a lesser extent to Dobel. Some similarities with Manombai, but intelligibility is lower than might be expected. Lorang people can speak several local languages to some degree and speak Dobel from childhood. Vigorous language use.

Manombai: also called Manobai, Wokam, Wamar. 7,475 speakers. Not inherently intelligible with Dobel. Vigorous language use.

Mariri: also called Mairiri. 390 speakers in eastern Aru on Mariri Island east of Kobroor Island, one village. Vigorous language use.

Tarangan, East: also called East Trangan, Tarangan Timur. 3,785 speakers on east coast of Tarangan Island, southern Aru Islands, and thirteen villages in Maikor Strait (Sungai Maikor). Vigorous language use.

Tarangan, West: also called West Trangan, Tarangan Barat. 6,480 speakers on west coast of Tarangan Island, southern Aru Islands. Largest language in the Aru Islands. Dialects are Southwestern Tarangan, North Central Tarangan. Two sharply distinct dialect groups, with minor variation within each. Vigorous language use. Trade language.

Ujir: also called Udjir. 975 speakers in two villages, Ujir on Ujir Island and Samang on the end of the western peninsula of Wokam Island, in northwestern Aru Islands. Bilingualism in Malay. Language use is declining in Ujir because of the influence of Malay spoken by an increasing number of outsiders. Less use reported in Samang than in Ujir.

B. GRIMES

ARUTANI-SAPE LANGUAGES. A group spoken on the eastern section of the Brazil-Venezuela border.

LANGUAGE LIST

Arutani: also called Auaqué, Auake, Awake, Aoaqui, Oewaku, Uruak, Urutani. 22 speakers in Brazil and Venezuela. In Brazil: 17 speakers remain in Roraima. The remaining speakers are bilingual in Ninam. Most are intermarried with the Ninam, some with the Pemon (Arecuna) and a few with the Sapi and do not speak Arutani fluently. In Venezuela: 5 speakers remain. Ethnic population: 30 or fewer as of 1977. Below the Sape of the Karum River area, state of Bolivar, headwaters of the Paraqua and Uraricáa Rivers. The remaining speakers are bilingual in Ninam. Most are intermarried with the Ninam, some with the Pemon (Arecuna), a few with the Sape, and they do not speak Arutani fluently.

Sapé: also called Kariana, Kaliána, Caliana, Chirichano. 5 speakers remain in Venezuela. Ethnic population: 25 or fewer as of 1977. Three small settlements on Paragua and Karuna Rivers. Some lexical correspondences with Warao (Isolate). Provisionally classified as Macro-Tucanoan. Most speakers have intermarried with Arecuna (Pemon) and a few with Arutani and Ninam. There are conflicting reports on the number of speakers and degree of bilingualism.

B. GRIMES

ASCOLI, GRAZIADIO ISAIA (1829–1907). Italian linguist (born at Gorizia under the Austro-Hungarian Empire). Ascoli was important both for his Indo-European studies (he established the correct reconstruction of the velars) and for his contributions to Romance linguistics and dialectology. While accepting some of the main tenets of the Neogrammarians, he pointed out that their views were less original than they appeared, and he had anticipated most of them.

ANNA MORPURGO DAVIES

ASL. *See* American Sign Language.

ASLIAN LANGUAGES. Part of the AUSTRO-ASIATIC family, probably as a top-level constituent of Mon-Khmer, Aslian languages are spoken primarily in western peninsular Malaysia.

FIGURE 1. *Subgrouping of Aslian Languages*

Jah Hut
North Aslian
  Chewong
  Eastern North Aslian
    Batek, Jehai, Minriq, Mintil
  Tonga
  Western North Aslian
    Kensiu, Kintaq
Senoic
  Lanoh, Sabüm, Semai, Semnam, Temiar
South Aslian
  Besisi, Semaq Beri, Semelai, Temoq

LANGUAGE LIST

Chewong: also called Cheq Wong, Che'wong, Siwang, Beri, Chuba. Ethnic population: 200 as of 2000. Just south of Semai, Pahang.

Batek: also called Bateq, Bateg, Batok, Kleb, Tomo, Nong. Ethnic population: 700 as of 2000. Northern Pahang, Kelantan, Trengganu. Dialects are Batek Teq (Teq), (Deq), Batek Iga, Batek Nong (Nong). Batek De' and Batek Nong may be separate languages.

Besisi: also called Mah Meri, Cellate. Ethnic population: 1,356. Selangor coast, Malacca. Dialects are Kuala Langot Besisi, Malakka Besisi, Ulu Langat Orang Bukit, Selangor Sakai, Betise' (Betisek), Sisi. One other dialect became extinct in late 19th century.

Jah Hut: also called Jah Het. Ethnic population: 2,442. Just south of main body of Semai, Kuala Krau, Pahang. Dialects are Kerdau, Krau, Ketiar Krau (Tengganu), Kuala Tembeling, Pulau Guai, Ulu Ceres (Cheres), Ulu Tembeling.

Jehai: also called Jahai, Pangan. 1,250 speakers in northeastern Perak and western Kelantan. Ethnic population: 1,375 as of 2000. Dialects are Jehai, Batek Teh.

Kensiu: also called Kenseu, Kensieu, Kensiw, Moniq, Monik, Mendi, Ngok Pa, Orang Bukit, Orang Liar. 3,300 speakers in peninsular Malaysia and Thailand. In peninsular Malaysia: 3,000 speakers. Northeastern Kedah, near Thai border. Overlaps slightly into southern Yala Province of Thailand. Dialects are Ijoh (Ijok), Jarum, Jeher (Sakai Tanjong of Temongoh), Kedah (Quedah), Plus, Ulu Selama, Kensiu Batu, Kensiu Siong, Kentaq Nakil. In Thailand: 300 speakers. Southern Yala Province, Phattaloong, Satun, Narathiwat provinces, Thai-Malay border. Some in a resettlement camp in Yala.

Kintaq: also called Kenta, Kintak, Kintaq Bong, Bong. 100 speakers remain in peninsular Malaysia and Thailand. In Malaysia: Kedah-Perak border area, Thai border. Overlaps slightly into Southern Yala Province of Thailand. In Thailand: Kedah-Perak border area, Thai border.

Lanoh: also called Jengjeng. Ethnic population: 224. North central Perak.

Minriq: also called Menriq, Menrik, Mendriq, Menraq, Menri. 125 speakers in southeastern Kelantan.

Mintil: also called Mitil. 40 speakers remain. Formerly spoken along Tamun River, Pahang.

Sabüm: Northern central Perak. Closest to Lanoh and Semnam; but not the same as Lanoh.

Semai: also called Central "Sakai," Senoi, Sengoi. Ethnic population: 18,327. Northwestern Pahang and southern Perak, Selangor, Negri Sembilan, central mountain area. Dialects are Jelai, Orang Tanjong of Ulu Langat, Sungkai, Perak I, Perak II, Cameron, Telom, Bidor, Betau, Lipis, Bil, Ulu Kampar (Kampar). Bilingualism in Malay.

Semaq Beri: also called Semaq Bri, Semoq Beri. Ethnic population: 2,078. Pahang, Trengganu, Kelantan. Two dialects.

Semelai: Ethnic population: 2,932. Between Segamat (Johore) and the Pahang River. Two dialects became extinct in the early 20th century.

Semnam: North central Perak. Close to Lanoh and Sabüm.

Temiar: also called Temer, Northern Sakai, Seroq, Pie. Ethnic population: 11,593. Mostly in Perak and Kelantan; also Pahang. Dialects are Grik, Kenderong, Kenering, Po-Klo (Sakai Bukit of Temongoh), Sakai of Plus Korbu, Sungai Piah, Tanjong Rambutan, Tembe' (Tembi), Ulu Kinta (Kinta Sakai), Lanoh Kobak.

Temoq: 350 speakers. Jeram River, southeastern Pahang.

Tonga: also called Mos. Spoken also in Thailand. In Thailand: Ethnic population: 300 as of 2000. Two areas in the south. Probably close to Kensiu. May be linguistically extinct. In peninsular Malaysia: northwestern tip north of Kaki. Probably close to Kensiu. May be linguistically extinct.

B. GRIMES

ASPECT. The term "aspect" designates the internal temporal organization of the situation described by a verb. The most common possibilities are the *perfective*, which indicate that the situation is to be viewed as a bounded whole, and the *imperfective*, which in one way or another looks inside the temporal boundaries of the situation. The latter may be divided into *habitual* and *progressive*.

These aspects are usually expressed by inflections, auxiliaries, or particles associated with the verb. In addition, the perfective/imperfective distinction may be derivational, as in the Slavic languages.

Other common derivational aspects, often called "Aktionsarten," are the *iterative*, indicating that the action of the verb is repeated; the *inceptive*, which signals the beginning of an action; and the *inchoative*, which indicates entrance into a state. In general, aspects and tenses cross-classify, except that it is most common for the perfective to be restricted to past tense.

[*See also* Semantics; Tense; *and* Verbs.]

BIBLIOGRAPHY

Comrie, Bernard. 1976. *Aspect: An introduction to the study of verbal aspect and related problems.* Cambridge and New York: Cambridge University Press.

Chung, Sandra, and Alan Timberlake. 1985. Tense, aspect, and mood. In *Language typology and syntactic description*, vol. 3, *Grammatical categories and the lexicon*, edited by Timothy Shopen, pp. 202–258. Cambridge and New York: Cambridge University Press.

Dahl, Östen. 1985. *Tense and aspect systems.* Oxford: Blackwell.

JOAN L. BYBEE

ASSESSMENT. *See* Language Testing.

ASSIMILATION. *See* Phonological Processes.

ATHABASKAN LANGUAGES. With a population of about 130,000 speakers, nearly three-quarters of whom speak Navajo, Athabaskan (also spelled Athabascan and Athapaskan) constitutes the most populous Native American language family of North America. It is widely distributed from Alaska to the US Southwest. Li 1946 on Chipewyan (now called Dëne Sųłiné) is a concise grammatical sketch; for more detailed grammars, see Golla 1970 on Hoopa, Cook 1984 on Sarcee (Tsúut'ina), Young and Morgan 1987 on Navajo, and Rice 1989 on Slavey. For historical-comparative studies, see Krauss 1973, Leer 1979, Krauss and Golla 1981, and Krauss and Leer 1981. Cook and Rice 1989 is a review of theoretical and analytical problems. Major dictionaries include Young and Morgan 1987, Kari 1990 (Ahtna), and Jetté and Jones 2000 (Koyukon).

1. History. The region comprising interior Alaska, the Yukon, and northern British Columbia, where the most diverse and conservative languages are found, is believed to have been the American homeland of the Athabaskans; this is further substantiated by Sapir 1936, on the linguistic evidence for the northern origin of the Navajo. Krauss and Golla 1981 list twenty-three N[orthern] A[thabaskan] languages spoken in Alaska and northwestern Canada (including the extinct Tsetsaut), as shown in Map 1. They recognize only eight P[acific] C[oast] A[thabaskan] languages—many fewer than the earlier classification shown in Map 2, and eliminating the language boundaries indicated there by broken lines. Most PCA languages of Oregon and California have become extinct (e.g. Kwalhioqua-Tlatskanai, known to have existed near the mouth of the Columbia River). Apachean, the southernmost group, consists of eight languages as shown in Map 3, including Navajo. Speculating that PCA is an earlier offshoot than Apachean, Krauss 1973 emphasized that much of Athabaskan is a dialect continuum with few abrupt boundaries; thus, its internal relationships may be better described in terms of a wave model than a tree model.

Athabaskan and Eyak descend from P[roto-] A[thabaskan-]E[yak], itself a branch of the controversial Na-Dené phylum (Sapir 1915); see Figure 1. The phonemic inventory of PAE (along with that of P[roto-] A[thabaskan]) has been reconstructed by Krauss and Leer 1981, who also offer what might be cognate items for PAE-Tlingit.

2. Phonology. The salient aspects of Athabaskan phonology can best be shown with reference to the PA phonemic inventory, based on work by Krauss and Leer, as shown in Table 1.

Of the seven core sets of obstruents, the dental and lateral sets are well preserved in the daughter languages; however, the remaining sets have either shifted forward or have merged into fewer sets. Patterns of forward shift (e.g. $*q > k$, $*k^y > *t\check{s}$, $*ts > t\theta$) and of mergers (e.g. $*(\check{s}, *t\check{s}^w > t\check{s})$, and loss of consonants in stem-final position, have been the most conspicuous diachronic processes; however, these have not affected the three-way contrasts between the plain, aspirated, and glottalized series. The development of labials from PA sibilants in some Slavey dialects and Dogrib, and from retroflexes in Tsetsaut, is exceptional.

Of the three nasal phonemes in Table 1, the status of $*n^y$ and $*m$ (which replace Leer's 1979 $*\bar{y}$ and $*\bar{w}$ respectively) is not yet fully understood. $*n^y$ must have had allophones ranging from palatals to velars (as in Carrier), and $*m$ must have alternated phonetically between an occlusive ([m]) and a glide ([w̃]). Syllable-final *n* is retained in some languages (e.g. Ahtna, Carrier); in others, it gave rise to nasalized vowels (e.g. Slavey, Dogrib) or dropped (Sarcee). A laryngeal feature ("constriction") is also reconstructed; parallel with the devel-

MAP 1. *Distribution of Northern Athabaskan Languages*

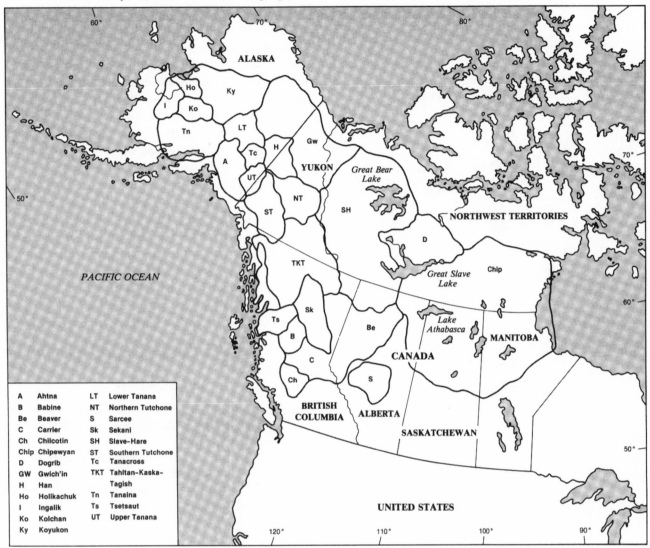

A	Ahtna	LT	Lower Tanana
B	Babine	NT	Northern Tutchone
Be	Beaver	S	Sarcee
C	Carrier	Sk	Sekani
Ch	Chilcotin	SH	Slave-Hare
Chip	Chipewyan	ST	Southern Tutchone
D	Dogrib	Tc	Tanacross
GW	Gwich'in	TKT	Tahltan-Kaska-
H	Han		Tagish
Ho	Holikachuk	Tn	Tanaina
I	Ingalik	Ts	Tsetsaut
Ko	Kolchan	UT	Upper Tanana
Ky	Koyukon		

opment of nasals, this has been developed to high tone (Slavey, Chipewyan) or to low tone (Dogrib, Navajo), or lost without a trace (PCA). Major synchronic processes include sibilant harmony; the "D-effect," by which a stem-initial consonant coalesces with a preceding *d*, e.g. $d + y \rightarrow d\check{z}$, $d + ? \rightarrow t$'; and gamma vocalization, i.e. $C\partial + \gamma\partial/\gamma^w\partial \rightarrow Ca/Cu$, which applies only across a conjunct boundary (see below).

3. Grammar. Verbs, nouns, postpositions, and particles are well-defined categories. A set of pronominal prefixes denotes both the possessors of nouns and the objects of postpositions; these show person and number, as in the Chipewyan paradigms in Table 2.

The verbal morphology is notable for its complexity: e.g., ten prefix positions were established for Chipewyan

by Li 1946, and many more (with sub-positions) for Ahtna by Kari 1979. The verb stem occurs in the right-most position (except for a few suffixes and enclitics in certain languages). The prefixes are divided into "conjunct" and "disjunct." The former are more tightly bound morphophonologically to the stem, and include such paradigmatic elements as subject and object (generally marking the same person and number categories as for nouns), and aspect/mode. The disjunct prefixes express such concepts as relation, manner, direction, location, and quantification, and include adverbials, incorporates, iterative/distributive elements, and other categories. Chipewyan prefix positions (based on Li) are shown in Table 3.

The verb stem consists historically of a root and a

MAP 2. *Distribution of Pacific Coast Athabaskan Languages*

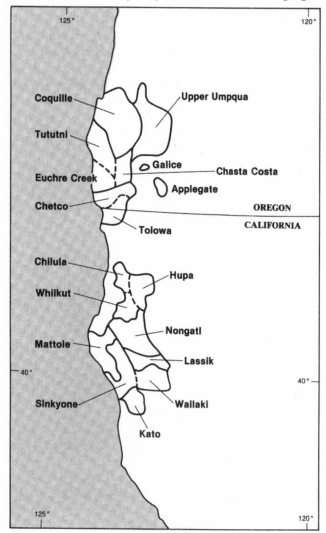

Characteristic of the Athabaskan family is a system of classificatory verbs. The existing analyses (e.g. Navajo by Davidson et al. 1963) indicate that there are co-occurrence restrictions between these verbs (with meanings such as 'be in position' and 'handle object') and the class of subject nouns (if intransitive) or object nouns (if transitive). The apparent co-occurrence restrictions are illustrated by one of four sets in Navajo; set A, given in Table 5, 'X is in a position of rest'. However, a careful examination of most innovative uses of the classificatory verbs reveals that the problem involved is not that of co-occurrence restrictions but that of semantics and pragmatics.

Athabaskan languages have basic S[ubject] O[bject] V[erb] word order; however, any NP, including the complement NP of a postpositional phrase (PP) may move to a focus position. The PP that is not a constituent of a complex verb may also move. NPs need not be overtly expressed, which is apparently correlated with the phenomenon that pronouns are inflectional categories of the verb.

[*See also* North American Languages.]

BIBLIOGRAPHY

Cook, Eung-Do. 1981. Athapaskan linguistics: Proto-Athapaskan phonology. *Annual Review of Anthropology* 10.253–273.

Cook, Eung-Do. 1984. *A Sarcee grammar*. Vancouver: University of British Columbia Press.

Cook, Eung-Do, and Keren D. Rice, eds. 1989. *Athapaskan linguistics: Current perspectives on a language family*. Berlin: Mouton de Gruyter.

Davidson, William, L. W. Elford, and Harry Hoijer. 1963. Athapaskan classificatory verbs. In *Studies in the Athapaskan languages* (University of California publications in linguistics, 29), by Harry Hoijer et al., pp. 30–41. Berkeley: University of California Press.

Golla, Victor K. 1970. *Hoopa grammar*. Berkeley: University of California, Berkeley, dissertation.

Jetté, Jules, and Eliza Jones. 2000. *Koyukon Athabaskan dictionary*. Fairbanks: Alaska Native Language Center.

Kari, James. 1979. *Athabaskan verb theme categories: Ahtna*. (Alaska Native Language Center research papers, 2.) Fairbanks: University of Alaska.

Kari, James. 1990. *Ahtna Athabaskan dictionary*. Fairbanks: Alaska Native Language Center.

Krauss, Michael E. 1973. Na-Dene. In *Current trends in linguistics*, vol. 10, *Linguistics in North America*, edited by Thomas A. Sebeok, pp. 903–978. The Hague: Mouton.

Krauss, Michael E., and Victor K. Golla. 1981. Northern Athapaskan languages. In *Handbook of North American*

mode/aspect suffix; this may combine with verbal prefixes to form the basic lexical representation of the verb (the "verb theme"). For example, the Ahtna root *de:tl'* occurs with four different sets of thematic elements representing four different themes: 'pl. walk', 'pl. fly', 'handle pl. objects quickly', and 'eat pl. objects'. In order to specify derivational relationships and lexical aspects (inherent or derived), verb themes can be organized into theme categories. Kari 1979 establishes ten basic theme categories for Ahtna. For example, the first lexical entry for *de:tl'* above belongs to the motion theme category and can be conjugated in five aspect paradigms: momentaneous, perambulative, reversative, continuative, and progressive. Table 4 shows two aspectual paradigms for Ahtna 'eat' (operative theme), conjugated in the durative and momentaneous aspects.

MAP 3. *Distribution of Apachean Languages*

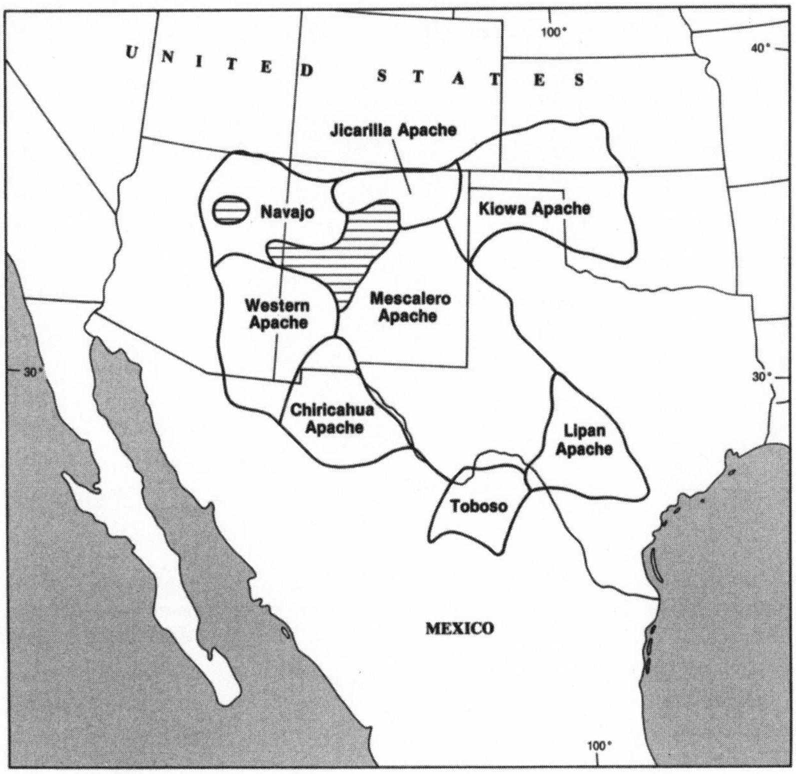

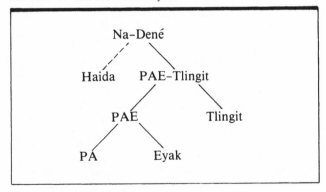

FIGURE 1. *The Na-Dené Phylum*

Na-Dené

Haida   PAE-Tlingit

PAE   Tlingit

PÁ   Eyak

Indians, vol. 6, *Subarctic*, edited by June Helm, pp. 67–85. Washington, D.C.: Smithsonian Institution.

Krauss, Michael E., and Jeff Leer. 1981. *Athabaskan, Eyak, and Tlingit sonorants*. (Alaska Native Language Center research paper 5.) Fairbanks: University of Alaska.

Leer, Jeff. 1979. *Proto-Athabaskan verb stem variation: Phonology*. (Alaska Native Language Center research paper 1.) Fairbanks: University of Alaska.

Li, Fang-Kuei. 1946. Chipewyan. In *Linguistic structures of Native America* (Viking Fund publications in anthropology, 6), by Harry Hoijer et al., pp. 398–423. New York.

Rice, Keren D. 1989. *A grammar of Slave*. Berlin: Mouton de Gruyter.

Sapir, Edward. 1915. The Na-dene languages: A preliminary report. *American Anthropologist* 17.534–558.

Sapir, Edward. 1936. Internal evidence suggestive of the northern origin of the Navajo. *American Anthropologist* 38. 224–235. Reprinted in Edward Sapir, *Selected Writings in language, culture, and personality*. (Berkeley: University of California Press, 1949), pp. 213–224.

Young, Robert D., and William Morgan. 1987. *The Navajo language: A grammar and colloquial dictionary*. Rev. ed. Albuquerque: University of New Mexico Press.

EUNG-DO COOK

LANGUAGE LIST

Ahtena: also called Atna, Ahtna, Copper River, Mednovskiy. 80 speakers remain in USA. Ethnic population: 500 as of 1995. Copper River above the Eyak River at its mouth, and upper Susitna and Nenana drainages. Eight communities. Bilingualism in English. Speakers are in their 50s or 60s and older.

Apache, Jicarilla: 812 speakers in USA. Ethnic population: 2,000 as of 1977. Northern New Mexico, area of Dulce.

TABLE 1. *Proto-Athabaskan Phonemic Inventory*

	Dental	Lateral	Alveolar	Alveopalatal	Labial/ Retroflex	Dorsopalatal	Uvular	Glottal
Occlusives								
Plain	d	dl	dz	dž	džʷ	gʸ	G	ʔ
Aspirated	t	tł	ts	tš	tšʷ	kʸ	q	
Glottalized	t'	tł'	ts'	tš'	tš'ʷ	k'ʸ	q'	
Fricatives								
Voiceless		ł	s	š	šʷ	xʸ	x	h
Voiced		l	z	ž	žʷ	γʸ	γ	

Sonorants	Labial			Dental			Dorsopalatal	
Oral	w						y	
Nasal	m			n			nʸ	

Vowels	Front				Back			
Full	i		e		a	u		
Reduced				ə	α	υ		

TABLE 2. *Person and Number Categories of Chipewyan in Nouns and Postpositions*

Categories	Noun Paradigm	Postposition Paradigm
1sg.	*se-lá* 'my hand'	*se-ts'ə́n* 'toward me'
2sg.	*ne-lá* 'your hand'	*ne-ts'ə́n* 'toward you'
3sg.	*be-lá* 'his/her hand'	*be-ts'ə́n* 'toward him/her'
4sg.	*ye-lá* 'the other's hand'	*ye-ts'ə́n* 'toward the other'
1/2pl.	*nuhe-lá* 'our hand'	*nuhe-ts'ə́n* 'toward us'
3pl.	*hube-lá* 'their hand'	*hube-ts'ə́n* 'toward them'
Indefinite/Areal	*ʔe-lá* 'someone's hand'	*ho-ts'ə́n* 'toward there/then'
Reflexive	*ʔede-lá* 'one's own hand'	*ʔede-ts'ə́n* 'toward oneself'
Reciprocal	*ʔełe-lá* 'each other's hand'	*ʔełe-ts'ə́n* 'toward each other'

TABLE 3. *Chipewyan Verb Prefix Positions*

```
10  Incorporated postposition ⎫
 9  Adverb                    ⎬ Disjunct
 8  Iterative                 ⎪
 7  Incorporated stem         ⎭
 6  Deictic/3rd person subject ⎫
 5  Object                     ⎪
 4  Mode                       ⎪
 3  Aspect                     ⎬ Conjunct
 2  1/2 person Subject         ⎪
 1  Classifier                 ⎪
 0  Stem                       ⎭
```

TABLE 4. *The Ahtna Verb 'eat' in Two Aspect Paradigms, Inflected for Four 'Modes'.* The final element in each form, set off by a hyphen, is the stem.

Mode	Durative	Momentaneous
Imperfective	*ʔes-ya·n* 'I'm eating it'	*q'eyi-di·s* 'he's finishing eating it'
Perfective	*γas-ya·n* 'I ate it'	*q'eyi-da·n* 'he's finished eating it'
Future	*txas-yi·ł* 'I'll eat it'	*q'eyta-di·ł* 'he'll finish eating it'
Optative	*γos-ya·n'* 'I should eat it'	*q'eyu-da·n'* 'he should finish eating it'

Many young adults may prefer English. As of 1998, most adults speak the language. Some children may speak the language; many can understand it, but tend to prefer English.

Apache, Kiowa: 18 speakers remain in USA. Ethnic population: 1,000 as of 1977. Western Oklahoma, Caddo County. Bilingualism in English.

Apache, Lipan: 2 speakers remain in USA. Ethnic population: 100 as of 1977. New Mexico, Mescalero Reservation. Bilingualism in English. Both speakers were elderly in 1981.

Apache, Mescalero-Chiricahua: 1,800 speakers in USA. Ethnic population: 2,000 as of 1977. Mescalero Reservation, New Mexico. A small number of Chiricahua at Fort Sill, Oklahoma. Dialects are Chiricahua, Mescalero. In

TABLE 5. *Navajo Classificatory Verb Stems, Set A*

Class of Subject/Object	Verb Stem
a single round solid object (e.g. a rock)	-ʔą́
a long slender rigid object (e.g. a stick)	-tą́
an animate being	-tį́
an aggregate of small objects (e.g. coins)	-nìl
a rigid container with content (e.g. a plateful)	-ką́
a fabric-like object (e.g. a blanket)	-tsòòz
a bulky object (e.g. a crate)	-žóód
a set of parallel long, rigid objects (e.g. logs)	-žòòž
a mass or collectivity (e.g. hay)	-džàà ʔ
a (ball-shaped?) wool-like mass	-džòòl
a rope-like object	-lá
a mud-like mass	-tłéé ʔ

Oklahoma most or all speakers are middle-aged or older. Vigorous language use in New Mexico.

Apache, Western: also called Coyotero. 12,693 speakers in USA. East central Arizona, several reservations. Dialects are White Mountain, San Carlos, Cibecue, Tonto. As of 1998, children were raised speaking the language. Vigorous language use.

Babine: also called Babine Carrier, Northern Carrier, Witswit'en. 500 speakers in Canada. Ethnic population: 2,200 according to 1982 and 1997 reports. Areas of Burns Lake, Babine Lake, Moricetown, Takla Lake area, west central British Columbia. Babine is still the principal means of communication among middle-aged adults and older. Children and young adults may speak Babine but prefer English.

Beaver: 300 speakers in Canada, reported to be highly bilingual in English.

Carrier: also called Central Carrier. 1,500 speakers in Canada. Ethnic population: 2,100 as of 1987. Central British Columbia, Stuart and Fraser Lake area. Bilingualism in English. Mainly adults. In some communities, vigorous language use among adults. Most children and young adults prefer English.

Carrier, Southern: 500 speakers in Canada. Central British Columbia, west of Quesnel and south of Cheslatta Lake, towards the Fraser and its tributaries, and Anahim Lake-Ulkatcho. Can use literature adapted from Central Carrier. Limited bilingualism. Vigorous language use.

Chetco: 5 speakers remain in USA. Ethnic population: 100 possibly as of 1977. Southern coast, Oregon. Bilingualism in English.

Chilcotin: also called Tzilkotin. 705 speakers in Canada. Ethnic population: 1,800 as of 1982. West of Williams Lake, south central British Columbia. Vigorous language use among adults. Many children prefer English.

Chipewyan: also called Dene. 4,000 speakers in Canada. Ethnic population: 6,000 as of 1995. As of 1995 also, speakers included children in some places.

Coquille: also called Upper Coquille, Mishikhwutmetunee. Formerly spoken in USA, southwestern Oregon, on upper Coquille River.

Degexit'an: also called Deg Xinag, Deg Xit'an. "Ingalik," "Ingalit" are derogatory names sometimes used. 20 speakers remain in USA. Ethnic population: 250 to 300 as of 1997. Alaska, Shageluk, Anvik, and Athabaskans at Holy Cross, below Grayling on the Yukon River. Bilingualism in English. Speakers are in their 50s or older.

Dogrib: 2,110 speakers in Canada. Ethnic population: 3,220 as of 2001. The Detah-Ndilo dialect developed from intermarriage between the Yellowknife subdivision of the Chipewyan and the Dogrib. 16% speak a little English; 37% speak both Dogrib and English, but speak Dogrib better; 14% speak both languages equally; 9% speak both, but speak English better; 7% speak English and a little Dogrib; 3% are monolingual in English (children and the elderly), 12% are monolingual in Dogrib. All ages. Adults prefer to use Dogrib in most contexts. One Dogrib band has frequent contact and close relationships with the Bear Lake (North Slavey) people of Fort Franklin. Relations with the Inuit and the Chipewyan have traditionally been strained.

Galice: formerly spoken in USA, southwestern Oregon.

Gwich'in: also called Kutchin, Loucheux. Around 700 speakers in Canada and USA. In Canada: 430 speakers. Ethnic population: 1,900 as of 1995, including 1,500 in Northwest Territories, 400 in Yukon. Between Old Crow, Yukon, and the lower Mackenzie River, Northwest Territories. Dialects are Fort Yukon Gwich'in, Arctic Village Gwich'in, Western Canada Gwich'in (Takudh, Tukudh, Loucheux), Arctic Red River. Most adults speak the language. In a few communities use of the language is vigorous by all ages. Elsewhere younger ones may speak the language, but tend to prefer English. In USA: 300 speakers. Ethnic population: 1,100 as of 1995. Northeastern Alaska on Yukon River and tributaries. Six villages. Dialects are Fort Yukon Gwich'in, Arctic Village Gwich'in, Western Canada Gwich'in (Takudh, Tukudh, Loucheux), Arctic Red River. Many young people prefer English. Many children only speak English. Generally most adults speak the language (parents and the elderly as of 1998). Vigorous language use in isolated communities.

Han: also called Han-Kutchin, Moosehide, Dawson. 7 speakers remain in USA and Canada. In USA: Ethnic population: 300 as of 1995. Yukon River in area of Alaska-Canada border, Eagle, Alaska. Bilingualism in English. As of 1997, the youngest speaker in Alaska was less than 60 years old. There is a Han textbook with tapes for teaching the language. In Canada: Yukon River area I on Alaska—Canada border,

Dawson. Bilingualism in English. As of 1995, all speakers were elderly.

Holikachuk: 12 speakers remain in USA. Ethnic population: 200 as of 1995. Village of Grayling on lower Yukon River, Alaska. Bilingualism in English. All speakers are probably over 60.

Hupa: also called Hoopa. 8 speakers remain in USA. Ethnic population: 2,000 as of 1998. Hoopa Valley Reservation, northwestern California. Bilingualism in English. Only elderly speakers left. Language revitalization effort is in progress. Adult classes, language immersion camps.

Kaska: also called Caska, Eastern Nahane, Nahane, Nahani. 400 speakers in Canada. Ethnic population: 900 as of 1995. Southeastern Yukon Territory and northern British Columbia border area, Watson Lake and Lower Post. Closely related to Tahltan. Bilingualism in English. Speakers are nearly middle aged, except at Ross River, where they may be younger.

Kato: also called Cahto, Batem-Da-Kai-Ee, Kai Po-Mo, Tlo-keang. Formerly spoken in USA. Laytonville Reservation, northwestern California. Bilingualism in English.

Koyukon: also called Ten'a. 300 speakers in USA. Ethnic population: 2,300 as of 1995. Alaska, Koyukuk and middle Yukon Rivers. Bilingualism in English. Speakers are 35, 40, 60, or older.

Mattole: formerly spoken in USA, northern California.

Navajo: also called Diné, Navaho. 148,530 speakers in USA. Ethnic population: 219,198 as of 1990. Northeastern Arizona, northwestern New Mexico, southeastern Utah, and a few speakers in Colorado. Vigorous language use, but as of 1998, mother tongue speakers among first graders were 30% versus 90% in 1968.

Sarsi: also called Sarcee. 50 speakers in Canada. Ethnic population: 600 as of 1977. Alberta, near Calgary. Bilingualism in English. All speakers are middle-aged or older.

Sekani: 30 speakers in Canada. Ethnic population: 600 according to studies done in 1982 and 1997. McLeod Lake and Ware (Finlay River), north central British Columbia. The majority are bilingual in English. Most speakers are middle-aged or older.

Slavey, North: also called Slavi, Dené, Mackenzian. "Slave" is a derogatory name sometimes used. 790 speakers in Canada. Ethnic population: 1,600 as of 1995. Dialects are Hare, Bearlake, Mountain. A separate language from South Slavey. All ages in some communities. Four or five communities have vigorous language use.

Slavey, South: also called Slavi, Dené, Mackenzian. "Slave" is a derogatory name sometimes used. 1,410 speakers in Canada. Ethnic population: 3,600 as of 1995. North and South Slavey are separate languages. Adults still use South Slavey in smaller, isolated communities, but there is serious attrition among children and young people.

Tagish: 2 speakers remain in Canada. Ethnic population: 400 possibly as of 1995. Southern Yukon, west or west-northwest of the Tlingit, with some at Carcross. Speakers are also fluent in Tlingit and speak English as second language. All are elderly.

Tahltan: 40 speakers remain in Canada. Ethnic population: 750 as of 1977. Telegraph Creek, northwestern British Columbia. Closely related to Kaska. Bilingualism in English. Only elderly speakers left as of 1991. Tahltan is seldom used.

Tanacross: 35 speakers remain in USA. Ethnic population: 120 as of 1997. Eastern Alaska, Tanacross, Healy Lake, Dot Lake, Tok. Dialects are Healy Lake, Mansfield-Ketchumstuck. Little dialect variation. Mansfield-Ketchumstuck is the most important politically and numerically. Closest to Upper Tanana, but they have different tone systems. Bilingualism in English, Upper Tanana. Youngest speakers in their 30s. Tanacross is spoken only between older adults in the home.

Tanaina: also called Dena'ina, Kinayskiy. 75 speakers in USA. Ethnic population: 900 as of 1997. Around Cook Inlet and adjacent area of southern Alaska. Dialects are Kenai Peninsula, Upper Inlet, Coastal-Inland, Stoney River. Bilingualism in English. Youngest speakers in their 20s at Lime Village, but elsewhere in their 50s and older. Kenai dialect is nearly extinct.

Tanana, Lower: also called Tanana. 30 speakers remain in USA. Ethnic population: 380 as of 1995. Tanana River below Fairbanks, Nenana, and Minto, central Alaska. Dialects include Chena River and Salcha-Goodpaster. Bilingualism in English. All speakers are near 60 or older. Chena River dialect became extinct in 1976 and Salcha-Goodpaster Rivers in 1993.

Tanana, Upper: also called Nabesna. 115 speakers remain in USA and Canada. In USA: 105 speakers. Ethnic population: 300 in USA as of 1995. Area of upper Tanana River, east central Alaska. Bilingualism in English. Youngest speakers are in their 20s at Tetlin, older elsewhere. In Canada: 10 speakers remain. Ethnic population: 40 as of 1995. Southwestern Yukon Territory, Beaver Creek. Speakers are bilingual in English.

Tolowa: also called Smith River. 4 speakers remain in USA, all elderly. Ethnic population: 1,000 as of 2000. Southwestern Oregon. Chasta Costa was a separate tribe in Oregon; now extinct. Language teaching, language materials development, recent book on the language.

Tsetsaut: formerly spoken in Canada. Portland Canal area, borderline to southwestern Alaska and British Columbia. Became extinct about 1930.

Tutchone, Northern: also called Selkirk. 200 speakers in Canada. Ethnic population: 1,000 as of 1995. Central Yukon, Mayo-Stewart, Selkirk-Pelly, Carmacks, and White River areas. Bilingualism in English. Youngest speakers are 30 to 40.

Tutchone, Southern: 200 speakers in Canada. Ethnic population: 1,400 as of 1995. Southwestern Yukon Territory, Whitehorse, Aishihik-Champagne-Klukwan, and Kluane-Burwash areas. Bilingualism in English. The youngest fluent speakers are 40 or 50.

Tututni: 10 speakers remain in USA, southwestern Oregon, as of 1962, all over 50 years old.

Upper Kuskokwim: also called Mcgrath Ingalik, Kolchan. 40 speakers remain in USA. Ethnic population: 160 as of 1995. Nikolai, Telida, McGrath, Upper Kuskokwim River, central Alaska. Bilingualism in English. Youngest speakers, average age 30.

Wailaki: formerly spoken in USA, Round Valley Reservation, northern California.   B. GRIMES

ATLANTIC LANGUAGES.

ATLANTIC LANGUAGES. Also called West Atlantic languages. They constitute one of the main branches of the NIGER-CONGO family. Atlantic languages are spoken primarily on the west cost of Africa from the Senegal River (i.e. the boundary of Mauritania and Senegal) to western Liberia; however, FULA, the Atlantic language with by far the largest number of speakers, has a substantial inland population as far east as Sudan.

LANGUAGE LIST

Badjara: also called Badara, Badian, Badyaranke, Pajade, Pajadinka, Gola, Bigola. 11,550 speakers in Guinea, Guinea-Bissau, and Senegal. In Guinea: 6,300 speakers in the Koundara region. In Guinea-Bissau: 3,750 speakers on the northeastern corner. The speakers may be bilingual in Mandinka. In Senegal: 1,500 speakers in the south central area, one village that is all Badjara. The speakers may use Mandinka as second language.

Baga Binari: also called Barka, Binari, Kalum, Mborin. Spoken in Guinea on the coast east of the Nunez River in Boké region. Close to Landoma and Temne. Bilingualism in Susu.

Baga Kaloum: formerly spoken in Guinea. The people now speak Susu.

Baga Koga: also called Barka, Koga, Koba. Spoken in Guinea on the coast between the Pongo and Konkouré Rivers, extending to the Œle de Kito. Close to Landoma and Themne. Bilingualism in Susu.

Baga Manduri: also called Barka, Mandari, Maduri, Manduri. Spoken in Guinea. Islands in Nunez River delta, around Dobale, Kanfarande subprefecture. Close to Landoma and Themne. Bilingualism in Susu.

Baga Mboteni: spoken in Guinea. Related to Nalu and Mbulungish. Bilingualism in Susu.

Baga Sitemu: also called Barka, Sitemuú, Tchitem, Stem Baga, Rio Pongo Baga. 32,100 speakers in Guinea on the southern bank of the Nunez River in the Boké and Boffa regions. Baga Marara is spoken on Marara islands south of the Rio Pongo Inlet. Close to Landoma and Themne. Bilingualism in Susu.

Baga Sobané: also called Barka, Sobané, Baga Kakissa. Formerly spoken in Guinea between the Kapatchez and Pongo Rivers. Was close to Landoma and Themne. Susu is the language used now.

Bainouk-Gunyaamolo: also called Banyum, Banyun, Bagnoun, Banhum, Bainuk, Banyuk, Banyung, Elomay, Elunay, Ñuñ. 5,000 speakers in Senegal and Gambia. In Senegal: North of the Casamance River in the triangle formed by the towns of Bignona, Tobor, and Niamone, north of Ziguinchor, across the Casamance River. Dialects are Gujaaxet, Gunyamoolo. Two dialects are intelligible to each other's speakers: the one around Niamone (Gunyaamolo) and the other around Tobor. Closely related to Kobiana and Kasanga of Guinea-Bissau. More closely related to the Tenda languages of eastern Senegal than to the neighboring Diola and Balanta-Kentohe. Gunyuño in Guinea-Bissau is distinct.

Bainouk-Gunyuño: also called Banyum, Banyun, Bagnoun, Banhum, Bainuk, Banyuk, Banyung, Elomay, Elunay. 7,260 speakers in Guinea-Bissau, south of the Casamance River. A distinct language from Bainouk-Gunyaamolo of Senegal and Gambia. Related to Kobiana and Kasanga of Senegal and Guinea-Bissau. More closely related to the Tenda languages of eastern Senegal than to Diola and Balanta-Kentohe.

Bainouk-Samik: 1,500 speakers in Senegal. A different language from Gunyaamolo-Bainouk in Senegal and Gambia, and Bainouk-Gunyuño in Guinea-Bissau.

Balanta-Ganja: also called Fjaa, Balant, Balante, Balanda, Ballante, Belante, Bulanda, Brassa, Alante, Fraase. 94,500 speakers in southwestern corner of Senegal, south of the Casamance River, between Goudomp and Tanaff, and south from there. Dialects are Fganja (Ganja), Fjaalib (Blip). A separate language from Balanta-Kentohe in Guinea-Bissau. Speakers are fairly bilingual in Mandinka.

Balanta-Kentohe: also called Balanta, Balant, Balante, Balanda, Ballante, Belante, Bulanda, Brassa, Alante, Frase. 326,700 speakers in Guinea-Bissau and Gambia. In Guinea-Bissau: North central and central coast. Dialects are Fora, Kantohe (Kentohe, Queuthoe), Naga, Mane. Naga, Mane, and Kantohe may be separate languages. A separate language from Balanta-Ganja in Senegal. Not intelligible with Mansoanka.

Bandial: also called Banjaal. 9,000 speakers in Senegal. Dialects are Affiniam, Elun (Hulon, Kuluunaay). More intelligible with Bandial than with Gusilay. Bilingualism in Jola-Fogny, Jola-Kasa, Mandinka, Pulaar, Wolof.

FIGURE 1. *Subgrouping of Atlantic Languages*

Bijago
  Bidyogo
Northern Atlantic
  Bak
    Balant-Ganja
      Balanta-Ganja, Balanta-Kentohe
    Jola
      Bayot
      Jola Proper
        Jola Central
          Gusilay
            Bandial, Gusilay
          Her-Ejamat
            Ejamat, Kerak
          Jola-Fogny
          Jola-Kasa
        Karon-Mlomp
          Karon, Mlomp
        Kwatay
          Kuwaataay
    Manjaku-Papel
      Mandjak, Mankanya, Papel
  Cangin
    Lehar, Ndut, Noon, Palor, Saafi-Saafi
  Eastern Senegal—Guinea
    Banyun
      Bainouk-Gunyaamolo, Bainouk-Gunyuño, Bainouk-Samik
    Nun
      Kasanga, Kobiana
    Tenda
      Badjara, Basari, Biafada, Budik, Wamey
  Mbulungish-Nalu
    Baga Mboteni, Mbulungish, Nalu
  Senegambian

Fula-Wolof
  Fulani
    East Central Fulani
      Central-Eastern Niger Fulfulde, Nigerian Fulfulde, Western Niger Fulfulde
    Eastern Fulani
      Adamawa Fulani, Bagirmi Fulani
    West-Central Fulani
      Benin-Togo Fulfulde, Maasina Fulfulde, Pular
    Western Fulani
      Pulaar
  Wolof
    Wolof, Gambian Wolof
  Serer
    Serer-Sine
Southern Atlantic
  Limba
    East Limba, West-Central Limba
  Mel
    Bullom-Kissi
      Bullom
        Northern Bullom
          Bom, Bullom So
        Southern Bullom
          Krim, Sherbro
      Kissi
        Southern Kisi, Northern Kissi
    Gola
    Temne
      Baga
        Baga Binari, Baga Kaloum, Baga Koga, Baga Manduri, Baga Sitemu, Baga Sobané, Landoma
      Temne-Banta
        Themne
  Sua
    Mansoanka

Basari: also called Bassari, Tenda Basari, Biyan, Onian, Ayan, Wo. 16,900 speakers in Senegal, Guinea, and Guinea-Bissau. In Senegal: 7,850 speakers. Southeastern, Upper Casamance, around Edun, border areas, Kedougou, Tambacounda. Closely related to Budik. In Guinea: 8,600 speakers. In Guinea-Bissau: Northeastern.

Bayot: also called Baiote, Baiot, Bayotte. 14,800 speakers in Senegal and Guinea-Bissau. In Senegal: 13,000 speakers. A cluster of villages about 12 km southwest of Ziguinchor, grouped around the village of Nyassia. Speakers use Jola-Kasa as second language, some Wolof, and perhaps Mankanya or Mandjak. In Guinea-Bissau: 1,800 speakers. Northwestern, along the border with Senegal.

Biafada: also called Beafada, Biafar, Bidyola, Bedfola, Dfola, Fada. 36,800 speakers in Guinea-Bissau. Central south, north of the Nalu.

Bidyogo: also called Bijogo, Bijago, Bijougot, Budjago, Bugago, Bijuga. 24,500 speakers in Guinea-Bissau. Dialects are Anhaqui (Anhaki), Kagbaaga, Kamona, Kajoko. Some intelligibility problems are reported between dialects, especially Kamona. Important grammatical differences between Kagbaaga and Anhaki, Kagbaaga and Kajoko. No information about dialects on Galinhas and Formosa Islands. Bilingualism in Crioulo.

Bom: also called Bome, Bum, Bomo. 250 speakers in Sierra Leone. Ethnic population: 5,000 as of 1991. Along the Bome River. Bilingualism in Mende.

Budik: also called Bedik, Tandanke, Tendanke, Tenda, Bande, Basari du Bandemba. 3,000 speakers in southeastern Senegal. Budik is close to Basari.

Bullom So: also called Northern Bullom, Bolom, Bulem, Bullun, Bullin, Mmani, Mandingi, Mandenyi. Spoken in

Sierra Leone and Guinea. In Sierra Leone: Ethnic population: 6,800 as of 1988. Along the coast from the Guinea border to the Sierra Leone River. Dialects are Mmani, Kafu. Bom is closely related. Little intelligibility with Sherbro, none with Krim. Speakers are switching to Themne. In Guinea: Along the coast from the Guinea border to the Sierra Leone River. Only elderly speakers.

Ejamat: also called Ediamat, Fulup, Feloup, Felup, Felupe, Floup, Flup. 21,350 speakers in Guinea-Bissau and Senegal. In Guinea-Bissau: 19,550 speakers. Northwestern corner, San Domingo district. In Senegal: 1,800 speakers. Extreme southern Senegal, a handful of villages 5 to 7 km due south of Oussouye, including Kahem, Efok, Youtou. A distinct language from other Jola varieties. 63% lexical similarity between Her-Ejamat and Jola-Fogny or Jola-Kasa; 50% with Gusilay or Elun. They may use Jola-Kasa and Wolof as second languages.

Fulfulde, Adamawa: also called Adamawa Fulani, Peul, Peulh, Ful, Fula, Fulbe, Boulbe, Eastern Fulani, Fulfulde, Foulfoulde, Pullo, Gapelta, Pelta Hay, Domona, Pladina, Palata, Paldida, Paldena, Dzemay, Zemay, Zaakosa, Pule, Taareyo, Sanyo, Biira. 760,000 speakers in Cameroon, Chad, Sudan, and Nigeria. In Cameroon: 668,700 speakers. It is spread all over the Far North, North, and Adamawa provinces. Dialects are Maroua, Garoua, Ngaondéré, Kambariire, Nomadic Fulfulde, Bilkire Fulani (Bilkiri). There are some serious problems in intelligibility among Cameroon dialects, and elsewhere with Cameroon dialects. Bilkire is spoken by second-language Fulfulde speakers. Trade language. In Chad: 128,000 speakers in the southwest, Mayo-Kebbi prefecture, around Léré. Dialects are Maroua, Garoua, Ngaoundéré, Kambariire, Nomadic Fulfulde, Bilkire Fulani (Bilkiri). In Sudan: 90,000 speakers. Northern Sudan, Blue Nile and Kordofan regions. Many speak Sudanese Arabic; some also speak Hausa and Songai as second languages. Mahdist group is bilingual in Fulfulde and Sudanese Spoken Arabic. Few monolinguals; most are children. In Nigeria: East central Nigeria, states of Taraba and Adamawa, center in Yola. National language.

Fulfulde, Bagirmi: also called Baghirmi Peul, Bagirmi Fula. 180,000 speakers in Chad and Central African Republic. In Chad: 24,000 speakers. West, Chari-Baguirmi prefecture, Massénya and Bokoro subprefectures, between Bokoro and Massénya. May be close to Bororo (Nigerian) Fulfulde; reported to be a nomadic group of Mbororo. Trade language. In Central African Republic: 156,000 speakers. Scattered. May be close to Bororo (Nigerian) Fulfulde; reported to be a nomadic group of Mbororo. Bilingualism in Sango.

Fulfulde, Benin-Togo: also called Peulh, Peul, Fulbe-Borgu. 328,000 speakers in Benin, Nigeria, and Togo. In Benin: 280,000 speakers. Dialects are Bakuure, Korakuure, Djougoure (Juguure), Tchabankeere (Caabankeere). Bilingualism in French. The Gando people speak Fulfulde, but are ethnically Boko and Baatonu (Bariba). In Togo: 48,200 speakers In the north. The Djougoure dialect may extend west into Togo.

Fulfulde, Central-Eastern Niger: also called Peul, Peulh, Fulani, Fula, Fulbe. 450,000 speakers in Niger. Central and eastern Niger, from around Dogondoutchi on eastward to the Chad border. Woodabe culture is distinct from other Fulfulde varieties. Many use Hausa as second language. The Fulbe (15,000,000) from Senegal to Sudan consider themselves to be one ethnic group and to speak one language, while acknowledging differences in speech. National language.

Fulfulde, Maasina: also called Peul, Macina. 919,700 speakers in Mali, Ivory Coast, and Ghana. In Mali: 911,200 speakers. Central Mali. The western dialect is spoken around Segou and Macina. The eastern dialect is spoken from north of Mopti to Boni in the east. Dialects are Western Macina, Eastern Macina. There are some dialect differences, but popular opinion is that all dialects in Mali are inherently intelligible. Substantial Bambara influence. There is skewing between the ethnic and linguistic relationships. Bilingualism in Bambara. All domains, local administration, trade language, some oral use in first two grades, oral and written use in religious services, oral use in business. Highly positive attitude toward Fulfulde. National language. In Ghana: Northern, in small groups. Bilingualism in Hausa.

Fulfulde, Nigerian: also called Kano-Katsina-Bororro Fulfulde. 7,611,000 speakers in Nigeria, Chad, and Cameroon. In Nigeria: Dialects are Kano-Katsina, Bororro (Bororo, Mbororo, Ako, Nomadic Fulfulde), Sokoto. In Chad: Dialects are Kano-Katsina, Bororro (Bororo, Mbororo, Ako, Nomadic Fulfulde). In Cameroon: Northern Cameroon. Dialects are Kano-Katsina, Bororro (Bororo, Mbororo, Ako, Nomadic Fulfulde).

Fulfulde, Western Niger: also called Peul, Peulh, Fulani, Fula, Fulbe. 1,150,000 speakers in Niger and Burkina Faso. In Niger: 400,000 speakers. Western Niger, from Burkina Faso border east to around Dogondoutchi. Dialects are Dallol, Bitinkoore. Many use Zarma as second language. The Fulbe from Senegal to Sudan consider themselves to be one ethnic group and to speak one language, while acknowledging differences in speech. In Burkina Faso: 750,000 speakers. Northeastern Burkina Faso corner. Dialects are Barani (Barain, Baraniire), Gourmantche, Bogandé, Jelgoore, Liptaakoore, Barkoundouba, Seeba-Yaga (Yaaga) Ouhiguyua, Fada Ngurma.

Gola: 107,300 speakers in Liberia and Sierra Leone. In Liberia: 99,300 speakers. Western Liberia, between the Mano and St. Paul Rivers. Dialects are Deng (Todii), Kongba, Senje. In Sierra Leone: 8,000 speakers. Along the border and a few miles into Sierra Leone. Dialects are De (Deng), Managobla (Gobla), Kongbaa, Kpo, Senje (Sene), Tee (Tege), Toldil (Toodii). Most Gola in Sierra Leone have become Mende speakers.

Gusilay: also called Kusiilaay, Gusilaay, Gusiilay, Kusilay. 12,400 speakers in Senegal. Village of Tionk Essil, between Tendouck and Mlomp-North. Bilingualism in Jola-Fogny, Wolof, Mandinka, Pulaar.

Jola-Fogny: also called Diola-Fogny, Dyola, Jóola, Jola. 313,000 speakers in Senegal, Gambia, and Guinea-Bissau. In Senegal: 260,000 speakers. Dialects are Buluf, Fogny, Kombo, Kalounaye, Narang. Gusilaay, Kuwaataay, Karon, Mlomp, Kerak, Ejamat, and Bayot are more distantly related languages, but they are close geographically. Jola-Fogny is the largest Jola variety and the most widely understood. Possibly less than 10% of speakers are monolingual. Over 90% of speakers also speak Wolof, French, or Mandinka. All domains, oral and written use in administration, informal use in education. Oral use in business, traditional religion, some use in other religious services, oral literature. Parents pass on Jola-Fogny to children. Recognized by the government as one of six national languages. Buluf seems to have many lexical items different from Fogny, but Buluf speakers are willing to learn to read Fogny. Speakers of Gusilay, Karon, Kuwaataay, Mlomp, and some Pulaar living in the area speak Jola-Fogny as second language. Very favorable attitude toward Jola-Fogny. National language. In Gambia: 53,000 speakers. Southwestern districts. Fogny is the largest and most widely understood Jola variety. In Guinea-Bissau: Fogny is the largest and most widely understood Jola variety.

Jola-Kasa: also called Diola-Kasa, Casa, Jóola-Kasa. 36,300 speakers in Senegal and Gambia. In Senegal: Dialects are Ayun, Esulalu (Esuulaalur, Oussouye, Mlomp South), Fluvial, Huluf, Selek, Bliss (Niomoun). Closely related to, but a distinct language from Jola-Fogny.

Karon: 9,300 speakers in Senegal and Gambia. In Senegal: 8,060 speakers. Bilingualism in Jola-Fogny, Wolof. In Gambia: 1,200 speakers. A distinct language from other Jola varieties.

Kasanga: also called Cassanga, Kassanga, I-Hadja, Haal. 600 speakers in Guinea-Bissau. A remnant are living near Felupe, in the northwest, in a sparsely populated border area. No speakers live in Senegal. Close to Bainouk-Gunyaamolo.

Kerak: also called Her, Keerak, Keeraku. 10,600 speakers in Senegal. A distinct language from other Jola varieties. Speakers may use French and Wolof as second languages.

Kissi, Northern: also called Gizi, Kisi, Kissien, Kisie. 326,500 speakers in Guinea and Sierra Leone. In Guinea: 286,500 speakers. South central, Kissidougou region. Dialects are Liaro, Kama, Teng, Tung. Closely related to Sherbro. Southern Kissi of Liberia and Sierra Leone is different. National language. In Sierra Leone: 40,000 speakers. Dialects are Liaro, Kama, Teng, Tung. Closely related to Sherbro. Southern Kissi is different. Bilingualism in Krio, Mende.

Kisi, Southern: also called Kissi, Gizi, Gisi, Kissien. 200,000 speakers in Liberia and Sierra Leone. In Liberia: 115,000 speakers. Lofa County, extreme northwest corner of Liberia. Dialects are Luangkori, Tengia, Warn. Different from Northern Kissi of Guinea. In Sierra Leone: 85,000 speakers.

Kobiana: also called Cobiana, Uboi, Buy. 600 speakers in Guinea-Bissau and Senegal. In Guinea-Bissau: Near Banyun. Closely related to Bainouk and Kasanga. Speakers are bilingual in Mandyak, but not vice versa. In Senegal: Closely related to Bainouk and Kasanga. Speakers are bilingual in Mandyak, but not vice versa.

Krim: also called Kim, Kittim, Kirim, Kimi. 500 speakers in Sierra Leone. Ethnic population: 10,000 as of 1990. On the coast between Sherbro and Vai, along the Krim River. The people are bilingual in Sherbro, and being absorbed into the Mende group. There are seven or eight towns where children and others speak Krim.

Kuwaataay: also called Kwatay. 5,000 speakers in Senegal. In Diembering, Bouyouye, Nyikine, Boukot-Diola and some other villages along the coast just south of the mouth of the Casamance River, and Dakar. A distinct language from other Jola varieties. Most speakers can speak or understand Jola-Kasa, Jola-Fogny, and some Wolof.

Landoma: also called Landouman, Landuma, Tyapi, Tyopi, Tiapi, Cocoli. 14,400 speakers in Guinea. Between the upper Nunez River and the upper Pongas River. Not in Guinea-Bissau. Close to Baga and Themne.

Lehar: also called Lala. 10,000 speakers in Senegal. North of Thies in west central Senegal, around the towns of Panbal, Mbaraglov, Dougnan. Inadequate intelligibility of Noon. Some bilingualism in Wolof. Some speakers are also bilingual in Noon, Ndut, or French.

Limba, East: also called Yimba, Yumba. 4,000 speakers in Guinea and Sierra Leone. In Guinea: Dialects are Northern Limba (Warawara, Ke-Woya-Yaka). In Sierra Leone: North central. Dialects are Northern Limba (Warawara, Ke-Woya-Yaka), Southern Limba (Biriwa-Saroko-Kalantuba-Sunko).

Limba, West-Central: also called Yimba, Yumba. 335,000 speakers in Sierra Leone, north central area north of Makeni. Dialects are Western Limba (Tonko, Sela), Central (Tamiso, Gbongogbo).

Mandjak: also called Mandjaque, Manjaca, Manjaco, Manjiak, Mandyak, Manjaku, Manjack, Ndyak, Mendyako, Kanyop. 253,350 speakers in Guinea-Bissau, Senegal, Gambia, and France. In Guinea-Bissau: 151,250 speakers. West and northwest of Bissau. Dialects are Bok (Babok, Sarar, Teixeira Pinto, Tsaam), Likes-Utsia (Baraa, Kalkus), Cur (Churo), Lund, Yu (Pecixe, Siis, Pulhilh). Important politically. Thousands have emigrated to France. In Senegal: 85,000 speakers in the southwest. Dialects are Bok (Kabok, Sara, Teixeira Pinto, Tsaam), Likes-Utsia (Baraa, Kalkus), Cur (Churo), Lund, Yu (Pecixe). Some dialects listed may be separate languages. Closely related to Mankanya and Papel. In Gambia: 17,100 speakers. Western, south of the

Gambia River. Dialects are Bok (Babok), Sarar, Teixeira Pinto, Tsaamo, Likes-Utsia (Baraa, Kalkus), Cur (Churo), Lund, Yu (Pecixe). Some dialects listed may be separate languages. Closely related to Mankanya and Papel.

Mankanya: also called Mankanha, Mancanha, Mancagne, Mancang, Bola. 61,000 speakers in Guinea-Bissau, Senegal, and Gambia. In Guinea-Bissau: 36,300 speakers northwest of Bissau. Dialects are Burama (Bulama, Buram, Brame), Shadal (Sadar). In Senegal: 23,500 speakers. Scattered. Dialects are Burama (Bulama, Buram, Brame), Shadal (Sadar). Related to Mandjak, in which there is extensive bilingualism. Speakers have a language association (PKUMEL), are developing an orthography and standardizing their language.

Mansoanka: also called Mansoanca, Maswanka, Sua, Kunant, Kunante. 12,700 speakers in Guinea-Bissau and Gambia. In Guinea-Bissau: North central. Not inherently intelligible with Balanta or Mandinka, although called "Mandinkanized Balanta."

Mbulungish: also called Baga Foré, Baga Monson, Monshon, Monchon, Bulunits, Longich, Black Baga. 5,000 speakers in Guinea in twenty-two villages. Related to Nalu and Baga Mboteni. Children were reported to be speaking the language actively in 1995–1996.

Mlomp: also called Mlomp North, Gulompaay. 4,350 speakers in Senegal. Many speak and understand Jola-Fogny as second language, some know Wolof, and a few may know Mandinka or Pulaar.

Nalu: also called Nalou. 20,250 speakers in Guinea and Guinea-Bissau. In Guinea: 13,000 speakers near Boke. Related to Mbulungish and Baga Mboteni. In Guinea-Bissau: 7,250 speakers southwest near the coast. Many are bilingual in Susu. Intermarriage in the border area with another group. Reported to be closed to outsiders.

Ndut: also called Ndoute. 25,350 speakers in Senegal. West central, northwest of Thiès. 32% intelligibility of Palor. Some bilingualism in Wolof. Some speakers are also bilingual in Lehar, Saafi-Saafi, or French.

Noon: also called None, Non, Serer-Noon. 26,500 speakers in Senegal. Surrounding and in Thiès. Dialects are Padee (in Fandene), Cangin (in Thiès), and Saawii north of Thiès). Noon is very different from Serer-Sine. 68% intelligibility of Lehar. Some bilingualism in Wolof, which they use to communicate with Lehar speakers and others. Some are also bilingual in French.

Palor: also called Falor, Sili, Sili-Sili, Waro. 8,600 speakers in Senegal. West central, west southwest of Thiès. 55% intelligibility of Ndut, 27% of Saafi-Saafi. Some bilingualism in Wolof. Some are also bilingual in Saafi-Saafi and French. Palor is used in the home.

Papel: also called Pepel, Papei, Moium, Oium. 114,000 speakers in Guinea-Bissau and Guinea. In Guinea-Bissau: 111,550 speakers on Bissau Island. Closely related to Mankanya and Mandyak. Three dialects.

Pulaar: also called Pulaar Fulfulde, Peul, Peulh. 2,921,300 speakers in Senegal, Gambia, Guinea-Bissau, Mali, Mauritania, and Guinea. In Senegal: 2,121,140 speakers. Dialects are Toucouleur (Tukolor, Tukulor, Tokilor, Pulaar, Haalpulaar, Fulbe Jeeri), Fulacunda (Fulakunda, Fulkunda). Fulbe Jeeri and Toucouleur (Haalpulaar'en) are separate ethnic groups speaking this form of Pulaar. Jeeri is a geographical region in which a large number of diverse lineages still follow a semi-nomadic life. There are three families subdivided into at least twenty lineages, each of which has some dialectal differences; all are inherently intelligible. Bunndu is a Fula geo-political state composed of a mix of Toucouleur and Fulbe Jeeri. Fuuta Tooro (Fouta Toro) was a major Toucouleur geo-political state, which has its seat in northern Senegal, and is also in Mauritania. Fulacunda is an ethnic group speaking a closely related dialect of Pulaar. Their region is called Fuladu in the Upper Casamance area of Senegal. Different enough from Pular to need separate literature. National language. In Gambia: 233,300 speakers. Dialects are Fulacunda (Fulakunda, Fulkunda), Toucouleur (Tukolor, Tukulor, Halpulaar, Haalpulaar). Bilingualism in Mandinka. Fulbe Jeeri, Toucouleur, and Fulacunda are ethnic groups that speak Pulaar. In Guinea-Bissau: 217,800 speakers. North central and northeastern Guinea-Bissau. Dialects are Fulacunda (Fulakunda, Fulkunda, Fula Preto, Fula Forro). There are five Fulfulde varieties in Guinea-Bissau. In Mali: 175,000 speakers. Settled primarily around Bandiagara and Ségou. Dialects are Toucouleur (Tukolor, Tukulor, Pulaar, Halpulaar, Haalpulaar, Fulbe Jeeri). Related to Maasina Fulfulde but distinct. The ethnic group Fulbe Jeeri speaks this language as mother tongue. In Mauritania: 150,000 speakers. Dialects are Toucouleur (Tukulor, Pulaar, Haalpulaar). In Guinea: One community near Dinguiray (Pulaar), and a few communities in the north near Sareboido. Dialects are Toucouleur (Tukulor, Tukolor, Pulaar), Fulacunda (Fulakunda, Fulkunda, Fula Preto). Different enough from Pular to need separate literature. The official orthography is different from that used elsewhere. National language.

Pular: also called Fuuta Jallon, Fouta Dyalon, Fulbe, Fullo Fuuta, Futa Fula, Foula Fouta, Fulfulde, Jalon, Pulaar. 2,900,000 speakers in Guinea, Sierra Leone, Senegal, Mali, Niger, and Nigeria. In Guinea: 2,550,000 speakers. Northwest, Fouta Djallon area. Dialects are Kebu Fula, Fula Peta. Different enough from Pulaar in Senegal to need separate literature. Many monolinguals. Maninka and Susu used as second language by others. Guinea had an extensive literature in Pular, but little still exists. Used in schools. Fuuta Jalon in Guinea is a major Pular geopolitical state. National language. In Sierra Leone: 178,400 speakers. Throughout the country but especially in the north. Dialects are Krio Fula, Kebu Fula. As of 1962, recent immigrants from Guinea speak the original Futa Jalon or the Kebu dialect. It is intelligible with Fula Peta of Guinea and with dialects of Guinea, Guinea-Bissau, and Senegal. A slightly modified form of Futa Jalon is known as Krio Fula with many loans from Sierra Leone languages. In Senegal: Speakers are looked upon as outsiders in Senegal. In Mali: Western Mali from Guinea up to about Keniéba, especially in the administrative arrondissements of Faléa and Faraba. Mali variety is completely intelligible with variety in Guinea.

Saafi-Saafi: also called Serer-Safen, Sereer-Saafen, Safi, Saafi, Safi-Safi, Safen. 104,000 speakers in Senegal. Dialects are Boukhou, Sebikotane, Sindia, Hasab, Diobass. Dialects are named after villages and a zone, Diobass. Some bilingualism in Wolof. Children and very few adults are monolingual. Some speakers are also bilingual in Ndut, French, Serer-Sine, English, Spanish, Pulaar, Palor. Wolof tends to be used in Muslim ceremonies. All domains, use with Saafi people, oral literature. Parents transmit it to children. Vigorous language use. Positive attitude toward Saafi-Saafi. Roman alphabet used.

Serer-Sine: also called Sérère-Sine, Serer, Serrer, Sereer, Seereer, Serer-Sin, Sine-Saloum, Seex, Sine-Sine. 1,051,200 speakers in Senegal and Gambia. In Senegal: 1,026,000 speakers. West central Senegal and the Sine and Saloum River valleys. Dialects are Segum, Fadyut-Palmerin, Sine, Dyegueme (Gyegem), Niominka. Niominka and Serere-Sine are inherently intelligible to each other's speakers. National language. In Gambia: Northwestern Gambia. Dialects are Segum, Fadyut-Palmerin, Sine, Dyegueme (Gyegem).

Sherbro: also called Southern Bullom, Shiba, Amampa, Mampa, Mampwa. 135,000 speakers in Sierra Leone. Southern Province adjoining the Western area; York district on western peninsula, Ribbi Shenge, Dima, Sicie, Timdel, Benducha, Nongoba. Dialects are Shenge Sherbro, Sitia Sherbro, Ndema Sherbro, Peninsula Sherbro. Not intelligible with Krim or Bullom So. 83% to 89% lexical similarity among dialects; 66% to 69% with Bullom So, 44% to 45% with Krim. Shenge Sherbro is the prestige dialect.

Themne: also called Temne, Timne, Timene, Timmannee, Temen. 1,200,000 speakers in Sierra Leone. Northern Province, west of Sewa River to Little Scarcie. Dialects are Banta, Konike, Yoni, Bombali, Western Temne (Pil), Sanda, Ribia, Kholifa, Koya, Masingbi, Malal. The people claim to understand all dialects. 25% use Krio, 5% use English as second language. A number of monolinguals. Used as a second language in parts of neighboring tribes. The primary language of central Sierra Leone. Trade language.

Wamey: also called Wamay, Wamei, Konyagi, Coniagui, Conhague, Koniagui. 20,120 speakers in Senegal and Guinea. In Senegal: 14,850 speakers in the southeast. Migration

from Guinea no longer taking place. In Guinea: 5,270 speakers in Koundara region and around Youkounkoun, extending to the Senegal border.

Wolof: also called Ouolof, Yallof, Walaf, Volof, Waro-Waro. 3,215,000 speakers in Senegal, Mali, Mauritania, Gambia, Guinea, Guinea-Bissau, and France. In Senegal: 3,170,200 speakers. Western and central, left bank of Senegal River to Cape Vert. May also be in Mali. Dialects are Baol, Cayor, Dyolof (Djolof, Jolof), Lebou (Lebu), Jander. Different from Gambian Wolof. Bilingualism in French, Arabic. The main African language of Senegal. Predominantly urban. National language. In Mauritania: Dialects are Baol, Cayor, Dyolof (Djolof, Jolof), Lebou, Ndyanger. Different from Wolof of Gambia. Language of wider communication. In Mali: Bamako. In Gambia: South bank of Gambia River.

Wolof, Gambian: 146,650 speakers in Gambia. Western division, southern and central banks of the Gambia River. Wolof on the northern bank speak Wolof of Senegal. Wolof of Senegal is not intelligible with that of Gambia.   B. GRIMES

ATTITUDES TO LANGUAGE. *See* Language Attitudes.

AUGMENTATIVES. *See* Diminutives.

AUSTIN, JOHN LANGSHAW (1911–1960). British philosopher, important in linguistics as the originator, in the 1950s, of the distinction between constative and performative utterances, and the definition of *felicity* as 'the requirement that the latter must meet'.

[*See also* Pragmatics and Contextual Semantics, *articles on* Implicature, Presupposition, *and* Speech Acts.]

ANNA MORPURGO DAVIES

AUSTRALIAN LANGUAGES. About 250 languages were spoken in Australia at the time of the European invasion in 1788. More than half of them are no longer spoken or remembered, and of the remainder no more than 20 are still being learned by children. There is good documentation for about half of the languages. (Of the 50 or so high-quality grammars available, the following can be particularly recommended: Dench 1995, Dixon 1972, Evans 1995, Merlan 1994, Nordlinger 1998, Rumsey 1982, and the grammars in Dixon and Blake 1979/2000.) For about 25 languages, there are only short word

lists, and for a further hundred, only partial grammars are available. For the languages on which data are scarce it is hard to make any judgment concerning their possible genetic relationships and typological profiles.

People first came to Australia (which was then joined to New Guinea and Tasmania) about fifty thousand years ago. They would soon have expanded to populate the whole continent, with tribes and languages splitting. At the end of the initial period of expansion, a family tree would have appropriately modeled the relationship between the languages, but then, for some tens of millennia, an equilibrium situation (Dixon 1997) prevailed across Australia, which became one large linguistic area.

About 40 low-level genetic subgroups can be recognized, most consisting of just two or three languages (see Table 1). These are the result of localized language splits in quite recent times and are likely to be due to such factors as population expansion into previously dry areas after water resources improved there.

A classification of Australian languages on lexicostatistic criteria (including "Pama-Nyungan" as one genetic family) appears in O'Grady, Voegelin, and Voegelin 1966. The sources used and lexical scores obtained were not made available, however, and this classification—although much quoted—has only occasional and accidental validity. All similarities between languages were looked on as indicators of genetic connection, but in fact most of them are due to the pervasive diffusion of phonological and grammatical features that characterizes the Australian linguistic area.

Dixon 2002 has, for ease of reference, divided the languages into 50 groups. Some of the groups are tentatively identified as low-level genetic subgroups; others are small linguistic areas within the large linguistic area that encompasses the whole of Australia; and the remainder consist of languages simply grouped together on a geographic basis.

This entry summarizes some of the typological parameters that characterize Australian languages, and in terms of which the languages vary. Almost all features are distributed on an areal basis, but independently of each other; that is, there is no bunching of isoglosses. (Dixon 2002 includes maps illustrating the areal distribution of more than 20 features.)

1. Phonology There are between four and six stops, with a nasal corresponding to each. All languages have a bilabial and a dorso-velar series. Some languages have

TABLE 1. *List of Australian Languages (Including Likely Low-Level Genetic Subgroups).* This provisional list contains the names of all of the known indigenous languages of Australia (excluding Tasmania); it is likely that there were further languages, which have been lost without trace. Only a few of the many alternative language and dialect names are included here.

An asterisk after a letter indicates that all the languages in this group probably make up a low-level genetic subgroup; e.g., B* shows that B is probably a subgroup, and Ba* that Ba is probably a subgroup within B. If two languages within a group are probably genetically related, an asterisk appears after each of their numbers, e.g. 1* and 2* within De (there is insufficient information on De3 to decide whether this belongs in the subgroup with De1 and De2).

A—1, West Torres (Papuan, with Australian substratum), 2, East Torres (Papuan)

B*—**Ba***: 1, Gudang; 2, Uradhi; 3, Wuthati; 4, Luthigh/Mpalitjanh; 5, Yinwum; 6, Anguthimri/Mpakwithi/Awngthim/Ntra'angith/Alngith/Linngithigh; 7, Ngkoth; 8, Aritinngithigh; 9, Mbiywom; 10, Andyingit

   Bb: Umpila/Kuuku-Ya'u/Kaantju

   Bc*: 1, Wik-Ngathrr; 2, Wik Me'nh/Wik Ep; 3, Wik-Mungknh (Wik-Munkan); 4, Kugu-Muminh (or Wik Muminh or Kugu/Wik Nganhcara); 5, Bakanha; 6, Ayabadhu

C—Umbindhamu

D—**Da***: 1, Morroba-Lama (or Umbuygamu); 2, Lama-Lama (or Mba Rumbathama)

   Db: 1, Rimang-Gudinhma; 2, Kuku-Wara

   Dc: 1, Flinders Island language (or Yalgawarra); 2, Marrett River language (or Tartalli)

   Dd: 1, Guugu Yimidhirr; 2, Barrow Point language

   De: 1*, Kuku-Thaypan; 2*, Kuku-Mini/Ikarranggal/Aghu Tharrnggala; 3, Takalak

   Df: Walangama

   Dg: Mbara

E—**Ea**: 1, Kuuk Thayorre; 2, Oykangand/Olgolo; 3, Ogh-Undjan

   Eb: 1, Yirr Yoront/Yir Thangedl; 2*, Koko Bera (or Kok Kaber); 3*, Kok Thawa

   Ec: Kok Narr (or Kok Nhang or Kundara)

   Ec*: 1, Kurtjar (or Gunggara); 2, Kuthant

   Ee: Kukatj (or Galibamu)

F—Kuku-Yalanji/Kuku-Njungkul/Wakura/Wakaman/Jangun/Muluridji

G*—1, Djabugay; 2, Yidinj/Gunggay/Wanjurru

H—1, Dyirbal/Girramay/Djiru/Gulngay/Mamu/Ngadjan; 2, Warrgamay/Biyay; 3, Nyawaygi; 4, Manbara/Wulgurukaba/Nhawalgaba

I—1, Cunningham; 2, Gorton; 3, O'Connor (all only from "Lower Burdekin" and "Mouths of Burdekin" vocabularies in Curr)

TABLE 1. *(continued)*

J—Ja*: 1, Bidjara/Marrganj/Gayiri/Dharawala/
Mandandanjdji/Guwamu/Gunggari/Nguri; 2, Biri/
Gangulu/Wirri/Yilba/Baradha/Yambina/Yetimarala/
Garingbal/Yangga; 3, Warungu/Gugu-Badhun/
Gudjala; 4, Ngaygungu; 5, Yirandhali

Jb: 1, Mbabaram; 2, Agwamin (or Wamin)

Jc: 1, Ngaro; 2, Giya

Jd: 1, Guwa; 2, Yanda

Je: 1, Kuungari; 2, Pirriya (or Bidia)

K*—1, Ngawun/Wunamara/Mayi-Thakurti/Mayi-Yapi/Mayi-
Kulan; 2, Mayi-Kutuna

L—1, Darambal; 2, Bayali

M—Ma: 1, Dappil; 2, Gureng-Gureng; 3, Gabi-Gabi/Badjala;
4, Waga-Waga/Duungidjawu

Mb: Yagara

Mc: Guwar

Md: Bigambal

Me: Yugambal/Ngarrabul (Ngarrbal)

Mf: Bandjalang/Yugumbir/Minjangbal/Gidabal/Wudjabal

Mg*: 1, Gumbaynggirr/Baanbay/Gambalamam; 2,
Yaygirr

N—Na*: 1, Awabagal/Cameeragal/Wonarua; 2, Gadjang/
Warimi/Birbay

Nb*: 1, Djan-gadi; 2, Nganjaywana (Aniwan)

Nc*: 1, Gamilaraay (Kamilaroi)/Yuwaalaraay/
Yuwaaliyaay (Euahlayi); 2, Wiradhurri; 3,
Ngiyambaa/Wangaaybuwan/Wayilwan

Nd: Muruwarri

Ne: Barranbinja

O*—1, Dharuk/Gamaraygal; 2, Darkinjung

P—Pa: 1, Gundungurra/Ngunawal; 2, Ngarigo

Pb: 1, Dharawal; 2, Dhurga/Tharumba; 3, Djirringanj; 4,
Thawa

Q—Muk-thang (Gaanay, Kurnai, Kunnai)/Bidhawal

R—1, Pallanmganmiddang; 2, Dhudhuroa/Yaithmathang

S—1, Yota-Yota (Bangerang); 2, Yabala-Yabala

T—Ta*: 1, Wemba-Wemba/Baraba-Baraba/Madhi-Madhi/
Ladji-Ladji/Wergaya/Djadjala/Jab-wurrong/Pirt-
Koopen-Noot/Jaja-wurrong; 2; Wadha-wurrung; 3,
Wuy-wurrung/Bun-wurrong/Dhagung-wurrong

Tb*: 1, Bungandik (or Bundanditj); 2, Kuurn-Kopan-Noot/
Peek-Whurrong/Dhautgart/Tjarcote (misnamed
Gournditch-Mara)

Tc: Kolakngat (or Kolijon)

U—1, Yaralde (or Ngarrindjeri or Narrinyeri); 2, Ngayawung;
3, Yuyu (or Ngarrket); 4, Keramin; 5, Yitha-Yitha/Dardi-
Dardi

V—Baagandji/Gurnu/Baarrundji/Barrindji/Marrawarra
(Maruara)

W—1, Kalkatungu; 2, Yalarnnga

X*—1, Waanji; 2, Garrwa (Garawa)

Y*—Ya*: 1, Dhuwal/Dhuwala (including Gupapuyngu,
Gumatj, Djambarrpuyngu); 2, Dhay'yi; 3,
Ritharngu (or Dhiyakuy)

Yb*: 1, Nhangu; 2, Dhangu; 3, Djangu

Yc*: 1, Djinang; 2, Djinba

TABLE 1. *(continued)*

WA—WAa: 1*, Pitta-Pitta (Pitha-Pitha); 2*, Wangka-Yutjuru;
3, Arabana-Wangkangurru

WAb: 1, Yandruwanhdha/Yawarawarga; 2*, Diyari/
Dhirari/Biladaba; 3*, Ngamini/Yarluyandi/
Karangura; 4, Midhaga/Karuwarli/Marulta

WAc: 1, Wangkumara/Punthamara; 2, Galali; 3, Badjiri

WAd: Maljangapa/Yardliyawara/Wardikali

WB—WBa: Kadli (Kaurna, Nantuwara, Ngadjuri, Narangka,
Nukunu)

WBb*: 1, Parnkala; 2, Adjnjamathanha/Guyani/Wailpi

WC—Wirangu/Nhawu

WD—The Western Desert language (dialects: Warnman,
Yulparitja, Manjtjiltjara, Kartutjarra, Kukatja, Pintupi,
Luritja, Ngaatjatjarra, Ngaanjatjarra, Wangkatha,
Wangatja, Ngaliya, Pitjantjatjarra, Yankunjtjatjarra,
Kukarta)

WE—1, Mirning; 2, Kalaaku (Ngadjunmaya); 3, Karlamay

WF—Nyungar (including Pipalman, Pindjarup, Whadjuk)

WG—WGa*: 1, Watjarri; 2, Parti-maya; 3, Cheangwa
language; 4, Nana-karti; 5, Natingero; 6,
Witjaari

WGb: Nhanta/Watchandi/Amangu

WGc: Malkana

WGd: Yingkarta

WH—WHa: Tharrkari/Warriyangka/Tjiwarli/Thiin

WHb: 1, Payungu/Purduna; 2, Thalantji/Pinikura

WHc: 1, Nhuwala; 2, Martuthunira; 3, Panjtjima; 4,
Yinjtjipartnti/Kurama; 5, Ngarluma; 6, Kariyara
(Kariera); 7, Tjururu; 8, Palyku/Nyiyapali; 9,
Nyamal; 10, Ngarla

WI—WIa*: 1, Njangumarta; 2, Karatjarri

WIb: Mangala

WJ*—WJa*: 1, Walmatjari/Tjuwalinj/Pililuna; 2, Djaru/
Wawari/Njininj; 3, Gurindji/Wanjdjirra/Malngin/
Wurlayi/Ngarinman/Pilinara; 4, Mudbura/
Karranga/Pinkangarna

WJb*: 1, Warlpiri/Ngaliya/Walmala/Ngardilpa; 2,
Ngardi; 3, Warlmanpa

WK—Warumungu

WL—1, Arrernte (Aranda) (including: Anmatjirra, Aljawarra,
Ayerrerenge, Antekerrepenhe, Ikngerripenhe, Pertami,
Alenjerntarrpe); 2, Kaytetj

WM*—WMa: Yanyuwa (or Yanyula)

WMb*: 1, Wagaya; 2, Bularnu/Dhidhanu/Injdjiladji;
3, Warluwara/Kapula/Parnkarra

NA*—NAa: Lardil

NAb*: 1, Kayardild/Yangkaal; 2, Yukulta (Kangkalita)/
Nguburindi

NAc: Minkin

NB—NBa, Mangarrayi (Ngarrabadji)

NBb*: 1, Marra; 2, Warndarrang (Wuyarrawala)

NBc*: 1, Rembarrnga/Kaltuy': 2, Ngalakan

NBd: 1, Ngandi; 2, Nunggubuyu (Wubuy, Yingkwira);
3, Aninhdhilyagwa

NBe: Dalabon (Dangbon)/Buwun/Ngalkbun (Ngalabun)

TABLE 1. *(continued)*

> **NBf*:** 1, Burarra/Gidjingaliya/Anbarra/Gun-nartpa; 2,
>   Gurrgoni; 3, Nakkara; 4, Ndjebbana (Kunibidji/
>   Gunavidji)
> **NBg:** 1, Gunwinjgu (Mayali, Bininj-gun-wok, Neinggu);
>   2, Gunbarlang
> **NBh:** 1, Jawoyn; 2, Warray
> **NBi:** Gungarakanj
> **NBj:** Uwinjmil (Awunjmil, Winjmil)
> **NBk:** Gaagudju
> **NBl*:** 1, Wagiman; 2, Wardaman/Dagoman/Yangman
> **NBm:** Alawa
> **NC*—NCa*:** 1, Djamindjung/Ngaliwuru; 2, Nungali
>   **NCb*:** 1, Djingulu (Djingili); 2, Ngarnga (Ngarndji);
>   3, Wambaya/Gudandji/Binbinka
> **ND*—**1, Kitja (Lunga); 2, Miriwung/Gajirrawung
> **NE*—**1, Njigina/Warrwa/Yawuru/Jukun; 2, Baardi/Jawi/Njul-
>   Njul/Jabirr-Jabirr/Ngumbarl/Nimanburru
> **NF*—**1, Bunuba; 2, Guniyandi
> **NG—**1, Worrorra/Unggumi; 2, Ungarrinyin; 3, Wunambal/
>   Gamberre/Kwini (Gunin)
> **NH—NHa:** Patjtjamalh/Kandjerramal (Pungu-Pungu)
>   **NHb*:** 1, Emmi/Merranunggu(Warrgat); 2, Marrithiyel/
>   Marri-Ammu/Marritjevin/Marridan/
>   Marramanindjdji; 3, Maringarr/Magati-ge
>   **NHc:** Malak-Malak
>   **NHd:** 1, Murrinh-patha; 2, Ngan.gi-tjemerri (Ngan.gi-
>   kurunggurr, Ngan.gi-wumeri)
>   **NHe*:** 1, Matngele; 2, Kamu
> **NI—NIa:** Umbugarla/Bugurndidja/Ngumbur
>   **NIb:** 1, Limilngan; 2, Wulna
>   **NIc:** Larrakiya (Gulumirrgin)
> **NJ—**Giimbiyu (including: Urningank, Mengerrdji, Erre)
> **NK*—NKa*:** 1, Mawung (Maung, Gun-marung)/Mananggari;
>   2, Iwaydja/Ilgar/Garik
>   **NKb:** Amurdag (Wardadjbak, A'mooridiyu)/Urrirk/
>   Didjurra
>   **NKc:** Marrgu (Terrutong, Yaako, Raffles Bay language,
>   Croker Island language)
>   **NKd:** Popham Bay language (Iyi, Limpapiu)
> **NL—**Tiwi

a single apical series (articulated with the tip of the tongue); languages in a large continuous area have a contrast between apico-alveolar and apico-post-alveolar (retroflex) stops and nasals. Some languages have a single laminal series (articulated with the blade of the tongue), but languages in two large and two small geographic regions show a contrast between lamino-dental and lamino-palatal stops and nasals. Languages in the east have a single lateral, an apico-alveolar, but other languages may have up to four laterals (one in each apical and laminal series). Just three languages have a contrast between lamino-dental and lamino-palatal semivowels;

other languages have a single laminal semivowel, *y*. All languages have a dorsal-labial semivowel, *w*. Stress is predictable and, in most languages, falls on the first syllable of a word.

Most languages have a single series to stops, and no fricatives. However, in about 60 languages, scattered across the continent, there is either a contrast between two stop series, or a contrast between stops and fricatives, or both. The stop contrast is basically fortis/lenis, realized as long/short in some languages and as voiceless/voiced in others (and by a combination of these features in a further group). About ten scattered languages have segmental glottal stop phoneme (resulting from recent sound changes), and a block of about seventeen languages have glottalization as an element of syllable prosody.

Most languages have two rhotic (grooved tongue) phonemes, one articulated further forward, with the tongue tip against the alveolar ridge (this is generally a trill, but can be a flap), and one articulated further back, with the tongue tip turned back to touch the base of the alveolar ridge or the hard palate (this is generally a continuant, sometimes a trill or flap). There are nine examples of systems with a single rhotic (mostly, just in one dialect of a language, where other dialects maintain two rhotics); and about 20 languages have three rhotics, the additional one being a voiceless apico-alveolar trill, an apico-alveolar flap, or an apico-post-alveolar flap.

There are two especially significant phonetic characteristics of Australian languages. One is the fact that, in a stressed syllable, the stress peak tends to occur relatively late in the syllable. This is responsible for initial consonants having been dropped from languages in separate regions. It can weaken the initial syllable so that stress shifts to the second syllable, and the vowel of the first syllable may then become lost, e.g. *bámba* > *ámba* > *ambá* > *mbá* in Mbabaram. What were phonologically conditioned allophones of a consonant or vowel in the second syllable of a word may now become contrastive phonemes owing to loss of the conditioning environment. This explains some developments of a stop contrast, of fricative phonemes, and of additional vowel contrasts.

The other significant characteristic is the fact that the lowering of the velum for nasal consonants tends to be delayed as long as possible. As a result, there is little phonetic nasalization of a vowel preceding a nasal consonant. In some languages, the lowering of the velum is delayed past the commencement of the consonant articulation, resulting in a prestopped nasal.

MAP 1. *Distribution of Some Languages of Australia*

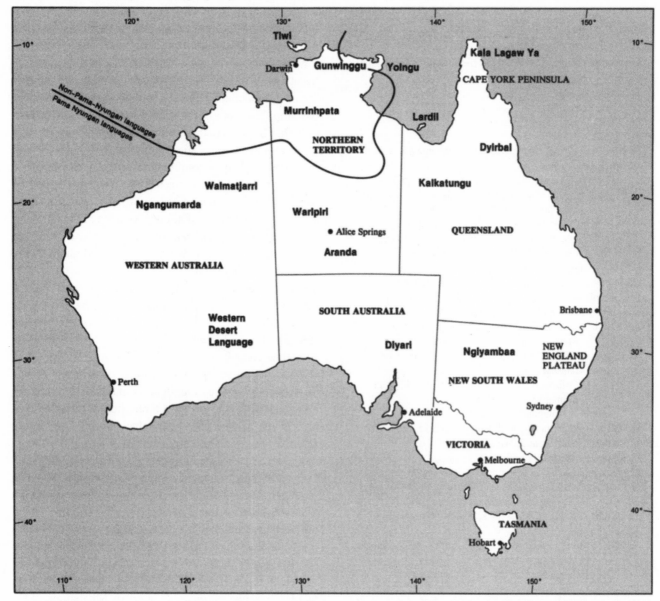

About two-thirds of the languages have a system of just three vowels: low *a*, high front unrounded *i*, and high back (sometimes rounded, some unrounded) *u*. A two-vowel system (*a* and *ə*) has been posited for three languages, and around 50 languages have larger systems with between four and eight vowels. It is likely that there was originally a length distinction in the initial, stressed syllable, but this is retained in only a few languages around the fringe of the continent. A number of languages have recently developed a length contrast, by a variety of means.

Most languages have words beginning with a single consonant and ending with a vowel or a single consonant.

However, owing to phonological changes, some languages have all words ending in a consonant, while others have all words ending in a vowel; a number have some words beginning with a vowel. In a few cases, what was a medial consonant cluster is now exposed into initial or final position.

2. Grammatical profile. It is likely that, at an earlier stage, Australian languages were mildly synthetic and fully agglutinative. There might have been no more than three or four suffixes added to nominals (marking function in a clause, and function in a noun phrase), and just a handful of verbal suffixes (marking tense, aspect, modality, imperative mood, or some combination of these). The languages have moved at varying rates toward a more synthetic profile. More nominal and verbal suffixes have evolved, in most cases separately in individual languages, as apparent from the difference in forms.

Australian languages typically have layered marking for syntactic function. For example, a possessor within a core noun phrase can take genitive marking (for its function in the phrase), followed by a marker of the function of the phrase in the clause (ergative, dative, etc.). In a few languages, a core noun phrase may take one suffix for its function in a subordinate clause, and one for the function of the subordinate clause in a main clause (Dench and Evans 1988). One pervasive feature of the Australian linguistic area is an "aversive" case function, marking a predicate argument whose referent has undesirable potential (for example, 'don't sit close to the fire *for fear of flying sparks*').

It is useful to distinguish intransitive subject (S) from transitive subject (A) and transitive object (O). Nouns and adjectives generally have absolutive (for S and O) and ergative (for A) inflections, while pronouns have nominative (S and A) and accusative (O) forms.

There is a strong tendency across the continent for free pronouns to give rise to bound pronominal enclitics, which may develop further into verbal suffixes. In one area in the central north there has been a radical change of profile with the development of prefixes to verbs. Each language in this area has pronominal prefixes (always for A and S functions, sometimes also for O), and some languages also have prefixes that mark direction, negation, and number.

Many languages have generic nouns, or nominal classifiers. These have been grammaticalized to become affixes marking noun classes, in two languages outside the prefixing area and in about 40 of the languages that have prefixes on verbs. Every language with prefixes to nominals also has prefixes to verbs, but not vice versa, suggesting that prefixes developed first on verbs and then spread—in just some languages—to nouns. Those languages where bound pronominal prefixes to the verb include information about noun class (in addition to person and number) have generally lost case marking on noun phrases and are now exclusively head-marking.

There are various types of system for 1st and 2nd person pronouns (3rd person is sometimes included in the same paradigm): (i) singular, dual and plural; (ii) the same, but with an inclusive/exclusive distinction for 1st dual and plural; and (iii) a set of minimal terms consisting of 1st singular, 2nd singular, and 'you and me', with further terms showing the addition of one participant or more than one participant to the minimal terms (called "unit augmented" and "augmented" respectively). Languages have changed between types, largely through reanalyzing the role of the 'you and me' form within the system.

Some languages have several hundred inflecting monomorphemic verbs, with just a dozen of them entering into compound constructions with members of a set of non-inflecting "coverbs"; for example, in Wardaman, coverb *ŋabŋab* 'unsteady' plus inflecting verb *-bu-* 'hit' gives compound verb *ŋabŋab -bu-* 'shoot at and miss'. In one set of languages, there are only a dozen or so inflecting verbs, each of which occurs in compounds with a fair number of coverbs. In other languages, coverb and inflecting verb have become fused into a single lexeme. (For details see Dixon 2002, chap. 6.)

3. Syntax. Because syntactic function is marked by case inflection and/or by cross-referencing elements in the verb, word order can be quite free. Most Australian languages have the underlying orders AOV for a transitive clause and SV for an intransitive clause, and noun followed by adjective within a noun phrase.

Many Australian languages, especially those outside the prefixing area, have syntactic devices to indicate coreferentiality of arguments within complex sentence constructions. A number of languages in a continuous region in the center and west show *switch-reference* marking: the verb of a subordinate clause bears one inflection if it has the same subject as the main clause, but a different inflection if their subjects differ (see Austin 1981).

A number of languages require that an argument be common to main and subordinate clauses in a complex sentence; in some, the shared argument must be in S or O function in each clause (an "S/O pivot"), and in others the shared argument must be in S or A function (an "S/A pivot"). All languages with an S/O pivot have an *antipassive* derivation by which an underlying argument in A function is placed in surface S function, to "feed" the pivot. Only some of the languages with an S/A pivot have a *passive* derivation to feed this pivot. (Useful surveys of the grammatical properties of Australian languages include Blake 1977, 1987, and Dixon 2002.)

4. Special styles. Perhaps every Australian language has a special speech style that must be used in the presence of a taboo relative (typically, son-in-law/mother-in-law). Sometimes the avoidance style involves only a few score special lexical forms, but one group of eastern tribes has a complete second vocabulary, with no lexical form common to avoidance and everyday styles (there is, in fact, a many-to-one correspondence between everyday and avoidance lexemes) (Dixon 1982:63–139; Alpher 1993).

Some tribes have "secret languages" confined to initiated males. Initiands of the Lardil tribe (NAa on the map) learn Damin, which has a quite different phonology from their everyday speech style; it involves nasalized clicks, an ingressive lateral fricative, and glottalized ejective stops.

Every Australian community has (or had) song styles, each with its own typical subject matter, accompaniment style, dance routine, and social role. These styles often use archaic words and slightly unusual grammatical conventions. The only full linguistic and musical study of a set of song styles is Dixon and Koch 1996.

5. Tasmanian. At the end of the 19th century, Tasmanians were believed to be non-Australian in physical type, culture, and language. Anthropologists have now reassessed the physical and cultural evidence; it is generally believed that the Tasmanians were a group of Australian Aborigines, isolated when their island was cut off by rising sea level about ten thousand years ago. Pitifully little information was gathered on Tasmanian languages before they ceased to be spoken more than a hundred years ago; there were probably eight to twelve distinct languages. Information on Tasmanian phonology suggests that the languages were typologically similar to those of Australia. No information on grammar is available. Only a few dubious cognates can be recognized between Tasmania and the mainland languages. For a full assessment see Crowley and Dixon 1981.

[*See also* Arandic Languages; Bunaban Languages; Burarran; Daly Languages; Djamindjungan Languages; Endangered Languages; Gunwingguan Languages; Karnic Languages; Laragiya; Maric Languages; Nyulnyulan Languages; Pama-Nyungan Languages; Southwest Pama-Nyungan Languages; West Barkly Languages; *and* Wororan Languages]

BIBLIOGRAPHY

Alpher, Barry. Out-of-the-ordinary ways of using a language. In *Language and culture in Aboriginal Australia*, edited by Michael Walsh and Colin Yallop, pp. 97–106. Canberra: Aboriginal Studies Press.

Austin, Peter. 1981. Switch-reference in Australia. *Language* 57.309–334.

Blake, Barry J. 1977. *Case marking in Australian languages.* Canberra: Australian Institute of Aboriginal Studies.

Blake, Barry, J. 1987. *Australian Aboriginal grammar.* London: Croom Helm.

Crowley, Terry, and R. M. W. Dixon. 1981. Tasmanian. In Dixon and Blake 1981, 394–421.

Dench, Alan Charles. 1995. *Martuthunira: A language of the Pilbara region of Western Australial.* Canberra: Pacific Linguistics.

Dench, Alan Charles, and Nicholas Evans. 1988. Multiple case marking in Australian languages. *Australian Journal of Linguistics* 8.1–47.

Dixon, R. M. W. 1972. *The Dyirbal language of North Queensland.* Cambridge: Cambridge University Press.

Dixon, R. M. W. 1982. *Where have all the adjectives gone? And other essays in semantics and syntax.* Berlin: Mouton.

Dixon, R. M. W. 1997. *The rise and fall of languages.* Cambridge: Cambridge University Press.

Dixon, R. M. W. 2002. *Australian languages: Their nature and development.* Cambridge: Cambridge University Press.

Dixon, R. M. W., and Barry J. Blake, eds. 1979–2000. *Handbook of Australian languages.* Vol. 1 (1979), vol. 2 (1981), vol. 3 (1983), Canberra: Australian National University Press and Amsterdam: Benjamins; vol. 4 (1991), vol. 5 (2000), Melbourne: Oxford University Press.

Dixon, R. M. W., and Grace Koch. 1996. *Dyirbal song poetry: The oral literature of an Australian rainforest people.* St. Lucia: University of Queensland Press.

Evans, Nicholas D. 1995. *A grammar of Kayardild, with historical-comparative notes on Tangkic.* Berlin: Mouton de Gruyter.

Merlan, Francesca. 1994. *A grammar of Wardaman, a language of the Northern Territory of Australia.* Berlin: Mouton de Gruyter.

Nordlinger, Rachel. 1988. *A grammar of Wambaya.* Canberra: Pacific Linguistics.

O'Grady, Geoffrey N., C. F. Voegelin, and F. M. Voegelin. 1996. *Languages of the world: Indo-Pacific Fascicle 6*, in Anthropological Linguistics,vol. 8, no. 2.

Rumsey, Alan. 1982. *An intra-sentence grammar of Ungarrinjin, north-western Australia.* Canberra: Pacific Linguistics.

R. M. W. DIXON

LANGUAGE LIST

[*For information on individual languages, see the following articles dealing with members of the proposed Australian language family:* Bunaban Languages, Burarran, Daly Languages, Djamindjungan Languages, Garawa, Giimbiyu, Gunwingguan Languages, Laragiya, Limilngan-Wulna, Nyulnyulan Languages, Pama-Nyungan Languages, Tiwi, Umbugarla-Ngumbur, West Barkly Languages, Wororan Languages, Yiwaidjan.]

B. GRIMES

AUSTRO-ASIATIC LANGUAGES.

A[ustro-]A[siatic] is probably the most "archaic" family in Southeast Asia and East India, in the sense that nearly all its languages are surrounded by more recent arrivals of the Austronesian, Tai-Kadai, Sino-Tibetan, and Indo-European families or are retreating under the advance of these languages. For useful literature, see Zide 1966 and Jenner et al. 1976; see also Map 1.

1. Subclassification. The primary split of AA is between the M[on-]K[hmer] and Munda families; the former are far more differentiated.

MK comprises well over one hundred languages. The mid-level subclassification of the family into some twelve branches is clear; however, there are uncertainties in the assignment of several of these branches to certain higher level divisions.

The Northern division of MK contains three branches: Khmuic, Palaungic, and Khasian. The Khmuic branch, found mostly in northern Laos and northern Thailand, includes the Khmu language with its many dialects, the Mal-Phrai languages, and Mlabri, spoken by hunter/gatherers nicknamed "Spirits of the yellow leaves."

The Palaungic branch is a very large subfamily, formerly called Palaung-Wa; it extends over northern Thailand and Laos, eastern Burma, and southwestern Yunnan. The Eastern sub-branch of Palaungic contains several Palaung languages, the Riang dialects, and Danau. The Western sub-branch contains three language groups: Waic, Angkuic, and Lametic. The most differentiated of these is the Waic group, which includes Bulang, the many Lawa dialects, and the Wa languages, totaling over half a million speakers. The Angkuic group includes several very small and nearly unknown languages: Angku, U, Hu, Mok, Man Met, and Kiorr.

The Khasian branch is found in northeastern India in the state of Meghalaya, where Khasi is the official language. Several so-called Khasi dialects, such as Synteng, Lyng-ngam, and Amwi (also called War), are clearly distinct but related languages.

To this North MK division may be added the very small Mang language located on the border of Vietnam and China.

The Eastern division of MK contains at least three branches: Khmeric, Bahnaric, and Katuic. The Khmeric branch contains a single language, Khmer, the national language of Cambodia, with Pre-Angkorian inscriptions beginning in the 6th century CE, and distinct dialects spoken in parts of Thailand and Vietnam.

The Bahnaric branch comprises about thirty-five languages located in central and southern Vietnam, southern Laos, and eastern Cambodia; it is divided into four parts. The South Bahnaric sub-branch constitutes a closely knit group of four languages—Srê, Mnong, Stieng, and Chrau, each with numerous dialects. Central Bahnaric includes Bahnar itself and several nearly unknown languages, such as Lamam and Tampuan. West Bahnaric is the least known sub-branch, including Brao, Nya-heuny, Oy, and at least six other languages of southern Laos. The North Bahnaric branch is better known and includes Monom, Kayong, Takua, Rengao, Sedang, Hrê, Jeh, Halang, and Cua. In the ethnographic literature, these are the "Montagnards" of the Vietnamese Highlands.

The languages of the Katuic branch are found in central Vietnam, central Laos, northeastern Thailand, and northern Cambodia. The West Katuic sub-branch includes Kuy, Bru, and Sô; the East Katuic sub-branch includes Katu, Pacoh, Ngeq, and the little-known Katang, Ta-oih, Yir, Klor, and Ong.

To this East MK division might be added the languages of the Pearic branch, spoken by very small groups in western Cambodia: the Samrê, Pear, Sa-och, and Chong. These languages have been heavily influenced by Khmer.

The Viet-Muong (Vietic) branch seems to form a division by itself, though there are signs that would favor including it in the East MK division. Besides Vietnamese, it comprises the Muong languages of northern Vietnam, plus two more distant subbranches—the Cuôi languages (Uy-Lô, Hung, Pọong, Không Khêng), and the Chứt languages (Arem, Sách, Mày, Rục). To these can be added Thavứng, Pakatan, Phon Soung, and a few others spoken across the border in northern Laos. In the past, the Vietnamese language has often been classified with Chinese, or even with the Tai languages; but more recent studies show that the Muong, Cuôi, and Chứt languages, obviously related to Vietnamese but much less Sinicized, offer decisive arguments for including Vietnamese in MK, or at least in AA.

The Palyu language, called Lai in Chinese, was recently discovered on the border of Guang Xi and Gui Zhou provinces; it may be a distant offshoot of the Viet-Muong branch—or, more probably, an isolate within Mon-Khmer.

Recent work shows that the Monic branch, contrary to earlier opinion, is rather distant from the languages of the East MK division. It comprises only two languages: Mon of Burma and Thailand (with Old Mon inscriptions beginning in the 6th c. CE), and Nyahkur, spoken in eastern central Thailand (Diffloth 1984).

MAP 1. *Distribution of Austro-Asiatic Languages*

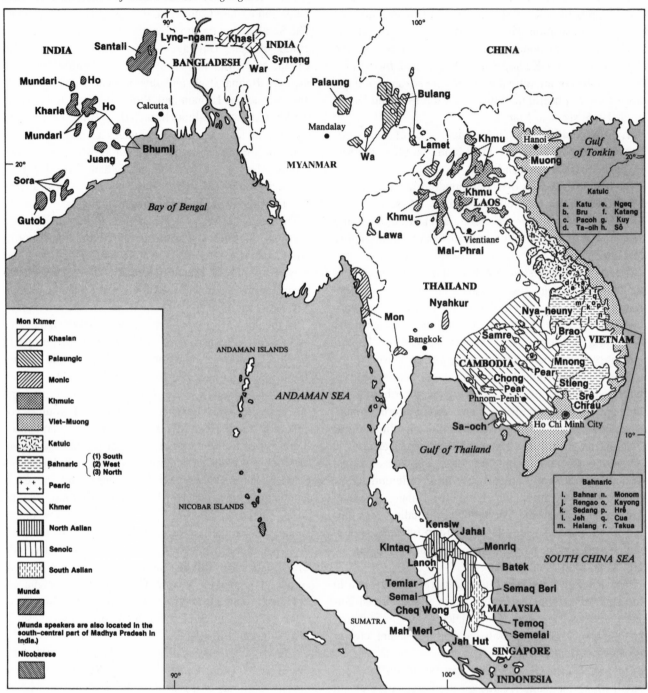

The Aslian branch of interior Malaysia is not a distant offshoot of AA, as previously thought; it clearly fits within MK and may actually form (together with Monic) a southern division of the family. Aslian comprises about sixteen languages: a Senoic sub-branch (Semai, Temiar, Lanoh, Semnam, Sabüm), previously known as Sakai; a North Aslian sub-branch (Kintaq, Kensiu, Menriq, Jehai, Batek, Cheq Wong), previously known as Semang; a

South Aslian sub-branch (Mah Meri, Semelai, Semaq Beri, Temoq); and Jah Hut as a subbranch by itself.

The languages of the Nicobar Islands, of at least four groups (Car, Nancowry, Great Nicobarese, and Chaura-Teressa), have also been considered a distant offshoot of AA. However, recent information suggests that they may form yet another branch of MK.

The Munda family is smaller and is located in eastern

India—primarily in the states of Bengal, Orissa, Bihar, and Andhra Pradesh. It is divided into North and South Munda subfamilies, which are quite different from each other. The North Munda languages are fairly closely related, in two branches: Korku and Kherwarian (which includes Santali, Mundari, and Ho). The South Munda subfamily consists of Kharia-Juang (Central Munda) and Koraput Munda; the latter branches into Gutob-Remo-Geta' and Sora-Juray-Gorum. There are about five million speakers of Munda languages; the great majority are of the North Munda group.

It is difficult to think of more different linguistic types than those represented by Munda and MK; for this reason, some linguists have questioned their genetic relationship. Yet there are several common or reconstructed features which probably go back to Proto-AA.

2. Features shared by the branches. A phonetic feature of nearly all AA languages is non-release of final stops; to be sure, this is the phonetic norm across language families in the Southeast Asian area, but it stands out as a characteristic feature of the Munda languages in the Indian linguistic area.

In phonology, both Munda and MK have complete sets of stops and nasals in root-final position in four places of articulation: velar, palatal, alveolar, and labial. In MK, but not necessarily in Munda, this position coincides with the end of the word. There is a dearth of spirants in the modern languages: typically, only *s* is found in Munda, and *s h* in MK. The canonical root forms of Proto-AA exclude final clusters, but require at least one final consonant. Many modern languages have relaxed this rule by losing final ?, thus allowing final open syllables. There is a great variety and frequency of consonant sequences word-initially. Attempts, notably by Schmidt 1907, to analyze complex initials as necessarily containing affixes, leaving only a single initial consonant per root, are no longer convincing: many of the purported affixes have no clearly recurrent meaning, or any other justification.

Morphologically, the nominalizing -*n*- infix is found in most AA languages, though it is much less common in Munda than in the rest of the family; the same is true of the causative labial prefix. Both these features are also old in Austronesian; this, among other things, led Schmidt to propose an Austric superstock which included AA and Austronesian.

Also common to MK and Munda is the presence of a basic lexical class of "expressives." Adverb-like, but without predicative force, these words are similar in some ways to African ideophones. They rely primarily on iconic means to evoke sensations of all kinds, especially in the domain of visual patterns. Their rich morphology is made of iconic diagrams—e.g. partial reduplications, substitutions, infixed copying and systematic distortions—often akin to deliberate language games.

3. Distinctive Mon-Khmer features. Characteristic of all MK languages, but never of Munda, are the presence of fixed ultimate-syllable stress, and the absence of suffixation. Apparent suffixes—found in Nicobarese, some Aslian languages, and Modern Spoken Mon—seem better described as phrase-final clitics. These two features concur in making the final, "major" syllable the richest and most stable part of the word; this is an areal feature of mainland Southeast Asian languages.

The non-final, "minor" syllables have a poor consonant inventory, as well as a vocalism which is reduced to a single possible vowel—except in Katuic and Aslian, where three or four different vowels are possible in this position. Most languages allow only one minor syllable to precede the major syllable, giving rise to a distinct language type termed "sesquisyllabic"; this is typologically halfway between the monosyllabic languages to the north and west of MK, and the disyllabic or polysyllabic languages to the south and east.

The most notable feature of MK phonology is the large number of possible vowels in major syllables. Systems are known with five degrees of height in the front, central, and back series; and systems with four are common. Diphthongized nuclei, broken vowels, and short vowels add to the inventory, as do nasalization and phonation types. All counted, sixty-eight contrastive vocalic nuclei, probably a world record, have been claimed for one variety of Bru. Vowel systems with twenty or more units are not unusual.

Phonological contrasts in the phonation-types of vowels, termed "voice-register" or simply "register," are also characteristic of MK languages. The most common is a two-way contrast of breathy vs. clear phonation, as in Paraok, Mon, Kuy, Bru, Jeh, Halang, and certain dialects of Western Khmer. However, three-way and even four-way register contrasts, as in Chong, have been recorded. Register can be accompanied by phonetic features of diphthongization, vowel height, and pitch. Some languages, e.g. Nyah Kur, appear to be in a transitional stage from register to tone and display both phenomena. Others, e.g. Vietnamese, are clearly tonal, but have distinct phonations which are redundantly tied to certain tones. However, the MK family has far more register languages than tone languages (the latter include U, Bulang, and Vietnamese).

Historically, the appearance of a breathy vs. clear

contrast in vowels is often the result of a devoicing of initial consonants; but there are other kinds of "registro-genesis." It is even possible that Proto-AA had a creaky vs. clear vowel contrast and was thus already a register language. The evolution of MK registers is intimately tied to the history of the large vowel systems, which remains mostly unknown at present.

In sharp contrast with the situation in Munda, MK morphology practically never indicates syntactic agreement. This morphology is usually derivational and non-productive—with a few exceptions, e.g. in the Aslian branch. Its typical function is to change the grammatical class or subclass of the base to which it is attached, e.g. from noun to verb, from intransitive to transitive and vice-versa, or from mass to count noun. There is a great semantic variety of causative formations and nominalizations.

The most original feature of the MK family is the presence of a great number and variety of infixes. These consist of a nasal, a liquid, or a simple vowel, inserted immediately after the first consonant of the base. It would be tempting to see here the result of an ancient process of metathesis and resyllabification, from original prefixed vocalic segments. However, there are examples of multiple infixations; and at least one non-vocalic infix, -p-, would be difficult to explain in this way. There are also a few languages—e.g. Lamet, Semai, Temiar, and Semelai—where practically any consonant can become an infix through a regular morphological process, which consists in copying the final consonant of the root and inserting it after the word-initial consonant: from a Semai root cəkɔt 'to tie' is derived cətkɔt 'to be tying'. This process is also found in Khmu expressives and may have its origin in deliberate iconic sound-play.

In languages where expressives have been described—e.g. Pacoh, Khmu, Bahnar, and Semai—this word class displays a profusion of morphological patterns, including different kinds of partial or modified reduplication. Numerous substitutions of segments are possible and convey gradations of meaning, especially with the many vowels available in such languages. It then becomes difficult to identify the root morpheme, or to describe these iconic patterns as instances of morphology. A theoretical solution to this problem would require the creation of an aesthetic component of grammar, in which iconic systems could be described.

In syntax, MK languages consistently place the object after the verb, the possessed after the possessor, the attribute after the noun, and deictics at the end of the noun phrase. This group of properties, which was iden-tified by Schmidt 1907, forms a coherent linguistic type found all over Southeast Asia. It is diametrically opposed to that found in the Munda languages, and more generally in the Indian linguistic area.

The place of the subject with respect to the verb is not so neatly patterned. Most languages have the order S[ubject] V[erb] O[bject] when O is expressed, agreeing in this with the pattern of the dominant Tai family. But when there is no O, several languages have the verb in first position. A few languages, e.g. in the Wa group, do this for all sentence types, at least as an option. Some others have "verb-first" as a basic order in certain con-structions, but disguise it by preposing an apparent sub-ject. Thus, in Khmer, what seems to be a SVO sentence— khñom chɨ: kba:l (lit. 'I sick head') 'I have a headache'— is actually an intransitive construction with the verb in first position chɨ: kba:l ('hurt + head'), and khñom 'I' preposed as an apparent subject. A closer translation would thus be 'My head hurts'. Since no neighboring language family provides a model for this pattern, there is a possibility that MK languages were originally "verb-first," at least as an option.

4. Distinctive Munda features include an elaborate system of demonstratives, found in some of the lan-guages, and the complex and productive morphology found in most. Certain functional properties, e.g. elabo-rate deixis, are common to the whole of Munda; but the systems are morphologically quite different from lan-guage to language and are only partly cognate in terms of reconstructible morphemes and constructions.

The most elaborate demonstrative systems are found in Santali (North Munda) and Gta? (South Munda). Number, gender (animate vs. inanimate), direct vs. lateral perception, sensory modality (visual vs. the rest), partic-ularizing, emphasis, and features relating to participants in the deictic scenario can be marked in one or both of these systems. In addition, expressive features (stem vowel lengthening, reduplication, and echoing) are used in forms heavily marked for the features listed above.

The Munda verb, very different in this regard from MK, marks a variety of verbal categories of tense, aspect, and mood. In South Munda, suffixation, infixation, and prefixation are used; in North Munda, suffixation is predominant. One characteristic of the South Munda verb is the presence of two sets of tense suffixes: one for intransitives, and the other for transitives. In Gta?, two "past" morphemes, -ge and -ke, are found; but they can mark any of a half-dozen or more different semantic features.

A negative conjugation can perhaps be reconstructed

for South Munda; it contains a negative element prefixed to the positive verb form. But strangely enough, the negatives are formed not from the corresponding positives, but rather from other tense/mood forms that seem to be selected arbitrarily. Thus, in Gta?, the negative of the past is formed by adding *ar-* to the "customary" positive verb form; the negative imperative is formed from the past, and so on.

[*See also* Aslian Languages; East Mon-Khmer Languages; Khmer; Munda Languages; Nicobarese Languages; North Mon-Khmer Languages; Viet-Muong Languages; *and* Vietnamese.]

BIBLIOGRAPHY

Diffloth, Gérard. 1984. *The Dvaravati Old Mon language and Nyah Kur.* Bangkok: Chulalongkorn University.

Jenner, Philip N., et al., eds. 1976. *Austroasiatic studies.* 2 vols. (*Oceanic Linguistics*, Special publication, 13.) Honolulu: University of Hawaii Press.

Schmidt, Wilhelm. 1907. *Die Mon-Khmer-Völker: Ein Bindeglied zwischen Völkern Zentralasiens und Austronesiens.* Braunschweig: Vieweg. Translated as *Les peuples mon-khmêr: Traît d'union entre les peuples de l'Asie centrale et de l'Austronésie* (Bulletin de l'École Française d'Extrême-Orient, 7–8; Hanoi, 1907).

Zide, Norman H., ed. 1966. *Studies in comparative Austroasiatic linguistics.* (Indo-Iranian monographs, 5.) The Hague: Mouton.

GÉRARD DIFFLOTH AND NORMAN ZIDE

LANGUAGE LIST

[*See the articles on* Mon-Khmer *and* Munda Languages.   B. GRIMES

AUSTRONESIAN LANGUAGES.

The Austronesian (AN) family (Latin *auster* 'south', Greek *nēsos* 'island') consists of several hundred languages spoken mainly on islands extending from Southeast Asia into the central Pacific, with a western outlier in Madagascar. (The term "Malayo-Polynesian" has also been used for this family, but see below for a more restricted usage.) Table 1 and Map 1 show the geographical distribution of AN languages and speakers. (For further geographical detail see Wurm and Hattori 1981–1984; Grimes et al. 1995 give a very detailed listing that arrives at considerably higher language numbers.)

Apart from colonial and trade languages, the Philippines, Madagascar, Micronesia, and Polynesia are entirely Austronesian-speaking. Indonesia-Malaysia and

TABLE 1. *Geographical Distribution of Austronesian Languages*

Area	Number of Languages	Number of Speakers
Taiwan (Formosa)	10	200,000
Philippines	70	40,000,000
Vietnam, Cambodia, China	7	700,000
Madagascar	1	8,000,000
Indonesia, Malaysia, Brunei[1]	300	130,000,000
Melanesia[2]	350	1,200,000
Micronesia[3]	12	200,000
Polynesia[4]	20	700,000
TOTAL	770	181,000,000

[1]Includes small communities in adjoining areas of Thailand and Burma.
[2]Papua New Guinea, Solomon Islands, Vanuatu, New Caledonia, and Fiji.
[3]Belau, Guam, Northern Marianas, Federated States of Micronesia, Marshall Islands, Kiribati, and Naura.
[4]Tuvalu, Tonga, Wallis and Futuna, Samoa, Tokelau, Niue, Hawaii, French Polynesia, Cook Islands, New Zealand, and Easter Island.

Melanesia are predominantly Austronesian, but they include two non-AN areas: the Aslian languages of the Malay peninsula, which belong to the Austro-Asiatic family, and the Papuan languages on the island of New Guinea and various smaller islands east and west of it, which comprise several distinct families. The Austronesian speakers in Vietnam, Cambodia, and China are small minority groups within states whose dominant languages are non-AN; likewise, the Austronesian-speaking aborigines of Taiwan are now vastly outnumbered by the Chinese who have settled the island during the past four centuries.

1. Comparative studies. From at least the early 18th century, various writers recognized that languages of Polynesia, island Southeast Asia, and Madagascar were related to one another, but systematic application of the comparative method to the family as a whole began with Otto Dempwolff, whose major work (1934–1938) remains the foundation of comparative AN linguistics. Among the main contributions to comparative studies of AN since Dempwolff's time have been those of Dyen 1965, Dahl 1976, and Blust 1983–1984. Although lexicostatistical studies have produced some strikingly divergent results (Dyen 1965), classical comparative reasoning has been the basis for most debate over AN subgrouping.

Figure 1 shows a subgrouping originally proposed by Blust and now widely accepted in its general outline (Blust 1999, Ross 1995). On the basis of certain phonemic mergers and changes in the pronouns, all AN languages outside Taiwan comprise a first-order subgroup

MAP 1. *Major Divisions of Austronesian Languages.*

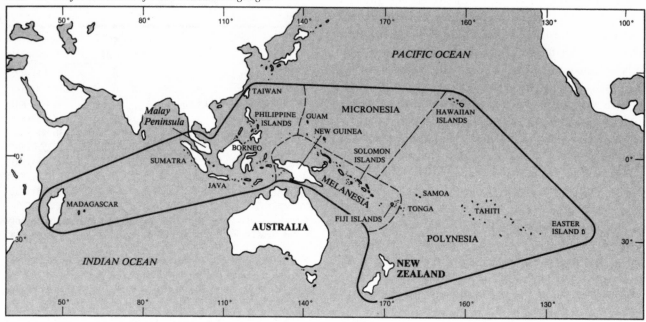

FIGURE 1. *Major Subgroups of Austronesian.* (Based on Blust 1983–1984.)

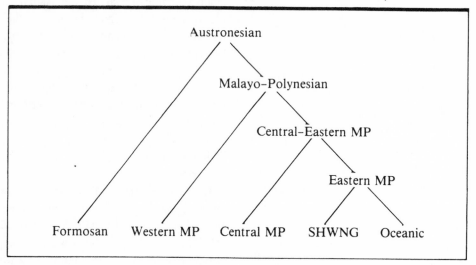

now termed M[alayo-]P[olynesian]. The Formosan languages may be divided into three (or more) first-order subgroups. MP divides into two groups, W[estern] MP (including the major languages of Indo-Malaysia and the Philippines) and C[entral-]E[astern] MP. CEMP branches into a Central MP group of perhaps 100 languages in the Moluccas and Lesser Sunda Islands, and this in turn into the South Halmahera-West New Guinea group (40 languages) and Oceanic.

First recognized by Dempwolff (under the name "Ur-melanesisch"), Oceanic includes all the AN languages of Melanesia, Micronesia, and Polynesia, with the exception of those in Irian Jaya (from Cenderawasih Bay westward), which belong to the South Halmahera-West New Guinea group, and Palauan and Chamorro in western Micronesia. (The latter two languages are MP but do not appear closely related to each other or to any other MP language.)

At least 80% of all AN languages fall into one of the two very large subgroups, WMP and Oceanic, each consisting of at least 400 languages. Oceanic is a classical subgroup, defined by a number of consonant mergers (see below) as well as lexical and grammatical changes. A dozen regional groups have been defined, though some are "linkages" resulting from differentiation of dialect chains rather than subgroups with universally shared innovations (Ross 1995).

At the eastern limit of AN, the Polynesian languages constitute a close-knit subgroup covering all of geographical Polynesia, and including also 15 small enclaves in Melanesia and Micronesia (the "Polynesian Outliers"). Polynesian's next of kin are Fijian and Rotuman, forming a Central Pacific subgroup. Central Pacific is one of a number of subgroups in the south and east of the Oceanic region that have been recognized for some time. Others are Nuclear Micronesian, Southeast Solomonic, North-Central Vanuatu, Southern Vanuatu, and New Caledonia–Loyalty Islands. Proposals for including several of these in a Remote Oceanic (Eastern Oceanic) and/or a Southern Oceanic group have been discussed for some time without achieving general consensus. In the western region (northwest Solomon Islands, Bismarck Archipelago, and New Guinea), Ross 1988 provides evidence for three large groups that he calls North New Guinea, Papuan Tip, and Meso-Melanesian, together comprising a Western Oceanic linkage. The languages of the Admiralty Islands appear to be a primary subgroup coordinate with the rest of Oceanic.

Western Malayo-Polynesian lacks the overall historic unity of Oceanic and may in fact be simply a residual group. Consensus has not yet been reached on higher-level groupings within WMP. Ross 1995 lists 24 local groups on which there would be considerable agreement. Of these, five are in the Philippines, six in Sulawesi, and six in Borneo. (Malagasy, despite its geographical separation, was shown by Dahl 1951 to subgroup most closely with the languages of southeast Borneo.) The Chamic group comprises the AN languages of Vietnam and Cambodia, together with Acehnese of north Sumatra and Tsat of Hainan Island. Malay, perhaps the best-known Austronesian language, has numerous highly distinctive local varieties and a few agreed close relatives, such as Minangkabau of central Sumatra. On one view, this Malayic group is most closely related to Chamic. Javanese, the largest AN language, has been linked with its eastern neighbors Balinese and Sasak; however, centuries of language contact in island Southeast Asia, and the political and cultural importance of Malay and Javanese, make it very difficult to distinguish common origin from later influence.

Proposals for wider connections of AN date back as far as Franz Bopp's proposal that it was related to Indo-European. The two most seriously considered today are "Austro-Tai," a connection with the Kam-Tai or Kadai family of the Southeast Asian mainland, most notably argued by Benedict 1975; and the "Austric" hypothesis of a group including AN and Austro-Asiatic, first proposed by Schmidt a century ago and recently explored further by Reid 1999.

2. Structural characteristics. Austronesian phoneme inventories are mainly medium-sized to small on a world scale, with extreme economy being reached in Polynesia. Thus, Maori, a typical Polynesian language, has ten consonants (*p t k f h m n ŋ r w*) and five vowels (*i e a o u*, with contrastive length). The east-west (WMP-Oceanic) division is reflected in different phonological tendencies, with the reconstructed P[roto-]AN phonology more faithfully retained in the west. The PAN four-vowel system *i a u ə* became P[roto-]Oc[eanic] *i e a o u*, through a shift of *ə* to *o* and fusion of a number of diphthongs. The PAN consonant system was simplified in Oceanic by the loss of voicing contrast in labial and velar stops, and merger of *d* to *r* and *Z* (a palatal stop) to *s*. However, POc developed a new series of prenasalized voiced consonants from original clusters, as well as a limited contrast between plain and velarized labials. Local developments in some areas, such as Micronesia and New Caledonia, have resulted in consonant and vowel systems considerably more complex than that of POc, including tone contrasts in some New Caledonian languages. A favored CVCVC shape for lexical morphemes is reconstructible for PAN, with some clusters permitted medially. Many Oceanic languages, and some in the west, have categorically lost word-final consonants.

Prefixing, suffixing, and infixing were all productive devices in PAN morphology. Affixes marking verbs for case orientation ("focus" or voice), transitivity, and nominalization are widespread; these have been reconstructed for PAN or other early stages. Reduplication also plays a part in most AN morphologies.

The distinction of inclusive and exclusive 1st person non-singular pronouns is a universal AN trait. Proto-Oceanic added a dual pronoun series (and possibly a trial) to the original singular/plural contrast. A distinction between proper nouns (personal pronouns and names) and common nouns is marked by articles in many languages. In PAN, pronominal possessors are marked by suffixes on the possessed noun, e.g. *maCa-ku* 'my eye'. Oceanic languages have elaborated this into a set of three or more contrasting categories of possession.

Two very different types of verbal syntax are found in modern AN languages. The "focus" type, typical of Philippine (e.g. Tagalog) and Formosan languages, marks a verb for one of (usually) four types of case orientation. The NP in the corresponding case relation is given a special marking of this privileged association with the verb, while any other NPs are marked to specify their case relationship. Word order is typically verb-initial, with free order of NPs. In the "transitive" type, typical of Oceanic languages, intransitive verbs are unmarked; transitive verbs are suffixed, sometimes with a choice of two suffixes to indicate case orientation to the object. Word order is typically Subject Verb Object; pronominal clitics index subject and object on the verb. The historical relation between these two types has been the subject of considerable debate, but the fact that the focus type occurs in both Formosan and non-Formosan (MP) languages, given the widely accepted subgrouping outlined above, argues for its greater antiquity (Pawley and Reid 1980).

[*See also* Malayo-Polynesian Languages; New Guinea Languages; Oceanic Languages; *and* Polynesian Languages.]

BIBLIOGRAPHY

Benedict, Paul K. 1975. *Austro-Thai language and culture, with a glossary of roots.* New Haven, Conn.: HRAF Press.

Blust, Robert. 1983–84. More on the position of the languages of eastern Indonesia. *Oceanic Linguistics* 22–23.1–28.

Blust, Robert. 1999. Subgrouping, circularity and extinction: some issues in Austronesian comparative linguistics. In Zeitoun and Li 1999, pp. 31–94.

Dahl, Otto C. 1951. *Malgache et manjaan.* Oslo: Egede-Instituttet.

Dahl, Otto C. 1976. *Proto-Austronesian.* 2d ed. Lund: Studentenlitteratur.

Dempwolff, Otto. 1934–38. *Vergleichende Lautlehre des austronesischen Wortschatzes.* 3 vols. Berlin: Reimer.

Dyen, Isidore. 1965. *A lexicostatistical classification of the Austronesian languages.* (Indiana University publications in anthropology and linguistics, memoir 19; International Journal of American Linguistics, 31:1, supplement). Baltimore, Md.

Grimes, Barbara F., Joseph E. Grimes, Malcolm Ross, Charles E. Grimes and Darrell T. Tryon. 1995. Listing of Austronesian languages. In Tryon 1995b, pp. 121–280.

Pawley, Andrew. 1999. Chasing rainbows: Implications of the rapid dispersal of Austronesian languages for subgrouping and reconstruction. In Zeitoun and Li 1999, pp. 95–138.

Pawley, Andrew, and Lawrence A. Reid. 1980. The evolution of transitive constructions in Austronesian. In *Austronesian studies* (Michigan papers on South and Southeast Asia, 15),
edited by Paz Buenaventura Naylor, pp. 103–130. Ann Arbor: University of Michigan.

Reid, Lawrence A. 1999. New linguistic evidence for the Austric hypothesis. In Zeitoun and Li, 1999, pp. 5–30.

Ross, Malcolm D. 1988. *Proto-Oceanic and the Austronesian languages of western Melanesia.* (Pacific Linguistics, C-98.) Canberra: Australian National University.

Ross, Malcolm. 1995. Some current issues in Austronesian linguistics. In Tryon 1995b, pp. 45–120.

Tryon, Darrell T. 1995a. The Austronesian languages. In Tryon 1995b, pp. 5–44.

Tryon, Darrell T., ed. 1995b. *Comparative Austronesian Dictionary: An introduction to Austronesian studies.* Berlin: Mouton de Gruyter.

Wurm, Stephen A., and Shiro Hattori. 1981–1984. *Language atlas of the Pacific area.* Canberra: Australian Academy of the Humanities.

Zeitoun, Elizabeth, and Paul Jen-kuei Li, eds. *Selected Papers from the Eighth International Conference on Austronesian Linguistics.* (Symposium series 1.) Taipei: Institute of Linguistics (Preparatory Office), Academia Sinica.

Ross Clark

LANGUAGE LIST

[*See the articles on* Formosan Languages *and* Malayo-Polynesian Languages.
                                                        B. Grimes

AUTISM. *See* Specific Language Impairment; Williams Syndrome and Down Syndrome: Cognitive Constraints on Language; *and* Developmental Language Disorder.

AUTOLEXICAL SYNTAX. Though the name implies a syntactic theory, Autolexical Syntax (ALS) is actually a view of the relationship between the various components of a grammar, only one of which is syntax. The name is justified, however, insofar as a great deal of what is included in syntax in more mainstream grammatical theories is seen in ALS as the province of other components, particularly of morphology or semantics. In ALS, distinct grammatical levels are described by autonomous grammars, called *modules*, each of which generates the set of well-formed representations at a single level.

The foundational article (Sadock 1985) considered mainly the syntactic and morphological levels, applying the idea of autonomous syntactic and morphological representations to the analysis of two phenomena: cliticization and incorporation. Both were taken to be cases of significant but allowable structural discrepancy be-

FIGURE 1.

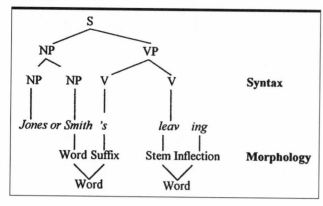

FIGURE 2.

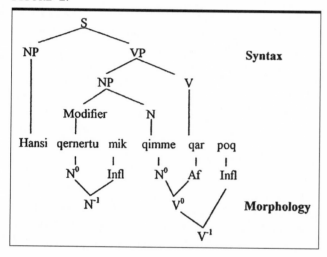

tween independent representations provided by the syntactic and the morphological modules. English auxiliary clitics, for example, were analyzed as syntactically identical to their free-verb counterparts, but, at the same time, as suffixes in the parallel morphology. The noun-incorporating suffixes of West Greenlandic Inuit were taken to be transitive verbs in the syntax and, at the same time, verb-forming suffixes in the morphology. The position of both clitics and incorporating affixes thus presented mismatches in two autonomous modules, as illustrated in Figures 1 and 2 and examples (1–2), which are typical of work in the ALS framework. They present the structure of expressions in the form of two (or more) simultaneous trees, each one corresponding to an analysis in a single module.

(1)   *Jones or Smith's leaving.*

(2)   *Hansi qernertu-mik   qimme-qar-poq*
       Hans   black-Instrumental/sg dog-have-Indicative/3sg
       'Hans has a black dog.'

One requirement for full grammaticality in this model is that an expression be properly analyzable with respect to each of the modules. In addition, ALS contains an interface component that ensures that various features of the autonomous representations correspond to some degree. Part of the interface includes the lexicon, since all of the representations of an expression must be compatible with the same set of lexical items. (Compare the idea of a "numeration" in the Minimalist Program.) In order to limit both the degree and the kinds of mismatches that the system allows, two quite specific interface constraints were suggested in Sadock 1985. Parts of morphological words are ordinarily not represented in the syntax at all, but if they are, the following interface principles were assumed (i) the Cliticization Principle, which requires that a host word and a morphological clitic be linearly adjacent in syntax; and (ii) the Incorporation Principle, which demands that a host stem and an affix or stem with which it combines morphologically be the head of a syntactic phrase and the head of its complement. (Compare head movement in the Government and Binding framework.) The interface was also charged with the task of adjudicating conflicts between modules. For example, one component may require the order B–A, and another the order A–B. A hierarchy of strength of components was proposed as the major feature of the system of conflict resolution, according to which morphology outranks syntax, and syntax outranks semantics.

Subsequent research turned up a number of phenomena that did not fit the stringent requirements of either the Cliticization or Incorporation principle. Smessaert 1996, for example, describes the system of West Flemish pronominal clitics, which attach to complementizers or to finite verbs even if the position of the free correspondent of the clitic is a considerable distance away, and even if there is an intervening head such as a preposition—as in (3), where the element *-der-* is a clitic in morphology and the syntactic object of the stranded preposition *mee,* which is two words away from where it would be found as an independent noun phrase:

(3)   *k-èn-der-ik   ol   mee èklapt*
       lsNOM-PrepObj-lsNOM already with talked
       'I have already talked to him/her.'

Based on such examples, the interface constraints were generalized (and weakened). In their place, Sadock 1991 suggested a Weak and Strong L(inearity) C(onstraint) demanding some degree of correspondence in linear order between independent representations, and a Weak and Strong C(onstructional) I(ntegrity) C(onstraint) enforcing some degree of match in terms of the hierarchical position of elements found in both the syntax and morphology. The Strong LC is similar to the older Cliticization Constraint, and the Strong CIC does much the same job as the Incorporation Constraint. Further examples have required even further generalization (and weakening) of the interface. In Sadock and Schiller 1993, all constraints on the interface were reduced to a single general principle, the Generalized Interface Principle, which requires all structural features of two independent representations of an expression—including linear order, hierarchical position, and category—to match as closely as the content of the levels and the demands of lexical items allow. Though attractive in its generality, this principle does not actually place any absolute limits on discrepancies between modular representations. It does, however, make mismatches costly in terms of the lexical and/or grammatical specifications that would be required to override the tendency toward full intermodular matching.

Subsequent work has made it clear that other levels of organization beyond the classical trio of syntax, semantics, and morphology need to be recognized. Woodbury 1996 and Chelliah 1996 draw an important distinction between morphology proper and morphophonology; and Faarlund 1996 suggests an independent module representing expressions in terms of predicates and thematic roles.

During the 1990s, the emphasis of work in ALS shifted from morphology vs. syntax discrepancies to syntax vs. semantics discrepancies, covering such topics as discussion of control phenomena, complementation, lexical categories, and compounding. More complex analyses that take account of the simultaneous interaction among three or more components have also appeared. A number of languages have been addressed from an ALS perspective, including English, French, Eskimo, Japanese, Hungarian, Norwegian, Circassian, Bangla, Welsh, Crow, and Hebrew.

Research in the late 1990s and early 2000s has emphasized individual constraints in addition to, or perhaps instead of, the system of rules that comprise the modules. Insofar as this work recognizes a number of distinct forces that compete for expression in surface form, it tends to resemble Optimality Theory, though in the ALS framework the constraints are weighted rather than ranked, and they can exhibit additive effects. Intermediate degrees of grammaticality are recognized as cases where conflicts among forces are unavoidable. The more serious the conflicting demands of the constraints are, the less acceptable the form is predicted to be.

[*See also* Clitics; Incorporation; Morphology; Optimality Theory; *and* Polysynthesis.]

BIBLIOGRAPHY

Chelliah, Shobhana L. 1996. An autolexical account of voicing assimilation in Manipuri. In Eric Schiller et al., pp. 11–30.

Faarlund, Jan Terje. 1995. Autostructural analysis of semantic roles. In Eric Schiller et al., pp. 31–86.

Sadock, Jerrold M. 1985. Autolexical syntax: A theory of noun incorporation and similar phenomena. *Natural Language and Linguistic Theory* 3.379–440.

Sadock, Jerrold M. 1991. *Autolexical syntax: A theory of parallel grammatical representations*. Chicago: University of Chicago Press.

Sadock, Jerrold M., and Eric Schiller. 1993. The generalized interface principle. *Proceedings of the Chicago Linguistic Society* 29.391–402.

Schiller, Eric, Elisa Steinberg, and Barbara Need, eds. 1996. *Autolexical theory: Ideas and methods*. Berlin: Mouton de Gruyter.

Smessaert, Hans. 1996. Pronominal cliticization in West Flemish. In Schiller et al., pp. 241–290.

Woodbury, Anthony C. 1996. On restricting the role of morphology in autolexical syntax. In Schiller et al., pp. 319–364.

JERROLD SADOCK

AUTOMATA THEORY. *See* Mathematical Linguistics.

AUTOSEGMENTAL PHONOLOGY. This theory of non-linear phonological representation was developed out of research in Generative Phonology at MIT in the mid and late 1970s, as a response to certain problems in the phonological theory of that time. Most previous research in phonology had been based on the view that speech is fundamentally linear in nature—i.e., that it consists, at the phonological level, of a single sequence of phonemes (often represented as unordered sets of distinctive features), which are separated by discrete boundaries. In the work of Roman Jakobson, Morris Halle, Noam Chomsky, and others, phonological form was represented in terms of two-dimensional feature

FIGURE 1. *Tonal Representation*

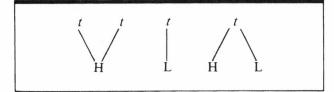

FIGURE 1. *Tonal Representation*

matrices, whose columns represented sequences of phonemes and whose rows represented their features. While
this account was adequate for most purposes of phonological description, it proved increasingly difficult to
reconcile with evidence that speech sounds are not discrete sequential entities, but show considerable overlap.

One source of such evidence came from the accumu-
lating descriptive literature on languages of Asia and
Africa, especially those in which *tone* plays a role. As
such systems became described in greater detail, it was
found that tone features showed patterns of distribution
and alternation which suggested that they were quite
loosely related to the segments that bear them, in contrast
to the more "tightly packed" sets of features that characterize vowels and consonants. Many linguists came to
believe that the theoretical implications of tone systems
should be examined more systematically; indeed, the
descriptivist H. A. Gleason went so far as to suggest
(1961:302) that "development of a theory better able to
handle tone will result automatically in a better theory
for all phonologic subsystems." For these and other
reasons—e.g. problems in the analysis of internally complex segments, long vowels and geminate consonants,
and processes carrying out "action at a distance"—an
increasing number of linguists came to believe that the
traditional segmental view of phonological representation
was in need of substantial revision.

1. Autosegmental treatment of tone. Autosegmental
phonology was initially developed in response to the
challenge of developing an adequate theory of tone. Its
immediate source of inspiration was the work of Williams
1971 and Leben 1973; these were the first to introduce
non-linear structures into generative phonology in their
treatments of tone systems in West African languages
such as Margi, Igbo, and Mende. In the model proposed
by these writers (termed "suprasegmental phonology" by
Leben), underlying tones were represented on separate
tiers from the feature matrices representing vowels and
consonants; they were subsequently *merged* with these
matrices by *tone mapping rules* that applied in the course
of derivation, creating single-tiered representations in

surface structure. This model went a considerable way
toward solving the descriptive problems mentioned earlier; e.g., it succeeded in showing how invariant lexical
tone melodies are distributed across words of varying
length.

The principal innovation of autosegmental phonology,
as presented in Goldsmith 1976, was the idea that tone
mapping rules do not merge tonal and segmental representations, but associate their elements by means of
formal entities known as *association lines*. In this framework, phonological representations consist of parallel
tiers of phonological segments, both tonal and segmental.
A typical tonal representation might have the form shown
in Figure 1, where H = high tone, L = low tone, and *t*
is any tone-bearing unit (e.g. vowel or syllable).

Elements of each tier, called *autosegments*, are sequentially ordered; elements of adjacent tiers are simultaneous
if and only if they are linked by association lines. As
Figure 1 shows, tones are not necessarily related to tone-
bearing units in a one-to-one fashion. Rather, one tone
may be linked to two or more tone-bearing units, and
one tone-bearing unit may be linked to two or more
tones—i.e. to a *contour*, such as a rising or falling tone.
Phonological rules may insert or delete elements on any
tier: since each tier is independent, deletion of an element
on one tier does not entail deletion of the element(s) to
which it is linked on another tier. In addition, phonological rules have the new function of creating and modifying
the patterns of association among elements of different
tiers. In this model, all tiers remain independent throughout derivations: at no point is the tonal tier merged with
the segmental tier.

A further innovation of autosegmental theory is the set
of universal principles termed *well-formedness conditions*, which govern the multi-tiered structure of the
representation. These principles not only define the set
of theoretically possible inter-tier configurations; they
also trigger the operation of a set of universal repair
mechanisms, often termed *association conventions*,
whenever configurations that violate them arise. One
important condition requires that association lines may
not cross. In the earliest version of the theory, further
conditions required that every element be linked to at
least one element on another tier at all stages of a
derivation (a condition satisfied in Figure 1). In later
work, however, it was shown that certain tones could
remain unlinked, accounting for the phenomenon of floating tones (Figure 2a). Further, some tone-bearing units
could be toneless, accounting for the phenomenon of

FIGURES 2a and 2b. *Floating Tones and Default Tones*

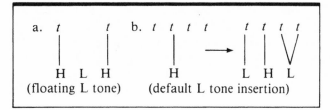

FIGURE 3. *Autosegmental Representation*

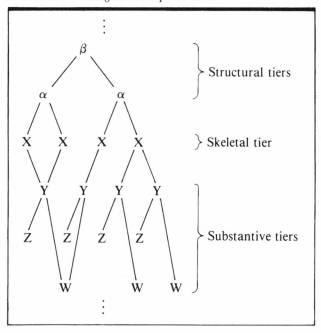

default tones—i.e. tones that are inserted into representations only after the initial mapping processes have been carried out, as in Figure 2b. (For further discussion, see Clements and Goldsmith 1984, Pulleyblank 1986.)

Goldsmith's original arguments for the autosegmental analysis of tone, drawn from a survey of well attested generalizations concerning tone systems, were widely accepted; they stimulated considerable further research, not only on tonal phonology, but also on non-tonal phenomena, as we will see below.

2. Generalized autosegmental phonology. In subsequent work, autosegmental phonology underwent further development; by the mid-1980s it could be considered a fully general theory of phonological representation, radically different from the linear representational systems of more traditional approaches. The general goal of research in autosegmental phonology, much like that of concurrent work in theoretical syntax, has been to reduce the power of phonological rules by developing an en-

riched theory of representation. Arbitrary rule-based descriptions of languages may then be replaced, to a great extent, by constrained accounts expressed in terms of simple, recurrent phonological parameters.

The primary innovation of the generalized model has been the view that not just tone and other so-called "prosodic" features, but *all* phonological features are arrayed on separate autosegmental tiers. In this conception, which draws upon earlier research in *metrical phonology* and *prosodic phonology*, phonological representations are three-dimensional structures involving numerous tiers whose feature content is linked, directly or indirectly, to a central organizational core or *skeleton* which consists of a sequence of abstract *timing units*. Some of these tiers have a substantive, phonetic content, providing feature information which is directly interpreted by rules of phonetic realization; others articulate the rhythmic structure characteristic of languages with stress systems; and others are purely formal and hierarchical, grouping phonetically defined features of the utterance together into higher-level structural units such as the syllable or foot. Sets of related tiers form *planes*. Rules of phonology continue to have the function of altering the content of each tier, or of readjusting the network of associations between units on related tiers. We may schematize this conception in terms of the fragment of a representation given in Figure 3; Greek letters designate structural units and Roman letters designate units with substantive content, such as features and feature classes.

This model extends the earlier tonal framework to a wide range of additional phenomena, including vowel harmony and segmental assimilation, syllable structure, phonological length, compensatory lengthening, and stress and intonation—in short, to the full domain of segmental and suprasegmental phonology.

A central notion in this conception is the *core* or prosodic skeleton, first proposed and elaborated in work on the root-and-pattern morphology of the Semitic languages by McCarthy 1979, 1981 (see also Halle and Vergnaud 1980). In Classical Arabic, the morphological structure of a word is distributed among three types of simultaneous phonological information: the sequence of consonants which provides the lexical content, the sequence of vowels which designates the aspect/voice category, and the canonic pattern of vowels and consonants which (independently of their segmental content) indicates the derivational category, or "measure." Thus, in a verb stem such as *kuutib,* the consonants [k..t..b] corre-

FIGURES 4a–4c. *Classical Arabic Morphology*

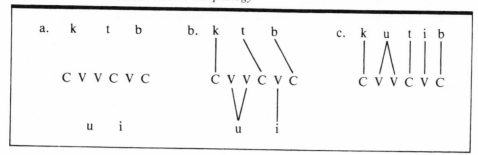

spond to the root meaning 'write', the vowel sequence [u..i] to the perfective passive, and the pattern CVVCVC to the "third measure." The descriptive problem posed by such morphological systems is to provide a principled way of accounting for the interlocking pattern of phonological information, without making use of ad-hoc constructs such as "discontinuous morphemes." McCarthy's solution follows from the universal postulate that the phonological content of each morpheme is represented on a separate tier, as in the lexical representation in Figure 4a. Autosegmental principles of association (identical to those assumed for tonal phonology) link the consonants and vowels to the respective C- and V-slots of the skeleton (Figure 4b). A later process of tier conflation (McCarthy 1986) collapses all segmental features into a single phonemic or "melody" tier, providing the surface representation (Figure 4c).

What is crucial for the present discussion is that the CV schema constitutes a separate autosegmental tier: the central core of the representation, around which vowels and consonants are articulated.

The prosodic skeleton plays not only a morphological role, but a phonological one as well. Clements and Keyser 1983 propose that the skeleton, which they term the "CV tier," forms part of universal phonological representation, where it serves multiple roles. First, it forms the basis of syllabification rules. V-elements on the skeletal tier are syllabified as syllable peaks; thus syllabic sounds (vowels and syllabic consonants) are dominated by V, and non-syllabic sounds (glides and non-syllabic consonants) are dominated by C. Second, it forms the basis of phonological quantity. Long segments are represented as single phonemes or "melody units," linked to two units of the CV tier; this accounts for the generalization that long segments count as one unit from the point of view of their segmental quality, but as two in regard to their quantity (see Kenstowicz 1982). Analogously, complex segments like affricates or prenasalized stops are repre-

FIGURE 5. *The CV Tier in English*

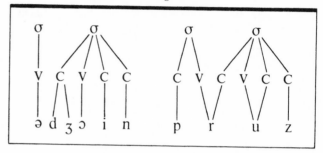

sented as two phonemes linked to a single CV tier unit; this accounts for the fact that they count as two units from the point of view of their feature substance, but as one from that of segmental quantity. All these points can be illustrated in the autosegmental representations of *adjoin* [ədžɔyn] and *peruse* [pruwz], as shown in Figure 5.

Additional evidence in favor of the phonological role of the prosodic skeleton comes from the phenomenon of *compensatory lengthening*, by which deletion of one segment is accompanied by the lengthening of another (usually adjacent) one. Under an autosegmental analysis, this is expressed as the spreading of a neighboring phoneme onto the skeletal position left vacant by the deleted one (Wetzels and Sezer 1986). Further, skeletal "slots" may be totally empty of segmental content; this accounts for the synchronic traces of historically deleted consonants, such as the *h aspiré* of French or the *yumuşak g* of standard Turkish. The formal nature of the prosodic skeleton has been a matter of controversy: some investigators prefer to regard it as a sequence of undifferentiated timing points, while others suggest that it may consist of a sequence of weight units or *moras*.

The phonemic segments displayed in Figures 4 and 5 are a shorthand notation for hierarchical feature complexes, arrayed on substantive tiers as suggested in Figure 3. This analysis is motivated by extensive evidence that segmental features are themselves autosegmental in nature. For example, an autosegmental description of vowel harmony systems, in which vowel features such as lip rounding or palatality are assigned to a separate tier, provides a straightforward account of so-called "long-distance assimilation" and related opacity effects (see Clements 1977). Furthermore, in many languages, certain subsets of features behave autonomously with respect to other subsets, as is shown by processes of partial deletion or partial assimilation; here again, we obtain a straightforward account if we assume that each such subset occupies an independent tier of its own (Thráinsson 1978). In the fully generalized model of subsegmental structure proposed in Clements 1985, all features are assigned to independent autosegmental tiers, where they form the terminal elements of feature trees. Such trees are dominated by a single node—the *root node*, which takes the place of the segmental distinctive feature matrix of earlier work. Intermediate nodes, called *class nodes*, serve a purely structural function: they group together functionally related subsets of features into subordinate hierarchical units. This model has been extended by Elizabeth Sagey, who proposes that the articulators—coronal, dorsal, labial, etc.—are not represented as terminal features of trees, but as *articulator nodes* dominating terminal features.

Further developments in autosegmental phonology include the grid-based theory of stress proposed by Halle and Vergnaud 1987, and the model of intonation and prosodic structure developed by Pierrehumbert and Beckman 1988. For a more recent overview and several new proposals, see Goldsmith 1990. As remarked by Van der Hulst and Smith 1982, progress in autosegmental phonology has owed much to its "problem-solving efficiency"—i.e. its success in finding solutions for previously unsolved representational problems, and integrating them into a consistent, over-all theoretical framework. In addition, it has had consequences in quite unexpected quarters: it has contributed to the development of the theory of non-concatenative morphology (see above); it has substantially reduced the abstractness required in earlier analyses; it has laid the basis for a substantive theory of "natural" or widely attested rule types; it has simplified the theory of rule application by eliminating the class of "non-local" rules; and it has stimulated new theories of phonetic features and of articulation-based speech synthesis.

[*See also* Generative Phonology; Intonation; Lexical Phonology; Metrical Phonology; Phonological Features; Phonology, *article on* Prosodic Phonology; Segments; Syllables; *and* Tone.]

BIBLIOGRAPHY

Clements, George N. 1977. The autosegmental treatment of vowel harmony. In *Phonologica 1976* (Innsbrucker Beiträge zur Sprachwissenschaft, 19), edited by Wolfgang U. Dressler and Oskar E. Pfeiffer, pp. 111–119. Innsbruck: Institut für Sprachwissenschaft der Universität.

Clements, George N. 1985. The geometry of phonological features. *Phonology Yearbook* 2.225–252.

Clements, George N., and John Goldsmith, eds. 1984. *Autosegmental studies in Bantu tone.* (Publications in African languages and linguistics, 3.) Dordrecht: Foris.

Clements, George N., and Samuel Jay Keyser. 1983. *CV Phonology: A generative theory of the syllable.* (Linguistic Inquiry monographs, 9.) Cambridge, Mass.: MIT Press.

Gleason, Henry Allan, Jr. 1961. Review of *African language studies*, vol. 1, edited by Malcolm Guthrie, and *The role of tone in Sųkúma*, by Irvine Richardson. *Language* 37.294–308.

Goldsmith, John. 1976. *Autosegmental phonology.* MIT dissertation. Published, New York: Garland, 1979.

Goldsmith, John. 1990. *Autosegmental and metrical phonology.* Oxford: Blackwell.

Halle, Morris, and Jean-Roger Vergnaud. 1980. Three-dimensional phonology. *Journal of Linguistic Research* 1: 1.83–105.

Halle, Morris, and Jean-Roger Vergnaud. 1987. *An essay on stress.* (Current studies in linguistics, 15.) Cambridge, Mass.: MIT Press.

Kenstowicz, Michael. 1982. Gemination and spirantization in Tigrinya. *Studies in the Linguistic Sciences* (University of Illinois) 12.103–122.

Leben, William R. 1973. *Suprasegmental phonology.* MIT dissertation. Published, New York: Garland, 1980.

McCarthy, John. 1979. *Formal problems in Semitic phonology and morphology.* Cambridge, Mass.: MIT dissertation. Published, New York: Garland, 1985.

McCarthy, John. 1981. A prosodic theory of non-concatenative morphology. *Linguistic Inquiry* 12.373–418.

McCarthy, John. 1986. OCP effects: Gemination and antigemination. *Linguistic Inquiry* 17.207–263.

Pierrehumbert, Janet, and Mary Beckman. 1988. *Japanese tone structure.* (Linguistic Inquiry monographs, 15.) Cambridge, Mass.: MIT Press.

Pulleyblank, Douglas. 1986. *Tone in lexical phonology.* Dordrecht: Reidel.

Thráinsson, Höskuldur. 1978. On the phonology of Icelandic preaspiration. *Nordic Journal of Linguistics* 1.3–54.

Van der Hulst, Harry, and Norval Smith. 1982. An overview of autosegmental and metrical phonology. In *The structure of phonological representations,* vol. 1, edited by Harry van der Hulst and Norval Smith, pp. 1–45. Dordrecht: Foris.

Wetzels, Leo, and Engin Sezer, eds. 1986. *Studies in compensatory lengthening.* (Publications in language sciences, 23.) Dordrecht: Foris.

Williams, Edwin. 1971. Underlying tone in Margi and Igbo. MS. Published in *Linguistic Inquiry* 7.463–484, 1976.

GEORGE N. CLEMENTS

AUXILIARIES. *See* Parts of Speech *and* Typology and Universals.

AYMARAN LANGUAGES. Spoken in the Andes Mountains, in Bolivia, Argentina, Chile, and Peru.

LANGUAGE LIST

Aymara, Central: Around 2,200,000 speakers in Bolivia, Peru, Chile, and Argentina. In Bolivia: 1,785,000 speakers. Whole Altiplano west of eastern Andes. Some migration to the yungas and the lowlands. All ages. In Peru: 300,000 speakers. Lake Titicaca area, Puno. Lupaca is the main literary dialect. All ages speak Central Aymara. In Chile: Ethnic population: 20,000 as of 1983. Mountains of extreme north, first region (Tarapáa); Arica, Parinacota, Iquique. Chilean Aymara is very close to La Paz, Bolivia, dialect. Bilingualism in Spanish.

Aymara, Southern: spoken in Peru. From Lake Titicaca toward ocean. Some important verb forms and vocabulary differences from Central Aymara. Dialect intelligibility needs investigation in Tacna and Moquegua. Limited bilingualism.

Jaqaru: also called Haqearu, Haqaru, Haq'aru, Aru. 736 speakers in Peru. Ethnic population: 2,000 as of 2000. Lima department, Yauyos Province, Tupe village (Jaqaru) and Cachuy village (Cauqui). Dialect is Cauqui (Kawki, Cachuy), nearly extinct. Most or all use Spanish as second language. There may still be a few monolinguals, all women. Adult speakers only of Jaqaru.   B. GRIMES

AZTEC. *See* Nahuatl.

B

BAAGANDJI LANGUAGES are a group spoken in New South Wales, Australia; they form a branch of the PAMA-NYUNGAN family of Australian languages.

LANGUAGE LIST

Bandjigali: also called Baarrundji, Barindji, Marrawarra, Maruara. One speaker remains. Formerly spoken in northwest, north and west of White Cliffs.

Darling: also called Kula, Baagandji, Southern Baagandji. 5 speakers remain. Formerly spoken along Darling River Basin. Dialects were Kula, Wiljakali (Wilyagali), Bagundji (Baagandji, Bagandji). B. GRIMES

BABAR LANGUAGES constitute a branch of CENTRAL MALAYO-POLYNESIAN. They are spoken on the Babar Islands in the south of the Indonesian province of Maluku.

LANGUAGE LIST

Babar, Northern: 1,500 speakers on northern Babar Islands, east of Timor, six villages. Reported dialect variation. Bilingualism in Malay. Vigorous language use.

Babar, Southeastern: 3,325 speakers. Southeastern Babar Island.

Dai: 808 speakers on South, Dai, and Babar Islands. Three villages. No dialect variation. Bilingualism in Malay. Vigorous language use.

Dawera-Daweloor: also called Davelor. 1,500 speakers in six villages on Dawera and Daweloor Islands, minor dialect differences. Bilingualism in Malay. Vigorous language use.

Emplawas: 250 speakers. Emplawas village, southwestern Babar Island.

Imroing: also called Imroin. 450 speakers in the village of Imroing, southwestern Babar Island.

Masela, Central: also called Central Marsela, Marsela-South Babar. 510 speakers in three villages on Marsela Island.

Masela, Eastern: also called East Marsela. 520 speakers in three villages on Marsela Island.

Masela, Western: also called West Marsela. 850 speakers in five villages on Marsela Island.

Serili: 330 speakers on northeastern Marsela Island.

Tela-Masbuar: also called Tela'a, Masbuar-Tela. 1,050 speakers in villages of Tela and Masbuar, southwestern Babar Island. B. GRIMES

FIGURE 1. *Subgrouping of Babar Languages*

North Babar
   Northern Babar, Dai, Dawera-Daweloor
South Babar
   Masela-South Babar
      Southeastern Babar, Central Masela, Eastern Masela, Western Masela, Serili
   Southwest Babar
      Emplawas, Imroing, Tela-Masbuar

BABBLING. *See* Acquisition of Language.

BACK FORMATION. *See* Abbreviation *and* Morphology.

BACKGROUNDING. *See* Discourse; Information Structure; *and* Semantics.

BACON, FRANCIS (1561–1626). English statesman and philosopher; Bacon counts as one of the first English empiricists and was a supporter of the inductive method (the "Baconian" method). He produced a strong critique of ordinary language, which he saw as a product of convention likely to lead to false classifications and analyses. Because of this, he was seen as an inspiration in the 17th-century search for a universal language.

[*See also* History of Linguistics]

ANNA MORPURGO DAVIES

BAKHTIN, MIKHAIL (1895–1975). Bakhtin was one of the most original thinkers in 20th-century Russia. His work was obstructed or suppressed under the Soviet regime but was seminal for semiotics and literary theory in the West, though it became known only after it was translated starting in the 1960s and 1970s; part of it was published posthumously. Some of his first books were published in collaboration with, or under the name of, others, such as V. N. Voloshinov and P. N. Medvedev: *Freudianism* (1927, transl. 1973), *Marxism and the philosophy of language* (1929, transl. 1973), *The formal method in literary scholarship* (1928, transl. 1978). His work on Rabelais and the carnivalesque (*Rabelais and his world*, 1984) and on Dostoevsky (*Problems of Dostoevsky's poetics*, 1984) is part of a larger concern for the theory of the novel (which, itself, is framed by larger questions of time and the imagination: *Speech genres and other late essays*, 1986, and *The dialogic imagination*, 1981). He was very much interested in the multiplicity of the construction of meaning ('heteroglossia'), dialogism, and the "polyphonic" novel.

[*See also* Discourse; Linguistics and Literature; *and* Text.]

ANNA MORPURGO DAVIES

BALI-SASAK LANGUAGES. These constitute a group spoken on Bali and adjacent islands of Indonesia. They form a branch of WESTERN MALAYO-POLYNESIAN.

LANGUAGE LIST

Bali: also called Balinese. 3,800,000 speakers on island of Bali, northern Nusapenida, 80,000 in western Lombok Islands, eastern Java, 40,000 in southern Sumatra, 60,000 in Sulawesi. Dialects are Lowland Bali (Klungkung, Karangasem, Buleleng, Gianyar, Tabanan, Jembrana, Badung), Highland Bali ("Bali Aga") Nusa Penida. Reported to be two distinct dialects: High Balinese is used in religion, but those who can handle it are diminishing. There are speech strata in several lowland varieties.

Sasak: also called Lombok. 2,100,000 speakers in Nusa Tenggara, Lombok Island. Dialects are Kuto-Kute (North Sasak), Ngeto-Ngete (Northeast Sasak), Meno-Mene (Central Sa-

sak), Ngeno-Ngene (Central East Sasak, Central West Sasak), Mriak-Mriku (Central South Sasak). Complex dialect network. Some "dialects" have difficult intelligibility with each other. Related to Sumbawa and Bali.

Sumbawa: also called Semawa, Sumbawarese. 300,000 speakers in Nusa Tenggara, western end of Sumbawa Island, west of the isthmus.

B. GRIMES

BALKAN LANGUAGES. The Balkan peninsula is a rugged, mountainous land mass in southeastern Europe, bounded by the lower Danube and Sava rivers to the north (though by some accounts beginning even farther north, in the vicinity of Vienna), by the Adriatic Sea to the west, and by the Black Sea up to the mouth of the Danube river to the east; it includes all of Greece to the south. It is home to a number of languages whose interrelationships are of great interest in regard to questions of language contact, language change, areal linguistics, and sociolinguistics. The languages in this area come mostly from several different branches of the I[ndo-]E[uropean] family, as listed in Figure 1. From the Altaic family (Turkic branch) comes Turkish.

The most significant fact about these languages is that various sets of them share certain structural and lexical features that do not, in the case of the IE languages, derive from their being genetically related. Such features do not represent common inheritances from Proto-IE; rather, they result from linguistic convergence over a period of intense, intimate contact among the speech communities in this area. Moreover, genetic relatedness could not possibly explain the similarities between Turkish and the IE languages of the Balkans. The languages which share significant numbers of these features are

FIGURE 1. *Subgrouping of Indo-European Branches of Balkan Languages*

Albanian
  Geg (in the north), Tosk (in the south)
Greek
  Ancient Greek, Modern Greek, Pontic, Tsakonian
Indic
  Romani (Gypsy)
    Balkan Romani, Carpathian Romani, Vlach Romani
Romance
  Aromanian (Vlach), Daco-Rumanian, Judeo-Spanish (also known as Ladino)
South Slavic
  Bulgarian, Macedonian, Bosnian-Croatian-Serbian (formerly known collectively as Serbo-Croatian)

often designated "Balkan languages" (Schaller 1975), as opposed to the merely geographic designation "languages of the Balkans"; the latter also include Slovenian, Armenian (spoken in Bulgaria), Circassian (Adygey, spoken in the Kosovo area), Ruthenian (Rusyn, spoken in the Vojvodina area of northern Serbia), and German and Hungarian (both spoken in Rumania).

This structural and lexical convergence has led to characterization of the Balkan languages as a *Sprachbund* ('linguistic league' or 'linguistic area'). This characterization—noted as early as Miklosich 1884, and systematically elaborated in the classic work of Sandfeld 1926, 1930—is based on the belief that the convergences observable in a comparison of these languages are not chance similarities, but instead are the natural consequence of the close contact among these speech communities. The most significant such features are listed below.

1. Phonological features include the following:

(a) A stressed mid-to-high central vowel is found in Albanian, Rumanian, Bulgarian, some dialects of Macedonian and Serbian, some Romani varieties, and Turkish.

(b) The vowel inventory contains *i e a o u*, without phonological contrasts of quantity, openness, or nasalization; this characteristic is found in Greek, Tosk Albanian, Rumanian, Macedonian, Bulgarian, some dialects of Serbian, and Romani.

2. Morphological features include the following:

(a) The nominal case system shows reduction—in particular, a falling together of the genitive and dative cases—in Greek, Albanian, Rumanian, Bulgarian, and Macedonian; the latter two have eliminated other case distinctions as well.

(b) A future tense based on a reduced, often invariant, form of the verb 'want' is found in Greek, Tosk Albanian, Rumanian, Macedonian, Bulgarian, Serbian, and Romani.

(c) An enclitic (postposed) definite article typically occurs after the first word in the noun phrase in Albanian, Rumanian, Macedonian, Bulgarian, and southeastern (Torlak) Serbian.

(d) The use of verbal forms to distinguish actions on the basis of the real or presumed source of information—commonly referred to as marking a witnessed/reported distinction, but also including nuances of surprise (admirative) and doubt (dubitative)—is found in Albanian, Bulgarian, Macedonian, and Turkish, and to a lesser extent in Romani, Serbian, and Rumanian (the presumptive; see Friedman 1981).

3. Syntactic features include the following:

(a) A non-finite verbal complement (generally called an "infinitive" in traditional grammar) is reduced in use, and is replaced by fully finite complement clauses (see Joseph 1983). This feature is found most intensively in Greek, Macedonian, Bulgarian, Serbian (especially the Torlak dialects), and Romani; it also occurs in Albanian (especially Tosk) and Rumanian.

(b) Analytic adjectival comparative structures are found in Greek, Albanian, Rumanian, Bulgarian, Macedonian, and Romani, as well as in Turkish.

(c) The pleonastic use of weak object pronominal forms in combination with full noun phrases for direct or indirect object is found in Greek, Albanian, Rumanian, Bulgarian, and Macedonian, dialectally in Serbian, and to a limited extent in Romani.

4. Lexical parallels are found throughout the area, including shared phraseology (e.g., a phrase that is lit. 'without (an)other' means 'without doubt'), and numerous shared loanwords, many from Turkish.

5. Processes. The above features, known as "Balkanisms," define the Balkan *Sprachbund*—even though not all are found in all the languages (see Hamp 1979, Hamp 1989). Most of these features represent synchronically valid statements about the superficial structure of these languages. However, several of them are diachronically oriented; over centuries of contact, the Balkan languages have moved away from stages in which they were typologically more different from one another, and toward their present state of structural convergence.

The causes of Balkan linguistic convergence must undoubtedly be sought in language contact, although some linguists have viewed various developments in each language as independent of those found in the others. The nature of the contact which led to convergence is a matter of some controversy. Some scholars opt for a substratum explanation which draws on facts about languages, e.g. Thracian and Illyrian, which were spoken in the Balkans in ancient times (see Katičić 1976). Others prefer an adstratum explanation, with the influence of Greek being especially important. Still others propose different models of contact, based, e.g., on bilingualism, or even on a form of pidginization. Before the matter can be fully understood, many details are still needed concerning the social situation in the medieval period, when the most significant contact occurred among these languages. (For further references, see Schaller 1977, Solta 1980, Assenova 1983, Banfi 1985, Feuillet 1986, Asenova 1989, and Demiraj 1994.)

[*See also* Albanian; Areal Linguistics; Bulgarian; Greek; Indo-European Languages; Rumanian; Serbo-Croatian; *and* Turkish.]

BIBLIOGRAPHY

Asenova, Petja, ed. 1983. *Linguistique balkanique: Bibliographie 1966–1975.* Sofia: Académie Bulgare des Sciences.

Asenova, Petja. 1989. *Balkansko ezikoznanie: Osnovni problemi na balkanskija ezikov săjuz.* Sofia: Izdatelstvo Nauka i Izkustvo.

Banfi, Emanuele. 1985. *Linguistica balcanica.* Bologna: Zanichelli.

Demiraj, Shaban. 1994. *Gjuhësi ballkanike.* Skopje: Logos-A.

Feuillet, Jack. 1986. *La linguistique balkanique.* (Cahiers balkaniques, 10). Paris: INALCO.

Friedman, Victor A. 1981. Admirativity and confirmativity. *Zeitschrift für Balkanologie* 17:1.12–28.

Hamp, Eric P. 1979. Linguistic areas or clusters? In *Quatrième Congrès International des Études du Sud-est Européen: Abrégés des communications,* pp. 282–283. Ankara: Türk Tarih Kurumu.

Hamp, Eric P. 1989. Yugoslavia—a crossroads of Sprachbünde. *Zeitschrift für Balkanologie* 25:1.44–47.

Joseph, Brian D. 1983. *The synchrony and diachrony of the Balkan infinitive: A study in areal, general, and historical linguistics.* (Cambridge studies in linguistics, Supplementary volume 1.) Cambridge and New York: Cambridge University Press.

Katičić, Radoslav. 1976. *Ancient languages of the Balkans,* vol. 1. (Trends in linguistics: State-of-the-Art reports, 4.) The Hague: Mouton.

Miklosich, Franz. 1884. Die türkischen Elemente in den südost- und osteuropäischen Sprachen. *Denkschriften der Kaiserlichen Akademie der Wissenschaften* (Vienna), Philosophisch-historische Klasse, 34.239–338.

Sandfeld, Kristian. 1926. *Balkanfilologien: En oversigt over dens resultater og problemer.* Copenhagen.

Sandfeld, Kristian. 1930. *Linguistique balkanique: Problèmes et résultats.* (Collection linguistique publiée de la Société de Linguistique de Paris, 31.) Paris: Champion.

Schaller, Helmut W. 1975. *Die Balkansprachen: Eine Einführung in die Balkanphilologie.* Heidelberg: Winter.

Schaller, Helmut W. 1977. *Bibliographie zur Balkanphilologie.* Heidelberg: Winter.

Solta, Georg R. 1980. *Einführung in die Balkanlinguistik, mit besonderer Berücksichtigung des Substrats und des Balkanlateinischen.* Darmstadt: Wissenschaftliche Buchgesellschaft.

BRIAN D. JOSEPH

BALTIC LANGUAGES. The Baltic family belongs to the *satem* branch of I[ndo-]E[uropean], along with Sl[avic], Indo-Iranian, and Armenian. Lithuanian, its most important member, was included in the *Comparative grammar* of Bopp 1833; the Baltic group was recognized by George Nesselmann in 1845. For reference, see Endzelīns 1923, 1971, Trautmann 1923, Fraenkel 1950, Senn 1957, Gimbutas 1963, Stang 1966, Schmalstieg 1974, and Dini 1997.

1. Membership. Baltic is divided into W[est] B[altic] and E[ast] B[altic]. WB is known from O[ld] P[russian], spoken formerly in East Prussia; it is attested from a 14th-century vocabulary list (Pomesan dialect) and from 16th-century catechisms (Samland dialect); it has been extinct since ca. 1700. Other Prussian ethnonyms sometimes cited, such as Pogesanian, Skalvian, and Jatvingian (Sudovian), are tribal groupings without known special linguistic features. EB includes Li[thuanian] and La[tvian], attested from the 16th century. Other EB languages sometimes mentioned—e.g. Kurish (Kuronian, Curonian), Zemgalian, and Selian—are known from names, borrowings, and substratum phenomena; none has known unique linguistic features. They are presumed to be transitional dialects, which were absorbed into either Li. or La. The East Latvian dialect area supports a separate literary language called Latgalian. Evidence also exists, from place names and other substratum phenomena, of a now-extinct Baltic language to the east, ranging as far as the territory of Moscow.

2. Classification. The shared features of Baltic and Slavic have led many scholars to propose an intermediate B[alto-]Sl[avic] family within IE; however, this view has been disputed by scholars who argue for a separate, if parallel, evolution of Baltic from IE. This issue remains open. Those who argue for a BSl. unity must account for very ancient differences between Baltic and Slavic. It is not possible to reconstruct a homogeneous Common Baltic; hence it cannot be possible to reconstruct a homogeneous BSl. However, those who oppose a BSl. unity must account for many shared features, including vocabulary, accent, and the development of IE syllabic sonorants. There has also been interest in the concept of a Baltic, Slavic, and Germanic community set off by an early Northern IE isogloss. Baltic can then be seen as a peripheral *satem* language, and as a transition to Germanic. There are old isoglosses which unite Baltic and Germanic, probably before 3000 BCE, and which are not shared by Sl. This suggests that BSl. unity, if real, could not have existed later than the 4th millennium BCE. Significantly, Baltic itself is actually divided by many old isoglosses—some shared with Slavic, and some with Germanic.

In general, Baltic is closer to the classical IE languages in its structure than to modern European languages; of living languages, Li. is the closest to "classical" reconstructed IE. Within Baltic, OPr. and Li. are conservative; but La. has developed in the analytic direction, with paradigmatic syncretism and loss. Changes in Li. have been much slower (e.g., the dual is attested and preserved in some dialects), and as much toward agglutination as analysis; the evolution of locative endings illustrates this. Modern Li. has not conserved the attested Old Li. locative endings, but neither does it follow the modern European pattern of merger and loss. Instead, there is retention of stem markers in both numbers, retention of -s as a plural marker, and generalization of -e as a mark of locative case in all declensions and numbers. By contrast, the OL sg./pl. endings for three stem classes are -ie/-uosu, -oj/-osu, -ej/-esu, while their modern counterparts are -e/-uose, -oje/-ose, -ėje/-ėse.

3. General features. Among the typological features of Baltic are the following:

(a) Preservation and expansion of IE vowel gradation (ablaut)

(b) The tendency to insert /k/ before consonant clusters beginning with a sibilant, cf. Li. krikštyti, OPr. crixtitwei 'baptize', La. pìrksts 'finger'

(c) A unique verb system, including lack of number contrast in the 3rd person—cf. Li. 3rd person pres. áuga 'grow(s)'; a simple past formed by adding *-ā and *-ē themes to stems (original root aorists, s-aorists, perfect, and imperfect are lost); and a present tense medial suffix -sta where the nasal infix (limited to canonical shape CVC) cannot occur

(d) Characteristic nominal elements, including great productivity for fem. -ē stems (cf. OPr. semme, Li. žẽmė, La. zeme 'earth', O[ld] C[hurch] S[lavic] *zemia); specifically Baltic diminutive and agentive suffixes; and personal names

(e) Characteristic Baltic vocabulary

Other features also justify a Baltic family; however, a reconstructed Common Baltic is more abstract than e.g. Common Slavic. Most typological features that divide the Baltic languages link one or another Baltic language with Slavic, or with branches of Slavic.

4. West Baltic features include the following:

(a) Possessive adjectives cognate with Slavic, cf. OPr. mais, twais, swais vs. OCS mojǐ, tvojǐ, svojǐ. By contrast, EB uses possessive pronouns based on the pronominal declension; cf. Li. màno, tàvo, sàvo.

(b) The preterit of 'be', OPr. bēi, be, cf. OCS běxŭ, bě. EB has only the stems es-, buv-.

(c) Preservation of the neuter gender in OPr.

(d) OPr. -o-stem genitive in -s; the EB and Sl. -o-stem genitive is based on the IE ablative in *-ā—cf. OPr. gen. deiwas, Li. diẽvo. The OPr. dative plural is -mans; cf. EB -mus, Sl. -mŭ.

(e) WB preserves an older separate pronominal declension, which has been nominalized in EB; cf. OPr. stas, gen. stessei, dat. stesmu, gen. pl. steison, dat. pl. steimans. Note also WB subs 'oneself', gen. subsai (EB pats, cf. Sanskrit páti, Greek pósis 'master'). The WB pronominal declension (like those of Sanskrit and Gothic) has a dative and locative element -sm-, whereas EB and Slavic have -m-.

(f) Present passive participle in -man-, whereas EB and Slavic have -m-. WB has a past active participle in -uns; cf. iduns 'having eaten' (EB -usi, Sl. -ьš- < *ŭsi-).

(g) WB has some significant old lexical contrasts with EB: cf. OPr. mentimai 'we tell lies' (Latin mentīre); seggit 'do' vs. Li. darýti; lauxnos 'stars', Li. žvaigždė; or emmens 'name', Li. var̃das. WB widdewu 'widow' is absent in EB. Note also, among number terms, OPr. ains (Li. víenas), OPr. newints (Li. deviñtas), OPr. tīrts (Li. trẽčias < *tretijas).

(h) IE *ei is reflected as ei everywhere in WB.

5. East Baltic. One can reconstruct a common EB as a fairly homogeneous language. Differences within EB have the character of a continuum, and are recent innovations (this is not true of differences between EB and WB). EB began to break up after about 600 CE, with the rapid phonological development of La.; but Li. remained conservative, or innovated differently and more slowly. The branches experienced different external influences from Germanic, Slavic, and Balto-Finnic. The phonological changes leading to La. were analogous to the changes which broke up Slavic unity during the same period (700–1100 CE), but they differ in details. These include: loss of final short vowels; shortening of long vowels; retraction and fixing of stress; iotations and palatalizations with varying structural results; and loss of tautosyllabic nasal consonants. In principle, these sound changes are spread out in continua in La. and Li. dialects. The most conservative dialects are in Li., and in the West. Li. and La. are further apart than the different Slavic languages: the two main Li. dialect groupings, Žemaitian and Aukštaitian, are as far apart as Eastern and Western Slavic.

[*See also* Indo-European Languages.]

BIBLIOGRAPHY

Ambrazas, Vytautas. 1997. *Lithuanian grammar.* Vilnius: Baltos Lankos.

Bopp, Franz. 1833. *Vergleichende Grammatik des Sanskrit, Zend, Griechischen, Lateinischen, Lithauischen, Gotischen und Deutschen,* vol. 1. Berlin: Dümmler.

Dini, Pietro V. 1997. *Le lingue baltiche.* Florence: La Nuova Italia.

Endzelīns, Jānis. 1923. *Lettische Grammatik.* Heidelberg: Winter.

Endzelīns, Jānis. 1971. *Comparative phonology and morphology of the Baltic languages.* The Hague: Mouton.

Fraenkel, Ernst. 1950. *Die baltischen Sprachen.* Heidelberg: Winter.

Gimbutas, Marija. 1963. *The Balts.* London: Thames and Hudson. New York: Praeger.

Schmalstieg, William R. 1974. *An Old Prussian grammar: The phonology and morphology of the three catechisms.* University Park: Pennsylvania State University Press.

Senn, Alfred. 1957. *Handbuch der litauischen Sprache,* vol. 1, *Grammatik.* Heidelberg: Winter.

Stang, Christian S. 1966. *Vergleichende Grammatik der baltischen Sprachen.* Oslo: Universitetsforlaget.

Trautmann, Reinhold. 1923. *Baltisch-slavisches Wörterbuch.* Göttingen: Vandenhoeck und Ruprecht.

JULES F. LEVIN

LANGUAGE LIST

Latvian: also called Latviska. "Lettish," "Lettisch" are derogatory names sometimes used. Over 1,500,000 speakers in Latvia, Estonia, Australia, Belarus, Brazil, Canada, Germany, Lithuania, New Zealand, European Russia, Sweden, Ukraine, United Kingdom, USA, and Venezuela. In Latvia: 1,394,000 speakers. Dialects are West Latvian (Central Latvian), East Latvian (High Latvian, Latgalian). Tamian is a subdialect of West Latvian. Roman script. National language. In Estonia: Ethnic population: 3,135 as of 1989.

Lithuanian: also called Liutuviskai, Lietuvi, Litovskiy, Litewski, Litauische. 4,000,000 speakers in Lithuania, Estonia, Argentina, Australia, Belarus, Brazil, Canada, Kazachstan, Kyrgyzstan, Latvia, Poland, European Russia, Sweden Tajikistan, Turkmenistan, United Kingdom, Uruguay, USA, and Uzbekistan. In Lithuania: 2,955,200 speakers. Dialects are Aukshtaitish (Aukshtaichiai, Aukstaitiskai, Highland Lithuanian), Dzukish (Dzukiskai), Shamaitish (Samogitian, Zhemaitish, Zemaitis, Zemaitiskai, Zemachiai, Lowland Lithuanian), Suvalkietiskai. Aukshtaitish speakers can understand Suvalkietiskai easily, Dzukish with a little diffi-culty, and Dzukish speakers can understand Aukshtaitish with a little difficulty. Shamaitish is difficult for all others to understand. Second languages Russian or English used with foreigners. All ages. All domains. Highlanders look down on lowlanders. Some speakers have reserved attitudes toward Russian and Polish. Roman script. National language. In Estonia: Ethnic population: 2,568 as of 1989.

Prussian: also called Old Prussian. Formerly spoken in Poland in eastern Prussia, which was formerly part of Germany, but is now part of Poland and Russia. Among other extinct Baltic languages are Selonian, Yotvingian, Semigallian, Curonian. Became extinct the end of the 17th or beginning of the 18th century.

B. GRIMES

BALTO-SLAVIC. *See* Baltic Languages *and* Slavic Languages.

BAMBARA-MANINKA-JULA. Bambara, Maninka (also spelled Mandinka), and Jula (also known as Malinke) are the three languages with the largest number of speakers of a group of languages collectively called Mandekan. They are spoken from the coast of Senegal into Burkina Faso, and from northern Mali to the coast of Côte d'Ivoire. They are part of the Northern Mande branch of Mande, a branch of Niger-Congo. Bambara, locally called Bamanakan, Maninka, and Jula (BMJ), are largely mutually intelligible, with up to 90% clear cognates in the core vocabulary. Bambara is spoken as a first language by approximately 3 million people, Maninka by 2.5 million, and Jula by 2.5 million; however, all three are used as languages of wider communication, so a conservative estimate is that 14 million people speak BMJ as either a first or auxiliary language. BMJ is spreading, with Bambara expanding in Mali and Jula in Côte d'Ivoire, replacing other languages for wider communication (e.g. Fula in Mali).

1. Writing systems. BMJ has been written in a variety of Latin-based alphabets since at least the 19th century, but the current phoneme-based writing system was first codified (for Bambara) in 1967, with a few subsequent modifications. In older texts, *è* or *ë* is used for ɛ; *ò* or *ö* is used for ɔ; *ng* is used for ŋ, and *ny* is used for ɲ; however, the current system uses the phonetic symbols rather than the accented letters, *ng*, and *ny*. In addition, the older system always used an *n* following a vowel to indicate that the vowel is nasal; the current system uses a following *n* to indicate nasality only when the vowel does not follow a nasal consonant. For example, the

FIGURE 1. *N'Ko Alphabet*

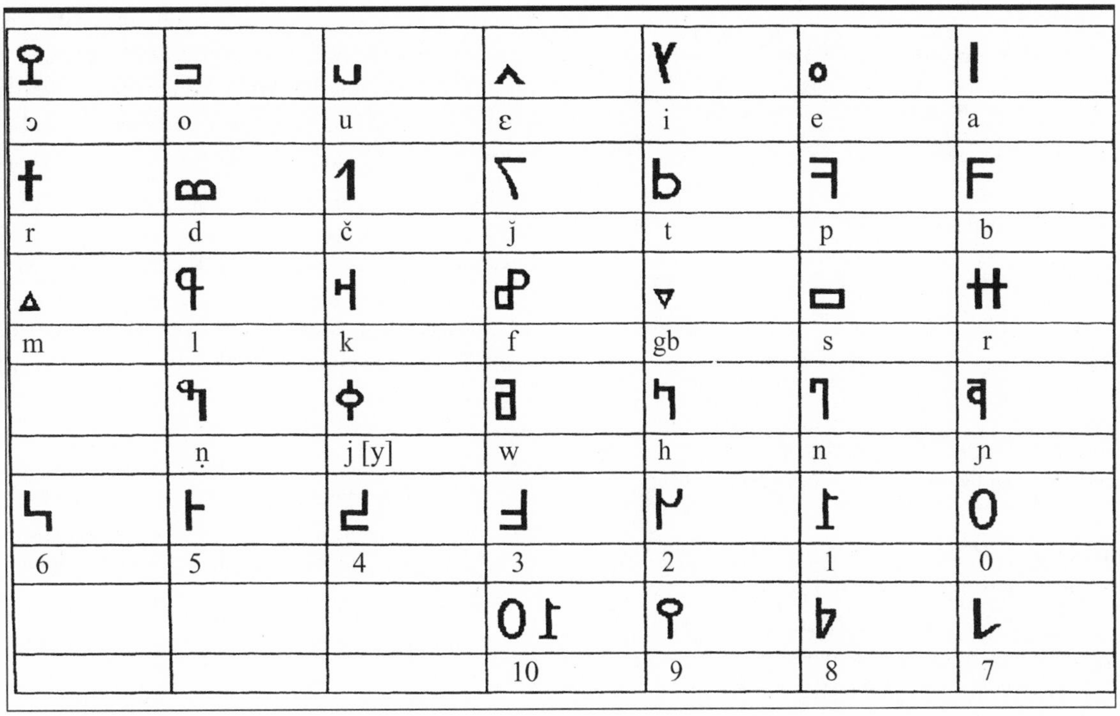

ɔ	o	u	ɛ	i	e	a
r	d	č	ǰ	t	p	b
m	l	k	f	gb	s	r
	n̦	j [y]	w	h	n	ɲ
6	5	4	3	2	1	0
			10	9	8	7

TABLE 1. *Consonants in BMJ*

	Labial	Alveolar	Alveo-palatal	Velar	Labio-velar	Glottal
Stops	p b	t d	c (j)	k,g	(gb)	
Fricatives	f (v)	s (z)	(sh)	(x)		h
Nasals	m	n	ɲ	ŋ	(ŋm)	
Liquids		l r				
Glides	w		y			

Bambara language name in the older system is spelled *bamanankan*, while it is *bamanakan* in the newer system. Tones are not indicated in this system.

In addition to the Latin-based alphabet, BMJ can be written in the N'Ko (literally 'I say') script, which was developed for Maninka in 1949 by Souleymane Kanté and has clear roots in both Arabic and Latin scripts. During the 1990s, it became increasingly popular through grass-roots literacy campaigns. Tones and vowel length are indicated by diacritics in this system.

2. Phonology. The segmental inventory of BMJ varies somewhat across dialects but is essentially as given in Tables 1 and 2. Segments subject to significant variation (i.e., that may or may not be present phonemically) are listed in parentheses. Vowel length is distinctive, with long vowels represented in the practical orthography by

TABLE 2. *Vowels in BMJ*

Front	Back
i, ii, in	u, uu, un
e, ee, en	o, oo, on
(ɛ, ɛɛ, ɛn)	(ɔ, ɔɔ, ɔn)
a, aa, an	

doubling the vowels. Nasal vowels can be phonemic, indicated by a following *n*.

BMJ are also tonal languages, with a system of two lexical tones. This tonal system shows little dialectal variation.

Syllables in BMJ are always open, with the exception of a syllabic nasal 1st person singular pronoun. Clusters of nasal plus homorganic stop or continuant occur

TABLE 3. *Number Systems of Bambara*

	Old	New
10	*tan*	*tan*
20	*mugan*	*mugan*
30	*mugan ni tan*	*bi-saba*
40	*dɛbɛ*	*bi-naani*
50	*dɛbɛ ni tan*	*bi-duuru*
60	*manin-kɛmɛ*	*bi-wɔɔrɔ*
70	*maninkɛmɛ*	*bi-wolonwula*
80	*kɛmɛ*	*bi-segin*
90	*kɛmɛ ni tan*	*bi-kɔnɔntɔn*
100	*kɛmɛ ni mugan*	*kɛmɛ*

syllable-initially, both word-initially and word-medially. Clusters of stop and continuant occur word-initially but not medially.

3. Morphology. BMJ is exclusively suffixing, but with little inflection, the only inflectional suffixes being aspect markers. There are no agreement, gender, class, or case markers. There is a more extensive system of some 25 derivational suffixes, used primarily for creating nouns from nouns, adjectives, and verbs.

One notable feature is an arguably passive alternation that is not indicated by any morphology, as shown in (1):

(1)   Active and "passive"
       Active
       n ma   jara faga
       I completive.negative lion kill
       'I didn't kill the lion.'

       Passive
       jara ma   faga
       lion completive.negative kill
       'The lion was not killed.'

Another feature of note is a reduplication construction *X o X* (e.g. *don o don* 'every/whatever day'), which was used in Culy 1985 to argue that the vocabulary of Bambara is not context-free.

4. Syntax. Word order in BMJ is very rigid. Sentence order is S Aux O V PP Adv. Just as the verb separates its modifiers, so too does the noun separate its modifiers, with the order Possessor N Adj Determiner Plural. Alienable possession is indicated by a linker between the possessor and the possessum; inalienable possession is indicated by juxtaposition. BMJ has postpositions, but subordinating conjunctions and complementizers precede their clauses, with complement clauses occurring clause-

finally. Relative clauses are primarily sentence-initial correlatives; sentence-final correlatives also occur. A sentence-internal relative is only rarely attested and may be a recent borrowing from French. Interrogative words are in situ. BMJ has distinct conjunctive ('and') coordinators for nouns (*ani, ni*) and verb phrases (*ka*, used only with a following non-finite verb). Finally, some varieties have no distinct reflexive pronouns, while others have only one (*i*, 'himself/herself'). Bambara examples follow:

(2)   *Madu be   saga ba   w   di jɔn ma*
      Madu incompletive sheep large plural give who to

      sini?
      tomorrow

      'Who will Madu give a sheep to tomorrow?'

(3)   *Mariama ani Madu be   taa sugu la ka*
      Mariama and Madu incompletive go market to and

      na.
      come

      'Mariama and Madu are going to the market and coming back.'

(4)   *den   min   y'   a   tigɛ, o*
      child relative completive (s)he cut   that

      ma   kasi.
      completive.negative cry

      'The child who cut himself/herself didn't cry.'

5. Number systems. The Bambara (see Table 3) and Maninka number systems illustrate some interesting points. The number systems have changed from base 80 (Bambara) and base 60 (Maninka) to base 100 over the past century or so. Both systems show the cognitive salience of the notion of base: the same word, *kɛmɛ*, is used for 80 in the old system and for 100 in the new. The older Bambara system also shows the cultural differentiation between Bambara and Maninka: the word for 60 in the older system is literally 'the *kɛmɛ* of the Maninka', showing that the Maninka used a base 60 number system.

[*See also* Mande Languages *and* Niger-Congo Languages.]

BIBLIOGRAPHY

Bimson, Kent D. Comparative reconstruction of Mandekan. *Studies in African Linguistics* 7.295–351.
Bird, Charles S. 1982. *The dialects of Mandekan.* Bloomington: Indiana University Press.
Bird, Charles, John Hutchison, and Mamadou Kanté. 1977. *An*

ka Bamanankan kalan: Beginning Bambara. Bloomington: Indiana University Linguistics Club.

Bird, Charles, and Mamadou Kanté. 1977. *An ka Bamanankan kalan: Intermediate Bambara*. Bloomington: Indiana University Linguistics Club.

Culy, Christopher. 1985. The complexity of the vocabulary of Bambara. *Linguistics and Philosophy* 8.345–351; repr. in *The formal complexity of language*, edited by Emmon Bach et al., pp. 349–357 (Boston: Dordrecht, 1987).

Dalby, David. 1969. Further indigenous scripts of West Africa: Manding, Wolof and Fula alphabets and Yoruba "holy" writing. *African Language Studies* 10.161–181.

Dumester, Gérard. 1998. Le bambara véhiculaire du Mali. *Faits de Languages* 11–12.121–28.

Rialland, Annie, and Mamadou Badjimé. 1989. Réanalyse des tons du bambara: Des tons du nom à l'organisation générale du système. *Studies in African Linguistics* 20.1–28.

CHRISTOPHER CULY

BANDJALANG is a language constituting an independent branch of the PAMA-NYUNGAN family, also called Bandjelang, Bogganger, Bundala, Gidabal, Yugumbe. 10 speakers remain in Australia in New South Wales, northeastern Woodenbong. Dialects are Gidabal (Gidhabal), Yugumbir. All speakers are bilingual in English.

B. GRIMES

BANTOID LANGUAGES. These constitute a group that covers most of Africa east and south of the southern part of the Nigeria-Cameroon border; they form one of the branches of the BENUE-CONGO LANGUAGES.

[*For language lists, see the entries on* North Bantoid Languages *and on* South Bantoid Languages.] The languages listed below are unclassified within Bantoid.

LANGUAGE LIST

Áncá: also called Bunta. Spoken in Nigeria in state of Taraba, Sardauna LGA, Antere, Nca village.

Buru: spoken in Nigeria in state of Taraba, Sardauna LGA, east of Baissa, a village near Batu.

Kwak: also called Bùkwák. Spoken in Nigeria in state of Taraba, Sardauna LGA, Antere.

Nshi: spoken in Nigeria in sate of Taraba, Sardauna LGA, Antere, Nkiri.

B. GRIMES

BANTU LANGUAGES. "Bantu" traditionally refers to the Narrow Bantu languages, which cover the southern half of Africa, extending from their presumed area of origin in eastern Nigeria to southern Somalia in the northeast, and southward to South Africa, including both the east and west coasts (see Map 1). Recently, "Bantu" has been extended to Narrow Bantu's closest relatives, the other South Bantoid languages, under the label "Wide Bantu" or "Broad Bantu." Its major groupings are Grassfields, Mbam, Beboid, and Mamfe in Cameroon, and Ekoid, Tivoid, Tikar, and Jarawan in Nigeria. The Narrow Bantu languages dominate central and southern Africa, comprising slightly less than a third of Africa's total population, with more than 400 language varieties, nearly 50 of them spoken by more than a million people each. Major languages include Bemba, Chokwe, Duala, Gikuyu (Kikuyu), Kamba, Kimbundu (Mbundu), Kongo, Lingala, Luba, Luganda (Ganda), Luhya (Luyia), Makua, Mongo, Nyamwezi-Sukuma, Nyanja, Nyarwanda (Rwanda), Rundi, Shona, Sotho, Swahili, Thonga (Tsonga), Tswana, Umbundu, Xhosa, Yao, and Zulu—mostly eastern or centrally located. Although these languages are not mutually intelligible, large areas within the Bantu realm form dialect continua. Bantu speakers generally recognize the linguistic affinity of their own languages to other Bantu languages, even without mutual intelligibility—in contrast to the coterritorial non-Bantu languages found in some areas. Swahili, Lingala, and Fanagalo (a pidginized form of Zulu) serve as lingua francas for large numbers of speakers. (For reference, see Doke 1945, Guthrie 1948, 1967–1971, Meussen 1967, Bryan 1959, Greenberg 1963, Welmers 1973, and Hinnebusch 1989.) The Broad Bantu languages show great diversity but are confined to southwestern Cameroon and adjacent eastern Nigeria. Among them, only Tiv in Nigeria and the Bamileke complex in Cameroon have more than a million speakers. The westernmost group, Jarawan, extends well into the Nigerian plateau.

Genetically, there is consensus that Bantu is a deep member of the Niger-Congo family. It can be classified within, successively, the Atlantic-Congo, Volta-Congo, Benue-Congo, Bantoid, and South Bantoid (Broad Bantu) groupings. The South Bantoid period of unity is assumed to have ended in the current Broad Bantu area around the Nigeria-Cameroon border long before the great southern and eastern spread and diversification of Narrow Bantu. Nevertheless, Narrow Bantu appears to preserve the earliest phonological and grammatical features of South Bantoid more generally than does Broad Bantu.

Historically, Bantu languages have a relatively simple phonology; words consist of open syllables, though a syllable may include prenasalized consonants like *mb* and *nd*. High and low tones are distinctive in most languages. Naturally, this reconstructed state of affairs

MAP 1. *Distribution of Major Bantu Languages.* Note that only languages mentioned in the text (over 1 million speakers) are indicated on the map. More than 100 other Bantu languages are spoken throughout the area by smaller populations. Only central locations of languages are indicated. Most are more widely spoken (or understood). Other languages (usually Bantu) are spoken in areas indicating a major Bantu language. As a second language, Swahili is spoken throughout East Africa as far west as eastern Zaire, north to southern coastal Somalia, south to northern Mozambique, and east to islands adjacent to the East African coast, including northern Madagascar.

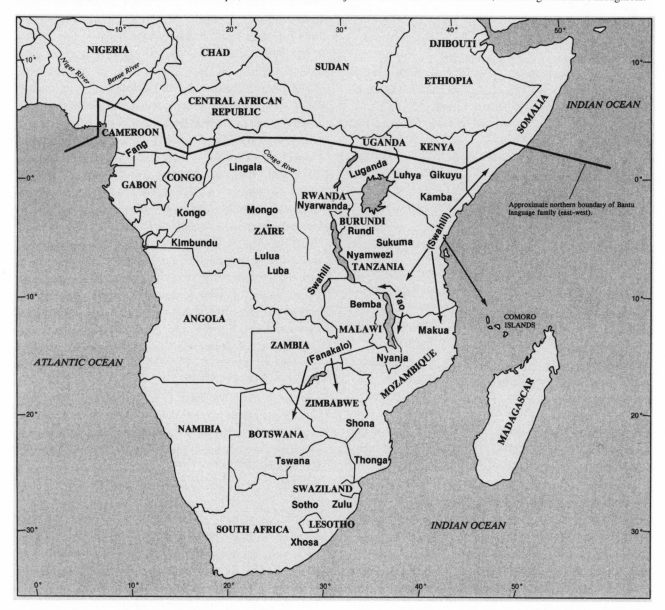

has been somewhat complicated by changes in individual languages. Yet most languages have simplified further by merging ancient long vowels with short ones, and by reducing the seven-vowel system to five. Even tone, once apparently distinctive for each syllable, has been reduced to one distinctive tone per word in many languages.

Despite the large geographical domain, most Bantu languages display a remarkable degree of grammatical homogeneity. Most characteristic are the classification of nouns into a large number of classes, the influence of these classes on concord in a number of other grammatical categories, and the inflectional and derivational complexity of the verb. For the most part, noun and verb morphology is transparently agglutinative.

The complexity of the noun class system and the principles of class concord are the features of Bantu which were earliest recognized by linguists. All Bantu languages have a set of noun classes, usually signaled by a class prefix marking a nominal stem. Many classes come in singular/plural pairs. Thus, in Gikuyu, *mũ-* is a common class prefix for singular human nouns, with a corresponding plural *a-,* e.g., *mũ-ndũ* 'person', *a-ndũ* 'people'; another pair is *kĩ-ndũ* 'thing', *i-ndũ* 'things'. Most languages have at least six pairs of classes. A semantic basis for the classes is discernible primarily in deverbal and other forms of nominal derivation (e.g. diminutive or augmentative), but is sometimes obscure for non-derived lexical items. By patterns of class concord, a morpheme phonologically identical or similar to a noun's class prefix is extended to cross-reference grammatical categories such as subject and object markers of a verb, or noun modifiers (e.g. demonstratives, quantifiers, numerals, and adjectives).

The morphological composition of the verb suggests that the word order S[ubject] O[bject] V[erb] AUX[iliary] can be reconstructed for Pre-Bantu. Thus the typical Bantu verb has an obligatory subject marker followed by one or more tense/aspect prefixes, (optionally) one or more derivational suffixes, (possibly) one or more aspect suffixes, and an obligatory modal marker which distinguishes subjunctive from other modalities. The verb prefixes are usually monosyllabic, and those cross-referencing nouns agree with the noun in class. Syntactically, Bantu word order is overwhelmingly, but not rigidly, S AUX V O and Head + Modifier.

Pervasive in Bantu is the dynamic role played by the word in many phonological and morphological processes. Phonologically, for most of Bantu, a form of vowel harmony applies to certain derivational suffixes: a mid-vowel suffix is selected following a mid-vowel verb stem. Thus, in Gikuyu, the reversive suffix *-ũra* applied to the verb root *hing-* 'close' results in *hing-ũra* 'open'; but applied to the verb *oh-* 'tie', it results in *oh-ora* 'untie'. Similarly, but in a more limited area, some languages display a dissimilation of voiceless stops in consecutive syllables (a pattern called Dahl's Law by Bantuists). Thus, in Gikuyu, the class prefix *kĩ-* (as in *kĩ-rĩma* 'mountain') becomes *gĩ-* as in *gĩ-kũyũ* 'Gikuyu'. Morphologically, the dynamic role played by the word is illustrated by the restriction of object and tense/aspect markers in Eastern Bantu. Originally, the number of object markers and tense/aspect prefixes which could be affixed to the verb was determined solely by the respective semantics of the verb and the clause. This is still true in many languages; e.g., in Umbundu, the object markers *-u-* 'him/her' and *-n-* 'me' can be concatenatively prefixed to a verb like *-lekisa* 'show' which allows two objects, resulting in *-u-n-dekisa* 'show him/her to me'. But most

Eastern coastal languages, including Swahili, allow only one object marker per verb. Similarly, verb derivational suffixes, also called "extensions," commonly concatenate where it is semantically appropriate. Thus, Swahili *chek-esh-ana* extends the verb root 'laugh' with the causative and reciprocal extensions to form 'make each other laugh'. Alone, the causative *chek-esha* means 'make laugh' and the reciprocal (or collective) *chek-ana* means 'laugh together' or 'laugh at each other'. Some Bantu languages also concatenate various tense/aspect prefixes, but many others restrict these prefixes to one per verb, using a preverbal auxiliary instead of a second prefix when necessary. For example, some Northern Swahili dialects concatenate *-li-* 'past' and *-ki-* 'imperfect', as in *a-li-ki-enda* 'he used to go', but most forms of Swahili use a compound verb construction in which the first prefix is attached to an auxiliary, in this case *(ki-)wa* 'be(come)', giving *a-li-kuwa a-ki-enda*.

Semantically, Bantu languages are notable for the number of distinctions made among tenses. Two degrees of past and future, 'near' and 'more remote', are very common. Up to four degrees of past are not rare—adding 'just past', and distinguishing 'today' from other 'near'.

[*See also* African Languages; Narrow Bantu Languages; Niger-Congo Languages; *and* Swahili.]

BIBLIOGRAPHY

Bastin, Yvonne. 1978. Les langues bantoues. In *Inventaire des études linguistiques sur les pays d'Afrique Noire d'expression française et sur Madagascar,* edited by Daniel Barreteau, pp. 123–186. Paris: Conseil International de la Langue Française.

Bryan, Margaret A., ed. 1959. *The Bantu languages of Africa.* London and New York: Oxford University Press.

Doke, Clement M. 1945. *Bantu: Modern grammatical, phonetical and lexicographical studies since 1860.* London: International African Institute. Reprinted, 1967.

Greenberg, Joseph H. 1963. *The languages of Africa.* (Indiana University Research Center in Anthropology, Folklore, and Linguistics, publication 25; International Journal of American Linguistics, 29:1, part 2.) Bloomington: Indiana University.

Guthrie, Malcolm. 1948. *The classification of Bantu languages.* London and New York: Oxford University Press. Reprinted, 1967.

Guthrie, Malcolm. 1967–1971. *Comparative Bantu.* 4 vols. Farnborough, England: Gregg.

Heine, Bernd, and Derek Nurse, eds. 2000. *African languages.* Cambridge: Cambridge University Press.

Hinnebusch, Thomas J. 1989. Bantu. In *The Niger-Congo languages,* edited by John Bendor-Samuel and Rhonda L. Hartell, pp. 450–473. Lanham, Md.: University Press of America.

Hombert, Jean-Marie, and Larry M. Hyman, eds. 1999. *Bantu*

historical linguistics: Theoretical and empirical perspectives. Stanford, Calif.: CSLI Publications.

Meussen, A. E. 1967. Bantu grammatical reconstructions. *Annalen van het Koninklijk Museum voor Midden-Afrika* 61.79–121.

Welmers, William E. 1973. *African language structures.* Berkeley: University of California Press.

BENJI WALD

LANGUAGE LIST

[*See the language lists under* Narrow Bantu, *which distinguish sixteen traditional 'zones' or subgroups, referred to by the letters A–H, J–N, P, R, and S.*] The languages listed below are unclassified within Narrow Bantu.

Bemba: also called Kinyabemba. Spoken in Democratic Republic of Congo, southern Kivu Province.

Isanzu: 32,400 speakers in Tanzania, Iramba district of Singida region.

Songa: also called Kisonga. Spoken in Democratic Republic of Congo, southern Kivu Province.

Songo: also called Kisongo, Itsong. Spoken in Democratic Republic of Congo, Bandundu Province, Bulungu territory. Possibly also in Angola.

B. GRIMES

BARBACOAN LANGUAGES. These constitute a language family spoken in Colombia and Ecuador.

LANGUAGE LIST

Andaqui: also called Andaki. Formerly spoken in Colombia in the southern highlands.

Awa-Cuaiquer: also called Coaiquer, Quaiquesar, Kwaiker, Cuaiquer, Awa, Awa Pit. 21,000 speakers in Colombia and Ecuador. In Colombia: 20,000 speakers. Pacific slopes of the Andes, Nariño, from Ecuador border north, near Barbacoas. Some bilingualism in Spanish. Mainly women and children speakers are monolingual. In Ecuador: 1,000 speakers. Ethnic population: 1,600 to 3,500 as of 2000. Extreme north, on the western slopes of the Andes, Colombia-Ecuador border, Carchi Province. More distantly related to Chachi and Colorado.

Barbacoas: formerly spoken in Colombia near the coastal town of Barbacoas, Nariño.

Chachi: also called Cayapa, Cha' Palaachi. 3,450 speakers in Ecuador. Ethnic population: as of 2000, estimated at either 3,500 to 5,000, or 7,000 to 8,000. Northern coastal jungle, Esmeraldas Province, Cayapas River and its tributaries (Onzole, Canandé, Sucio, Cojimíes, and others). Some bilingualism in Spanish. Women, older people, and those living in the isolated headwaters of the river are less bilingual in Spanish.

FIGURE 1. *Subgrouping of Barbacoan Languages*

Andaqui
Cayapa-Colorado
Chachi, Colorado
Coconucan
Guambiano, Totoro
Pasto
Awa-Cuaiquer, Barbacoas

Colorado: also called Tsachila, Tsafiki. 2,300 speakers in Ecuador. Ethnic population: 2,300 as of 2000. Northwestern jungle west of Quito, around Santo Domingo de los Colorados.

Guambiano: also called Namdrik, Guambia, Moguex. 12,000 speakers in Colombia. Ethnic population: 12,000 to 15,000 as of 2000. Central Andes Range near Popayán, Caucá, in concentrated areas. Fewer than 10% are monolingual, over 90% also speak limited Spanish. All domains, including oral and written local administration. Parents transmit Guambiano to children. People support the language.

Totoro: 4 speakers in Colombia. Ethnic population: 3,650 as of 1998. 17 km west of Silvia, Cauca, in town of Totoro.

B. GRIMES

BARITO LANGUAGES. These languages are spoken in the southeast of the island of Borneo (Kalimantan, Indonesia), but also include Malagasy (Madagascar). They form a branch of the BORNEO LANGUAGES.

LANGUAGE LIST

Ampanang: 30,000 speakers in east central Kalimantan, southeast of Tunjung, around Jambu and Lamper.

Bakumpai: also called Bara-Jida. 40,000 speakers in Kalimantan, Kapuas and Barito Rivers, northeast of Kualakapuas. Dialects are Bakumpai, Mengkatip (Mangkatip, Oloh Mengkatip). Related to Ngaju, Kahayan, Katingan.

Bushi: also called Shibushi, Kibushi, Kibuki, Sakalava, Antalaotra. 39,200 speakers in Mayotte. Dialects are Kibushi Kiatalaotsy, Kibushi Kimaore (Shibushi Shimaore). Kibushi is the Malagasy variety spoken in Mayotte. There are two to four dialects.

Dohoi: also called Ot Danum, Uut Danum, Uud Danum. 80,000 speakers in Kalimantan, extensive area south of the Schwaner Range on the upper reaches of south Borneo rivers. The Ulu Ai' are on the Mandai River with seven villages. Dialects are Ot Balawan, Ot Banu'u, Ot Murung 1 (Murung 1, Punan Ratah), Ot Olang, Ot Tuhup, Sarawai (Melawi), Dohoi, Ulu Ai' (Da'an).

Dusun Deyah: also called Deah, Dejah. 20,000 speakers in

FIGURE 1. *Subgrouping of Barito Languages*

East Barito
  Central-South Barito
    Central Barito
      Dusun Deyah
    South Barito
      Dusun Malang, Dusun Witu, Ma'anyan, Paku
  Malagasy
    Bushi, Antankarana Malagasy, Baba Malagasy, Northern
  Malagasy
    Betsimisaraka, Southern Malagasy Betsimisaraka,
  Masikoro Malagasy, Merina
      Malagasy, Northern Malagasy Sakalava, Southern
  Malagasy, Tandroy Malagasy, Tsimehety Malagasy
  North Barito
    Lawangan
Mahakam
  Ampanang, Tunjung
West Barito
  North West Barito
    Dohoi, Kohin, Siang
  South West Barito
    Bakumpai, Kahayan, Katingan, Ngaju

southeastern Kalimantan, Tabalong River northeast of Bongkang.

Dusun Malang: 10,000 speakers in east central Kalimantan, west of Muarainu, northeast of Muarateweh. Closest to Ma'anyan, Paku, Dusun Witu, and Malagasy.

Dusun Witu: 25,000 speakers in southeastern Kalimantan, regions of Pendang and Buntokecil; south of Muarateweh. Closest to Ma'anyan, Paku, Dusun Malang, Malagasy.

Kahayan: also called Kahaian, Kahajan. 45,000 speakers in Kalimantan, Kapuas and Kahayan Rivers, south central, northeast of Ngaju. Related to Ngaju, Katingan, and Bakumpai.

Katingan: 45,000 speakers in Kalimantan, south central Katingan River. Related to Ngaju, Kahayan, and Bakumpai.

Kohin: also called Seruyan. 3,000 speakers in Kalimantan, Kotawaringin Timur district, along the central and northern Seruyan River, ten villages.

Lawangan: also called Luwangan, Northeast Barito. 120,000 speakers in east central Kalimantan, around the Karau River. Dialects are Tabuyan (Taboyan, Tabojan, Tabojan Tongka), Ajuh, Bakoi (Lampung), Bantian (Bentian), Banuwang, Bawu, Kali, Karau (Beloh), Lawa, Lolang, Mantararen, Njumit, Purai, Purung, Tuwang, Pasir, Benua.

Ma'anyan: also called Maanyak Dayak, Ma'anjan, Siang. 70,000 speakers in southern Kalimantan around Tamianglayang, area of the drainage of Patai River. Dialects are Samihim (Buluh Kuning), Sihong (Siong), Dusun Balangan. Related to Merina Malagasy in Madagascar, Africa.

Malagasy, Antankarana: also called Antankarana, Antankarina-Malagasy. 88,000 speakers in northern tip of Madagascar, Antananarivo.

Malagasy, Baba: 520,000 speakers in southern Madagascar.

Malagasy, Masikoro: also called Masikoro-Malagasy. 90,000 speakers in southwestern Madagascar, Toliara Province, Toliara and Morombe districts.

Malagasy, Merina: also called Malgache, Standard Malagasy, Merina-Malagasy. 5,130,700 speakers in Madagascar, Comoros Islands, and Réunion. In Madagascar: 5,122,000 speakers on the central part of the Island. Dialects are Merina, Taisaka (Antaisaka, Tesaka), Tsimanambondro (Antaimanambondro), Sahafatra, Taifasy (Tefasy, Antaifasy), Tambahoaka (Antambahoaka), Zafisoro, Sihanaka, Bezanozano (Antaiva, Antanka, Tankay), Tanala (Antanala, Menabe-Ikongo), Betsileo, Tañalaña, Antankarana (Tankarana), Taimoro (Antaimoro, Temoro). The closest language outside of Madagascar is Ma'anyan in southern Borneo (Kalimantan, Indonesia). The Merina dialect was the first to be written in Latin characters and it has become the literary dialect. National language. In Comoros Islands: Most are bilingual in Comorian. It is spoken by a substantial number of residents of Madagascar origin.

Malagasy, Southern: also called Southern-Malagasy. 1,586,000 speakers on southern tip of Madagascar. Dialects are Tanosy, Vezo, Mahafaly, Karimbola, Ta-Flala-Fla.

Malagasy, Tandroy: also called Ntandroy, Antandroy, Tandroy-Malagasy. 500,000 speakers in southern Madagascar, Toliara Province, Beloha, Tsihombe, and Ambovombe, Bekily districts.

Malagasy, Tsimehety: also called Tsimihety, Tsimehetry, Tsimihety-Malagasy. 1,016,000 speakers in north central Madagascar.

Malagasy Betsimisaraka, Northern: 900,000 speakers on east coast of Madagascar, Toamasina Province, Mananara, Avaratra, Soanierana Ivongo, Fenoarivo Antsinana, Vavatenina, Toamasina districts.

Malagasy Betsimisaraka, Southern: 600,000 speakers on east coast of Madagascar, Toamasina Province, Mahanoro district; Fianarantsoa Province, Nosy Varika, Mananjary, Manakara Atsimo districts.

Malagasy Sakalava, Northern: also called Northern Sakalava-Malagasy. 350,000 speakers in Madagascar.

Ngaju: also called Ngadju, Ngaju Dayak, Biadju, Southwest Barito. 250,000 speakers in Kalimantan, Kapuas, Kahayan, Katingan, and Mentaya Rivers, south. Dialects are Pulopetak, Kapuas (Ngaju, Bara-Dia), Ba'amang (Bara-Bare, Sampit), Mantangai (Oloh Mangtangai). Related to Katingan, Kahayan, Bakumpai. Trade language for most of Kalimantan, from the Barito to the Sampit Rivers, east of the Barito languages, and north in the Malawi River region. Trade language.

Paku: 20,000 speakers in southeastern Kalimantan, south of

Ampah. Closest to Ma'anyan, Malagasy, Dusun Malang, Dusun Witu.

Siang: also called Ot Siang. 60,000 speakers in central Kalimantan, east of Dohoi. Dialects are Siang, Murung 2. Related to Dohoi.

Tunjung: also called Tunjung Dayak. 50,000 speakers in east central Kalimantan, between Adas, Dempar, Melak, and east around the lake; south around Muntaiwan. Dialects are Tunjung (Tunjung Tengah), Tunjung Londong, Tunjung Linggang, Pahu.   B. GRIMES

BARRIERS. *See* Principles and Parameters.

BASE. *See* Morphology; Formal Grammar; *and* Transformations.

BASQUE. A non-Indo-European language, Basque is spoken by close to 1 million people in the western Pyrenees—more precisely, in a 50-kilometer coastal strip extending from Bayonne, France, to Bilbao, Spain (see Map 1). For all the ink spent on its genetic affiliations over the past hundred years, the matter is still unclear. A few scholars hold Basque to be related to Afroasiatic (Hamito-Semitic); others (cf. Lafon 1972) claim genetic ties with the Kartvelian languages of the Caucasus. Most experts remain skeptical of both proposals. The once popular notion that Basque was a close relative of ancient Iberian has largely been abandoned; existing analogies seem to reflect areal phenomena rather than family resemblance. (For reference, see Lafon 1972, Michelena 1977, Echenique 1983, Rebuschi 1984, 1997, Aulestia 1989, Hualde and Ortiz de Urbina 1990, Hualde, Lakarra, and Trask 1995, Trask 1997.)

Of the eight Basque dialects, four have been used in literature: Guipuzcoan, Biscayan, Navarro-Labourdin, and Souletin. Adult speakers today are bilingual, their other language being that of their official nationality, French or Spanish. In the New World, to which many Basques have emigrated, Basque/English bilingualism occurs.

Numerous loanwords have been integrated into Basque, mainly but not exclusively from Latin and the surrounding Romance languages: e.g. *errege* 'king', *lege* 'law', *eliza* 'church', *liburu* 'book', *zeru* 'sky', *dorre* 'tower', *katu* 'cat', *gaztelu* 'castle'. There are also a number of early loans from Celtic, e.g. *adar* 'horn', *hartz* 'bear',

maite 'dear', *mando* 'mule', *hogei* 'twenty', *-tegi* 'hut'. The language still occasionally resorts to borrowing to cope with the novelties of modern life. However, its rich system of nominal derivation and composition generally succeeds in creating satisfactory terms to express new concepts in science and technology.

The rise of a standard language dates from 1968, when the Basque Academy, guided by the eminent linguist Luis Michelena (1915–1987), set out to create a standard dialect for written communication. This is called *Euskara Batua* "unified Basque." Since 1980, more than 80% of all Basque publications have been in this variety. With time, it may become a spoken standard as well; but given the strong attachment of most speakers to their local varieties, such a process is likely to take several generations.

1. Phonology. The Basque vowel system is very much like that of Castilian Spanish: *a e i o u*, without distinctive length. Only the northeastern varieties of Basque have developed a sixth vowel, *ü*. There are six diphthongs, all falling: *au eu ai ei oi ui*. The consonant system is shown in Table 1. (See Michelena 1976.)

Voiced *b d g* are subject to intervocalic spirantization and final devoicing. The nasals *m n* are neutralized in syllable-final position, where the result is dental, unless the following consonant determines otherwise. In most of the Basque-speaking area, an intervocalic nasal or lateral is realized as palatal after *i*. Otherwise, palatal *ñ* and *ll* occur only in place names and expressive forms.

The opposition between *rr* and *r* is quite similar to that of the corresponding phonemes in Castilian Spanish; they contrast only in intervocalic position. A noteworthy difference from Castilian is that Basque vibrants cannot begin a word (thus *Erroma* 'Rome'); this peculiarity is shared with the neighboring Romance dialects, Gascon and Aragonese.

A notable characteristic of Basque phonemics is the three-way contrast among sibilants and affricates. All sibilants and affricates are normally voiceless. The non-palatal affricates *tz ts* can be syllable-initial, but not word-initial.

The remaining consonants, *f j,* are restricted to syllable-initial position. Of the multifarious local pronunciations of *j*, two are common in the literary standard: semivocalic, like Eng. *y,* spread by Basque television; and velar, like Sp. *j*, borrowed from the Guipuzcoan dialect.

Dialects north of the French/Spanish border have a phoneme *h*, pronounced as in English; it occurs fre-

MAP 1. *Location of the Basque Language*

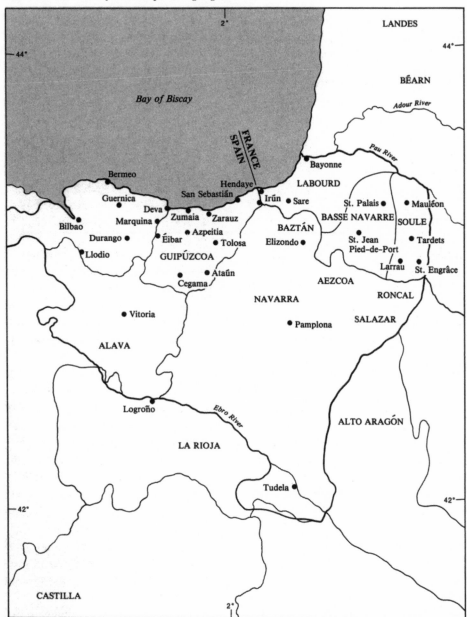

quently, but with fairly restricted distribution. Unless word-initial, it must follow a vowel, liquid, or *n*. In the same dialects, voiceless plosives can be aspirated in certain positions, usually at the beginning of the first or second syllable. The syllable division shows that the aspirates are not to be analyzed as clusters: *a-pho* 'toad' vs. *ol-ho* 'oats'. Since the great majority of Basque speakers lack *h*, the 1968 decision of the Basque Academy to include the letter in its standard orthography stirred controversy—even though the Academy agreed

to ban the writing of post-consonantal *h*, leaving it only in word-initial or intervocalic positions.

The eastern dialects have a stress system, the details of which vary considerably according to region. The sociolinguistically more important western dialects, Biscayan and Guipuzcoan, have a tonal system, remarkably uniform over the area; every phonological phrase shows either an unmarked level toneme or a marked falling one.

2. Nominal inflection operates through suffixation to an invariable base. Nouns and adjectives do not distin-

TABLE 1. *Basque Consonants in Standard Orthography*

	Labial	Dental	Dorso-alveolar	Apico-alveolar	Palatal	Velar	Glottal
Occlusives							
Voiceless	p	t	tz	ts	tx	k	
Voiced	b	d				g	
Fricatives	f		z	s	x		(h)
Nasals	m	n			(ñ)		
Vibrants							
Flap				r			
Trill				rr			
Lateral				l	(ll)		
Semivowel					j		

TABLE 2. *Basque Forms of* katu *'cat'*

	Indefinite	Definite Singular	Definite Plural
Absolute	*katu*	*katua*	*katuak*
Ergative	*katuk*	*katuak*	*katuek*
Dative	*katuri*	*katuari*	*katuei*
Genitive	*katuren*	*katuaren*	*katuen*
Benefactive	*katurentzat*	*katuarentzat*	*katuentzat*
Motivational	*katurengatik*	*katuarengatik*	*katuengatik*
Sociative	*katurekin*	*katuarekin*	*katuekin*
Instrumental	*katuz*	*katuaz*	*katuez*

TABLE 3. *Basque Locative Cases of* gaztelu *'castle' and* katu *'cat'*

	Indefinite	Definite Singular	Definite Plural
Inanimate nouns			
Inessive	*gaztelutan*	*gazteluan*	*gazteluetan*
Elative	*gaztelutatik*	*gaztelutik*	*gazteluetatik*
Allative	*gaztelutara*	*gaztelura*	*gazteluetara*
Terminal	*gaztelutaraino*	*gazteluraino*	*gazteluetaraino*
Tendential	*gaztelutarantz*	*gaztelurantz*	*gazteluetarantz*
Animate nouns			
Inessive	*katurengan*	*katuarengan*	*katuengan*
Elative	*katurengandik*	*katuarengandik*	*katuengandik*
Allative	*katurengana*	*katuarengana*	*katuengana*
Terminal	*katurenganaino*	*katuarenganaino*	*katuenganaino*
Tendential	*katurenganantz*	*katuarenganantz*	*katuenganantz*

guish gender or number; but articles and demonstratives display a singular/plural contrast. Thus, for each case inflection, there are an indefinite, a definite singular, and a definite plural form. In the non-locative cases, the indefinite marker is Ø, the definite marker is *-a,* and the plural marker is *-g* (elided with intervocalic, devoiced to *-k* in final position); the inflection of *katu* 'cat' is shown in Table 2. (See Aulestia 1989.)

Table 3 shows that, in the locative cases of inanimate nouns, the indefinite marker is *-ta-,* the definite marker Ø, and the plural marker *-eta*; however, the locative cases of animate nouns take a suffix *-gan* preceding these and affixed to the genitive, thus following the system of Table 2. (The "terminal" case can be glossed 'up to, until', and the tendential as 'toward'.)

Finally, the partitive case ending *-(r)ik* is reserved for otherwise absolutive indefinite N[oun] P[hrase]s in negative, interrogative, or conditional contexts:

TABLE 4. *Basque Verb Forms.* 'It' subsumes 'him' and 'her', 'he' subsumes 'she' and 'it'.

n-a-tor	*n-a-kar*	*da-kar-t*
'I'm coming'	'he's bringing me'	'I'm bringing it'
h-a-tor	*h-a-kar*	*da-kar-k*
'you're coming'	'he's bringing you'	'you're bringing it'
da-tor	*da-kar*	*da-kar*
'he's coming'	'he's bringing it'	'he's bringing it'

(1) *Hemen ez dago gaztelurik.*
     'There is no castle here.'

(2) *Ohostu al duzu katurik?*
     'Have you stolen any cat?'

Case endings in Basque do not percolate down into the constituent parts of a NP. Only the last word is inflected: *katu beltz batengatik* 'because of a black cat' (where the numeral *bat* 'one' serves as an indefinite article), *gaztelu zahar batzuetan* 'in some old castles'.

The genitive case, being adjectival, can be followed by the definite article *-a*; this serves as a pronoun whose reference is to be inferred from the context, e.g. *katuarena* 'the one of the cat'. The resulting NP may in turn take any case ending, including the genitive: *katuarenarekin* 'with the one of the cat', *katuarenarenei* 'to the ones of the one of the cat'. This kind of recursion has been misleadingly styled "hyperdeclension."

Spatial relationships are expressed by locative case forms of locational nouns, e.g. *aurre* 'front', *atze* 'back', and *ondo* 'proximity', constructed with the genitive: *gazteluaren aurrean* 'in front of the castle', *gaztelu baten ondoan* 'next to a castle', *katuen atzean* 'behind the cats', *katuen atzetik* 'after the cats'.

Gradable adjectives have a comparative form in *-ago,* a superlative in *-en,* and an excessive in *-egi*: *hotz* 'cold', *Bilbo baino hotzago* 'colder than Bilbao', *hotzena* 'the coldest', *hotzegi* 'too cold'.

3. Ergativity and verbal morphology. Before delving into the riches of verbal morphology—an 18th-century grammarian counted no fewer than 30,952 forms of a single verb—it must be noted that Basque is an ergative language. Subjects of intransitive verbs and direct objects of transitive ones are in the unmarked absolutive case; subjects of transitive verbs are in the ergative case, marked with *-(e)k*:

(3) *Jon dator* 'John is coming.'

(4) *Jonek Xixili dakar* 'John is bringing Cecily.'

The observation by Levin 1983 that all Basque intransitives with absolutive subject are "unaccusative" (cf. Perlmutter 1978) suggests that Basque ergativity stems from the absence of a mechanism to alter the initial object case of unaccusative objects. Some objectless verbs which require ergative subjects (e.g. *iraun* 'to last', *irakin* 'to boil', *distiratu* 'to glitter') are then explainable as 'unergative' verbs which take the regular subject case, i.e. the ergative.

Basque ergativity is not syntactic: in embeddings, co-ordinate clauses, reflexives, reciprocals, etc., absolutive subjects pair with ergative subjects, not with absolutive objects. However, the ergative is not restricted to case-marking; it also governs verbal morphology. The pattern of Table 4 is typical.

The prefixed absolutive markers *n- h- g- z-* derive from the personal pronouns: *ni* 'I', *hi* 'you (familiar)', *gu* 'we', *zu* 'you (polite)'. (Third person *da-* is a tense marker.) Ergative markers are suffixes: *-t* (from *-da*), *-k* (from *-ga*), *-gu, -zu.* This is the only area where gender is relevant: when the 2nd person familiar is female, the suffix *-na* appears instead of the unmarked *-ga* (used even by females soliloquizing).

Pervasive in the present tense, the ergative pattern is interrupted in the past tense and in tenses based on it; this has been interpreted by Heath 1977:197 as a relic of a former antipassivization rule. Little happens as long as the direct object remains 1st or 2nd person; but when it is 3rd person, the absolutive marker drops, and the ergative subject is marked by a prefix—thus *nekarren* 'I brought him', *genekarren* 'we brought him', *zenekarren* 'you brought him', as opposed to the ergative pattern of *nindekarzun* 'you brought me'. This morphological antipassivization, however, has no clause-level effects, since it affects neither word order nor case-marking.

Multipersonal verb agreement is characteristic of Basque: any finite verb form must agree in person and number with its subject, its direct object, and (in most dialects) also its indirect object. Since non-emphatic personal pronouns serving these functions are omitted, a finite verb preceded by the affirmative particle *ba-* or the negation *ez* can constitute a complete sentence:

(5a)   *Badakar* 'He is bringing it.'
(5b)   *Badakarte* 'They are bringing it.'
(5c)   *Badakartza* 'He is bringing them.'
(5d)   *Badakartzate* 'They are bringing them.'

An indirect object may also be expressed in the verb alone:

(6a)   *Badakarkio* 'He is bringing it to him.'
(6b)   *Badakarkiote* 'They are bringing it to him.'
(6c)   *Badakarzkio* 'He is bringing them to him.'
(6d)   *Badakarzkiote* 'They are bringing them to him.'

If the indirect object is plural, *e* is substituted for *o*.

The dative markers have the same shape as the ergative ones, except for the 3rd person: dative *-o* and ergative Ø for the singular, and dative *-e* (variant *-ote*), ergative *-te* for the plural. Some verbs add the dative marker directly to the stem; others, like *ekarri* 'to bring', use an intervening segment *-ki-*. The dative marker always precedes the ergative when both are present:

(7)   *Badakarkizugu* 'We're bringing it to you.'

With such verbal morphology, it is hardly surprising that Basque speakers use the dative as much as possible, e.g. preferring the "possessive dative" *Katua hil zaigu* 'The cat has died on us' to *Gure katua hil da* 'Our cat has died.'

The verb *ekarri* 'to bring' is special in having synthetic forms. Most verbs have only a periphrastic conjugation, consisting of a non-finite verb form and a conjugated auxiliary. In Basque as commonly spoken, only about twelve verbs are "strong," i.e. allow synthetic forms. There used to be more; but even in the 16th century, their number did not exceed 50, as seen in Leizárraga's New Testament translation (1571) and other texts. In today's literary language, synthetic forms function as indicators of style: the loftier the style, the more synthetic forms appear, including some that are entirely innovative.

Except for one or two defective verbs, all strong verbs have periphrastic forms as well, constructed with the following non-finite verb forms:

(a)   An adjectival past participle (the citation form of the verb), often characterized by a suffix *-i* or *-tu*: *ekarri* 'brought', *hartu* 'taken', *jakin* 'known', *hil* 'died'
(b)   A gerund, consisting of the verbal noun (in *-te* or *-tze*) plus an inessive ending *-n*: *ekartzen* 'bringing', *hartzen* 'taking', *jakiten* 'knowing', *hiltzen* 'dying'
(c)   A future participle, consisting of the past participle plus a suffix *-ko*, or (in the eastern dialects) an indefinite genitive ending *-ren*: *ekarriko* (*ekarriren*), *hartuko* (*harturen*), *jakingo* (*jakinen*), *hilko* (*hilen*)
(d)   A radical, consisting of the past participle minus the suffix *-i* or *-tu*: *ekar, har, jakin, hil*

To show how the periphrastic conjugation system is constructed, we break it down into five moods: indicative, conditional, subjunctive, imperative, and potential. The indicative has six major tenses:

(a)   Present imperfect = gerund + present tense auxiliary: *ekartzen du* 'he brings it'
(b)   Past imperfect = gerund + past tense auxiliary: *ekartzen zuen* 'he brought it, he used to bring it'
(c)   Present perfect = past participle + present tense auxiliary: *ekarri du* 'he has brought it'
(d)   Past perfect = past participle + past tense auxiliary: *ekarri zuen* 'he brought it, he had brought it'
(e)   Future = future participle + present tense auxiliary: *ekarriko du* 'he will bring it'
(f)   Past future = future participle + past tense auxiliary: *ekarriko zuen* 'he would bring it'

Strong verbs also have a simple present, e.g. *dakar* 'he is bringing it', and a simple past, *zekarren* 'he was bringing it'. Simple forms in colloquial use express momentaneous action, while the imperfect tenses express habitual action or background activity. There is also a synthetic future tense, little used except in the northeastern dialects: *dakarke* 'he will (probably) bring it'.

By adding non-finite forms of the auxiliary to the periphrastic verb forms, "hyperperiphrastic" tenses have been created in some dialects, calqued on certain compound tense forms of Romance.

In the conditional, strong verbs have three synthetic forms: a protasis form with the conditional prefix *ba-* (*balekar* 'if he were to bring it'); an imperfect apodosis form with the irrealis suffix *-ke* (*lekarke* 'he would bring it'); and a perfect apodosis form with the past tense suffix *-en* added to *-ke* (*zekarkeen* 'he would have brought it').

Except in the northern dialects, which follow a slightly

different system, conditionals have four periphrastic tense forms:

(a) Imperfect protasis = future participle + protasis form of the auxiliary: *ekarriko balu* 'if he were to bring it'
(b) Perfect protasis = past participle of main verb, optionally followed by the past participle of the auxiliary + the protasis form of the auxiliary: *ekarri (izan) balu* 'if he had brought it'
(c) Imperfect apodosis = future participle + imperfect apodosis form of the auxiliary: *ekarriko luke* 'he would bring it'
(d) Perfect apodosis = future participle + perfect apodosis form of the auxiliary: *ekarriko zukeen* 'he would have brought it'

The subjunctive has two tenses, present and past. The older language also had an irrealis, now obsolete. For most strong verbs, the subjunctive is formed from the simple indicative by adding the unmarked complementizer *-la*—or, in purpose clauses and the like, the relativizer *-n*: *dakargun* 'let us bring it', *dakarrela* 'let him bring it'. The two auxiliaries have irregular subjunctives: intransitive *izan* 'to be' has a subjunctive stem *-di-*, and transitive **edun* 'to have' has *-za-*. The periphrastic present/past subjunctive consists of a radical + present or past subjunctive auxiliary: *ekar dezan* 'that he may bring it', *ekar zezan* 'that he might bring it'.

The imperative mood has only one tense, e.g. *ekarzu* '(you) bring it!' There is also a 3rd person jussive form distinct from the subjunctive: *bekar* 'let him bring it!' The periphrastic imperative consists of a radical + imperative auxiliary: *ekar ezazu* '(you) bring it!', *ekar beza* 'let him bring it!'

The potential has three tenses: present (*dakarke* 'he can bring it'), conditional (*lekarke* 'he could bring it'), and past (*zekarkeen* 'he could have brought it'). The periphrastic potential consists of the radical + one of the auxiliary potential forms: *ekar dezake* 'he can bring it', *ekar lezake* 'he could bring it', *ekar zezakeen* 'he could have brought it'.

Within these sixteen periphrastic tenses, together with the twelve simple tenses for the strong verbs, multiple agreement operates to yield a plethora of possible verbal forms. The number is again more than doubled by a pragmatic process of addressee agreement, which gives rise to allocutive forms, a salient feature of Basque. Whenever the familiar form of address corresponding to the pronoun *hi* 'you (fam.)' is used, all non-subordinate verbs must agree with the sex of the addressee. Thus, in the central dialects, the phrase 'I know (it)' is *badakit* (unmarked), *bazekiat* (male addressee), or *bazekinat* (female addressee). In the northeastern dialects, addressee agreement also involves the *zu* (singular polite) forms.

Most (perhaps all) periphrastic transitive verb forms can be made impersonal by substituting the corresponding intransitive auxiliary for the transitive one. Thus, beside *ekartzen du* 'he brings it', we have *ekartzen da* 'it is being brought'; beside *ematen digu* 'he gives it to us', *ematen zaigu* 'it is being given to us'. These impersonals do not allow ergative subjects; they function like the agentless passives of other languages.

4. Syntax. As regards complementation, Basque verbs of communication and appearance require finite complements; verbs of perception and cognition take finite complements or gerunds; verbs of volition and command take finite subjunctive or non-finite complements; and other verbs take non-finite complements or nominalizations, as in *Badaiteke katua etortzea* 'It may be that the cat is coming.'

Standard Basque has two finite complementizers, which are realized as suffixes to the subordinate verb: a WH-complementizer *-n*, and a regular complementizer *-la*:

(8)   *Ez dakit katua nork dakarren.*
      'I don't know who is bringing the cat.'
(9)   *Ez dakit katua datorren*(or: *datorrenentz*).
      'I don't know whether the cat is coming.'
(10) *Badakit katua ez datorrela.*
      'I know that the cat is not coming.'
(11) *Katuak ez dirudi datorrela.*
      'The cat does not seem to be coming' (lit. 'does not seem that he is coming').

Relativization operates by deletion of the lower NP together with its case endings. The relative clause, which must end in a finite verb bearing a relativizing suffix *-n* (homonymous with both the inessive ending and the WH-complementizer), directly precedes the antecedent in modern usage:

(12) *Sarri joaten naizen gaztelua urruti dago.*
      'The castle I often go to is far.'

Finite adverbial clauses are characterized by a suffix on the subordinate verb. They are mostly derived from adjectival clauses modifying an abstract noun; the suffix is often analyzable as a relativizer followed by a case ending. Thus *gaztelura joaten naizenean* 'when I go to the castle' derives from the less common, but equally grammatical, *gaztelura joaten naizen orduan* 'at the time (*ordu*) that I go to the castle'. Likewise, *katua datorre-lakoan* 'under the impression that the cat is coming' derives from *katua datorrelako ustean* 'in the belief (*uste*) that the cat is coming'.

This discussion has focused on finite clauses; however, non-finite constructions of various types involving past participles, gerunds, and verbal nouns (as well as other nominalizations) are extremely common in Basque, and occur freely in conversational speech.

Among the few monographs on Basque syntax, Rebuschi 1984 and Ortiz de Urbina 1989 deserve special mention; Lafitte 1979 and Saltarelli et al. 1988 also contain interesting observations.

5. Typology and word order. Basque is postpositional and has predominantly Subject Object Verb order, with the genitive preceding the noun and the adjective following it.

The order of constituents within a NP is: (i) relative clause; (ii) genitive; (iii) postpositional phrase followed by *-ko*; (iv) numeral; (v) head noun; (vi) adjective; (vii) determiner. All these may occur in one phrase:

(13) *gaur heldu dire-n   ama-ren   atzerriko*
      today arrived they.are-REL mother-POSS from.abroad

      hiru adiskide aberats horiek
      three friends   rich   those

      'those three rich friends of mother's from abroad who arrived today'

A postpositional phrase cannot directly modify a NP (de Rijk 1988), but requires the adjectival suffix *-ko*: *gazte-lurako bidea* 'the road to the castle' (in *atzerriko* 'from abroad' in 13, the ablative ending *-tik* has been deleted before *-ko*).

The underlying constituent order of Basque can be argued to be Subject + Indirect Object + Direct Object + Verb; this is also the predominant surface order. However, there is no rigid constraint on order, and all 24 possible permutations are found. Surface constituent order is largely determined by pragmatics: topic position is at the beginning of the sentence, and focus position immediately before the verb. Question words must be in focus position, but need not be sentence-initial:

(14) *Jonek zer ikusi du?*
      'What has John seen?'

(15) *Jonek katu beltza ikusi du.*
      'John has seen a black cat.'

Here *Jon* is topic, *katu beltza* is focus. Focus is doubly marked: by preverbal position, and by comparatively higher-pitched intonation.

The auxiliary immediately follows the main verb, except in negative sentences (and in some dialects, except in emphatic positives):

(16) *Jon Mirenekin etorri da gaur.*
      'John has come today with Miren.'

(17) *Jon ez da gaur Mirenekin etorri.*
      'John has not come with Miren today.'

BIBLIOGRAPHY

Aulestia, Gorka. 1989. *Basque–English dictionary.* Reno: University of Nevada Press.

Aulestia, Gorka. 1990. *English–Basque dictionary.* Reno: University of Nevada Press.

de Rijk, Rudolf P. G. 1988. Basque syntax and universal grammar. In *Euskara Biltzarra / Conference on the Basque Language,* vol. 1, pp. 69–88. Vitoria, Spain: Eusko Jaurlaritzaren Argitalpen-Zerbitzu Nagusia.

de Rijk, Rudolf P. G. 1999. *De lingua Vasconum: Selected writings.* Bilbao: Universidad del País Vasco.

Echenique Elizondo, María Teresa. 1987. *Historia lingüística vasco-románica.* Revised ed. Madrid: Paraninfo.

Heath, Jeffrey. 1977. Remarks on Basque verbal morphology. In *Anglo-American contributions to Basque studies: Essays in honor of Jon Bilbao,* edited by William A. Douglass et al., pp. 193–201. Reno, Nev.: Desert Research Institute.

Hualde, José Ignacio, and Jon Ortiz de Urbina, eds. 1990. *Generative studies in Basque linguistics.* Amsterdam: Benjamins.

Hualde, José Ignacio, Joseba Andoni Lakarra, and R. Larry Trask, eds. 1995. *Towards a history of the Basque language.* Amsterdam and Philadelphia: Benjamins.

Lafitte, Pierre. 1979. *Grammaire basque (navarro-labourdin littéraire).* Revised ed. San Sebastian: Elkar.

Lafon, René. 1972. The Basque language. In *Current trends in linguistics,* edited by Thomas A. Sebeok, vol. 9, *Linguistics in Western Europe,* pp. 1744–1792. The Hague: Mouton.

Levin, Beth C. 1983. Unaccusative verbs in Basque. *North Eastern Linguistic Society* 13.129–143.

Michelena, Luis. 1976. *Fonética histórica vasca.* Revised ed. San Sebastián: Imprenta de la Diputación de Guipúzcoa.

Michelena, Luis. 1977. Basque. *Encyclopaedia Britannica* 2.762–764.

N'Diaye, Geneviève. 1970. *Structure du dialecte basque de*

Maya. (Janua linguarum, Series practica, 86.) The Hague: Mouton.

Ortiz de Urbina, Jon. 1989. *Some parameters in the grammar of Basque.* Dordrecht: Foris.

Perlmutter, David M. 1978. Impersonal passives and the unaccusative hypothesis. *Berkeley Linguistics Society* 4.157–189.

Rebuschi, Georges. 1984. *Structure de l'énoncé en basque.* (L'Europe de tradition orale, 3.) Paris: Société d'Études Linguistiques et Anthropologiques de France.

Rebuschi, Georges. 1997. *Essais de Linguistique basque.* Bilbao: Universidad del País Vasco.

Saltarelli, Mario, et al. 1988. *Basque.* London: Croom Helm.

Trask, R. Larry. 1997. *The history of Basque.* London: Routledge.

RUDOLF P. G. DE RIJK

BAUDOUIN DE COURTENAY, JAN (1845–1929). Polish linguist. His contribution to phonology, originally in collaboration with his shorter-lived pupil Mikołai Kruszewski (1850–1887), was fundamental to the development of structural linguistics in Europe, especially as furthered by Saussure and by the work of the Prague School in the 1930s.

[*See also* Phonology.]

ANNA MORPURGO DAVIES

BAYONO-AWBONO LANGUAGES are spoken in the west of the Indonesian province of East Papua.

LANGUAGE LIST

Awbono: 100 speakers south of Tokuni on the Modera River. The dialect, Kvolyab, is spoken on the south coast, northwest of Korowai. Not related to Ok, Asmat, Awyu-Dumut, Momuna, or highland languages like Dani or Mek. No bilinguals among the Kvolyab speakers.

Bayono: 100 speakers south of Tokuni on the Steenboom River. Not related to Ok, Asmat, Awyu-Dumut, Momuna, or highlands languages like Dani or Mek.   B. GRIMES

BEBOID LANGUAGES. These languages are spoken in western Cameroon with some spillover into Nigeria; they form a branch of SOUTH BANTOID.

LANGUAGE LIST

Abar: also called Mijong, Missong. 2,000 speakers in Cameroon centered around village of Missong, including villages of Munken, Abar, Mundabi; Wum subdivision, Menchum division, North West Province.

Bebe: also called Yi Be Wu, Naami. 2,500 speakers in Came-

FIGURE 1. *Subgrouping of Beboid Languages*

Bukwen
Mashi
Eastern Beboid
    Bebe, Cung, Kemezung, Mungong, Naki, Ncane, Noone, Nsari
Western Beboid
    Abar, Fang, Koskin, Mbu', Mundabli

roon, west of Nkambe and north of Ring Road, west part of Ako subdivision, Donga-Mangung division, North West Province.

Bukwen: spoken in Nigeria, in the state of Taraba, near Takum, one village.

Cung: 2,000 speakers in Cameroon, northeast of Wum, west of Nkambe, Menchum division, North West Province.

Fang: 2,400 speakers in Cameroon, village of Fang, northeast of Wum; Wum subdivision, Menchum division, North West Province.

Kemezung: also called Dumbo, Dzumbo, Kumaju. 4,500 speakers in Cameroon, northwest of Nkambe, southwest corner of Ako subdivision, Donga-Mantung division, North West Province.

Koskin: also called Kosin, Kaw. 1,000 speakers in Cameroon, village of Koshin, Wum subdivisions, North West Province.

Mashi: spoken in Nigeria, in the state of Taraba, near Takum.

Mbu': 1,000 speakers in Cameroon, village of Mbu', northeast of Wum; Wum subdivision, Menchum division, North West Province.

Mundabli: also called Bu. 1,000 speakers in Cameroon, villages of Mundabli, Bu, and Ngwen, northeast of Wum, Wum subdivision, Menchum division, North West Province.

Mungong: also called Mungom. 1,500 speakers in Cameroon, village of Mungong, northeast of Wum, west of Nkambe, Menchum division, North West Province. Linguistically close to Noone and Ncane.

Naki: also called Mekaf, Munkaf, Nkap, Bunaki. 3,000 speakers in Cameroon, Naki, Mekaf, Bukpang II and Lebo villages, Nse chiefdom, Furu-Awa subdivision, Menchum division, North West Province. In Nse chiefdom they speak Nsaa and are called "Bunsaa." Limited bilingualism in Nse and Lebo, although Jukun is the trade language. In Bukpang II few speak Jukun. Pidgin is used in the area.

Ncane: also called Nchanti, Ntshanti, Cane. 14,500 speakers in Cameroon, in and south of Misaje village, western Nkambe subdivision, Donga-Mantung division, North West Province.

Noone: also called Noni, Nooni. 35,000 speakers in Cameroon, northwestern Kumbo subdivision, Bui division, North West Province.

Nsari: also called Akweto, Pesaa, Sali. 7,000 speakers in Cameroon, on both sides of Ring Road between Misaje and

Nkambe, western part of Nkambe subdivision, Donga-Mantung division, North West Province.   B. GRIMES

BENGALI. In 1989, Bengali was reported to have some 162 million speakers, making it a major language of the world. It is the national language of Bangladesh, where some two-thirds of its speakers reside. Most of the remainder inhabit the contiguous state of West Bengal, India. Within these boundaries, the language shows considerable dialect variation, the full extent of which is not yet adequately surveyed.

Bengali is characterized by diglossia: distinctive language styles are used in formal vs. informal social contexts. The more conservative literary or "pundit language" (*sadhu bhasa*) prevails in formal and written discourse. However, since the early 20th century, such functions have begun to accrue to the colloquial style or "current language" (*colit bhasa*); see Dimock 1960. The standard of colloquial spoken Bengali is identified with the speech of Calcutta, West Bengal. (For general reference, see Dimock et al. 1964, Ray et al. 1966, Čižikova and Ferguson 1969, Bender and Riccardi 1978, and Klaiman 1987.)

1. History. Bengali belongs to the Magadhan subfamily of the Indo-Aryan branch of Indo-European. The unattested ancestor of the Magadhan languages, attributed to the Middle period of Common Indo-Aryan, is called Eastern or Magadhan Apabhramsa. Bengali's closest relatives are, in order, Assamese and Oriya. Bengali has evolved in three major historical stages, designated by Chatterji 1926:130 as Old, Middle, and Modern. The sole surviving Old Bengali literary text, a collection of nearly 50 short Buddhist songs called the Caryāpada hymns, was composed sometime between 1000 and 1200 CE. The earliest surviving text of the Middle period is a much longer narrative collection of over 400 songs composed by the poet Baṛu Caṇḍīdāsa, known as Srīkṛṣṇa-kīrtana. Opinions differ about its dating, but Chatterji assigns it to the late 14th century. According to him, the start of the Modern period coincides with the rise of literary interest in prose, about the beginning of the 18th century. Westerners are most likely to be acquainted with the name of Rabindranath Tagore (Ṭhākur) as a craftsman of prose and poetry in Modern Bengali, although superlative modern writers are numerous.

Over 90% of Modern Bengali vocabulary is Indo-Aryan, but the lexicon also shows significant foreign influences. For about 600 years, from the beginning of

TABLE 1. *Consonant Phonemes of Bengali*

	Labial	Dental	Retroflex	Palatal	Velar	Glottal
Obstruents						
Voiceless						
Unaspirated	p	t	ṭ	c	k	
Aspirated	ph	th	ṭh	ch	kh	
Voiced						
Unaspirated	b	d	ḍ	j	g	
Aspirated	bh	dh	ḍh	jh	gh	
Spirants				s		h
Nasals	m	n	ṇ			
Flaps		r	ṛ			
Lateral		l				

the 13th century, Bengal was dominated by Islamic invaders from the northwest; they were supplanted by the British in the mid-18th century. According to Chatterji 1926:218, some 3.3% of Modern Bengali vocabulary consists of Persian/Arabic borrowings; about another 1% is from English. In addition, the influence of indigenous tribal languages—still spoken in and around the Gangetic delta—is inferable not only in Bengali vocabulary, but also in other features to be mentioned below. In light of the region's recent political history, it is noteworthy that current spoken Bengali shows minimal influences from Hindi, the national language of India, or from Urdu, the national language of Pakistan.

2. Phonology. Table 1 displays the consonant phonemes of Modern Bengali (cf. Chatterji 1921, Ferguson and Chowdhury 1960). Bengali has inherited from earlier Indo-Aryan the distinctions of aspirated vs. non-aspirated and of voiced vs. voiceless obstruents, as well as the distribution of these segments over five principal points of articulation. Modern Bengali has only one sibilant phoneme (Sanskrit had three); it is peculiar in being palatal, though realized as dental before *t th n r l*. The vowels are *i e æ a ɔ o u*. All vowels may occur with distinctive nasalization—*ĩ ẽ*, etc.

Major phonological processes involve vowels more often than consonants in Modern Bengali. One, Vowel Raising, neutralizes the close/open distinction in the mid vowels, predominantly in unstressed syllables. Since stress regularly falls on the initial syllable, the effects of vowel raising are, for the most part, observed only in non-initial position. A few illustrations appear in Table 2, Part A.

A second process, Vowel Height Assimilation, is significant for morphophonemic alternations in verbal bases. In this process, a non-high vowel other than /a/ assimi-

TABLE 2. *Bengali Phonological Processes Affecting Vowel Height*

A. Vowel Raising			
mɔl	'dirt'	ɔmol	'pure'
sɔ	'hundred'	ækso	'one hundred'
æk	'one'	ɔnek	'many'
B. Vowel Height Assimilation			
æk	'one'	ekṭi	'one' (plus classifier -ṭi)
lɔjja	'shame'	lojjito	'ashamed'
nɔṭ	'actor'	noṭi	'actress'
æk	'one'	ekṭu	'a little, a bit'
tɔbe	'then'	tobu	'but (then)'

TABLE 3a. *Traditional Order of Bengali Vowels (Initial Forms)*

Symbol	Transcription	Symbol	Transcription
অ	ɔ	ঋ	r̥ (/ri/)
আ	a	এ	e
ই	i	ঐ	oy
ঈ	ī (/i/)	ও	o
উ	u	ঔ	ow
ঊ	ū (/u/)		

lates to the height of the nearest succeeding [+high] vowel segment within the phonological word. Outside of verbal morphophonemics, the most common manifestations of the process involve neutralizations of the close/open distinction in the mid vowels before /i u/ in the following syllable. Some illustrations appear in Table 2, Part B.

3. Script. Like all other modern writing systems indigenous to the Indian subcontinent, that of Bengali is

TABLE 4. *Bengali Nominal Declension*

	Singular	Plural
Nominative	Ø	-ra/-era; -gulo
Objective	-ke	-der(ke)/-eder(ke); -guloke
Genitive	-r/-er	-der/-eder; -gulor
Locative/Instrumental	-te/-e or -ete	-gulote

derived from the ancient Brāhmī script. The modern characters, shown in Tables 3a–b, are peculiar to Bengali and (with a few differences) Assamese. This script is read from left to right, and is "alpha-syllabic" rather than segmental.

4. Morphology. A chart of declension for nouns appears in Table 4. It is notable that Modern Bengali lacks many of the declensional parameters of the noun which occur in earlier I[ndo]-A[ryan], such as the original system of eight cases and three genders in the noun and adjective. Modern Bengali adjectives are not declined at all. Moreover, the plural is usually marked only in nouns which have animate and/or definite reference—failing which, the singular/plural distinction tends to be neutralized.

Verbal inflection is summarized in Table 5 (cf. Ferguson 1945, Sarkar 1976). Like the noun, the verb lacks inflectional number. However, three distinctions of status—despective, ordinary, and honorific—are made inflectionally in the 2nd and 3rd persons; the honorific inflections are derived from earlier Indo-Aryan plural terminations. The shapes of inflections in the table depend on the shapes of the verbal stems to which they are added.

Table 6 presents a sample conjugation for the root *dækh-* 'see'. The alternation shown in the height of the

TABLE 3b. *Traditional Order of Bengali Consonants (Initial Forms)*

	Occlusives				Nasals	
	Voiceless		Voiced			
	Unaspirated	Aspirated	Unaspirated	Aspirated		
Velar	ক k	খ kh	গ g	ঘ gh	ঙ ŋ	
Palatal	চ c	ছ ch	জ j	ঝ jh	ঞ ñ	
Retroflex	ট ṭ	ঠ ṭh	ড ḍ	ঢ ḍh	ণ ṇ	
Dental	ত t	থ th	দ d	ধ dh	ন n	
Labial	প p	ফ ph	ব b	ভ bh	ম m	
Resonants:	য y (/j/)	র r	ল l			
Spirants:	শ ś (/s/)	ষ ṣ (/s/)	স s (/s/)	হ h		

TABLE 5. *Bengali Verbal Inflection*

		Despective		Ordinary		Honorific
	1st Person	2nd Person		2nd Person	3rd Person	2nd/3rd Person
Present Imperative	—	Ø		-o	-uk	-un
Unmarked Indicative						
and -(c)ch stems	-i	-is		-o	-e	-en
-b stems	-o	-i		-e	-e	-en
-t and -l stems	-am	-i		-e	-o	-en

TABLE 6. *Sample Verbal Conjugation of Bengali* dækh-*'see'*

1. Verbal noun[1]	*dækha*	'seeing'
2. Present indicative	*dækhe*	'sees'
3. Present imperative	*dekhuk*	'let him/her/ them see!'
4. Present continuous	*dekhche*	'is seeing'
5. Future indicative/imperative	*dekhbe*	'will see/ must see!'
6. Infinitive[1]	*dekhte*	'to see'
7. Perfect conditional/ Past habitual	*dekhto*	'would see'
8. Imperfect conditional[1]	*dekhle*	'if/when one sees'
9. Ordinary past	*dekhlo*	'saw'
10. Past continuous[2]	*dekhchilo*	'was seeing'
11. Conjunctive participle[1]	*dekhe*	'having seen'
12. Present perfect[2]	*dekheche*	'has seen'
13. Past perfect[2]	*dekhechilo*	'had seen'

[1] Non-inflecting verbal forms with invariant or zero termination.
[2] Stems formed with two or three successive stem-forming affixes.

vowel *æ* exemplifies the pattern of morphophonemic alternation discussed above (cf. Dimock 1957). This can be considered a conditioned phonological process, provided that the stem-forming affixes in lines 4–13 are assumed to have an underlying initial high vowel, as a required condition for Vowel Height Assimilation. In fact, a high vowel /i/ does occur initially in these stem affixes when they are added to a few monosyllabic verbal bases ending in ɔ *a*; e.g. *ga-* 'sing', *gaibe* 'will sing', *gaite* 'to sing', *gaile* 'if/when one sang'.

5. Syntax. The dominant word order in Modern Bengali sentences is Subject + Indirect Object + Direct Object + Oblique Object + Verb. Subordinate clauses which contain non-inflecting or invariant verbal forms, such as conditionals and infinitives, precede finite clauses:

(1a) *Se ele   klas suru   hɔbe.*

he when.comes class beginning will.be
'When he comes, class will start.'

(1b) *Se aste   klas suru   holo.*
he come.INF class beginning was
'On his coming, class started.'

Finite subordinate clauses are also usually initial:

(2) *Jodi se asbe   (tɔbe) klas suru   hɔbe.*
when he will.come then   class beginning will.be
'When he comes, (then) class will start.'

However, the finite complement construction beginning with *je* 'that' is sentence-final. It often alternates with an initial construction in *bole*. Thus both these sentences mean 'I know that you will come':

(3a) *Ami jani je   tumi asbe.*
   I   know that you will.come

(3b) *Tumi asbe   bole ami jani.*
   you will.come COMP I   know

Conjunctive clauses also precede finite main clauses:

(4) *Bose se khabar khelo.*
   sitting he food   ate
   'He sat and ate.'

The conjunctive form of a main verb may also appear in verbal compounds in which the succeeding finite verb aspectually modifies the main verb (such compounds are a frequent IA feature). The aspectual verbs comprise a limited set, including *phæl-* (lit. 'throw'), which indicates completion of activity (e.g. *kha-* 'eat', *kheye phæl-* 'eat up'), as well as *ja-* lit. 'go', indicating motion from a point (e.g. *pa-* 'receive', *peye ja-* 'walk off with').

6. Diffusion. In some syntactic characteristics, Bengali diverges from the norms of earlier Indo-Aryan, and approaches the general types of modern South Asian languages irrespective of genetic affiliation. Thus Bengali has several dozen predicates which require subjects marked with the genitive case (rather than the more typical nominative), and which lack the otherwise usual subject/verb agreement (Klaiman 1981). Such "indirect" subjects are typically associated with sensory, mental, emotional, corporeal, and other characteristically human experiences, e.g. thinking or recalling:

(5)   *Baba-r   toma-ke mon-e   holo.*
      of-father to-you   in-mind became
      'Father thought of you.'

Constructions like these are rare in earlier Indo-Aryan, although they typify modern South Asian languages (Masica 1976:169). Other non-Aryan traits in Bengali that suggest external influences include word-initial stress, absence of grammatical gender, post-verbal negatives, negative existential verbs, and a proliferation in varieties of non-finite complements and subordinate clauses.

Bengali has also apparently absorbed two non-Aryan lexical features of the greater South Asian region. It has about a dozen numeral classifiers, such as *jon* denoting human referents (e.g. *tin jon sikkhok* 'three CLF teacher', i.e. 'three teachers'), or *khana* denoting flat objects (e.g. *du khana boi* 'two CLF book', i.e. 'two books'). It also has a class of reduplicative expressives, e.g. *kickic* suggesting grittiness, *miṭmiṭ* suggesting flickering, and *t-ɔlmɔl* suggesting overflowing or a fluid state. The modern language has dozens of such expressives, in contrast to earlier Indo-Aryan, in which they were largely lacking. It seems likely that these and other features entered Bengali after its separation from the other Modern Indo-Aryan languages. They may have originated with non-Aryan languages which were gradually absorbed when Bengali became the dominant speech of the greater Gangetic delta.

[*See also* Indo-Aryan Languages.]

BIBLIOGRAPHY

Bender, Ernest, and T. Riccardi, Jr. 1978. *An advanced course in Bengali*. Philadelphia: South Asia Regional Studies, University of Pennsylvania.

Chatterji, Suniti Kumar. 1921. Bengali phonetics. *Bulletin of the School of Oriental and African Studies,* University of London, 2.1–25.

Chatterji, Suniti Kumar. 1926. *The origin and development of the Bengali language*. 2 vols. London: Allen and Unwin. Reprinted with supplementary volume, 1970–1972.

Čižikova, Ksenija L., and Charles A. Ferguson. 1969. Bibliographical review of Bengali studies. In *Current trends in linguistics,* vol. 5, *Linguistics in South Asia,* edited by Thomas A. Sebeok, pp. 85–98. The Hague: Mouton.

Dimock, Edward C., Jr. 1957. Notes on stem-vowel alternation in the Bengali verb. *Indian Linguistics* 17.173–177.

Dimock, Edward C., Jr. 1960. Literary and colloquial Bengali in modern Bengali prose. In *Linguistic diversity in South Asia: Studies in regional, social and functional variation* (Indiana University Research Center in Anthropology, Folklore, and Linguistics, Publication 13; International Journal of American Linguistics 26:3, part 3), edited by Charles A. Ferguson and John J. Gumperz, pp. 43–63. Bloomington: Indiana University.

Dimock, Edward C., Jr., et al. 1964. *Introduction to Bengali,* vol. 1. Honolulu: East-West Center Press. Reprinted, Columbia, Mo.: South Asia Books, 1976.

Ferguson, Charles A. 1945. A chart of the Bengali verb. *Journal of the American Oriental Society* 65.54–55.

Ferguson, Charles A., and Munier Chowdhury. 1960. The phonemes of Bengali. *Language* 36.22–59.

Klaiman, Miriam H. 1981. *Volitionality and subject in Bengali: A study of semantic parameters in grammatical processes.* Bloomington: Indiana University Linguistics Club.

Klaiman, Miriam H. 1987. Bengali. In *The world's major languages,* edited by Bernard Comrie, pp. 490–513. London: Croom Helm. New York: Oxford University Press.

Masica, Colin P. 1976. *Defining a linguistic area: South Asia.* Chicago: University of Chicago Press.

Ray, Punya Sloka, et al. 1966. *Bengali language handbook.* Washington, D.C.: Center for Applied Linguistics.

Sarkar, Pabitra. 1976. The Bengali verb. *International Journal of Dravidian Linguistics* 5.274–297.

M. H. KLAIMAN

BENUE-CONGO LANGUAGES. These languages constitute one of the main branches of the NIGER-CONGO family; they are spoken from the Benin-Nigeria border eastward and southward to cover most of the rest of the continent, except the southwestern corner.

[*For language lists, refer to the following articles on subgroups within Benue-Congo:* Bantoid Languages, Cross River Languages, Defoid Languages, Edoid Languages, Idomoid Languages, Igboid Languages, Kainji Languages, Nupoid Languages, Platoid Languages.] The language list below includes Akpes, Oko-Eni-Osayen (Oko), and Ukaan, single languages each forming a separate branch of Benue-Congo, and three languages that are unclassified within Benue-Congo.

LANGUAGE LIST

Akpes: also called Ibaram-Efifa. 10,000 speakers in Nigeria in state of Ondo, Akoko North LGA. Dialects are Akunnu (Akpes), Ase, Daja, Efifa, Esuku (Echuku), Gedegede, Ikorom, Ibaram, Iyani. A dialect cluster. Yoruba is the lingua franca.

Fali of Baissa: spoken in Nigeria, in south of state of Taraba, Falinga Plateau region.

Koro Ija: also called Koro Afiki. Spoken in Nigeria, Federal Capital Territory, south of Abuja, north of the Minna Suleja road. Listed as separate by some. Different from Koro Zuba, Koro of Lafia, Begbere-Ejar, or Tanjijili. "Koro" is used as a cover term for several languages.

Koro Zuba: spoken in Nigeria, Federal Capital Territory, near Zuba, north of the Minna Suleja road. Listed as separate language by some. Different from Koro Ija, Koro of Lafia, Begbere-Ejar, or Tanjijili. "Koro" is used as a cover term for several languages.

Oko-Eni-Osayen: also called Oko, Ogori-Magongo. 10,000 speakers in Nigeria, state of Kogi, Okene LGA, Ogori and Magongo towns, ten miles south southwest of Okene. Dialects are Oko (Ogori, Uku), Osayen (Magongo, Osanyin), Eni. A dialect cluster. It seems to be equally distantly related to Yoruba, Ebira, Edo, Igbo, and Idoma.

Ukaan: also called Ikan, Anyaran, Auga, Kakumo. 18,000 speakers in Nigeria, state of Ondo, Akoko North LGA, towns of Kakumo-Akoko, Auga, Ishe; state of Edo, Akoko Edo LGA, town of Anyaran, Kakumo-Aworo. Dialects are Ishe, Kakumo, Auga. Yoruba is the lingua franca.

B. GRIMES

BENVENISTE, ÉMILE (1902–1976).

French Indo-Europeanist and general linguist. His works on Indo-European include an elegant theory of the structure of the root (1935), an account of agentive nouns and action nouns (1948), and two brilliant volumes (1969) on the nature of the Indo-European institutions as revealed by inherited vocabulary, together with a long series of monographs and articles on the major Indo-European languages (especially Iranian and Hittite).

[*See also* History of Linguistics *and* Indo-European Lanugages.]

ANNA MORPURGO DAVIES

BERBER LANGUAGES.

The Berber language family constitutes a separate branch of the Afroasiatic language phylum. Berber languages are spoken in a discontinuous area stretching from the Atlantic Ocean in the west to the Egyptian oasis of Siwa in the east, and from the Mediterranean in the north to the Niger River in the south. The languages are closely related; in fact, French linguistic tradition has long preferred to call them "dialects" rather than separate languages. This position, however, understates the differentiation inside the Berber language group: there is no mutual intelligibility between, for instance, Figuig Berber (eastern Morocco) and Tashelhiyt (southwestern Morocco), and the differences between these two languages and Tuareg are even greater.

Berber has a long but weak tradition of writing. In Roman times, the Libyan alphabet was used for inscriptions. This alphabet survived with the Tuaregs, where it is called *tifinaɣ*. In southern Morocco, there has been a continuous tradition of writing Tashelhiyt Berber in Arabic script at least from the 11th century CE. Sporadic writings of Berber in Arabic script are found elsewhere too, but nowhere does this tradition seem to have had the same extent as in Tashelhiyt. In colonial and post-colonial times, Berber has been written with Arabic or Latin characters, as well as in a recently refurbished and reintroduced version of the *tifinaɣ* alphabet.

A number of Berber-speaking people call their language *Tamaziɣt* or use a related term, such as Tuareg *Tamašəq* and *Tamahaq*. Many partisans of the Berber cause prefer this term to "Berber." In the linguistic tradition, the term *Tamaziɣt* is often restricted to the language of central Morocco.

Berber, specifically Tuareg, is a national language in Mali and Niger. In the Maghreb countries of North Africa, Berber has no official status.

1. Phonology. Berber languages distinguish short (or lax) consonants from long (or tense) consonants (see Tables 1 and 2). In addition to length, other phonetic features can be markers of this phonological contrast. All Berber languages distinguish pharyngealized from nonpharyngealized consonants. Two of these, z (and its long counterpart zz) and d (and its long counterpart tt) belong to the Proto-Berber consonant inventory. The other pharyngealized consonants are either borrowed from Arabic or result from secondary developments.

Vowel systems (Table 3) differ greatly among the languages. The northern languages have three plain vowels plus a short central vowel, $ə$, whose status as a phoneme is questionable. Tashelhiyt (southwestern Morocco) is unique in that $ə$ has no phonemic status, and syllabification is ruled entirely by inherent qualities of the consonants. Tuareg and Ghadames Berber have an entirely different system with seven vowel qualities. The

TABLE 1. *Phoneme Inventory of Tashelhiyt Short Consonants (after Galand 1988)*

	f	t	s	š	k	x	ḥ
b		d	z	ž	g	ɣ	ʕ
		(ṭ)	ṣ		kʷ	xʷ	
		ḍ	ẓ		gʷ	ɣʷ	
m		n					
(w)				(y)			(h)
		r					
		(ṛ)					
		l					

TABLE 2. *Phoneme Inventory of Tashelhiyt Long Consonants (after Galand 1988)*

	ff	tt	ss	šš	kk	qq	xx	ḥḥ
bb		dd	zz	žž	gg		(ɣɣ)	ʕʕ
		ṭṭ	ṣṣ	(ṣ̌ṣ̌)	kkʷ	qqʷ	xxʷ	
		ḍḍ	ẓẓ	(ẓ̌ẓ̌)	ggʷ		(ɣɣʷ)	
mm		nn						
ww				yy				(hh)
		rr						
		(ṛṛ)						
		ll						
		(ḷḷ)						

TABLE 3. *Vowel Inventories of Tashelhiyt and Tuareg.* The two Tuareg central vowels /ə/ and /ä/ are often analyzed as short vowels; this would mean that Tuareg would have a threefold vowel length contrast, short, long, and overlong.

Tashelhiyt							
i		u					
	a						
Tuareg							
i			u	ii			uu
	e	ə	o		ee		oo
		ä					
		a			aa		

TABLE 4. *Free and Annexed State Forms in Figuig ("Regular" Forms)*

masc.	singular	plural	
Free	a-funas	i-funas-ən	'ox'
Annexed	u-funas	i-funas-ən	
fem.	**singular**	**plural**	
Free	ta-funas-t	ti-funas-in	'cow'
Annexed	t-funas-t	t-funas-in	

two central vowel qualities correspond to *ə* or the absence of a vowel in the northern languages, while the five non-central qualities correspond to the three plain vowels in Northern Berber. In addition, Tuareg has five long vowels, corresponding in quality to the five non-central vowels.

2. Morphology. Berber morphology is built on affixation (mainly prefixation) and on apophony, including consonant lengthening. Compounding and stem reduplication are not commonly used as morphological processes. The nominal plural is marked in the nominal prefix and by suffixation and/or apophony. Nouns distinguish two genders, masculine and feminine; the feminine is used for female persons and animals as well as for small(er) objects. The productive derivation masculine

→ feminine is quite regular morphologically, using noun prefixes and noun suffixes.

Nouns distinguish two cases, called "states," expressed in the nominal prefix (Table 4). In most languages, the relative case ("annexed state") is used after most prepositions and after numerals, as well as when the lexical subject follows the verb. The absolute case ("free state") is used in all other contexts, including the citation form. All other case relations are expressed by means of prepositions.

In the verb, most Berber languages distinguish four or five aspectual stems, differentiated by means of apophony (Table 5). Two stems are used exclusively after the negative particle. In the Northern Berber languages, there

TABLE 5. *Verb Stem Apophony in Figuig*

	'to steal'	'to live in'	'to kill'	'to be thirsty'
Aorist	ašər	zdəɣ	nəɣ	fad
Perfective ('prétérit')	usər	zdəɣ	nɣi/u/ə*	fad
Imperfective ('aoriste intensif')	ttašər	zəddəɣ	nəqq	ttifad
Negative Perfective	ušir	zdiɣ	nɣi	fad
Negative Imperfective	ttišər	zəddəɣ	nəqq	ttifad

*The vocalization depends on the person of the verb.

is considerable homophony between some of the aspectual stems, which is entirely predictable from the formal structure of the verb.

Berber languages have certain prefixal stem derivations that change the valency of the verb. Of special interest is the fact that a large proportion of underived verbs in Berber can be used as intransitives with a patient subject, as well as as transitives with an agent subject. This does not rule out the possibility of applying transitivizing and intransitivizing derivations to these double-valency verbs.

Person, gender, and number of the subject are expressed by affixes to the verb. Depending on the language, there are either two sets of affixes (indicative and imperative) or three sets (normal indicative, stative, and imperative). In addition to these finite forms, there exists a relative form, called a "participle" in spite of its verbal nature, which is used when the antecedent is the subject of a relative clause.

There are several series of clitic pronouns, as well as a set of independent pronouns. A typologically interesting feature in some of these series is the distinction between masculine and feminine in all persons except the 1st person singular.

3. Syntax. Berber noun phrases are head-initial: adjectives, relative clauses, and prepositional complements always follow the head noun. Berber languages are, in principle, verb-initial. Before the initial verb, elements can be fronted to a topicalization position. Typically, topicalized subjects have the "free state":

(1)   Figuig Berber
       i-nna   yidd   u-məddukəl   inux . . .
       3sm-said to.me Annexed.State-friend my
       'My friend said to me . . . ' (subject not topicalized)

(2)   *a-məddukəl*   inux i-nna   yidd . . .
       Free.State-friend   my   3sm-said to.me
       'My friend said to me. . . . ' (subject topicalized)

In 'be'-phrases, normally a non-verbal construction is used, in which there is no connecting element between the subject and the predicate when the predicate is a prepositional phrase or an adverb. In many languages, a particle *d* is inserted before the predicate if the predicate is a noun (substantive or adjective) or an independent pronoun. As with verbal sentences, the lexical subject can be absent in non-verbal sentences.

Clitics normally follow the verb. In some syntactic contexts, however, the full clitic chain is fronted to the position immediately preceding the verb. This occurs in relative clauses and after certain particles (esp. the "nonreal" particle *ad* and the negative particle *wer*).

Berber rarely uses nominalization as a syntactic device. Constructions that in European languages would be infinitival or "small clauses" are full sentential clauses in Berber:

(3)   Figuig Berber
       i-xəs   a   dd   y-as
       3sm-want prospective hither 3sm-come
       'he wants to come' (lit. 'he wants he will come')

(4)   *i-dwəl   dd   i-žžəy*
       he-became hither he-recovered
       'he became healthy again'

       yy-ən   t   d lmalik
       made-they him   is king
       'they made him king'

The second clauses of these sentences could be used as separate sentences, i.e. *a dd y-as* 'he will come', *i-žžəy* 'he (is) recovered', *d lmalik* 'it is a/the king'.

[*See also* Afroasiatic Languages.]

BIBLIOGRAPHY

Bougchiche, Lamara. 1997. *Langues et littératures berbères des origines à nos jours: Bibliographie internationale*. Paris: Ibis.

Chaker, Salem. 1983. *Un parler berbère d'Algérie (Kabylie) (syntaxe)*. Aix-Marseilles: Université de Provence.

Galand, Lionel. 1988. Le berbère. In *Les langues dans le monde ancien et moderne; troisième partie, les langues chamito-sémitiques (textes réunis par David Cohen)*, edited by Jean Perrot, pp. 207–242. Paris: CNRS.

Kossmann, Maarten. 1997. *Grammaire du parler berbère de Figuig (Maroc oriental)*. Paris and Louvain: Peeters.

Penchoen, Thomas G. 1973. *Tamazight of the Ayt Ndhir*. Los Angeles: Undena.

MAARTEN KOSSMANN

LANGUAGE LIST

Awjilah: also called Aujila, Augila, Aoudjila. 3,000 speakers in Cyrenaica, eastern Libya. Most men are bilingual in Libyan Spoken Arabic. Women are monolingual.

Chenoua: 15,000 speakers in Algeria, towns are Cherchell, Hamadia, Gouraya, Damous, Oued Damous, Larhat, Marceau, Sidi Amar, Nador, Tipaza, Sidi Mousa, Ain Tagourirt. Men and young people use Algerian Spoken Arabic as second language.

Ghadamès: 4,000 speakers in Libya and Tunisia. In Libya: 2,000 speakers in Ghadamès, a small oasis near the Algeria-Tunisia border. Dialects are Ayt Waziten, Elt Ulid. In Tunisia: 2,000 speakers.

Ghomara: formerly spoken in Morocco. North and west of Tamazight, a small region near Chechaouen, western Rif Mountains, Oued Laou Valley. Said to be intelligible with Tarifit. The ethnic group now speaks only Moroccan Spoken Arabic.

Guanche: formerly spoken in Canary Islands, Spain. Its relation to Berber has been questioned. Extinct in the 16th century.

Judeo-Berber: 2,000 speakers in Israel. Formerly spoken in High Atlas range, Tifnut, and other communities in Morocco. Speakers went to Israel from 1950 to 1960. Monolingual communities may have disappeared before 1930 in Morocco. Speakers also formerly used Judeo-Arabic. As of 1992, all were elderly. Hebrew script used.

Kabyle: 3,123,000 speakers in Algeria, France, and Belgium. In Algeria: 2,537,000 speakers in the Grande Kabylie Mountain range, western Kabylia. Dialects are Greater Kabyle, Lesser Kabyle. French is often used by men in trade and correspondence. Arabic is also used as second language. Kabyle is used in the home and market. Speakers have pride in Kabyle and resistance to Arabic. Roman script. In France: 537,000 speakers.

Nafusi: also called Djerbi, Nefusi, Jabal Nafusi, Jebel Nefusi, Jbel Nafusi. 167,000 speakers in Libya and Tunisia. In Libya: 141,000 speakers. Tripolitania, western Libya, isolated area around the towns of Nalut and Yafran, Jabal Nafusah region, coastal area around Zuara, west of Tripoli. Dialects are Zuara (Zouara, Zuwarah, Zwara, Zuraa), Tamezret (Duwinna), Jerbi (Jerba). Zuara dialect well-known in Jebel Nafusa area and in Jerba Tunisia. Some visit Zuara, but not vice versa. Dialect of Matmata and Tatawine area less well understood by speakers in Jerba or Zuara. Speakers in Zuara and Jebel areas understand Jerba stories well. Pre-school children are monolingual in Nafusi. All ages. In Nafusi villages they speak Nafusi among themselves. In towns they speak it among friends and families, most exclusively at home. They are not ashamed of Nafusi. In Tunisia: 26,000 speakers. Dialects are Tamezret (Duwinna), Jerba (Djerba, Guelili). Spoken only in the home.

Sawknah: also called Sokna. Spoken in Tripoli, Libya. The language may be extinct.

Sened: formerly spoken in Tunisia, in Sened and Tmagourt villages, northwest of Gabès, southern Tunisia. Dialects are Tmagourt (Tmagurt), Sened. Only a few elderly people still remember a few words.

FIGURE 1. *Subgrouping of Berber Languages*

Eastern Berber
  Awjila-Sokna
    Awjilah, Sawknah
  Siwa
    Siwi
Guanche
Northern Berber
  Chenoua
  Atlas Berber
    Judeo-Berber
    Tachelhit
    Central Atlas Tamazight
  Kabyle
  Zenati
    East Zenati
      Ghadamès, Nafusi, Sened
    Ghomara
    Mzab-Wargla
      Tagargrent, Taznatit, Temacine Tamazight, Tumzabt
    Riff
      Senhaja de Srair, Tarifit
    Shawiya
      Tachawit
    Tidikelt
      Tidikelt Tamazight
Tamasheq
  Northern Tamasheq
    Tahaggart Tamahaq
  Southern Tamasheq
    Tawallammat Tamajaq, Tayart Tamajeq, Tamasheq
Zenaga

Senhaja de Srair: also called Sanhaja of Srair. Formerly spoken in northern Morocco, west of Tarifit. Said to have been a separate language from Tarifit. The ethnic group now speaks only Moroccan Spoken Arabic.

Siwi: also called Siwa, Sioua, Oasis Berber, Zenati. 5,000 speakers in the northwestern desert of Egypt, Siwa Oasis, several isolated villages in the western oasis. Not closely related to other Berber languages. Bilingualism in Arabic.

Tachawit: also called Chaouia, Shawiya, Shawia. 1,400,000 speakers in Algeria, south and southeast of Grand Kabylie in the Aurès Mountains. One of the major Berber languages.

Tachelhit: also called Tashilheet, Tachilhit, Tashelhit, Tasoussit, Shilha, Susiua, Southern Shilha. 3,500,000 speakers in Morocco, Algeria, and France. In Morocco: 3,000,000 speakers. Many men are bilingual in Arabic. Many women do not learn Arabic. In Algeria: Southern Algeria near the Moroccan border around Tabelbala. Dialects are Susiua (Sus, Sousse). Many men are bilingual in Arabic, but many women do not learn Arabic. One of the major Berber languages.

Tagargrent: also called Ouargla, Ouargli, Wargla. 5,000 speakers in Algeria, south of Constantine, near Mzab. Ouargla and Ngouça are the main centers. Dialects are Ouedghir (Wadi), Temacin, Tariyit. Related to Tumzabt, Temacine Tamazight, and Taznatit. Status as a language or dialect has not been decided. Tariyit is a possible dialect spoken by the Haratine (former slaves of the Ouargli people). Positive language and cultural attitudes.

Tahaggart Tamahaq: also called Tamachek, Tamashekin, Tomachek, Tuareg, Touareg, Tourage. 62,000 speakers in Algeria, Niger, and Libya. In Algeria: 25,000 speakers. Dialects are Hoggar (Ahaggaren, Ajjer, Tahaggart), Ghat (Ganet, Djanet). In Niger: 20,000 speakers. Dialects are Hoggar (Ahaggaren, Ajjer, Tahaggart), Ghat (Ganet, Djanet). Traditional script called *Shifinagh*. In Libya: 17,000 speakers. Dialects are Hoggar (Ahaggaren, Ajjer, Tahaggart), Ghat (Ganet, Djanet).

Tamasheq: also called Kidal Tamasheq, Tomacheck, Tamashekin, Timbuktu, Kidal. "Tuareg" is a derogatory name sometimes used. 270,000 speakers in Mali, Burkina Faso, and Algeria. In Mali: 250,000 speakers. Central, Timbuktu area, and northeastern Mali. Dialects are Timbuktu (Tombouctou, Tanaslamt) and Tadhaq (Kidal), which may be two separate languages. In Burkina Faso: 20,000 speakers in Oudalan Province. Dialects are Timbuktu (Tombouctou, Tanaslamt) and Tadghaq (Kidal). Theses two dialects may also be separate languages.

Tamazight, Central Atlas: also called Central Shilha, Middle Atlas Berber, Shilha. 3,500,000 speakers in Morocco Algeria, and France. In Morocco: 3,000,000 speakers. Dialects are Central Atlas, South Oran. 40% monolingual. Others use Arabic as second language. One of the major Berber languages. In Algeria: Western Algeria mountain area of Atlas and adjacent valleys to Taza, in the vicinity of Rabat, south near the Moroccan border.

Tamazight, Temacine: also called Tougourt, Touggourt, Tugurt. 6,000 speakers in Algeria, in the vicinity of Temacine, Tamelhat, Ghomra, and Meggarin. Related to Tumzabt, Tagargrent, and Taznatit. Possibly a dialect of Tagargrent, but not likely. People may have shifted to Arabic.

Tamazight, Tidikelt: 9,000 speakers in Algeria, in Tidikelt, in the vicinity of Salah, and Tit in southern Algeria. Dialects are Tidikelt, Tit. People may have shifted to Arabic.

Tarifit: also called Rifi, Rifia, Northern Shilha, Shilha. 2,000,000 speakers in Morocco, Algeria, France, and the Netherlands. In Morocco: 1,500,000 speakers in the north. The dialects listed are near Al Hoceima. They are Urrighel and Beni Iznassen. The chief differences between the dialects are phonological. There may be other dialects. Senhaja de Srair was said to be a separate language in 1939. In Algeria: Along the coast, eastern Alteria to Arzeu. Dialects are Arzeu, Igzennaian, Iznacen (Beni Iznassen).

Tawallammat Tamajaq: also called Tamasheq, Tamachek, Tomacheck, Tamashekin, Tuareg, Touareg, Tourage, Amazigh, Tahoua, Tewellemet, Tahoua Tamajeq. Over 640,000 speakers in Niger, Mali, and Nigeria. In Niger: 450,000 speakers. Dialects are Tawallammat Tan Dannag (Ioullemmeden), Tawallammat Tan Ataram. Traditional script called *Shifinagh*. National language of Niger. In Mali: 190,000 speakers. East Mali, Menaka, and Gao regions. Dialects are Tawallammet Tan Dannag (Ioullemmeden), Tawallammat Tan Ataram. In Nigeria: It may be the eastern rather than the western dialect in Nigeria.

Tayart Tamajeq: also called Tamachek, Tomacheck, Amazigh, Tuareg, Touareg. 250,000 speakers in central Niger, Agadez area. Dialects are Air (Agadez, Tayart, Tayert, Tamestayert), Tanassfarwat (Tamagarast). Traditional script called *Shifinagh*.

Taznatit: 40,000 speakers in Algeria. Isolated, around Timimoun, near the Touat region and around 400 miles southwest of the Mzab. Dialects are Gourara (Gurara), Touat (Tuat, Tuwat). Related to Tumzabt, Tagargrent, and Temacine Tamazight. Low intelligibility with other Tamazight speech forms, including Tumzabt and Tagargrent. Vigorous language use.

Tumzabt: also called Mzab, Mzabi, Ghardaia. 70,000 speakers in Algeria, in the Mzab region, 330 miles south of Algiers in seven oases; Ghardaia being the principal one. Only minor dialect variations. Related to Tagargrent, Temacine Tamzight, and Taznatit. Some speakers are probably bilingual in Arabic, French, or Spanish. Women virtually monolingual in Tumzabt. Vigorous language use.

Zenaga: 200 speakers in Mauritania between Mederdra and the Atlantic coast, southern Mauritania. The language is related to other Berber languages in basic structure, though specific features differ. Bilingualism in Hassaniyya. It is reported that adult speakers are not teaching it to their children.

B. GRIMES

BILINGUALISM AND MULTILINGUALISM.

[*This entry includes the following subentries:*
Overview
Bilingual Education
Multilingualism
Brain Structures in Bilingualism]

Overview

As a term, "bilingualism" has been applied to individuals as well as to groups and institutions. The issues raised by scholars describing individuals have been primarily psycholinguistic and social-psychological (Grosjean 1982, Baetens Beardsmore 1986). At the group level, the concept has raised sociolinguistic, educational, and political considerations (Fishman 1978). In popular usage and debate about the merits of bilingualism, considerable confusion is caused by unclear specification of whether one is referring to individuals or to social categories.

1. Definitions. A bilingual individual is someone who controls two or more languages. Beyond this simple definition, considerable fuzziness arises from the difficulty of defining what it means to control a language. Using a loose criterion, such as the ability to utter or comprehend some minimal range of sentences, the majority of the world's population would be considered bilingual. However, a strict criterion of native-like control would severely limit this number. The definitional problem is further complicated because control of language can vary as a function of the domain of language use—and because, within any domain, skill in the language can undergo development or attrition. Although there is disagreement on criteria, scholars agree on the existence of these variabilities (Haugen 1973).

Several typologies of bilingual individuals have been proposed. The best known is Weinreich's 1953 distinction between *compound* and *coordinate* bilingualism, referring to the lexical organization of two languages with respect to the concepts they represent. This is determined by the extent to which the languages are segregated in contexts of acquisition and usage: a compound organization integrates the languages under a single concept, whereas coordinate organization maintains separate concepts. Other distinctions refer to the age at which bilingualism is attained: thus *simultaneous* vs. *sequential* bilingualism distinguishes whether the two languages are learned at the same time, or whether the second language is acquired after the primary language has been established (starting at about age three). *Early* vs. *late* bilingualism has been also used to refer to this distinction, but also serves to distinguish between sequential bilinguals who attained their second language at different ages.

Bilingualism at the group level is more complex, because it can refer to a wide range of entities—including speech communities, schools, and governments. Important here is the degree and nature of functional separation granted the two languages within these groups.

Ferguson's 1959 notion of diglossia has been usefully applied to some settings of stable bilingualism, where more conservative and more innovative language varieties function as *formal* and *informal* varieties, respectively, e.g. Classical Arabic vs. Colloquial Arabic. Many sociolinguists believe that, in the absence of diglossia, bilingualism will result in language shift. An important distinction which incorporates the notion of majority and minority languages is that between *additive* and *subtractive* bilingualism—also referred to as *elite* vs. *folk* bilingualism. In additive bilingualism, as in the case of Canadian Anglophones who learn French, the majority group learns the minority language without fearing loss of the native language. Subtractive bilingualism describes the situation of language minority groups in the United States, where the second language eventually replaces the native language.

2. Developmental processes. The development of simultaneous bilingualism has been described in a number of case studies—most prominently a study by Leopold 1939–1949 of his daughter, who was raised speaking German and English. Functional separation of the two linguistic systems appears early in development, although not without cross-over between languages. Some observers report delays in vocabulary development at the early stages, but with few long-term effects; however, neither observation has been substantiated against normative data. For optimal development, a one-parent/one-language method is commonly prescribed, in which each parent uses one language consistently; but practical problems are acknowledged. Long-term studies suggest that bilingualism has no harmful effects on overall linguistic or cognitive development, and possibly has beneficial effects.

Sequential bilingualism has been studied most intensively from the perspectives of phonological, morphological, and syntactic development. The driving question has been the extent to which characteristics of the *first* or *native language* (L1) predict outcomes in acquisition of the *second language* (L2); this question has been associated with *contrastive analysis*. Phonological development can be described, though by no means wholly, in terms of L1 influences, particularly among adults. Morphological and syntactic aspects of L2 acquisition show far fewer effects of L1, particularly with respect to the types of errors in production. Thus L2 acquisition is governed primarily by the properties of the target language, although L1 provides the learner with a source of hypotheses about L2.

Statements about discourse factors are limited by the

theoretical status of contrastive studies in this area. Theoretical approaches to L2 acquisition have tended to mimic those in L1 acquisition research, with recent interests arising in universal grammar and learnability theory.

3. Constraints on development. Unlike L1 acquisition, L2 acquisition is characterized by differential success, with often imperfect approximations to the target language. Selinker (1972) has introduced the term *fossilization*, which has been widely accepted to refer to *arrest* along the developmental continuum. A variety of factors, ranging from biological to situational variables, supposedly modulate the occurrence of this process. Many theorists have used the age of the learner as a global variable, and generally have assumed this to be equivalent to biological maturation. But the picture is considerably more complex: cognitive, social, and emotional factors also covary with age, and not all of these have wholly biological bases.

Studies have tested the truth of folk observations that, with respect to L2 acquisition, "The younger the better." Such observations are supported to a limited extent, particularly with respect to pronunciation, by studies of L2 learners with more than five years' opportunity to learn the L2. However, the exact shape of the declining function with age is unclear; e.g., we do not know whether it is linear, non-linear, or discontinuous. Puberty is frequently claimed to be an important breaking point, particularly by supporters of a critical period for L2 acquisition; but evidence is sparse. An advantage for older learners has also been found with respect to the rate of acquisition when exposure levels are limited.

Research which looks at individual differences in L2 acquisition within specified age groups has turned up a number of interesting factors. In addition to the variable of *language aptitude* (often equated with verbal intelligence), Lambert 1972 and other works have shown the importance of *motivational variables*—such as positive attitudes toward speakers of the target language, or instrumental goals to be attained through its acquisition. While language aptitude accounts for performance on primarily academic assessments of L2 acquisition, motivational variables account for performance on listening comprehension, and on more communicatively driven tasks. Other researchers have pointed to personality variables such as field-independence, extroversion, and other learning styles as positively contributing to L2 acquisition. Another important consideration is the *cultural orientation* of the learner, particularly in classroom situations. This complex area suggests that important interaction effects exist between predispositions of learners and the nature of the learning situation.

4. Consequences of bilingualism. Early work conducted in the psychological tradition of mental measurement gave rise to the alarming conclusion that bilingualism could have harmful effects on mental and social development. This substantial literature is notable for its flaws in subject selection, and its failure to control background variables in comparisons. When background factors are controlled, a large number of studies have shown a positive correlation between bilingualism and performance on a wide variety of tests of cognitive flexibility. Several studies have suggested that the direction of causality is complex; but they support the argument that bilingualism, especially when additive, fosters cognitive skills. The studies, in any event, suggest no negative effects associated with bilingualism.

5. Cognitive and neurological processes. The issue of whether compound and coordinate bilinguals show different patterns for processing information has generated a sizeable but inconclusive literature. Some researchers have avoided the problem of individual differences, and have instead focused on the organization of the mental lexicon in the two languages. Studies support the view that the two lexicons of most bilinguals are interdependent; thus, in memory experiments, they behave as though word equivalents in the two languages are repetitions in the same language. However, some experimental protocols continue to yield data for memory of the particular language of presentation—suggesting that, in certain contexts, the form of the presentation is retained in memory.

Studies of the neurofunctional bases of language organization in bilinguals are intriguing, particularly those which suggest that the two languages might be localized differently. There is also preliminary evidence for considerable right-hemisphere involvement in the early stages of second-language acquisition.

6. Social processes. Conversations among bilinguals typically involve *code-switching*, and a useful distinction can be drawn between situational and conversational varieties. *Situational switching* refers to differential use of the languages depending on the situation, whereas *conversational switching* is the change of languages within conversational episodes, often intrasententially. Bilinguals use code-switching for various expressive functions, including emphasis and the marking of group identity. Researchers emphasize that code-switching is the result neither of inadequate competence in the two languages, nor of confusion between them; rather, the languages are situation-bound.

Language as a marker of ethnic identity is important in marking in-group and out-group membership. Elaborate social psychological models have been developed, taking account of sociological factors such as the dominance relations between the in-group and out-group, to predict convergence or divergence of linguistic markers in intergroup contact. Empirical support for such models is still sketchy, but promising.

7. Bilingualism and education. Issues surrounding bilingual education programs for language majority students need to be distinguished from those surrounding programs for language minority students. In programs for majority students, the goal is additive bilingualism: the L2 is an enrichment, and there is no threat to the status of the L1. In minority language programs, the primary concern is the development of the majority language, with secondary concern, to varying degrees, for the maintenance of the L1.

Considerable research investment has been made in evaluating *immersion* education programs for majority students, particularly in Canada. In such programs, the majority students receive instruction exclusively in the L2 from the early elementary grades, with later introduction of language arts in their L1. Immersion programs are more effective than traditional foreign language programs, and students maintain age-appropriate levels of performance in the L1.

Bilingual education programs for minority students vary in their philosophy toward maintaining the students' native language and culture. In some programs, the L1 is used only until students have sufficient control of L2, often within two to five years, to receive instruction exclusively through the majority language. In other programs which attempt maintenance, the goal is to enhance and maintain the L1, even after the majority language has been acquired. Regardless of program orientation, such special programs for immigrant and guest-worker children are in many countries a focal point for public attitudes concerning immigration and demographic change.

Much of the debate on these programs focuses on the length of time it takes for minority students to learn the new target language and on the relative amounts of school-time exposure they should have to the target language as compared to their native language. In reality, a number of external factors contribute to a student's rate of acquisition of a second language, including the student's level of proficiency in the native language on immigration, family socioeconomic status, and age of immigration.

8. Politics and demographics. The degree to which bilingualism becomes a political issue is related to the activism and critical mass of the minority language groups. Bilingualism at the societal level is not the root cause of political difficulties, as in Quebec or in Belgium; but the symbolic politics of language can be powerful, and often linguistic unity is equated with political unity and nationalism. In many parts of Western Europe, as well as in North America, linguistic minorities in the schools have increased to the point where minorities are about to become a majority. In the United States, such demographic changes have been accompanied by attempts to legislate language through a constitutional declaration for an official language. Such movements attempt to restrict ethnic language usage among minorities. However, attempts to impose language politically have not been very successful in the past. Language shift, e.g. in the United States, is governed more by linguistic minorities' choice to gain access to the economic and political power held by speakers of the majority language.

[*See also* Applied Linguistics; Code-Switching; Diglossia; Social Variation; *and* Sociolinguistics.]

BIBLIOGRAPHY

Baetens Beardsmore, Hugo. 1986. *Bilingualism: Basic principles.* 2d ed. Clevedon, Avon, England: Multilingual Matters.

Ferguson, Charles A. 1959. Diglossia. *Word* 15.325–340.

Fishman, Joshua A., ed. 1978. *Advances in the study of societal multilingualism.* The Hague: Mouton.

Grosjean, François. 1982. *Life with two languages.* Cambridge, Mass.: Harvard University Press.

Hamers, Josiane F., and Michel Blanc. 1989. *Bilinguality and bilingualism.* New York: Cambridge University Press.

Haugen, Einar. 1973. Bilingualism, language contact, and immigrant languages in the United States: A research report, 1956–1970. In *Current trends in linguistics,* edited by Thomas A. Sebeok, vol. 10, *Linguistics in North America,* pp. 505–591. The Hague: Mouton.

Lambert, Wallace E. 1972. *Language, psychology, and culture: Essays.* Stanford, Calif.: Stanford University Press.

Leopold, Werner F. 1939–1949. *Speech development of a bilingual child: A linguist's record.* 4 vols. Evanston, Ill.: Northwestern University Press.

Romaine, Suzanne. 1995. *Bilingualism.* 2d ed. Cambridge, Mass.: Blackwell.

Selinker, Larry. 1972. Interlanguage. *International Review of Applied Linguistics* 10.219–231.

Weinreich, Uriel. 1953. *Languages in contact: Findings and problems.* New York: Linguistic Circle of New York. Reprinted, The Hague: Mouton, 1974.

KENJI HAKUTA

Bilingual Education

"Bilingual education" usually refers to the use of two languages of instruction at some point in the student's career. In other words, it is defined in terms of the means through which particular educational goals are achieved. Proficiency in two languages is not necessarily a goal of bilingual education in this sense. For example, in some contexts bilingual instruction is employed as a temporary measure to help students from linguistic minority groups make a transition between the language of the home and the language of the school without falling behind in the mastery of subject matter. When it is assumed that students have attained sufficient proficiency in the school language to follow instruction in it, home-language instruction is discontinued. However, the term "bilingual education" is sometimes defined in terms of goals, to refer to educational programs that are designed to promote bilingual skills among students. When used in this broader sense, "bilingual education" may entail instruction primarily or exclusively through only one language, e.g. when instruction is delivered through a minority language in order to give students the maximum opportunity to learn that language. Second-language *immersion* programs of this type are implemented widely in certain countries, e.g. Canada's French immersion programs. (For general reference, see Paulston 1980, Spolsky 1986.)

1. Issues. Within the general area of bilingual education, issues that are of particular relevance to applied linguistics include the following:

(a) The consequences of different forms of bilingual education for language learning and academic achievement, in both first language (L1) and second language (L2)

(b) The impact of bilingual education on attitudes toward and use of languages by students and their parents outside the school

(c) Within the general sphere of *language planning*, the role of bilingual education in conferring status and power on the ethnolinguistic groups whose languages receive institutional recognition in the public education system.

This last aspect of bilingual education involves both sociological and applied-linguistic concerns; it accounts for the considerable controversy that bilingual education policies have engendered in many countries. In the United States, for example, although bilingual education is designed to promote educational equity for minority students, it has frequently been characterized by media and political commentators as socially divisive and "un-American." Critics fear that the institutionalization of minority languages in public education may encourage the continued use of those languages outside the school, and may retard the assimilation of minority populations, particularly the rapidly increasing Hispanic population, into the American mainstream.

2. Classification of bilingual education. Various typologies of bilingual education have been proposed. The most elaborate is that of Mackey 1972, which distinguishes ninety different potential varieties, depending on the intersection of languages of the home, neighborhood, and country. By contrast, the more limited sociolinguistic typology of Fishman 1976 distinguishes the following four types of bilingual education for minority students, based primarily on program objectives:

(a) *Transitional bilingualism* refers to programs that use the minority language to the extent necessary to help students master subject matter until their skills in the majority language are developed to the point where it alone can be used as the medium of instruction.

(b) *Monoliterate bilingualism* programs are intermediate in orientation between language shift and language maintenance: they encourage the continued development of aural/oral skills in the minority language, but concern themselves with literacy only in the majority language.

(c) *Partial biliterate bilingualism* programs aim at fluency and literacy in both languages, but literacy in the L1 is restricted to certain subject matter, generally that related to the ethnic group and its cultural heritage.

(d) *Full biliterate bilingualism* programs attempt to develop all skills in both languages in all domains.

Skutnabb-Kangas 1984 has developed a typology that focuses on the relationship of program organization to linguistic and societal goals for both minority and majority students. According to this typology, the medium of instruction can be primarily the majority language, the minority language, or both. The program can be designed for the majority (dominant) group, the minority (subordinate) group, or both together (a "two-way" or integrated program). Societal goals of bilingual education can include direct assimilation of minority students, segregation and possible repatriation of minority students, or enrichment and/or instrumental benefits (e.g. jobs) for both minority and majority students. Finally, the linguistic aims include producing students who are (i) monolingual or strongly dominant in the majority language, e.g. US transitional bilingual programs; (ii) monolingual or strongly dominant in the minority language, e.g. some primarily L1 programs for guest-worker children in Europe; and (iii) bilinguals.

This typology is useful in considering some of the current controversies about bilingual education, insofar as it captures the direct relationship between interethnic power relations and program organization. The scope of the typology could be broadened by elaborating the "societal goals" category into educational goals, sociolinguistics goals, and socio-political goals. Educational goals include: (i) *equity* vis-à-vis academic achievement and (ii) *enrichment*—access to two languages and cultures. Sociolinguistic goals refer to promoting access to a language of wider communication, usually a language of economic or political power, versus promoting access to a less used language, usually a "heritage" language whose survival is threatened. Finally, socio-political goals refer to the status and modes of participation envisaged for students upon graduation into the wider society—for example, total assimilation into the mainstream culture, integration that permits maintenance of some bicultural allegiance, or segregation. Sociolinguistic and socio-political goals can overlap, as when proficiency in a heritage or threatened language is made a condition of employment for certain government occupational categories (e.g. Irish in Ireland, Basque in the Basque country).

3. The outcomes of bilingual education. Although there is considerable variation among types of bilingual education, some general patterns have emerged consistently in the research results. First, for both majority and minority students, instruction through the medium of a minority language appears to entail no long-term delay in the development of academic skills in the majority language. Thus, students from anglophone home backgrounds in Canada who are instructed during the early grades largely through the medium of French perform as well in English academic skills as students instructed

entirely through English. By the same token, minority francophone students in Canada who are instructed largely through French perform as well in English as do similar students instructed largely through English. The same pattern emerges in the United States for Hispanic students, and in many other countries. This pattern has been attributed to a 'common underlying proficiency' or interdependence that facilitates transfer of academic or conceptual knowledge across languages (Skutnabb-Kangas 1984, Cummins 2000).

A second general finding is that, for minority students who are at risk of school failure, strong promotion of the students' L1 in school often results in significantly better academic progress in the majority language than does instruction primarily through the majority language. It has been argued that this pattern depends on a variety of factors that operate together with the medium of instruction—e.g. the extent to which the program validates minority students' cultural identity, and the extent of minority community involvement—as well as general pedagogical and assessment practices (Skutnabb-Kangas 1984, Cummins 1986, Hakuta 1986).

Finally, research consistently shows that use of the target language as a medium of instruction is highly effective in developing students' proficiency in that language. However, research data are considerably sparser on the effects of bilingual education on language attitudes and use. Some studies (cf. Ireland 1975) have reported that positive attitudes toward the minority language, and actual use of it, are significantly related to previous participation in bilingual or minority language immersion programs. It appears likely that bilingual education is associated with increased proficiency in and generally positive attitudes toward the target language (Lambert and Tucker 1972); but proficiency and positive attitudes by themselves, although necessary, are not sufficient to guarantee extensive use of the language after leaving school.

In conclusion, the research data on bilingual education are considerably more clear-cut than the public debate might suggest. Results support the view that properly implemented bilingual programs can contribute both to equity for minority students and to the enrichment of educational experience, involving access to two languages and cultures, for both minority and majority students. Implementation of such programs, however, also changes the status quo with respect to the power relations (e.g. employment prospects) between different ethnolinguistic groups. In the public debate, the educational merits of different program options often become obscured by the intensity of competing vested interests.

[*See also* Applied Linguistics; Code-Switching; Diglossia; Language Planning; Social Variation; Sociolinguistics.]

BIBLIOGRAPHY

Cummins, Jim. 1986. Empowering minority students: A framework for intervention. *Harvard Educational Review* 56.18–36.

Cummins, Jim. 2000. *Language, power and pedagogy: Bilingual children in the crossfire*. Clevedon, Avon, England: Multilingual Matters.

Fishman, Joshua A. 1976. *Bilingual education: An international sociological perspective*. Rowley, Mass.: Newbury House.

Hakuta, Kenji. 1986. *Mirror of language: The debate on bilingualism*. New York: Basic Books.

Ireland. 1975. *Report of the Committee on Irish Language Attitudes Research*. Dublin: Minister for the Gaeltacht.

Lambert, Wallace E., and G. Richard Tucker. 1972. *Bilingual education of children: The St. Lambert experiment*. Rowley, Mass.: Newbury House.

Mackey, William F. 1972. A typology of bilingual education. In *Advances in the sociology of language*, vol. 2, *Selected studies and applications*, edited by Joshua A. Fishman, pp. 413–432. The Hague: Mouton.

Paulston, Christina Bratt. 1980. *Bilingual education: Theories and issues*. Rowley, Mass.: Newbury House.

Skutnabb-Kangas, Tove. 1984. *Bilingualism or not: The education of minorities*. (Multilingual matters, 7.) Clevedon, Avon, England: Multilingual Matters.

Spolsky, Bernard, ed. 1986. *Language and education in multilingual settings*. Clevedon, Avon, England: Multilingual Matters.

JIM CUMMINS

Multilingualism

Multilingualism, the simultaneous existence of more than one linguistic variety, can occur at both personal and group levels. The former always implies some degree of fluency in more than one variety; the latter may or may not involve more than monolingual individual abilities. This simple distinction accounts for large variations among multilingual societies, but in practice, the distinction is never so simple. Some societies are made up largely of people who are multilingual, and some are explicit or implicit federal arrangements that politically unite different speech communities; however, there are very few societies so homogeneous that only one variety can be heard in them. Similarly, some societies are

multilingual by law, while others extract a single official variety from a de facto multilingualism. Perhaps of greatest social interest and importance are official stances on language matters, which build on historical and traditional patterns of power and tolerance, and which suggest, for instance, underlying conceptions of diversity and pluralism, illuminating the treatment of minority groups and revealing attitudes about linguistic usage and aspirations. In both democratic societies and dictatorial ones, reaction to linguistic heterogeneity can have real and immediate consequences. Multilingual realities trigger different responses in different settings—including desires for monolingualism—but all rest on the acknowledgment of diversity and the social accommodations this suggests. (Even where diversity is not valued, or where harmonious accommodation is neither sought nor desired, responses still derive from this acknowledgment: linguistic diversity is usually, after all, a patent fact of social life.)

Worldwide, multilingualism is clearly a more prevalent condition than monolingualism, a fact easily forgotten by those who speak a 'big' language. Around five thousand languages exist in a world divided into only about two hundred states; at official levels, however, only about one-quarter of those states recognize more than one language. Even where multilingualism has legal standing, one language is likely to be more equal than the other(s) or varieties dominate in particular regions, or socioeconomic power adheres more closely to some forms than to others. The relationships among German, French, Italian, and Romansch in Switzerland are illustrative. Another sort of situation is represented by Ireland, where both Irish and English are officially sanctioned, but the former is limited increasingly to symbolic significance.

The relationship between policy and usage is not always clear. Multilingual encounters may be less frequent in countries that recognize more than one language (if, e.g., the recognition is territorially limited) than in officially monolingual states. Thus, Nigeria formally sanctions only English, but its 80 million people speak around 400 languages. Much depends on individual and group needs and desires. In India, where 15 languages have legal status, one could live out one's days monolingually, but there are multilingual *possibilities* that could not exist in more homogeneous surroundings:

A Bombay spice merchant has, as his maternal variety, a Kathiawari dialect of Gujerati, but at work he most often uses Kacchi. In the marketplace he speaks Marathi and, at the railway station, Hindustani. On internal air flights English is used, and he may watch English-language films at the cinema. He reads a Gujerati newspaper written in a dialect more standard than his own. (Edwards 1994:2)

Simple mobility in a multilingual environment necessitates this sort of linguistic flexibility. Less immediately obvious, but of considerable importance, is that multiple fluencies are rarely (if ever) equally developed. It would be uneconomical to 'overdevelop' them beyond the needs associated with each: the Bombay citizen knows just enough Marathi to buy rice, but his Gujerati is a fuller competence. And, given that the rice-seller or the railway worker may have a linguistic repertoire at least as rich, 'overlaps' can occur; these enable and sometimes directly encourage *code-switching* exchanges. "Sometimes," to quote Poplack 1980, "I'll start a sentence in English *y terminó en español.*"

How does multilingualism arise? The underlying dynamic is mobility and contact. Immigrants bring their varieties together and into contact with those of the receiving society. Other sorts of expansion—territorial, colonial, imperialist, and mercantile—may produce similar effects. It is not always necessary for great numbers of people to move physically; for instance, military and economic pressures involving only a handful of soldiers, bureaucrats, and traders can create cultural and linguistic contacts that give rise to multilingual adaptations. Original exigencies can then fade away, leaving such adaptations in place. A foreign, intrusive language may leave various residues of status, culture, or international access that continue to support multilingualism long after the imperial armies have gone home.

Another common scenario that leads to multilingualism is political union among speech communities, as in Belgium, Canada, and Switzerland. Such unions need not involve partners equal in numbers or power; even within the three democracies mentioned, real or perceived imbalances find linguistic expression. For example, degrees of bilingual competence among francophone Canadians reflect different backgrounds, requirements, and aspirations than among anglophones. There are other, more pointed examples of asymmetrical unions. Federations may be built on arbitrary and involuntary amalgamations. Thus, the Canada that unites the two 'charter' groups, the two 'founding peoples', *also* incorporates a million members of the indigenous 'First Nations'. Welsh- and Gaelic-speaking parts of the United Kingdom remind us of another sort of incorporation. Colonial boundary marking

and state creation as carried out in Africa, Asia, and South America provide even more egregious examples of imposed associations that have had linguistic consequences.

Beyond geographical and political motivations, cultural and educational goals can also expand linguistic repertoires, even if there is no desire or opportunity to use the new ability in ordinary conversation. Nonetheless, there is a perceived necessity, though subtler and less immediately practical.

One response to the communicative problems created by multilingualism is multilingualism itself. Faced with a diversity of languages, one could urge the expansion of individual repertoires: if there are a dozen varieties spoken in a region, and if everyone there knows all of them, there is no problem. This, however ignores practical facts: not everyone may need to know all twelve languages; some languages will be restricted in scope by their speakers' status, or by accepted domain limitations; and it would probably be unproductive to aim for nativelike fluency in all cases. There are more problems. Where does 'your' region end? Why stop at the border within which these dozen languages are found? Won't you ever need to deal with the state next door, where there are another dozen varieties?

Certain remarkable demonstrations of competence imply a much broader linguistic potential than most of us even dream about. Giuseppe Mezzofanti, a Vatican curator in the early 19th century, was reportedly fluent in 60 languages; James Murray, the editor of the *Oxford English Dictionary*, indicated in an application letter of 1866 that he knew at least 20; the Victorian scholar-explorer Sir Richard Burton spoke about 25. Linguistically narrower but still impressive are people like Vladimir Nabokov and George Steiner, moving effortlessly through the highest literary reaches of several languages—both, in fact, claimed to be maternally trilingual. More ordinary mortals often have studied a language or two at school or have expanded their repertoires in more informal or desultory fashion. Clearly, given sufficient motivation and time, multilingual capabilities can be greatly increased; yet even if we were all Mezzofantis and Murrays, communicative difficulties would remain. Sixty languages are still only a small percentage of five thousand. Other responses to multilingualism are required.

The two basic ways to cross the barriers of a multilingual world involve either translation or some sort of lingua franca. *Link languages* fall into three categories:

(i) powerful 'natural' languages that have, in one way or another, risen to prominence, sometimes referred to as 'languages of wider communication'; (ii) restricted or simplified forms of languages, alone or in combination, whose limited scope is easy to master yet sufficient for circumscribed communicative purposes; and (iii) constructed languages, sometimes called (but never by their adherents) 'artificial' varieties.

Throughout history, dominant varieties have served as bridges between language communities. Their power derives not from any inherent linguistic qualities, but from the military, political, or economic might of their speakers. If cultural elite status underpins a lingua franca, it has usually grown out of these more blatant potencies. The muscle behind lingua francas derives from their native speakers' control of important commodities—wealth, prestige, or scholarship—that others desire.

Greek and Latin are the prime examples of classical lingua francas, but there are many others, past and present, including Italian, Arabic, Malay, Chinese, and Hindi. Lingua franca status is an impermanent quantity, waxing or waning with the fortunes of the dominant culture. Where are Latin and Greek today? Where, indeed, is French, relative to its recent overarching importance in global intercourse? Contemporary French frustrations and the linguistic machinations they lead to are heightened by the fact that history records no example of a lingua franca that has regained lost status. (I prescind here from discussion of the possibly unique circumstances surrounding Hebrew.) Today English is clearly *the* global lingua franca; its ubiquity and penetration make it by far the most powerful lingua franca ever seen. Whereas earlier link languages tended to coexist with more localized varieties, some think that English threatens to push the others off the stage altogether. Where a strong language virtually eliminates a weaker one, the former necessarily ceases to be merely a lingua franca, a language of intergroup convenience, and coexistence yields to outright replacement.

A second category of link languages comprises pidgins and creoles. The former involves some sort of mixture between varieties—an indigenous language and a colonial one, for instance, in contact occasioned by mercantile expansion and exploration. The resulting vocabularies and grammars are usually very restricted, intended only to allow simple communication. It is easy to see that some pidgins would have a relatively short existence, while others might be required for a long time. Some,

like Tok Pisin in New Guinea, eventually achieve official recognition. Prolonged contact can lead to other possibilities, too. As communicative requirements expand, one group may increasingly adopt the other's language. Alternatively, a pidgin may evolve into a creole. This happens when those born in pidgin-speaking communities begin to develop this part of their linguistic inheritance; the simplified pidgin, insufficiently nuanced, is 'creolized' to become richer and more expressive. In effect, a new mother tongue is born, and the child is more competent in it than the parent. In Sierra Leone, Krio is a national language, the maternal variety of some and a second medium for many others; in fact, Krio is now a partner in the production of new pidgins. (This is a good reminder, incidentally, of the historically dynamic course of all language varieties.)

Constructed languages can also act as lingua francas. Esperanto is the best-known example, but hundreds have been built. In most instances, the initial desire has been to produce some sort of neutral auxiliary that everyone could agree to learn as a second (or subsequent) language. Maternal languages would not be threatened, this auxiliary form being a simple facilitator of global communication. The argument has often been made that powerful 'natural' languages cannot have this desired neutrality (because they are tinged by an imperial or colonial past, e.g.), and the way is theoretically clear for some Esperanto to fill a large and bothersome gap. Most architects of constructed languages have had broader aspirations than simply supplying a universal instrumental medium; they have often seen their creations as a contribution to the 'internationalizing' of identity and the encouragement of global peace and harmony. No constructed language, however, has yet managed more than a peripheral existence. There are several reasons for this, but the chief difficulty is that they are always up against existing lingua francas, powerful natural varieties possessing full historical pedigrees.

The other broad approach to multilingual matters is translation. A large literature exists on perspectives and methods, but the basic idea is simplicity itself: individuals who have a foot in two (or more) linguistic camps can be bridges between them, relieving members of each community of the need to expand their own repertoires. Translation is admittedly an unwieldy process, and it works best when relatively infrequent contact is involved, or when the translation can achieve permanence through print or other permanent record. Translating between languages—at least, when we go beyond simple word-for-word exercises, which are almost useless—always involves interpretation (indeed, even within the same language, communication implies interpretation: we 'read between the lines' in all our interactions). Admonished since Cicero's time not to translate *verbum pro verbo* ('word for word'), we immediately sense the subjectivity and the detail involved in going from one language to another. Huge possibilities loom for mistakes, but also for more intentional manipulation and selectivity.

This is why perceptions of translation and translators are more complicated than might first be thought. Translation can mean the revealing of deep matters to outsiders, and this is not to be taken lightly. The translator, whose multilingual abilities allow the necessary straddling of boundaries, can be a type of quisling—but a quisling who must be accepted, whose spying is needed for obvious and practical purposes. Just to acknowledge this is to sense the historical uneasiness about translation, and to understand the Italian phrase *traduttori, traditori* ('translators, traitors'). As Steiner points out, "there is in every act of translation—and specially where it succeeds—a touch of treason. Hoarded dreams, patents of life are being taken across the frontier" (1992:244). A contemporary reflection of this is found in 'voice appropriation', the telling of native stories by outsiders. In many cultures, particularly those with rich oral traditions, stories are regarded as property of the group or of designated storytellers within it.

It is easy to understand that the forms and consequences of multilingual contact can be especially important among groups of unequal status. Where minority-language populations are involved, concerns about linguistic and cultural survival are intimately entwined with the use of a lingua franca or the scope of translation. In fact, since minority status implies limited power, the agendas for cross-group communication are usually set by others. Lingua francas, as we have seen, are usually the languages of powerful communities, and they may elbow other varieties out of their indigenous niches—a constant worry among minority-group members. Similarly, translations involving 'small' languages will inevitably decrease in quantity—and in appeal—as the languages themselves retreat before powerful neighbors. The overall danger is an accelerating downward spiral, the logical conclusion of which is one ultimate answer to multilingualism: monolingualism. If everyone speaks the lingua franca, then outright replacement of smaller varieties becomes a real possibility. This is an unacceptable solution to many people, particularly those whose languages are threatened. Consequently, predictable efforts are made on behalf of *language maintenance*, in situations in which *language shift* is a looming possibility; sometimes, if matters have become sufficiently grave, attempts at *language revival* may be indicated. Each of these phenomena now reflects an important subfield of linguistic inquiry.

Language maintenance, shift, and revival are among the most dramatic consequences of multilingual contact—important and far-reaching phenomena in themselves, and interesting perspectives from which to understand something of the poignancy of minority–majority relations. In addition to their bearing on the obvious communicative functions of language and what they reveal about social power, the existence of maintenance and revival efforts—and the fervor with which they are undertaken, and the sacrifices that may be made for them—reminds us of the formidable power of language as a marker of group identity. Why would people struggle so long and so passionately for a purely instrumental medium? The symbolic aspects of language, its role as mediator of cultures and civilizations, its literary expression, its central position in nationalist politics—these, too, are part of the broader story of a multilingual world.

[*See also* Applied Linguistics; Language Planning; Code-Switching; Diglossia; Pidgins and Creoles; Social Variation; Sociolingusitics; *and* Translation and Interpretation.]

BIBLIOGRAPHY

Baker, Colin, and Sylvia Prys Jones. 1998. *Encyclopedia of bilingualism and bilingual education.* Clevedon, Avon, England: Multilingual Matters.

Edwards, John. 1985. *Language, society and identity.* Oxford: Blackwell.

Edwards, John. 1994. *Multilingualism.* London: Routledge.

Grenoble, Lenore, and Lindsay Whaley. 1998. *Endangered languages.* Cambridge: Cambridge University Press.

Kaplan, Robert, and Richard Baldauf. 1997. *Language planning: From practice to theory.* Clevedon, Avon, England: Multilingual Matters.

Paulston, Christina, ed. 1988. *International handbook of bilingualism and bilingual education.* Westport, Conn.: Greenwood.

Poplack, Shana. 1980. Sometimes I'll start a sentence in English *y terminó en español. Linguistics* 18.581–616.

Steiner, George, 1992. *After Babel: Aspects of language and translation.* 2d ed. Oxford: Oxford University Press.

Wardhaugh, Ronald. 1987. *Language in competition.* Oxford: Blackwell.

JOHN EDWARDS

Brain Structures in Bilingualism

To study brain organization for two or more languages, one employs observation of breakdown in aphasia, as well as more modern instrumental and imaging techniques. Most bilingual or multilingual aphasics lose and recover their languages in similar fashion, and to the extent that they knew them before the aphasia-producing incident. However, for an interesting subset of bilingual aphasic patients, there is an unexpected recovery pattern. Rarely, a different sort of aphasia may be seen in each of two or more languages in a patient with a single lesion of the dominant hemisphere (Albert and Obler 1978). Somewhat more frequently, the severity of the aphasic symptoms is markedly greater in one language than in another. Paradis 1977, 1987 has described eight types of recovery from aphasia in bilinguals or multilinguals: parallel, differential, successive, antagonistic, mixed, selective, and alternating antagonistic. The discrepancies in all but the parallel form suggest that there is at least partially differentiated organization in the brain of the two or more languages. (For general reference, see Vaid 1986 and Fabbro 1999.)

Three types of explanation have been proposed for differential recovery. Ribot 1882 argued that the first-learned language was most likely to return first. Pitres 1895 observed that the language most practiced around the time of the aphasia-producing accident would return first. Others have argued that affective factors influence the patient for or against using a particular language. Affect can be used to explain any recovery pattern; however, Pitres's rule holds with an accuracy greater than chance, while that of Ribot does not (Obler and Albert 1977).

It is possible that representation of the languages themselves is not differentially impaired, but rather that *access* to one of them is worse. For example, researchers have posited a "switch mechanism" that might itself be damaged—resulting in the common pattern of differential recovery, in which one language is nearly impossible to produce, while the other is produced in aphasic fashion. However, efforts to localize the switch have proven fruitless, as damage in the clearest cases ranges throughout the language and non-language areas of the brain, from frontal through parietal to temporal lobes.

Few features of aphasia are exclusive to bilinguals, except for differential recovery. In *demented* bilinguals, however, inappropriate choice of language occurs in a number of patients, and some reseachers argue that normal code-switching constraints may be violated. Most striking are the changes in language choice: the healthy bilingual virtually never chooses to use a language with an interlocutor who cannot understand it, and is quickly able to self-correct if this is done inadvertently. The cognitive loss in demented patients seems to impair this sophisticated pragmatic mechanism; monolingual interlocutors may be addressed in code-switching style, or simply in a language they do not know—usually the patient's first language.

Studies of lateral dominance for language in bilinguals have suggested somewhat greater bilateral organization for both their languages, as compared to that of monolinguals—and greater bilateral organization for the second language, as compared to the first. However, these findings are disputed in other studies that suggest no difference in lateral dominance between bilinguals and monolinguals, or between the languages of bilinguals. Tachistoscopic and dichotic studies provide most of the fuel for this debate, but none serves as a frank replication of another study: they invariably differ in factors presumed to affect brain organization (e.g. age or manner of second-language acquisition). Furthermore, there is often inadequate control for factors pertinent to instrumental laterality studies per se, e.g. measures of relative dominance, or equivalent difficulty between stimulus sets in the two languages. Sodium amytal studies or split-brain studies might be more convincing measures of lateral dominance, but these have yet to be systematically carried out on bilingual subjects. Anecdotal reports from researchers involved with such patients indicate no evidence for differential lateral organization for the two languages. Crossed aphasia originally appeared to occur with higher incidence among bilinguals, which would suggest greater bilateral organization for language among bilinguals than among monolinguals. The consensus now is that such cases were simply more likely to be reported for bilingual aphasics.

There is some evidence from normal bilinguals that the critical period at puberty for second-language (L2) acquisition (Lenneberg 1967) affects the lateral organization for language (cf. Vaid 1983). These findings contrast with the "stage" hypothesis: this proposes that, in the early stages of L2 acquisition, more right-hemisphere skills are required—while by later stages, left-hemisphere dominance is more marked. However, some talented L2 learners manage to escape the constraints of a critical period, and learn a second language with apparent native-like proficiency, perhaps as a result of unusual cortical cellular organization (Novoa et al. 1988). In addition, the notion of a critical period, or even a sensitive period, has been questioned in light of studies like those of Johnson and Newport that show decline in morphosyntactic competence from acquisition ages well before puberty.

Cortical stimulation studies of bilinguals (Ojemann and Whitaker 1978) suggest partial but incomplete overlap of organization of the two languages within the left hemisphere. Brain-imaging studies (see Abutalebi et al. 2001) suggest that any differential distribution within the language areas of the left hemisphere is associated primarily with language production rather than with comprehension, and is linked to lower proficiency in the L2, and perhaps less exposure to it.

Certain psycholinguistic mechanisms posited for bilinguals imply neurolinguistic structures yet to be substantiated. For example, the notion of a monitor to direct incoming speech for processing via the appropriate language would suggest interaction of frontal as well as temporal lobe structures. The distinction of *compound* vs. *coordinate* implies that cortical representation of the lexica of subgroups of bilinguals is distributed differently, depending on language-learning history, patterns of use, and proficiency. Moreover, Kroll and his colleagues have reported directional asymmetries in accessing meaning directly or via a more proficient language. Like the older notions of transfer and interference, such processes must be instantiated in neuronal activity, one way or another.

[*See also* Aphasia; Neurolinguistics; *and* Psycholinguistics.]

BIBLIOGRAPHY

Abutalebi, Jubin, et al. 2001. The bilingual brain as revealed by functional neuroimaging. *Bilingualism: Language and Cognition* 4.179–190.

Albert, Martin L., and Loraine K. Obler. 1978. *The bilingual brain: Neuropsychological and neurolinguistic aspects of bilingualism.* New York: Academic Press.

Fabbro, Fabbro. 1999. *The neurolinguistics of bilingualism: An introduction.* Hove, UK: Psychology Press.

Lenneberg, Eric H. 1967. *Biological foundations of language.* New York: Wiley.

Novoa, Loriana, et al. 1988. Talent in foreign languages: A case study. In *The exceptional brain: Neuropsychology of talent and special abilities,* edited by Loraine K. Obler and Deborah Fein, pp. 294–302. New York: Guilford.

Obler, Loraine K., and Martin L. Albert. 1977. Influence of aging on recovery from aphasia in polyglots. *Brain and Language* 4.460–463.

Ojemann, George, and Harry A. Whitaker. 1978. The bilingual brain. *Archives of Neurology* 35.409–412.

Paradis, Michel. 1977. Bilingualism and aphasia. In *Studies in neurolinguistics,* vol. 3, edited by Haiganoosh Whitaker and Harry A. Whitaker, pp. 65–121. New York: Academic Press.

Paradis, Michel. 1987. *The assessment of bilingual aphasia.* Hillsdale, N.J.: Erlbaum.

Pitres, A. 1895. Étude sur l'aphasie chez les polyglottes. *Revue de Médecine* 15.873–889.

Ribot, Theodule. 1882. *Diseases of memory: An essay in the positive psychology.* London: Paul. New York: Appleton.

Vaid, Jyotsna. 1983. Bilingualism and brain lateralization. In *Language functions and brain organization,* edited by Sidney J. Segalowitz, pp. 315–339. New York: Academic Press.

Vaid, Jyotsna, ed. 1986. *Language processing in bilinguals: Psycholinguistic and neuropsychological perspectives.* Hillsdale, N.J.: Erlbaum.

LORAINE K. OBLER

BIMA-SUMBA LANGUAGES are spoken on islands in the Flores and Savu Seas, Nusa Tenggara, Indonesia; they constitute a branch of CENTRAL MALAYO-POLYNESIAN. Of the languages listed below, Ende, Keo, Li'o, and Nage form an Ende-Lio group.

LANGUAGE LIST

Anakalangu: also called Anakalang. 14,000 speakers. Ethnic population: 14,000 as of 1981. Spoken on Sumba Island, southwestern coast, east of Wanukaka. Closely related to, but unintelligible to speakers of Wejewa, Mamboru, Wanukaka, and Lamboya.

Bima: also called Bimanese. 500,000 speakers on Sunda Islands, eastern Sumbawa Island, east of the isthmus. Dialects are Kolo, Sangar (Sanggar), Toloweri, Bima, Mbojo.

Eastern Ngad'a: also called Southeastern Ngada. 5,000 speakers. Minor dialectal variation.

Ende: also called Endeh. 87,000 speakers on south central Flores, west of Sikka, Lesser Sundas. Dialects are Ende (Endeh, Ja'o, Djau), Nga'o (Ngao, West Ende). Dialect chain. Li'o is on the border between a separate language or dialect of Ende.

Kambera: also called Sumbanese, East Sumbanese, Oost-Sumbaas, Humba, Hilu Humba, East Sumba, Sumba. 200,000 speakers. Ethnic population: 200,000 as of 1989.

Spoken on the eastern half of Sumba Island, south of Flores, Lesser Sundas. Dialects are Kambera, Melolo, Uma Ratu Nggai (Umbu Ratu Nggai), Lewa, Kanatang, Mangili-Waijelo (Wai Jilu, Waidjelu, Rindi, Waijelo), Southern Sumba. Dialect network Kambera dialect is widely understood. Speakers of Lewa and Uma Ratu Nggai have difficulty understanding those from Mangili in many speech domains.

Keo: 40,000 speakers. Ethnic population: 40,000. Distinct from Nage. Close to Nage, Ngada, Ende, Lio, Palu'e, Riung. 02% are fluent in Indonesian. Keo migrants in towns and larger, more accessible places are tending to teach children Indonesian instead of Keo. All ages. All domains with Keo speakers. Ceremonies, personal letter writing in Keo, but Indonesian viewed as the proper language for writing and using with outsiders. Speakers view Indonesian as the prestige language that children need to speak to obtain better jobs. They view Nage and Ngad'a as superior to Keo, because of a cultural belief that mountain languages are more refined. English is viewed as a very prestigious language.

Kepo': also called Kepoq. Spoken in central Flores, between Manggarai and Rembong, with a separate enclave between Manggarai and Wae Rana. May be intelligible with one of the surrounding languages.

Kodi: also called Kudi. 40,000 speakers in West Sumba, Lesser Sundas. Dialects are Kodi Bokol, Kodi Bangedo, Nggaro (Nggaura). May be closest to Wejewa.

Komodo: spoken on Komodo Island and western coast of Flores. Not on Timor. Considered to be a separate language from Manggarai.

Lamboya: 25,000 speakers on Sumba Island, southwestern coast, southwest of Waikabubak. Dialects are Lamboya, Nggaura. Closely related to, but unintelligible to speakers of Wejewa, Mamboru, Wanukaka, and Anakalangu.

Laura: also called Laora. 10,000 speakers in northwestern Sumba between Kodi and Mamboru. Dialects are Laura, Mbukambero (Bukambero). Not intelligible with Kodi.

Li'o: also called Lio, Aku, Tanah Kunu, Lionese. 130,000 speakers on central Flores, west of Sikka around Paga and Dondo, Lesser Sundas. Palu'e is borderline between language and dialect with Li'o.

Mamboru: also called Memboro. 16,000 speakers on northwestern Sumba Island, coast around Memboro. Closely related to, but unintelligible to speakers of Wejewa, Wanukaka, Lamboya, and Anakalangu.

Manggarai: 500,000 speakers on western third of Flores Island and northern central Flores, Lesser Sundas. Dialects are Western Manggarai, Central Manggarai (Ruteng), West-Central Manggarai, Eastern Manggarai, Far-East Manggarai. Around forty-three subdialects. Closely related to Riung.

Nage: also called Nagé, Nage-Keo. 50,000 speakers on central Flores, northeast of Ngad'a, on the northern and western slopes of Ebu Lobo volcano.

Ndao: also called Ndaonese, Ndaundau, Dao. 5,000 speakers on island of Ndao, scattered on Rote, and Timor. Related to Sabu, but a distinct language. Difficult phonology.

Ngad'a: also called Ngadha, Ngada, Nad'a, Nga'da, Bajava, Badjava, Bajawa, Rokka. 60,000 speakers on southern central Flores, between Manggarai and Ende and Li'o. Dialects are Central Ngada, Bajawa, South Ngada. Dialect diversity.

Palu'e: also called Palue, Lu'a, Paluqe. 10,000 speakers on Palu Island, north of central Flores. Also the village of Nangahure on the northern coast of the Flores mainland northwest of Maumere. Dialect chain with Ende-Lio; marginal intelligibility with Li'o.

Rajong: also called Razong. Spoken on central Flores, two enclaves between Manggarai, Wae Rana, Ngad'a, and Rembong.

Rembong: spoken on northern central Flores, between Eastern Manggarai and Riung. Dialects are Rembong, Wangka, Namu.

Riung: also called Far Eastern Manggarai. 14,000 speakers on northern central Flores Island, Kecamatan Riung in Kaupaten Ngada, Lesser Sundas. Closely related to Manggarai; but marginal intelligibility.

Rongga: spoken on southern central Flores, between Manggarai and Ngad'a, and south of Wae Rana.

Sabu: also called Hawu, Havunese, Savu, Sawu, Sawunese, Savunese. 110,000 speakers. Dialects are Seba (Heba), Timu (Dimu), Liae, Mesara (Mehara), Raijua (Raidjua). Related to Ndao.

So'a: also called Soa. 10,000 speakers on central Flores, central Kabupaten Ngada, between Ngad'a and Riung. Closely related to Ngad'a.

Wae Rana: also called Waerana. Spoken on southern central Flores, between Manggarai and Ngad'a.

Wanukaka: also called Wanokaka. 10,000 speakers on Sumba Island, southwestern coast, east of Lamboya. Dialects are Wanukaka, Rua. Closely related to, but unintelligible to speakers of Wejewa, Mamboru, Lamboya, and Anakalangu. Intelligibility with varieties in east Sumba and Kambera uncertain.

Wejewa: also called Wewewa, Wajewa, Wewjewa, Waidjewa, West Sumbanese, Weyewa, Veveva. 65,000 speakers in interior of western Sumba Island, Lesser Sundas. Dialects are Weyewa, Lauli (Loli), Tana Righu.   B. GRIMES

BINARY FEATURES. See Phonological Features; Phonology; Semantics; Ethnosemantics; Componential Analysis; History of Linguistics; *and* Syntactic Features.

BINDING. *See* Anaphora.

BIOLOGY OF LANGUAGE. *See* Neurolinguistics; Evolution and Language; Acquisition of Language; Specific Language Impairment; *and* Williams Syndrome and Down Syndrome: Cognitive Constraints on Language.

BIU-MANDARA LANGUAGES. These are spoken in northeastern Nigeria and northern Cameroon, with some overspill into Chad. These languages form a top-level constituent of the CHADIC branch of Afro-Asiatic.

LANGUAGE LIST

Afade: also called Affade, Afadeh, Afada, Kotoko, Mogari. 25,000 speakers in Nigeria and Cameroon. In Nigeria: State of Borno, Ngala LGA, twelve dense villages. All Kotoko-language speakers in Nigeria may speak Afade. In Cameroon: Centered around Afade in the southern part of Makari subdivision, Logone-and-Chari division, Far North Province. It is unclear if the high comprehension of Mpade is attributable to dialectal closeness or bilingualism.

Bacama: also called Bachama, Bashamma, Abacama, Besema, Bwareba, Gboare. 150,000 speakers in Nigeria, state of Adamawa, Numan and Guyuk LGAs, state of Kaduna, northeast of Kaduna town. Dialects are Mulyen (Mulwyin, Mwulyin), Opalo, Wa-Duku. In Bata dialect cluster. Trade language.

Baldamu: also called Mbazla. Spoken in Cameroon. Diamare division, Far North Province.

Bana: also called Baza, Koma, Ka-Bana, Parole des Bana, Mizeran. 13,000 speakers in Cameroon on Nigerian border, north and northeast of Bourrah, Bourrah subdivision, Mayo-Tsanaga division, Far North Province. Dialects are Gamboura, Gili (Guili). Closely related to Psikye and Hya in Cameroon and Kamwe in Nigeria.

Bata: also called Gbwata, Batta, Demsa Bata, Gboati, Gbwate, Bete, Birsa, Dunu. 152,500 speakers in Nigeria and Cameroon. In Nigeria: 150,000 speakers. State of Adamawa, Numan, Song, Fufore, and Mubi LGAs. Dialects are Zumu (Zomo, Jimo), Wadi (Wa'i), Malabu, Kobotachi, Ribaw, Demsa, Garoua, Jirai. Closely related languages: Bacama, Gude, Nzanyi, Vin, Ziziliveken. They have joined with the Bacama in the Bwatiye Association. In Cameroon: "Demsa" may be an alternate name or dialect. Bacama is spoken only in Nigeria.

Boga: also called Boka. Spoken in Nigeria, state of Adamawa, Gombi LGA.

Buduma: also called Boudouma, Yidena, Yedima, Yedina, Yidana. 58,800 speakers in Chad, Nigeria, Cameroon, and Niger. In Chad: 51,600 speakers in the west, Lac prefecture, Bol subprefecture, islands and northern shore of Lake Chad. Dialects are Southern Buduma, Northern Buduma. 90% inherent intelligiblity between the dialects. 66.6% have good to excellent oral proficiency in Kanembu as second lan-

FIGURE 1. *Subgrouping of Biu-Mandara Languages*

Subgroup A
  Family A.1
    Eastern A.1
      Boga, Ga'anda, Hwana
    Western A.1
      Jara, Tera
  Family A.2
    Nggwahyi
    Subfamily 1
      Bura-Pabir, Cibak, Kofa, Putai
    Subfamily 2
      Huba, Central Marghi, South Marghi
  Family A.3
    Bana, Hya, Kamwe, Psikye
  Family A.4
    Lamang
      Lamang, Vemgo-Mabas, Hdi
    Mandara Proper
      Glavda
        Cineni, Dghwede, Glavda, Guduf-Gava, Gvoko
      Mandara
        Wandala
      Podoko
        Parkwa
  Family A.5
    Baldamu, Cuvok, Dugwor, Gaduwa, Gemzek, North Giziga, South Giziga, Mada, Mafa, Matal, Mbuko, Mefele, Moloko, Merey, North Mofu, Mofu-Gudur, Muyang, Pelasla, Wuzlam, Zulgwa
  Family A.6
    Sukur
  Family A.7
    Buwal, Daba, Gavar, Mbedam, Mina
  Family A.8
    Bacama, Bata, Fali, Gude, Gudu, Holma, Jimi, Ngwaba, Nzanyi, Sharwa, Tsuvan, Zizilivakan
Subgroup B
  Family B.1
    Jilbe
    Buduma
    Jina
      Jina, Majera
    Kotoko Proper
      Afade, Lagwan, Malgbe, Maslam, Mpade, Mser
  Family B.2
    Mbara, Musgu, Muskum
Subgroup C
  Gidar

guage, about 50% in Kanuri. Some can use Arabic. Used in the home and traditional livelihoods. Vigorous language use. In Nigeria: 3,000 speakers in state of Borno, on islands in Lake Chad. Dialects are Buduma, Kuri (Kouri, Kakaa). In Cameroon: Islands of Lake Chad, Logone and Chari division, Far North Province. In Niger: Seasonally some are in

Niger in Nguigmi, on the islands, and as far up the Koma-dougou River as Diffa. National language of Niger.

Bura-Pabir: also called Bura, Burra, Bourrah, Pabir, Babir, Babur, Barburr, Mya Bura, Kwojeffa, Huve, Huviya. 250,000 speakers in Nigeria, state of Borno, Biu and Askira-Uba LGAs; state of Adamawa, Gombi LGA. Dialects are Pela (Bura Pela, Hill Bura), Hyil Hawul (Bura Hyilhawul, Plain Bura). Kofa may be a related language.

Buwal: also called Ma Buwal, Bual, Gadala. 5,000 speakers in Cameroon. In and around Gadala, Mokolo subdivision, Mayo-Tsanaga division, Far North Province. May be intel-ligible with Gavar. Speakers closer to Mofu or Gavar regions claim to understand those languages. Fulfulde and French bilingualism is limited. Buwal is used in church.

Cibak: also called Chibuk, Chibok, Chibbak, Chibbuk, Kyi-baku, Kibbaku, Kikuk. 100,000 speakers in Nigeria, state of Borno, Damboa LGA.

Cineni: 3,000 speakers in Nigeria, state of Borno, Gwoza LGA, Cineni village. Closely related to Guduf, but it appears to be a separate language.

Cuvok: also called Tchouvok. 5,000 speakers in Cameroon in and around Tchouvok, Matakam South Canton, near Zamay, Mokolo subdivision, Maya-Tsanaga division, Far North Province. There is interpretation from Fulfulde into Cuvok in churches. Limited use of Fulfulde with outsiders and French by the few who have gone to school. Most do not know nearby languages well (Mefele, Mofu South, Mafa). Cuvok used in home, village, and market.

Daba: also called Dabba. 36,700 speakers in Cameroon and Nigeria. In Cameroon: 35,700 speakers. Dialects are Nive, Pologozom, Kola (Daba Kola, Kpala), Musgoi (Musgoy, Mazagway, Daba Mousgoy). In Nigeria: State of Adamawa, Mubi LGA, between Mubi and Bahuli, one village.

Dghwede: also called Hude, Johode, Traude, Dehoxde, Tghu-ade, Toghwede, Wa'a, Azaghvana, Zaghvana. 30,000 speak-ers in Nigeria, state of Borno, Gwoza LGA.

Dugwor: also called Dougour. Spoken in Cameroon. West of Tchere Canton between Maroua and Meri, Meri subdivision, Diamare division, Far North Province.

Fali: also called Fali of Mubi, Fali of Muchella, Vimtim, Yimtim. 20,000 speakers in Nigeria, state of Adamawa, Mubi and Michjika LGAs, four principal villages. Dialects are Vin (Uroovin, Uvin, Vimtim), Huli (Bahuli, Urahuli), Madzarin (Ura Madzarin, Muchella), Bween (Urambween, Bagira). Dialects are named after villages. Bilingualism in Fulfulde, Hausa.

Ga'anda: also called Ga'andu, Ganda, Mokar, Makwar. 43,000 speakers in Nigeria, state of Adamawa, Gombi LGA. Some also in Song, Guyuk, and Mubi LGAs, and state of Borno, Biu LGA. Dialects are Ga'anda, Gabin. Bilingualism in Hausa, Fulfulde.

Gaduwa: spoken in Cameroon, southwestern corner of Mayo-

Sava division, Far North Province, one village. May be a dialect of Gemzek.

Gavar: also called Gawar, Gouwar, Gauar, Rtchi, Kortchi. 5,000 speakers in Cameroon. Gavar may be intelligible with Buwal, but speakers consider Buwal speakers to be different. The Gavar Hossere use Fulfulde in the market and for outside contacts. French is learned by the few who go to school. Comprehension of surrounding languages is limited (South Mofu, Mafa, Daba). The Gavar Hossere use their language in home and village. The Gavar Hossere speak Gavar; the Gavar Fulfulde speak Fulfulde.

Gemzek: also called Gemjek, Guemshek. 8,000 speakers in Cameroon on the eastern edge of the Mandara Mountains, north of Meri, Tokombere subdivision, Mayo-Sava division, Far North Province, sixteen villages. Slight dialectal differ-ences between villages. Related to Zulgwa. Gaduwa may be a dialect. Fulfulde often used in church, but interpreted into Gemzek or Zulgwa. If Zulgwa is used in church, interpre-tation is not given into Gemzek. Speakers appear to be bilingual in Zulgwa.

Gidar: also called Guider, Guidar, Gidder, Kada, Baynawa. 65,687 speakers in Cameroon and Chad. In Cameroon: 54,000 speakers. Guider and Figuil subdivisions, Mayo-Louti division, North Province; a small section of Diamare division, Far North Province. In Chad: 11,687 speakers in the southwestern Mayo-Kebbi prefecture, Léré subprefec-ture, northwest of Léré in Chad to Guider in Cameroon, at least twenty-five villages.

Giziga, North: also called Guiziga, Gisiga, Gisika, Tchere, Mi Marva, Giziga De Maroua, Dogba. 20,000 speakers in Cameroon, north and west of Maroua, in Tchere and Mo-gazang massifs and neighboring Dogba plains, Meri subdi-vision, Diamare division, Far North Province.

Giziga, South: also called Guiziga, Gisiga, Gisika. 60,000 speakers in Cameroon southwest of Maroua, in Diamare plains, Diamare and Kaele divisions, Far North Province. Dialects are Muturami (Muturwa, Muturua, Giziga de Mou-touroua, Loulou), Mi Mijivin (Giziga de Midjivin), Rum.

Glavda: also called Galavda, Gelebda, Glanda, Guelebda, Galvaxdaxa. 22,800 speakers in Nigeria and Cameroon. In Nigeria: 20,000 speakers in the state of Borno, Gwoza LGA, mainly in Nggoshe village (different from Ngoshi), and in Agapalawa, Amuda, Vale, Ashigashiya, Kerawa, Pelekwa villages. Dialects are Bokwa, Ngoshie (Ngweshe), Glavda. Closely related to Guduf. In Cameroon: 2,800 speakers around the village of Gelvaxdaxa, south of Ashigashia, on the Nigerian Border, Koza subdivision, Mayo-Tsanaga di-vision, Far North Province. Separated linguistically in 1971 from Guduf and Gvoko. Closely related to Guduf.

Gude: also called Goude, Cheke, Tchade, Shede, Mapodi, Mapuda, Mudaye, Mocigin, Motchekin. 96,000 speakers in Nigeria and Cameroon. In Nigeria: 68,000 speakers in the state of Adamawa, Mubi LGA; state of Borno, Askira-Uba LGA. Different dialects are spoken in Cameroon and Nigeria but they are inherently intelligible. Bilingualism in Hausa, Nzanyi, Fulfulde, English. In Cameroon: 28,000 speakers.

Gudu: also called Gudo, Gutu. 5,000 speakers in Nigeria in the state of Adamawa, Song LGA.

Guduf-Gava: also called Gudupe, Afkabiye. 22,500 speakers in Nigeria and Cameroon. In Nigeria: 20,000 speakers in the state of Borno, Gwoza LGA, mainly in Gava, Cikide, and Guduf. Dialects are Cikide (Chikide), Guduf, Gava (Yaghwatadaxa, Yawotataxa). Closely related to Glavda. Hdi speakers have 35% intelligibility of Guduf. Guduf was separated linguistically in 1971 from Gvoko and Glavda. In Cameroon: 2,500 speakers on the Nigerian border, Cikide and Guduf, Mokolo subdivision, Mayo-Tsanaga division, Far North Province. Dialects are Cikide (Chikide), Guduf, Gava (Yaghwatadaxa, Yawotataxa). Closely related to Glavda. Hdi speakers have 35% intelligibility of Guduf.

Gvoko: also called Gevoko, Ghboko, Gavoko, Kuvoko, Ngossi, Ngoshi, Ngoshe-Ndhang, Ngweshe-Ndaghan, Ngoshe Sama, Nggweshe. 20,000 speakers in Nigeria and Cameroon. In Nigeria: State of Borno, Gwoza LGA; state of Adamawa, Michika LGA. A separate but related language to Glavda and Guduf. In Cameroon: Ngoshi village (different from Nggoshe), north of Tourou, Mololo subdivision, Mayo-Tsanaga division, Far North Province. Linguistically separated from Guduf and Glavda in 1971.

Hdi: also called Xedi, Hedi, Hide, Turu-Hide, Xadi. 28,000 speakers in Cameroon and Nigeria. In Cameroon: 25,000 speakers in fifteen villages on Nigerian border northwest of Mokolo, Mokolo subdivision, Mayo-Tsanaga division, Far North Province. Dialects are Tur (Turu, Tourou, Ftour). 51% intelligibility of Mabas, 48% of Lamang, 35% of Gvoko. In Nigeria: 3,000 speakers in the state of Borno, Gwoza LGA; state of Adamawa, Michika LGA; along the Cameroon border, across from Tourou; part of one village.

Holma: also called Da Holmaci, Bali Holma. 4 speakers in Nigeria. Formerly spoken in state of Adamawa, north of Sorau on the Cameroon border. Related to Nzanyi. Being replaced by Fulfulde.

Huba: also called Kilba, Chobba. 175,000 speakers in Nigeria in the state of Adamawa, Hong, Maiha, Gombi, and Mubi LGAs. Bilingualism in Hausa, Fulfulde.

Hwana: also called Hwona, Hona, Tuftera, Fiterya. 32,000 speakers in Nigeria, in the state of Adamawa, Gombi LGA, and some in Song and Hong LGAs. Bilingualism in Fulfulde, Hausa, Kilba, Gaanda.

Hya: also called Ghye, Za. Spoken in Cameroon. Only in Amsa on the Nigerian border, Mokolo subdivision, Mayo-Tsanaga division, Far North Province. Closely related to Kamwe of Nigeria and Psikye of Cameroon.

Jara: also called Jera. 4,000 speakers in Nigeria in the state of Borno, Biu and Kwaya-Kusar LGAs; state of Gombei, Akko and Yamaltu-Deba LGAs. Jara is being replaced by Fulfulde and Hausa.

Jilbe: also called Zoulbou. 100 speakers in Nigeria in the state of Borno, Jilbe town, on the border of Cameroon across from the town of Dabanga in one village only. Speakers of Kotoko languages in Cameroon and Chad consistently report low intelligibility with Jilbe. Not the same as Zizilivakan.

Jimi: also called Djimi, Jimjimen, 'Um Falin. 3,500 speakers in Cameroon on the Nigerian border in and around Bourrha, Mayo-Tsanaga division, Far North Province. Dialects are Djimi, Zumo (Zumu, Zomo, Zame), Jimo, Wadi (Wa'i), Malabu.

Jina: also called Zina. Spoken in Cameroon around Zina and east of Waza near the south of Logone-Birni subdivision, Logone-and-Chari division, Far North Province. Dialects are Jina (Zine), Sarassara, Tchide (Sede), Muxule (Muxuli, Ngodeni), Mae. People in Zina say they understand Lagwan and Musgu better than Muxule.

Kamwe: also called Higi, Hiji, Higgi, Vacamwe. 300,000 speakers in Nigeria in the state of Adamawa, Michika LGA, in the Mandara Mountains. Dialects are Nkafa, Dakwa (Bazza), Sina, Wula, Futu, Tili Pte, Fali of Kiriya, Fali of Mijilu. Closely related to Psikye and Hya of Cameroon.

Kofa: also called Kota. Spoken in Nigeria in the state of Adamawa, Song LGA, north of Betul road and Yola. Reported to be a separate language from Bura-Pabir.

Lagwan: also called Kotoko-Logone, Logone, Lagwane, Lagouane. 38,500 speakers in Cameroon, Nigeria, and Chad. In Cameroon: Dialects are Logone-Birni, Logone-Gana (Kotoko-Gana). Related to Afade, Mser, Malgbe, Maslam, and Mpade. In Nigeria: 25,000 speakers in the state of Borno, Dikwa and Ngala LGAs. Dialects are Logone-Birni, Logone-Gana (Kotoko-Gana). Related to Afade, Mser, Malgbe, Maslam, and Mpade. In Chad: In the west, Chari-Baguirmi prefecture, N'Djaména subprefecture, south of N'Djaména along the Logone River, in the vicinity of Logone-Gana. Dialects are Logone-Birni, Logone-Gana (Kotoko-Gana).

Lamang: also called Laamang, Gbuhwe, Waha. 40,000 speakers in Nigeria in the state of Borno, Gwoza LGA; state of Adamawa, Michika LGA. Dialects are North Laamang, Central Laamang, South Laamang. Speakers have 37% intelligibility of Mabas, 31% of Hedi. Subdialects of North Lamang: Zaladeva (Alataghwa), Dzuba, Leghva (Luhuva), Gwoza-Wakane; of Central Lamang: Hedkala (Hidkala, Xidkala, Hitkala, Hitkalanchi), Waga (Waha, Woga, Wagga), Dlige; of South Lamang: Ghudavan.

Mada: 17,000 speakers in Cameroon on the Mada massif at edge of Mandara Mountains and neighboring plain, Tokombere subdivision, Mayo-Sava division, Far North Province.

Mafa: also called Mofa, Natakan. "Matakam" is a derogatory name sometimes used. 138,000 speakers in Cameroon and Nigeria. In Cameroon: 136,000 speakers. From Mokolo north in Mayo-Tsanaga division, Far North Province. Dialects are West Mafa, Central Mafa, East Mafa. Muktele may be a separate language. Subdialects of West Mafa: Magoumaz, Mavoumay; Central Mafa: Ouzal, Koza, Mokola, Mokolo, Ldamtsai; East Mafa: Soulede, Roua. In Nigeria: State of Borno, Gwoza LGA.

Majera: also called Midah, Mida'a, Da'a. 5,000 speakers in Cameroon and Chad. In Cameroon: Around Majera in extreme southern Logone-Birni subdivision, Logone-and-Chari division, Far North Province. Dialects are Majera (Mazra), Kajire-'dulo, Hwalem (Holom). In Chad: West, Mayo-Kebbi prefecture, Bongor subprefecture, north of Gelengdeng, Dogwea village. Dialects are Majera (Mazra), Kajire-'dulo, Hwalem (Holom).

Malgbe: also called Malgwe, Gulfe, Gulfei, Goulfei, Sanbalbe, Malbe, Ngwalkwe. 36,000 speakers in Cameroon and Chad. In Cameroon: North of Kousseri in a town of Goulfey and Goulfey subdivision, along the Chari River, Logone-and-Chari division, Far North Province. Dialects are Malgbe (Goulfei), Mara, Dro, Douguia. Related to Afade, Mser, Lagwan, Maslam, and Mpade. In Chad: Dialects are Goulfey, Walia, Mara, Douguia. Related to other Kotoko ethnic and linguistic groups: Afade, Lagwan, Maslam, Mpade, Mser, and Jilbe (of Nigeria).

Marghi, Central: also called Marghi, Margi. 135,000 speakers in Nigeria in the state of Borno, Askira-Uba and Damboa LGAs; state of Adamawa, Mubi and Michika LGAs. Dialects are Lassa (Babal), Gulak (Dzerngu), Madube (Gwara), Mulgwe (Malgwa), Wurga.

Marghi, South: spoken in Nigeria in the state of Borno, Askira-Uba LGA; state of Adamawa, Mubi and Michika LGAs. Dialects are Wamdiu, Hildi. South Marghi, Central Marghi, and Putai form a language cluster. South Marghi was related to Huba rather than to Central Marghi in 1963.

Maslam: 5,000 speakers in Cameroon and Chad. In Cameroon: In Maltam and Saho northwest of Kousseri, Makari subdivision, Logone-and-Chari division, Far North Province. Dialects are Maslam (Maltam), Sao (Sahu). Related to Afade, Mser, Lagwan, Malgbe, and Mpade. Speakers may be able to use literature in one of those languages. In Chad: Dialects are Maslam (Maltam), Sao (Sahu). In the Kotoko ethnic and linguistic group. Closest to Afade.

Matal: also called Mouktele, Muktile, Muktele, Balda. 18,000 speakers in Cameroon. Eastern edge of Mandara Mountains, to the south, southwest of Mora, Mora subdivision, Mayo-Sava division, Far North Province.

Mbara: also called Massa de Guelengdeng, Guelengdeng, G'kelendeng, G'kelendeg. 1,000 speakers in Chad.

Mbedam: spoken in Cameroon northeast of Hina, Mokolo subdivision, Mayo-Tsanaga division, Far North Province.

Mbuko: also called Mbuku, Mboku, Mbokou. 6,700 speakers in Cameroon on Mbuko massif and neighboring Mayo-Raneo plain, Meri subdivision east of Meri, Diamare division, Far North Province.

Mefele: also called Bula, Bulahai, Boulahay. 10,000 speakers in Cameroon south and east of Mokolo, Mokolo subdivision, Mayo-Tsanaga division, Far North Province, six villages. Dialects are Mefele, Serak (Sirak), Muhura (Mouhour), Shugule (Chougoule). Bilingualism in Fulfulde is increasing among those who travel, and in French among the few children in school. Bilingualism in Mafa appears to be increasing among the children, who learn it at school and market. Vigorous language use in family and village life.

Merey: also called Meri, Mere, Mofu de Meri. 10,000 speakers in Cameroon west of Meri on Meri massif, Diamare division, Far North Province.

Mina: also called Hina, Besleri. 8,000 speakers in Cameroon south of Mokolo, Hina subdivision, Mayo-Tsanaga division, Far North Province, twenty villages. Dialects are Besleri, Jingjing (Dzumdzum), Gamdugun. Fulfulde is used at the market. French is learned in school, but few children attend school. Speakers are not generally bilingual in Daba. All ages. Vigorous language use in daily life.

Mofu-Gudur: also called Mofou, Mofou de Goudour, Mofu-Sud, Mofu South. 60,000 speakers in Cameroon. Massifs south of Tsanaga River to the Mayo-Louti, Mokolo subdivision, Mayo-Tsanaga division extending into Diamare division, Far North Province. Dialects are Mokong, Gudur, Zidim, Dimeo, Massagal (Massakal), Njeleng.

Moloko: also called Molokwo, Melokwo, Mokyo, Molkoa, Molkwo, Molo. 8,500 speakers in Cameroon on Melokwo Mountain and in the plains around its base, Makalingay Canton, Tokombere subdivision, Mayo-Sava division, Far North Province. Only one dialect. Surrounded by four related languages (including Muyang, North Giziga, and the Mikiri dialect of Dugwor) plus one other. Little bilingualism except in outlying areas where there has been intermarriage with speakers of other languages. Fulfulde is used in the market, but interpretation is necessary when it is used in church. A few educated speakers can use French. Moloko is used in all domains of daily living.

Mpade: also called Makari, Makary, Mendage, Mandage, Mandagué. 12,000 speakers in Cameroon, Nigeria, and Chad. In Cameroon: Centered around Makari next to Lake Chad, and Goulfey along the Chari River, Logone-and-Chari division, Far North Province. Dialects are Shoe (Shawe, Chaoue, Schoe, Mani), Mpade (Makari), Bodo, Woulki, Digam. Shoe dialect is only in Cameroon. Close to Lagwan. Related to Afade, Mser, Malgbe, and Maslam. In Nigeria: State of Borno. In Chad: In the west, Chari-Baguirmi prefecture, N'Djaména subprefecture, south of Lake Chad, in and around Mani on the Logone River, north of N'Djaména. Dialects are Makari, Shoe (Shawe, Chaoue, Mani), Bodo, Woulki, Digam.

Mser: also called Kotoko-Kuseri, Kuseri, Kouseri, Koussseri, Mandage. 2,100 speakers in Cameroon and Chad. In Cameroon: Kousseri subdivision, Logone-and-Chari division, Far North Province. Dialects are Mser (Kousseri), Kalo (Kalakafra), Gawi, Houlouf, Kabe. Related to Afade, Lagwan, Malgbe, Maslam, and Mpade. In Chad: In the west, Chari-Baguirmi prefecture, N'Djaména subprefecture, Cameroon border near N'Djaména. Dialects are Mser (Kousseri, Msir), Kalo (Kalakafra), Gawi, Houlouf, Kabe. The majority are bilingual in Chadian Arabic. Kanuri is also used. The people of Klesem village no longer speak Mser.

Musgu: also called Mousgou, Mousgoun, Musgum, Mousgoum, Musuk, Muzuk, Munjuk, Mulwi. 85,908 speakers in Cameroon and Chad. In Cameroon: 61,500 speakers in the entire Maga subdivision, Mayo-Danay division, Far North Province. Dialects are Mpus (Pus, Pouss, Mousgoum de Pouss), Beege (Jafga), Vulum (Vlum, Mulwi), Ngilemong, Luggoy, Maniling (Mani-Iling), Muzuk (Mousgoum de Guirvidig). Vulum dialect is mainly in Chad. In Chad: 24,408 speakers. Dialects are Mpus (Pus, Pouss, Mousgoum de Pouss, Musgum-Pouss), Beege (Jafga), Vulum (Vlum, Mulwi-Mogroum), Muzuk (Mousgoum de Guirvidig, Mousgoum de Guirvidik, Guirvidig). The Vulum dialect is mainly in Chad.

Muskum: also called Muzgum. Formerly spoken in Chad. In the west, Mayo-Kebbi prefecture, Bongor subprefecture along the Logone River, west of Guélengdeng, village of Muskum (Mouskoun), 10 km north of Katoa. There was one speaker in 1976. Because of intermarriage, speakers eventually shifted to the Vulum dialect of Musgu.

Muyang: also called Myau, Myenge, Muyenge, Mouyenge, Mouyengue. 15,000 speakers in Cameroon on the Muyang, Mougouba, Gouadagouada, and Palbarar massifs, northeast of Tokombere, Mayo-Sava division, Far North Province.

Nggwahyi: also called Ngwaxi, Ngwohi. 2,000 speakers in Nigeria in the state of Borno, Askira-Uba LGA.

Ngwaba: also called Gombi, Goba. 10,000 speakers in Nigeria in the state of Adamawa, Gombi LGA at Fachi and Guduniya, and Hong LGA in two villages. Bilingualism in Fulfulde, Hausa, Gudu, Nzanyi.

North Mofu: also called Mofu-Douvangar, Douvangar, Mofu-Nord. 27,500 speakers in Cameroon on the massifs south of Meri, Diamare division, Far North Province. Dialects are Douroun (Mofu de Douroum, Durum), Wazan (Wazang).

Nzanyi: also called Njanyi, Nzangi, Njai, Njeny, Zani, Zany, Jeng, Jenge, Njei, Njeing, Kobotshi. 86,000 speakers in Nigeria and Cameroon. In Nigeria: 77,000 speakers in the state of Adamawa, Maiha LGA. Dialects are Paka, Rogede, Nggwoli, Hoode, Maiha, Magara, Dede, Mutidi, Lovi. In Cameroon: 9,000 speakers west of Dourbeye near Nigerian

border in Doumo region, Mayo-Oulo subdivision, Mayo-Louti division, North Province.

Parkwa: also called Podoko, Paduko, Podokwo, Podogo, Padogo, Padokwa, Pawdawkwa, Parekwa, Gwadi Parekwa, Kudala. 30,000 speakers in Cameroon west and southwest of Mora, Mora subdivision, Mayo-Sava division, Far North Province.

Pelasla: also called Maslava, Vame. 8,500 speakers in Cameroon on the southern Mora massif south of Mora, Mora and Tokombere subdivisions, Mayo-Sava division, Far North Province. Dialects are Mayo-Plata (Pelasla, Plasla, Platla, Plata, Gwendele, Damlale), Mberem (Mbreme, Maslava), Demwa (Dmwa, Doume), Hurza (Hurzo, Ourza, Ourzo, Ouzza), Ndreme. The five dialects are inherently intelligible to each other's speakers. Mayo-Plata is closer to Wuzlam than the other dialects are to Wuzlam. Few know Fulfulde except some in the Hurza area. Wandala is also used.

Psikye: also called Kapsiki, Kamsiki, Ptsake. 52,500 speakers in Cameroon and Nigeria. In Cameroon: 40,500 speakers in the southwestern part of Mokolo subdivision, Mayo-Tsanaga division, Far North Province. Some in Nigeria. Dialects are Psikye (Kapsiki, Kamu), Zlenge, Wula (Oula, Ula-Xangku). Closely related to Hya and Kamwe of Nigeria. In Nigeria: 12,000 speakers in the state of Adamawa, north and east of Michika, south of Madagali, in the Mandara Mountains. Dialects are Psikye (Kapsiki, Kamu), Zlenge, Wula (Oula, Ula-Xangku, Lying). The Wula dialect is in Nigeria. Closely related to Hya and Kamwe of Nigeria.

Putai: also called Marghi West. Spoken in Nigeria in the state of Borno, Damboa LGA. Bilingualism in Kanuri.

Sharwa: also called Tchevi, Sherwin. Spoken in Cameroon in the southern Bourrah subdivision, Mayo-Tsanaga division, Far North Province; a few in Mayo-Louti division, North Province.

Sukur: also called Sugur, Adikimmu Sukur, Gemasakun, Sakul. 14,779 speakers in Nigeria. at the northern tip of state of Adamawa, Michika LGA, Mandara Mountains. Perhaps in Cameroon. Speakers use Fulfulde, Hausa, Wula (dialect of Psikyye), Kamwe, or some English as second languages. Hausa used in most churches.

Tera: 50,000 speakers in Nigeria in the state of Bauchi, Yamaltu-Deba LGA; state of Borno, Kwayakusar LGA. Dialects are Nyimatli (Nyemathi, Yamaltu, Nimalto, Nyimatali), Pidlimdi (Hina, Hinna, Ghuna, Ghena), Bura Kokura. Dialect cluster. Bilingualism in Hausa.

Tsuvan: also called Matsuvan, Motsuvan, Terki, Teleki, Telaki, Tchede. Spoken in Cameroon.

Vemgo-Mabas: 15,000 speakers in Nigeria and Cameroon. In Nigeria: 10,000 speakers in the state of Adamawa, Michika LGA, Madagali district. Dialects are Vemgo, Mabas, Visik (Vizik). 56% intelligibility of Lamang, 36% intelligibility of Hedi. Speakers use Fulfulde, Mafa, or Wula (a dialect of

Psikye) as second language. Some speak Hdi. In Cameroon: 5,000 speakers in the village of Mabas on Nigerian border northwest of Mokolo, Mayo-Tsanaga division, Far North Province. Dialects are Vemgo, Mabas. 56% intelligibility of Lamang, 36% of Hdi. Possibly intelligible with Mafa. Speakers may be bilingual in Mafa or Lamang. Some people speak Hdi.

Wandala: also called Mandara, Ndara, Mandara Montagnard. 43,500 speakers in Cameroon and Nigeria. In Cameroon: 23,500 speakers. Dialects are Kamburwama, Masfeima, Jampalam, Ziogba, Mazagwa, Gwanje, Wandala (Mandara), Mura (Kirdi-Mora, Mora Brousse, Mora Massif, Duwe), Gamargu (Gamergou, Gamergu, Malgo, Malgwa). A dialect cluster. Some speak French or Fulani. All domains. Used in church services, oral use in business. It is transmitted by parents to children. The Pelasla speak it as second language. People have a positive attitude toward Wandala. Trade language. In Nigeria: 20,000 speakers in the state of Borno, Damboa, Bama, Gwoza, and Konduga LGAs. Dialects are Kamburwama, Masfeima, Jampalam, Ziogba, Mazagwa, Gwanje, Gamargu (Gamergu, Malgo, Malgwa), Kirawa. Dialect cluster. Some speak Hausa or English. It is transmitted by parents to children.

Wuzlam: also called Uldeme, Ouldeme, Uzam, Udlam, Uzlam, Mizlime. 10,500 speakers in Cameroon on the Wuzlam Massif south of Mora, Tokombere subdivision, Mayo-Sava division, Far North Province.

Zizilivakan: also called Ziziliveken, Ziliva, Àmzírív, Fali of Jilbu. Spoken in Cameroon and Nigeria. In Cameroon: Near Nigerian border, Bourrah subdivision, Mayo-Tsanaga division, Far North Province. In Nigeria: In the state of Adamawa, Mubi LGA, Jilbu town, near Cameroon border.

Zulgwa: also called Zulgo, Zoulgo, Zelgwa, Mineo, Minew. 18,000 speakers in Cameroon. Dialects are Zelgwa, Minew (Zulgwa, Zulgo, Mukuno, Minewe, Mineo).

B. GRIMES

BLACK ENGLISH. *See* African American Vernacular English.

BLOCKING. *See* Morphology.

BLOOMFIELD, LEONARD. Bloomfield was born in Chicago on 1 April 1887, and died at New Haven, Connecticut, on 13 April 1949. He received the A.B. at Harvard in 1906, and the Ph.D. at Chicago in 1909. Bloomfield taught at Cincinnnati (1909–1910), Illinois (1910–1921), Ohio State (1921–1927), Chicago (1927–1940) and, as Sterling Professor of Linguistics, at Yale (1940–1949). His main fields of endeavor were Germanic, Malayo-Polynesian (Tagalog), American Indian languages (especially comparative Algonkian), and general linguistics. Bloomfield's influence was broadest in the last area, through his widely read *Language* (1933).

Bloomfield and his contemporary Edward Sapir were the first influential American linguists to emphasize the importance of a structuralist approach to language, both for descriptive work and as a necessary preliminary to historical and comparative linguistics. Bloomfield's work on Tagalog and Menomini led him in the 1920s and 1930s to a type of structural analysis, especially in phonemics, parallel to but largely independent of that of the Prague School. In Comparative linguistics, Bloomfield was a strong defender of the principle of *regularity* in phonemic change. His postulation of a unique Proto-Algonkian cluster *$/çk/$, based on incomplete evidence, was later vindicated by data he gathered on Swampy Cree.

In Bloomfield 1933, younger scholars found both a thorough theoretical orientation and a manual of analytical procedure for all levels of linguistic structure, including syntax. Bloomfield fully recognized the importance of semantics in linguistic analysis, but he was skeptical of its amenability to scientific treatment. In this, in his early adherence to the doctrine of immediate constituent analysis in syntax, and in his rejection of linguistic synonymity, he continued to advocate positions he had adopted from Wilhelm Wundt's system of psychology (Fought 1999a), although Bloomfield gave up the rest of Wundt's dualism. In the 1920s, under the influence of the psychologist Albert P. Weiss, Bloomfield argued that it was unnecessary to postulate a non-physical "mind," or to follow any given school of psychology in order to describe and analyze language. He also accepted the idea, then widely held, of society as "superorganic"—that societies are actual "organisms" held together by the use of language, as individual bodies are coordinated by the brain and central nervous system.

Since some of Bloomfield's views about language were contrary to widely held opinions concerning the nature of meaning and the importance of "mind," his 1933 *Language* aroused opposition even during his lifetime. Some of his followers later exaggerated his positions, causing stronger rejection of "Bloomfieldian" views in the 1960s and 1970s, and leading to gross misunderstandings and misinterpretations; however, a more balanced view came gradually to prevail in the 1980s. (See Hockett 1970, Hall 1987, 1990. Fought, 1999a, b.)

[*See also* History of Linguistics, *articles on* American Structuralism *and* The Prague School; *and* Sapir, Edward.]

BIBLIOGRAPHY

Bloomfield, Leonard. 1914. *An introduction to the study of language.* New York: Holt. Reprinted, with a foreword by Joseph F. Kess. Amsterdam: Benjamins, 1983.

Bloomfield, Leonard. 1933. *Language.* New York: Holt. Reprinted, with a foreword by Charles F. Hockett. Chicago: University of Chicago Press, 1984.

Fought, John G. 1999a. Leonard Bloomfield's linguistic legacy: Later uses of some technical features. *Historiographia Linguistica* 26.313–332.

Fought, John G, ed. 1999b. *Leonard Bloomfield: Critical assessments of leading linguists.* 3 vols. London: Routledge.

Hall, Robert A., Jr., ed. 1987. *Leonard Bloomfield: Essays on his life and work.* Historiographia Linguistica 14.1–2. Amsterdam: Benjamins.

Hall, Robert A., Jr. 1990. *A life for language: A biographical memoir of Leonard Bloomfield.* Amsterdam: Benjamins.

Hockett, Charles F., ed. 1970. *A Leonard Bloomfield anthology.* Bloomington: Indiana University Press.

Sapir, Edward. 1931. The concept of phonetic law as tested in primitive languages by Leonard Bloomfield. In *Methods in social science: A case book*, edited by Stuart A. Rice, pp. 297–306. Chicago: University of Chicago Press.

ROBERT A. HALL, JR. AND JOHN FOUGHT

BOAS, FRANZ (1858–1942). American anthropologist (born and educated in Germany). Boas was the teacher of Edward Sapir and other eminent scholars in both linguistics and anthropology, and, more than any other before or since, the founder and organizer of linguistic fieldwork in the United States.

[*See also* Anthropological Linguistics *and* History of Linguistics, *article on* American Structuralism.]

ANNA MORPURGO DAVIES

BOPP, FRANZ (1791–1867). German linguist. Bopp was one of the founders of I[ndo]-E[uropean] comparative linguistics, and author of the first IE comparative grammar.

When Bopp was still a boy, his family moved from Mainz to Aschaffenburg, following the Elector's court in the aftermath of the French occupation. There he attended the Gymnasium and, inspired by K. Windischmann, developed an interest in Oriental languages and literatures. To pursue this, it was necessary for him to leave Germany; from 1812 to 1817, he studied Sanskrit in Paris. He then visited London in order to study Sanskrit manuscripts; during his stay, he made the acquaintance of Wilhelm von Humboldt, to whom he gave instruction in Sanskrit, and who became a firm friend. In 1820, Bopp returned to Germany, taking up residence in Göttingen. In 1821, largely because of the influence of Wilhelm and Alexander Von Humboldt, Bopp was appointed Professor of Oriental Literature and General Philology in Berlin, where he remained until his death.

Bopp has often been hailed as the founder of comparative linguistics, and many consider that the publication of his *Conjugationssystem* (1816) marks the beginning of the discipline, though the comparative element acquired prominence only in the 1820 adaptation (Rousseau 2001). That Sanskrit was related to Latin, Greek, and other languages of Europe was by this time well known; in 1808, Friedrich von Schlegel (in his influential *Über die Sprache und Weisheit der Indier*) had suggested that a "comparative grammar" would "lead to new conclusions about the genealogy of languages." Bopp, however, was the first to carry out a systematic and detailed comparison of morphological forms. His investigations culminated in the first IE comparative grammar, his *Vergleichende Grammatik* (1833–1852). Further contributions to IE linguistics include works on Celtic, Albanian, Old Prussian, and comparative accentuation. Bopp also developed an interest in Malayo-Polynesian and Caucasian languages and attempted to show that these too were related to Sanskrit.

Today, Bopp is a somewhat controversial figure. On the one hand, he was influenced by exponents of Romanticism, in particular by Schlegel. On the other hand, his concern to discover the "physical and mechanical laws" of languages makes him seem more of a rationalist. His methodology involved the *Zergliederung* ('dissection') and comparison of forms, on the basis of which he was able to attribute particular roots and inflections to the parent language; these could then be further analysed and explained. One of his central ideas was that endings arose by agglutination of meaningful elements; thus he considered that the personal endings of the verb arose by agglutination of forms of the verb 'to be' and personal pronouns.

Bopp is also remembered for his contribution to the teaching of Sanskrit. His grammars, written along European rather than Indian lines, together with his publication of relatively easy texts with translations, made the language more accessible to European students. In this way too, his work was of importance in the development of IE studies.

[*See also* History of Linguistics, *article on* Comparative-Historical Linguistics *and* Indo-European Languages.]

BIBLIOGRAPHY

Bopp, Franz. 1816. *Über das Conjugationssystem der Sanskritsprache in Vergleichung mit jenem der griechischen, lateinischen, persischen und germanischen Sprache.* Frankfurt am Main: Andreä. Excerpts translated in *A reader in nineteenth century Indo-European historical linguistics,* edited by Winfred P. Lehmann (Bloomington: Indiana University Press, 1967), pp. 38–45.

Bopp, Franz. 1820. Analytical comparison of the Sanskrit, Greek, Latin and Teutonic languages, shewing the original identity of their grammatical structure. *Annals of Oriental Literature* (London) 1:1.1–64. New edition, edited by E. F. K. Koerner, Amsterdam: Benjamins, 1974.

Bopp, Franz. 1833–1852. *Vergleichende Grammatik des Sanskrit, Zend, Griechischen, Lateinischen, Lithauischen, Gothischen und Deutschen.* 2 vols. Berlin: Dümmler. 2d ed., 1857–1861; 3rd posthumous ed., 1868–1871. Translation, London: Madden and Malcolm, 1845–1853.

Guigniaut, Joseph D. 1877. Notice historique sur la vie et les travaux de M. François Bopp. *Mémoires de l'Académie des Inscriptions et Belles-Lettres* 29:1.201–224. Reprinted in Bopp [1820] 1974, pp. xv–xxxviii.

Koerner, Konrad. 1989. Franz Bopp (1791–1867). In *Practicing Linguistic Historiography,* edited by Konrad Koerner, pp. 291–302. Amsterdam: Benjamins.

Lefman, Salomon. 1891. *Franz Bopp, sein Leben und seine Wissenschaft.* 2 vols. Berlin: Reimer.

Martineau, Russell. 1867. Obituary of Franz Bopp. *Transactions of the Philological Society* 1867:305–312. Reprinted in Sebeok 1966, vol. 1, pp. 200–206.

Morpurgo Davies, Anna. 1987. 'Organic' and 'organism' in Franz Bopp. In *Biological metaphor and cladistic classification,* edited by Henry M. Hoenigswald and L. F. Wiener, pp. 81–107. London: Pinter.

Morpurgo Davies, Anna. 1998. Nineteenth century linguistics. In *History of Linguistics,* edited by Giulio Lepschy, vol. 4. London: Longman.

Rousseau, Jean. 2001. La genèse de la grammaire comparée. In *History of the Language Sciences,* edited by Sylvain Auroux et al., vol. 1/2, pp. 1197–1210. Berlin and New York: de Gruyter.

Schmitter, Peter. 1996. Bopp, Franz. In *Lexicon Grammaticorum,* edited by Hanso Stammerjohann, pp. 120–121. Tübingen: Niemeyer.

Sebeok, Thomas A., ed. 1966. *Portraits of linguists.* 2 vols. Bloomington: Indiana University Press.

Sternemann, Reinhard. 1984. *Franz Bopp und die vergleichende indoeuropäische Sprachwissenschaft.* (Innsbrucker Beiträge zur Sprachwissenschaft, Vorträge und Kleinere Schriften, 33.) Innsbruck: Institut für Sprachwissenschaft.

Verburg, P. A. 1950. The background to the linguistic conceptions of Franz Bopp. *Lingua* 2.438–468. Reprinted in Sebeok 1966, vol. 1, pp. 221–250.

KATRINA M. HAYWARD

BORNEO LANGUAGES. These languages are spoken on the island of Borneo and form a branch of WESTERN MALAYO-POLYNESIAN.

[*For language lists, see the articles on* Apo Duat Languages, Barito Languages, Kayan-Kenyah Languages, Land Dayak Languages, Northeast Borneo Languages, Punan-Nibong Languages, *and* Rejang-Baram Languages.]

B. GRIMES

BORROWING. [*This entry includes the following subentries:*

Overview

Loanword Phonology]

Overview

The term *borrowing* has been used with varying scope in linguistics. It has sometimes been applied broadly to the transfer of features from any language into another. More often, it is used to refer specifically to speakers' adoption of foreign features into their mother tongue. In this sense, it is distinct from the changes introduced by non-native speakers shifting to a new language.

Borrowing first took on theoretical importance in the 19th century as linguists began to look on their work as a science. Comparativists observing regular sound correspondences across related languages captured the regularities in sound laws meant to represent the phonological changes that had occurred in each language. Numerous apparent exceptions to the laws could be explained by the recognition of borrowing: words that failed to exhibit the predicted sound changes simply had not been part of the language at the time of the changes. Such words were first called *loanwords* by A. H. Sayce in his *Principles of comparative philology* (1874:200fn), modeling the term on German *Lehnwort*.

The recognition of lexical borrowing as a factor in language change was unproblematic, but acceptance of the possibility of grammatical borrowing was not. It was felt that the borrowing of grammatical elements or patterns is not a part of normal language development and would result in "mixed languages," a threat to the current understanding of genetic relationships in terms of the family tree model. Max Müller, a popularizer of linguistics, declared that mixed languages do not exist (1864). The American Sanskritist William Dwight Whitney echoed his view: "Such a thing as a language with a mixed grammatical apparatus has never come under the cognizance of linguistic students; it would be to them a monstrosity, it seems an impossibility" (1867:199). In 1872, Johannes Schmidt introduced his Wave Theory, which explained certain previously intractable exceptions to Indo-European sound laws by the diffusion of morphological entities and patterns among neighboring languages: case endings with *m* instead of the expected *bh*, passives ending in *r*, the prefix *e-* in past tenses, feminine nouns with masculine suffixes, and the use of original perfects as general past tenses. The Wave Theory held appeal for Hugo Schuchardt, a German scholar working in Graz, Austria, who was acutely aware of the effects of contact on language development from his studies of the origins of Vulgar Latin, of creoles in West Africa, India, and the Philippines, and of European languages in the Austro-Hungarian Empire. He maintained that there are no fully unmixed languages (1884:6).

Comparativists were not yet ready, however, to admit that structural diffusion could play a significant role in the development of language. The Frenchman Antoine Meillet emphasized the fact that phonology, morphology, and syntax constitute closed systems, unlike the lexicon, and that these systems resist disturbance from the outside (1921:84). It was recognized that sounds and morphemes can be diffused secondarily, riding into a language on loanwords, but this effect was assumed to be superficial.

The view that structure is not borrowed had an impact on work on genetic classification. By the end of the 19th century, the several hundred languages of North America had been classified into 58 distinct families by the Bureau of American Ethnology under the direction of John Wesley Powell (1891). In 1921, Edward Sapir proposed an overarching scheme grouping these families into just six superstocks on the basis of perceived structural similarities alone (1921a). Sapir wrote, "So long as such direct historical testimony as we have gives us no really convincing examples of profound morphological influence by diffusion, we shall do well not to put too much reliance in diffusion theories" (1921b:206). His teacher Franz Boas and others felt it premature to rule out the possibility of grammatical borrowing and voiced serious reservations about Sapir's classification. In an article on Spanish elements in modern Nahuatl, a Uto-Aztecan language of Mexico, Boas noted that because of long contact, there was not only substantial lexical borrowing, but also "the syntax has undergone great simplification. It is particularly noticeable that the old type of coordination and subordination of clauses has disappeared and Spanish conjunctions are of frequent occurrence" (1930:85).

Over the 20th century, progress was made in distinguishing the kinds of borrowing that affect vocabulary. In his 1933 textbook *Language*, Leonard Bloomfield illustrated several types. The term "loanword" had already been established to designate vocabulary whose basic form and meaning are taken directly from another language, then integrated with lesser or greater fidelity into the phonological and grammatical systems of the matrix language, like English *czar* from Russian or *kindergarten* from German. The Spanish loans in Nahuatl cited by Boas show considerable integration, appearing in native morphological structures such as *i-burro* 'his donkey' and *łech-servir-oa* 'it serves us'. A *loanblend* consists of a combination of native and borrowed morphological material, such as English *washable*, formed from the native root *wash* and the borrowed suffix *-able*, which had come into English on loanwords from Latin and French. Boas lists such Nahuatl blends as *quahui-tero* 'woodchopper' and *łona-nita* 'a little old woman' with Nahuatl roots and Spanish derivational suffixes. A *loan translation*, also called a *calque*, consists of a morpheme-by-morpheme translation of a morphologically complex expression from the source language. Oft-cited examples are the German and French terms for 'skyscraper', based on the English: German *Wolkenkratzer* ('cloud-scratch-er') and French *gratte-ciel* ('scratch-sky'). Many loan translations in European languages are based on Latin terms, such as *paeninsula*, the basis for German *Halbinsel* ('half-island') and French *presqu'île* ('almost-island'). Finally, a *loanshift* represents a purely semantic transfer, consisting entirely of native material whose meaning has been shifted to encompass an introduced concept. A familiar example is English *heaven*, which originally meant simply 'sky'. With the introduction of Christianity, its meaning was extended to include the modern religious sense. A new term, *sky*, was subsequently borrowed into English from Scandinavian and took over the original meaning of *heaven*, leaving the religious sense of the latter as primary.

Bloomfield also distinguished types of borrowing according to the social conditions under which they take place: cultural borrowing, intimate borrowing, and dialect borrowing. Cultural borrowing occurs between languages spoken in separate geographical areas. It can be bidirectional, but the nature and extent of borrowing on each side is determined by the nature of the contact. When new material goods and concepts are introduced by one group to another, names for them may be introduced as well. One can thus often infer the nature of contact long after the fact by examining the content of loans. Bloomfield cites German loanwords in English for certain foods (*frankfurter, sauerkraut, pretzel*) and for philosophical and scientific concepts (*zeitgeist, wanderlust*), and Italian musical terms (*piano, sonata, scherzo*). Boas 1930 cites Spanish loans in Nahuatl pertaining to religion and the church (*dios, santo, ángelis*), political organization (*nación, rey, prefectura, policías, justicia*), ranch life (*hacienda, rancho, corral, patio*), horses (*cahuayo, jáquima, cordel*), money and measures (*semana, peso, centavo*), numerals, garments, implements and utensils, games, and others. The second type, intimate borrowing, occurs between languages spoken in "what is topographically and politically a single community," a situation that often arises by immigration or conquest. It is predominantly one-sided: most items are borrowed by the lower group, the immigrants or the conquered, from the language of the dominant or privileged group. New immigrants need names for the many new objects and institutions they encounter in their new home (*baseball, alderman, boss*), and conquered populations may seek to use terms with more prestige. The third type, dialect borrowing, takes place across varieties of a single language. Forms may arise in the speech of a prestigious town, group, or individual, then be adopted by those in contact and gradually spread over an ever-increasing area. Such innovations are not limited to words but may include phonetic variants and turns of speech.

Betz 1949 devised a detailed framework for classifying borrowings in his work on medieval Latin loans in trans-

lations into Old High German. He contrasted *Lehnwörter*, loanwords proper, with *Lehnbildunge* or 'loan formations', constructions resulting from foreign influence. The latter were in turn classified into loan-translations, loan-transfers, loan-creations, loan-expressions, loan-meanings, and loan-syntax.

The Norwegian-American Einar Haugen investigated the effects of American English on the Norwegian of immigrants from Norway to the United States and produced rich studies of the structural and social details of the process, particularly *The Norwegian language in America* (1953). Haugen pointed to the role of bilingualism in diffusion, an important factor not always noted in earlier work, and emphasized that American Norwegian was not a "mixed language": at any given time, speakers were consciously speaking either Norwegian or English.

Attention to the level of bilingualism can often point to multiple layers of borrowing over time. For example, speakers of Central Pomo, a language of northern California, first encountered Europeans in the early 19th century, when Spanish-speaking missionaries and colonists began to arrive (Mithun 1990). At the earliest stage of cultural contact, before bilingualism was extensive, Central Pomo speakers created descriptive names for introduced goods, which remain today: *hts'ím q^{h}ale* 'by poking-to.stick with' = 'fork'; *šakú hsáq' q^{h}ale* 'leg by.poking-to.push with' = 'pants'. With the arrival of more Spanish-speaking colonists, Central Pomo speakers, who had always been multilingual, learned some Mexican Spanish and borrowed words for introduced goods, such as *kúčiiya* 'knife' (from Spanish *cuchilla*) and *máayiš* 'corn' (from *maíz*). The borrowed terms, primarily nouns, were fully integrated into Central Pomo phonologically and grammatically; speakers altered their shapes to conform to their own sound patterns, substituting sounds and giving them initial stress: *páaka* 'cow' (from Spanish *vaca*), *'ádiina* 'flour' (from Spanish *harina*). Many of the words did not actually enter Central Pomo directly from Spanish, but rather through neighboring California languages whose speakers were first in contact with Spanish speakers at the missions. For example, Central Pomo contains the vowel [o], equivalent to Spanish *o*, but many Spanish loans show a substitution of [u] for [o], adjustments made by other groups: *péesu* 'money' (from Spanish *peso*), *káwaayu* 'horse' (from *caballo*). Spanish loans in Central Pomo appear in compounds with native terms, like *kóoči p'še* 'pork' (from Spanish *coche* 'pig' and Central Pomo *p'še* 'deer/meat'). They also appear with native derivational and inflectional morphology:

wáalsa=wi šdétč'ič'in 'pocket=in carrying.around' = 'carrying them around in their pockets' (from Spanish *bolsa*). At midcentury, the land was transferred from Mexico to the United States, and English-speaking ranchers began to arrive. By 1910, half of the Central Pomo children were enrolled in school; by 1935, Central Pomo was used at home only by the elderly; and by the mid-20th century, there were few monolingual speakers. This contact situation resulted in another layer of borrowing that differs in nature from the first. English loanwords include not only nouns in a variety of domains but also verbs and adjectives. They show the American English pronunciation of the community, because speakers are bilingual. They are fully integrated into the grammar morphologically and syntactically, which can result in complex constructions: *learnčikaw* '[she] taught [me]' (*learn-či-ka-w* 'learn-*semelfactive-causative-perfective*').

There had always been an awareness among linguists that linguistic elements differ in their susceptibility to borrowing. Whitney 1881 noted that words are most easily borrowed (and among words, nouns), then suffixes, then inflections, and then sounds, with the last two carried in only on loanwords: "Whatever is more formal or structural in character remains in that degree free from the intrusion of foreign material." Haugen 1950 maintained that "all linguistic features can be borrowed, but they are distributed along a *scale of adoptability* which somehow is correlated to the structural organization." (1950:224). In his own corpus of American Norwegian, he found that 75.5% of the loanwords were nouns, 18.4% verbs, 3.4% adjectives, 1.4% interjections, and 1.2% adverbs and prepositions. He explained that while vocabulary is added throughout the lifetime of the speaker, structural features are established in early childhood and frequently repeated: "The more habitual and subconscious a feature of language is, the harder it will be to change" (1950:224).

Structuralist approaches to language led to interest in delimiting the possible extent of structural borrowing. Roman Jakobson of the Prague School, sharing the traditional view that structural changes are introduced only in loanwords, proposed that such changes are always typologically consistent with the native pattern of the language: "Language accepts foreign structural elements only when these correspond to its own developmental tendencies" ([1938] 1962:240).

Uriel Weinreich's influential *Languages in contact* (1953) provided an important framework for the study of diffusion. On the prerequisite of typological fit, he re-marked, "Indeed, it stands very much to reason that the transfer of morphemes is facilitated between highly congruent structures; for a highly bound morpheme is so dependent on its grammatical function (as opposed to its designative value) that it is useless in an alien system unless there is a ready function for it" (1953:33). He proposed a set of structural constraints on morphological borrowing: (i) grammatical categories are typically not borrowed, but rather, morphemes are borrowed to designate existing categories; (ii) borrowed morphemes typically add substance, in that non-zero morphemes replace zero morphemes, and long forms replace short ones; (iii) free morphemes tend to replace bound ones; (iv) a morpheme with a single, invariant form is likely to replace one with multiple allomorphs; (v) morphemes with complex grammatical functions deeply embedded in the grammar are unlikely to be transferred; and (vi) affective morphological processes, like diminutive formation, are especially susceptible to borrowing.

Weinreich emphasized, however, that interference cannot be accounted for solely in terms of structure. The speaker's ability to keep languages apart, relative proficiency in each, manner of learning each, and attitude toward each, as well as the domains of use of each, relative numbers of speakers of each, and tolerance for code-switching, all affect the kinds of transfer that take place. Words are borrowed not just to designate new objects, persons, places, or concepts, but also to provide terms that carry connotations associated with the source culture (prestigious or otherwise), to express perceived distinctions lacking in the borrowing language, to resolve clashes between homophones, and to fill gaps as affective words lose their expressive force over time.

In a fine study of diffusion among languages in Arnhem Land in northern Australia, Heath 1978 investigated the spread of structural features in light of current proposed constraints. The populations of speakers of the languages under study were small and strictly exogamous. Multilingualism was the norm: brides usually took up residence with their husbands' people, so children learned at least two languages, that of their mother and that of their community. In this situation, Heath found that the structural constraint on phonology proposed by Meillet and Jakobson—that languages will accept only those loans that are consistent with their current topologies—did not determine which structural elements were borrowed, though it did affect the kinds of subsequent internal readjustments motivated by the loans. Many of the structural constraints on morphology suggested by Weinreich also failed. First, new categories were created by morphemic diffusion, such as an ergative-instrumental case marker. Second, most morphemic borrowing resulted in replacing a native form with a borrowed form of the same size: the ablative suffixes *-wala* and *-yani*, for example, were borrowed back and forth. In one case, a shorter form replaced a longer one: a genitive-dative-purposive suffix *-gu* replaced the native *-guŋuŋ*. Third, there was little evidence that free morphemes replace bound ones, since the borrowed morphemes were nearly all bound. Fourth, morphemes with multiple allomorphs were borrowed to replace native morphemes with a single form. Weinreich's final two hypotheses were borne out, however: morphemes with opaque grammatical functions were not borrowed, and affective morphological processes—in particular, diminutives—were borrowed. Overall, Heath found that affixes marking case, number, noun class, diminutives, and negation were diffusable, as were an inchoative verbalizer, thematizing augment, and postpositions. By contrast, independent pronouns, bound pronominals, verbal inflectional affixes, demonstrative stems, and demonstrative adverbs were not. Certain factors favored diffusability for morphemes, in particular syllabicity, sharpness of boundaries between morphemes, unifunctionality, categorical clarity, and analogical freedom. Morphemes forming relatively closed systems, such as case suffixes, were less susceptible to transfer.

Moravcsik 1978 surveyed the literature on attested patterns of diffusion and considered their implications for possible constraints on the process. She listed seven that appear to hold: (i) no non-lexical feature is borrowed before words; (ii) no phrasally unaccented material is borrowed before accented material, so that affixes, clitics, and parts of compounds are not borrowed before full words; (iii) nouns are borrowed before other kinds of words; (iv) verbs are not borrowed as verbs; (v) inflection is not borrowed before derivation; (vi) grammatical morphemes are not borrowed without the order in which they occur, so that a preposition would not be borrowed and postposed; and (vii) if some native members of a lexical category carry no inflectional ending, then at least some borrowed members of that category will also carry no inflectional ending, like neuter nouns in German.

In a masterful work on language contact, Thomason and Kaufman 1988 examined a tremendous body of descriptions of contact phenomena and proposals on constraints on the potential outcome. In the tradition of Weinreich, they demonstrated that ultimately any linguistic feature can be diffused, given particular social circumstances. Determinants of contact-induced change are primarily social and secondarily structural. Most important is the distinction between contact with language maintenance and contact with language shift. Contact-induced change with language maintenance is borrowing narrowly defined, instigated by native speakers. It involves the adoption of foreign vocabulary first, then of structure only under increasing cultural pressure. The intensity of cultural pressure depends on the length of contact and degree of bilingualism. The second kind of contact-induced change, which takes place under language shift, is instigated by second-language learners who do not fully master the new language. It typically involves the transfer of structure first, as non-native speakers consciously use the vocabulary of the new language but fail to adjust some structural features of their original grammar.

On this basis, Thomason and Kaufman set up a scale of borrowability in the narrow sense, proposing that "the more internal structure a subsystem of language has, the more intense the contact must be in order to result in structural borrowing" (1988:73). Their scale distinguishes five degrees of contact. (i) Under casual contact, there is lexical borrowing only, which is limited to content words (such as nouns and verbs) that are not part of core vocabulary. (ii) Under slightly more intense contact, some function words are borrowed, such as conjunctions and adverbial particles, along with minor phonological, syntactic, and lexical-semantic features within the loanwords. (iii) Under more intense contact, personal and demonstrative pronouns and adpositions may be borrowed, and more structural borrowing can be seen, including derivational affixes abstracted from borrowed words and extended to native vocabulary. Inflectional affixes may enter on loanwords. There may be phonemicization of previous allophones and minor word-order shifts, as from postpositions to prepositions or the reverse. (iv) Under strong cultural pressure, structural features may be borrowed that cause little typological change. New distinctive phonological features may appear, as well as new syllable structures and extensive word order changes. Borrowed inflectional affixes and categories may be added to native words. (v) Finally, under very strong cultural pressure, there is heavy structural borrowing, which may result in significant typological disruption. There may be loss of phonological contrasts, changes in word structure (such as the addition of prefixes to a previously suffixing language), shift from more flectional toward agglutinating morphology, development of new case patterns such as ergativity, new concord rules, and the addition of pronominal affixes. All these situations are richly illustrated with examples from languages around the world. The work of Thomason and Kaufman is generally considered to represent the current state of knowledge in the area of borrowing.

[*See also* Bilingualism and Multilingualism; Historical Linguistics; Language Change; *and* Pidgins and Creoles.]

BIBLIOGRAPHY

Betz, Werner. 1949. *Deutsch und Lateinisch: Die Lehnbildungen der althochdeutschen Benediktinerregel.* Bonn: Bouvier.

Bloomfield, Leonard. 1933. *Language.* New York: Holt, Rinehart and Winston.

Boas, Franz. 1930. Spanish elements in modern Nahuatl. In *Todd Memorial Volumes: Philological studies*, edited by John D. Fitz-Gerald and Pauline Taylor, pp. 85–89. Freeport, N.Y.: Books for Libraries Press.

Haugen, Einar. 1950. The analysis of linguistic borrowing. *Language* 26.210–231.

Haugen, Einar. 1953. *The Norwegian language in America: A study in bilingual behavior.* 2 vols. Philadelphia: University of Pennsylvania Press; repr. Bloomington: Indiana University Press, 1969.

Heath, Jeffrey. 1978. *Linguistic diffusion in Arnhem Land.* Canberra: Australian Institute of Aboriginal Studies.

Jakobson, Roman. 1938. Sur la théorie des affinités phonologiques entre les langues. *Actes du quatrième Congrès International de Linguistes*, pp. 48–59. Copenhagen: Einar Munksgaard. Repr. in *Selected writings of Roman Jakobson* vol. 1., pp. 234–246. The Hague: Mouton.

Meillet, Antoine. 1921. Le problème de la parenté des langues. In his *Linguistique historique et linguistique générale*, vol. 1, p. 84. Paris: Champion.

Mithun, Marianne. 1990. Language obsolescence and grammatical description. *International Journal of American Linguistics* 56.1–26.

Moravcsik, Edith. 1978. Language contact. In *Universals of human language*, vol. 1, edited by Joseph Greenberg, pp. 93–122. Stanford, Calif.: Stanford University Press.

Müller, Max. 1861–1864. *Lectures on the science of language* 2 vols. Bern: Francke.

Powell, John Wesley. 1891. Indian linguistic families of America north of Mexico. In *Seventh Annual Report, Bureau of American Ethnology*, pp. 1–142. Washington, D.C.: Government Printing Office. Repr. in *American Indian languages*, edited by Preston Holder, pp. 82–218. Lincoln: University of Nebraska Press.

Sayce, A. H. 1874. *The principles of comparative philology.* London: Trübner.

Sapir, Edward. 1921a. A bird's-eye view of American languages north of Mexico. *Science* n.s. 54.408. Reprinted in *The collected works of Edward Sapir* vol. 5, edited by William Bright, pp. 93–94. Berlin: Mouton de Gruyter, 1990.

Sapir, Edward. 1921b. *Language.* New York: Harcourt, Brace, and World.

Schmidt, Johannes. 1872. *Die Verwandtschaftsverhältnisse der indogermanischen Sprachen.* Weimar: Böhlau.

Schuchardt, Hugo. 1884. *Slawo-deutsches und Slawoitalienisches.* (Slawisches Propyläen, 66.) Graz: Leuschner and Lubensky. Repr. Munich: Fink, 1971.

Weinreich, Uriel. 1953. *Languages in contact: Findings and problems.* New York: Linguistic Circle of New York.

Whitney, William Dwight. 1867. *Language and the study of language.* New York: Scribners.

Whitney, William Dwight. 1881. On mixture in language. *Transactions of the American Philological Association* 12.5–26. Repr. in *Whitney on language*, edited by Michael Silverstein, pp. 170–191. Cambridge, Mass.: MIT Press, 1971.

EINAR HAUGEN AND MARIANNE MITHUN

Loanword Phonology

Words borrowed from one language into another are typically altered to conform to the phonological canons of the borrowing language, in ways that range from changes in individual segments to more global deformations of structure. Loan phonology is often quite revealing of the grammatical constraints and processes of the borrowing language. Complete systematicity is not to be expected, however, since loanwords may enter a language either through orthography or through pronunciation; they may be borrowed at different points in the history of a language; and they may be affected by such factors as the degree of *bilingualism* in the borrowing community, or the similarity of the loanword to taboo words in the recipient language. (For general reference, see Haugen 1950, Weinreich 1953, Byarushengo 1976, Holden 1976, Paradis and LaCharité 1996.) It is not uncommon to find groups of loanwords comprising a subsystem within a language, with phonological properties that are not shared with the rest of the vocabulary. In English, for example, we find an alternation of *k* and *s* in Latinate vocabulary (such as *electric/electricity*) that is not found in Germanic vocabulary. In Japanese, we find three distinct strata: Yamato (native) vocabulary, Sino-Japanese roots, and recently borrowed foreign vocabulary. Vocabulary of each stratum obeys different (though sometimes overlapping) sets of restrictions: for example, only Yamato words are subject to the restriction that a word may contain no more than one voiced obstruent, while Yamato and Sino-Japanese words, but not more recent borrowings, are subject to the restriction that geminate obstruents must be voiceless (Ito and Mester 1995).

Perhaps the most obvious alteration in loanwords is the replacement of single segments, often called *phoneme substitution*. This process subjects the loanword to the borrowing language's restrictions on possible phonemes and their distribution; thus, in English, the replacement of the velar fricative by *h* or *k* (as in *Chanukah* and *Bach* respectively) is subject to the restriction that *h* may not occur syllable-finally in English. The allophonic restrictions of the recipient language are also generally obeyed; Spanish *estufa* 'stove' becomes Yaqui *ehtupa,* where nonoccurring *f* is replaced by *p,* but *s,* which does occur in Yaqui, is realized as *h,* the appropriate positional variant before *t* (Haugen 1950).

The choice of a replacement phoneme is often assumed to be determined by phonetic similarity, though it is not clear which aspect of a given sound will be perceived as most salient by speakers of a particular language. For example, among languages which lack θ but employ both *s* and *t* as phonemes, some typically replace English θ by *s* and some by *t,* for no obvious phonetic reason (Hyman 1970a).

One question that arises in connection with phoneme substitution is whether borrowers actually perceive contrasts that are lacking in their native language. Thus, Silverman 1992 argues that the Cantonese pronunciation [sap] 'sharp' is evidence that Cantonese speakers simply do not hear a contrast between alveolar and alveopalatal fricatives. However, in Tagalog, which like Cantonese lacks a contrast between *s* and *ʃ,* the borrowed form 'shopping' may be pronounced in its reduplicated form as [sa-ʃapŋ] (Ross 1996), indicating that even speakers who correctly produce the non-native phoneme simplify it in a context where preservation of the original pronunciation is a lower priority.

Loanwords also commonly conform to constraints on prosodic organization as well as on segmental structure. Constraints on syllable structure are typically maintained by the insertion of vowels, as in Samoan *sipuni* 'spoon', which obeys the Samoan requirement that syllables consist maximally of one consonant followed by one vowel. However, additional strategies may be used, such as the deletion of a consonant (e.g. loss of *p* in *pneumonia*); or reordering of segments as in the common rendering by American news reporters of *Tbilisi* as [tiblisi].

In addition to constraints on syllable structure, borrowing languages commonly enforce restrictions on possible word structure; in Arabic, for example, monosyllabic nouns and verbs must consist of a syllable which is either closed by two consonants, or which contains a long vowel followed by a consonant, so that borrowed *bus* becomes either [ba:s] or [bass]. Borrowing languages also tend to translate the prosodic structure of the loanword into native prosodic configurations.

While nativization is clearly a strong factor in loanword transformation, some patterns seem rooted in neither the borrowing nor the recipient language, but rather in universal preferences for less marked configurations. Thus, while Lovins 1975 argues that in Japanese borrowings from English the pitch accent of the borrowed word is determined by the position of stress in the English pronunciation, Katayama 1998 suggests that what appears to be transfer from English stress is actually reversion to a universally preferred, unmarked accent pattern. The effect of universal markedness patterns may also be seen in the fact that a number of languages with no word-initial consonant sequences in native vocabulary tend to insert a vowel inside initial clusters of rising sonority (as in Egyptian Arabic [bilastik] 'plastic') but before the clusters of falling sonority (as in Egyptian Arabic [sikii] 'ski', Broselow 1992). Because the borrowing languages have no initial clusters at all, the distinction between the two cluster types is not explainable in terms of the structure of the native languages, but may be related to the greater markedness of falling sonority onset clusters. In opposition to the tendencies to nativize borrowed words or to transform them in accord with universally unmarked patterns, we may also find a tendency to mark borrowed words as foreign in their prosody: for example, although the late Syrian leader's name *Assad* is pronounced in Arabic with stress on its initial syllable, American newscasters often pronounce it with stress on the final syllable, a pattern that (because less common in English) is apparently seen as more authentically foreign.

The recasting of loanwords into forms consistent with the phonology of the borrowing language has the consequence that loan phonology may serve as a useful testing ground for hypotheses about the grammar of the borrowing language. For example, the alterations of metrical structure discussed above provide a diagnostic for the recipient language's constraints on syllable and word structure. Another sort of example involves Nupe, a Nigerian language, in which consonants occurring before non-low front vowels *i e* are palatalized, while consonants occurring before back vowels *u o* are not. However, both palatalized and non-palatalized consonants occur before the back vowel *a.* Hyman 1970b argues that, in the optimal grammar of Nupe, palatalized consonants derive from a rule which palatalizes a consonant before a front vowel; surface *a* following a palatalized consonant is derived from underlying front ɛ by an absolute neutralization rule that transforms ɛ to *a* after palatalization has taken place. This sort of analysis is supported by the Nupe rendering of Yoruba loans like *kɛkɛ* 'bicycle' as *kyakya,* where all palatalized consonants are derived from underlying front vowels. More recently, loan vocabulary has been used to argue in favor of the hypothesis that grammars consist of a set of universal constraints on surface structure; Yip 1993, Broselow 1999, and Jacobs and Gussenhoven 2000 all provide cases in which loanword adaptations are consistent with the predictions of the native-language constraint rankings, even where some of these predictions are untestable on the more restricted range of native-language inputs.

[*See also* Bilingualism and Multilingualism; Markedness; Phonology; *and* Syllables.]

BIBLIOGRAPHY

Broselow, Ellen. 1992. Language transfer and universals in second language epenthesis. In *Language transfer and language learning*, edited by Susan Gass and Larry Selinker, pp. 71–86. Amsterdam: John Benjamins.

Broselow, Ellen. 1999. Stress, epenthesis, and segment transformation in Selayarese loans. In *Berkeley Linguistics Society* 25.211–225.

Byarushengo, Ernest R. 1976. Strategies in loan phonology. *Berkeley Linguistics Society.* 2.78–88.

Haugen, Einar. 1950. The analysis of linguistic borrowing. *Language.* 26.210–231.

Holden, Kyril. 1976. Assimilation rates of borrowings and phonological productivity. *Language.* 52.131–147.

Hyman, Larry M. 1970a. The role of borrowing in the justification of phonological grammars. *Studies in African Linguistics.* 1.1–48.

Hyman, Larry M. 1970b. How concrete is phonology? *Language.* 46.58–76.

Itô, Junko and Armin Mester. 1995. Japanese phonology. In *The handbook of phonological theory*, edited by John A. Goldsmith, pp. 817–838. Oxford: Blackwell.

Jacobs, Haike, and Carlos Gussenhoven. 2000. Loan phonology: Perception, salience, the lexicon and OT. In *Optimality Theory: phonology, syntax, and acquisition*, edited by Joost Dekkers et al., pp. 193–210. Oxford: Oxford University Press.

Katayama, Motoko. 1998. *Optimality Theory and Japanese loanword phonology.* University of California at Santa Cruz dissertation.

Lovins, Julie B. 1975. *Loanwords and the phonological structure of Japanese.* Bloomington: Indiana University Linguistics Club.

Paradis, Carole, and Darlene LaCharité. 1997. Preservation and minimality in loanword adaptation. *Journal of Linguistics.* 33.379–430.

Ross, Kie. 1996. Floating phonotacics: variability in infixation and reduplication of Tagalog loanwords. M.A. thesis, University of California, Los Angeles.

Silverman, Daniel. 1992. Multiple scansions in loanword phonology: Evidence from Cantonese. *Phonology.* 9.289–328.

Weinreich, Uriel. 1953. *Languages in contact.* New York: Linguistic Circle of New York. Reprinted, The Hague: Mouton, 1974.

Yip, Moira. 1993. Cantonese loanword phonology and Optimality Theory. *Journal of East Asian Linguistics.* 2.261–91.

ELLEN BROSELOW

BOUND. *See* Anaphora; Morpheme; Morphology; *and* Semantics.

BOUNDARY. *See* Sentence Phonology.

BRAIN AND LANGUAGE. *See* Aphasia; Bilingualism and Multilingualism; Neurolinguistics; Evolution and Language; Psycholinguistics; *and* Writing and Written Language.

BRÉAL, MICHEL (1832–1915). Pioneer of comparative-historical linguistics in France, and a scholar with more general interests. His *Essai de sémantique* (1897) is a general introduction to grammatical and lexical theory, influential in particular for its treatment of changes in the meanings of words. We owe to him the first use of the term *sémantique.*

[*See also* History of Linguistics *and* Semantics.]

ANNA MORPURGO DAVIES

BRUGMANN, KARL (1849–1919). German Indo-Europeanist and a founder of the Neogrammarian movement. He wrote a monumental *Handbook of Indo-European* (*Grundriss der vergleichenden Grammatik der indogermanischen Sprachen,* 2d ed. 1897–1916) that is still regularly consulted.

[*See also* History of Linguistics, *article on* Comparative-Historical Linguistics.]

ANNA MORPURGO DAVIES

BÜHLER, KARL (1879–1963). Psychologist. Bühler was a professor at the University of Vienna from 1922 to 1938, where his views influenced the thinking of Nikolai Trubetzkoy and other members of the Prague School.

[*See also* History of Linguistics, *article on* The Prague School.]

ANNA MORPURGO DAVIES

BULGARIAN. The official language of the Republic of Bulgaria, where it has about 7,600,000 speakers (approximately 88% of the total population of 8,612,757, July 1996 estimate). A South Slavic language, it forms a dialect continuum with Macedonian and Eastern Serbo-Croatian dialects. Bulgarian is also a member of the Balkan language area.

Among works published in English. Rå Hauge 1999, DeBray 1980, and Scatton 1984 are general grammars covering all aspects of the language. Aronson 1968 is a structuralist analysis of inflectional morphophonology. Alexander and Mladenova 2000 is a thorough textbook treatment of Bulgarian grammar that presupposes no prior knowledge of Bulgarian or another Slavic language. Atanassova et al. 1995 and Rankova et al. 1987–1988 are comprehensive bilingual dictionaries. Scatton 1975 gives a generative analysis of Bulgarian phonology; Aronson 1967 presents a structuralist analysis of the grammatical categories of the Bulgarian verb; Rudin 1986 is an analysis combining Revised Extended Standard Theory and Government and Binding; and Fielder 1993 deals with aspect selection from a functionalist-structuralist point of view.

1. Phonology. Literary Bulgarian has a six-vowel system, with binary distinctions of front/back, rounded/unrounded, and higher/lower. The phonemes are *i e ə a u o*. Stress is distinctive; unstressed position is characterized by greater or lesser degrees of neutralization of the opposition high/low, in the direction of high.

Among the consonants, the major contrasts are voiced/voiceless and palatalized/non-palatalized. The latter is syntagmatically weakly implemented: palatalization is distinctive only before back vowels—in native words, most commonly before *a*, and before *ə* at morpheme boundaries. The consonantal phonemes are shown in Table 1.

Bulgarian is written in the Cyrillic alphabet in a form close to that used for Russian. The letter щ is pronounced *št*; the symbol Ъ represents the vowel *ə*.

TABLE 1. *Bulgarian Consonant Phonemes*

	Labial	Dental	Palatal	Velar
Stops				
Voiceless				
Plain	p	t		k
Palatalized	p'	t'		k'
Voiced				
Plain	b	d		g
Palatalized	b'	d'		g'
Affricates				
Voiceless				
Plain		c	č	
Palatalized		c'		
Voiced (Plain)			ǰ	
Fricatives				
Voiceless				
Plain	f	s	š	x
Palatalized	f'	s'		
Voiced				
Plain	v	z	ž	
Palatalized	v'	z'		
Nasals				
Plain	m	n		
Palatalized	m'	n'		
Vibrants				
Plain		r		
Palatalized		r'		
Laterals				
Plain		l		
Palatalized		l'		
Glide			j	

2. Morphophonology (see Aronson 1968). Bulgarian has regressive assimilation of voicing; e.g.,

(1) /gradové/ 'cities'   /grát/ 'city'
     /lovéc/ 'hunter'   /lofcí/ 'hunters'
     /otparíš/ 'from Paris' /odbəlgárija/ 'from Bulgaria'

Morphologically conditioned alternations in the nominal system include the following.

(a) Vowel/zero alternation:

(2) *dvoréc* 'palace', def. *dvorécət*,
          but pl. *dvorcí*

(3) *knižóven* 'literary (masc.)',
          but fem. *knižóvna*, neu. *knižóvno*

(b) The alternations *k~c, g~z, x~s* in the plurals of masculine nouns:

(4) *vojník* 'soldier'   pl. *vojníci*

antropológ 'anthropologist' pl. *antropolózi*
monáx 'monk'   pl. *monási*

(c) Stress alternations from the stem to the singular definite article (masc., fem.) and to the plural desinence (masc., neu.), and from the desinence to the stem in the vocative (fem.)

Alternations in the verbal system include the following:

(d) Alternation of *k~č, g~ž* before *e*:

(5) *peká* 'I bake', but 2sg. *pečéš*, 3sg. *pečé*

(6) *móga* 'I can', but 2sg. *móžeš*, 3sg. *móže*

(e) Stress alternations from the stem to the desinence in the imperative, from the ending to the stem in the aorist, and optionally from the stem to the desinence in some aorists.

Peculiar to Bulgarian is the so-called *jat*-umlaut, where some occurrences of *á* after soft consonants alternate with *e* under the following circumstances:

(i) When the vowel loses stress:

(7) *mjásto* 'place', pl. *mestá*

(ii) When the vowel is followed by a syllable which begins with a palatal(ized) consonant or contains a front vowel:

(8) *vljáza* 'I enter', *vlézeš* 'you enter'

(9) *mljáko* 'milk', adj. *mléčen*

(10) *djásna* 'right' (fem.), *djásno* (neu.), but masc. *désen*, pl. *désni*

3. Noun morphology.

Bulgarian has a contrast of three genders—masculine, feminine, and neuter—marked by the adjective:

(11) masc. *tózi nóv véstnik*   'this new newspaper'
      fem. *tázi nóva kníga*   'this new book'
      neu. *tová nóvo spisánie*   'this new magazine'

In the plural, there are no gender oppositions: *tézi nóvi véstnici, kníg i, spisánija* 'these new newspapers, books, magazines'.

As in Macedonian (but not the other Slavic literary languages), Bulgarian substantives and adjectives lack case. However, a definite article is postposed to the first substantive or adjective in the noun phrase:

(12a) *véstnik* 'newspaper', *véstnikət* 'the newspaper'
       véstnici 'newspapers', *véstnicite* 'the newspapers'

(12b) *kníga(ta)* '(the) book,' *kníg i(te)* '(the) books'

(12c) *spisánie(to)* '(the) magazine', *spisanija(ta)* '(the) magazines'

(12d) *nóv(ijat) véstnik* '(the) new newspaper', *nóvi(te) véstnici* '(the) new newspapers'

The masculine article *-ət* has, in the normative language, an 'accusative' form in *-a, -ja*:

(13) *Lékarjat vížda véstnika.*
      'The doctor sees the newspaper.'

The substantive (and masc. adjective) also has a vocative form:

(14) *drág prijátel* 'dear friend', voc. *drági prijátelju*

Most masc. substantives distinguish two plural forms: the "quantified plural" is used after numerals and other quantifiers, and the other is used in all other environments:

(15) *tézi pét véstnika* 'these five newspapers'
      tézi stári véstnici 'these old newspapers'

Personal nouns tend not to take the quantified plural.

Comparison of adjectives and adverbs is by means of the stressed prefixes *pó-* 'more', *náj-* 'most':

(16) *mlád* 'young', *pó-mlád* 'younger', *náj-mlád(ijat)* '(the) youngest'

(17) *dobré* 'well', *pó-dobré* 'better', *náj-dobré* 'best'

Numerals show an opposition of virile (masc. personal) vs. non-virile:

(18) *tríma məžé* 'three men'
      tri žení 'three women'
      tri véstnika 'three newspapers'

4. Pronominal morphology.

The stressed forms of personal pronouns oppose the cases NOM and OBL[ique] (= DAT-ACC); clitic forms have either one OBL, or separate DAT and ACC. The forms are shown in Table 2.

The DAT clitic forms are used to mark possession:

(19) *knígata mu* 'his book'
      véstnikət ni 'our newspaper'

TABLE 2. *Bulgarian Pronoun Forms*

	Stressed		Unstressed	
	Nom	Obl	Dat	Acc
1sg.	*áz*	*méne*	*mi*	*me*
2sg.	*tí*	*tébe*	*ti*	*te*
1pl.	*níe*	*nás*	*ni*	
2pl.	*víe*	*vás*	*vi*	
3sg.masc.	*tój*	*négo*	*mu*	*go*
3sg.neu.	*tó*	*négo*	*mu*	*go*
3sg.fem.	*tjá*	*néja*	*ì*	*ja*
3pl.	*té*	*tjáx*	*im*	*gi*
Reflexive	—	*sébe (si)*	*si*	*se*

TABLE 3. *First Person Singular Verb Forms of Bulgarian*

	Perfective	Derived Imperfective
Simplex forms		
Non-past	*opíša*	*opísvam*
Imperfect	*opíšex*	*opísvax*
Aorist	*opísax*	*opísvax*
Pluperfect₁	*bjáx opísal*	*bjáx opísval*
Forms with the future particle *šte*		
Future	*šte opíša*	*šte opísvam*
Future preterit	*štjáx da opíša*	*štjáx da opísvam*
Perfect forms (with the auxiliary *səm* 'be')		
Present perfect	*opísal səm*	*opísval səm*
Pluperfect₂	*bíl səm opísal*	*bíl səm opísval*
Future perfect	*šte səm opísal*	*šte səm opísval*
Conditional	*bíx opísal*	*bíx opísval*

TABLE 4. *Other Verb Forms of Bulgarian*

	Perfective	Derived Imperfective
Imperative	*opiší, opišéte*	*opísvaj, opísvajte*
Pres. act. participle	——	*opísvašt*
Past act. participle	*opísal*	——
Past pass. participle	*opísan*	*opísvan*
Gerund	——	*opísvajki*
Verbal noun	——	*opísvane*

In addition, there are stressed possessive adjectives.

5. Verbal morphology. Bulgarian possesses one of the most complex verbal systems in Slavic. In addition to the superordinated, grammatical opposition of perfective/derived imperfective, Bulgarian has the "screeves" shown below; these are paradigmatic tense/aspect sets varying only in person and number, or in person, number, and gender. Table 3 gives examples of the 1sg. form of the (perfective) verb *opíša* 'describe', derived imperfective *opísvam*. Other forms, which do not have complete paradigms, are shown in Table 4.

Within the past tense, the aorist and imperfect are opposed to each other in aspect: the imperfect denotes an event that occupies more than one moment in the past.

Central to the Bulgarian verbal system is the category of *status*, which indicates how the speaker vouches for the reality of the event described. The aorist and imperfect are *confirmative* forms, generally used to mark witnessed events. The perfect forms are basically *nonconfirmative;* they are widely used to mark non-witnessed events, either reported or inferred. With the meaning 'reported', the 3rd person auxiliaries *e, sa* 'be' are often dropped.

6. Syntax. Like other Balkan languages, Bulgarian replaces the infinitive constructions of Western European and most other Slavic languages with an analytic conjunctive; this consists of the particle *da* followed by a finite form of the verb, e.g.:

(20) *Ískam da govórja s   lékarja.*
      I.want that I.speak with the.doctor
      'I want to speak with the doctor.'

Possession is normally indicated with the preposition *na*, or by clitic dative pronouns:

(21a) *knígata   na   lékarja*
       the.book of   the.doctor
(21b) *knígata   mu*
       book.the to-him = 'his book'

The preposition *na* and the DAT clitics also serve to mark the indirect object:

(22a) *Dádox knígata na lékarja.*
       'I gave the book to the doctor.'
(22b) *Dádox mu knígata.*
       'I gave him the book.'

Subject/direct object relations are expressed primarily through word order—normally Subject Verb Object—and by concord in person, number, and gender between the subject and the verb. Object reduplication, through the clitic DAT and ACC pronouns in the verb phrase, can serve to mark subject/object relations:

(23) *Maríja ja vidjá včéra.*
Mary her-ACC s/he.saw yesterday
'S/he saw Mary yesterday.'

[*See also* Balkan Languages *and* Slavic Languages.]

BIBLIOGRAPHY

Alexander, Ronelle, and Olga M. Mladenova. 2000. *Intensive Bulgarian: A textbook and reference grammar.* Madison: University of Wisconsin Press.

Aronson, Howard I. 1967. The grammatical categories of the indicative in the contemporary Bulgarian literary language. In *To honor Roman Jakobson: Essays on the occasion of his seventieth birthday* (Janua linguarum, Series maior, 31), vol. 1, pp. 82–98. The Hague: Mouton.

Aronson, Howard I. 1968. *Bulgarian inflectional morphophonology.* (Slavistic printings and reprintings, 70.) The Hague: Mouton.

Atanassova, Theodora, et al. 1995. *Bulgarian-English dictionary.* Sofia: Nauka i Izkustvo.

De Bray, Reginald G. A. 1980. Bulgarian. In his *Guide to the South Slavonic languages,* pp. 78–136. Columbus, Ohio: Slavica.

Fielder, Grace E. 1993. *Semantics and pragmatics of verbal categories in Bulgarian.* Lewiston, N.Y.: Edwin Mellem.

Rå Hauge, Kjetil. 1999. *A Short Grammar of Conetmporary Bulgarian.* Bloomington, Ind.: Slavica.

Rankova, Marija, Teodora Atanasova, and Ivanka Kharlakova. 1987–1988. *Anglijsko-bëlgarski rečnik.* Sofia: Nauka i izkustvo.

Rudin, Catherine. 1986. *Aspects of Bulgarian syntax: Complementizers and WH constructions.* Columbus, Ohio: Slavica.

Scatton, Ernest A. 1975. *Bulgarian phonology.* Cambridge, Mass.: Slavica.

Scatton, Ernest A. 1984. *A reference grammar of modern Bulgarian.* Columbus, Ohio: Slavica.

HOWARD I. ARONSON

BUNABAN LANGUAGES.
These languages constitute a branch of the proposed AUSTRALIAN language family and are spoken in northern Western Australia.

LANGUAGE LIST

Bunaba: also called Punapa, Bunuba. 50 speakers in Fitzroy Crossing area. Bilingualism in Kriol. Only old people speak Bunaba. Children only know a few words; their first language is Kriol.

Gooniyandi: also called Guniyandi, Guniandi, Gunian, Kunian, Kuniyan, Guniyan, Guniyn, Kunan, Koneyandi, Konejandi. 100 speakers in Gogo, Fossil Downs, Louisa, and Margaret River stations. Bilingualism in Kriol. Said to be nearly extinct. People generally speak Kriol.
B. GRIMES

BUNGKU-TOLAKI LANGUAGES.
These constitute a subgroup within the SULAWESI LANGUAGES and are spoken on the southeastern peninsula and offshore islands of Sulawesi Island, Indonesia.

LANGUAGE LIST

Bahonsuai: 200 speakers in central Sulawesi, Bungku Tengah subdistrict, Bahonsuai village on the east coast.

Bungku: also called Nahine. 21,500 speakers. Dialects are Bungku, Routa, Tulambatu, Torete (To Rete), Landawe, Waia. Bungku was a language of wider communication before independence. Torete is not becoming extinct as reported earlier.

Kodeoha: also called Kondeha. 1,500 speakers in southeastern Sulawesi, Kolaka district, Lasusua subdistrict, west coast of Kolaka. Bilingualism in Bugis.

Koroni: 500 speakers in central Sulawesi, Bungku Tengah subdistrict, Unsongi village on the east coast 12 km south of Bungku town.

Kulisusu: also called Kalisusu, Kolinsusu, Kolensusu. 22,000 speakers in southeastern Sulawesi, Kulisusu, and Bonegunu subdistricts on the northeastern corner of Buton Island.

Mori Atas: also called West Mori, Upper Mori. 12,000 speakers.

Mori Bawah: also called East Mori, Lower Mori, Nahina. 12,000 speakers in central Sulawesi at the neck of the southeastern peninsula; Petasia and Lembo subdistricts in twenty-four villages or parts of villages. Also in southern Sulawesi. Dialects are Tambe'e, Nahina, Petasia, Soroako, Karonsie.

Moronene: also called Maronene. 37,000 speakers. Dialects

FIGURE 1. *Subgrouping of Bungku-Tolaki Languages*

Eastern Bungku-Tolaki
  East Coast Eastern Bungku-Tolaki
    Bahonsuai
    Bungku
    Mori Bawah
    Wawonii
  Kulisusu
    Koroni, Kulisusu, Taloki
  Southwest Eastern Bungku-Tolaki
    Moronene
Western Bungku-Tolaki
  Interior Western Bungku-Tolaki
    Mori Atas, Padoe, Tomadino
  West Coast Western Bungku-Tolaki
    Kodeoha, Rahambuu, Tolaki, Waru

are Wita Ea (Rumbia, Poleang, Moronene), Tokotu'a (Kabaena). Some bilingualism in Indonesian. 5% are monolingual, some also speak Bugis. All domains. Oral use in local administration, occasional oral use in church, letter writing. Vigorous language use. Parents transmit it to children. Many Bugis and Muna speakers living in Moronene villages can speak Moronene with varying degrees of fluency. Speakers have positive attitude toward Moronene.

Padoe: also called South Mori, Padoé, Alalao. 6,000 speakers. Two dialects. Some bilingualism in Indonesian. Vigorous language use.

Rahambuu: also called Wiau, Wiaoe. 5,000 speakers in southeastern Sulawesi, Kolaka district, Pakue subdistrict, west coast north of the Kodeoha.

Taloki: also called Taluki. 500 speakers all reported to have a high bilingualism in Muna.

Tolaki: also called To'olaki, Lolaki, Lalaki, Laki, Kolaka. "Noie," "Noihe," "Nehina," "Nohina," "Nahina," "Akido" are derogatory names sometimes used. 281,000 speakers in southeastern Sulawesi, Kendari and Kolaka districts. Mekongga are in the Mekongga Mountains on the western edge of the group near Soroako. Dialects are Wiwirano, Asera, Konawe (Kendari), Mekongga (Bingkokak), Norio, Konio, Tamboki (Tambbuoki), Laiwui (Kioki). Wiwirano dialect is spoken only by older people.

Tomadino: 600 speakers in central Sulawesi, Bungku Tengah subdistrict, Sakita village on the east coast, outskirts of Bungku town. 71% lexical similarity with Bahonsuai, 68% with Mori Atas, Mori Bawah, and Padoe. Bilingualism in Bungku.

Waru: also called Mopute, Mapute. 350 speakers in southeastern Sulawesi, Kendari district, Asera subdistrict, Mopute village by the Lindu River. Dialects are Waru, Lalomerui.

Wawonii: also called Wowonii. 22,000 speakers in southeastern Sulawesi, Wawonii, and Menui I Islands near Kendari. Dialects are Wawonii, Menui.   B. GRIMES

BURARRAN LANGUAGES constitute a branch of the proposed AUSTRALIAN language family and are spoken in Arnhem Land, Northern Territory, Australia.

LANGUAGE LIST

Burarra: also called Anbarra, Burada, Bureda, Burera, Barera, Bawera, Gidjingaliya, Gujingalia, Gujalabiya, Gun-Guragone, Jikai, Tchikai. 400 speakers in Maningrida. Gunardba (Gun-nartpa) is a related language that may be extinct, or may be an alternate name.

Djeebbana: also called Ndjébbana, Gunavidji. 100 speakers on the northern coast around Maningrida. Not closely related to other languages. Most speakers also speak Gunwinjku and another Burarran language.

Guragone: also called Gurrgoni, Gurrogone, Gorogone, Gun-Guragone, Gungorogone, Gunagoragone, Gutjertabia. 20 speakers south of Maningrida, along the Mann River, northwest of the Rembarrnga language, east of the Gunwinygu language. All speakers are bilingual in Burarra or Gunwingku.

Nakara: also called Kokori, Nagara, Nakkara. 75 speakers in Maningrida, Goulburn Island. People generally speak Burarra or Djeebbana.   B. GRIMES

BURMESE. The first language of the majority of the nearly 50 million inhabitants of Burma (Myanmar), Burmese is also a lingua franca for many of the ethnic minorities that make up about a third of that number. The language of the Irrawaddy valley is considered the national standard; other dialects are spoken in peripheral regions, e.g. Arakan and Tenasserim. The dialects differ mostly in pronunciation and lexical choice rather than in grammatical structure (see Okell 1995). Structural differences added to lexical then distinguish Burmese dialects from closely related "Burmish" languages such as Atsi (Tsaiwa) and Maru (Lawng). At greater depth, the Burmish group belongs to the Lolo-Burmese (Burmese-Yipho) branch of the T[ibeto-]B[urman] family. (For general reference, see Okell 1969, 1994; Wheatley 1995, 2001.)

The earliest records of Burmese are stone inscriptions and captions on temple paintings from the central Burmese kingdom of Pagan. These date from the early 12th century and appear in conjunction with a written tradition in which Mon (a Mon-Khmer language) predominated, but which also included Pali and occasionally Pyu (thought to have been TB, but even then nearing extinction). The best-known example of early writing is the Myazedi inscription, dated 1113 CE, which records an act of merit in four languages, Pyu, Pali, Mon, and Burmese. By the end of the 12th century, most writing in Pagan is in Burmese. Mon and Burmese contact was close enough to have allowed the spread of significant linguistic and cultural features, including a script probably adopted directly from Mon for the writing of Burmese.

The large body of stone inscriptions and other writing dating from the 12th to the 15th century can be called "Old Burmese." The modern orthography ("Written Burmese") can be regarded as the partial reflection of a later Middle Burmese period. By the late 18th century, the language was close to its modern form.

TABLE 1. *Burmese Consonant Phonemes.* Parentheses enclose rare or restricted phonemes: *r* occurs in loanwords, and *hw* is used mostly in onomatopoeia. The contrast of *f* and *ð* is barely functional.

	Labial	Interdental	Alveolar	Palatal	Velar	Glottal
Occlusives						
Aspirated	hp		ht	hc	hk	ʔ
Plain	p		t	c	k	
Voiced	b		d	j	g	
Fricatives						
Aspirated			hs			
Plain		θ	s			h
Voiced		(ð)	z			
Nasals						
Voiceless	hm		hn	hɲ	hŋ	
Voiced	m		n	ɲ	ŋ	
Lateral						
Voiceless			hl			
Voiced			l			
Approximants						
Voiceless	(hw)			hy [š]		
Voiced	w		(r)	y		

The major source of learned words was, and continues to be, Pali, the language of the Theravada scriptures. Many terms must have come directly from Pali texts, but sometimes the spelling shows evidence of transmission through Mon.

British rule over Burma, beginning in the 19th century, resulted in the use of a large number of English loanwords. Many of these were abandoned after the resumption of independence, but English continues to be a source for technical and commercial vocabulary (Wheatley 1999).

1. Phonology. While Indic loans form a prominent layer of polysyllabic vocabulary, native morphemes are almost always monosyllabic or "sesquisyllabic." The latter contain an unstressed "minor" syllable followed by a stressed "major" one. The bulk of sesquisyllabic words in Burmese contain derivational prefixes; others represent the reduction of first syllables in compounds. Some words contain two minor syllables followed by a major; these derive from compounds in which the first constituent is itself sesquisyllabic (e.g. *htəmìn* 'rice', *htəmənè* 'a sticky rice pudding'.)

Major syllables have five possible elements: initial, post-initial, and final consonants, vowel, and tone. Of these, initial (including ʔ-), vowel, and tone are always present. The only post-initial consonants found in the modern standard are -*y*- (after labials) and -*w*-; the only final consonants are -ʔ and -*n* (often just nasalization).

The phonetic realization of phonological units in these positions is partly determined by the nature of the syllable boundary. At least two extremes of juncture need to be recognized: "open juncture" between syllables, characterized by a minimal degree of assimilation; and "close juncture," by a maximal degree. Close juncture is common in disyllabic nouns (but not verbs), as well as in certain grammatical environments, e.g. noun + adjectival modifier. Juncture differences are reflected most noticeably by morphophonemic alternation at the initial (e.g., voiceless stops varying with voiced), and by allophonic variation at the final.

The consonant phonemes of Burmese are shown in Table 1; the transcription is based in part on morphological considerations. The series with prescript *h*- alternates with the series without it in about 100 pairs of verbs, in which the *h*- members are generally transitive and the non-*h* intransitive: *cuʔ, hcuʔ* 'to come off', 'to take off'; *nwè, hnwè* 'to be warm', 'to heat'. This process is no longer productive; it reflects an earlier sibilant "transitivizing" prefix. This prefix is more directly attested by the "irregular" pair *ʔeʔ, θeʔ* 'to sleep', 'to put to sleep', in which a favorable phonetic environment allowed the prefix to pre-empt the glottal initial (and later to join in the regular shift to interdental).

The distribution of the voiced stops *b d j g* is defective: in absolute initial position (i.e. excluding those that result from close juncture), they appear almost exclusively in

TABLE 2. *Burmese Vowel Phonemes*. The vowel ɛ occurs only in syllables of form CV, CVʔ; ɔ occurs only in CV; *ai au* occur only in CVN, CVʔ.

	Front	Mid	Back
High	i		u
Higher mid	e		o
Lower mid	ɛ		ɔ
Low		a	
Diphthongs	ai		au

nouns. Some of these items are loanwords; others suggest the effect of derivational processes such as prefixation. The distribution reflects the fact that, with few exceptions, neither borrowing nor prefixation gives rise to verbs.

Vowel contrasts vary according to syllable type, as indicated in Table 2. In the modern languages, the [ɔ] of open syllables is in complementary distribution with both [ai] and [au] of closed syllables. The orthography identifies [ɔ] with [au]; here we follow established usage, and write all three. The neutralization of vocalic contrasts in minor syllables is realized as a mid central vowel ə.

Burmese can be called a "pitch-register" language. The "low" tone, left unmarked in the transcription, and the "heavy" tone, marked here with the grave accent, are distinguished primarily by pitch (though as the name suggests, the heavy is also more intense and sometimes slightly breathy). The "creaky" tone, marked here with an acute accent, and the "checked" tone, with final ʔ, are distinguished from the others mainly by their glottality— and from each other by the presence of creaky (or tense) voicing in the first vs. clear voicing with abrupt glottal closure in the second.

2. Writing system. The Mon-Burmese script has South Indian antecedents and retains typical features of Indian "alpha-syllabic" systems, including consonant signs that contain an inherent *a*-vowel. Certain features of the Indian system have been adapted to Burmese conditions, e.g. the use of the long vs. short vowel signs to indicate tonal distinctions in certain syllables. Other signs, such as those for the Indic retroflex and voiced aspirate consonant series, have been retained mostly for Indic loans.

Originally, the script must have represented the Burmese of the day fairly directly. Sound changes occurring since then have multiplied the values of written signs, most notably the vowels; e.g., written ⟨i⟩ is read as *i* in (written) open syllables, *e* in (written) closed; and written

⟨u⟩ is *u* or *o*. Other changes, such as the shift of *s* to θ, are revealed only by comparing modern pronunciation with the Indic or Mon values of the letters.

The writing system is illustrated in Tables 3a–b. The usual transliteration (cf. Okell 1971) goes beyond the internal evidence of the script and assigns Indian (Pali) values to the letters. The spelling of Burmese shows complete sets of final oral and nasal stops, including palatal ⟨c⟩ and ⟨ñ⟩, which are found only with the ⟨a⟩ vowel. Each set is reduced to a single contrast in the spoken language, symbolized -ʔ and -*n*; in isolation, -*n* is realized only as nasalization on the vowel.

3. Morphology. Burmese morphology is mainly derivational in function. An exception is the use of creaky tone with pronouns and nouns of personal reference to indicate certain grammatical roles, such as possession (reflecting an original creaky-toned possessive particle) and object.

Derivation involves mainly prefixation or reduplication. Thus nouns are frequently derived from verbs by the addition of the prefix ʔə-; adverbials may be derived by verbal reduplication, or by prefixation of ʔə-.

Compounding is much utilized to create new lexical material, and is preferred over the adaptation of foreign words. As a result, technical vocabulary is often beautifully transparent; 'iron-follow' for 'magnet', 'hand-press-machine' for 'typewriter'.

Word building may also serve aesthetic functions. Many verbs have pleonastic alternates formed by adding (usually afterward) a synonym, or a semantically empty riming or chiming (alliterative) syllable. In nouns or adverbials, such processes give rise to rhythmically and euphonically balanced four-syllable expressions of a type well known in Southeast Asian languages. Similar processes probably account for the proliferation of variants ("word families") that are so common to the region.

4. Major word classes. Nouns and verbs are clearly demarcated; very few words function as both. The class of "verb" includes adjectival verbs. Nouns are counted by means of *classifiers* which often reflect some physical feature of their referents. In combination with numerals, classifiers may serve pronominal functions of reference. The small set of true pronouns is supplemented by certain nouns which index social information while signaling reference.

Few words are specialized for the adverbial function; most adverbials are derived from verbs by productive processes. The work of indicating grammatical relation-

TABLE 3a. *Traditional Order of Burmese Consonants.* Voiceless aspirates are here given in the conventional transliteration as *kh*, etc., corresponding to the alternative transcription with *hk*, etc. Symbols for voiced aspirates, used only in Pali words, are pronounced in Burmese as simple voiced stops. Palatal occlusives are pronounced as alveolar sibilants in Burmese. Retroflex consonants in Pali words are pronounced as dentals.

	Occlusives				Nasals	
	Voiceless		Voiced			
	Unaspirated	Aspirated	Unaspirated	Aspirated		
Velar	က k	ခ k kh	ဂ g	ဃ gh	င	ŋ
Palatal	စ c (= /s/)	ဆ ch (= /hs/)	ဇ j (= /z/)	ဈ jh (= /z/)	ည	ɲ
Retroflex	ဋ ṭ	ဌ ṭh	ဍ ḍ	ဎ ḍh	ဏ	ṇ
Dental	တ t	ထ th	ဒ d	ဓ dh	န	n
Labial	ပ p	ဖ ph	ဗ b	ဘ bh	မ	m
Resonants:	ယ y	ရ r (= /y/)	လ l	ဝ w		
Others:	သ s (= /θ/)	ဟ h	ဠ ḷ (= /l/)	အ ʔ		

ships and functions is performed by specialized nouns or particles.

5. Syntax. The following sentence illustrates some of the syntactic features discussed in this section. The particle *-dɛ́* is "realis," with creaky tone signaling subordination; postnominal *-bɛ̀* is emphatic or restrictive:

(1) ʔɛ̀di hpòndɔ̀jì hɔ̀-dɛ́   gahta hye hniʔ
     this monk   preach-PCPL verse long two

    poʔ-ko-lɛ̀-bɛ̀   θwà
    stanza-OBJ-also-PTCL go

    yè-pè-laiʔ-pa.
    write-(give)-(follow)-(include)

    'And please just go and write down (for me) the
    two long verses that the monk recited.'

Apart from a subset of "nominal clauses"—which, in positive form, usually appear without a copular verb—clauses end with a verbal phrase. Minimally, this may consist of only a verb followed by one of a small set of "clause particles." (The lack of such a particle, as in the example, signals "positive imperative.") In negative sentences, these mark only the distinction of declarative vs. imperative mood; but in positive declarative sentences, additional aspectual distinctions between realis, irrealis, and punctative are possible. Punctative sentences relate a change of state expressed by the verb in relation to a particular time, usually the time of speaking: *tɔ* 'to be

TABLE 3b. *Traditional Order of Burmese Vowels.* The initial consonant အ/ʔ/ is used for illustration. Note that some tones are associated with choice of vowel symbol. Also note that tones not "built into" a vowel (or combination of vowel + final consonant) are indicated by a subscript dot for the creaky tone, and by a following double dot for the heavy tone, e.g. ေအ ေအ ʔé, ေအး ʔè.

Symbol	Transcription	Symbol	Transcription
အ	ʔá	ေအ	ʔe
အာ	ʔa	အဲ	ʔɛ̀
အိ	ʔí	ေအာ	ʔɔ
အိ	ʔi	ေအာ့	ʔo
အု	ʔú		
အူ	ʔu		

sufficient', *tɔ-bi* 'That's enough'; *sà* 'to eat', *sà-bi* 'We've started eating.'

The verb phrase usually consists of a string of morphemes whose grammatical properties lie hidden beneath a uniform syntax of juxtaposition. In historical terms, many such morphemes can be related to verbs; but synchronically, the verbal connection may be difficult to perceive. In (1), the meanings in parentheses are those of the putative verbal prototypes; however, when subordinated to a verb, *pè* indicates that the verbal action benefits someone else ('for'); *laiʔ*, that it requires little effort ('just'); and *pa* shows consideration on the part of the speaker toward the addressee ('please').

Generally, when a morpheme seems closely connected to an independent verb, it appears relatively leftward in the verbal phrase. Such semantic judgments are supported by certain syntactic and phonological features; e.g., the further to the left, the more likely a morpheme is to be directly negatable (in our example, *yè* and *pè* may be negated, but not *lai*ʔ), or explicitly conjoined (*θwà* and *yè* only.) A categorial distinction between verb and particle is useful; however, the various criteria for distinguishing the two classes do not completely coincide, so at some point the division is arbitrary.

Within the noun phrase, the order is generally modifier before modified: demonstratives, genitive phrases, nominal attributes, and relative clauses all precede the head noun. Classifier phrases, consisting of numeral + classifier, *follow* their head nouns (preceding case marking and other particles), but the relationship is appositional. The chief exception to the modifier + modified ordering involves adjectival modifiers (e.g. *hye* above), which generally follow their heads. Particles come last in the phrase; those that mark case roles (-*ko* above) precede those that perform quantificational functions (-*lè*, -*bè*).

Burmese allows core constituents of clause structure to be omitted in contexts where they are recoverable; thus the minimal declarative clause may consist of only a verb and a clause particle. There is no fixed order for preverbal elements, though certain arrangements are more common than others: manner adverbials and WH-question words almost always appear directly before the verb, and objects frequently do so. Subjects, as well as temporal and locative phrases, are likely to be topical. Object Subject Verb order can be found, but is not common.

The semantic roles of clause constituents are indicated by postpositional particles. Adjuncts are almost always marked, but subject and object need not be.

Clause subordination is illustrated by the following sentence, which contains a clausal subject marked by the realis nominalizer -*da,* and a causal subordinate clause, marked by -*ló*:

(2) *Luwu*ʔ-*nɛ́*   *ne-yá-da*   *mə-pyɔ-ló*   *hpònjì*
layman-with   stay-must-NOM not-happy-because monk

pyan   *wu*ʔ-*θwà-dɛ.*
return wear-go-REAL

'Because he was not happy as a layman, he donned (the robes of) monkhood again.'

6. Literary Burmese. Like the orthography, Burmese writing conserves many features of earlier stages of the language. Nowadays, the most prominent differences between written and spoken styles involve substitution of particles and some other grammatical words: e.g. spoken -*hma,* but written ⟨nhuik⟩ (read -*hnai*ʔ) 'at'; spoken -*hpó,* but written ⟨ran⟩ (-*yan*) 'purpose'. Writing based entirely on spoken forms is becoming more common, but it lacks the impersonal, timeless qualities associated with the literary forms, and is still felt inappropriate for serious genres.

[*See also* Pali; Sino-Tibetan Languages; *and* Southeast Asian Languages.]

BIBLIOGRAPHY

Okell, John. 1969. *A reference grammar of colloquial Burmese.* 2 vols. (London Oriental series, 11.) London: Oxford University Press.

Okell, John. 1971. *A guide to the romanization of Burmese.* London: Luzac.

Okell, John. 1994. *Burmese: An introduction to the literary style.* (Southeast Asian language text series.) DeKalb, Ill.: Center for Southeast Asian Studies, Northern Illinois University.

Okell, John. 1995. Three Burmese dialects. In *Papers in South-East Asian linguistics,* edited by David Bradley (*Pacific Linguistics,* A-83), pp. 1–138. Canberra, Australia: ANU.

Wheatley, Julian K. 1995. Burmese writing. In *The world's writing systems,* edited by Peter T. Daniels and William Bright, pp. 450–456. Oxford: Oxford University Press.

Wheatley, Julian K. 2003. Burmese. In *The Sino-Tibetan languages,* edited by Graham Thurgood and Randy LaPolla, pp. 195–207. Richmond, England: Curzon Press.

Wheatley, Julian K., with San San Hnin Tun. 1999. Languages in contact: The case of English and Burmese. *Journal of Burma Studies* 4.61–99.

JULIAN K. WHEATLEY

C

CADDOAN LANGUAGES. A family of the Great Plains in the United States.

LANGUAGE LIST

Arikara: also called Arikari, Arikaris, Arikaree, Ree, Ris. 20 speakers remain in USA. Ethnic population: 3,000 as of 1997. On Fort Berthold Reservation, North Dakota. Not inherently intelligible with Pawnee. Bilingualism in English. Most or all speakers are middle-aged or older. Arikara instructional material has been published for use in a language teaching program.

Caddo: also called Kado, Caddoe, Kadohadacho. 25 speakers remain in USA. Ethnic population: 3,371 as of 1997. Western Oklahoma, Caddo County. Formerly in northeastern Texas, extending into southwestern Arkansas. Related to Pawnee, Wichita, and two extinct languages, Kitsai and Adai. Bilingualism in English. No monolinguals as of 2000. Youngest speakers are 70 as of 2000.

Kitsai: also called Kichai. Formerly spoken in USA. Ethnic population: 2,000 as of 1997. West central Oklahoma among the Caddo, Caddo County. Closer to Pawnee than to Wichita.

Pawnee: 20 speakers remain in USA. Ethnic population: 2,500 as of 1997 in north central Oklahoma. Dialects are South Band, Skiri (Skidi). Closely related to Arikara, but not inherently intelligible with it. Kitsai is between Pawnee and Wichita, but closer to Pawnee. Bilingualism in English. All speakers are elderly.

Wichita: 3 speakers remain in USA. Ethnic population: 1,400

FIGURE 1. *Subgrouping of Caddoan Languages*

Northern Caddoan
Pawnee-Kitsai
Kitsai
Pawnee
Arikara, Pawnee
Wichita
Southern Caddoan
Caddo

as of 2000. West central Oklahoma. Dialects are Waco, Tawakoni. Close to Kitsai and Pawnee. Bilingualism in English. Youngest speakers are 80 years old.   B. GRIMES

CAHUAPANAN LANGUAGES. A family of northern Peru.

LANGUAGE LIST

Chayahuita: also called Chayawita, Chawi, Tshaahui, Chayhuita, Chayabita, Shayabit, Balsapuertino, Paranapura, Cahuapa. 10,000 speakers along Paranapura, Cahuapanas, Sillay and Shanusi Rivers. Dialects are Chayahuita, Cahuapana. Very slight intelligibility with Jebero. Some bilingualism in Spanish. All ages.

Jebero: also called Xebero, Chebero, Xihuila. Ethnic population: 2,000 to 3,000 as of 2000. District of Jebero. Widespread use of Spanish. Only older adults. Interest in language revival.   B. GRIMES

CAMBODIAN. *See* Khmer.

CARIBAN LANGUAGES. The Cariban Languages constitute one of the large linguistic families of South America. The comparative study of this family is two centuries old, and has amassed a wealth of data; its grammatical studies have contributed significantly to linguistic typology.

The Cariban family is named after one of its members, the language of the Caribs. These Indians live near the northern coast of the continent, in an area extending from northeast Brazil through the coastal plains of French Guiana, Surinam, and Guyana to Venezuela. Most of their linguistic relatives live in southern Venezuela, Guy-

259

MAP 1. *Distribution of Cariban Languages*

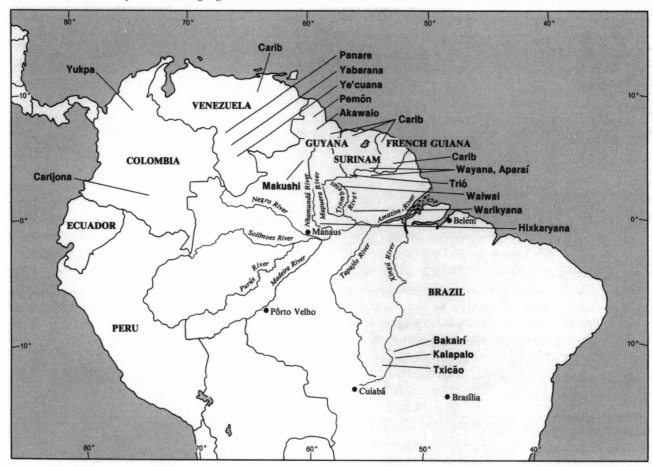

ana, and Surinam, and in the adjacent parts of Brazil; as shown in Map 1. The languages in this area include the following: in southeastern Venezuela, Panare, Yabarana, and Ye'cuana; in the Venezuelan/Guyanese/Brazilian border area, Pemón, Makushi, and Akawaio; somewhat farther south, in Brazil, Waiwai, Hixkaryâna, and Warikyana; in Surinam and in adjacent parts of Brazil and French Guiana, Trió, Wayana, and Aparai. A few Cariban tribes have strayed far from this central area: Yukpa in northwestern Venezuela; Carijona in Ecuador and Colombia; and Bakairí, Txicão, and Kalapalo/Kuikuro at the headwaters of the Xingu River in southern Brazil.

This list of 18 languages accounts for the main extant Cariban-speaking tribes. If smaller groups and finer linguistic distinctions were considered, it would be twice as long. In addition, written data have been salvaged for 20 extinct languages. Comparative Cariban linguistics deals, in all, with some 60 individual languages and dialects.

Finally, mention should be made of a language which is also called "Carib" or "Island Carib," and which used to be spoken on a number of Caribbean islands. The original name of this language was Iñeri; it belongs to the Arawakan family. It came to be called "Carib" after the conquest of the islands by Carib settlers from the mainland, who imposed their nationality and name—which eventually inspired the modern geographical name of the area; however, they failed to displace the native Iñeri language (cf. Taylor and Hoff 1980). A descendant of Island Carib is still spoken in Central America (Belize and Honduras) under the name of "Black Carib" or Garífuna.

1. Comparative studies in Cariban made a very early start with the work of Filippo Salvadore Gilij in 1782; the contributions of missionaries, explorers, and professional linguists have accumulated ever since. Published work on the subclassification of the family tends to give little actual language data as evidence; subgroupings are proposed and reshuffled with summary discussion, or none at all. However, in terms of bibliographical exploration alone, a tremendous amount of work has been done by a small number of people: the sources have at least been discovered and saved, and a great many cognate pairs have been recognized. A project for the systematic collection of data—the South American Indian Languages Documentation Project, directed by Brent Berlin of the University of California, Berkeley—will, when completed, give new impetus to the internal classification of the family.

The external relationships of Cariban became a research goal after World War II. In the classification of Greenberg 1987, Cariban is grouped most closely with Andoke, Bora, Kukura, Uitoto, and Yagua; and then with Macro-Gê and Macro-Panoan. However, Rodrigues 1985 has demonstrated a relationship to Tupian.

Recent book-length grammars are available for Carib (Hoff 1968) and Hixkaryâna (Derbyshire 1985). Other important references are Basso 1977, Fock 1963, Koelewijn 1987, and Payne 1990.

2. Phonology. Carib, as spoken in western Surinam, has the following phonemes: /a e o i u ï au ai ei oi ui ïi/ (for long vowels see below), /p t k/, marginal /b d g/, /m n/, /w y/, /r/ (flap), and /s/. A second fricative, /x/, has a distinct status distributionally and historically (see below). Sequences of vowels and of some consonants are permitted, but a regular alternation of V and C predominates. No consonants except nasals occur in word-final position. The Hixkaryâna system is similar but somewhat richer, containing palatal consonants, /φ/, and /h/.

In Carib and many of its relatives, word-medial syllables of the proto-language have been lost. This process has left different residues in different languages and dialects. In the Carib dialect of the Saramacca River, Surinam, the residue is breathiness of the preceding vowel; e.g., *wapoto 'fire' became wa:ʰto. Abundant instances are provided by synchronic morphophonemics: pe:kï 'to sink it' + imperative -ko gives i-pe:ʰ-ko 'sink it!' This breathiness corresponds, in other dialects of Carib, to a clear vowel followed by a velar fricative: waxto, i-pex-ko.

Carib vowel length is largely prosodic: either the second and the fourth vowel of a word, or the first and the third, are long, provided that they are present, non-final, and not followed by two consonants, e.g. asa:pará:pi 'species of fish', ka:rawá:si 'species of tree'. Similar rules have been reported for Makushi and Hixkaryâna. Word stress is on the second heavy syllable (containing a long vowel, diphthong, or VC), counted from the left; if there is none, stress is final.

3. Grammar. Many Cariban languages have rich morphologies. In Carib, six word classes have characteristic morphological properties: verbs, nouns, postpositions, adjectives/adverbs, numerals, and demonstratives. Modal particles (e.g. *painare* 'perhaps') and non-modal particles (*era:pa* 'too') constitute separate word classes: syntactically, these have nothing in common with the adverbs, and little with each other. There are no conjunctions, relative pronouns, or complementizers. Dependent clauses contain a non-finite verb, and relate directly to a head in the main clause.

In Carib, Hixkaryâna, and other languages, each transitive finite verb form contains a prefix which identifies both agent and patient (*s-e:ne-i* 'I have seen him', *y-e:ne-i* 'he has seen me'). Such verbs frequently occur as complete utterances, but may of course be complemented by separate nominals.

At a time when typologists still doubted the occurrence of O[bject] V[erb] S[ubject] as an unmarked, "basic" constituent order, Derbyshire 1977 demonstrated that Hixkaryâna constitutes an instance of precisely this. In the following decade, the ensuing discussion provided the starting points for promising further research in three directions:

(a) OVS order was sought and found in other languages of the area, both Cariban and non-Cariban.

(b) Attempts were initiated to relate the rise of OVS in these languages, and the preservation of SOV in others, to other grammatical properties of the languages concerned, such as ergativity.

(c) Interest was stimulated in discourse factors and information structure, as relevant to patterns of constituent order and their change.

[*See also* Arawakan Languages *and* South American Languages.]

BIBLIOGRAPHY

Basso, Ellen B., ed. 1977. *Carib-speaking Indians: Culture, society, and language.* Tucson: University of Arizona Press.

Derbyshire, Desmond C. 1977. Word order universals and the existence of OVS languages. *Linguistic Inquiry* 8.590–599.

Derbyshire, Desmond C. 1985. *Hixkaryana and linguistic typology.* (Summer Institute of Linguistics publications in linguistics, 76.) Dallas: Summer Institute of Linguistics.

Fock, Niels. 1963. *Waiwai: Religion and society of an Amazonian tribe.* (Etnografisk række, 8.) Copenhagen: National Museum.

Greenberg, Joseph H. 1987. *Language in the Americas.* Stanford, Calif.: Stanford University Press.

Hoff, Berend J. 1968. *The Carib language: Phonology, morphonology, morphology, texts and word index.* (Verhandelingen van het Koninklijk Instituut voor Taal-, Land-, en Volkenkunde, 55.) The Hague: Nijhoff.

Koelewijn, Cees. 1987. *Oral literature of the Trio Indians of Surinam.* (Verhandelingen van het Koninklijk Instituut voor

Taal-, Land-, en Volkenkunde, Caribbean series, 6.) Dordrecht: Foris.

Payne, Doris Lander, ed. 1990. *Amazonian linguistics: Studies in lowland South American languages.* Austin: University of Texas Press.

Rodrigues, Aryon Dall'Igna. 1985. Evidence for Tupi-Carib relationships. In *South American Indian languages: Retrospect and prospect,* edited by Harriet E. Manelis Klein and Louisa R. Stark, pp. 371–404. Austin: University of Texas Press.

Taylor, Douglas R., and Berend J. Hoff. 1980. The linguistic repertory of the Island-Carib in the seventeenth century: The men's language—a Carib pidgin? *International Journal of American Linguistics* 46.301–312.

BEREND J. HOFF

LANGUAGE LIST

Akawaio: also called Acewaio, Akawai, Acahuayo, Kapon. 4,300 speakers in Guyana, Brazil, and Venezuela. In Guyana: Around 3,800 speakers. West central, north of Patamona. In Brazil: 500 speakers in Roraima and Rio Branco. Close to Macushi and Arecuna. Limited bilingualism. In Venezuela: Bolivar. Close to Macushi but not inherently intelligible. Marginally intelligible with Arecuna. Limited bilingualism. Ethnic pride.

Akurio: also called Akoerio, Akuri, Akurijo, Akuriyo, Akuliyo, Wama, Wayaricuri, Oyaricoulet, Triometesem, Triometesen. 44 speakers remain in Suriname, in the southeastern jungle. Related to, but not inherently intelligible with, Trió. Dialects or related languages: Urukuyana, Kumayena. All but one group is living with the Trió and bilingual in Trió. Children speak Trió. The Trió respect the Akurio for their knowledge of the forest, but look down on them and their language.

Apalaí: also called Aparai, Apalay. 450 speakers remain in Brazil in Pará, mainly on the Paru Leste River with fringe groups on the Jari and Citare Rivers in twenty villages. 75% bilingualism in Wayana, 25% monolingualism.

Atruahí: also called Atroaí, Atroarí, Atrowari, Atroahy, Ki'nya. 350 speakers in Brazil. Dialects are Atruahi, Waimirí, (Uaimirí, Wahmirí, Jawaperi (Yauaperi). Dialects or related languages: Sapara, Pauxiana, Piriutite, and Tiquiriá.

Bakairí: also called Bacairí, Kurâ. 570 speakers in Brazil in nine or ten villages of state of Mato Grosso. Speakers are somewhat bilingual in Portuguese.

Carib: also called Caribe, Cariñ, Kalihna, Kalinya, Galibi. 10,000 speakers in Venezuela, Suriname, French Guiana, and Guyana. In Venezuela: 4,000 speakers. Monagas and Anzoategui states, northeast near mouth of Orinoco River, plus a few communities in state of Bolivar, just south of Orinoco. The very old and very young are monolingual. Well integrated into Venezuelan culture, though they do speak their own language among themselves. In Suriname: 2,390 speakers. Dialects are Murato (Myrato, Western Carib), Tyrewuju (Eastern Carib). Speakers of the central dialect are reported to be bilingual and switching to Sranan. They also speak Dutch as second language. All ages in some areas. The eastern dialect is the prestige dialect in Suriname. In French Guiana: 1,200 speakers in the coastal areas. In Guyana: Ethnic population: 2,700 as of 1990. West coast and northwest. Dialects are Murato (Myrato, Western Carib). In Brazil: State of Amapá.

Carijona: also called Karijona, Carihona, Omagua, Umawa, Hianacoto-Umaua. 140 speakers remain in Colombia. Upper Vaupés, Yarí, and lower Caquetá Rivers, one hour by motorized canoe; two to three hours by canoe south of Miraflores, around Puerto Nare. Possibly two separate languages, Hianacoto-Umaua and Carijona. The two groups have not had contact for many years. Some bilingualism in Spanish. Intermarrying with other tribes.

Chaima: also called Chayma, Sayma, Warapiche, Guaga-Tagare. Spoken in eastern Venezuela coastal region. Speakers may all be bilingual or monolingual in Spanish.

Coyaima: formerly spoken in Colombia, Tolima region. Said to have been a variety of Yukpa. The tribe still exists as an entity, but has not spoken the language for several generations. Spanish is now spoken.

Cumanagoto: formerly spoken in eastern Venezuela coastal region.

Hixkaryána: also called Hixkariana, Hishkaryana, Parukoto-Charuma, Parucutu, Chawiyana, Kumiyana, Sokaka, Wabui, Faruaru, Sherewyana, Xerewyana, Xereu, Hichkaryana. 600 speakers remain in Brazil. Ethnic population: 600 as of 2000. Amazonas, upper Nhamunda River to Mapuera and Jatapú Rivers. Close to Waiwai. No dialectal variation. The Sherewyana speak the same language but some live with the Waiwai. Some bilingualism in Portuguese.

Ikpeng: also called Txikão, Txikãn, Chicao, Tunuli, Tonore. 146 speakers remain in Brazil. Xingú Park, Mato Grosso. A separate language, similar to Arara of Pará. Bilingualism is limited.

Japrería: also called Yaprería. 80 speakers remain in Venezuela in the northern region of Sierra de Perija, state of Zulia. Not inherently intelligible with other Carib languages of the area.

Kaxuiâna: also called Kashuyana, Kashujana, Kachuana, Warikyana, Warikiana, Kaxûyana. 434 speakers remain in Brazil. There is a fair amount of bilingualism between some speakers of Trio and Kaxuiâna.

Kuikúro-Kalapálo: also called Kuikuru, Guicurú, Kurkuro, Cuicutl, Kalapalo, Apalakiri, Apalaquiri. 526 speakers in Brazil in Xingú Park, Mato Grosso. The Kuikúru and the Kalapálo speak the same language, but are separate ethnically. Limited bilingualism.

Macushi: also called Makushi, Makuxi, Macusi, Macussi,

Teweya, Teueia. 11,400 speakers in Guyana, Brazil, and Venezuela. In Guyana: 7,000 speakers in the southwestern border area, Rupununi north savannahs. Spread out in small settlements up to the foothills of the Pakaraima Mountains. Close to, but not intelligible with, Patamona. The second language is English in Guyana, Portuguese in Brazil, Spanish in Venezuela. In Brazil: 3,800 speakers. Contingo, Quino, Pium, and Mau Rivers, northeastern Roraima and Rio Branco. Not intelligible with Arecuna or Patamona. Bilingualism increasing in Portuguese. In Venezuela: 600 speakers in the eastern border area. Close to, but not intelligible with Patamona. Some from Guyana in state of Bolivar speak English as second language.

Mapoyo: also called Mapayo, Mapoye, Mopoi, Nepoye, Wanai. 3 speakers remain in Venezuela. Ethnic population: 120 as of 1977. Suapure River, 100 km north of La Urbana, Amazonas. Closely related to Yabarana. Bilingualism in Spanish. Speakers are 70 to 100 years old.

Maquiritari: also called Maiongong, Maquiritare, Yekuana, De'cuana, Ye'cuana, Maquiritai, Soto, Cunuana, Pawana. 5,240 speakers in Venezuela and Brazil. In Venezuela: 4,970 speakers. In Brazil: 270 speakers in Roraima. Dialects are Cunuana, De'cuana (Wainungomo), Ihuruana, Maitsi, Mayongong (Ye'cuana, Yekuana).

Matipuhy: also called Matipu, Mariape-Nahuqua. 40 speakers remain in Brazil. Xingú Park, Mato Grosso. Dialects are Matipuhy, Ñahukuá (Nakukwa, Nafukwá, Nahuqua). Kuikúro-Kalapá is said to be a dialect of Nahukuá. May also be intelligible with Kuikúro.

Panare: also called Panari, Abira, Eye. 1,200 speakers in Venezuela. 150- mile perimeter south of Caicaro de Orinoco basin of the Cuchivero River, state of Bolivar. Two groups: jungle and highland. Nearly all are monolingual.

Pará Arara: also called Ajujure. 110 speakers remain in two villages in Brazil. The closest extant languages are Txikão and Bakairí. A few can speak a little Portuguese.

Patamona: also called Ingariko, Eremagok, Kapon. 4,700 speakers in west central Guyana,. in about thirteen villages. Close to Macushi but not inherently intelligible. Marginally intelligible with Arecuna. Closest to Akawaio, but vocabulary differences and language attitudes make separate literature necessary.

Pemon: also called Pemong. Approximately 6,004 speakers in Venezuela, Guyana, and Brazil. In Venezuela: 5,000 speakers. Ethnic population: 18,871 as of 1993 census that may include Macushi. State of Bolivar, Gran Sabana and adjacent areas, southeastern Venezuela. Dialects are Camaracoto, Taurepan (Taulipang), Arecuna (Aricuna, Arekuna, Jaricuna, Pemon, Daigok, Potsawugok, Pishauco, Purucoto, Kamaragakok). Marginally intelligible with Akawaio and Patamona. Camaracoto may be distinct. 5,000, the large majority, were monolingual as of 2001. In some areas most children have Spanish as mother tongue. Some children can understand Pemon but are ashamed to speak it. In Brazil: 679 speakers. Rio Branco, near Guyana border, Roraima. Dialects are Taulipang (Taurepan), Camaracota (Ipuricoto), Arecuna (Aricuna, Arekuna, Jaricuna). In Guyana: 475 speakers. Paruima settlement. Dialects are Camaracoto, Taurepan (Taulipang), Arecuna (Aricuna, Arekuna, Jaricuna). Marginally intelligible with Patamona and Akawaio. Camaracoto may be a separate language.

Salumá: spoken in Brazil. Northwestern Pará, on the upper Anamu River, source of the Trombetas, along the Suriname border.

Sikiana: also called Sikiâna, Shikiana, Chiquiana, Chikena, Chiquena, Xikujana, Xikiyana. 33 speakers remain in Brazil and Venezuela. In Brazil: Northwestern Pará, between the Rio Cafuini and the headwaters of the Turuna and Itapi Rivers, near the Suriname border. Close to Salumá.

Tamanaku: formerly spoken in Venezuela. Near other related languages. Similar to Panare.

Trió: also called Tirió. 1,151 speakers remain in Suriname and Brazil. In Suriname: 822 speakers. South central, villages of Tepoe and Alalapadu. All domains: home, school, playground, church, administration. Speakers are proud of Trió, but do not consider it to be appropriate for study or instruction in school. The purer Trió is considered to be spoken by the older men and storytellers, and not by most of the younger men, those who have lived in town, or children of mixed marriages. In Brazil: 329 speakers in Pará, Rio Mapari.

Waiwai: also called Uaiuai, Uaieue, Ouayeone. 770 speakers in Brazil and Guyana. In Brazil: 571 speakers in Amazonas, Pará, Roraima. Dialects are Katawian (Katwena, Katawina, Catawian, Catauian, Parucutu, Parukutu, Katuena, Cachuena). Dialect or related language: Salumá. Some consider Katawian to be a separate language. In Guyana: 200 speakers in southwestern Guyana, headwaters of the Essequibo River. Dialects are Katawian (Katwena, Katawina).

Wayana: also called Oayana, Wajana, Uaiana, Oyana, Oiana, Alukuyana, Upurui, Roucouyenne. 750 speakers remain in Suriname, French Guiana, and Brazil. In Suriname: 397 speakers in villages in the southeast. In French Guiana: 200 speakers in the southwestern border area. In Brazil: 150 speakers in Amapá, among the Apalaí. Dialects are Rucuyen (Roucouyenne), Urucuiana (Urucena). Partially intelligible with Apalaí.

Yabarana: also called Yauarana, Yawarana. 20 speakers remain in Venezuela. North central, Nueva Esparta, area of the Manapiare River basin above the village of San Juan de Manapiare, Amazonas. Dialects are Curasicana, Wokiare (Uaiquiare, Guayqueri). Closely related to Mapoyo.

Yarumá: also called Jarumá, Waiku. Spoken in Brazil in Xingú Park, state of Mato Grosso.

Yukpa: also called Yuko, Yuco, Yupa, Yucpa, Northern Motilón, Carib Motilón. 3,000 speakers in Colombia and Venezuela.

In Colombia: 2,500 speakers. Ethnic population: 3,530 as of 1998. Dialects are Río Casacará (Iroka), Río Maracas, Caño Padilla-La Laguna, Coyaima. At least five extant dialects including two in Venezuela. Coyaima is said to have been a dialect. Río Cascará and Río Maracas dialects are probably the largest ones, and different enough to probably be separate languages. Venezuela dialects seem more similar to Río Maracas. Relations between speakers of different dialects have sometimes been hostile in the past. Presently they have little contact with each other. Unrelated to Chibchan Motilón. Men can use Spanish for buying and selling only. Vigorous language use. In Venezuela: 500 speakers. Areas adjacent to Colombia border, state of Zulia. Dialects are Yrapa, Río Negro.   B. GRIMES

CASE. [*This entry includes the following subentries:*
Overview
Case Theory
Case Alignment]

Overview

Case is a notoriously ambiguous notion. The traditional notion of *morphological case* refers to an inflectional category; however, particular case markers are also referred to with the term "case." (For references, see Lyons 1968.) Case markers normally appear on nouns, but they may also occur with N[oun] P[hrase]s. In NPs, two different case categories can sometimes be distinguished: one case is directly governed by the syntactically superordinate unit, while the other appears as a mark of agreement. In adjectives, case is often a mark of agreement. The number of case-markers varies from language to language. Thus there are two cases in Old French, three in Hindi and Rumanian, five in Ancient Greek, seven in Latin, ten in Russian, eighteen in Hungarian, twenty-six in Andi and Archi, and forty-six in Tabassarian (Mel'čuk 1986). However, it is not always clear what should be considered a case-marker; consequently, scholars may differ as to the number of them in a given language.

Morphological cases can be classified in various ways. Each nominal case marks a dependent syntactic role of the noun, and sometimes the meaning of the case is confined to this syntactic role (grammatical case). Typical cases marking syntactic roles in accusative-type languages, such as those of the Indo-European family, are as follows:

(a) Nominative: grammatical subject
(b) Accusative: direct object
(c) Dative: indirect object
(d) Instrumental: instrument or means
(e) Genitive: adnominal attribute

Overlap between these functions is not rare. In Russian and Sanskrit, the instrumental also marks the agent; in Hungarian and Latin, instrumental function merges with the comitative ('along with X'). This merging of functions is called *case syncretism*. Among the adverbial cases, the local cases (locational and directional), which express localization with respect to the object denoted by the noun, form a particularly rich system. Typical localizations expressed by means of cases are within an object, on/over its upper surface, on/under its lower surface, on its side, behind it, in front of it, near it, or between two objects. In addition, localization can be specified with respect to movement: being at a place, traveling to it, traveling out of or from it, traveling through it, or traveling toward it. The combination of eight localizations with five types of movements produces forty local cases. Actually, more distinctions are made in some languages. For example, a local case may also express the spatial relation of the object to the speaker an/or hearer. Other types of cases may not form such neat systems (Mel'čuk 1986).

Some languages (e.g. Old Georgian, Chukchi, Daghestanian) show double case: in adnominal possessive constructions the possessor NP is case-marked to indicate the possessive relationship with the head noun and in addition agrees in case with this head noun. This phenomenon, dubbed "Suffixaufnahme," is due to agreement (Plank 1995). In many cases Suffixaufnahme can be explained if it is assumed that the genitive/possessive suffix is a derivational adjectivalizing affix or the adnominal NP is an anaphorically interpreted headless possessor in apposition.

The term "case" is sometimes used to denote *deep case*, the semantic relations between a predicate and its arguments (Fillmore 1968). The system of deep case has become one of the modules of generative Government/Binding theory, under the name of *theta theory*, or the theory of *thematic roles* (Chomsky 1981). Thematic roles include *agent, patient* (or *theme*), and *goal*. There is no general agreement as to how many thematic roles are required for the description of predicate/argument structure. A thematic role may correlate in surface structure with various phenomena: syntactic position, adpositions, inflectional suffixes, etc.

Case theory is a theory about abstract cases: it requires phonetically non-empty NPs to be governed by a unique case-assigner. For example, in English, the subject of a tensed clause receives the nominative case from the tensed VP; the possessive NP in a NP receives genitive case from the noun; and the object of a preposition receives accusative case from the preposition. Abstract case need not be morphologically marked; in fact, a language may neutralize all case distinctions. In English, the overt morphological realization in full lexical noun phrases is restricted to the genitive case, the overt distinction of nominative and accusative forms appears in the pronominal system only. Other languages, like Latin or Hungarian, have a morphologically rich case system where distinct cases are overtly marked on nouns, adjectives, determiners, etc. as well as on pronouns. All languages have a fully fledged system of abstract case, which is thus part of universal grammar, but the degree of morphological realization of abstract case varies parametrically from one language to another. Case theory is an important part of Government/and Binding Theory. *Syntactic case* is associated with a particular syntactic configuration; in contrast, *lexical case* is assigned to a NP on the basis of lexical information associated with the predicate. Lexical case must be realized morphologically or syntactically in surface structure (cf. Riemsdijk and Williams 1986).

[*See also* Formal Grammar; Principles and Parameters; Morphology; *and* Semantics.]

BIBLIOGRAPHY

Chomsky, Noam. 1981. *Lectures on government and binding.* (Studies in generative grammar, 9.) Dordrecht: Foris.

Fillmore, Charles J. 1968. The case for case. In *Universals in linguistic theory,* edited by Emmon Bach and Robert T. Harms, pp. 1–88. New York: Holt, Rinehart and Winston.

Lyons, John. 1968. *Introduction to theoretical linguistics.* London: Cambridge University Press.

Mel'čuk, Igor A. 1986. Toward a definition of case. In *Case in Slavic: Studies dedicated to the memory of Roman O. Jakobson,* edited by Richard D. Brecht and James S. Levine, pp. 35–85. Columbus, Ohio: Slavica.

Plank, Frans, ed. 1995. *Double case: agreement by Suffixaufnahme.* New York and Oxford: Oxford University Press.

Riemsdijk, Henk C. van, and Edwin Williams. 1986. *Introduction to the theory of grammar.* (Current studies in linguistics series, 12.) Cambridge, Mass.: MIT Press.

FERENC KIEFER

Case Theory

The notion of case is as old as the scientific study of grammar. Medieval grammarians had elaborate conceptions of grammatical case and the domains (of *rectio* 'government') where it manifests itself. Latin, Greek, and Hebrew, all carefully studied languages of the time, had manifest case markings, as in the Latin declensions. Much later, structuralist linguists, such as Louis Hjelmslev, gave accurate descriptions of the phenomenon across several languages, along with definitions of government. From the traditional perspective, case can be seen as a morphological mark that appears, in some languages, in nominal elements (nouns and adjectives) in the government context of non-nominal items (verbs and prepositions): note the contrast between *he* and *him* in *he saw him*. A puzzle already noted by medieval theorists is that "external" cases (nominative in the verbal system, genitive in the nominal one) do not fit this picture, and so they were supposed to be assigned under *concors* ('agreement'). Case first entered generative grammar through Charles Fillmore's theory. The main contribution of his approach was to provide a justification for the phenomenon of case from the perspective of thematic roles or predicate valences. In this view, the reason case exists in the system has to do with marking valences, in an approximately bijective fashion. This notion of case has survived in terms of what is usually referred to as "lexical" or "inherent" case, of the sort witnessed in the German expression *ihn sehen* 'him-ACC see' vs. *ihm helfen* 'him-DAT help'. Here, accusative case correlates with a theme role in the object of *sehen*, while dative case correlates with a benefactive role in the object of *helfen*.

The most influential generative proposal regarding case came from Jean-Roger Vergnaud, who realized the filtering effect of case. His proposal was made in the context of the Extended Standard Theory, at a time when linguists were exploring ways of limiting the generative power of transformational grammars. In particular, Vergnaud showed how some of Chomsky and Lasnik's 1977 ad-hoc filters can be deduced from the requirement that noun phrases be case-marked. This turns out to be true regardless of whether or not case manifests itself morphologically; for this reason, this notion of case came to be known as "structural" or "abstract" Case, capitalizing the term to distinguish it from the traditional notion. A typical Vergnaud argument runs as follows. Descriptively, it is known that noun phrases can appear as subjects of finite clauses, as in *he is a liar*, but somewhat surprisingly, not as subjects of infinitival clauses: **him to be a liar* (*is regrettable*). Apparently unrelated to this is the similarly surprising fact that certain complementizer-infinitival sequences are impossible, for example **for to be a liar* (*is regrettable*). Two separate stipulations could be added to the theory in order to ban each sort of ungrammaticality. However, Vergnaud's theory suggests an immediate correlation: a noun phrase like *him* requires Case, which it cannot receive as the subject of an infinitival expression; in turn, a complementizer-preposition like *for* assigns Case. As a result, an expression like *for him to be a liar* (*is regrettable*) meets both sorts of requirements: *him* receives the Case that *for* assigns. Both of the ungrammatical expressions owe their deviance to the same underlying principle.

That sort of reasoning is central to the Government and Binding (GB) program developed by Noam Chomsky and others in the early 1980s. Case was considered a central module in that approach, entering into the characterization of a variety of phenomena that could be unified, in large part, in terms of their motivation as Case-theoretical: passive, raising, clitic placement, and even expletive-associate agreement were all argued to be cued by Case demands. Typically, noun phrase *X* starts its derivational history in a position *Y* in which Case is not assigned and gets displaced to a site *Z* where Case is provided. For example, *Y* can be the subject of the infinitival [*Y to be a liar*], and this sentence can be the complement to a passive expression like *was believed*. In such an instance, the subject *Z* of [*Z was believed . . .*] is both a position where Case is assigned (nominative) and a site that, because of properties of the passive voice, carries no thematic properties and is thus semantically empty. *Z* is then an ideal target for *Y*, which upon moving in subject-to-subject fashion will obtain its required Case, yielding *He was believed to be a liar*. It can be argued, then, that the need for the pronoun to obtain some form of Case drives the displacement from *Y* to *Z*. Similar arguments can be constructed for other sorts of transformations that fall under the rubric of what is referred to as A[rgument]-movement.

In the GB context, much energy went into characterizing the domains under which (abstract) Case assignment is possible, which was largely akin to determining a definition of government. At this point, the old puzzle of Case being assigned (internally) under government and (externally) under agreement was elevated to the category of a disjunction in the theory. Various attempts were made to subsume agreement under government, but serious formal problems remained, particularly with the notion of Exceptional Case Marking (ECM). In these instances, Case is assigned by a verb or preposition that bears absolutely no thematic relation to the Case recipient, as in *I believe him to be a liar* (where *him* is obviously the thematic subject of *be a liar*, and cannot in any sense be a thematic object of *believe*, yet acts clearly as its grammatical object, for instance receiving accusative Case from the verb). Any attempt to generalize government to cover this sort of instance resulted in many unwanted consequences and complicated the definition of that structural notion to the point that it became obvious that government ought to follow from deeper principles.

It was also not clear in GB theory what the elements are that require structural Case, and why they do. For some analysts, Case is a property of morphologically expressed noun phrases, and thus not of null categories like PRO—the implicit subject of infinitivals like *PRO to be a liar* (*must be exhausting*)—or the trace *t* of a moved noun phrase, which ought to be in a non-Case position (if Case drives movement in a sentence like *he was believed t to be a liar*, the source *t* of movement must not be Case-marked). However, traces of operator movement (e.g. a question word or a relative pronoun) clearly occupy a Case position, and in fact they are ungrammatical in Caseless positions (e.g., **I know the man (who) it seems [t to be a liar]*). Given that counter-example to the idea that only morphologically realized elements exhibit Case properties, some other theorists take Case to be a property of arguments. That is consistent with the suggestion that traces of operators (interpreted as variables) should need Case, because they are arguments, whereas traces of A-movements do not. At the same time, from this perspective, PRO (an argument) must receive Case, despite appearances to the contrary. In turn, pleonastic elements like *there* in *there is a man in the room*, which clearly require Case (**there to be a man in the room* (*would be surprising*)) do so not because of their argumental properties (they have none), but because of those of their agreeing associate, *a man*. For this element to be in a Case configuration, it must be covertly displaced to the site of the pleonastic, yielding [[*there*[*a man*]] *is t in the room*] as its LF representation. This analysis, called Expletive Replacement, entails that Case satisfaction is an LF property, as is expected if the requirement is not morphological but instead is an abstract characteristic of arguments.

The abandonment of government as a primitive notion, and Expletive Replacement with its consequence of Case as an LF property, are central traits of the Minimalist program. In this theoretical perspective, there is no module of Case theory as such; rather, Case properties are coded as values for features of noun phrases that must be determined in given configurations. Absent government, the relevant configurations must be somewhat local, and they entail a generalization of the Expletive Replacement analysis to all instances of Case licensing, now systematically assumed to be executed abstractly in the LF component. In Minimalist terms, functional categories like Tense or abstract agreement markers are taken to be the sites where Case is determined (through agreement). The fact that Case in some languages is also manifested in morphological terms (*he* vs. *him*, etc.) is reconciled with the LF-movement analysis by assuming that Case is not assigned but is actually checked, or sanctioned, in appropriate sites, with relevant forms originating as pronounced already in the lexicon. Much debate has ensued on whether it is Case per se that drives LF-movement, or whether Case checking is a byproduct of movement for other reasons (e.g. agreement). Important questions also arise as to whether noun phrases are accessible to further transformations after their Case is checked, and if not, why. The issue is simply posed by such ungrammatical examples as *there seems to a man that he is a liar*, where it is not obvious why *a man* cannot be the associate of the pleonastic. If *a man* can get its Case checked within the domain of the dative preposition *to*, it arguably cannot associate to *there* in subject position, under the assumption that this association is established in circumstances of (e.g. nominative) Case checking. This fact led Chomsky to suggest that Case may well be a mechanism that grammars possess to signal items that can undergo transformations, which become inactive after their Case requirement is appropriately checked. That novel idea shows how a topic that has been studied for centuries still has surprises to offer.

[*See also* Formal Grammar; Logical Form; Minimalist Program; Nouns; Principles and Parameters; Pronouns; *and* Traces.]

BIBLIOGRAPHY

Chomsky, Noam. 1981. *Lectures on government and binding.* Dordrecht: Foris.

Chomsky, Noam. 1986. *Knowledge of language.* New York: Praeger.

Chomsky, Noam. 1995. *The Minimalist program.* Cambridge, Mass.: MIT Press.

Chomsky, Noam, and Howard Lasnik. 1977. Filters and control. *Linguistic Inquiry* 8.425–504.

Covington, Michael. 1984. *Syntactic theory in the High Middle Ages: Modistic models of sentence structure.* New York: Cambridge University Press.

Fillmore, Charles. 1968. The case for case. In *Universals in linguistic theory,* edited by Emmon Bach and Robert T. Harms, pp. 1–88. New York: Holt, Rinehart and Winston.

Hjelmslev, Louis. 1937. La catégorie des cas. Repr. Munich: Wilhem Fink, 1972.

Vergnaud, Jean-Roger. 1985. *Dépendances et niveaux de représentation en syntaxe.* Amsterdam: John Benjamins.

JUAN URIAGEREKA

Case Alignment

A central issue in linguistic typology and functional approaches to grammar is the coding of the clausal *nuclear arguments*: intransitive S[ubject], transitive subject or A[gent], and transitive object or P[atient]. Languages typically code nuclear arguments according to a restricted set of patterns, despite the diverse range of predicate meanings and actual coding strategies; the latter may include nominal case marking, cross-referencing, verbal agreement, or word order. This article surveys coding patterns and the functional explanations that have been proposed for them. (For reference, see Comrie 1978, 1981, Dixon 1979, Hopper and Thompson 1980, Mallinson and Blake 1981, Foley and Van Valin 1984, Du Bois 1987.)

The most common pattern is the (nominative-) ACCUSATIVE, in which S and A are coded alike by nominative case, while P is distinguished by accusative case. Another pattern is the ERGATIVE(-absolutive), in which S and P are coded alike by absolutive case, but A is distinguished by ergative case. (Small capitals are used here to refer to a coding pattern, while lowercase type is used for the actual noun cases.)

The logical possibilities of coding S, A, and P are given in Figure 1, where a circle around a group indicates that they are coded alike. Of these five types, I–II are by far the most common; III is common in restricted coding

FIGURE 1. *Possible Coding Types*

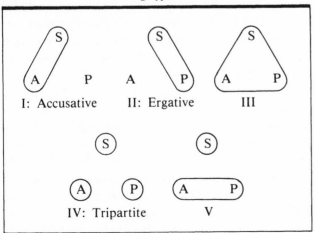

I: Accusative   II: Ergative   III

IV: Tripartite   V

domains (e.g. for case-marking); the tripartite system (type IV) is unusual; and V is rarer still.

The ergative pattern is illustrated in the following well-known examples from Dyirbal (Australia; Dixon 1972: 130), in which -ŋgu marks the ergative case, while the absolutive case is unmarked:

(1) *Balan d⁰ugumbil baŋgul yaṛa-ŋgu   balgan.*
     DET   woman.ABS DET   man-ERG   hit
     'The man hit the woman.'

(2) *Bayi yaṛa   baninʸu.*
     DET   man.ABS   came.here
     'The man came here.'

Examples (1–2) illustrate a general principle: the more general case (absolutive or nominative) is formally unmarked, while the more restricted (ergative or accusative) is marked.

It is unusual for languages to apply one coding pattern rigorously to all nominals in all clauses. Some languages use a combination of ERGATIVE and ACCUSATIVE patterns, giving the SPLIT ERGATIVE type. Other languages mix I and III: their accusative case is not always formally distinct from the nominative. Certain factors favor ACCUSATIVE, and others favor ERGATIVE, specifically, (i) perfective aspect or past tense favors ergative, and imperfective or non-past favors accusative. However, (ii) argument nominals of high inherent topicality (e.g. pronouns, names, and definites) favor accusative coding; those of lower inherent topicality (e.g. inanimates and indefinites) favor ergative coding. This phenomenon has been referred to in the literature as the "agency hierarchy," the "animacy hierarchy," or the "topicality hierarchy"—each term implying a particular explanation of the phenomenon.

Much research has been devoted to these correlations, with most attention paid to (ii). Explanations for (ii) usually take one of the following approaches.

(a) Distinguishing accounts: The principal purpose of argument coding is to distinguish the syntactic function of arguments. Given that A and P may need to be distinguished, it is efficient to treat S like either one of these two—hence the ACCUSATIVE or ERGATIVE systems. The rarity of patterns IV and V is predicted—since, in these, S is treated differently from both A and P.

(b) Characterizing accounts in terms of semantic roles: Coding expresses semantic generalizations about arguments; the absolutive codes Ps, while the nominative codes As. From this perspective, ERGATIVE languages may be claimed to have a passive character, because they generalize the role of P. Patterns IV and V are rare because they do not capture any semantic generalization. In SPLIT ERGATIVE languages, the preferred case-marking system is determined by the potential agency of a nominal: nominals higher in potency are preferably coded accusatively, while those lower in potency are treated ergatively.

(c) Characterizing accounts in terms of discourse markedness: Coding systems indicate the markedness of nominals in serving particular functions. As usually have high "topic continuity," so As of inherently low topic continuity are marked as ERGATIVE. Conversely, Ps of inherently high topicality are marked as ACCUSATIVE. This accounts for the SPLIT ERGATIVE nominal hierarchies. The coding characterizes the likelihood that a nominal will occupy a particular argument role in discourse. The appeal in semantic accounts to "prototypical" or "potential" agents is thus misdirected; more to the point is a characterization in terms of preferred discourse function. "Prototypical agent" is in fact a frequent or predictable topic in actual discourse.

In the late 1980s, there was a tendency to focus on the characterizing functions of argument coding based on detailed discourse studies, with a steady move away from purely distinguishing or semantic accounts. Studies have shown that P and S share important discourse properties: they are the preferred locus of new mentions, and of full noun phrase expressions. In contrast, A and S form the locus of nominals with established topicality and higher continuity in the discourse. This suggests an explanation in which the primary function of argument coding systems is to characterize the informational status of arguments, rather than to distinguish them or characterize their semantic properties.

In terms of this trend, it is instructive to consider the SPLIT-S or ACTIVE coding type, in which S is not treated coherently, but is coded like A for some intransitive predicates and like P for others (see Durie 1985 for a description of an active language). It used to be thought that the split in such cases was based solely upon the lexical semantics of the predicate—hence the term "active" (the relevant contrast is often event vs. state, or volition vs. non-volition). However, the irregularity which often complicates the lexical semantics of such splits suggests that a distinguishing explanation in terms of discourse functions may prove more general. The semantic correlations would then be a secondary effect.

Work on argument coding systems has stimulated related research into syntactic patterning. Languages differ in the way in which they treat S, A, and P in syntactic processes; ERGATIVE, ACCUSATIVE, and SPLIT-S patterning are reported.

[*See also* Clause; Functional Linguistics; Morphology; *and* Transitivity and Voice.]

BIBLIOGRAPHY

Comrie, Bernard. 1978. Ergativity. In *Syntactic typology: Studies in the phenomenology of language,* edited by Winfred P. Lehmann, pp. 329–394. Austin: University of Texas Press.

Comrie, Bernard. 1981. *Language universals and linguistic typology: Syntax and morphology.* Oxford: Blackwell.

Dixon, Robert M. W. 1972. *The Dyirbal language of North Queensland.* (Cambridge studies in linguistics, 9.) London: Cambridge University Press.

Dixon, Robert M. W. 1979. Ergativity. *Language* 55.59–138.

Du Bois, John W. 1987. The discourse basis of ergativity. *Language* 63.805–855.

Durie, Mark. 1985. *A grammar of Acehnese on the basis of the dialect of north Aceh.* (Koninklijk Instituut voor Taal-, Land- en Volkenkunde, Verhandelingen, 112.) Dordrecht: Foris.

Foley, William A., and Robert D. Van Valin, Jr. 1984. *Functional syntax and universal grammar.* (Cambridge studies in linguistics, 38.) Cambridge and New York: Cambridge University Press.

Hopper, Paul, and Sandra A. Thompson. 1980. Transitivity in grammar and discourse. *Language* 56.251–299.

Mallinson, Graham, and Barry J. Blake. 1981. *Language typology: Cross-linguistic studies in syntax.* (North-Holland linguistic series, 46.) Amsterdam: North-Holland.

MARK DURIE

CASE GRAMMAR. *See* Case; Principles and Parameters; *and* Formal Grammar.

CATEGORIAL GRAMMAR. This framework for grammatical analysis has its historical roots in philosophical and logical investigations of compositional relations between syntactic structure and semantic interpretation. Characteristically, a categorial system **C** consists of a vocabulary *V,* a type structure *T,* and a categorial calculus *C.* Each vocabulary element *v* is associated with one or more types in *T.* The combinatorial properties of each pair $\langle v,t \rangle$ are determined by the structure of *t* and the type calculus *C.* Moreover, if **C** is interpreted, the interpretation of $\langle v,t \rangle$ must meet constraints imposed by the choice of *t.* Thus the type structure plays a central role in grammatical composition.

The type structure *T* is based on a set of primitive types (such as S[entence], N[oun] P[hrase], and N[oun]) and a set of type-forming operators (such as the binary operators '/' and '\'). We can form new types by combining already given types with the type-forming operators, yielding types NP\S, N/N, (NP\S)/NP, etc. Informally, we may think of the type-forming operators '/' and '\' in a number of ways; for example, we may think of an expression e_1 of type α/β or $\beta\backslash\alpha$ as something which combines with an expression e_2 of type β to its right or left, respectively, to form an expression e_1e_2 or e_2e_1, respectively, of type α. Alternatively, when *e* is assigned to the type α/β or $\beta\backslash\alpha$, we may identify e_1 with a function which maps any element e_2 of type β to the element e_1e_2 or e_2e_1, respectively, of type α. (Relative to these conventions, if *the* is of type NP/N and *sensible world* is of type N, the expression *the sensible world* is of type NP.) The formal characterization of the type-forming operators is given by the calculus *C,* which defines a set of valid *arrows,* typically of the form $\alpha_1, \ldots, \alpha_k \to \beta$. Given a valid arrow of this form, any sequence $e_1, \ldots, e_k$ of *k* expressions associated with types $\alpha_1, \ldots, \alpha_k$, respectively, is assigned to the type β.

For example, the categorial system **AB** (based on Ajdukiewicz 1935, and proved equivalent in weak generative capacity to context-free grammars by Bar-Hillel 1964) has a type structure based on the operators '/' and '\', and a type calculus which defines the class of valid arrows by the axioms

(1) $\alpha \to \alpha$

(2) $\alpha/\beta, \beta \to \alpha$

(3) $\beta, \beta\backslash\alpha \to \alpha$

with the rule of substitution: if 4a-b are valid, then 5 is valid (where Δ, Φ, and ψ represent sequences of types, Δ non-empty):

(4a) $\Delta \to \alpha$

(4b) $\Phi, \alpha, \psi \to \beta$

(5) $\Phi, \Delta, \psi \to \beta$

In this system, NP, (NP\S)/NP, NP $\to$ S is a valid arrow: apply the substitution rule to the two valid premises

(6) $(NP\backslash S)/NP, NP \rightarrow NP\backslash S$

(7) $NP, NP\backslash S \rightarrow S$

Thus, if *nature, inspires,* and *wonder* are elements of *V* assigned to NP, $(NP\backslash S)/NP$, and NP, respectively, then *Nature inspires wonder* $\rightarrow$ S in **AB**.

This simple example illustrates one characteristic of categorial grammar: subcategorization information can be encoded directly into the structure of syntactic types. A second characteristic is the possibility of higher-order types: a type such as VP/(VP/NP) can be assigned to an element which combines with a VP lacking an NP, to form a VP (such as the accusative clitics in the Romance languages or, with modifications, adjectives like *tough* in *English is tough to learn*). A third syntactic characteristic is the possibility of flexible type-assignment: the validity of the arrow $(NP\backslash S)/NP \rightarrow NP\backslash(S/NP)$ would allow a transitive verb to combine with two flanking NP arguments in two different ways.

An elegant way to interpret the system **AB** defined over primitive types S, NP, and N involves a model structure $\mathcal{M}$ which contains a distinguished substructure t' for every type in *T,* in a way compatible with the arrows valid in **AB**. Let *A* be a set of individuals and 2 be the set of truth values {*true, false*}. Let $\mathcal{M}$ be the smallest set which contains *A* and 2—and which, when it contains α and β, contains the set α^β of functions from β to α. We associate each type *t* in *T* with a substructure t' in $\mathcal{M}$ as follows, where simple types are handled by clauses 8–10 and complex types by clause 11 (see Montague 1974, Bentham 1986):

(8) $S' = 2$

(9) $NP' = A$

(10) $N' = 2^{bA}$

(11) $(\alpha/\beta)' = (\beta\backslash\alpha)' = \alpha'^\beta$

There are many extensions of the simple example discussed here, deriving both from abstract considerations and from empirical problems. The arrows $\alpha/\beta,\beta \rightarrow \alpha$ and $\beta,\beta\backslash\alpha \rightarrow \alpha$ have analogs in the logical principle "Modus ponens" (in the tautological form $(p\wedge(p \Rightarrow q)) \Rightarrow q$), and in the application of a function $f : \beta \rightarrow \alpha$ to an argument of type β to yield a value of type α. This leads to the construction and investigation of categorial calculi with broader classes of valid arrows. Notable examples of such calculi include Associative Syntactic Calculus **L** (Lambek 1958), Lambda-Categorial Languages (Cresswell 1973), and Combinatory Grammars (Steedman 1988). See also the work of Buszkowski 1989 and Moortgat 1989.

While these "extended" categorial grammars have direct application to linguistic phenomena such as morphological bracketing "paradoxes" (Hoeksema 1984), empirical problems have provided the impetus for theoretical innovations. This has led to the introduction of different systems of basic types (Steele 1988); to unification-based categorial systems in which the basic categories are themselves structured objects (Haddock et al. 1987, Klein and Benthem 1987); and to new kinds of type-forming operators (Moortgat 1989).

One result of these innovations is the increasingly sophisticated adaptation of categorial grammars to the syntactic and semantic properties of natural languages (Steedman 1996, 2000; Carpenter 1997). Another is the realization that the perspective developed within categorial grammar—the study of syntactic and semantic composition as an integrated system—is applicable more generally to the class of problems involving the interaction of properties from different linguistic dimensions. Examples of such problems of 'generalized compositionality' are well-known; they include the interaction of syntactic, semantic, and phonological properties in morphology, the interaction of syntax and phonology in sandhi rules, and the syntactic and interpretive constraints on intonational phrasing. Current interest in issues seemingly so remote from its philosophical and logical roots is a sign of categorial grammar's coming of age.

Recent developments (Morrill 1994, Moortgat 1997) have generalized the basic properties of categorial grammars described above, strengthening the intrinsic connections between categorial grammar and logic, and dramatically extending the empirical reach of current systems.

The earliest systems of categorial grammar characterize grammatical systems in which there is a single mode of composition; *multi-modal* systems now make it possible to characterize grammatical systems with a variety of ways of putting expressions together. As a result, categorial grammars are no longer restricted to problems of the sort $\Sigma \rightarrow A$, with *A* being a type and Σ a single data-structure (such as sequences, binary-bracketed sequences of types, multisets, ...). Instead, the basic problem can be represented by arrows of the form $C(t_1, \ldots, t_k) \rightarrow A$, with $C(t_1, \ldots, t_k)$ a structured configuration of types (or lexical elements standing for types they are lexically associated with), built up from a stock of available modes of composition. To adapt this set-up to a system of grammatical deduction, one must connect modes of composition with type-structure.

Each mode of composition has distinguishable properties. A basic property of a mode is its *arity*—the number of arguments it acts on. Strings and binary trees, for example, can be constructed using a binary operator. Although modes of higher arity are possible, the focus here is on unary and binary modes. Each mode of arity k is assigned a distinct family of type-constructors, each of arity k as well, consisting of a product operator and k corresponding implications. For example, if $- \circ_i -$ is a binary mode, its corresponding family of type-constructors can be represented by the binary product $- \bullet_i -$ and the binary implicational operators $- /_i -$ and $- \backslash_i -$. If $\langle - \rangle_j$ is a unary mode, its corresponding family of type-constructors can be represented by the unary product $\Diamond_j -$ and the unary implication $\Box_j -$.

Now, fix a set $\mathcal{M}$ of modes and a set $\mathcal{A}$ of atomic types. The set $\mathcal{T}$ of *types* is the smallest set containing $\mathcal{A}$ and closed under the operations of every type-constructor associated with any element of $\mathcal{M}$. The set of Σ of *structures* is the smallest set containing $\mathcal{T}$ and closed under the elements of $\mathcal{M}$. An *arrow* is a pair (σ, A), with σ a structure and A a type. As usual, we write $\sigma \to A$ for such a pair.

The arrow $\sigma \to A$ is to be interpreted as the claim that every instance of the structure σ is an instance of the type A. It is immediate that for any type A, the Identity Arrow $A \to A$ is valid. Equally, if $\tau \to A$ holds and $\sigma [A] \to B$ holds (where $\sigma [A]$ is a structure σ containing a designated occurrence of A), then $\sigma [\tau] \to B$ holds as well (where $\sigma [\tau]$ is the result of replacing the designated occurrence of A in $\sigma [A]$ with τ), since $\sigma [\tau]$ is an instance of $\sigma [A]$ and, by assumption, any instance of $\sigma [\tau]$ is an instance of B. This is the Cut Rule.

There are two other significant sources of valid inference rules, following a distinction introduced by Gentzen 1934: logical rules and structural rules. *Logical rules* govern the members of each family of type-constructors. Each implicational operator is assumed to be right adjoint to the corresponding product. For the unary types, this means that $\Diamond_j B \to C$ is valid iff $B \to \Box_j C$ is valid. For binary types, there are two cases: $A \to C\backslash B$ iff $A \bullet_i B \to C$ iff $B \to A\backslash_i C$. It is easy to see that the binary case is essentially the same as the unary case: take $A \bullet_i -$ as a unary product operator with corresponding implication

$A\backslash_i -$, then one can see the similarity between the unary and binary cases by writing one of the binary cases as

$$\boxed{A \bullet_i} B \to C \text{ iff } B \to \boxed{A\backslash_i} C$$

The other binary case is the same, with $- \bullet_i B$ as the unary product and $-/_i B$ as its corresponding implication.

Together with Identity and Cut, the logical rules that derive directly from the adjointness laws yield many consequences. For example, by Adjointness, $A/B \bullet_i B \to B$ iff $A/_i B \to A/_i B$. But the right-hand side of this biconditional holds by Identity. Thus the *modus ponens* cancellation law on the left-hand side is derivable. Similarly, one derives $A \bullet_i A\backslash_i B \to B$ and, using the same reasoning, the unary form of *modus ponens*, $\Diamond \Box A \to A$. Thus, the consequences of adjointness can be used *synthetically* to solve for the unknown x in problems of the form $\sigma \to x$. On the other hand, using the adjointness laws in the other direction makes it possible to take apart product structures *analytically*, yielding solutions to problems of the form $\sigma [x] \to A$, where $\sigma [x]$ is a product structure containing the unknown x (as exemplified linguistically by the problem of assigning syntactic properties to newly encountered expressions in otherwise familiar contexts).

Adjoint pairs arise naturally in many different data structures—as MacLane 1971 says, "Adjoints occur almost everywhere in many branches of Mathematics." Maps from one data-type to another data-type that preserve adjointness are capable of carrying significant information reliably. Thus, adjointness provides a suitable level of abstractness to interpret grammatical structures compositionally—that is, in a such a way that the interpretation of a valid arrow depends on its proof. The role of the λ-calculus in the Curry-Howard semantics for conjunctive/implicational logics offers an example of this perspective (Girard et al. 1989).

An important second source of valid inference rules is what Gentzen called *structural rules*. These reflect further properties of individual modes of composition and their interaction. For example, a binary mode of composition $\circ_a$ may be associative (rendering $(\rho \circ_a \sigma_a) \circ_a \tau$ and $\rho \circ_a (\sigma \circ_a \tau)$ equivalent); or commutative (rendering $\sigma \circ_a \rho$ and $\rho \circ_c \sigma$ equivalent). Other structural rules deal with multiplicities of occurrence and with monotonicity properties of inference. There is a corresponding range of possibilities for unary modes.

If we restrict our attention to systems with a single family $\{\bullet, /, \backslash\}$ of binary type-constructors, one can see immediately that, in general, adding a structural rule of inference makes more arrows provable. For example, associativity makes it possible to prove the arrows of Composition ($A/B{\circ}B/C \to A/C$) and Division ($A/B \to (A/C)/(B/C)$); commutativity makes it possible to prove $A/B \to B\backslash A$; and in the presence of commutativity and associativity, one may prove $(A/B)/C \to (A/C)/B$. This leads to a hierarchy of conjunctive/implicational logics, stretching from the non-associative Lambek calculus **NL** (no structural rules), to the associative Lambek calculus **L** (associativity), to the Lambek/van Benthem calculus **LP** (associativity and commutativity; equivalent for present purposes with the Multiplicative fragment **MLL** of Linear Logic), to various relevant logics (associativity, commutativity, and contraction), to intuitionistic logic (adding the monotonicity rule). (For details, see Došen and Schroeder-Heister 1993 and Restall 2000.)

On the other hand, adding structural rules leads to a loss of structural discrimination: in the presence of associativity, for example, one cannot use bracketing to distinguish different structures, and in the presence of associativity and commutativity, any string is equivalent to any of its permutations. In a system with a single binary mode and its associated family of type constructors, structural rules represent absolute choices: if one accepts a given structural option in order to gain access to a richer deductive setting, one must accept the global loss of structural discrimination that comes with it. This feature of single-mode inference systems seems alien to natural language, where one typically finds selective, local access to structural options: word order may be strictly enforced in some contexts, yet loosened in others; clause-union structures (which display formal affinities with associativity) may be possible for some verbs, impossible for others, and obligatory for still others.

In the multi-modal setting, it is possible to characterize this controlled access to structural rule options by a simple combination of structural declarations dependent only on the logical constants of the type system and judicious type-declarations. As an example, consider the variety of filler-gap dependencies displayed in English indirect questions: *she wondered . . . who knocked*; . . . *who Kim saw*; . . . *who Kim sent to Sandy*: . . . *who Kim showed a picture of to Sandy*: . . . *who Kim insisted that Sandy had called*, and so on. Let q be the type of indirect questions (so *wondered* has type $(np\backslash s) /_k q$ for some mode $\circ_k$, about which we need make no special assumptions. We would like to assign the critical element *who* a

type that will form an embedded question if it finds on its right a sentence missing an *np*. As a first attempt, we might try $q/(np\backslash_k s)$, but this is too weak, and if we attempt to strengthen it by adding postulates ensuring the associativity and commutativity of $\circ_k$, the overall system suffers from a massive loss of discrimination. But suppose we postulate the type $q/_k ((\Diamond \Box np)\backslash_k s)$. The unary *modus ponens* already gives us $\Diamond \Box np \to np$. Taking *knocked* to have type $np\backslash_k s$, this is already enough to account for embedded questions like *who knocked*: given the type for *who*, *who* will combine with *knocked* to yield type q if *knocked* $\to (\Diamond \Box np)\backslash_k s$; but since *knocked* $\to np\backslash_k s$, by adjointness, $np\bullet_k$ *knocked* $\to s$; and this, with $\Diamond \Box np \to np$, yields by Cut the desired *knocked* $\to (\Diamond \Box np)\backslash_k s$.

To deal with *who Kim saw*, we need the structural transition:

$$\frac{\sigma[\tau \circ_k (\rho \circ_k \Diamond A)] \to C}{\sigma[\Diamond A \circ_k (\tau \circ_k \rho)] \to C} R0$$

This rule allows the hypothetical $\Diamond \Box np$ to look for its gap in the *vp*-final position. One gets all the remaining cases mentioned above by adding rules that pass an appropriately modally decorated type down one or another right branch:

$$\frac{\sigma[(\tau \circ_k \Diamond A)\circ_k \rho] \to C}{\sigma[(\tau \circ_k \rho)\circ_k \Diamond A] \to C} R1 \quad \frac{\sigma[\tau \circ_k (\rho \circ_k \Diamond A)] \to C}{\sigma[(\tau \circ_k \rho)\circ_k \Diamond A] \to C} R2$$

This simple set of structural postulates is not a complete account of embedded questions, but it covers an impressive range of cases and gains additional plausibility from a number of factors. First, the rules are directly motivated by empirical examples of intuitively increasing complexity. Second, if $\circ_k$ is not associative, the structural rules above do not allow embedded questions that violate the '*that*-trace filter' (such as **who Kim said that knocked*; though more must be said about the acceptability of the complementizerless case *who Kim said knocked*). Third, it is adaptable to languages other than English. In Dutch, corresponding coverage may be attained by dropping rule $R0$ and substituting $L1$ and $L2$ for their symmetrical counterparts $R1$ and $R2$:

$$\frac{\sigma[(\Diamond A \circ_k \tau) \circ_k \rho] \to C}{\sigma[\Diamond A \circ_k (\tau \circ_k \rho)] \to C} L1 \quad \frac{\sigma[\tau \circ_k (\Diamond A \circ_k \rho)] \to C}{\sigma[\Diamond A \circ_k (\tau \circ_k \rho)] \to C} L2$$

With these rules, violations of the *that*-trace filter are inevitable. Interestingly enough, they form an attested property of Dutch extraction constructions. Moreover, comparing these two sets of structural rule packages for English and Dutch, one finds the basis for other noteworthy typological distinctions: the *R*-rules allow extraction from prepositional phrases, the *L*-rules do not; the *R*-rules disallow extraction of a determiner, the *L*-rules permit it (as in Dutch *wat ben je toch dom!* 'how dumb you are!').

The discussion above shows how multi-modal categorial grammar brings together a variety of modes of composition, the logical properties that adjointness confers upon their corresponding families of type-constructors, and the linguistic advantages that flow from the controlled access to structural reasoning inherent in this perspective. The result is a system of grammatical logic—a system of resource-sensitive deduction that characterizes classes of linguistic structures—that allows one to study properties of grammatical composition abstractly, empirically, and computationally.

[*See also* Formal Grammar; Learnability; *and* Mathematical Linguistics.]

BIBLIOGRAPHY

Ajdukiewicz, Kazimierz. 1935. Die syntaktische Konnexität. *Studia Philosophica* 1.1–27. Translated in *Polish logic,* edited by Storrs McCall (Oxford and New York: Oxford University Press, 1967), pp. 207–231.

Bar-Hillel, Yehoshua. 1964. *Language and information.* Reading, Mass.: Addison-Wesley.

Benthem, Johan van. 1986. *Essays in logical semantics.* (Studies in linguistics and philosophy, 29.) Dordrecht: Reidel.

Buszkowski, Wojciech. 1989. *Logiczne podstawy gramatyk kategorialnych Ajdukiewicza-Lambeka.* Warsaw: PWN.

Buszkowski, Wojciech, et al., eds. 1988. *Categorial Grammar.* (Linguistic and literary studies in Eastern Europe, 25.) Amsterdam: Benjamins.

Carpenter, Bob. 1997. *Type-logical semantics.* Cambridge, Mass, and London: MIT Press.

Cresswell, Maxwell J. 1973. *Logics and languages.* London: Methuen.

Došen, Kota, and Peter Schroeder-Heister, eds. 1993. *Substructural logics.* Oxford: Clarendon Press.

Gentzen, Gerhard. 1934. Untersuchungen über das logische Schliessen. *Mathematische Zeitschrift* 39.176–210, 405–431. English translation in M. E. Szabo, ed., *The Collected Papers of Gerhard Gentzen*, pp. 68–131. Amsterdam, New York, and Oxford: North-Holland, 1969.

Girard, Jean-Yves; Yves Lafont, and Paul Taylor. 1989. *Proofs and types.* Cambridge: Cambridge University Press.

Haddock, Nicholas, et al., eds. 1987. *Categorial Grammar, Unification Grammar, and parsing.* (Edinburgh working papers in cognitive science, 1.) Edinburgh: Centre for Cognitive Science, University of Edinburgh.

Hoeksema, Jack. 1984. *Categorial morphology.* University of Groningen dissertation. Published, New York: Garland, 1985.

Klein, Ewan, and Johan van Benthem, eds. 1987. *Categories, polymorphism, and unification.* Edinburgh: Centre for Cognitive Science, University of Edinburgh.

Lambek, Joachim. 1958. The mathematics of sentence structure. *American Mathematical Monthly.* 65.154–170. Reprinted in Buszkowski et al. 1988, pp. 153–172.

MacLane, Saunders. 1971. *Categories for the working mathematician.* Berlin: Springer.

Montague, Richard. 1974. *Formal philosophy: Selected papers.* Edited by Richmond Thomason. New Haven, Conn.: Yale University Press.

Moortgat, Michael. 1989. *Categorial investigations.* Dordrecht: Foris.

Moortgat, Michael. 1997. *Categorial type logics.* In *Handbook of Logic and Language*, edited by Johan van Benthem and Alice ter Meulen. Amsterdam: Elsevier.

Morrill, Glyn. 1994. *Type logical grammar.* Dordrecht: Klumer.

Oehrle, Richard, et al., eds. 1988. *Categorial Grammars and natural language structures.* (Studies in linguistics and philosophy, 32.) Dordrecht: Reidel.

Restall, Greg. 2000. *An introduction to substructural logics.* London and New York: Routledge.

Steedman, Mark. 1988. Combinators and grammars. In Oehrle et al. 1988, pp. 417–442.

Steedman, Mark. 1996. *Surface structure and interpretation.* Cambridge, Mass., and London: MIT Press.

Steedman, Mark. 2000. *The syntactic process.* Cambridge, Mass., and London: MIT Press.

Steele, Susan. 1988. A typology of functors and categories. In Oehrle et al. 1988, pp. 443–466.

RICHARD T. OEHRLE

CAUCASIAN LANGUAGES. The 38 indigenous languages of the Caucasus can be grouped into four families, which take their names from the geographical regions in which their members are spoken: N[orth] W[est] C[aucasian], N[orth] C[entral] C[aucasian], N[orth] E[ast] C[aucasian], and S[outh] C[aucasian]. (See Map 1.) The three northern families may be genetically related in a North Caucasian group (especially NCC and NEC) (see Nikolayev and Starostin 1994); however, all attempts to establish such a relationship between SC and any other language or family must be judged unconvincing. NWC

MAP 1. *Politico-Linguistic Divisions in the Caucasus*

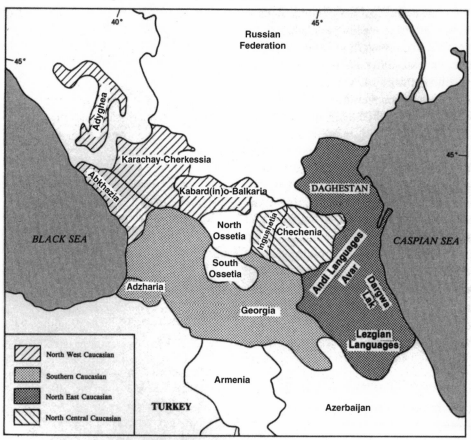

MAP 2. *Distribution of South Caucasian Languages*

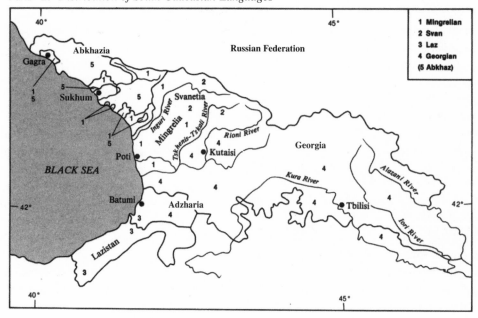

Ubykh, spoken only in Turkey since the migration of the entire population in 1864, is now extinct, and the future of several other languages is precarious; Hinukh was estimated in 1992 to have only 500 speakers (van den Berg 1995).

Typical areal features, though not necessarily characteristic of all languages and dialects, include ejective consonants, predominantly vigesimal counting systems, agglutination, ergativity (cf. Boeder 1979, Catford 1976), triple deixis, an inferential mood, and use of speech particles to mark direct speech. Except in SC, subordinating conjunctions are typically absent, and non-finite verb forms are used in subordinate "clauses."

Within the former Soviet Union, the following were literary languages: Georgian, Abkhaz, Abaza, Adyghe, Kabardian, Chechen, Ingush, Lak, Dargwa, Avar, Lezgi, and Tabassaran; attempts have recently been made to create orthographies for some other NEC languages, such as Aghul, Tsakhur, and Rutul. General references are Catford 1977, Greppin 1989, and Hewitt 1981.

1. South Caucasian (also called Kartvelian) consists of Georgian (see Hewitt 1995), Svan, Mingrelian, and Laz; the last two are sometimes known jointly as Zan. (See Map 2.) Laz is spoken in Turkey, and the Ingilo dialect of Georgian in Azerbaijan; otherwise, the family is spoken in Georgia. Georgian is the best known and most widely spoken of all Caucasian languages, with a literary tradition of fifteen centuries in its own alphabet. The most divergent is Svan, in northwestern Georgia. Mingrelian is spoken in lowland western Georgia.

1.1. *Phonology.* To the phoneme inventory of Georgian, Mingrelian adds *ə* and *ʔ*, while Svan adds a variety of long and umlauted vowels. The singularity of Kartvelian lies in its great tolerance of consonant clusters. Disregarding sequences which incorporate a morpheme boundary, Georgian has 740 initial clusters; of these, 233 have two elements, 334 three elements, 148 four elements, 21 five elements, and 4 have six elements. Out of 244 final clusters, 148 are biphonemic, 82 triphonemic, and 14 quadriphonemic (Vogt 1958).

1.2. *Morphology.* Case systems are roughly comparable throughout the family, though Laz lacks the Adverbial. A distinct Ergative morph seems to have developed independently in each language, since Georgian *-m(a(n))* and Zan *-k* cannot reflect a single proto-form. Among a variety of Ergative exponents in Svan, a clue to the proto-SC system may be seen in the pattern which uses *-d* jointly in Ergative/Adverbial function; cf. Adverbial *-(a)d, -o(t)* in Georgian and

Mingrelian respectively. The precise number of "screeves" (i.e. tense/aspect/modal paradigms) differs from language to language. Mingrelian is particularly rich in Inferentials, and distinguishes simple from potential intransitives, as in (1a–b) vs. (2a–b):

(1a) Absolute
    i-č'ar-u 'it is being written'

(1b) Relative
    Ø-a-č'ar-u 'it is being written to/for/on X'

(2a) Absolute
    i-č'ar-e 'it can be written'

(2b) Relative
    Ø-a-č'ar-e 'X can write it' (Ø = I[ndirect] O[bject])

Verbs can agree with S[ubject]s, D[irect] O[bject]s, and IOs by means of two sets of personal affixes (designated sets A and B); however, there can be no more than two such morphological exponents in a single verb, regardless of that verb's syntactic valency; minimally, a verb requires a Set A affix. Preverbs indicate direction with motion verbs, and perfective aspect elsewhere.

Zan has an extremely rich preverbal system. That of Svan is more simple; but like Old Georgian, it allows "tmesis," i.e. the separation of the preverb from the rest of the verbal complex. Complexes may also incorporate a causative suffix and a *ver[sion]* prefix; version vowels indicate a variety of relationships between verbal arguments, such as location, possession, and benefaction (Deeters 1930:70 ff.). A certain number of suppletive verb roots exist, determined by such factors as the screeve, singularity vs. plurality, or animacy vs. inanimacy of the intransitive S or DO; e.g. in Svan:

(3a) *x-uɣv-a*
    3-VER-have-3.INAN
    's/he has it'

(3b) *x-a-q'-a*
    3-VER-have-3.AN
    's/he has him/her'

In the Present subseries, 'to convey' is realized by the addition of the appropriate directional *prev[erb]* to the basic expression for 'to have'; e.g., in the Lent'ex dialect of Svan:

(4a) *a-x-u-ɣv-a*
    PREV-3-have-3.INAN
    's/he brings it'

(4b) *a-x-a-q'-a*
      PREV-3-VER-have-3.AN
      's/he brings him/her'

1.3. Syntax. Word order patterns include A[djective] + N[oun], G[enitive] + N (Old Georgian had NA, NG), N[oun] P[hrase] + Postposition, and S[ubject] O[bject] V[erb] (fluctuating with SVO). Case-marking for the central arguments of the verb varies according to which screeve series is employed. Svan essentially mirrors Georgian, while Zan has enlarged the role of its Ergative (in *-k*) in two directions:

(a) Laz uses the Ergative for transitive Ss in all series, with new non-inverted forms to rival the older inverted ones in Series III (Čikobava 1936:103).

(b) Mingrelian uses the Ergative for all forms in Series II, to give the following *Accusative* configuration:

(5) *k'oč-(i)-k c'eril-i   do-Ø-č'ar-u.*
     man-NOM letter-ACC PREV-it-write-he.AOR
     'The man wrote the letter.'

(6) *c'eril(i)-k d-i-č'ar-u.*
     letter-NOM PREV-PASS-write-it.AOR
     'The letter was written.'

Note also the Series II pattern for Indirect verbs (i.e. those with Dative S in all series; see Hewitt 1987:336):

(7) *k'o(č(i))-s k-Ø-e-ʔorop(-u)*
     man-DAT   PREV-he-VER-fall.in.love.with-her.AOR

     osur-k.
     woman-NOM

     'The man fell in love with the woman.'

Transitive verbal nouns display nominal governance by taking objective Genitives—though Old Georgian had an infinitive with verbal governance, whose object stood in either of the language's DO cases (Dative and Nominative). SC subordinate clauses tend to behave like their Indo-European counterparts, as in this Mingrelian relative:

(8) *b-jir-i   jɣab-i, namu-t i-bir-d-ə.*
     I-see-AOR girl   who-REL ver-sing-IMPF-she
     'I saw the girl who was singing.'

But several alternatives also exist to complicate this picture:

(9) *b-jir-i jɣab-i, namu-t i-bir-d-ə-ni* (with subordinator *-ni*)

(10) *i-bir-d-ə(-ni) (peri) jɣab-i b-jir-i* (with *peri* 'like')

In Laz, case endings or postpositions are attached to finite clauses, with or without the general subordinator, to produce a range of adverbial clauses:

(11) [*sum c'an-er-i   b-or-t'-i*]-*ši*
     three year-DER-ADJ I-be-IMPF-INDIC-GEN
     'when I was three, . . .'

(12) [*bere k'itx-er-i-na   t'-u*]-*šeni*
     child read-PPL-ADJ-SUB be.IMPF-it-for
     'Since the child was educated, . . .'

2. North West Caucasian (see Map 3) is divided as follows:

(a) Abkhaz, in Abkhazia and Abaza, in Karachay-Cherkessia

(b) West Circassian or Adyghe, in Adyghea; and East Circassian (Kabardian, Kabardo-Cherkess), in Kabard(in)o-Balkaria and Karachay-Cherkessia

(c) Ubykh (extinct; formerly spoken on the eastern coast of the Black Sea)

Well over half a million ethnic NW Caucasians are found throughout the Near East, predominantly in Turkey (Smeets 1984:51).

2.1. Phonology. Large consonant inventories combine with minimal ("vertical") vowel-systems. Despite the attempt of Kuipers 1960 to prove that there is no phonemic opposition between vowels and consonants in Kabardian, most commentators accept at least *ə* and *a* for these languages. Consonant phonemes range from 45 (Literary Kabardian) to 83 (Ubykh), if one includes three phonemes attested only in loans. The Bzyp dialect of Abkhaz demonstrates NWC's use of secondary features, as shown in Table 1.

2.2. Morphology. Case systems are impoverished: Abkhaz formally marks only its adverbial case. The oppositions indefinite vs. definite (generic, for Abkhaz) and singular vs. plural are observed. Possession is always marked on the possessed noun by a personal prefix correlating with the possessor (Adyghe distinguishes alienable vs. inalienable possession); this is paralleled by the NP-postposition relationship. Verbs

Map 3. *North West Caucasian Tribes circa 1880*

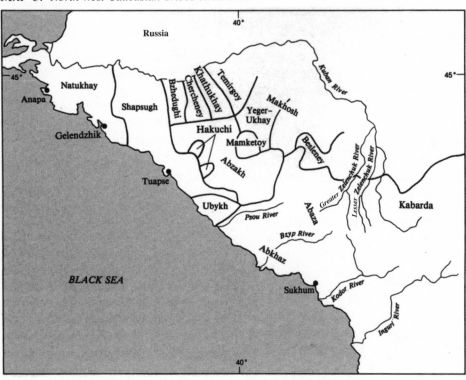

differentiate "dynamic" from "stative" categories, and (especially in Abkhaz-Abaza) "finite" from "non-finite." The exponents which build the polysynthetic verb complexes of NWC, discounting tense/mood/aspect formants, include three sets of pronominal prefixes; these are differentiated, if not always formally, by their positions in the complex. Abkhaz-Abaza has human/non-human, masculine/feminine oppositions in part of the pronominal system. There is also a bewildering array of locational preverbs; relative, relational, reflexive, reciprocal, and causative prefixes; potential, orientational, and adverbial affixes; subordinating and interrogative particles; emphatics; and negatives.

2.3. Syntax. Word order patterns include SOV, NP + Postposition, GN, and NA (but a few easily characterizable adjectives stand first, e.g. ethnonyms). Relatives are preposed, though Circassian and Ubykh (perhaps less commonly, Abkhaz too) allow the notional head NP to be placed in the adverbial case, and then to stand within the clause. These examples are from Adyghe, both meaning 'The man who killed the woman is coming':

(13) ɕ°əzə-r   Ø-zə-wəč'ə-ɣe   ʼlʼə-r
      woman-the.ABS her-who-kill-PAST.NONFIN man-the.ABS

Ø-qe-k'°e.
he-PREV-come.PRES

(14) ʼlʼ-ew   ɕ°əzə-r   Ø-zə-wλč'ə-ɣe-r
      man-ADVL woman-ABS her-who-kill-PAST.NONFIN-the.ABS

Ø-qe-k'°e.
he-PREV-come.PRES

Affixal agreement—Set A for intransitive Ss and DOs, B for IOs, and C for transitive Ss—is supported by case-marking, where that exists. It shows ergative patterning, e.g. in Ubykh:

(15) wa-tət   (a-)k''a-n.
      that-man.ABS he(A)-go-PRES
      'That man is going.'

(16) yə-tətə-n   yə-məzə-n   za-m̃a
      this-man-OBL this-child-OBL an-apple.ABS

Ø-(ə-)n-t°ə-n.
it(A)-to.him(B)-he(C)-give-PRES

'This man gives an apple to this child.'

TABLE 1. *Abkhaz Consonants*

	Labial	Alveolar	Retroflex	Alveo-palatal	Palatal	Velar	Uvular	Pharyngeal
Stops								
Voiced								
Plain	b	d				g		
Labialized		d°				g°		
Palatalized						g′		
Voiceless								
Plain	p	t				k		
Labialized		t°				k°		
Palatalized						k′		
Glottalized								
Plain	p'	t'				k'	q'	
Labialized		t'°				k'°	q'°	
Palatalized						k''	q''	
Affricates								
Voiceless								
Plain		c	ç	tç	č			
Labialized				tç°				
Voiced								
Plain		3	3̣	dʑ	ǰ			
Labialized				dʑ°				
Glottalized								
Plain		c'	ç'	tç'	č'			
Labialized				tç'°				
Fricatives								
Voiceless								
Plain	f	s	ṣ	ç	š	x	X	ħ
Labialized				ç°	š°	x°	X°	ħ°
Palatalized						x′		
Voiced								
Plain	v	z	ẓ	ʑ	ž	γ		
Labialized				ʑ°	ž°	γ°		
Palatalized						γ′		
Nasals	m	n						
Vibrant		r						
Lateral		l						
Semivowels								
Plain	w				y			
Labialized					y°			

A few Circassian roots permit two constructions: (unmarked) S-OBL + O-ABS + V vs. (marked, "anti-passive") S-ABS + O-OBL + V. Many more "labile" roots may be either transitive or intransitive, depending on deletion of S or DO. Questions are formed by particles. Subordination is by non-finite verb plus subordinating particle. Both these constructions are illustrated below for Abkhaz:

(17) *s-y°ə́za   y-an*
      my-friend his-mother

      d-anə̀-tç̌'a-Ø,   *warà*
      she(A)-when-fall.asleep-AOR.NONFIN you.MASC

wə-cà-Ø-ma   *nàsg'ə*
you(A)-go-AOR.NONFIN-Q   and

yə-wə̀-c-ca-Ø-da.
who-you-with-go-AOR.NONFIN-who?

'When my friend's mother fell asleep, did you go and who went with you?'

3. North Central and North East Caucasian.
NCC, also known as Nakh or Veinakh, consists of Chechen and Ingush (in Chechenia and Ingushetia, united for at least the latter half of the Soviet period as the Chechen-Ingush

TABLE 2. *Botlikh Consonants*

	Labial	Alveolar	Palato-Alveolar	Palatal	Lateral	Velar	Uvular	Pharyngeal	Laryngeal
Stops									
Voiced	b	d				g			
Voiceless									
Plain	p	t				k	q		ʔ
Long						k:			
Glottalized									
Plain		t'				k'	q'		
Long						k':			
Affricates									
Voiced			ǰ						
Voiceless									
Plain		c	č						
Long		c:	č:		kɬ:				
Glottalized									
Plain		c'	č'						
Long		c':	č':		kɬ:'				
Fricatives									
Voiced		z	ž		l				
Voiceless									
Plain		s	š	x′	ɬ		X		h
Long		s:	š:		ɬ:		X:	ħ:	
Nasals	m	n							
Vibrant		r							
Semivowels	w			y					

ASSR), and Bats or Tsova-Tush (in the Georgian village of Zemo Alvani).

NEC has three divisions:

(a) Avar-Andi-Dido consists of Avar itself; eight Andi languages (Andi proper, Botlikh, Ghodoberi, Karata, Chamalal, Tindi, Bagvalal, and Akhvakh); and five Dido (Tsez) languages (Dido proper, Hinukh, Khvarshi, Bezhta, and Hunzib).

(b) The Lak-Dargwa division contains only Lak and Dargwa, in southern Daghestan; Kubachi is sometimes treated as a separate language.

(c) The Lezgian languages include Lezgi, Tabassaran, Aghul, Tsakhur, and Rutul as well as Udi, Budukh, Khinalugh, Kryts, and Archi. Their range is centered on Daghestan, with extensions into Azerbaijan, Georgia, and Chechenia.

3.1. Phonology. Vowel systems can be complicated by diphthongs, length, umlaut, nasalization, and pharyngealization. Strong or geminate consonants are general, and laterals abound in the Avar-Andi-Dido group. The Botlikh consonant system is shown in Table 2.

Tonal accent has been noted for a number of NEC languages (Kibrik et al. 1978). Four tones are the maximum observed. Four accentual patterns can occur:

(a) The prosodic scheme of the word is defined as a sequence of tonal characteristics of its constituent syllables, as in the Gigatl dialect of Chamalal.

(b) The tone of one syllable predetermines that of another, as in Bezhta.

(c) Tone and stress combine, as in Rutul.

(d) Dynamic stress occurs, as in Lezgi.

3.2. Morphology. Relatively simple verb structures are offset by rich case systems, whose complexity arises from their variety of locatives. The system in Andi has been described as follows: for each of seven series, there are essive, allative, and elative forms. The series signify 'on' (horizontal), 'on' (vertical), comitative, 'in' (spatial, sg. objects), 'beneath', 'in' (masses), and 'in' (spatial, pl. objects).

Noun classes, essentially covert, range from zero (Udi) to two (N. Tabassaran), three (Avar), four (Lak), five (Chamalal), six (Chechen), and eight (Bats). In some languages, verbs do not agree with any NP (Aghul, Lezgi); in others, there is personal agreement (Udi); in still others, agreement of person and class (Bats, Lak, Dargwa, Tabassaran); finally, in some there is class-agreement only. Subordination is achieved by the use of non-finite verbs. Five-way deixis is not unknown. Bats idiosyncratically extends its vigesimal numeral system beyond the usual '99', so that '10,321' = '(25×20×20)+(16×20)+1'.

3.3. Syntax. Patterns of word-order are SOV, GN, AN, NP + postposition, and relative + head. Variety in case-marking patterns for the central arguments of the verb depends on whether the verb is intransitive, transitive, affective, of perception, or of possession, as in Avar:

(18) *yas   yekerula.*
     girl.ABS run.PRES
     'The girl runs away.'

(19) *ins:uc:a vas   vecula.*
     father.ERG son.ABS praise.PRES
     'The father praises (his) son.'

(20) *ins:uye vasul   rok'l:'ula.*
     father.DAT sons.ABS love.PRES
     'The father loves (his) sons.'

(21) *ins:uda ču   bix'ula.*
     father.LOC horse.ABS see.PRES
     'The father sees (a) horse.'

(22) *ins:ul   yas   yigo.*
     father.GEN daughter.ABS be
     'The father has a daughter.'

The basic ergative pattern is sometimes subject to variation; thus antipassives occur, as in Dargwa:

(23) *nu-ni žuz   b-uč'ul-ra.*
     I-ERG book.ABS it-read-I
     'I read the book.'

(24) *nu   žuz-li   Ø-uč'ul-ra.*
     I.ABS book-ERG I-read-I
     'I am reading the book.'

The "double absolutive" configuration is widespread, though apparently limited to analytic verb-forms (Kibrik 1979), where a choice of constructions is sometimes possible, as in Chechen:

(25) *so   bolx   b-eš   v-u.*
     I.ABS work.ABS it-doing I-be
     'I habitually work.'

(26) *bolx   as   b-eš   b-u.*
     work.ABS I.ERG it-doing it-be
     'I am engaged in (some specific) work.'

(27) *as   bolx   b-o.*
     I.ERG work.ABS it-do
     'I work.'

Bats has adapted its basic ergative configuration in certain interesting contexts (Holisky 1984:184–187):

(a) A few intransitives (e.g. 'run', 'pray', 'fight') require 1st/2nd person subjects to be ergative; some other intransitives permit ergative or absolutive subjects, with the latter marked for non-agentivity.

(b) Among dative-S affective verbs, three ('hate', 'forget', and 'like') allow 1st/2nd person DOs to be either absolutive or ergative; the latter stresses the DO's desire to induce the relevant feeling.

(c) Among dative-S perception verbs, two ('see' and 'know') take ergative subjects in perfective aspectual forms, when some effort is involved on the subject's part.

[*See also* Georgian; North Caucasian Languages; *and* South Caucasian Languages.]

BIBLIOGRAPHY

Boeder, Winfried. 1979. Ergative syntax and morphology in language change: The South Caucasian languages. In Plank 1979, pp. 435–480.

Catford, John C. 1976. Ergativity in Caucasian languages. *North Eastern Linguistic Society* 6.37–48.

Catford, John C. 1977. Mountain of tongues: The languages of the Caucasus. *Annual Review of Anthropology* 6.283–314.

Čikobava, Arnold S. 1936. *Č'anuris gramat'ik'uli analizi* [The grammatical analysis of Laz]. Tbilisi: Academy Press.

Deeters, Gerhard. 1930. *Das kharthwelische Verbum.* Leipzig: Markert and Petters.

Greppin, John A. C., ed. 1989. *The indigenous languages of the Caucasus,* vol. 1, *South Caucasian* (edited by Alice C. Harris); vol. 2, *North West Caucasian* (edited by B. G. Hewitt); vol. 3, *North Central and North East Caucasian* (edited by Rieks Smeets and D. M. Job). New York: Caravan Books.

Hewitt, B. G. 1981. Caucasian languages. In *Languages of the*

Soviet Union, edited by Bernard Comrie et al., pp. 196–237. Cambridge and New York: Cambridge University Press.

Hewitt, B. G. 1987. Georgian: Ergative or active? *Lingua* 71.319–340.

Hewitt, B. G. 1995. *Georgian: A structural reference grammar.* Amsterdam: John Benjamins.

Holisky, Dee Ann. 1984. Anomalies in the use of the ergative case in Tsova-Tush (Batsbi). *Folia Slavica* 7.181–194.

Kibrik, Aleksandr E. 1979. Canonical ergativity and Daghestani languages. In Plank 1979, pp. 61–77.

Kibrik, Aleksandr E., et al. 1978. O prosodičeskoj strukture slov v dagestanskix jazykax. [On the prosodic structure of words in Daghestanian languages]. *Institut Russkogo Jazyka AN SSSR, Predvaritel'nye publikacii,* vypusk 115:1.5–26.

Kuipers, Aert H. 1960. *Phoneme and morpheme in Kabardian (Eastern Adyghe).* (Janua linguarum, Series minor, 8.) The Hague: Mouton.

Nikolayev, S. L., and S. A. Starostin. 1994. *A North Caucasian etymological dictionary.* Moscow: Asterisk.

Plank, Frans, ed. 1979. *Ergativity: Towards a theory of grammatical relations.* London: Academic Press.

Smeets, Henricus J. 1984. *Studies in West Circassian phonology and morphology.* Leiden: Hakuchi.

Van Den Berg, Helma. 1995. *A grammar of Hunzib (with texts and lexicon).* Munich and Newcastle: Lincom Europa.

Vogt, Hans. 1958. *Structure phonémique du géorgien.* (Norsk Tidsskrift for Sprogvidenskap, 18.) Oslo: Universitetsforlaget.

B. G. Hewitt

LANGUAGE LIST

[*For data on individual languages, see* Kartvelian Languages, Nakh-Daghestanian Languages, *and* Abkhaz-Adyghe Languages.]   B. Grimes

CAUSATIVE. While the term "causative construction" could in principle refer to any grammatical device that encodes causation, in practice the term has come to be used to express the kind of construction found in Turkish (2), where the verb expresses the notion of causation:

(1)   *Hasan öl-dü.*
     H.   die-PAST
     'Hasan died.'

(2)   *Ali   Hasan-ı öl-dür-dü.*
     A.   H.-ACC die-CAUS-PAST
     'Ali caused Hasan to die, killed Hasan.'

In (2), causation is expressed by means of a productive suffix; this is called a "morphological" causative. Cau-

sation can also be expressed periphrastically, as in the so-called "analytic" causative of English:

(3)   *Ned made his dog run.*

In Japanese, causation is sometimes expressed by a completely different lexical item, referred to as a "lexical" causative:

(4)   *Taroo   ga   sin-da.*
     T.   NOM   die-PAST
     'Taro died.'

(5)   *Ziroo   ga   Taroo   o   korosi-ta.*
     J.   NOM T.   ACC kill-PAST
     'Jiro killed Taro.'

In addition to these clearly defined types, there are intermediate varieties. Thus the French construction with *faire* 'to make' is formally analytic; however, it has many syntactic properties of a morphological causative, in that the sequence *faire* plus infinitive behaves like a single verb:

(6)   *Paul a   fait   venir   les enfants.*
     Paul has made come-INF the children
     'Paul has made the children come.'

Here *les enfants* must follow the whole sequence *faire* plus infinitive (as if object of the whole sequence), rather than occurring between *faire* and the infinitive (as if it were the object of *faire* or the subject of the infinitive).

In Japanese, the productive causative suffix *-(s)ase* produces morphological causatives; however, non-productive derivational patterns give rise to lexical causatives, e.g. *tome-* 'stop (tr.)' as lexical causative of *tomar-* 'stop (intr.)':

(7)   *Taroo   ga   Ziroo o   zibun no uti   no mae de*
     T.   NOM J.   ACC self GEN house GEN front at

     tomar-ase-ta.
     stop-CAUS-PAST

     'Taro caused Jiro to stop in front of his (Taro's/Jiro's) house.'

(8)   *Taroo   ga   Ziroo o   zibun no uti   no mae de*
     T.   NOM J.   ACC self GEN house GEN front at

     tome-ta.
     stop-PAST

'Taro stopped Jiro in front of his (Taro's/Jiro's) house.'

(In Japanese, the reflexive pronoun can refer back to the subject of the corresponding non-causative of a morphological causative, but not of a lexical causative.) The scale "lexical, morphological, analytic" corresponds to a semantic scale of cohesion between causing and caused events; for example, English *kill* implies a closer relation between cause and effect than does *cause to die*.

Cross-linguistically, causative constructions, in particular of the morphological type, show surprisingly similar syntactic and semantic patterns. Syntactically, if we assume a hierarchy of grammatical relations "subject, direct object, indirect object, other," then the grammatical relation assumed by the causee (i.e. the subject of the corresponding non-causative) tends to occupy the highest position on the hierarchy that is not otherwise occupied (Comrie 1975). This can be seen by comparing Turkish (2) above with the following additional sentences:

(9)   *Dişçi   mektub-u müdür-e   imzala-t-tı.*
      dentist letter-ACC director-DAT sign-CAUS-PAST
      'The dentist got the director to sign the letter.'

(10) *Dişçi Hasan-a mektub-u   müdür   tarafından*
      dentist H.-DAT letter-ACC   director by

      göster-t-ti.
      show-CAUS-PAST

      'The dentist got the director to show the letter to Hasan.'

The pattern illustrated by Turkish is by far the most widespread single pattern across the world's languages. However, exceptions to it are found in various languages, in which a causee of the types in (2) or (9) receives a lower ranking—as in Finnish, where the causee appears in a locative case:

(11) *Minä   rakennut-i-n   talo-n   muurare-i-lla.*
      I   build.CAUS-PAST-1.SG house-ACC bricklayer-PL-on
      'I got the bricklayers to build the house.'

In Sanskrit, two accusative noun phrases may occur, though detailed studies of such "doubling" in various languages suggest that only one is a syntactic direct object.

(12) *Rāma-ḥ   bhṛtya-ṃ   kaṭa-ṃ   kār-aya-ti.*
      Rama-NOM servant-ACC mat-ACC prepare-CAUS- SG.
      'Rama got the servant to prepare the mat.'

Some languages allow alternative grammatical expressions of the causee in certain cases, and these often correlate with semantic distinctions (Cole 1983). In Kannaḍa, for instance, the causative of a transitive construction may have its causee either in the dative, in accordance with the above pattern, or in the instrumental. Use of the dative implies that the causee has less control over whether the situation comes about, while use of the instrumental implies greater control:

(13) *Avanu nana-ge   biskeṭ-annu tinn-is-id-anu.*
      he   I-DAT   biscuit-ACC eat-CAUS-PAST- SG.
      'He fed me the biscuit.'
(14) *Avanu nann-inda biskeṭ-annu tinn-is-id-anu.*
      he   I-INSTR   biscuit-ACC eat-CAUS-PAST- SG.
      'He got me to eat the biscuit.'

A similar opposition is expressed in Japanese by the alternation of accusative and dative case markers:

(15) *Taroo ga Ziroo o   ik-ase-ta.*
      T.   NOM J.   ACC   go-CAUS-PAST
      'Taro made Jiro go.'
(16) *Taroo ga Ziroo ni   ik-ase-ta.*
      T.   NOM J.   DAT   go-CAUS-PAST
      'Taro got Jiro to go.'

A range of articles treating theoretical and descriptive aspects of causative constructions is found in Shibatani 1976, and a set of more recent articles in Comrie and Polinsky 1993. Song 1996 is a recent survey of the field.

[*See also* Clause; Morphology; Semantics; *and* Transitivity and Voice.]

BIBLIOGRAPHY

Cole, Peter. 1983. The grammatical role of the causee in universal grammar. *International Journal of American Linguistics* 49.115–133.

Comrie, Bernard. 1975. Causatives and universal grammar. *Transactions of the Philological Society* 1974:1–32.

Comrie, Bernard, and Maria Polinsky, eds. 1993. *Causatives and transitivity.* Amsterdam and Philadelphia: Benjamins.

Shibatani, Masayoshi, ed. 1976. *The grammar of causative constructions.* (Syntax and semantics, 6.) New York: Academic Press.

Song, Jae Jung. 1996. *Causatives and causation.* London and New York: Longman.

BERNARD COMRIE

C-COMMAND. Certain relations and dependencies between phrases in a S[entence] are sensitive to the hierarchical organization of constituents of the sentence, e.g. the following:

(a) The relation between a pronoun used as a bound variable and its antecedent: the condition on pronominal binding states that a pronoun must be c-commanded by its antecedent.

(b) The relation between a *wh*-phrase and the position it binds: the condition on proper binding states that the trace of a *wh*-phrase must be c-commanded by the *wh*-phrase.

(c) The relation between a reflexive or a reciprocal anaphor and its antecedent: Principle A of the Binding Theory states that an anaphor must be c-commanded by its antecedent in a local domain.

(d) The relation between a name and a coreferential pronoun: Principle C of the Binding Theory states that a name cannot be c-commanded by a pronoun coreferential with it.

(e) Scope relations in general, the scope of negation in particular, and the distribution of negative polarity items (which must be c-commanded by the negative element).

Naturally, there is considerable discussion as to the appropriate characterization of the c-command relation—and as to whether the same notion is at work in all of the above cases, and any other relevant ones. C-command is a member of a family of *command relations,* which share the following general idea: Node A commands node B in a tree representation if there is a constituent C which meets property P and contains both A and B. It is usually stipulated that command relations are not reflexive; i.e., a node does not command itself.

The various definitions found in the literature differ on how they state property P. For c-command—introduced under the name "in construction with" by Klima 1964, to treat relations as in (e) above—P reads: C is the first constituent containing A and some other material (i.e., C is the first branching node over A). Langacker 1969 takes P to be: C is the first S node containing A. Lasnik 1976 modifies this to: C is the first cyclic node containing A.

Langacker and Lasnik are concerned mostly with relations of type (d) above.

C-command was rediscovered in a slightly different form by Reinhart 1983, who is also responsible for the name; she deals mostly with relations as in (d) above. She states P as: C is the first branching node over A, or the node immediately above it if both nodes are of the same syntactic category.

M-command is introduced by Aoun and Sportiche 1982 (with a review of several other notions), in the context of a discussion of the Government relation. They state P as: C is the first maximal projection containing A. I-command is also sometimes argued for in the literature, and states P as: C is the first node containing A.

Naturally, the correct formulation of the relation depends on a fine analysis of constituent structure. Much debate continues in this area.

[*See also* Anaphora *and* Phrase Structure.]

BIBLIOGRAPHY

Aoun, Joseph, and Dominique Sportiche. 1982. On the formal theory of government. *Linguistic Review* 2.211–236.

Klima, Edward S. 1964. Negation in English. In *The structure of language,* edited by Jerry A. Fodor and Jerrold J. Katz, pp. 246–323. Englewood Cliffs, N.J.: Prentice-Hall.

Langacker, Ronald. 1969. On pronominalization and the chain of command. In *Modern studies in English: Readings in transformational grammar,* edited by David A. Reibel and Sanford A. Schane, pp. 160–186. Englewood Cliffs, N.J.: Prentice-Hall.

Lasnik, Howard. 1976. Remarks on coreference. *Linguistic Analysis* 2.1–22.

Reinhart, Tanya. 1983. *Anaphora and semantic interpretation.* London: Croom Helm. Chicago: University of Chicago Press.

HILDA KOOPMAN

CELTIC LANGUAGES. The earliest Celts are associated with two major Central European Iron Age cultures—Halstatt, dated to the 7th century BCE, and La Tène, dated to the 5th century BCE. From this central location, the Celts spread throughout Europe in different migrations: southeast through the Balkans and into Asia Minor; south into Italy (they captured Rome in 390 BCE); west into the Iberian peninsula; and north to the Atlantic coast and across into Britain and Ireland, where they were dominant by the 3rd century BCE. Today, the surviving Celtic-speaking communities are located in the peripheries of states with other majority languages: Brittany, Wales, and Ireland each claim around half a million speakers, and about 80,000 speakers remain in northwest Scotland. Many emigrant Celts are dispersed among other majority populations, especially in the New World. Ethnic communities were established in America, notably by Scottish Gaels in Nova Scotia, from the late 18th century, and by Welsh settlers in Argentine Patagonia in 1865. A few native speakers of Patagonian Welsh and Cape Breton Gaelic still remain.

1. Continental Celtic (see Evans 1981). The first direct mentions of the Celts are to be found in the writings of Greek and Roman ethnographers and historians, who identified them as a separate people speaking a distinctive tongue. This language, Continental or Common Celtic, has been partially reconstructed from place names, inscriptions, and references in Latin texts, and has long been established as a member of the I[ndo-] E[uropean] family. It is distinguished by, e.g., its loss of IE *p*: cf. Latin *pater,* Gaelic *athair* 'father'. There seems to have been a range of Celtic dialects even in the earliest period; these are reflected in the remains of Gaulish, Celtiberian, and Lepontic (northern Italy), though the evidence is limited, and some of it is strongly in dispute. No direct evidence of Galatian (Asia Minor) remains, though it survived until the 5th century CE.

2. Insular Celtic. Apart from possible enclaves, Celtic speech appears to have died out on the European continent by 500 CE. In Britain, however, Celtic languages survived the Roman occupation. Scotland north of the Forth-Clyde line (the domain of the Picts) had avoided Romanization, and Ireland had not undergone Roman occupation at all. The modern Celtic languages derive from Insular Celtic (see Schmidt 1993). There are two branches: *Brythonic* or *British* (rarely called "Gallo-Britonnic," Britain being regarded as on a continuum with Gaul), and *Goedelic* or *Gaelic.* These are differentiated by, e.g., their treatments of IE *kʷ,* which became *p* in British (and Gaulish), and eventually *k* in Gaelic. In the ancient Ogam script, which was based on the Latin alphabet, the symbol for this labiovelar is transliterated by scholars as *q*; thus Old Welsh *map* 'son' is in Ogam Irish *maqq-.*

The two branches are usually referred to as *P-Celtic* and *Q-Celtic* (Schmidt 1993). To P-Celtic belong Welsh (Northern British) (Thomas 1992), Pictish (as far as the evidence shows), and Cornish (George 1993), which died out in the 18th century. The ancestors of the Bretons emigrated from southwestern Britain in the 5th century. They may have amalgamated with surviving Celtic speakers in northwestern Gaul; the evidence is disputed. (On Breton, see Stephens 1993.) Q-Celtic is divided into two groups: Western Gaelic, represented by Irish (Ó Murchú 1985); and Eastern Gaelic, including Scottish Gaelic (MacAulay 1992) and Manx (the last speaker of which died in 1974; see Broderick 1984). Each of the extant languages has a range of dialects.

3. Typological affinities and distinctive features. Typologically, Celtic languages show affinities with the Western European languages with which they have long had contact. In constructions and vocabulary, they show evidence of scholarly influence from Latin; Welsh also reflects its ancient contact with that language as well as the modern influence of English. The Gaelic languages contain many English calques and borrowings; Breton shows strong influences from French in the same areas—with additional phonological relationships, such as comparable loss of final nasals.

Modern Celtic languages also have features which distinguish them from their neighbors. Their basic word order is Verb + Subject + Object (or Complement)—though this was not the case in Continental Celtic, as far as we can judge. For example, 'Tom is in the house' has the following shapes:

(1)   Scottish: *Tha Tom anns an taigh.*
       Irish: *Tá Tom san tigh.*
       Welsh: *Mae Tom yn y tŷ.*
       Breton: *Emañ Tom en ti.*

The order of elements above is Verb + Subject + Complement (Prepositional Phrase). Items may be highlighted by placing them at the front of the sentence. This was originally accomplished by means of a preceding verbal element and a following main verb in the relative form, as in Scottish:

(2)   *(Se) Tom a leughas an leabhar.*
       '(It is) Tom who reads the book.'

But such a construction has come to be the neutral word order in Breton:

(3)   *Tom   a   lenn   al   levr.*
       T.   REL   read   the   book
       'Tom is reading the book.'

TABLE 1. *Celtic Mutation*

	'dog'	'his dog'	'her dog'
Scottish	*cù* /ku:/	*a chù* /ə xu:/	*a cù* /əku:/
Irish	*cú* /ku:/	*a chú* /ə xu:/	*a cú* /ə ku:/
Welsh	*ci* /ki:/	*ei gi* /i gi:/	*ei chi* /i xi:/
Breton	*ki* /ki:/	*e gi* /e gi:/	*e c'hi* /e xi:/

Celtic languages have no verb 'have'. Possession is expressed by the verb 'to be' + Possessed[SUBJ] + Possessor[LOC], as in Irish:

(4) *Tá an leabhar ag Tom.*
     is the book   at T.
     'Tom has the book.'

Some modern dialects construct their progressive, perfective, and prospective aspects by means of prepositional phrases with verbal nouns as heads:

(5a) Scottish: *Tha Tom a' leughadh an leabhair.*
(5b) Welsh: *Mae Tom yn darllen y llyfr.*
                is   T.   at/in reading the book.GEN
                'Tom is reading the book.'

When the object is pronominal, it precedes the verbal noun, as in Welsh:

(6) *Mae Tom yn ei   ddarllen.*
     is   T.   in its.MASC reading
     'Tom is reading it.'

However, Breton, and optionally Irish, construct the perfective by using 'have' (i.e. 'be' with a locative possessor) with a past participle.

One notable feature of Celtic languages is the extensive use of initial consonant *mutation* to carry morphological distinctions. We can illustrate some aspects of this complex phenomenon by looking at noun phrases consisting of possessive pronoun + 'dog', shown in Table 1.

The change stop → nasal is the third type of change affecting stops; it occurs after the Welsh 1st person possessive (*fy nghi* /və ŋhi:/ 'my dog'), and after the 3pl. possessive in some Gaelic dialects (*an cù* /ə ŋku:/ 'their dog'). In Breton, nasal mutation affects only initial *d*: *an nor* (*<dor*) /ə nɔ:r/ 'the door'. The mutations function differently in the different languages.

[*See also* Indo-European Languages.]

BIBLIOGRAPHY

Broderick, George. 1984. *A handbook of late spoken Manx.* 3 vols. Tubingen: Niemeyer.

Evans, D. Ellis. 1981. *The labyrinth of Continental Celtic.* London: British Academy.

George, Ken. 1993. Cornish. In *The Celtic languages*, edited by Martin Ball, pp. 410–468. London: Routledge.

Jackson, Kenneth H. 1953. *Language and history in early Britain.* Edinburgh: Edinburgh University Press.

MacAulay, Donald. 1992. The Scottish Gaelic language. In *The Celtic languages*, edited by Donald MacAulay, pp. 137–248. Cambridge: Cambridge University Press.

Ó Murchú, Mairtin. 1985. *The Irish language.* (Gnéithe dar nDúchas, 10.) Dublin: Department of Foreign Affairs.

Russell, Paul. 1995. *An introduction to the Celtic languages.* London: Longmans.

Schmidt, Karl Horst. 1993. Insular Celtic: P and Q Celtic*. In *The Celtic languages*, edited by Martin Ball, pp. 64–99. London: Routledge.

Stephens, Janig. 1993. Breton. In *The Celtic languages*, edited by Martin Ball, pp. 349–409. London: Routledge.

Thomas, Alan R. 1992. The Welsh Language. In *The Celtic languages*, edited by Donald MacAulay, pp. 215–345. Cambridge: Cambridge University Press.

DONALD MACAULAY

LANGUAGE LIST

Breton: also called Brezhoneg. Over 500,000 speakers in France and USA. In France: Western Brittany, and dispersed in eastern Brittany and Breton emigrant communities throughout the world. Dialects are Leonais, Tregorrois, Vannetais, Cornouaillais. Some claim to be monolingual in Breton. As of 1974, 18,000 speakers were children under 14 years; 56,250 between 15 and 24; 423,000 between 25 and 64; 168,000 over 65. No official status. Strong nationalistic movement demanding recognition, a place in the schools, media, and public life. In USA: 32,722 speakers.

Cornish: also called Curnoack, Kernewek. Spoken in United Kingdom. Ethnic population: 468,425 as of 1991. Duchy of Cornwall, southwest of England. A few in Canada and Australia. Related to Breton, Welsh, Gaulish (extinct), Irish Gaelic, Manx Gaelic, Scots Gaelic. Bilingualism in English. Some children grow up bilingual. Church services are held in Cornish. There are evening classes, correspondence courses, summer camps, children's play groups. There is a Cornish Language Board. It became extinct as a first language from 1777 to 1894, but is being revived. Two spelling systems are in use.

Gaelic, Hiberno-Scottish: also called Gaoidhealg, Hiberno-Scottish Classical Common Gaelic. Formerly spoken in United Kingdom, in Ireland and Scotland. Archaic literary language based on 12th-century Irish, formerly used by professional classes in Ireland until the 17th century and Scotland until the 18th century. Printed in Roman script for use in Scotland.

Gaelic, Irish: also called Irish, Erse, Gaeilge. 260,000 speakers in Ireland, Northern Ireland, Scotland, Isle of Man, and USA. In Ireland: Western isles, northwest and southwest coasts; Galway, part of Mayo, Kerry, Donegal, Meath, Cork, Waterford, Scotland (Albain). Dialects are Munster-Leinster (Southern Irish), Connacht (Western Irish), Donegal (Ulster, Northern Irish). Bilingualism in English. National language. In United Kingdom: Belfast and counties of Fermanagh and Armagh, Northern Ireland. In USA: Boston, Massachusetts.

Gaelic, Scottish: also called Gàidhlig, Gaelic, Gaidhlig Albannach, Erse, Scots Gaelic. 94,000 speakers in United Kingdom, Canada, Australia, and USA. In United Kingdom: 88,892 speakers. North and central counties of Ross, islands of Hebrides and Skye, Glasgow. Church Gaelic is based on the Perthshire dialect of two hundred years ago and is at a distance from spoken dialects. East Sutherlandshire dialect is so different from other spoken dialects as to be a barrier to communication. In some communities it is primarily used in the home, in church, and for social purposes. Books and journals are produced on various topics. Resurgence of interest in Scots Gaelic in the 1990s has been given a boost by the establishment of Scotland's own Parliament, for the first time in three hundred years. In Canada: 5,000 speakers. Nova Scotia, Cape Breton, Prince Edward Island. In Australia: New South Wales.

Manx: also called Gaelg, Gailck, Manx Gaelic. Formerly spoken in United Kingdom. Closely related to Scottish Gaelic. It became extinct during this century as a first language. There are efforts to revive it. Second language for 200 to 300 who have mainly learned it as adults. Used for some public functions. Different from Scottish Gaelic orthography.

Welsh: also called Cymraeg. 580,000 speakers in United Kingdom, Argentina, and Canada. In United Kingdom: 508,098 speakers. Northern, western, and southern Wales. Dialects are Northern Welsh, Southern Welsh, Patagonian Welsh. As of 1991, 44,600 between 5 and 9 years old spoke Welsh, 47,100 between 10 and 14 years old. As of 1998, 19% of the Welsh population speak the language, and 33% are able to understand it. Literature is being produced. The Royal National Eisteddfod meets annually. 88% of those questioned believe they should be proud of Welsh, and that it should be treated equally with English. There is an increase in the number of parents choosing a Welsh-medium education for their children. Official language. In Argentina: Patagonia, Chubut territory. Bilingualism in Spanish. As of 1998, there were first or second language speakers. Spoken here since around 1891.

B. GRIMES

CENTRAL AND SOUTHERN NEW GUINEA-KUTUBUAN LANGUAGES.

A branch of the Central and Western Main Section of the proposed TRANS-NEW GUINEA phylum. They are spoken in a broad belt from western Papua, Indonesia, into western and southern Papua New Guinea.

LANGUAGE LIST

Aekyom: also called Awin, Aiwin, Akium, West Awin. 8,000 speakers in Papua New Guinea, Western Province, Kiunga area. Dialects are North Awin, South Awin, East Awin.

Aghu: 3,000 speakers in Papua, Indonesia, the southern coastal area along the Digul River west of the Mandobo language, Merauke Kabupaten, Jair Kecamatan.

Aimele: also called Kware. 500 speakers in Papua New Guinea.

Asmat, Casuarina Coast: also called Kaweinag. 9,000 speakers in Papua, Indonesia. Dialects are Matia, Sapan (Safan).

Asmat, Central: also called Manowee, Jas, Yas. 7,000 speakers in Papua, Indonesia. Dialects are Simai (Simay), Misman, Ajam (Ayam). North Asmat is the most distinct dialect. Related to the Sempan language north of the rivers. Close to Kamoro and Citak. Many are becoming bilingual in Indonesian; some in neighboring languages.

Asmat, North: also called Keenok. 1,000 speakers in Papua, Indonesia.

Asmat, Yaosakor: also called Yaosakor, Asmat Pendalaman, Asomot. 2,000 speakers in Papua, Indonesia, the southern coast along the Sirac River, Merauke Kabupaten, Agats and Atsy Kecamatans.

Awyu, Miaro: also called Miaro, Pisa. 3,500 speakers in Papua, Indonesia, the southern coastal area, southwest of Wildeman River and east of Kampong River, inland from Pirimapun. Closely related to Siagha-Yenimu. A separate language from Nohon Awyu.

Awyu, Nohon: also called Auyu, Awya, Awju, Ajau, Avio, Nohon. 18,000 speakers in Papua, Indonesia. A separate language from Miaro Awyu. About nine dialects. Many becoming bilingual in Indonesian.

Bainapi: also called Pikiwa, Dibiasu, Turumasa. 400 speakers in Papua New Guinea, Western Province, villages of Makapa, Pikiwa, and Bamustu, via Balimo.

Beami: also called Bedamini, Bedamuni, Mougulu. 4,200 speakers in Papua New Guinea, Western Province, east of Nomad, extending into Southern Highlands Province. Dialects are Komofio, North Beami.

Bimin: 2,000 speakers in Papua New Guinea, Sandaun Province, Bak-Bimin district, and Western Province. Dialects are Bim, Nimtep Weng. Closely related to Faiwol.

Bogaya: also called Pogaya, Bogaia. 300 speakers in Papua New Guinea, Western Province, some also in base of northern neck of Southern Highlands Province.

FIGURE 1. *Subgrouping of Central and Southern New Guinea-Kutubuan Languages*

```
Central and South New Guinea
  Asmat-Kamoro
    Casuarina Coast Asmat, Central Asmat, North Asmat,
    Yaosakor Asmat, Buruwai, Citak, Tamnim Citak, Diuwe,
    Kamberau, Kamoro, Sempan
  Awin-Pare
    Aekyom, Kamula, Pare
  Awyu-Dumut
    Awyu
      Miaro Awyu
      Nohon Awyu
      Jair
      Siagha-Yenimu
      Aghu
        Aghu, Tsakwambo
    Dumut
      Kombai, Mandobo, Wambon
    Sawi
    Unclassified Awyu-Dumut
      Korowai, North Korowai
  Bosavi
    Aimele, Bainapi, Beami, Edolo, Kaluli, Kasua,
    Onobasulu, Sonia
  Duna-Bogaya
    Bogaya, Duna
  East Strickland
    Fembe, Gobasi, Konai, Kubo, Odoodee, Samo
  Mombum
    Koneraw, Momina
  Ok
    Lowland Ok
      Iwur, Ninggerum, Yongkom
    Mountain Ok
      Bimin, Faiwol, Mian, Nakai, Ngalum, Setaman,
    Suganga, Telefol, Tifal, Urapmin
      Western Ok
        Burumakok, Kopkaka, Kwer, Marub, Tokuni
  Kutubuan
    East Kutubuan
      Fiwaga, Foi
    West Kutubuan
      Fasu
```

Burumakok: 40 speakers in Papua, Indonesia. Some bilingual ability. All ages.

Buruwai: also called Asienara, Asianara, Karufa, Madidwana, Sabakor. 700 speakers in Papua, Indonesia.

Citak: also called Cicak, Tjitak, Tjitjak, Kaunak, Amat Darat. 8,000 speakers in Papua, Indonesia. Dialects are Senggo, Komasma, Bubis, Esaun, Pirabanak, Vakam, Tiau. A closely related language to Asmat. Bilingual level estimates for Indonesian are 0 90%, 1 10%, 2 0%, 3 0%, 4 0%, 5 0%. Vigorous language use.

Citak, Tamnim: also called Tamnim, Asmat Darat. 290 speakers in Papua, Indonesia, near Senggo, villages of Tamnim, Epem, Zinak, Wowi. Merauke Kabupaten, Citak-Mitak Kecamatan. May be linguistically closer to Asmat, but the speakers want to be called Citak, not Asmat. Vigorous language use.

Diuwe: 100 speakers in Papua, Indonesia, 12 miles southwest of Sumo, east of the Catalina River.

Duna: also called Yuna. 11,000 speakers in Papua New Guinea, Southern Highlands Province, Lake Kopiago and Koroba districts, some in Western Highlands Province.

Edolo: also called Etoro, Edolo Ado, Etolo. 1,300 speakers in Papua New Guinea, Southern Highlands Province, Tari district, and Western Province, Nomad district; southwest of Mt. Sisa, 16 villages. Dialects are Eastern Edolo, Western Edolo. 60% are monolingual, 30% can use Huli, Onobasulu, or Beami as second language. All ages. All domains. Spoken and some written use in religious services, Local use in business. Vigorous language use. Parents transmit it to children. Positive attitude.

Faiwol: also called Faiwolmin, Fegolmin, Unkia, Kauwol, Kawol, Kavwol. 4,500 speakers in Papua New Guinea, Western Province, Tabubil district, at the headwaters of the Fly and Palmer Rivers. Not in Papua, Indonesia. Dialects are Wopkeimin, Ankiyakmin.

Fasu: also called Namome. 1,200 speakers in Papua New Guinea, Southern Highlands Province, Nipa district, south into Gulf Province and west to the Kikori River in Western Province. Dialects are Some, Kaibu (Kaipu), Namome (Namumi, Namuni).

Fembe: also called Sinale, Agala. 350 speakers in Papua New Guinea, Western Province, Upper Strickland River. Closest to Odoodee and Konai.

Fiwaga: also called Fimaga, Fiwage. 300 speakers in Papua New Guinea, Southern Highlands Province, northeast of Tama.

Foi: also called Foe, Mubi River. 2,800 speakers in Papua New Guinea, Southern Highlands Province, east and south of Lake Kutubu and Mubi River. Dialects are Ifigi, Kafa, Kutubu, Mubi.

Gobasi: also called Nomad. 1,100 speakers in Papua New Guinea, Western Province. Dialects are Gobasi (Bibo), Honibo, Oibae (Oiba). Related to Samo and Kubo.

Iwur: also called Iwoer. 1,000 speakers in Papua, Indonesia, border area in valley of Iwur River, Ok Iwur and east to Ok Denom.

Jair: also called Dyair, Djair, Yair, Awyu. 1,500 speakers in Papua, Indonesia, the southern coastal west side of Digul River, south of Kombai, east of Awyu.

Kaluli: also called Bosavi. 2,500 speakers in Papua New

Guinea, Southern Highlands Province, extending into Western Province, on the northern and western slopes of Mt. Bosavi. Dialects are Ologo, Kaluli, Walulu, Kugenesi. No significant dialect differences. Closely related to but different from Kasua. Bilingual level estimates are Tok Pisin: 0 60%, 1 20%, 2 15%, 3 5%, 4 0%, 5 0%; English: 0 89%, 1 8%, 2–5 3%. Some speakers between 15 and 25 years old speak a little Tok Pisin for common topics.

Kamberau: also called Kamrau, Iria. 1,570 speakers in Papua, Indonesia, southeastern Bomberai Peninsula around Kamrau Bay, villages of Ubia-Seramuku, Bahomia, Waho, Wamoma, Inari, Tanggaromi, Koi, Wamesa, Coa. Closely related to Buruwai.

Kamoro: also called Kamora, Mimika, Lakahia, Nagramadu, Umari, Mukamuga, Neferipi, Nefarpi, Nafarpi, Kaokonau. 8,000 speakers in Papua, Indonesia, the southern coast from Etna Bay to Mukamuga River. Dialects are Tarya, Yamur. Four other dialects. Many becoming bilingual in Indonesian.

Kamula: also called Wawoi. 800 speakers in Papua New Guinea, villages of Kamiyami (Wasapea), Aramia River area, and villages of Keseki and Somokopa, Wawoi Falls area, Western Province. The closest language is Pare. Speakers are basically monolingual. Some use Gogodala or Doso as second language.

Kasua: 600 speakers in Papua New Guinea, Southern Highlands Province, east and south of Mt. Bosavi, northeastern corner of Western Province, and northwestern corner of Gulf Province.

Kombai: also called Komboy. 5,000 speakers in Papua, Indonesia, the southern coastal area east of Senggo around Boma. Dialects are Wanggom (Wanggo, Wangom), Central Kombai, Tayan. Closely related to Wambon, Mandobo.

Konai: also called Mirapmin. 600 speakers in Papua New Guinea, Western Province, western side of Upper Strickland River. Closest to Odoodee and Fembe.

Koneraw: 200 speakers in Papua, Indonesia, the southern coast of Frederik Hendrik Island.

Kopkaka: also called Kopka. 250 speakers in Papua, Indonesia. Closely related to Kwer. No bilingual ability.

Korowai: also called Kolufaup. 700 speakers in Papua, Indonesia, the southern coastal area, north of Boma, east of Senggo. Younger speakers use Indonesian as second language.

Korowai, North: 100 speakers in Papua, Indonesia, north of Korowai area, southeast of Siradala, west of Awimbon.

Kubo: 1,000 speakers in Papua New Guinea, Western Province, Lake Murray district, northern half of Upper Strickland Census district, east of Strickland River, north of the Samo. A separate language from Samo and Gobasi, but related.

Kwer: 100 speakers in Papua, Indonesia. Closely related to Kopkaka. All ages.

Mandobo: also called Nub, Dumut, Mandobbo. "Kaeti" is a derogatory name sometimes used. 10,000 speakers in Papua, Indonesia, and Papua New Guinea. In Papua, Indonesia: Border area near Fly River on eastern side of Digul River between Tanahmerah and Mindiptanah. In Papua New Guinea: Western Province, east of Fly River around Maporoan and Kwem.

Marub: 100 speakers in Papua, Indonesia, between Kwer and Tokuni on the western bank of the Sirec River.

Mian: also called Mianmin. 2,200 speakers in Papua New Guinea. Dialects are Upper August River, Usage, Mianmin.

Mombum: also called Kemelom. 250 speakers in Papua, Indonesia, an island next to the southeastern coast of Frederik Hendrik Island. Closest to Koneraw.

Momina: 200 speakers in Papua, Indonesia, the lowlands just south of main ranges extending from south of Silimo east to south of Una language, Samboka village.

Momuna: also called Somahai, Somage, Sumohai. 2,000 speakers in Papua, Indonesia, the lowlands just south of main ranges extending from south of Silimo east to south of Una language. No bilinguals.

Nakai: 700 speakers in Papua, Indonesia. They report difficulty in understanding Indonesian or Malay.

Ngalum: 18,000 speakers in Papua, Indonesia, and Papua New Guinea. In Papua, Indonesia: 10,000 speakers in the valleys of Ok Sibil, Ok Tsop, and perhaps Ok Bon, border area in main range north of Muyu (Yongkom) and Iwur languages, northeast of Nakai. Dialects are Ngalum, Apmisibil, Sibil. In Papua New Guinea: 8,000 speakers in Sandaun Province. Dialects are Ngalum, Apmisibil, Sibil.

Ninggerum: also called Ninggrum, Ninggirum, Ningerum, Niyium, Kativa, Kasiwa, Obgwo, Tedi, Tidi. 4,000 speakers in Papua New Guinea and Papua, Indonesia. In Papua New Guinea: 3,000 speakers. Dialects are Kasuwa, Daupka. 40% are monolingual. 10% can speak Hiri Motu, 5% English, 50% Tok Pisin, 5% also speak neighboring languages (Yongkom, Faiwol, Telefol). All ages. All domains. Used in preschool and first two grades, oral use in church, songs, local business. Vigorous language use. Parents transmit it to children. Speakers are very positive toward Ninggerum. In Papua, Indonesia: 1,000 speakers at the border area and in Papua New Guinea between the Ok Birim and Ok Tedi Rivers.

Odoodee: also called Kalamo, Nomad, Tomu, Tomu River, Ododei. 410 speakers in Papua New Guinea. Closest to Samo-Kubo and Konai.

Onobasulu: also called Onabasulu. 700 speakers in Papua New Guinea, Southern Highlands Province midway between Mt. Sisa and Mt. Bosavi. 50% are monolingual. Others use Kaluli, Edolo, or Tok Pisin as second languages. All ages. It is the first language children learn. Also used by Edolo speakers as a second language. All domains. Oral and written use in preschool and adult literacy. Vigorous language use. Parents transmit it to children. Speakers have a very positive attitude toward Onabasulu.

Pare: also called Pa, Akium-Pare. 2,000 speakers in Papua New Guinea, Western Province.

Samo: also called Daba, Nomad, Supei. 900 speakers in Papua New Guinea, Western Province, Lake Murray district, southern Upper Strickland Census district, east of the Strickland River, north of Nomad. Bilingualism in Hiri Motu.

Sawi: also called Sawuy, Aejauroh. 3,500 speakers in Papua, Indonesia. Closest to Awyu. Bilingual level estimates for Indonesian are 0 75%, 1 25%, 2 0%, 3 0%, 4 0%, 5 0%.

Sempan: also called Nararapi. 1,000 speakers in Papua, Indonesia, the mid southern coast, between Kokonao and Agats, east of Kamoro and west of Asmat languages. Close to Kamoro.

Setaman: 200 speakers in Papua New Guinea, Sandaun Province.

Siagha-Yenimu: also called Siagha, Syiagha, Sjiagha, Sijagha, Oser, Yenimu, Jenimu. 3,000 speakers in southeastern Papua, Indonesia, near the coast, north of lower Digul River.

Sonia: 300 speakers in Papua New Guinea, Western Province and Southern Highlands Province, 10 to 20 miles west and southwest of Bosavi.

Suganga: also called Wagarabai, North Mianmin. 700 speakers in Papua New Guinea. Sandaun Province, Amanab district. Closely related to Mianmin.

Telefol: also called Telefomin, Telefolmin, Teleefool. 5,400 speakers in Papua New Guinea. Sandaun Province, Telefomin district. Dialects are Telefol, Feramin.

Tifal: also called Tifalmin. 3,200 speakers in Papua New Guinea, Sandaun Province, Telefomin district. Dialects are Tifal, Asbalmin. None are monolingual. They use Tok Pisin, Telefol, Faiwol, or Opti as second languages. All ages. All domains. Used in preschool. Oral and written use in churches. Oral use in local business. Personal letters. Vigorous language use. Parents transmit it to children. Speakers are eager to use and preserve the language.

Tokuni: 100 speakers in Papua, Indonesia, the lowlands just south of main ranges, south of Momina and Kopkaka, Tokuni village. Dialect chain running east and west. Closely related to Kopkaka. No bilingual speakers.

Tsakwambo: also called Kotogüt, Tsokwambo. 500 speakers in Papua, Indonesia, the southern coastal area on upper Digul River north of Mandobo language. Dialects or related languages: Ederah, Kia, Upper Digul, Upper Kaeme.

Urapmin: 395 speakers in Papua New Guinea, Sandaun Province, Telefomin district.

Wambon: 3,000 speakers in Papua, Indonesia, the southern coastal area northeast of Mandobo language.

Yongkom: also called Yongom, Yonggom. 6,000 speakers in Papua New Guinea and Papua, Indonesia. In Papua New Guinea: 4,000 speakers. In Papua, Indonesia: 2,000 speakers

on the southern coastal border area just north of where Fly River forms border between Papua and Papua New Guinea. Dialects are Northern Muyu (North Kati, North Moejoe, Niinati, Ninatie, Kati-Ninanti, Kataut), Southern Muyu (South Kati, South Moejoe, Digoel, Digul, Metomka, Kati Metomka, Ok Bari). B. GRIMES

CENTRAL-EASTERN MALAYO-POLYNESIAN LANGUAGES. These constitute one of the two main branches of Malayo-Polynesian within the AUSTRONESIAN family.

LANGUAGE LIST

[*See the language lists for* Central Malayo-Polynesian languages *and* Eastern Malayo-Polynesian languages.]

Unclassified Central–Eastern Malayo-Polynesian Languages

Adabe: also called Ataura, Atauru, Atauro, Raklu-Un, Raklu Un. 1,000 speakers in Timor Lorosae. Ethnic population: 1,000 (1981), Atauro Island, north of Dili on Timor Island. Reported to be different from Galoli dialects on Atauro.

Kuri: also called Modan, Nabi. 500 speakers in Papua, Indonesia, on southwestern Bomberai Peninsula, along Nabi (Kuri) River west from Wandamen Bay, sixteen villages. Closely related to Irarutu. B. GRIMES

CENTRAL-EASTERN OCEANIC LANGUAGES. These form a branch of OCEANIC.

[*For language lists, consult the articles on* Remote Oceanic Languages, South Vanuatu Languages, *and* Southeast Solomonic Languages.] B. GRIMES

CENTRAL INDO-ARYAN LANGUAGES. A subgroup of INDO-ARYAN LANGUAGES. They are spoken predominantly in western and central India, extending into Nepal and Pakistan; they also include the Romani (Gypsy) languages spoken in Europe and the Americas.

LANGUAGE LIST

Aer: 100 speakers remain in Pakistan. Dialects are Jikrio Goth Aer, Jamesabad Aer. They also speak Sindhi (adult men only for common topics), Panjabi (adult men of Jikrio Goth only for common topics), and have worship songs in Gujarati. Women are monolingual. 100% of boys and 25% of

FIGURE 1. *Subgrouping of Central Indo-Aryan Languages*

Bhil
Barli Bareli, Palya Bareli, Rathwi Bareli, Bauria, Bhilali, Bhili, Bhilori, Chodri, Dhodia, Dubli, Dungra Bhil, Gamit, Adiwasi Garasia, Rajput Garasia, Mawchi, Pardhi, Rathawi, Wagdi

Dom
Domari

Gujarati
Aer, Gujarati, Jandavra, Kachi Koli, Parkari Koli, Wadiyara Koli, Saurashtra, Vaghri, Vasavi

Khandesi
Ahirani, Dhanki, Khandesi

Panjabi
Eastern Panjabi

Rajasthani
  Marwari
    Dhatki, Goaria, Loarki, Marwari, Marwari, Mewari
  Unclassified Rajasthani
    Bagri, Gujari, Gurgula, Harauti, Lambadi, Gade Lohar, Malvi, Nimadi

Romani
Balkan Romani
  Northern Romani
    Baltic Romani, Carpathian Romani, Kalo Finnish Romani, Sinte Romani, Welsh Romani
Vlax Romani

Western Hindi
Bundeli
  Hindustani
    Hindi
    Urdu
    Sansi
      Kabutra, Sansi
  Unclassified Western Hindi
    Bhaya, Braj Bhasha, Chamari, Ghera, Gowli, Haryanvi, Kanauji

Unclassified Central Indo-Aryan
Parya, Sonha, Dangaura Tharu, Kathoriya Tharu

girls attend Sindhi medium schools. All ages. Aer is used within the group. Sindhi-based script.

Ahirani: also called Ahiri. 779,000 speakers in India, in Maharashtra; Gujarat. Preliminary findings are that it is distinct from Khandesi.

Bagri: also called Bagari, Bagria, Bagris, Baorias, Bahgri. 2,007,000 speakers in India and Pakistan. In India: 1,807,000 speakers in Punjab, Rajasthan, Haryana, Madhya Pradesh. In Pakistan: 200,000 speakers in the Sindh and Punjab. Related to Bhil groups and Marwari. Does not seem close to any other language. They speak some Sindhi and understand some Urdu.

Bareli, Barli: also called Barewali, Bareli Pauri. 150,000 speakers in India. Bareli Barli not intelligible with Rathwi Bareli or Palya Bareli. Dialect center in Maharashtra, Nandurbar district, Dhadgaon tahsil. Bilingualism in Hindi, Marathi, Ahirani, Nimadi is very limited. All domains except education. Vigorous language use. Strong and positive attitude toward Bareli Barli.

Bareli, Palya: also called Pali, Palodi, Palya Bareli. 10,000 speakers in India. Bareli Palya not intelligible with Rathwi Bareli or Barli Bareli. Dialect center in Madhya Pradesh, Barwani district, Rajpur tahsil, Choutharya village. Bilingualism in Hindi, Marathi, Ahirani, Nimadi is limited. All domains except education. Vigorous language use. Strong and positive attitude toward Bareli Palya.

Bareli, Rathwi: also called Barel, Pauri, Pawri, Pawari, Rathwi Pauri, Rathi, Rathia. 1,100,000 speakers in India. Rawthi Bareli not intelligible with Palya Bareli or Barli Bareli. Bareli Barli and Rathwi Bareli not intelligible with Vasavi or Bhilori. Bilingualism in Hindi, Marathi, Ahirani is limited. All domains except education. Vigorous language use. Strong and positive attitudes toward Bareli Rathwi. Modified Devanagari alphabet.

Bauria: also called Badak, Babri, Basria, Bawari, Bawaria, Bhoria, Vaghri, Baori. 247,872 speakers in India: Punjab, Himachal Pradesh, Delhi, Haryana, Chandigarh, Rajasthan, Uttar Pradesh.

Bhaya: 70 speakers remain in Pakistan. Similarity of key morphemes: The possessive postposition with g- contrasts with all other languages in the area. Gender endings match Rajasthani. This might be the same as Bhoyari (a dialect of Malvi) in India. It may be in the Western Hindi group.

Bhilali: also called Bhilala. 1,000,000 speakers in India.

Bhili: also called Bhilbari, Bhilboli, Bhilla, Bhil, Vil, Bhagoria, Lengotia. 1,300,000 speakers in India. Dialects are Ahiri, Anarya (Pahadi), Barel, Bhim, Charani, Chodhri, Dehawali, Chodia, Dubli, Gamti, Girasia, Habura, Konkani, Kotali, Kotvali (Kotwalia), Magra Ki Boli, Nahari (Baglani) Naikdi, Panchali, Pawri, Ranawat, Rani Bhil, Rathvi, Siyalgir, Wagdi. Patelia in Gujarat is inherently intelligible with Bhili. Bhili of Ratlam district in Madhya Pradesh is inherently intelligible with Wagdi. Connecting link between Gujarati and Rajasthani (Marwari). Bhili is a Scheduled Tribe in Rajasthan, Gujarat, Maharashtra, Madhya Pradesh, Tripura; Kotvali is a Scheduled Tribe in Gujarat and Maharashtra. Limited proficiency in Hindi. Spoken as mother tongue by the Patelia in Madhya Pradesh.

Bhilori: also called Bhilodi, Patelia. 100,000 speakers in India in Maharashtra, northern Dhule district, around Dhadgaon; Gujarat. Dialects are Bhilodi, Noiri (Satpuda Noiri). Noiri may be the same as Nora. 60% intelligibility with Marathi, 50% with Vasavi. Might be intelligible with Dungra Bhil. Limited bilingual proficiency in Marathi. Spoken as mother tongue by the Patelia in Gujarat.

Braj Bhasha: also called Braj, Braj Bhakha, Brij Bhasha, Antarbedi, Antarvedi, Bijbhasha, Bri, Briju, Bruj. 44,000 speakers in India, in Uttar Pradesh, Agra region; Rajasthan, Bharatpur, Sawai Madhopur districts; Haryana, Gurgaon district; Bihar; Madhya Pradesh; Delhi. Dialects are Braj Bhasha, Antarbedi, Bhuksa, Sikarwari, Jadobafi, Dangi. Bhuksa is sometimes mentioned as a dialect of Kanauji.

Bundeli: also called Bundel Khandi. 644,000 speakers in India. Dialects are Standard Bundeli, Pawari (Powari), Lodhanti (Rathora), Khatola, Banaphari, Kundri, Nibhatta, Tirhari, Bhadauri (Towargarhi), Lodhi, Kosti, Kumbhari, Gaoli, Kirari, Raghobansi, Nagpuri Hindi, Chhindwara Bundeli. Intelligibility testing of Standard varieties gave 83%, 92%, and 98%. Chhatapur dialect is widely understood. Other dialects listed are Standard Braj of Mathura, Aligarh, western Agra; Standard Braj of Bulandshahr; Standard Braj of eastern Agra, southern Morena, southern Bharatpur; Braj merging into Kanauji in Etah, Mainpuri, Budaun, and Bareilly; Braj merging into the Bhadauri subdialect in northern Morena; Braj merging into Jaipuri (Rajasthani) in northern Bharatpur and Sawai Uradhopur; Bhuksa in southern Nainital. The uneducated have limited ability in Hindi. Bundeli is used in the home. There is ethnic pride in the language and culture. Favorable attitudes toward Chhatapur dialect.

Chamari: also called Chamar, Chambhar Boli, Chambhari. 5,325 speakers in India in Madhya Pradesh, Uttar Pradesh, Maharashtra.

Chodri: also called Chaudri, Chodhari, Chaudhari, Choudhary, Choudhara. 226,534 speakers in India, mainly in Gujarat, Broach and Dangs districts. Some in Maharashtra, Karnataka, Rajasthan.

Dhanki: also called Dhanka, Dangi, Dangri, Dangs Bhil, Tadavi, Tadvi Bhil, Kakachhu-Ki Boli. 138,000 speakers in India, in Gujarat, Dangs district; Maharashtra, Jalgaon district; Karnataka; Rajasthan. Bilingualism in Gujarati. Trade language.

Dhatki: also called Dhati. 200,000 speakers in Pakistan in Lower Sind in Tharparkar and Sanghar districts. Dialects are Eastern Dhatki, Southern Dhatki, Central Dhatki, Barage, Malhi. Varies considerably from northern Marwari, although they claim to understand one another. The Malhi are an ethnic group living in three main areas. Those in the Kunri-Pithoro-Noakot-Mithi area speak a dialect with 80% lexical similarity to Dhatki, 74% to Sindhi, and work as water-drawers. People also speak some Sindhi and Urdu. Dhatki of Rajasthan and Dhatki of Thar are 88% lexically similar. Sindhi-based script.

Dhodia: also called Dhori, Dhore, Dhowari, Doria. 139,000 speakers in India, in. Gujarat, Surat and Valsad districts, Daman and Diu, Dadra and Nagar Haveli; Madhya Pradesh; Maharashtra; Karnataka; Rajasthan. Bilingualism in Gujarati.

Domari: also called Middle Eastern Romani, Tsigene, Gypsy. 500,000 speakers in Iran, Iraq, European Turkey, Syria, Israel, Jordan, European Russia, Palestinian West Bank and Gaza, Lybia, Uzbekistan, India, and Egypt. In Iran: 80,000 speakers. Kurbati dialect is in western Iran, Karachi in northern Iran. Dialects are Kurbati (Ghorbati), Qinati, Yürük, Koli, Karachi, Luli, Maznoug, Nawar. In Iraq: 50,000 speakers. In European Turkey: Mainly in western Turkey, some in eastern Turkey. Dialects are Karachi, Beludji, Marashi. In Syria: Dialects are Nawar, Kurbati, Beirut, Nablos, Barake. In Israel: Mainly Jerusalem (Old City), Bir Zeit near Ramallah. Not intelligible to Romani speakers. Bilingualism in South Levantine Spoken Arabic. The first language of children in some places. In European Russia: Karachi dialect is in the Caucasus, Luli and Maznoug in Uzbekistan. Dialects are Karachi, Luli, Maznoug. In Palestinian West Bank and Gaza: Gaza and Bir Zeit near Ramallah. Not intelligible to Romani speakers. Bilingualism in South Levantine Spoken Arabic. The first language of children in some places. In Jordan: Dialects are Nawar, Kurbat, Barake. In India: Bihar, Saran and Champaran districts. Dialects are Domaki, Wogri-Boli. A Gypsy language partly used for in-group identification. In Egypt: The Ghagar live mainly in Dakahlia Governorate, north of Cairo. Dialects are Nawar (Ghagar), Helebi. Reports that many now speak Arabic.

Dubli: also called Dubala, Dubla, Rathod, Talavia. 202,000 speakers in India.

Dungra Bhil: 200,000 speakers in India, in Gujarat, Baroda district; Madhya Pradesh; Maharashtra. 84% to 89% intelligibility with Bhilori of Maharashtra.

Eastern Panjabi: also called Punjabi, Gurmukhi, Gurumukhi. 27,109,000 speakers in India, Kenya, Singapore, Fiji, Bangladesh, Canada, Malalysia, Mauritius, United Arab Emirates, United Kingdom, and USA. In India: Dialects are Panjabi Proper, Majhi, Doab, Bhatyiana (Bhatneri, Bhatti), Powadhi, Malwa, Bathi. Western Panjabi is distinct from Eastern Panjabi, although there is a chain of dialects to Western Hindi (Urdu). Bhatyiana considered to be a mixture of Panjabi and Rajasthani. See separate entry for Dogri-Kangri. Gurmukhi script, a variant of Devanagari; Bhatyiana uses Devanagari script. National language. In Kenya: Nairobi. In Singapore: Ethnic population: 14,000 as of 1993. In Fiji: Ethnic population: 1,167.

Garasia, Adiwasi: also called Adiwasi Girasia, Girasia, Adiwasi Gujarati. 100,000 speakers in India in northern Gujarat, Banaskantha and Sabarkantha districts. Not intelligible with Rajput Girasia or Dungari Garasia. Gujarati proficiency is limited.

Garasia, Rajput: also called Rajput Garasia, Girasia, Grasia, Dungri Grasia, Dhungri Garasia, Dungari Garasia. 62,000 speakers in India in Rajasthan, Sirchi, Pali, and Udaipur districts; Gujarat. Not intelligible with Adiwasi Garasia.

Proficiency in Hindi and Gujarati is limited. Positive attitude toward Garasia. Some negative attitudes toward Adiwasi Garasia and Bhili. Gujarati and Devanagari scripts.

Gade Lohar: also called Gaduliya Lohar, Lohpitta Rajput Lohar, Bagri Lohar, Bhubaliya Lohar, Lohari, Gara, Domba, Dombiali, Chitodi Lohar, Panchal Lohar, Belani, Dhunkuria Kanwar Khati. 500 speakers in India. Rajasthan, Gujarat, Madhya Pradesh, Maharashtra, Uttar Pradesh, Delhi, Haryana, Punjab. No significant dialect differences. May be the same as Loarki listed in Pakistan. Considered by others to be low caste. Devanagari script.

Gamit: also called Gamati, Gamti, Gamta, Gavit, Gamith, Gameti. 233,000 speakers in India, in Gujarat, mainly Surat district, some in Bharuch, Dangs, and Valsad districts. Similar to Mawchi. Barati script.

Ghera: also called Sindhi Ghera, Bara. 10,000 speakers in Pakistan. Quite different grammatically from Gurgula and similar to Urdu. Widespread multilingualism among both sexes with both Sindhi and Urdu. 25% of boys and some girls attend Sindhi medium schools.

Goaria: 20,000 speakers in Pakistan. This might be the same as Sadri, a dialect of Maithili in India. Adults speak Sindhi and other local languages for trade, Hindi for worship. All ages. Goaria used in all domains except religion. Sindhi-based script.

Gowli: also called Nand. 35,000 speakers in India, in Madhya Pradesh; Maharashtra, Amravati district. Dialects are Nand, Ranya, Lingaayat, Khamla. Nand subdialects have 93% or higher intelligibility of the Khamla dialect. Dialect used in Madhya Pradesh appears closer to Marathi (southern zone) than to Hindi (central zone). Many have some understanding of Marathi and Hindi. Nand Gowli is the primary language used in the home.

Gujarati: also called Gujrathi, Gujerati, Gujerathi. 46,100,000 speakers in India, Tanzania, Kenya, Malawi, Singapore, Fiji, Pakistan, Bangladesh, Malawi, Mauritius, Oman, Réunion, South Africa, Uganda, United Kingdom, USA, Zambia, and Zimbabwe. In India: 45,479,000 speakers in Gujarat; Maharashtra; Rajasthan; Karnataka; Madhya Pradesh. Dialects are Standard Gujarati (Saurashtra Standard, Nagari, Bombay Gujarati, Patnuli), Gamadia (Gramya, Surati, Anawla, Brathela, Eastern Broach Gujarati, Charotari, Patidari, Vadodari, Ahmedabad Gamadia, Patani), Parsi, Kathiyawadi (Jhalawadi, Sorathi, Holadi, Gohilwadi, Bhawnagari), Kharwa, Kakari, Tarimuki (Ghisadi). Spoken as mother tongue by the Keer. Gujarati script. National language. In Tanzania: Small communities. Vigorous language use. In Kenya: Mainly in Nairobi. In Malawi: The second main language of Asians in Malawi. In Singapore: Ethnic population: 1,619 as of 1985. In Fiji: Ethnic population: 6,203. In Pakistan: Lower Punjab, Sindh. Some Pakistani dialects are closer to standard Gujarati than others. Pakistani Gujarati is probably a subdialect of Gamadia. The Memoni ethnic group in Karachi, Hyderabad, Sukkur, and other parts of Pakistan are reported to speak a variety closer to Gujarati, while those in India are reported to speak a variety of Kachchi. All Parsi (5,000), many Ismaili Muslims, and many Hindu sweepers (10,000 to 100,000) speak Gujarati. Many Parsi and Ismaili Muslims are literate in Gujarati. There seems to be a shift to Urdu among many Gujarati-speaking sweepers.

Gujari: also called Gujuri, Gujer, Gujar, Gujjari, Gurjar, Gojri, Gogri, Kashmir Gujuri, Rajasthani Gujuri, Gojari. 1,400,000 speakers in India, Pakistan, and Afghanistan. In India: 600,000 speakers in Himachal Pradesh, Madhya Pradesh, Uttar Pradesh, Jammu and Kashmir, and Haryana; also northwestern India and into Pakistan and northeastern Afghanistan. Poonch may be understood by others and form the basis for a standard dialect. Bilingualism in Hindi. Urdu, Kumauni, Garwhali, Kullu, Jaunsari, Kashmiri, Dogri also used. At home, with other Gujars, about 50% for religion. In general, the Hindu agriculturalists have not retained the Gujari language and culture, whereas the Muslim Gujari have. They perceive Gujari as one people and one language. Positive attitude toward Gujari, and toward second languages if it is advantageous to use them. Nastaliq and Devanagari. In Pakistan: 300,000 speakers. Dialects are Western Gujari, Eastern Gujari. Eastern Gujari appears closer to Northern Hindko or Pahari-Potwari. Western Gujari speakers appear to understand the Eastern dialect better than vice versa. Comparison with India varieties is needed. It is reported that most Gujars in Pakistani Punjab have shifted to Panjabi. Spoken in some pockets of Punjab by immigrants from elsewhere. Some unpublished literature. In Afghanistan: Nomads traveling in the summer in the valleys of eastern Afghanistan.

Gurgula: also called Marwari Ghera. 30,000 speakers in Pakistan. Ghera is quite different gramatically. Widespread multilingualism in Sindhi, Urdu, some Gujarati among all ages and sexes as needed, with men being the most proficient. They speak Gurgula among themselves. They are proud of Gurgula. Sindhi-based script.

Harauti: also called Hadauti, Hadoti, Hadothi, Piploda. 572,000 speakers in India. Rajasthan, Kota district; Madhya Pradesh. Dialects are Sipari, Harauti. Mother tongue of the ethnic Saharia of Rajasthan.

Haryanvi: also called Bangaru, Banger, Bangri, Bangru, Haryani, Hariyani, Hariani, Desari, Chamarwa. 13,000,000 speakers in India. Ethnic population: 16,000,000 as of 1992. Haryana, Punjab, Karnataka, Delhi, Himachal Pradesh, Uttar Pradesh. Dialects are Bangaru Proper, Deswali, Bagdi, Mewati. "Bagdi" is the variety used around Fatehabad and Sirsa, and south of Bhiwani (distinct from the Wagdi language in southern Rajasthan). Needs comparison with Bagri. Intelligibility among dialects is good, but Haryanvi is not intelligible with Hindi, the closest language. Closest to Braj Bhasha. Hindi is used as second language; proficiency higher among educated speakers than uneducated ones. Some bilingual ability in all social groups for education and contact with non-Haryanvi speakers. All ages. At home and for religion. Positive attitudes toward Haryanvi.

Hindi: also called Khari Boli, Khadi Boli. 366,000,000 speakers in India, South Africa, Nepal, Bangladesh, Belize, Botswana, Germany, Kenya, New Zealand, Philippines, Singapore, Uganda, United Arab Emirates, United Kingdom, USA, Yemen, and Zambia. In India: 180,000,000 speakers. Ethnic population: 363,839,000 as of 1997. Throughout northern India: Delhi; Uttar Pradesh; Rajasthan; Punjab; Madhya Pradesh; northern Bihar; Himachal Pradesh. Formal vocabulary is borrowed from Sanskrit, de-Persianized, de-Arabicized. Literary Hindi, or Hindi-Urdu, has four varieties: Hindi (High Hindi, Nagari Hindi, Literary Hindi, Standard Hindi); Urdu; Dakhini; Rekhta. State language of Delhi, Uttar Pradesh, Rajasthan, Madhya Pradesh, Bihar, Himachal Pradesh. Languages and dialects in the Western Hindi group are Hindustani, Haryanvi, Braj Bhasha, Kanauji, Bundeli; see separate entries. Spoken as mother tongue by the Saharia in Madhya Pradesh. Hindi, Hindustani, Urdu could be considered co-dialects, but have important sociolinguistic differences. Devanagari script. National language. In South Africa: Mainly in Natal. In Nepal: Southern strip of low country. Language of wider communication.

Jandavra: also called Jhandoria. 5,000 speakers in Pakistan in. southern Sindh Province from Hyderabad to east of Mirpur Khas. Reported to be many more in Jodhpur, Rajasthan, India. Men tend to be conversant in Sindhi and Urdu, at least on a basic level, but women are not. All ages.

Kabutra: also called Nat, Natra. 1,000 speakers in Pakistan, in Sindh, some concentrations around Umerkot, Kunri, and Nara Dhoro. Speakers say that 90% of the people remain in the Zal area of Marwar, India. Speakers report they have inherent intelligibility of Sansi and Sochi, and use Kabutra when speaking to them. All ages and sexes speak Urdu for most common topics, some Sindhi. Women speak Urdu better than in most Hindu groups. They speak Kabutra among themselves.

Kanauji: also called Bhakha, Braj Kanauji, Braj. 6,000,000 speakers in India in Uttar Pradesh. Dialects are Kanauji Proper, Tirhari, Transitional Kanauji. Transitional Kanauji dialect is between Kanauji and Awadhi.

Khandesi: also called Khandeshi, Khandish, Dhed Gujari. 1,579,000 speakers in India, in Maharashtra; Gujarat. Dialects are Kunbi (Kunbau), Rangari, Khandesi, Kotali Bhil.

Koli, Kachi: also called Kuchi, Kachi, Katchi, Koli, Kohli, Kolhi, Kori, Vagari, Vagaria, Kachi Gujarati. 570,000 speakers in Pakistan and India. In Pakistan: 170,000 speakers. Dialects are Kachi, Rabari (Rahabari), Kachi Bhil, Vagri (Kachi Meghwar), Katai Meghwar, Zalavaria Koli. Intermediate between Sindhi and Gujarati; it is becoming more like Sindhi. Complex situation: people with basically the same language are socially quite distinct. Based on Sindhi, based in turn on Arabic. Some older people use Gujarati script, related to Devanagari. In India: 400,000 speakers. There may be a group in India, concentrated in their ancestral homeland centered around Bhuj, in the Rann of Kach, Gujarat. Dialects are Kachi, Rabari (Rahabari), Kachi Bhil, Vagri (Kachi Meghwar), Katai Meghwar, Zalavaria Koli. Intermediate between Sindhi and Gujarati; it is becoming more like Sindhi.

Koli, Parkari: also called Parkari. 250,000 speakers in Pakistan. Based on Sindhi, which is based in turn on Arabic.

Koli, Wadiyara: also called Wadaria, Wadhiara. 350,000 speakers in Pakistan and India. In Pakistan: 175,000 speakers in Sind in an area bounded by Hyderabad, Tando Allahyar, and Mirpur Khas in the north, and Matli and Jamesabad in the south. Dialects are Mewasi (Mayvasi Koli), Wadiyara Koli, Nairya Koli, Tharadari Koli, Tharadari Bhil, Hasoria Koli, Hasoria Bhil, Rardro Bhil. Mewasi and Wadiyara are almost the same linguistically and are coming together as a caste. Dialects listed are distinct sociolinguistic endogamous ethnic groups. There is an incipient, gradual breakdown of some strict caste rules concerning intermarriage and interdining: possibly "lower" groups wishing to move "up," and barriers in "close" castes breaking down. In India: 175,000 speakers.

Lambadi: also called Lamani, Lamadi, Lambani, Labhani, Lambara, Lavani, Lemadi, Lumadale, Labhani Muka, Banjara, Banjari, Bangala, Banjori, Banjuri, Brinjari, Gohar-Herkeri, Goola, Gurmarti, Gormati, Kora, Singali, Sugali, Sukali, Tanda, Vanjari, Wanji. 2,867,000 speakers in India in Andhra Pradesh, Madhra Pradesh, Himachal Pradesh, Gujarat, Tamil Nadu, Maharashtra, Karnataka, Orissa, West Bengal. Dialects are Maharashtra Lambadi, Karnataka Lambadi, (Mysore Lambadi), Andhra Pradesh Lambadi (Telugu Lambadi). Bilingualism in Telugu, Kannada, Marathi. Each of the three dialects needs a different script: Maharashtra uses Devanagari script, Karnataka uses Kannada script, Andhra Pradesh uses Telugu script.

Loarki: 20,000 speakers in Pakistan, Sindh Province, rural. 500 to 750 speakers in India. Probably the same as Gade Lohar in Rajasthan, India, a Rajasthani language. All ages and sexes speak Sindhi; the educated or those working outside the community speak Urdu for most common topics. All ages. Loarki is used for all in-group functions.

Malvi: also called Malwada, Mallow, Ujjaini, Malwi, Malavi. 1,102,000 speakers in India. Northwest Madhya Pradesh, Maharashtra, Rajasthan, Gujarat. Dialects are Bachadi, Bhoyari, Dholewari, Hoshangabad, Jamral, Katiyai, Malvi Proper, Patvi, Rangari, Rangri, Sondwari (Soudhwari). Considered the standard dialect of Southeastern Rajasthani.

Marwari: also called Merwari, Rajasthani, Marwari Meghwar, Jaiselmer, Marawar, Marwari Bhil. 220,000 speakers in Pakistan. Dialects are Northern Marwari, Southern Marwari,

Marwari Bhil, Marwari Meghwar, Marwari Bhat. Northern and Southern Marwari are inherently intelligible to speakers. May or may not be the same as Marwari in Rajasthan, India. Speakers are moderately bilingual in Sindhi. Educated speakers are trilingual in Urdu. The literary language of Rajasthan is Hindi. One sweeper community of 10,000 to 100,000 identifies itself as Marwari, but is undergoing rapid shift to Urdu. Marwari is not usually written. Sindhi and Urdu scripts.

Marwari: also called Rajasthani, Merwari, Marvari. 12,963,000 speakers in India and Nepal. In India: Gujarat, Rajasthan, Madhya Pradesh, Punjab, Delhi, Haryana, Uttar Pradesh, throughout India. Dialects are Standard Marwari, Jaipuri, Shekawati, Dhundhari, Bikaneri. The standard form of Rajasthani. 23 dialects. It is not clear if Mewari is a dialect of Marwari or separate language (see Mewari language entry). Different from Mewati, dialect of Haryanvi. May or may not be different from Marwari of Pakistan. Devanagari script. In Nepal: Mechi Zone, Jhapa District; Koshi Zone, Morang and Sunsari districts; Narayani Zone, Parsa District, some in Kathmandu. The names of other dialects not known.

Mawchi: also called Mauchi, Mavchi, Mawachi, Mowchi, Mawchi Bhil. 76,000 speakers in India in southwestern Gujarat; Maharashtra, Dhule district. Dialects are Mawchi, Padvi.

Mewari: also called Mewadi. 1,220,000 speakers in India, in Rajasthan, Udaipur, Bhilwara, Chitorgarh districts. It is not clear if Mewari is a dialect of Marwari or separate language (see Marwari language entry). Devanagari script.

Nimadi: also called Nemadi, Nimari, Nimiadi. 1,359,000 speakers in India. Madhya Pradesh, Khandwa, Khargone, Barwani, and southern Dhar districts; Uttar Pradesh; Maharashtra. 90% to 100% intelligibility among dialects. No prestige dialect identified. Limited Hindi proficiency. Hindi used in education. All domains except with government officials. Actively used by majority. Positive attitudes toward Nimadi.

Pardhi: also called Bahelia, Chita Pardhi, Lango Pardhi, Paidia, Paradi, Paria, Phans Pardhi, Takankar, Takia. 18,000 speakers in India in Andhra Pradesh; Madhya Pradesh; Gujarat; Maharashtra; scattered over wide area. Dialects are Neelishikari, Pittala Bhasha, Takari. Thought to be more than one language.

Parya: also called Afghana-Yi Nasfurush, Afghana-Yi Siyarui, Laghmani, Pbharya. 1,000 speakers in Tajikistan, Uzbekistan, and Afghanistan. In Tajikistan: Hissar Valley in Tajikistan and some in the upper part of the Surkhandarya Valley in Uzbekistan. It may be a dialect of Marwari, related to Panjabi, or the Laghman dialect of Southeast Pashayi of Afghanistan. Subgroups: Kalu, Jitain, Juni, Maggar, Bisiyan, Mussali, Shuiya. Bilingualism in Tajiki. Parya remains the exclusive language within the home. Uzbek and Tajiki men who marry Parya women learn Parya and become assimilated into the community. In Afghanistan: It may be related to Panjabi, or the Laghman dialect of Southeast Pashayi of Afghanistan. Bilingualism in Tajiki. Parya remains the exclusive language within the home.

Rathawi: also called Kohelia, Bal-La. 308,640 speakers in India, in Gujarat, Baroda, and Panchmahals districts. 76% intelligibility with Bhilali. There is a dialect continuum from Bhilali to Rathawa, but the extremes have limited intelligibility with each other. Bilingualism in Gujarati.

Romani, Balkan: 1,000,000 speakers in Yugoslavia, Bulgaria, Macedonia, Greece, Moldova, France, Germany, USA, Romania, Iran, Hungary, Italy, European Turkey, and Ukraine. In Yugoslavia: 120,000 speakers. Balkans, Kosovo. Dialects are Arlija, Dzambazi, Tinners Romani. The Arlija dialect (252,000 to 367,000 total) is understood by Greek Romani and Dzambazi speakers. In Bulgaria: 187,900 speakers between Sofia and the Black Sea (Central dialect). The Tinsmiths dialect is in central and northwest Bulgaria; Arlija is in the Sofia region. Dialects are Arlija, Tinners Romani, Greek Romani, Dzambazi, East Bulgarian Romani, Paspatian, Ironworker Romani. In Macedonia: 120,000 speakers in the Balkans region of Macedonia. Dialects are Arlija, Dzambazi, Tinners Romani. The Arlija dialect (252,000 to 367,000 total) is understood by Greek Romani and Dzambazi speakers. In Greece: Agia Varvara, a suburb of Athens. Dialects are Greek Romani, Arlija (Erli). Bilingualism in Greek. In Moldova: Moldova; Crimean Peninsula, Ukraine. In France: Dialects are Arlija, Dzambazi. In Germany: Dialects are Arlija (Erli), Dzambazi. The Arlija dialect is understood by Dzambazi speakers. In USA: Brooklyn and Queens, NY. In Romania: Black sea region. In Iran: 2 communities.

Romani, Baltic: 100,000 speakers in Poland, Asian Russia, Latvia, Estonia, Belarus, Lithuania, and Ukraine. In Poland: 30,000 speakers in the Baltic region, central and southern parts. Dialects are Latvian Romani (Lettish Romani), North Russian Romani, White Russian Romani, Estonian Romani, Polish Romani. In Asian Russia: 20,000 speakers in Siberia, Podolia. In Latvia: 8,000 speakers. Dialects are Latvian Romani (Lettish Romani), North Russian Romani, White Russia Romani, Estonian Romani, Polish Romani. In Estonia: Ethnic population: 665 as of 1989.

Romani, Carpathian: also called Bashaldo, Romungro, Hungarian-Slovak Romani. 241,000 speakers in Czech Republic, USA, Hungary, Slovakia, Rumania, Poland, and Ukraine. In Czech Republic: 220,000 speakers. Central, Bohemia, and Moravia. Dialects are Moravian Romani, East Slovakian Romani, West Slovakian Romani. Not intelligible with Vlax Romani or Angloromani. Speakers do not interact socially with speakers of Vlach Romani or Angloromani. In USA:

18,000 speakers in the north and northeast. In Hungary: Dialects are Galician, Transylvanian. In Slovakia: Northern, eastern, and southern Slovakia. Dialects are Moravian Romani, East Slovakian Romani, West Slovakian Romani. Not intelligible with Vlax Romani or Angloromani, and speakers do not interact socially with speakers of those languages. In Rumania: One dialect is in Transylvania. Dialects are Galician, Transylvanian. In Poland: One dialect is in southern Poland, eastern Hungary, and Galicia; another in Transylvania, Rumania; others in Czech Republic and Slovakia, Ukraine, USA.

Romani, Kalo Finnish: also called Fíntika Rómma, Gypsy. 5,000 speakers in Finland and Sweden. In Finland: 4,000 speakers in the west and south. Not inherently intelligible with Traveller Swedish, Traveller Norwegian, Traveller Danish, or Angloromani. In Sweden: 1,000 speakers.

Romani, Sinte: also called Rommanes, Sinte, Sinti. 200,000 speakers in Yugoslavia, Germany, Switzerland, Italy, France, Poland, Kazakhstan, Hungary, Czech Republic, Austria, Croatia, and Netherlands. In Yugoslavia: 31,000 speakers in Kosovo. Dialects are Abbruzzesi, Slovenian-Croatian Romani, Serbian Romani. Croatian, Slovenian, and Serbian Romani speakers understand each other. Those varieties may be quite distinct from the German varieties. Sinte Romani is characterized by German influence. In Germany: 30,500 speakers in Hamburg and colonies in the south. Dialects are Gadschkene, Estracharia, Krantiki, Kranaria, Eftawagaria, Praistiki. All dialects in Germany are inherently intelligible, but possibly not with Yugoslavian dialects. Not intelligible with Vlax Romani. Most use Sinte Romani. In Switzerland: 21,000 speakers. In Italy: 14,000 speakers in northern Italy. Dialects are Piedmont Sintí, Slovenian-Croatian, Manouche. Not intelligible with Vlax Romani. In France: The dialect is Manouche (Manuche, Manush). Not intelligible with Vlax Romani. In Poland: Not intelligible with Vlax Romani. In Kazakhstan: (formerly Volga area until 1941) Not intelligible with Vlax Romani. In Hungary: Eastern Hungary. Not intelligible with Vlax Romani. A Gypsy language. In Czech Republic: Not intelligible with Vlax Romani.

Romani, Vlax: also called Gypsy, Tsigene, Romanese, Vlax Romany, Danubian. 1,500,000 speakers in Rumania, USA, France, European Russia, Germany, Hungary, Italy, Greece, Netherlands, Slovakia, Sweden, Ukraine, Bosnia-Herzegovina, United Kingdom, Chile, Argentina, Albania, Norway, Brazil, Bulgaria, Canada, Colombia, Mexico, Moldova, Norway, and Portugal. In Rumania: 200,000 speakers. Dialects are Sedentary Romania, Kalderash (Kelderashícko, Coppersmith), Ukraine-Moldavia, Eastern, Churari (Churarícko, Sievemakers), Lovari (Lovarícko), Machvano (Machvanmcko), North Albanian, South Albanian, Serbo-Bosnian, Zagundzi, Sedentary Bulgaria, Ghagar, Grekurja

(Greco). Vlax developed from the Romani spoken when they were slaves in Rumania for five hundred years. There were migrations out of Rumania from the mid-14th to mid-19th centuries. Those who left earlier have less Rumanian influence in their dialects. Kalderash, Ursari, Churari are occupational ethnonyms; Machvano is a geographical one. Other names are Argintari 'silversmith', and Lingurari 'spoonmakers'. Machvano and Serbian Kalderash have a south Slavic superstratum; Russian Kalderash is influenced by east Slavic, mainly Russian; Lovari is influenced by Hungarian; Grekurja is probably Turkish influenced and is distinct from the Greek Romani dialect of Balkan Romani. All twenty or more Vlax dialects are inherently intelligible; the differences are mainly lexical and sociolinguistic. In USA: 650,000 speakers. In France: Dialects are Kalderash, Lovari. Vlax and Kalderash are understood by the Lovari. In European Russia: Russian SFSR, Odessa, Transcarpathia. Dialects are Central Vlax Romani, Kalderash. In Germany: Dialects are Lovari, Kalderash. In Hungary: Dialects are Lovari, Churari. In Italy: Dialects are Kalderash, Lovari. In Greece: They can understand Manus (Manuche) only with difficulty. Settled Gypsies are bilingual. In Netherlands: Dialects are Kalderash, Lovari. In Slovakia: Dialects are Lovari, Kalderash (Kaldarári). Kalderash is reported to be understood by the Lovari. In Sweden: Dialects are Kalderash, Lovari. In Ukraine: Eastern and western Ukraine, Odessa, Transcarpathia. Dialects are Ukrainian Vlax Romani, Central Vlax Romani, Kalderash. In Bosnia-Herzegovina: Dialects are Serbo-Bosnian (Machwaya, Machvano), Kalderash, Southern Vlax. In United Kingdom: Dialects are Kalderash, Lovari. Vlax and Kalderash are understood by the Lovari. In Chile: Dialects are Jorajane, Leasi.

Romani, Welsh: spoken in United Kingdom. England and Wales. Not inherently intelligible with Angloromani.

Sansi: also called Bhilki. 242,000 speakers in India and Pakistan. In India: 231,893 speakers in Punjab: Rajasthan, Haryana, Delhi, Jammu, and Kashmir, Madhya Pradesh, Karnataka, and Uttar Pradesh. Reported to be related to Rajasthani, Sindhi, and between Punjabi and Hindustani. They sometimes identify themselves as Marwari. Second language is Sindhi, followed by Urdu, Panjabi, and Saraiki. In Pakistan: Northern Sindh Province, main town, and some in Karachi. The Sochi, who live throughout Sindh, (population 100,000), speak a related variety. They sometimes identify themselves as Sansi or Marwari. Second language is Sindhi, followed by Urdu, Panjabi, and Saraiki.

Saurashtra: also called Saurashtri, Sourashtra, Sowrashtra, Patnuli. 310,000 speakers in India. Dialects are Southern Saurashtra, Northern Saurashtra. Indo-Aryan elements in its deep structure reveal Gujarati relationship. Has borrowed some structure from Dravidian, lexicon from Telugu and

Tamil. An Indo-European island surrounded by Dravidian languages. The three main populations in Salem, Thanjavur, and Madurai cities had between 67% and 97% inherent intelligibility. Most adults speak Tamil in public and Saurashtra in private. Used at home and in prayer. Vigorous language use. Has had its own script for centuries. A modern version developed in the late 1800s. Since the end of the 19th century, books have been printed using Telugu, Tamil, Devanagari, and Saurashtra scripts. Currently an adapted Tamil script is most commonly employed, using superscript numbers and a colon to show sounds not used in Tamil.

Sonha: also called Sonahaa. 10,000 speakers in Nepal along the Karnali River in western Nepal, Kailali district, Seti zone; Bheri River, Bheri zone, Mahakali River, Mahakali zone. Close to Dangura Tharu; 80% intelligibility.

Tharu, Dangaura: also called Dang Tharu. 343,000 speakers in Nepal and India. In Nepal: 300,000 speakers in the Rapti zone, Dang district. Also in other areas of the Tarai, like Bardiya, Banke, Kailali, and Kanchanpur districts. 68% to 91% intelligibility of Rana Tharu, 95% to 97% of Kathoriya Tharu. Some varieties listed as dialects have only 71% to 79% intelligibility of others. Some intelligibility difficulty with speakers from India. Closest to Mari Tharu. Possibly Eastern Hindi Group. Educated people tend to be more bilingual in Nepali, men more than women, young people more than older people. Hindi and Maithili are also used. All ages. Dangaura Tharu is used almost exclusively in the family, with older people, children, and mainly with village leaders. They usually use Tharu with other Tharu, but sometimes Nepali. Vigorous language use. The Rana Tharu and Dangaura Tharu are well known, but the Kathoriya Tharu and other smaller groups are often unknown. Devanagari script. In India: 31,000 speakers in Uttar Pradesh, along the border in Nighasan Tahsil of Kheri district and Tulsipur Tahsil of Gonda district. Hindi bilingual proficiency is limited among the 70% to 90% who are uneducated.

Tharu, Kathoriya: also called Kathariya. 60,000 speakers in Nepal and India. In Nepal: Seti zone, Kailali district. There appear to be differences in speech between Nepal and India dialects. Possibly Eastern Hindi Group. Bilingualism in Nepali. Hindi also used. In India: Uttar Pradesh, Kheri and Gonda districts.

Urdu: 60,290,000 speakers in Pakistan, India, South Africa, Mauritius, Thailand, Guyana, Fiji, Afghanistan, Bahrain, Bangladesh, Botswana, Germany, Malawi, Nepal, Norway, Oman, Qatar, Saudi Arabia, Thailand, United Arab Emirates, United Kingdom, and Zambia. In Pakistan: 10,719,000 speakers. Intelligible with Hindi, but has formal vocabulary borrowed from Arabic and Persian. The second or third language of most Pakistanis for whom it is not the mother tongue. Arabic script in Nastaliq style with several extra characters used. National language. In India: 48,062,000 speakers. Jammu and Kashmir and by Muslims in many parts of India. Dialects are Dakhini (Dakani, Deccan, Desia, Mirgan), Pinjari, Rekhta (Rekhti). Dakhini is freer of Persian and Arabic loans than Urdu. Rekhta is a form of Urdu used in poetry. Arabic script for both Urdu and Dakhini. National language. In South Africa: Along the Natal coast and urban areas around Durban, Transvaal surrounding Johannesburg, and scattered smaller towns. Most speak English. In Mauritius: Often used in government and politics. In Thailand: Bangkok, Mookherji area. In Guyana: Older Muslims. In Fiji: Ethnic population: 3,562 as of 1980.

Vaghri: also called Vaghri Koli, Salavta, Bavri. 10,000 speakers in Pakistan. Reported to be related to the language spoken by the Kukar people living near Chanesar Halt, Mehmoodabad in Karachi. They speak some Sindhi, Urdu, and Gujarati.

Vasavi: also called Vasave, Vasava, Vasava Bhil. 900,000 speakers in India. Dialects are Dehvali (Ambodi), Dungri (Dogri). Not intelligible with Rathwi Bareli or Bhilori. 77% to 93% intelligibility between Dungri, Khatali, Dehvali, Dubli, and Kotni varieties. Bilingual proficiency in Marathi is limited. Gujarati and Marathi scripts.

Wagdi: also called Wagadi, Vagdi, Vagadi, Vagari, Vageri, Vaged, Vagi, Wagari, Waghari, Wagri, Wagholi, Mina Bhil, Bhili. 1,621,000 speakers in India, in Rajasthan, southern Udaipur district, Dungarpur and Banswara; Gujarat, Sabarkantha and Panch Mahals; Andhra Pradesh, Hyderabad. Dialects are Kherwara, Sagwara, Adivasi Wagdi. Intelligibility among dialects is above 95%. Second language is Hindi; proficiency is adequate for market and other common topics; used with people not speakers of Wagdi. A regional language in Vagad Desh. Merchants and government workers use it as second language. No feeling of inferiority attached to Wagdi. Devanagari script. Language of wider communication.

B. GRIMES

CENTRAL MALAYO-POLYNESIAN LANGUAGES.

One of the two main branches of Central-Eastern Malayo-Polynesian languages within the Malayo-Polynesian branch of the AUSTRONESIAN family.

[*For language lists, consult the articles on* Aru Languages, Babar Languages, Bima-Sumba Languages, Central Maluku Languages, North Bomberai Languages, South Bomberai Languages, Southeastern Maluku Languages, Teor-Kur Languages, Timor Languages, *and* West Damar Languages.]

B. GRIMES

CENTRAL MALUKU LANGUAGES.

Spoken on the islands of Seram and Buru and on the Sula Islands in the Indonesian provinces of Maluku and North Maluku. They form a branch of CENTRAL MALAYO-POLYNESIAN.

FIGURE 1. *Subgrouping of Central Maluku Languages*

Ambelau	**Saparua**
Buru	Latu, Saparua
Buru, Lisela, Moksela, Palumata	Kamarian
East Central Maluku	**West Piru Bay**
Banda-Geser	**Asilulu**
Banda	Asilulu
Geser-Gorom	**Hoamoal**
Bati, Geser-Gorom, Watubela	**East Hoamoal**
Seram	Boano, Larike-Wakasihu
Bobot	**West Hoamoal**
East Seram	Luhu, Manipa
Hoti	**Three Rivers**
Manusela-Seti	Yalahatan
Benggoi, Huaulu, Liana-Seti, Manusela, Salas	**Amalumute**
Masiwang	**Northwest Seram**
Nunusaku	Horuru
Kayeli	Hulung
Piru Bay	Lisabata-Nuniali
Haruku	**Loun**
East Piru Bay	Piru
Kaibobo	**Ulat-Inai**
Sepa	Alune, Naka'ela
Teluti	**Wemale**
Seram Straits	North Wemale, South Wemale
Ambon	**Sawai-Nuaulu**
Hitu, Laha, Seit-Kaitetu, Tulehu	North Nuaulu, South Nuaulu, Saleman
Solehua	**Sula**
Paulohi	Mangole
Uliase	Sula
Hatuhaha	**Taliabo**
Elpaputi	Kadai, Taliabu
Amahai, Elpaputih, Nusa Laut	

LANGUAGE LIST

Alune: also called Sapalewa, Patasiwa Alfoeren. 13,000 speakers in Maluku, five villages in Seram Barat district, and twenty-two villages in Kairatu and Taniwel districts, western Seram, central Maluku. Dialects are Kairatu, Central West Alune (Niniari-Piru-Riring-Lumoli), South Alune (Rambatu-Manussa-Rumberu), North Coastal Alune (Nikulkan-Murnaten-Wakolo), Central East Alune (Buriah-Weth-Laturake). Rambatu dialect is reported to be prestigious. Kawe may be a dialect. Related to Naka'ela and Lisabata-Nuniali. The largest language in western Seram. The people in the interior, who are the majority, use the language daily. Usage in the coastal villages is not as vigorous. The southern dialect in Kairatu village is nearly extinct.

Amahai: also called Amahei. 50 speakers in Maluku, four villages near Masohi, southwestern Seram, central Maluku. Dialects are Makariki, Rutah, Soahuku. Language chain with Iha and Kaibobo. Also related to Elpaputih and Nusa Laut.

Ambelau: also called Amblau. 5,700 speakers in central Maluku. Ethnic population: 5,700. Spoken on Ambelau Island off the southeastern coast of Buru Island, Wae Tawa village on the coast of Buru, opposite Ambelau, eight villages. Not intelligible with Buru.

Asilulu: 8,750 speakers in Maluku. Dialects are Asilulu, Ureng, Negeri Lima (Lima, Henalima). Trade language.

Banda: 3,000 speakers in Maluku. Dialects are Eli, Elat. Different from other languages of southern Maluku. Bilingualism in Kei. Banda used for all purposes among themselves.

Bati: also called Gah. 3,500 speakers in Maluku, eastern Seram Island along the coast between Kian Darat and Keleser, and in the interior. Related to Geser and Watubela. Many claim to be bilingual in Geser. Strong separation of ethnolinguistic identity from Geser-Gorom.

Benggoi: also called Bengoi, Kobi-Benggoi, Uhei-Kaclakin, Uhei Kachlakan, Uhei-Kahlakim, Isal. 350 speakers in central Maluku, the northern coast, Werinama and Bula districts, eastern Seram, three villages (Benggoi, Balakeo, Lesa). Dialects are Lesa, Benggoi, Balakeo.

Boano: also called Buano. 3,240 speakers in central Maluku, Boano Island west of Seram, mainly in North Buano village. Related to Larike-Wakasihu. Vigorous language use in North Boano. South Boano may be extinct.

Bobot: also called Werinama, Hatumeten, Atiahu, Ahtiago, Ntau. 4,500 speakers in central Maluku, southeastern Seram, Werinama district, from the village of Atiahu to Kota Baru, and Tunsai village in the Liana area.

Buru: also called Boeroe, Buruese. 33,000 speakers in Maluku and Netherlands. In Maluku: 32,980 speakers on southern, southeastern, and central Buru Island, central Maluku, Ambon, Jakarta, 70 villages. Dialects are Masarete (South Buru), Wae Sama (Waesama), Central Buru (Rana, Wae Geren, Wae Kabo), Fogi (Li Emteban, Tomahu). Li Garan is a special taboo dialect spoken by the Rana people (3,000 to 5,000 users). Bilingual level estimates are Ambonese Malay: 0 15%, 1 20%, 2 50%, 3 10%, 4 5%, 5 0%; Indonesian: 0 15%, 1 40%, 2 35%, 3 7%, 4 3%, 5 0%. All ages. All domains. Vigorous language use in most areas. Parents transmit Buru to children. Fogi (500 in ethnic group) has apparently undergone complete shift to Ambonese Malay. Roman alphabet used.

Elpaputih: also called Elpaputi. Spoken in central Maluku, western Seram. Closest to Nusalaut, Amahai.

Geser-Gorom: also called Geser, Gesa, Gorom, Goram, Goran, Gorong, Seram, Seran, Seran Laut. 36,500 speakers in Maluku, the eastern end of Seram, and the Gorom Islands. Dialects are Goram Laut, Mina Mina Gorong, Kelimuri. Watubela speakers use this as second language.

Haruku: 18,219 speakers in central Maluku, Haruku Island, Lease Islands. Dialects are Hulaliu, Pelauw, Kailolo, Rohomoni. Each village is a separate dialect. Bilingualism in Ambonese Malay.

Hitu: 15,965 speakers in Maluku, five villages: Wakal, Hitu, Mamala, Morela, and Hila; Hitu Peninsula, Ambon Island. Dialects are Wakal, Morela, Mamala, Hitu, Hila. Moderate to vigorous.

Horuru: spoken in central Maluku, Seram. Hulung may be related. This may be an alternate name for another language.

Hoti: 10 speakers remain in central Maluku, eastern Seram. In 1987, all were elderly.

Huaulu: also called Alakamat, Bahasa Asli. 300 speakers in central Maluku, eastern Seram, northwest of Manusela, ten villages.

Hulung: 10 speakers remain in central Maluku, Hulung village, and Sauweli hamlet, western Seram.

Kadai: 300 speakers in North Maluku, Sula Islands, Taliabu Island, interior mountains. Possibly also in the mountains of Mangole Island. May be intelligible with Taliabu.

Kaibobo: also called Kaibubu. 500 speakers in Maluku. Dialects are Kaibobo, Hatusua. Related to Lisabata-Nuniali. Bilingualism in Ambonese Malay. Language use may be shifting to Ambonese Malay in some villages.

Kamarian: also called Kamariang, Seruawan. 10 speakers remain in central Maluku. Ethnic population: 6,000 in the village as of 1987. Spoken on western Seram, Kamarian village on the southern coast of Seram, at the eastern end of Piru Bay.

Kayeli: also called Kajeli, Cajeli, Caeli, Gaeli. 3 speakers remain in central Maluku. Ethnic population: 800 as of 1995. Spoken on southern Namlea Bay, northern Buru Island. Dialects are Kayeli, Leliali (Liliali), Lumaete (Lumaiti, Mumaite, Lumara). Bilingualism in Ambonese Malay. Speakers are over 60 years old. Others have completely shifted to Ambonese Malay as first language. Lumaete became extinct recently and Leliali became extinct in March 1989.

Laha: also called Central Ambon. 3,900 speakers in central Maluku, Laha village, and several nearby smaller villages, southern central coast of Ambon Island. Related to Seram languages, but distinct from Manusela. Bilingualism in Ambonese Malay. All ages. Parents encourage children to speak Laha.

Larike-Wakasihu: 12,557 speakers in Maluku, Larike, Wakasihu, Tapi, Allang, and Lai villages, southwestern Hitu Peninsula, Ambon Island. Dialects are Allang, Wakasihu, Larike. Wakasihu may need separate literature from Larike. The western end of the Ambon dialect chain. Vigorous language use in Larike and Wakasihu, weak in Allang. Only older people in Allang, Allang Asaude, Uraur, and Urusana still speak Allang, but apparently do not use it.

Latu: 2,135 speakers in central Maluku, Latu village, Elpaputih Bay, southwestern Seram Island, central.

Liana-Seti: also called Liana, Lianan, Uhei Kaclakin, Uhei Kachlakan, Uhei Kahlakim, Teula, Liambata-Kobi. 3,000 speakers in central Maluku, eastern Teluti Bay to the northern coast, districts of Seram, Bula, Werinama, and Tehoru, eight villages. Dialects are "Seti," Wahakaim, Kobi. Seti use Teluti as second language. Vigorous language use.

Lisabata-Nuniali: also called Lisabata, Nuniali, Noniali. 1,830 speakers in central Maluku, spread across the northern coast of western and northern Seram, five villages. Dialects are Lisabata-Timur, Nuniali, Sukaraja, Kawa. Bilingualism in Ambonese Malay. Vigorous language use except in Kawa.

Lisela: also called Buru, North Buru, Li Enyorot, Liet Enjorot, Wayapo. 11,922 speakers in Maluku. Dialects are Lisela (Licela, Licella), Tagalisa. Bilingualism in Ambonese Malay. Language use not vigorous; a shift to Ambonese Malay is taking place.

Loun: spoken in central Maluku, northern central Seram.

Luhu: 6,500 speakers in Maluku, Luhu village on Hoamoal Peninsula, western Seram Island, and Boano and Kelang islands, off of western Seram. Dialects are Luhu, Batu Merah, Kelang. Related to Manipa. Vigorous language use. Batu Merah dialect spoken on Ambon Island is nearly extinct.

Mangole: also called Mangoli, Sula Mangoli. 4,000 speakers in North Maluku, southern coast of Mangole Island and northern tip of Sulabesi of the Sula Islands.

Manipa: also called Soow Huhelia. 1,500 speakers in central Maluku, Manipa Island west of Seram, four villages.

Manusela: also called Wahai, Wahinama. 7,000 speakers in central Maluku, 30 villages, Manusela mountains of northern Seram, and along Teluti Bay in southern Seram. Dialects are Kanikeh, Hatuolu, Maneo, South Manusela. Bilingualism in Teluti. Vigorous language use.

Masiwang: also called Bonfia. 1,000 speakers in Indonesia (Maluku). Seram Island, Waru Bay area, Bula district, central Maluku. Some use Geser-Gorom as second language. Used by Salas as second language.

Moksela: also called Maksela, Opselan. Formerly spoken in central Maluku, possibly eastern Buru Island, near Kayeli. Last speaker died in 1974.

Naka'ela: 5 speakers remain in central Maluku, Kairatu village, northwestern Seram. 71% lexical similarity with Lisabata-Nuniali, 66% with Hulung, 63% with Alune.

Nuaulu, North: also called Nuaulu, Patakai, Fatakai. 500 speakers in central Maluku, two villages on the northern coast of central Seram Island.

Nuaulu, South: also called Nuaulu, Patakai, Fatakai. 1,500 speakers in central Maluku, six villages on the southern coast and interior of Amahai district, Seram Island. Many use Sepa as second language. Some people do not speak Indonesian. Vigorous language use.

Nusa Laut: also called Nusalaut. 10 speakers remain in central Maluku. Ethnic population: 2,226 as of 1989. Spoken in Titawai village, Nusa Laut Island, Lease Islands. Barely used, and only by a few older people.

Palumata: also called Palamata, Balamata. Formerly spoken in central Maluku, northwestern Buru Island.

Paulohi: 50 speakers in central Maluku, western Seram, western shore of Elpaputih Bay in southern central Seram Island, two villages, Kecamatan Amahai.

Piru: 10 speakers remain in central Maluku, one village, on western Seram Island. People use Ambonese Malay as first or second language.

Salas: also called Liambata, Lenkaitahe, Salas Gunung. 50 speakers in central Maluku, Salas Gunung village, Seram Island, Waru Bay. Most use Masiwang as second language.

Saleman: also called Sawai, Seleman, Hatue, Wahai. 4,800 speakers in central Maluku, five villages (Saleman, Pasanea, Sawai, Besi, Wahai), northern central Seram. Vigorous language use except in Wahai.

Saparua: 10,200 speakers in Maluku. Dialects are Kulur, Iha-Saparua, Iha-Seram, Siri-Sori. Each village is a dialect.

Seit-Kaitetu: also called Hila-Kaitetu. 10,171 speakers in central Maluku, Seit (Seith) and Kaitetu villages, northern coast of Ambon Island. Dialects are Seit (Seith), Kaitetu. Bilingualism in Ambonese Malay. Vigorous language use.

Sepa: also called Tamilouw. 2,600 speakers in central Maluku, Sepa village, Seram Island. Used as a second language by South Nuaulu speakers. Trade language.

Sula: also called Sanana. 20,000 speakers in Maluku. Dialects are Fagudu, Falahu, Facei (Facé). Mangole is closely related. Vigorous language use in daily communication.

Taliabu: also called Taliabo. 2,500 speakers in North Maluku, Taliabu Island and northwestern Mangole, Sula Islands. Dialects are Padang (Samada), Mananga, Mangei (Mange'e, Mange, Mang, Soboyo, Sobojo). Language attitudes are positive.

Teluti: also called Taluti, Tihoru, Tehoru, Silen, Wolu. 17,000 speakers in central Maluku, southern Seram Island, Teluti Bay. Dialects are West Teluti (Haya, Wolu, Tehoru, Tehua), Laha Serani. Used as second language by many Manusela and Seti speakers in the area. Trade language.

Tulehu: also called Northeast Ambon. 18,840 speakers in central Maluku, four villages on the coast of northeastern Ambon Island. Dialects are Tulehu, Liang, Tengah-Tengah, Tial. Each dialect is in a separate village. Eastern end of Ambon dialect chain. Vigorous language use.

Watubela: also called Snabi Watubela, Kasiui, Kesui, Kasui, Wesi, Esiriun, Matabello. 4,000 speakers in eastern central Maluku, Watubela Islands, north of Kur Island. Dialects are Tamher Timur, Sulmelang. Many claim to use Geser-Gorom as second language.

Wemale, North: 4,930 speakers in Maluku spread along the northern coast of Taniwel district, east of Taniwel, and in the westernmost part of eastern Seram district, 24 villages. Dialects are Horale, Kasieh, Uwenpantai. Kawe may be a dialect. Language used in church. Vigorous language use.

Wemale, South: also called Tala, Honitetu. 3,725 speakers in central Maluku, western Seram, 15 villages; 13 in Kairatu, mainly in the interior, and two westernmost coastal villages of Amahai district. Dialect chain between Horale, Kasieh, Uwenpantai, and Honitetu. Kawe may be a dialect. Vigorous language use.

Yalahatan: also called Atamanu, Jahalatan, Jahalatane, Awaiya. 800 speakers in central Maluku, western Seram, villages of Yalahatan and Haruru. Slight dialect differences reported between the two villages.

B. GRIMES

CENTRAL PACIFIC LANGUAGES. These constitute a branch of REMOTE OCEANIC.

[*For language lists, consult the articles on* East Fijian-Polynesian Languages *and* West Fijian-Rotuman Languages.]

B. GRIMES

CENTRAL SUDAN LANGUAGES. A branch of the proposed NILO-SAHARAN family. They are spoken in

FIGURE 1. *Subgrouping of Central Sudan Languages*

East Central Sudanic
  Lendu
    Bendi, Lendu, Ngiti
  Mangbetu
    Asoa, Lombi, Mangbetu
  Mangbutu-Efe
    Efe, Lese, Mamvu, Mangbutu, Mvuba, Ndo
  Moru-Madi
    Central Moru-Madi
      Aringa, Avokaya, Keliko, Logo, Lugbara, Omi
    Northern Moru-Madi
      Moru
    Southern Moru-Madi
      Ma'di, Southern Ma'di, Olu'bo
West Central Sudanic
  Bongo-Bagirmi
    Bongo-Baka
      Baka
      Bongo
      Morokodo-Beli
        Beli
        Jur Modo
        Mittu
        Morokodo-Mo'da
          Mo'da, Morokodo, Nyamusa-Molo
    Kara
      Furu, Gula, Yulu
    Sara-Bagirmi
      Birri
      Fongoro
      Bagirmi
        Bagirmi, Berakou, Bernde, Disa, Gula, Jaya, Kenga,
        Naba
    Sara
      Sara Proper
        Bedjond
        Dagba
        Gor
        Gulay
        Horo
        Kaba
        Laka
        Mango
        Mbay
        Ngam
        Ngambay
        Sar
        Sara Kaba
          Kaba Deme, Kaba Na, Kulfa, Sara Dunjo, Sara
          Kaba
        Vale
          Lutos, Vale
        Sinyar
    Kresh
      Aja, Gbaya

two separate geographical areas; the western area includes parts of Sudan, Democratic Republic of Congo, Chad, and the Central African Republic; the eastern comprises parts of Democratic Republic of Congo and adjacent parts of Sudan and Uganda.

LANGUAGE LIST

Aja: also called Ajja, Adja. 200 speakers in southern Sudan, Western Bahr al-Ghazal Province. Also reported to be in the western Central African Republic, along the Sudan border, near the Shinko and Sapo rivers. They consider themselves to be a Kresh tribe, but their language is not intelligible to the Kresh. Santandrea reports it to be halfway between Banda and Gbaya; nearer to Banda in vocabulary and Gbaya in structure. Speakers are mostly bilingual in Gbaya (Kresh).

Aringa: also called Low Lugbara. 588,830 speakers in Uganda, northwestern corner, north of Lake Albert, Aringa county, north of Lugbara, west of Ma'di. Not in Sudan. The speakers of Lugbara and Ma'di both consider Aringa to be a separate but related language.

Asoa: also called Asua, Asuati, Asuae, Aka. Spoken in Democratic Republic of Congo, Orientale Province, Rungu territory, Ituri forest, among Mangbetu groups Maele, Meje, Aberu, and Popoi. Not inherently intelligible to Meje (dialect of Mangbetu) speakers. Some Asoa learn Meje. Mangbetu men sometimes take Asoa wives, but Mangbetu women do not ordinarily marry Asoa men.

Avokaya: also called Abukeia, Avukaya. 40,000 speakers in Democratic Republic of Congo and Sudan. In Democratic Republic of Congo: 25,000 speakers. Orientale Province, Faradje territory, close to Sudan border. Dialects are Ojila, Ajugu, Northern Ogambi, Avokaya Pur. Avokaya Pur near Faradje is closer to Logo than to the Ojila dialect of Sudan. In Sudan: 15,000 speakers. Dialects are Ojila (Odzila, Odziliwa), Ajugu (Adjiga, Ojiga, Agamoru), Pur. Closely related to Logo. There is intermarriage and bilingualism with the Baka and Mundu, especially near Maridi. Some speakers are bilingual in Zande.

Bagirmi: also called Baguirmi, Baghirmi, Baguirme, Tar Barma, Barma, Mbarma, Tar Bagrimma, Bagrimma, Lis, Lisi. 44,761 speakers in Chad and Nigeria. In Chad: Dialects are Gol, Kibar, Bangri, Dam. Many dialects. The majority use Arabic as second language. It was the language of the ancient Bagirmi kingdom. It is widely spoken as a second language. Trade language. In Nigeria: State of Borno, Maiduguri LGA.

Baka: also called Tara Baaka. 26,300 speakers in Sudan and Democratic Republic of Congo. In Sudan: 25,000 speakers in southern Sudan, Western Equatoria Province, south and west of Maridi, northwest of Yei. Sudanese Creole Arabic is the main second language. Zande is taught in school and used in Episcopalin church. Some speakers intermarry with the Avokaya and Mundu and are bilingual in those languages. Moru also used. In Democratic Republic of Congo: Orientale Province, between Garamba National Park and Sudan border. A few among the Logo.

Bedjond: also called Mbay Bediondo, Mbay Bejondo, Bediondo Mbai, Bédjonde, Bedjondo, Bediondo, Nangnda. 36,000 speakers in southwestern Chad. Moyen-Chari prefecture, Koumra and Moïssala subprefectures, centered around Bediondo. West of the Day. Dialects are Bedjond, Bébote, Yom.

Beli: also called Behli, Beili, Jur Beli, 'Beli. 6,600 speakers in Sudan. Dialects are Wulu, Bahri Girinti, Sopi (Supi).

Bendi: also called Mabendi, Mabeni. 32,000 speakers in Democratic Republic of Congo, Orientale Province, Djugu territory, midway between Bunia and Djalasiga.

Berakou: also called Babalia, Bubalia. 2 speakers remain in Chad. Dialects are Bolo Djarma, Mondogossou, Manawadji, Yiryo. Bilingualism in Chadian Arabic, Babalia Arabic. As of 1995, speakers were in their 60s. During the last century the Babalia have been shifting to Chadian Arabic or Kotoko languages.

Bernde: also called Morom, Tar Murba. 2,000 speakers in central Chad, Guéra prefecture, Bitkine subprefecture, west of the village of Bolong to the border of Chari Baguirmi prefecture. Dialects are Morom, Morbo, Bayo, Bolong (Tar Bolongo).

Birri: also called Biri, Viri, Bviri. 200 speakers in Central African Republic. Ethnic population: 5,000. Extinct in Sudan as of 1993. Scattered throughout southwestern corner of Central African Republic, and formerly in Deim Zubeir, Bahr al-Ghazal Province, Sudan. Dialects are Mboto, Munga. Only one dialect spoken in Central African Republic. The people are bilingual in Zande. They may be assimilated by the larger Zande people through marriage.

Bongo: also called Bungu, Dor. 5,000 speakers in Sudan. A large sparsely populated area reaching from Tonj and Wau on the north, the Beli on the east, the Zande on the south, and the Bor on the west. Dialects are Busere Bongo, Tonj Bongo, Bungo. Slight dialect differences between those on the River Busere, who have had Zande influence, and those around Tonj. Bungo dialect has minor differences. Close to the Jur Beli cluster. Bilingualism in Jur Beli is low. Generally, adults understand Zande, and adult males understand Dinka Rek. Younger people do not understand Zande or Dinka because education is mostly in Arabic with some English. Many students drop out of school because they cannot understand the language being used.

Dagba: 40,000 speakers in Central African Republic and Chad. In Central African Republic: Batangafo, Kabo, and Bossangoa subprefectures. May be intelligible with Kaba. In Chad: May be intelligible with Kaba.

Disa: spoken in southern Chad, Moyen-Chari prefecture, Kyabé subprefecture, northwest of Lake Iro.

Efe: 20,000 speakers in Democratic Republic of Congo, Orientale Province, Mambasa, Watsa, Irumu, and Djugu territories. Related to Lese. A separate language from Mamvu.

Fongoro: also called Gele, Kole. 1,000 speakers in Chad. The people have shifted to Fur linguistically and culturally. There may be a few elderly speakers left and some living in isolated places. Apparently extinct in Sudan.

Furu: also called Bagero, Bagiro, Baguero, Baguiro. 16,000 speakers in Democratic Republic of Congo and Central African Republic. In Democratic Republic of Congo: 12,000 speakers in Equateur Province, Nord Ubangi, east of Bosobolo in Bosobolo and Mobaye territories. Most are bilingual in Lingala, Sango, Mono, or Gbanziri. Lingala comprehension is limited. In Central African Republic: 4,000 speakers. Mobaye subprefecture, eleven villages. Bilingualism in Sango, Mono.

Gbaya: also called Kresh, Kreish, Kreich, Kredj, Kparla, Kpala, Kpara. 16,000 speakers in Sudan and Central African Republic. In Sudan: Dialects are Naka (Kresh-Boro), Gbaya-Ndogo (Kresh-Ndogo), Gbaya-Ngbongbo (Kresh-Hofra), Gbaya-Gboko, Orlo (Woro), Gbaya-Dara, Dongo. Eight tribes and dialects. Gbaya-Ndogo is prestigious and understood by all. Naka is largest and also well understood. Men and those who have been to school speak Sudanese Arabic as second language for most common topics. They do not accept Standard Arabic, except for a few who have been to school.

Gor: also called Bodo. 75,000 speakers in Chad, Logone Oriental Prefecture, Doba subprefecture, centered around Bodo. Dialects are Bodo, Yamod. Close to Bedjond, with high inherent intelligibility. There is a Gor Language Committee. The speakers have a clear understanding of their identity as separate from Mango and Bedjond.

Gula: also called Kara of Sudan, Kara de Soudan, Kara, Tar Gula, Gula du Mamoun, Goula, Yamegi. 13,000 speakers in Central African Republic and Sudan. In Central African Republic: Birao subprefecture, near Sudan border at Kafia Kingi. Dialects are Molo, Mele, Mot-Mar (Moto-Mara), Sar (Sara), Mere, Zura (Koto). In Sudan: Southern Sudan at Kafia Kingi in extreme western Bahr alGhazal Province and at Kata. Dialects are Gula (Goula), Nguru (Bubu, Koyo). Many in Sudan are reported to be bilingual in Kresh or Arabic.

Gula: also called Sara Goula, Sara Gula, Goula. Spoken in Chad, Moyen-Chari prefecture, Kyabé subprefecture, northwest of Lake Iro. Probably related to Disa.

Gulay: also called Goulai, Goulei, Gulei, Gulai, Goulaye. 163,271 speakers in southwestern Chad. Moyen-Chari (six cantons), Logone Oriental (one canton) and Tandjilé (one canton) prefectures, between Koumra, Laï, and Doba. Dialects are Gulay, Pen (Peni). Sar is the lingua franca.

Horo: also called Hor. Formerly spoken in Chad. Béhor north of Sarh on the Chari River. Extinct. The ethnic group now speaks the Kle dialect of Ngam.

Jaya: 2,200 speakers in central Chad, Guéra prefecture, Bitkine subprefecture, 50 km north-northwest of Bitkine. Not inherently intelligible with Kenga.

Jur Modo: also called Modo, Jur. 100,000 speakers in Sudan, southern Sudan, vicinity of Mvolo and on the Naam (Olo) River. Dialects are Lori, Modo (Jur Modo, Modo Lali), Wira, Wetu. Many speak Arabic, Dinka, Moru, Baka, or Zande as second language. All domains, oral and written use in administration, business, written use in folk stories, keeping of family records. Parents pass on Jur Modo to children. The Wetu dialect is not extinct. Positive attitude toward Jur Modo.

Kaba: also called Kabba, Sara Kaba, Sara. 84,000 speakers in Central African Republic and Chad. In Central African Republic: 72,000 speakers in Paoua and Marounda subprefectures. In Chad: 11,000 speakers in the southwest, Logone Oriental Prefecture, Goré subprefecture, around Goré and to the southeast.

Kaba Deme: also called Kaba Demi, Kaba 'Dem, Tà Sàra. Sara Kaba Dem. 40,000 speakers in Chad. Dialects are Siime, Mara, Kuruwer.

Kaba Na: also called Kaba Nar, Kaba Naa, Na, Dana, Sara Kaba, Sara Kaba Naa. 35,000 speakers in southeastern Chad, Moyen-Chari prefecture, Kyabé subprefecture, centered in Kyabé. Dialects are Dunje (Dendje, Dindje, Dinje, Denje, Dounje), Na, Banga (Mbanga), Tie (Tiye). Dunje may be the same as Kaba Dunjo of Central African Republic. Kaba Na may be the same as Sara Kaba of Central African Republic.

Keliko: also called Kaliko. 22,500 speakers in Sudan, Democratic Republic of Congo, and Uganda. In Sudan: 10,000 speakers in southern Sudan, southern part of Yei district. Dialects are Eastern Kaliko, Western Kaliko. The two dialects in Sudan are inherently intelligible to each other's speakers. In Democratic Republic of Congo: 7,500 speakers in Orientale Province, northern Aru territory, along the Sudan border. Dialects are Didi, Dogo. The two dialects in Democratic Republic of Congo are inherently intelligible. Dogo dialect is more like Sudanese Keliko. In Uganda: 5,000 speakers.

Kenga: also called Kenge, Cenge. 40,000 speakers in central Chad, Guéra prefecture, Bitkine subprefecture, around Bitkine, fifty-two villages, including Bolongo, Bokiyo. Dialects are Cenge (Tar Cenge), Banama (Tar Banama), Bidjir, Banala (Tar Banala). Related to Naba, and Jaya, but not inherently intelligible. The majority of men use Chadian Arabic as second language for trade. Speakers have a positive attitude toward Kenga and Kenga literacy.

Kulfa: also called Kulfe, Kurmi, Kurumi. ëKaba Soí is a derogatory name sometimes used. Spoken in southeastern Chad, Moyen Chari prefecture, Kyabé subprefecture, southwest of Lake Iro. Centered in Alako, Male, and Moufa. Dialects are Kurmi, So (Suka, Souka, Soko).

Laka: also called Kabba Laka. 57,200 speakers in Chad and Central African Republic. In Chad: 55,143 speakers. Dialects are Mang, Bémour, Maïngao, Goula, Paï. Some consider it to be a dialect of Ngambai. In Central African Republic: Bocaranga subprefecture, nine villages at the Chad border. Some consider it to be a dialect of Ngambai.

Lendu: also called Bbadha, Bbaledha, Kilendu, Baletha, Batha, Balendru, Bale, Hema-Nord, Kihema-Nord. 760,000 speakers in Democratic Republic of Congo and Uganda. In Democratic Republic of Congo: 750,000 speakers in Orientale Province, Ituri district, Djugu territory, west and northwest of Lake Albert. Dialects are Djadha, Tadha, Pidha, Ddralo, Njawlo, Gegere. Tadha is the standard dialect. Djadha is the largest dialect and the one used for literature. Gegere is spoken by the ethnic Hema. Bilingualism in Swahili. Spoken as mother tongue by people from four ethnic backgrounds: Lendu, Hema-North, Alur, and Okebu.

Lese: also called Lesa, Lesse, Lissi, Walisi, Walese, Balese, Mbuti. 50,000 speakers in Democratic Republic of Congo, Orientale Province, Watsa, Djugu, Irumu, and Mambasa territories. Dialects are Lese Karo, Arumbi (Upstream Lese), Ndese (Lese Dese), Vukutu (Vonkutu, Obi), Fare. Closely related to Mamvu, Bendi, Mangbutu, and Efe. Congo Swahili (Kingwana) and Bangala are the lingua francas, but their use is somewhat limited, especially among the women.

Logo: also called Logoti. 210,000 speakers in Democratic Republic of Congo, Orientale Province, Faradje territory and Watsa town. Dialects are Ogambi (Ogamaru, Northern Logo), Doka, Lolya, Obilebha (Obelebha, Obileba), Bhagira (Bagela), Bari (Bari-Logo, Bariti). A dialect cluster, with Lolya as central. Closely related to Avokaya and Omi. Avokaya in Democratic Republic of Congo spoken in the northern Ogambi Area, may be closer to Logo than to Avokaya in Sudan.

Lombi: also called Lumbi, Rombi, Rumli, Odyalombito. 12,000 speakers in Democratic Republic of Congo, Orientale Province, Tshopo district, Bafwasende territory, Barumi and Bekeni collectivités. Opienge, Banguruye, and Bangolu are centers. Closely related to Mangbetu, but not as close as Mangbetu dialects are to each other.

Lugbara: also called High Lugbara. 488,000 speakers in Uganda and Democratic Republic of Congo. In Uganda: 200,000 speakers in the northwest, western Nile district. Dialects are Arua (Standard Lugbara), Maracha, Terego (Omugo). In Democratic Republic of Congo: 288,000 speakers in Orientale Province, Aru territory, six collectivités. Dialects are Zaki, Abedju-Azaki, Lu, Aluru, Nio, Otsho.

Lutos: also called Ruto. 19,000 speakers in Central African

Republic and Chad. In Central African Republic: 17,000 speakers in Ndélé, Kaga Andoro, and Kabo subprefectures. Dialects are Nduka (Ndouka, Ndoukwa), Lutos (Ruto, Routo, Rito, Luto, Louto), Wada (Wad), Nduga (Ngougua), Konga. In Chad: 1,978 speakers in the southwest, Moyen-Chari prefecture, Maro subprefecture, south of the Ngam. Dialects are Ruto (Routo, Rito, Louto, Luto). Only Lutos dialect is in Chad; Ruto and Nduka dialects are in Central African Republic. Not intelligible with Sar or Ngambai.

Ma'di: also called Ma'adi, Ma'diti. Around 150,000 speakers in Uganda and Sudan. In Uganda: 130,558 speakers. Dialects are Moyo, Adjumani (Oyuwi). In Sudan: 18,000 speakers in southern Sudan, Equatoria Province, Madi subdistrict, Opari district, West Nile district. Dialects are Pandikeri, Lokai, 'Burulo.

Ma'di, Southern: 48,000 speakers in Uganda, Okollo dounty, on the west bank of the Nile River. Okollo town is the administrative center. Dialects are Okollo, Ogoko, Rigbo. Closer to Lugbara than to Moyo (dialect of Ma'di), which they do not understand. Ogoko and Rigbo are closer to Lugbara than Okollo is; intelligibility testing needed. Okollo dialect is considered more "pure" than the others.

Mamvu: also called Tengo. 60,000 speakers in Democratic Republic of Congo, Orientale Province, west and southwest of Watsa in Watsa territory. Possibly some speakers in Uganda. Dialects are Amengi, Mamvu (Momvu, Momfu).

Mangbetu: also called Nemangbetu, Mangbettu, Mambetto, Amangbetu, Kingbetu. 650,000 speakers in Democratic Republic of Congo. Dialects are Meje (Medje), Mangbetu, Makere, Malele, Popoi. The Meje dialect is reported to have the most speakers, and is the most widely understood. Lombi and Asoa are related separate languages. Perhaps 50% know Bangala, another 10% know a limited amount. Popoi and Aberu are in Swahili-speaking areas. Both are made up of people who live in Swahili-speaking areas.

Mangbutu: also called Mombuttu, Wambutu, Mangu-Ngutu. 15,000 speakers in Democratic Republic of Congo, Orientale Province, south of the Kibali River and east of the Moto River in Watsa territory. Dialects are Andinai, Makutana, Angwe (Andali). The Andinai are separated from the other Mangbutu by the Lese. The Andali are a clan speaking the Angwe dialect.

Mango: also called Mongo, Mbay Doba, Doba. 50,000 speakers in Chad, Logone Oriental Prefecture, Doba subprefecture, centered around Bodo. Close to Bedjond and Gor, with high inherent intelligibility. There is a Mango Language Committee. The speakers have a clear understanding of their identity as separate from Gor and Bedjond.

Mbay: also called Mbai, Mbaye, Sara Mbai, Moissala Mbai, Mbay Moissala. 100,000 speakers in Chad, Central African Republic, and Nigeria. In Chad: Southwest, Moyen-Chari prefecture, Moïssala subprefecture. Around Moïssala. The traditional area is on the border of Chad and Central African Republic. Dialects are Bédjou, Kan (Mbay-Kan), Ngoka (Mbang), Bédégué, Mougo, Bbate. In Central African Republic: 8,300 speakers. Markounda and Batangafo subprefectures. In Nigeria: State of Borno.

Mittu: formerly spoken in southern Sudan.

Mo'da: also called Gberi, Gweri, Gbara, Muda. 600 speakers in southern Sudan, northwest of Mvolo on both sides of the border of Lakes and Western Equatoria provinces.

Morokodo: also called Ma'di. 3,400 speakers in southern Sudan, in the area between Amadi and Maridi. Dialects are Biti, Ma'du, Morokodo. A dialect cluster. Many use Moru as second language. As of 1984, Ma'du may be extinct.

Moru: also called Kala Moru. 70,000 speakers in Sudan, in southern Sudan, Mundri district, Equatoria Province. Dialects are Agi, Andri, 'Bali'ba, Kadiro, Lakama'di, Miza, Moruwa'di. Andri and 'Bali'ba dialects are similar, Kadiro and Lakama'di are nearly identical. Orthography problems.

Mvuba: also called Mbuba, Bambuba, Bamvuba, Mvuba-A, Obiye. 5,000 speakers in Democratic Republic of Congo and Uganda. In Democratic Republic of Congo: Nord-Kivu Province, Beni territory, around Oicha. Closely related to Lese.

Naba: 232,448 speakers in Chad. Dialects are Bilala (Bilaala, Boulala, Bulala, Mage, Ma), Kuka (Kouka, Lisi), Medogo (Modogo, Mud). Related but not inherently intelligible with Berakou or Kenga. Some use Chadian Arabic as second language. One part of the Kuka ethnic group, who live near Oum Hadjer, have shifted from the Naba language to Chadian Arabic.

Ndo: also called Ke'bu, Oke'bu, Kebutu, Ndu. 300,000 speakers in Democratic Republic of Congo and Uganda. In Democratic Republic of Congo: 100,000 speakers. Dialects are Avari (Avare, Avere, Aviritu), Oke'bu, Membi (Membitu, Meembi, Mombi, Ndo). Bilingualism in Bangala, Swahili. Vigorous language use. In Uganda: 200,000 speakers. Northwestern. Mahigi is the center. Dialects are Avari (Aviritu, Avere), Oke'bu (Ndo Oke'bu, Kebutu, Kebu), Membi.

Ngam: also called Ngama, Sarngam, Ngahm. 61,400 speakers in Chad and Central African Republic. In Chad: 43,743 speakers. Dialects are Ngam Tel, Ngam Tira, Kon Ngam, Kle, Ngam Gir Bor. Sara Madjingay is the lingua franca. In Central African Republic: 17,700 speakers in Kabo subprefecture.

Ngambay: also called Sara, Sara Ngambai, Gamba, Gambaye, Gamblai, Ngambai. 750,000 speakers in Chad and 2 other countries. In Chad: Dialects are Lara, Benoye, Murum (Mouroum), Kere, Bemar (Daba de Goré). The dialects are reported to be completely intelligible with each other. The Laka language is considered by some to be a dialect of Ngambay. Largest language of the Sara-Bagirmi group. Trade language.

Ngiti: also called Kingiti, Ngeti, Kingeti, Ndruna, Druna, Bindi, Lendu-Sud. 100,000 speakers in Democratic Republic of Congo, Orientale Province, Irumu territory, south of Bunia.

Nyamusa-Molo: 1,200 speakers in southern Sudan, western Equatoria Province, southeast of Beli, northeast of Morokodo. Dialects are Nyamusa, Molo.

Olu'bo: also called Lulubo, Luluba, Olubogo, Oluboti, Ondoe, Lolubo. 15,000 speakers in Sudan, southern Sudan, eastern Equatoria Province, about 30 miles east of the Nile River. Many are bilingual in Bari (dialect of Logo). There is strong interest in using Olu'bo for education.

Omi: also called Kaliko-Omi. 39,500 speakers in Democratic Republic of Congo, Orientale Province, Aru territory, between the Nzoro and Lowa rivers along the Aru to Aba road. Closely related to Keliko, but not close enough to Keliko or Ma'di to use literature in those languages. Previously considered to be a Keliko dialect. An important language.

Sar: also called Sara, Sara Madjingay. 183,471 speakers in Chad. Dialects are Majingai (Majinngay, Madjingaye, Madjingay, Madja Ngai), Nar, No. The principal language of Sarh. Trade language.

Sara Dunjo: also called Kaba Dunjo, Sara Dinjo. 4,000 speakers in Central African Republic, Ndélé subprefecture, close to the Chadian border in nine villages. May be the same as Kaba Na of Chad. May be intelligible with Sara.

Sara Kaba: also called Ta Sara. 13,600 speakers in Central African Republic, Ndélé and Birao subprefectures. May be intelligible with Sara Dunjo of Central African Republic or Kaba Na of Chad.

Sinyar: also called Sinya, Shemya, Shamya, Symiarta, Shamyan, Zimirra, Taar Shamyan. 5,000 speakers in Chad and Sudan. In Chad: East, Ouaddaï prefecture, Goz-Beïda subprefecture, north of Mongororo, near the confluence of the Kaja, Azum, and Salih Rivers. People are generally trilingual in Sinyar, Fur, and Chadian Arabic. Many speak Daju or Masalit. The language is not dying out. In Sudan: The main center is at Foro Boranga. Speakers are geographically cut off from speakers of other Bongo-Bagirmi languages.

Vale: 5,400 speakers in Central African Republic, in Batangafo, Kabo, and Kaga Bandoro subprefectures. Not in Chad. Dialects are Vale, Tana (Tane, Tele). Related to Lutos. Not intelligible with Sara or Ngambai. High bilingualism in Sango.

Yulu: also called Youlou. 7,000 speakers in Central African Republic, and 2 other countries. In Central African Republic: 4,000 speakers. Ouadda-DjaléI and Ouadda subprefectures. Yulu are in Central African Republic and Sudan; Binga are in Sudan and Democratic Republic of Congo. Dialects are Binga, Yulu. Many are bilingual in Gbaya or Arabic in Sudan. In Sudan: 3,000 speakers.   B. GRIMES

CHADIC LANGUAGES. The Chadic family includes some 150 languages spoken in sub-Saharan Africa to the west, south, and east of Lake Chad. Excluding Hausa, the Chadic language area can be described roughly as a rectangle extending from 9° to 13° N and from 9° to 19° E (see Map 1). The best-known and most populous Chadic language is Hausa. The other languages, some now endangered, range in size from under one-half million to as few as 50 speakers. Many of these have never been described beyond short word lists, although for some (e.g. Margi and Miya), first-rate descriptive grammars exist. Most Chadic languages are still unwritten, apart from short scriptural texts prepared by Protestant missionaries.

Chadic is a constituent of the Afroasiatic (AA) phylum. Resemblances between individual Chadic languages and other AA languages had been noted since the mid-19th century, but the relationship was not generally accepted until a century later, following the overall classification of the languages of Africa by Greenberg 1963. According to the now standard internal classification (Newman 1990, building on the pioneer work of Lukas 1936 and Newman and Ma 1966), Chadic languages fall into three large branches—West, Biu-Mandara (= Central), and East—plus the isolated Masa cluster. A comprehensive list of languages in the family is given in Figure 1.

Chadic languages typically have many consonants and few vowels. Four positions of articulation are the norm: labial, alveolar, palatal, and velar (including labialized velar). A common pattern is to have a set of glottalized (implosive and/or ejective) obstruents alongside the voiced and voiceless ones. (Glottal stop, however, is not a characteristic Chadic phoneme.) Many languages also have a full set of prenasalized phonemes. Thus, a four-way phonation distinction is commonplace, at least in the labial and alveolar positions, e.g. /t d ɗ nd/. Another typical feature is the presence of lateral fricatives, voiceless, voiced, and (much less often) ejective, e.g., /ɬ ɮ ɬ'/. Bura and closely related languages are unusual in having simultaneously articulated labial-alveolar and labial-palatal consonants, e.g., / ɓɗ bz pč /.

Vowel systems typically range from two vowels, as in Mandara, consisting simply of high (/ə/) vs. low (/a/), to seven vowels, as in Dangaleat. The most common patterns are / i (e) a (o) u ə /, with /e/ and /o/ often being marginal, and /i e a o u/. The only diphthongs that occur are /ai/ and /au/. Distinctive vowel length is widespread in the family; it is usually limited to word-medial position. Contrary to a common AA pattern, most Chadic

MAP 1. *Distribution of Major Groups of Chadic Languages*

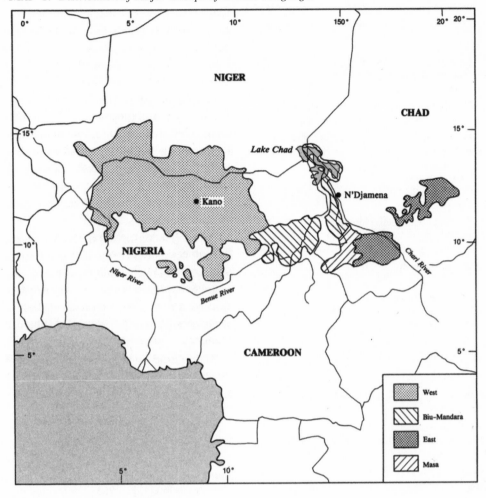

languages allow vowel-initial words. Nasal vowels are practically nonexistent in the family. Vowel harmony is rare, although a fully fledged nine-vowel ATR-type system occurs in Tangale.

All Chadic languages are tonal. Both two-tone and three-tone systems are common, often accompanied by distinctive downstep. The lexical functional load of tone is usually slight; its major role is usually grammatical, e.g. in marking tense/aspect distinctions.

Grammatical gender is commonplace though not omnipresent. There are always two genders, masculine and feminine, with no distinction in the plural. In grammatical morphemes, the masculine and plural markers are often phonologically identical, or nearly so, whereas the feminine is different, for example, *n/t/n* or *ka/ta/ku* ('masc./fem./pl.'). Pronouns distinguish gender in both 2nd and 3rd persons.

Chadic languages exhibit a multiplicity of noun plural formations involving various suffixes (some relating to Proto-Chadic *-aki*, *-Vn*, and *-i*), and/or internal vowel changes, including the insertion of internal -a-. Many languages also have "pluractional" verbs, which indicate an action done many times or affecting a multiplicity of subjects (if intransitive) or objects (if transitive). These pluractionals are typically formed by vocalic ablaut, gemination, or partial reduplication. Grammatical number agreement with the subject is rare, although it is found in a few languages belonging to the Bole group.

Verbs typically allow one or more suffixal extensions that express action in, toward, down, away (= "efferential"), as well as partially, totally, or well done. Some of the extensions are grammatical in nature, indicating benefaction, transitivization, or perfectivity. The causative is usually expressed syntactically rather than by means of a morphological extension.

The most common word order in the family is S[ubject]

FIGURE 1. *Subgrouping of Chadic Languages*

West Branch:
  Subgroup A
    A.1. Gwandara, Hausa
    A.2. Bele, Bole, Deno, Galambu, Gera, Geruma, Kanakuru, Karekare, Kirfi, Kubi, Kupto, Kushi, Kwami, Maha, Ngamo, Pero, Piya, Tangale
    A.3. Angas, Chip, Gerka, Goemai, Jorto, Koenoem, Kofyar, Montol, Mupun, Pyapun, Sura, Tal
    A.4. Fyer, Karfa, Kulere, Mundat, Ron, Sha, Shagawu, Tambas
  Subgroup B
    B1. Bade, Duwai, Ngizim
    B.2. Diri, Jimbin, Kariya, Mburku, Miya, Pa'a, Siri, Tsagu, Warji
    B.3. Boghom, Buli, Dass, Geji, Guruntum, Jimi, Ju, Mangas, Polci, Saya, Zangwal, Zeem

Biu-Mandara (Central) Branch:
  Subgroup A
    A.1. Ga'anda, Hona, Jara, Tera
    A.2. Bura-Pabir, Chibak, Kilba, Margi, Putai
    A.3. Bana, Higi-Kapsiki
    A.4. Dghwede, Glavda, Guduf, Gvoko, Lamang, Mabas, Mandara, Podoko
    A.5. Balda, Cuvok, Dugwor, Gisiga, Hurza, Mada, Matakam, Mboku, Mefele, Merey, Mofu, Moloko, Muktele, Muyang, Ndreme, Ouldeme, Zulgo
    A.6. Sukur
    A.7. Buwal, Daba, Gawar, Hina
    A.8. Bachama-Bata, Gude, Gudu, Ngwaba, Nzanyi
  Subgroup B
    B.1. Buduma, Kotoko, Logone, Midah
    B.2. Mbara, Musgu
  Subgroup C
    Gidar

East Branch:
  Subgroup A
    A.1. Gadang, Miltu, Mod, Ndam, Sarwa, Somrai, Tumak
    A.2. Gabri, Kabalai, Kimre, Lele, Nancere, Tobanga
    A.3. Kera, Kwang
  Subgroup B
    B.1. Bidiyo, Birgit, Dangaleat, Jegu, Kujarke, Mahwa, Migama, Mogum, Mubi, Toram
    B.2. Mukulu
    B.3. Barain, Saba, Sokoro

Masa Branch
    Lame, Marba-Monogoy, Masa, Mesme, Musey, Peve, Zime, Zumaya

V[erb] O[bject]. Pronoun indirect objects commonly cliticize to the verb, whereas noun indirect objects appear as prepositional phrases after the direct object. A small number of Biu-Mandara languages spoken in the Nigeria-Cameroon border area are VSO, probably the result of a geographically shared innovation rather than reflecting an archaism going back to Proto-Chadic. All Chadic languages are prepositional. Negation is most often indicated by a particle at the end of the sentence, sometimes co-occurring with a preverbal negative particle, for example, Margi *Ni nda wi mai* 'I didn't run' (lit. I NEG run NEG). Reflexives are most often built on the body parts 'head' and 'body', for example, 'ourselves' is Hausa *kanmu* (lit. 'head of us'), Tera *vami* (lit. 'body of us').

Within the noun phrase, the noun is generally followed by numerals, adjectives, and demonstratives. In possessive constructions (including part-of relationships), the possessed precedes the possessor, often with an overt genitive marker between the constituents. Most Chadic languages (apart from Hausa) distinguish alienable from inalienable possession.

[*See also* Afroasiatic Languages; Biu-Mandara Languages; East Chadic Languages; Hausa; Masa Languages; *and* West Chadic Languages.]

BIBLIOGRAPHY

Frajzyngier, Zygmunt. 1996. *Grammaticalization of the complex sentence: A case study in Chadic.* Amsterdam: Benjamins.

Greenberg, Joseph H. 1963. *The languages of Africa.* (Indiana University Research Center in Anthropology, Folklore, and Linguistics, publication 25; *International Journal of American Linguistics,* 29:1, part 2.) Bloomington: Indiana University.

Hoffmann, Carl. 1963. *A grammar of the Margi language.* London: Oxford University Press.

Jungraithmayr, Herrmann, and Dymitr Ibriszimow. 1994. *Chadic lexical roots.* Vol. 1: *Tentative reconstruction, grading, distribution and comments.* Vol. 2: *Documentation.* (Sprache und Oralität in Afrika, 20.) Berlin: Dietrich Reimer.

Lukas, Johannes. 1936. The linguistic situation in the Lake Chad area in Central Africa. *Africa* 9:332–349.

Newman, Paul. 1977. *Chadic classification and reconstructions.* (*Afroasiatic Linguistics* 5/1.) Malibu: Undena Publications.

Newman, Paul. 1980. *The classification of Chadic within Afroasiatic.* Leiden: Universitaire Pers.

Newman, Paul. 1990. *Nominal and verbal plurality in Chadic.* Dordrecht: Foris Publications.

Newman, Paul. 1996. *Hausa and the Chadic language family: A bibliography.* (African linguistic bibliographies, 6.) Cologne: Rüdiger Köppe.

Newman, Paul, and Roxana Ma. 1966. Comparative Chadic: Phonology and lexicon. *Journal of African Languages* 5.218–251.

Pawlak, Nina. 1994. *Syntactic markers in Chadic: A study on development of grammatical morphemes.* Warsaw: Instytut Orientalistyczny, Uniwersytetu Warszawskiego.

Schuh, Russell G. 1998. *A grammar of Miya.* (University of California Publications in Linguistics, 130.) Berkeley and Los Angeles: University of California Press.

Stolbova, Olga V. 1996. *Studies in Chadic comparative phonology.* Moscow: Diaphragma Publishers.

PAUL NEWMAN

CHAMORRO.

A branch of WESTERN MALAYO-POLYNESIAN; also called Tjamoro. Around 78,000 speakers in Guam and Northern Mariana Islands. In Guam: 62,500 speakers. Dialects are Chamorro, Rotanese Chamorro. Active language use. Language gaining in importance. Taught at the University of Guam. National language. In Northern Mariana Islands: 14,205 speakers on Alamagan Island. Slight dialect differences. Some bilingualism in English. It is a trade language on Saipan. National language.

B. GRIMES

CHAPACURA-WANHAM LANGUAGES.

A group spoken in northeastern Bolivia and adjacent parts of Brazil.

LANGUAGE LIST

Itene: also called Iteneo, Itenez, More. Formerly spoken in Bolivia. Ethnic population: 108 as of 2000. North central Beni department at junction of Mamoré and Itenez Rivers. Children were not speaking Itene and only some of the older people were actively using it 30 years ago. They speak Spanish. Related languages: Chapacura, Quitemoca, Cujuna, Cumana, Mataua, Uanham, Urunumacan; probably all extinct.

Kabixí: also called Cabichí, Cabishi. 100 speakers in Brazil on the slopes of Planalto dos Parecís, right bank of upper Guaporé, near Vila Bela, Mato Grosso. Related to Cujuna, Cumana, Mataua, Wanham, Urunumacan. Both people and language may be extinct.

Oro Win: 5 speakers remain in Brazil. Ethnic population: 55

FIGURE 1. *Subgrouping of Chapacura-Wanham Languages*

| **Guapore** |
| Itene, Kabixí |
| **Madeira** |
| Oro Win, Pakaásnovos, Torá |

as of 1998. Headwaters of the Pacaas-Novos River, a tributary of the Mamoré River, along the Brazil–Bolivia border. Related to Tora, Itene (More), and Wari (Pakaasnovos), but not inherently intelligible with them. Bilingualism in Wari. As of 1986, all speakers were over 40 years old.

Pakaásnovos: also called Jaru, Uomo, Pakaanovas, Pacaas-Novos, Pakaanova, Pacahanovo, Oro Wari, Wari. 1,833 speakers in Brazil, in Rondônia, seven villages.

Torá: also called Toraz. 40 speakers remain in Brazil. Ethnic population: 120 as of 1990. Amazonas, on the lower Rio Marmelos, tributary of the Rio Madeira.

B. GRIMES

CHIAPANEC-MANGUE LANGUAGES.

A branch of the OTO-MANGUEAN family. They are or were spoken in Chiapas state, Mexico, and in Costa Rica and Nicaragua.

LANGUAGE LIST

Chiapaneco: 150 speakers in Mexico in the state of Chiapas, El Bosque, Las Margaritas, Ocosingo, Palenque, Sabanilla. Reported to be quite similar to Chorotega of Costa Rica and El Salvador.

Chorotega: also called Choluteca, Mangue, Diria, Orotina. Formerly spoken in Costa Rica and Nicaragua. Ethnic population: 795 as of 2000. Dialects are Chorotega, Diria, Nagrandan, Nicoya, Orisi, Orotinya (Orotina). Became extinct in Costa Rica by the end of the 18th century, in Nicaragua in the 19th century.

B. GRIMES

CHIBCHAN LANGUAGES.

A family of southern Central America and northernmost South America.

LANGUAGE LIST

Boruca: also called Borunca, Burunca, Brunca, Brunka. 5 speakers remain in Costa Rica. Ethnic population: 1,000 as of 1991. Southern coast between Playa Bonita and Golfito. Nearly all speak only Spanish.

Bribri: also called Talamanca. 9,000 speakers in Costa Rica. Ethnic population: 12,172 as of 2000. Southern, along Lari, Telire, and Uren Rivers, canton of Talamanca, Limón Province; canton of Buenos Aires, Puntarenas Province. Dialects are Salitre-Cabagra, Amubre-Katsi, Coroma. Closest to, but unintelligible to speakers of Cabécar, Guatuso, and Teribe. The three major dialects are inherently intelligible to each others' speakers. Bilingualism in Spanish. All ages. Bribri spoken in the home.

Buglere: also called Bokota, Bogota, Bofota, Bobota, Bocota, Bukueta, Nortenyo, Murire, Veraguas Sabanero. 2,500 speakers in mountains of western Panama. Dialects are

FIGURE 1. *Subgrouping of Chibchan Languages*

Aruak
    Cogui, Ica, Malayo
Chibchan Proper
    Chibcha
    Tunebo
        Angosturas Tunebo, Barro Negro Tunebo, Central
        Tunebo, Western Tunebo
Cofan
    Cofán
Guaymi
    Buglere, Ngäbere
Kuna
    Border Kuna, San Blas Kuna
Motilon
    Motilón
Paya
    Pech
Rama
    Maléku Jaíka, Rama
Talamanca
    Boruca, Bribri, Cabécar, Teribe
Unclassified
    Chimila

Sabanero, Bokotá. Speakers of Sabanero are few and integrated among the Guaymí.

Cabécar: also called Chirripó. 8,840 speakers in Costa Rica. Ethnic population: 9,308 as of 2000. Turrialba region. Dialects are Chirripó, Telire, Estrella, Ujarrás. Some bilingualism in Spanish. 80% are monolingual. 95% of the ethnic group are speakers.

Chibcha: also called Muisca, Mosca. Formerly spoken in central highlands of Colombia. The Chibcha people are still located near the towns of Tocancipa, Cota, Gachancipa, and Tenjo. No speakers are left.

Chimila: also called Caca Weranos, San Jorge, Shimizya. 2,000 speakers in Colombia, the lowlands south and west of Fundación, and scattered in the central part of department of Magdalena. Vigorous language use. Limited Spanish is used as second language.

Cofán: also called Kofán, Kofane, A'i, A'ingae. 1,500 speakers in Ecuador and Colombia. In Ecuador: 900 speakers. Ethnic population: 900. as of 2000. Chibchan with Western Tucanoan features, though others theorize Barbacoan or Jivaroan features. Some bilingualism in Spanish. 800 are monolingual, 700 have elementary knowledge of Spanish. 50 may also know Siona, Secoya, or Lowland Quichua. Schools are in Spanish, except for early grades that are bilingual. Speakers also speak Siona, Secoya, Lowland Quichua. All ages. All domains. Spoken and written use in religious services. Parents transmit Cofán to children. Some Siona and Secoya have learned Cofán because of intermarriage, and their children

learn Cofán. People are proud of Cofá. Roman alphabet used. Official language. In Colombia: 600 speakers. Ethnic population: 600 as of 2000. Colombia-Ecuador border area, Putumayo Province. Dialects are Aguarico, Santa Rosa. Fairly monolingual. Some children not learning Cofán.

Cogui: also called Kogui, Coghui, Kogi, Kagaba, Kaggaba. 9,770 speakers in Colombia. Ethnic population: 11,000 as of 1998. Northern, eastern, and western slopes of Sierra Nevada de Santa Marta. Some bilingualism in Spanish. Malayo also used.

Ica: also called Aruaco, Arhuaco, Bintuk, Bíntukua, Bintucua, Ijca, Ijka, Ika, Ike. 14,301 speakers in Colombia. Ethnic population: 14,301 as of 1998. Southern slopes of Sierra Nevada de Santa Marta. 90% are monolingual. A few use Spanish as second language. All ages.

Kuna, Border: also called Colombia Cuna, Caiman Nuevo, Cuna, Paya-Pucuro. 1,300 speakers in Colombia and Panama. In Colombia: 600 speakers in northern coastal region near the Panama isthmus. In Panama: 700 speakers in southeastern Panama, villages of Paya and Pucuro. Classification of Kuna is uncertain; it may be an isolate with certain Chibchan features. Some bilingualism in Spanish.

Kuna, San Blas: also called San Blas Cuna. 50,000 speakers in Panama on San Blas Islands and on the mainland. Dialects are Chuana, Cueva, Bayano (Alto Bayano, Maje). Some bilingualism in Spanish. English also used.

Malayo: also called Marocasero, Maracasero, Sanja, Sanka, Sancá, Arosario, Arsario, Guamaka, Guamaca, Wiwa. 3,225 speakers in Colombia on the southern and eastern slopes of Sierra Nevada de Santa Marta.

Maléku Jaíka: also called Guatuso. 750 speakers in Costa Rica. Ethnic population: 1,074 as of 2000. Northern Costa Rica. Some bilingualism in Spanish.

Motilóón: also called Bari, Motilone. 1,500 speakers in Colombia and Venezuela. In Colombia: Oro River and Catatumbo River region. In Venezuela: 850 speakers on Venezuelan and Colombian border, state of Zulia. One scholar questions its classification as Chibchan; another classifies it as Arawakan.

Ngäbere: also called Valiente, Chiriqui, Ngobere, Guaymí. 133,000 speakers in Panama and Costa Rica. In Panama: 128,000 speakers in northeastern Chiriqui, Bocas del Toro, western Veraguas (western provinces). Dialects are Valiente, Eastern Guaymí (Tolé), Chiriquí. Some bilingualism in Spanish. English Creole also used. In Costa Rica: Ethnic population: 5,360 as of 2000. 95% of the ethnic group are speakers.

Pech: also called Paya, Seco. 994 speakers in Honduras. Ethnic population: 2,586 as of 1993. Bilingualism in Spanish. The youngest speakers are 40 years old, but most are over 60. Speakers are more active in using Pech in Agua Amarilla and La Laguna in El Carbó, and use Spanish less often.

Rama: 24 speakers remain in Nicaragua. Ethnic population: 900 as of 2000. Rama Cay, 30-mile radius. Most people now speak Rama Cay Creole.

Teribe: also called Terraba, Tiribi, Tirribi, Nortenyo, Quequexque, Naso. 3,000 speakers in Panama and Costa Rica. In Panama: Northwestern area, Changuinola, Teribe River. Bilingualism in Spanish. In Costa Rica: Ethnic population: 35 to 300 as of 1991, Southeastern, north coast. Terraba in Costa Rica who knew only a little of this language wanted to relearn the language and culture in 1991.

Tunebo, Angosturas: spoken in Colombia. 71% intelligibility between Eastern and Angosturas Tunebo. Some amount of mutual intelligibility.

Tunebo, Barro Negro: also called Eastern Tunebo. 300 speakers in Colombia. 62% intelligibility with Central Tunebo. Partly bilingualism, some acculturation. Tunebo is used exclusively in the home.

Tunebo, Central: also called Cobaría Tunebo, U'wa. 2,500 speakers in Colombia and Venezuela. In Colombia: Northern slopes of Sierra Nevada de Cocuy, Boyaca and Arauca regions; Satocá, Calafita, Tegría (Boyacá), Cobaría (Boyacá). Some bilingualism in Spanish. All ages. In Venezuela: state of Apure.

Tunebo, Western: also called Aguas Blancas, U'wa. 700 speakers in Santander del Sur, Colombia. The most divergent of the Tunebo languages. Limited bilingualism.

B. GRIMES

CHILD LANGUAGE. *See* Acquisition of Language; Evolution of Language; Formal Grammar; Psycholinguistics; *and* Sociolinguistics.

CHIMAKUAN LANGUAGES constitute a language family of northwestern Washington, United States. Of the two languages in the family, Chimakum, formerly spoken on the Puget Sound side of the Olympic Peninsula, is extinct.

LANGUAGE LIST

Quileute: 10 speakers remain in USA. Ethnic population: 300 as of 1977. Pacific side of Olympic Peninsula in Washington. Dialects are Quileute, Hoh. Bilingualism in English.

B. GRIMES

CHINANTECAN LANGUAGES. A branch of the OTO-MANGUEAN family. They are spoken in Oaxaca state, Mexico.

LANGUAGE LIST

Chinanteco, Chiltepec: 1,000 speakers in Oaxaca, San José Chiltepec. 76% intelligibility of Tlacoatzintepec Chinanteco (closest), 20% of Usila and Ojitlán Chinanteco, 13% of Valle Nacional Chinanteco. Speakers use Spanish as second language, but outlying towns are not as bilingual as the center.

Chinanteco, Comaltepec: 2,000 speakers. Ethnic population: 2,000. 69% intelligibility of Quiotepec Chinanteco (closest), 7% of Tepetotutla Chinanteco. Bilingualism level estimates for Spanish are 0 5%, 1 15%, 2 30%, 3 30%, 4 19%, 5 1%. 25% of speakers are monolingual. All ages. All domains. Oral use in local administration, pre-school, religion. Written use to record customs, traditions, history. Vigorous language use. Parents transmit it to children. Speakers want to preserve their language.

Chinanteco, Lalana: 10,500 speakers at the Oaxaca-Veracruz border, 25 towns. 87% intelligibility of Tepinapa Chinanteco (closest, but lower in outlying areas), 43% of Ozumacín, 24% of Lealao Chinanteco. Bilingual level estimates for Spanish are 0 50%, 1 29%, 2 10%, 3 10%, 4 1%, 5 0%.

Chinanteco, Lealao: also called San Juan Lealao Chinanteco. 2,000 speakers in northeastern Oaxaca, San Juan Lealao, Latani, Tres Arroyos, and La Hondura. Considered the most divergent of the Chinantec languages. Some bilingualism in Spanish. 500 speakers are monolingual. 1,200 are bilingual in Spanish. There is also some bilingualism in Zapoteco. All ages. All domains. Oral and written use in religious services. Oral use in local business. Vigorous language use. Parents transmit it to children. Speakers consider it to be inferior to Spanish, but they continue to use it.

Chinanteco, Ojitlán: 22,000 speakers. 49% intelligibility of Sochiapan Chinanteco (closest), 43% of Usila Chinanteco, 39% of Palantla Chianteco, 31% of Chiltepec Chinanteco.

Chinanteco, Ozumacín: also called Juujmii. 5,000 speakers in northeastern Oaxaca, three towns: San Pedro Ozumacín, Auyotzintepec, Santiago Progreso. Ozumacín town has slight dialect difference from others. 63% intelligibility of Palantla Chinanteco (closest), 22% of Lalana Chinanteco and Valle Nacional Chinanteco. 1,500 monolinguals. 3,500 speak some Spanish. Some speak some Palantla Chinanteco. All ages. Oral use in local administration, business, some in religious services. Half of parents transmit it to children. Speakers view Chinanteco as inferior to Spanish, but continue to use it.

Chinanteco, Palantla: 12,000 speakers in Oaxaca, San Juan Palantla plus 13 towns. 78% intelligibility of Tepetotutla Chinanteco (closest), 72% of Valle Nacional Chinanteco, 69% of Usila Chinanteco, 54% of Ozumacín Chinanteco. Bilingual level estimates for Spanish are 0 10%, 1 25%, 2 35%, 3 25%, 4 5%, 5 0%.

Chinanteco, Quiotepec: also called Highland Chinanteco. 8,000 speakers. 87% intelligibility of Comaltepec Chinanteco (closest, lower in outlying areas), 7% of Tepetotutla Chinanteco. The highland Chinanteco languages share a complexity of vowel length and tone extensions that Tepetotutla and Palantla do not have. Some bilingualism in Spanish.

Chinanteco, Sochiapan: 5,800 speakers. Ethnic population: 6,000. North Oaxaca, Cuic: San Pedro Sochiapan, Retumbadero, San Juan Zautla, Santiago Quetzalapa, San Juan Zapotitlán. 66% intelligibility of Tlacoatzintepec Chinanteco (closest), 56% of Chiltepec Chinanteco, 45% of Usila Chinanteco, 11% of Tepetotutla Chinanteco. Some bilingualism in Spanish. About 15% are monolingual, 85% use Spanish as second language. 10 to 20 people know some English. All ages. All domains. Oral use in local administration, business. A few teachers try to teach it in school. Oral and written use in church. Vigorous language use. Parents transmit it to children. Speakers have a positive attitude toward it.

Chinanteco, Tepetotutla: 2,000 speakers in northern Oaxaca, Santa Cruz Tepetotutla, San Antonio del Barrio, San Pedro Tlatepusco, Santo Tomás Texas, Vega del Sol, El Naranjal. 60% intelligibility of Quiotepec Chinanteco, 59% of Palantla Chinanteco, 48% of Yolox.

Chinanteco, Tepinapa: 8,000 speakers. 79% intelligibility of Comaltepec Chinanteco, 87% to 68% of Lalana Chinanteco, 24% of Lealao Chinanteco, 23% of Ozumacín. Limited bilingualism in Spanish. Most children are monolingual when they start school. Vigorous language use.

Chinanteco, Tlacoatzintepec: 2,000 speakers in Oaxaca, San Juan Bautista Tlacoatzintepec, San Pedro Alianza, Santiago Quetzalapa, San Juan Zapotitlán. 85% intelligibility of Chiltepec Chinanteco (closest, lower in outlying areas), 84% of Usila Chinanteco, 74% of Sochiapan Chinanteco, 15% of Tepetotutla Chinanteco. Some bilingualism in Spanish.

Chinanteco, Usila: 9,000 speakers in Oaxaca, San Felipe Usila plus 12 towns, and one in Veracruz (Pueblo Doce). 48% intelligibility of Tlacoatzintepec Chinanteco (closest), 33% of Palantla Chinanteco, 32% of Sochiapan Chinanteco, 31% of Ojitlán Chinanteco. Some bilingualism in Spanish.

Chinanteco, Valle Nacional: 1,000 speakers in northern Oaxaca, San Juan Bautista Valle Nacional and mainly in San Mateo Yetla. 71% intelligibility of Chiltepec Chinanteco (closest), 70% of Palantla Chinanteco, 53% of Ozumacín Chinanteco, 40% of Tepetotutla Chinanteco. Bilingualism in Spanish.

B. GRIMES

CHINESE.

As a language name, "Chinese" is highly ambiguous. It is used to designate any of the following spoken languages: the official spoken language of the People's Republic of China, where the language is called Pǔtōnghuà; the official spoken language of Taiwan (*Guóyǔ*); one of the official languages of Singapore (*Huáyǔ*); or any of the hundreds of regional variants ("dialects") spoken in China. It may also refer to various versions of the written language of an enormous body of literature. Some of this literature represents the vernacular language of different historical periods, and some represents highly stylized written languages used exclusively in certain literary genres. (For reference, see Wáng 1947, 1957–1958, Forrest 1948, Karlgren 1949, Chao 1968, Li and Thompson 1978, 1981, DeFrancis 1984, Ramsey 1987, and Norman 1988.)

There is, however, a significant degree of commonality behind the diverse reality of the Chinese language. This commonality is manifested in these facts:

(a) The vast majority of the people of China speak one of the Mandarin dialects.
(b) The Mandarin dialects are by and large mutually intelligible.
(c) The official spoken languages of China, Taiwan, and Singapore are all based on the Běijīng dialect of the Mandarin group.
(d) The contemporary written language used by the Chinese people is primarily based on the Běijīng dialect.

1. Genetic classification and dialects. The various forms of spoken Chinese, which will be designated as "dialects" in this article, constitute an independent branch of the Sino-Tibetan language family. Parallel to Chinese, but distantly related to it, is the Tibeto-Burman subfamily, with the Karen languages sometimes considered a third subfamily rather than a branch of Tibeto-Burman. Within the Chinese branch are hundreds of dialects, many of them mutually unintelligible. These dialects are classified into seven groups, primarily on the basis of phonological evidence, as listed below (see Map 1).

1.1. *Mandarin* dialects are spoken natively by about two-thirds of the one billion people in China. The geographical range of Mandarin includes all of north China, west China, part of central China, and the Sìchuān basin, as well as Guìzhōu and Yúnnán provinces in the south. This large dialect group is often divided into four subgroups, according to their phonological and lexical affinities and their geographical range: (i) Northern Mandarin, (ii) Northwestern Mandarin, (iii) Southwestern Mandarin, and (iv) Eastern or Lower Yángzě River Mandarin. The common characteristics of the Mandarin dialects are: the absence of voiced stops [b d g]; the absence of syllable-final consonants [p t k m]; and a relatively simple system of tones (usually four), with fewer tone sandhi

MAP 1. *Distribution of Dialects of Chinese*

rules. (In the standard Pīnyīn transcription of Mandarin, the symbols *b d g* represent voiceless unaspirated stops, while *p t k* are aspirated.)

1.2. Wú dialects are spoken around the coastal area of the lower Yángzě River and its tributaries, in the provinces of Jiāngsū, Zhèjiāng, and Ānhuī. Speakers of Wú occupy an area roughly the size of the state of Illinois. The most important feature of Wú dialects is the three-

way phonemic distinction between voiced stops, voiceless unaspirated stops, and voiceless aspirated stops in syllable-initial position: [b d g] vs. [p t k] vs. [p' t' k']. This three-way contrast of stops is attested in M[iddle] C[hinese] (7th c. BCE).

1.3. Gàn dialects are spoken primarily in Jiāngxī province, to the southwest of the Wú area. The region and its dialect group are named after the Gàn River, which traverses the province from north to south. Some linguists consider Gàn a subgroup of Mandarin. The major difference between Mandarin and Gàn lies in the historical development of the MC voiced stops [b d g]. In Gàn, these have become voiceless aspirated stops [p' t' k']. (In Mandarin, the historical development of the voiced stops is more varied.)

1.4. Xiāng dialects are spoken in Húnán province, to the immediate west of the Gàn dialect area. The name Xiāng refers to a river which runs from north to south in Húnán province, as a tributary of the Yángzě. There are two dialect groups, "Old" and "New." Old Xiāng, like Wú, preserves the MC voiced stops [b d g]. But unlike the Northern Wú dialects—which typically associate these voiced stops with some sort of laryngeal activity, described as "murmuring"—the voiced stops in Old Xiāng do not have any unusual phonetic property. New Xiāng, like Mandarin, has lost the series of voiced stops. (In fact, there is no systematic distinction between New Xiāng and Mandarin, which have a greater degree of mutual intelligibility than Old Xiāng and New Xiāng.) Old Xiāng is spoken primarily in rural communities, and New Xiāng in northwest Húnán, as well as in urban areas all over the province. It is likely that New Xiāng has become more and more distant from Old Xiāng because of contact with Mandarin.

1.5. Mǐn is spoken in the southern coastal province of Fújiàn and the island of Taiwan, as well as the northern coast, the Léizhōu peninsula, and Hǎinán island of Guǎngdōng province. Mǐn dialects are numerous, and often mutually unintelligible: in Fújiàn province alone, nine mutually unintelligible subgroups of dialects have been reported. In addition, the dialects of northern coastal Guǎngdōng and of Hǎinán island (Mǐn Nán or Southern Min) are significantly different from the Mǐn dialects of other areas. The definitive characteristic of Mǐn is the contrast between the voiceless aspirated dental stop [t'] and voiceless unaspirated [t] in a particular set of words meaning, e.g., 'tree', 'know', 'hail', and 'insect'.

1.6. Yuè dialects occupy most of Guǎngdōng and Guǎngxī provinces. The standard dialect is the speech of the city of Guǎngzhōu, known as Cantonese; this is also the language of Hong Kong, and of many overseas Chinese settlements in North America, Europe, and Southeast Asia. Yuè dialects preserve all the MC syllable-final consonants [p t k m n ŋ]. (See O. Y. Hashimoto 1971.)

1.7. Kèjiā or Hakka dialects are distributed throughout southeastern China, in small agricultural communities in Yuè and Mǐn dialect areas. Historically, they were northerners who moved south during several waves of migration. The name Hakka is a word of Cantonese origin, meaning 'guests'; Kèjiā is the pronunciation of Hakka in Beijing Mandarin. The Kèjiā dialects share with the Gàn dialects the feature that MC voiced stops have developed into corresponding voiceless aspirated stops [p' t' k']. But differences in other phonological features, as well as in lexicon, keep the two groups separate. It has been assumed that the Kèjiā dialects are relatively homogeneous; however, as new information emerges, this assumption may prove wrong. (See M. J. Hashimoto 1973.)

Although Chinese dialects are numerous and their geographical spread enormous, they share a number of grammatical features; those described below are salient (see Yuán et al. 1960).

2. Tone. In Chinese, every syllable which is not de-stressed has a contrastive pitch pattern, called its *tone*. This pattern is significant because it distinguishes the meanings of words with the same segmental composition, as in the following example from Běijīng Mandarin (the numbers indicate pitch levels, with 5 representing the highest pitch and 1 the lowest):

	Word	Tone	Gloss
(1)	*tōng*	high level (55)	'to open up'
	tóng	high rising (35)	'copper'
	tǒng	low falling-rising (214)	'tub'
	tòng	high falling (51)	'to ache'

Tonal variation accounts for the most common differences among the dialects. With four tones, Běijīng Mandarin has one of the simplest tone systems. In general, the dialects of Wú, Yuè, Mǐn, and Kèjiā tend to have more complex tone systems than Mandarin, Gàn, or Xiāng (see Ballard 1988).

The complexity of the tone system of a Chinese dialect is indicated not only by the number of tones, but also by the phenomenon of "tone sandhi," i.e. a change of tones when two or more syllables are chained in speech. The most complicated tone sandhi phenomena are found in the Wú and Mǐn dialects. For example, in Cháozhōu, a southern Mǐn dialect, there are eight tones for syllables in isolation. When a syllable is followed by another syllable in Cháozhōu, its "isolation tone" is changed to a different "combination" tone. The following table illustrates the Cháozhōu isolation tones and their corresponding combination tones (the numbers represent pitch levels as before):

(2) Isolation: 5 2 33 11 35 53 213 55
     Combination: 3 5 33 11 31 35 53   13

It should be noted that the presence of tones in Chinese does not imply the absence of intonation and stress. In fact, the Chinese dialects include stress-timed languages, in which stresses typically recur at regular time intervals during speech, as well as syllable-timed languages. Thus Mandarin dialects are stress-timed, whereas Yuè dialects are syllable-timed.

3. Chinese as an isolating language. Most Chinese words have one immutable form which does not change according to number, gender, tense, mood, case, or any other inflectional category (although there is a morphological category of verbal aspect). These categories are either indicated by lexical choice, or are inferred from the discourse context. Concomitant with the absence of inflectional morphology are three other characteristics.

3.1. Grammatical relations such as subject, direct object, and indirect object play no significant role. Word order may be used to distinguish agent from patient, as shown in (3–4) from Běijīng Mandarin. However, sentences like (5) are perfectly natural and commonplace.

(3) *Wǒ mà   tā   le.*
     1.SG scold 3.SG PERF
     'I scolded him.'

(4) *Tā   mà   wǒ   le.*
     3.SG scold 1.SG PERF
     'He scolded me.'

(5) *Yú   chī le.*
     fish eat PERF
     '(Someone) ate the fish; The fish has eaten.'

As the two readings of (5) indicate, the noun *yú* 'fish', preceding the verb, may be understood as either agent or patient. This type of sentence is called the *topic-comment* construction. Its common occurrence in Chinese discourse is correlated with the deemphasis of grammatical relations in the structure of the language.

3.2. There are no overt markers signaling subordination, parataxis, or coordination in "serial verb constructions." The serial verb construction in Chinese contains two or more predicates, juxtaposed without any morphological marker to indicate either the relationship between the nouns and the predicates, or that between the predicates. Sentences which in other languages might have subject complementation, object complementation, purposive clauses, conjoined clauses, or other complex struc-

tures, are rendered into serial verb constructions in Chinese. The following examples are from Běijīng Mandarin.
Subject complementation:

(6) *Tā   bù   lái   shàngbān shì hěn qíguài.*
     3.SG NEG come work   be very strange
     'It is strange that he does not come to work.'

Object complementation:

(7) *Wǒ zhīdào tā   bù   zài   jiā.*
     1.SG know 3.SG NEG be.at home
     'I know that he is not home.'

Purposive clause:

(8) *Tā   zuò-shēnyi zhuàn qián.*
     3.SG do-business make money
     'He is engaged in business in order to make money.'

"Pivotal" construction:

(9) *Wǒ qǐng tā   chī-fàn.*
     1.SG invite 3.SG eat-meal
     'I invited him to have a
      meal.'

"Descriptive" clauses:

(10) *Wǒ mǎi-le   yījiàn yīfu tài dà.*
     1.SG buy-PERF one   outfit too big
     'I bought an outfit that was too big.'

"Circumstantial Adjunct":

(11) *Tā   tǎng zài chuáng-shàng kàn shū*
     3.SG lie at bed-on   read book
     'He lay in bed reading a book.'

Conjoined predicates:

(12) *Tā   tiāntiān chōuyēn hējiǔ.*
     3.SG daily   smoke   drink
     'He drinks and smokes daily.'

3.3. Chinese discourse, whether written or oral, is characterized by an abundance of zero pronouns, i.e. ones that are understood and have no overt realization (Li and Thompson 1979.). They should be considered the norm in Chinese discourse: it is the occurrence, rather than the absence, of a pronoun that calls for an explanation. The interpretation of the referent for the unrealized pronoun is inferred from discourse principles and from pragmatic knowledge, rather than from the grammatical structure of individual sentences:

I. Two friends, A and B, meet on the street:

A: *Hǎojiǔ   bù   jiàn! zěme-yàng? Hái   hǎo   ma?*
   long.time NEG see how   rather well   Q
   'I haven't seen you for a long time. How is it? Are you well?'

B: *Ài . . .   máng de   yàomìng! xiànzài lián háizi*
   Well   busy ADV extreme now   even child

   dǒu   méi   kòng   chàogù.
   all   not.have free.time look.after

   'Well, I have been extremely busy! These days I don't even have time to look after my children.'

II. Two colleagues, X and Y, are discussing how Mr. Wang is irresponsible and uncooperative:

X: *Zhèyang de rén,   nǐ   shuō zěme bàn?*
   this.kind of person 2.SG say   how do
   'A person of this sort! What do you think (we) can do?'

Y: *Shì a,   yòu   bù gōngzuò, yòu   méi*
   be PCLE not.only NEG work   but.also not.have

   wénhuà.   Chèzhí ba!
   civilization dismiss PCLE

   'Indeed, not only does he not work, but he is also uncivilized. Let (us) fire (him)!'

4. The written language. A fully developed Chinese writing system first appeared in the late Shang Dynasty (14th–11th c. BCE), as inscriptions on oracle bones and bronze vessels. Each symbol of the Chinese writing system is called a *character* or *logograph*. It is always pronounced in one syllable, and it usually represents a single morpheme, either synchronically or diachronically. The forms of the characters have undergone several stages of development during the past three millennia. The most recent change took place in the 1950s, when the government of the People's Republic of China began to introduce simplified characters to replace characters which are too complex. Currently the list of simplified characters contains some 2,238 entries. During the same period, the government also authorized an alphabetical writing

system, called *Pīnyīn,* which is used for the Mandarin examples in this article.

Historically, there are five processes by which characters were created:

4.1. *Pictographs* originated as the pictorial representation of objects. An example is the character 日 *ri*, meaning 'sun': its original form, several millennia ago, was ☉, which is clearly a picture of the sun.

4.2. *Ideographs* are characters derived from diagrams symbolizing ideas or abstract notions. For example, the diagrams ⊥ and ⊤ were created to symbolize the notions 'above' and 'below'; they have become formalized into the characters 上 *shàng* 'above' and 下 *xià* 'below', respectively.

4.3. *Compound ideographs* are characters whose meaning is in some way represented by the combination of the meanings of their parts. Thus the character 明 *míng* 'bright' is a compound of the characters 日 *rì* 'sun' and 月 *yuè* 'moon'.

4.4. *Loan characters* result from borrowing a character for a morpheme which is homophonous with another morpheme already represented by that character. For example, in an earlier stage of the Chinese language, the character 易 *yì* 'scorpion' was borrowed to represent the morpheme meaning 'easy', because 'easy' and 'scorpion' were homophonous. In modern Chinese, a new character stands for 'scorpion', obscuring the historical origin of the character 易 'easy'.

4.5. *Phonetic compounds* are combinations of two characters—one representing a semantic feature of the morpheme, and the other representing its pronunciation. For example, the character 铀 *yóu* 'uranium' is composed of the two characters 金 *jīn* and 由 *yóu*. The first means 'metal'; the second has a pronunciation which approximates the first syllable of the English word *uranium*.

5. Contact with minority languages. China is often erroneously perceived and portrayed as a nation composed of a monolithic ethnic group speaking a monolithic language. In fact, not only does Chinese have hundreds of different dialects, but China also has more than 55 minority nationalities—speaking scores of different languages belonging to such families as Altaic, Tibeto-Burman, Tai, and Hmong-Mien. Historically, the minority nationalities were the sole inhabitants of more than 60% of the territory of China; many of them were once more than equal to the Chinese in terms of military and political dominance in East Asia. Thus the complex ethnic and socio-political situation in China over the past three millennia fostered contact between Chinese and the minority languages. A good part of the differences between northern Chinese (Mandarin) and southern dialects (Yuè, Mǐn and Kèjiā) is the result of contact; see Hashimoto 1976. For example, Altaic probably influenced such northern features as the simpler tone systems, the simplified classifier systems, the exclusive/inclusive distinction in the 1pl. pronoun, and the presence of certain sentential constructions favoring the verb-final word order. In the south, the dialects tend to have more complex tone systems, richer classifier systems, syllable-timed prosody, and word orders that are more strictly verb-medial, with some cases of modifiers following the modified. All these features may be in part the result of influence from Tai and Hmong-Mien languages. One notable feature of Chinese contact with minority languages is that loanwords from the latter are relatively rare; this is one reason why the influence of minority languages on Chinese did not receive much scholarly attention until recent years.

[See also Sino-Tibetan Languages and Tone.]

BIBLIOGRAPHY

Ballard, William L. 1988. *The history and development of tonal systems and tone alternations in South China.* (Study of languages and cultures of Asia and Africa monograph series, 22.) Tokyo: Institute for the Study of Languages and Cultures of Asia and Africa, University of Foreign Studies.

Chao, Yuen Ren. 1968. *A grammar of spoken Chinese.* Berkeley: University of California Press.

DeFrancis, John. 1984. *The Chinese language: Fact and fantasy.* Honolulu: University of Hawaii Press.

Forrest, Robert A. D. 1948. *The Chinese language.* London: Faber and Faber.

Hashimoto, Mantaro J. 1973. *The Hakka dialect: a linguistic study of its phonology, syntax, and lexicon.* (Princeton-Cambridge studies in Chinese linguistics, 5.) Cambridge: Cambridge University Press.

Hashimoto, Mantaro J. 1976. Language diffusion on the Asian continent. *Computational analyses of Asian and African Languages* 3.49–66.

Hashimoto, Oi-kan Yue. 1971. *Phonology of Cantonese,* vol. 1, *Studies in Yue dialects.* (Princeton-Cambridge studies in Chinese linguistics, 3.) Cambridge: Cambridge University Press.

Karlgren, Bernhard. 1949. *The Chinese language.* New York: Ronald Press.

Li, Charles N., and Sandra A. Thompson. 1978. An exploration of Mandarin Chinese. In *Syntactic typology,* edited by Winfred Lehmann, pp. 223–266. Austin: University of Texas Press.

Li, Charles N., and Sandra A. Thompson. 1979. Third-person pronouns and zero-anaphora in Chinese discourse. In *Discourse and syntax* (Syntax and semantics, 12), edited by Talmy Givón, pp. 311–335. New York: Academic Press.

Li, Charles N., and Sandra A. Thompson. 1981. *Mandarin Chinese: A functional reference grammar.* Berkeley: University of California Press.

Norman, Jerry. 1988. *Chinese.* Cambridge and New York: Cambridge University Press.

Ramsey, S. Robert. 1987. *The languages of China.* Princeton, N.J.: Princeton University Press.

Wáng, Lì. 1947. *Zhōngguó xiàndài yǔfǎ* [The grammar of modern Chinese]. Shanghai: Zhōnghuá Shūjú.

Wáng, Lì. 1957–58. *Hànyǔshǐgǎo* [A draft history of the Chinese language]. 2 vols. Beijing: Zhōnghuá Shūjú.

Yuán, Jiāhuá et al. 1960. *Hànyǔ fānyán gàiyào* [An outline of the Chinese dialects]. Beijing: Wénzì Gǎigé Chūbǎn-shè.

CHARLES N. LI

LANGUAGE LIST

Chinese, Gan: also called Gan, Kan. 20,580,000 speakers in China. Dialects are Chang-Jing, Yi-Liu, Ji-Cha, Fu-Guang, Ying-Yi. Marginally intelligible with Mandarin Chinese and Wu Chinese. Speakers are reported to be sufficiently bilingual in Standard Chinese (Mandarin) to use that literature. No written form apart from Standard Chinese.

Chinese, Hakka: also called Hakka, Hokka, Kejia, Kechia, Ke, Xinminhua, Majiahua, Tu Guangdonghua. 33,000,000 speakers in China, Taiwan, Singapore, Thailand, Panama, Suriname, South Africa, French Guiana, Brunei, French Polynesia, Indonesia, Malaysia, Mauritius, New Zealand, United Kingdom, and USA. In China: 25,725,000 speakers. Dialects are Yue-Tai (Meixian, Raoping, Taiwan Kejia), Yuezhong (Central Guangdong), Huizhou, Yuebei (Northern Guangdong), Tingzhou (Min-Ke), Ning-Long (Longnan), Yugui, Tonggu. Meixian is now the standard dialect. In Taiwan: 2,366,000 speakers in Taoyuan, Hsinchu, Miaoli, Pingtung counties. Shi Xien is in northern and southern Taiwan, Hi-Lu is central and north central. Dialects are Hailu (Hoiluk, Hoilluk, Hi-Lu), Sanhsien (Shigen, Shixien, Shi Xien). Sanhsien closely resembles Yuetai of Mainland China. Hailu closely resembles Yong-Ting or Yuqui of Mainland China. In Singapore: Ethnic population: 151,000 in Singapore as of 1993. In Thailand: Cities. In Panama: Ethnic population: 30,000 to 60,000 including Cantonese as of 1981. Panama City, Colón, larger towns of interior. Bilingualism in Spanish. In Suriname: Ethnic population: 12,000 Chinese, including Yue, as of 1971. In South Africa: Natal coast. In French Guiana: Bilingual. They have preserved their language.

Chinese, Huizhou: also called Huizhou. Spoken in China in southern Anhui Province and northern Zhejiang Province. Dialects are Jixi, Xiuyi, Qide, Yanzhou, Jingzhan. Formerly considered to be part of the Jianghuai dialect of Mandarin, but now considered by many to be a separate major variety of Chinese. Dialects are reported to differ greatly from each other. Different from the Huizhou dialect of Hakka. Speakers are reported to be sufficiently bilingual in Standard Chinese to use that literature. No written form apart from Standard Chinese.

Chinese, Jinyu: also called Jinyu. 45,000,000 speakers in China, mainly in Shanxi Province, with some in Shaanxi and Henan Provinces. Formerly considered to be part of the Xibei Guanhua dialect of Mandarin, but now considered by many to be a separate major variety of Chinese. Unlike Mandarin in having contrastive glottal checked syllables and other distinctive features. Speakers are reported to be sufficiently bilingual in Standard Chinese to use that literature. No written form apart from Standard Chinese.

Chinese, Mandarin: also called Mandarin, Guanhua, Beifang Fangyan, Northern Chinese, Guoyu, Standard Chinese, Putonghua, Hanyu. 874,000,000 speakers in China, Taiwan, Indonesia, Malaysia, Singapore, Mongolia, Thailand, Brunei, Cambodia, Laos, Mauritius, Philippines, Asian Russia, United Kingdom, USA, and Vietnam. In China: 867,200,000 speakers. Dialects are Huabei Guanhua (Northern Mandarin), Xibei Guanhua (Northwestern Mandarin), Xinan Guanhua (Southwestern Mandarin), Jianghuai Guanhua (Jiangxia Guanhua, Lower Yangze Mandarin). Wenli is a literary form. Written Chinese is based on the Beijing dialect, but has been heavily influenced by other varieties of Northern Mandarin. Putonghua is the official form taught in schools. Hezhouhoua is spoken in the Linxia Hui Autonomous Prefecture and Gannan Tibetan Autonomous Prefecture of southern Gansu Province, and in neighboring areas in Qinghai Province. The grammar is basically Altaic or Tibetan, while the vocabulary and phonology is basically Northwestern Mandarin, or a relexified variety of Tibetan. More investigation is needed. Putonghua is inherently intelligible with the Beijing dialect and other Mandarin varieties in the northeast. Mandarin varieties in the Lower Plateau in Shaanxi are not readily intelligible with Putonghua. Mandarin varieties of Guilin and Kunming are inherently unintelligible to speakers of Putonghua. Taibei Mandarin and Beijing Mandarin are fully inherently intelligible to each other's speakers. Few speakers are bilingual. All ages. All domains, administration, education, religion, business, media, traditional literature. Vigorous language use. Parents transmit it to children. Many speakers of other languages use it as second language. The Hui are non-Turkic, non-Mongolian Muslims who speak Mandarin as first language. Hui is a separate official nationality. The Hui correspond ethnically to "Khoton," "Hoton," or "Qotong" in Mongolia, 20,000 Muslim Chinese in Taiwan, and the Hui in Thailand. Several hundred Chinese Jews in Kaifeng city, Henan Province, are largely assimilated to the Han or Hui Chinese, and

speak Mandarin. They are officially recognized. Most speakers live in monolingual areas, so are not conscious of other languages. They do recognize the difference between standard Mandarin (Putonghua), and approve its use, especially in northern areas. Chinese characters. Official language. In Taiwan: Mainly in Taipei and five provincial cities. Fully inherently intelligible with Putonghua in China, but intelligible with Benjing dialect with some difficulty. Nearly all mother tongue speakers in Taiwan speak with Min-influenced grammar and various degrees of Min-influenced pronunciation. Many of the educated strive to cultivate standard pronunciation. Grammatical differences of the Taiwan variety often appear in writing. Many of the 30- to 50-year-old generation in Taiwan are also fluent in Taiwan Min. National language. In Java and Bali, Indonesia: Scattered throughout Indonesia. Of the five to six million ethnic Chinese in Indonesia (per 1979 estimate; 5,500,000 in 1976 or 4% of total population according to United Nations), 65% (3,500,000 to 4,000,000) speak Indonesian in the home, 35% (2,000,000) speak five Chinese languages in the home. In peninsular Malaysia: Sabah, and Sarawak. In Singapore: 44% also use other Chinese varieties at home; 12% use English at home. Increasing use. National language. In Mongolia: Northwestern Mongolia, Uvs Aimag. Bilingualism in Halh Mongolian. In Thailand: Bangkok, provincial towns, and Kra Peninsula in the south. Dialects are Ho (Haw, Cin Haw, Yunnanese, Western Mandarin, Hui, Hui-Tze, Hwei, Panghse, Pantha, Panthe, Pathee).

Chinese, Min Bei: also called Northern Min, Min Pei. 10,537,000 speakers in China and Singapore. In China: 10,290,000 speakers in northern Fujian Province in seven counties around Jian'ou. The Chinese now divide Chinese Min into five major varieties: Min Nan, Min Bei, Min Dong, Min Zhong, and Pu-Xian. Others say there are at least nine varieties that are inherently unintelligible to each other's speakers. In Singapore: Ethnic population: 11,000 in Singapore as of 1985.

Chinese, Min Dong: also called Eastern Min. 247,000 speakers in China, Malaysia, Indonesia, Singapore, Thailand, and Brunei. In China: Area from Fu'an in northeastern Fujian to Fuzhou in east central Fujian. The dialect is Fuzhou (Fuchow, Foochow, Guxhou). The prestige variety is that spoken in Fujian. Speakers are reported to be adequately bilingual in Standard Chinese. In peninsular Malaysia: : 206,013 speakers. In Java and Bali, Indonesia: 20,000 speakers. In Singapore: 15,000 speakers. Ethnic population: 31,391 as of 1985, mainly in China. The dialect is Fuzhou (Fuchow, Foochow, Guxhou). In Thailand: The dialect is Fuzhou (Fuchow, Foochow).

Chinese, Min Nan: also called Southern Min, Minnan. 45,000,000 speakers in China, Taiwan, Malaysia, Thailand, Indonesia, Brunei, Philippines, Singapore, and USA. In

China: 25,725,000 speakers. Dialects are Xiamen (Amoy), Leizhou (Lei Hua, Li Hua), Chao-Shan (Choushan, Chaozhou), Hainan (Hainanese, Qiongwen Hua, Wenchang), Longdu, Zhenan Min. Xiamen has subdialects Amoy, Fujian (Fukien, Hokkian, Taiwanese). Amoy is the prestige dialect. Amoy and Taiwanese are easily intelligible to each other. Chao-Shan has subdialects Chaoshou (Chaochow, Teochow, Teochew) and Shantou (Swatow). Chao-Shan, including Swatow, has very difficult intelligibility with Amoy. Sanjiang is somewhat difficult for other dialect speakers. Hainan is quite different from other dialects. Min Nan is the most widely distributed and influential Min variety. Chao-shan speakers may speak Mandarin, Cantonese, or English for buying and selling, Mandarin to outside Chinese and government purposes, Cantonese to those people, English to foreigners. Those under 30 are more bilingual. All ages. Most domains. Speakers of other languages use this for business. Shantou and Chenhai varieties of the Chao-shan dialect are considered to be cultured. In Taiwan: 15,000,000 speakers in Tainan, Penghu Archipelago, cities on the east coast, western plain except for a few Hakka pockets. The dialect is Amoy (Taiwanese, Formosan). Taiwanese is close to Amoy dialect; intelligibility is not very difficult. There are two subdialects in Taiwan: Sanso and Chaenzo, with some difficulty in intelligibility. Mandarin is used as second language. Those over 60 also speak Japanese. In peninsular Malaysia: Dialects are Fukienese (Amoy, Fujianese, Hokkien), Hainanese, Chaochow (Teochow, Teochew). In Singapore: Ethnic population: 1,482,000 as of 1993, including 884,000 Hokkien, 452,000 Teochew, and 146,000 Hainanese. Dialects are Hokkien (Fukienese, Fujian, Amoy, Xiamen), Teochew (Chaochow, Chaozhou, Taechew), Hainanese. Speakers report Hokkien and Teochew to be intelligible with each other, but not Hainanese. Mandarin, English, and other Chinese varieties are also used at home. Hokkien is the most widely understood language in Singapore. Trade language. In Thailand: Cities. Dialects are Chaozhou (Chaochow, Tiuchiu, Teochow, Techu), Shantou (Swatow), Hainan, Fujian (Fukien, Hokkien). Most Min Nan speakers in Thailand speak Chaochow. In Java and Bali, Indonesia: Pontianak in West Borneo and elsewhere. Dialects are Fujian (Hokkien), Chaochow (Tiu Chiu). In Brunei: Dialects are Chaochow (Tiuchiu, Teochow), Hainan, Fujian (Hokkien).

Chinese, Min Zhong: also called Central Min. Spoken in China around Yong'an, Sanming, and Shaxian in central Fujian Province. Speakers are reported to be adequately bilingual in Standard Chinese to use that literature.

Chinese, Pu-Xian: 6,000 speakers in China, Singapore, and Malaysia. In China: Putian and Xianyou counties of east central Fujian Province. Dialects are Putian (Putten, Xinghua, Hinghua, Henghua, Hsinghua), Xianyou (Hsienyu). Speakers are reported to be adequately bilingual in Standard Chinese. In Singapore: Ethnic population: 12,902 as of 1985. The dialect is Henghua (Hinghua, Xinghua). In Malaysia: Peninsular Malaysia and Sarawak. The dialect is Xinghua (Hsinghua, Hinghua).

Chinese, Wu: also called Wu. 77,175,000 speakers in China. Dialects are Taihu, Jinhua (Kinhwa), Taizhou, Oujiang, Wuzhou, Chuqu, Xuanzhou. Subdialects of the Taihu dialect are Piling, Su-Hu-Jia, Tiaoxi, Hangzhou, Lin-Shao, Yongjiang. Chuqu subdialects are Chuzhou, Longqu. Xuanzhou subdialects are Tongjing, Taigao, Shiling. Mandarin is used for news and official broadcasts.

Chinese, Xiang: also called Hunan, Hunanese, Xiang, Hsiang. 36,015,000 speakers in China, Hunan Province, over twenty counties in Sichuan, and parts of Guangxi and Guangdong Provinces. Dialects are Changyi, Luoshao, Jishu. Linguistically between Mandarin and Wu Chinese and marginally intelligible with them. Sufficiently bilingual in Standard Chinese to use that literature. Xiang has no written form apart from Standard Chinese.

Chinese, Yue: also called Yuet Yue, Gwong Dung Waa, Cantonese, Yue, Yueh, Yueyu, Baihua. 71,000,000 speakers in China, Vietnam, Malaysia, Singapore, Canada, South Africa, Costa Rica, Honduras, Panama, USA, Australia, Brunei, Mauritius, Nauru, Netherlands, New Zealand, Philippines, Singapore, Thailand, and United Kingdom. In China: 52,000,000 speakers. Dialects are Yuehai (Guangfu, Hong Kong Cantonese, Macau Cantonese, Shatou, Shiqi, Wancheng), Siyi (Seiyap, Taishan, Toisan, Hoisan, Schleiyip), Gaolei (Gaoyang), Qinlian, Guinan. The Guangzhou variety is considered the standard. Subdialects of Yuehai are Xiangshan, spoken around Zhongshan and Shuhai, and Wanbao around Dongwan City and Bao'an County. Outside of mainland China, many Cantonese-specific characters are used in the writing system. Official language. In Vietnam: Thành Phố Hồ Chí Minh, Hà Noi, Hau Giang, Hai Phòng, Cuu Long Provinces. Chinese calligraphy. In peninsular Malaysia: Dialects are Cantonese, Toishanese. In Singapore: Ethnic population: 338,000 as of 1993. In Canada: Vancouver, Toronto, Montreal, and small numbers elsewhere. In South Africa: Natal coast. In Costa Rica: Limòn, Guanacaste, Puntarenas, San José. In Honduras: Tegucigalpa. Not bilingual. In Australia: Sydney, Melbourne, and elsewhere. In Panama: Panama City, Colón, larger towns of interior. Bilingualism in Spanish. In USA: Hawaii and mainland.

Dungan: also called Dzhunyan, Tungan, Huizu, Zwn'jan, Kwuizwu. 49,400 speakers in Kyrgyzstan, Kazakhstan, Tajikistan, Turkmenistan, and Uzbekistan. In Kyrgyzstan: 38,000 speakers. Ethnic population: 52,000, as of 1979, to 100,000. The Gansu dialect is mainly in Prschewalsk and Osh, Kyrgyzstan, the Shaanxi dialect in Kazakhstan, and in Fergana, Uzbekistan. Dialects are Ganzu (Gansu), Shaanxi

(Shensi), Yage. Speakers of the Shaanxi and Ganzu varieties have difficult inherent intelligibility with each other. Dungan has three tones (Standard Mandarin tones 1 and 2 are merged), but they are not indicated in writing. Also different from Mandarin in phonology and lexicon. Bilingualism in Russian. Those under 50 to 55 are reported to speak Russian as mother tongue. Cyrillic script. In Kazakhstan: Speakers of the Shaanxi and Ganzu varieties of Dungan have difficult inherent intelligibility with each other.   B. GRIMES

CHOCO LANGUAGES.
A family of the Pacific coast of Colombia, with some overspill into Panama and Ecuador.

LANGUAGE LIST

Anserma: also called Anserna. Formerly spoken in Colombia. Related to Cauca, Arma (both extinct), and Caramanta.

Arma: formerly spoken in Colombia. People spoke either Cenu or Cauca (both extinct).

Emberá-Baudó: also called Baudó, Catrú: 5,000 speakers in Colombia, Baudó River basin and northern Pacific coastal rivers between Cabo Corrientes and the south of the San Juan River, near Northern Emberá. Somewhat intelligible with Northern Emberá and other southern Emberá languages.

Emberá-Catío: also called Catio, Katio, Embena, Eyabida. 15,000 speakers in Colombia and Panama. In Colombia: Upper Sinu, San Jorge, San Pedro, Murri Rivers. 90% to 95% are monolingual, a few use Spanish as second language.

Emberá-Chamí: also called Chami. 11,000 speakers in Colombia, departments of Risaralda, Caldas, Antioquí, Valle, including the *municipio* of Caramanta.

Emberá-Saija: also called Saija, Epená Saija, Epea Pedée, Southern Embera, Southern Empera, Cholo. 9,000 speakers in Colombia, Ecuador, and Panama. In Colombia: 8,000 speakers on southern Pacific coast, Caucá, Nariño, Chocó departments. Some bilingualism in Spanish. No speakers are monolingual. All speak Spanish, and some speak Woun Meu. There is intermarriage with speakers of Woun Meu. Saija is used in the home and traditional religion. Vernacular language and culture strong. Most parents transmit Saija to children. People are proud of their language. In Ecuador: Borbó, northern Pacific coast. In Panama: Southern Pacific coast, Caucá, Nariñ, Chocó departments. Some bilingualism in Spanish.

Emberá-Tadó: also called Embená Tadó. 1,000 speakers in Colombia, upper San Juan River region, Andes, Risaralda region, near the Chamí.

Northern Emberá: also called Empera, Ebera, Bedea, Atrato, Darien, Dariena, Panama Embera, Cholo, Eerã. 20,000 speakers in Panama and Colombia. In Panama: 7,000 speak-

FIGURE 1. *Subgrouping of Choco Languages*

Anserma
Arma
Runa
Woun Meu
Embera
  Northern Embera
    Northern Emberá, Emberá-Catío
  Southern Embera
    Emberá-Baudó, Emberá-Chamí, Emberá-Saija, Emberá-Tadó

ers in southeastern Panama, Darién area, lowland jungle. Some bilingualism in Spanish. In Colombia: 13,000 speakers in Atrato River basin in Chocó department, Pacific coastal rivers from Cabo Corrientes (5'30"N), to Antioquia (Rio Verde) department. Related languages in order of closeness: Emberá-Catío, Emberá-Baudó, Emberá-Tadó, Epena Saija, Embera-Chamí, and Wounmeu. Panama and Colombia dialects are inherently intelligible. Northern Emberá of the Upper Baudó area and downriver Emberá-Baudó are inherently intelligible.

Runa: formerly spoken in Colombia.

Woun Meu: also called Waun Meo, Waunana, Waumeo, Wounmeu, Wounaan, Noanama, Noenama, Nonama, Chocama, Chanco. 6,000 speakers in Panama and Colombia. In Panama: 3,000 speakers. Southeastern Panama, lowlands. Some bilingualism in Spanish. In Colombia: 3,000 speakers in San Juan River basin.   B. GRIMES

CHOMSKY HIERARCHY.
See Mathematical Linguistics.

CHOMSKY, NOAM.
See Formal Grammar; History of Linguistics; Principles and Parameters; *and* Minimalist Program.

CHON LANGUAGES.
Also called Patagon, these constitute a language family of southern Argentina and adjacent parts of Chile.

LANGUAGE LIST

Ona: also called Aona, Selknam, Shelknam. 1 speaker remains. Formerly spoken in Patagonia, Tierra del Fuego. Also formerly in Chile. There was bilingualism in Spanish.

Tehuelche: also called Aoniken, Gunua-Kena, Gununa-Kena, Inaquen. 4 speakers remain in Argentina. Ethnic population: 200 as of 2000. Formerly spoken in Patagonia.   B. GRIMES

CHRYSIPPUS (ca. 280–ca. 207 BCE). Came to Athens from Cilicia in Anatolia, was the third head of the Stoic philosophical school, wrote a number of books on philosophical problems, on cases, parts of speech, and so on. Since most of his written work is lost, it is difficult to know what parts of the Stoic theory of language should be attributed to him and what parts to his successors, but he is credited with an interest in dialectics and with having considered the problems of language from a logical point of view.

[*See also* Diogenes of Babylonia; History of Linguistics, *article on* Ancient Greece and Rome; *and* Stoics.]

ANNA MORPURGO DAVIES

CHUKOTKO-KAMCHATKAN LANGUAGES. A

family of the Chukotka and Kamchatka Peninsulas in the far east of Russia.

LANGUAGE LIST

Alutor: also called Alyutor, Aliutor, Olyutor. 100 speakers. Ethnic population: 2,000 as of 1997. Dialects are Alutorskij (Alutor Proper), Karaginskij (Karaga), Palanskij (Palana). Considered a dialect of Koryak until recently. Bilingualism in Russian. Senior citizens speak Alutor actively and some are monolinguals; the middle-aged know it passively; those younger than 35 know only Russian according to a study done in 1997. Second language used for most domains except perhaps family. Thought to be headed toward extinction.

Chukot: also called Chukcha, Chuchee, Chukchee, Luoravetlan, Chukchi. 10,000 speakers. Ethnic population: 15,184 as of 1989. Maritime Chukchi 25% of population, Raindeer Chukchi 75%. Chukchi Peninsula, Chukot and Koryak National Okrug, northern Yakutia, northeastern Siberia. Dialects are Uellanskij, Pevekskij, Enmylinskij, Nunligranskij, Xatyrskij, Chaun, Enurmin, Yanrakinot. Bilingualism in Russian, Yakut, Lamut, Yukagir. Nomadic groups have adult and some children speakers. Settled groups have few or no children speakers. Second language used for most domains except perhaps family. 60% of the Chuckchi speak Chukot. Although those under 50 speak Russian with varying proficiency, nomadic groups resist Russian language and culture. People are mildly to strongly supportive toward Chukot.

Itelmen: also called Itelymem, Western Itelmen, Kamchadal, Kamchatka. 60 speakers remain. Ethnic population: 2,481 as of 1989. Dialects are Sedanka, Kharyuz, Itelmen, Xajrjuzovskij, Napanskij, Sopocnovskij. Bilingualism in Russian. Speakers are primarily the older generation. Itelmen not

FIGURE 1. *Subgrouping of Chukotko-Kamchatkan Languages*

Northern Chukotko-Kamchatkan
  Chukot
Koryak-Alutor
    Alutor, Kerek, Koryak
Southern
  Itelmen

used except perhaps in family. Under 10% of ethnic population speak Itelmen. People are neutral to mildly supportive toward Itelmen.

Kerek: 2 speakers remain. Ethnic population: 100 to 400, according to studies done in 1990 and 1997. Formerly spoken on Cape Navarin, in Chukot villages. Dialects are Mainypilgino (Majna-Pil'ginskij), Khatyrka (Xatyrskij). Previously considered a dialect of Chukot, Kerek is now classified as a separate language. Speakers are now assimilated into Chukot. All are senior citizens. Kerek not used except perhaps in family. Under 10% of the ethnic group speak Kerek.

Koryak: also called Nymylan. 4,847 speakers. Ethnic population: 9,242 as of 1989. Koryak National Okrug, south of the Chukot; northern half of Kamchatka Peninsula and adjacent continent. Dialects are Cavcuvenskij (Chavchuven), Apokinskij (Apukin), Kamenskij (Kamen), Xatyrskij, Paren, Itkan, Palan, Gin. Chavchuven, Palan, and Kamen are apparently not inherently intelligible. Bilingualism in Russian. A few children speak Koryak. Second language used for most key domains. 30% to 50% of the ethnic group speak Koryak. Neutral to mildly supportive attitude toward Koryak.

B. GRIMES

CHUMASHAN LANGUAGES constitute a family

formerly spoken near Santa Barbara in southern California.

LANGUAGE LIST

Barbareño: No longer spoken; was not intelligible with other Chumash varieties.

Chumash: No longer spoken. Ethnic population: 156 as of 2000. Inherently unintelligible Chumash varieties formerly spoken included Obispeño, Ineseño, Purisimeño, Barbareño, Ventureño, and Cruzeño (Island Chumash, Isleño), named after the missions to which they were brought. Said not to be the same as Hokan. Extinct since 1965.

Cruzeño: also called Island Chumash, Isleño. No longer spoken. Was not intelligible with other Chumash varieties. Had multiple dialects.

Ineseño: No longer spoken. Was not intelligible with other Chumash varieties.

Obispeño: No longer spoken. Was the northernmost Chumash language. Not inherently intelligible with other Chumash varieties.

Purisimeño: No longer spoken. Was not intelligible with other Chumash varieties.

Ventureño: No longer spoken. Was not intelligible with other Chumash varieties. Had multiple dialects.   B. GRIMES

CLASSIFIERS. *See* Agreement *and* Semantics.

CLASSROOM RESEARCH. *See* Institutional Linguistics *and* Pedagogical Grammar.

CLAUSE. [*This entry includes the following subentries:*
Overview
Clause-Combining Constructions
Complementation]

Overview

The clause, along with the word and the syntactic phrase, is one of the most basic grammatical units of human language. Like the others, it is not sharply definable in terms of structural criteria, either within or across languages. It is impossible to identify the functional basis of the clause: to communicate an event, that is, some situation unfolding in time, with or without discernible change (cf. Croft 1998). Events are cognitively complex, consisting of entities (participants) and their relations to one another. The clause in human language is an expressive device that allows us to select some facets of our experience in the form of a manageable chunk that conveys an integrated situation involving one or more participants in the event, and some predication about those participants. The cognitive processes involved in making this selection out of the flux of experience, and the precise relation of those processes to language (in general, and to the particular language of expression), are vastly complex and still little understood. What we do know is that all languages have some unit with observable structural characteristics, even if not inviolable ones, that can occur as a stand-alone expression of an integrated event.

Crucial to a clause is the presence of a predicate functioning as the head of the clause; this is typically a verb, although other units are possible, such as predicate nominals and adjectives. A great many languages show a distinction between *finite* and *non-finite* clauses. Finite clauses are free-standing, non-dependent clauses with verbs that are inflected for major verbal categories (most commonly, tense/aspect) and with potential expression of the nominal participants involved in the events (in the form of nominals, pronominals, or agreement marking). Non-finite clauses are grammatically dependent and lack to some degree the full range of expression of event structure that is possible with a finite clause: they may lack the expression of verbal categories required by finite verbs, or otherwise required clausal participants. For example, in a non-finite clause, participles and infinitives can be the principal verb (the head) of the clause, but they lack the category inflection characteristic of a finite clause and are often restricted with regard to the expression or interpretation of the nominal participants in the event they express.

Another common distinction in languages is between *independent* and *dependent* clauses: independent clauses (finite by definition) can occur alone, while dependent clauses cannot. (Usually the term "dependent clause" excludes non-finite clauses, although these are, strictly speaking, dependent.) In languages where finite verbs appear in sequence (serial verbs), it can be difficult to determine clause boundaries—that is, to distinguish between a case of separate, independent clause, each headed by a verb, and a clause with main and dependent verbs. There are many other cases where determining clause boundaries is not straightforward and requires analysis; in general, these exhibit indeterminate or partially fused event structure. However, it appears that all languages have simple finite clauses whose elements can be clearly related to simple event structures composed of predicates and their associated participants.

Several types of simple (clause: event structure) relations are found cross-linguistically and appear to be universal; these can be called "basic" clause types. The most important of the basic clause types are *transitive* and *intransitive* clauses, two simple clause types distinguished by the presence of an object complement. Other structural criteria are associated with these types within and across languages, and the actual range of clause types is gradient, ranging from clauses that have all the structural concomitants of transitive clauses to those that have all the properties associated with intransitive clauses (Hopper and Thompson 1984). Nevertheless, each of the two types appears to be anchored semantically in a specific event structure that is maximally differentiated from the other. The intransitive clause type is based on the semantic prototype of a one-participant event, and the transitive clause rests on the prototypical conception of an event with two participants, one acting on the other (Comrie 1981, Givón 1984). Each of these types appears to be associated with a semantic predicate type or types (Kemmer 1993): transitive clauses and their two-participant prototype event structure are associated cross-linguistically with verbs of transmission of physical force, and intransitive clauses are associated with verbs of animate motion and of location. Predicates falling outside these classes display greater variation within and across languages with regard to the type of basic clause in which they characteristically occur.

The two basic transitivity clause types are "un-marked" according to the markedness criteria given in Greenberg 1966 and Croft 1990. A third basic clause type that is "marked" in terms of these criteria is the *di-transitive* clause, which is everywhere far less frequent than the other two types and more restrictive in the predicates it admits. This type has two objects and expresses three-participant events; it appears to be most strongly associated with the predicates of transfer of possession ('give') and/or induced change of location ('send', 'throw').

Many other marked clause structures exist, but it is debatable whether any of them should be considered a basic clause type, because it is hard to make a case for universality of structure. For example, *reflexive* clauses are marked clause structures, and they correspond to a definable event type in terms of the relation between the participants: the initiating participant in the action chain is the same as the endpoint entity (Kemmer 1993, Langacker 1991). However, it is difficult to identify reflexives cross-linguistically with a single "clause type," given that reflexive events are associated with two major types of marked structure—one in which the clause is basically transitive (those with nominal/pronominal reflexive objects), and another in which it is intransitive (reflexive-marked intransitive verbs), in keeping with its intermediate event structure (Kemmer 2002). A similar case is the *passive*, equally widespread in human languages and also a definable event structure, but one that is expressed in a number of different marked structural clause types. It is fair to say that there exists a wide range of simple event structure types that correspond, but not one-to-one, with marked clause types in the languages of the world;

and all these event types depart in some measure from the one-participant and two-participant prototypes that appear to be the most basic and deeply entrenched event types underlying clause structure in human language.

[*See also* Functional Linguistics; Control; *and* Transitivity and Voice.]

BIBLIOGRAPHY

Comrie, Bernard. 1981. *Language universals and linguistic typology.* Chicago: University of Chicago Press.

Croft, William. 1990. *Typology and universals.* Cambridge: Cambridge University Press.

Croft, William. 1998. The structure of events and the structure of language. In *The new psychology of language*, vol. 1, edited by Michael Tomasello, pp. 67–92. Mahwah, N.J.: Lawrence Erlbaum.

Givón, Talmy. 1984. *Syntax: A functional-typological introduction*, vol. 1. Amsterdam: Benjamins.

Greenberg, Joseph H. 1966. *Language universals, with special reference to feature hierarchies.* (Janua linguarum, Series minor, 59.) The Hague: Mouton.

Hopper, Paul, and Sandra Thompson. 1980. Transitivity in grammar and discourse. *Language* 56.251–259.

Kemmer, Suzanne. 1993. *The middle voice.* Amsterdam: Benjamins.

Kemmer, Suzanne. 2002. Human cognition and the elaboration of events: Some universal conceptual categories. In *The New psychology of language*, vol. 2, edited by Michael Tomasello. Mahwah, N.J.: Lawrence Erlbaum.

Langacker, Ronald. 1991. *Foundations of cognitive grammar*, vol. 2. Stanford, Calif.: Stanford University Press.

SUZANNE KEMMER

Clause-Combining Constructions

In any sort of discourse, individual clauses are combined into larger structures. Different languages afford their speakers various grammatical means to indicate that a clause is closely associated with, but not a part of, another clause or other clauses within a larger unit, which may be thought of as a sentence. The different types of complex constructions that are associated with that kind of clause-combining are of general interest, for they raise questions related to such areas of research as clause structure, coreference across clause boundaries, and the relationships among syntax, semantics, and pragmatics. These constructions have received special attention from those who approach linguistics from functional and typological perspectives: functionalists have generally looked at language in actual use, where wide ranges of clause combinations occur; typologists have generally looked at ways in which languages may vary, and languages vary greatly in the ways in which they combine clauses (Haiman and Thompson 1988).

Morphological and/or phonological (often intonational) cues may indicate that a clause is part of a larger structure. The clauses within that structure may bear any of a large number of semantic or pragmatic relationships to one another: e.g., the actions or states described in the clauses may occur or exist sequentially, simultaneously, or in alternation; one clause may present a cause, a result, or a purpose of another; one clause may give a condition for another, or describe the manner in which some action is done. Grammatical particles or specific construction types may indicate the relationship that holds between the clauses, or may limit the range of possible relationships between the clauses; but there may be no overt sign of precisely how the clauses are to be interpreted. Particular interpretations of strings of clauses, then, will often depend upon context (Stump 1985).

In some languages, like English and other familiar Indo-European languages, a distinction may be made between *coordinate* combinations, in which both clauses are relatively independent of each other, and *subordinate* combinations in which one is more or less dependent, semantically or grammatically, on the other, independent clause. In some languages, including Hua (Haiman 1980) and other languages of New Guinea (Longacre 1972), it is more useful to describe clause combination in terms of *clause-chaining* constructions. In still other languages, such as Mandarin (Li and Thompson 1981), West African languages, and creole languages (Sebba 1987), there is not always a clear distinction between subordinate and coordinate clauses; instead, serial verb constructions are used.

1. Coordination and subordination. In those languages that may clearly be analyzed as distinguishing subordinate from coordinate constructions, coordinate constructions will include clauses which may stand alone, by some criteria, and which are either juxtaposed or connected by a conjunction. Ex. (1) is composed of two coordinate clauses, connected with the conjunction *or*:

(1)   *She'll give you a call or I'll send you a message.*

Subordinate clauses may be distinguished from independent clauses by special subordinating morphemes, by special word order, by special verb forms (often called

participles), or by a restricted distribution of the categories of tense, aspect, or mood (Thompson and Longacre 1985). Some subordinate clauses are often referred to as *adverbial* because they function in ways similar to adverbs. For example, they may give time of, manner of, or reason for an action or state described in another clause. (2) contains a main clause followed by a subordinate clause which gives information about the time of the action expressed in the first clause; the subordinate clause is introduced by *while*:

(2)   *I did a lot of sightseeing while I was in the States.*

Subordinate clauses vary in the extent to which they are bound to the clauses on which they depend. They may serve as topics or otherwise provide a framework for the information contained in the main clause, and they often present information which is unfamiliar in its context (Haiman 1978, Chafe 1984).

2. Clause chaining. In a typical string of clauses in a typical clause-chaining language, every clause except the last is marked for *switch-reference* (Jacobsen 1967); that is, it indicates whether its subject is the same as the subject of the following clause, using S[ame] S[ubject] marking, or different from it, using D[ifferent] S[ubject] marking. The last verb of the chain is called the "final" verb; nonfinal verbs are called "medial" verbs. Exx. (3–4) are from Koita, a Papuan language (Dutton 1975, cited by Lynch 1983:210). In each example, the first verb appears with a suffix which indicates switch-reference—SS in (3), and DS in (4):

(3)   *daka   oro-γo-i   era-γa-nu.*
       I   come-SG-SS   see-SG-PAST
       'I came and saw him.'

(4)   *daka   oro-γo-nuge   auki da   era-γa-nu.*
       I   come-SG-DS   he   me   see-SG-PAST
       'I came and he saw me.'

The clauses in a chain may be semantically related to one another in ways that are characterized by both coordinating and subordinating constructions in other languages (Longacre 1985).

Switch-reference systems are not limited to clause-chaining languages. Switch-reference is a typically verbal category which serves to keep track of the referents in a discourse. On a very general discourse level, SS markers may be seen as marking a kind of referent continuity, and DS markers as marking a kind of discontinuity.

Traditionally, switch-reference marking is considered sensitive to the identity of syntactic subjects; a clause will be marked for switch reference with respect to a clause which is on its own syntactic level or on a higher syntactic level. Whether switch-reference should be regarded as syntactic or pragmatic is a matter of controversy (see Finer 1984, Roberts 1988). Many historical sources for switch-reference markers have been proposed; such markers are themselves prone to reanalysis. (See Haiman and Munro 1983 for further discussion.)

3. Serial verbs. In serial verb constructions, two clauses, or two verb phrases—or two finite, relatively independent verbs, which may share arguments—are juxtaposed, with the precise relationship between them generally left unmarked. Exx. (5–6) are from Twi, a Kwa language of West Africa (Sebba 1987:175); they each show two finite verbs which share an agentive argument. No conjunction separates the verbs:

(5) *Kofi de   pono no baae.*
     K.   take.PAST table the come.PAST
     'Kofi brought the table.'

(6) *ɔyɛɛ adwuma mã   ne nua.*
     he.do work   give his brother
     'He works for his brother.'

In (7), from Mandarin (Li and Thompson 1981:595), the two juxtaposed verb phrases *mǎi piào* and *jìn-qu* may be understood to be related in two different ways:

(7) *wǒ mǎi piào   jìn-qu.*
     I   buy   ticket enter-go
     'I bought a ticket and went in'; 'I bought a ticket to go in.'

Several different types of serial verb constructions may be found in a given language. Two verbs may have the status of a single lexical item; one verb (often meaning 'give' or 'take') may increase the valence of another; one verb may be analyzed as an auxiliary verb; or two verbs may express relations that are expressed by subordinate and coordinate constructions in other languages. Verb serialization in a wide range of languages is discussed by Foley and Olson 1985 and by Sebba 1987.

The evolution of serial verb constructions has been widely discussed; serial verbs have been suggested as the sources of prepositions (Lord 1973, Givón 1975, Li and Thompson 1974) and of classifiers (Seiler 1986) in various languages.

[*See also* Functional Linguistics; Incorporation; Objects; Polysynthesis; Relative Clauses; *and* Subjects.]

BIBLIOGRAPHY

Chafe, Wallace L. 1984. How people use adverbial clauses. *Berkeley Linguistics Society* 10.437–449.

Dutton, Tom E. 1975. A Koita grammar sketch and vocabulary. In *Studies in languages of central and south-east Papua* (Pacific Linguistics, C-29), edited by T. E. Dutton, pp. 281–412. Canberra: School of Pacific Studies, Australian National University.

Finer, Daniel. 1984. *The formal grammar of switch-reference.* MIT dissertation. Published, New York: Garland, 1985.

Foley, William A., and Mike Olson. 1985. Clausehood and verb serialization. In *Grammar inside and outside the clause: Some approaches to theory from the field,* edited by Johanna Nichols and Anthony C. Woodbury, pp. 17–60. Cambridge and New York: Cambridge University Press.

Givón, Talmy. 1975. Serial verbs and syntactic change: Niger-Congo. In *Word order and word order change,* edited by Charles N. Li, pp. 47–112. Austin: University of Texas Press.

Haiman, John. 1978. Conditionals are topics. *Language* 54.564–589.

Haiman, John. 1980. *Hua: A Papuan language of the eastern highlands of New Guinea.* (*Studies in Language*, Companion series, 5.) Amsterdam: Benjamins.

Haiman, John, and Pamela Munro, eds. 1983. *Switch-reference and universal grammar.* (Typological studies in language, 2.) Amsterdam: Benjamins.

Haiman, John, and Sandra A. Thompson, eds. 1988. *Clause combining in grammar and discourse.* (Typological studies in language, 18.) Amsterdam: Benjamins.

Jacobsen, William, Jr. 1967. Switch-reference in Hokan-Coahuiltecan. In *Studies in Southwestern Ethnolinguistics,* edited by Dell Hymes, pp. 238–263. The Hague: Mouton.

Li, Charles N., and Sandra A. Thompson. 1974. Co-verbs in Mandarin Chinese: Verbs or prepositions? *Journal of Chinese Linguistics* 2.257–278.

Li, Charles N., and Sandra A. Thompson. 1981. *Mandarin Chinese: A functional reference grammar.* Berkeley: University of California Press.

Longacre, Robert E. 1972. *Hierarchy and universality of discourse constituents in New Guinea languages: Discussion.* 2 vols. Washington, D.C.: Georgetown University Press.

Longacre, Robert E. 1985. Sentences as combinations of clauses. In Shopen 1985, pp. 235–286.

Lord, Carol. 1973. Serial verbs in transition. *Studies in African Linguistics* 4.269–296.

Lynch, John. 1983. Switch-reference in Lenakel. In Haiman and Munro 1983, pp. 209–221.

Roberts, John R. 1988. Amele switch-reference and the theory of grammar. *Linguistic Inquiry* 19.45–63.

Sebba, Mark. 1987. *The syntax of serial verbs: An investigation into serialisation in Sranan and other languages.* (Creole language library, 2.) Amsterdam: Benjamins.

Seiler, W. 1986. Noun-classificatory verbal prefixes as reanalysed serial verbs. *Lingua* 68.189–207.

Shopen, Timothy, ed. 1985. *Language typology and syntactic description,* vol. 2, *Complex constructions.* Cambridge and New York: Cambridge University Press.

Stump, Gregory T. 1985. *The semantic variability of absolute constructions.* (*Synthèse* language library, 25.) Dordrecht: Reidel.

Thompson, Sandra A., and Robert E. Longacre. 1985. Adverbial clauses. In Shopen 1985, pp. 171–234.

JANINE SCANCARELLI

Complementation

In approaches to linguistics within, or influenced by, the generative tradition, the term "complementation" has come to refer to the syntactic state of affairs where a notional sentence or predication functions as an argument of a predicate, that is, as a subject or object. The complements are in small capitals below:

(1)   THAT ROY FELL OFF HIS HORSE *surprised Dale.*

(2)   ROY'S FALLING OFF HIS HORSE *surprised Dale.*

(3)   FOR ROY TO FALL OFF HIS HORSE *would surprise Dale.*

Relative clauses, absolutes, and clauses of purpose, manner, time, or place are not considered complements because they are not arguments.

Even within a single language, complements can take a variety of syntactic shapes, referred to as "complement types." Examples (1–3) above illustrate three different complement types for English—a sentence-like complement (1), a nominalization such as a *gerund* (2), and an *infinitive* (3). All languages seem to have at least two complement types; the maximum seems to be about five. (For reference, see Givón 1980, Noonan 1985, Ransom 1986, and Dixon 1991.)

1. Complement types are identified by the following:

(a) The morphology of the predicate, that is, its part of speech or, if it is a verb, its grammatical mood

(b) The sorts of syntactic relations the predicate has with its arguments, for example, whether the agent has a subject relation to the predicate, as in (1), or a genitive relation to it, as in (2)

(c) The external syntactic relations of the complement as a whole, for example, whether the complement has a subordinate or coordinate relation to the main (or matrix) clause

Some complement types are regularly accompanied by a *complementizer*—a word, clitic, or affix whose function is to identify the construction as a complement. Example (1) contains the complementizer *that.* Example (2) has no complementizer: neither derivational morphology (the gerund suffix *-ing*) nor inflectional morphology (the genitive *-'s*) are properly complementizers. Example (3) has the complementizer *to.*

Complement types may be either S[entence]-like or non-S-like. Complementizers aside, S-like complement types have roughly the same syntactic form as a main clause, but non-S-like complement types may differ considerably from main clauses in their syntax. Further, non-S-like complement types, regardless of the part of speech of their predicates, are typically reduced or *desententialized*, in that they may not have the full range of grammatical and inflectional possibilities available to main clauses and S-like complements. For example, neither the infinitive nor the gerund in English can be inflected for primary tense—though secondary tenses, for example, the perfect, are available to these forms. All languages seem to have at least one S-like complement type.

One way in which complement types can be reduced is that there may be limitations on the sorts of grammatical relations that can hold between predicates and their arguments. The most common limitations affect the relation between a predicate and its notional subject: with infinitives, notional subjects are either *raised* (4), *equideleted* (5), or made into objects of adpositions (6):

(4)   *We wanted* ZEKE TO EAT LEEKS.

(5)   *We wanted* Ø TO EAT LEEKS.

(6)   FOR ZEKE TO EAT LEEKS *would please Zelda.*

"Raising" refers to the situation where the notional subject of the complement is treated syntactically as the direct object of the matrix clause: in (4), if *Zeke* is replaced by a pronoun, it is replaced by the objective case *him* and not the subjective *he.* In (5), the notional subject of the complement is *we,* coreferential with the subject of the matrix clause; it is said to be "equi-deleted" under identity with the matrix subject.

2. Features of complement types. Some of the more important features of the most common complement types are summarized below.

(a) *Indicative*: Predicate is a verb. The syntactic relation of subject to predicate is the same as in the main clause. The range of inflectional categories is the same as for the main clause. The S-like form is (nearly) identical to a declarative main clause.

(b) *Subjunctive*: Predicate is a verb. The syntactic relation of subject to predicate is the same as in the main clause. The range of inflectional categories is typically reduced. The S-like form differs from a declarative main clause; when it is itself a main clause, it is often used in hortative or imperative sentences.

(c) *Paratactic*: Predicate is a verb; it may agree with the subject, but does not form a constituent with it. The range of inflectional categories is the same as for the indicative. The construction is interpreted as a separate assertion; syntactically, it is not a subordinate clause, and cannot take a complementizer.

(d) *Infinitive*: Predicate is a verb, but cannot form a constituent with the subject. The range of inflectional categories is reduced, with no subject/verb agreement. Relations with the object are the same as in the indicative.

(e) *Nominalization*: Predicate is a noun; there is an associative relation between the subject and predicate. Inflectional categories are reduced, but as a noun, the predicate may be marked for nominal categories such as case and number. The construction may have the internal structure of a noun phrase; there is often gradation between nominalizations and infinitives.

(f) *Participle*: Predicate is an adjective. The subject is the head, while the rest of the predication is syntactically a modifier. Inflectional categories are reduced; the construction may take adjectival inflections when it agrees with the subject. Syntactically, it may conform to principles governing adjectives.

3. Choice of complement type, in any given situation, is determined by the meaning of the complement type in that language, together with the meaning of the predicate in the matrix clause. For example, in English, gerunds are used to express complement predications treated as facts, whereas infinitives are used to express complement predications treated as potential, projected events. *Remember* is compatible with both, since one can remember both a fact and a projected event:

(7)   *Alvin remembered* WASHING THE DOG. (gerund)

(8)   *Alvin remembered* TO WASH THE DOG. (infinitive)

Want, however, is compatible only with projected events; what one wants cannot have occurred prior to wanting it. Therefore, *want* is compatible with the infinitive, but not with the gerund:

(9)   **Alvin wanted* WASHING THE DOG. (gerund)

(10)   *Alvin wanted* TO WASH THE DOG. (infinitive)

Few grammatical principles, if any, are specific to complementation; and though complementation can be given a workable definition, the definition is semantic rather than grammatical. For example, all the complement types have functions both inside and outside the complement system, and their properties cannot be characterized solely by reference to complementation. Complementation can be understood as one mode of clause-combining.

[*See also* Control; Functional Linguistics; *and* Phrase Structure.]

BIBLIOGRAPHY

Dixon, R. M. W. 1991. *A new approach to English grammar, on semantic principles.* Oxford: Clarendon Press.

Givón, Talmy. 1980. The binding hierarchy and the typology of complements. *Studies in Language* 4.333–377.

Noonan, Michael. 1985. Complementation. In *Language typology and syntactic description,* edited by Timothy Shopen, vol. 2, *Complex constructions,* pp. 42–140. Cambridge and New York: Cambridge University Press.

Ransom, Evelyn N. 1986. *Complementation: Its meanings and forms.* (Typological studies in language, 10.) Amsterdam: Benjamins.

MICHAEL NOONAN

CLAUSE CHAINING. *See* Clause.

CLINICAL LINGUISTICS. *See* Neurolinguistics; Aphasia; Williams Syndrome and Down Syndrome: Cognitive Constraints on Language; *and* Specific Language Impairment.

CLITICS. [*This entry includes the following subentries:*
Overview
Pronominal Clitics]

Overview

"Clitic" is a term conventionally applied as a generalization of the traditional categories *proclitic* and *enclitic* (for clitics appearing at the beginning and end, respectively, of an associated host word or phrase). The interest of the category derives from the fact that clitics appear to partake of both the properties of independent words and those of affixes. (For references, see Anderson 1992, 2000, Everett 1996, Kaisse 1985, Klavans 1985, Zwicky 1977, 1985, and Zwicky and Pullum 1983.)

This single category conceals two logically distinct linguistic notions, each with its own research history. The first is rooted in traditional grammar: in standard descriptions, enclitics and proclitics are identified as accentless words (or particles) that depend accentually (or "lean," hence the name, from Greek *kli:no* 'lean') on an adjacent accented word, and form a prosodic unit together with it. Apart from their defining accentual characteristics, these clitics might show other behaviors as a class: for example, Wackernagel 1892 showed that, in several ancient Indo-European languages (and probably in Proto-Indo-European as well), clitics clustered immediately after the first word of their containing sentence, regardless of their individual function.

A second research tradition originates in the related observation that some "little" words in some languages appear in positions where the normal syntax of the corresponding syntactic category would not be expected to put them. Most notable among these elements are the pronominal clitics found in the Romance languages and elsewhere (discussed in the following subentry); and since these are also generally unaccented, the term "clitic" came to be used to describe that behavior as well.

Because the unusual properties of clitics (in both of the senses identified above) are bound up with their ambiguous status between affixes and words, we may consider some criteria that distinguish affixes (which are determined, bound, and reduced) from words (undetermined, free, and full):

(a) The typical word, but not the typical affix, has an independent accent.

(b) The phonological shape of a word must be listed in the lexicon, but the phonology of an affix is described, in general, by saying how the shape of some stem is altered (so that affixes can have "process," as well as affix, realizations).

(c) Separate, language-specific restrictions can govern the possible phonological shapes of words vs. affixes. In particular, affixes, but not words, are often nonsyllabic.

(d) Syntactically, words belong to (lexical) categories,

i.e. word classes, but the assignment of affixes to such categories is problematic.

(e) Syntactic rules introduce word classes as co-constituents with other syntactic categories, but an affix is syntactically dependent, described by rules that locate it by reference to syntactic elements (e.g. on nouns, on the head of a verb phrase, in the first word of the sentence, at the right edge of a noun phrase).

(f) For each affix, morphological rules specify the class of words with which it can occur, and the properties of the resultant combination, but the syntactic rules distributing words typically make reference to phrasal categories rather than to word classes. From this, it follows that affixes are typically very selective in the word classes with which they occur, but words are unconstrained with respect to the word classes that happen to occur adjacent to them.

(g) Syntactic rules cannot alter morphological structure. In particular, syntactic rules cannot allow a word to interrupt a stem + affix combination; a word attached to such a combination must have edge position.

(h) Syntactic rules that introduce a lexical category are blind to the morphology and phonology of its co-constituents, but rules that introduce an affix may be contingent on such properties of its stem. From this, it follows that there can be arbitrary gaps and morphophonological idiosyncrasies, including suppletion, in the set of stem + affix combinations, but not in the set of word + word combinations.

(i) Alternative orders of words within a constituent are common, but the ordering of an affix—with respect to its stem, and to other such affixes—is fixed. However, the same affixes may combine in different orders to express different meanings; e.g., the passive of a causative is not the same as the causative of a passive, and the affixers involved may reflect this in their ordering.

Various mixtures of these properties are possible. Syntactically dependent words, or *quasi-clitics* are words by all but criterion (e)—e.g. accented Latin adverbs that are located in "second position" in the sentence. Prosodically dependent words, or "leaners," are words by all but criterion (a)—e.g. the English infinitive marker *to*. Phrasal affixes are affixes by all but criteria (f) and (g), e.g. the possessive markers in English and Finnish.

A number of types of bound words can be distinguished, although the analytic status of the distinctions is not clear. Optionally bound words, such as the English auxiliary clitics, are in stylistic alternation with independent words in the language, and so behave like words on criterion (e); other bound words, in contrast, behave like inflections in this respect. Permutable bound words, such as Tagalog particle clitics, have some ordering freedom with respect to one another and so behave like words on criterion (i); other bound words then behave like affixes. Head-bound words, such as the object pronoun clitics in most Romance language, attach to words from a single class (verbs), and so behave like inflections on criterion (f); other bound words here behave like words. The Finnish particle clitics belong to none of these subtypes; they are words on criteria (b) and (d)–(g), but affixes on criteria (a), (c), (e), and (i)—and they can be taken as unmarked representatives of the set of bound words.

From these considerations, we can see that it is useful to distinguish two dimensions of clitic-hood: a phonological one and a morphosyntactic one. The phonological sense of "clitic" is that of an element which, in contrast with normal lexical items, is prosodically subordinate to adjacent material. The morphosyntactic sense is that of an element whose positioning within a larger syntactic construction is determined by principles other than those of the language's normal syntax—principles that bear close similarity to those of morphological affixation. Following Zwicky 1977, we can refer to items displaying these two sorts of property as *simple clitics* and *special clitics*, respectively. Most special clitics are also prosodically dependent, and hence simple clitics as well, though this is not always the case: the Latin adverbs referred to above would appear to be special, but not simple, clitics.

Phonologically dependent elements can be regarded as segments, as syllables, or perhaps even as metrical feet, which do not have a lexically assigned organization into a prosodic word. As a result of this orphan status, they are necessarily incorporated into an adjacent word by the language's rule(s) of "Stray Adjunction," and they form a prosodic unit with that word. The principles of Stray Adjunction often result in a clitic's attaching to a word with which it has no (or even a counter-intuitive) syntactic affiliation. In Kʷakʷ'ala, for example, determiner clitics at the left edge of nominal expressions attach to the word on their left, resulting in a situation in which each constituent appears to terminate in a marker for the case and deictic status of the *following* nominal.

The morphosyntactic dimension of clitic status has been treated in various ways within different theoretical frameworks. Syntacticians have commonly regarded pronominal clitics as syntactically homogeneous with other nominals, generated in the corresponding positions and then moved (e.g., in French, to a position immediately preceding the inflected verb of the clause by syntactic mechanisms that are somehow sensitive to the item's clitic status. Others, however, have preferred to treat clitics of this sort as introduced directly in their surface position within the phonological form of a sentence by mechanisms closer to those of morphology than to those of syntax (reflecting their similarity to affixes, as opposed to words).

In this connection, we can observe that there is a fairly narrow range of positions in which special clitics can appear. These positions can be characterized by three basic parameters (following Klavans 1985 and Anderson 1992):

(a) The clitic is located within the phonological realization of some specific syntactic constituent.
(b) The clitic can be located with respect to the leftmost element, the rightmost element, or the structural head of the constituent within which it occurs.
(c) The clitic may precede or follow the element with respect to which it is located.

These positions are essentially the same as those that can be occupied by affixes within a word, providing some of the motivation for preferring an account outside of normal syntax. The familiar category of "second position" clitics identified by Wackernagel 1892, for instance, is parallel to infixes that come immediately after a word-initial segment, vowel, syllable, etc. (e.g. Kamhmu *srnal* 'earlobe adornment'; cf. *sal* 'to place in ear'). Each can be identified by fixing the domain (sentence, word), the anchoring position (initial word, initial consonant), and the position with respect to that element (following, in both cases). The initial element with respect to which second position clitics are placed is, at least in some cases (e.g. Hittite, some forms of Serbo-Croatian, and most of the examples cited by Wackernagel 1892), the first word rather than the first syntactic phrase within the domain. This fact further suggests that mechanisms other than those of syntax might be required for the description of special clitics and their placement (cf. Anderson 2000). Similarly, the fact that clitics typically display fixed order (as long as meaning remains unchanged), even in languages with considerable freedom of syntactic word order, makes them seem more affix-like; see criterion (i) above.

The semantic interest of clitics arises from the fact that a syntactically dependent item (like *'s* in *the man with the hat's problems* or *The man with the hat's going*) is semantically interpreted with respect to the whole constituent on which it is dependent, not the word to which it happens to be attached.

[*See also* Affixation; Incorporation; Inflection; Metrical Phonology; Morphology, *article on* Morphology and Syntax; Parts of Speech; Polysynthesis; Stem and Root; *and* Words.]

BIBLIOGRAPHY

Anderson, Stephen R. 1992. *A-morphous morphology.* Cambridge: Cambridge University Press.

Anderson, Stephen R. 2000. Towards an optimal account of second position phenomena." In *Optimality Theory: Syntax, phonology and acquisition*, edited by J. Dekkers et al., pp. 302–333. Oxford: Oxford University Press.

Everett, Daniel. 1996. *Why there are no clitics.* Dallas, Tex.: Summer Institute of Linguistics and the University of Texas at Arlington Series in Linguistics.

Kaisse, Ellen M. 1985. *Connected speech: The interaction of syntax and phonology.* Orlando, Fla.: Academic Press.

Klavans, Judith L. 1985. The independence of syntax and phonology in cliticization. *Language* 61.95–120.

Wackernagel, Jakob. 1892. Über ein Gesetz der indogermanischen Wortselling. *Indogermanische Forschungen* 1.333–436.

Zwicky, Arnold M. 1977. *On clitics.* Bloomington Indiana University Linguistics Club.

Zwicky, Arnold M. 1985. Clitics and particles. *Language.* 61.283–305.

Zwicky, Arnold M., and Geoffrey K. Pullum. 1983. Cliticization vs. inflection: English *n't. Language* 59.502–513.

STEPHEN R. ANDERSON AND ARNOLD M. ZWICKY

Pronominal Clitics

The term *clitics* is commonly used to denote elements that serve as syntactic constituents, but that are not phonologically independent words. A primary example of such elements are pronominal clitics (PC), as they are found, for example, in the Romance, Slavic, and Semitic languages. Since PCs enter both the syntactic and the morphological component, they offer an important insight into the nature of syntactic and lexical phenomena, and the interactions between the two.

Arguably, many of the morphophonological properties of PCs are best captured if we assume that, as with affixes, they are attached to their host by a morphological rule, the output being a word. If this is true, then, according to some syntactic models (notably those assuming the correctness of the Lexical Integrity Hypothesis), cliticization can only be characterized as a lexical phenomenon. This direction has been pursued by Andrews 1982 and Grimshaw 1982, within the framework of Lexical-Functional Grammar.

Alongside the morphophonological properties of PCs, they also have many syntactic properties. Chiefly, PCs satisfy both categorial and thematic selection requirements of predicates; they normally occur in complementary distribution with the syntactic phrase that their host predicate selects. Categorial requirements are traditionally met by phrasal categories, but any attempt to accommodate PCs within such phrasal statements requires another mechanism.

Grammatical models that assume movement and empty categories have typically utilized movement to state the relations between PCs and the subcategorized positions (originating with Kayne 1975). The output of such a movement of the French object clitic *les* is depicted in ex. (1):

(1) $[_{VP} [_V les_i + V] [_{NP} e_i]]$

Recent reformulations of this idea, utilizing functional structure, subscribe to the view that PCs are the realization of some functional node within the phrase selected by the predicate, typically D, which moves to attach to the host (cf. Torrego 1998, Uriagereka 1995), as depicted in (2):

(2) $[_{FP} les_i + F(V) [_{VP} (e_i/V) [_{DP} e_i [_{NP} \ldots]]]]$

Within Chomsky's Bare Phrase Structural approach, note that if a phrase dominates PC exclusively, PC is both a maximal projection (X^{max}) and a minimal projection (X^{min}), thereby doing away with the potential conflict between the head status of PC and the phrasal status of selected complements.

Alternatively (cf. Jaeggli 1982), it has been suggested that, in a structure like (1), a base-generated PC can be linked to an empty category in the subcategorized position. Recent reformulation of this idea, again utilizing a richer functional structure, postulates the base-generation of PC as agreement markers (typically associated either with a subject agreement or an object agreement phrase), and binding a null pronominal, *pro,* in the position that satisfies selection requirements (see Borer and Wexler 1992, Sportiche 1995), as schematized in (3):

(3) $[_{agr}P \ [_{agr}' \ les_i + F(V) \ [_{VP} \ [_{v}' \ (e_v/V) \ [_{DP} \ pro \ ]]]$

Various structural constraints have been discovered to apply to the relations between the clitic and its corresponding empty category. Kayne 1975 argues that the relationship is constrained by the Specified Subject Condition. Borer 1984 contends that it is constrained by government, while Aoun 1985 argues for an A'-binding relation. Identification relations have also been proposed, on the assumption that the clitic identifies a null pronominal PRO or *pro* in the empty subject or object position. Within approaches that postulate direct movement of the PC to its final position, such locality constraints are reducible to independent conditions on movement. Within approaches that postulate base-generation, such locality constraints are met by the movement of the phrasal projection containing PRO or *pro* (see arrows in [3]).

Research on PCs typically addresses questions concerning their interaction with argument structure and their relations with their hosts. Thus, it is commonly assumed that PCs may absorb assignment features such as abstract Case and theta-role (cf. Jaeggli 1982, Borer 1984, Aoun 1985). Such absorption results in the unavailability of an overt complement for the predicate in question, explaining the complementary distribution between clitics and, for example, selected arguments. However, at least with abstract Case, if an independent Case assigner is available, its co-occurrence with a clitic may result in the surfacing of the missing argument. This leads to the phenomenon of *clitic doubling*, exemplified here from Rumanian (OM = Object Marker):

(4) I_iam vazut pe $Popescu_1$
       him_1-I.have seen OM $Popescu_1$
       'I have seen Popescu.'

The reader should consult Brandi and Cordin 1989 and Rizzi 1986 on the interaction between PCs and null subjects. Grimshaw 1982 and Belletti 1982 offer differing analyses of reflexive clitics, specifically in Romance. For a comprehensive survey of work on PCs in the 1980s, see Borer 1986; for work in the 1990s, see Riemsdijk 1999.

[*See also* Anaphora and Binding; Lexical-Functional Grammar; Principles and Parameters; Predication; Pronouns, *article on* Pronominals; *and* Subcategorization and Selection.]

BIBLIOGRAPHY

Andrews, Avery D. 1982. The representation of case in Modern Icelandic. In Bresnan 1982, pp. 427–503.

Aoun, Joseph. 1985. *A grammar of anaphora.* (Linguistic Inquiry monographs, 11.) Cambridge, Mass.: MIT Press.

Belletti, Adriana. 1982. On the anaphoric status of the reciprocal construction in Italian. *Linguistic Review* 2.101–137.

Borer, Hagit. 1984. *Parametric syntax: Case studies in Semitic and Romance languages.* (Studies in generative grammar, 13.) Dordrecht: Foris.

Borer, Hagit, ed. 1986. *The syntax of pronominal clitics.* (Syntax and semantics, 19.) Orlando, Fla.: Academic Press.

Borer, Hagit, and Kenneth Wexler. 1992. Bi-unique relations and the maturation of grammatical principles. *Natural Language and Linguistic Theory* 10.2.

Brandi, Paula, and Patricia Cordin. 1989. Two Italian dialects and the null subject parameter. In Jaeggli and Safir.

Bresnan, Joan, ed. 1982. *The mental representation of grammatical relations.* Cambridge, Mass.: MIT Press.

Grimshaw, Jane. 1982. On the lexical representation of Romance reflexive clitics. In Bresnan 1982, pp. 87–148.

Jaeggli, Osvaldo. 1982. *Topics in Romance syntax.* (Studies in generative grammar, 12.) Dordrecht: Foris.

Jaeggli, Osvaldo, and Kenneth Safir, eds. 1989. *The null subject parameter.* Dordrecht: Kluwer.

Kayne, Richard S. 1975. *French syntax: The transformational cycle.* (Current studies in linguistics series, 6.) Cambridge, Mass.: MIT Press.

Riemsdijk, Henk van. 1999. *Language typology: Clitics in the languages of Europe.* Berlin: Mouton de Gruyter.

Rizzi, Luigi. 1986. On chain formation. In Borer 1986, pp. 65–95.

Rooryck, Johan, and Laurie Zaring, eds. 1995. *Phrase structure and the lexicon.* Doredrecht: Kluwer.

Sportiche, Dominique. 1995. Clitic constructions. In Rooryck and Zaring 1995.

Torrego, Esther. 1998. *The dependencies of objects.* (Linguistic inquiry monograph, 34.)

Uriagereka, Juan. 1995. Aspects of the syntax of clitic placement in Western Romance. *Linguistic Inquiry* 26.79–123.

HAGIT BORER

COAHUILTECAN LANGUAGES.
Formerly spoken in southern Texas and northwestern Mexico. Only Tonkawa is reasonably well documented; other known languages of the family are Coahuilteco, Comecrudo, Cotoname, and Karankawa.

LANGUAGE LIST

Tonkawa: formerly spoken in north central Oklahoma. The ethnic group speaks English as mother tongue.

B. GRIMES

COARTICULATION AND TIMING. "Coarticulation" refers to the overlap of articulatory gestures associated with separate speech segments, and by extension to its acoustic effects. An articulation that nominally belongs to one segment occurs in part during another segment. As a result of coarticulation, segments vary according to their contexts. Thus the /t/ in *tea* may be produced with spread lips, but the /t/ in *two* with more rounded lips, anticipating the rounding of the following vowel. Similarly, the /u/ in *choose* may have a more fronted tongue position, because of the surrounding consonants, than does the /u/ in *poof*; the vowel in *man* may be nasalized, unlike that in *bad*. The term "coarticulation" was originated in the 1930s by P. Menzerath, who (like others before him, especially E. W. Scripture), argued against the view that successive speech sounds consist of discrete steady states and transitions. Hardcastle 1981 provides a history of early work on coarticulation.

Coarticulation refers primarily to the relative timing of articulations; however, it can also involve contextual effects on the spatial extent of articulations, such as reductions in articulatory gestures at faster rates of speech. Such effects eliminate extreme articulatory movements; thus coarticulation has been linked to ease of articulation.

The term "coarticulation" is sometimes used interchangeably with "assimilation." However, Menzerath apparently meant to call attention to the physiological basis of assimilation: coarticulation is the cause, and assimilation the effect. Nonetheless, there are many types of assimilation, not all of them articulatory; and today there are many different opinions on the relation between coarticulation and assimilation (see Farnetani 1997 for a review).

Many models of coarticulation have been proposed (See Farnetani 1997; Farnetani and Recasens 1999; and other chapters in Hardcastle and Hewlett 1999). One (by Menzerath, but also independently influential later) is that articulations begin as early as possible; another is that vowel articulations begin during consonants, and vice versa. Alternatively, certain articulations begin at a fixed amount of time before others. It has also been proposed that higher levels of structure, such as syllables, words, or phrases, are involved in coarticulation.

Other studies of coarticulation, dating back to the earliest work, have been concerned with possible differences across languages—and more recently, with general principles that would account for such differences (see Manuel 1999). A related question concerns the acquisition of coarticulation: if languages differ, then speakers must learn language-specific patterns.

The study of timing in speech can also involve the measurement of durations of particular events or units, in either physiological or acoustic records (Lehiste 1970). Because coarticulation blurs boundaries between segments, measurements of segment durations are necessarily arbitrary, but have been shown to vary systematically across contexts, both the segmental context, and the prosodic/phrasal context (Lehiste 1970, Fletcher and Harrington 1999). Segment durations can vary both because durations of individual articulations vary, and because measured durations of segments reflect the extent to which they overlap. Variation in articulation durations is often described in a dynamical systems framework (see Saltzman and Munhall 1989, Lofqvist 1997).

In addition to references cited above, most work on coarticulation has been published in the major phonetics and speech science journals; the *Journal of Phonetics* has published several review and debate papers since 1977.

[*See also* Articulatory Phonetics.]

BIBLIOGRAPHY

Farnetani, Edda. 1997. Coarticulation and connected speech processes. In Hardcastle and Laver 1997, pp. 371–404.

Farnetani, Edda, and Daniel Recasens. 1999. Coarticulation models in recent speech production theories. In Hardcastle and Hewlett 1999, pp. 31–68.

Fletcher, Janet, and Jonathan Harrington. 1999. Lip and jaw coarticulation. In Hardcastle and Hewlett 1999, pp. 164–175.

Hardcastle, William J. 1981. Experimental studies in lingual coarticulation. In *Towards a history of phonetics*, edited by Ronald E. Asher and Eugenie J. A. Henderson, pp. 50–66. Edinburgh: Edinburgh University Press.

Hardcastle, William J., and Nigel Hewlett, eds. 1999. *Coarticulation: Theory, data, and techniques.* (Cambridge studies in speech science and communication.) Cambridge: Cambridge University Press.

Hardcastle, William J., and John Laver, eds. 1997. *The handbook of phonetic sciences.* Oxford and Cambridge, Mass.: Blackwell.

Lehiste, Ilse. 1970. *Suprasegmentals.* Cambridge, Mass.: MIT Press.

Lofqvist, Anders. 1997. Theories and models of speech production. In Hardcastle and Laver 1997, pp. 405–426.

Manuel, Sharon. 1999. Cross-language studies: Relating language-particular coarticulation patterns to other language-particular data. In Hardcastle and Hewlett 1999, pp. 179–198.

Saltzman, Elliot, and Kevin Munhall. 1989. A dynamical approach to gestural patterning in speech production. *Ecological Psychology* 1.333–382.

PATRICIA A. KEATING

CODA. *See* Syllables.

CODE-SWITCHING. Code-switching (*hereafter CS*) refers to "the juxtaposition within the same speech exchange of passages of speech belonging to two grammatical systems or subsystems" (Gumperz 1982: 56) and affects more or less everyone who speaks several languages or dialects. This typical exchange was recorded in Alsace, where French is spoken alongside the regional variety of German:

A: Ja, j'ai joué la semaine dernière, **verdeckel dü!** Deux jours, hein, courbaturé! **Ich maan, ich bin verschlawe worre.**
*Yes, I played last week, **damn it!** Two days, eh, stiff as a poker! I felt I had been beaten.*
B: Tu m'étonnes, hé, **wenn d'so lang spielsch . . .**
*You (don't) surprise me, **when you play for so long . . .***

Primarily characteristic of informal speech, in many communities CS becomes systematic. Written examples, though rarer, are also found. CS is commonplace in multilingual regions where several unstandardized varieties co-exist (e.g. India, Africa, or the Caribbean), but also among regional minorities and communities of immigrant origin. CS is, both in theory and in practice, closely interlinked with other developments within bilingual communities: borrowing, language shift, and pidginization. It has parallels in "monolingual" areas in dialect-switching and style-shifting.

1. Defining CS. The term "code-switching" was first used in the 1940s in a technical sense in Information Technology, and only later in linguistics, with "code" meaning "linguistic variety." Much discussion revolves around the relationship between CS and other outcomes of language contact, especially borrowing, but is hampered by a lack of terminological clarity.

As code-switching implies that there is alternation between two *discrete* varieties, some have reserved the term for cases where such alternation appears to occur and used another term—for example, "code-mixing," where there is convergence between the two systems (Muysken 2000). Others have continued using CS as the umbrella term for a variety of contact phenomena, either out of inertia, as CS is the more widely used term, or because bilingualism is seldom a stable state of affairs and some degree of integration usually takes place when the phenomenon is viewed diachronically. There is evidence in some cases of a chronological progression from a type of CS in which there are clear reasons for individual switches, to a mixed mode, in which frequent CS is a community norm, but the switches themselves appear arbitrary, to the establishment of new mixed varieties.

Language contact is now seen as a crucial factor in language change, not only in the case of pidgins, creoles, and mixed languages previously considered exotic or marginal. Even a standard world language like English has evolved from contact between Celtic, Anglo-Saxon, Latin, and Norman French. Since CS occurs alongside borrowing and so on, in many contexts where language change is clearly occurring, it should be considered alongside these in discussions of language change.

Language Interaction has been proposed as an umbrella term to replace CS and include all the linguistic results of contact (LIPPS Group 2000); if generally adopted, it may help solve the difficulty illustrated in Milroy and Muysken 1995, where each contributing author had to individually explain his or her use of the terms.

CS has been studied from three main perspectives.

1.1. Psycholinguistic. It was originally assumed that something resembling an electric switch operated when bilinguals changed languages. Psycholinguists in the 1950s through the 1970s first proposed a "single switch model," in which, when one of the bilingual's languages was activated, the other automatically disengaged, then a "2-switch model," which hypothesized that different mechanisms control input (listening/understanding) and output (speaking). Nowadays, the control system is thought of as flexible, and sensitive to changes in the linguistic and the non-linguistic environment. In CS, the output is free to vary according to which words reach threshold first. Grosjean 2000 concludes from various experiments that no specific switch/monitor mechanism is needed to account for bilingual processing, but that bilinguals may be operating in *monolingual* or *bilingual mode* at any given moment. Variations on switching behavior have been observed in bilingual children and in cases of language pathology. Attempts to establish whether bilinguals differ from monolinguals in terms of hemispheric lateralization do not point to any fundamental differences between monolingual and bilingual functioning.

1.2. Sociolinguistic. Until CS began to be studied systematically in the 1970s, normative attitudes condemning any mixing of languages prevailed among linguists. Nowadays, they are still found in popular attitudes to CS, even among speakers who code-switch regularly themselves. In fact, most CS occurs in "native" bilinguals—people for whom both languages represent "mother-tongues." Consequently, what are separate languages for the observer should not necessarily be seen as such for the speaker. Gumperz warned against confusing the grammarian's notion of language and the speaker's notion of code (1982:99). Auer argues that certainty that two languages are separate for the speaker depends on showing that they contrast meaningfully in conversation (1998: 13).

One explanation for CS is "lexical need"—that is, lack of access to a word/expression in the other language, or lack of precise equivalent (Poplack's *mot juste* switching). But such cases represent a small minority of instances of CS for fluent bilinguals, who may use the same word within the same utterance, first in one language and then the other. Often, two words considered as translation equivalents acquire complementary meanings in CS. Moreover, some people in bilingual communities never speak other than in a code-switching mode. The latter takes its place among the options available in the linguistic marketplace and is related to macrolinguistic parameters on the same basis as the available monolingual varieties (Heller 1988).

In his earlier work, Gumperz distinguished *situational* and *conversational* CS. Situational CS coincides with a change in topic/speaker/setting; conversational CS occurs without such changes but fulfils various conversational functions—for example, the *metaphorical* function of introducing connotations of language A into a conversation in language B. Only situational CS is possible in diglossic communities: when varieties are strictly allocated to different domains, CS constitutes a *marked choice*—that is, involves redefining the current set of rights and obligations. It constitutes the *unmarked choice* where speakers draw on a dual identity and most conversations involve using both varieties—for example, in Alsace, where speaking "pure" French or Alsatian may be a political statement.

Auer 1998 describes CS as the most significant discourse marker in bilingual conversation, constituting a "contextualization cue" which makes relevant/maintains/revises/cancels some aspect of context responsible for the interpretation of an utterance. Using the "dispreferred language" may serve to show disagreement or as an avoidance strategy (Li Wei 2000). CS may mark off asides/empasize/quote/draw attention to a particular passage—for example, either in combination with, or instead of, techniques available to monolingual speakers.

1.3. Grammatical. Muysken 2000 claims that the study of CS can uniquely contribute to resolving one of the crucial debates in linguistics, "the division of labour between the lexicon and grammar of a language." Grammatical studies of CS have, however, so far been characterized by an apparently fruitless search for universal rules or constraints.

Sankoff and Poplack 1981 proposed two constraints on where CS could occur in the sentence, based on Spanish-English CS in New York:

a. The *equivalence constraint:* CS could only occur at points where the grammars of the two languages were equivalent.

b. The *free morpheme constraint:* no switch could occur between bound morphemes of a single word.

Other data-sets, however, provided numerous counterexamples. In some communities, adapting lexical items morphologically to the surrounding language is one of the most productive forms of CS.

Further constraints, proposed by others, were also not upheld by the evidence. For example, it was proposed that there could be no switching between elements related by Government: along with the categorical/semantic features of a lexical head, the prediction was that a language index would also be projected on the constituent. But as Muysken later pointed out, very common switches are ruled out by this (e.g., "I saw *la casa*"–verbs govern their noun phrases, so the article *la* should be in English). Similarly, Arabic-Dutch CS data contains verbal and prepositional noun phrases in a different language from the governing verb or preposition.

Myers-Scotton's Matrix Language Frame (*MLF*) model 1993 integrates psycholinguistic and grammatical explanations for CS. The sociolinguistically "unmarked" variety for a particular interaction type is presumed the most *activated* at a psycholinguistic level; this is the ML (matrix language). Changes in ML only coincide with major changes in the situation; all system morphemes (or closed class words) are in the ML, which also determines morpheme order in the sentence. Where stretches of speech contain system morphemes from the EL (embedded language), or following EL word order, these are termed "EL islands."

The problem is establishing which is the ML in a noncircular way. The ML is said to provide more morphemes than the EL—but where does one begin and end counting? Furthermore, in some multilingual situations, many morphemes are shared between the two varieties, and cannot be assigned exclusively to either.

Summarizing these findings, Muysken says that none of the constraint-systems proposed holds good in all cases. Instead, various mechanisms play a role in different CS situations. He identifies three main processes, each of which is related both to structural and sociolinguistic conditions:

1. Insertion (of lexical items or constituents from variety A into variety B).
2. Alternation (between structures).
3. "Congruent lexicalization": two varieties share a grammatical structure, which can be filled lexically with elements from either.

Further work is needed to tie-in CS patterns with structural and sociolinguistic parameters. Another promising line involves looking at the various processes used by bilinguals to facilitate transitions between the two systems. Research on CS is crucial in linguistics because it shows that grammars are accessed via a series of sociolinguistic factors, which determine when and how they apply.

[*See also* Bilingualism and Multilingualism; Diglossia; *and* Sociolinguistics.]

BIBLIOGRAPHY

Auer, Peter. 1998. *Code-switching in conversation: Language, interaction and identity.* London: Routledge.

Grosjean, François. 1996. *Processing mixed language: issues, findings, models.* In *Tutorials in bilingualism: psycholinguistic perspectives,* edited by Annet de Groot and Judith Kroll, pp. 225–254. Hillsdale, N.J.: Erlbaum.

Gumperz, John. 1982. *Discourse strategies.* Cambridge: Cambridge University Press.

Heller, Monica. 1988. *Code-switching: Anthropological and sociolinguistic perspectives.* Berlin: Mouton de Gruyter.

Li Wei. 2000. *The bilingualism reader.* London: Routledge.

LIPPS Group (*Language Interaction in Plurilingual and Plurilectal Speakers*). 2000. The LIDES coding manual: A document for preparing and analysing language interaction data. *International Journal of Bilingualism,* Special Issue, June 2000.

Milroy, Lesley, and Pieter Muysken. 1995. *One speaker, two languages: Cross-disciplinary perspectives on code-switching.* Cambridge: Cambridge University Press.

Muysken, Pieter. 2000. *Bilingual speech: A typology of code-mixing.* Cambridge: Cambridge University Press.

Myers-Scotton, Carol. 1993. *Duelling languages: Grammatical structure in codeswitching.* Oxford: Clarendon Press.

Sankoff, David, and Shana Poplack. 1981. A formal grammar for code-switching. *Papers in Linguistics* 14:1.3–46.

PENELOPE GARDNER-CHLOROS

COGNITIVE GRAMMAR. C[ognitive] G[rammar] is a linguistic model developed by Ronald W. Langacker (Langacker 1987, 1990, 1991, 1999, among others). Its main goal is to express the semiotic function of language, namely to allow the symbolization of conceptualizations by means of phonological sequences. A CG grammar is best described as a structured inventory of symbolic units that represents the speaker's knowledge of established linguistic conventions. Three kinds of units are posited: phonological, semantic, and symbolic units. A symbolic unit consists of the symbolic association between a semantic unit (its semantic pole), and a phonological unit (its phonological pole). In this view, the lexicon, morphology, and syntax form a continuum of symbolic units that cannot be naturally divided into separate components.

The only entities available for the description of any level of linguistic organization are "i) semantic, phonological or symbolic units which are (part of) occurring expressions, ii) schematizations of permitted structures, iii) categorizing relations between permitted structures" (Langacker 1987:488). Grammatical constructions take the form of templates that represent the schematization of actually occurring expressions and sanction the use of novel ones. They are also symbolic in nature, and thus meaningful, even though their meaning is usually more abstract than that of lexical items. Constructions co-exist in the grammar with their instantiations. They both capture different facets of the speaker's linguistic knowledge. This "usage-based" conception of language constitutes "a nonreductive approach to linguistic structure that employs fully articulated schematic networks and emphasizes the importance of low-level schemas" (Langacker 1987:494).

Because of their symbolic status, linguistic expressions of any level of complexity have a semantic pole. The exploration of their meaning thus constitutes an important facet of their description. In CG, meaning is equated with conceptualization, or in other words with the human interpretation of the world. It is subjective, anthropocentric, and reflects dominant cultural concerns and culture-specific modes of interaction, as well as features of the world as such. Ultimately, conceptualization needs to be explicated in terms of cognitive processing. Langacker 1988:6 writes: "Entertaining a particular conceptualization, or having a certain mental experience, resides in the occurrence of some complex 'cognitive event'. An established concept is simply a cognitive routine, i.e. a cognitive event (or event type) sufficiently well-entrenched to be elicited as an integrated whole."

The meaning of a linguistic expression is characterized as the particular construal it imposes on a scene. A central manifestation of construal concerns the "profile" expressions impose on their conceptual "base." The base consists of one or more "cognitive domains" (Langacker 1987:147–166), and the profile designates a specific substructure within the base. Any knowledge system or conceptualization can function as a domain regardless of its complexity or abstractness. For example, *father* designates and makes salient a specific subsection of a network of kinship relations. Different expressions can share the same base and only differ as to the nature of their profile. *Mother,* for example, designates another subsection of the same conceptual base as *father.* Importantly, because profiling is a matter of construal, the use of a given expression to code a particular scene reflects the speaker's choice to structure that scene in a specific way, rather than its intrinsic properties.

The notion of profiling also affords a semantic characterization of grammatical categories. According to the nature of their profile, the entities described by linguistic expressions can be divided into "things" and "relations." Nouns profile things. A thing represents "a region in some domain" (Langacker 1987:189), and a "region" is defined as "a set of interconnected entities" (Langacker 1987:198). The other grammatical categories (prepositions, adjectives, participles, adverbs, and verbs) are relational in character. Relational expressions profile "the interconnections between two or more conceived entities" (Langacker 1987:215). Verbs represent a particular kind of complex relation because they profile the successive configurations between their participants as evolving through conceived time. They are therefore said to have a "temporal profile." Here again, because the grammatical categories are characterized in terms of their profile, each one of them reflects a specific construal of the conceptualized scene.

The CG model has been used to insightfully describe a large number of linguistic phenomena in numerous languages. These include, among others, anaphora (van Hoek 1997), case marking (Cook 1988, Dabrowska 1997, Janda 1993, Smith 1994), complementation (Achard 1998), discontinuous morphology (Rubba 1993), negative polarity (Israel 1998), raising (Newman 1981, Langacker 1995), middle constructions (Maldonado 1999, Manney 2000), spatial constructions (Vandeloise 1986, Lindner 1981, Casad and Langacker 1985), and transitivity (Tuggy 1981, Rice, 1987).

[*See also* Functional Linguistics; Metaphor and Semantics; Psycholinguistics; Semantics; *and* Semiotics.]

BIBLIOGRAPHY

Achard, Michel. 1998. *Representation of cognitive structures: Syntax and semantics of French sentential complements.* (Cognitive linguistics research, 11.) Berlin and New York: Mouton de Gruyter.

Casad, Eugene, and Ronald W. Langacker. 1985. Inside outside in Cora grammar. *International Journal of American Linguistics* 51:247–281.

Cook, Kenneth. 1988. *A cognitive analysis of grammatical relations, case, and transitivity in Samoan.* San Diego: University of California dissertation.

Dabrowska, Ewa. 1997. *Cognitive semantics and the Polish dative.* (Cognitive linguistics research, 9.) Berlin and New York: Mouton de Gruyter.

Israel, Michael. 1998. *The rhethoric of grammar: Scalar reasoning and polarity sensitivity.* San Diego: University of California dissertation.

Janda, Laura A. 1993. *A geography of case semantics: The Czech dative and the Russian instrumental.* (Cognitive linguistics research, 4.) Berlin and New York: Mouton de Gruyter.

Langacker, Ronald W. 1987. *Foundations of cognitive grammar,* vol. 1, *Theoretical prerequisites.* Stanford, Calif.: Stanford University Press.

Langacker, Ronald W. 1988. An overview of cognitive grammar. In *Topics in cognitive linguistics,* edited by Brydgida Rudzka-Ostyn, pp. 3–48. Amsterdam and Philadelphia: Benjamins.

Langacker, Ronald W. 1990. *Concept, image, and symbol. The cognitive basis of grammar.* (Cognitive linguistics research, 1.) Berlin and New York: Mouton de Gruyter.

Langacker, Ronald W. 1991. *Foundations of cognitive grammar,* vol. 2, *Descriptive applications.* Stanford: Stanford University Press.

Langacker, Ronald W. 1995. Raising and transparency. *Language* 71.1–62.

Langacker, Ronald W. 1999. *Grammar and conceptualization.* (Cognitive linguistic research, 14.) Berlin and New York: Mouton de Gruyter.

Lindner, Susan. 1981. *A lexico-semantic analysis of English verb-particle constructions with UP and OUT.* San Diego: University of California dissertation.

Maldonado, Ricardo. 1999. *A media voz. Problemas conceptuales del clítico se.* Universidad Nacional Autónoma de México.

Manney, Linda. 2000. *Middle voice in modern Greek: Meaning and function of an inflectional category.* (*Studies in Language*, Companion series, 48.) Amsterdam and Philadelphia: Benjamins.

Newman, John. 1981. *The semantics of raising constructions.* San Diego: University of California dissertation.

Rice, Sally. 1987. *Toward a cognitive model of transitivity.* San Diego: University of California dissertation.

Rubba, Joanna. 1993. *Discontinuous morphology in modern Aramaic.* San Diego: University of California dissertation.

Smith, Michael. 1994. Agreement and iconicity in Russian impersonal constructions. *Cognitive Linguistics* 5:5–56.

Tuggy, David. 1981. *The transitivity-related morphology of Tetelcingo Nahuatl: An exploration in space grammar.* San Diego: University of California dissertation.

Vandeloise, Claude. 1986. *L'espace en français.* Paris: Éditions du Seuil.

van Hoek, Karen. 1997. *Anaphora and conceptual structure.* Chicago and London: University of Chicago Press.

MICHEL ACHARD

COGNITIVE LINGUISTICS. *See* Cognitive Grammar; Semantics; Metaphor and Semantics; *and* Scripts, Frames, and Schemas.

COGNITIVE SCIENCE. The field of cognitive science is the interdisciplinary study of intelligent devices—actual (e.g. thermostats and other "smart" devices) or virtual (design specifications for abstract machines or other such system blueprints), inorganic (computers and software), and organic (brains). All such devices are studied from the viewpoint that they process information by using representations, and they manipulate this information in a mechanized, systematic way. Cognitive science might thus be said to be the discipline that studies computational minds in all their manifestations—their design, explanation, implementation, development, and breakdown (Wilson and Keil 1999, Lepore and Pylyshyn 1999).

Cognitive science has emerged out of the convergence of at least seven fields studying representational issues: linguistics, psychology, computer science, neuroscience, philosophy, biology, and anthropology. These disciplines have contributed to cognitive science via their subfields directly concerned with intelligent, representation-using devices. Linguistics informs cognitive science through formal and functional linguistics and other theoretical pursuits dedicated to discovering the nature of a grammar; psycholinguistics, neurolinguistics, and computational linguistics play a role through their focus on the development and processing of linguistic representations. Cognitive psychology, especially cognitive neuroscience, informs the field through empirical studies of memory, learning, and development, and through accounts of how of mental information-processing systems are linked to brain systems. In computer science, natural language processing, artificial intelligence, machine learning, and learnability theory bear on cognitive science through the study of knowledge representation, parsing, language recognition and generation, computational architectures, and formal learning systems. Neuroscience, particularly computational neuroscience, provides material on the components of the organic machines that subserve mind—neurons and their assembly into brains. Philosophy of mind and philosophy of science contribute by analyzing what a mind could logically be, and how a justifiable scientific explanation of a mind might be formulated. Evolutionary biology offers information on the range of organic intelligent devices (human and animal minds) and the ways they emerge in ecological niches, given conditions on adaptation. Like evolutionary biology, anthropology contributes by examining evolutionary questions, but social and cultural anthropology also play a role in cognitive science via cognitive anthropology, the study of culture as a mental representation (Osherson 1995–2000, Bechtel and Graham 1999).

The range of fields that bear on cognitive science can be breathtaking. How could a single person ever know enough to be a cognitive scientist? This is an intrinsically collaborative field, where individuals who are expert in one or more subfields combine efforts toward a single research program. For example, a phonologist and a cognitive neuroscientist might join forces to identify the cognitive and brain mechanisms that support the mental representation of sound systems. Because of the collaborative nature of the field and the multiplicity of viewpoints, cognitive science is often referred to in the plural as "the cognitive sciences."

Despite the diversity of inquiry, collaborators share a number of common principles that raise cognitive science to the level of an overarching explanatory pursuit. Just as evolution is the explanatory mechanism that gives order to the various findings within the biological sciences, so cognitive science is a unifying metadiscipline for the mind sciences, providing not only explanations for phenomena within contributing disciplines but also ways of arbitrating theoretical disputes.

Suppose, for instance, that a linguist discovers that the grammars of all human languages have a certain property—say, that the rules of language are structure-dependent and refer to abstract categories (like NP or INFL) that are invisible on the surface of language. She might ask: "Why this property and not others?" The answer can be found outside linguistics proper and in the overriding theory of computational mind: information systems that run in real time on things like brains require stored programs with variables like NP and INFL in order to respond consistently to changing input. The linguistic phenomenon of structure-dependence is a consequence of the way intelligent devices are designed. Now suppose that another linguist discovers a counter-property—say, that the rules of language do not refer to abstract structures like NP and INFL but are statistical regularities computed over frequencies of co-occurrence, making NP an emergent regularity of certain words appearing in the speech stream with other words. She asks: "Which account is correct for human language—structure dependence or statistical calculation?" The answer to this linguistic question, again, would lie in the metatheory of cognitive science, where debates are raised over whether intelligent linguistic devices are abstract code-crunching machines or statistical processors (Marcus 2000). In this case, cognitive science resolves a disciplinary clash not by eliminating one hypothesis in favor of another, but by synthesizing and rising above the theoretical fray—a classic function of metatheory. In looking beyond itself to a unifying theory for explanations and resolutions of scientific disputes, linguistics is a branch of cognitive science in the same way that particle physics is a branch of cosmology.

What are the common principles that make cognitive science an overarching explanatory pursuit? How does linguistics borrow from these principles and contribute to them?

1. Levels of explanation. To be complete, accounts of phenomena relevant to cognitive science should provide an explanation at three levels: what the intelligent device is doing (its tasks or ecology), what mechanisms it uses to do what it is doing (its algorithms or knowledge), and what physical device or machine supports the mechanisms that allow the device to do what it is doing (its hardware or "wetware") (Marr 1982). This explanatory heuristic—"the device is doing X by means of Y running

on Z"—unifies the various cognitive sciences *in a single pursuit* (functional systems) and circumscribes a mode of inquiry. By studying functional representation machines at three levels, cognitive science cuts a path between the physical sciences on the one hand and the social sciences on the other. Adherence to the three levels, properly aligned, is a responsibility often carried out more in principle than in practice, given the difficulty of fully stating information at all three levels; however, it is an acknowledged constraint on theorizing in cognitive science.

Failure to appreciate all levels and their proper alignment can lead to problems. Exposing this failure, Calvin (1996:34–36) pokes fun at mathematicians and physicists who have gotten heavily into the cognitive science industry by arguing that the human brain is a quantum computer to be explained by the properties of atoms in chemical exchange, chaos theory, and other mathematical characterizations of dynamic systems. This sort of explanation poses alignment problems: how does quantum mechanics support the computational mechanisms that yield behavior?

In contrast, good cases of alignment are instructive. We are now learning a great deal about how Williams syndrome, caused by a genetic deletion within a stretch of 83 kilobases on chromosome 7 (Frangiskakis et al. 1996), involves fairly selective difficulty with the cognitive mechanisms for the visual integration of objects, yet surprisingly preserves aspects of language (Frawley 2002). Cognitive science lacks some of the specifics of level alignment in Williams syndrome—e.g., how the failed protein expression from the genetic deletions affects the cognitive—but at least the story has begun to be told in a complete and constrained way, from subcellular code affecting the expression of protein in neurons to instructions for visual processing and to task failures.

2. Representation. Mind is the evolutionary outcrop of the increasing growth of mechanisms intervening between input and output. *Informational throughput* gives organisms the ability to defer reaction and to plan or act for an apparent purpose. Cognitive science investigates *mediated* input-output systems. Fodor 1983 calls the mediating code a "language of thought" because the requisite properties of the code needed to perform its tasks appear to be properties of a natural language in the abstract: system, structure, dependency, and productivity. Although there is continuing debate over whether the code is language-like, even the major counters to Fodor

FIGURE 1. *Symbolic Account of Innovative Suffixation*

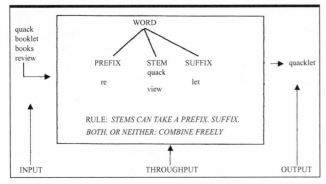

presume some mediating representational system that constructs new information on the basis of old, and does so systematically and productively (Clark 2001).

The evident necessity of representation does not mean that everyone agrees on what the right code is. The available models fall into two large competing classes: *symbols* and *pattern associations*. The differences between these two come down to disputes over the abstractness of the content of the code and the explicitness of regularities and patterns in it.

2.1. Symbols. Some cognitive scientists hold that mental code is abstract and independent of properties of the input—i.e., not driven by learning—and that regularities in behavior are a consequence of explicitly stated regularities in the mediating code. In this view, the relation between input and throughput is indirect, and representation involves *recoding* of input. Such a picture downplays learning (insofar as "learning" means decision-making or behavioral change based on properties of the input), since mental work is done by the abstract representations themselves, which filter, ignore, restate, and otherwise supersede properties of the input. Moreover, the manipulation of these representations and the systematic and productive behavior that such manipulation yields are the result of regularities *overtly stated* in the mental code. Mind is symbols operated on by rules, much as a program in any standard programming language (see Pinker 1994, 1997).

Why believe symbolism? Consider an example. When my daughter was two years old, she called a little duck a *quacklet*. This expression was not learned or input-driven, but evidently derived from the manipulation of formulas with variables like stem (core of the word) and suffix (attachment to the end of the core). *Quacklet* is a regular consequence of her too freely applied rules for words as data structures. Her error is in the unconstrained

power of her algorithms. We might, then, picture her symbolic process as a kind of abstract, rule-and-category, analysis-and-synthesis system, as shown in Figure 1.

2.2. Pattern association. Opponents of symbolism claim that it is not empirically feasible. When you look at the platform (the brain) on which language runs, you see no symbols and rules, just patterns of electrical activity. You do not need abstract symbolic code to mediate input and output in order to capture systematic and productive behavior. What you need is a *good learning mechanism:* some minimal coding scheme that picks up patterns in the input and generalizes by analogy across these patterns. You need a big—if representationally shallow—memory.

Pattern association, usually via its more popular names—*connectionism, neural networks,* or *parallel distributed processing* (PDP)—asserts that symbol processors have the design specifications wrong. Instead of a relatively small set of abstract, explicit data structures and rules mediating input and output, you can get by with a lot of simple recording devices that recode input minimally and keep track of one another's current states to see what has been recorded: a network of nodes and connections. In this way, regularities—which are, in any model, statements about expectations across states of the mediating code—become properties of the interaction (connections) of the recording devices (nodes) as they settle into a constant state of cross-check. Rules or regularities are *distributed* across the system and are *emergent properties* of the system as a whole. Mind is an activated network of distributed regularities, not data structures and algorithms explicitly stated (see Elman et al. 1996, Ellis and Humphreys 1999).

Now reconsider *quacklet*, this time as a consequence of learned features of input, emergent properties of a network, and distributed regularities in nodes and associations. My daughter has been exposed to a lot of words, some of them *quacklet*-like. Her brain has recorded all of them, and even weighted them for the number of times they have appeared alone and with each other. These words have also developed cross-checks with one another that are weighted as they turn one another on and off, given more and different exposures—i.e., as she has more experiences. Moreover, the cross-checks themselves and overall activation patterns of the input can give rise to new, intermediate patterns (called "hidden layers" in connectionist terminology), and these can enter into the overall behavior of the network, too.

The output of the association network as a whole

FIGURE 2. *Pattern Association Account of Innovative Suffixation*

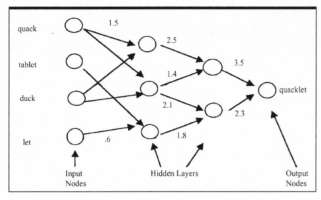

produces *quacklet*, but does so as a consequence of exposure to words recorded essentially as they are (not abstracted), and as they enter into probabilistic dependencies with one another; see Figure 2.

Quacklet is a possible word because it is in accord with the distributed regularities of the system. Given the kinds and number of exposures the system has had to all words and the chances it has had at making cross-checks in the associations, *quacklet* is a natural consequence of the relatively stable states that the network has come to settle in. The "procedure" that generates *quacklet* is an emergent property of the network, not an explicitly stated rule. Even though *quacklet* is a natural consequence of an emergent regularity, it is still novel and coined, precisely because the forms in the input that ultimately converge on *quacklet* as output have low probability (e.g. *tablet*).

There are many more subtle aspects of pattern association, but here it is enough to see that the alternative to input-free, abstract coding and explicit statement of regularities can be input-sensitive, shallow coding with emergent regularities in an activated network. All varieties of pattern associators put their bets on representation as vectors of activation, and so construe the mediating code as an analog or continuous representation system, in contrast to the digitized symbolic code envisioned by the competing view.

Which, then, is the right model to meet the commitment to representation in cognitive science: abstract symbolic code, or shallow pattern association? Both, it turns out—a point acknowledged by some members of both camps—and this yields two lessons. First, each kind of code might be better for a different kind of representational demand. Pattern associators are suited to perceptual learning, where the relation between code and input must be shallow, and where abstract categories and stated rules are less necessary. For example, much of the phonetic structure of language—speech as mechanical energy—can be captured in a multidimensional vector space representing the physical properties of the speech signal. However, it is difficult to see how the more abstract properties of language, like subject-verb agreement and grammatical relationships, can be discerned in this sort of analog code (cf., however, Elman et al. 1996). Some regularities, no matter how ostensibly driven by analogy and correlated with other features of the input, seem to be formed by the extraction of relevant *pieces* of the input and their abstract recombination (Marcus 2001).

Second, one way of linking the two kinds of representation is to say that connectionism is the implementation of what symbolic explanations provide. Symbolic code explains the algorithmic or mechanism level; pattern association explains the machine level. The real challenge, then, is to state how data structures and rules can be converted into association patterns. This kind of talk pleases the symbolists because it seems to make the explanatory war a non-issue, deferring the problems and solutions to the imagination of computer scientists. But it is not clear what should be done, even if connectionism is the implementation of symbolic structures. What happens to the symbols, then? Suppose there is a way to completely reduce *quacklet* to patterns of association. Should linguistics then abandon the vocabulary of explanation that relies on stems, prefixes, and suffixes? If your calculator is just running through electrical patterns that go proxy for adding, should we then say that insofar as all adding is an implementation, there is no such thing as adding?

3. Computation. To compute is to execute functions, or mappings between two states (Churchland and Sejnowski 1992:62). More technically, computation is the mediation of input and output by effective procedures that manipulate interpretable formal objects by virtue of their shape, structure, or arrangement—their syntax—and not necessarily by what they refer to. *Effective procedures* are precise and mechanical mapping operations (when such procedures always halt, they are called *algorithms*). The execution of functions places limits on what can be represented, processed, and learned at all.

FIGURE 3. *String Solution by Differences*

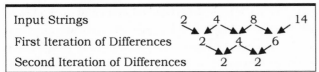

In attributing computation to a system, it is important to keep in mind the locale of the execution of procedures. From an external standpoint, one might say that a tree is computing simply by growing, since it may be described as mapping between two growth states—but then everything seems computational. More critical is internal computation, in which a system actually runs effective procedures, or can be explained as doing so. Representation-using input-output devices—minds—compute in this sense.

Suppose that that a system receives as input a string of items—2, 4, 8, 14—and its task is to determine a pattern in the input that solves the string and all future strings of like sequence. How could the system halt computing (develop an algorithm) so that it decides all input of this type? This task is, in essence, the learnability problem for all formal systems. The system might double the current input to produce the next, but this procedure would fail at 14. If, however, it were to take the difference between later numbers and earlier ones, and do this in successive iterations, it would ultimately come to a point where the different output is constant at 2, as shown in Figure 3.

When the system arrives at the constant, we may say that it has "learned" the input: it has decided a grammar for these strings. Moreover, it has done this computationally because its decision procedure is a function that maps from string to string. The direct analogy to language input should be clear. How does a language-learning system decide the patterns in input strings? Grammar is a solution to input cast in terms of effective procedures.

Many questions arise at this point. How regular are the input strings? Can language be learned from its input alone? What is the system equipped with to start the decision procedure? Can the learning mechanism be simple? Does one need to recast the input in terms of abstract representations for the learning to occur? These are genuine issues in cognitive science, but not ones directly challenging computation. Even accounts of mind and language that lack representations altogether, and in

which knowledge is developed and deployed "on the fly," such as Dynamical Systems Theory, are compatible with computation (van Gelder 1998).

4. Architecture. How does computation flow? Does all information have access to or affect all other information? How is the system managed? Are representations processed singly or in groups? Do different kinds of processes and code affect one another? These are questions about the *architecture*, the overall organization of the input-throughput-output system.

Architecture can be understood as the relationship between two parameters:

- How many representations can be computed at a time? Answers to this question yield the difference between *serial* and *parallel* architectures.
- How do computed representations interact? Answers to this question yield *modular* or *interactive* architectures.

Do mental devices work serially, computing one thing at a time, finishing one task first and sending it off before doing anything else? Such processing would seem to take too much time, but perhaps some representationally mediated input-output systems are just *very fast* serial processors. Still, a brain runs slowly because its connectivity is built on neurochemical transfer, measured roughly by the millisecond (10^{-3}). How could you get 100 billion slow things done at a fast rate? The answer is to do the computations simultaneously, in parallel, cutting the time by the factor that constitutes the simultaneity.

The second architectural parameter turns on how the interactions of representations are managed. Do computations run independently, with no interactive feedback among them ? Or do they converge as they run, intruding on and affecting one another's output? In modular architectures, computations, are *encapsulated*, *domain-specific*, and *specialized*: they have their own areas of operation and talk to one another to coordinate activity via special sets of cross-domain code (interfaces), not via constant feedback and interaction. In an interactive architecture, however, information from one domain can evoke and intrude on the information in another while the processing is active. Interactive architectures are *unencapsulated*. Information of a particular kind might be domain-specific, but the computations of one domain are not immune to intrusions of information from another domain. This is not to say that information processing is not specialized—only that the division of labor that

340   COGNITIVE SCIENCE

FIGURE 4. *Kinds of Architectures*

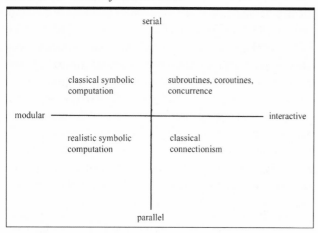

characterizes modular systems artificially limits the processing space.

The two basic parameters of architecture—serial vs. parallel and modular vs. interactive—are orthogonal. By combining number of representations computed at a time with kind of interaction of representations, we can generate four possible classes of architecture, as shown in Figure 4.

If representations are computed in a stepwise fashion and organized into encapsulated modules, we get classical symbolic computation, in which programs run sequentially and different chunks of programs are executed without interference with other chunks; this is a *serial modular* architecture. But we can preserve serial processing and loosen modularity by running chunks of programs and code to varying degrees of simultaneity, via such things as subroutines, coroutines, and concurrence. This kind of *serial interactive* architecture is a way of introducing a connectionist flavor into serial processing by mimicking interactivity. We could also allow many representations to be computed at once and let them interact as they will; this results in a *parallel interactive* architecture, of which classical connectionism is the prime illustration—a fully recurrent network with all parts, in principle, running and affecting one another at once. Finally, we could preserve parallel computation of representations but restrict their interaction to domain-specific computation, resulting in *parallel modular* architecture. In spite of partisanship in the field for pure modularity or pure connectionism, this last combination of the two seems to be the solution that nature has selected in making organic architectures. Mental devices divide the labor into dedicated processing areas, thereby solving

the management and resource issue by building in control, but allowing the specialized computational areas to run at once (Calvin 1996, Jackendoff 2002).

These four possible categories of architecture are compatible with any representation scheme. Although it would seem natural to link parallel interactive architectures with pattern association, and serial modular architectures with symbolic code, neither marriage is preordained. For example, constraint satisfaction systems have had increasing influence in cognitive science because of their flexibility, generality, and openness to including a wide range of heterogeneous constraints interactively determining an optimal solution. Optimal constraint satisfaction systems have been used widely in advances in linguistics (e.g. Optimality Theory; Kager 1999) and in modeling face recognition (Churchland 1996:38–49). The kinds of representations that comprise the constraints to be satisfied can have any form: explicit symbolic rules, probabilistic input-sensitive association patterns, or both. This flexibility is often claimed by opponents to be a fatal flaw, but the larger lesson is that the nature of the code to be computed is independent of the format of the computation over that code. The number of computations to be performed at any one time and their style of interaction are not reducible to the form the representations must take.

In the end, architectures may actually be the *effects* of the nature, sequencing, and interactions of computed representations themselves, not of some explicit organization in the processing system (Tanenhaus and Lucas 1987). In a modular architecture, representations are discrete and interact indirectly; one representation is computed completely, and any other representation provides the computational context for the first either before or after the fact, not during the processing of the first. In an interactive architecture, however, because the computation of representations is interleaved, one representation provides the computational context for another while the latter is processed. Modularity and connectionism are thus claims about the computational context for a representation.

If this view of data flow as computational-representational effect is true, then the issue for architecture turns on discovering which kinds of knowledge domains and their representations are organized and computed as discrete packages, and which are organized and computed as interleaving bundles. There is evidence for each.

Calvin 1996:96 observes that for sudden limb movements, which would require the computational interaction of perceptual and motor representations, the time needed to execute the movement is so short that feedback and interaction from the perceptual domains during the assessment of the movement would simply be ineffective; therefore, some aspects of motor knowledge must be prepackaged. Similar results hold for language, where modular architectures have been extensively studied (Jackendoff 1997, 2002). Individuals known as Broca's aphasics, who have a lesion in the left temporal cortex, often lose the ability to speak, but they can sing! Moreover, breakdowns within the language module—e.g., the loss of phonological, grammatical, or semantic processing as a consequence of stroke—do not always ramify across language as a whole, as if the module of language is further modularized into smaller, more specialized dedicated processing areas. Broca's aphasics have difficulty speaking, but they generally can comprehend speech, which suggests that the sound and grammar systems that underlie the production of language are architecturally separate from the meaning system, which underlies comprehension.

In contrast, the computation of information about faces appears to be more interactive, again as a consequence of how the representations are organized and processed, not because of some imposed architecture. Face knowledge is computed out of six features: forehead line, eyes and their surround, nose width, mouth features, chin, and vertical orientation of those five. These features work as complexes (or "holons"; Churchland 1996) and interact to produce a kind of generic gestalt face. Because the representations are global, they interact closely in processing, and the actual face to be recognized falls out as an emergent regularity of the interaction of these six features as constraints. A face is a distributed regularity, not a prepackaged solution.

In the end, these considerations and their implications for the format of data flow return us to the core of cognitive science: computation and representation. What is the organization of the inner code, and how do the processing operations that run the code yield the architecture? Linguistics fits snugly into the debates over this question as a science that takes code and processing as givens and studies computed representations in their own right.

5. Future directions. Where are cognitive science and linguistics heading? Substantial work continues to be done on representation systems of language: their formal and computational properties, their processing character-

istics, and their developmental aspects, including both growth in acquisition and loss under disorder (e.g. Crain and Lillo-Martin 1999, Baker 2001, Smith and Tsimpli 1995). Perhaps the most ambitious work, though, concerns the biological plausibility of the genetic predisposition to learn language. In terms more apposite to cognitive science, how representationally rich is the language device in its initial state? There is the usual range of positions in answer to this question (Deacon 1997, Jackendoff 2002, Elman et al. 1996), but what is most promising about this work is that the study of the origins and evolution of language, once purged from linguistics as a defective, dead-end pursuit, has gained new credibility, in large measure because of the linking of linguistics and cognitive science. It is again vital to ask why did we turn out to be this kind of computational device?

[*See also* Acquisition of Languages; Connectionism; Computational Linguistics; Evolution and Language; Learnability; Neurolinguistics; Parsing; Philosophy of Language; Psycholinguistics.]

BIBLIOGRAPHY

Baker, Mark. 2001. *The atoms of language.* New York: Basic Books.

Bechtel, William, and G. Graham, eds. 1999. *A companion to cognitive science.* Oxford: Blackwell.

Calvin, William. 1996. *How brains think.* New York: Basic Books.

Churchland, Patricia, and Terrence Sejnowski. 1992. *The computational brain.* Cambridge, Mass.: MIT Press.

Churchland, Paul. 1996. *The engine of reason, the seat of the soul.* Cambridge, Mass.: MIT Press.

Clark, Andy. 2001. *Mindware.* Oxford: Oxford University Press.

Crain, Stephen, and Diane Lillo-Martin. 1999. *An introduction to linguistic theory and language acquisition.* Oxford: Blackwell.

Deacon, Terrence. 1997. *The symbolic species.* New York: Norton.

Elman, Jeffrey, et al. 1996. *Rethinking innateness.* Cambridge, Mass.: MIT Press.

Fodor, Jerry. 1983. *Modularity of mind.* Cambridge, Mass.: MIT Press.

Frangiskakis, J., et al. 1996. Lim-kinase hemizygosity implicated in impaired visuospatial constructive cognition. *Cell* 86.59–69.

Frawley, William. 2002. Control and cross-domain mental computation: Evidence from language breakdown. *Computational Intelligence* 18.1–28.

Jackendoff, Ray. 1997. *The architecture of the language faculty.* Cambridge, Mass.: MIT Press.

Jackendoff, Ray. 2002. *Foundations of language.* Oxford: Oxford University Press.

Kager, René. 1999. *Optimality Theory.* Cambridge: Cambridge University Press.

Lepore, Ernest, and Zenon Pylyshyn, eds. 1999. *What is cognitive science?* Oxford: Blackwell.

Marcus, Gary. 2001. *The algebraic mind.* Cambridge, Mass.: MIT Press.

Marr, David. 1982. *Vision.* Cambridge, Mass.: MIT Press.

Osherson, Daniel, ed. 1995–2000. *An invitation to cognitive science.* 4 vols. Cambridge, Mass.: MIT Press.

Pinker, Stephen. 1994. *The language instinct.* New York: William Morrow.

Pinker, Stephen. 1999. *Words and rules.* New York: Basic Books.

Smith, Niel, and Ianthi-Marion Tsimpli. 1995. *The mind of a savant.* Oxford: Blackwell.

Tanenhaus, Michael, and Margery Lucas. 1987. Context effects in lexical processing. *Cognition* 25.213–234.

van Gelder, Timothy. 1998. The dynamical hypothesis in cognitive science. *Behavioral and Brain Sciences* 21.615–665.

Wilson, Robert, and Frank Keil, eds. 1999. *The MIT encyclopedia of the cognitive sciences.* Cambridge, Mass.: MIT Press.

WILLIAM FRAWLEY

COGNITIVE SEMANTICS. *See* Semantics; Cognitive Grammar; Metaphor and Semantics; *and* Scripts, Frames, and Schemas.

COHESION. *See* Text.

CO-INDEXING. *See* Anaphora and Binding *and* C-Command.

COMMAND. *See* C-Command.

COMMUNICATIVE COMPETENCE. *See* Sociolinguistics; Acquisition of Language; Discourse; *and* Psycholinguistics.

COMP. *Notation for* Complement. *See* Phrase Structure.

COMPARATIVE-HISTORICAL LINGUISTICS. *See* Historical Linguistics.

COMPARATIVE METHOD. The comparative method examines items (e.g. phonemes, morphemes, or syntactic constructions) from two or more languages to establish genetic relationship and reconstruct ancestral forms. Unlike typological comparison, which ignores genetic affiliation, the comparative method assumes that the languages compared are (or may be) cognate languages: the descendants of a common ancestor. The ancestor, or *proto-language*, may be unattested (e.g. Proto-Germanic, the ancestor of the Germanic languages), or attested in some of its varieties (e.g. Classical Latin, the literary variety of the language from which the Romance languages are descended). The present discussion will concentrate on phonology and morphology, the two areas that depend on regular sound correspondences; however, the comparative method has been used with considerable success in reconstructing syntax and semantics. (For general reference, see Meillet 1925, Bloomfield 1933:297–320, Campbell 1999:108–149, Hoenigswald 1950, 1960:119–143, Bynon 1977:45–57, Lass 1997.)

The comparative method makes three assumptions:

(a) The relationship between sound and meaning is arbitrary; therefore, widespread similarity in form and meaning between two languages cannot be accidental.

(b) Corresponding features of cognate languages continue features inherited from an ancestral stage or proto-language.

(c) Completed sound changes are exceptionless.

1. Similarity and genetic relationship. The first step in the method is to compile a list of potential cognates. A list of words from several modern Germanic languages, for example, yields many striking similarities of form and meaning (Table 1).

Similarities among these languages are not confined to the words on this list; indeed, the list could be extended greatly. The languages also show many grammatical similarities; for example, each has some verbs with preterits and past participles formed by adding a suffix containing a dental or alveolar (as in Eng. *work, worked*), and other verbs with preterits and past participles formed by changing the stem vowel (e.g. Eng. *sing, sang, sung*). Grammatical similarities even extend to irregular and

TABLE 1. *Cognates from Modern Germanic Languages*

English	Dutch	German	Icelandic
blood	*bloed*	*Blut*	*blóð*
glass	*glas*	*Glas*	*glas*
(to) hold	*houden*	*halten*	*halda*
foot	*voet*	*Fuss*	*fótur*
side	*zijde*	*Seite*	*síða*
warm	*warm*	*warm*	*varmur*
work	*werk*	*Werk*	*verk*
cold	*koud*	*kalt*	*kaldur*
calf	*kalf*	*Kalb*	*kálfur*
under	*onder*	*unter*	*undir*

suppletive forms. For example, all the languages make a regular comparative by adding a suffix containing *r* to the positive stem, and a regular superlative by adding a suffix with *-st* (e.g. Eng. *sweet, sweeter, sweetest*); but in each a small set of very common adjectives has suppletive comparatives (e.g. Eng. *good, better, best,* Ger. *gut, besser, am besten*). Similarities so pervasive, extending to so much basic vocabulary and to so many detailed points of grammar, have only one explanation: the languages must be genetically related—the descendants of a common ancestor, Proto-Germanic.

However, languages can resemble each other for other reasons. Onomatopoetic words, "baby-talk," and words showing sound symbolism are excluded from consideration: in these, the relationship between sound and meaning is not entirely arbitrary. Similarity can result from borrowing and other effects of language contact, or even from sheer chance—factors which must be eliminated in a list of potential cognates.

Sometimes knowledge of the external history of a language allows us to exclude borrowing as a cause of similarity. For example, we know that many English words resemble French words because English has borrowed extensively from French since the 11th century. Where language contact is less well documented or prehistoric, similarity resulting from borrowing can be excluded with reasonable certainty by selecting items unlikely to have been borrowed. For instance, words referring to technology or material culture, which are often borrowed along with cultural or technological innovations, may make poor candidates for comparison. By contrast, basic vocabulary—kinship terms, numerals, pronouns, pre- and postpositions, and common verbs, adverbs, adjectives, and nouns—are less likely under most circumstances to be borrowed, and are usually more helpful to the comparativist.

There may, however, be exceptions to this generalization, even in core vocabulary. The English third person plural pronoun *they*, for example was borrowed from Scandinavian. Matisoff, describing Southeast Asia as "a region that is home to several quite distinct but highly ramified language families that have undergone mutual influence for millennia," notes that languages in this area have borrowed not only core vocabulary from each other, but also such features as tone systems and monosyllabicity.

Since the relation between sound and meaning is arbitrary, and the phonological inventory of a language is finite, while the number of potential meanings is in principle infinite, we expect a few chance resemblances between any two unrelated languages. For example, in Kaqchikel (a Mayan Language) the word *mes*, 'mess, disorder, garbage' resembles the English word *mess*. However, the similarity, while striking, is not evidence for genetic relationship. As Lyle Campbell 1999:114 observes, English initial *m-*: Kaqchikel *m-* "does not recur and is not a true correspondence." By contrast, resemblances among the Germanic languages embrace most of the basic vocabulary. The difference is important: sheer number of resemblances allows us to exclude chance with virtual certainty—because chance, as Thieme 1964:587 observes, "does not repeat itself indefinitely."

Length and complexity of sequences are also important. Similarities between whole morphemes or words are far more probative in establishing genetic relationship than are similarities between short sequences of sounds, since the latter are more likely to be accidental. Shared irregularities are very important, especially in morphology or syntax, because languages in intimate contact may come to resemble each other in morphology or surface syntax and resemblance in syntax sometimes reflects typological universals. This is a chief reason why approaches such as mass, or multilateral, comparison, in which short sequences from a large number of language families are inspected for resemblances in order to establish super families such as Nostratic or Proto-Amerinel are open to debate. In critiquing such approaches as applied to Nostratic, Brent Vine 1991:16 writes that ". . . the minimal body of reconstructed Nostratic morphemes opens up vast possibilities for chance correspondences . . ." Irregularity, however, is usually not transmitted in contact situations; and it is language-specific, not universal. Com-

TABLE 2. *Sound Correspondences from Modern Germanic Languages*

English	Dutch	German	Icelandic
s-	z-	s- /z-/	s-
-l-	-l-	-l-	-l-
-l-	-u-	-l-	-l-
-d(-)	-d(-)	-t(-)	-d(-)

TABLE 3. *Conditioned and Unconditioned Merger*

	Gothic	Old English (West Saxon)	Old High German (9th c. Frankish)	
A.	*hēr*	*hēr*	*hiar*	'here'
	Krēks	*Crēcas*	*Kriahha*	'Greeks'
B.	*gadēþs*	*dǣd*	*tāt*	'deed'
	swērs	*swǣr*	*swārs*	'honored, heavy'
	swēs	*swǣs*	*swās*	'one's own'
C.	*fōtus*	*fōt*	*fuoz*	'foot'
	blōþ	*blōd*	*bluot*	'blood'
D.	*mēna*	*mōna*	*māno*	'moon'
	nēmun	*nōmon*	*nāmun*	'they took'

parisons of words or morphemes that are not members of productive paradigms are especially useful, since the sound correspondences in these are unlikely to have been disrupted by analogy.

2. Sound correspondences and methodology. To confirm genetic relationship and reconstruct proto-languages, the comparative method uses regular sound correspondences. This makes the comparative method a precise historical tool, rather than a mere cataloging of similarities; and it permits reconstruction of proto-languages even when resemblances among cognate languages are less obvious than those within Germanic.

From the list of Germanic cognates, we can extract the sound correspondences in Table 2 (among others). More data would show that each correspondence recurs.

The correspondence of Eng. -*l*-, Dutch -*l*-, Ger. -*l*-, and Ic. -*l*- only allows us to reconstruct Gmc. *-*l*-; but correspondences that differ (e.g. Eng. -*l*-, Dutch -*u*-, Ger. -*l*-, Ic. -*l*-) imply phonological change in one or more languages. The choice of what to reconstruct depends on the distribution of correspondences, and therefore on the distribution of sounds in each language. In these data, Du. -*u*- occurs only in the sequence *oud* (cf. Eng. *old*,

Ger. *alt,* Ic. *ald*), but the distribution of -*l*- is not so restricted: it is apparent that Du. *u* originated as a vocalized allophone of *l* (other data confirm that the preceding vowel was *o*, and show that *l* was also vocalized before *t*). We can reconstruct the following change:

(1) $*l > u / o$ ‗‗‗‗ $\{t, d\}$

Since correspondences and reconstructions are statements about historical events, they are independent of notation (Hoenigswald 1973:56). Thus the correspondence of Eng. -*l*-, Du. -*u*-, Ger. -*l*-, Ic. -*l*- could be represented by distinctive feature matrices. This approach might have the advantage of showing clearly that the Dutch sound change involved vocalization ([−vocalic] > [+vocalic]), but it would not change the facts.

To the extent that completed sound change is regular, correspondences should also be regular. The *regularity principle* gives the comparative method a great deal of practical and predictive power. It allows, for example, the prediction of cognates, and it permits the exclusion of similarities resulting from borrowing. For instance, regular correspondences between Eng. /š/ and Ic. /sk/ (e.g. Eng. *ship*, Ic. *skip*) reflect a late Old English sound change /sk/ > /š/. Other words, however, show a correspondence Eng. /sk/ : Ic. /sk/ (e.g. Eng. *skin*, Ic. *skinn*), which betrays them as medieval borrowings from Scandinavian dialects closely related to Icelandic.

Unlike *internal reconstruction*, the other major method in historical linguistics, the comparative method recovers both conditioned and unconditioned merger (Hoenigswald 1973:56), as shown in Table 3. Correspondences for the vowels of the words in A and B show two sounds in O[ld] E[nglish] and O[ld] H[igh] G[erman] that correspond to a single long vowel in Gothic: Go. *ē*, OE *ǣ*, *ē*, OHG *ā*, *ia*. But a contrast in one or more descendants of a proto-language should continue, in some form, a contrast in the proto-language. Therefore, the OE contrast of *ǣ* and *ē* (note *swǣr* vs. *hēr*), and of OHG *ā* and *ia* (note *swārs* vs. *hiar*) reveals a Common Germanic contrast between two front vowel phonemes which have merged in Gothic, and which we will provisionally transcribe as $*\bar{e}_1$ (= OE *ǣ*, OHG *ā*) and $*\bar{e}_2$ (= OE *ē*, OHG *ia*). Since phonemes do not undergo random, unconditioned split, we can exclude the possibility that Gothic reflects the original situation, and that a single phoneme has split into two in Old English and Old High German; i.e., to posit $*\bar{e} >$ OE *ǣ*/*ē* in *swǣr/hēr* and $*\bar{e} >$ OHG *ā*/*ia* in *swārs/hiar* would violate the regularity principle.

TABLE 4. *Phonological Split*

Gothic	Old English	Old High German	
dōmjan	*dēman*	*tuomen*	'to judge'
fōdjan	*dēdan*	*fuoten*	'to feed'
dōmida	*dēmde*	*tuomit*	'(s)he judged'

TABLE 5. *Anatolian Reflexes of IE Labio-Velars*

Indo-European	Cuneiform Luvian	Hieroglyphic Luvian	Lycian
$*k^w$	k^w	k^w (*ku*)	*t-*
$*k^w i/o$-	*$k^w is$*	*kumana*	*ti*
interrog. pronoun	rel./interrog. pron.	'when, while'	rel. pron.
$*g^w$	*w*	*w*	*w*
$g^w ou$-		*wawa-*	*wawa-*
'cow, ox'			
$*g^w en$-eh_2-	*wana-(tti-)*		
'woman'			

The correspondence of Go. *ō*, OE *ō*, and OHG *uo* in section C continues Gmc. *$*ō$ (the earliest OHG documents also have *ō*); but Go. *ē*, OHG *ā* in section D should point to Gmc. *$*ē_1$ as it does in section B. OE *ǣ* and *ō* do not contrast before nasals, but they do contrast elsewhere (e.g. *blōd* 'blood' vs. *dǣd* 'deed'). We would therefore reconstruct *$*ē_1$ for the words in C, positing merger of Gmc. *$*ē_1$ and *$*ō$ before nasals in Old English:

(2) $\{*ē_1, *ō\} > ō$ / ___ [+nasal]

A major advantage of the comparative method is that it recovers phonological split, even when the conditioning for such split has been lost through further sound change; cf. Table 4.

The correspondence of Go. *ō*, OHG *uo* should reflect Gmc. *$*ō$ as in Table 3, section C; but OE cognates have *ē*, not *ō*. Apparently Gmc. *$*ō$ suffered conditioned split in Old English; but Gothic, not Old English, reveals the conditioning. Wherever the correspondence Go. *ō*, OE *ē*, OHG *uo* occurs, Gothic has *i* or *j* ([i̯]) in the next syllable; but wherever Go. *ō*, OE *ō*, OHG *uo* occurs, the Gothic word lacks *i/j*. Therefore, the split must have involved fronting of Gmc. *$*ō$ to *ē* (through an intermediate stage *ǽ*, attested in some early documents) when the next syllable contained *i/j*:

(3) *$*dōm(i)jan$ > *$*dǽmjan$
*$*dōmidē$ > *$*dǽmidē$

But the *i/j* was later lost through conditioned sound change:

(4) *$*dǽmjan$ > *dēman*
*$*dǽmidē$ > *$*dēmde$

Knowing that the correspondence OE *ē*, Go. *ō*, OHG *uo* points to Gmc. *$*ō$ followed by a syllable containing *i/j* even allows us to reconstruct Gmc. *$*ō$ when *i/j* has also been lost in Gothic. For example, Go. *ō*, OE *ē* in Go. *brōþr* 'brother' (dat. sg.), OE *brēþer* (id.) points to a Gmc. *$*brōþri$ in which *i* conditioned OE fronting (OE *-er-* points to an intermediate stage *$*brǽþr̥$ with *$*r̥$ > *er*).

"Reconstructing forward"—starting with a known feature of the proto-language, and reconstructing the changes that produced the attested features of its daughters—can be a valuable technique when the phonology or morphology of the proto-language is well understood, but the details of development in its daughters are obscure. This is an especially useful technique in Anatolian—where, because of the limitations of the syllabaries used for Hittite, Cuneiform Luvian, and Hieroglyphic Luvian, the phonology of Proto-Anatolian is sometimes better known than the phonology of its daughters. It is, for example, unclear whether Hittite, Cuneiform Luvian, and Hieroglyphic Luvian preserved the I[ndo-]E[uropean] distinction (reconstructed on the basis of sound correspondences among the other IE languages) between initial voiced and voiceless stops. (Lycian, written in an alphabet, has only voiceless stops word-initially.) We do know, however, that Proto-Anatolian retained the voicing distinction, because the languages of the Luvian branch have distinct reflexes for initial *$*k^w$ and *$*g^w$ (Table 5).

Contrast in daughter languages implies contrast in the proto-language; the contrasting reflexes imply a voicing contrast in Proto-Anatolian and Proto-Luvian: IE *$*k^w$ > PAn. *$*k^w$ > PLu. *$*k^w$ (> Lyc. *t*); IE *$*g^w$ > PAn. *$*g^w$ > PLu. *$*w$ (> Lyc. *w*).

3. Reconstructing morphology. Reconstruction of morphology depends upon phonological reconstruction, although analogic creation and leveling must often be taken into consideration. Ideally, the regularity principle provides a check on reconstruction, helping to separate phonologically regular descendants of morphemes from

TABLE 6. *Neuter S-Stems in Several IE Languages*

	Sanskrit	Greek	Latin	Gothic	Hittite
Nom./ Acc.	*nábh-as* 'cloud'	*nép^h-os* 'cloud'	*gen-us* 'race'	*riq-is* 'darkness'	*nēb-is* 'heaven'
Oblique Stem	*nábh-as-*	*nép^h-e-*	*gen-er-*	*riq-iz-*	*nēb-is-*

TABLE 7. *Correspondences among Morphemes*

	Sanskrit	Greek	Latin	Gothic	Hittite
Nom./Acc.	*-as*	*-os*	*-us*	*-is*	*-is*
Oblique	*-as-*	*-e-*	*-er-*	*-iz-*	*-is-*

those with analogical changes. Neuter *s*-stems in several IE languages illustrate both possibilities (Table 6). Once we establish the segmentation of stem, suffix, and ending in each language, we can set up correspondences among morphemes (Table 7).

Morphological correspondences consist of phonological ones. In the suffix of the oblique stem, regular sound change is implied by the correspondences Skt. *a*, Gk. *e*, La. *e*, Go. *i*, Hitt. *i* (IE *e*), and Skt. *s*, Gk. Ø, La. *r*, Go. *z*, Hitt. *s* (IE *s*). This allows us to reconstruct a suffix *-es-*.

The sound changes implied by these correspondences also permit the reconstruction of additional details of the IE paradigm. In Hittite, IE *e* splits, becoming *ē* when accented and *i* when unaccented. Go. *z* results from the Germanic sound change known as Verner's Law, by which IE *s* became Gmc. *z* when not immediately preceded by the accent. Hittite and Gothic, then, confirm the root accent of Sanskrit and Greek as an inheritance from IE. Accordingly, we can reconstruct an IE oblique stem, *Root(accented)-es-* (e.g. *nébh-es-*).

The nominative/accusative in each language is simply the root plus suffix. For the suffix, all the languages agree in showing final *-s*, and we reconstruct IE *s* (actually, Go. *-s* is the reflex of Gmc. *-z* via devoicing). Correspondences for the vowel preceding the *-s* are not regular, however. Greek and Latin agree in showing IE *o* (for Gk. *o*, La. *u* in final syllables, cf. Gk. *zdugón* 'yoke', La. *jugum* < IE *yugom*). However, Gothic and Hittite have reflexes of unaccented *e*. (Skt. *-as* is ambiguous, since IE *e* and *o* merge in closed syllables in Sanskrit.) Here we must invoke analogy to explain the divergences. Go. *-is* and Hitt. *-is* can easily result from independent generalizations of the suffix of the oblique

stem, but Gk. *-os* and La. *-us* cannot be explained as analogical; therefore, we reconstruct an IE nominative/ accusative *-os* (e.g. *nébh-os*).

4. Limitations. The comparative method has limitations, some of which are inherent in the assumptions it makes. It does not recognize similarities resulting from contact, or from convergent but independent development after a proto-language breaks up. The method is most accurate, therefore, when a speech community breaks up suddenly—e.g., after a group has migrated out of the original community—and the resulting groups have little subsequent contact. The method works well with completed sound changes that have attained a high degree of regularity; but it cannot accurately handle changes that spread unevenly via geographic or sociolinguistic diffusion.

The time depth of reconstructions is not great. The earliest texts in IE languages, for example, date from the second millennium BCE, and reconstructed Indo-European reflects a language spoken in about the fourth millennium. In language families without written records before the 19th or 20th centuries (e.g. most languages of Africa and the Americas), the absolute time depth of reconstructions may be much shallower, although the relative gap between the proto-language and the attestation of its daughters could well be comparable (Haas 1969:27–30).

Other limitations lie not in the method, but in the data with which it works. Because changes accumulate with time, the longer cognate languages have been separated, the less they tend to resemble each other. The comparative method has had its greatest successes in cases where the separation between languages is recent. The break-up of the IE speech community in the fourth millennium BCE is a "recent" event in human history, but accumulated phonological and morphological changes make resemblances less clear, and genetic relationship less easy to demonstrate, when the gap between separation and attestation is greater or the relationship more distant.

The plausibility of reconstructions depends on the quality of data. Sometimes gaps in the data hinder reconstruction. Traits may be lost and, therefore, unrecoverable. When working with extinct languages, it may be difficult to find cognates with secure etymologies. For example, although we can reconstruct an initial voicing contrast *k^w* : *g^w* for Proto-Anatolian and Luvian, it is unclear whether Hittite preserved the contrast, because the most reliable potential cognates with IE *g^w* : *g^wou-* 'ox' and *g^wen (eh-)* 'women' were written as Sumerian ideographs *GUD* and *MUNUS*. Often we can reconstruct the phonology of a proto-language, but not phonetic details. For example, as we saw above, contrast between OE *ǣ* and *ē* and between OHG *ā* and *ia* requires us to reconstruct two Proto-Germanic vowels. However, as long as we choose distinct symbols to represent the phonemic distinction, any reconstruction of the phonetic details of the two phonemes is essentially an educated guess. We might, for example, reconstruct open */ɛ̄/ for *$\bar{e}_1$ (= Go. *ē*, OE *ǣ*, OHG *ā*) vs. close */ē/ for *$\bar{e}_2$ (= Go. *ē*, OE *ē*, OHG *ia*)—a typologically common opposition that easily explains the sound changes in each language. However, nothing in the comparative method gives us any reason to prefer */ɛ̄/ and */ē/ over, say, */ǣ/ vs. */ē/, or any other typologically possible pair. In fact, early Proto-Germanic probably had no single entity *$\bar{e}_2$. Instead, several minor sound changes may have produced a long vowel distinct from *$\bar{e}_1$ in North and West Germanic.

Although it has been claimed that the comparative method assumes a uniform proto-language lacking sociolinguistic and dialect variation, this assumption is simply the result of the incomplete data the method uses. A proto-language is, in essence, an idealized artifact constructed from competing statements about etymologies, phonological correspondences, and sound changes. It usually cannot capture much of the rich variation of a living language. However, if sufficient data have been preserved, the comparative method can indeed recover some types of linguistic variation.

5. Conclusion. While the comparative method is one of the supreme intellectual achievements of the 19th century, it is by no means an object of mere antiquarian interest; it remains the surest method for demonstrating genetic relationship and for reconstructing the prehistory of languages. Its usefulness is certainly not confined to Indo-European or other language families with long written traditions (see especially Haas 1969). Even within Indo-European, it has been the surest guide we have had in reconstructing Anatolian phonology. Because it permits reconstruction of unrecorded ancestral stages, it can be used, often with great precision, to recover details of vernacular varieties of languages attested only in literary form. This is a property well known to Romance philologists, and one exploited with considerable success by Harris 1987, in his use of data from Atlantic Creoles to reconstruct front-raising of Early Modern English /a/.

[*See also* Historical Linguistics; Internal Reconstruction; Phonological Change; Semantic Reconstruction; *and* Stylistic Reconstruction.]

BIBLIOGRAPHY

Bloomfield, Leonard. 1933. *Language.* New York: Holt.

Bynon, Theodora. 1977. *Historical linguistics.* Cambridge and New York: Cambridge University Press.

Campbell, Lyle. 1999. *Historical linguistics: An introduction.* Cambridge, Mass.: MIT Press.

Haas, Mary R. 1969. *The prehistory of languages.* (Janua linguarum, Series minor, 57.) The Hague: Mouton.

Harris, John. 1987. On doing comparative reconstruction with genetically unrelated languages. In *Papers from the Seventh International Conference on Historical Linguistics,* edited by Anna G. Ramat et al., pp. 267–282. Amsterdam: Benjamins.

Hoenigswald, Henry M. 1950. The principal step in comparative grammar. *Language* 26.357–364.

Hoenigswald, Henry M. 1960. *Language change and linguistic reconstruction.* Chicago: University of Chicago Press.

Hoenigswald, Henry M. 1973. The comparative method. In *Current trends in linguistics,* vol. 11, *Diachronic, areal, and typological linguistics,* edited by Thomas A. Sebeok, pp. 51–62. The Hague: Mouton.

Lass, Roger. *Historical linguistics and language change.* Cambridge, UK: Cambridge University Press.

Matisoff, James A. 1990. On megalocomparison. *Language* 66.1.106–120.

Matisoff, James A. 1990. Bulging monosyllables: Areal tendencies in Southeast Asian diachrony. In Kira Hall et al., eds., *Proceedings of the Sixteenth Annual Meeting of the Berkeley Linguistics Society,* pp. 543–559.

Meillet, Antoine. 1925. *La méthode comparative en linguistique historique.* Oslo: Aschehoug. Reprinted, Paris: Champion, 1966.

Thieme, Paul. 1964. The comparative method for reconstruction. In *Language in culture and society: A reader in linguistics and anthropology,* edited by Dell Hymes, pp. 585–598. New York: Harper and Row.

Vine, Brent. 1991. Indo-European and Nostratic. Indogermanische Forschungen 96:9–35.

Sara E. Kimball

COMPARATIVE PHILOLOGY. *See* Historical Linguistics; Language Change; *and* Reconstruction.

COMPARATIVES. *See* Parts of Speech *and* Typology and Universals.

COMPETENCE. *See* Formal Grammar; Psycholinguistics; Sociolinguistics; Acquisition of Language; *and* Neurolinguistics.

COMPLEMENT. *See* Clause; Adjunction; Subcategorization and Selection; *and* Phrase Structure.

COMPLEMENTARY DISTRIBUTION. *See* Phonology.

COMPLEMENTATION. *See* Clause.

COMPLEMENTIZER. *See* Clause; Typology and Universals; *and* Grammaticalization.

COMPONENTIAL ANALYSIS. Also called "lexical decomposition." C[omponential] A[nalysis] has its roots in two structuralist traditions: that of the European post-Saussureans (e.g. Hjelmslev 1943), and that of the American anthropological linguists (e.g. Lounsbury 1956). Both groups wanted to show the semantic relationships of formally unrelated words, much as phonologists brought out shared properties among different sounds by decomposing them into distinctive features such as [voiceless], [stop], and [bilabial]. They thus sought to characterize the meaning of sets of semantically related items in terms of semantic components—variously called semes, classemes, distinguishers, semantic markers, semantic features, or semantic primitives. As a simple example, consider the set of words in Table 1.

CA would define these words in terms of a smaller set of semantic components: for example, a species term (e.g. OVINE), MALE VS. FEMALE, and MATURE VS. YOUNG.

In addition, linguists and anthropologists often need to define words of other languages, but the nearest translation equivalent is often inexact; a kin term might apply to ego's father, paternal grandfather, and fathers' brothers. Therefore, it was necessary to create a metalanguage that was free of translation problems. Analyses for kin terms in all languages were proposed in terms of components such as PARENT OF, SIBLING OF, CHILD OF, CONSANGUINEAL, AFFINAL, MALE, FEMALE, and a few others, together with rules for combination and recursion.

Although many linguists and anthropologists have used semantic components, theories of CA have perhaps been worked out in most detail by Katz (e.g. Katz and Fodor 1963, Katz 1972), Jackendoff (e.g. 1983, 1990), and

TABLE 1. *Domestic Animals in English*

sheep	ram	ewe	lamb
horse	stallion	mare	foal
chicken	rooster	hen	chick

Wierzbicka (e.g. 1985, 1996). In Katz's theory, intended to be the semantic counterpart of Chomsky's 1965 syntactic theory, each item is to be decomposed into semantic markers, many of which have considerable internal structure. Jackendoff also works within a generative framework and, like Katz, has developed systems and hierarchies of semantic components and machinery for combining them and for accounting for a variety of semantic properties and relations of sentences. Wierzbicka's analysis into components is the most radical, since she attempts, in the spirit of Leibniz, to reduce the meanings of linguistic items to a small number of indefinable semantic primitives (currently around sixty): examples are I, YOU, THINK, DO, HAPPEN, THIS, ALL, GOOD, BAD, BIG, SMALL, NOW, HERE, BECAUSE, IF, NOT. Full definitions in this approach can accordingly be quite long.

Despite a shared commitment to semantic decomposition, practitioners of CA in fact differ widely in assumptions, methods, and goals. While most analysts assume that CA is applicable to all areas of a language, some (e.g. Hjelmslev) have held a more restricted view. In terms of the depth of semantic description sought, some approaches have explicitly been content with a limited analysis sufficient to distinguish lexical items in a given field; others have in practice focused on broad aspects of the meanings of words close to the interface with syntax, thus producing at best partial semantic descriptions (cf. the criticisms of Bolinger 1965 and Taylor 1996). Wierzbicka, by contrast, strives for completeness in this respect. As for the nature of components, some regard these as meanings of words, either of a given language (e.g. Hjelmslev) or else assumed to be universally present in all languages (e.g. Wierzbicka); other approaches have treated them as psychological entities, or as purely theoretical constructs.

CA is appealing for several reasons. First, CA can be used to show explicitly many semantic correlations in a language and to formalize certain semantic relations. Second, it is potentially a useful descriptive device for comparative lexicology: semantic fields in different languages can be compared and contrasted in terms of a relevant set of components. More widely, it provides the potential for a universal metalanguage that could be used to define all items in all languages. This in turn would provide a basis for a theory of translation, in that it would be possible to show explicitly by means of components that some translation equivalents are exact, while others differ.

Nevertheless, CA can be questioned on various grounds. First, it remains far from clear that CA is suitable for the full semantic analysis of all parts of the vocabulary. As indicated above, comprehensive analyses remain few, and applications have been limited to a relatively small number of semantic fields. CA is deficient, for example, in dealing with scalar terms and various kinds of opposites (Lyons 1977, Lehrer and Lehrer 1982), which suggests that it may constitute at best one ingredient of a full semantic theory. A second problem is that semantic components may prove not to be universal. This is a matter for ongoing empirical investigation and, while lack of universality does not invalidate using CA for individual languages, it reduces its appeal for comparative lexicology. There remains the additional question of the empirical status of components (cf. Lyons 1977). As we have seen, some versions of CA regard them as the meanings of words, but in many approaches they are treated as elements of a theoretical metalanguage. Any metalanguage needs an interpretation, and as Allan 2001 points out, for most purposes the metalanguage must be interpreted in terms of some natural language(s) to be used and understood. Where the precise relationship of components to the meanings of actual words is not made explicit, the proposed analyses are not testable against speakers' semantic intuitions, and their validity is accordingly unverifiable.

[See also Semantics and Ethnosemantics.]

BIBLIOGRAPHY

Allan, Keith. 2001. *Natural language semantics*. Oxford: Blackwell.

Bolinger, Dwight. 1965. The atomicity of meaning. *Language* 41.555–573.

Chomsky, Noam. 1965. *Aspects of the theory of syntax*. Cambridge, Mass.: MIT Press.

Hjelmslev, Louis. 1943. *Omkring sprogteoriens grundlaeggelse*. Copenhagen: Lunos. Translated as *Prologomena to a theory of language*. Madison: University of Wisconsin Press, 1961.

Jackendoff, Ray. 1983. *Semantics and cognition*. Cambridge, Mass.: MIT Press.

Jackendoff, Ray. 1990. *Semantic structures*. Cambridge, Mass.: MIT Press.

Katz, Jerrold J. 1972. *Semantic theory*. New York: Harper and Row.

Katz, Jerrold J., and Jerry A. Fodor. 1963. The structure of a semantic theory. *Language* 39.170–210.

Lehrer, Adrienne, and Keith Lehrer. 1982. Antonymy. *Linguistics and Philosophy* 5.483–501.

Lounsbury, Floyd. 1956. A semantic analysis of the Pawnee kinship usage. *Language* 37.158–194.

Lyons, John. 1977. *Semantics*. 2 vols. Cambridge: Cambridge University Press.

Taylor, John R. 1996. On running and jogging. *Cognitive Linguistics* 7.21–34.

Wierzbicka, Anna. 1985. *Lexicography and conceptual analysis*. Ann Arbor: Karoma.

Wierzbicka, Anna. 1996. *Semantics: Primes and universals*. Oxford and New York: Oxford University Press.

ADRIENNE LEHRER AND ANTHONY E. BACKHOUSE

COMPOSITIONALITY. *See* Connectionism; Formal Grammar; Cognitive Sciences; Philosophy of Language; *and* Semantics.

COMPOUNDING. A prototypical compound is a morphologically complex word containing at least two elements which can otherwise occur as free forms, i.e. as independent words—Eng. *steamboat, delivery van, head-hunter, snow-white, Polish-German*. Thus compounding essentially represents a grammatical device by which complex words can be formed from smaller elements which, under normal circumstances, have word status. Compounding differs from affixation in that the latter involves morphemes which cannot have word status. Affixal morphemes are basically of two types, derivational as in *read-er,* and inflectional as in *(he) read-s*; neither type can be freely distributed as independent words.

1. Word properties. An important indication that a string of elements constitutes a compound is its word-like behavior. Thus parts of compounds cannot be rearranged without a change in meaning (*flower garden* vs. *garden flower*), although rearrangement of constituents might otherwise be possible in a given language. Furthermore, compounds are like words in that their constituents cannot generally be separated by intervening material. Compounds also typically receive stress like that of words, not of syntactic phrases. Thus the German compound *Starkbier* 'strong-beer' has initial stress, which is common in words; but the phrase *starkes Bier* 'strong beer' has phrasal stress, with prosodic prominence on *Bier*. In many languages, compounds are characterized by the occurrence of special morphological elements between the parts of a compound, e.g. *-o-* in Czech *vod-o-pád* 'water-fall' and in Russian *čern-o-zem* 'black-soil'. The Slavic linking morpheme (or interfix) *-o-* is typical of compounds; it appears neither in words derived by affixation nor in syntactic phrases. German linking morphemes, such as *-s-* in *Beobachtung-s-turm* 'observation-tower', can be traced historically to case inflection; however, their distribution and meaning in compounds radically differ from those of contemporary case morphemes. Thus one must again speak of a trait characteristic of compounding.

2. Relations between parts. Two basic relations between parts of compounds are generally recognized: *determination* and *coordination*. In the first case, there is a *modifier* (determinans) and a *modified element* (determinatum); this is characteristic of so-called determinative compounds like *steamboat*. In the second case, represented by *coordinative* (copulative) compounds such as *Polish-German*, no part is subordinate to another. This classification is based on the semantic intuition that the modified part of a determinative compound names a set of denotata, while the modifier restricts it to a subset. Thus *boat* in *steamboat* names a set of denotata called 'boats'; *steam* restricts it to a subset, namely 'boats driven by steam'. A coordinative compound, by contrast, typically names a conjunction of sets of denotata named by the subparts of the compound. Thus, in *mother-child relationship,* the hyphenated part is a coordinative compound denoting a conjunction of sets of denotata. The entire phrase, however, is a determinative compound, in which the coordinative subpart functions as a modifier of relationship.

3. Headedness. Since the early 1980s, scholars have stressed the importance of the notion of *heads* in word formation, including compounding (Williams 1981). The head of a word, or more generally of a syntactic construction, is that part which determines the morphosyntactic properties of the entire word. Recourse to this notion is useful because "head" is a category in general theories of phrase structure (such as X-bar theory), and thus is independent of word-formation. However, the definition of head employed in theories of word-structure is not quite the same as in theories of syntactic structure. In particular, it is suggested that the head in word-formation

is defined in terms of the positional notions 'right' and 'left'—rather than in terms of the level of projection, as is common in syntactic phrases. In languages like German or English, words are generally right-headed; thus, in *steamboat,* the noun *boat* is termed the head of the entire compound.

In certain subtypes of compounds, the notion of "head" is not applicable without problems. Thus, in Eng. *pickpocket,* it is not clear to what degree *pocket* should be viewed as determining the category of the entire compound. As far as semantics is concerned, the compound certainly denotes neither a type of pocket nor a type of picking. Compounds such as these have traditionally been called exocentric in contrast to endocentric; an example of the latter is regular determinative compounds. Another type of compound traditionally described as exocentric is represented by Eng. *redskin* and Ger. *Blauhemd* 'blue-shirt', i.e. a soldier wearing a blue uniform. However, although *redskin* does not denote a type of skin, nor *Blauhemd* a type of shirt, a purely morphosyntactic definition of head requires us to regard them as endocentric, despite traditional classification. This is best illustrated by data from German, where the right-hand element determines the gender of the entire compound: thus *Blauhemd* is neuter, like *Hemd*.

4. Internal structure. Compounds, like syntactic phrases, may have a complex internal structure. This is so because each constituent of a compound can be in itself internally complex. In particular, nominal compounds in languages like German can develop a complex internal structure; e.g.,

[[[[[*Ober*][*schul*]][*lehrer*]][*witwen*]][*verein*]]
'high-school-teacher-widow-union'.

In this sense, compounding rules have a certain recursive property. Complex internal structure is also found in compounds which accommodate material with phrasal properties: *an area-by-area directory, a once-in-a-lifetime opportunity, a what-I-don't-know-won't-hurt-me attitude.*

5. Categories involved in compounding. Depending on the syntactic category of lexical morphemes involved, a variety of combinations, and hence a variety of compounds, can be obtained—including noun + noun compounds (*steamboat*), verb + noun compounds (*hover-boat*), adjective + noun compounds (*snow-white*), etc. Typically, these combinations differ in productivity. Whereas noun + noun compounding is fairly productive in English, compounds of noun + verb *(to baby-sit)* or verb + verb *(to hop-skip)* are not productive. Patterns with minor lexical categories such as prepositions *(onto, undergarment)* are also of rather limited productivity.

6. Semantic relations between parts. Much attention has been paid to the classification of compounds on the basis of the semantic roles which may be satisfied by their subparts. One type of semantic role includes agent, theme, experiencer, and location, which are typically involved in compounds containing verbs and adjectives. In particular, compounds which incorporate verbs, either as pure roots or as nominalizations, have been classified in accordance with these relations. Thus, in German *Putzfrau* 'cleaning lady', the nominal constituent may be interpreted as filling the agent role of *putzen* 'to clean', and in *Trinkwasser* 'drinking water' as filling the role of theme of the verb *trinken* 'to drink'. For compounds without overt predicates, such as noun + noun compounds, scholars have proposed a variety of semantic relations holding between the subparts, in addition to the above semantic roles—including relations such as class-inclusion *(pathway)* and similarity *(blood orange)*.

Rather than classifying compounds on the basis of semantic relations, generative studies (Selkirk 1982, Lieber 1983, Boase-Beier et al. 1986) have focused on principles which regulate the distribution of semantic roles in compounds, and have attempted to relate these principles to the so-called theory of thematic roles (θ-theory).

7. Cross-linguistic variation. Both similarity and variation can be detected in compounding in various languages, as is the case with word-formation in general (cf. Anderson 1985). A major distinction concerns the position of the head of the compound. For instance, in Germanic, Slavic, and Finno-Ugric languages, the head typically follows the modifier. Romance languages, on the other hand, display patterns in which the head precedes the modifier; thus Italian *caffellatte* (i.e. *caffè +latte* 'coffee-milk') denotes a type of coffee, not a type of milk. Variation in the position of the head is also found when types of phrases other than compounds are compared.

Another major distinction concerns the productivity of compounding in different languages. Germanic languages utilize compounding extensively, Slavic and Romance languages to a much lesser degree. Typically, even languages which exploit compounding only to a limited degree still have several highly productive compounding patterns. Thus, in Czech, an adjective + noun compound can be formed from any proper name of the form adjective + noun; cf. *Staré Zámky* (lit. 'Old Castles'), *starozámecký* 'pertaining to Staré Zámky'. But other compounding patterns, such as noun + noun or verb + noun, are uncommon. It has been assumed that the presence of compounding in the grammar of a language, or of particular patterns, should be contingent on other properties of the language; but this point has not yet been satisfactorily explicated.

8. History of research. Ancient Indian grammarians, including Pāṇini (5th c. BCE) and Patañjali (2nd c. BCE), are the first linguists known to have dealt with compounding. They studied Sanskrit compounds and presented a classification based on semantic criteria (Mahavir 1978). Some of their terminology—dvandva compounds for coordinative compounds, bahuvrihi compounds for a type of exocentric compounds—is still used. In the European tradition, J. G. Schottelius (1612–1676) noted the distinction between the modifying and the modified element in German compounds.

In the 20th century a rich descriptive tradition as well as a variety of theoretical approaches developed. One example of a descriptive approach is that of Marchand 1969. Other approaches include generative grammar (Selkirk 1982, Lieber 1983, Toman 1983, Di Sciullo and Williams 1987), categorial grammar (Hoeksema 1984), and natural morphology (Dressler 1987). Compounds have also been studied from specialized points of view, including their use in situational contexts (Downing 1977), in poetic language (Boase-Beier 1987), and many others.

[*See also* Derivational Morphology; Generative Morphology; Heads; Inflection; Natural Morphology; *and* Semantics.]

BIBLIOGRAPHY

Anderson, Stephen R. 1985. Typological distinctions in word formation. In *Language typology and syntactic description,* vol. 3, *Grammatical categories and the lexicon,* edited by Timothy Shopen, pp. 3–56. Cambridge and New York: Cambridge University Press.

Boase-Beier, Jean. 1987. *Poetic compounds: The principles of poetic language in modern English poetry.* (Linguistische Arbeiten, 179.) Tübingen: Niemeyer.

Boase-Beier, Jean, and Jindřich Toman. 1986. On θ-role assignment in German compounds. *Folia Linguistica* 20.319–340.

Di Sciullo, Anne-Marie, and Edwin Williams. 1987. *On the definition of word.* (*Linguistic Inquiry* monographs, 14.) Cambridge, Mass.: MIT Press.

Downing, Pamela. 1977. On the creation and use of English compound nouns. *Language* 53.810–842.

Dressler, Wolfgang U. 1987. Word formation as part of Natural Morphology. In *Leitmotifs in Natural Morphology* (*Studies in Language*, Companion series, 10), edited by Wolfgang U. Dressler et al., pp. 99–126. Amsterdam: Benjamins.

Hoeksema, Jack. 1984. *Categorial morphology.* University of Groningen dissertation. Published, New York: Garland, 1985.

Lieber, Rochelle. 1983. Argument linking and compounds in English. *Linguistic Inquiry* 14.251–285.

Mahavir. 1978. *Pāṇini as a grammarian, with special reference to compound formations.* Delhi: Bharatiya Vidya Prakashan.

Marchand, Hans. 1969. *The categories and types of present-day English word-formation: A synchronic-diachronic approach.* 2d ed. Munich: Beck.

Selkirk, Elisabeth O. 1982. *The syntax of words.* (*Linguistic Inquiry* monographs, 7.) Cambridge, Mass.: MIT Press.

Spencer, Andrew, and Arnold Zwicky, eds. 1998. *Handbook of Morphology.* Oxford: Blackwell.

Toman, Jindřich. 1983. *Wortsyntax: Eine Diskussion ausgewählter Probleme deutscher Wortbildung.* (Linguistische Arbeiten, 137.) Tübingen: Niemeyer.

Williams, Edwin. 1981. Argument structure and morphology. *Linguistic Review* 1.81–114.

JINDŘICH TOMAN

COMPREHENSION. *See* Acquisition of Language; Neurolinguistics; *and* Psycholinguistics.

COMPUTATIONAL LINGUISTICS. [*This entry includes the following subentries:*

Overview

The history of automatic N[atural] L[anguage] P[rocessing] can be divided into four phases: the first from the late 1940s to the late 1960s, the second from the late 1960s to the late 1970s, the third to the late 1980s, and the fourth to the end of the century.

1. Phase 1: Late 1940s to late 1960s. The work of the first phase was focused on M[achine] T[ranslation]. Following a few early swallows, including A. D. Booth and R. H. Richens's investigations and Weaver's influential memorandum on translation of 1949 (Locke and Booth 1955, Hutchins 2000), research on NLP began in earnest in the 1950s. Automatic translation from Russian to English, in a very rudimentary form and limited experiment, was exhibited in the IBM-Georgetown Demonstration of 1954. The journal *MT (Mechanical Translation),* the ancestor of *Computational Linguistics,* also began publication in 1954. The first international conference on MT was held in 1952, the second in 1956 (the year of the first artificial intelligence conference); at the important Washington International Conference on Scientific Information of 1958 language processing was linked with information retrieval, for example in the use of a thesaurus, Marvin Minsky drew attention to artificial intelligence, and H. P. Luhn provided auto-abstracts (actually extracts) for one session's papers. The Teddington International Conference on Machine Translation of Languages and Applied Language Analysis in 1961 was perhaps the high point of this first phase: it reported work done in many countries on many aspects of NLP including morphology, syntax, and semantics, in both interpretation and generation, and ranging from formal theory to hardware.

This first phase was a period of enthusiasm and optimism. It is notable not only because those engaged attacked a very difficult NLP task, and so encountered the problems of syntactic and semantic processing, and of linguistic variety, in all their force; they were seeking to use a new tool, computers, for non-numerical, data-processing purposes when data-processing itself was not well established. It is essential to remember how primitive the available computing resources were. This was the era of punched cards and batch processing. There were no suitable higher-level languages and programming was virtually all in assembler. Access to machines was often restricted; they had very limited storage, and were extremely slow. Plath 1967 reports processing speeds like 7 minutes for long sentences, even with the most advanced algorithms and on the best machines then available. Vast amounts of programming effort were devoted to bit-packing to save space and time. It is remarkable how much was done with such poor resources, for example in grammar and lexicon building: some of the grammars and dictionaries of the early 1960s were very large even by current standards.

Research in this period was thoroughly international, with considerable activity in the USSR as well as in the United States and Europe, and some in Japan. US grant funding increased after Sputnik 1, but the work had begun before. Russian and English were the dominant languages, but others, including Chinese, were involved (Booth 1967, Hutchins 1986).

Though the period ended under the cloud of the 1966 ALPAC Report, most of those engaged were neither crooks nor bozos. Many came to NLP research with a background and established status in linguistics and language study, and were motivated by the belief that something practically useful could be achieved, even though the strategies adopted were crude and the results not of high quality. The first major question was whether even to obtain only limited results, principled methods based on generalization were required, or whether ad hoc particularization would suffice. The second issue was the relative emphasis to be placed, in either case, on syntax and on semantics. The third problem was the actual value of the results, especially when balanced against pre- or post-editing requirements.

The main line of work during this period can be summarized as starting with translation as lookup, in dictionary-based word-for-word processing. The need to resolve syntactic and semantic ambiguity, and the former in particular because it is not open to fudging through the use of broad output equivalents, led to ambiguity resolution strategies based on local context, so dictionary entries became in effect individual procedures. Semantic resolution involved both specific word, and semantic category, collocation. But long-distance dependencies, the lack of a transparent word order in languages like German, and also the need for a whole-sentence structure characterization to obtain properly ordered output, as well as a perceived value in generalization, led to the development of autonomous sentence grammars and parsers.

Most of the NLP research done in this period was focused on syntax, partly because syntactic processing was manifestly necessary, and partly through implicit or explicit endorsement of the idea of syntax-driven processing. The really new experience in this work, and its contribution to linguistics in general, came from recognizing the implications of computing represented by the need not only for an explicit, precise, and complete characterization of language, but for a well-founded or formal characterization and, even more importantly, for algorithms to apply this description. Plath's 1967 account of NLP research at Harvard shows this development of computational grammar with its lexicon and parsing strategy very clearly. But as Plath also makes clear, those concentrating on syntax did not suppose that this was all there was to it: the semantic problems and needs of NLP were only too obvious to those aiming, as many MT workers were, at the translation of unrestricted real texts like scientific papers. The strategy was rather to tackle syntax first, if only because semantic ambiguity resolution might be finessed by using words with broad meanings as output; these could be given the necessary more specific interpretations in context.

There were however some workers who concentrated on semantics because they saw it as the really challenging problem, or assumed semantically driven processing. Thus Margaret Masterman's and Silvio Ceccato's groups, for example, exploited semantic pattern matching using semantic categories and semantic case frames, and Ceccato's approach (1967) also involved the use of world knowledge to extend linguistic semantics, along with that of semantic networks as a device for knowledge representation.

MT research was almost killed by the 1966 ALPAC Report, which concluded that MT was nowhere near achievement and led to funding cuts especially in the most active country, the United States, even though it recommended support for computational linguistics. But it is important to recognize what these first NLP workers did achieve. They recognized, and attempted to meet, the requirements of computational language processing, particularly in relation to syntactic analysis, and indeed successfully parsed and characterized sentences. They investigated many aspects of language, like polysemy, and of processing, including generation. They addressed the issues of overall system architectures and processing strategies, for example in direct, interlingual or transfer translation. They began to develop formalisms and tools, and some influential ideas first appeared, like the use of logic for representation (cf. Yngve 1967). Some groups were also established, developing resources like grammars and gaining experience, as at the Rand Corporation.

There was little work, on the other hand, on some important problems that have since attracted attention, like anaphor resolution, since though text was being translated it was treated as a sequence of independent sentences, or on the function of language, since the work was mainly on single-source discourse. There was little attempt to incorporate world knowledge, and to relate this non-linguistic to linguistic knowledge, though some world knowledge was smuggled in under the heading of semantics. The belief, or challenge, was that one could get far enough with essentially linguistic, and therefore shallow, processing not involving reasoning on world models. The research of this period did not produce any systems of scope or quality, though by the end of the 1960s there were MT production systems providing output of use to their customers (Hutchins 1986). There was more merit in the work of the period, and more continuity, through individuals, with later effort, than subsequent myths allow, though the early literature was inaccessible and little used. But perhaps the best comment is Bledsoe's (1986) on the value, for artificial intelligence as a whole, of the early MT workers' head-on attempt to do something really hard.

Work on the use of computers for literary and linguistic study also began in this period, but it has never been closely linked with that in NLP.

2. Phase 2: Late 1960s to late 1970s. The second phase of NLP work was A[rtificial] I[ntelligence]-flavored, with much more emphasis on world knowledge and on its role in the construction and manipulation of meaning representations. Pioneering work influenced by AI on the problems of addressing and contructing data or knowledge bases began as early as 1961, with the BASEBALL question-answering system (Green et al. 1961). The actual input to these systems was restricted and the language processing involved very simple compared with contemporary MT analysis, but the systems described by Minsky 1968, and Raphael's SIR in particular, recognized and provided for the need for inference on a knowledge base in interpreting and responding to language input.

Woods et al.'s LUNAR (1978) and Winograd's SHRDLU (1973) were the natural successors of these systems, but they were widely seen at the time as representing a step up in sophistication, in terms both of their linguistic and their task-processing capabilities. Though differing in many ways they shared a procedural style, and were perceived as having overall coherence as systems and a genuinely computational character. The dominant linguistic theory of the late 1960s, T[ransformational] G[rammar], was seen both as fundamentally unsuited to computation and particularly to analysis, even though TG was formally oriented and there was at least one serious transformational parser,

and as offering nothing on semantics, which had to be tackled for any actual NLP system. The computational confidence illustrated by Woods's and Winograd's work, and the range of experiment it promoted, while drawing on previous work, are well shown by the varied research reported in Rustin 1973.

The view that current linguistics had nothing to contribute, and the feeling that AI was liberating, were also apparent in Schank's work (1980), which explicitly emphasized semantics in the use both of general-purpose semantics with case structures for representation and of semantically driven processing. The community's concern, illustrated by Winograd and Schank alike, with meaning representation and the use of world knowledge then became an argument, reflecting a widespread feeling in AI stimulated by Minsky's promulgation of frames, for the use of a larger-scale organization of knowledge than that represented in NLP by verb case frames or propositional units: this large-scale organization would characterize the different relationships among the elements of a whole universe of discourse, and would support the inferences, including default inferences, needed especially in interpreting longer discourse and dialog. NLP would deliver deep representations integrating and filling out individual inputs to form a whole constituting an instantiation of a generic world model. Schank's arguments for the Yale group's use of more event-oriented scripts developed this line in the context of earlier work, by linking individual propositional case frames with the larger structures via their semantic primitives (cf. Cullingford 1981). Semantic networks (Bobrow and Collins 1975, Findler 1979) were similarly proposed as a third variant on this theme, offering a range of options from associative lexical networks only weakly and implicitly embodying world knowledge, to alternative notations for frames. These types of knowledge representation linked NLP with mainstream AI, and their descriptive and functional status, for example in relation to logic, was and has remained a matter for debate.

Semantic primitives seen, as in Schank's Conceptual Dependency, as having a representational and not just a selective role, also appeared to fit naturally with the need to capture underlying conceptual relations and identities in discourse processing, particularly for types of material or task where fine distinctions do not figure. Their status too was a matter for controversy, but they have continued in use, supplemented by or sometimes in the form of domain-specific categories, in application systems. They have also had a significant role in the more conventional form of selectional restrictions, even when semantic driving has been abandoned.

The general confidence of those working in the field, and the widespread belief that progress could be and was being made, was apparent on the one hand in the ARPA S[peech] U[nderstanding] R[esearch] project (Lea 1980), and on the other in some major system development projects building database front ends. Several of the SUR projects were ambitious attempts to build genuinely integrated systems combining top-down with bottom-up processing, though unfortunately the best performing system against the target measurements was the least theoretically interesting.

The front end projects (see e.g. Hendrix et al. 1978) were intended to go significantly beyond LUNAR in interfacing to large autonomous (and therefore not controlled) databases, and in being more robust under the pressures of "ill-formed" input; and the confidence on which they were based drove other work including that on the first significant commercial front end, INTEL-LECT (Harris 1984). But these projects unfortunately also showed that even an apparently straightforward, and perhaps the simplest because naturally constrained, NLP task was far more difficult than it seemed to be. NLP workers have been struggling ever since with the problems on the one hand of constructing general-purpose transportable front ends and of providing for the acquisition of application-specific knowledge, and on the other of handling the user's real needs in dialog. The former has led to the development of modular architectures, general-purpose formalisms, and toolkits, typically for supplying a specialized lexicon, semantics, and domain and database model on top of standard syntax, following the sublanguage approach which had been pioneered for text processing by Sager's NYU group (in Kittredge and Lehrberger 1982), but sometimes supplying a specialized syntax as well. The latter has stimulated research on the identification of the user's beliefs, goals, and plans, which is also and more fully needed for dynamic and extended interaction with expert systems for consultation and command, where the system's responses should be cooperative.

The need to identify the language user's goals and plans was early recognized by the Yale group, and has become a major trend in NLP research since that time, along with a more careful treatment of speech acts. Work on interactive dialog in particular, from the second half of the 1970s, has emphasized the communicative function of language, and the indirect function and underlying meaning, as well as direct function and surface meaning, of linguistic expressions. At the same time work on discourse understanding in the 1970s, whether on single-source texts like stories or reports, or on dialog, stimulated research on anaphor resolution and on the construction, maintenance, and use of discourse models not relying only on prior scenarios like scripts; and some useful progress was made with the development of notions of discourse or focus spaces and of resolution algorithms tied to these (Joshi et al. 1981, Brady and Berwick 1983, Grosz et al. 1986).

3. Phase 3: Late 1970s to late 1980s. It was nevertheless apparent by the early 1980s that it was much harder to build well-founded, i.e. predictable and extensible, NLP systems even for heavily restricted applications than had been supposed, and that systems for more challenging applications, in terms of processing tasks or discourse domains, could not generally be built in an ad hoc and aggregative way, though claims were made for this as a possible strategy for utilitarian MT, given enough investment of effort.

If the second phase of NLP work was AI-flavored and semantics-oriented, in a broad sense of "semantic," the third phase can be described, in reference to its dominant style, as a grammatico-logical phase. This trend was a response to the failures of practical system building which was stimulated by the development of grammatical theory among linguists during the 1970s, and by the move toward the use of logic for knowledge representation and reasoning in AI. Following Augmented Transition Networks as computational grammars in a theoretical as well as practical sense, linguists developed a whole range of grammar types, for example functional, categorial, and generalized phrase structure which, because they are oriented toward computability as an abstract principle, are also relevant to actual parsing, particularly since they also tend to have a context-free base supporting efficient parsing algorithms. The emphasis was also on a declarative approach and on unification as the fundamental process, which fitted naturally with a general trend in computing in this period associated with, for example, the growth of logic programming. The processing paradigm for analysis in particular was therefore syntax-driven compositional interpretation into logical forms.

Computational grammar theory became a very active area of research, linked with logics for meaning and knowledge representation able to deal with the user's beliefs and intentions, and with discourse features and functions like emphasis and theme. Capturing the refinements of linguistic expressions indicating time and mood, and of large-scale discourse and dialogue structure, remain challenges for this paradigm, but the grammatico-logical approach led by the end of the decade to powerful general-purpose sentence processors like SRI's Core Language Engine (Alshawi 1992), and Discourse Representation Theory (Kamp and Reyle 1993) offered a means of tackling more extended discourse within the grammatico-logical framework.

The grammatico-logical approach also encouraged a more general, if informal, use of predicate calculus-style meaning representations, and it led, via work on system building, to a shift in the meaning of "semantic" and "pragmatic" and a redistribution of effort within a system as a whole. The linguistic process of semantic interpretation was restricted, and the full meaning of expressions could be derived only by reference to the (application-specific) pragmatic context, which subsumed both prior discourse context and the application's domain, or world model.

Altogether, the period was one of growing confidence and consolidation, and also an expanding community. Practical resources (e.g. grammars) and tools (e.g. parsers) became available (Alvey Natural Language Tools, http://www.cl.cam.ac.uk/Research/NL/anlt.html). There were more operational and commercial systems, such as for database query. There was a conspicuous revival of work on MT, especially in Europe and Japan, often with a heavy application-specific emphasis. New tasks were addressed, such as message understanding (information extraction). These developments were reflected by the ACL's Applied NLP Conferences from 1983, and were significantly promoted by the beginning of the US technology development and evaluation programs in speech and language processing. The (D)ARPA speech recognition and message understanding conferences were important not only for the tasks they addressed but also for their emphasis on rigorous evaluation, initiating a major trend of the 1990s.

There was also, following the early work of the 1970s, a practically motivated surge of research on discourse, especially dialog, and on generation, particularly multisentence text generation. These were connected because cooperative response (e.g. in advice-giving systems) depends on modeling the participant's beliefs, goals, and plans, and it can naturally lead to paragraph-length out-

puts, for instance in providing explanations. Work on user modeling (Kobsa and Wahlster 1989) was one strand in research on language processing for such active communication, and on discourse structure serving this (Cohen et al. 1990). At the same time, as McKeown 1985 showed, rhetorical schemas could be useful recipes for producing both linguistically coherent and communicatively effective text.

Outside the main line, research on connectionist approaches to NLP signaled important topics for the future, notably word sense disambiguation (Small et al. 1988) and, via probabilistic networks, statistically colored NLP. The final trend of the 1980s, work on the lexicon, also pointed in this direction. This was stimulated by the important role the lexicon plays in the grammatico-logical approach, by MT requirements, and by practical needs for transportable or readily customizable systems. Serious attempts were made to exploit commercial dictionaries in machine-readable form, which in turn led to work using test corpora to validate or enhance existing lexical data, and also to projects to define formalisms—for example, exploiting feature structures—that can both capture rich lexical information and permit its direct use, including inferential use, within a formal processing context.

4. Phase 4: The 1990s. The lexicalist approach to grammar that appeared in the 1980s has become increasingly influential. The lexicon has taken over much of what was formerly assigned to the syntactic component, leaving the latter with a few general rules. Parsing with head phrase-structure grammars, for instance, is a compositional operation on large blocks of constituent feature data, with corresponding semantic rules delivering logical forms as before. Lexicalized tree-adjoining grammars illustrate the same trend. However, there has been a competitive revival, stimulated by practical tasks like information extraction from news material, of simple finite-state methods, and formal linguistic modeling has come under general attack from statistical approaches to data characterization and processing.

Statistical language processing was the most striking feature of the 1990s (Manning and Schuetze 1999). This involved not only data analysis (e.g. for semantic classification), an old idea rejuvenated by the arrival of vast quantities of machine-readable data and the machine power to handle it. It has involved more significantly the direct application of statistical methods to NLP itself, as for probabilistic parsing. The two are combined in machine learning from corpus data—for example, to derive both syntactic rules and their probabilities. This development was partly a response to the challenges presented by the rich, varied, and unpredictable material, like news text, to which translation systems were to be applied and for which absolutist approaches are manifestly unsuited. It was also a response to the successes of Hidden Markov Modeling in speech recognition.

A third feature of the 1990s was significant progress in practical tasks, especially those for which shallow processing methods (e.g. using finite-state parsing and surface patterns) can deliver useful output. The vast quantities of text flooding the World Wide Web have stimulated work on tasks for managing this flood, notably by information extraction and automatic summarizing, and on sufficient-to-the-day strategies for these tasks—for instance, text extraction using word frequency and discourse structure cues. For the first time, these tasks have also seriously involved spoken language. Speech recognition (transcription) technology has advanced rapidly, and natural (albeit very simple) speech dialog systems are now commercial realities; more ambitious ones involving translation, like Verbmobil (Wahlster 2000), are beginning to appear. The shallow processing approach has been extended to dialog structure through the use of conversational games rather than intensional user modeling. These developments (cf. Cole et al. 1998) are reflected in the use of "language engineering" as distinct from either "computational linguistics" or "natural language processing."

This emphasis on language technology naturally has been associated with the fourth major trend of the decade, evaluation (Spärck Jones and Galliers 1996). US government programs, extended over an increasing range of tasks, have played a significant part, through carefully designed and challenging evaluations, in stimulating work on generic task systems and general-purpose components. They have placed particular emphasis on robustness and portability, on systems that either do not require heavy domain knowledge or can be customized easily. Similar European initiatives have focused largely on multi-lingual tasks and issues. This concern with evaluation has been associated with a conspicuous growth of interest in the design and provision of linguistic resources, for example the British National Corpus and WordNet (Fellbaum 1999), and test tools like the Penn Treebank, which has annotations allowing parser performance assessment. Public domain processing tools, such as taggers, are now available, allowing rapid prototype system assembly using modular architectures.

5. Conclusion. Natural language processing is currently flourishing. Information technology developments are encouraging work on a broad range of tasks designed to find, digest, package, and represent speech or text-derived information. Some kind of MT, for instance, is now a routine offering by search engines, and is more useful because better NLP systems will appear. At the same time, foundational work continues, seeking to combine the formally sound with the computationally real. One important aspect of this, which Sparck Jones et al. 2000 mark as a trend for the next decade, is how to combine formal theories and statistical data in a principled and practical way for NLP.

[*See also* Computational Morphology; Parsing; Generalized Phrase Structure Grammar; Lexical-Functional Grammar; Mathematical Linguistics; Speech Recognition; Statistical Linguistics; Cognitive Science; Computational Morphology; Computational Phonology; *and* Machine Translation.]

BIBLIOGRAPHY

ALPAC. 1966. *Language and machines: Computers in translation and linguistics.* A report by the Automatic Language Processing Advisory Committee, Division of Biological Sciences, National Academy of Sciences. Washington, D.C.

Alshawi, Hiyan, ed. 1992. *The core language engine.* Cambridge, Mass.: MIT Press.

Alvey Natural Language Tools. http://www.cl.cam.ac.uk/Research/NL/anlt.html.

Bledsoe, Woodrow. 1986. I had a dream: AAAI Presidential Address, 19 August 1985. *AI Magazine* 7:1.57–61.

Bobrow, Daniel G., and Allan Collins, eds. 1975. *Representation and understanding: Studies in cognitive science.* New York: Academic Press.

Booth, Andrew D., ed. 1967. *Machine translation.* Amsterdam: North Holland.

Brady, Michael, and Robert C. Berwick, eds. 1983. *Computational models of discourse.* Cambridge, Mass.: MIT Press.

British National Corpus. http://info.ox.ac.uk/bnc/.

Ceccato, Silvio. 1967. Correlational analysis and mechanical translation. In Booth 1967, pp. 77–135,

Cohen, Paul R., Jerry Morgan, and Martha E. Pollack, eds. 1990. *Intentions in communication.* Cambridge, Mass.: MIT Press.

Cole, Ronald, et al., eds. 1998. *Survey of the state of the art in human language technology.* Cambridge: Cambridge University Press.

Cullingford, Richard. 1981. SAM. Reprinted in Grosz et al. 1986, pp. 627–649.

Fellbaum, Christian D., ed. 1999. *WordNet: An electronic lexical database and some of its applications.* Cambridge, Mass.: MIT Press.

Findler, Nicholas V., ed. 1979. *Associative networks: Representation and use of knowledge in computers*. New York: Academic Press.

Green, Bert F., et al. 1961. BASEBALL: An automatic question answerer. Reprinted in Grosz et al. 1986, pp. 545–549.

Grosz, Barbara J., Karen Sparck Jones, and Bonnie L. Webber, eds. 1986. *Readings in natural language processing*. Los Altos, Calif.: Kaufmann.

Harris, Larry R. 1984. Experience with INTELLECT. *AI Magazine* 5:2.3–50.

Hendrix, Gary G., et al. 1978. Developing a natural language interface to complex data. Reprinted in Grosz et al. 1986, pp. 563–584.

Hutchins, William John. 1986. *Machine translation: Past, present and future*. Chichester, UK: Ellis Horwood.

Hutchins, William John, ed. 2000. *Early years in machine translation: Memoirs and biographies of pioneers*. Amsterdam: Benjamins.

Joshi, Aravind K., et al., eds. 1981. *Elements of discourse understanding*. Cambridge and New York: Cambridge University Press.

Kamp, Hans, and Uwe Reyle. 1993. *From discourse to logic*. Dordrecht: Kluwer.

Kittredge, Richard, and John Lehrberger, eds. 1982. *Sublanguage: Studies of language in restricted semantic domains*. Berlin: de Gruyter.

Kobsa, Alfred, and Wolfgang Wahlster, eds. 1989. *Use models in dialog systems*. Berlin: Springer.

Lea, Wayne A., ed. 1980. *Trends in speech recognition*. Englewood Cliffs, N.J.: Prentice-Hall.

Locke, William N., and Andrew D. Booth, eds. 1955. *Machine translation of languages*. New York: Wiley.

Manning, Christopher D., and Hinrich Schuetze. 1999. *Foundations of statistical language processing*. Cambridge, Mass.: MIT Press.

McKeown, Kathleen R. 1985. *Text generation*. Cambridge: Cambridge University Press.

Minsky, Marvin, ed. 1968. *Semantic information processing*. Cambridge, Mass.: MIT Press.

Penn Treebank. http://www.cis.upenn.edu/~treebank/.

Plath, Warren. 1967. Multiple-path analysis and automatic translation. In Booth 1967, pp. 267–315.

Rustin, Randall, ed. 1973. *Natural language processing*. New York: Algorithmics Press.

Schank, Roger C. 1980. Language and memory. Reprinted in Grosz et al. 1986, pp. 171–191.

Small, Steven L., Garrison W. Cottrell, and Michael K. Tanenhaus, eds. 1988. *Lexical ambiguity resolution*. San Mateo, Calif.: Morgan Kaufman.

Spärck Jones, Karen, and Julia R. Galliers. 1996. *Evaluating natural language processing systems*. Berlin: Springer.

Spärck Jones, Karen, Gerald J. M. Gazdar, and Roger M.

Needham, eds. 2000. Computers, language and speech: Formal theories and statistical data. *Philosophical Transactions of the Royal Society*, Series A, 358:1769.1225–1431.

Wahlster, Wolfgang, ed. 2000. *Verbmobil: Foundations of speech-to-speech translation*. Berlin: Springer.

Winograd, Terry. 1973. A procedural model of language understanding. Reprinted in Grosz et al. 1986, pp. 249–266.

Woods, William A. 1978. Semantics and quantification in natural language question answering. Reprinted in Grosz et al. 1986, pp. 205–248.

Yngve, Victor H. 1967. MT at M.I.T. 1965. In Booth 1967, pp. 451–523.

KAREN SPÄRCK JONES

Architectures

A language processing system has many components, both knowledge sources and processors; for example for syntactic analysis it needs a *grammar* and a *parser*. What these components are and how they should be organized for effective and efficient processing is a serious, unsolved problem. A system architecture has to specify the *structural relations* between the components, and the *flow of control* from one to another during processing.

1. Data Representation. In addition to specifying structural relationships and control flow between components of a language processing system, an architecture should also make clear the data protocols governing the form and content of representations passed between components. This facilitates the substitution of one component by another, which may extend the first or may perform the same function in a different manner (e.g. using a different algorithm or different knowledge sources). The semantics of these representations will, in most cases, depend on the linguistic theory that the system implements (e.g., the tag set for a part-of-speech tagger, the feature set for a feature-based grammar, or the logic for a semantic analyzer); it is useful, however, to adopt certain conventions about the syntax of the representations and, in the case of analysis systems, how the results of analysis are to be related to the linguistic objects (text or speech signal) they describe.

More specifically, annotations containing information about a particular linguistic object may be embedded in that object but distinguished from it using a markup language, such as the Standard General Markup Language (Goldfarb 1990). As an alternative, annotations may be held separately and related to the underlying language stream by indices based on character or time offset information (Grishman 1995). Each approach has its advantages and its advocates. Although agreement at such a low and linguistically uninteresting level may not seem significant, it is nonetheless essential and has critical implications for the design of system components and the ease with which large, complex language processing systems can be assembled and modified.

2. Structural Organization and Flow of Control. A simple *linear* model for sentence *interpretation* (e.g. Woods 1978) would specify a *morphological analyzer* exploiting lexicon and morphological rules, a *syntactic analyzer* applying lexical information and grammar rules, and a *semantic analyzer* using word meaning information in conjunction with selection restrictions. The first two processors build intermediate representations of the input sentence showing its lexical elements and structural character; the final processor output is the sentence's *meaning representation*. Designing systems thus requires appropriate choices of representation to pass between processors.

A corresponding linear model for sentence *generation* would start with a meaning representation, derive a language-specific linguistic structure with lexical elements, and then express this as a word string.

But these simple models are not sufficient, even for very restricted purposes like database access. It is also necessary for interpretation to have a *pragmatic processor* to determine underlying speech acts, for example, and a *domain processor* to apply knowledge of the system's reference world, in order to achieve a fully resolved and explicit representation of the meaning of an input with quantifiers correctly scoped, anaphor resolved, and so forth. In many cases a specific *task processor* is also required to transform the meaning representation to meet a particular application need, for example to search a database.

In the necessary broader context, further points arise. Thus it is clear from work on translation, for example, that interpretation and generation may involve distinct grammars; the same grammatical information may indeed be organized differently in a monolingual system. Linguistic processes may invoke non-linguistic ones, notably reasoning on domain knowledge, for example to interpret a compound noun. Interpretation and generation, as linguistically motivated activities, may be separated by an arbitrary amount of non-linguistic computation, for example to determine the answer to a question. Language

processing systems may moreover be components of other systems, rather than free-standing as is usual in translation, for example be front ends to expert systems; interpretation and generation may then be quite distinct, and independently driven generation may be a more complex formulation and expression process than in the simple case, demanding a *strategic* as well as *tactical* processor, for instance to choose a paragraph structure. Finally, when sentence processing is embedded in longer discourse or dialog processing, a *discourse processor* is required, e.g. for inter-sentential reference determination; this would be applied in interpretation following pragmatic processing, and would use a discourse model as knowledge source. A sentence meaning representation is then itself also transient, as it is used to extend or modify the discourse model, which is viewed as the discourse representation. Thus for all but the most trivial application, the linear model needs to be extended over a whole series of modules with their respective processors, knowledge sources, and representations.

A linear architecture has many advantages for system development, because modules can be built and changed independently. But it is unsatisfactory in two ways. It is psychologically implausible. It is difficult to believe that human beings complete syntactic analysis before embarking on semantic processing or, particularly in the case of speech, that lexical processing is independent of discourse context; and psycholinguistic experiment indeed suggests that all sources of information are jointly applied to the incoming word (Marslen-Wilson and Tyler 1981), implying an incremental model of interpretation. The linear model also has computational disadvantages: the general view of interpretation is of a progressive resolution of ambiguity: alternative word categories are weeded by syntax, alternative structures by semantics, and so forth. Though there is no requirement that a particular ambiguity, for example of pronoun reference, should be resolved at a particular stage, it must be resolved somewhere along the line. But there is always a danger that information available at an earlier stage has become inaccessible, for example information about input constituent order in a multi-stage translation program; and the computational cost of carrying forward and examining many alternatives, particularly in earlier stages, is very high.

It is however possible to modify the crude linear architecture by *cascading* or *interleaving*, where candidate syntactic constituents for instance are passed to a semantic processor (Bobrow and Webber 1980), and semantically acceptable constituents may in turn be checked by a discourse or dialog processor; or by *rule pairing* so, for example, syntactic constituents are semantically interpreted as they are built. This gives orderly, and in these cases syntax-initiated, processing.

But processing like this is still very constrained, and the alternative architecture is therefore some form of *unordered conjoint processing*. But this in turn raises further issues: should each processor interact with all the others; and should processing be *need-* or *data-driven*? The linear model naturally presupposes particular choices here. Communication is restricted, since each processor communicates directly only with its predecessor and successor, though some information may in fact be simply forwarded for use further down the line (e.g. the actual input word form in translation); and processing as a whole is data-driven in that the activity of each processor is determined by what is passed to it, though the internal operation of a processor may be *top-down*, i.e. need-driven, or *bottom-up*, i.e. data-driven.

It is not clear, particularly in speech processing, that every processor could usefully receive information from, or send it to, every other processor: for example a string of phonemes would ordinarily not be relevant to the pragmatic processor. Need-, or expectation-, driven processing implies a dominance relation between components: for instance applying standard message scenarios or scripts to inputs may imply searching for items with particular semantic or referential properties (Schank and Riesbeck 1981). But this can force premature and incorrect decisions which have to be unpicked, or simply lose information altogether. In general, processing becomes unacceptably complex when relationships between many processors have to be managed through a predetermined control structure, since this may not fit some particular input very well.

Blackboard architectures have been proposed to overcome this problem (Erman et al. 1980). Individual processors post outputs (hypotheses about the discourse) on a board from which they may be read independently by any others, at any time, though in practice boards may be divided into subboards for particular subsets of processors. This architecture seems particularly suited to (real-time) speech processing, and to specific needs like anaphor resolution, where what will arrive may not be predictable and individual processors should be allowed to work on incoming data as they can. But this does not

eliminate the control problem: processors have tasks, and there must be some means of ordering these, i.e. of scheduling and rescheduling items on the system's global or processors' local *agendas*. The control flow is not predetermined in detail, but the system has to apply evaluation criteria to decide which tasks to execute given the context supplied by the data; it can then focus on tasks associated with the currently most productive hypothesis about the input. But scheduling is still complex, and an alternative much simpler form of interaction between processors in a speech understanding system, via specialized question-answer channels, has been proposed by Briscoe and Boguraev 1984.

Connectionist architectures (Waltz and Pollack 1985, McClelland and Kawamoto 1986) can be seen as devices for further weakening control in a completely data-driven manner. Individual processing units define possible descriptive properties, e.g. specific phonemes, word senses, or case roles, and are positively or negatively connected with others to form a *constraint network*, e.g. a word sense may be positively linked with a syntactic category and negatively linked with an alternative sense. In interpreting an input, represented by some particular set of units, the system works from these in parallel attempting to satisfy multiple constraints, with responses by each processor propagating to others over the network so the overall outcome is determined by the cumulative bias of the responses and not necessarily by any individual one. Given feedback the outcome is the stable state reached after iterative propagation. When the units are in layers with feedback between them, so for example a layer of semantic units and a layer of syntactic units reinforce each other's decisions, we have a relaxed version of the usual blackboard architecture. *Input sampling*, as in speech analysis, adds repetition to the basic reinforcement strategy, so connectionist architectures look natural for speech processing. In fine-grained parallelism, conventional units like syntactic categories may themselves have a distributed representation over a set of feature-defining processor units.

In all of these architectures, processors or sets of processors are distinguished by the type of information they deploy. There is a *syntactic processor* or, in the connectionist case a set of syntactic processors individually or collectively applying a single rule. In *lexicalist* or *word expert* architectures processing, and specifically interpretation, is done through a set of individual processors, one for each word (Small 1981). A word's expert embodies all the information required to determine its sense and contribution to the overall sentence, so interpretation is a mutual interaction among experts seeking to match their individual requirements. In *functional* architectures each component may be very different in character: thus Hirst 1987 combines conventional syntactic and semantic processing with marker passing through an associative lexical network. In the word expert model all the processors are of the same type, and typically do not separate knowledge source from process but mix the two.

Most implemented systems, especially for applications, have had a linear architecture: it is straightforward, and its limitations are less obvious for restricted domains or tasks where, for example, syntactic choices can be ordered by likelihood, or some processes like speech act determination are not required. Non-linear architectures have some attractive properties, but are harder to design and implement, and need much more investigation.

3. Reference Architectures. As awareness has grown of the difficulty of building large-scale, robust language processing systems, whether for application or linguistic research, so has awareness of the necessity of reusing and sharing components and knowledge sources across systems. This awareness has led to the creation of architectures not only for individual systems but also for classes for systems. Such general architectures, or reference architectures, do not supply specific components for language processing, but rather provide specifications, in some cases implemented, for the way in which components are to be linked together to build language processing systems.

For instance, GATE, the General Architecture for Text Engineering (Cunningham et al. 1997) aims to support developers of language analysis systems. It provides services for managing document collections and for managing annotations on portions of documents, documents, and document collections (using the indexed annotation model), services for registering and executing processing components within a larger system, and services for viewing the results of running components against documents.

RAGS, the Reference Architecture for Generation Systems (Mellish et al. 2000), aims to support developers of language generation systems. RAGS provides a layered representation scheme and an inter-module communication scheme based on a whiteboard (a cumulative blackboard, where data are not deleted or changed, but explic-

itly revised). The representation scheme allows for the construction of most common data structures used in language processing; in addition, it supports specific relations between such data structures, such as that one data structure realizes (is more concrete than) another, revises another, or co-refers (shares structure with) another. Such relations are particularly useful in generation systems where one processing module (e.g. a text-planning module) may contribute to multiple data representations at different levels (e.g. semantic and rhetorical) and each data representation (e.g. syntactic) is incrementally completed by successive modules (e.g. centering and lexical choice). The whiteboard model can be used to implement pipeline or asynchronous control flow models.

Such general architectures remain under debate and development. If consensus concerning them can be obtained, then language system researchers and developers will possess powerful, ready-made system architectures into which they can slot their new or modified language processing components, building on well-tested foundations.

[*See also* Parsing; Cognitive Science; Philosophy of Language; Connectionism; *and* Statistical Linguistics.]

BIBLIOGRAPHY

Bobrow, Rusty J., and Bonnie L. Webber. 1980. Knowledge representation for syntactic/semantic processing. In *Proceedings, First Annual National Conference on Artificial Intelligence,* American Association for Artificial Intelligence, pp. 316–323. Los Altos, Calif.: Kaufman.

Briscoe, Edward J., and Branimir K. Boguraev. 1984. Control structures and theories of interaction in speech understanding systems. In *Proceedings of COLING 84* (Tenth International Conference on Computational Linguistics), pp. 259–266. Morristown, N.J.: Association for Computational Linguistics.

Cunningham, Hamish, Kevin Humphreys, Robert Gaizauskas, and Yorick Wilks. 1997. Software infrastructure for natural language processing. In *Proceedings of the Fifth ACL Conference on Applied Natural Language Processing (ANLP-97),* pp. 237–244. Washington, D.C.

Erman, Lee D., et al. 1980. The Hearsay-II speech understanding system: Integrating knowledge to resolve uncertainty. *Computing Surveys* 12.213–253.

Goldfarb, Charles F. 1990. *The SGML handbook.* Oxford: Oxford University Press.

Grishman, R. 1995. TIPSTER phase II architecture design document (Tinman architecture) version 1.52. http://www.cs.nyu.edu/tipster.

Hirst, Graeme. 1987. *Semantic interpretation and the resolution of ambiguity.* Cambridge and New York: Cambridge University Press.

Marslen-Wilson, William D., and Loraine K. Tyler. 1981. Central processes in speech understanding. *Philosophical Transactions of the Royal Society,* Series B, 295.317–332.

McClelland, James L., and Alan H. Kawamoto. 1986. Mechanisms of sentence processing: Assigning roles to constituents. In *Parallel distributed processing: Explorations in the microstructure of cognition,* vol. 2, *Psychological and biological models,* edited by David E. Rumelhart, James L. McClelland et al., pp. 272–325. Cambridge, Mass.: MIT Press.

Mellish, Christopher, Roger Evans; Lynne Cahill, Christie Doran, Daniel Paiva, Mike Reape, Donia Scott, and Neil Tipper. 2000. A representation for complex and evolving data dependencies in generation. In *Proceedings of the Sixth Applied Natural Language Processing Conference (ANLP-2000),* pp. 119–126. Seattle: Association for Computational Linguistics.

Schank, Roger C., and Christopher K. Riesbeck. 1981. *Inside computer understanding.* Hillsdale, N.J.: Erlbaum.

Small, S. 1981. Viewing word expert parsing as linguistic theory. In *Proceedings of the Seventh International Joint Conference on Artificial Intelligence,* pp. 70–76. Los Altos, Calif.: Kaufmann.

Waltz, David L., and Jordan B. Pollack. 1985. Massively parallel parsing: A strongly interactive model of natural language interpretation. *Cognitive Science* 9.51–74.

Woods, William A. 1978. Semantics and quantification in natural language question answering. In *Advances in computers,* vol. 17, edited by Marshall C. Yovits, pp. 1–87. New York: Academic Press.

KAREN SPÄRCK JONES AND ROBERT GAIZAUSKAS

Generation

Natural language generation is the production of linguistic utterances guided by communicative intentions. There are two main forms, speaking and writing; the producing agencies can be people or computers. In practice, however, the term "N[atural] L[anguage] G[eneration]" refers to the composition of printed text by computers. The length and complexity of the texts may vary from elliptical answers to questions (e.g. in a natural language dialog system), to multi-paragraph reports (e.g. in an explanation facility which forms part of an expert system). There is also growing interest in the automatic generation of spoken language. Theoretical and practical work in this area aims at the integrated design of generators capable of converting communicative intentions into high-quality, prosodically well-formed speech (as opposed to bipartite designs consisting of a printed-text generator which feeds into a text-to-speech converter).

The overall architecture of the language generation process can be explained with reference to the following outline (based on Levelt 1989 and using his terminology wherever applicable). It features the principal components that would be needed in a full-fledged language generator. The list reflects a decomposition of the language generation process which is emerging from both computational and psycholinguistic work.

Processing components of natural-language generators

A. Conceptualizer
   A.1. Macroplanner (communicative intentions ⇒ illocutionary acts):
        Discourse plans (rhetorical structure)
        Pragmatic goals (social, emotional, etc.; rhetorical effects)
   A.2. Microplanner (illocutionary acts ⇒ preverbal messages):
        Reference (referential expressions, surface speech acts)
        Information-processing factors (topic, focus, prominence)
B. Formulator
   B.1. Grammatical Encoder (preverbal messages ⇒ surface structures):
        Lexicalization (lemma selection)
        Syntactic tree formation (functional and positional trees)
   B.2. Phonological Encoder (surface structures ⇒ phonetic plans):
        Lexicalization (selection of phonological word-forms)
        Prosodic planning (intonation contour, metrical structure)

The *conceptualizer* is responsible for planning the meaning content and rhetorical organization of a text. The *formulator* prepares the grammatical and phonetic shape of individual sentences. The conceptualizer delivers a text in the form of a sequence of preverbal messages which is fed into the formulator. A preverbal message specifies all information that the formulator needs in order to convert the message into a sentential or subsentential (elliptical) expression. Not shown in this outline is an *output* component which realizes utterances phonetically or orthographically.

Each main component consists of two cooperating subcomponents, the first one having a more global span of control than the second. The *macroplanner* is capable of structuring the contents of possibly extensive discourse units. The *microplanner* deals with a few adjacent preverbal messages at a time. Within the formulator, global control is exercised by the *grammatical encoder* while constructing full sentences. The *phonological encoder* needs simultaneous access to no more than a few successive syntactic constituents.

The macroplanner receives as input communicative intentions generated by an expert system, a question-answering system, or some other application program. A communicative intention specifies a desired mental state in the addressee (e.g. knowledge, belief, or intention). In response, the macroplanner starts composing a *plan* which will bring about the goal state. The resulting plan is a sequence of one or more illocutionary acts—speech acts such as 'inform somebody of something', 'request somebody to do something', etc. This planning activity requires powerful reasoning methods tuned to the logical structure of the content domain; it must be sensitive to the knowledge that is already available to the addressee and his/her emotional state.

Within the conceptualizer, illocutionary acts are represented as expressions over a "private" vocabulary of terms which denote actions, objects, states of affairs, events, etc. To make these "referents" recognizable for the addressee, the microplanner forms conceptual (descriptive, referential) expressions. For example, 'person25', a referent, is replaced by the conceptual expression underlying noun phrases such as *the vice president* or *your boss,* depending on the addressee. In addition, the microplanner attempts to facilitate the addressee's interpretive task in various ways:

(a) It assigns prominence to descriptions of newly introduced referents, thus influencing pitch accent placement during later phonological encoding.

(b) It marks some description as topic. This often causes it to be grammatically encoded as the subject of the sentence. The addressee takes the topic's referent as the best memory location to store the information expressed in the remainder of the sentence.

(c) The microplanner maintains a list of referents which are in focus, i.e., currently being attended to. It will refer to focused referents by anaphorical expressions (e.g. *he/him* as subsequent reference to person25). Or it can signal to the addressee that a new referent is brought into focus, e.g. by using indefinite reference as in *He had an accident.*

The conceptual structures delivered by the conceptualizer are fed into the formulator. These preverbal messages trigger abstract (pre-phonological) lexical items of the target language. These items are called *lemmas*. On the basis of their syntactic properties, the grammatical encoder attaches them as terminal nodes to tree-like structures specifying constituent hierarchy, grammatical functions, and left-to-right position. These surface structures serve as input to the phonological encoder, which fleshes them out with information determining the global sound shape of the final utterance. This activity includes replacing lemmas by phonologically specified word forms, and computing prosodic patterns.

Although, viewed globally, the four subcomponents operate in series, there is ample opportunity for parallel processing. For instance, the grammatical encoder need not wait for the microplanner to deliver a complete preverbal message. Grammatical encoding can begin upon receipt of a partial message. This will result in a syntactic fragment to be completed as soon as further parts of the preverbal message have been elaborated; this is termed *incremental production* (Kempen and Hoenkamp 1987). Thus the microplanner and the grammatical encoder may be working simultaneously on the same sentence, although on different parts. A comparable situation holds for other processing components. However, the occurrence of incomplete inputs has a drawback: it increases the probability for the generator "to talk itself into a corner." This circumstance is one of the reasons for including a *monitor* in the generator's design. Its task is to diagnose troubles incurred by any component, and to reactivate earlier components with modified inputs.

The oldest natural language generators date from the early 1970s. They generated isolated English sentences from a shallow meaning representation, using A[ugmented] T[ransition] N[etwork]s as central grammatical formalism. Being too rigid, ATNs quickly fell into disuse and were replaced by more flexible formalisms, in particular Systemic Grammar, H[ead-driven] P[hrase] S[tructure] G[rammar] and T[ree] A[djoining] G[rammar]. In the 1980s and 1990s, extensive "surface generation" grammars were developed for a range of modern languages. In the same period, the problem of generating connected discourse gained ever-increasing importance. The design of discourse generators capable of coherent and cohesive text output was founded on theoretical work by, among others, Grosz and Sidner 1986—who proposed a conjoined treatment of discourse structure and focusing—Mann and Thompson 1987 (Rhetorical Structure theory), and Kamp and Reyle 1993 (Discourse Representation theory). Generators dealing with various aspects of discourse were implemented by McDonald 1983, McKeown 1985, Dale 1992, and Hovy 1993.

Around the turn of the century, NLG technology was approaching the level of practical applicability, in particular in the areas of

- message and report generation (object descriptions, help and error messages, technical documentation, weather forecasts, database content presentation, expert system explanation)
- text critiquing
- machine translation
- natural-language dialog systems
- authoring support (systems that assist writers of routine documents, text critiquing, and rephrasing)

A practical handbook for the implementation of NLG systems has recently been published (Reiter and Dale 2000).

Special research topics address the role that NLG can play in other computer applications:

- discourse planning in multimedia (multimodal) information systems (e.g. Maybury 1993)
- multilingual spoken dialog and translation systems (e.g. Wahlster 2000)
- automated summarization (e.g. Mani and Maybury 2000)
- interleaving language generation and parsing (for generating non-ambiguous text and for text revision support; e.g., Neumann 1998)

[*See also* Discourse; Pragmatics and Contextual Semantics, *articles on* Implicature *and* Presupposition; Semantics; Speech Synthesis; *and* Text, *article on* Text Understanding.]

BIBLIOGRAPHY

Dale, Robert. 1992. *Generating referring expressions: Constructing descriptions in a domain of objects and processes.* Cambridge, Mass.: MIT Press.

Grosz, Barbara J., and Candace L. Sidner. 1986. Attention, intentions, and the structure of discourse. *Computational Linguistics* 12.175–204.

Hovy, Eduard. 1993. Automated discourse generation using discourse relations. *Artificial Intelligence* 63:341–385.

Kamp, Hans, and Uwe Reyle. 1993. *From discourse to logic.* Dordrecht: Kluwer.

Kempen, Gerard A. M., ed. 1987. *Natural language generation: New results in artificial intelligence, psychology, and linguistics.* Dordrecht: Kluwer.

Kempen, Gerard A. M., and Eduard Hoenkamp. 1987. An incremental procedural grammar for sentence formulation. *Cognitive Science* 11.201–58.

Levelt, Willem J. M. 1989. *Speaking: From intention to articulation.* Cambridge, Mass.: MIT Press.

Mann, William C., and Sandra A. Thompson. 1987. Rhetorical structure theory: Description and construction of text structures. In Kempen 1987, pp. 85–95.

Mani, Inderjeet, and Mark T. Maybury, eds. 1999. *Advances in automatic text summarization.* Cambridge, Mass.: MIT Press.

Maybury, Mark T., ed. 1993. *Intelligent multimedia interfaces.* Menlo Park, Calif.: AAAI Press.

McDonald, David D. 1983. Natural language generation as a computational problem: An introduction. In *Computational models of discourse,* edited by Michael Brady and Robert C. Berwick, pp. 209–265. Cambridge, Mass.: MIT Press.

McKeown, Kathleen R. 1985. *Text generation: Using discourse strategies and focus constraints to generate natural language text.* Cambridge and New York: Cambridge University Press.

Neumann, Günter. 1998. Interleaving natural language parsing and generation through uniform processing. *Artificial Intelligence* 99.121–163.

Reiter, Ehud, and Robert Dale. 2000. *Building natural language generation systems.* Cambridge: Cambridge University Press.

Wahlster, Wolfgang, ed. 2000. *Verbmobil: Foundations of speech-to-speech translation.* Berlin: Springer.

GERARD A. M. KEMPEN

Word-Sense Ambiguity

Ambiguity of word meaning is pervasive in language, with the most frequent words having the greatest multiplicity of meanings. The problems this introduces have long been recognized, particularly with regard to automatic language understanding: in a 1949 memorandum, the ground-breaking mathematician Warren Weaver noted that, without sufficient context, " 'Fast' may mean 'rapid'; or it may mean 'motionless'; and there is no way of telling which" (cited in Silberman 2000). Similarly, Bar-Hillel's 1964 famous example, "The box is in the pen," was contrived to illustrate the extent to which world knowledge and context are necessary to distinguish *pen* 'writing instrument' from *pen* 'enclosure'.

Within computational linguistics, computational *lexicons*—repositories of information about words—frequently catalog information about word meanings in ways similar to traditional dictionaries, distinguishing parts of speech and subcategorization information, and enumerating lists of shallow hierarchies of word meanings, often called *senses*. *Homonyms* are generally considered to be words that are unrelated in meaning or related only by distant etymology, such as BANK$_1$ 'financial institution' and BANK$_2$ 'river edge'. In contrast, a single word with multiple, more closely related meanings is referred to as *polysemous*; for example, LINE$_1$ 'geometrical object' and LINE$_2$ 'written mark'. (Some authors use the term "polysemy" more generally, to include homonymy.) Models within artificial intelligence, natural language processing, and psycholinguistics sometimes organize word meanings into hierarchies or graphs called *semantic networks* (e.g. Collins and Loftus 1975, Quillian 1968).

Some linguists have proposed cross-linguistic relationships as a basis for justifying word sense distinctions, arguing, for example, that the reality of the distinction between DRUG$_1$ 'medicine' and DRUG$_2$ 'narcotic' is supported by the fact that these concepts are lexicalized differently in French (as *medicament* and *drogue*), as well as in German, Italian, and Japanese (Dagan and Itai 1994, Ide 1999, Resnik and Yarowsky 1999). Alternative attempts to characterize word meaning distinctions include partial or total decomposition into related semantic representations. For example, Levin and Rappaport-Hovav 1995 propose that a verb like *dry* in *The paint dried* is represented as [BECOME Y (DRY)], while *dry* in *Steve dried his hair* would be represented as [X ACT [CAUSE [BECOME Y (DRY)]]] (see also Jackendoff 1983, Dorr and Olsen 1996).

Still other approaches reject entirely the idea that word senses can be enumerated. Generative Lexicon theory proposes a model in which multiple meanings emerge from interactions among underspecified lexical representations; for example, this accounts for the way underspecified *fast* captures different meanings in *fast typewriter*, *fast road*, and *fast meal*, and for "regular polysemy relationships" between meanings like LAMB$_1$ 'mammal' and LAMB$_2$ 'meat' (Pustejovsky 1996). Prototype theory suggests a representational space in which meanings are closer to or more distant from prototypical concepts, capturing the fact that *robin* is more central to the concept

BIRD than is *penguin* (Rosch et al. 1976). Corpus-based techniques have been used to represent words as points in a vector space and to produce meaning-like clusters on the basis of distributional co-occurrence (e.g. Lee 1997, Schuetze 1997).

Word sense disambiguation (WSD) is the problem of selecting one or more senses for a word in the context in which it appears—for example, deciding that *line* in *He drew a neat line through the incorrect answer* refers to 'written mark' rather than some other sense. Traditionally, this has been viewed as a problem of assigning a single sense tag to a word, much like part-of-speech tagging, but some have argued that it is better viewed as the more general problem of assigning a probability distribution over all possible senses, or in terms of more general semantic annotation (Light 1997). WSD is often approached as a *classification* problem (Mitchell 1997) in which the goal is to classify an ambiguous instance into the best category *c*, given a representation of the instance as a collection of features. In *supervised* approaches to WSD, algorithms learn from training data annotated with correct word senses (Escudero et al. 2000, Yarowsky 1993). *Unsupervised* approaches make no use of training data, relying instead on lexical knowledge sources such as dictionary definitions and semantic networks (Lesk 1986, Richardson and Smeaton 1995). WSD algorithms are evaluated on the basis of accuracy against a manually annotated test set, usually in comparison with the agreement rate of independent human annotators (Kilgarriff and Palmer 2000).

[*See also* Lexicon; Machine Translation; Semantics; *and* Parsing.]

BIBLIOGRAPHY

Bar-Hillel, Y. 1964. *Language and information*. Reading, Mass.: Addison-Wesley.

Collins, A., and E. Loftus. 1975. A spreading activation theory of semantic processing. *Psychological Review* 82.407–428.

Dagan, Ido, and Alon Itai. 1994. Word sense disambiguation using a second language monolingual corpus. *Computational Linguistics* 20.563–596.

Dorr, Bonnie J., and Mari Broman Olsen. 1996. Multilingual generation: The role of telicity in lexical choice and syntactic realization. *Machine Translation* 11.37–74.

Escudero, Gerard; Lluís Marquez; and German Rigan. 2000. A comparison between supervised learning algorithms for word sense disambiguation. In *Proceedings of CoNLL-2000 and LLL-2000, Lisbon, Portugal*, pp. 33–36.

Ide, Nancy. 1999. Parallel translations as sense discriminators.

In *Proceedings of SIGLEX99: Standardizing lexical resources*, edited by M. Palmer, pp. 52–61. ACL '99 Workshop: College Park, Md.

Jackendoff, Ray. 1983. *Semantics and cognition.* Cambridge, Mass.: MIT Press.

Kilgarriff, Adam, and Martha Palmer. 2000. Introduction to the special issue on SENSEVAL. *Computers and the Humanities* 34.1–2.

Lee, Lillian. 1997. *Similarity-based approaches to natural language processing.* Cambridge, Mass: Harvard University dissertation. Published, Harvard University Technical Report TR-11-97.

Lesk, M. E. 1986. Automatic sense disambiguation using machine readable dictionaries: How to tell a pine cone from an ice cream cone. In *Proceedings of the 1986 SIGDOC Conference, Toronto, Ontario, June 1986,* pp. 24–26. New York: Association for Computing Machinery.

Levin, Beth, and Malka Rappaport-Hovav. 1995. *Unaccusativity: At the syntax-lexical semantics interface.* Cambridge, Mass.: MIT Press.

Light, Marc, ed. 1997. Tagging text with lexical semantics: Why, what, and how? In *ACL/SIGLEX Workshop, Washington, D.C., April 4–5, 1997.*

Mitchell, Tom. 1997. *Machine learning.* New York: McGraw-Hill.

Quillian, M. Ross. 1968. Semantic memory. In *Semantic information processing,* edited by Marvin Minsky, pp. 216–270. Cambridge, Mass.: MIT Press.

Pedersen, T., and R. Bruce. 1997. Distinguishing word senses in untagged text. In *Proceedings of the Second Conference on Empirical Methods in Natural Language Processing, Providence, R.I., August 1997,* pp. 197–207.

Pustejovsky, James. 1996. *The generative lexicon.* Cambridge, Mass.: MIT Press.

Resnik, Philip, and David Yarowsky. 1999. Distinguishing systems and distinguishing senses: New evaluation methods for word sense disambiguation. *Natural Language Engineering* 5.113–133.

Richardson, R., and A. Smeaton. 1995. Using WordNet in a knowledge-based approach to information retrieval. In *Proceedings of the 17th BCS-IRSG Colloquium, Crewe.*

Rosch, Eleanor; Carolyn Mervis; Wayne Gray; David Johnson; and Penny Boyes-Braem. 1976. Basic objects in natural categories. *Cognitive Psychology* 8.387–439.

Schuetze, Hinrich. 1997. *Ambiguity resolution in language learning.* Chicago: University of Chicago Press.

Silberman, S. 2000. Talking to strangers. *Wired* 8.05, May 2000, p. 5. Available at http://www.wired.com/wired/archive/8.05/translation_pr.html.

Yarowsky, David. 1993. One sense per collocation. In *Proceedings of the ARPA Human Language Technology Workshop,* Princeton, N.J., 1993, pp. 266–271.

PHILIP RESNIK

Part of Speech Tagging and Phrasal Chunking

Syntactic analysis is an important precursor to many natural language applications, including text understanding, grammar checking, machine translation, and deep information retrieval. Full syntactic parsing provides valuable linguistic information for such applications, but creating a parser is a difficult, time-consuming task. Although there has been a great deal of recent progress in parser development, broad-coverage parsers are still typically slow and prone to errors. Part of speech taggers and phrasal chunkers both provide a useful subset of information found in a syntactic parse, with the advantage that fast and accurate programs can be built easily to perform both of these tasks.

1. Part of speech tagging is the task of assigning syntactic labels (such as noun, verb, adjective) to lexical items. It is usually assumed that a dictionary is available that lists the allowable tags for words. The two challenges in tagging are then (i) choosing between multiple allowable tags for a word, based on context (*The race/noun ended*, vs. *The boys race/verb*) and (ii) determining the part of speech of a word not in the dictionary. Manually constructed taggers date back to the 1960s, with one of the earliest described by Zellig Harris (Harris 1962). In Harris's system, each word was initially assigned all allowable parts of speech, and then rules applied that eliminated certain tags in certain contexts (for example, eliminating the "verb" tag as a possibility if the word appears after a determiner). These elimination rules were written by hand.

The creation of part-of-speech tagged corpora, such as the one-million-word Brown Corpus (Kucera and Francis 1967), led people to explore techniques for automatically training taggers from these corpora. Ken Church's 1988 demonstration of the efficacy of a simple model known as a Markov model for tagging served as a catalyst for a decade of intense research

FIGURE 1. *A Markov Model for Part of Speech Tagging*

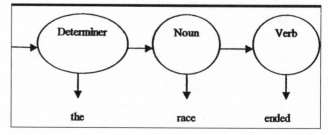

activity in this area. The simplest effective Markov model tagger is the bi-gram tagger. This can be conceptually viewed as a model of language production where text is generated by going to a particular part-of-speech state, then outputting a word from that state according to a probability distribution, then moving to a new part-of-speech state according to another probability distribution, and so forth. The goal of tagging is then to guess what state sequence was traversed given an observed word sequence. (See Figure 1.) Given a sufficiently large corpus of correctly tagged text (typically 10^5–10^6 words), such a part-of-speech tagger can achieve a rate of accuracy above 96% when trained and tested on similar material (e.g., training and testing on newspaper text), typically dropping 1–2% lower when training and testing on different material (e.g., training on newspaper text and testing on novels).

Subsequent to development of Markov model taggers, a large number of taggers have been developed based on a diverse set of machine learning techniques, for example transformation-based learning (Brill 1995) and maximum entropy models (Ratnaparkhi 1998). All of these techniques can be broken down into two components: the features and the algorithm used for learning. Remarkably, there is very little variety in the features used across the machine-learned taggers. The feature set used by virtually all taggers consists of the words and parts of speech of words in a very local neighborhood (typically +/− 2 or 3 words) to the word being tagged, roughly the same features used in Harris's early hand-constructed tagger. In addition to automatically trained taggers, very successful taggers have been built by hand using constraint-based grammars that describe those contexts in which different tags are not permitted to appear (Voutilainen 1995), which is similar in spirit to the tag deletion rules of Harris's system.

2. Phrasal chunking, also called *Partial Parsing*, is the task of finding the major non-overlapping phrases in a sentence and is closely related to the problem of named entity recognition. Phrasal chunking provides much of the non-hierarchical phrasal information found in full parses. Most recent work in this area has concentrated on noun phrase chunking, that is, finding all maximal noun phrases in a sentence. The approaches that have been applied to this problem have been heavily influenced by the success of part-of-speech taggers. In fact, most phrasal chunkers treat the problem as a slight variant of part-of-speech tagging. As in tagging, phrasal chunkers assign labels to words, but instead of labels such as Noun and Verb, phrasal chunkers assign labels that indicate whether a word is inside or outside of a phrase. One of the first systems that took this approach was created by L. Ramshaw and M. Marcus (Ramshaw and Marcus 1995). They trained a system to assign one of three labels to a word: I, O, or B. "I" means a word is inside a phrase, "O" means a word is outside, and "B" means a word is at the boundary of two contiguous phrases. For instance, for a noun phrase chunker, the sentence

[NP *The big elephant*] *gave* [NP *the monkey*] [NP *an orange*].

would be represented as:

The/I*big*/I*elephant*/I *gave*/O *the*/I *monkey*/I *an*/B *orange*/I.

This formulation is identical to the part-of-speech tagging problem, but with different labels. Indeed, Ramshaw and Marcus built their noun phrase chunker using part-of-speech tagging software. Phrasal chunkers usually apply after text has been part-of-speech tagged. The appropriate chunk label for a word is decided based on surrounding words, part of speech tags, and surrounding chunk labels.

As is the case for part of speech tagging, chunking has been a ripe domain for machine learning. The best noun phrase chunkers currently attain about 95% precision and recall (meaning 95% of the returned chunks are valid, and 95% of the chunks in the test set are found) when trained and tested on similar text.

While both part of speech taggers and phrasal chunkers are able to achieve high accuracy, they are still not perfect. Further gains in accuracy are likely once we learn how to effectively incorporate richer linguistic features into the learning algorithms.

[*See also* Parsing; Parts of Speech; Statistical Linguistics; Mathematical Linguistics; Learnability.]

BIBLIOGRAPHY

Brill, E. 1995. Transformation-based error-driven learning and natural language processing: A case study in part-of-speech tagging. *Computational Linguistics* 21.543–565.

Church, K. 1988. A stochastic parts program and noun phrase parser for unrestricted text. In *The Second Conference on Applied Natural Language Processing*, pp. 136–143.

Harris, Z. 1962. *String analysis of language structure.* The Hague: Mouton.

Kucera, H., and W. N. Francis. 1967. *Computational analysis of present-day American English*. Providence, R.I.: Brown University Press.

Ramshaw, L., and M. Marcus. 1995. Text chunking using transformation based learning. In *Proceedings of the Third Annual Workshop on Very Large Corpora*, pp. 82–94.

Ratnaparkhi, A. 1998. A maximum entropy model for part-of-speech tagging. In EMPNLP 1, pp. 133–142.

Voutilainen, A. 1995. A syntax-based part of speech analyzer. In EACL 8, pp. 157–164.

ERIC BRILL

Grammar Formalisms

The term *grammar formalisms* denotes artificial languages whose purpose is to characterize precisely other artificial or natural languages. They are used descriptively in linguistics for characterizing, and thereby under certain assumptions explaining the properties of fragments of particular natural languages. They are used normatively in computer science for characterizing, and thereby providing a reference standard for, computer languages, especially programming languages. Their application to N[atural] L[anguage] P[rocessing] combines aspects of both these uses; grammars for this latter purpose require descriptive accuracy, yet serve as a precise norm to which computers must adhere.

Formalisms for NLP can be evaluated according to the following criteria:

(a) *Linguistic felicity*: The degree to which descriptions can be directly (or indirectly) stated as linguists tend to state them.

(b) *Expressiveness*: Which class of analyses can be stated at all in the formalism.

(c) *Computational effectiveness*: Whether there exist computational devices for interpreting the grammars expressed in the formalism—and, if such devices do exist, what computational limitations inhere in them.

The trade-offs among these criteria typically preclude their coexisting optimally within any single formalism. For instance, as the expressiveness of the formalism grows, algorithms that are efficient enough for parsing may no longer exist. Alternatively, as a formalism becomes oriented toward the style of analysis of one particular linguistic theory, the class of expressible analyses may diminish. Furthermore, the use to which the formalism is to be put may argue for quite different weightings of these criteria. For instance, linguistic theories typically minimize expressiveness in the effort to explain learnability. NLP formalisms, by contrast, may maximize the expressiveness of formalisms as a means of gaining flexibility.

Grammar formalisms can characterize languages *procedurally*, by providing a method or algorithm for generating all of the strings of the language; or *declaratively*, by providing a direct description of the language elements. Further, a procedural description can be *synthetic*, in that the algorithm specifies how the strings of the language can be constructed; or *analytic*, if the algorithm specifies how the strings can be recognized.

Grammar formalisms also provide a structure upon which statistical models may be built. The structural elements that a formalism makes available may be associated with probabilities or other statistical parameters. For instance, hidden Markov models are essentially a probabilistic variant of finite state grammars and context-free grammars have a probabilistic variant as well. Such models are widely used in corpus processing and natural language processing applications, and the algorithms devised for efficiently computing probabilities associated with strings are typically direct analogs of corresponding algorithms for parsing sentences.

1. The rewriting hierarchy. Early research on formal language theory, motivated by problems in linguistics, led to the codification of a series of four language classes, each a strict subset of the previous one. Each member of the so-called *Chomsky hierarchy* of four language classes corresponds to a different grammatical formalism, in particular a rewriting system. A *rewriting system* is a grammar formalism that defines languages procedurally (in fact, synthetically) by giving rules for substituting one substring for another in a given string. Of particular interest is the formalism corresponding to Type 2 rewrite rules, the so-called C[ontext-] F[ree] G[rammar]s. The CFG formalism was developed as a codification of the type of immediate-constituent analysis found in structural linguistics; CFGs have served as components of later formalisms in linguistics (e.g. the base component of a transformational grammar) and NLP. The languages defined by these grammars are specified procedurally as the output of a string-generating algorithm. However, the more restrictive (non-type-0) classes have an alternative declarative interpretation under which the rules are viewed as admissibility conditions for sets of nodes in parse trees. This distinction in the interpretation method for grammars can have mathematical ramifications—Peters and Ritchie 1973 demonstrated that Type 1 grammars under the admissibility interpretation can express only Type 2 languages—and therefore highlights the importance of distinguishing procedural and declarative formalisms.

The four formalisms characterizing the Chomsky hierarchy do not exhaust the possibilities for formalism expressiveness. For instance, the formalism of tree-adjoining grammars, which is based on the rewriting of tree structures rather than strings, falls between Type 1 and Type 2 systems in expressiveness.

Greibach 1981 provides a detailed history of the origins of formal language theory, including the development of the rewriting hierarchy and Categorial Grammars, and their relationship to mathematical and computational linguistics.

2. Grammar formalisms in linguistic theory. After the pioneering work on the rewriting hierarchy and its relation to classes of automata, the design of grammatical formalisms diverged in the fields of computer science and linguistics—and, within computer science, between those engaged in the study of formal language theory and those interested in NLP. Nonetheless, many NLP researchers have attempted to use formalisms from linguistic theory directly for the purpose of automatic processing of natural language.

Chomsky's immediate use of his results from formal language theory was to motivate the necessity for the more powerful formalism implicit in standard theory transformational grammar, which augments a context-free or context-sensitive string-rewriting component with tree-rewriting rules of a certain sort, called *transformations*. Many NLP projects have attempted to make use of transformational grammars (e.g. Zwicky et al. 1965), in spite of the discovered difficulty of "reversing transformations" (see Petrick 1971 and references therein). The theories of G[eneralized] P[hrase-] S[tructure] G[rammar], L[exical-]F[unctional] G[rammar], and H[ead-Driven] P[hrase-]S[tructure] G[rammar] incorporate grammar formalisms without transformations; they have also been used for NLP tasks.

Not all linguistic theories incorporate a grammar formalism. Relational Grammar and Government and Binding Theory are examples of theories which make both language-particular and language-universal statements in a natural as opposed to artificial metalanguage.

3. Grammar formalisms in NLP. In parallel with the development of grammar formalisms in linguistic theory, several formalisms have been designed specifically for the task of NLP. In the 1950s, Yngve 1958 developed the COMIT programming language as a powerful procedural analytic system for linguists to use in describing natural-language structure to a computer. The language was the precursor of string-processing computer languages such as SNOBOL, whose use went well beyond NLP tasks.

The A[ugmented] T[ransition] N[etwork] formalism is a procedural analytic formalism based on the augmentation of pushdown automata (the automaton equivalent of CFGs) with a procedural language for assigning values to registers.

This theme of augmenting CFGs with registers or features that can take on values permeates the computer-science work on grammar formalisms, both for NLP and for computer-language specification—as well as linguistic formalisms such as GPSG, LFG, and HPSG. Other procedural NLP formalisms participating in this theme include the Dialogic formalism (Robinson 1982) used to build the large Diagram grammar of English; the Linguistic String Project system (Sager 1981); Wilensky's phrasal grammar (Wilensky and Arens 1980); and the Lingol formalism (Pratt 1973). (In this last case, however, the augmentations are restricted to being used for preferences among rules, and for syntax-directed translation into a semantic representation.) Thus the Dialogic formalism allows context-free rules to be augmented with *constructors* that encode, in an extension of the LISP programming language, constraints on features associated with the constituents. Sentence formation rule no. 1 found in the ATN in the Parsing entry, augmented with person and number agreement, might be roughly recast in Dialogic as follows:

```
(1)    (S1 S = NP VP;
           CONSTRUCTOR
           (PROGN
             (OR (AGREE NBR NP VP)
                 (F.REJECT 'F.NUMAGR))
             (OR (AGREE PER NP VP)
                 (F.REJECT 'F.PERAGR))
             (OR (@ VP TENSED)
                 (F.REJECT 'F.UNTENSEDS))
             (@SET TYPE 'DECLARATIVE)))
```

Another important strain of NLP research concerns the development of highly procedurally oriented formalisms that are intended specifically to allow the stating of performance, rather than competence, models of a language. Marcus's PIDGIN formalism (1980) is primary among these efforts. Grammars in the formalism are comprised of instructions as to what actions (such as node creation or attachment) to perform on particular data structures for parsing in particular situations. Marcus used the formalism to define a grammar which models, among other phenomena, the psycholinguistic phenomenon of garden-path sentences.

The move toward context-free-based formalisms augmented with nonterminals, structured as sets of features and values, led in the mid-1980s to the development of a set of *declarative* (as opposed to the previously discussed procedural) formalisms: the so-called *complex-feature-based* or *unification-based* formalisms. These include the linguistic formalisms used in GPSG, LFG, and HPSG, as well as the NLP formalisms Functional Unification Grammar and PATR-II. These formalisms rely on structured information associated with phrases (as in categorial grammars), as opposed to unstructured symbols (as in CFGs). This set of structures can be thought of as the union of a primitive set of *atomic structures* with the set of finite *functions* whose domain is a set of features and whose range is the set of structures itself. These structures—called variously *f-structures* (in LFG), *feature bundles, feature matrices*, or *categories* (in GPSG), *attribute-value matrices* (in HPSG), or *feature structures*—can be modeled mathematically in various ways: as finite functions, as graph structures of a certain sort, or as finite automata. Typically, formalisms use these structures by allowing grammars to specify constraints on the structures, e.g. as equations. The PATR-II formalism, perhaps the simplest of the class, allows rules to be augmented with equational constraints. For instance, a rule for sentence formation with an added constraint of agreement of subject and predicate could be stated as:

(2)   S → NP VP
⟨NP agreement⟩ = ⟨VP agreement⟩
⟨VP tensed⟩ = yes
⟨S type⟩ = declarative

Closely related to the unification-based grammar formalisms are the *logic grammar* formalisms such as D[efinite-]C[lause] G[rammars] (Pereira and Warren 1980), Extraposition Grammars, Slot Grammars, and Gapping Grammars. In these, the structured nonterminals are typically first-order terms, and the effect of equational constraints is achieved by the sharing of variables. For example, a DCG rule for sentence formation might be:

(3)   s(Agr, decl) → np(Agr), vp(Agr, yes).

Here the sentence-term arguments correspond to agreement and type, respectively; the NP argument to agreement alone; and the VP arguments to agreement and tensedness. Shieber 1986 gives references for unification-based and logic-grammar formalisms.

4. Comparing formalisms. In addition to true expressive differences among grammatical formalisms, notational differences are important: they determine the ease of use of the formalism, and may push one toward certain styles of analysis. However, the import of such notational distinctions should not overwhelm that of the analyses. One way to understand the relationships among notationally distinct formalisms is to map from one notation to another. A mapping is revealing, however, only if it preserves some important aspect of the grammars—ideally, their interpretation. To rigorously demonstrate such semantic invariance, the input and output formalisms must have explicit semantics defining the interpretations of grammars. This area of research is only beginning to receive attention. Nonetheless, at least informal work on notational reduction has begun. As a greater understanding of the relationships among grammar formalisms is achieved, it will be possible to place them in their rightful role as ancillary devices, secondary to the linguistic analyses that they are used to encode.

[*See also* Categorial Grammar; Generalized Phrase Structure Grammar; Learnability, *article on* Mathematical Aspects; Lexical-Functional Grammar; Parsing; Phrase Structure; Formal Grammar; Mathematical Linguistics; *and* Transformations.]

BIBLIOGRAPHY

Greibach, Sheila A. 1981. Formal languages: Origins and directions. *Annals of the History of Computing* 3.14–41.

Marcus, Mitchell P. 1980. *A theory of syntactic recognition for natural language.* Cambridge, Mass.: MIT Press.

Pereira, Fernando C. N., and David H. D. Warren. 1980. Definite-clause grammars for natural language analysis: A survey of the formalism and a comparison with augmented transition networks. *Artificial Intelligence* 13:3.231–278.

Peters, P. Stanley, and Robert W. Ritchie. 1973. On the generative power of transformational grammars. *Information Sciences* 6.40–83.

Petrick, Stanley R. 1971. Transformational analysis. In *Natural language processing,* edited by Randall Rustin, pp. 27–42. New York: Algorithmics Press.

Pratt, Vaughan R. 1973. A linguistics oriented programming language. In *Proceedings of the Third International Conference on Artificial Intelligence,* Stanford, Calif., pp. 372–381.

Robinson, Jane J. 1982. DIAGRAM: A grammar for dialogues.

Communications of the Association for Computing Machinery 25.27–47.

Sager, Naomi. 1981. *Natural language information processing: A computer grammar of English and its applications.* Reading, Mass.: Addison-Wesley.

Shieber, Stuart M. 1986. *An introduction to unification-based approaches to grammar.* (CSLI lecture note series, 4.) Stanford, Calif.: Center for the Study of Language and Information.

Wilensky, Robert, and Yigal Arens. 1980. *PHRAN: A knowledge-based approach to natural language analysis.* (Electronics Research Laboratory, Memorandum No. UCB/ERL M80/34.) Berkeley: University of California.

Yngve, Victor H. 1958. A programming language for mechanical translation. *Mechanical Translation* 5:1.25–41.

Zwicky, Arnold M., et al. 1965. The Mitre syntactic analysis procedure for transformational grammars. In *American Federation of Information Processing Societies Conference Proceedings* (1965 Fall Joint Computer Conference), 27:1.317–326. New York: Spartan Books.

Stuart M. Shieber

Pragmatics and Discourse

To design computer systems capable of engaging in extended dialogs with their users or processing complex texts, it is necessary to understand the influence of contextual information on the interpretation and production of multi-sentence, multi-speaker discourses. "Contextual" information is information that is not contained in a single sentence but instead depends on the circumstances in which it occurs: the topic of the text or conversation, the task being accomplished, the previous discourse, and so on. Some key issues that must be resolved by application of such information are:

(a) Reference of noun phrases: For example, *John can open Bill's safe.* **He knows the combination**.

(b) Word senses: *John withdrew cash from the* **bank.**

(c) Syntactic ambiguity: *John saw* **the man on the hill with a telescope**.

(d) Compound nominals: *Horse shoes* are shoes for horses, but *alligator shoes* are shoes made of alligator skin.

(e) Metonymy: *He read all of* **Shakespeare** *over the summer.*

(f) Ellipsis: *The next flight to Boston?*

(g) Quantifier scoping: *There is a chair in every corner of the room* (meaning 'one chair per corner').

(h) Interclause relation: Compare *Open the door. I don't have a key* with *Open the door. The key is on the table.*

(i) Speaker attitude: *It's cold here* looks like an assertion but may be used as a request.

These problems have been addressed mainly through the application of a combination of constraints on the structure of the domain and on the discourse itself. The first constraints are between predicates and their arguments. In its simplest form, the *new selectional restrictions* technique partitions the domain of discourse into a number of sorts of basic objects, assigns nouns to one or more sorts, and restricts the arguments of adjectives and verbs to certain sorts.

The entities mentioned in a discourse and their salience also constrain interpretation of subsequent referring expressions. The simplest method of representing salience is as a list, called a *history list*, of all entities (objects, classes, types, events, etc.) mentioned in a text, often in order of recency of appearance. Various refinements of the structure of history lists have been proposed, based on features of sentences (topicalization, subject/object position, and structure of the discourse, sometimes marked by phrases such as *Now* and *In any case*) (see Sidner 1983 and Walker et al. 1998). Inspired by Montague semantics, *Discourse Representation Theory* attempts to extend single-sentence semantic theory to deal with multi-sentence and contextual phenomena, such as interclause anaphora, tense, and aspect (Kamp and Reyle 1993).

The third kind of constraint is provided by the possible (or probable) sequences of events in the domain being discussed (in the case of a narrative) or in the task in which the participants are engaged (in the case of a dialog). *Scripts* are encodings of stereotypical relations between events. If we have a script about restaurants that describes a normal episode there as consisting of entering the restaurant, being seated, ordering from the waiter, paying him, and leaving, we can then infer from a text such as *Bill went to a restaurant. He ordered a hamburger, which was brought to him cold* that the unmentioned waiter was the recipient of the order and the implicit subject of the bringing. Matching events in a text with events in some script allows inferring, by default, information not explicitly mentioned.

Initially, scripts were limited to linear sequences of actions, but more structured versions were later developed by borrowing from artificial intelligence (AI) theory the notion of a *plan*, or hierarchical decomposition of actions into subactions. The plan of a task being performed jointly by two participants has been used to structure the set of salient entities in the dialog they conduct during the task. Grosz 1978 contains an example of a naturally occurring dialog showing that an occurrence of the word *it* at the end of a 30-minute dialog is easily recognized as referring to an object that was mentioned once very early, even though several entities mentioned more recently satisfy all the required selectional constraints. The natural breakdown of the task into subtasks allowed some entities mentioned early still to be salient at the end.

It is tempting to try to extend the notion of task structure to dialog structure. Script- and plan-based models for dialogs have been proposed, generally relying on classifying sentences in dialogs as "actions" or "moves," such as questions, answers, challenges, or evidence. However, it is not possible to do this classification on the basis of form alone, given the frequency of nonliteral, indirect, ironic, and insincere uses. The relation between the form of an utterance, the kinds of actions it can be used to perform, and the consequences of these actions for the participants is the central problem of *speech act theory*.

Much of the early development of this area is owed to ordinary-language philosophers, in particular to John Searle, influenced by J. L. Austin and H. P. Grice. Though fertile in intuitions, this work is largely descriptive and informal. Its major focus is the identification of necessary and sufficient conditions for the performance of the central class of speech acts, the *illocutionary acts*, such as asserting, requesting, and promising. However, the proposed definitions are both too simple and too complicated, in part because of a lack of grounding in precise theories of action, mental state, and observation. The main contribution of researchers in AI and computational linguistics has been to begin the development of such theories, along with algorithms for reasoning about these concepts to both interpret and generate utterances. (For references, see Cohen et al. 1990.)

Logics beyond the well-known predicate logics and their associated reasoning methods have found increasing application to problems in pragmatics. *Modal logics* are used in theories of belief, knowledge, and intention, and in theories of action (e.g. Moore 1985). *Abductive reasoning*, which allows the inference of $p(a)$ from $q(a)$ and $\forall x.p(x) \rightarrow q(x)$ is the basis for several accounts of interpretation in context, which view it as the problem of providing the "best possible explanation" for the utterance—that is, the change in the common information of the conversational participants that is maximally informative but makes the fewest assumptions (Hobbs et al. 1993). *Nonmonotonic reasoning*, in which the addition of new information may invalidate previous conclusions, plays an important role in theories of action, plan recognition, knowledge and belief, speech acts, and presuppositions (Ginsberg 1987).

[*See also* Pragmatics and Contextual Semantics; Semantics; Information Structure; *and* Discourse.]

BIBLIOGRAPHY

Allen, James F. 1995. *Natural language processing*. 2d ed. Menlo Park, Calif.: Benjamin/Cummings.

Brady, Michael, and Robert Berwick, eds. 1983. *Computational models of discourse*. Cambridge, Mass.: MIT Press.

Cohen, Philip R., Jerry Morgan, and Martha E. Pollack, eds. 1990. *Intentions incommunication*. Cambridge, Mass.: MIT Press.

Ginsberg, Matthew L., ed. 1987. *Readings in nonmonotonic reasoning*. Los Altos, Calif.: Morgan Kaufmann.

Grosz, Barbara J. 1978. Discourse analysis. In Walker 1978, pp. 235–268.

Grosz, Barbara. J., Karen Spärck Jones, and Bonnie L. Webber, eds. 1986. *Readings in natural language processing*. Los Altos, Calif.: Morgan Kaufmann.

Hobbs, Jerry R., and Robert C. Moore, eds. 1985. *Formal theories of the commonsense world*. Norwood, N.J.: Ablex.

Hobbs, Jerry R., Mark E. Stickel, Douglas E. Appelt, and Paul Martin. 1993. Interpretation as abduction. *Artificial Intelligence* 63:1–2.69–142.

Joshi, Aravind, Bonnie L. Webber, and Ivan Sag, eds. 1981. *Elements of discourse understanding*. Cambridge: Cambridge University Press.

Kamp, Hans, and Uve Reyle. 1993. *From discourse to logic: Introduction to model-theoretic semantics of natural language, formal logic and discourse representation theory*. Dordrecht: Kluwer.

Lehnert, Wendy G., and Martin H. Ringle, eds. 1982. *Strategies for natural language processing*. Hillsdale, N.J.: Lawrence Erlbaum.

Moore, Robert, C. 1985. A formal theory of knowledge and action. In Hobbs and Moore 1985, pp. 319–358.

Sidner, Candace. 1983. Focusing in the comprehension of definite anaphora. In Brady and Berwick 1983, pp. 267–230.

Walker, Donald E., ed. 1978. *Understanding spoken language*. New York: North Holland.

Walker, Marilyn A., Aravind K. Joshi, and Ellen F. Prince, eds. 1998. *Centering theory in discourse*. New York: Oxford University Press.

C. RAYMOND PERRAULT

Semantics and Knowledge Representation

In a N[atural] L[anguage] P[rocessing] context, the terms "semantics" and "semantic interpretation" usually refer to methods of representing the meanings of natural language expressions and of computing such meaning representations. This brand of "syntactic semantics" is distinct from the notion of denotational semantics as understood in formal logic. (This is not to say that the latter notion is irrelevant; see below.)

Semantic interpretation in many NLP systems can be viewed as involving three interleaved phases: determination of a preliminary, underspecified semantic representation of the input; disambiguation of this representation; and inference of implicit or "missing" information, notably connections between causes and effects, between means and ends (goals), and between parts and wholes (things, episodes, plans). Other kinds of implicit information that need to be extracted for genuine discourse understanding are implicatures, presuppositions, and inferences about the speaker's or author's knowledge, goals, and plans, and about the structure of the discourse and context.

In *syntax-directed* (or syntax-driven) systems, the preliminary representation is derived from a syntactic analysis of the input, using rules that relate components of the syntactic analysis to components of the meaning representation. In *semantically directed* systems, text is mapped directly into parts of meaning representations, often using *meaning templates* associated with particular words, and procedures that seek fillers for the parts of those templates.

Disambiguation includes choosing among alternative preliminary representations (corresponding to alternative syntactic analyses), selecting word senses, scoping quantifiers, resolving anaphora, and choosing among alternative ways of filling in implicit connections.

The recognition that inference of implicit connections plays a central role in language understanding is one of the main insights that has emerged from NLP research. Understanding is thought to be achieved by processes that match input information against stored knowledge (axioms, rules, plans, "frames," "scripts," etc.; see below), allowing the new information to be elaborated and linked with previously given or derived information. It remains unclear what general principles guide these processes; one suggestion is that the overall goal is to find the "least costly" (or most probable) explanation of what has been said (or why it was said) (see Hobbs et al. 1993).

Experience in NLP indicates that the requisite body of of knowledge—about word meanings, about discourse conventions, and most of all, about the "world" (the domain of discourse)—is very large for non-trivial domains.

Besides the distinction between syntax-directed and semantically directed systems, another major distinction among interpretive strategies concerns the way in which they treat semantic coherency constraints such as selectional restrictions. They may be treated as axiomatic knowledge, as constraints on syntax-semantics mapping, or as constraints on syntactic form (as in so-called semantic grammars). A good general source of information on semantic interpretation is Allen 1995, parts 2 and 3.

1. The form of semantic representation. The sketch of the semantic interpretation process above leaves open the question of what form the semantic representation of an input, and the knowledge needed to compute it, should take. Semantic representation and knowledge representation have generally been assumed to require a well-defined symbolism, along with a theory of how this symbolism can express information about a domain of discourse. However, a general distinction is made between *declarative* representations and *procedural* ones. Declarative representations are thought of as encoding propositions (facts, beliefs, etc.), while procedural representations encode potential behaviors (methods, skills, techniques, etc.). Most frameworks for knowledge representation allow for both types of representation, though they may bias implementation choices one way or the other.

In discussions of declarative representations, two major controversies surface repeatedly. One is whether such a representation should admit a Tarski-style denotational semantics and theory of truth. "Logicists" insist that it should, if it is to be comprehensible and if it is to support theories of sound inference. Their opponents question the feasibility and usefulness of the logicist enterprise and seek to justify representational choices either in terms of procedural efficacy or in terms of cognitive and linguistic consideration (see Jackendoff 1990 for the latter perspective).

The other controversial issue is whether word meanings should be decomposed into "primitive" elements in the process of mapping natural language input into an internal representation. It is argued that decomposition is required in order to capture shared inferences, such as that both eating and drinking result in a transfer of material to the inside of the agent (as may be inferred from decompositions based on an INGEST primitive). A counter-argument is that such generalizations can just as well be captured by axioms relating specific predicates (such as EAT and DRINK) to more general ones (such as INGEST). This avoids the problematic assumption that word meanings are definable in terms of a relatively small number of primitives.

2. Common types of representation. Perhaps the simplest declarative representations are those based on sets of *attribute-value* pairs attached to objects (words, things, facts, events). Several early question-answering systems used this type of representation, and many of the more advanced types of declarative representation can be viewed as elaborations of attribute-value representations.

Relational databases, from the present perspective, are essentially large-scale attribute-value tables. They have been the focus of much activity in NLP because of the attractiveness of natural-language access to information in existing databases, and the relative ease of interpreting and answering questions confined to database contents. Moreover, the importation of AI techniques into database systems, and vice versa, has led to a convergence toward a common "knowledge base" area (see, e.g., articles in von Luck and Marburger 1994).

Logical representations, whose origins lie in the traditions of philosophical and mathematical logic, were proposed early, both as semantic representations and as representations for common-sense knowledge, including knowledge about actions, abilities, goals, and causes. Early work on NLP tended to view the mapping from the syntactic form of sentences to their underlying logical form as rather haphazard and complex. Several later developments shed new light on this mapping and facilitated computational realizations. Montague Grammar illuminated intensional locutions (such as *seeks a unicorn*) and showed how to derive logical forms from syntactic forms compositionally, in node-by-node fashion. The combination of Montague's ideas with new grammatical frameworks such as Generalized Phrase Structure Grammar, Head-Driven Phrase Structure Grammar, and Categorial Grammar proved particularly fruitful for computational linguists. Situation Semantics has clarified the relation between sentences and the situations they describe, along the way providing an account of how logically equivalent sentences can differ in meaning; various versions of its metalanguage for specifying and relating situations have been developed into meaning representations for use in NLP work. Discourse Repre-

sentation Theory (DRT) tackles other longstanding problems, including that of providing a formal account of anaphoric dependencies in multi-sentence texts, and more generally that of explicating the way in which utterances depend on and add to the meaning of the prior discourse. DRT has also given rise to many implementations. There is also a clear trend toward amalgamation of ideas from various approaches to representation, including those just mentioned, into more comprehensive frameworks and computational systems. Logic programming has also facilitated the syntax-semantics transduction by allowing all types of knowledge needed for interpretation—about syntax, semantics, pragmatics, and the world—to be logically encoded.

Like logical representations, *procedural representations* have some philosophical precedent, particularly in logical positivism and Ludwig Wittgenstein's view of language as a communicative game. Semantic interpretation of an input, on the procedural view, involves construction of an executable command, such as an information storage or retrieval request. Many database-oriented systems have interpreted inputs in this way, including LUNAR (Woods 1977) and its many descendants. LUNAR also encodes grammatical knowledge procedurally; the "blocks world" program SHRDLU (Winograd 1972) took the further step of proceduralizing world knowledge. Thus, the fact that all (toy) blocks are manipulable was recast imperatively as "If you wish to show that x is manipulable, try showing that x is a block," or alternatively as "Upon learning that x is a block, conclude that x is manipulable." A more recent development is the attempt to use schematic descriptions of sensory-motor processes not only as a means of specifying an agent's behavior but also as a basis for interpreting language (Narayanan 1997).

Semantic nets originated in psychologically oriented studies of language understanding but have also found application in many practically oriented projects (e.g., Lehmann 1992). They are characterized by (i) a graph-theoretic propositional syntax closely related to logical syntax (though perhaps motivated by cognitive or linguistic hypotheses); (ii) a *property structure* organization that makes propositions about a thing directly accessible from a token for that thing; and (iii) processes such as *spreading activation* from referenced nodes (as a basis for semantic disambiguation) and *property inheritance* in generalization hierarchies. It should be mentioned that some form of (ii) and (iii) is found in most natural language understanding systems; furthermore, whether or not a computerized propositional representation is seen as graph-theoretic is to some extent in the eye of the beholder.

Frames are structures encoding knowledge about stereotyped kinds of objects or situations, with special provision for the "roles" played by their parts or participants (Minsky 1975). Frames used in semantic representation are often termed *case frames*, reflecting the influence of theories of *case relations*. When used in conjunction with semantically directed interpreters (as is common), case frames are instantiated by procedures that seek semantically appropriate fillers for the case roles. Frames are also in common use for world knowledge representation, especially for specifying hierarchies of concepts and their roles, with semantic-net-like property inheritance. As such, their usefulness lies in the systematic way in which they encode general expectations about the attributes possessed by concepts, including the default values of those attributes. Closely related to frames, in this respect, are *scripts* and *plans,* structures that provide general expectations about how familiar kinds of events typically unfold and how familiar kinds of goals are typically pursued (Schank and Abelson 1977).

Finally, specialized representations for taxonomic, spatial, temporal, numeric, and other pervasive types of relationships appear to be indispensable for building NLP systems with human-like inferential capabilities. Such representations can be viewed as analogs, in certain crucial respects, of the relations they model. The practical advantages of such representations have long been recognized, and there appears to be evidence for their psychological plausibility as well (e.g. Johnson-Laird 1983).

3. Research issues. Most of the topics touched on here remain under intensive investigation in 2002. As far as methodological issues are concerned—and these include the viability of logicism, of decompositional approaches to word meaning, and of various declarative and procedural formalisms—no resolution or consensus can be expected on any theoretical grounds. Experience with more powerful NLP systems will be the final arbiter.

In the meantime, all proposals for semantic representation still confront many specific difficulties, such as the representation of tense and aspect, adjectival and adverbial modification, nominalization, generic sentences, propositional attitudes, counterfactual conditionals, comparatives, and generalized quantifiers. Consequently,

rules for obtaining preliminary semantic representations of natural texts can be given only for very restricted subsets of natural languages. As a result, much practically oriented research has focused on the development of techniques for extracting very specific information items from text corpora by pattern-matching techniques that do not depend on deriving a full semantic representation, or on making inferences. Similarly, many aspects of the disambiguation process remain obscure, though statistical approaches to this problem have made significant headway in recent years on both structural and word-sense disambiguation. The inference of implicit causal connections, plans, goals, reasons, and so on remains a refractory problem.

The number of semantic and factual details underlying interpretation and understanding is so huge that much current research looks toward *learning,* often based on scanning large computerized corpora of annotated or unannotated texts, as a way of bootstrapping NLP systems toward levels of increased competence.

[*See also* Pragmatics and Contextual Semantics; Cognitive Science; Sociolinguistics; Scripts, Frames, and Schemas; *and* Semantics.]

BIBLIOGRAPHY

Allen, James. 1995. *Natural language understanding.* Redwood City, Calif.: Benjamin/Cummings.

Dalrymple, Mary, John Lamping, Fernando C. N. Pereira, and Vijay Saraswat. 1995. Linear logic for meaning assembly. Workshop on Computational Logic for Natural Language Processing (CLNLP-95), Apr. 3–5, Edinburgh.

Hobbs, Jerry R., Mark E. Stickel, Douglas E. Appelt, and Paul Martin. 1993. Interpretation as abduction. *Artificial Intelligence* 63.69–142.

Jackendoff, Ray. 1990. *Language and cognition.* Cambridge, Mass.: MIT Press.

Johnson-Laird, Phillip N. 1983. *Mental models.* Cambridge, Mass.: Harvard University Press.

Lehmann, Fritz, ed. 1992. *Semantic networks in artificial intelligence.* Oxford: Pergamon Press.

Minsky, Marvin. 1975. A framework for representing knowledge. In *The psychology of computer vision,* edited by Patrick H. Winston, pp. 211–280. New York: McGraw-Hill.

Narayanan, Srinivasan. 1997. *Knowledge-based Action Representation for Metaphor and Aspect (KARMA).* Berkeley: University of California dissertation.

Schank, Roger C., and Robert P. Abelson. 1977. *Scripts, plans, goals and understanding: An inquiry into human knowledge structures.* Hillsdale, N.J.: Lawrence Erlbaum.

von Luck, Kai, and Heinz Marburger, eds. 1994. Management and processing of complex data structures. In *Third Workshop on Information Systems and Artificial Intelligence,* Hamburg, Germany, February 28–March 2, Proceedings. (*Lecture Notes in Computer Science*, 777.) New York: Springer.

Winograd, Terry. 1972. *Understanding natural language.* New York: Academic Press.

Woods, William. 1977. Lunar rocks in English: Explorations in natural language question answering. In *Linguistic structures processing* (Fundamental studies in computer science, 5), edited by A. Zampolli, pp. 521–569. Amsterdam: North-Holland.

LENHART K. SCHUBERT

Applications of Language Technology

HAL, the computer in Stanley Kubrick's *2001: A Space Odyssey*, is in some respects the ultimate natural language application: a conversational computer, capable of interacting with human beings in the most human of ways. This kind of application has been a goal of computer science since the advent of computing (Turing 1950), but language, and therefore linguistics, is the key to this interaction. The conversational computer paradigm provides a way to articulate the properties and challenges of natural language applications and the ways those challenges are being addressed within the field of computational linguistics (Cole et al. 1996).

One notable property of language applications is that they involve not just language per se, but also *interactions* between linguistic knowledge and other forms of knowledge. At one end of the spectrum, *automatic speech recognition* (ASR) applications are relatively "pure" in their focus on language, having as their goal the accurate transcription of spoken utterances. The conversational computer must determine *what* was said, which in practice involves the training of probabilistic models using large samples of transcribed speech. This requires less linguistic knowledge and large computational power. In contrast, in dialogue-based applications (e.g., for assisting human users in performing tasks such as answering questions automatically), language-focused components must interact with general world knowledge, domain-and task-specific knowledge, and user-focused knowledge. The fully conversational computer must not only recognize the words but also interpret them syntactically, semantically, and pragmatically, and then reason about the utterance. Finally, it must generate appropriate responses in either text or synthesized speech.

A second variable in computational linguistic applications is the extent to which there is a human "in the loop." The process of information retrieval (IR), for example, can be viewed either as finding documents relevant to an individual query, or as part of a more general process of query formulation, retrieval, and refinement. Text retrieval systems provide a good test bed for language processing technologies because qualitative or quantitative aspects of language (e.g. morphology, syntax, semantics, and pragmatics) can be used in varying degrees, with ways for humans to supply feedback as part of the process. Similarly, applications in translation can be viewed purely as a problem of automatic machine translation (MT), or as a problem of helping the user in an interaction supporting machine-assisted human translation or human-assisted machine translation. For these computational linguistics applications, issues of world knowledge also interact with task and domain, as well as requiring user models.

A third crucial consideration in language applications is the question of how systems are evaluated. In optical character recognition (OCR), for example, success is determined by the rate at which characters or words are misrecognized, which can be measured against a "gold standard" that represents the objective truth for a particular test case. However, for many computational linguistics applications, such as machine translation or summarization, objective truth is more difficult to determine. For example, in evaluations of automatic summarization systems, human judgments differ about what is the desired standard, and so system accuracy must be compared with the inter-judge agreement rate for human judgments on the same task. This agreement rate is often used to estimate upper bounds on system performance, under the assumption that a machine could not be expected to perform better than a human. At the same time, low inter-judge agreement can be viewed as evidence that a task is poorly defined. The conversational computer may eventually be judged on the extent to which it seems to be human, but at present, language-technology components continue to be evaluated in terms of performance on specialized tasks. Thus, evaluation of larger applications continues to be difficult because the performance of individual components does not constitute full application evaluation.

The techniques used in applications involving computational linguistics have seen a shift since the field of computer science started dealing with language data in the 1940s. In the initial years, statistical models were predominant (Shannon and Weaver 1949). As the field evolved, particularly under the influence of generative syntactic theory and symbolic artificial intelligence developed in the 1960s and 1970s, many rule-based applications were built based on these theories. The goals of these applications were to push the limits of computational power at the time by building applications that would function accurately and thoroughly. However, the fact that these systems were often computationally inefficient led to the partial reintroduction of statistical techniques. Thus, in the 1970s and 1980s, the balance began to shift from the development of systems based primarily on manually constructed rules, often with domain-specific knowledge, to applications that brought in quantitative data and techniques.

Applications in the late 1980s that combined statistical and rule-based techniques first used large text corpora as knowledge sources. In the late 1980s and early 1990s, hybrid systems began to dominate (Klavans and Resnik 1996), leading to the development of commercially viable applications. Large corpora of standardized tools and resources, such as WordNet (Miller 1990), combined with common test beds, led to a rapid growth in the number of interchangeable tools. Soon the development of a wide range of new Internet-based technologies created a need for new language applications. For example, the inability of search engines to accurately locate information on the World Wide Web exposed many more people to the need for effective linguistic applications. Another example is the Global Positioning System, which can use speech recognition and text-to-speech, combined with dialog technology. Other opportunities include hand-held dictation and transcription devices useful in medicine or emergency situations. Growth in computational linguistic applications seems to occur with every new technology introduced.

[*See also* Machine Translation; Parsing; Speech Recognition; Statistical Linguistics; Corpus Processing; *and* Speech Synthesis.]

BIBLIOGRAPHY

Cole, R., J. Mariani, H. Uszkoreit, A. Zaenen, and Victor Zue, eds. 1996. *Survey of the state of the art in human language technology.* New York: Cambridge University Press.
Klavans, Judith, and Philip Resnik, eds. 1996. *The balancing act: Combining symbolic and statistical approaches to language.* Cambridge, Mass.: MIT Press.
Miller, George. 1990. WordNet: An on-line lexical database. *International Journal of Lexicography* 3.235–312.
Shannon, C. E., and W. Weaver. 1949. *The mathematical theory of communication.* Urbana: University of Illinois Press.
Turing, Alan. 1950. Computing machinery and intelligence. *Mind* 59.433–460.

Philip Resnik and Judith Klavans

COMPUTATIONAL MORPHOLOGY. This method creates and implements models of word formation, i.e. inflection, derivation, and compounding. Typical applications are systems for word-form recognition and generation. *Recognition* involves finding the underlying lexemes and grammatical forms of actual inflected (or compounded, or derived) word forms. *Word-form generation* goes in the opposite direction, producing desired grammatical forms of given lexemes.

A theoretical goal of computational morphology is linguistic—acquiring better and more explicit understanding of morphology. However, computational morphology is used in practical tasks, for example in processing and indexing large corpora of texts, spelling checking, and information retrieval. Computational morphology interfaces with syntactic analysis (and sentence generation) on one hand, and with speech recognition and synthesis on the other.

Some languages, e.g. English, have hardly any inflection. In practical N[atural] L[anguage] P[rocessing] systems, inflection is often ignored by listing all forms of words in the lexicon as such. Other languages (e.g. Greek, Sanskrit, Arabic, or Russian) have more extensive inflection, and the full listing approach is less feasible. In Finnish, for example, each noun has some two thousand distinct inflectional forms, and each verb more than twelve thousand, because of the several layers of endings: nominalization, comparison, number, case, possessive suffixes, and clitic particles. Regular word derivation and compounding increase these figures by several magnitudes.

1. Overview. Word-form recognition (or generation) consists of several tasks:

(a) Coping with phonological and morphophonological processes which cause variation in surface phonemes (or letters, in written language). This corresponds to the domain of phonology.

(b) Identification of underlying morphemes of stems and various affixes (prefixes, infixes, suffixes, or other inflectional or derivational elements).

(c) Description of possible morphotactic structures of word

FIGURE 1. *Framework for Computational Morphology*

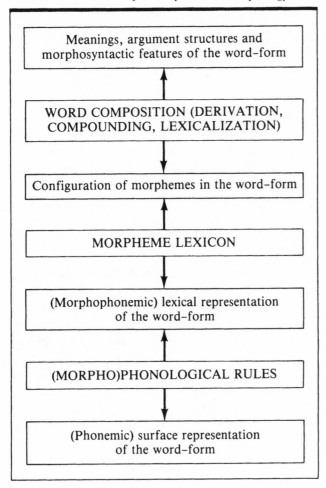

Meanings, argument structures and morphosyntactic features of the word-form

WORD COMPOSITION (DERIVATION, COMPOUNDING, LEXICALIZATION)

Configuration of morphemes in the word-form

MORPHEME LEXICON

(Morphophonemic) lexical representation of the word-form

(MORPHO)PHONOLOGICAL RULES

(Phonemic) surface representation of the word-form

FIGURE 2. *Finite-State Transducer*

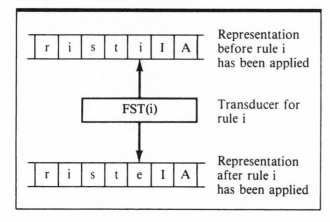

| r | i | s | t | i | I | A |

Representation before rule i has been applied

FST(i)

Transducer for rule i

| r | i | s | t | e | I | A |

Representation after rule i has been applied

forms—possible sequences and combinations of morphemes—i.e. how word roots, prefixes, suffixes, etc. may be combined to form full words.

(d)   Identifying morphosyntactic features and semantic de-

scriptions of full word forms from descriptions of component morphemes (e.g. roots and affixes).

(e)   Describing lexicalization, where certain configurations of morphemes have properties that cannot be deduced from the corresponding properties of the individual components.

Figure 1 sketches the domain of morphological analysis and generation by dividing it into four representations, and three modules relating them. Particular models may ignore some of these representations and merge the corresponding modules. The topmost module is often assigned to the syntactic component. Word-form recognition corresponds to the upward direction, while generation goes the opposite way.

2. Finite-state phonology. Phonological rules define the relation between the underlying form and the surface form of the word. Douglas Johnson noted in 1972 that phonological rules correspond closely to *finite-state transducers*. Ronald Kaplan and Martin Kay noted in 1981 (and published in 1994) that rules of generative phonology can be compiled into a *cascade* of transducers, where the output tape of one transducer is the input tape of the next (Figure 2). These transducers are bidirectional; i.e., they operate in the directions of both recognition and generation. Implementing cascaded transducers depends on the possibility of composing a chain of transducers into a single larger one. For languages with complex phonology, this composition is not practical because of the size of the result. Even then, the combination of the rules and the lexicon may be reasonable in size.

The two-level model of Koskenniemi 1983 differs from rewriting systems and from the cascaded design by describing the relation between lexical and surface forms directly, without any intermediate stages. All rules are thus parallel and independent of one another.

Two-level rules describe what kinds of alternations occur in the surface forms of morphemes as they occur in different contexts. Thus the Finnish nouns *koira* 'dog' and *risti* 'cross' have the plural inessive (*-I-ssA*) forms *koir+i+ssa* 'in dogs' and *riste+i+ssä* 'in crosses'. Stem alternations correspond roughly to rules $a: \emptyset \Leftrightarrow$ ___ *I*: and *i:e* $\Leftrightarrow$ ___ *I*: where, e.g., the latter reads as 'A lexical *i* corresponds to a surface *e* if and only if it is followed by a plural *I*.' The plural *I* itself corresponds usually to surface *i*; but if it is surrounded by vowels on the surface, it will correspond to *j*, i.e. *I:j* $\Leftrightarrow$:*Vowel* ___ :*Vowel*.

Two-level rules are logical statements defining acceptable correspondences between the two representations; they may be implemented in various ways. Methods for compiling two-level rules into finite-state transducers, which can be used in actual recognition and production programs, have been developed by Koskenniemi 1984 and by Karttunen et al. 1987.

Finite-state automata and transducers are extremely simple and rather well understood formal devices. Finite-state morphology often relies on non-deterministic processes which drive the automata; this entails a source of possible computational complexity. In principle, the formalisms alone do not exclude the possibility of exponentially complex processing. Natural languages, however, seem to have certain characteristics that exclude such behavior. (Most alternations are triggered by strictly local contexts; only a few alternations, i.e. from zero to two, depend on long-range contexts, e.g. vowel harmony.)

Not all alternations need be described in the rule component. For instance, complex endings in fusional languages like Latin may be treated as portmanteau morphs if there is no transparent way to segment them into further components.

3. Alternative models. Many word-form recognition systems have been developed with the idea of procedurally undoing phonological alternations while stripping endings from inflected forms. This often leads to unidirectional and language-specific models.

Even in many heavily inflected languages, there is no technical need to incorporate a phonological component in a recognition system. One may list possible allomorphs of each morpheme, and describe combinatory restrictions in some way. It is not clear whether any computational efficiency can be gained in this way.

Several language-specific systems have been developed for heuristic segmentation of inflectional endings on words in running text. Many programs also assign part-of-speech tags to words. Most models operate without a dictionary and are stochastic in nature.

Programs have also been developed for deducing word entries out of sorted word-frequency lists of large text corpora. The occurrence of a set of consistent inflectional forms in a list is used as a basis for proposing base forms, part-of-speech codes, and inflectional classes for underlying word entries.

4. Structure of the lexicon and structure of complex words. The lexicon is often considered to be a list of entries. In practical recognition systems, it usually has the form of a *letter tree* to permit fast incremental look-up.

The *morpheme lexicon* relates configurations of mor-phemes to lexical representations. The set of all feasible lexical representations is defined through it. Grammatically correct sequences of morphemes may be partly defined by the lexicon through its division into sublexicons of different classes of morphemes, and by markings of possible continuations to further sublexicons. In addition to this, or instead of it, the morphotactic structure may be controlled, e.g. by Context-Free or Categorial Unification-Based Grammar (see Shieber 1986).

Trees or sets of linked trees are special cases of *finite-state transition networks*. Word roots in Semitic languages usually consist of three consonants, and inflectional elements of vowels and consonants intercalate with the root elements. Such phenomena may be described as intersections of root and inflection lexicons, represented as transition networks. Kay 1987 has described the morphology of Arabic in the spirit of autosegmental phonology, using a four-tape transducer. An alternative, multitiered but closely related model has been proposed by Kiraz 2000. His model is especially suited for Semitic and other languages with complex morphology (see also Sproat 1992).

Attribute-value descriptions and unification, which are widely used in NLP grammar formalisms, seem to be suitable for defining feature structures of complex word-forms. In addition, such feature calculi may be used for defining which combinations of morphemes are grammatical and which are not, especially when the lexicon itself has no continuation facility according to morpheme classes (Russell et al. 1986).

[*See also* Computational Phonology; Computational Linguistics; Mathematical Linguistics; Morphology; *and* Natural Language Processing.]

BIBLIOGRAPHY

Kaplan, Ronald, and Martin Kay. 1994. Regular models of phonological rule systems. *Computational Linguistics* 20.331–378.

Karttunen, Lauri, Kimmo Koskenniemi, and Ronald Kaplan. 1987. A compiler for two-level phonological rules. In *Tools for morphological analysis* (Report no. CSLI-87–108, Center for the Study of Language and Information), edited by Mary Dalrymple et al. Stanford, Calif.: Stanford University.

Kay, Martin. 1987. Non-concatenative finite-state morphology. In *Third Conference of the European Chapter of the Association for Computational Linguistics: Proceedings*, pp. 2–10. Morristown, N.J.: Association for Computational Linguistics.

Kiraz, George. 2000. Multitiered non-linear morphology using multitape finite automata: A case study on Syriac and Arabic. *Computational Linguistics* 26.77–105.

Koskenniemi, Kimmo. 1983. *Two-level morphology: A general computational module for word-form recognition and production.* (Department of Linguistics, Publications, 11.) Helsinki: University of Helsinki.

Koskenniemi, Kimmo. 1984. A general computational model for word-form recognition and production. In *Tenth International Conference on Computational Linguistics: Proceedings of COLING 84,* pp. 178–181. Morristown, N.J.: Association for Computational Linguistics.

Russell, Graham J., et al. 1986. A dictionary and morphological analyser for English. In *Proceedings of COLING 86,* pp. 277–279. Morristown, N.J.: Association for Computational Linguistics.

Sproat, Richard. 1992. *Morphology and computation.* Cambridge, Mass.: MIT Press.

Shieber, Stuart M. 1986. *An introduction to unification-based approaches to grammar.* (CSLI lecture notes, 4.) Stanford, Calif.: Center for the Study of Language and Information.

KIMMO KOSKENNIEMI

COMPUTATIONAL PHONOLOGY. Phonology, as it is practiced, is deeply computational. Phonological analysis is data-intensive, and the resulting models are nothing other than specialized data structures and algorithms. In the past, phonological computation—managing data and developing analyses—was done manually with pencil and paper. Increasingly, with the proliferation of affordable computers, IPA fonts, and drawing software, phonologists are seeking to move their computation work online. Computational phonology provides the theoretical and technological framework for this migration, building on methodologies and tools from computational linguistics.

1. Documentation and description. Phonological data are essentially three types: *texts, wordlists,* and *paradigms.* A text is any phonetically transcribed narrative or conversation. A wordlist is any compilation of linguistic forms that can be uttered in isolation, with information about pronunciation and meaning. A paradigm is broadly construed to mean any tabulation of words or phrases that illustrates contrasts and systematic variation. Any of these data types may be *annotated* with more abstract information originating from a phonological theory, such as syllable boundaries, stress marks, and prosodic structure. Additionally, any of these data types may be associated with recordings of audio, video, or physiological signals. Digitizing this documentation and description brings all the different media types together, makes the cross-links navigable, and opens up many new possibilities for management, access, and preservation.

2. Exploration and analysis. The data types described above are closely interconnected in phonological practice. For instance, the discovery of a new word in a text may require an update to the lexicon and the construction of a new paradigm (e.g., to classify the word correctly). Fresh insights may lead to new annotations and further elicitation, closing the loop in this perpetual exploratory process. Phonological analysis typically involves defining a formal model, systematically testing it against data, and comparing it with other models. (In some cases, the model may be incorporated into a software system, e.g. for generating natural intonation in a text-to-speech system.) In this exploration and analysis—sorting, searching, tabulating, defining, testing, and comparing—the principal task is computational.

Perhaps the earliest work in computational phonology was Bobrow and Fraser's 1968 *Phonological rule tester,* an implementation of *The sound pattern of English* (*SPE*) (Chomsky and Halle 1968) designed to "alleviate the problem of rule evaluation." Shortly afterward, Johnson 1972 showed that, while *SPE* rules resemble general rewriting systems at the top of the Chomsky hierarchy, the way *SPE* rules are used in practice requires only finite-state power. Independently, Kaplan and Kay 1994 discovered the connections between *SPE* grammars and finite-state transducers in the 1970s and 1980s and laid down a complete algebraic foundation. Significant implementations followed, including Koskenniemi 1983 and Beesley and Karttunen 2002. Attempts to apply finite-state devices to Autosegmental Phonology have largely foundered, but applications to Optimality Theory are thriving.

While finite-state phonology fixated on *SPE,* Generative Phonology continued its rapid evolution. The discovery of rule "conspiracies" (Kisseberth 1970) and the abstractness controversy (Koutsoudas et al. 1974) led to calls for the reintroduction of *surface structure constraints.* Many theories arose from the fallout; most notable for its computational ramifications was Montague Phonology (Wheeler 1981). This model adapted new lexicalist formalisms from syntax and semantics, providing a *declarative* (as opposed to *procedural*) account of phonological well-formedness, and providing the first computational account of underspecification (in which the phonological content of a lexical entry is incompletely specified, to be filled in during derivation). From these beginnings, *Declarative Phonology* was born, and subsequent work provided a mathematical foundation in first-order logic (Bird 1995), as well as phonetic interpretation with links to Firthian prosodic analysis and speech synthesis (Coleman 1997); implementations generally are in the Prolog programming language.

A third major strand of development, complementing the finite-state and declarative models, is best characterized as statistical. It seeks to apply neural networks, information theory, and weighted automata in the automatic discovery of phonological information. Gasser 1992 trained a recurrent neural network to recognize syllables and to repair ill-formed syllables. Ellison 1992 showed how a technique from information theory called MDL—*minimum description length*—could be applied to identify syllable boundaries automatically in phonetically transcribed texts. Many researchers apply Markov models (a kind of weighted automata) in speech recognition, mapping speech recordings to phonetic transcriptions and thence to orthographic words, using large, phonetically annotated corpora as training data (e.g. TIMIT; Garofolo et al. 1986)).

Four key areas of ongoing research in computational phonology are in Optimality Theory, automatic learning, interfaces to grammar and phonetics, and supporting phonological description in the field. Comprehensive references to online research papers in this areas may be found on the SIGPHON website.

Computational phonology is generating sophisticated and rigorous ways of creating, exploring, and disseminating multidimensional phonological information, encompassing primary recordings, texts, wordlists, paradigms, theories, and analyses. As phonologists adopt the computational methods described above, extending and adapting them as needed, the consequences for the discipline will be increased accessibility, accountability, and stability of empirical research.

3. Resources. The Association for Computational Linguistics (ACL) has a special-interest group in computational phonology (SIGPHON) with a homepage at http://www.cogsci.ed.ac.uk/sigphon/. The website contains online proceedings for SIGPHON workshops and information about relevant books, dissertations, and articles. A special issue of *Computational Linguistics* devoted to computational phonology was published in 1994 (Bird 1994).

[*See also* Generative Phonology; Hidden Markov Models; Mathematical Linguistics; Speech Recognition; Computational Linguistics; *and* Computational Morphology.]

BIBLIOGRAPHY

Beesley, K. R., and L. Karttunen. 2002. *Finite-state morphology: Xerox tools and techniques.* Cambridge: Cambridge University Press.

Bird, S., ed. 1994. *Computational linguistics 20.3: special issue on computational phonology.*

Bird, S. 1995. *Computational phonology: A constraint-based approach.* Cambridge: Cambridge University Press.

Bobrow, D. G., and J. B. Fraser. 1968. A phonological rule tester. *Communications of the ACM* 11.766–772.

Chomsky, Noam, and Morris Halle. 1968. *The Sound pattern of English.* New York: Harper and Row.

Coleman, J. S. 1997. *Phonological representations—their names, forms and powers.* Cambridge University Press.

Ellison, T. M. 1992. *Machine learning of phonological structure.* Crawley: University of Western Australia dissertation.

Garofolo, J. S., L. F. Lamel, W. M. Fisher, J. G. Fiscus, D. S. Pallett, and N. L. Dahlgren. 1986. *The DARPA TIMIT Acoustic-Phonetic continuous speech corpus CDROM.*NIST. http://www.ldc.upenn.edu/Catalog/LDC93S1.html.

Gasser, M. 1992. Learning distributed representations for syllables. In *Proceedings of the Fourteenth Annual Conference of the Cognitive Science Society*, pp. 396–401. Hillsdale N.J.: Lawrence Erlbaum Associates.

Johnson, C. D. 1972. *Formal aspects of phonological description.* The Hague: Mouton.

Kaplan, R. M., and M. Kay. 1994. Regular models of phonological rule systems. *Computational Linguistics* 20.331–378.

Kisseberth, C. W. 1970. On the functional unity of phonological rules. *Linguistic Inquiry* 1.291–306.

Koskenniemi, K. 1983. *Two-level morphology: A general computational model for word-form recognition and production.* Helsinki, Finland: University of Helsinki dissertation.

Koutsoudas, A., G. Sanders, and C. Noll. 1974. The application of phonological rules. *Language* 50.1–28.

Wheeler, D. W. 1981. *Aspects of a categorial theory of phonology.* Amherst, Mass.: University of Massachusetts dissertation.

STEVEN BIRD

COMPUTER-ASSISTED INSTRUCTION.

Computer-assisted language learning (CALL), defined as "the search for and study of applications of the computer in language teaching and learning" (Levy 1997: 1), in the past was the concern of only a few language teachers interested in experimenting with the use of technology.

Examples of early experiments are those that used software designed for a stand-alone computer explicitly to teach a particular aspect of grammar or to provide a set of texts that learners could explore by searching for key grammatical features. The expanding role of technology throughout society has now resulted in teachers' and learners' daily use of computers—for example, to communicate through the Internet; as a consequence, all language teachers face questions about how computers can best be used for language learning. Teachers observe the attraction that technology holds for language learners, the enthusiasm with which many learners contribute to electronic discussion and the variety of interesting target-language input to which learners have access on the Internet.

At the same time, critical analysis of learners' language experiences on the Internet points out that the amount of language exposure should not be equated with the quality of time spent on language learning. As a consequence, the primary problem for theory and practice in CALL is to inform the development of computer-based language learning tasks that take advantage of the inherent attractions of the technology while incorporating appropriate second language pedagogy. For example, learners can identify for themselves Web pages containing interesting material, but the pedagogical CALL task must require them to use the information in a way that prompts them to attend to and examine the language in a more than superficial way. This suggestion is drawn directly from the claim from research in second language acquisition "that subliminal language learning is impossible, and that [what might be learned] is what learners consciously notice" (Schmidt 1990:149). This claim is consistent with findings indicating that acquisition requires interaction with the target language rather than exposure to input alone (Long 1996, Gass 1997). Recognition of the importance of interaction for prompting noticing, in addition to an expanded view of factors related to selection of classroom materials (Doughty and Williams 1998, Skehan 1998), has prompted those who work with CALL to formulate guiding principles for pedagogy.

A number of these pedagogical principles define criteria for ideal CALL tasks that capitalize on research on second language learning and the observations from use of CALL (Chapelle 2001). The first principle is that CALL tasks should have *language learning potential* (i.e., they should be expected to be beneficial for language learning, rather than simply a means of communication). The second one, *learner fit*, refers to the appropriate fit of CALL materials to learners' level of linguistic ability and their individual characteristics. The third, *meaning focus*, denotes the direction of learners' attention primarily toward the meaning of the language required to accomplish the task. The fourth, *authenticity* refers to the degree of correspondence between a CALL task and the language use the learner is likely to engage in outside the classroom. The fifth, *positive impact* of a CALL task, refers to its effects beyond its language learning potential. Finally, *practicality* denotes the ease with which learners and teachers can implement the CALL task within the particular constraints of a class or language program.

These qualities can be judged tentatively by teachers as they plan tasks for second language learners; ideally, however, research will help to substantiate the value of particular types of CALL tasks relative to these criteria. For example, a study of language learning potential yielded results favoring CALL materials in which linguistic form (e.g. the relative clause) was highlighted to help learners notice this form in a text that they were reading for meaning (Doughty 1991). Another found vocabulary gains for second language learners when they had access to hyperlinked annotations that provided the opportunity for interaction during reading (Chun and Plass 1996). A third found that access on demand to first language subtitles was associated with learners' ability to use the second language that they had listened to in a CALL task (Borrás and Lafayette 1994). Evidence for learner fit and meaning focus has been identified through analysis of the semantic content and linguistic features of the language of electronic discussion in classroom environments (Lamy and Goodfellow 1999, Kern 1995).

These research results begin to demonstrate the ways in which CALL can contribute to second language learning, but this is unquestionably an area in need of much investigation. In particular, teachers and researchers need to understand better how to investigate the ways in which CALL tasks can have a positive impact on learners and teachers (Warschauer 1998). Ideally future investigation of CALL will be undertaken in view of perspectives from second language classroom research, because CALL has now become commonplace for second language learners.

[*See also* Acquisition of Language, *article on* Second Language Acquisition; Pedagogical Grammar; *and* Applied Linguistics.]

BIBLIOGRAPHY

Borrás, I., and R. C. Lafayette. 1994. Effects of multimedia courseware subtitling on the speaking performance of college students of French. *Modern Language Journal* 78.61–75.

Chapelle, C. A. 2001. *Computer applications in second language acquisition: Foundations for teaching, testing and research*. Cambridge: Cambridge University Press.

Chun, D. M., and J. L. Plass. 1996. Effects of multimedia annotations on vocabulary acquisition. *Modern Language Journal* 80.183–198.

Doughty, C. 1991. Second language instruction does make a difference: Evidence from an empirical study of SL relativization. *Studies in Second Language Acquisition* 13.431–469.

Doughty, C., and J. Williams. 1998. Pedagogical choices in focus on form. In *Focus on form in classroom second language acquisition*, edited by C. Doughty and J. Williams, pp. 197–261. Cambridge: Cambridge University Press.

Gass, S. 1997. *Input, interaction, and the second language learner*. Mahwah, N.J.: Lawrence Erlbaum.

Kern, R. G. 1995. Restructuring classroom interaction with networked computers: Effects on quantity and characteristics of language production. *Modern Language Journal* 79.457–476.

Lamy, M. N., and R. Goodfellow. 1999. Reflective conversation in the virtual language classroom. *Language Learning and Technology* 2.43–61.

Levy, M. 1997. *Computer-assisted language learning: Context and conceptualization*. Oxford: Clarendon Press.

Long, M. H. 1996. The role of linguistic environment in second language acquisition. In *Handbook of second language acquisition*, edited by W. C. Ritchie and T. K. Bhatia, pp. 413–468. San Diego, Calif.: Academic Press.

Schmidt, R. W. 1990. The role of consciousness in second language learning. *Applied Linguistics* 11.129–158.

Skehan, P. 1998. *A cognitive approach to language learning*. Oxford: Oxford University Press.

Warschauer, M. 1998. Researching technology in TESOL: Determinist, instrumental, and critical approaches. *TESOL Quarterly* 32.757–761.

CAROL A. CHAPELLE

CONCEPTUAL SEMANTICS. *See* Semantics; Cognitive Grammar; Metaphor and Semantics; *and* Scripts, Frames, and Schemas.

CONCORD. *See* Agreement.

CONDILLAC, ÉTIENNE BONNOT DE (1714–1780), French philosopher. Condillac was influenced by British empiricism and in his turn had considerable influence on French linguistic thought down to the Idéologues. He saw the origin of ideas in sensation and language as a precondition of thought, especially theoretical thought.

[*See also* History of Linguistics, *article on* Seventeenth- and Eighteenth-Century Europe.]

ANNA MORPURGO DAVIES

CONDITIONAL. *See* Mood; Typology and Universals; *and* Clause.

CONGO LANGUAGES. *See* Niger-Congo Languages *and* Benue-Congo Languages.

CONJUNCTION. *See* Parts of Speech; Typology and Universals; Clause; *and* Coordination.

CONNECTIONISM. This computational framework for cognitive modeling is based on numerical computation rather than on symbol manipulation. Inspired by mathematical models of neural processes and by associationist psychology, variations of the connectionist approach over several decades have been termed *cybernetics, perceptrons, neural networks*, and *P[arallel] D[istributed] P[rocessing]* (Rumelhart et al. 1986, Anderson and Rosenfeld 1988, Grossberg 1988, Arbib 1995, Christiansen and Chater 2001). Connectionism may hold the potential for a unified framework within which to address disparate aspects of linguistics, though this goal will require overcoming a number of serious problems (Pinker and Mehler 1988).

A typical connectionist computational system is a network of simple numerical processing *units—nodes* or *neurons*; each has an *activation value* which it computes, according to some simple numerical formula, from the activation values of the other units to which it is connected; see Figure 1. A connection from unit 1 to unit 2 has a positive or negative numerical *strength* or *weight*, which governs whether activity at unit 1 will increase or decrease activity at unit 2—i.e., whether it will *excite* or *inhibit* it—and to what degree. All the processing units compute at once, in parallel. The pattern of activity of all the units in the network represents the *data* currently being operated upon by the network; the connection strengths constitute the *program* (or knowledge) which governs the processing of these data. A pattern of activity

FIGURE 1. *A Connectionist Network.* Here activity flows from the four input units to the six hidden units, among which it circulates through the lateral connections. From the hidden units, activity flows to the two output units. If a series of inputs is presented over time on the input units, the recurrent activity in the hidden units allows the output at any given time to be sensitive not just to the current input, but also to the previous inputs.

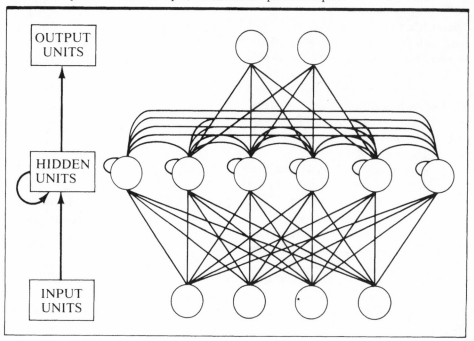

encoding an input is presented on the input units, and activity flows through the network (typically through intermediate *hidden* units) until a pattern of activity encoding the output develops on the output units. Connectionist networks often program themselves: during *training,* they are shown examples of the desired input/output pairs; and on the basis of numerical *learning algorithms,* they iteratively modify their connections to more closely approximate the desired computation. Connection strengths change slowly enough that they are essentially constant during the computation of output activity patterns from input activity patterns.

1. Representations used in connectionist cognitive models are typically presumed to lie at a level higher than that corresponding to actual neurons in the human brain. The representations which encode inputs and outputs are explicitly designed by the modeler; by contrast, the meaning of the activity of a hidden unit—the situations in which it is active, and the consequences of its activity—is determined by its connections.

Network units often correspond to identifiable hypotheses about the data being processed; the activity of such a unit encodes the current degree to which the network accepts the hypothesis. For interpreting acoustic speech input, two such hypotheses about an utterance might be: (a) that the first segment is voiced, and (b) that there is a vowel preceded by a dental. These two hypotheses illustrate a general approach to the representation of structured information—a particularly important problem for connectionist models of language. Structures can be represented with units denoting the conjunction of a property of a constituent with a property of the role it plays; for the structure of a sequence of phonetic segments, the two hypotheses above illustrate such conjunctions: (i) voiced segment and initial position, and (ii) vocalic segment and post-dental position (Smolensky 1990).

Representation poses central challenges for connectionist models of language. Particularly important is the adequate representation of embedded structure. A second, more general problem is that after learning (if any) is completed, the meaning of each unit is fixed during computations of outputs from inputs. Networks must be extremely large, so they can be set up in advance to accommodate any possible piece of data in a large space.

This obstacle might be overcome through networks in which the connections to a unit effectively change during activation computation; in such networks, the meaning of hidden units can effectively be determined dynamically during the processing of an input.

Network-defined representations that arise in hidden units through learning are typically difficult to interpret; except in isolated (but often quite interesting) cases, the connection pattern of a hidden unit rarely supports a simple interpretation. In many cases, it is not the activity of an individual unit, but rather the activity pattern over a set of units, that supports a given interpretation: this is *distributed representation*. Insights into such representations can be extracted using statistical techniques such as hierarchical clustering and factor analysis, and linear algebra techniques such as matrix decomposition. Elman 1990 demonstrated a network which learned, solely from the distribution of unanalyzed words in sentences, an internal representation of those words in which hidden-unit activities clustered hierarchically into such classes as nouns, verbs, animate nouns, etc.; the network invented this classification itself. (Figure 1 shows the structure of this network.)

2. Activation computation. The flow of activation in connectionist networks may contain closed loops ("feed-back," as in Figure 1), or no such loops ("feed-forward"). A variety of equations are used for computing activation values. The equations may be designed to implement statistical inference or plausible reasoning; thus the activation value of a unit represents the probability or plausibility of a hypothesis, given the evidence provided by other units' activities. Each connection in such a framework constitutes a *soft constraint*: e.g., a negative connection from unit 1 to unit 2 asserts that, if hypothesis 1 is accepted, hypothesis 2 should be rejected. This constraint can be overruled by those embodied in the other connections to unit 2. The activation equations may involve random decisions. Such models (e.g. Boltzmann machines) often have a "computational temperature" parameter that controls the degree of randomness; this decreases during the computation of an output ("simulated annealing"). In many models, a *harmony* or "energy" value corresponds to each activity pattern of a network; states of greatest harmony (lowest energy) represent maximally self-consistent values for the units' hypotheses, and activation equations drive the network toward such states.

In a *harmonic grammar,* numerically weighted rules assess harmony penalties to ill-formed configurations, and the grammatical structural descriptions are those that maximize harmony (Legendre et al. 1990; see also Goldsmith 1993).

3. Learning. Algorithms for learning are typically designed to minimize the total error made by the network on its training examples. These algorithms perform a complex kind of statistical induction from the observed training set to unseen inputs; we are only now beginning to understand this induction. Training consists in the presentation of example inputs, together with: (i) the corresponding desired output ("supervised learning," e.g. the back-propagation algorithm); or (ii) a global positive/ negative reinforcement signal ("reinforcement learning"); or (iii) no additional information ("unsupervised learning"). Some of these learning algorithms can be applied to training from positive examples only; such algorithms can allow a network to judge a novel example as either positive or negative, even though the training set includes no negative examples (Plunkett 1998). These methods have close connections to those of statistical computational linguistics.

4. Connectionism and associationism. Contemporary connectionism distinguishes itself from its simpler associationist precursors in several ways. There is a major emphasis on internal representation, and considerable interest in how these representations relate to the theoretical abstractions of linguistics and other areas of cognitive science. Distributed representations have constituent structure, unlike the simplest associationist representations, which are atomic. Distributed representations, and the techniques of statistical inference embodied in connectionist computation and learning, lie in new mathematical territory whose power and limits are only beginning to be explored (Smolensky et al. 1996).

5. Optimality Theory. High-level properties of connectionist computation suggest a number of principles forming the basis of Optimality Theory (Prince and Smolensky 1993, 1997). These properties include:

(a) *Optimality:* The correct output representation is the one that maximizes Harmony.
(b) *Containment:* Competition for optimality is between outputs that include the given input. (Clamping the input units restricts the optimization in a network to those patterns including the input.)
(c) *Parallelism:* Harmony measures the degree of simultaneous satisfaction of constraints. (Connectionist

optimization is parallel: the constraints encoded in the connections all apply simultaneously to a potential output.)

(d) *Interactionism:* The complexity of patterns of grammaticality comes not from individual constraints, which are relatively simple and general, but from the mutual interaction of multiple constraints. (Each connection in a network is a simple, general constraint on the co-activity of the units it connects; complex behavior emerges only from the interaction of many constraints.)

(e) *Conflict:* Constraints conflict; it is typically impossible to simultaneously satisfy them all. (Positive and negative connections typically put conflicting pressures on a unit's activity.)

(f) *Domination:* Constraint conflict is resolved via a notion of differential strength; stronger constraints prevail over weaker ones in cases of conflict.

(g) *Minimal violability:* Correct outputs typically violate some constraints (because of conflict), but do so only to the minimal degree needed to satisfy stronger constraints.

(h) *Learning:* requires determination of constraint strengths; acquiring the grammar of a particular language requires determining the relative strengths of constraints in the target language.

Other central principles of Optimality Theory are quite unexpected from a connectionist perspective:

(i) *Strict domination:* Each constraint is stronger than all weaker constraints combined. (This corresponds to a strong restriction on the numerical constraint strengths; it enables optimality to be determined without numerical computation.)

(j) *Universality:* The constraints are the same in all human grammars. (This corresponds to a strong restriction on the content of the constraints embodied in network connections, presumably to be explained eventually by the interaction of certain innate biases and experience.)

Attempting to reconcile these fundamental principles of grammar with those of neural computation may lead to future breakthroughs in both connectionist and linguistic theory (Smolensky and Legendre 2003).

[*See also* Cognitive Science; Computational Linguistics; Optimality Theory; Psycholinguistics; Neurolinguistics; Philosophy of Language; *and* Learnability.]

BIBLIOGRAPHY

Anderson, James A., and Edward Rosenfeld, eds. 1988. *Neurocomputing: Foundations of research.* Cambridge, Mass.: MIT Press.

Arbib, Michael A. ed. 1995. *The Handbook of brain theory and neural networks.* Cambridge, Mass.: MIT Press/Bradford Books.

Christiansen, Morten H., and Nick Chater, eds. 2001. *Connectionist psycholinguistics.* Westport, Conn.: Ablex.

Elman, J. L. 1990. Finding structure in time. *Cognitive Science* 14.179–211.

Goldsmith, John A. 1993. Harmonic phonology. In *The last phonological rule,* edited by John A. Goldsmith. Chicago: University of Chicago Press.

Grossberg, Stephen. 1988. *Neural networks and natural intelligence.* Cambridge, Mass.: MIT Press.

Legendre, Geraldine, Yoshiro Miyata, and Paul Smolensky. 1990. Can connectionism contribute to syntax? Harmonic grammar, with an application. *Chicago Linguistic Society* 26.

Pinker, Steven, and Jacques Mehler, eds. 1988. *Connections and symbols.* Cambridge, Mass.: MIT Press.

Plunkett, Kim, ed. 1998. *Language acquisition and connectionism.* New York: Taylor and Francis.

Prince, Alan, and Paul Smolensky. 1993. Optimality Theory: Constraint interaction in generative grammar (Technical Report). Rutgers University, New Brunswick, N.J., and University of Colorado, Boulder, Colo.

Prince, Alan, and Paul Smolensky. 1997. Optimality: From neural networks to universal grammar. *Science* 275.1604–1610.

Rumelhart, David E., James L. McClelland, et al. 1986. *Parallel distributed processing: Explorations in the microstructure of cognition,* vol. 1, *Foundations*; vol. 2, *Psychological and biological models.* Cambridge, Mass.: MIT Press.

Smolensky, Paul. 1990. Tensor product variable binding and the representation of symbolic structures in connectionist networks. *Artificial Intelligence* 46.159–216.

Smolensky, Paul, and Géraldine Legendre. 2003. *The harmonic mind: From neural computation to Optimality-Theoretic Grammar.* Cambridge, Mass.: Blackwell.

Smolensky, Paul, Michael C. Mozer, and David E. Rumelhart, eds. 1996. *Mathematical perspectives on neural networks.* Mahwah, N.J.: Lawrence Erlbaum.

PAUL SMOLENSKY

CONNOTATION. *See* Semantics.

CONSONANT HARMONY. *See* Phonological Processes.

CONSONANTS. *See* Phonetics *and* Phonology.

CONSTITUENT. *See* Phrase Structure.

CONSTRAINTS. *See* Psycholinguistics; Optimality Theory; Minimalist Program; Acquisition of Language; Learnability; Formal Grammar; Subjacency; Evolution and Language; Cognitive Science; Filters; Principles and Parameters; Mathematical Linguistics; *and* Connectionism.

CONSTRUCTION GRAMMAR (CG). A family of approaches to the writing of grammars that gives central importance to the concept of construction. A grammatical construction is defined as a set of constraints, expressible as a feature structure, that partially determines a class of well-formed expressions (constructs) in the language and their meanings. A complete CG analysis of a linguistic expression is a display of the assembly of articulated constructions that jointly license all of the grammatical and semantic properties of the expression. At the intuitive level, this can be seen as fitting pieces together: some patterns provide slots requiring linguistic objects of particular kinds; linguistic objects come with properties that satisfy requirements of certain structures and may impose requirements on their own contexts.

An indefinite determiner requires a nominal expression headed by a singular count noun; a preposition requires a full noun phrase (NP) as its object; a singular count noun can only participate in a full NP if it is paired with some kind of determiner; and so on. In short, the features grammatically associated with a linguistic expression (word or phrase) identify (i) what it is independent of context (*a hat* in *she wore a hat* is a singular indefinite maximal NP), (ii) what contextual requirements it imposes (*wear* in that sentence requires a subject and an object), and (iii) what properties it acquires from its context (*she*, by its position, has grammatical function "Subject" and is nominative, and *a hat* has grammatical function "Object").

Historically CG has distinguished itself from other unification-based, non-derivational, generative grammars (such as H[ead-driven] P[hrase] S[tructure] G[rammar]) more by the interests of its practitioners than by the architecture of its formalisms. The construction gram-

marian's preoccupation with what is idiosyncratic in language has always aimed toward developing a uniform mechanism to account for both the specialized constructions and the general-purpose or "core" constructions. A grammar is the irreducible set of constructions needed for explaining the structures and meanings of the expressions in the language. The work of doing a detailed CG analysis of a candidate construction is precisely that of determining just which parts of it cannot be accounted for as instances of independently known constructions. To say that CG is non-derivational means that it does not propose different layers of structure separating interpretation from form, and that no phonetically empty constituents are introduced in the analysis of a sentence; to say that it is unificational means that the full parse, syntactic and semantic, of a construct is explained in terms of mutual constraint-satisfaction of the constructions that license it.

Grammar and lexicon are represented in uniform ways. Constructions can be purely lexical, the simplest being a feature structure specifying phonological form, meaning, gross or fine syntactic category membership, and, for a predicating word, its valence. The valence information identifies minimally those semantic role combinations upon which valence constructions can assign syntactic properties (grammatical function, phrase type). The linking constructions that fill in such syntactic information do so independently of the constructions that provide constituent structure and phrase order.

Phrasal constructions provide the means by which the valence requirements of a lexical predictor can be satisfied as phrases in the environment of the predicator. These are of such types as Complementation (in English, providing places for some of the valence elements as right sisters of a lexical head), Co-instantiation (by which a valence element of one predicate also satisfies a requirement of another that is embedded in it), Extraction (by which a valence item is realized externally to the constituent headed by the predicate, typically as subject, interrogative or relative PRO-word, topicalized constituent, and so on), and Null Instantiation (by which, under specific types of interpretation, valence elements can be "conceptually present but unexpressed"). Other construction types include Coordination of various kinds and Modification (by which the properties of the modifier are unified with properties of the head).

Some constructions are completely general, applying to almost every sentence (e.g. Complementation); some

FIGURE 1. *Constituent Structure of the Correlative Conditional Sentence*

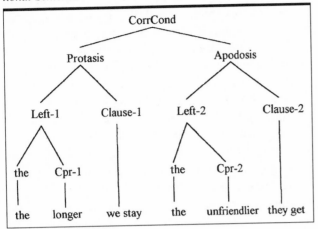

are completely special, covering a small and limited repertory of phrases with limited functions (e.g. formulas for telling clock-time). CG has given special emphasis to complex structures that exhibit articulations of both general patterns and special conditions, and to situations in which semantic structures associated with a construction interact with the semantic properties of lexical items that participate in it. (For the former, see Kay and Fillmore 1999, Michaelis and Lambrecht 1966a,b; for the latter, see Goldberg 1995.)

An example of a particularly elaborate construction with unusual syntax and unusual semantics is what might be called the Correlative Conditional Sentence, having roughly the constituent structure indicated in Figure 1. The labels in the figure are for immediate convenience only: a CG description of the construction has a feature structure at each node that gives the constraints on each constituent. (The most detailed description of the facts is in Culicover and Jackendoff 1999.)

An informal description of the features of this construction is as follows:

- The labels "Protasis" and "Apodosis" are to distinguish the two main segments of the correlative conditional and to associate them with the two parts of a conditional sentence. The interpretation is conditional: *If we stay longer, they will become less friendly.*
- The constituents labeled "Left" are headed by comparative phrases (Cpr-1, Cpr-2), and these can be of any part of speech within which morphological or phrasal comparison is possible; hence we cannot give a grammatical category label to the "Left" segments.

We can find adverbs, as in *the longer we stay*, adjectives, as in *the unfriendlier they get*, and nominals, as in *the more beans you eat* (where the morphological comparative is a quantifier) or *the more you say*. The form of the comparative can also be phrasal, thus allowing both positive and negative comparison: *the more friendly, the less carefully*.

- No grammatical category is assigned to the *the*, though we could speak of *the* in these phrases as specifiers, having position and functions similar to *how much (longer)* and *that much (unfriendlier)*. In any case, this is a construction-specific use of *the*, and no generalization would be served by identifying it as the definite determiner.
- The "Left" constituents are realizations of some valence requirement in a predicate in the following open clause: compare *we stay longer, they get unfriendlier*. The relation between the "Left" constituents and their clauses can be a "long distance" one in the usual sense: it is possible to say *the more beer you think they are willing to drink*, where *the more beer* satisfies a requirement of the embedded verb *drink*.
- The verbal forms of the two paired clauses match patterns found in ordinary non-counterfactual conditional sentences: thus, one pattern has the futurate present in the protasis, and the *will* future in the apodosis. *The sooner they arrive, the sooner we'll be able to start.* (Not *the sooner they'll arrive.*)
- The first clause is a negative polarity context, the second is not. Thus, *the more often anybody complains* is a possible Protasis, but not a possible Apodosis in this construction. (The presence of the *less* comparative would create its own negative polarity context, of course.)
- The second clause, but not the first, permits a stylistic inversion: *the sooner will she be willing to go out with you* is a possible Clause-2, not a possible Clause-1.
- But the content of the constituent clauses is limited only by constraints on ordinary finite sentences.

Construction grammar works in a bottom-up inductive manner in the inquiry stage. If there are specific universals of grammatical organization, CG is in a position to discover them. Ongoing research is of the expected kind: patterns earlier thought to need treatment as instances of a special construction can be shown to follow from independently needed constructions; ordinary patterns can be shown to have unexpected properties that suggest the need for special treatment. Typological characteristics should be expressible within the system of constructional inheritance: for example, to say that English is a "head-first" language is to say that complementation structures have the lexical head as their first constituent, and this can be accomplished by declaring that the complementation constructions inherit an abstract phrase-building construction regarding lexical heads.

[*See also* Heads; Phrase Structure; *and* Functional Linguistics.]

BIBLIOGRAPHY

Culicover, Peter, and Ray Jackendoff. 1999. The view from the periphery: The English comparative correlative. *Linguistic Inquiry* 30.543–571.

Goldberg, Adele. 1995. *Grammatical constructions.* Chicago: The University of Chicago Press.

Kay, Paul, and Charles J. Fillmore. 1999. Grammatical constructions and linguistic generalizations: The what's X doing Y? construction. *Language* 75.1–33.

Michaelis, Laura, and Knud Lambrecht. 1996a. Toward a construction-based theory of language-function: The case of nominal extraposition. *Language* 72.215–247.

Michaelis, Laura, and Knud Lambrecht. 1996b. The exclamative sentence type in English. In *Conceptual structure, discourse and language,* edited by Adele Goldberg, pp. 375–389. Stanford Calif.: Center for the Study of Language and Information.

Zwicky, Arnold. 1994. Dealing out meaning: Fundamentals of syntactic constructions. In *Proceedings of the Twentieth Annual Meeting of the Berkeley Linguistics Society*, edited by Susanne Gahl et al., pp. 611–625. Berkeley, Calif.: Berkeley Linguistics Society.

CHARLES J. FILLMORE

CONTEXT. *See* Pragmatics and Contextual Semantics; Sociolinguistics; Semantics; Computational Linguistics; Psycholinguistics; Discourse; *and* Acquisition of Language.

CONTEXT-FREE GRAMMARS. *See* Mathematical Linguistics.

CONTEXT-SENSITIVE GRAMMARS. *See* Mathematical Linguistics.

CONTINUITY HYPOTHESIS. *See* Evolution and Language *and* Acquisition of Language.

CONTOUR. *See* Intonation.

CONTRACTION. *See* Ellipsis.

CONTRADICTION. *See* Semantics.

CONTRASTIVE ANALYSIS. *See* Applied Linguistics *and* Text.

CONTRASTIVE RHETORIC. *See* Text.

CONTROL. The phenomenon of control is illustrated in the following examples:

(1a)   *George persuaded his friends* [*to vote for him*].

(1b)   *George hoped* [*to become President*].

(1c)   *Paul tried* [*to stop the argument*].

(1d)   [*To pass the exam*] *would please me.*

In these structures, a verb takes a non-finite complement that has no apparent subject, e.g. [*to vote for him*] in ex. (1a). Although these complements appear to lack subjects, they are understood as if they did have subjects, the interpretation of which is supplied by some N[oun] P[hrase] that is an argument of the matrix predicate—the object NP *his friends* in (1a), the matrix subject in (1b), and so on.

The relation between such an understood subject and the argument that supplies its interpretation is the relation of *control*. One says that the complement subject is *controlled* by a matrix argument; that argument is in turn known as the *controller* of the complement subject.

Three important issues have dominated research in this area: (i) How are the formal constraints on the Control relation to be accounted for? (ii) What principles determine which matrix argument controls an implicit subject? (iii) What are the semantic and referential properties of the implicit subject of the complement clause?

1. The controlled NP. In English, complements headed by infinitive verbs may have controlled subjects (as seen in ex. 1a–d). Complements whose verb is an *-ing* participial may also have controlled subjects:

(2a)   *I accused him* [*of being insincere*].

(2b)   *I denied* [*stealing the documents*].

(2c)   [*Being poor*] *depressed them.*

But finite complements do not allow control:

(3a)   *I wanted [should go home].

(3b)   *I hoped [would become president].

(3c)   *Failed the exam [depressed them].

This restriction constitutes a central puzzle: Why should it be that the control relation can reach only into non-finite complements, and never into finite complements?

Furthermore, only subjects may be controlled; this condition is met in (1–3). In (4), however, non-subjects are controlled:

(4a)   *George persuaded his friends (for) them to like.

(4b)   *Paul tried (for) his colleagues to respect.

Most theoretical work on control, then, has assumed that only subjects of non-finite clauses may be controlled, and has sought to construct an explanation for this observation.

2. Selection of controller. Depending on the matrix predicate, either a subject (as in 5a), a direct object (as in 5b), an indirect object (as in 5c), or an oblique argument (as in 5d) may function as controller:

(5a)   GEORGE promised (his wife) [to quit smoking].

(5b)   George persuaded his BROTHER [to quit smoking].

(5c)   Paul shouted to GEORGE [to be quiet].

(5d)   It is impossible for PEOPLE these days [to get ahead].

There are also cases in which the controller argument is itself implicit:

(6a)   It is immoral [to question authority].

(6b)   It's fun [to trick people].

Such examples are instances of so-called *arbitrary control*, in which the implicit subject of the complement is assigned an interpretation commonly called "generic" or "arbitrary." In most if not all such cases, the matrix predicate has an implicit *benefactive* argument that can be viewed as the controller.

3. Early analyses. The earliest generative analyses of this phenomenon were transformational. In this conception, non-finite complements are derived from full clauses which have fully specified subjects; if identical to, and coreferential with, a matrix NP, those subjects are deleted by a transformation known as Equi-NP-Deletion. An example like (1c), for instance, would be derived roughly as follows:

(7)   Paul$_j$ tried [$_s$ Paul$_j$ stop the argument].
⇓
Paul$_j$ tried [$_s$ Ø stop the argument].

The condition that the deleted element must be the subject of a non-finite clause is stipulated.

This analysis brings with it an elaborate theory of *rule governance*, since application of Equi-NP-Deletion depends on the presence of particular predicates in the matrix. The rule is obligatory for some (see 8), optional for others (9), and inapplicable for still others (10):

(8a)   Jim tried [to be good].

(8b)   *Jim$_j$ tried [(for) him(self)$_j$ to be good].

(8c)   *Jim$_j$ tried [(that) he$_j$ be good].

(8d)   *Jim$_j$ tried [(that) the students like him$_j$].

(9a)   Bill wanted [to have a good marriage].

(9b)   ??Bill$_j$ wanted [himself$_j$ to have a good marriage].

(9c)   Bill$_j$ wanted [that he$_j$ should have a good marriage].

(9d)   Bill wanted [that everyone have a good time].

(10a)   *Paul screamed [to open the door].

(10b)   Paul screamed [for George to open the door].

(10c)   *Paul$_j$ screamed [for him$_j$ to open the door].

The problem is a complex one. The verb *try*, in this conception, has the property that it must be inserted into a syntactic structure in which Equi-NP-Deletion will apply. The verb *want* may (but is not required to) appear in an environment in which Equi-NP-Deletion can apply. The verb *scream* must be inserted into a syntactic structure of such a kind that Equi-NP-Deletion cannot apply to it.

4. Subcategorization analyses (see Brame 1976, Bresnan 1982, Dowty 1985, Gazdar et al. 1985). Partly because of the complexity of the system of rule governance that the transformational analysis made necessary, a number of theorists proposed in the mid-1970s to eliminate the transformation of Equi-NP-Deletion in favor of an analysis of control phenomena in terms of direct *lexical subcategorization*. The general strategy behind this approach is to maintain that the complement of a control-verb like *try* is a V[erb] P[hrase] at every level of syntactic representation, and that it is simply a lexical property of *try* that it demands a VP complement. Neither the deletion transformation nor the associated apparatus of rule governance is now necessary; (8b–d) are ungrammatical because they violate lexical requirements of *try*. It follows directly that only subjects may be controlled.

VP complements are supplied with subjects from the argument structure of the matrix predicate—that is, they are supplied with controllers, either by means of *lexical rules* (Bresnan 1982), rules of *semantic composition* (Gazdar et al. 1985), or by *Meaning Postulates* (Dowty 1985). This general approach to the problem of control is a feature, in one version or another, of Generalized Phrase-Structure Grammar (Gazdar et al. 1985), Lexical-Functional Grammar (Bresnan 1982), and Categorial Grammar (Dowty 1985). It has been criticized on two main grounds. First, it leaves unexplained the fact that only a non-finite VP may be a subcategorized complement. That is, there is no account of the observation that only the subjects of non-finite complements may be controlled. Second, it has been argued that control complements exhibit the syntactic characteristics of full clauses, rather than those of VPs (see Koster and May 1982).

Partially cross-cutting this syntactic debate about the category of the control complement, there is a debate about the semantic properties of the control complement. Those who have maintained that control complements are clausal in their syntax typically also maintain that they are propositional in their semantics. An alternative view (Bach 1979, 1982; Williams 1980; Dowty 1985; Chierchia 1984, 1989, 1990; Clark 1990) is that control complements denote unsaturated predicates or properties.

An important challenge to this line of argument comes from Landau 2000, who proposes to rethink the typology of control constructions in such a way that a previously noticed but largely neglected type of control turns out to be pervasive. This is the phenomenon of "partial control," as seen in (11):

(11)   John wanted to meet at 6:00.

In a case such as (11), the individual denoted by the matrix subject is interpreted as being properly contained within the group denoted by the complement (controlled) subject. Landau argues that the phenomenon of partial control is much more widespread than previously thought, and that it is characteristic of contexts in which control is obligatory. He also believes that this conclusion is incompatible with the idea that control complements denote predicates or properties. These considerations, if correct, also tell against the movement analysis of control urged by Hornstein 1999.

5. PRO and the PRO-Theorem (see Chomsky 1981, Manzini 1983). Accounts of the phenomenon of control within Chomsky's Extended Standard Theory and its successor, Government/Binding Theory are also non-transformational. These theories assume, however, that control complements are full clauses at every level of representation. Furthermore, they have syntactic subjects; their subject position is occupied by a phonetically null pronoun with quite particular properties. This element, known as PRO, is anaphorically linked with a matrix antecedent:

(11)   *Paul$_i$ tried* [$_s$ PRO$_i$ [*to* [$_{vp}$ *stop the argument*]]].

The postulation of the silent syntactic subject is consistent with, and required by, the Projection Principle—a consequence of which is that, if a structure has a subject argument for semantic purposes, then it must also have a subject argument at every syntactic level of representation.

The question of why only subjects of non-finite clauses can be controlled becomes the question of why PRO may appear only in this position. This restriction is analyzed as deriving from the anomalous character of PRO with respect to Binding Theory. The element PRO shows the typical characteristics both of *anaphors* and of *pronominals* (Chomsky 1986:125–131). Being an anaphor, it is subject to Condition A of the Binding Theory, which requires it to be *bound* in its governing category. Being a pronominal, it is subject to Condition B of the Binding Theory, which requires it to be *unbound* in its governing category. These conflicting requirements can be resolved if PRO has *no* governing category; and this can hold true only if PRO has no governor. Therefore, PRO may appear only in ungoverned positions. All non-subject argument positions are governed by lexical categories; the subject position of a finite clause is governed, and Case is assigned to it by the element INFL, which defines a clause as finite. The only argument position which is systematically ungoverned is the subject position of a non-finite clause. Thus PRO may appear there, but not in other argument positions.

This analysis has been challenged on the grounds that its crucial step, the assignment of the element PRO simultaneously to the categories of anaphor and pronominal, is unmotivated—and furthermore, that the distinction between subjects of finite clauses and subjects of non-finite clauses in terms of government is artifactual.

The problem of selecting a controller for PRO in a given structure is assigned to the separate subtheory of control. At the time of writing, the content of this subtheory remains poorly understood (Chomsky 1986:124–31).

[*See also* Anaphora and Binding; Categorial Grammar; Clause; Deletion; Generalized Phrase-Structure Grammar; Government and Binding; Lexical-Functional Grammar; Pronouns; Recoverability; *and* Subcategorization and Selection.]

BIBLIOGRAPHY

Bach, Emmon. 1979. Control in Montague Grammar. *Linguistic Inquiry* 10.515–531.

Bach, Emmon. 1982. Purpose clauses and control. In *The nature of syntactic representation*, edited by Pauline Jacobson and Geoffrey Pullum, pp. 35–57. Dordrecht: D. Reidel.

Brame, Michael K. 1976. *Conjectures and refutations in syntax and semantics*. New York: North-Holland.

Bresnan, Joan, ed. 1982. *The mental representation of grammatical relations*. Cambridge, Mass.: MIT Press.

Chierchia, Gennaro. 1984. *Topics in the syntax and semantics of infinitives and gerunds*. Amherst, Mass.: University of Massachusetts dissertation, distributed by Graduate Linguistic Students Association, University of Massachusetts, Amherst.

Chierchia, Gennaro. 1989. Structured meanings, thematic roles, and control. In *Properties, types, and meanings*, vol. 2, *Semantic issues*, edited by Gennaro Chierchia et al., pp. 131–166. Dordrecht: Kluwer.

Chierchia, Gennaro. 1990. Anaphora and attitudes *de se*. In *Semantics and contextual expression*, edited by Renate Barsche et al., pp. 1–32. Dordrecht: Foris.

Chomsky, Noam. 1981. *Lectures on government and binding*. (Studies in generative grammar, 9.) Dordrecht: Foris.

Chomsky, Noam. 1986. *Knowledge of language: Its nature, origins, and use*. New York: Praeger.

Clark, Robin. 1990. *Thematic theory in syntax and interpretation*. London: Routledge.

Dowty, David R. 1985. On recent analyses of the semantics of control. *Linguistics and Philosophy* 8.291–331.

Gazdar, Gerald, Ewan Klein, Geoffrey K. Pullum, and Ivan A. Sag. 1985. *Generalized Phrase Structure Grammar*. Oxford: Blackwell. Cambridge, Mass.: Harvard University Press.

Hornstein, Norbert. 1999. Movement and control. *Linguistic Inquiry* 30.69–96.

Koster, Jan, and Robert May. 1982. On the constituency of infinitives. *Language* 58.117–143.

Landau, Idan. 2000. *Elements of control*. Dordrecht: Kluwer.

Manzini, Maria Rita. 1983. On control and control theory. *Linguistic Inquiry* 14.421–446.

Rosenbaum, Peter S. 1967. *The grammar of English predicate complement constructions*. Cambridge, Mass.: MIT Press.

Williams, Edwin. 1980. Predication. *Linguistic Inquiry* 11.203–238.

JAMES MCCLOSKEY

CONVENTIONAL IMPLICATURE. See Pragmatics and Contextual Semantics, *article on* Implicature.

CONVERGENCE. *See* Dialectology; Historical Linguistics; Areal Linguistics; *and* Etymology.

CONVERSATIONAL IMPLICATURE. *See* Pragmatics and Contextual Semantics.

CONVERSATION ANALYSIS. *See* Discourse.

CONVERSION. Also known as functional shift or zero derivation. This is the process whereby a new word is derived by change in part of speech, without adding a derivational affix; e.g. $cheat_V > cheat_N$ 'someone who cheats' (= $sing_V > sing\text{-}er_N$), $gas_N > gas_V$ 'treat with gas' (=$alcohol_N > alcohol\text{-}ize_V$), $clean_{ADJ} > clean_V$ 'make clean' (= $legal_{ADJ} > legalize_V$).

Several theoretical approaches exist. In one approach, no derivational process is assumed: words may have multiple class membership (Nida 1948:434–436; Vogel 1996); or there are special overlapping classes NV, AV, NAV (Hockett 1958:225–227); or separate lexical entries are related only in the semantic component by a directional or non-directional redundancy rule (Lieber 1981: 119–139).

In another approach, a directional derivational relationship is assumed, which can take one of the following forms:

(a) Conversion is treated as a syntactic phenomenon— as a simple change of class, typical of languages (such as English) that lack inflectional word-class characteristics; thus German $laufen_V$ 'to run' > $Lauf_N$ '(a) run', $Salz_N$ 'salt' > $salzen_V$ 'to salt' would not count as conversions (Kruisinga 1932:96–161).

(b) Conversion is treated as parallel to explicit suffixation, with the same semantic properties. The suffix takes the form of zero, i.e. *cheat-$\emptyset_N$*, *clean-$\emptyset_V$*, thus preserving the binary structure of word-formation syntagmas (Marchand 1969:359–389).

(c) Conversion is treated as a special "headless" morphological rule that does not involve any branching (Williams 1981:247, 250, 257).

(d) Conversion is treated as a special derivational process whose output, a *contextual*, is semantically vague, and derives its concrete meaning by pragmatic factors from the context (Clark and Clark 1979).

[*See also* Morphology; Derivational Morphology; Heads; *and* Lexicon.]

BIBLIOGRAPHY

Clark, Eve V., and Herbert H. Clark. 1979. When nouns surface as verbs. *Language* 55.767–811.

Hockett, Charles F. 1958. *A course in modern linguistics.* New York: Macmillan.

Kruisinga, Etsko. 1932. *A handbook of present-day English,* part 2, *English accidence and syntax,* vol. 3. Groningen: Noordhoff.

Lieber, Rochelle. 1981. *On the organization of the lexicon.* Bloomington: Indiana University Linguistics Club.

Marchand, Hans. 1969. *The categories and types of present-day English word-formation: A synchronic-diachronic approach.* 2d ed. Munich: Beck.

Nida, Eugene A. 1948. The identification of morphemes. *Language* 24.414–441.

Vogel, Petra M. 1996. *Wortarten und Wortartenwechsel: Zu Konversion und verwandten Erscheinungen im Deutschen und in anderen Sprachen.* Berlin and New York: de Gruyter.

Williams, Edwin S. 1981. On the notions "lexically related" and "head of a word." *Linguistic Inquiry* 12.245–274.

DIETER KASTOVSKY

COOPERATIVE PRINCIPLE. *See* Pragmatics and Contextual Semantics.

COORDINATION. Constructions in which two or more parts of the sentence are conjoined by words like *and* or *or,* as in ex. (1), are generally referred to by the term *coordination*:

(1a)   *John {and/or} Mary went to the park.*

(1b)   *John ate dinner {and/or} read a book.*

There have long been two main formal approaches to this area of grammar. The first proceeds from the observation that a sequence such as N[oun] P[hrase] *and* NP may appear wherever a simple NP is permitted. This generalization may be formalized as the following phrase structure rule, where α is any phrasal or lexical category:

(2) $\alpha \rightarrow \alpha$ {*and/or*} α

For ex. (1a), α equals NP; for (1b), it equals V[erb] P[hrase]. Coordinate structures are thus base-generated in this approach, sometimes called *phrasal conjunction*.

The second approach to coordination develops the idea that sentences like (1a–b) are reduced from the following:

(3a)   *John went to the park {and/or} Mary went to the park.*

(3b)   *John ate dinner {and/or} John read a book.*

In this approach, sometimes called *derived* or *sentential conjunction*, only sentences are conjoined in underlying structure; a process of *Conjunction Reduction* then applies to produce the observed surface structures. Occasionally both phrasal conjunction and derived conjunction are adopted within a single analysis, but more often, one or the other approach is chosen.

One reason that both approaches have coexisted for so long is that each is faced with difficult prima-facie problems. A phrasal conjunction approach as in (2), for instance, must deal with cases in which conjoined elements may not be constituents:

(4)   Mary bought [the newspaper on Tuesday] and [the magazine on Wednesday]

Whether or not sentences like (4) pose a problem, however, clearly depends on the clausal constituent structure that one adopts.

Another potential problem for phrasal conjunction arises in cases, such as (5), which appear to involve VP-conjunction:

(5a)   *John insulted Bill and was hit by Mary.*

(5b)   *Tom lives in Paris and seems to be happy.*

If one assumes an NP-movement analysis of passive and raising constructions, then the object of *hit* in (5a) and the subject of *be happy* in (5b) seem simply to have disappeared rather than moved. Burton and Grimshaw 1992 and McNally 1992, however, point out that the VP-internal subject hypothesis allows one to reanalyze sentences like (5) as instances of Across-the-Board movement (see below).

The derived conjunction approach also presents some difficulties. Given an underlying structure as in (6a), stipulations may be required to prevent derivation of the ungrammatical sentence (6b), in which the conjuncts are of differing syntactic categories:

(6a)   *John sang the song and John sang at home.*

(6b)   **John sang the song and at home.*

These facts illustrate what is known as the Law of the Coordination of Likes, which states that only like categories may be conjoined, a condition that (6b) violates.

In addition to these specific problems, there is also a range of complex facts associated with coordination that present a descriptive challenge to any approach. One such set of facts involves extraction processes such as WH-movement. Ross 1967 noted that extraction is not permitted out of a coordinate structure (his Coordinate Structure Constraint), as in (8a), unless the extraction affects all the conjuncts, as in (8b):

(8a)   **This is the book which John read ___ and Mary wrote an article.*

(8b)   *This is the book which John read ___ and Mary wrote.*

The latter case, known as Across-the-Board extraction, appears to be subject to its own particular constraints. Specifically, if we extract an element from the matrix subject position of one conjunct, we must do the same in all conjuncts; for example,

(9a)   *This is the book which ___ appeared on the shelves last week and ___ costs $20.*

(9b)   **This is the book which John read ___ and ___ appeared on the shelves last week.*

Aside from this, extraction is not required to apply to parallel positions in each conjunct:

(10)   *This is the book which John read ___ and Mary hopes ___ will be a best-seller.*

The peculiar patterning of facts in (8b), (9), and (10) is sometimes referred to as an "asymmetry" in Across-the-Board extraction.

Other areas of investigation within coordination include *Gapping*, as in (11), where the verb in the second of two conjoined sentences is omitted; and *Right Node Raising*, as in (12), where the rightmost constituent of two conjoined sentences appears to their right:

(11)   *John read the book, and Mary the newspaper.*

(12)   *John read, and Mary bought, the new book which appeared last week.*

Each of these constructions is subject to a complex set of constraints. Another active area of study has been the interaction of coordination with case and agreement systems.

A major focus of research on coordination has been the question of the extent to which coordinate structures are like other, more intensively studied structures. Early work in Generalized Phrase Structure Grammar, for instance, argued that major properties of coordination follow if one adopts a rule such as (2) together with the independently needed notion of slash categories. Within the principle and parameters framework, Munn 1993 and Johannessen 1998 have proposed that coordinate structures may be profitably accommodated within X'-theory, with the conjunction as the head of the phrase. Other researchers, however, have suggested that coordination involves structural relations different from those involved in the more widely studied cases of subordination. Goodall 1987, Moltmann 1992, and Muadz 1991, for instance, argue for a representation of coordinate structures in which the conjuncts appear in parallel planes.

[*See also* Clause; Deletion; Ellipsis; *and* Parasitic Gaps.]

BIBLIOGRAPHY

Burton, Strang, and Jane Grimshaw, 1992. Coordination and VP-internal subjects. *Linguistic Inquiry* 23.305–313.

Gazdar, Gerald, Ewan Klein, Geoffrey K. Pullum, and Ivan Sag. 1985. *Generalized Phrase Structure Grammar.* Oxford: Blackwell. Cambridge, Mass.: Harvard University Press.

Goodall, Grant. 1987. *Parallel structures in syntax: Coordination, causatives, and restructuring.* (Cambridge studies in linguistics, 46.) Cambridge and New York: Cambridge University Press.

Johannessen, Janne Bondi, 1998. *Coordination.* Oxford: Oxford University Press.

McNally, Louise. 1992. VP coordination and the VP-internal subject hypothesis. *Linguistic Inquiry* 23.329–335.

Moltmann, Friederike. 1992. *Coordination and comparatives.* Cambridge, Mass.: MIT dissertation.

Muadz, H. 1991. *A Planar theory of coordination.* University of Arizona dissertation.

Munn, Alan. 1993. *Topics in the syntax and semantics of coordinate structures.* College Park, Md.: University of Maryland dissertation.

Oirsouw, Robert R. van. 1987. *The syntax of coordination.* London: Croom Helm.

Ross, John Robert. 1967. *Constraints on variables in syntax.* Cambridge, Mass.: MIT dissertation. Published as *Infinite syntax.* Norwood, N.J.: Ablex, 1986.

GRANT GOODALL

COPULA. *See* Parts of Speech; Typology and Universals; *and* Verbs.

CO-REFERENCE. *See* Anaphora and Binding *and* Control.

CORPUS PROCESSING. A computer corpus is a large body of naturally occurring computer-readable texts or text-extracts used for research, and especially for the development of N[atural] L[anguage] P]rocessing] software.

Historically, it became feasible for computers to store and manipulate such large quantities of natural language text in the early 1960s; the first well-known example was the corpus of modern American written text extracts known as the Brown Corpus, compiled at Brown University (see Francis and Kučera 1964, 1982), consisting of over one million text words ("word tokens"). Since that time many computer corpora have been assembled—representing different languages, or different varieties of the same language (e.g. British, American, and Indian English), or encoding different kinds of information about written and spoken texts.

In size, corpora can vary greatly for practical and technical reasons. To build even a relatively small corpus of spoken discourse in reliably detailed transcription may require thousands of hours of transcription by skilled phoneticians. (See Svartvik et al. 1982 and Knowles et al. 1996 for details on two corpora of this kind.) However, as a result of advances in optical character recognition, and the availability of machine-readable text from various electronic sources, such as the Internet, it is now technically relatively easy to amass a vast corpus, of the order of 300–500 million words of printed text.

In spite of this massive increase in the availability of machine-readable text over the past forty years, the opportunities for using such resources for research have been little exploited until recently, for three main reasons. First, whereas computer corpora of written language exist in abundance, there is still a shortage of corpora of spoken language; yet it is speech technology—for example, in the development of spoken dialogue systems—that has most to gain from corpus-based research.

Second, the availability of corpora for research in a technical sense does not entail availability in a legal sense. In practice, restrictions of copyright and other proprietary rights impede the average researcher's access to corpus data.

Third, it is argued (e.g. in Aarts and Van den Heuvel 1985 and in Garside et al. 1987:16–29) that the value of computer corpora for research has been recognized belatedly and insufficiently in computational linguistics. This is partly because of an unappealing research style: the work of the corpus linguist is strongly data-oriented and labor-intensive. Another reason relates to the evolving state of the art: up to the 1990s, computational linguists were able to avoid confronting the multitudinous messiness of unrestricted natural language use by concentrating on the development of computer systems (sometimes disparagingly called "toy systems") designed for artificially selected or domain-restricted data. Only comparatively recently has NLP research advanced so far as to need testing of grammars, parsers, etc., against non-pre-selected data; this is precisely the point at which the computer corpus comes to be seen as a valuable, if not indispensable, tool.

The computer corpus satisfies the need for access to a wide range of actually occurring instances of language use when developing wide-coverage tools of language description, such as a dictionary or a grammar. Dictionaries and grammars may exist in the form of printed books (see Sinclair 1987 on the use of a large corpus in the compilation of a printed dictionary). For the present purpose, however, we may focus on machine-readable "computer grammars" and "computer dictionaries" (lexicons) used for NLP.

To be useful, the corpus itself has to undergo various kinds of computer processing or analysis. We will discuss four models of the role of corpus processing:

MODEL A. In the linguistic *information retrieval* model, the computer's role is subservient to the analysis carried out by the human user. The computer sorts, counts, arranges (e.g. by concordance), and presents linguistic data; the human analyst may then use the output for formulating, checking, or testing rules or generalizations about the language.

MODEL B. In the *induction* model, the computer is a means of deriving ("inducing") generalizations automatically from data. The generalizations, in this case, will be stated in terms of frequency or probability, since induction is essentially a statistical process.

MODEL C. The *automatic corpus processing* model increases the value of processing for both Model A and Model B by "annotating" the corpus with descriptive information over and above that found in the original (see Garside et al. 1997). One useful kind of information is provided by the part-of-speech (POS) tagging of the corpus: to each text word is attached a label, or *tag*, indicating its grammatical class. In principle, such tags could be added manually; but in practice, the tagging of any sizeable corpus requires an automatic system which will accomplish the task largely by machine.

Many corpora or partial corpora are now undergoing a further stage of annotation, namely parsing. The resulting parsed corpus, or *treebank*, is extremely laborious to compile by hand, and so the development of an automatic corpus parser is required (although manual post-editing is also normally necessary). An example of a large treebank generally available for research is the Penn Treebank, compiled by Marcus et al. 1993. Because of the unrestricted nature of the text, corpus tagging and parsing systems have special requirements, such as an ability to cope with a large and open-ended vocabulary. They often rely on probabilistic methods, which are approximative but preeminently robust.

MODEL D. The *self-organizing* model addresses a current major problem of Model C: that corpus processing systems such as probabilistic parsers require a large body of already analyzed text on which to be "trained"—that is, to be given adequate frequency statistics for the automatic analysis of further text. Thus a treebank of several million words may be needed to produce frequency data adequate for a probabilistic parser. But compiling such a treebank manually is beyond the bounds of practicality. This problem can be overcome by a self-organizing methodology (Jelinek 1998), using a statistical method which enables the computer to "learn" by interaction with the text data. The computer system, beginning with crude estimates, is able to train itself by progressive approximation to the frequencies inherent in the text data being analyzed.

It will now be evident that Models A–D are closely interdependent. They add up to an extensive and challenging research program which is of interest to linguists, and which also has applications in areas such as speech synthesis, text checking, machine translation, information extraction, and spoken dialogue systems.

Useful introductions to corpus processing are found in McEnery and Wilson 1996, Biber et al. 1998, and Kennedy 1998.

[*See also* Machine Translation; Text; Computational Linguistics; *and* Lexicography.]

BIBLIOGRAPHY

Aarts, Jan, and Theo Van den Heuvel. 1985. Computational tools for the syntactic analysis of corpora. *Linguistics* 23.303–335.

Biber, Douglas, Susan Conrad, and Randi Reppen. 1998. *Corpus linguistics: Investigating language structure and use.* Cambridge: Cambridge University Press.

Francis, W. Nelson, and Henry Kučera. 1964. *Manual of information to accompany a standard sample of present-day edited American English, for use with digital computers.* Providence, R.I.: Department of Linguistics, Brown University. 3d ed., 1979.

Francis, W. Nelson, and Henry Kučera. 1982. *Frequency analysis of English usage: Lexicon and grammar.* Boston: Houghton Mifflin.

Garside, Roger, Geoffrey Leech, and Geoffrey Sampson, eds. 1987. *The computational analysis of English: A corpus-based approach.* London: Longman.

Garside, Roger, Geoffrey Leech, and Anthony McEnery. 1997. *Corpus annotation.* London: Longman.

Jelinek, Frederick. 1998. *Statistical methods for speech recognition.* Cambridge, Mass.: The MIT Press.

Kennedy, Graeme. 1998. *An introduction to corpus linguistics.* London: Longman.

Knowles, Gerry, Brony Williams, and Peter Alderson. 1996. *A corpus of formal British English speech.* London: Longman.

Marcus, Mitchell, Beatrice Santorini, and Mary Marcinkiewicz. 1994. Building a large annotated corpus of English: The Penn Treebank. *Computational Linguistics.* 19.313–330.

McEnery, Tony, and Andrew Wilson. 1996. *Corpus linguistics.* Edinburgh: Edinburgh University Press.

Sinclair, John M., ed. 1987. *Looking up: An account of the COBUILD project.* London: Collins ELT.

Svartvik, Jan, et al. 1982. *Survey of spoken English: Report on research, 1975–1981.* (Lund studies in English, 63.) Lund: Gleerup.

GEOFFREY LEECH

COUNTABILITY. *See* Nouns *and* Semantics.

CREOLES. *See* Pidgins and Creoles.

CRITICAL LINGUISTICS. The term *critical linguistics* was first used by a group, mainly of linguists, at the

University of East Anglia in the 1970s (Fowler et al. 1979). Their linguistics was "critical" in the sense that it set out to reveal hidden power relations and ideological processes which were at work in linguistic texts. Following the common practice, this article extends the term to other schools who share these objectives; however, some of them prefer to describe themselves as "discourse analysts," "pragmaticists" (Mey 1985), or simply "sociolinguists." (For general reference, see Fairclough 1989.)

Critical linguists see their work as a departure from "mainstream" linguistics. They criticize the latter for a preoccupation with form and formalism at the expense of social function, for describing the linguistic practices of a society without attempting to explain them socially, and for taking such practices at face value in ways which obscure their ideological and political investment. Much critical linguistics is critical *discourse analysis*—that is, analysis of spoken or written texts in relation to the social context of their production and interpretation. Other work is concerned, for example, with finding socially satisfactory bases for grammar, with studies of language standardization as a facet of social or class struggle, or with more critical approaches to language education. This article will focus on critical discourse analysis.

The emergence of critical linguistics is associated with the prominence given to language in recent social theory, which is sometimes said to have undergone a "linguistic turn." Major theorists like Michel Foucault and Jürgen Habermas give language a central place in the production and reproduction of society, and in the constitution of relations of power. Developments in the theory of ideology, associated especially with Antonio Gramsci and Louis Althusser, see ideologies as embedded in social practices and as part of "common sense"; this view has suggested to others a focus upon language practices as the main locus of ideology. Althusser and Foucault have also contributed to a new view of the social subject as non-unitary, constituted in social practice (including language), and constantly open to reconstitution. Other significant influences on critical linguistics include semiology (notably the work of Roland Barthes), and the rediscovery, mainly via literary theory, of the early Soviet critical work of Mikhail Bakhtin and V. N. Voloshinov.

Michel Pêcheux and the French school of discourse analysis—working within the structuralist articulation of Marxism, linguistics, and psychoanalysis (specifically that of Lacan) which developed in the 1960s and 1970s in France—have highlighted the linguistic dimensions of ideology and of the constitution of subjects, through conceptualizing "discourse" as the specifically linguistic material form of ideology. Althusser was the main theoretical influence in the earlier work of this school; more recently, they have drawn increasingly upon the theorization of discourse in the work of Foucault. Pêcheux emphasizes semantics and the variability of word meaning according to ideology, associating different "discursive formations" with different "ideological formations"; he deals mainly with written political discourse, but more recent French work addresses other linguistic levels and discourse types (Maingueneau 1987).

Pêcheux's method aims to reconstruct discursive formations from corpora of texts, not to analyze specific texts; in contrast, text analysis is primary for the East Anglia group, who aim to provide a critical resource usable by non-linguists. From Michael A. K. Halliday they have inherited a concern to combine close formal analysis of texts with social analysis. They focus on written mass-media texts, and on the analysis of grammar: choices in transitivity and modality, for example, are treated as ideologically determined. Members of the East Anglia group, in collaboration with semioticians and still under the influence of Halliday, have more recently been involved in developing a "social semiotics" approach in Australia; this approach investigates non-verbal as well as verbal semiotic codes within a critical framework (Hodge and Kress 1988).

More recently, several new positions have developed within critical discourse analysis (Fairclough and Wodak 1997). Some recent research aims at making a specifically discourse-analytical contribution to social research on the major transformations affecting the contemporary world ("globalization," the restructuring of capitalism, and their ramifications throughout social life). This is leading to a more intensive dialogue between critical discourse analysis and social theory and research about the nature of discourse and its relationship to other aspects of social life, about whether and how discourse "constitutes" or "constructs" the social, and so forth (Chouliaraki and Fairclough 1999). Many social researchers now analyze discourse, but few of them analyze linguistic texts and interactions in any detail. What critical discourse analysis can perhaps best contribute to social research is new resources for analysis that are better fitted to the concerns of the latter than existing analytical frameworks developed within linguistics.

[*See also* Discourse, *article on* Critical Discourse Analysis; Power and Language; Pragmatics and Contextual Semantics; Semiotics; Linguistics and Literature; *and* Sociolinguistics.]

BIBLIOGRAPHY

Chouliaraki, Lilie, and Norman Fairclough. 1999. *Discourse in late modernity.* Edinburgh: Edinburgh University Press.

Fairclough, Norman. 1989. *Language and power.* London: Longman.

Fairclough, Norman, and Ruth Wodak. 1997. Critical discourse analysis. In *Discourse as Social interaction,* edited by Tenn van Dijk. London: Sage.

Fowler, Roger, et al. 1979. *Language and control.* London: Routledge and Kegan Paul.

Hodge, Robert, and Gunther Kress. 1988. *Social semiotics.* Cambridge: Polity Press. Ithaca, N.Y.: Cornell University Press.

Maingueneau, Dominique. 1987. *Nouvelles tendances en analyse du discours.* Paris: Hachette.

Mey, Jacob L. 1985. *Whose language? A study in linguistic pragmatics.* Amsterdam: Benjamins.

NORMAN FAIRCLOUGH

CRITICAL PERIODS. *See* Acquisition of Language; Evolution and Language; *and* Cognitive Science.

CROCE, BENEDETTO (1866–1952). Italian idealist philosopher. Croce's treatise *Estetica* (1902) develops aesthetics as a science of expression with which general linguistic theory is identified. Language is seen as "perpetual creation," and individual expression represents the reality of language. Grammar and other systems are merely artificial creations of linguists. In his antipositivistic attitudes, Croce was very influential in Italy and also in France.

ANNA MORPURGO DAVIES

CROSS RIVER LANGUAGES. Spoken in southeastern Nigeria, with some overspill into Cameroon; they form a branch of BENUE-CONGO.

LANGUAGE LIST

Abua: also called Abuan. 25,000 speakers in Nigeria, in Rivers state, Degema and Ahoada LGAs. Dialects are Central Abuan, Emughan, Otabha (Otapha), Okpeden. The central dialect is understood by all others. Odual is the most closely related language.

Agoi: also called Wagoi, Ro Bambami, Wa Bambani, Ibami. 12,000 speakers in Nigeria, Cross River state, Obubra LGA, Agoi-Ekpo, Ekom-Agoi, Agoi-Ibami, and Itu-Agoi towns.

Agwagwune: also called Agwaguna, Gwune, Akurakura, Okurikan. "Akunakuna" is a derogatory name sometimes used. 20,000 speakers in Nigeria, Cross River state, Akamkpa LGA. Dialects are Abayongo (Bayono, Bayino), Abini (Obini, Abiri), Adim (Odim, Dim), Orum, Erei (Enna, Ezei), Agwagwune, Etono (Etuno). A dialect cluster.

Alege: also called Alegi, Uge, Ugbe. 1,200 speakers in Nigeria, Cross River state, Obudu LGA. Related to Gayi (Bisu of Obanliku cluster) of Nigeria and Cameroon.

Anaang: also called Anang, Annang. 1,000,000 speakers in Nigeria, Akwa Ibom state, Ikot Ekpene, Essien Udim, Abak, Ukanafun, and Oruk-Anam LGAs. Dialects are Ikot Ekpene, Abak, Ukanafun.

Baan: also called Baan-Ogoi, Goi, Ogoi. 5,000 speakers in Nigeria, Rivers state, Gokana, Tai, and Eleme LGAs, Ban-Ogoi plus villages. Dialects are Ka-Ban, Kesari.

Bakpinka: also called Begbungba, Uwet, Iyongiyong, Iyoniyong. Spoken in Nigeria. Cross River state, Akamkpa LGA. Reported to be dying out.

Bekwarra: also called Ebekwara, Bekworra, Yakoro. 100,000 speakers in Nigeria, Cross River state, Ogoja LGA.

Bete-Bendi: also called Bette-Bendi, Dama. 36,800 speakers in Nigeria, Cross River state, Obudu LGA. Dialects are Bete (Bette, Mbete), Bendi.

Bokyi: also called Boki, Nki, Okii, Uki, Nfua, Osikom, Osukam, Vaaneroki. 144,000 speakers in Nigeria and Cameroon. In Nigeria: 140,000 speakers. Cross River state, Ikom, Obudu, and Ogoja LGAs. Dialects are Basua (Bashua), Irruan (Erwan, Eerwee), Boje (Bojie), Kwakwagom, Nsadop, Osokom, Wula (Baswo, Okundi, Kecwan), Oku, Boorim, Oyokom, Abo (Abu), Eastern Bokyi (East Boki). Important district language. In Cameroon: Along Nigerian border northwest of Mamfe, Akwaya Subdivision, Manyu Division, South West Province. Dialects are Basua, Boki, Iruan.

Bumaji: spoken in Nigeria. Cross River state, Obudu LGA, Bumaji town.

Cross River Mbembe: also called Okam, Oderiga, Wakande, Ifunubwa, Ekokoma, Ofunobwam. 100,000 speakers in Nigeria, Cross River state, Obubra and Ikom LGAs; Anambra state, Abakaliki LGA. Dialects are Okom (Eghom, Ohana-Onyen), Apiapum, Adun, Osopong (Osophong, Ezopong), Ofombonga (Ewumbonga), Ofonokpan, Ekama (Ekamu), Oferikpe.

Doko-Uyanga: also called Uyanga, Dosanga, Basanga, Iko. Spoken in Nigeria, Cross River state, Akamkpa LGA, several towns.

Ebughu: also called Oron. 5,000 speakers in Nigeria, Akwa Ibom state, Mbo and Oron LGAs. Listed separately in Crozier and Blench 1992.

FIGURE1. *Subgrouping of Cross River Languages*

Bendi
  Alege, Bekwarra, Bete-Bendi, Bokyi, Bumaji, Obanliku, Putukwam, Ubang, Ukpe-Bayobiri
Delta-Cross
  Central Delta
    Abua-Odual
      Abua, Odual
    Kugbo
      Kugbo, Mini, Obulom, Ogbia, Ogbogolo, Ogbronuagum
  Lower Cross
    Obolo
      Eki
      Idere
      Obolo
      Ebughu
      Efai
    Efik
      Anaang, Efik, Ibibio, Ukwa
    Ekit
      Ekit, Etebi
    Enwang-Uda
      Enwan, Uda
    Ibino
    Ibuoro
      Ibuoro, Ito, Itu Mbon Uzo, Nkari
    Iko
    Ilue
    Okobo
    Oro
    Usaghade
Ogoni

East Ogoni
  Gokana, Khana
West Ogoni
  Baan, Eleme
Upper Cross
  Agoi-Doko-Iyoniyong
    Agoi, Bakpinka, Doko-Uyanga
  Akpet
    Ukpet-Ehom
  Central Upper Cross
    East-West Central Upper Cross
      Ikom
        Olulumo-Ikom
      Loko
        Lokaa, Lubila, Nkukoli
      Mbembe-Legbo
      Legbo
        Legbo, Lenyima, Leyigha
      Mbembe
        Cross River Mbembe
    North-South Upper Cross
    Koring-Kukele
      Koring
        Oring
      Kukele
        Kukele, Uzekwe
    Ubaghara-Kohumono
      Kohumono
        Agwagwune, Kohumono, Umon
        Ubaghara
Kiong-Korop
  Kiong, Korop, Odut

Efai: also called Effiat. 5,000 speakers in Nigeria and Cameroon. In Nigeria: Akwa Ibom state, Mbo LGA. Listed separately in Crozier and Blench 1992. In Cameroon: Isangele subdivision.

Efik: also called Calabar. 400,000 speakers in Nigeria. Cross River state, Calabar municipality, Odukpani and Akamkpa LGAs. Akwa Ibom Stete, Itu town. The major dialect and language of the Ibibio-Efik group. Used in adult education, university courses. Decreasing in use as a second language. Roman alphabet. National language.

Eki: 5,000 speakers in Nigeria, Cross River state, northeast of Efik, south of Idere. Probably Central Lower Cross, related to Anaang. Close to Idere.

Ekit: also called Eket. 200,000 speakers in Nigeria, Akwa Ibom state, Uquo Ibeno and Eket LGAs. Some dialect variation.

Eleme: 58,000 speakers in Nigeria, Rivers state, Otelga LGA.

Enwan: also called Oron. 15,000 speakers in Nigeria, Akwa Ibom state, Mbo LGA.

Etebi: 15,000 speakers in Nigeria, Akwa Ibom state, Uquo Ibeno LGA.

Gokana: 100,000 speakers in Nigeria, Rivers state, Gokana, Tai, and Eleme LGAs.

Ibibio: 1,500,000 speakers in Nigeria. Akwa Ibom state, Itu, Uyo, Etinan, Ikot Abasi, Ikono, Ekpe-Atai, Uruan, Onna, Nsit-Ubium, and Mkpat Enin LGAs. Dialects are Enyong, Central Ibibio, Itak, Nsit. Several dialects. Efik is decreasing in use as literary language. Ibibio is the main trade language of Akwa Ibom state. Used in university courses. Roman alphabet. Trade language.

Ibino: also called Ibeno, Ibuno. 10,000 speakers in Nigeria, Akwa Ibom state, Uquo-Ibeno LGA.

Ibuoro: 5,000 speakers in Nigeria, Akwa Ibom state, Itu and Ikono LGAs.

Idere: 5,000 speakers in Nigeria, Akwa Ibom state, Itu LGA. Probably Central Lower Cross, related to Anaang. Close to Eki.

Iko: 5,000 speakers in Nigeria, Akwa Ibom state, Ikot Abasi

LGA, three villages. Culturally they consider themselves Obolo, but they cannot use Obolo literature. The language is closer to other Lower Cross languages than to Obolo.

Ilue: also called Idua. 5,000 speakers in Nigeria, Akwa Ibom state, Oron LGA. Generally not used by younger people. Diminishing in size. Reported to be giving way to Efik or Oron.

Ito: 5,000 speakers in Nigeria. Akwa Ibom state, Akamkpa LGA.

Itu Mbon Uzo: also called Itu Mbon Uso, Itu Mbuzo. 5,000 speakers in Nigeria, Akwa Ibom state, Ikono and Itu LGAs.

Khana: also called Kana, Ogoni. 200,000 speakers in Nigeria, Rivers state, Khana, Gokana, and Iyigbo LGAs. Dialects are Tai, Yeghe, Norkhana, Ken-Khana, Boúe. Closely related to Gokana, Eleme. Important district language.

Kiong: also called Akayon, Akoiyang, Okonyong, Okoyong, Iyoniyong. Spoken in Nigeria, Cross River state, Odukpani and Akampka LGAs. Bilingualism in Efik. Spoken only by elderly people; the younger generation speaks Efik. For several generations before now, the people were bilingual in Kiong and Efik.

Kohumono: also called Bahumono, Ohumono, Ediba, Humono, Ekumuru. 30,000 speakers in Nigeria, Cross River state, Obubra LGA.

Korop: also called Ododop, Durop, Kurop. 12,500 speakers in Nigeria and Cameroon. In Nigeria: Cross River state, Odukpani and Akampka LGAs. Speakers in Nigeria are reported to be mostly bilingual in Efik. In Cameroon: Northwest of Mundemba, along Nigerian border, Ndian division, South West Province.

Kugbo: 2,000 speakers in Nigeria. Rivers state, Brass LGA.

Kukele: also called Ukele, Bakele. 95,000 speakers in Nigeria, Cross River state, Ogoja LGA; Ebonyi state, Abakaliki LGA; Benue state, Okpokwu and Oju LGAs. Dialects are Mtezi, Ugbala, Iteeji. Four dialects in the north, three in the south, besides those named.

Legbo: also called Agbo, Gbo, Igbo, Imaban, Itigidi. 60,000 speakers in Nigeria, Cross River state, Obubra LGA; Ebonyi state, Afikpo LGA.

Lenyima: also called Anyima, Inyima. Spoken in Nigeria, Cross River state, Obubra LGA.

Leyigha: also called Asiga, Assiga, Ayigha, Ayiga, Yigha. 10,000 speakers in Nigeria, Cross River state, Obubra LGA.

Lokaa: also called Yakurr, Yakö, Loko, Loke, Luko. 120,000 speakers in Nigeria, Cross River state, Obubra LGA. Dialects are Ugep, Nkpam.

Lubila: also called Lubilo, Kabila, Kabire, Ojor, Ofor. Spoken in Nigeria, Cross River state, Akamkpa LGA, at Ojo Nkomba and Ojo Akangba.

Mini: spoken in Nigeria. Rivers state, Brass LGA, three villages.

Nkari: 5,000 speakers in Nigeria, Akwa Ibom state, Ikono LGA. Formerly thought to be a dialect of Ibibio. Ibibio is the main trade language of Akwa Ibom state.

Nkukoli: also called Lokoli, Lokukoli, Nkokolle, Ekuri. 1,000 speakers in Nigeria, Cross River state, at the juncture of Ikom, Obubra and Akamkpa LGAs, Iko Ekperem Development Area.

Obanliku: also called Abanliku. 65,000 speakers in Nigeria, Cross River state, Obudu LGA. Dialects are Bebi, Busi, Basang, Bisu (Gayi), Bishiri. Dialect cluster. Related to Alege.

Obolo: also called Andoni, Andone, Andonni. 100,000 speakers in Nigeria. Dialects are Ngo, Ataba, Unyeada, Okoroete, Ibot Obolo. Ngo is the prestige dialect. Ibibio and Ibo are the trade languages. English is learned in school. In the east there is a movement toward establishing a stronger Obolo ethnic identity and getting rid of borrowed words from Ibibio.

Obulom: also called Abuloma. Spoken in Nigeria, Rivers state, Okrika LGA, Abuloma town.

Odual: also called Saka. 18,000 speakers in Nigeria, Rivers state, Ahoada LGA. Dialects are Arughaunya, Adibom.

Odut: 20 speakers remain in Nigeria, Cross River state, Odukpani LGA.

Ogbia: also called Ogbinya. 200,000 speakers in Nigeria, Bayelsa state, Brass LGA. Dialects are Kolo, Oloibiri, Anyama. Dialect cluster but all inherently intelligible. English making little impact.

Ogbogolo: also called Obogolo. 10,000 speakers in Nigeria, Rivers state, Ahoada LGA, one town.

Ogbronuagum: also called Bukuma. 12,000 speakers in Nigeria. Ethnic population: 12,000 as of 2000. Rivers state, Degema LGA, Bukuma village near Buguma.

Okobo: 50,000 speakers in Nigeria, Akwa Ibom state, Okobo LGA. Possibly two dialects.

Olulumo-Ikom: also called Lulumo. 30,000 speakers in Nigeria, Cross River state, Ikom LGA. May also be in Cameroon. Dialects are Okuni, Olulumo, Ikom.

Oring: also called Orri, Orrin, Orringorrin, Koring. 75,000 speakers in Nigeria, Benue state, Okpokwu LGA; Ebonyi state, Ishielu LGA. Dialects are Okpoto, Ufia (Utonkon), Ufiom (Effium).

Oro: also called Oron. 75,000 speakers in Nigeria, Akwa-Ibom state, Oron LGA. Some dialect variation.

Putukwam: also called Utugwang, Mbe Afal, Mbube Eastern. 12,000 speakers in Nigeria, Cross River state, Obudu and Ogoja LGAs. Dialects are Utugwang (Otukwang), Okorogung, Okorotung, Afrike (Aferike), Obe (Mbe East), Oboso. Member of the Obe cluster. Speakers are reported to understand Bekwarra well.

Ubaghara: 30,000 speakers in Nigeria, Cross River state, Akampka LGA. Dialects are Biakpan, Ikun, Etono, Ugbem, Utuma (Utama, Utamu). Dialect cluster.

Ubang: spoken in Nigeria, Cross River state, Obudu LGA.

Uda: 10,000 speakers in Nigeria, Akwa Ibom state, Mbo LGA.

Ukpe-Bayobiri: 12,000 speakers in Nigeria, Cross River state,

Obudu and Ikom LGAs. Dialects are Ukpe, Bayobiri. Dialect cluster.

Ukpet-Ehom: also called Akpet-Ehom. Spoken in Nigeria, Cross River state, Akamkpa LGA. Dialects are Ukpet (Akpet), Ehom (Ubeteng, Ebeteng). A dialect cluster.

Ukwa: spoken in Nigeria, Cross River state, Akampka LGA.

Umon: also called Amon. 20,000 speakers in Nigeria, Cross River state, Akampka LGA, 25 villages.

Usaghade: also called Usakade, Usakedet, Isangele. 10,000 speakers in Cameroon and Nigeria. In Cameroon: Mainly in Cameroon, Isangele subdivision. A separate language from Efik. In Nigeria: Cross River state, Odukpani LGA, half of a village. In and around Calabar.

Uzekwe: also called Ezekwe. 5,000 speakers in Nigeria, Cross River state, Ogoja LGA.

B. GRIMES

CUNEIFORM, lit. 'wedge-shaped' writing (from Latin *cuneus* 'wedge'), was used in the Near East from ca. 2900 BCE to the 1st century CE; its earliest examples have been found in Uruk (now Warka, ca. 250 km southeast of Baghdad). It was used primarily in Mesopotamia, the area between the Euphrates and Tigris Rivers in present-day Iraq. Cuneiform texts have also been found in southwestern Iran at Susa; in Syria at Ugarit, Ebla, and Emar; in Turkey at Boghazköy; in Palestine at Megiddo; and in Egypt at Tell el-Amarna. The great majority of these texts are written in Sumerian, an isolated language, or in Akkadian (also known as Assyro-Babylonian), a Semitic language. However, many other languages from various linguistic families used the same system through the centuries, including Eblaite, Elamite, Hurrian and Urartian, Ugartian, Ugaritic, Old Persian, Hittite, Palaic, and Luvian. All these languages use basically the same inventory of signs; only Ugaritic and Old Persian created their own sign systems.

The normal medium was clay tablets, on which wedge-shaped impressions were made with a stylus. Cuneiform writing could also be carved on stone—or, rarely, painted, for example, on bricks or ceramics. Documents on perishable materials, such as wood, leather, or papyrus, are known to have existed, but have not survived, except for a few examples on wooden boards covered with wax. As many as 375,000 tablets are now preserved in museums, and more come to light every year in archaeological digs. (For general reference, see Civil 1973, Reiner 1973, Diakonoff 1975, Borger 1981, Edzard 1980, 1982, and Walker 1987.)

1. Decipherment. The existence of cuneiform writing was forgotten in the Western scholarly world—in contrast to the more visually appealing Egyptian hieroglyphs, which were never completely forgotten—and was rediscovered by European travelers only in the 17th century. In 1802, G. F. Grotefend succeeded in reading the royal names in a trilingual (Akkadian-Elamite-Persian) inscription. Progress was rapid, and the process of decipherment, which included Akkadian, can be considered completed by 1857. In that year, H. C. Rawlinson, Edward Hincks, W. H. Fox Talbot, and Jules Oppert presented independent and sealed translations of the same text to the Royal Asiatic Society in London; when opened, the four translations were found to be essentially in agreement. In present-day studies, determination of the meanings and phonetic shapes of cuneiform signs is solidly based on native word lists used for scribal training. Lexical collections—mostly Sumero-Akkadian bilinguals with tens of thousands of words, arranged either by sign shapes or thematically—have been reconstructed from school exercises. In their most complete form, the lexical entries include several columns, as shown in the example in Figure 1: (a) the phonological description of the Sumerian word in terms of a set of basic syllabograms; (b) the

FIGURE 1. *Sumero-Akkadian Lexical Entries*

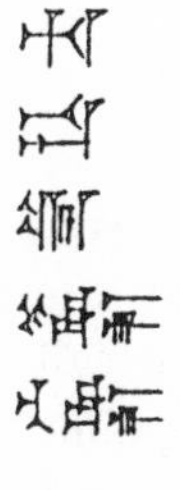

(a)	(b)	(c)	
mu-še-en	(MUŠEN)	*iṣ-ṣu-ru*	'bird'
gu-up	(DU)	*ú-zu-uz-zu*	'to stand up'
pe-eš	(ŠÀXA)	*e-ru-ú*	'to be pregnant'
na-qa	(NAGA)	*uh-hu-lu*	'vegetable ashes'
ši-ni-ik	(ŠINIG)	*bi-i-nu*	'tamarisk tree'

corresponding logogram, conventionally transcribed in small capitals; and (c) the syllabically written Akkadian translation.

The meanings of the Akkadian words in column (c) are suggested by comparison with closely related languages of the Semitic family, and are confirmed by contextual analysis. The phonological shapes of syllabograms were first established in transliterations of foreign words, and were subsequently refined by comparative Semitic sound correspondences. Frequent alternative spellings, for example, *ka-al-bu* and *kal-bu* (both representing /kalbu/ 'dog'), provide confirmation. The same syllabograms are used to give the phonemic forms of Sumerian words; however, distortions in the cross-language representation of sounds, and the lack of comparative material, result in a less precise definition of the Sumerian phonemic inventory.

2. The system. Cuneiform signs have three main functions:

(a) As *syllabograms*, they represent a word, or part of it, on a phonemic level.
(b) As *logograms*, they represent an entire word on a lexical level.
(c) As *classificators* or *determinatives*, they assign the word to a semantic set with no direct phonological connotation.

Some syllabograms ("polyphonic signs") may have more than one pronunciation; thus the same syllabogram may be read *ne, dè, bí,* or *bil,* depending on its context. Conversely, different signs can have apparently homophonous readings, which are indicated in transliteration by accents or subscripts. The homophony sometimes is the result of our imprecise knowledge of the phonemic systems, especially the Sumerian. A logogram can have several different meanings, and consequently different phonemic connotations. The system has devices to reduce ambiguity to reasonable levels. In general, a word can be written syllabically or logographically, depending on the language of the text, and on scribal habits and traditions. Examples of syllabically written words are *še-er-ha-an* 'ornament' in Sumerian and *ni-ik-nu-kà-kum-ma* 'we sealed it for you' in Akkadian. A sign used as a logogram, for example, ŠINIG in Figure 1, can be read either as Sumerian /šinik/ or Akkadian /bīnu/, depending on the language of the reader. As a consequence, some texts can be, and in ancient times undoubtedly were, read indifferently in Sumerian or Akkadian.

Uncertainties about readings and meanings are dis-

pelled partly by the context, and partly by the writing system itself, through the use of classificators and "phonetic indicators." Thus, when used as a classificator, the sign GIŠ assigns the word following it to the class of trees or wooden objects. About twenty of these signs are in common use, mostly designating physical classes: raw materials, zoological and botanical types, toponyms, and so on. There is one to indicate human professions or conditions, one for the female gender, and one for divine beings. A "phonetic indicator" is a syllabogram, used mostly in Sumerian, which is added to a logogram to give its pronunciation, partially or in toto. Such signs are in principle optional, but tradition dictates their use within relatively narrow limits; for instance:

$$\textit{ú} + \textsc{naga} + \textit{ga} + \textsc{mušen}$$

(The phonetic complements, the only parts which are "read," are in lower case.) The logogram transliterated NAGA is read /uga/ when it means 'raven'. It will normally be followed by the classificator MUŠEN to show that the word belongs to the lexical set of birds. Traditionally, but not always, it is accompanied by the syllabograms *ú* and *ga* to specify its pronunciation and to prevent ambiguity. With other classificators, the same logogram has different meanings with different readings: /naga/ 'vegetable ashes' with the classificator for vegetables, /teme/ 'a plant, *Salsola* sp.' with the sign for plants, /ereš/ (a toponym) with the sign for town, and /nidaba/ (a goddess) with the classificator of divine beings. Phonetic complements are less frequent, and more variable, in Akkadian.

Although the cuneiform signs are the same for Sumerian and Akkadian, they are used in different ways. Sumerian is essentially logographic, using syllabograms to represent proper names, loanwords, and bound morphemes. Examples of Sumerian texts entirely written in syllabograms, perhaps for didactic purposes or because of the scribe's unfamiliarity with the standard system, are secondary and relatively rare. But Akkadian uses predominantly syllabograms and reserves logograms for convenient abbreviations. In technical or repetitious texts, the number of logograms can be quite high. In a typical letter, for instance, only 3–5% of the signs will be logograms; but in long, repetitious lists of omens, the logograms can constitute more than 80% of the total number of signs. The other languages (Hurrian, Hittite, and so on) use syllabic cuneiform. In addition, Hittite uses syllabically written Akkadian words as logograms ('Akkadograms').

3. History. In their earliest form, cuneiform signs were

FIGURE 2. *Evolution of Cuneiform*

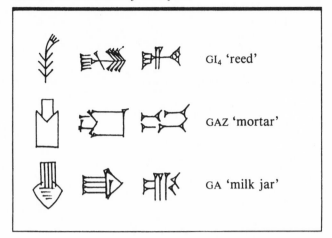

pictographic, that is, representations of physical objects. The curved lines were later replaced by straight stylus impressions, and the shapes were progressively simplified; this culminated in the Neo-Assyrian script, in which only a limited number of wedge shapes are admitted, and every wedge is significant. In earlier, intermediate stages, only the general form of the sign is significant, and there is a certain latitude in the number of strokes of the stylus. To recognize the objects originally depicted, the reader must be aware that, in modern editions, most texts have to be rotated 90 degrees to the right to reposition the signs in their initial orientation. Figure 2 illustrates the historical evolution of cuneiform signs.

The oldest texts (Early Dynastic Period, 2900–2350 BCE) present two unexpected features. First, texts are divided into "cases," each of which contains a phrase or clause. The arrangement of signs within a case is free; that is, the signs do not follow the syntactic sequence, which suggests that scribes represented speech at the sentence level. For instance, the phrase *si gù ba-ni-in-ra* 'he sounded there the horn' can be written:

si	*gù*	or as	*gù*	*si*
ra ba			*ba ra*	

or in any other arrangement. This example also illustrates a second feature: sentence elements, mostly bound morphemes, that could be predicted from the context (here the locative infix *-ni-* and the 3rd person agent mark *-n-*) are omitted, to be supplied by the reader. After the 24th century BCE, morphemes are represented in their proper sequence, and very few syllabograms are omitted. Up to the beginning of the Old Babylonian period (19th century BCE), syllabic writings tend to omit final consonants in

certain cases, as in *é-ba* 'pair' or *ma-sá* 'a basket' (for later *é-ba-an* and *ma-sá-ab*).

4. Writing and phonology. In older texts, syllabograms tend to represent the consonants in an underdifferentiated way; thus a single sign stands for the voiced and the voiceless homorganic stop (and in Akkadian, also the emphatic plosive)—that is, the same sign represents /da/, /ta/, and /ṭa/. No conclusions as to the phonemic inventory of a language can be inferred from this purely graphic simplification. The existence of a voicing rule, demonstrably present in the case of Sumerian, seems sufficient to account for this scribal practice. A peculiarity attested so far only in texts from Ebla, ca. 2400 BCE, is the optional omission of the consonant *l*. Alternative writings show that it is a graphic feature of no phonological significance. Similar considerations apply to the occasional use of *l*-signs to represent *r*. In more recent texts, writing seems to render phonological shapes adequately—controllable in the case of Akkadian by comparative etymologies. There are, however, three exceptions:

(a) It is possible that the loss of Semitic laryngeals in Akkadian texts does not properly reflect the linguistic situation; such consonants may simply have been omitted in writing—perhaps because of their absence from the Sumerian phonemic inventory, and the subsequent lack of traditional signs to represent them.

(b) The second exception results from an inherent limitation of a syllabic system: initial and final consonant clusters cannot be directly represented, and the scribe has to add prothetic or epenthetic vowels. Thus a theoretical */pras/ would have to be written *pa-ra-as*. In rare cases, especially in early periods, a cluster C_1C_2 is written C_2, even in medial position.

(c) Finally, in Sumerian and in a few cases in Akkadian, the scribes used morphophonemic representations. For instance, the Sumerian subjunctive/optative verbal prefix is subject to vowel harmony, with the allomorphs *ha-*, *he-*, and *hu-*. In early periods, *ha-* may be written before syllables with *u*, where later texts consistently write *hu-*.

5. Derived systems (Ugaritic, Old Persian). During the 13th–14th centuries BCE, scribes in Ugarit (present Ras Shamra on the Syrian coast) used a system based on the traditional clay and stylus, but radically different in its representation of the language. It consists of thirty purely consonantal signs, with the exception of three which represent the voiceless glottal stop (aleph) followed by the vowels *a, u,* or *i*. It thus belongs to the

FIGURE 3. *Sumerian Writing (Fable of 17th Century BCE)*

kur-gi₄^{mušen}e ^{ú}NAGA$^{ga\ mušen}$

mu-na-ni-ib-gi₄-gi₄

mušen-dù-e sa ma-ná-e

kurgi-e uga mu-na-ni-b-gi-gi mušendu-e sa ma-na-e
'Crane answered Raven: "The fowler will lay down a net against me." '

FIGURE 4. *Akkadian Writing (Code of Hammurabi, ca. 1775 BCE)*

šum-ma DUMU a-ba-šu

im-ta-ha-aṣ

KIŠIB.LÁ-šu

i-na-ak-ki-su

šumma mārum abašu imtahaṣ rittašu inakkisu
'If a son strikes his father, they will cut off his hand (lit. 'fist').'

northwestern Semitic tradition and is functionally similar to Aramaic and Phoenician. In the 6th century BCE, in a different reaction to the complexity of the traditional Sumero-Akkadian system, Old Persian was written with a syllabary of thirty-six new simple signs, completed by half a dozen logograms and auxiliary signs.

6. Writing samples are given in Figures 3–4. Classificators and phonetic complements are written in superscripts; accents and subscripts are used to distinguish homophonous signs. In the Sumerian transcription, hyphens separate morphemes.

[*See also* Akkadian; Decipherment; Elamite; History of Linguistics, *article on* Babylonian Grammatical Tradition; Hittite; Hurrian and Urartian; *and* Writing and Written Language, *article on* Writing Systems.]

BIBLIOGRAPHY

Borger, Rykle. 1981. *Assyrisch-babylonische Zeichenliste.* (Alter Orient und Altes Testament, 33/33A.) Neukirchen-Vluyn: Neukirchener Verlag.

Civil, Miguel. 1973. The Sumerian writing system: Some problems. *Orientalia* n.s. 42.21–34.

Diakonoff, Igor M. 1975. Ancient writing and ancient written language: Pitfalls and peculiarities in the study of Sumerian. In *Sumeriological studies in honor of Thorkild Jacobsen on his seventieth birthday* (Assyriological studies, 20), pp. 99–121. Chicago: University of Chicago Press.

Edzard, Dietz O. 1980. Keilschrift. In *Reallexikon der Assyriologie* 5.544–568. Berlin: de Gruyter.

Edzard, Dietz O. 1982. Der Aufbau des Syllabars 'Proto-Ea'. In *Societes and languages of the ancient Near East: Studies in honour of I. M. Diakonoff,* edited by M. A. Dandamayev et al., pp. 42–61. Warminster, England: Aris and Phillips.

Reiner, Erica. 1973. How we read cuneiform texts. *Journal of Cuneiform Studies* 25.3–58.

Walker, Christopher B. F. 1987. *Reading the past: Cuneiform.* London: British Museum.

MIGUEL CIVIL

CUSHITIC LANGUAGES. The term "Cushitic" is applied to a group of some 50 languages which make up one of the sub-families of Afroasiatic. The territory of Cushitic comprises the northern Sudan from the Egyptian border, the republics of Djibouti and Somalia, a large part of Ethiopia and Kenya, and some isolated areas of northern Tanzania (see Map 1).

The Cushitic language family consists of the subgroups

MAP 1. *Distribution of Cushitic Languages*

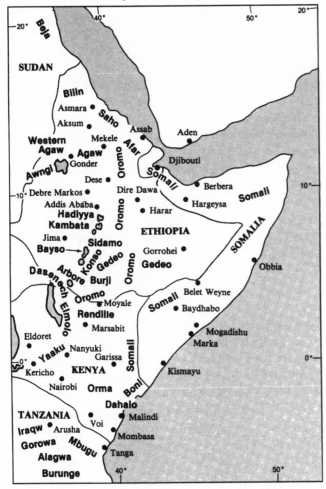

FIGURE 1. *Subgroups of the Cushitic Language Family*

Central Cushitic (Agaw)
    Western Agaw (including Kemant and Quara), Awngi, Bilin, Khamtanga
Eastern Cushitic
    Dullay
        Dihina, Dobase, Gaba, Gawwada, Gergere, Gobeze, Gollango, Gorose, Harso, Tsamai
    Highland East Cushitic
        Alaba, Burji, Gedeo, Hadiyya, Kambata, Sidamo
    Konso-Gidole
    Oromo
    Rendille-Boni
    Saho-Afar
    Somali
    Western Omo-Tana
        Arbore, Bayso, Dasenech, Elmolo
    Yaaku
Northern Cushitic
    Beja
Southern Cushitic
    Aasáx, Alagwa, Burunge, Dahalo, Iraqw, Kw'adza

shown in Figure 1, with their territories indicated in parentheses, with names of some individual languages.

A group of languages considered by some scholars to constitute a West Cushitic branch is regarded by others as constituting a separate Omotic branch within Afroasiatic. Some scholars have cast doubt on the classification of Northern and Southern Cushitic, suggesting rather that Beja is an independent branch of Afroasiatic, and Southern Cushitic a subbranch of Eastern Cushitic (Hetzron 1980).

Until the 1960s, Cushitic was a neglected area of linguistic research. Since then, however, interest in the investigation of these languages has increased greatly; most of the languages are now documented by modern grammars, or at least by sketches. Some of the minor languages remain undescribed. There is still no general introduction to the study of Cushitic languages; for more limited surveys, see Zaborski 1976, Sasse 1981, 1987; for Central Cushitic, see Hetzron 1976. Comparative work includes Sasse 1979 on Eastern Cushitic, and Ehret 1980 and Kiessling 2002 on Southern Cushitic; for reconstruction of the phonology and vocabulary of Proto-Cushitic as a whole, see Ehret 1987.

Characteristic features of the Cushitic phoneme inventory include glottalized consonants, pharyngeals, rounded velars, and (in a restricted area) vowel harmony. Glottalized consonants appear in many variants: the entire series may be ejective (*p' t' k' . . .*) or implosive (*b' d' g' . . .*); *d'* is sometimes retroflex, and *k'* tends to be uvular. The pharyngeals [ḥ ʕ], very rarely found in languages outside Afroasiatic, are fricatives articulated by constricting the pharynx. Vowel harmony occurs in Somali, Boni, and Rendille; these languages possess two varieties of each vowel quality, the distinctive feature being advanced vs. retracted tongue root. All vowels in a word normally belong to the same harmonic category.

In almost all the languages, tonal differentiations play a distinctive role. In contrast to typical tone languages, Cushitic tones are determined primarily by morphosyntax. Generally, two levels are distinguished—high and low—the high tone being the marked member of the opposition. Many grammatical categories (e.g. gender, number, case, mood, focus, and aspect) are marked either by tone alone, or by a combination of a specific tone pattern with a segmental marker. Hyman 1981 has argued that some Cushitic tone systems are so deviant both from the regular "stress" accent systems and from regular "pitch" systems found in the tone languages of West Africa and Asia that a third category of "tone-accent systems" could be justified.

Cushitic morphology is highly synthetic and fusional. Most languages are characterized by extremely complex inflectional systems which use all types of morphemes: prefixes, suffixes, infixes, reduplication, iteration, alternation of stem consonants and vowels, and suprasegmental changes of tone pattern, glottalization, or quantity. Moreover, a tendency toward morphophonemic complexity results in the formation of inflectional classes ("declensions" and "conjugations"). The abundance of clitics, and the tendency in some languages to incorporate nominals into the phonological verb word, result in a somewhat polysynthetic character. The complexity of inflection pertains equally to all inflected word classes. Hence the number of morphologically marked grammatical categories is relatively high, and morphological distinctions among word classes are accordingly great: nouns, verbs, and pronouns differ considerably both in their categories and in their inflectional behavior. Word class distinctions are further supported by rich category-changing derivational morphology (nominalization and verbalization). Only the word class of adjectives is comparatively marginal; it is sometimes entirely lacking, or at best constitutes a closed class with a limited number of members.

Nouns generally distinguish gender, number, and case. Gender is twofold, masculine and feminine, but often does not correspond with sex. In some languages, gender is more or less arbitrarily distributed, mostly on the basis of derivational (or stem-building) affixes which have inherent gender; in others, there is a semantic principle according to which masculine is connected with bigness and importance, and feminine with smallness and insignificance. Number categories are singular, plural, collective, and singulative (i.e. a single element of a collective). Number marking is often derivational rather than inflectional; its morphological means are manifold and heterogeneous, including tone, suffixes, and internal changes. Many nouns are number-indifferent, especially in East Cushitic. The morphologically and semantically defined plural category does not always correspond to a plural category defined on the basis of agreement behavior. Many formally plural nouns do not agree with plural verb forms, but with singular forms, mainly of the opposite gender ("polarity"). Hayward (1981:127ff.) was the first to suggest a solution to this problem: plural *formation* is regarded as part of the derivational system, and plural *agreement* as belonging to the grammatical gender system.

The original Proto-Cushitic case system distinguished two basic case forms: an absolute (the citation form of the noun, predicate, and object case), and a nominative (the subject case). There may also have been a genitive case, as in most modern languages. South Cushitic has totally abandoned case inflection, but many other Cushitic languages have enlarged the case inventory, chiefly by agglutinating postpositions. In Agaw languages, at least seven cases are distinguished (nominative, accusative, comitative, dative, genitive, directive, and ablative). Moreover, the genitive agrees with its head noun in gender, number, and case. Definiteness, deictic categories, and possessive affixes are also part of noun inflection in many languages.

A classical study of Cushitic verb morphology is Zaborski 1976. The basic categories are aspect, tense, and mood; affirmative and negative verb forms are often morphologically distinguished. The original system consisted of four paradigms—imperfective, perfective, subjunctive, and imperative—but this has been enlarged in various ways by different languages. The most conspicuous development has taken place in Agaw, where cliticized conjunctions and auxiliary elements have fused with the personal endings to form a system of 50 or more "tenses." The normal Cushitic paradigm consists of seven forms: three persons each for singular and plural, with a gender distinction in the third person singular. Pronominal markers are prefixed in an archaic conjugation type preserved in some languages; otherwise, they are suffixed. The derivational system exhibits a rich array of categories: different types of causatives, a frequentive, a middle voice, a passive, etc. Many languages of the Eastern and Southern branches have developed a larger verb complex (often called "verbal piece"), with focus markers, negation, subject and object pronouns, preverbs indicating case relations of arguments (locative, instrumental, benefactive, etc.), and occasionally, additional tense markers cliticized to the inflected core verb form.

Cushitic syntax is predominantly discourse-oriented. The discourse categories of topic and focus play a prominent role (for Somali, see Saeed 1984). Grammatical relations such as subject and object are less marked. In many sentences, case distinctions are neutralized; thus, in Somali, the absolutive/nominative distinction is preserved only if the subject is not focused or left-dislocated. In Northern Cushitic languages, there is a tendency toward unmarked S[ubject] O[bject] V[erb] word order, and the NP is head-final. The other languages normally vary their word order according to pragmatic principles, but the verb is generally sentence-final. The only SVO language is Yaaku.

[*See also* African Languages; Afroasiatic Languages; Omotic Languages; *and* Somali.]

BIBLIOGRAPHY

Ehret, Christopher. 1980. *The historical reconstruction of Southern Cushitic Phonology and vocabulary.* (Kölner Beiträge zur Afrikanistik, 5.) Berlin: Reimer.

Ehret, Christopher. 1987. Proto-Cushitic reconstruction. *Sprache und Geschichte in Afrika* 8.7–180.

Hayward, Richard J. 1981. Nominal suffixes in Dirayta (Gidole). *Bulletin of the School of Oriental and African Studies,* University of London, 44.126–144.

Hetzron, Robert. 1976. *The Agaw languages.* (Afroasiatic linguistics, 3:3.) Malibu, Calif.: Undena.

Hetzron, Robert. 1980. The limits of Cushitic. *Sprache und Geschichte in Afrika* 2.7–126.

Hyman, Larry M. 1981. Tonal accent in Somali. *Studies in African Linguistics* 12.97–124.

Kiessling, Roland. 2002. *Die Rekonstrucktion der südkuschitischen Sprachen (West-Rift)* (Cushitic Language Studies.) Cologne: Köppe.

Saeed, John I. 1984. *The syntax of focus and topic in Somali.* (Kuschitische Sprachstudien, 3.) Hamburg: Buske.

Sasse, Hans-Jürgen. 1979. The consonant phonemes of Proto-East. Cushitic (PEC): A first approximation. *Afroasiatic Linguistics* 7.1–67.

Sasse, Hans-Jürgen. 1981. Die kuschitischen Sprachen. In *Die Sprachen Afrikas,* edited by Bernd Heine et al., pp. 187–215. Hamburg: Buske.

Sasse, Hans-Jürgen. 1987. Kuschitische Sprachen. *Studium Linguistik* 21.78–99.

Zaborski, Andrzej. 1976. Cushitic overview. In *The non-Semitic languages of Ethiopia,* edited by Marvin Lionel Bender, pp. 67–84. East Lansing: African Studies Center, Michigan State University.

HANS-JÜRGEN SASSE

LANGUAGE LIST

Aasáx: also called Asax, Aasá, Assa, Asak, Lamanik, Il Konono. "Ndorobo," "Dorobo" are derogatory names sometimes used. 350 speakers in Tanzania. Ethnic population: 350 or slightly more as of 1991. They speak Maasai with the Maasai, on whom they are economically dependent. Reported in 1999 to still be spoken in the central Massai steppe. It became linguistically extinct in the eastern Maasai steppe in 1976. Speakers became absorbed into the Maasai and nearby Bantu groups. In Landenai and Ndovu Okutu, they are looked down on by others as low-ranking non-cattle owners.

Afar: also called Afaraf, Afar Af, Adal. "Danakil," "Denkel" are derogatory names sometimes used. 1,579,367 speakers in Ethiopia, Eritrea, and Djibouti; also possibly Somalia. In Ethiopia: 979,367 speakers. Ethnic population: 967,367 as of 1998. Eastern lowlands, Afar region. May also be in Somalia. Dialects are Northern Afar, Central Afar, Aussa, Ba'adu. Saho is related but distinct. Bilingualism in Arabic. In Eritrea: 300,000 speakers in southern Eritrea. Dialects are Central Afar, Northern Afar, Aussa, Ba'adu. Bilingualism in Arabic. In Djibouti: 300,000 speakers.

Alaba: also called Allaaba, Halaba. 126,257 speakers in Ethiopia. Ethnic population: 125,900 as of 1998. Rift Valley southwest of Lake Shala. Separated by a river from the Kambatta. There is interest in using Alaba for primary education.

Alagwa: also called Wasi, Alagwase, Alawa, Chasi, Uwassi, Asi. 30,000 speakers in Tanzania, Dodoma region, Kondoa district, Central Province, in the Rangi chiefdom. Related to Iraqw, but not inherently intelligible. Also close to Burunge and Gorowa. Nearly all are bilingual in Rangi for trade and some in Swahili for administration. Children tend to speak Rangi among themselves. All members of the ethnic group have a fairly good command of the language.

Arbore: also called Arbora, Erbore, Irbore. 4,441 speakers in Ethiopia. Ethnic population: 6,559 as of 1998. Extreme southwest, Omo region, near Lake Stefanie. Komso is the lingua franca.

Awngi: also called Awiya, Awi, Agaw, Agau, Agew, Agow, Awawar, Damot, Kwollanyoch. 356,980 speakers in Ethiopia. Ethnic population: 397,491 as of 1998. Amhara region and widely scattered parts of Agew Midir and Metekel, southwest of Lake Tana. A separate language. 80% to 90% of speakers use Amharic as second language.

Baiso: also called Bayso, Alkali. 1,010 speakers in Ethiopia. Ethnic population: 3,260 as of 1994. Older people and those living on Gidicho Island speak Afan Oromo as second language, younger people have better proficiency in Gamo and Wolaytta, and little knowledge of Afan Oromo. Most children learn Bayso. Speakers use Baiso in most domains. The people have resisted extinction for at least one thousand years. They are positive toward the idea of Baiso literature.

Bedawi: also called Beja, Bedawiye, Bedauye, To-Bedawie, Bedja. 1,148,000 speakers in Sudan, Eritrea, and Egypt. In Sudan: 951,000 speakers in northeastern Sudan along the Red Sea coast. Dialects are Hadendoa (Hadendowa, Hadendiwa), Hadareb (Hadaareb), Bisharin (Bisariab), Beni-Amir. Little vocabulary in common with other Cushitic languages, but a great deal of the verbal morphology is similar. Bilingualism in Arabic, Tigre. In Eritrea: 120,000 speakers. Dialects are Hadareb (Hadaareb), Bisharin (Bisarin, Bisariab), Hadendoa (Hadendowa), Beni-Amir, Ababda, Amara. In Egypt: 77,000 speakers.

Bilen: also called Bogo, Bogos, Bilayn, Bilin, Balen, Beleni, Belen, Bilein, Bileno, North Agaw. 70,000 speakers in Eritrea, in central Eritrea, in and around the town of Keren. 60% of the Christians are partly bilingual in Tigrinya, 70%

of the Muslims appear to be bilingual in Tigré. The younger generation mixes their speech with Arabic. Some are bilingual in Nara or Kunama.

Boni: also called Aweera, Aweer, Waata, Wata, Sanye, Wasanye, Waboni, Bon, Ogoda, Wata-Bala. 5,000 speakers in Kenya and Somalia. In Kenya: 3,500 speakers in forest hinterland behind Lamu, Lamu and Tana River districts, Coast Province; Garissa district, North-Eastern Province. At least eleven villages. Close to Garre of Somalia. Many are monolingual. Some are bilingual in Somali, Orma, or Swahili. In Somalia: Reported to be linguistically close to Garre of Somalia, but not close in culture or appearance.

Boon: also called Af-Boon. Spoken in Somalia, Jilib district, Middle Jubba region speakers are scattered in the bush and live in settlements of two or three houses with their closest relatives. There are similarities to Somali. All speakers over 60 years old as of 1986. In recent decades they have shifted to the Maay dialect of Jilib.

Burji: also called Bambala, Bembala, Daashi. 42,731 speakers in Ethiopia and Kenya. In Ethiopia: 35,731 speakers. Ethnic population: 46,565 (1998 census). South of Lake Ciamo. Many speakers in Ethiopia are older. In Kenya: 7,000 speakers mainly around Marsabit township, Moyale. Kenyan resident Burji below 40 years are apparently functionally bilingual in Boran. Speakers are more than 20 years old. Those below 20 do not speak Burji. Ethiopia is considered the traditional home territory, but some migration occurs between the two countries.

Burunge: also called Bulunge, Mbulugwe. 31,000 speakers in Tanzania in Central Province, Kondoa district, Dodoma region, southeast of the Rangi, Goima, Chambalo, and Mirambu villages. Closely related to Wasi, Gorowa, Iraqw. They also speak Swahili and Rangi as second languages.

Bussa: also called Dobase, D'oopace, D'opaasunte, Lohu, Mashile, Mashelle, Masholle, Mosiye, Musiye, Gobeze, Gowase, Goraze, Orase. 6,624 speakers in Ethiopia. Ethnic population: 9,207 as of 1998. Omo region, west of Lake Chamo. There is a dialect chain with Komso-Dirasha-Dobase. Bilingualism reinforces intelligibility of Komso and Dirasha.

Daasanach: also called Dasenech, Daasanech, Dathanaik, Dathanaic, Dathanik, Gheleba, Geleba, Geleb, Gelebinya, Gallab, Galuba, Gelab, Gelubba, Dama, Marille, Merile, Merille, Morille, Reshiat, Russia. "Shangilla" is a derogatory name sometimes used. 34,564 speakers in Ethiopia and Kenya. In Ethiopia: 32,064 speakers. Ethnic population: 32,099 as of 1998. Lower Omo River, along Lake Turkana, extending into Kenya. In Kenya: 2,500 speakers on the northeastern shore of Lake Turkana, around Illeret, Marsabit district, Eastern Province.

Dabarre: also called Af-Dabarre. 20,000 speakers in Somalia. Dialects are Dabarre, Iroole (Af-Iroole). A very distinctive language in the Digil clan family.

Dahalo: also called Sanye, Guo Garimani. 3,000 speakers in Kenya, near the mouth of the Tana River, Lamu and Tana River districts, Coast Province. The language has clicks, although unrelated to Khoisan languages. Highly assimilated and bilingual in Swahili.

Dirasha: also called Dhirasha, Diraasha, Dirayta, Gardulla, Ghidole, Gidole. 50,328 speakers in Ethiopia. Ethnic population: 54,354 as of 1998. Omo region, in the hills west of Lake Chamo, around Gidole town. Part of a dialect chain with Komso and Bussa. Many are bilingual in Oromo or Komso.

El Molo: also called Elmolo, Fura-Pawa, Ldes, Dehes. "Ndorobo" is a derogatory name sometimes used. 8 speakers remain in Kenya. Ethnic population: 400 as of 2000. Formerly spoken along the southeastern shore of Lake Turkana, Elmolo Bay, Marsabit district, Eastern Province. The original language is close to Daasanach. Most of the ethnic group now speak Samburu. They are affiliated with the Samburu. As of 1994, all were over 50 years old.

Garre: also called Af-Garre. 50,000 speakers in Somalia. Reported to be linguistically close to Boni.

Garreh-Ajuran: 128,000 speakers in Kenya, Mandera and Wajir districts, North-Eastern Province. Dialects are Garreh (Gurreh, Garre, Gari), Ajuran (Ajuuraan, Ujuuraan). Part of a dialect cluster. The Ajuran in Kenya speak Somali as second language. Swahili is also used, and some can also speak the Garre of Somalia, which their ancestors spoke. In Somalia (not Kenya) the Ajuran ethnic group speaks a variety of Common Somali as mother tongue, and the Garre ethnic group apparently speaks a language related to Somali.

Gawwada: also called Gauwada, Gawata, Kawwad'a, Kawwada. 32,698 speakers in Ethiopia. Ethnic population: 33,971 as of 1998. Omo region, west of Lake Chamo. Dialects are Dihina (Tihina, Tihinte), Gergere (K'ark'arte), Gobeze, Gollango (Kollanko), Gorose (Gorrose, Korrose), Harso (Worase). Amharic and Oromo are used as second languages. Leaders use Komso.

Gedeo: also called Geddeo, Deresa, Derasa, Darasa, Derasanya, Darassa. 637,082 speakers in Ethiopia. Ethnic population: 639,905 as of 1998. Central highland area, southwest of Dilla and east of Lake Abaya.

Gorowa: also called Goroa, Gorwaa, Fiome. 50,000 speakers in Tanzania, Arusha region, Mbulu district, Dodoma region, Kondoa district, near Babati, around Mt. Ufiome. Closely related to Burunge, Wasi, and Iraqw. May be a dialect of Iraqw. They speak Iraqw and Swahili as second languages.

Hadiyya: also called Adiya, Adiye, Hadiya, Hadya, Adea, Hadia. 923,958 speakers in Ethiopia. Ethnic population: 927,933 as of 1998. Gurage, Kambaata, Hadiyya region, between the Omo and Billate Rivers, in and around Hosaina town. Dialects are Leemo, Soro. Bilingualism in Amharic.

Iraqw: also called Mbulu, Mbulunge, Erokh, Iraku. 365,000 speakers in Tanzania, Arusha region, Mbulu district, highlands southwest of Arusha in north. Asa may be a separate language.

Jiiddu: also called Jiddu, Af-Jiiddu. 20,000 speakers in Somalia. Lower Shabeelle Bay and Middle Jubba regions, Qoryooley, Dhiinsoor, Jilib, and Buurhakaba districts. A distinct language from Somali and Tunni, usually grouped under the Digil dialects or languages. Different sentence structure and phonology from Somali. Closer to Somali than to Baiso. Some similarities to Konsoid languages, and to Gedeo, Alaba, Hadiyya, and Kambaata. Spoken by the Jiiddu clan. Ethnic Jiiddu in Bale Province, Ethiopia, speak Oromo as mother tongue.

Kambaata: also called Kambatta, Kambata, Kembata, Kemata, Kambara, Donga. 606,241 speakers in Ethiopia. Ethnic population: 621,407 as of 1998. Southwestern Gurage, Kambaata, Hadiyya region. Durame is the main town. Dialects are Tambaro, Timbaro (Timbara, Timbaaro), Qebena (Qabena, Kebena, K'abena). Qebena may be a separate language.

Komso: also called Konso, Conso, Gato, Af-Kareti, Karate, Kareti. 149,508 speakers in Ethiopia. Ethnic population: 153,419 as of 1998. South of Lake Ciamo in the bend of the Sagan River. A few migrants in Kenya.

Kunfal: also called Kunfel, Kunfel, Kumfel. 2,000 speakers in Ethiopia east of Lake Tana. Related to Awngi. The people are fairly bilingual in Amharic.

Kw'adza: also called Qwadza. Formerly spoken in Tanzania, Mbulu district. Related to Iraqw, but a separate language. C. Ehret was reported to be working with the last speaker in 1976.

Libido: also called Maraqo, Marako. 36,612 speakers in Ethiopia. Ethnic population: 38,096 as of 1998. Hadiyya, Kambaata, Gurage region, northeast of Hosaina. Syntactic, morphological, and lexical differences from Hadiyya.

Maay: also called Af-Maay Tiri, Af-Maay, Af-May, Af-Maymay, Rahanween, Rahanweyn. 500,000 speakers in Somalia, in southern Somalia, Gedo region, Middle and Lower Shabeelle, Middle and Lower Jubba, Baay, and Bakool regions. It may be more than one language; the dialects form a continuum. Standard Somali is difficult or unintelligible to Maay speakers, except for those who have learned it through mass communications, urbanization, and internal movement. Different sentence structure and phonology from Somali. The Rahanwiin (Rahanweyn) clan confederacy speak various Maay dialects or languages. Af-Helledi is a Maay secret language used by hunters. Used by the Tunni, Jiiddu, Garre, and Dabarre as second language.

Orma: also called Uardai, Wadai, Warday, Wardei. 55,000 speakers in Kenya. Dialects are Munyo (Korokoro, Munyo Yaya), Waata (Sanye), Orma. A distinct language from Boran. Munyoyaya is an ethnic group speaking a dialect of Orma.

Oromo, Borama-Arso-Giji: also called Afan Oromo, Southern Oromo. "Galla," "Gallinya," "Galligna" are derogatory names sometimes used. 3,786,000 speakers in Ethiopia, Kenya, and Somalia. In Ethiopia: 3,634,000 speakers in southern Oromo region. Dialects are Borana (Boran, Borena), Arsi (Arussi, Arusi), Guji (Gujji, Jemjem), Kereyu, Salale (Selale), Gabra (Gabbra, Gebra). Harar is closely related, but distinct enough to need separate literature. Oromo is viewed as one people speaking one language. In Kenya: Marsabit and Isiolo districts, Eastern Province. Dialects are Boran, Gabra (Gabbra, Gebra), Sakuye (Saguye). Gabra and Sakuye may have significant dialect and language attitude differences from Borana. Also spoken by the younger Burji population around Marsabit and Moyale. In Somalia: Gedo region. Dialects are Borana (Booran, Boran).

Oromo, Eastern: also called Harar, Harer, Ittu. "Qotu," "Qottu," "Quottu," "Qwottu," "Kwottu" are derogatory names sometimes used. 4,526,000 speakers in Ethiopia. eastern and western Hararghe zone in northern Bale zone. Closely related to Borana Oromo, but also different. Bilingualism in Amharic. The Oromo view themselves as one people speaking one language.

Oromo, West-Central: also called Afan Oromo, Oromiffa, Oromoo. "Galla" is a derogatory name sometimes used. 8,920,000 speakers in Ethiopia and Egypt. In Ethiopia: Oromo region, eastern and central Ethiopia, and along the Rift Valley escarpment east of Dessie and Woldiya. Dialects are Western Oromo, Central Oromo. Subdialects are Mecha (Maccha, Wellaga, Wallaga, Wollega), Raya, Wello (Wollo), Tulema (Tulama, Shoa, Shewa). Harar and Boran are different enough to need separate literature. Used by regional and national government, public media, national business, education to eighth grade, variety of literature. The Oromo are viewed as one people speaking one language. Roman alphabet. Trade language.

Rendille: also called Rendile, Randile. 32,000 speakers in Kenya. Marsabit district, between Lake Turkana and Marsabit Mountain, Eastern Province.

Saho: also called Sao, Shaho, Shoho, Shiho. 166,759 speakers in Eritrea and Ethiopia. In Eritrea: 144,000 speakers in southern Eritrea. Very close to Afar. The Irob dialect is only in Ethiopia. In Ethiopia: 22,759 speakers. Tigray. Very close to Afar. The Irob dialect is only in Tigray. They are inhospitable to outsiders.

Sanye: also called Sanya, Wasanye, Ariangulu, Langulo, Waata, Waat. 5,000 speakers in Kenya, lower parts of Tana River, Lamu district, Coast Province.

Sidamo: also called Sidámo 'Afó, Sidaminya. 1,876,329 speakers in Ethiopia. Ethnic population: 1,842,314 as of 1998. South central Ethiopia, northeast of Lake Abaya and southeast of Lake Awasa (Sidamo Awraja). Awasa is the capital of the Sidama region.

Somali: also called Af-Soomaali, Af-Maxaad Tiri, Common Somali, Standard Somali. 9,472,000 speakers in Somalia,

Ethiopia, Kenya, Yemen, Djibouti, Finland, Italy, Oman, Saudi Arabia, Sweden, United Arab Emirates, United Kingdom, and Yemen. In Somalia: 5,400,000 speakers throughout the country. Dialects are Northern Common Somali, Benaadir, Af-Ashraaf (Ashraaf). Northern Somali is the basis for Standard (or Common) Somali. It is readily intelligible to speakers of Benaadir Somali, but difficult or unintelligible to Maay and Digil speakers, except for those who have learned it through mass communications, urbanization, and internal movement. The Rahanwiin (Rahanweyn) are a large clan confederacy in southern Somalia, speaking various Maay dialects or languages (Central Somali). The Digil are a clan confederacy speaking Central Somali varieties. Daarood is a large clan family in northeastern Somalia and the Ogaadeen region of Ethiopia, extreme southern Somalia, and northeastern Kenya, which speaks several different dialects. Dir is a clan family with various clans in Djibouti, Ethiopia, throughout Somalia, and northeast Kenya. The Gadabuursi are a section of the Dir living in northwestern Somalia and adjoining parts of Djibouti and Ethiopia, and speaking Northern Common Somali. The Isxaaq are a major clan grouping in northeastern Somalia, some in Djibouti and Ethiopia, speaking Northern Common Somali. The Hawiye are a major clan family living in central southern Somalia, parts of Ethiopia, and extreme northeast Kenya. Hawiye northern clans (Habar Gidir) speak a dialect of Common Somali similar to the adjacent Daarood clans, while Hawiye southern clans (especially Abgaal and Gaaljaal) speak the Benaadir dialect of Common Somali. Ogaadeen is the largest clan within the Daarood clan family, living in eastern Ethiopia, extreme southern Somalia, and northeastern Kenya, speaking various forms of Northern Common Somali. *Sab* is an ambiguous term used by some scholars to refer to various lower caste clans. "Medibaan" is a low-caste clan within the Hawiye. "Benaadir" as an ethnic group refers to the residents of the coastal cities. Those in Merka and Muqdisho speak Af-Ashraaf, a distinct variety that may have limited inherent intelligibility to speakers of Standard Somali. Most of these fled to Kenya during the recent fighting. Bilingualism in Arabic, Italian. The language of most of the people of the country. The government adopted the Roman script in 1972. The Osmania script is no longer used. National language of Somalia. In Ethiopia: 3,187,053 speakers. Ethnic population: 3,160,540 as of 1998. Southeastern Ethiopia, Somali region. 10% use Amharic or Arabic as second language. In Kenya: Northeastern Province around Wajir. Dialects are Degodia, Ogaden. Dialect differences cut across clan differences. In Yemen: Mainly in camps near Aden. In Djibouti: Various dialects.

Tsamai: also called Ts'amay, S'amai, Tamaha, Tsamako, Tsamakko, Bago S'aamakk-Ulo, Kuile, Kule, Cule. 8,621 speakers in Ethiopia. Ethnic population: 9,702 as of 1998. Omo region, lowlands west of Lake Chamo. The Tsamai say Gawwada is difficult to understand. Possibly related to Birale. The most aberrant Dullay variety. They use Komso for trade.

Tunni: also called Af-Tunni. 20,000 speakers in Somalia, in lower Shabeelle and Middle Jubba regions, Dhiinsoor, Baraawe, and Jilib districts. A distinct language from Somali or Jiiddu, usually grouped under the Digil dialects or languages. Different sentence structure and phonology from Somali.

Western Agaw: 1,650 speakers in Ethiopia and Eritrea. In Ethiopia: Ethnic population: 172,327 as of 1998. Northwestern Amhara Region, north of Lake Tana. Communities of Qwara or Kayla are near Addis Ababa and in Eritrea. None in Sudan. Dialects are Qimant (Kemant, Kimant, Kemanat, Kamant, Chemant, Qemant), Dembiya (Dembya, Dambya), Hwarasa (Qwara, Qwarina, "kara"), Kayla, Semyen, Achpar, Kwolasa (Kwolacha). A separate language from Awngi, Bilen, and Xamtanga. It is reported that all Qimant are bilingual in Amharic. Ge'ez is used as liturgical language, but many use a few Hebrew words in prayer. Qwara is extinct.

Xamtanga: also called Khamtanga, Simt'anga, Agawinya, Xamta, Xamir. 143,369 speakers in Ethiopia. Ethnic population: 158,231 as of 1998. North Amhara Region, Avergele district and Lasta and Waag zones, 100 km north of Weldiya. Inherent intelligibility is inadequate with Qimant. The monolinguals are older people or women. Others are bilingual in Amharic. A few Xamir do not speak Xamtanga, but most do and have a strong desire for literature. There is an association of Xamtanga speakers in Weldiya.

Yaaku: also called Mukogodo, Mogogodo, Mukoquodo, Siegu, Yaakua. "Ndorobo" is a derogatory name sometimes used. 50 speakers in Kenya. Ethnic population: 250 as of 1983. Laikipia district, Mukogodo division, Mukogodo Forest west of Doldol, foothills north of Mt. Kenya. Yaaku may be Konsoid, Dullay rather than Oromo. Most or all "Ndorobo" groups are highly bilingual in an adopted language. As of 1983, all were over 40 years old. Yaaku not used in many domains. Negative attitude toward Yaaku.   B. GRIMES

CV. *Abbreviation for* Consonant and Vowel. *See* Syllables.

CYCLE. *See* Formal Grammar; Phonological Derivations; Transformations; *and* Lexical Phonology.

CZECH AND SLOVAK. These two languages are members of the West Slavonic subfamily of Slavic languages, along with Polish, Upper and Lower Sorbian, and extinct Polabian. They are, respectively, the official languages of the Czech Republic (which consists of the provinces of Bohemia and Moravia, the latter including part of southern Silesia), and of Slovakia; prior to 1993 they were equal official languages throughout Czechoslovakia. Czech is spoken by about ten million people, and Slovak by about five million, with several hundred thousand more speakers in enclaves elsewhere in eastern and southeastern Europe, and in more or less cohesive 19th- and 20th-century migrant communities, especially in German-speaking Europe and the Americas.

The two languages are, potentially, mutually intelligible, but parallel texts can be created, based on not entirely peripheral vocabulary, where the coincidence would be far lower than the 90% average traditionally quoted.

For pedagogical grammars with reference sections on Czech, see Heim 1982, Naughton 1998, and Short 1993 (all frequently reprinted); on Slovak, Baláž et al. 1976 and Naughton 1997. Survey grammars are given for Czech by Kavka 1988 and Short 1993a; for Slovak, by Bartoš and Gagnaire 1972, Mistrík 1983, and Short 1993a. The historical grammar of Czech is covered by Mann 1957. The most recent reference grammar of Czech is Karlík et al. 1995; Grepl and Karlík 1998 gives a new presentation of Czech syntax.

1. Dialects and history. Both languages show considerable dialect variation. Bohemia has only minor distinctive dialects at the fringes; Moravia has greater variation, chiefly through different degrees of phonological conservatism. The most striking dialects are in southern Silesia, and are transitional to Polish. Slovak's three main divisions—Eastern, Central, and Western—are further fragmented by the many mountain ranges and rivers. Western Slovak shares some features with Moravian Czech, and Eastern Slovak with Polish—but also with Western Slovak, supporting the theory that Central Slovakia was colonized later, splitting East from West.

Modern Standard Czech emerged during the national revival of the early 19th century, largely through the work of Josef Dobrovský and Josef Jungmann. In many respects, it is an archaic formation, largely modeled on the "ideal" of 16th-century Humanist Czech. While this standard is broadly observed in the media, in education, and in other appropriate circumstances, it coexists with "Common Czech"—a version of the language which has evolved since the 16th century, with some phonological and syntactic differences from the standard, and considerable morphological and lexical differences. For an account of one of its variants, see Townsend 1990. Rooted in Central Bohemia, it has spread elsewhere, interacting with other regional (especially urban) dialects; some features are assertive enough even to penetrate colloquial registers of the standard language. Daneš 1997 contains a range of studies on how the language is evolving at the turn of the 21st century.

Standard Slovak is also a semi-artificial creation, codified by Ľudovít Štúr in the 1840s, with later refinements. However, it is at least based on a modern form (Central Slovak, with some West Slovak features), and thus is in a sense less conservative than Czech. An earlier attempt by Anton Bernolák to codify Slovak, using a West Slovak dialect as the basis, failed to win general acceptance. An unhappy attempt at the beginning of the 20th century to create an additional language based on Eastern Slovak, and called "Slovjak," was short-lived.

The lexicon has a common core, shared with the other Slavonic languages, but with critical cases of "false friendship" (e.g. Cz. *statek* 'farm', pl. 'property', Slo. *statok* 'cattle'). There are some differences within the core vocabulary (e.g. Cz. *vepřové maso*, Slo. *bravčové mäso* 'pork'; Cz. *vteřina*, Slo. *sekunda* 'second'; and the month terms, Cz. *leden, únor, březen . . .*, Slo. *januar, februar, marec . . .*). Lexical divergence is greatest among loanwords: Slovak has long been influenced by Hungarian; there is also an element from Rumanian, chiefly connected with upland sheep-farming. Both languages have borrowed heavily from German, but the standing of German loans differs—owing, in particular, to recurrent bouts of purism among the Czechs. Terminologies coincide only partially, and even recent items may differ, e.g. Cz. *dálnice* 'motorway', a native neologism analogous to *silnice* 'main road', Slo. *autostráda*, a loanword. However, the 1970s and 1980s showed an increasing tendency toward convergence and/or interference; hence *autostráda* is commonly replaced, at least colloquially, by *dial'nica*, the phonological counterpart to *dálnice*. Generally, codifiers and some users of Slovak resist obvious Bohemicisms, which can be quite frequent in daily, unguarded discourse; the controversial Slovak post-independence language legislation of the 1990s was highly protective of the language, now official in the new Slovak state, in terms of both its purity and its use (in part to the exclusion of others). The influence of Slovak on Czech is weaker, but perhaps more insidious.

2. Phonology (cf. Král' and Sabol 1989, Palková 1994, and Rubach 1993. The main distinctive consonantal features of Czech and Slovak—voiced $h < g$ and (Czech only) $\check{r} < r'$—had already developed before the start of the long Czech written tradition, which goes back to the

TABLE 1. *Czech and Slovak Consonant Phonemes.* Orthographic equivalents are in italics.

	Labial	Apical	Palatal	Velar	Laryngeal
Occlusives					
Voiceless	p	t	c ⟨*ť*⟩	k	
Voiced	b	d	ɟ ⟨*ď*⟩	g	
Affricates					
Voiceless		ts ⟨*c*⟩	tʃ ⟨*č*⟩		
Voiced		dz	dʒ ⟨*dž*⟩		
Fricatives					
Voiceless	f	s	ʃ ⟨*š*⟩	x ⟨*ch*⟩	
Voiced	v	z	ʒ⟨*ž*⟩		h
Nasals	m	n	ɲ ⟨*ň*⟩		
Lateral		l	ʎ ⟨*ľ*⟩		
Vibrants					
Plain		r			
Fricative		ř			
Semivowel			j		

TABLE 2. *Czech and Slovak Vowels*

	Front	Mid	Back
High	i ⟨*i/y*⟩		u
Mid	e		o
Low	æ ⟨*ä*⟩	a	

13th century; other details of the modern consonantism were established by the 16th century. Important to both systems, though operating in different ways, are the voiced/voiceless and palatal/non-palatal oppositions. For the consonant phonemes, see Table 1. Note that the palatal lateral occurs only in Slovak, as do the voiced affricates (in Czech, mere allophones of /ts/ /tʃ/). Phonemic /ce ci ca co cu c/ are spelled *tě* (*te* in Slovak) *ti ťa ťo ťu ť,* and similarly for /ɟ/ and Slo. /ʎ/; for /ɲ/ the form is *ně ni ňa ňo ňu ň.*

In the vocalism, the main phonological developments of Cz. are the 14th-century umlauts of /a/ > /ę/, /a:/ > /ie/ (later > /i:/), /u/ > /i/, /u:/ > /i:/, plus the more restricted /o/ > /ę/ and /o:/ > /ie/ (later > /i:/), in certain well-defined environments. These changes, eventually followed by the merger of /ę/ with /e/, underlie many of the morphological differences between the two languages. Slo. is conspicuous for its diphthongs, which are involved in oppositions over and above the general long/short opposition. Slo. also has a "law of rhythmical shortening": in a sequence of two (historically) long syllables, the second loses its length, hence Slo. *krásny* 'beautiful' but Cz. *krásný.* The modern vowel phonemes are shown in Table 2. Note that the vowel /æ/ occurs in Slovak only, where,

however, it is used by only a tiny minority of the population; the majority replace it with /e/ (both are codified). Long vowels are written with acute accents (and Cz. /ú/ is also written as *ů*). Diphthongs include, in Cz., *ou*; in Slo., *ia ie ô* (= /uo/) and *iu*; the chain *ou* in Slovak (see occurrences in Tables 3 and 4) is evaluated as /o + [w]/. Long /o:/ and diphthongs *au eu* occur only in loans. Both languages have syllabic *l* and *r*, which in Slo. may, like the vowels, be both short and long.

3. Morphology. Cz. and Slo. are inflecting languages with complex morphology to express seven cases—nominative, vocative (absent from Slovak), accusative, genitive, dative, locative or prepositional, and instrumental. (For Czech, see Karlík et al. 1995, Kavka 1988, and Short 1993a; for Slovak, Bartoš and Gagnaire 1971 and Short 1993a.) There are singular and plural numbers; some conservative remnants of the dual in Czech are now treated as anomalous plurals. The genders are masculine, feminine, and neuter. Masculine is subdivided into animate and inanimate, but the scope of the distinction differs between the two languages. In the singular, any masculine noun denoting a living creature is "animate" in both languages (expressed by having acc. = gen., and by distinctive dat./loc. forms). In the plural, the same range of nouns is covered in Czech, which has a distinctive nom. for animates; in Slovak, animacy is confined to nouns denoting male humans, which are morphologically marked in both nom. and acc. (= gen. as in sg.). The patterns are shown in Table 3.

The effect of the 14th-century Czech umlauts, by which the "soft" declensions moved further away from their "hard" counterparts, is shown in Table 4. The Czech suffixes should be compared with the equivalent forms of *žena* in Table 3, and with the parallel Slovak, in which no umlaut occurred. Tables 3–4 give some indication of how history has produced varying degrees of case homonymy and syncretism in the many paradigms. This is most marked in the singular of Cz. *paní* 'lady, Mrs.', Slo. *pani* 'Mrs.', which evince no distinct case forms at all.

Adjectival declension is in origin a compound form, and differs completely from nominal types; pronominal declensions vary greatly.

There are three main verb conjugations, in *-e-, -á-,* and *-í-*; these have several subtypes (notably a productive class in *-uje-*) and phonologically conditioned variants. Samples are given in Table 5.

The past tense in both languages is formed by means of an earlier participle in *-l*, with added gender/number markers, and with the present tense of *být/byť* 'be' as

TABLE 3. *"Hard" Noun Declensions in Czech and Slovak*

	Czech		Slovak	
	Singular	Plural	Singular	Plural
"Hard" masculine animate: *pán* 'gentleman'				
Nom.	*pán*	*pánové/páni*	*pán*	*páni*
Voc.	*pane*	*pánové/páni*	—	—
Acc.	*pána*	*pány*	*pána*	*pánov*
Gen.	*pána*	*pánů*	*pána*	*pánov*
Dat.	*pánu/pánovi*	*pánům*	*pánovi*	*pánom*
Loc.	*pánu/pánovi*	*pánech*	*pánovi*	*pánoch*
Instr.	*pánem*	*pány*	*pánom*	*pánmi*
"Hard" feminine: *žena* 'woman'				
Nom.	*žena*	*ženy*	*žena*	*ženy*
Voc.	*ženo*	*ženy*	—	—
Acc.	*ženu*	*ženy*	*ženu*	*ženy*
Gen.	*ženy*	*žen*	*ženy*	*žien*
Dat.	*ženě*	*ženám*	*žene*	*ženám*
Loc.	*ženě*	*ženách*	*žene*	*ženách*
Instr.	*ženou*	*ženami*	*ženou*	*ženami*
"Hard" neuter: *slovo* 'word'				
Nom.	*slovo*	*slova*	*slovo*	*slová*
Voc.	*slovo*	*slova*	—	—
Acc.	*slovo*	*slova*	*slovo*	*slová*
Gen.	*slova*	*slov*	*slova*	*slov*
Dat.	*slovu*	*slovům*	*slovu*	*slovám*
Loc.	*slově*	*slovech*	*slove*	*slovách*
Instr.	*slovem*	*slovy*	*slovom*	*slovami*

auxiliary. The conditional is formed analogously, but using a former aorist of *být/byť* as auxiliary. Sample forms are shown in Table 6. Note that singular endings are masc. *-l*, fem. *-la*, neut. *-lo*. Plural endings are Czech masc. anim. *-li*, masc. inan. or fem. *-ly*, neut. *-la*. (Slovak does not discriminate gender in the plural). The written Czech distinction of *-li* vs. *-ly* is not reflected in pronunciation. Polite 2nd person singular address is expressed in Czech by the singular form of the *l-* participle and the plural form of the auxiliary; Slovak uses the same form

TABLE 4. *"Soft" Noun Declension in Czech and Slovak:* duše/duša *'soul' (feminine)*

	Czech		Slovak	
	Singular	Plural	Singular	Plural
Nom.	*duše*	*duše*	*duša*	*duše*
Voc.	*duše*	*duše*	—	—
Acc.	*duši*	*duše*	*dušu*	*duše*
Gen.	*duše*	*duší*	*duše*	*dúš*
Dat.	*duši*	*duším*	*duši*	*dušiam*
Loc.	*duši*	*duších*	*duši*	*dušiach*
Instr.	*duší*	*dušemi*	*dušou*	*dušami*

TABLE 5. *Present Tense Verb Forms of Czech and Slovak.* The Czech alternative 1sg. and 3pl. forms are newer variants, used in more colloquial registers.

		Czech		Slovak	
Infinitive		*psát* 'write'	*dát* 'give, put'	*písať*	*dať*
Singular	1	*píši/-u*	*dám*	*píšem*	*dám*
	2	*píšeš*	*dáš*	*píšeš*	*dáš*
	3	*píše*	*dá*	*píše*	*dá*
Plural	1	*píšeme*	*dáme*	*píšeme*	*dáme*
	2	*píšete*	*dáte*	*píšete*	*dáte*
	3	*píší/-ou*	*dají*	*píšu*	*dajú*
Infinitive		*myslet* 'think'	*pracovat* 'work'	*mysliet'*	*pracovať*
Singular	1	*myslím*	*pracuji/-u*	*myslím*	*pracujem*
	2	*myslíš*	*pracuješ*	*myslíš*	*pracuješ*
	3	*myslí*	*pracuje*	*myslí*	*pracuje*
Plural	1	*myslíme*	*pracujeme*	*myslíme*	*pracujeme*
	2	*myslíte*	*pracujete*	*myslíte*	*pracujete*
	3	*myslí*	*pracují/-ou*	*myslia*	*pracujú*

TABLE 6. *Past and Conditional Verb Forms of Czech and Slovak* dát/dať *'to give'*

Czech		Slovak	
Past	Conditional	Past	Conditional
dal/-a jsem	*dal/-a bych*	*dal/-a som*	*dal/-a by som*
dal/-a jsi	*dal/-a bys*	*dal/-a si*	*dal/-a by si*
dal/-a/-o	*dal/-a/-o by*	*dal/-a/-o*	*dal/-a/-o by*
dali/-y jsme	*dali/-y bychom*	*dali sme*	*dali by sme*
dali/-y jste	*dali/-y byste*	*dali ste*	*dali by ste*
dali/-y/-a	*dali/-y/-a by*	*dali*	*dali by*

as 2nd person plural. Note (from Tables 5 and 6) the variety in the markers for 1sg. in Czech (*-u, -i, -Vm, -ch*), while Slovak has generalized *-Vm* in all paradigms.

The paucity of tenses is compensated for, in both languages, by aspect. The present tense form of an "imperfective" verb expresses present meaning; that of a "perfective" verb, a future meaning, but also various kinds of nontopical present. Future imperfective is expressed by the imperfective infinitive plus the future of *být/byť* as auxiliary. Verbs, except those of state and some others, must be learned in pairs, which differ either by a perfectivizing prefix (Cz. *psát* > *napsat*, Slo. *písať* > *napísať*), or by a secondary imperfectivizing suffix (Cz. *přepisovat* < *přepsat*, Slovak *prepisovať* < *prepísať* 're-write'), often with concomitant stem and conjugation changes.

4. Syntax. Czech and Slovak are fundamentally S[ubject] V[erb] O[bject] languages, but the exigencies of enclitic-placing rules and of functional sentence perspective create considerable variation in word order. The main enclitics are the past and conditional auxiliaries, unstressed personal pronouns, and the indefinite pronoun *to* 'it/this/that'. Relative freedom of order accounts for the low incidence of the periphrastic passive, since 'Peter was killed by Paul' becomes 'Peter(ACC) killed Paul(NOM).' Expression of the passive, especially the impersonal type, is generally by means of reflexive verb phrases containing the pronominal particle Cz. *se,* Slo. *sa*; the reflexive verb phrase expresses numerous shades of meaning, and thus is of high frequency. Czech and Slovak differ from western European languages in having no rule of "sequence of tenses"; thus 'She said she was ill' is expressed as Cz. *Řekla, že je nemocná,* Slo. *Povedala, že je chorá* 'She said she is ill.' Hence, in subordinate clauses after verbs of speaking or perceiving, the present, past, and future express simultaneity, anteriority, or posteriority of the action vis-à-vis that of the governing clause, whatever the tense of the latter.

[*See also* Slavic Languages.]

BIBLIOGRAPHY

Baláž, Peter, et al. 1976. *Slovak for Slavicists.* Bratislava: Slovenské Pedagogické Nakladateľstvo. 2d ed., 1985.

Bartoš, Jozef, and Gagnaire, Joseph. 1972. *Grammaire de la langue slovaque.* Paris: Institut d'Études Slaves, and Bratislava: Matica Slovenská.

Daneš, František, et al. 1997. *Český jazyk na přelomu tisíciletí.* Prague: Academia.

Grepl, Miroslav, and Karlík, Petr. 1998. *Skladba češtiny.* Olomouc: Votobia.

Heim, Michael. 1982. *Contemporary Czech.* Columbus, Ohio: Slavica.

Karlík, Petr, et al. 1995. *Příruční mluvnice češtiny.* Prague: Lidové Noviny.

Kavka, Stanislav. 1988. *An outline of Modern Czech grammar.* Uppsala: Slaviska Institutionen, Uppsala Universitet.

Kráľ, Ábel, and Sabol, Ján. 1989. *Fonetika a fonológia.* Bratislava: Slovenské Pedagogické Nakladateľstvo.

Mann, Stuart E. 1957. *Czech historical grammar.* London: Athlone. Revised ed., Hamburg: Buske, 1977.

Mistrík, Jozef. 1983. *A grammar of contemporary Slovak.* Bratislava: Slovenské Pedagogické Nakladateľstvo. 2d ed, 1987.

Naughton, James D. 1987. *Colloquial Czech.* London and New York: Routledge. Revised ed., 1999.

Naughton, James D. 1997. *Colloquial Slovak.* London and New York: Routledge.

Paľková, Zdena. 1994. *Fonetika a fonologie češtiny.* Prague: Univerzita Karlova.

Rubach, Jerzy. 1993. *The lexical phonology of Slovak.* Oxford: Clarendon Press.

Short, David. 1993. *Teach yourself Czech.* London: Hodder and Stoughton, 1994. Lincolnwood, Ill.: NTC.

Short, David. 1993a. Czech; Slovak. In *The Slavonic languages,* edited by Bernard Comrie and Greville G. Corbett, pp. 455–532, 533–592. London, New York: Routledge.

Townsend, Charles E. 1990. *A description of Prague spoken Czech.* Columbus, Ohio: Slavica.

DAVID SHORT

D

DALY LANGUAGES. The Daly languages constitute a branch of the proposed AUSTRALIAN language family and are spoken in the Daly River area, in the northern part of the Northern Territory, Australia.

LANGUAGE LIST

Ami: also called Ame, Amijangal. 30 speakers remain. Formerly spoken along the coast of Anson Bay, southwest of Darwin. May be intelligible with Wadjiginy. Bilingualism in Kriol.

Giyug: 2 speakers remain. Formerly spoken on Peron Islands in Anson Bay, southwest of Darwin.

Kamu: also called Gamor. 2 speakers remain. Formerly spoken south of Darwin, east of Daly River.

Kuwama: also called Pungupungu, Patjtjamalh, Kandjerramal. 2 speakers remain. Formerly spoken near mouth of Muldiva River, southwest of Darwin.

Madngele: also called Matngele, Matngala, Warat, Madngela, Maangella, Mandella, Muttangulla. 15 speakers remain. Formerly spoken south of Darwin and Daly River, west bank of Muldiva River. Related to Kamu and Yunggor, which may be extinct.

Manda: 25 speakers remain. Formerly spoken on the coast southwest of Anson Bay, southwest of Darwin. Bilingualism in Kriol, English.

Maranunggu: also called Merranunggu, Emmi, Warrgat. 15 speakers remain. Formerly spoken southwest of Darwin, inland from Anson Bay, east of Manda. Young people speak Kriol.

Maridan: also called Meradan. 20 speakers remain. Formerly spoken southwest of Darwin, north of Moyle River, east of Magadige.

Maridjabin: also called Maretyabin, Maridyerbin, Maredyerbin. 20 speakers remain. Formerly spoken inland from Anson Bay, south of Mariyedi and Manda, southwest of Darwin. May be intelligible with Marithiel or Maringarr. Bilingualism in Kriol.

Marimanindji: also called Maramarandji, Maramanandji, Mar-

imanindu, Murinmanindji, Marramaninjsji. 15 speakers remain. Formerly spoken south of Darwin and Daly River, west of Muldiva River, near headwaters.

Maringarr: also called Marenggar, Maringa. 30 speakers remain. Formerly spoken south of Moyle River, southwest of Darwin. Dialects are Maranunggu (Marranunga, Maramanunggu, Merranunggu, Warrgat). May be intelligible with other Bringen languages. Bilingualism in Kriol.

Marithiel: also called Maridhiyel, Marithiyel, Marrithiyel, Maridhiel, Berringen. "Brinken", "Bringen" are derogatory names sometimes used. 25 speakers remain. Formerly spoken 30 to 50 miles south of Daly River and central Daly River; Daly River Mission, Bagot, Delissaville, Roper River Mission, Northern Territory. Dialects were Marithiel, Nganygit, Mare-Ammu (Mari-Ammu). People generally speak Kriol.

Mariyedi: 20 speakers remain. Formerly spoken inland from Anson Bay, south of Manda, southwest of Darwin.

Marti Ke: also called Magati-Ge, Magadige, Mati Ke, Marti Ke, Magati Gair. 10 speakers remain. Ethnic population: 100 as of 2001. Formerly spoken in Wadeye, the coast south from Moyle River estuary to Port Keat, southwest of Darwin. Close to Maringarr, Marithiel. Bilingualism in Murrinh

FIGURE 1. *Subgrouping of Daly Languages*

Bringen-Wagaydj
Bringen
Marti Ke, Maridan, Maridjabin, Marimanindji,
Maringarr, Marithiel, Mariyedi
Wagaydj
Ami, Giyug, Kuwama, Manda, Maranunggu, Wadjiginy
Malgmalag
Daly Proper
Kamu, Madngele
Malagmalag Proper
Mullukmulluk, Tyaraity
Murrinh-Patha
Murrinh-Patha, Nangikurrunggurr

Patha, Kriol, English. Speakers are 40 to 100 years old. 50 people speak it as their second or third language.

Mullukmulluk: also called Malak-Malak, Malagmalag, Ngolak-Wonga, Nguluwongga. 9 speakers remain. Formerly spoken on the northern bank of Daly River. People generally speak Kriol.

Murrinh-Patha: also called Murinbada, Murinbata, Garama. 900 speakers in Port Keats area, Wadeye. Dialects are Murrinhpatha, Murrinhkura, Murrinhdiminin. Related to Ngan'gitjemerri, which may be extinct. In Port Keats about 90% of speakers speak English and other Aboriginal languages.

Nangikurrunggurr: also called Ngenkikurrunggur, Ngangi-karangurr, Ngankikurrunkurr, Nangikurunggurr. 275 speakers at the junction of Flora and Daly Rivers, Daly River Mission, Tipperary Station. Dialects are Tyemeri (Moil, Ngangi-Tjemerri, Ngankikurrunggurr), Ngangi-Wumeri (Nangumiri, Nangiomeri, Angomerry, Marewumiri, Nangimera, Ngangomori). Bilingualism in Kriol, English. Main language in Daly River group.

Tyaraity: also called Dyeraidy, Daktjerat, Tjerait, Djeradj, Djerag, Kuwema. Spoken in Delissaville. Speakers were originally near the mouth of the Reynold River. All or most are bilingual in English.

Wadjiginy: also called Wogaity, Wagaydy. 12 speakers. Formerly spoken southwest of Darwin along coast and inland along Finniss River. The people speak Kriol but understand Wadjiginy when the older people speak it.   B. GRIMES

DANI-KWERBA LANGUAGES form a branch of the Central and Western Main Section of the proposed TRANS-NEW GUINEA phylum. They are spoken in the northern center of the Papua district in Indonesia.

LANGUAGE LIST

Airoran: also called Aeroran, Adora, Iriemkena. 400 speakers.

Bagusa: also called Kapeso, Suaseso. 300 speakers east of Mamberamo, Lake Rombebai, north of Kauwera language. Jayapura Kabupaten, Mamberamo Tengah Kecamatan. All ages. Vigorous language use.

Dani, Lower Grand Valley: also called Balim Selatan. 20,000 speakers in central highlands, Baliem Grand Valley and upper gorge. Dialects are Lower Grand Valley Hitigima (Dani-Kurima, Kurima), Upper Bele, Lower Bele, Lower Kimbin (Kibin), Upper Pyramid.

Dani, Mid Grand Valley: also called Tulem, Central Grand Valley Dani, Baliem Valley Dani, Balim Tengah. 50,000 speakers in Baliem Valley.

Dani, Upper Grand Valley: also called Balim Atas, Wosi. 20,000 speakers in central highlands, Baliem Grand Valley and upper gorge.

FIGURE 1. *Subgrouping of Dani-Kerba Languages*

Northern Dani-Kwerba
  Isirawa
  Kwerba
    Airoran, Bagusa, Kauwera, Kwerba, Kwerba Mamberamo, Trimuris
  Massep
  Samarokena
Southern Dani-Kwerba
  Dani
    Lower Grand Valley Dani, Mid Grand Valley Dani, Upper Grand Valley Dani, Western Dani, Hupla, Nggem, Walak
  Ngalik-Nduga
    Nduga, Silimo, Angguruk Yali, Pass Valley Yali, Southern Yali
  Wano

Dani, Western: also called Dani Barat, Ilaga Western Dani, Lani, Laany, Oeringoep, Timorini. 180,000 speakers in central highlands, west of Baliem Grand Valley and east from upper Kemandoga Valley. Dialects are Western Dani of Pyramid, Western Dani of Bokondini. Many other dialects are not as distinct as those listed.

Hupla: also called Soba, Balim Selatan. 3,000 speakers in central highlands area near eastern side of Baliem gorge. Closely related to Lower Grand Valley Dani.

Isirawa: also called Saweri, Saberi, Okwasar. 1,800 speakers. Dialects are Western Isirawa, Eastern Isirawa. Close to Kwerba. The dialects are very close. Bilingual level estimates for Indonesian are 0 0%, 1 30%, 2 40%, 3 30%, 4 0%, 5 0%. Vigorous language use. Trade language.

Kauwera: also called Kauwerawec, Kauwerawetj, Kaowerawedj. 400 speakers east of mid Mamberamo, north and south of Kasonaweja. Vigorous language use.

Kwerba Mamberamo: also called Nopukw, Nopuk, Nobuk. 300 speakers east of Mamberamo River, in the mountains between the villages of Kwerba, Edifalen, and Marinafalen, south of Kasonaweja. All ages. Vigorous language use.

Kwerba: also called Airmati, Naibedj, Tekutameso. 2,500 speakers. Dialects are Serikenam, Sasawa, Nogukwabai.

Massep: also called Masep. 25 speakers on northern coast east of Mamberamo River mouth and west of Sarmi, near Apauwer River. No children or a few speak Massep. Not used except perhaps in family. 30% or less of the ethnic group speak Massep.

Nduga: also called Ndugwa, Ndauwa, Dauwa, Dawa, Pesechem, Pesecham, Pesegem. 10,000 speakers in Jayawijaya, Tiom, central highlands, south of high ranges, south of Western Dani, north of Asmat. Widely scattered. Dialects are Sinak Nduga, Hitadipa Nduga. Bilingual level estimates for Dani are 0 60%, 1 10%, 2 20%, 3 0%, 4 0%, 5 10%. Some speak Damal, Moni, Indonesian.

Nggem: 3,000 speakers along the middle Haflifoeri River, north of Wamena. Closely related to Walak.

Samarokena: also called Samarkena, Karfasia, Tamaya, Tamaja. 400 speakers on northern coast inland just east of Apawar River, west of Sarmi, villages of Karfasia, Samarkena, Maseb, Tamaya. Speakers bilingual in Airoran, Isirawa, and some in Kwerba.

Silimo: also called South Ngalik, Paiyage. 5,000 speakers in central highlands south of the range immediately west of the Baliem River, Amo, Kiniage valleys.

Trimuris: 300 speakers on the eastern bank of the Mamberamo River between Kauwera and Bagusa languages, Jayapura Kabupaten, Mamberamo Tengah Kecamatan. They do not understand Kwerba very well. All ages. Vigorous language use.

Walak: also called Lower Pyramid, Wodo. 1,500 speakers in villages of Ilugwa, Wodo, Bugi, Mogonik, Wurigelebut.

Wano: 7,000 speakers. Closely related to Nggem, Walak. Western Dani, Dem, Moni, or Indonesian spoken by leaders, men, adults, young people, those who have been to school, about common topics, because of intermarriage.

Yali, Angguruk: also called Northern Yali, Angguruk, Yalimo, Yali Tengah. 15,000 speakers in the central highlands area northwest of Nalca, east of Grand Valley Dani. Different from Yali of Ninia and Yali of Pass Valley, but related.

Yali, Pass Valley: also called Western Yali, Pass Valley, Abendago, Yali Utara. 5,000 speakers in central highlands, east of Angguruk and northwest of Naltya, Jayawijaya, Kurulu, and Kurima. Dialects are Pass Valley, Landikma, Apahapsili. Different from Yali of Ninia and Yali of Angguruk, but related.

Yali, Southern: also called Ninia, Yali, Yali Selatan, Jaly, Jalè, North Ngalik. 10,000 speakers. Different from Yali of Pass Valley, Yali of Angguruk, and Hupla, but closely related.

B. GRIMES

DATIVE. *See* Case.

DECIPHERMENT. In a technical linguistic sense, "decipherment" refers to the decoding of a writing system which is no longer in use and no longer comprehensible. It is usual to distinguish decipherment from cryptoanalysis or cryptology; the latter aims at understanding special writing codes or ciphers devised to disguise the meaning of a message. We also distinguish decipherment from interpretation: a text written in an obscure language but in a known script (e.g. the Latin alphabet) requires interpretation, not decipherment.

Some of these definitions and distinctions are less sharp than we would hope. First, the concept of decipherment is tied to the concept of writing, but it is not always obvious what counts as writing. Second, cryptoanalysis and decipherment often overlap in their techniques. Third, the interpretation of texts is the only test of decipherment: if the language is known, no problems arise—but if it is not, interpretation is necessary for decipherment. Fourth, we often hesitate between the use of "decipherment" and "interpretation." Lycian was an Anatolian language of the 1st millennium BCE, written in an alphabet borrowed from Greek; yet the phonetic values of some of its signs differ from those of Greek, and there are additional signs not found in Greek. If we succeed in understanding these texts, is it decipherment or interpretation? (For general reference on scripts and decipherment, see Gelb 1952, Cohen 1958, Voegelin and Voegelin 1963, Friedrich 1966a,b, and Trager 1974.)

1. History of decipherment. Decipherment is normally required for scripts which fell out of use, either because they were employed for languages which also became extinct (e.g. Akkadian Cuneiform), or because literacy disappeared (Linear B), or because they were replaced by other forms of writing (Syllabic Cypriot). Modern scholarship has been immensely successful in deciphering all such types; but there are still many scripts (or supposed scripts) for which no full and generally accepted decipherment is available. They include the Indus Valley script of the 3rd millennium BCE, Cretan Hieroglyphic of the 2nd millennium BCE, the Easter Island script of the 19th century, and a number of others (see Gelb 1973:266, RAS 1975, Leclant 1975, Daniels and Bright 1996:139–188).

1.1. *Early steps.* Interest in ancient scripts goes back to the Renaissance and earlier (Pope 1999). Evidence for languages and scripts was extensively collected in the 16th and 17th centuries, when languages like Coptic (a form of Neo-Egyptian) were rescued. In the 17th century, the interest in universal languages also led to discussions about universal writing, which helped to establish a typology of writing. However, the first serious decipherments belong to the 18th century. In 1754, two scholars—J. Swinton and the abbé Barthélemy—independently deciphered the Aramaic script used in the Palmyra inscriptions of the 3rd century CE; in 1787, A.-I. Silvestre de Sacy deciphered Sassanian, the script used in Persia to write the Middle Iranian language of the Sassanid dynasty. In both instances, the script was a form of the Aramaic alphabet, closely related to the Syriac writing which was already known. Both decipherments were based on bilingual texts that included Greek versions. The first methodological principles were also established in the 18th century. As early as 1714, Leibniz had advocated the use of personal names to establish the necessary links between the known and undeciphered parts of a bilingual text. Personal names were important in the decipherment of Palmyrene and Sassanian and played an essential role in later decipherments.

In the 19th century, the prerequisites for decipherment—extensive knowledge of scripts, adequate editions of texts, philological skills, and ability to reconstruct linguistic forms from limited evidence—became more widely available. Two great decipherments opened the way to further successes: that of the Egyptian Hieroglyphs, and that of the Old Persian Cuneiform.

1.2. *Egyptian hieroglyphs.* For a long time, mystery had surrounded the hieroglyphic script attested in Egypt from the 3rd millennium BCE to the 4th century CE. Later it was assumed that each pictographic sign represented a word or a notion. The decipherment was made possible by the discovery of an Egyptian stele, the Rosetta Stone, dated from 196 BCE, which contained three versions of a decree in honor of King Ptolemy V. One version was in Greek; the other two were written in hieroglyphic and in demotic (a very cursive version of the Egyptian script, often mistaken for alphabetic by early decipherers). Sequences of signs equivalent to the personal names of the Greek version were identified in the demotic, and in one instance (the name *Ptolemaios*) in the hieroglyphic part. The most impressive contributions came from a young Frenchman, Jean-François Champollion (1790–1832), who had prepared himself for the task almost from childhood, through a series of philological studies of the Egyptian evidence (including Coptic). He succeeded in showing that a number of names were written with signs which had phonetic values. This was announced in 1822; in his later work, through a simple count of the number of signs in the hieroglyphic part of the Rosetta Stone and of the number of words in the Greek part, Champollion discredited the old view that, except for personal names, each "hieroglyph" corresponded to a word. Some of the hieroglyphs indeed had logographic functions, but others had a phonetic value; a word could be indicated by both logographic and phonetic signs. Thus the phonetic values puzzled out on the basis of personal names could also be exploited elsewhere; further, some morphemes seemed to be related to the corresponding Coptic forms. What emerged from the work which followed Champollion's results was a

complicated writing system which included logographic signs, determinatives, and phonetic signs corresponding to one or more consonants (see Friedrich 1966a:4–25, Pope 1999:43–84).

1.3. *Cuneiform writing* was unknown to the West until the 17th century. The first reliable copies of the Persepolis cuneiform inscriptions were published in the second half of the 18th century; some (connected with the Achaemenid kings of Persia, who reigned in the 5th century BCE) were multilingual, with three versions of the same text in different cuneiform scripts used for different languages. At the beginning of the 19th century, a German schoolteacher interested in cryptoanalysis, G. F. Grotefend (1775–1853), recognized (as others had before him) the sign that divided words; he concluded from the number of the signs and the length of the words that the script was alphabetic or semi-alphabetic; he guessed from the pattern of repeated sequences that the text included the formula found in later Sassanian inscriptions ("X, great king, king of kings, son of Y, Achaemenid . . ."); and finally, he recognized the names of the king Darius and his son Xerxes. The first phonetic values could then be assigned, but Grotefend was prevented from going much farther by his insufficient linguistic knowledge. In 1826, the great comparativist Rasmus Rask identified the ending of the genitive plural in the phrase "king of kings" and compared it with the genitive plural of Sanskrit. It then became clear that Old Persian was closely related to Sanskrit and to Avestan; this led to further identification of sign values and allowed scholars to determine through comparison the meanings of a number of words. An Englishman, Henry Rawlinson (1810–1895), succeeded in reading the great Behistun inscription of Darius; on the basis of that evidence, he produced a new decipherment of the Old Persian texts, which partly overlapped with that of Grotefend, but went much further.

The decipherment of Old Persian was crucial: first, it was achieved without the help of a version in a known language; second, it opened the way to the even more important decipherment of Akkadian (Assyro-Babylonian) cuneiform (also started by Rawlinson). The script and language were used in one of the versions of the Persian texts—but also in innumerable clay tablets which formed the archives, recently discovered, of the main Near Eastern centers during the 3rd to 1st millennia BCE. The Old Persian version gave no help with the sign values, but it provided the necessary bilingual material and the personal names likely to be found in both versions. The language was found to be Semitic, and comparative

Semitic evidence was invaluable in defining the meaning of a number of roots. Like the Egyptian hieroglyphic script, the writing system included logograms, determinatives, and phonetic signs; the last were all syllabic, and indicated a V[owel], C[onsonant]+V, V+C, or (more rarely) C+V+C. The knowledge of the new writing system led to the understanding of a number of ancient Near Eastern languages whose existence had been barely suspected: most important was Sumerian, the non-Indo-European and non-Semitic language attested in Mesopotamia from the late 4th millennium BCE, for which the first forms of cuneiform writing were probably devised. Also important was Hittite, which was written in Anatolia during the 2nd millennium BCE. Most of the texts were written in a form of cuneiform similar to Akkadian; they were easy to read, but they remained incomprehensible until it was discovered that the language was Indo-European (indeed the oldest attested Indo-European language), and until a combination of contextual and etymological work led to the understanding of both grammar and vocabulary (Friedrich 1966a: 27–71, Pope 1999:85–122).

1.4. *Linear B*. The most celebrated decipherment of this century was that of Linear B, a script written on clay tablets in Crete and in mainland Greece in the latter part of the 2nd millennium BCE. The decipherment, announced in 1952, was the work of a young architect, Michael Ventris, who in the last stages of his work had the help of the linguist John Chadwick. It built on earlier discoveries (especially by the American Alice Kober): given the number of signs, the script was likely to be syllabic, possibly with V or CV signs like the obviously related Syllabic Cypriot; and the language was inflected, since the final parts of words showed regular types of alternations. On the basis of these alternations, Ventris established a grid of signs which had either the same vowel or the same consonant (though their values remained unknown). He then guessed the values of some signs on the basis of various criteria: identification of Cretan place names in the Cretan tablets; graphic similarity between the Linear B signs and the signs of the Cypriot syllabary; and the assumption that the sign most frequently found in word-initial position represented the [a] vowel. The grid was used to test these suggestions and to define the values of other signs. From his first tentative readings, Ventris was unwillingly led to the correct conclusion that most of the words and most of the patterns of word-formation had to be Greek. The script was shown to be syllabic, with approximately eighty phonetic signs of the type V or CV, and with logograms used separately from the phonetic signs (see Chadwick 1973).

2. Methods. The work just exemplified led to two immediate results: first, the typology of writing was better understood than previously; second, a rudimentary methodology for decipherment was developed. Yet it is doubtful that there ever was a logical decipherment in which guesswork did not play a considerable part; even now, there is no known recipe for decipherment. What we have is a series of heuristic devices, some of which are mentioned below (see Aalto 1945, Friedrich 1966a:134–39, Gelb 1973, 1974).

The importance of preparatory work has been underlined. The decipherer needs to know as much as possible about the linguistic and historical data relevant to the period and area to which the texts belong. Accurate drawings, photographs, or "squeezes" (moldings or casts) of the texts are also necessary—as well as a first-hand acquaintance with the monuments, if possible, and an understanding of their relative chronology. The direction of writing, and as many external features of the script as possible, must be identified. Above all, are there word-dividers or any other features which can distinguish words? The next task (only feasible if there are sufficient texts) is to separate the functionally distinct signs (graphemes) from the individual or distributional variants: for example, in English, the graphic distinction between *a* and *o* is significant, but *z* and *ʒ* are merely graphic variants of the same letter. The total number of graphemes then helps to determine the nature of the writing system. A system with fewer than thirty signs is likely to be alphabetic, while one with fifty to one hundred signs is probably syllabic. Some two hundred to four hundred signs normally point to a system with both logographic and phonetic signs.

It is essential to study the frequency and distribution of the signs (Koskenniemi et al. 1970). It is also necessary to compare similar sequences of signs in the hope of recognizing grammatical features such as prefixation or affixation. Computers may be invaluable for this type of work (Packard 1971). In a simple syllabic system, the decipherer may be able to establish a grid of the type set up by Ventris for Linear B.

The crucial step is identification of the language, and the attribution of meanings and/or phonetic values to the signs or sequences of signs. When there is a bilingual document, those elements which are likely to recur in comparable phonetic forms in both texts (personal names, place names, etc.) must be identified. It may then become possible to recognize other forms; and it may become clear whether the script conceals a known language. If the language is not known, interpretation is still possible if there are sufficient texts, and if the bilingual evidence is adequate. It is also possible that the language, though unknown, is related to known languages; if so, a judicious use of the combinatory method (a contextual approach) and of the etymological method can lead to satisfactory results. A pure etymological approach is in general dangerous and ought to be avoided.

In the absence of a bilingual document, information about the content of the text can be provided by the typology of the texts themselves—funerary monuments, dedications, royal statements, and so on—and by their historical background. Some logographic elements may be immediately interpretable (e.g. numbers, or logograms for men and women); some formulae may be expected. Comparison of the signs with formally similar signs of other scripts must be done with extreme caution, but it may sometimes be useful. Yet even if some of the signs can be assigned phonetic values, there is no guarantee of interpretation if the language is not known.

A decipherment must be tested not on the basis of the method used to achieve it, but on its results. If correct, it must permit an interpretation of the text which does not contradict expectations based on external or internal factors: typology of the monument, historical considerations, arrangement of the text, pictograms, numerals, and so on. The text should be linguistically coherent. A decipherment of chronologically and geographically coherent texts which yields a mixture of early and late forms, or of geographically incompatible features, is suspect.

In general, the decipherment of a script used for a known language is possible if the body of evidence is not too small; alphabets and simple syllabic systems are easier to decipher than logographic-syllabic systems. It is far more difficult (and sometimes impossible) to decipher a script used for an unknown language. In favorable circumstances, a decipherment may be possible, but it is not always the case that all signs can be assigned a value, and that all texts can be fully interpreted. Contrary to usual belief, most decipherments do not result from the sudden cracking of codes by isolated geniuses who rely exclusively on the sheer power of their intelligence and erudition. In a number of instances, the process of decipherment is extremely slow, and advances are made through the cumulative efforts of a number of experts.

Thus the study of the so-called Hieroglyphic Hittite (now Luwian), a logographic-syllabic script used to write an Indo-European language in Anatolia and Syria of the 2nd to 1st millennia BCE, started in the 1910s, obtained considerable results in the 1930s, most of which were confirmed by the discovery of a bilingual text in the 1940s. This led to the first glossary and full list of signs in the 1960s. The work gained new impetus in the 1970s and 1980s with the attribution of new values to some very frequent signs, and with a number of new editions of texts. Decipherment of the script of the 1st millennium is now almost complete, barring unexpected developments (Friedrich 1966a:72–84, Pope 1999:136–145, Hawkins et al. 1974, Hawkins 2000).

Hieroglyphic Luwian is not unique; a similar account could be given for numerous other decipherments.

3. Recent achievements. Two very recent decipherments, also due to cumulative work by more than one scholar, provide good examples of different approaches to the problem. The Maya glyphs were written from before the beginning of our era to one or two centuries after the Spanish conquest on different material (stone, wood, bark, pots, codices) by peoples inhabiting El Salvador, Belize, Guatemala, Honduras, and parts of Southern Mexico. There was resistance to the idea that the glyphs were in fact forms of writing and even stronger resistance to the suggestion that they might be used for phonetic writing. In the 19th century, a copy of a 16th-century account by Diego de Landa, a Franciscan friar (subsequently a bishop), of the so-called Mayan alphabet was found. This turned out to provide very difficult and sometimes hopeless evidence which, however, was crucial in the first steps of the decipherment. A helpful factor was that, though the Mayan language of the pre-Conquest period was not independently known, the descendant and related languages still survive. The two breakthroughs in the decipherment were (a) the discovery that a number of texts have historical value and (b) the demonstration that the glyphs were used as logograms but also as phonetic determiners in connection with a logogram or as syllabic signs in sequences used to render words in entirely phonetic form. In the middle of the 20th century, the starting point for the decipherment was the combination of pictorial signs that were clearly recognizable (e.g. a turkey or a dog) with glyphs for which (on the basis of Diego de Landa's "alphabet") it was possible to suggest syllabic values that fit with the words for *turkey* or *dog* known from the later language. After the first values were established, the 1980s and 1990s witnessed increasingly fast progress in determining the values of the individual glyphs (Pope 1999:195–203, Justeson and Campbell 1979, Bricker 1986, Macri 1996, Coe 2000).

For the Mayan glyphs, the main question was whether they were a form of phonetic writing; for the badly attested Carian script, that was never doubted but the breakthrough came when it became clear that some of the alphabetic values that had been taken for granted had to be abandoned. The Carians inhabited southwest Anatolia in the 1st millennium BCE and spoke a language that was soon replaced by Greek. They left short inscriptions datable from the 7th to 4th century BCE found partly in Anatolia, partly (and mostly) in Egypt, where there were a number of Carian mercenaries. The script is very close to the Greek alphabet but has a number of different signs, which at some point were taken as syllabic. Naturally the letters that matched Greek letters were assigned the same values, but this did not lead to any coherent interpretation of the texts. The first attempts to focus on the Carian texts of Egypt and to find in Carian the equivalents of Egyptian names date from the 1970s, but the most detailed and successful work was that of the Cambridge Egyptologist John Ray, who in the 1980s and 1990s used the comparison with Egyptian material to assign new values to the Carian letters; the work was continued independently in the 1990s by a young Spanish linguist, I.-J. Adiego, and by a German, Diether Schürr. The end result was a set of alphabetic values (no question of syllabic signs) which only partly matched those of the Greek alphabet; see, in addition to Pope 1999:192–194, Ray 1981, 1987, Adiego 1993, Schürr 1992, Giannotta 1994. The new values have now been proved to be correct thanks to the 1996 discovery and fast publication of a short Greek/Carian bilingual inscription (Frei and Marek 1997), which seems also to provide enough evidence to show that the language belonged to the Anatolian branch of Indo-European. The lesson once again is that even in related scripts similarity of letter shapes does not necessarily mean similarity of phonetic values.

[*See also* Cuneiform; Egyptian; Mayan Languages; and Writing and Written Language.]

BIBLIOGRAPHY

Aalto, Pentti. 1945. *Notes on methods of decipherment of unknown writings and languages.* (Studia orientalia, 11:4.) Helsinki: Societas Linguistica Fennica.

Adiego Lajara, Ignacio-Javier. 1993. *Studia Carica: investigaciones sobre la escritura y lengua Carias.* Barcelona: Promociones y Publicaciones Universitarias.

Bricker, Victoria R. 1986. *A grammar of Mayan hieroglyphs.* (Middle American Research Institute, Publication 56.) New Orleans: Tulane University Press.

Chadwick, John. 1973. Linear B. In *Current trends in linguistics,* vol. 11, *Diachronic, areal, and typological linguistics,* edited by Thomas A. Sebeok, pp. 537–568. The Hague: Mouton.

Coe, Michael D. 1992. *Breaking the Maya code.* London: Thames and Hudson. Revised ed., 2000.

Coe, Michael D., and Mark Van Stone. 2001. *Reading the Mayan glyphs.* London: Thames and Hudson.

Cohen, Marcel. 1958. *La grande invention de l'écriture et son évolution.* 3 vols. Paris: Klincksieck.

Daniels, Peter T., and William Bright, eds. 1996. *The world's writing systems.* New York and Oxford: Oxford University Press.

Frei, Peter, and Christian Marek. 1997. Die Karische-Griechische Bilingue von Kaunos. *Kadmos* 36.1–89.

Friedrich, Johannes. 1966a. *Entzifferung verschollener Schriften und Sprachen.* 2d ed. Berlin: Springer. Translated as *Extinct languages.* New York: Philosophical Library; London: P. Owen, 1957.

Friedrich, Johannes. 1966b. *Geschichte der Schrift.* Heidelberg: Winter.

Gelb, Ignace J. 1952. *A study of writing: The foundations of grammatology.* Chicago: University of Chicago Press. Revised ed., 1963.

Gelb, Ignace J. 1973. Written records and decipherment. In *Current trends in linguistics,* vol. 11, *Diachronic, areal, and typological linguistics,* edited by Thomas A. Sebeok, pp. 253–284. The Hague: Mouton.

Gelb, Ignace J. 1974. Records, writing, and decipherment. *Visible Language* 8.293–318.

Giannotta, M. E., et al., eds. 1994. *La decifrazione del Cario.* Rome: Consiglio Nazionale delle Ricerche.

Hawkins, (John) David. 2000. *Corpus of hieroglyphic Luwian inscriptions,* vol. 1, *Inscriptions of the Iron Age.* 3 Parts. Berlin: de Gruyter.

Hawkins, (John) David, Anna Morpurgo Davies, and Günter Neumann. 1974. *Hittite hieroglyphs and Luwian: New evidence for the connection.* (Nachrichten der Akademie der Wissenschaften in Göttingen, Philosophisch-historische Klasse, 1973:6.) Göttingen: Vandenhoeck and Ruprecht.

Justeson, John S., and Lyle Campbell, eds. 1979. *Phoneticism in Mayan hieroglyphic writing.* (Institute for Mesoamerican Studies, Publication 9.) Albany: State University of New York.

Koskenniemi, Seppo, et al. 1970. A method to classify characters of unknown ancient scripts. *Linguistics* 61.65–91.

Leclant, Jean, ed. 1975. *Le déchiffrement des écritures et des langues: Colloque du XXIX congrès des Orientalistes, Paris, juillet 1973.* Paris: L'Asiathèque.

Macri, Martha J. 1996. Maya and other mesoamerican scripts. In Daniels and Bright 1996, pp. 172–182.

Packard, David W. 1971. Computer techniques in the study of the Minoan Linear script A. *Kadmos* 10.52–59.

Pope, Maurice. 1999, 1st ed. 1975. *The story of decipherment: From Egyptian hieroglyphic to Linear B.* New York: Scribners. Revised edition, London: Thames and Hudson.

RAS. 1975. *Proceedings of the symposium on the undeciphered languages, held in London 25–27 July 1973.* London: Royal Asiatic Society. (*Journal of the Royal Asiatic Society*, 1975: 2.)

Ray, John. 1981. An approach to the Carian script. *Kadmos* 20.150–162.

Ray, John 1987. The Egyptian approach to Carian. *Kadmos* 26.98–103.

Schürr, Diether. 1992. Zur Bestimmung der Lautwerte des Karischen Alphabets 1971–1991. *Kadmos* 31.127–160.

Trager, George L. 1974. Writing and writing systems. In *Current trends in linguistics,* vol. 12, *Linguistics and adjacent arts and sciences,* edited by Thomas A. Sebeok, pp. 373–496. The Hague: Mouton.

Voegelin, C. F., and F. M. Voegelin. 1963. Patterns of discovery in the decipherment of different types of alphabets. *American Anthropologist* 65.1231–1253.

ANNA MORPURGO DAVIES

DECLARATIVE. *See* Pragmatics and Contextual Semantics; Clause; Systemic Grammar; Computational Linguistics; *and* Mood.

DEEP STRUCTURE. *See* Formal Grammar *and* Levels of Representation.

DEFINITENESS. *See* Anaphora; Deixis; Discourse; Philosophy of Language; Pragmatics and Contextual Semantics; Semantics; *and* Typology and Universals.

DEFOID LANGUAGES. These languages, also called Yoruba-Akokoid languages, constitute a group spoken in Benin, in Togo, and in southwestern Nigeria. They form a branch of BENUE-CONGO.

LANGUAGE LIST

Arigidi: also called North Akoko. 48,000 speakers in Nigeria, in. Ondo state, Akoko North LGA; Kogi state, Kogi LGA.

FIGURE 1. *Subgrouping of Defoid Languages*

Akokoid
    Arigidi
Ayere-Ahan
    Àhàn, Ayere
Yoruboid
    Edekiri
        Cabe, Ica, Idaca, Ifè, Ije, Isekiri, Kambolé, Lucumi, Mokole, Nago, Ulukwumi, Yoruba
    Igala

Dialects are Oyin, Uro, Arigidí, Erúsú (Erushu), Ojo, Udo (Ido, Òwnòn Üdò, Üdò Oke-Agbe), Afa (Affa, Òwòn Àfá, Oke-Agbe), Òge (Òwòn Ògè), Aje, Ese (Òwòn Èsé), Igasi (Ìgàshí, Òwòn Ìgásí). A dialect cluster.

Àhàn: also called Ahaan. 300 speakers in Nigeria, in Ondo state, Ekiti LGA, Ajowa, Igashi, and Omou towns.

Ayere: 3,000 speakers in Nigeria, in Kwara state, Oyi LGA, Kabba district.

Cabe: also called Caabe, Ede Cabe. 80,000 speakers in Benin, Borgou, and Zou provinces. Bilingualism in Ewe, Fon, Yoruba.

Ica: also called Ede Ica. 39,000 speakers in Benin and Togo. In Benin: Zou Province. In Togo: Dadja.

Idaca: also called Idaaca, Ede Idaca. 30,000 speakers in Benin, Zou Province. Bilingualism in Yoruba.

Ifè: also called Baate, Ana, Ana-Ife, Anago, Ede Ife. 155,000 speakers in Benin and Togo. In Benin: 80,000 speakers in Zou Province. Bilingualism in Yoruba. In Togo: 74,000 speakers in southeast central, Ogou Province. The main centers are Atakpamé, Kamina, and Dadja. Also in the town of Ese-Ana in southern Togo. Dialects are Tschetti, Djama, Dadja. Some bilingualism in Éwé in the south and Yoruba in the north. Some also know French.

Igala: also called Igara. 800,000 speakers in Nigeria, in Kogi state, Ankpa, Idah, Dekina, and Bassa LGAs; Edo state, Oshimili LGA; Anambra state, Anambra LGA. Dialects are Ebu, Idah, Ankpa, Ogugu, Ibaji, Ife, Anyugba. Speakers are able to converse in most common topics in Idoma and Agatu. Agatu, Idoma, and Bassa people use Igala for attending Ika Bible School.

Ije: also called Holi, Ede Ije. 20,000 speakers in Benin, Zou Province. Bilingualism in Yoruba.

Isekiri: also called Itsekiri, Ishekiri, Shekiri, Jekri, Chekiri, Iwere, Irhobo, Warri, Iselema-Otu, Selemo. 510,000 speakers in Nigeria, in Delta state, Warri, Bomadi, and Ethiope LGAs. Closely related to Yoruba.

Kambolé: also called Southwest Ede. 20,000 speakers in Togo, east central in the town of Kambolé and a few surrounding villages. Closely related to Ifé. Bilingualism in French, Yoruba.

Lucumi: spoken in Cuba. A secret language used for ritual by the Santeria religion.

Mokole: also called Mokollé, Mokwale, Monkole, Féri. 65,500 speakers in Benin, in Borgou Province, Kandi and villages to the north and east. Language related to Yoruba, but culture to Baatonu (Bariba), among whom they live. Bilingualism in French.

Nago: also called Nagots, Nagot, Ede Nago. 175,000 speakers in Benin, in Weme and Atakora Provinces. Some speakers are bilingual in Yoruba.

Ulukwumi: 10,000 speakers in Nigeria, in Delta state, Aniocha and Oshimili LGAs.

Yoruba: also called Yooba, Yariba. 20,000,000 speakers in Nigeria, Benin, Togo, United Kingdom, and USA. In Nigeria: 18,850,000 speakers in most of Oyo, Ogun, Ondo Osun, Kwara, and Lagos states; and western LGAs of Kogi state. Dialects are Oyo, Ijesha, Ila, Ijebu, Ondo, Wo, Owe, Jumu, Iworro, Igbonna, Yagba, Gbedde, Egba, Akono, Aworo, Bunu (Bini), Ekiti, Ilaje, Ikale, Awori. Roman alphabet. Official language. In Benin: Zou and Ouéme Provinces. Bilingualism in French.   B. GRIMES

DEIXIS.

Expressions whose reference or extension is systematically determined by aspects of the speech situation (words like *I, you, now, this,* and *here*) are called *deictic* or *indexical* terms. Sometimes they denote aspects of the speech situation itself (as with *I*), but sometimes what they denote is only partially determined by reference to the speech situation (as in *local pub, long ago, next year, distant planet, the late president*).

Linguists tend to think of deixis as a unitary field, anchored around the speech event, embracing *person deixis* (1st and 2d person pronouns and forms of address); *spatial deixis* (demonstratives, locative adverbs like *here,* relational positionals like *in front of*); *temporal deixis* (tense, adverbials like *today, now,* and *next week*); as well as *social deixis* (e.g. honorifics) and *discourse deixis* (like *the latter, the aforesaid*). Typically, the unmarked "anchor" or deictic center is the current spatio-temporal locus of the speaker. Thus, in many languages a demonstrative like *that* can be glossed as distal from the speaker, but in some languages the addressee (or other participants) may play a subsidiary role; thus Japanese *sore* 'that' must be glossed as proximal to the addressee. Hence, as speakers alternate in conversation, the reference of the same deictic expressions tends to change, making acquisition of these terms difficult for children (Tanz 1980; Wales 1986).

Confusingly, philosophers sometimes oppose the terms *indexical* and *deictic*, so that indexical expressions denote aspects of the speech event as above, while 3d person pronouns (not deictic in the linguistic sense) are termed deictic wherever they are not anaphoric. One should note, too, a divergent conception of indexicality in the work of Charles S. Peirce. Philosophers also tend to think of demonstratives as distinct from spatial indexicals, while linguists tend to merge the two classes.

Deixis has a fundamental importance for theories of meaning, because it relativizes the content of utterances to the situation of the utterance; in short, deixis makes it necessary to talk about the interpretation of utterances, not of sentences in the abstract (*I am thirty-three* will be true only if said by certain speakers at certain times). This context-relativity of interpretation proves pervasive; thus, in the familiar European languages (but not in Chinese), virtually all sentences, even if they lack indexical words, have tense and are thus interpreted relative to the time of speaking. Other languages force other kinds of obligatory deictic relativity; for example, Kwakiutl requires all N[oun] P[hrase]s to be marked for visibility/invisibility from the speaker's locus, while Javanese forces encoding of the social rank of speaker relative to addressee in most sentences. In general, there is a great deal of cross-linguistic variability in deictic categories. Taking systems of demonstratives and locative adverbs as an example: Malagasy encodes seven degrees of extension away from the speaker; Samal appears to encode proximity to speaker vs. addressee vs. non-addressed participant vs. non-participant; and Dyirbal encodes 'above', 'below', 'level with speaker', and 'upriver' vs. 'downriver from speaker' (see Anderson and Keenan 1985, Fillmore 1997).

It is becoming increasingly clear that theorists have underestimated both the complexity and the extent of deixis (for the range of problems, see Fillmore 1997, Jarvella and Klein 1982, and Levinson 1983, 1988). Thus *behind* looks like a two-place relation (*The cat is behind the car*), but it has a covert third deictic argument (*The cat is behind the car from the speaker's locus or the car's intrinsic front*). More generally, NPs may always have deictic elements: definite NPs presuppose contextual uniqueness; quantified NPs presuppose a contextually given domain of discourse; many NPs may have implicit temporal reference (*the president of the United States*); and even proper names rarely refer uniquely without implicit reference to speakers' connections to entities around them. Another problem is that many deictic anchorings can be shifted from the speech situation to narrative reference points (*John realized that now that he was here in the countryside the local pubs were far away).* All this means that the treatments of deixis in formal semantic theories like that of Montague are hopelessly inadequate. This has led to new theories, especially Situation Semantics (Barwise and Perry 1983), where a more serious attempt is made to capture the contextual relativity of semantic interpretation.

[*See also* Pragmatics and Contextual Semantics *and* Semantics.]

BIBLIOGRAPHY

Anderson, Stephen R., and Edward L. Keenan. 1985. Deixis. In *Language typology and syntactic description,* vol. 3, *Grammatical categories and the lexicon,* edited by Timothy Shopen, pp. 259–308. Cambridge and New York: Cambridge University Press.

Barwise, Jon, and John Perry. 1983. *Situations and attitudes.* Cambridge, Mass.: MIT Press.

Fillmore, Charles J. 1997. *Lectures on deixis.* Stanford, Calif.: CSLI Publications.

Jarvella, Robert J., and Wolfgang Klein, eds. 1982. *Speech, place and action: Studies of deixis and related topics.* New York: Wiley.

Levinson, Stephen C. 1983. *Pragmatics.* Cambridge and New York: Cambridge University Press.

Levinson, Stephen C. 1988. Putting linguistics on a proper footing. In *Erving Goffman,* edited by P. Drew and A. Wootton, pp. 161–227. Cambridge: Polity Press.

Lyons, John. 1977. *Semantics.* 2 vols. Cambridge and New York: Cambridge University Press.

Tanz, Christine. 1980. *Studies in the acquisition of deictic terms.* (Cambridge studies in linguistics, 26.) Cambridge and New York: Cambridge University Press.

Wales, Roger. 1986. Deixis. In *Language acquisition,* 2d ed., edited by Paul Fletcher and Michael Garman, pp. 401–428. Cambridge and New York: Cambridge University Press.

STEPHEN C. LEVINSON

DELETION. Throughout the history of generative grammar (Chomsky 1957 onward), various phenomena have been argued to involve deletion transformations. Deletion rules were invoked to account for the disparity between deep structures and their syntactically "reduced" surface strings. For example, Katz and Postal 1964 accounted for the properties of English imperatives by proposing deletion of an underlying *you will*; and Ross 1967 proposed a set of rules (including VP Deletion, Sluicing and One's Deletion) to delete constituents under identity with an antecedent. Ross also proposed a "pruning" mechanism whereby empty nodes could be deleted prior to the surface level. In addition, Rosenbaum 1967 accounted for the interpretation of coreferential complement subjects by positing that they were derived from full N[oun] P[hrase]s deleted by Equi NP-Deletion. Postal 1970, 1972 provided a similar account of the interpretation of pronouns, arguing that they derived from deep-structure full NPs in which One's Deletion had applied. (For further discussion of early approaches to deletion see Hankamer 1971, Ross 1969, and Grinder and Postal 1971.)

Debates concerning the descriptive adequacy of deletion rules centered on the interpretation of deleted constituents. Thus Jackendoff 1972 noted certain problems in using deletion to account for the interpretation of pronouns and complement subjects; he proposed an alternative analysis where both pronouns and empty complement subject NPs could be base-generated, and coindexed with an appropriate antecedent for interpretation. Wasow 1972 observed analogous problems with a deletion account of ellipted VPs; he argued for a similar "interpretive" approach where empty VPs, like empty complement subjects, could be base-generated and coindexed with an antecedent (cf. Williams 1977; and see Sag 1976, Hankamer and Sag 1976 for an alternative analysis).

In the late 1970s, the notion that constituents could be generated empty and coindexed with an antecedent was extended to account for the relation of categories derived by movement, i.e. *traces,* to their antecedents. Moreover, Chomsky 1977 observed that certain constraints, applying to the distribution of base-generated empty categories, also constrain the distribution of trace—and that certain deletion operations can even be argued to be derived by movement. Chomsky argued (contra Bresnan 1973, 1975) that sentences like *John is taller than Ron is* involve movement rather than deletion. He also discarded unconstrained pruning mechanisms in favor of a number of specific deletions typically involving COMP— S' Deletion and Complementizer Deletion—which are required for particular grammars (see also Chomsky 1981). Work of the late 1980s continues to reflect the idea of parallel constraints on base-generated empty categories and traces; thus Zagona 1988 argues that ellipted VPs, like traces, are subject to Chomsky's 1981 Empty Category Principle—a proposal extended by Lobeck 1987 to constrain ellipsis across categories in general (see also Chao 1988). Lasnik and Saito 1984 propose a general rule of *Affect* (move or delete) *alpha,* which can result in the deletion of a trace in the syntax or at L(ogical) F(orm).

Deletion of traces is also possible in Chomsky's 1995 Minimalist framework, as is deletion of features, at P(honological) F(orm) or at LF. Other work in the 1990s brought a resurgence of interest in ellipsis as deletion. Tancredi 1992 proposes that VP Ellipsis involves PF deletion of a deaccented VP, a position also taken by Chomsky and Lasnik 1993.

[*See also* Clause; Control; Coordination; Ellipsis; Principles and Parameters; Recoverability; *and* Traces.]

BIBLIOGRAPHY

Bresnan, Joan. 1973. Syntax of the comparative clause construction in English. *Linguistic Inquiry* 4.275–343.

Bresnan, Joan. 1975. Comparative deletion and constraints on transformation. *Linguistic Analysis* 1.25–74.

Chao, Wynn. 1988. *On ellipsis.* New York: Garland.

Chomsky, Noam. 1957. *Syntactic structures.* (Janua linguarum, Series minor, 4.) The Hague: Mouton.

Chomsky, Noam. 1977. On WH-movement. In *Formal syntax,* edited by Peter Culicover et al., pp. 71–132. New York: Academic Press.

Chomsky, Noam. 1981. *Lectures on government and binding.* (Studies in generative grammar, 9.) Dordrecht: Foris.

Chomsky, Noam, and Howard Lasnik. 1993. The theory of principles and parameters. In *Syntax: An international handbook of contemporary research*, vol. 1, edited by Joachim Jacobs et al., pp. 506–569. Berlin: Walter de Gruyter.

Grinder, John, and Paul Postal. 1971. Missing antecedents. *Linguistic Inquiry* 2.269–312.

Hankamer, Jorge. 1971. *Constraints on deletion in syntax.* New Haven, Conn.: Yale University dissertation.

Hankamer, Jorge, and Ivan A. Sag. 1976. Deep and surface anaphora. *Linguistic Inquiry* 7.391–428.

Jackendoff, Ray. 1972. *Semantic interpretation in generative grammar.* (Studies in linguistics series, 2.) Cambridge, Mass.: MIT Press.

Katz, Jerrold J., and Paul M. Postal. 1964. *An integrated theory of linguistic descriptions.* Cambridge, Mass.: MIT Press.

Lasnik, Howard, and Mamoru Saito. 1984. On the nature of proper government. *Linguistic Inquiry* 15.235–290.

Lobeck, Anne C. 1987. *Syntactic constraints on VP ellipsis.* Bloomington: Indiana University Linguistics Club.

Postal, Paul M. 1970. On coreferential complement subject deletion. *Linguistic Inquiry* 1.439–500.

Postal, Paul M. 1972. Some further limitations of interpretive theories of anaphora. *Linguistic Inquiry* 3.349–371.

Rosenbaum, Peter S. 1967. *The grammar of English predicate complement constructions.* Cambridge, Mass.: MIT Press.

Ross, John R. 1967. *Constraints on variables in syntax.* Cambridge, Mass.: MIT dissertation. Published as *Infinite syntax,* Norwood, N.J.: Ablex, 1986.

Sag, Ivan A. 1976. *Deletion and Logical Form.* Cambridge, Mass.: MIT dissertation. Published, New York: Garland, 1979.

Tancredi, Chris. 1992. *Deletion, deaccenting, and presupposition.* Cambridge, Mass.: MIT dissertation.

Wasow, Thomas. 1972. *Anaphoric relations in English.* Cambridge, Mass.: MIT dissertation. Revised as *Anaphora in generative grammar* (Ghent: Story-Scientia, 1979).

Williams, Edwin S. 1977. Discourse and Logical Form. *Linguistic Inquiry* 8.103–139.

Zagona, Karen. 1988. Proper government of antecedentless VP in English and Spanish. *Natural Language and Linguistic Theory* 6.95–128.

ANNE LOBECK

DEMENTIA AND LANGUAGE. "Dementia" currently refers to cognitive loss resulting from certain diseases, e.g. Alzheimer's disease, or from other biological states, e.g. malnutrition or depression. Changes in language use are characteristic of the syndromes of dementia, as are memory decline, behavioral changes, and difficulty in simple problem-solving.

The linguistic performance traditionally associated with dementia includes naming disturbance, empty speech, press of speech (logorrhea), repetitions (echolalia and palilalia), and muteness. For most of the past two centuries, demented behavior was considered a psychiatric disorder, and attempts were made to classify its linguistic manifestations in relation to those of other psychiatric disturbances (e.g. Séglas 1892).

Since the 1970s increasing Western medical study has resulted in clearer understanding of the neurological bases of dementia. Some of these involve primarily *cortical* damage, e.g. A[lzheimer's] D[ementia], Pick's disease, and multi-infarct dementia; others involve primarily *subcortical* damage, e.g. the dementia seen in one-third of patients with Parkinson's disease. In the subcortical dementias, motor performance is primarily affected—e.g. in dysarthria, acceleration (festination) of speech, or illegible handwriting; in the cortical dementias, language performance is affected. (For reference, see Irigaray 1973, Bayles and Kaszniak 1987, Kempler and Zelinski 1994.)

During the progressive decline involved in AD, scores on naming tests decrease, and responses become semantically farther from the target; comprehension of oral and written materials deteriorates, especially for longer and/or more complex materials; and discourse becomes increasingly devoid of content. However, phonological and syntactic production are relatively spared, as is the ability to read aloud. Automatic speech tasks—e.g. reciting known series, such as the days of the week—soon show omissions or additions. Certain pragmatic abilities are spared until late in the course of dementia, e.g. use of social formulas; others decline early, e.g. appreciating inference. Metalinguistic abilities appear to decline; one cannot engage patients in the tasks.

A stage model of progressive decline has proven useful in projecting the language changes of the cortical dementias, especially AD. In the early stages, patients resemble anomic aphasics; by the middle stages, they closely resemble those with Wernicke's aphasia or transcortical sensory aphasia (most strikingly with regard to empty speech, logorrhea, and poor comprehension). By the later stages, we find echolalia, then palilalia, then muteness; and other non-language behavioral deficits render confusion with aphasia unlikely.

Distinguishing the linguistic performance of early- and mid-stage AD from that of certain aphasic syndromes is difficult; thus the question arises as to whether the linguistic disturbance results from damage to brain areas associated with language, or whether language similar to that in aphasia can result from damage to areas responsible for non-language cognitive abilities, such as ideation, memory, attention, and self-monitoring.

Bayles and Kaszniak 1987 argue that disturbance of semantic memory accounts for the breakdown of language and communication in AD; others (e.g. Obler and Albert 1985) maintain that the predilection for cellular damage to frontal and temporal areas of the brain in AD makes the language areas particularly vulnerable to deficit, especially in conjunction with the decline in the other non-language cognitive mechanisms listed above.

The lexicon is the linguistic level that has received the most experimental study in the dementias. Evidence exists to show primary breakdown in lexical access, with secondary breakdown in lexical representation, and also in visual identification of the objects to be named. The evidence for breakdown at the stage of lexical access or recall comes from naming studies which find that demented patients make errors related semantically to the target—or use circumlocutions to explain what the object to be named does, instead of naming it. Such responses suggest that knowledge of what the item is remains intact. However, problems with subordinate categories, as compared to superordinate information, argue for a degree of semantic or conceptual breakdown as well. In "semantic dementia" they are paramount (see Garrard and Hodges 1999).

The relation of age at the onset of dementia to the degree and pace (but not the type) of linguistic impairment, remains controversial. Presenile AD, with onset prior to age sixty-five, appears to show earlier and more severe linguistic disturbance than does senile AD. In the rare cases of strong familial AD, with onset in the thirties and forties, language/communication disturbance appears strikingly early in the course of decline.

Lay belief assumes that the behavioral changes of dementia simply represent normal or accelerated aging ("senility"); however, certain admittedly infrequent behaviors—e.g. "klang"-association, i.e. compulsive phonologically motivated response to phonological cues on a naming task—are seen only in the language of demented patients. Pragmatic breakdown, too, can be quite severe in dementia (e.g., demented bilinguals' inappropriate choice of language or code-switching with a monolingual interlocutor).

[See also Aphasia; Bilingualism and Multilingualism; and Neurolinguistics.]

BIBLIOGRAPHY

Au, Rhoda, et al. 1988. The relation of aphasia to dementia. *Aphasiology* 2.161–173.

Bayles, Kathryn A., and Alfred W. Kaszniak. 1987. *Communication and cognition in normal aging and dementia.* Boston: Little, Brown.

Garrard, Peter, and John Hodges. 1999. Semantic dementia: Implications for the neural basis of language and meaning. *Aphasiology* 13.609–623.

Kempler, Daniel, and Elizabeth M. Zelinski. 1994. Language in dementia and normal aging. In *Dementia and normal aging*, edited by F. A. Huppert et al., pp. 331–365. Cambridge: Cambridge University Press.

Obler, Loraine K., and Martin L. Albert. 1985. Language skills across adulthood. In *Handbook on the psychology of aging*, 2d ed., edited by James E. Birren and K. Warner Schaie, pp. 463–473. New York: Van Nostrand Reinhold.

Séglas, Jules. 1892. *Des troubles du langage chez les aliénés.* Paris: Rueff.

LORAINE K. OBLER

DEMONSTRATIVES. See Deixis; Discourse; Philosophy of Language; Pragmatics and Contextual Semantics; Semantics; and Typology and Universals.

DENOTATION. See Semantics and Philosophy of Language.

DEONTIC MODALITY. See Modality.

DERIVATIONAL MORPHOLOGY. The theory of derivational morphology is empirically based on D[erivational] affixes, i.e. morphemes which are bound and placed before I[nflectional] affixes, in cases where the lexical category requires inflection. (For general reference, see Motsch 1988, 1999.)

1. Definitions. Derivational morphology rests on the following abstract system of definitions:

(a) A *word form* is a word plus one or more I-affixes.
(b) A *word* is (i) a root, (ii) a root plus a D-affix, (iii) a root plus a root, (iv) a word plus a D-affix, or (v) a word plus a word. In addition, a root or a word which is a co-constituent of a D-affix is called a *base*.

In this definition, I-affix, D-affix, and root are primitive terms, empirically motivated by restrictions on ordering (I-affixes vs. words) or occurrence (affixes vs. roots). If we assume that I-affixes, D-affixes, and roots are separate categories of word structure, then I-morphology, D-morphology, and compounding may be considered as different branches of morphology, dealing respectively with three separate types of systematic relations between words and I-affixes, between bases and D-affixes, and between words within a word. However, there are several problems with this distinction. For instance, it has been argued that both I-morphology and D-morphology require the same sort of formal processes (cf. Lieber 1980).

A category-based distinction between root and D-affix, and consequently a fundamental difference between D-morphology and compounding, is argued explicitly by Selkirk 1982, but has been denied by Höhle 1982. However, there is a widely shared view that the distinction between prefix and suffix is not a categorial one; prefixation and suffixation are assumed to be governed by the same types of rules.

The restriction of D-morphology to D-affixes presupposes an essential difference between affixation and other techniques involved in morphological processes, such as *conversion*, *ablaut*, and *reduplication*. These techniques, however, differ only in the way in which semantic processes of the same kind are realized linguistically (see Dressler 1977).

2. Rules and productivity. From a grammatical point of view, derivatives are essentially considered to be the products of rules. This is in keeping with the general assumption that complex linguistic forms of a language may be reduced to units and rules of some type. *W[ord]-F[ormation] R[ule]s*, then, are rules that combine word structure units to form new complex words. Complex words typically serve to enrich the permanent vocabulary of a language. Other functions are recategorization (e.g. pure nominalization in languages like English, German, or Russian), and stylistic variation (such as diminutives).

As a result of the first function, the vocabulary of a language includes many derived words from earlier periods of the language, which are related to rules only in a rather limited way. Such limited regularities are covered by the concept of *R[edundancy] rules*. R-rules of the kind proposed by Jackendoff 1975 allow for explicit description of the dependent information, i.e. of (sub)regularities, in the representation of the lexical entries which are part of the permanent lexicon of a language. Such rules account for all types of restrictions which run counter to full regularity. As a borderline case, these rules may be identical to those which form new derivatives, i.e. to WFRs which involve affixes.

The study of WFRs is concerned only with that part of the lexicon which is covered by R-rules which correspond to WFRs, and ad-hoc formations in texts which are presumably the products of WFRs. On one hand, the analysis of lexicalized complex words presupposes the study of the general grammatical properties of WFRs; on the other, it goes beyond the types of regularities relevant to the grammar.

Characteristic of many D-processes are the greater or lesser restrictions on the class of base words which belong to a given process (cf. Aronoff 1976). Often it is not possible to restrict the class using only syntactic and morphological categories. In some cases, it is scarcely possible even to find a proper non-ad-hoc semantic description. There is another peculiarity, labeled the *productivity* of a certain type of D-process; some new words predicted by a tentative WFR, abstracted from lexical entries with the same kind of dependent information, come up against acceptability restrictions. Different proposals have been made to account for productivity (Aronoff 1976, Górska 1982, Dressler et al. 1987:87 ff., 112 ff.).

Productivity is frequently considered to be a mere performance phenomenon, to be ignored in grammatical analysis. Some approaches claim a correspondence between productivity and the restrictedness of a class of bases (cf. Aronoff 1976). One promising way to account for these phenomena might be to elaborate on Hermann Paul's reflections on analogy in morphological processes. A suitable program could be sketched as follows: productivity and acceptability are phenomena which depend on different degrees of transparency of dependent information in lexicalized derivatives. The highest degree of transparency is achieved in R-rules corresponding to productive WFRs, and the lowest in the analysis of a simple lexical entry like German *einsam* 'lonely', which is semantically opaque (similar to Eng. *on+ly*). Nevertheless, *zweisam* 'two alone' has been coined by analogy with *einsam*. The main task is to discover what kinds of deviations from properties of productive rules affect the transparency of dependent information to a greater or lesser extent. The explanatory basis of this description is probably to be found in the psychological mechanisms of analogy.

3. Derivational processes. In general, it is claimed that the study of the rules which underlie D-processes in a particular language has to account for all general and particular language-specific properties of such rules, as well as for universal constraints on the form of derivational rules. The formal description of D-processes has to provide the following sorts of information: (i) phonological form of the affix, (ii) syntactic category and subcategory frame of the derivative, (iii) restrictions defining the class of bases available to the affix, (iv) diacritical features of the derivative, and (v) semantic form of the derivative.

Since (ii) and (v) show significant relations to the same sort of information in the representation of the corresponding base, it is necessary to analyze in detail the systematic aspects of "argument inheritance," or the rebuilding of argument structure in derived words, as well as types of semantic amalgamation.

Traditional linguistic approaches to D-morphology postulated a separate component dealing with word formation. In earlier versions of generative grammar, D-processes as well as compounding were treated as syntactic transformations. According to this concept, word formation is only a special case of the construction of syntactic phrases. The transformationalist position, however, has been criticized as inadequate on empirical and theoretical grounds. The general requirement on the study of D-processes since the end of the 1970s has been to find a few simple principles which will enable the linguist to explain the complex phenomena which can be observed in word structures. Besides grammatical principles, semantic and pragmatic ones must be taken into account. A favorite topic is the question of whether there are separate principles which govern word structure.

In all mainstream approaches, special rules defining the grammatical properties of derivatives have been elaborated. However, views differ both on the form of WFRs

and on their underlying grammatical principles. The most prominent positions are the following.

3.1. WFRs include all aspects of D-processes: the internal morphological structure, the external properties, and the semantic structure of the derived word. Examples are the WFRs and R-rules proposed by Aronoff 1976 and Jackendoff 1975, respectively. Aronoff takes the view that WFRs are constrained by general principles of word structure, such as the Word-Based Hypothesis, the Unitary Base Hypothesis, and the Binary Branching Hypothesis (cf. Scalise 1984).

3.2. WFRs determine the syntax of words; and this in turn is the basis of semantic interpretation (cf. Lieber 1980, Selkirk 1982, Toman 1987). Within this general framework, however, there are different views concerning the principles that govern word syntax. Some linguists argue that syntactic principles (such as X-bar Theory or the θ-criterion) also apply to word structure. Another line of argument stresses the difference between phrase structure and word structure, although similarities are admitted (cf. Selkirk 1982).

3.3. Possible words are defined by general principles of semantic interpretation. The interesting properties of word structure, like argument inheritance and categorial restrictions, can be explained on the basis of these principles. The remaining syntactic properties are very trivial (cf. Fanselow 1988).

3.4. In a further approach, Beard 1986 proposes a strict separation of lexeme and morpheme, as units belonging to entirely different subsystems of the grammar. According to Beard, the structure of lexemes is determined by rules operating on semantic and syntactic properties of lexical entries. By contrast, the properties of morphemes (e.g. suffixes) are governed by entirely separate principles.

4. Semantic properties. Until now, semantic properties of D-processes have been analyzed more or less on an observational level. In the traditional study of word formation, for example, the meaning of affixes has been described more or less intuitively. The same is true of semantically based classifications like nomina agentis, nomina actionis, resultatives, diminutives, collectives, etc. Semantic considerations also include the distinction between modification and transposition, which has been adopted in many works by Soviet linguists on word formation. Diminutives are a typical example of modification; here the concept denoted by the base is semantically modified by the concept denoted by the affix. Transposition encompasses all other types of semantic processes involved in D-rules. In the 1990s, semantic studies have been extended—for example, in the description of German verbal prefixes and particles based on logical sense (Stiebels 1997) and the presentation of semantic patterns underlying German word formation (Motsch 1999).

A more precise and theoretically elaborated analysis of D-processes is an important desideratum. Unresolved problems include:

(a) The design of a proper semantic representation of the meaning of derivatives, especially of D-affixes.

(b) The analysis of different kinds of amalgamation, including semantic aspects of argument inheritance and the creation of argument structures conveyed by affixes.

(c) The analysis of operations which will give explicit statements of encyclopedic knowledge, as part of the processes of semantic interpretation.

(d) The search for semantic peculiarities of D-affixes as opposed to other types of linguistic expressions, such as I-affixes, function words, or roots. Aspects of this problem are discussed by Bybee 1985.

[*See also* Affixation; Conversion; Diminutives; Generative Morphology; Reduplication; Stem and Root; *and* Words.]

BIBLIOGRAPHY

Aronoff, Mark. 1976. *Word formation in generative grammar.* (Linguistic Inquiry monographs, 1.) Cambridge, Mass.: MIT Press.

Beard, Robert. 1986. *On the separation of derivation from morphology.* Bloomington: Indiana University Linguistics Club.

Bybee, Joan L. 1985. *Morphology: A study of the relation between meaning and form.* (Typological studies in language, 9.) Amsterdam: Benjamins.

Dressler, Wolfgang U. 1977. *Grundfragen der Morphonologie.* Vienna: Verlag der Österreichischen Akademie der Wissenschaften.

Dressler, Wolfgang U., et al. 1987. *Leitmotifs in Natural Morphology.* (Studies in Language, Companion series, 10.) Amsterdam: Benjamins.

Fanselow, Gisbert. 1988. Word formation and the human conceptual system. In Motsch 1988, pp. 31–52.

Górska, Elżbieta. 1982. Formal and functional restrictions on the productivity of word formation rules. *Folia Linguistica* 16.149–162.

Höhle, Tilman N. 1982. Über Komposition und Derivation: Zur Konstituentenstruktur von Wortbildungsprodukten im Deutschen. *Zeitschrift für Sprachwissenschaft* 1.76–112.

Jackendoff, Ray. 1975. Morphological and semantic regularities in the lexicon. *Language* 51.639–671.

Lieber, Rochelle. 1980. *On the organization of the lexicon.* MIT dissertation. Published, Bloomington: Indiana University Linguistics Club, 1981.

Motsch, Wolfgang, ed. 1988. *The contribution of word structure theories to the study of word formation.* (Linguistische Studien, Reihe A, 179.) Berlin: Zentralinstitut für Sprachwissenschaften, Akademie der Wissenschaften der DDR.

Motsch, Wolfgang. 1999. *Deutsche Wortbildung in Grundzügen.* Berlin and New York: de Gruyter.

Scalise, Sergio. 1984. *Generative morphology.* (Studies in generative grammar, 18.) Dordrecht: Foris.

Selkirk, Elisabeth O. 1982. *The syntax of words.* (Linguistic Inquiry monographs, 7.) Cambridge, Mass.: MIT Press.

Stiebels, Barbara. 1996. *Lexikalische Argumente und Adjunkte: Zum semantischen Beitrag von verbalen Präfixen und Partikelen.* Berlin and New York: Mouton de Gruyter.

Toman, Jindřich. 1987. *Wortsyntax: Eine Diskussion ausgewählter Probleme deutscher Wortbildung.* 2d ed. (Linguistische Arbeiten, 137.) Tübingen: Niemeyer.

WOLFGANG MOTSCH

DETERMINERS. *See* Phrase Structure.

DEVELOPMENTAL DYSPHASIA. *See* Developmental Language Disorder; Specific Language Impairment; *and* Williams Syndrome and Down Syndrome: Cognitive Constraints on Language.

DEVELOPMENTAL LANGUAGE DISORDER. Delayed and difficult acquisition of language that is not caused by brain injury, mental retardation, hearing loss, or any other clear cause has been known variously as developmental language disorder, developmental aphasia, and congenital aphasia; it is discussed in the entry Specific Language Impairment, the current term for the disorder. Other disorders of language associated with two well-studied genetic syndromes are discussed in the entry Williams Syndrome and Down Syndrome: Cognitive Constraints on Language.

DEVELOPMENTAL LINGUISTICS. *See* Neurolinguistics; Psycholinguistics; Aphasia; *and* Acquisition of Language.

DIACHRONIC LINGUISTICS. *See* Historical Linguistics *and* Comparative Method.

DIALECTOLOGY. One branch of linguistics that deals with the nature and distribution of variation in language is known as dialectology. It has not been easy to define "dialect" or to distinguish it from "language." One of the more successful definitions is that of Ammon (1983:64):

> A dialect is a language such that (i) there is at least one other language with which it has a high degree of similarity; (ii) there is no language which is regionally included within it as a proper part; and (iii) neither its writing system nor its pronunciation nor its lexicon nor its syntax is officially normalized.

(For general reference, see Kurath 1972, Chambers and Trudgill 1980, Francis 1983, Trudgill 1983, Kirk et al. 1985, Cassidy 1985, 1991, 1996, Carver 1987, Trudgill 1990.)

1. History. Although dialectology did not become a formal discipline until the middle of the 19th century, knowledge and illustration of dialect differences go far back in linguistic and literary history. In Classical Greek, certain dialects were recognized as the appropriate media for certain types of literature: Ionic for epic, dating from Homer; Doric for odes, as in Pindar; Aeolic for lyric poetry; and Attic for drama—not to mention the use of her native dialect by Sappho of Lesbos. In English, Chaucer made comic use of Northern English in his "Reeve's Tale," and Shakespeare identified the Welshman Fluellen by his curious phonology. But it was not until the latter part of the 19th century that serious study of dialect began. Notable were Ellis's extensive survey (1889) of the contemporary phonology of English dialects, and Winteler's study (1876) of the Kerenzen dialect of Switzerland; the latter strongly influenced the Neogrammarians Osthof and Brugmann.

The hypothesis of the Neogrammarians that sound change was exceptionless inspired one of the most ambitious dialect surveys ever undertaken—Georg Wenker's *Deutscher Sprachatlas,* begun in 1876, and in a sense still continuing. Starting as a modest attempt to study the boundary between High and Low German, this was ultimately extended to cover all Germany and Austria. Wenker used the method of translation: he sent out his list of forty model sentences to nearly fifty thousand schoolmasters, asking them to translate the sentences into local dialects with the help of native-speaking pupils.

One unexpected result was the discovery of the so-called Rhenish Fan, a spreading pattern of *isoglosses,* which seems to refute the hypothesis that sound changes are without exception.

Twenty years after Wenker began his work, another great pioneering linguistic survey was begun: the *Atlas linguistique de la France,* conducted by the Swiss dialectologist Jules Gilliéron and his indefatigable fieldworker Edmond Edmont. It established what has come to be the favored method of dialect collection, in face-to-face interviews with native speakers by a trained phonetician, eliciting items from a set questionnaire. In only four years, Edmont visited more than six hundred localities throughout France, eliciting nearly two thousand items from each. The results were published as maps in thirteen large volumes (Gilliéron and Edmont 1902–1913). This work has been a primary influence on subsequent dialectological surveys the world over. There are now dialect atlases on this model from most countries of Europe, including Italy, Switzerland, Spain, Rumania, the Scandinavian countries, and even tiny Andorra.

2. Methodology. There are basically two types of dialect survey. The first and older type, often called "traditional," is based on regional distribution, in the manner of Wenker and Gilliéron; this is often called *dialect geography.* The more recent type emphasizes variation in speech according to social level, often concentrating on a few selected features; it is called *sociolinguistic* dialectology. Labov 1966, a study of sociolinguistic variation in New York City, is often cited as the first work of this type, although some of the methods had been used earlier. It has largely superseded the traditional type; however, important regional surveys are still being conducted.

Both methods require a large body of language—a *corpus*—as a basis for description and analysis. The corpus to be used consists of a sample of the particular feature or features of the dialect which are to be studied. These may include phonology or pronunciation, morphology, lexicon or vocabulary, and syntax or grammar. Sociolinguistic surveys in particular may also be concerned with informants' attitudes toward their dialect and that of others, and in the cultural interests and values which dialect reveals. The corpus must be gathered with care, to assure that it is representative of the population chosen for investigation.

3. Geographical dialectology. There are two different methods of collecting the data. As in Wenker's survey, questionnaires may be sent to various localities, to be

FIGURE 1. *List of Responses.* (Orton and Halliday 1963:726)

BOOTS*

Q. What do you call those things that you are wearing?

Rr. (STRONG) BOOTS/SHOES, HIGH BOOTS/TIES

Note 1—Sometimes the f.ws. had to press for the wanted word, and sometimes they omitted to rec. it.

Note 2—Forms of BOOT also occur at VI.14.25 and IX.8.6.

1 Nb   1 bɪɣts   2 bu:ts   3 bɪöts   4 ᐃbɪɣt   5 bɪəts   6 bjɣts   7 bɪəts   8 bɪøts   9 bɪəts

2 Cu   1 ʃɒɷz   2 sʈɹaŋ bɪɷts   3 bɪɷts   4 bu:ts   5 bɪəts   6 p. bɪu:ts [not used]

3 Du   1 bjɒts, ᵒ~¹   2 bjɣts   3 bɪəts   4–5 bjɣts   6 bɪöts, ᵒbɪu:ts²

4 We   1 sʈɹaŋ bɪəts   2 straŋ ʃᵒu:z, p. bɪəts [rare]   3 bɪəts   4 bɷəts

5 La   1 ʃu:z, bu:ts   2 bu:ts   3 bɷəts   4 bu:ts   5 böuts   6 ɛɪ bu:ts [lastɪksaɪdɪd bu:ts *elastic-sided boots*]   7 sʈɹɒŋ ʃu:n   8 ʃᵒu:n, bɣ:ts ["modern"]   9 ʃɒn: ["older"], bᵒu:ts ["newer"]   10 ʃᵒü:n [old word], p. bᵒü:ts   11 bᵒu:ts   12 bɣ:ts   13 sʈɹɒŋ ʃɣ:z, p.p bɣ:ts [not used]   14 bᵒü:ts

---

filled in by a responsible person such as the local school-teacher or clergyman—who may not, in fact, be a speaker of the local dialect. Or, as with the French atlas, the collection may be done in person by a fieldworker, who records data either in writing or on a tape-recorder. The advantage of the former, "postal" method, which has been used less often in modern surveys, is that it can reach a larger number of sources, and thus can produce a large corpus at relatively low expense. The disadvantage is that it relies on amateurs who may not be actual speakers of the dialect, and who may have no training in phonetic transcription or other phases of language study. The advantage of the interview method is that the interviewer can make sure that the consultants are true speakers of the dialect, that they understand what is being asked, and that their answers are relevant and authentic. Its principal disadvantage is that it is both expensive and time-consuming, and thus results in a more restricted corpus.

Traditional dialect surveys have usually attempted to collect a corpus of the indigenous local dialect of ordinary speakers, who are familiar with it from childhood, and who use it regularly (at least in informal conversation among themselves). Such a dialect is sometimes called a *basilect*. It is not difficult to find and elicit, as long as one is dealing with a stable community, e.g. a small village whose inhabitants are not highly educated or well traveled, and who pursue occupations that do not bring them into frequent contact with speakers of a standard or cultivated variety of the language. Such communities were quite common in Europe at the time of Wenker and Gilliéron. But in modern times, with greater mobility and communication—and with the growth of urban centers which draw population from throughout a country, and even from beyond its borders—the situation is much altered. This has led to objections that traditional surveys are not representative of the actual language of the majority of the population. However, the method has been defended, chiefly on historical grounds; thus it is felt that the *patois* of French villages, now rapidly disappearing, is a sort of endangered species which, if it cannot be preserved, can at least be recorded for the benefit of future historians of the language. The traditional dialectologist is thus a kind of antiquary, collecting and recording the speech of the past.

Once the corpus of the basilect has been assembled, the question arises of how it is to be made public. The two common methods are lists and maps; more recently, tape-recordings of the original interviews have been made available. A list gives the responses from all localities, usually in geographic order. For example, Figure 1 (from Orton and Halliday 1963) lists the responses from five

MAP 1. *Diphthongs in Northern England* (Kolb 1966:199)

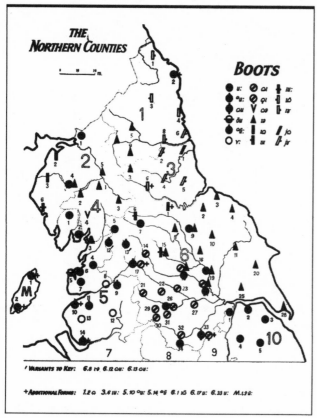

MAP 2. *'Child' versus 'Bairn' in England* (Upton et al. 1987: 50)

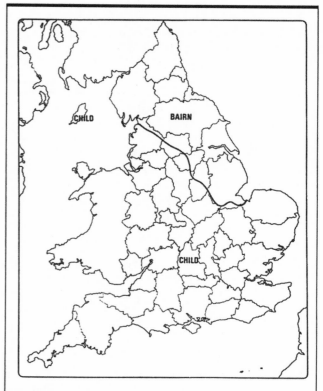

northern counties of England for the word *boots.* Only two lexical items appear: *boots* and *shoes*; the phrase *strong shoes,* reported from some localities, contrasts with *slender shoes* for ordinary footwear. Of particular interest is the variety of pronunciations of the vowel or diphthong in *boots.*

Lists have the obvious advantage of being easy and cheap to produce. Their principal shortcoming is that only the person intimately familiar with the geography can picture the regional distribution of the forms. Others will have to mark the variants on an outline map.

Maps, gathered into atlases, perform this function for the student. Map 1 shows, by means of symbols, the distribution of diphthongs in *boots* in the north of England (from Kolb 1966). The northeastern section has diphthongs that begin with a front vowel or glide, while the southwestern section has diphthongs that begin with a high back round vowel.

A refinement in the making of distributional maps uses isoglosses. An *isogloss* is a line that marks the extent of the area in which a particular feature appears, or an

approximate boundary between two variants of the same feature. Map 2 is an isogloss map of England with a line that separates southern *child* from northern *bairn* (from Upton et al. 1987). Both are Old English words; but it is clear that, in the northern area of Scandinavian settlement, *bairn* has been reinforced by Old Norse *barn* (still Norwegian for 'child'). This map is of historical interest, since the isogloss runs parallel to (but a bit north of) the line established under King Alfred in the 9th century to mark the southern limit of the Danelaw, or area of Danish dominance.

Isogloss maps are rarely so simple; often the isoglosses are elaborately convoluted, as in Map 3, which shows two variant terms for 'molars' (from Orton and Wright 1974). Areas marked "1" have some form of *axle-teeth*; those marked "2" have *grinders*; and unmarked areas have either standard *molars,* or some other term like *double-teeth.* To fill in the unmarked areas, one would have to resort to lists like that in Figure 1. Maps 2–3 are from a type of publication called a *word geography,* which presents lexical variation but disregards phonetic detail. Computerization of cartography has enabled cre-

MAP 3. *Terms for 'Molars' in England.* (Orton and Wright 1974:179)

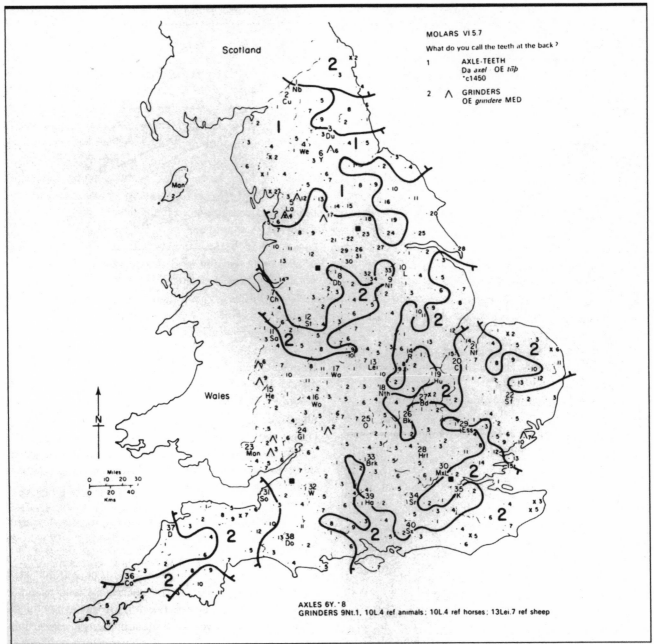

ation of sophisticated projections of results of dialect research.

4. Social dialectology. Sociolinguistic dialect surveys differ from traditional ones primarily in their purpose. While the latter are preoccupied with a basilect, which may be used by only a minority of the population, the former is concerned with the language of larger groups in its chosen locality. Instead of attempting to deal with a large sample of the lexicon and the total phonology, the sociolinguistic survey concentrates on features which preliminary research has suggested will show significant variation. The variation in these features is correlated with socially significant variables, such as class, age, race, ethnicity, sex, and the circumstances and types of discourse in which the forms occurred.

William Labov, a pioneer in urban dialect studies, used

simple averages in studying linguistic variables correlated with variation in social status in style (Labov 1966). More recent sociolinguistic studies of dialects use more complicated statistical procedures done with computers. Thus, in the Tyneside Linguistic Survey in England, both social stratification and multiple linguistic features were subjected to *cluster analysis* (Jones-Sargent 1983). The application of statistics to dialect study is described by Davis (1983:69–84).

5. Dialectometry. A statistical method of dialect analysis developed during the 1970s and 1980s was called "dialectometry" by its originator, French dialectologist Jean Séguy (e.g. 1973). It has been further developed in Austria by Hans Goebl, and in Germany by Wolfgang Viereck. The method is directed at measuring the "linguistic distance" between individual localities in a dialect region, by counting the number of contrasts in a large sample of linguistic features. Although Séguy's dialect atlas of Gascony was prepared manually, the large number of comparisons involved makes the use of a computer a virtual necessity. This method gives promise of identifying dialect areas by methods more objective than those of traditional linguistic geography.

6. Conclusions. It remains to inquire what use is to be made of the products of dialectological research, whether traditional or sociolinguistic. Obviously, they have added greatly to our knowledge of language—both as a system in itself, and as a major element of human culture and psychology. Traditional dialectology has also established precise scientific methods for identifying and describing the variability which is recognized as an essential attribute of language. It has contributed to historical linguistics by showing that inherent variability is a major source of language change (Weinreich et al. 1968).

Sociolinguistic dialectology has helped to integrate language, perhaps the most characteristic feature of humanity, into the over-all pattern of human culture; and it has contributed to a growing understanding of the diversity of culture. By establishing that dialects are language systems in their own right—rather than degenerate forms of a literate standard, to be eradicated by schooling or even by fiat—it has given them dignity and importance. Indeed, results of dialect studies have increasingly been taken into account in school curriculum design. Dialectology, once the hobby of amateur collectors of odd words, has taken a major position within linguistics; this makes it an important field of study not only for linguists, but for all educated persons.

[*See also* Historical Linguistics; History of Linguistics, *article on* Comparative-Historical Linguistics; Language Change; Social Variation, *article on* Social Dialects; Sociolinguistics.]

BIBLIOGRAPHY

Ammon, Ulrich. 1983. Vorbereitung einer Explizit-Definition von 'Dialekt' und benachbarten Begriffen mit Mitteln der formalen Logik. In *Aspekte der Dialekttheorie,* edited by Klaus J. Mattheier, pp. 27–68. Tübingen: Niemeyer.

Carver, Craig. 1987. *American regional dialects: A word geography.* Ann Arbor: University of Michigan Press.

Cassidy, Frederic, ed. 1985, 1991, 1996. *Dictionary of American regional English.* Vols. 1–3. Cambridge, Mass.: Harvard University Press, Belknap.

Chambers, J. K., and Peter Trudgill. 1980. *Dialectology.* Cambridge and New York: Cambridge University Press.

Davis, Lawrence. 1983. *English dialectology: An introduction.* University, Ala.: University of Alabama Press.

Ellis, Alexander J. 1889. *The existing phonology of English dialects.* London: Trübner.

Francis, W. Nelson. 1983. *Dialectology: An introduction.* London: Longman.

Gilliéron, Jules, and Edmond Edmont. 1902–1913. *Atlas linguistique de la France.* 13 vols. Paris: Champion.

Jones-Sargent, Val. 1983. *Tyne bytes: A computerised sociolinguistic study of Tyneside.* Frankfurt: Lang.

Kirk, John M., et al. 1985. *Studies in linguistic geography: The dialects of Britain and Ireland.* London: Croom Helm.

Kolb, Eduard. 1966. *Linguistic atlas of England: Phonological atlas of the northern region.* Bern: Francke.

Kurath, Hans. 1972. *Studies in area linguistics.* Bloomington: Indiana University Press.

Labov, William. 1966. *The social stratification of English in New York City.* Washington, D.C.: Center for Applied Linguistics.

Orton, Harold, and Wilfrid J. Halliday. 1963. *Survey of English dialects,* vol. 1, *The six northern counties and the Isle of Man.* Leeds: Arnold.

Orton, Harold, and Nathalia Wright. 1974. *A word geography of England.* London: Seminar Press.

Séguy, Jean. 1973. La dialectométrie dans l'Atlas linguistique de la Gascogne. *Revue de Linguistique Romane* 35.335–357.

Trudgill, Peter. 1983. *On dialect: Social and historical perspectives.* Oxford: Blackwell.

Trudgill, Peter. 1990. *The dialects of England.* Cambridge, Mass.: Blackwell.

Upton, Clive, et al. 1987. *Word maps: A dialect atlas of England.* London: Croom Helm.

Weinreich, Uriel, William Labov, and Marvin I. Herzog. 1968. Empirical foundations for a theory of linguistic change. In *Directions for historical linguistics,* edited by Winfred P.

Lehmann and Yakov Malkiel, pp. 97–195. Austin: University of Texas Press.

Wenker, Georg, et al. 1876–1956. *Deutscher Sprachatlas*. Marburg: Elwert.

Winteler, Jost. 1876. *Die Kerenzer Mundart des Kantons Glarus*. Leipzig: Winter.

W. Nelson Francis

DIALECTS. *See* Dialectology; Social Variations; Sociolinguistics; *and* Historical Linguistics.

DICTIONARIES. *See* Lexicography; Lexicon; *and* Semantics.

DIGLOSSIA. The concept of diglossia has remained at the heart of debates in sociolinguistics and in studies of language contact for almost five decades.

1. Classic definition. The classic concept of diglossia, first formulated by Ferguson 1959, refers to a highly specific sociolinguistic situation in which there is strict functional differentiation between two varieties of the same language, with a H[igh] variety reserved for use in formal, institutional settings, and a L[ow] variety for use in informal home and community settings. Ferguson 1959 distinguished between diglossia and the more common situation in which a standard language coexists with dialects, noting that "no segment of the linguistic community in diglossia regularly uses H as a medium of ordinary conversation" (1959:337). He also made a clear distinction between diglossia and bilingual situations "where two distinct (related or unrelated) languages are used side by side throughout a speech community with a clearly defined role" (325, n. 2). For Ferguson, the initial formulation of the concept of diglossia was part of a broader intellectual project of establishing a taxonomy of the major types of sociolinguistic situations. This would then contribute to the construction of a general theory about the relationship between change in the social organization of speech communities and in the social functions of language, and about change in language varieties and sociolinguistic repertoires (Ferguson 1959, 1991).

The four "clear cases" of diglossia cited by Ferguson in his original article were Arabic speakers in Cairo, Greek speakers in Athens, speakers of Haitian Creole in Port-au-Prince, and speakers of Swiss German in Zurich. Three decades later, Ferguson emphasized that, with respect to the communities cited in his 1959 study, he was interested in language use and language attitudes as well as language structure (1991:221). His concern with all three dimensions is evident in the nine defining characteristics of diglossia specified in his original article, which follow.

1.1. *Function.* This dimension of diglossia is central in Ferguson's model. He emphasizes the complementarity of H and L varieties, arguing that "in one set of situations, only H is appropriate and in another only L, with the two sets overlapping only very slightly" (1959:328). Complementarity of functions is illustrated by "situations" where an H or L variety might be used, as in Table 1.

1.2. *Prestige.* Under this heading, Ferguson draws attention to the way diglossia is sustained by speakers' valorizations of H and L. H is seen as superior to L and is often evaluated as more beautiful or more logical. Sometimes, as with Arabic, religion is a key source of prestige for the H variety.

1.3. *Literary heritage.* One defining characteristic of the H variety in diglossia, for Ferguson, is the existence of a substantial body of literature in this variety. In all four "clear cases" in his model, the H variety is associated with an extensive literary heritage extending over a long time period.

1.4. *Acquisition.* Another defining attribute of the H variety is that it is not used in ordinary, everyday conversation, as in the home. It can be learned only in formal educational contexts. Access to this variety is therefore related to access to education.

1.5. *Standardization.* Ferguson also notes that, in addition to having a long literary heritage, the H variety is

TABLE 1. *Use of H and L Varieties across Different Types of Situations.* (Ferguson, 1959:329)

	H	L
Sermon in church or mosque	x	
Instructions to servants, waiters, workmen, clerks		x
Personal letter		x
Speech in parliament, political speech	x	
University lecture	x	
Conversation with family, friends, colleagues		x
News broadcast	x	
Radio soap opera		x
Newspaper editorial, news story, photo caption	x	
Caption on political cartoon		x
Poetry	x	
Folk literature		x

likely to be highly codified, whereas the L variety is not codified. However, he acknowledges that standard forms of one or more L varieties may emerge over time, based on usage in influential urban centers. For example, in the case of Greek diglossia, Athenian *dhimotiki* (vernacular) emerged as a single standard variety of L; in Arabic diglossia, different regional standards emerged in cities such as Cairo and Damascus.

1.6. *Stability.* Again citing Arabic and Greek, Ferguson points out that diglossia can persist for several hundred years or even longer. He hypothesizes that a diglossic order is most likely to emerge in societies with an entrenched social hierarchy and where literacy is limited to a small elite. His 1959 predictions regarding the decline of diglossia are therefore linked to the leveling of social boundaries, to democratization of access to formal education and other formal institutional domains, to the opening of new channels of communication between social groups, and to the mobilization of the wider population around unifying symbols of nationhood, such as an L variety. He sees the spread of literacy as playing a key role in these social and historical processes.

1.7. *Grammar.* According to Ferguson, one of the principal ways in which the H and L varieties are differentiated is by grammatical forms (1959:333). He also argues that, at least for three of his "clear cases," the grammars of the L varieties are characterized by greater simplicity than those of the H varieties. He also suggests that this may be a general attribute of diglossic situations.

1.8. *Lexicon.* Ferguson observes that a major proportion of the lexis of H and L would be shared because the varieties evolved within the same broad linguistic tradition; however, the lexicon of the H variety would include a quantity of technical and/or specialized vocabulary. In addition, he draws attention to the existence of "paired items" in Arabic, Greek, and Haitian Creole (1959:334–335)—lexical items associated with either H or L varieties, respectively, but with broadly the same range of meaning.

1.9. *Phonology.* This is one area where Ferguson encountered more variability in his four defining languages and language varieties, and so he is not able to make clear assertions. He does, however, suggest that the phonology of the L variety might be the basic system, with features of the H variety constituting a subsystem (1959:335).

2. Extended definitions of diglossia. Since Ferguson's original formulation of the classic diglossia concept, there have been numerous attempts to refine, adapt,

and extend it (e.g. Abdulaziz-Mkilifi 1978, Deuchar 1978, Fasold 1984, Fishman 1967, Khubchandani 1985, Pauwels 1986, Platt 1977, Timm 1981, and Winford 1985). The contribution that has had the greatest impact thus far is Fishman's (1967) paper on the relationship between bilingualism and diglossia, along with his subsequent writing on this topic (Fishman 1972, 1980).

Fishman 1967 extends the classic notion of diglossia to encompass bilingual and multilingual situations, where two or more languages are functionally differentiated, as well as the highly specific types of diglossia described by Ferguson 1959. Fishman sees diglossia as a primarily social phenomenon, and he associates bilingualism with the actual language practices (or behavior) of individuals. Like Ferguson, Fishman places the functional complementarity of the languages in diglossia at the center of his model. Fishman also characterizes diglossia as a stable sociolinguistic phenomenon, stretching over at least three generations, whereas bilingualism is more ephemeral and susceptible to change, even within an individual lifespan.

Fishman 1967 proposes that the relationship between diglossia and bilingualism can be understood in four broad ways, as shown in Table 2. The first quadrant in the table represents sociolinguistic situations in which all or most speakers are bilingual, and there is a broad functional differentiation of language across domains of language use, with the H language reserved for use in formal, institutional domains. For example, in Paraguay, a significant proportion of the urban population speak Guarani (an indigenous language), but Spanish is the superposed H language and is used in many institutional domains.

The second quadrant represents situations with a diglossic social order but where bilingualism is relatively rare. This type is likely to emerge in highly stratified societies where social groups remain largely segregated from each other and each group speaks a different language; an example is tsarist Russia before World War I, where the elite used French and the masses used Russian. In such situations, intergroup communication was made possible by small numbers of bilingual interpreters.

The third quadrant reveals Fishman's concern with identifying social conditions that can contribute to the demise of a diglossic order. He predicts that situations of bilingualism without diglossia are likely to arise as a result of major social and historical processes of change like urbanization and migration, because such processes can lead to a dislocation of norms and values. One

TABLE 2. *Relationships between Diglossia and Bilingualism.* (Fishman 1967:30)

1.) Both diglossia and bilingualism	2.) Bilingualism without diglossia
3.) Diglossia without bilingualism	4.) Neither diglossia nor bilingualism

consequence of this, he argues, is that there would no longer be any societal consensus governing the use of different languages, and the continued use of the L language would be threatened. He makes an explicit link with the process of language shift.

The fourth quadrant represents a hypothetical situation. It is virtually impossible to identify communities where there is no functional differentiation of language varieties, whether languages, dialects, or registers.

There are some conceptual commonalities in Ferguson 1959 and Fishman 1967. The models have four features in common: both are broadly taxonomic; both give primacy to the complementarity of the functions of H and L varieties; both represent the L variety as being acquired in informal lifeworlds (home and community contexts), with the H variety acquired later in formal institutional contexts; and, finally, in both there is a concern with identifying the social conditions that give rise to diglossia and those that lead to its demise.

There are two major differences between the models. First, Fishman allows not only for bilingualism (including in genetically unrelated languages) but also for functional differentiation of a much wider range of varieties, including dialects, registers, or functionally differentiated varieties of any kind (1972:92). Second, Fishman allows for two different kinds of social conditions for diglossia: first, situations where two (or more) languages or varieties are used within a single community but remain functionally differentiated; and second, situations where there is a hierarchy of primarily monolingual communities within a single polity (as in the second quadrant in Table 2, diglossia without bilingualism).

Fishman's extension of the classic diglossia model provided the starting point for sociolinguistic research across a range of bilingual and multilingual settings. However, as researchers grappled with the task of applying the model to the particularities and complexities of sociolinguistic variation in specific social and historical contexts, they felt the need to adapt, refine, and extend the model. The binary distinction in the term "diglossia" was found too restrictive. For example, in Tanzania,

Abdulaziz-Mkilifi 1978 found that Kiswahili stood in symbolic opposition to other languages in two main ways: first as an L variety with respect to English, the superposed H and former colonial language; and second as an H variety with respect to the regional languages of Tanzania. Abdulaziz-Mkilifi's term for this phenomenon is "triglossia"; Fasold 1984 refers to this case as "overlapping diglossia," to foreground the two-way symbolic opposition that has emerged historically in the Tanzanian context.

Some researchers have drawn attention to the ways in which a classic diglossia situation is embedded in a wider multilingual context with diglossic features. In a study carried out with English-educated Chinese in Malaysia, Platt 1977 introduces the term "polyglossia" to capture the complexity of the relationship between the different languages and language varieties within their communicative repertoires. He shows that there is a polyglossic relationship between the different varieties of Chinese spoken locally, and that, in addition, Mandarin functions as a distant "dummy H": that is, as a language perceived as highly prestigious but not widely used locally in any domain. This polyglossic relationship among the Chinese varieties is, at the same time, embedded within a further polyglossic order where Malaysian English and Bahasa Malaysia, the national language, are the H varieties. Bazaar Malay, a local contact language, is an L variety.

Some writers have called for a move away from a strict application of one of the defining features of diglossia—the complementarity of language functions. Fasold (1984:53), for example, introduces a looser notion of "broad diglossia." Drawing on her empirical work with bilingual minorities of European origin in Australia, Pauwels 1986 proposes a fluid definition of diglossia "where several functions are less rigidly attached to a particular code" (15). She has also entertained the possibility of a range of diglossic situations, with more or less strict functional differentiation of languages.

3. Advantages and disadvantages of extending the classic model. As the classic notion of diglossia has been extended to take account of increasingly diverse multilingual settings, considerable ambiguity and diffuseness have become associated with it, so that it has been said that some of Ferguson's original aims have been neglected (Timm 1981). Arguing for retaining Ferguson's original definition of diglossia, Hudson 1991a draws attention to the fact that the outcomes of the decline of diglossia in classic diglossia situations are often different from the outcomes documented for diglossia-like situations of societal bilingualism. In the former, the L often displaces the H variety; in the latter, H often ends up displacing L.

Calls continue for a return to a narrower definition of diglossia. However, in considering the feasibility of a return to a definition based on Fergusonian principles, one has to take account of the fact that the extended versions of diglossia formed the conceptual basis of a very large body of research on bilingualism and multilingualism from the 1960s onwards, whose validity would be challenged if the notion were redefined.

4. Future directions. There is still ample room for refining and strengthening both the original Fergusonian notion of diglossia and the extended versions. As Ferguson 1991 points out, one task that lies ahead is that of fine-tuning the classic definition of diglossia, because "the original conceptualisation had a number of weaknesses" (1991:232). Ferguson here identifies seven points relating to both the social and the linguistic dimensions of diglossia that he would have dealt with differently if he had been writing the article in the 1990s rather than in the late 1950s.

The overall strengthening of research in this field will require a move away from a strict taxonomic approach to the description and analysis of sociolinguistic situations, which seeks only to identify what counts as an instance of diglossia on the basis of predetermined checklists of criteria. Two kinds of studies have provided the greatest insights thus far: those that focus on social, linguistic, and ideological particularities, attempting to throw light on the ways in which the symbolic oppositions between H and L varieties emerge and then change over time (e.g. Eckert 1980); and those that investigate the ways in which H varieties come to be vested with legitimacy (e.g. Errington 1998). Studies such as these have been conducted at one point in time, reconstructing illuminating historical detail and drawing on contemporary evidence; however, there is also a need for longitudinal studies, to document periods of rapid social and linguistic change. Ferguson 1991 calls for this type of research on diglossia, as he sketches what he feels to be the most fruitful avenues for future research.

[*See also* Bilingualism and Multilingualism; Code-Switching; Language Attitudes; Pidgins and Creoles; Power and Language; Social Variation; *and* Sociolinguistics.]

BIBLIOGRAPHY

Abdulaziz-Mkilifi, M. H. 1978. Triglossia and Swahili-English bilingualism in Tanzania. In *Advances in the study of societal multilingualism,* edited by Joshua A. Fishman, pp. 129–149. The Hague: Mouton.

Deuchar, M. 1978. *Diglossia and British Sign Language.* (Working Papers in Sociolinguistics, 46.) Austin: University of Texas.

Eckert, Penelope. 1980. Diglossia: Separate and unequal. *Linguistics* 18.1053–1064.

Errington, J. J. 1998. *Shifting languages.* Cambridge: Cambridge University Press.

Fasold, R. 1984. *The sociolinguistics of society.* Oxford: Basil Blackwell.

Ferguson, Charles A. 1959. Diglossia. *Word* 15.325–340.

Ferguson, Charles A. 1991. Epilogue: Diglossia revisited. In Hudson 1991b, pp. 214–234.

Fishman, Joshua A. 1967. Bilingualism with and without diglossia; diglossia with and without bilingualism. *Journal of Social Issues* 23.29–38.

Fishman, Joshua A. 1972. Societal bilingualism: Stable or transitional. In *Language in sociocultural change: Essays by J. A. Fishman,* edited by A. Dil. Stanford: Stanford University Press.

Fishman, Joshua A. 1980. Bilingualism and biculturism as individual and as societal phenomena. *Journal of Multilingual and Multicultural Development* 1.1–15.

Hudson, A. 1991a. Towards the systematic study of diglossia. In Hudson 1991b, pp. 1–22.

Hudson, A., ed. 1991b. *Studies in diglossia.* Special issue of *Journal of the Linguistic Association of the Southwest* 10.1.

Khubchandani, L. M. 1985. Diglossia revisited. *Oceanic Linguistics* 20.199–211.

Pauwels, A. 1986. Diglossia, immigrant dialects and language maintenance in Australia: The case of Limburgs and Swabian. *Journal of Multilingual and Multicultural Development* 7.13–30.

Platt, J. T. 1977. A model for polyglossia and multilingualism with reference to Singapore and Malaysia. *Language in Society* 6.361–378.

Timm, L. A. 1981. Diglossia old and new: A critique. *Anthropological Linguistics* 23.356–367.

Winford, D. 1985. The concept of "diglossia" in Caribbean Creole situations. *Language in Society* 14.345–356.

MARILYN MARTIN-JONES

DIMINUTIVES. This category of derivational morphology is characterized by a basic denotative meaning of smallness, and potentially by a variety of connotative meanings—for example, endearment, as in English *doggie,* or depreciation, as in Italian *attric-etta* 'starlet'. (For general reference, see Hasselrot 1957, Wierzbicka 1984, Volek 1987, Rainer 1993, Dressler and Merlini Barbaresi 1994, 2001, Dal 1997.)

Diminutives are mostly effected by suffixation, with an iconic tendency towards palatal phonemes: for example, English *-ie, -ette*; German *-chen, -lein*; French *-et(te), -on*; Spanish *-ito, -ico, -illo*; Italian *-ino, -etto, -ello*; Russian *-ak, -(č)ik*, etc. (Hasselrot 1957:283 ff.). In some cases, suffixes are applied recursively, for example, Spanish *-it-iqui-it-ico*.

Diminutive formation preferentially applies to noun bases, and more rarely to adjectives, adverbs, and verbs—for example, It. *magr-ino* (or, with interfix *-ol, magr-ol-ino*) 'rather thin'; French *touss-et-er* 'to cough lightly and repeatedly'. It normally does not change the class of the base, and so is often referred to as 'modification' (Ettinger 1974:112), or even excluded from derivational morphology (Scalise 1984).

Some languages, such as Russian and Italian, use different suffixes to distinguish connotative nuances, for example, It. pejorative/depreciative *donn-etta* 'woman of mean spirit' vs. *donn-ina* 'dear little woman'. Alternatively, with polysemous suffixes, meaning may have to be pragmatically determined. Thus Polish *śnieżek* 'little snow' is used only by children, or by adults addressing children, and this favors a connotation of familiarity and reassurance (Wierzbicka 1984).

Related derivatives, but with the opposite denotation of bigness and with mostly pejorative connotations, are *augmentatives*, for example, *donn-ona* 'big, unattractive woman'.

BIBLIOGRAPHY

Dal, Georgette. 1997. *Grammaire du suffixe -et(te)*. Paris: Didier.

Dressler, Wolfgang, and Lavinia Merlini Barbaresi. 1994. *Morphopragmatics*. Berlin: Mouton de Gruyter.

Dressler, Wolfgang, and Lavinia Merlini Barbaresi. 2001. Morphopragmatics of diminutives and augmentatives: On the priority of pragmatics over semantics. In *Perspectives on semantics, pragmatics, and discourse: A festschrift for Ferenc Kiefer,* edited by István Kenesei and Robert M. Harnish. Amsterdam: Benjamins.

Ettinger, Stefan. 1974. *Form und Funktion in der Wortbildung.* (Beiträge zur Linguistik, 47.) Tübingen: Narr.

Hasselrot, Bengt. 1957. *Études sur la formation diminutive dans les langues romanes.* Uppsala: Almqvist and Wiksell.

Rainer, Franz. 1993. *Spanische Wortbildungslehre*. Tübingen: Niemeyer.

Scalise, Sergio. 1984. *Generative morphology.* (Studies in generative grammar, 18.) Dordrecht: Foris.

Volek, Bronislawa. 1987. *Emotive signs in languages and semantic functioning of derived nouns in Russian.* Amsterdam: Benjamins.

Wierzbicka, Anna. 1984. Diminutives and depreciatives: Semantic representation for derivational categories. *Quaderni di Semantica* 5.123–130.

LAVINIA MERLINI BARBARESI

DIOGENES OF BABYLONIA (c. 240–c. 152 BCE). Pupil of Chrysippus in Athens who like him became the head of the Stoa. His visit to Rome in 156–155 BCE contributed to the diffusion of Stoic theories outside Greece. His book *On language (Peri phōnēs)* apparently reflects Chrysippus' thought; it is lost but is summarized (through yet another intermediary) by Diogenes Laertius in his *Lives of philosophers* (VII.55ff.).

[*See also* Chrysippus; History of Linguistics, *article on* Ancient World: Ancient Greece and Rome; *and* Stoics.]

ANNA MORPURGO DAVIES

DIONYSIUS THRAX (c. 170–c. 90 BCE). Scholar trained in Alexandria, later settled in Rhodes. He authored a famous grammar of Greek, the *Technē grammatikē*. It is not clear whether the text that we have is a much later compilation or contains parts at least of what he originally wrote.

[*See also* History of Linguistics, *article on* Ancient Greece and Rome.]

ANNA MORPURGO DAVIES

DIRECT OBJECT. See Objects *and* Grammatical Relations.

DISCOURSE. [*This entry includes the following sub-entries:*

Overview
Narrative in Conversation
Transcription
Critical Discourse Analysis
Discourse and Interactional Sociolinguistics
Conversation Analysis]

Overview

The term *discourse* is used in somewhat different ways by different scholars, but underlying the differences is a common concern for language beyond the boundaries of isolated sentences. The term *text* is used in similar ways.

Both terms may refer to a unit of language larger than the sentence: one may speak of "a discourse" or "a text." "Discourse" may also refer to the study of such a unit, a branch of linguistics coordinate with morphology or syntax. One may speak of a linguist who specializes in discourse, for example. Often the terms *discourse* (or *text*) *analysis*, or *discourse* (or *text*) *linguistics*, are used in this way.

The study of discourse has emerged as a distinct and established branch of linguistics only since the 1970s. Within the period between 1977 and 1983, there appeared two major journals, *Discourse Processes* (1978) and *Text* (1981), and at least five major textbooks (Beaugrande and Dressler 1981, Brown and Yule 1983, Coulthard 1977, Edmondson 1981, Stubbs 1983). Published shortly afterward was the four-volume *Handbook of discourse analysis* (van Dijk 1985). Since then, the journals *Discourse and Society* and *Discourse Studies* have been added, along with the comprehensive survey *Approaches to discourse* (Schiffrin 1994) and *The handbook of discourse analysis* (Schiffrin, Tannen, and Hamilton 2001).

Journal articles, textbooks, and contributions to anthologies on discourse show a great heterogeneity of approaches. The data investigated, the theoretical positions taken, and the overlap with other disciplines are diverse enough to suggest that discourse constitutes more than one distinct subfield of linguistics. Nevertheless, most approaches that look beyond the boundaries of sentences have shared certain research experiences; these have led to some agreement on the general kinds of data that are of interest, appropriate methodologies for handling and interpreting those data, the kinds of explanation that are regarded as significant, and even the kinds of questions that are worth asking.

With respect to data, while sentence-based studies of language have most commonly focused on invented sentences and intuitive judgments of their grammaticality or acceptability, the same procedure is more questionable when applied to discourse. A procedure of inventing whole texts and judging their acceptability has not found widespread application. There is, therefore, a strong tendency for discourse analysts to rely more heavily on observations of naturally occurring language. Conversely, scholars who wish to theorize on the basis of naturally occurring language have inevitably been led beyond the boundaries of sentences, since natural language rarely occurs in isolated sentence form. In pursuing natural language data, discourse analysts have also become more conscious of differences among diverse styles, genres, and modes of language use. Considerable attention has

been paid, for example, to possible differences between spoken and written language. Although many discourse studies have focused exclusively on one or the other of these two modes, there has been increasing interest in comparisons between the two.

With respect to methodology, research on spoken discourse has benefited immeasurably from the availability of the tape recorder, which allows easy storage and retrieval of discourse samples. The processing of tape-recorded data raises interesting questions regarding the conversion of sound into writing for research purposes. Because discourse research deals with large bodies of diverse data, it lends itself to quantitative methods, drawing especially on techniques developed in psychology, sociology, and statistical studies of texts. At the same time, textual studies profit from more humanistically oriented techniques of interpretation—for example, of the type that have been labeled *hermeneutics*. The breadth and depth of discourse phenomena militate against exclusive commitment to any single mode of analysis.

With respect to explanation, discourse studies have in general focused less on abstract formalisms, and more on some variety of functional explanation. If there is a principle whereby increasingly larger units of language are decreasingly constrained by factors purely internal to language, on a scale from phonology to morphology to syntax to discourse, then discourse constitutes the area of language most subject to influence from psychological and social factors. This realization that discourse cannot be understood apart from its psychological and social contexts can contribute substantially to the more thoroughly studied aspects of language, such as morphology and syntax. It would appear, for example, that discourse considerations are essential to a fuller understanding of such familiar topics as anaphora and word order.

Finally, with respect to questions that are seen to be worth asking, discourse analysts tend to be driven to understand how naturally occurring language is determined by, and in turn determines, the ways in which knowledge is acquired, stored, and used by the human mind—as well as how language shapes and is shaped by the ways in which people interact with one another within their social and cultural contexts.

While it is difficult to deal with isolated sentences except in terms of grammar and lexicon, discourse can be studied in terms as varied as are the forces and functions responsible for language itself. In line with the interests sketched above, major areas of research have included the extension of grammar beyond the boundaries of the sentence; the use of discourse to illuminate psychological structures and processes; and the study of discourse as a way of gaining insights into social interaction.

Earlier interests in more restricted areas of grammatical structure have been extended by some linguists into the area of discourse. Early work of this kind included that of Harris 1952, and the ambitious project of Pike 1967. Besides Pike, other researchers associated with the Summer Institute of Linguistics have continued to make important contributions to discourse studies. Especially noteworthy have been the studies of Grimes 1975 and Longacre 1983. Other influential grammarians who have extended their work to discourse are represented by Fillmore 1985, Givón 1983, and Halliday 1985.

The British psychologist Bartlett (1932) used textual material to demonstrate the relevance of knowledge patterns or *schemata* to memory. The revival of his findings within cognitive psychology has resulted in an extension of the phrase structure model of sentence structure to larger schemata identified as *story grammars.* Constructs of this kind have been exploited in psychological research where, as models of knowledge representation, they have been interpreted as shedding light on the nature of memory and language development (see Mandler and Johnson 1977).

The relevance of discourse to cognitive structures and processes has also emerged in studies of *information flow*—changes in the cognitive status of knowledge as language is produced and comprehended through time. For example, changes in the newness or givenness of information or the identifiability of referents may determine such basic grammatical phenomena as pronominalization, intonation, word order, and the use of definite and indefinite articles. Tracking such elements in discourse can in turn provide insights into ongoing mental processing.

A different and very active branch of discourse study has directed its attention to language as a vehicle of social interaction. Much of this work comes out of, or is relevant to, sociological concerns; in fact, most of sociolinguistics can be seen as a branch of discourse analysis. Here belong, for example, the detailed analyses of recorded conversations that have been conducted in the styles of two rather different traditions: *conversation analysis*, an outgrowth of ethnomethodology, and what is here called *interactional sociolinguistics*, in the tradition of Gumperz 1982. Here belongs also the work of William Labov on the negotiation of social meaning through the use of evaluative devices. The analysis of conversations has shed new light on grammatical elements of the type identified

as *discourse markers* and has highlighted the important role of *formulaic speech* in everyday language. Of particular social relevance has been the study of gender asymmetries in language use. Other studies have investigated the development of discourse competence in children.

Many anthropologically oriented studies of discourse have been pursued under the heading *ethnography of speaking*, where speaking is seen as one of the principal elements of culturally determined behavior. More humanistically oriented approaches are represented in the work of Becker 1979, Friedrich 1986, and Tedlock 1983.

Finally, because discourse studies aim at an understanding of language in its great variety of natural settings, a number of discourse studies have looked at language use during interactions between clients and the practitioners of various professions. Discourse analysts also concern themselves with language in such domains as education, politics, and advertising.

The diversity of discourse linguistics reflects the richness of its subject matter. Increased understanding of language in actual use calls for the examination of a maximally wide range of data, as well as free access to an unrestricted arsenal of methods and theoretical approaches (Chafe 1986). Discourse provides a focus and meeting ground for all investigations of language as it really is. Its diversity, reflecting as it does the diversity of language and the human mind, offers a liberating challenge to a linguistics freed of the bonds of parochial concerns.

[*See also* Conversation Analysis; Discourse Markers; Ethnography of Speaking; Information Structure; Institutional Linguistics; Ritual Language; Sociolinguistics; Text; Tagmemics; Verbal Play; *and* Writing and Written Language.]

BIBLIOGRAPHY

Bartlett, Frederic C. 1932. *Remembering: A study in experimental and social psychology.* Cambridge: Cambridge University Press.

Beaugrande, Robert-Alain de, and Wolfgang U. Dressler. 1981. *Introduction to text linguistics.* (Longman linguistics library, 26.) London: Longman.

Becker, Alton L. 1979. Text-building, epistemology, and aesthetics in Javanese shadow theatre. In *The imagination of reality: Essays in Southeast Asian coherence systems,* edited by Alton L. Becker and Aram A. Yengoyan, pp. 211–243. Norwood, N.J.: Ablex.

Brown, Gillian, and George Yule. 1983. *Discourse analysis.* Cambridge and New York: Cambridge University Press.

Chafe, Wallace L. 1986. How we know things about language: A plea for Catholicism. In *Languages and linguistics: The interdependence of theory, data, and application* (36th Georgetown University Round Table, 1985), edited by Deborah Tannen and James E. Alatis, pp. 214–225. Washington, D.C.: Georgetown University Press.

Coulthard, Malcolm. 1977. *An introduction to discourse analysis,* 2d ed. London: Longman, 1985.

Edmondson, Willis. 1981. *Spoken discourse: A model for analysis.* (Longman linguistics library, 27.) London: Longman.

Fillmore, Charles J. 1985. Linguistics as a tool for discourse analysis. In van Dijk 1985, vol. 1, pp. 11–39.

Friedrich, Paul. 1986. *The language parallax: Linguistic relativism and poetic indeterminacy.* Austin: University of Texas Press.

Givón, Talmy, ed. 1983. *Topic continuity in discourse: A quantitative cross-language study.* (Typological studies in language, 3.) Amsterdam: Benjamins.

Grimes, Joseph E. 1975. *The thread of discourse.* (Janua linguarum, Series minor, 207.) The Hague: Mouton.

Gumperz, John J. 1982. *Discourse strategies.* (Studies in interactional sociolinguistics, 1.) Cambridge and New York: Cambridge University Press.

Halliday, Michael A. K. 1985. Dimensions of discourse analysis: Grammar. In van Dijk 1985, vol. 2, pp. 29–56.

Harris, Zellig S. 1952. Discourse analysis. *Language* 28.1–30.

Longacre, Robert E. 1983. *The grammar of discourse.* New York: Plenum.

Mandler, Jean M., and Nancy S. Johnson. 1977. Remembrance of things parsed: Story structure and recall. *Cognitive Psychology* 9.111–151.

Pike, Kenneth L. 1967. *Language in relation to a unified theory of the structure of human behavior,* 2d ed. (Janua linguarum, Series maior, 24.) The Hague: Mouton.

Schiffrin, Deborah. 1994. *Approaches to discourse.* Oxford: Blackwell.

Schiffrin, Deborah, Deborah Tannen, and Heidi E. Hamilton. 2001. *The handbook of discourse analysis.* Oxford: Blackwell.

Stubbs, Michael. 1983. *Discourse analysis: The sociolinguistic analysis of natural language.* (Language in society, 4.) Oxford: Blackwell. Chicago: University of Chicago Press.

Tedlock, Dennis. 1983. *The spoken word and the work of interpretation.* Philadelphia: University of Pennsylvania Press.

van Dijk, Teun A., ed. 1985. *Handbook of discourse analysis.* 4 vols. London and Orlando: Academic Press.

WALLACE CHAFE

Narrative in Conversation

The use of oral narrative in conversation is a key issue for discourse analysis because it occurs at the intersection of structural and functional studies of language. The structure of narrative is better understood than that of any other discourse unit. Moreover, narrative structure forms the basis of many other oral discourse units, such as spatial descriptions, explanations, task directions, and hypothesizing of future events. Narratives occur not only in speech but also in other genres, such as writing and film. The use of narratives is developmentally early: although the construction of narrative is initially scaffolded by adults, children learn it as one of their first discourse units. Finally, narratives are an important site for social exchange, in which self-presentation, group membership, and agreement on values can be negotiated between interlocutors.

The most influential definition of narrative is that it is one method of recapitulating past experience by matching a verbal sequence of clauses to the sequence of events that (it is inferred) actually occurred (Labov 1972). According to Labov, the parts of a narrative are (i) an optional *abstract*, a summary of the whole story; (ii) the *orientation*, or description of time, place, persons, and situation; (iii) *complicating action*, simple past-tense clauses interpreted as having the temporal ordering of the events they report (called "narrative clauses"); (iv) an optional *coda*, a formal marking of the end of the narrative that may also bring the action up to the time of narration; and (v) the *evaluation*, used to indicate the point of the narrative and how it is to be understood.

There have been a number of critiques of this definition and additions to it. One is that narratives need not be in the past tense; they may also be hypothetical, habitual, or inferentially future. It has also been argued that a simple sequence of clauses is not sufficient to establish a narrative; it must also be possible to infer socially coherent relations between the clauses. There have been challenges to the realist assumption that events have an independent existence prior to the social act of narration; such arguments claim that events should be seen not as existing independently in the world, but rather as created by the act of narration.

Expanding the data from narratives recorded in interviews to narratives in spontaneous social interactions challenges the assumption of a single speaker as the creator of a narrative. Although narrative in conversation is still a structural unit, it is more an interactional achievement than an individual performance. On this view, narrative is a unit co-constructed by all the members of the immediate interaction, a response to immediately prior conversation, and a continuation of the interlocutors' history of conversations. In most narratives studied, there is still a main speaker, with contributions from additional interlocutors; however, spouses or other close associates may produce narratives that are essentially duets. Berman's (1998) study of low-status Javanese women's narrative shows an extensive case of co-construction in which topic, orientation, events narrated, and evaluation can all be jointly constructed by a group of interlocutors.

In narratives with a single main narrator, each structural component permits or requires specific types of responses from interlocutors. The most interactionally salient and demanding part of narrative, the evaluation, consists of those elements of the narrative that provide meaning by demonstrating how the events of the narrative show the way the world is or ought to be, what proper behavior is, and the kind of people the speaker and interlocutors are. An extremely common form of evaluation is the demonstration that the speaker is a good person who acted correctly under the circumstances. Even in narratives that recount the speakers doing something presented as bad, the act of narration remedies the trespass because the narrator recognizes the breach of moral order, even if the protagonist—the narrator in the past—did not. Indeed, one way to justify the apparent egotism of holding the floor with a personal story is to frame it as universally applicable, an account of what any reasonable person would do in such a situation.

The meaning of evaluation is produced not just by the speaker but by a process of negotiation between speaker and interlocutors. Narrative clauses focus on what is asserted to have happened. Because the events are usually best known to the narrator, they demand little agreement from an interlocutor. However, because the evaluation presents a claim about why the narrated events are important and what they mean, the evaluation is intrinsically interactional: it permits, and often requires, the interlocutor to agree that the proposed story is worth telling, and to agree or disagree with the proposed meaning of the events.

An interlocutor may show agreement with the main speaker's evaluative construction by providing evaluation in the course of the story, after it, or by following it with a second story with the same evaluative point. An interlocutor may disagree with the speaker's proposed meaning and supply an alternative evaluation for the same events. If this happens, the speaker and interlocutors must then negotiate what the point of the story will be on this occasion of telling. Polanyi 1989 shows how this can

result in a radical change in the evaluation. In other cases, it may be impossible for storytelling to proceed if the interlocutors do not share a basic agreement on meaning. Negotiation on evaluation throughout a narration can therefore bring about a reconstitution of the audience, as in Goodwin's (1986) analysis, in which only one of several initial interlocutors remains—the one who agrees with the speaker's proposed characterization of the events narrated.

Speakers evaluate not only the moral meaning of the events narrated, but also their *reportability* (see Labov 1997). Reportability contrasts the expectable with the extraordinary. Completely expectable events cannot be made into a narrative because the speaker's claim to hold the floor may be challenged with some version of the formulaic response "So what?" Thus, an apparently ordinary event must be known—or shown—to be somehow out of the ordinary before its narration can be justified. Yet there is no fixed scale to determine how reportable a sequence of events must be. Reportability is both determined by, and partially constitutive of, the relationship between interlocutors: the closer the relationship and the more frequent the communication, the less reportable the events need to be. Thus, the story of today's traffic jam is reportable to a person one sees every day, but it is inappropriate as the main topic of a conversation between people who meet once a year. Persons who are socially close but geographically distant may assume that no major reportable events have happened since their last contact because their relationship dictates that if something highly reportable had happened, it would have been reported.

The degree of reportability is also affected by the person of the narrative's protagonist. The events of third-person narratives are either more unusual or more closely occasioned by the preceding conversation than those of first-person narratives, because the narration of events involving an absent third person requires more justification than those involving the parties present. Second-person narratives are rare: the normal assumption is that people are the best authorities on their own lives. Cases in which the speakers are not taken as the final authority on their own life events include parents telling children about their behavior as infants (a common way of imparting to children "mythologies" about their characters), speakers recounting events in their lives that addressees do not remember, or interlocutors providing a different interpretation for events remembered by the main narrator.

Within literate societies, narratives play an important role in the creation of a personal and shared sense of continuity and history. Some narratives are ephemeral, reportable for a day or two after the occurrence of their reported events; others are reportable for a long time, forming part of the speaker's life story—a discontinuous, composite unit consisting of the aggregate of all such narratives, including their revisions and changes, over the speaker's entire life (Linde 1993). Such narratives constitute a presentation of self: who the speaker is, what the speaker has done, and what the addressee must know in order to know the speaker. They conventionally include accounts of culturally defined major life events, such as schooling, marriage, military service, childbirth, and career choice, as well as idiosyncratic events that the speaker constructs as central for the creation of personal meaning. It requires individual creativity to form these stories and the relations between them coherently in order to define for others what one's life has meant.

Creation of coherence in life-story narratives is not entirely an individual task, however; coherence must depend on shared meaning. Any culture makes available to its members systems of beliefs and relations between beliefs that serve as the background assumptions permitting individual creativity. The most widely used and least obvious system is "common sense"—beliefs that can be assumed to be known, if not shared, by everyone in a given culture or subculture. In addition, there are special coherence systems: popular versions of expert explanatory systems such as religious, political, or ideological systems, psychology, astrology, and so on. Such shared coherence systems provide the background assumptions for what is an expectable event or reaction, for what may count as an explanation, and for what may function as an evaluation within a given culture.

This discussion has taken conversation as the most salient context for the analysis of narrative. Conversation may be understood in ordinary terms as informal oral exchange, or technically—as in Conversation Analysis, where it is defined as that form of interaction in which the order of turns, size of turns, and content of turns are not preassigned but are negotiated from moment to moment during the ongoing interaction. However, there are also long-term relational and institutional contexts that structure both conversations and the narratives within them. Institutions such as corporations, universities, and families maintain a variety of forms of official and semi-official narratives in a variety of media, including spontaneous narration and scripted speeches, written histories and biographies, filmed historical presentations, and photographic images (Linde 2000). Institutions differ in the number of narratives maintained, the occasions for telling narratives, preferred and dispreferred events and evaluations for narratives, and the identity of preferred and dispreferred speakers for given narratives (the allocation of storytelling rights).

Within institutions, these group narratives perform a significant part of the work of social reproduction: maintaining institutional identity and continuity, negotiating power relations, managing change, and establishing individual membership and identity, as well as transacting the daily business of the organization. In addition, individual narratives establish part of their meaning by their location within an ecology of narratives. Thus, a story told in a corporation has a very different meaning if it supports or contradicts the values of that corporation's story, or the official narrative of the predictable events and stages of a successful career. To understand the meaning of a story about a member, it is necessary to understand whether it is to be heard as an instance of an approved career course, or as a sad example of how not to act within that institution.

[See also Linguistics and Literature; Text.]

BIBLIOGRAPHY

Bamberg, Michael, ed. 1997. *Oral versions of personal experience: Three decades of narrative analysis.* (Special Issue, *Journal of Narrative and Life History,* 7.1–4) Mahwah, N.J.: Lawrence Erlbaum.

Berman, Laine. 1998. Speaking through the silence: Narratives, social conventions, and power in Java. In *Oxford studies in anthropological linguistics,* edited by William Bright. New York and Oxford: Oxford University Press.

Goodwin, Charles. 1986. Audience diversity, participation and interpretation. *Text* 6.283–316.

Goodwin, Majorie Harness. 1990. *He-said-she-said: Talk as social organization among black children.* Bloomington: Indiana University Press.

Labov, William. 1972. The transformation of experience in narrative syntax, in William Labov, *Language in the inner city,* pp. 354–396. University Park: University of Pennsylvania Press.

Labov, William. 1997. Further steps in narrative analysis. In Bamberg 1997, pp. 395–415.

Linde, Charlotte. 1993. *Life stories: The creation of coherence.* New York: Oxford University Press.

Linde, Charlotte. 2000. The acquisition of a speaker by a story: How history becomes memory and identity. *Ethos* 28.

Linde, Charlotte. To appear. *Working the past: Narrative and institutional memory.* New York: Oxford University Press. *Ethos* 8.608–632.

Orr, Julian. 1990. Sharing knowledge, celebrating identity:

Community memory in a service culture. In *Collective remembering*, edited by David Middleton and Derek Edwards, pp. 169–189. London and Thousand Oaks, Calif.: Sage.

Polanyi, Livia. 1989. *The American story*. Cambridge, Mass.: MIT Press.

Sacks, Harvey. 1992. *Lectures on conversation*. Edited by Gail Jefferson. Oxford: Blackwell.

CHARLOTTE LINDE

Transcription

For linguists who work with data from ordinary conversation, transcription has become such a commonplace tool that one can easily forget that it is an artifact. The transcript is necessarily selective and interpretive, rather than exhaustive and objective. It is not a direct mirror of reality; it is a translation of a selected set of spatio-temporally organized oral and gestural events into a written medium with properties of its own. Communicative gestalts are analyzed into components, such as gestures, words, or prosodics; continua are divided into discrete categories, for example, pitch or stress levels, pause lengths, and intonation contours; and logical and temporal interrelationships among these parts are signaled by a handful of visually processed cues—spatial positioning and proximity, relative visual prominence (font size, upper vs. lower case, parentheses), and explicit labeling with alphabetic and non-alphabetic characters.

When complementary to discourse type, research topic, and theoretical perspective, transcription is a tremendously effective research tool; it can freeze in time a relevant subset of normally transient events, expressed in the researcher's own categories, and free of extraneous detail. When this is not the case, the transcript may give rise to irrelevant or misleading perceptions and may actually hinder the detection of interesting regularities. For example, Ochs 1979 noted that, when turns at talk are printed one beneath the other, the eye is biased to perceive the speakers' turns as mutually contingent. To capture the much more asymmetrical structuring of early child/adult discourse, which is child-centered and child-controlled, Ochs advocated isolating the utterances of adult and child in separate columns, with the child's column to the left to enhance its perceived dominance in the interaction (considering the left-right bias of reading).

For other discourse types, or other research purposes, different conventions may be preferable. Discourse theory provides little guidance in these matters, partly because some of the biases arise from competing influences

TABLE 1. *Shortcomings of Eye-Dialect*

	Eye-Dialect	Standard English Spelling
Inconsistency	*of, uv*	*of*
	cuz, excuz	*'cause, excuse*
Ambiguity	*go::d*	*God* (rather than *goad* or *goed*)
Uninformativeness	*wuz, uv*	*was, of*
False Phonetics	*brou:ght*	*brought* (with lengthened vowel)
	askedche	*asked you* (rather than *asktche*)
	dz, wz, w'z, sm	*does, was, some*
	difference:	(entire last syllable lengthened)
Poor Readability	*tih, ahhndh, iht*	*to, and, it* (extra aspiration)
	bighta lunch, doo	*bite of lunch, to*

at the written/spatial level. Transcription methods must therefore be devised inductively, subject to change with subsequent screenings of the recorded data—which are primary. Crucial for minimizing bias is an awareness of the alternatives, and of what each implies interpretively. The following discussion surveys alternatives concerning words and larger units of the discourse, pauses, prosodics, nonverbal phenomena, contextual notes, and suitability for computer-assisted analysis. (For fuller discussion and examples, see Edwards 2001 and Edwards and Lampert 1993).

1. The words. The syllables and words spoken in an interaction are usually transcribed in standard orthography, sometimes supplemented by phonetic transcription (International Phonetic Alphabet, or IPA) when finer distinctions are necessary. However, conversation analysts trained in sociology use a third method, an impressionistic extension of English spelling known as *eye-dialect*:

(1)   It's <u>r</u>illy <u>i</u>ntresti:ng:: (0.2) I showed <u>T</u>om how tuh pro-
      (.) how doo uh: program a: hhh the computer doo:
      make a ra:ndom <u>n</u>umber CHA:RT EHHEH! ·HH!
      (Davidson 1984: 122)

Eye-dialect is more accessible to non-linguists than IPA, but it is also less systematic in its sound-to-grapheme correspondences, giving rise to problems of uninformativeness, inconsistency, ambiguity, faulty phonetics, and poor readability, especially for non-native English speakers. Table 1 contains examples from published work (mostly from Atkinson and Heritage 1984), which demonstrate these faults.

Since the distorted spellings do not enter into the analyses, eye-dialect seems intended to give the general flavor of the dialect without being precise. Contextual notes are preferable for this purpose, since they avoid the false impression of precision. Where precision is needed, it is preferable to use IPA-related conventions like those of Labov 1973—not only for scientific reasons, but also because they avoid the cartoon-like stereotypes reinforced by eye-dialect, which makes nonstandard dialects appear substandard, and their speakers lower-class or unintelligent (Preston 1985).

2. Larger units. The literary model of the dramatic play is sometimes adopted in preserving conversation data:

(2)   Woody Allen: *I finished my first film,* Take the Money and Run, *in 1968 or something, and the day that I was through that—put it out in movie theaters, I never, ever looked at it again, nor have I looked at any of them again.*
Morley Safer: *Really?* (official transcript of CBS, *60 Minutes*, December 13, 1987)

However, this is inadequate for discourse analysis, because it is biased toward the written rather than the spoken language. Its units are syntactically rather than intonationally defined, and its punctuation captures only partially the prosodic contours of spoken discourse (Chafe 1987, Tedlock 1983).

Preferable for discourse analysis are systems which are organized around intonation or tone units:

(3)   *And he comes down,*
       .. from the ladder,
       [1.1] *and he's wearing an apron,*
       that holds the pears,
       in deep pockets.
       And he dumps them [.45] *into some baskets .. that he has.* (Chafe 1980: 34)

Here punctuation marks unit-final prosodic contours, such as falling, rising, continuing (actually non-falling/non-rising), extra-low falling, and disrupted intonation. These decisions may rest on acoustic similarity to a set of contours that are believed to be socio-culturally relevant to the speaker. The alternative is to examine larger stretches of speech by the speaker, attempting to infer from the context of use which contour serves which function for the speaker. Neither method is strictly objective. Since the prosodic contours for different discourse functions (question, statement, etc.) vary across cultures and languages, Du Bois et al. 1990 mark both the contours and the functions. The prosodic systems of Du Bois et al. 1990 and also Cruttenden 1997 have accompanying audiocassettes, which are highly useful for training transcribers to make prosodic distinctions reliably.

For narrative discourse, the *episode* is a useful unit; but it may have fuzzy boundaries because of anaphoric ties to earlier parts of the discourse. The *turn* is a useful unit where multiple speakers are involved; but it is not objectively delimitable where there is much overlapping talk. When overlap involves entire utterances by different speakers, the decision of whose utterance is leftmost or topmost is arbitrary; but it has implications for perceived priority, because of the direction-of-reading bias. When an overlap ends because one speaker seems to drop out in mid-utterance, some researchers mark it "interrupted." This is useful for locating points of difficulty in an interaction, but it involves interpretive leaps with respect to (i) judged incompletion and (ii) attribution of cause or even blame.

3. Pauses. What is considered a 'short' pause is found to vary interestingly with research purposes. It tends to be 0.5 seconds or less for sociolinguists, but 0.2 seconds or less for those investigating more intra-individual processes, such as the packaging of information in narratives.

A particular pause is known to seem longer or shorter depending on its position in the discourse (mid-utterance vs. between-turns) as well as on the influence of other acoustic features such as syllable lengthening and deceleration (O'Connell and Kowal 1983). With socio-culturally similar speakers, where intonational fine-tuning may carry much communicative weight, more context-sensitive categories seem preferable, assuming that the researcher's categories are the right ones. For cross-linguistic research, objective measurement may be preferable, since it highlights the specific acoustic cues which are interpreted differently by various cultural groups.

An inter-turn pause may be placed in any of three locations: at the end of the pre-pause utterance, at the beginning of the post-pause utterance, or on a line in between. The third implies most clearly the shared responsibility of interactants for the length of such pauses. Where a speaker resumes a turn after an exceptionally long pause, that pause may be perceived as an intra-turn pause. Transcribing such a pause instead as a 'silent turn' by the other speaker (Labov and Fanshel 1977) may be an effective method for indicating speaker reticence; but it is clearly an interpretive judgment, as Tannen 1981 observes.

4. Prosodics. Some systems mark distinctions in intonation and tempo more finely. In the following example, capital letters indicate the nucleus of the tone unit; hollow arrows signal the relative pitch register; line arrows signal rising, falling, and level tone; double and single quotes signal stress; and dashes and dots signal pauses (London/Lund Corpus S.1.10, Svartvik and Quirk 1979: 256).

(4)　**A** ³⁶⁴ ▪[m̀]▪ - - - ³⁶⁵ ▪but [ə:m] · you ▪know it's △very
　　▷ĪNTERESTING [ə:m]▪ · ³⁶⁶ [ə:] a ▪great 'great 'flap
　　and ge△fuffle 'went ÓN [əm]▪³⁶⁷ when ·▪SĔSAME
　　'Street {▪came to Aus'tralian △TĒLEVISION▪} ▪·
　　b ³⁶⁸ [m]
　　A ³⁶⁹ ▪everyone ▷SĀID▪ ³⁷⁰ ▪▪HĔAVENS you KNÓW▪
　　³⁷¹ ▪what a DRĔADFUL THĪNG▪ ³⁷² our ▪children will
　　'now talk A△MĔRICAN▪

The decisions involved in such a transcription take time, and are not needed for all research questions.

Many of these conventions involve subdividing dimensions into discrete categories. In the 1950s, American "levels" theorists marked four distinct pitch levels and four distinct stress levels in an attempt at precise description. British "configurationalists," concerned with effective foreign-language training, criticized the approach as overly atomistic; they noted that it overlooked the fact that many non-identical contours (e.g. /4 1/ and /3 1/) function equivalently in discourse, that is, as falling contours (Ladd 1980). This controversy has been replaced by "levels" vs. "movements" approaches, represented by the ToBI (Tone and Break Index) system, and the "British school," respectively. These are described from contrasting viewpoints by Ladd 1996 and Cruttenden 1997, who also list partial correspondences between the two systems.

5. Nonverbal phenomena. Coughs, laughs, and yawns are often noted within brackets, directly on the utterance line. This preserves the temporal ordering of verbal and nonverbal events, while implying the subordination of nonverbal to verbal. More detailed descriptions of nonverbal events are generally placed on a separate line, co-indexed at the relevant point on the verbal line. Transcription methods and typologies for gaze, gesture, and posture are found in the intra-individually oriented approach of Ekman and Friesen 1969, and in the more discourse-oriented approaches of Erickson and Shultz 1982 and Heath 1986.

6. Contextual notes. For some analyses, the transcript is useless without adequate ethnographic information concerning the participants, their relationships, and the context of data-gathering. Although such information is of far less relevance to Conversation Analysis than it is to sociolinguistics, its inclusion is expedient, especially in an era of increasing collaboration and data-sharing among researchers with different theoretical perspectives.

7. Transcription for computer search. The following are necessary for efficient and exhaustive computer-assisted search of patterns (words, phrases, or codes) in the data:

(a) systematic differentiation of speakers
(b) systematic differentiation of speech from non-speech events (e.g. comments or contextual notes)
(c) associating a standard version with each nonstandard (IPA or eye-dialect) variant in the corpus ('normalization')

The first two requirements are satisfied in practically all systems; but the third is still infrequent. Diacritics can be suppressed en masse as special characters, but no such filtering is possible for nonstandard spellings and IPA variants. Unless the researcher is able to anticipate all nonstandard variants in the data, the retrieved instances may constitute a partial and potentially biased sample. For example, to locate all instances of *the* in a corpus, the researcher would need to think of looking also for any and all other nonstandard spellings or IPA variants of *the* (e.g. [dhi]) which might also be present in the data. There are various ways of tying a nonstandard item to its normalization. Regardless of the method chosen, it is best to normalize during initial data entry, before the human eye becomes habituated to interpretively inconsequential surface differences which the computer will take quite literally. Data entry and analysis are greatly speeded by computer interfaces such as "Transcriber" (Barras et al. 2001), which enable efficient typing, flexible playback of digitized recordings, and systematic linkage of transcript to audio.

Choices among such alternatives as those surveyed here may facilitate the perception of some types of structure in the data, but may hinder the perception of others. Thus a transcript simultaneously embodies and influences the analyst's perspectives on the data. To minimize misleading biases in a transcript, it is important to choose carefully among alternatives, with awareness of what each of them implies; and to view each stage of the transcript as provisional and derived—subject to change with subsequent screenings of the recorded data, which are primary.

BIBLIOGRAPHY

Atkinson, J. Maxwell, and John Heritage, eds. 1984. *Structures of social action: Studies in conversation analysis.* Cambridge and New York: Cambridge University Press.

Barras, Claude, Edouard Geoffrois, Zhibiao Wu, and Mark Liberman. 2001. Transcriber: Development and use of a tool for assisting speech corpora production. *Speech Communication* 33.5–22.

Chafe, Wallace L., ed. 1980. *The pear stories: Cognitive, cultural, and linguistic aspects of narrative production.* (Advances in discourse processes, 3.) Norwood, N.J.: Ablex.

Chafe, Wallace L. 1987. Cognitive constraints on information flow. In *Coherence and grounding in discourse* (Typological studies in language, 11), edited by Russell S. Tomlin, pp. 21–51. Amsterdam: Benjamins.

Cruttenden, Alan. 1997. *Intonation.* 2d ed. Cambridge: Cambridge University Press.

Davidson, Judy. 1984. Subsequent versions of invitations, offers, requests, and proposals dealing with potential or actual rejection. In Atkinson and Heritage 1984, pp. 102–128.

Du Bois, John W., et al. 1993. Outline of discourse transcription. In *Talking data: Transcription and coding methods in discourse research,* edited by Jane A. Edwards and Martin D. Lampert, pp. 45–89. Hillsdale, N.J.: Erlbaum.

Edwards, Jane A. 2001. The transcription of discourse. In *The handbook of discourse analysis,* edited by Deborah Schiffrin, Deborah Tannen, and Heidi Hamilton, pp. 321–348. New York: Blackwell.

Edwards, Jane A., and Martin D. Lampert, eds. 1993. *Talking data: Transcription and coding in discourse research.* New York: Erlbaum.

Ekman, Paul, and Wallace V. Friesen. 1969. The repertoire of nonverbal behavior: Categories, origins, usage, and coding. *Semiotica* 1.49–98.

Erickson, Frederick, and Jeffrey J. Shultz. 1982. *The counselor as gatekeeper: Social interaction in interviews.* New York: Academic Press.

Heath, Christian. 1986. *Body movement and speech in medical interaction.* Cambridge and New York: Cambridge University Press.

Labov, William. 1973. *Language in the inner city: Studies in the Black English vernacular.* Philadelphia: University of Pennsylvania Press.

Labov, William, and David Fanshel. 1977. *Therapeutic discourse: Psychotherapy as conversation.* New York: Academic Press.

Ladd, D. Robert, Jr. 1980. *The structure of intonational meaning: Evidence from English.* Bloomington: Indiana University Press.

Ladd, D. Robert. 1996. *Intonational phonology.* Cambridge: Cambridge University Press.

Ochs, Elinor. 1979. Transcription as theory. In *Developmental pragmatics,* edited by Elinor Ochs and Bambi B. Schieffelin, pp. 43–72. New York: Academic Press.

O'Connell, Daniel C., and Sabine Kowal. 1983. Pausology. In *Computers in language research,* vol. 2, *Notating the language of music, and the (pause) rhythms of speech* (Trends in linguistics, Studies and monographs, 19), edited by Walter A. Sedelow Jr. and Sally Y. Sedelow, pp. 221–301. Berlin: Mouton.

Preston, Dennis R. 1985. The Li'l Abner Syndrome: Written representations of speech. *American Speech* 60.328–336.

Svartvik, Jan, and Randolph Quirk, eds. 1979. *A corpus of English conversation.* (Lund studies in English, 56.) Lund: Gleerup.

Tannen, Deborah. 1981. Review of Labov and Fanshel 1977. *Language* 57.481–486.

Tedlock, Dennis. 1983. *The spoken word and the work of interpretation.* Philadelphia: University of Pennsylvania Press.

JANE ANNE EDWARDS

Critical Discourse Analysis

The terms *critical linguistics* (CL) and *critical discourse analysis* (CDA) are often used interchangeably, although recently CDA has been preferred, used to denote the theory formerly identified as CL. CDA sees language as social practice (Fairclough and Wodak 1997) and regards as crucial the consideration of the context of language use (Wodak 2000, Benke 2000), particularly the contextual relation of language and power. CDA also refers to the critical linguistic approach of scholars who find the larger discursive unit of text to be the basic unit of communication. This research specifically considers institutional, political, gender, and media discourses that show more or less overt relations of struggle and conflict. The heterogeneity of methodological and theoretical approaches in CDA confirms van Dijk's point that CDA and CL "are at most a shared perspective on doing linguistic, semiotic or discourse analysis" (1993:131).

The notion of *critique* inherent in CDA's program has a variety of senses. Some adhere to that of the Frankfurt School, some to the literary critical notion, and some to those of Marx (Reisigl and Wodak 2001). For all approaches to CDA, however, application of results is important—from practical seminars for teachers, doctors, and bureaucrats to the writing of expert opinions or devising schoolbooks.

The notions *critical* and *ideology* and the role of critical theory are important to CDA (Anthonissen 2001). Thompson 1990 discusses the relationship between ideology and *culture* and points out that the concept of ideology first appeared in late 18th-century France. The term has been given different functions and meanings at different times. For Thompson, *ideology* refers to social forms and processes within which, and by means of which, symbolic forms circulate in the social world.

Critical theory is afforded special standing as a guide for human action, aimed at producing enlightenment and emancipation. Such theory seeks not only to describe and explain but also to root out a particular kind of delusion. Despite its differing concepts of ideology, critical theory intends to create awareness in agents of how they are deceived about their own needs and interests. This explains why CL often chooses the perspective of those who suffer and critically analyzes the language use of those in power, who are responsible for the existence of inequalities and who also have the means and opportunity to improve conditions. In agreement with its critical theoretic predecessors, CDA emphasizes the need for interdisciplinary work to gain understanding of how language functions in constituting and transmitting knowledge, in organizing social institutions, and in exercising power.

An important characteristic of CDA is that much of the work is multiply authored. In texts, discursive differences are negotiated and governed by differences in power, which are themselves in part encoded in and determined by discourse and by genre. Therefore, texts are often sites of struggle in that they show traces of differing discourses and ideologies contending and struggling for dominance. Power is about relations of difference, and particularly about the effects of differences in social structures. The constant unity of language and other social matters ensures that language is entwined with social power in a number of ways: language indexes power, expresses power, and is involved where there is contention over and challenge to power. Power does not derive from language, but language can be used to challenge power, to subvert it, and to alter distributions of power in the short and long term. Language provides a finely articulated means for differences in power in social hierarchical structures. Very few linguistic forms have not, at some stage, been pressed into the service of the expression of power by a process of syntactic or textual metaphor.

The roots of CDA lie in classical rhetoric, text linguistics, and sociolinguistics, as well as in applied linguistics and pragmatics. The notions of ideology, power, hierarchy, and gender, and static sociological variables have all been seen as relevant for the interpretation or explanation of text. Gender issues, racism, media discourses, and identity research have become prominent (Blommaert and Verschueren 1998, Billig and Schegloff 1999). Methodologies vary greatly, as well, from small qualitative case studies to large data corpora drawn from fieldwork and ethnographic research.

1. Principles. Fairclough and Wodak 1997 established eleven basic principles of a CDA program (see also Wodak 2001).

1. The approach is interdisciplinary.

2. Interdisciplinarity is located at several levels: in theory, in the work itself, in teams, and in practice.

3. The approach is problem-oriented, not focused on specific linguistic items.

4. The theory and the methodology are eclectic; theories and methods are integrated in understanding and explaining the object under investigation.

5. The study always incorporates fieldwork and ethnography to explore the object under investigation (study from the inside) as a precondition for any further analysis and theorizing.

6. The approach is abductive: a constant movement back and forth between theory and empirical data is necessary.

7. Multiple genres and multiple public spaces are studied, and intertextual and interdiscursive relationships are investigated. Recontextualization is the most important process in connecting these genres as well as topics and arguments (*topoi*).

8. The historical context is always analyzed and integrated into the interpretation of discourses and texts.

9. The categories and tools for the analysis are defined according to all these steps and procedures, as well as to the specific problem under investigation.

10. "Grand theories" serve as a foundation; in the spe-

cific analysis, "middle-range theories" serve the aims better.

11. Practice is aimed at: the results should be made available to experts in different fields and then applied, with the goal of changing certain discursive and social practices.

2. Main research agenda. Taking up the tradition of Michel Foucault, Norman Fairclough sets out the social theories underpinning CDA, and, as in other early critical linguistic work, analyzes a variety of textual examples to illustrate the field, its aims, and its methods of analysis. Fairclough 1992 and Chouliaraki and Fairclough 1999 explain and elaborate some advances in CDA, showing not only how the analytical framework for researching language in relation to power and ideology has developed, but also how CDA is useful in disclosing the discursive nature of much contemporary social and cultural change.

The language of the mass media is particularly scrutinized as a site of power and struggle where language is often seemingly transparent. Media institutions purport to be neutral in that they provide space for public discourse, reflect states of affairs disinterestedly, and give the perceptions and arguments of the newsmakers. Fairclough shows the falseness of these assumptions and illustrates the mediating and constructing role of the media.

Also strongly influenced by Foucault is the Duisburg School. Jäger 1993 is concerned with linguistic and iconic characteristics of discourse, focusing on "collective symbols" (*topoi*) that possess important cohesive functions in texts. Discourse is seen as the flow of text and speech through time (Jäger 1993:6). Discourses have historical roots and are interwoven. Jäger has developed an explicit research program and methodology that allows analysis in several steps; its main topics of research have been right-wing discourses in Germany and tabloids.

The mediation of discourse and society through a sociocognitive model was first provided by van Dijk, who, along with Kintsch 1983, considered the relevance of discourse to the study of language processing. Their development of a cognitive model of discourse understanding in individuals gradually developed into cognitive models for explaining the construction of meaning on a societal level.

van Dijk has now turned specifically to media discourse, both reflecting on communication in the mass media and bringing together the theories and applications of various scholars interested in the production, uses, and functions of media discourses. In critically analyzing various kinds of discourses that encode prejudice, his interest is in developing a theoretical model that will explain cognitive discourse processing mechanisms (Wodak and van Dijk 2000) and racism and ideology.

By the end of the 1980s, CDA was able to describe its aims, research interests, chosen perspective, and methods more specifically and rigidly. Wodak 2001 lists, explains, and illustrates the most important characteristics of critical linguistic research as established in research—for example, investigating language use in institutional settings, and a new focus on the necessity for historical perspective. Various research projects have followed into discursive practices in institutional contexts that would assist in developing an integrated theory of critical discourse analysis.

Another important research agenda is the study of racism and anti-Semitism (Wodak and van Dijk 2000). The "discourse historical approach" (Reisigl and Wodak 2001), fundamentally an interdisciplinary and theory-oriented methodology, was first used in the study of the Kurt Waldheim affair (1986) and the rise of public anti-Semitic discourses in Austria.

Recognition of the contribution of all aspects of the communicative context to text meaning, as well as a growing awareness in general media studies of the importance of nonverbal aspects of texts, has turned attention to semiotic devices in discourse other than the linguistic ones. Pioneering work on the interaction between the verbal and visual in texts and discourse, as well as on the meaning of images, has been done by van Leeuwen (Kress and van Leeuwen 1996), and this provides a useful framework for considering the communicative potential of visual devices in the media.

[*See also* Language and Power *and* Sociolinguistics, *article on* Sociology of Language.]

BIBLIOGRAPHY

Anthonissen, C. 2001. On the effectivity of media censorship: An analysis of linguistic, paralinguistic and other communicative devices used to defy media restrictions. Dissertation, University of Vienna.

Billig, M., and E. A. Schegloff. 1999. Debate: Critical discourse analysis and conversation analysis. *Discourse and Society* 10.543–582.

Blommaert, Jan, and Jef Verschueren. 1999. *The diversity debate.* London: Routledge.

Chouliaraki, L., and Norman Fairclough. 1999. *Discourse in late modernity: Rethinking critical discourse analysis.* Edinburgh: Edinburgh University Press.

Fairclough, Norman, and Ruth Wodak. 1997. Critical discourse analysis. In *Introduction to discourse analysis,* edited by T. A. van Dijk, pp. 258–284. London: Sage.

Jäger, S. 1993. Kritische Diskursanalyse: Eine Einführung. Dissertation, Duisburg.

Kress, G., and T. van Leeuwen. 1996. *Reading usages.* London: Routledge.

Muntigl, Peter, Gilbert Weiss, and Ruth Wodak. 2000. *European Union discourses on unemployment: An interdisciplinary approach to employment policy-making and organizational change.* Amsterdam: Benjamins.

Reisigl, Martin, and Ruth Wodak. 2001. *Discourse and discrimination.* London: Routledge.

Thompson, J. B. 1990. *Ideology and modern culture.* Cambridge: Polity Press.

van Dijk, T. A. 1993. Principles of critical discourse analysis. *Discourse and Society* 4.249–283.

van Dijk, T. A., and W. Kintsch. 1983. *Strategies of discourse comprehension.* New York: Academic Press.

Wodak, Ruth. 1996. *Disorders in discourse.* London: Longman.

Wodak, Ruth. 2001. What CDA is about—a summary of its history, important concepts and its developments. In *Methods of critical discourse analysis*, edited by R. Wodak and M. Meyer, pp. 1–14. London: Sage.

Wodak, Ruth, and T. A. van Dijk, eds. 2000. *Racism at the top.* Klagenfurt: Drava.

Ruth Wodak

Discourse and Interactional Sociolinguistics

With the rise of interest in discourse analysis, a growing number of linguists have turned to analyzing the language of face-to-face interaction. The form of interaction most commonly studied in this framework is ordinary conversation; but research has also focused on other speech genres, such as interviews, public lectures, and classroom discourse, and on specific strategies, such as asking questions and telling stories. Work in this area can be distinguished by its relative focus either on the linguistic phenomena or on the interaction. Some linguists use the tape-recorded language of real interaction as a source of data for linguistic analysis, the main goal of which is understanding the linguistic structures found in the transcript. Work in this branch of discourse analysis is an extension of grammatical analysis beyond the sentence level. Others use their knowledge of linguistic phenomena to account for the processes and outcomes of interaction.

This branch of discourse analysis may be called I[nteractional] S[ociolinguistics]. In contrast to *conversation analysis*—a subdiscipline of ethnomethodological sociology whose primary concern is demonstrating the universal orderliness of everyday behavior—IS is associated with anthropology, and is frequently concerned with culturally identified interactional strategies.

The backbone of IS is the detailed transcription of audio- or video-taped interaction. Transcription systems vary, depending on conventions established in particular disciplines and the requirements of particular theoretical assumptions and methodological practices. However, most interactional sociolinguists attempt to represent intonational and prosodic contours in the transcription, since these are often crucial for analysis.

A theoretical framework influencing some of the research in IS is the schematization of politeness phenomena. Goffman 1967 observed that speakers serve two "face" requirements: the *positive face* needed to show involvement with others, and the *negative face* needed not to offend others. Lakoff 1979 sees linguistic choices as resulting from the application of underlying *rules of rapport*. Brown and Levinson 1987 have formalized and elaborated these schemas as *universals of politeness* phenomena. Matsumoto 1988, Pan 2000, and others working on non-Western languages have questioned the universality of Brown and Levinson's schema. Tannen 1994 emphasizes that linguistic means of serving positive and negative face, or power and solidarity, are inherently ambiguous and polysemous.

Gumperz 1982, 1999 shows that speakers use *contextualization* cues—prosodic and paralinguistic features, familiar formulaic expressions and conversational routines, and identifiable conventions for organizing and sequencing information—to signal not only what they mean to say, but also what *speech activity* they are engaged in, that is, what they think they are doing at each point in the interaction. Gumperz departs from immediately preceding linguistic theory by placing at the core of his theoretical framework "paralinguistic and prosodic features" that had previously been dismissed as marginal to the linguistic system.

In giving prominence to the notion of speech activity, IS builds directly on Bateson's 1972 notion of *framing*. Bateson points out that no message (the meaning of words or utterances) can be interpreted without reference to a metamessage about the frame. For example, any utterance can mean the opposite of what it says if the speaker is operating in a frame of play, irony, joking, or teasing. A formidable, multi-layered schema for frame analysis is presented by Goffman 1974. IS sees the language produced in interaction as the means for accomplishing continual shifts in *footing* among participants (Goffman 1981, Tannen and Wallat 1987).

Another key element in Gumperz's theoretical framework is *conversational inference*: not only do participants glean meaning from words and phrases as they occur, but they also make active predictions about what will come next, based on the line of interpretation suggested by ongoing talk as measured against prior interactive experience. In Gumperz's view, speakers do not follow conversational rules, but rather are guided by interpretive norms which are continually reinforced or revised in the light of ongoing interpretation. The analyst's task, then, becomes one of interpreting specific instances of discourse, giving rise to the label *hermeneutic* for this approach.

Much of the work of Gumperz (and those influenced by him) uses cross-cultural communication as a heuristic site. We can examine conversations in which the interaction of different signaling systems leads to misinterpretation of others' abilities and intentions; this affords insight into the processes of signaling and interpreting meaning which go unnoticed in successful interactions.

Gumperz has analyzed interaction between inner-city black and middle-class white Americans, as well as British English-speaking and Indian English-speaking Londoners, by following these steps:

(a) Tape-recording and transcribing interaction among speakers of different cultural or subcultural backgrounds

(b) Interviewing participants separately to gain insight into their interpretations of the interaction, and to identify the linguistic phenomena which led to their interpretations

(c) When possible, comparing instances of cross-cultural communication with recordings of similar speech events involving participants of a single cultural background

(d) Examining the tape and transcript to identify the linguistic strategies for signaling frames, and identifying speech activities which were differentially interpreted by the culturally different participants

(e) Explaining how the cultural differences in interpretive norms led to the differing interpretations, and consequently the breakdown in communication

(f) Checking the cultural basis of interpretive norms by playing segments of the interaction for other members of the cultural groups represented, to see if their reported interpretations follow patterns similar to those identified for participants

Tannen 1984 extends the paradigm of cross-cultural communication to account for conversation among Americans of different subcultural backgrounds. Individuals develop unique blends of signaling habits as they learn from peers in a particular speech community—influenced by numerous factors including regional, ethnic, class, age, and gender differences. These habits, which together make up an individual's conversational style, amount to slightly or grossly different systems used to signal meaning and to accomplish framing in interaction. When systems are relatively similar, participants share interpretive norms; so meaning is likely to be understood as intended. But when systems are relatively different, participants have different norms, and intentions are likely to be misjudged. A simple example with reference to the turn-taking system is the situation in which speakers have different expectations about the appropriate length of inter-turn pauses. The speaker who expects shorter pauses repeatedly but unintentionally "cuts off" the one who expects longer pauses. The shorter-pausing speaker interprets the "silence" of the other as evidence of having no intention to speak.

Analysis of the language of face-to-face interaction has not been confined to linguistic and paralinguistic features, but has included kinesic and rhythmic phenomena (Auer, Couper-Kuhlen, and Müller 1999). Successful conversation is characterized by a finely tuned synchrony and microsynchrony, both within the behavior of a speaker and among participants. This shared *rhythm* amounts to a musical component of language which allows participants to show *listenership*, to move between speaking and listening, to emphasize points, to establish cohesion and coherence, and to predict where important information is likely to come, all in a smooth and seamless way. When rhythm is not shared, speakers cannot participate comfortably, or may not be able to participate at all; they may either miss information entirely, or misjudge its relative significance. Erickson and Shultz 1982 document this process in *gatekeeping encounters*—speech events in which only one of the participants has much at stake— between college counselors and students who have different subcultural backgrounds.

Influenced by the conversation analysts Harvey Sacks and Emanuel Schegloff, much study has addressed the turn-taking system. In contrast to that ethnomethodological approach, interactional sociolinguists claim that, whereas instances of observable phenomena can be assigned to a descriptive category such as "overlap" without reference to interpretive norms, they can only be assigned to interactionally significant categories, such as "interruption," by understanding the perceived rights and obligations of the participants (Bennett 1981, James and Clarke 1993), and by reference to their conversational styles (Tannen 1984, 1994).

Research in IS often focuses on linguistic devices and strategies. Much attention has been paid to *narrative* and questions. Approaches to the analysis of such strategies are also influenced by the *ethnography of speaking*, which has supplied an invaluable source of cross-cultural evidence as an antidote to hasty claims for universality. For example, questions have been much studied as powerful interactional devices because they strongly favor a response. The analysis of questions as prime devices for implicature or indirect communication is supported by ethnographic accounts of cultures in which questions are routinely interpreted as hinting unstated meaning rather than directly requesting information (Goody 1978, Scollon and Scollon 1981).

Other devices and strategies that fall within the purview of IS include silence, hesitation phenomena, discourse markers, topic, power and solidarity, figures of speech, *formulaic speech*, repetition (Tannen 1989), and reported speech, or dialogue.

A central concern of IS is the interactive nature of conversation. The model of language as produced by a speaker alone is questioned; rather, listening and speaking are seen as inextricably intertwined. Thus any utterance by any participant in a conversation is a joint production, influenced by speaker, listener, and audience (including the investigators or their equipment). For this reason, research has also focused on listenership behavior. Among the more frequently studied of such phenomena is *backchanneling*. This includes minimal responses such as *Mhm* and *Uhuh,* lax tokens such as *Yeah,* one-word responses such as *Right,* phrases such as *I see what you mean,* repetitions and sentence completions, and short ratifying utterances. Using a method similar to that of Gumperz, Erickson 1986 demonstrates that, when nonverbal listenership behavior is not shared, unexpected patterns of listenership create gross changes in speaker behavior. For example, a speaker who does not receive a steady *gaze*, with nodding at key phrase boundaries, gets the impression that the listener is not attending, or not

understanding; the speaker consequently recycles utterances in succeedingly more simplified form, with the result of seeming to "talk down" to a fully comprehending listener.

One effect of the shift from the intuited data of syntactic studies to the language of real interaction is a corresponding shift in the conception of language. The syntactician's data typically consist of a sentence; however, investigators who have examined transcripts of naturally occurring spoken discourse have observed that the minimal unit of spoken language is not the sentence, but the *utterance* or *intonation unit*. This is a phrase averaging six or seven words, always characterized by an identifiable intonational contour and often bounded by a pause, particle, or hesitation marker; it represents a single focus of consciousness (Chafe 1986). Some linguists find that analysis of conversational data suggests that the sentence is an idealization created by written language. Moreover, examining the language of actual interaction has called into question the generative basis of grammar—suggesting that language is more a matter of arranging preformed phrases and utterances, rather than of arranging words (Bolinger 1976, Pawley 1986).

In sum, IS is a major field of research at the intersection of linguistics and anthropology. Because it frequently identifies discourse strategies as associated with culturally identifiable speakers, and examines the effects on interaction of the differing strategies of culturally different speakers, IS is a branch of linguistics that promises to help solve real-world problems involving communication. In addition, it contributes to theoretical issues in linguistics by shedding light on the nature of meaning in language, and on the nature of language in interaction.

[*See also* Anthropological Linguistics; Discourse Markers; Ethnography of Speaking; Nonverbal Communication; Sociolinguistics; Text; *and* Writing and Written Language.]

BIBLIOGRAPHY

Auer, Peter, Elizabeth Couper-Kuhlen, and Frank Müller. 1999. *Language in time: The rhythm and tempo of spoken interaction.* New York and Oxford: Oxford University Press.

Bateson, Gregory. 1972. *Steps to an ecology of mind.* New York: Ballantine.

Bennett, Adrian. 1981. Interruptions and the interpretation of conversation. *Discourse Processes* 4.171–188.

Bolinger, Dwight. 1976. Meaning and memory. *Forum Linguisticum* 1:1.1–14.

Brown, Penelope, and Stephen C. Levinson. 1987. *Politeness:*

Some universals in language usage. (Studies in interactional sociolinguistics, 4.) Cambridge and New York: Cambridge University Press.

Chafe, Wallace. 1986. How we know things about language: A plea for Catholicism. In *Languages and linguistics: The interdependence of theory, data, and application* (Thirty-sixth Georgetown University Round Table, 1985), edited by Deborah Tannen and James E. Alatis, pp. 214–225. Washington, D.C.: Georgetown University Press.

Erickson, Frederick. 1986. Listening and speaking. In *Languages and linguistics: The interdependence of theory, data, and application,* edited by Deborah Tannen, pp. 294–319. Washington, D.C.: Georgetown University Press.

Erickson, Frederick, and Jeffrey Shultz. 1982. *The counselor as gatekeeper: Social interaction in interviews.* New York: Academic Press.

Goffman, Erving. 1967. The nature of deference and demeanor. In Erving Goffman, *Interaction ritual: Essays in face-to-face behavior,* pp. 47–95. New York: Anchor Books.

Goffman, Erving. 1974. *Frame analysis: An essay on the organization of experience.* New York: Harper and Row.

Goffman, Erving. 1981. Footing. In Erving Goffman, *Forms of talk,* pp. 124–159. Philadelphia: University of Pennsylvania Press.

Goody, Esther N. 1978. Towards a theory of questions. In *Questions and politeness: Strategies in social interaction* (Cambridge papers in social anthropology, 8), edited by Esther N. Goody, pp. 17–43. Cambridge and New York: Cambridge University Press.

Gumperz, John J. 1982. *Discourse strategies.* (Studies in interactional sociolinguistics, 1.) Cambridge and New York: Cambridge University Press.

Gumperz, John J. 1999. On interactional sociolinguistic method. In *Talk, work, and institutional order: Discourse in medical, mediation and management settings,* edited by Srikant Sarangi and Celia Roberts, pp. 453–471. Berlin: Mouton de Gruyter.

James, Deborah, and Sandra Clarke. 1993. Women, men and interruptions: A critical review. In *Gender and conversational interaction,* edited by Deborah Tannen, pp. 231–280. New York and Oxford: Oxford University Press.

Lakoff, Robin Tolmach. 1979. Stylistic strategies within a grammar of style. In *Language, sex, and gender* (Annals of the New York Academy of Science, 327), edited by Judith Orasanu et al., pp. 53–78. New York.

Matsumoto, Yoshiko. 1988. Reexamination of the universality of face: Politeness phenomena in Japanese. *Journal of Pragmatics* 12.403–426.

Pan, Yuling. 2000. *Politeness in Chinese face-to-face interaction.* Stamford, CT: Ablex.

Pawley, Andrew. 1986. Lexicalization. In *Languages and linguistics: The interdependence of theory, data, and application* (Thirty-sixth Georgetown University Round Table, 1985), edited by Deborah Tannen and James E. Alatis, pp. 98–120. Washington, D.C.: Georgetown University Press.

Scollon, Ron, and Suzanne B. K. Scollon. 1981. *Narrative, literacy, and face in interethnic communication.* Norwood, N.J.: Ablex.

Tannen, Deborah. 1984. *Conversational style: Analyzing talk among friends.* Norwood, N.J.: Ablex.

Tannen, Deborah. 1989. *Talking voices: Repetition, dialogue and imagery in conversational discourse.* (Studies in interactional sociolinguistics, 6.) Cambridge and New York: Cambridge University Press.

Tannen, Deborah. 1994. The relativity of linguistic strategies: Rethinking power and solidarity in gender and dominance. In *Gender and discourse,* pp. 19–52. New York and Oxford: Oxford University Press.

Tannen, Deborah, and Cynthia Wallat. 1987. Interactive frames and knowledge schemas in interaction: Examples from a medical examination/interview. *Social Psychology Quarterly* 50:2.205–216.

DEBORAH TANNEN

Conversation Analysis

In its vernacular usage, the term *conversation* usually refers to casual, informal talk between two or more people. This definition identifies a pervasive type of speech situation but, unfortunately, excludes other types of verbal interchange, such as interviews and meetings; moreover, it fails to encompass the range of subject matter addressed by the practitioners of C[onversation] A[nalysis]. Schegloff (1987:101) uses the more comprehensive term *talk-in-interaction* to cover the scope of CA inquiry. CA is concerned with the discovery and description of the methods or procedures that speakers use systematically to assemble recognizable *actions* using embodied language in conversation and other forms of social interaction involving language. Such procedures constitute a ubiquitous and fundamental form of social organization.

Other approaches to language use—sociolinguistics, for example—study the influence of variables such as race, class, gender, and other social constraints on speech practices. Scholars of communication measure the communicative competence of speakers and determine how these skills affect persuasive communication or conversational control. Discourse analysts, continuing the linguistic tradition by devising concepts and methodology for units larger than the clause, address issues of cohesion and coherence between the utterances and underlying actions that constitute spoken discourse; or they study information flow, anaphora, and so on.

Critical discourse analysis (CDA) approaches talk and text with an interest in issues of ideology and power relationships. All of these approaches utilize some form of spoken or written language as data, but, with few exceptions, they do not address talk *as* action; or, if they do so, they do not approach its technical specification or its endogenous organization.

This entry is concerned with CA not merely as a descriptive term, specifying a commonsensically defined subject matter, but in the more restrictive sense of a subdiscipline within sociology, with relevance to linguistics. It has a distinctive focus: the full resources of spoken language, including gaze, gesture, and paralinguistic conduct, as a vehicle of action and social interaction.

1. Turn-taking. Fundamental to the focus of CA is the assumption that conversation as an interactional activity displays features that can be analyzed as the specific achievements of speakers and hearers, employing general procedures to manage the local contingencies of interactions. One such set of procedures—the mechanisms for *turn-taking* in conversation—provides a useful example of conversation-analytic concerns. In an important and influential paper, Sacks et al. 1974 proposed that any model of turn-taking must account for several observable facts about conversation, for example:

(a) At least one, but not more than one, person speaks at a time.
(b) Turn order, turn size, and turn content are free to vary.
(c) Length of conversation is not predetermined.
(d) The number of participants is free to vary.
(e) The distribution of turns (in multi-party conversation) is not prespecified.

If conversation is an orderly activity, there must be some systematic way in which participants manage actual conversations to achieve the particular distribution of turns, turn-length, turn-order, etc., which characterize any given conversation. Sacks et al. 1974 developed a model that operates by a set of general trans-situationally stable procedures by which turns are interactionally constructed and allocated. These procedures are employed to manage turn-taking on a *local* basis; that is, although they are general, they are adaptable to the specific purposes and identities of the parties present, to their actual social

circumstances, and to the particular contingencies of the situation.

Turns are principally constructed of sequentially relevant clausal, phrasal, lexical, or other elements; non-lexical vocal elements and gestures are other possible turn-constructional components. Unit boundaries can be anticipated and are thereby usable by participants to predict points of possible transition. Turns are allocated by an interactionally constrained, temporally ordered set of options (Sacks et al. 1974:703–706), which provide for possible turn transition at or near the possible turn boundary.

The model set forth in Sacks et al. 1974 constituted an initial attempt to address the endogenous organization of turn-taking, not the final word on the topic. For example, although the model is designed to produce and thus account for one person speaking at a time, actual conversation displays many instances of simultaneous talk. This fact is sometimes treated as a challenge to the model. Although brief simultaneity is often generated by the operation of the system (Sacks et al. 1974:706–708), the occurrence and systematics of overlapping talk require attention. Schegloff 2000 describes an important mechanism by which overlapping talk is systematically pursued or resolved by the parties to the talk.

The turn-constructional component of the 1974 model was originally treated as largely, but not exclusively, syntactic. Schegloff (1996:55) suggests that the turn is a natural setting for syntactic objects such as sentences, and that such units should be understood as "adaptations to that environment." He then suggests the notion of "positionally sensitive grammar(s)": the types of utterances or utterance fragments that make up a T[urn] C[onstructional] U[nit] may be distributed relative to their position within it. Hence, it is possible to ask "whether there is a describable orderliness between *types of positions* in a turn and *types of units* occupying those positions" (1996:64). Moreover, an element within a TCU may involve extra-turn considerations such as sequence and interactional juncture.

Thus, although TCUs in the original model were defined in terms of syntactic units, a deeper understanding of the relationship between grammar and interaction leads to the view that "the grammatical structures of language should . . . be understood as at least partially shaped by interactional considerations. . . . And one locus of those considerations will be the organization of the turn, the organization unit which 'houses' grammatical units"

(Schegloff 1996:55). The recognition that grammar and interaction enter into mutually determinative relations is reflected in work that can be characterized as a form of "interactional linguistics" (see Couper-Kuhlen and Selting 2001, Ford et al. 2002).

A related issue concerns how the elements of TCUs are assembled to project its terminal boundary for turn transition purposes. Ford and Thompson 1996 identify the syntactic, prosodic, and pragmatic features speakers use to produce and recognize points of possible completion and to evaluate quantitatively the function of these features in actual turn transition. They explicitly provide for the convergence of syntactic, prosodic, and pragmatic (action) elements ("complex transition relevance places") of TCUs to organize turn transition. Their research thus refines the model by more precisely integrating grammatical and interactional processes.

Turn-taking is not the sole focus of CA, although it is one of the central organizing elements of talk-in-interaction. Moreover, turn-taking has a commonsense construal that presumes a certain transparency—for example, that it is a means of maintaining a "clear channel" of communication, or a form of politeness. However, as Schegloff (1988:97–98) proposes, a society without an organized mechanism for turn-taking would not be particularly impolite; rather, in it the possibility of concerted, responsive action would be foreclosed. Turn-taking provides a means of *ordering* the actions undertaken in turns at talk, thereby furnishing a space designed for response, as well as a place for the current speaker to display a grasp of the type of action constituted in the preceding turn.

2. Other forms of organization. *Sequential organization* is a central mechanism of talk-in-interaction. Such organization encompasses the production and recognition of successive turns, where a subsequent turn stands in some specifiable relationship to the prior beyond mere serial placement. Examples include invitations and their subsequent acceptance or decline; the initiation of repair by another in the next turn when the prior speaker has not self-corrected; a second assessment to a first; and opening or closing sequences.

One form of sequence organization is *adjacency pair* organization (Schegloff and Sacks 1973; Heritage 1984: 245–253; Levinson 1983:303–308). This deals with the relationship of adjacent turns where an initial turn is of a particular type. The type of the initial turn constrains some designated part to produce a second, adjacent turn of a type matched to the first.

Other work has identified procedures for opening conversations and establishing the aligning identities; the initiation, management, and closure of topics; for the organization of *repair* activities addressing a broad range of conversational "troubles"; for *preference* organization—the structural allocation of preferred (immediate, direct, and unmitigated) and dispreferred (delayed, indirect, and mitigated) turn types in response to different sequences, such as in repair or adjacency pair organization (inviting, requesting, or complimenting). Other work has identified procedures for *opening* conversations and for *closing*, or achieving a coordinated exit from talk. The list could be extended.

Spoken interaction, whether in ordinary conversation or institutional settings, is seen as exhibiting features that are *produced* and *oriented to* by participants as orderly and informative, and that are relied upon as a basis for further inference and action. Indeed, it is the fact that participants themselves *locate* these features (e.g., through behaviors subsequently addressed to them) that warrants regarding them as relevant to conversational activity. The course of conversational interaction is thus managed on a turn-by-turn basis, with the sequential environment providing the primary context for participants' understanding, appreciation, and use of what is being done and said in the talk (Schegloff and Sacks 1973:234).

3. Institutional talk. When conversational analysts turn to the study of spoken interaction in institutional settings (courtrooms, physicians' offices, news interviews, etc.), they focus on how the features of mundane conversation are modified and adapted to the tasks in the setting—for example, how turn-taking is modified to achieve a unified focus of attention. The features of these interactions *constitute* the setting as much as they are occasioned by it (Heritage 1984:231–240).

As one example, when various parameters of the turn-taking system are constrained in some way, the occasion and the talk within it are transformed. When the turn order, the number or social category of participants, and the turn content or type are pre-specified, a different mode of organizing spoken interaction comes into operation: a different *speech exchange system* (Sacks et al. 1974:729–731). In news interviews, for example, turn types (questions and answers, respectively) are pre-allocated to specified categories of participants, the interviewers and interviewees. Among other consequences, this limits or prescribes who may initiate what type of action to what type of recipient, and when (Heritage and Greatbatch 1990).

Various forms of spoken interaction, then, may reflect systematic modifications of the organization of turn-taking found in ordinary conversation. These modifications are not the only means by which institutional settings are "talked into being" (Heritage 1984:290). Formal activities may be accomplished through lexical choice (lay vs. professional vocabularies), turn design, overall structural organization, and other means (Drew and Heritage 1992:29–53). Detailed observations of ordinary conversations have yielded not only a model of turn-taking and variant speech exchange systems, but also an empirically based characterization of the primary subject matter (mundane conversation) and a means of systematically identifying and comparing different types of spoken interaction in society, including institutionally organized activities.

4. CA and social order. The view that spoken interaction, as a domain of social action, exhibits a high measure of orderliness, and that this order is produced and oriented to by speakers and hearers, requires further comment, particularly in relation to the usual interests of sociologists. Sociology seeks its orderly phenomena in group, institutional, or societal patterns emerging from aggregate behaviors. The identification and analysis of these socially organized patterns are thought to require the respecification of observed, reported, or recorded social activities in terms of analytical categories or variables that permit the investigator to link seemingly disparate concrete events. Such analytic moves are thought necessary for the extraction of abstract but orderly patterns out of what is otherwise a confusing array of concrete particulars. Thus, the concrete occasions of everyday activities are not a promising site for the study of social order.

The purpose for turning to the study of conversation was to reorient sociology as "a natural observational science" (Sacks 1984:21; see also Sacks, 1992a,b). In this view, sociological inquiry should strive to observe, analyze, and account for the particulars of everyday behavior as deeply and finely organized social conduct. Accordingly, CA considers these details as matters to be accounted for as the workings of a socially organized "machinery," operating at the level of the most mundane and singular face-to-face interactions. This view runs counter to the conventional wisdom of social science.

Thus, CA holds itself analytically responsible for the particulars of interactions. Its formulations must be ca-

pable of recovering these details through close description of the methods by which interactants produce them. Its data are the features of naturally occurring talk (contrived or invented discourse is avoided) in which participants are free to employ the resources of conversation's organization to deal with the interactional and situational contingencies of the occasion.

[*See also* Discourse Markers; Ethnography of Speaking; *and* Social Variation.]

BIBLIOGRAPHY

Atkinson, J. Maxwell, and John C. Heritage, eds. 1984. *Structures of social action: Studies in conversational analysis.* Cambridge and New York: Cambridge University Press.

Boden, Deirdre, and Don H. Zimmerman. 1990. *Talk and social structure.* Cambridge: Polity Press.

Couper-Kuhlen, Elizabeth, and Margaret Selting, eds. 2001. *Studies in interactional linguistics.* Amsterdam: Benjamins.

Drew, Paul, and John Heritage 1992. Analyzing talk at work: An introduction. In Drew and Heritage 1992, pp. 3–65.

Drew, Paul, and John Heritage, eds. 1992. *Talk at work.* Cambridge: Cambridge University Press.

Drew, Paul, and Anthony Wootton, eds. 1988. *Erving Goffman: Exploring the interaction order.* Cambridge: Polity Press.

Ford, Cecelia, Barbara Fox, and Sandra A. Thompson, eds. 2002. *The language of turn and sequence.* Oxford: Oxford University Press.

Heritage, John. 1984. *Garfinkel and ethnomethodology.* Cambridge: Polity Press.

Heritage, John, and David Greatbatch 1990. On the institutional character of institutional talk. In Boden and Zimmerman 1990, pp. 93–137.

Levinson, Stephen C. 1983. *Pragmatics.* Cambridge and New York: Cambridge University Press.

Ochs, Eleanor, Emanuel A. Schegloff, and Sandra A. Thompson, eds. 1996. *Interaction and grammar.* Oxford: Oxford University Press.

Sacks, Harvey. 1984. Notes on methodology. In Atkinson and Heritage 1984, pp. 21–27.

Sacks, Harvey. 1992a. *Lectures on conversation: Vol. 1.* Oxford: Oxford University Press.

Sacks, Harvey, 1992b. *Lectures on conversation: Vol. 2.* Oxford: Oxford University Press.

Sacks, Harvey, Emanuel A. Schegloff, and Gail Jefferson. 1974. Simplest systematics for the organization of turntaking for conversation. *Language* 50.696–735.

Schegloff, Emanuel A. 1986. The routine as achievement. *Human Studies* 9.111–152.

Schegloff, Emanuel A. 1987. Analyzing single episodes of interaction: An exercise in conversation analysis. *Social Psychology Quarterly* 50.101–114.

Schegloff, Emanuel A. 1988. Goffman and the analysis of conversation. In Drew and Wootton 1988, pp. 89–135.

Schegloff, Emanuel A. 1996. Turn organization: One intersection of grammar and interaction. In Ochs, Schegloff, and Thompson, 1996, pp. 52–133.

Schegloff, Emanuel A. 2000. Overlapping talk and the organization of turn-taking for conversation. *Language in Society* 29.1–63.

Schegloff, Emanuel A., and Harvey Sacks. 1973. Opening up closings. *Semiotica* 8.289–327.

DON H. ZIMMERMAN

DISCOURSE ANALYSIS. *See* Discourse.

DISCOURSE MARKERS.

The production and interpretation of coherent discourse is an interactive process that requires speakers and hearers to draw upon several different types of knowledge. One type of competence is *social* and expressive—the ability to use language to display personal and social identities, to perform actions, and to negotiate relationships between self and other. Still other types of competence are *cognitive*, for example, the ability to organize conceptual information and to represent it through language, and *textual*, for example, the ability to create and understand messages within units of language longer than a single sentence.

One set of linguistic items that function in the cognitive, social, expressive, and textual domains is commonly referred to as D[iscourse] M[arker]s: sequentially dependent elements which bracket units of talk (Schiffrin 1987a:31). Examples are connectives (*and, but, or*), particles (*oh, well*), adverbs (*now, then*), and lexicalized phrases (*y'know, I mean*). DMs function in relation to aspects of language that can be defined only through discourse per se (a linguistic unit larger than the sentence) and in relation to communicative processes underlying (and realized through) situated language use. Sometimes the unit being marked is a sentence; at other times, the unit is defined as an action, an idea unit, or a turn at talk (Schiffrin 1987a:31–36). The functions of the markers are always relative to the form and meaning of both prior and upcoming discourse. The particular aspect of discourse to which they pertain, however, varies for different markers; for example, *oh* pertains most to the distribution and management of information, while *I mean* and *y'know* pertain most to the organization of participation and involvement (Schiffrin 1987a:chap. 10).

Although there were scattered studies of discourse markers in the 1980s, their study in the past 10 years has abounded in various branches of linguistics and allied fields. Markers have been studied in a variety of languages, including Chinese, Danish, Finnish, French, German, Hebrew, Hungarian, Indonesian, Italian, Japanese, Korean, Latin, Mayan, Portuguese, and Spanish (see Jucker and Ziv 1998 for a range of languages; Schiffrin 2001 for specific citations). Markers have been examined in a variety of genres and interactive contexts, including narratives, political interviews, health care consultations, games, computer-generated tutorial sessions, newspapers, radio talk, classrooms, and service encounters (see Schiffrin 2001 for citations), in a number of different language contact situations (e.g. Maschler 2000). Synchronic studies have been supplemented by diachronic analyses of first- (e.g. Meng and Sromqvist 1999) and second-language acquisition (Flowerdew and Tauroza 1995), as well as language change (Brinton 1996).

The application of different perspectives to the study of DMs means the influence of different theoretical assumptions and frameworks, and the use of different methods of analysis. Not surprisingly, some studies result in different substantive findings (see Carlson 1984, Jucker 1993, Schiffrin 1987a:chap. 5, Schoroup 2001), and different conclusions about their specific role in theories of language and communication.

Despite differences in individual studies, we can draw some general conclusions about the relationship of DMs to language structure and use. Research reveals that such markers both reflect and create the interpretive and interactive contexts in which discourse is constructed. In fact, the use of DMs is not only a part of what makes a way of speaking seem natural and appropriate to its context, but also a part of what makes language seem distinctly human—in the terms of Wierzbicka (1986:519), what "distinguishes human language from the language of robots." These interdependencies mean that the study of DMs is quite central to our understanding of communicative competence—how our cognitive, social, expressive, and textual knowledge allows us to use language in culturally appropriate ways.

The analysis of DMs contributes in still other ways to our understanding of language structure and use. DMs whose function is based on their semantic meaning (e.g. *and, or*) often figure critically in ideational aspects of discourse coherence—in the indication of semantic relationships between different propositions. Such DMs, as well as others whose meaning is not propositionally based, also help to segment discourse into smaller chunks, for example, idea units, which are cognitively differentiated from one another as separate foci of attention (Chafe 1994); or into smaller chunks which are structurally and/or functionally different from one another, but nevertheless interrelated (Hymes 1981, Sherzer 1982). Thus many DMs bracket small chunks of discourse that are cognitively and textually organized in speakers' competence.

Other DMs bracket units of talk that function in more social and expressive domains. Thus the markers *I mean, y'know,* and *now* are important means of displaying speaker attitude and subjective orientation toward what is being said and to whom. Markers such as *so, then,* and *well* have a role in solving both mechanical problems (e.g. turn-taking, topic transition) and interpersonal problems of conversational management. Still other DMs work in both cognitive and social domains; thus *oh* as a marker of information receipt displays a transfer of information during clarification sequences in conversation (Heritage 1998; Schiffrin 1987a:chap. 4). That DMs have these functions means that their study is important not only for our understanding of communicative competence, but also for our understanding of meaning (as conveyed through situated utterances) and of conversational organization.

Most DMs frequently have several simultaneous functions. Thus, *well* may convey the fulfillment of a conversational obligation, for example, an answer to a question, at the same time that it conveys speaker attitude, for example, distance from a proposition (Schiffrin 1987a: chap. 5). Multifunctionality is central to our understanding of form/function relationships and the development of functionalist models of language. It also bears directly on models developed within cognitive semantics (e.g. the important notions of polysemy and radial categories; Fischer 2000, Sweetser 1990). Detailed analyses of the multiple functions of individual markers suggest that the processes through which coherent discourse is constructed are essentially *integrative:* processes in which meanings, actions, and structures must be synthesized with one another in the service of sense-making and message formation.

The discussion thus far has assumed that DMs can be considered a set of some kind, despite the fact that the linguistic items serving as markers are members of word classes as various as conjunctions, interjections, and adverbs. Since words that function as discourse markers are derived from a variety of words and phrases within one language, as well as a variety of word types across languages, their status as a word class has been open to

closer scrutiny. Although most scholars combine function and form, no set of features that combine to define markers as a single class—and exclude other words from that class—has yet been agreed upon. Nor has the terminology remained consistent. Although "marker" continues to be widespread, some scholars (e.g. Fischer 2000) prefer the term "particle." Whereas "particles" facilitates the inclusion of modal and epistemic terms, as well as freer movement within a host clause, "markers" focuses more on the structural segmentation of discourse units and is more restricted to initial position. Terms like "cue phrases" (Hirschberg and Litman 1993) focus on the signaling function of markers in relation to propositional meanings that accrue across clauses.

The potential openness in the category of DMs might suggest that our definitions are inadequate; and that the category itself is too fuzzy or imprecise to allow rigorous analysis. However, this openness actually reflects a duality in the definition of discourse itself. That is, discourse is defined both as structural—a unit of language larger than a sentence—and as pragmatic, that is, language in use. Thus it is not surprising that DMs, as terms that define units of discourse, can also be identified as both text- and speaker-based. Likewise, it should not be surprising that the actual contribution of DMs to discourse can vary (compare the coordinator *and* with the metalinguistic *I mean*) depending on the meaning and/or formal properties that the individual marker brings to the discourse.

At another level, the potential openness of the class of DMs may reflect on-going semantic transitions from propositional meanings grounded in relatively objective situations, to textual meanings grounded in text, to expressive meanings grounded in speakers' attitudes to what is said (Onodera 1995, Traugott 1995). Thus the discourse marker *then* may be seen as a synchronic reflection of a change from a word with basically propositional meaning (referring to the time of events), to one marking discourse connections between temporally successive textual units, to one functioning in an expressive (perhaps epistemic) domain to indicate a recently warranted inference (Schiffrin 1992). Such changes figure in grammaticalization, the historical process whereby lexical items acquire a new status as grammatical, morphosyntactic forms. Studies of grammaticalization have done a great deal to challenge more conventionally held views of grammar as a static, closed system with discretely bound categories (Hopper 1988). If DMs do reflect, or participate in, processes of grammaticalization, then their analysis can be relevant not only to functionalist models of language and communication, but also to formalist models of language and grammar.

In sum, DMs have been characterized as "linguistic Cinderellas: familiar, drab, hard-worked, and lacking in morphological, phonological, and etymological glamour" (Enkvist 1972:95). Research on their function, however, reveals not only that they are important for the construction of coherent discourse and the organization of communicative competence, but also that their analysis may be relevant to debates about the structure of grammar.

Finally, the analysis of DMs can also contribute to the development of sociolinguistic theory. Schiffrin (1987a: chap. 10) suggests that, despite the individual functions served by different markers, a very general shared function is *indexical*: markers point to the "contextual coordinates," both textual and pragmatic, in which utterances are produced and in which speakers intend them to be interpreted. DMs share their indexical function with two key sociolinguistic constructs—contextualization cues and sociolinguistic variables—which point not to discourse, but to utterance interpretation and social meaning, respectively (Schiffrin 1987b). Contextualization cues are verbal and non-verbal elements of behavior which point to the culturally schematized frameworks in which utterances are understood as messages. Sociolinguistic variables are alternative realizations of linguistic form which point to the circumstances in which an utterance is produced, for example, speaker identity or definition of the situation. The shared indexical functions of DMs, contextualization cues, and sociolinguistic variables provide a valuable link among different levels of sociolinguistic inquiry whose relationships have not often been apparent: discourse, utterance interpretation, and social meaning. Establishing such links can be one step in developing a sociolinguistic theory to explain how utterances (their structure and their use) are socially constituted.

[*See also* Sociolinguistics; Pragmatics and Contextual Semantics; Discourse; Grammaticalization; Sociolinguistics; *and* Text.]

BIBLIOGRAPHY

Brinton, Laurel. 1996. *Pragmatic markers in English: Grammaticalization and discourse functions.* The Hague: Mouton de Gruyter.

Carlson, Lauri. 1984. *'Well' in dialogue games: A discourse analysis of the interjection 'well' in idealized conversation.* (Pragmatics and beyond, 6.) Amsterdam: Benjamins.

Chafe, Wallace. 1994. *Discourse, consciousness and time.* Chicago: University of Chicago Press.

Enkvist, Nils Erik. 1972. Old English adverbial *þā*—an action marker? *Neuphilologische Mitteilungen* 73.90–96.

Fischer, Kerstin. 2000. *From cognitive semantics to lexical pragmatics.* Berlin and New York: Mouton de Gruyter.

Flowerdew, J., and S. Tauroza. 1995. The effect of discourse markers on second language lecture comprehension. *Studies in Second Language Acquisition* 17:4.435–458.

Heritage, John. 1998. *Oh*-prefaced responses to inquiry. *Language in Society* 27:3.291–334.

Hirschberg, Julia, and Diane Litman. 1993. Empirical studies on the disambiguation of cue phrases. *Computational Linguistics* 19:3.501–530.

Hopper, Paul. 1988. Emergent grammar and the a priori Grammar Postulate. In *Linguistics in context: Connecting observation and understanding* (Advances in discourse processes, 29), edited by Deborah Tannen, pp. 117–134. Norwood, N.J.: Ablex.

Hymes, Dell. 1981. *'In vain I tried to tell you': Studies in Native American ethnopoetics.* Philadelphia: University of Pennsylvania Press.

Jucker, Andreas. 1993. The discourse marker *well*: A relevance-theoretical account. *Journal of Pragmatics* 19.435–452.

Jucker, Andreas, and Yael Ziv, eds. 1998. *Discourse markers: Description and theory.* Amsterdam and Philadelphia: Benjamins.

Maschler, Yael. 2000. *Discourse markers in bilingual conversation.* Special issue of *The International Journal of Bilingualism* 4:4. London: Kingston Press.

Meng Katharina, and Sven Sromqvist, eds. 1999. *Discourse markers in language acquisition* Special issue of *Journal of Pragmatics* 3110.

Onodera, Noriko. 1995. Diachronic analysis of Japanese discourse markers. In *Historical pragmatics,* edited by Andreas Jucker, pp. 393–437. Amsterdam and Philadelphia: Benjamins.

Schiffrin, Deborah. 1987a. *Discourse markers.* Cambridge and New York: Cambridge University Press.

Schiffrin, Deborah. 1987b. Discovering the context of an utterance. *Linguistics* 25.11–32.

Schiffrin, Deborah. 1992. Anaphoric *then*: Aspectual, textual and epistemic meaning. *Linguistics* 30:4.753–792.

Schiffrin, Deborah. 2001. Discourse markers: Language, meaning and context. In *Handbook of discourse analysis*, edited by Deborah Schiffrin, Deborah Tannen, and Heidi Hamilton, pp. 54–75. Oxford: Blackwell.

Schourop, Lawrence. 2001. Rethinking 'well.' *Journal of Pragmatics* 33.1025–1060.

Sherzer, Joel. 1982. Poetic structuring of Kuna discourse: The line. *Language in Society* 11.371–390.

Sweetser, Eve. 1990. *From etymology to pragmatics.* Cambridge: Cambridge University Press.

Traugott, Elizabeth. 1995. The role of the development of discourse markers in a theory of grammaticalization. In *12th International Conference on Historical Linguistics*. http://www.stanford.edu/~traugott/papers/discourse.pdf.

Wierzbicka, Anna. 1986. Introduction to special issue on "particles." *Journal of Pragmatics* 10.519–534.

DEBORAH SCHIFFRIN

DISCOURSE REPRESENTATION THEORY. *See* Semantics.

DISSIMILATION. *See* Phonological Processes.

DISTINCTIVE FEATURES. *See* Phonological Features.

DISTRIBUTED MORPHOLOGY. *See* Generative Morphology.

DJAMINDJUNGAN LANGUAGES. The Djamindjungan languages constitute a branch of the proposed AUSTRALIAN language family and are spoken in the northwestern part of the Northern Territory, Australia.

LANGUAGE LIST

Djamindjung: also called Jaminjung. 30 speakers along the Victoria River. Reports indicate that Djamindjung and Ngaliwuru are so close as to be one language; only some elderly people can distinguish the difference. No monolinguals. Ngarinman or Kriol are the second languages.

Nungali: 2 speakers remain in Australia. Formerly spoken in upper Daly River area.   B. GRIMES

DJERAGAN LANGUAGES. These constitute a family of the northern part of Western Australia and the Northern Territory.

LANGUAGE LIST

Gadjerawang: also called Gadjerong, Kajirrawung. 3 speakers remain. Formerly spoken on north coast from Wyndham to mouth of Victoria River and inland.

Kitja: also called Kija, Gidja, Kidja. 100 speakers near Hall's Creek and Turkey Creek. Closest to Miriwung. Related to

Kuluwarrang (Guluwarin, Guluwarung). Bilingualism in Kriol. Kriol is Kitja children's mother tongue, and adults are bilingual in Kriol.

Miriwung: also called Mirung, Merong, Miriwun, Miriwoong. 10 speakers remain. Formerly spoken at Kununurra and Turkey Creek. Some older people speak Miriwung. The young people use only Kriol. Most older people speak Kriol.

B. GRIMES

DONATUS, AELIUS (4th c. CE). Roman grammarian. His works include a compendium of Latin grammar (the *Ars maior* 'Larger skill') and a catechism on the parts of speech and their different forms or "accidents" (the *Ars minor* or 'smaller skill'), which were to have an immense influence, directly and through their role as a model for other grammarians, throughout the medieval period and into the modern.

[*See also* History of Linguistics, *article on* Ancient Greece and Rome.]

ANNA MORPURGO DAVIES

DOWNSTEP AND DOWNDRIFT. *See* Tone.

DOWN SYNDROME. *See* Williams Syndrome and Down Syndrome: Cognitive Constraints on Language.

DRAVIDIAN LANGUAGES. More than 25 languages of the Dravidian family are spoken in India, Pakistan, and Sri Lanka (see Map 1); they are divided into four geographic/genetic groups, as shown in Figure 1. Of the above, Tamil, Malayalam, Kannada, and Telugu are literary languages; the rest have oral traditions.

1. Historical relationships. Various scholars have proposed a major subgrouping including South-Central and Central Dravidian (Krishnamurti 1961). However, there is now better evidence to group South and South-Central into a major subgroup vis-à-vis Central and North. The main isoglosses supporting the present subgrouping are given below. (Citations of *DEDR* refer to Burrow and Emeneau 1984.)

(a) $*i\ u > *e\ o\ /\ (C)\_Ca$

(b) The back-formation of $*ñ\bar{a}n$ 'I' (*DEDR* 5160) from $*ñ\bar{a}m$ 'we (inclusive)' (*DEDR* 3647) beside PDr. $*y\bar{a}n$ 'I' (*DEDR* 5160)

Map 1. *Distribution of Languages in South Asia*

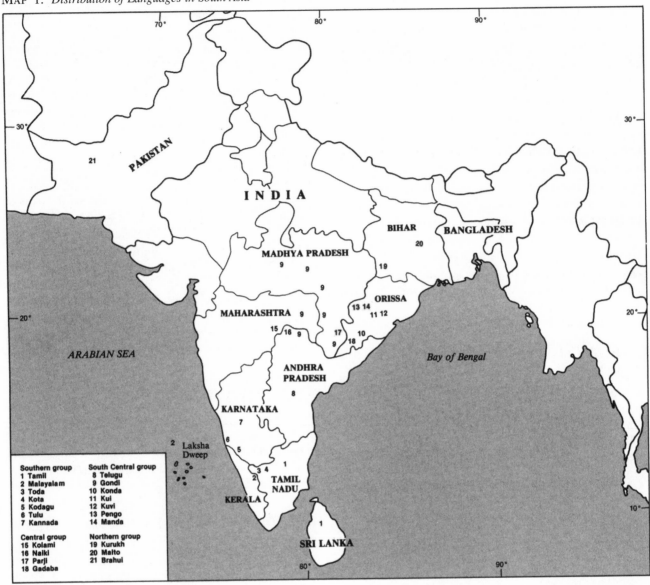

Southern group
1 Tamil
2 Malayalam
3 Toda
4 Kota
5 Kodagu
6 Tulu
7 Kannada

South Central group
8 Telugu
9 Gondi
10 Konda
11 Kui
12 Kuvi
13 Pengo
14 Manda

Central group
15 Kolami
16 Naiki
17 Parji
18 Gadaba

Northern group
19 Kurukh
20 Malto
21 Brahui

Figure 1. *Subgroupings of Dravidian Languages*

Central Dravidian
    Gadaba, Kolami, Naiki, Ollari, Parji
Northern Dravidian
    Brahui, Kurux, Malto
South-Central Dravidian
    Gondi (including Koya), Konda, Kui, Kuvi, Manda, Pengo, Telugu
Southern Dravidian
    Irula, Kannada, Kodagu, Kota, Malayalam, Tamil, Toda, Tulu

(c) The change *c > s > h > Ø in South and South-Central

South Dravidian is distinguished by the innovation of *awaḷ 'she (far)' *iwaḷ 'she (near)' (*DEDR* 1, 410) representing feminine gender, and the loss of the final syllable in *awaṇtu (*DEDR* 1), *iwaṇtu 'he' (*DEDR* 410). Changes such as *ṭ > d, ḍ / V__(V), and the innovation of derived numerals in the female category (e.g. *īr-aḷ 'two women', *DEDR* 474, *mū-aḷ 'three women' *DEDR* 5052) distinguish the Central subgroup from the others. The sound change *k > x / #__V (V = all but i ī) characterizes North Dravidian.

Contact between Old Indo-Aryan-speaking peoples and native Dravidians dates to the middle of the 2nd millennium BCE. Bilingualism through the ages has led not only to extensive lexical borrowing between Dravidian and Indo-Aryan, but also to convergence in several phonological, morphological, and syntactic features (Emeneau 1980). Diffusion from Dravidian into Indo-Aryan is thought to be responsible for the progressive increase in the incidence of retroflex consonants in later Indo-Aryan; the increased use of echo-words and onomatopoetic expressions; compound verbs; dative subject constructions; and changes in noun declension.

Attempts have been made to discover distant relationships of Dravidian with Uralic (Ural-Altaic), Proto-Elamite—or, more recently, Japanese; however, none of these has been established beyond reasonable doubt (Krishnamurti 1969, 1985).

2. Phonology. P[roto-]D[ravidian] had ten vowels, i e a o u plus their long counterparts, and seventeen consonants, including a laryngeal *H as shown in Table 1.

There are no prefixes. Alveolar and retroflex consonants do not begin a root or word. All consonants except r and ẓ can be geminated postvocalically. The vowel-ending roots may take formative suffixes of the shape C, CV, CCV, CCCV. Roots ending in C take formative suffixes of the above types preceded by V_2 = a, i, u. A base-final stop is followed by u. There are no consonant clusters word-initially. Postvocalic clusters are either geminates or sequences of nasal + stop (+ stop).

The obstruents, when intervocalic, had lenis allophones [w d r̠ ḍ s g]; after a nasal, they were voiced stops, and geminates were always voiceless. The descendant languages have maintained this pattern, but have also developed word-initial voicing and aspiration through sound changes and borrowing from Indo-Aryan.

3. Grammar. The following are the shared native syntactic and morphological features of the Dravidian languages. (For reference, see Caldwell 1856, Shanmugam 1971, Subrahmanyam 1971, and Zvelebil 1978).

Dravidian languages are verb-final (SOV); adverbs precede verbs, and adjectives precede nouns; auxiliaries follow the main verb.

A sentence may have a VP or NP predicate, i.e. S → NP + PRED; and PRED → {VP, NP}. The finite verb, inflected for tense, carries agreement with the subject in G[ender/]N[umber]/P[erson] in the 3rd person, but only in number and person in the 1st and 2nd persons. A predicate NP also carries subject agreement in many cases.

The main clause ends in a finite verb with the internal structure stem + tense/mode + GNP; subordinate clauses end in non-finite verbs, such as perfective, durative, conditional, and concessive. A NP + NP clause becomes subordinate when a non-finite form of the verb *ā 'to be' (DEDR 333) or *aHn 'to say' (DEDR 868) is added to it. Quotatives carry the perfective participle of *aHn 'having said' as a complementizer. Sometimes two main verbs are fused as the predicate in a simple sentence (Steever 1988).

Interrogative sentences are formed either by the use of question words, or by adding (in the yes-no type) a question particle *ā to the phrase or clause questioned.

Relative clauses are formed by changing the finite verb to a participle (stem + tense + adjectival suffix), and shifting the head noun to the position following the participle.

In verbal predications, negation can be a part of verb inflection; in nominal predications, use is made of a negative inflected form of *ā, *man 'to be' (DEDR 333, 4778), or of a negative verb *cil 'to be not' (DEDR 2559).

The major grammatical categories are nouns (including pronouns and numerals) and verbs. Most adjectives are nouns in the genitive. There are some basic adjectives which often occur in compounds, e.g. *kem 'red' (DEDR 1931), *weḷ 'white' (DEDR 5496a), *kiṯu 'small' (DEDR 1594). The deictic bases *ā/*aH 'that' (DEDR 1), *ī/*iH 'this' (DEDR 140), *ū/*uH 'yonder' (DEDR 557a), and *yā/*yaH 'which' (DEDR 5151) are used only as modifiers. Demonstrative pronouns denoting person, time, place, quantity, etc. are derived from these roots; e.g. PD *awantu 'that man', *atu 'that woman, thing', *appōẓ(u) 'then' (DEDR 1); *iwantu 'this man', *itu 'this woman, thing', *ippōẓ(u) 'now' (DEDR 410).

Nouns carry gender and number; in the Southern group, a three-way distinction of gender occurs in the singular, e.g. *awan 'he', *awaḷ 'she', *atu 'it'; in plural *awar 'they (human)' and *away 'they (non-human)' are distinguished. South-Central and Central Dravidian show a two-way distinction in the singular and plural: *awantu 'he', *atu 'she, it'; *awar 'they (men, or men and women)'; *away 'they (non-human, or women)'. Telugu and North Dravidian deviate from the above in the plural, i.e. *awar 'they (men and/or women)', *away 'they (non-human)'. It is assumed that South Dravidian innovated *awaḷ in the singular, whereas North Dravidian and Telugu independently added an exclusive semantic cate-

TABLE 1. *Proto-Dravidian Consonants*

	Labial	Dental	Alveolar	Retroflex	Palatal	Velar	Glottal
Obstruents	p	t	t̲	ṭ	c	k	
Nasals	m	n		ṇ	ñ		
Laterals			l	ḷ			
Vibrant			r				
Glides	w			ẓ	y		H

gory of 'women' under *awar*. North Dravidian (Kurux and Malto) also introduced gender in the 1st and 2nd persons through contact with Indo-Aryan. There are two numbers, singular (unmarked) and plural: human *-(V)r* vs. non-human *-k(V)*, *-nk(V)*, *-nkk(V)*; *-ḷ*; *-V(n)kaḷ* (the last is a sequence of two underlying plural morphemes).

Non-nominative cases are added to the oblique stem (formed with one or more of the suffixes *tt, *n, *i, *a*), which also functions as the genitive. The cases reconstructible for PD are nominative (unmarked), accusative, dative, and possibly genitive. Instrumental/locative, sociative, and ablative cases also exist, but are not clearly reconstructible to Proto-Dravidian. A number of postpositions denoting cause, purpose, direction, etc., which are grammaticalized words, are also used in different languages.

The numerals 1 to 5 and 8 to 10 consist of a root + a fused neuter morpheme *t, *tt, *k*, e.g. *on-tu* 'one' (*DEDR* 990), *ir-aṇtu* 'two' (*DEDR* 474), *mū-ntu* 'three' (*DEDR* 5052), *nāl-(k)ku* 'four' (*DEDR* 3655), *caym-tu* 'five' (*DEDR* 2826), *eṇ-ṭṭu* 'eight' (*DEDR* 784), *toḷ-/ *toṇ-* 'nine' (*DEDR* 3532), *paH-tu* 'ten' (*DEDR* 3918); the forms *cātu* 'six' (*DEDR* 2485) and *ēẓ* 'seven' (*DEDR* 910) are also used with neuter (non-human) agreement; a human suffix *-war* is added to the numeral roots when they qualify human nouns, e.g. *mūwar* 'three persons', *mūntu* 'three (non-human)'.

An inflected finite verb consists of a verb stem (simple or complex) + (modal auxiliary) + tense + GNP. An extended verb stem may contain transitive/causative marker + reflexive. There are at least two tenses reconstructible to PD: past and non-past. The NPs which are the constituents of a VP carry case morphemes denoting object, instrument, source, location, etc. generally interpreted in terms of the semantic structure of the verb.

There are many clitics, of which two are reconstructible: *-ā* interrogative and *-ē* emphatic. Each language and subgroup has evolved many others, mostly representing contraction of finite verbs.

Adverbs of time and place are inflected for case like noun stems, but do not carry number and gender. Adverbs are also formed from descriptive adjectives by adding an inflected verb 'to be'. Onomatopoetic words and echo words generally function as adverbs.

[*See also* Kannada; Malayalam; South Asian Languages; Tamil; *and* Telugu.]

BIBLIOGRAPHY

Burrow, Thomas, and Murray B. Emeneau. 1984. *A Dravidian etymological dictionary*. 2d ed. Oxford: Clarendon Press.

Caldwell, Robert. 1856. *A comparative grammar of the Dravidian or South-Indian family of languages*. London: Harrison. 3d ed., London: Routledge and Kegan Paul, 1913. Reprinted, Madras: University of Madras, 1956.

Emeneau, Murray B. 1980. *Language and linguistic area*. Stanford, Calif.: Stanford University Press.

Krishnamurti, Bh. 1961. *Telugu verbal bases: A comparative and descriptive study*. (University of California publications in linguistics, 24.) Berkeley: University of California Press.

Krishnamurti, Bh. 1969. Comparative Dravidian studies. In *Current trends in linguistics*, vol. 5, *Linguistics in South Asia*, edited by Thomas A. Sebeok, pp. 309–333. The Hague: Mouton.

Krishnamurti, Bh. 1985. An overview of comparative Dravidian studies since *Current trends 5* (1969). In *For Gordon H. Fairbanks* (Oceanic Linguistics, Special publication no. 20), edited by Veneeta Z. Acson and Richard L. Leed, pp. 212–231. Honolulu: University of Hawaii Press.

Krishnamurti, Bh. 1997. Proto-Dravidian Laryngeal *H revisited. *PILC Journal of Dravidic Studies* 7.145–65.

Krishnamurti, Bh. 2001. *Comparative Dravidian Linguistics: Current perspectives*. London: Oxford University Press.

Shanmugam, S. V. 1971. *Dravidian nouns: A comparative study*. Annamalainagar: Annamalai University.

Steever, Sanford B. 1988. *The serial verb formation in the Dravidian languages*. (Motilal Banarsi Dass series in linguistics, 4.) Delhi: Motilal Banarsi Dass.

Subrahmanyam, P. S. 1971. *Dravidian verb morphology: A comparative study*. Annamalainagar: Annamalai University.

Zvelebil, Kamil. 1978. *A sketch of comparative Dravidian*

morphology, vol. 1. (Janua linguarum, Series practica, 180.) The Hague: Mouton.

BH. KRISHNAMURTI

LANGUAGE LIST

Allar: also called Chatans. 350 speakers in India. Kerala, Palghat district.

Aranadan: also called Eranadans. 236 speakers remain in India, in Tamil Nadu; Karnataka; Kerala, Calicut and Palghat districts. Bilingualism in Malayalam.

Badaga: also called Badag, Badagu, Badugu, Baduga, Vadagu. 171,000 speakers in India, in Tamil Nadu, Madras-Nilgiri, Kunda hills. 200 villages. May be a dialect of Kannada.

Bazigar: 100 speakers in India, in Gujarat; Himachal Pradesh; Jammu and Kashmir; Madhya Pradesh; Karnataka.

Bellari: spoken in India. Related to Tulu and Koraga languages.

Bharia: also called Bhar, Bharat, Bhumia, Bhumiya, Paliha. 196,512 speakers in India. reported to speak a variety of Hindi. Devanagari script is used.

Brahui: also called Brahuidi, Birahui, Brahuigi, Kur Galli. 2,210,000 speakers in Pakistan, Afghanistan, Iran, and Turkmenistan. In Pakistan: 2,000,000 speakers, south central, Quetta and Kalat regions, east Baluchistan and Sind Provinces. Dialects are Jharawan, Kalat, Sarawan. Kalat is the standard dialect, Jharawan is spoken in the lowland. Some bilingualism in Western Balochi. Nastaliq script is used. In Afghanistan: 200,000 speakers among the Baluchi in the south, from Shorawak to Chakhansoor. In Iran: Eastern. Dialects are Jharawan, Kalat, Sarawan. Brahui in Iran are reported to speak Western Balochi now.

Chenchu: also called Chenchucoolam, Chenchwar, Chenswar, Choncharu. 28,754 speakers in India, in Andhra Pradesh, highest concentration in Kurnool district, Nallamalla hills; Karnataka; Orissa. Entirely monolingual. Telugu script is used.

Duruwa: also called Dhurwa, Dhruva, Durva, Parji, Parjhi, Paraja, Parajhi, Thakara, Tagara, Tugara. 90,000 speakers in India. Ethnic population: 100,000 as of 1986, 2/3 in Bastar, 1/3 in Koraput. Madhya Pradesh, Bastar district, southeastern Jagdalpur Tahsil; Orissa, Koraput district. Dialects are Tiriya, Nethanar, Dharba, Kukanar, all inherently intelligible. Nethanar dialect is central. Monolinguals include children. Halbi is the second language. Part of the ethnic group speaks Halbi as first language (around Jagdalpur, Bastar district); 1% speak Oriya; less than 2% use Bhatri (northern Bastar district). Hindi is the state language, but it is not well known except by the educated. 90% of the ethnic group speak Parji as mother tongue. Parji is spoken by the Madiya for communicating with the Dhurwa people. Devanagari and Oriya scripts are used.

Gadaba Ollar, Pottangi: also called Ollar Gadaba, Ollari, Ollaro, Hallari, Allar, Hollar Gadbas, San Gadaba, Gadba, Sano, Kondekar, Kondkor. 15,000 speakers in India, in Orissa, Koraput districts, Pottangi and Nandapur blocks. Adivasi Oriya is the main second language. Bilingual proficiency in Oriya is limited. Telugu is also used. Speakers have a positive attitude toward Gadaba. Oriya script is used in Orissa, Telugu script in Andhra Pradesh.

Gadaba Ollar, Salur: 10,000 speakers in India, in Andhra Pradesh, Vizianagaram, Vishakapatnam, and Srikakulam districts. 93% to 98% intelligibility among dialects. Bilingual proficiency in Telugu is limited. Used at home, in the village, for religion. Positive attitudes toward this language. Telugu script is used.

Gondi, Northern: also called Gondi, Gaudi, Gondiva, Gondwadi, Goondile, Goudwal, Ghond, Godi, Gondu, Goudi. 1,954,000 speakers in India in Madhya Pradesh, Betul, Chindwara, Seoni, Mandla, Balaghat districts; state of Maharashtra, Amravati, Wardha, Nagpur, Bhandara, Yavatmal districts. Dialects are Betul, Chindwara, Mandla, Seoni, Amravati, Bhandara, Nagpur, Yavatmal. Inherent intelligibility between dialects 94% to 97%. Speakers tested in some other dialects understood Amravati 94% to 97%; Betul 83% to 96%, and Seoni 82% to 97%. 58% to 78% intelligibility of Southern Gondi. Some bilingualism in Hindi in Madhya Pradesh, and Marathi in Maharashtra, but proficiency is not very high. All ages. Speakers have a positive attitude toward Gondi.

Gondi, Southern: also called Telugu Gondi. 600,000 speakers in India in Andhra Pradesh, Adilabad district; Maharashtra; southern Yavatmal; southern Chandrapur; and southeastern Garhichiroli districts. Dialects are Sironcha, Nirmal (Adilabad), Bhamragarh, Utnoor, Aheri, Rajura, Etapally Gondi. Sironcha is the dialect understood best by the others, with 90% to 98% intelligibility. 49% to 58% intelligibility of Northern Gondi. Telugu script is used.

Holiya: also called Holar, Holari, Hole, Holian, Holu, Golari-Kannada, Gohllaru. 8,000 speakers in India in Madhya Pradesh; Maharashtra; Karnataka. It is reported that 50% of Holiya speakers speak some Telugu as second language: 60% of speakers are adults, 30% children.

Irula: also called Eravallan, Erukala, Irava, Irular, Irular Mozhi, Iruliga, Iruligar, Korava, Kad Chensu. 75,000 speakers in India, in Tamil Nadu, Nilgiri, Coimbatore, Periyar, Salem, Chengai Anna districts; Karnataka; Kerala, Palghat district; Andhra Pradesh. Dialects are Mele Nadu Irula, Vette Kada Irula, Irula Pallar, Northern Irula. Vette Kada had 73% intelligibility with Mele Nadu, Northern Irula had 83% intelligibility with Mele Nadu. Irula is not inherently intelligible with Tamil. Nearly all speak some Tamil, 44% Kannada, 32% Badaga. Tamil proficiency is limited. Irula is used in the home, village, in market and politics with other Irula people, and for praying. Speakers have a positive attitude toward Irula, and literature development.

Kadar: also called Kada, Kadir. 2,265 speakers in India, in

Kerala, Ernakulam, Palghat, and Trichur districts; Andhra Pradesh; Tamil Nadu, Coimbatore district. In 1975 described as close to Malayalam, but a separate language. In 1994 described as close to Tamil. Malayalam or Tamil spoken with outsiders.

Kaikadi: also called Kokadi, Kaikai, Kaikadia. 11,846 speakers in India, in Maharashtra, Jalgaon district; Karnataka.

Kamar: 23,456 speakers in India, in Madhya Pradesh, Raipur and Rewa districts; Maharashtra. Speakers are reported to speak Chhattisgarhi among themselves and Hindi with others.

Kanikkaran: also called Kanikkar, Kannikan, Kannikaran, Kannikharan, Malampashi. 25,000 speakers in India, in Kerala, Calicut, Ernakulam, Quilon, Trivandrum districts, Neyyattinkara and Nedumangadu Taluks; Tamil Nadu, Tirunelveli district. 90% of the people use Malayalam as second language, 10% use Tamil.

Kannada: also called Kanarese, Canarese, Banglori, Madrassi. 35,346,000 speakers in India, in Karnataka; Andhra Pradesh; Tamil Nadu; Maharashtra. Dialects include Bijapur, Jeinu Kuruba, Aine Kuruba. About twenty dialects; Badaga may be one. Kannada script is similar to Telugu script. National language.

Khirwar: also called Khirwara, Kherwari. 34,250 speakers in India, in Madhya Pradesh.

Kodagu: also called Coorge, Kadagi, Khurgi, Kotagu, Kurja, Kurug, Kodava Thak. 122,000 speakers in India, in Karnataka, Coorg (Kodagu) district, around Mercara, bordering on Malayalam to the south. May be more than one language. 66% intelligibility of Malappuram Paniya. 80% of speakers use Kannada as second language. Kannada script is used.

Kolami, Northwestern: also called Kolamboli, Kulme, Kolam, Kolmi, Kolamy. 50,000 speakers in India, in Maharashtra, Yavatmal, Wardha, and Nanded districts; Andhra Pradesh; Madhya Pradesh. Dialects are Madka-Kinwat, Pulgaon, Wani, Maregaon. Northwestern and Southeastern Kolami are not inherently intelligible. Northwestern Kolami is probably not intelligible with Duruwa, Sallur Gadaba Ollar languages, or Pottangi Gadaba Ollar. Nearly all adults are somewhat bilingual in Marathi, Telugu, or Southern/Northern Gondi. Proficiency is limited in Marathi; actually a nonstandard Marathi, also used by mother tongue Marathi speakers in the region. Northwestern Kolami is used within the caste; the state language for outside communication.

Kolami, Southeastern: 10,000 speakers in India, in Andhra Pradesh, Adilabad district; Maharashtra, Chandrapur, and Nanded districts. Dialects are Metla—Kinwat, Utnur, Asifabad, Naiki. Not intelligible with Northwestern Kolami. In 1950 another dialect was reported in Chinnoor and Sirpur Taluks of Adilabad district. Naiki is different from Naikri. People in Maharashtra are not functionally bilingual in Telugu or Marathi. The Arakh speak the Naiki dialect as mother tongue.

Konda-Dora: also called Porja. 32,000 speakers in India, in Konda-Dora in Andhra Pradesh, Visianagaram, Srikakulam, East Godavari districts; Kubi in Orissa, Koraput district; Assam. Dialects are Konda-Dora (Konda), Kubi, which are inherently intelligible with each other. Bilingualism is limited in Telugu. Many speakers along roads through Araku are competent in Adiwasi Oriya, others are more limited.

Koraga, Korra: also called Koragar, Koragara, Korangi, Korra. Spoken in India. Karnataka, Dakshin Kannad district; Kerala, Cannanore and Kasargod districts; Tamil Nadu. Related to Tulu and Bellari. Not intelligible with Mudu Koraga, Tulu, or Kannada. Structural differences in phonology with Mudu Koraga.

Koraga, Mudu: also called Mu:du. Spoken in India. Kerala. Not intelligible with Korra Koraga, Tulu, or Kannada. Structural differences in phonology with Korra Koraga.

Kota: also called Kotta, Kowe-Adiwasi, Kother-Tamil. 2,000 speakers in India, Tamil Nadu, Madras; Nilgiri hills, Trichikadi village, and a few others around Kokkal Kotagiri. Tamil script is used.

Koya: also called Koi, Koi Gondi, Kavor, Koa, Koitar, Koyato, Kaya, Koyi, Raj Koya. 330,000 speakers in India. Dialects are Malakanagiri Koya, Podia Koya (Gotte Koya), Chintoor Koya (Dorla Koitur), Jaganathapuram Koya (Gommu Koya, Godavari Koya), Dorli (Korla, Dora, Dor Koi, Dora Koi, Dorla Koitur, Dorla Koya). Chintoor is the linguistic center. The Malakanagiri and Podia varieties are more divergent. Telugu is the second language but bilingual proficiency is low. Telugu, Oriya, and Devanagari scripts are used. Roman script is reportedly preferred by Koya leaders.

Kudiya: 2,462 speakers in India, in Kerala, Cannanore district; Karnataka, Coorg and South Kannara districts; Tamil Nadu. Tulu, Kodagu, Kannada, Malayalam spoken with outsiders. Kannada and Malayalam scripts.

Kui: also called Kandh, Khondi, Khond, Khondo, Kanda, Kodu, Kodulu, Kuinga, Kuy. 717,000 speakers in India, in Orissa, Phulbani, Koraput, Ganjam districts, Udayagiri area in Ganjam; Andhra Pradesh; Madhya Pradesh; Tamil Nadu. Dialects are Khondi, Gumsai. Spoken by the Dal and Sitha Kandha as mother tongue.

Kurichiya: also called Kurichia, Kurichchia. 29,375 speakers in India, in Kerala, Wynad, Cannanore districts; Tamil Nadu, Dharampuri district. Language shift taking place to Malayalam in Kerala and Kannada in Tamil Nadu. Listed as an endangered language. Further study is being done at Annamalai University.

Kurumba: also called Korambar, Kuramwari, Kurumar, Kurumbar, Kuruba, Kurumvari, Kuremban, Kurubas Kuruban, Kurubar, Kuruma, Kuruman, Kurumans, Kurumbas, Kurumban, Palu Kurumba, Nonstandard Kannada, Southern Kannada, Canarese. 150,000 speakers in India. Dialects are inherently intelligible among speakers. Limited bilingual proficiency in Tamil and Kannada.

Kurumba, Alu: also called Alu Kurumba Nonstandard Kannada, Pal Kurumba, Hal Kurumba. 2,500 speakers in India, in Tamil Nadu, eastern side of Nilgiri hills. Limited bilingualism in Tamil, Kannada, and Southern Kannada.

Kurumba, Betta: also called Betta Kurumba Nonstandard Tamil, Kadu Kurumba, Urali Kurumba. 10,000 speakers in India, in Tamil Nadu, Nilgiri district; Karnataka, Mysore district, north side of Nilgiri hills, just east of Kerala border; Kerala, Wynad district. A nonstandard variety of Tamil or Kannada. May or may not be the same as Betta Kuruba in Coorg district. Betta Kurumba has been listed as endangered. It is being studied at Annamalai University.

Kurumba, Jennu: also called Jennu Kurumba Nonstandard Kannada, Jen Kurumba, Ten Kurumba, Jennu Nudi, Naikan, Kattu Nayaka, Naik Kurumba. 35,000 speakers in India. May or may not be the same as Jeinu Kuruba, a variety of Kannada. Limited bilingual proficiency in Kannada, Malayalam, and Tamil. Speakers have a positive attitude toward Kurumba.

Kurumba, Mullu: 6,000 speakers in India, in Tamil Nadu, Nilgiri district; Kerala, Wynad district.

Kurux: also called Uraon, Kurukh, Kunrukh, Kadukali, Kurka, Oraon, Urang, Kisan, Kunha, Kunhar, Kunuk, Kunna, Kuda, Kora, Koda, Kola, Morva, Birhor. 2,053,000 speakers in India and Bangladesh. In India: Bihar; Madhya Pradesh; Western Bengal; Orissa; Assam; Tripura. Dialects are Oraon, Kisan. Kisan and Oraon have 73% intelligibility. Oraon is becoming standardized. Related to Kumarbhag Paharia. Different from Nepali Kurux. In Bangladesh: Distinct from Nepali Kurux.

Kurux, Nepali: also called Dhangar, Jhanger, Janghard, Jangad, Uraon, Orau, Oraon. Spoken in Nepal in eastern Terai, Janakpur zone, Dhanusa district. Different from Kurux of India and Bangladesh. Bilingualism in whatever Indo-Aryan language is spoken in area, for example, Maithili, Nagpuri, Bhojpuri, Assamese, and so on.

Kuvi: also called Kuwi, Kuvinga, Kuvi Kond, Kond, Khondi, Khondh, Jatapu. 300,000 speakers in India, in Orissa, mainly Koraput district, also Kalahandi, Ganjam, and Phulbani districts; Andhra Pradesh, Visakhapatnam, Vizianagaram, Srikakkulam districts. The Dongria and Kuvi subgroups speak Kuvi as mother tongue.

Malankuravan: also called Malaikuravan, Male Kuravan, Malankudi. 7,339 speakers in India, in Tamil Nadu, Kanyakumari district; Kerala. Bilingualism in Tamil.

Malapandaram: also called Malapantaram, Malepantaram, Hill Pantaram, Pandaram Basha. 3,147 speakers in India, in Kerala, Kottayam, Ernakulam, and Quilon districts; Tamil Nadu.

Malaryan: also called Malai Arayan, Maley Arayan, Male Arayans, Malayarayan, Arayans, Karingal, Vazhiyammar. 27,716 speakers in India, in Kerala, Ernakulam, Kottayam, and Trichur districts; Tamil Nadu. Bilingualism in Malayalam.

Malavedan: also called Malavetan, Towetan, Vedans. 9,533 speakers in India, in Kerala, Ernakulam, Kottayam, Quilon, Trivandrum districts; Tamil Nadu, Kanyakumari, and Tirunelveli districts. Dialects are Vetan, Vettuvan. Bilingualism in Tamil.

Malayalam: also called Alealum, Malayalani, Malayali, Malean, Maliyad, Mallealle, Mopla. 35,706,000 speakers in India, Singapore, Fiji, Malaysia, Qatar, Bahrain, Israel, Singapore, United Arab Emirates, United Kingdom. In India: 35,351,000 speakers in Kerala, Laccadive Islands, and neighboring states. Dialects are Malabar, Nagari-Malayalam, Malayalam, South Kerala, Central Kerala, North Kerala, Kayavar, Namboodiri, Moplah, Pulaya, Nasrani, Nayar. Caste and communal dialects: Namboodiri, Nayar, Moplah, Pulaya, Nasrani. State language of Kerala. The Cochin Jews in Kerala speak Malayalam. Malayalam script is used. National language. In Singapore: Ethnic population: 14,000 as of 1993. In Fiji: Ethnic population: 313.

Manda: spoken in India in Orissa, Kalahandi district.

Manna-Dora: 18,964 speakers in India in Andhra Pradesh, East Godavari, Srikakulam, Visakhapatnam districts; Tamil Nadu. Telugu script is used.

Mannan: also called Manne, Mannyod. 58,028 speakers in India in Kerala, Idukki district, Devikulam Taluk; Tamil Nadu, Kanyakumari and Tirunelvgeli districts. 70% intelligibility with Malayalam.

Maria: also called Hill Maria, Madi, Madiya, Madia, Modh, Modi. 134,000 speakers in India. Dialects are Abujmaria (Abujhmadia, Abujmariya, Abujhmaria, Abujmar Maria), Bhamani Maria (Bhamani), Adewada, Etapally Maria. Etapally Maria is apparently understood by all. 76% to 77% intelligibility of other Gondi varieties. Muria Gondi is intelligible to Abujmaria around Narainpur area, but not elsewhere and is said to be distinct from Maria of Chanda district in Maharashtra. Maria is intelligible with Abujmaria, and the speech of the Gatte Maria, an ethnic group. Most men can speak some Muria, Halbi, or Hindi. Used nearly always in all domains. Speakers have negative attitudes toward the Gondi varieties mentioned above.

Maria, Dandami: also called Bison Horn Maria, Maria Gond, Madiya, Dhuru, Dandami Madiya. 150,000 speakers in India in Madhya Pradesh, central and southern Bastar district, Dantewara Tahsil. Dialects are Geedam, Sukma (Suka). May be more than one language. A separate language from Northern Gondi, Southern Gondi, Abujmaria, and Koya. Spoken by all ages.

Mukha-Dora: also called Reddi-Dora, Conta-Reddi, Reddi, Riddi, Nuka-Dora, Nooka Dora, Mukha Dhora. 17,456 speakers in India in Andhra Pradesh, Vishakhapatnam, Srikakulam, Vizianagaram districts. Bilingualism in Adivasi Oriya.

Muria, Eastern: spoken in India in Madhya Pradesh, Northeastern Bastar district, northwestern Koraput district. Dialects are Raigarh, Lanjoda. 95% intelligibility between dialects; 73% to 83% of Western Muria; 19% to 34% of Northern Gondi; 35% of Dandami Maria. All ages. All domains.

Muria, Far Western: spoken in India in Maharashtra, northern Garhichiroli district, Kurkhed Taluk. 79% to 88% intelligibility of other Muria languages; 74% of Dandami Maria, 0% to 34% of Northern Gondi, 6% to 50% of Southern Gondi, 2% to 70% of Maria. All ages. All domains.

Muria, Western: also called Jhoria, Mudia, Muria Gondi. 12,898 speakers in India, in Madhya Pradesh, northern and western Bastar district. Dialects are Sonapal, Banchapai, Dhanora. 80% to 96% intelligibility among dialects, 69% to 73% with Eastern Muria; 51% to 78% with Far Western Muria. Not inherently intelligible with Dandami Maria, Northern Gondi, Southern Gondi, or Maria. All ages. All domains.

Muthuvan: also called Mudavan, Muduvar, Mudugar, Mutuvar, Muduvan, Muduva. 12,219 speakers in India. 80% intelligibility with Malayalam.

Nagarchal: also called Nagar, Nagarchi. 7,100 speakers in India in Madhya Pradesh; Maharashtra; Rajasthan.

Paharia, Kumarbhag: also called Malto, Malti, Maltu, Maler, Mal, Mad, Paharia, Pahariya, Kumar. 12,000 speakers in India. Inherent intelligibility with Mal Paharia is inadequate [*see* Bengali-Assamese]. Related to Kurux. Low bilingualism in Hindi and Bengali. Kumarbhag Paharia is actively used in all domains. Speakers have a positive attitude toward this language.

Paharia, Sauria: also called Malto, Malti, Maltu, Maler, Sawriya Malto. 74,000 speakers in India. Dialects are Sahibganj, Godda, Hiranpur, Litipara (Chatgam). Inherent intelligibility with Kumarbhag Paharia is inadequate. Related to Kurux.

Paliyan: also called Palaya, Palayan, Paliyar, Palliyar, Poliyar, Palleyan, Palani, Makkal, Malai, Seramar. 5,438 speakers in India in Kerala, Idukki district; Tamil Nadu, Nadyraum Tahavur, Pudukkotai, Tiruneveli, Coimbatore districts.

Paniya: also called Pania, Paniyan, Panyah, Nil. 63,827 speakers in India in Kerala, Wynad, Kozhikode, Cannanore, Malapuram districts; Tamil Nadu, west of Nilgiris hills; Karnataka. Intelligibility of Malappura Paniya by Kodagu is 66%. State languages: Malayalam, Tamil, or Kannada used with non-Paniya speakers. Paniya used with Paniya speakers at home and for religion. Christians pray in Malayalam. Malayalam script is used in Kerala, Tamil script in Tamil Nadu, Kannada script in Karnataka.

Pardhan: also called Pradhan, Pradhani. 116,919 speakers in India. Probably more than one language. Most speak Hindi in Madhya Pradesh, Marathi in Maharashtra.

Pengo: also called Pengu, Hengo. 1,254 speakers in India, in Orissa, Koraput district, Kashipur, Pappadahandi, Nowrangapur, and Nandapur Tahsils, Kalahandi district. Dialects are Indi, Awe, Manda.

Ravula: also called Adiya, Adiyan, Yoruba, Yerava, Panjiri Yerava. 27,413 speakers in India, in Karnataka, Coorg (Kodagu) district; Kerala, Wayanad, and Cannanore districts. 93% to 94% dialect intelligibility between Yerava and Adiya dialects. Bilingual proficiency in Kannada (in Karnataka) and Malayalam (in Kerala) is limited. Vigorous language use. Speakers have positive attitudes toward Ravula. Kannada script is used in Karnataka; Malayalam script in Kerala.

Savara: spoken in India in Andhra Pradesh; Orissa. Savara indigenous, Oriya, Telugu scripts are used.

Sholaga: also called Sholiga, Sholigar, Kadu Sholigar, Soliga, Solaga, Soligar. 24,000 speakers in India in Karnataka, Mysore district, Biligiri Rangana hills; Tamil Nadu.

Tamil: also called Tamalsan, Tambul, Tamili, Tamal, Damulian. 66,000,000 speakers in India, Sri Lanka, Malaysia, Singapore, Mauritius, Fiji, Bahrain, Germany, Netherlands, Qatar, Réunion, South Africa, Thailand, United Arab Emirates, and United Kingdom. In India: 61,527,000 speakers in Tamil Nadu and neighboring states. Dialects are Adi Dravida, Aiyar, Aiyangar, Arava, Burgandi, Kasuva, Kongar, Madrasi, Pattapu Bhasha, Tamil, Sri Lanka Tamil, Malaya Tamil, Burma Tamil, South Africa Tamil, Tigalu, Harijan, Sanketi, Hebbar, Mandyam Brahmin, Secunderabad Brahmin. Kasuva is a jungle tribe dialect. Burgandi speakers are nomadic. Aiyar and Aiyangar are Brahmin dialects. National language. In Sri Lanka: Northern and northeastern coasts, a few pockets in the south. In Peninsular Malaysia: Bilingualism in Malay, English. In Singapore: Ethnic population: 111,000 as of 1993. 19% speak English at home. National language. In Mauritius: Often used in government and politics. In Fiji: Ethnic population: 6,631.

Telugu: also called Telegu, Andhra, Gentoo, Tailangi, Telangire, Telgi, Tengu, Terangi, Tolangan. 69,666,000 speakers in India, Fiji, Bahrain, Malaysia, Bahrain, Singapore, and United Arab Emirates. In India: 69,634,000 speakers in Andhra Pradesh and neighboring states. Dialects are Berad, Dasari, Dommara, Golari, Kamathi, Komtao, Konda-Reddi, Salewari, Telangana, Telugu, Vadaga, Srikakula, Vishakapatnam, East Godaveri, Rayalseema, Nellore, Guntur. Yanadi and Bagata are ethnic groups speaking Telugu as mother tongue. Telugu script is used. National language. In Fiji: Ethnic population: 2,008.

Toda: also called Todi, Tuda. 600 speakers in India, in Orissa; Tamil Nadu, Nilgiri hills, Kunda hills.

Tulu: also called Tal, Thalu, Tilu, Tuluva Bhasa, Tullu, Thulu. 1,949,000 speakers in India, in Andhra Pradesh; Kerala; Tamil Nadu; Maharashtra; Karnataka; Meghalaya. Dialects are Tulu, Bellari. Bellari may be a separate language.

Ullatan: also called Katan, Kattalan, Kochuvelan, Ulladan.

12,687 speakers in India, in Kerala, Palghat, Trichur, Ernakulam, Kottayam, Quilon, Alleppey, Trivandrum districts.

Urali: also called Oorazhi, Uraly, Urli. 18,257 speakers in India, in Tamil Nadu, Periyar district, Sathayamangalam area, east of Nilgiri district; Kerala, Idukki, Wynad districts. Reported in 1991 to be a distinct speech variety, sharing features with Tamil, Irula, and Kannada.

Vishavan: also called Malarkuti. 150 speakers in India, in Kerala, Ernakulam, Kottayam, Trichur districts.

Waddar: also called Vadari, Werder. 61,000 speakers in India, in Andhra Pradesh; Karnataka; Maharashtra, Jalgaon district.

Yerukula: also called Yerukala, Yarukula, Yerkula, Yerukla, Erukala, Korava, Yerukala-Korava, Yerukula-Bhasha, Eruku Bhasha, Korchi, Kurutha, Kurru Bhasha. 300,000 speakers in India. Closely related to Ravula and Irula. Some regions have low bilingual proficiency in Telugu—higher in Andhra Pradesh and among educated adults. In Andhra Pradesh, increasing use in home, among friends, religion. In Rayalseema and Telengana regions, use is even greater. Fairly vigorous language use. Strong positive attitude toward Yerukula. Telugu script is used.   B. Grimes

D-STRUCTURE. *See* Levels of Representation.

DUAL. *See* Number; Agreement; Semantics; *and* Morphology.

DURATIVE. *See* Aspect.

DUTCH. Modern Standard Dutch is the official language of the Netherlands, and one of the official languages of Belgium—where it is often called *Flemish,* and competes with French. Afrikaans, spoken in South Africa, is a direct descendant of Dutch. The number of native speakers in Holland and Belgium together is approximately twenty million. Dutch is also spoken to some extent in Surinam (formerly Dutch Guyana) and in the Netherlands Antilles. It had some influence on the creole languages in those areas; it also influenced the standardized form of Malay that is now the official language of Indonesia.

In the Netherlands, the usage of standard Dutch is widespread. There still exists a remarkable variety of dialects, but active dialect speakers are declining in numbers. (The same is true of Frisian, the only other language spoken in the Netherlands.) Politically as well as linguistically, the situation in Belgium is more complex. Present-day Dutch in the Netherlands is the outcome of two major developments: the rise of Amsterdam as the political center of the Dutch Republic, and the mass immigrations of speakers of southern dialects after the fall of Antwerp in 1585.

Historically (cf. van Loey 1970), Dutch belongs to the so-called Low German dialects, and contrasts with the varieties of High German that formed the standard language of Germany; cf. Dutch *appel,* English *apple,* but German *Apfel* with [pf]. With German, however, Dutch shares the devoicing of word-final consonants: Dutch *rond* 'round' (adjective) and Ger. *rund* with final [t], but Eng. *round* with final [d]. A peculiar development is the change of Germanic [g] to the velar fricative [x]: Dutch *goed* 'good' [xut], but Ger. *gut* [gut] and Eng. *good* [gud]. Dutch retained many Germanic words that have disappeared from English, but the number of words of Romance origin in its vocabulary is also considerable. Sometimes a Germanic and a Romance word coexist: *verhouding* and *relatie* 'relation'.

In its morphology, Dutch is similar to English in the loss of inflectional endings and case endings. In the syntax of words, phrases, and clauses, it is similar to German in all fundamental respects.

A comprehensive survey of Dutch grammar is Haeseryn et al. 1997. A useful practical grammar is Donaldson 1996.

1. Phonology. The vowels and consonants of Dutch are shown in Tables 1 and 2, respectively.

The consonant system is comparatively simple. Word-final devoicing leads to morphophonemic alternations in the nominal and verbal paradigms; the feature [voice] also plays an important role in rules for assimilation in compound words and across word boundaries.

The difference between long and short vowels is contrastive with mid and low vowels: *boom* 'tree' vs. *bom* 'bomb'; *baas* 'boss' vs. *bas* 'bass'; *beek* 'brook' vs. *bek* 'beak'. The diphthongs are rising: [ɛi] is the counterpart of Eng. and Ger. [ai], as in *rijden* 'ride', Ger. *reiten*.

2. Morphology. Nominal as well as verbal paradigms have been drastically simplified since the period of Middle Dutch. Case endings are absent, except for the occasional use of the genitive *'s,* and gender distinctions have been reduced to two. The majority of nouns select the determiner *de,* but original neuters select the determiner *het.* The distinction between strong and weak inflection is preserved to some extent; adjectives take the strong

TABLE 1. *Consonant Phonemes of Dutch.* Common orthographic equivalents are given in brackets.

	Labial	Alveolar	Palatal	Velar	Uvular	Glottal
Stops						
Voiceless	p	t		k		
Voiced	b	d				
Fricatives						
Voiceless	f	s		x ⟨ch⟩		h
Voiced	v	z		γ ⟨g⟩		
Nasal	m	n		ŋ ⟨ng⟩		
Liquid		l			ʀ ⟨r⟩	
Glide	ʋ ⟨w⟩		j			

TABLE 2. *Vowel Phonemes of Dutch*

	Front		Central		Back	
	Unrounded	Rounded	Unrounded	Rounded	Unrounded	Rounded
High	i	ü				u
Higher mid	ɪ	ö				o
Lower mid	e		ə	œ		ɔ
Low	ε		a		ɑ	
Diphthongs	εi			ʌü		ɑu

(non-suffixed) form only in noun phrases with the indefinite determiner *een* when the noun is of the neuter category. Compare:

(1a)   *het grote paard*   *de grote koe*
       'the big horse'   'the big cow'

(1b)   *een groot paard*   *een grote koe*
       'a big horse'   'a big cow'

(1c)   *de grote paarden*   *de grote koeien*
       'the big horses'   'the big cows'

The plural of nouns is formed by adding *-en* to the stem; it is usually pronounced without the final *-n.* The ending *-s* has replaced *-en* in a number of native words and is common in loanwords. Dutch orthography preserves the distinction between word-final plosives that are underlyingly voiced, and those that are voiceless throughout.

The paradigm of the present and past tenses of the regular (or weak) verb *spelen* 'to play' is given in Table 3.

After stems ending in a voiceless consonant, the ending of the past tense is *-te,* and that of the past participle is *-t:* thus *ik gokte* 'I gambled', *ik heb gegokt* 'I have gambled'. As in other Germanic languages, so-called strong verbs form their past tense by vowel change—e.g.

TABLE 3. *Present Tense and Past Tense in Dutch*

	Present	Past
Singular		
ik	*speel*	*speelde*
jij/u	*speelt*	*speelde*
hij/zij/het	*speelt*	*speelde*
Plural		
wij	*spelen*	*speelden*
jullie	*spelen*	*speelden*
zij	*spelen*	*speelden*
Participle		
	spelend	*gespeeld*

geven, gaf, gegeven, corresponding to Eng. *give, gave, given.*

Word formation is of a mixed type. Inflection and derivation are predominantly suffixal, but many derivations are lexicalized and non-productive. One of the most productive suffixal derivations is the formation of diminutives, e.g. *paard+je* 'small horse'. Prefixation is more transparent, and occurs frequently in the formation of verbs. The following verbs are all derived from the intransitive verb *werk+en* 'to work': *be+werken* 'to work (the land), to adapt (a text)'; *ver+werken* 'to process, to digest'; *door+werken* 'to work one's way through'; *te-*

gen+werken 'to obstruct'. Nominal compounding is frequent and productive, e.g. *huis* 'house', *huis+dier* 'domestic animal, pet'.

3. Syntax. In the structure of its sentences, Dutch is a typical continental Germanic language. In declarative sentences, the finite verb (which agrees in number with the subject) is in second position in the main clause, and is typically separated by adverbials from its immediate complements. This "Verb Second" phenomenon also occurs in Scandinavian languages, but is more conspicuous in Dutch and German.

(2a) *Jan wast de auto.*
      'John washes the car.'
(2b) *Jan wast morgen de auto.*
      'John will wash the car tomorrow.'
(2c) *Jan heeft de auto gewassen.*
      'John has washed the car.'

The structure of these sentences becomes transparent under the assumption that the clause is basically verb-final—which is the ordering that actually occurs in the dependent clause:

(3a) *omdat Jan de auto wast*
      'because John washes the car'
(3b) *omdat Jan morgen de auto wast*
      'because John will wash the car tomorrow'
(3c) *omdat Jan de auto heeft gewassen*
      'because John has washed the car'

In dependent clauses, constituents are ordered from right to left, with the main verb as the focal point; in the independent clause, that ordering is broken up by moving the finite verb. Thus compare:

(4a) *Jan   gaat morgen   met de   auto naar*
      John goes tomorrow with the car to

      Amsterdam.
      A.

(4b) *als Jan morgen   met de   auto naar*
      when John tomorrow with the car to

      Amsterdam gaat
      A.   goes

In complex sentences, verbs from different clauses are strung together—a phenomenon known as Clause Union

or Verb Raising. This is obligatory with some verbs, and optional with others. Thus either (5b) or (5c) are acceptable:

(5a) *Jan   probeerde* [*de auto te besturen*].
      John tried   the car to steer
      'John tried to drive the car.'
(5b) *Jan   heeft geprobeerd* [*de auto te besturen*].
      John has   tried   the car to steer
(5c) *Jan   heeft de   auto* [*proberen te besturen*].
      John has   the car   try   to steer

Ex. 5c also shows another particularity: when verbs are strung together, the infinitive replaces the past participle in the perfect tense.

In declarative main clauses, the sentence-initial position can be occupied either by the grammatical subject or by other constituents. Under appropriate contextual conditions, the following sentences are equally acceptable in the meaning 'I have given that book to John':

(6a) *Ik heb aan Jan dat boek gegeven.*
(6b) *Dat boek heb ik aan Jan gegeven.*
(6c) *Aan Jan heb ik dat boek gegeven.*

The finite verb stays in second position; otherwise, word order is quite free, and is subject to much stylistic variation. Prepositional phrases can also move to a position after the main verb, but noun phrase complements cannot. Compare these sentences meaning 'I have bought that book for John':

(7a) *Ik heb voor Jan dat boek gekocht.*
(7b) *Ik heb dat boek gekocht voor Jan.*
(7c) **Ik heb voor Jan gekocht dat boek.*

[*See also* Germanic Languages.]

BIBLIOGRAPHY

Donaldson, Bruce C. 1996. *Colloquial Dutch, the complete course for beginners.* London and New York: Routledge.
Haeseryn, W., et al. 1997. *Algemene Nederlandse spraakkunst.* Second, revised edition. Groningen: Wolters-Noordhoff.
van Loey, Adolphe. 1970. *Schönfelds historische grammatica van het Nederlands.* 8th ed. Zutphen: Thieme.

JAN G. KOOIJ

DYANGADI LANGUAGES

DYANGADI LANGUAGES are a group spoken in New South Wales, Australia; they form a branch of the PAMA-NYUNGAN family of AUSTRALIAN languages.

LANGUAGE LIST

Dyangandi: also called Djan-Gadi, Dainggati, Dangadi, Dangati, Danggadi, Danggetti, Ghangatty, Tangetti, Thangatti, Thangatty, Boorkutti, Burgadi. 5 speakers remain. Formerly spoken in Kempsey area, Armidale, Macleay River.

Nganyaywana: also called Nganjaywana, Aniwan. Formerly spoken in northeastern New South Wales, between Inverell, Ashford, and Glen Innes. Said to be extinct as of 1987.

B. GRIMES

DYIRBALIC LANGUAGES

DYIRBALIC LANGUAGES. A branch of the PAMA-NYUNGAN family of AUSTRALIAN languages spoken in northern Queensland, Australia.

LANGUAGE LIST

Dyirbal: also called Djirubal. 40 speakers remain. Formerly spoken in Herberton south to headwaters of Herbert River, to Cashmere, at Ravenshoe, Millaa Millaa, and Woodleigh, east to Tully Falls. Dialects were Dyiru, Girramay (Keramai), Gulnguy (Gulngay), Mamu, Ngadjan (Ngatjan). Related to Manbara, Wulgurukaba, Nhawalgaba.

Nyawaygi: also called Nawagi. 1 speaker remains.

Warrgamay: also called Biyay. 3 speakers remain. Formerly spoken on coast south of Hinchinbrook Island, and inland along Herbert River.

B. GRIMES

DYSLEXIA

DYSLEXIA. The term "dyslexia" refers to a continuum of severe impairments related to written language, which may include problems in accuracy and fluency in reading, spelling, or writing, or all of these. *Developmental dyslexia* involves problems in the acquisition and development of reading, with performance typically one and one-half to two years or more below the level appropriate to age. *Acquired dyslexia*, also called *alexia* and described under that heading in this encyclopedia, is the loss of written language skills as a result of specific brain lesions.

1. Definitions and incidence. Definitions of dyslexia vary. Many are intentionally exclusionary and further define the syndrome as having no instructional, environmental, intellectual, emotional, or gross neurological basis for the impairments. For example, *discrepancy-based definitions* use a regression formula to calculate whether there is a discrepancy between the child's IQ-derived reading age and the actual reading level; only children who exhibit this discrepancy are considered dyslexic, and not those whose slow reading is commensurate with their IQ level. The latter children have been called "garden-variety poor readers" or "non-discrepancy-based poor readers." More inclusionary definitions of dyslexia emphasize only severely impaired levels in reading performance. These definitions have the advantage of permitting schools to provide special services to children whose reading is poor but who show no discrepancy. The disadvantage of the sole use of a reading-performance criterion is that it excludes some children whose reading deficits appear only in the context of a discrepancy with their potential. The most comprehensive definitions define as dyslexic children who fulfill either or both of these criteria.

The incidence of dyslexia in the population is estimated at between 5 and 20 percent, depending on the definition used and the writing system of the language. Incidence is affected by the regularity, or *transparency,* of the orthography and writing system. Thus, higher rates of dyslexia appear for more irregular orthographies, like that of English, which require a greater number of possible letter-to-sound rules, called "grapheme-phoneme correspondence rules." The English-speaking child must learn more rules and also many exceptional words with letter patterns that obey no such rules (e.g. *yacht, who*).

Common characteristics of dyslexia include delayed speech development; a familial history of dyslexia; difficulty in phoneme awareness (the understanding that words are composed of small units of sound) and in naming speed (slowed retrieval of names for visual stimuli like common objects, letters, and numbers); sequencing problems; weaknesses in mathematics and/or writing; short-term memory problems; and directional confusions. The typical dyslexic child has great difficulty in learning to read, to spell, and often to write, despite average to superior intelligence and adequate instruction and opportunities.

2. Early history of research. For most of its early history, dyslexia was considered a visually based problem. Adolf Kussmaul, a 19th-century neurologist, first used the term "word-blindness" to describe reading-impaired adults with discrete brain lesions. Other 19th-century neurologists, including Rudolf Berlin and J. J. Déjerine, used the terms "dyslexia" (<Greek 'bad' + 'word') and "alexia" ('not' + 'word') to describe *acquired* reading loss. Childhood cases were discovered in the late 19th century by the British physicians James

Kerr and Pringle Morgan; these were thought to be the developmental analog of acquired reading disorders in adults. In the early 20th century, the Scottish ophthalmologist James Hinshelwood renamed the syndrome "congenital word-blindness." Hinshelwood was the first to emphasize the presence of dyslexia in children of normal or above-average intelligence, and its high incidence in boys.

In the 1930s, Samuel T. Orton renamed the syndrome "strephosymbolia" (<Gr. 'twisted' + 'symbol'), based on the following hypotheses:

(a) The cerebral hemispheres contain mirror images of the same information (e.g. *bud* vs. *dub*).
(b) In dyslexia, cerebral dominance is incomplete.
(c) Because visual information competes between hemispheres, images and symbols are reversed for dyslexics, leading to frequent letter reversals in dyslexia.

Although Orton's view of brain function and reversals was incorrect, his extensive work contributed both to later neuropsychological theories and to a major method of remediation, the Orton-Gillingham method, which emphasizes the need to learn systematic grapheme-phoneme correspondence rules.

3. Modern history of research. Since Orton, there has been an exponential increase in theoretical knowledge about the cognitive and linguistic structure of reading, its development, and its breakdown. Reading came to be depicted as a complex, interactive ensemble of multiple perceptual, cognitive, and linguistic sub-processes, each requiring a rapid (or automatic) rate of processing, attention, and memory (see Adams 1990). A focus on the centrality of language sub-processes, particularly phonological processes, began with the psycholinguistic work of Shankweiler and Liberman 1972 which represented a major step in understanding reading acquisition and reading failure. These researchers and their colleagues demonstrated the connections between a child's evolving ability to perceive phonemes and the ability to learn the grapheme-phoneme correspondence rules that are essential to learning to read. Children's ability to learn the alphabetic principle underlying reading requires that they understand, first, that words are made up of individual sounds, and second, that each of these sounds has corresponding letters.

Advances in understanding the reading process led to similar advances in understanding dyslexia. Chall 1983 and Frith 1985 described in detail the systematic changes in the development over time of reading skills and their underlying processes. Vellutino 1979 exemplified the move from a "perceptual deficit" view of dyslexia to one giving centrality to linguistic deficits. Over the next 20 years, extensive studies showed phonological processing deficits, as indexed by phoneme awareness tasks, to be a major indicator of dyslexia (Torgesen et al. 1994). The phonological-core deficit perspective (Stanovich 1986) became the basis for great strides in the diagnosis and treatment of dyslexia.

Parallel research in the cognitive neurosciences confirmed the extraordinary underlying complexity of the reading process. For example, brain-imaging research (Shaywitz et al. 1998) indicates the activation of multiple regions across the brain during reading. Such research also suggests that phonological deficits are but one source of breakdown in impaired readers. Research in the neurosciences on reading pathology has occurred at the behavioral, neuronal, and structural levels.

At the behavioral level, Geschwind 1974 and Denckla and Rudel 1976 described how the cognitive, perceptual, linguistic, and motor processes that underlie naming speed closely correspond to the same processes that underlie reading. Studies across many language systems demonstrate that naming-speed deficits represent a second core deficit in dyslexia that is especially pronounced in more regular orthographies. Based on work on deficits in naming speed and phonological deficits, Wolf and Bowers 1999 proposed the "double-deficit hypothesis": that phonological and naming-speed deficits, either singly or in combination, contribute to three of the most common subtypes of dyslexia.

The earliest dyslexia research at the neuronal level was by Norman Geschwind, Albert Galaburda, Thomas Kemper, and their colleagues, who demonstrated anatomical differences in dyslexic brains, originating during fetal development. A long series of architectonic studies indicated aberrant neuronal organization in particular language areas (e.g., area Tpt, in the left planum temporale, the magnocellular system in the lateral and medial geniculate nuclei in the thalamus), with cell migration into inappropriate neuronal layers, and cortical thinning in other areas (for a review, see Rosen et al. 2001).

Structural-level neuroscientific work in dyslexia involves the sophisticated application of various brain-imaging technologies, such as functional Magnetic Resonance Imaging, Computerized Axial Tomography scans, Event-Related Potentials, Magneto-EncephaloGraphy, and Diffusion Tensor Imaging. Computerized images are used to study the activation of the brain as it reads and to detect possible differences in brain structure and activation patterns during reading-related tasks.

4. Diagnosis and remediation. The intrinsic complexity of the reading process, the consequent heterogeneity of reading disorders, and the lack of consensus about definition have made the actual diagnosis of developmental dyslexia difficult. The identification and early prediction of reading problems are more straightforward, however, owing to extensive late-20th-century research. Before reading begins, the most predictive tests of later reading performance are phoneme-awareness tasks (e.g., the tester asks a child to say the word *dog* without the /d/) and naming-speed tasks (e.g., the child is asked to name, as quickly as possible, an array of letters, numbers, colors, or common objects). After reading instruction has begun, typical tests measure word identification skills, word attack (where nonsense words based on known letter patterns measure knowledge of decoding skills without context), oral reading and oral reading rate, and passage comprehension. Children whose accuracy and/or fluency are one to two years behind their age level (in some cases, reading age level as derived from IQ scores) are considered to be reading-impaired.

Considerable advances in remediation have occurred over the same period, based on research on the better-understood core deficits in phonological processes and the fluency, or rate-related, processes underlying naming speed. For example, theoretically based programs in phoneme awareness training have been successful in kindergarten and first grade in preventing many cases of reading failure (Adams 1990). Instruction for children with reading disabilities must provide systematic, developmentally sequenced training in the alphabetic principle (i.e. early emphasis on phoneme awareness and phonics) alongside consistent work in vocabulary growth and reading vocabulary-controlled words in context. Practice is imperative; some children need multiple exposures to every letter pattern.

Children with dyslexia require careful diagnosis to establish their individual profile of strengths and weaknesses as a basis for remediation. For example, research by Wolf and Bowers 1999 and their colleagues has shown that one subtype with reading fluency and comprehension problems has little difficulty in phonological processes but requires heavy emphasis on increasing the rate of processing in all underlying reading skills.

The most insidious and often-ignored component of severe reading disability is the children's belief that their inability to read means that they lack intelligence. Successful reading programs directly address phonological, orthographic, semantic, *and* affective processes, an insight originally offered by Orton. Such programs contain a strong developmental component, such that the evolving requirements of the educational system (e.g. increasingly sophisticated inferential demands in text, writing requirements, increased fluency) are addressed at each stage of the child's development.

5. Future directions. As knowledge increases about brain structure and brain-activation differences among dyslexic readers, there is also growing application of imaging techniques to evaluate reading intervention. Evidence is emerging that reading gains made during successful intervention programs are reflected in activation-pattern changes in specific brain regions. A second major direction involves a movement to assess the remarkable strengths of the many successful, highly visible dyslexic individuals, particularly in fields that require skills in macro-pattern analysis such as architecture, radiology, finance, and computer science.

[*See also* Alexia and Agraphia; Developmental Language Disorders; Neurolinguistics; Specific Language Impairment; Text; *and* Writing and Written Language.]

BIBLIOGRAPHY

Adams, Marilyn. 1990. *Beginning to read: Thinking and learning about print.* Cambridge, Mass.: MIT Press.

Chall, Jeanne S. 1983. *Stages of reading development.* New York: McGraw-Hill.

Denckla, M. B., and R. G. Rudel. 1976. Rapid automized naming (R.A.N.): Dyslexia differentiated from other learning disabilities. *Neuropsychologia* 14.471–479.

Frith, Uta. 1985. Beneath the surface of developmental dyslexia. In *Surface dyslexia: Neuropsychological and cognitive studies of phonological reading,* edited by Karalyn E. Patterson et al., pp. 301–330. London: Erlbaum.

Geschwind, Norman. 1974. *Selected papers on language and the brain.* Boston: Reidel.

Rosen, G., R. H. Fitch, M. Clark, J. J. Lo Turco, G. Sherman, and A. Galaburda. 2001. Animal models of developmental dyslexia. In *Dyslexia, fluency, and the brain,* edited by M. Wolf, pp. 129–157. Timonium, Md.: York Press.

Shankweiler, Donald, and Isabelle Y. Liberman. 1972. Misreading: A search for causes. In *Language by ear and by eye: The relationships between speech and reading,* edited by James F. Kavanagh and Ignatius G. Mattingly, pp. 293–317. Cambridge, Mass.: MIT Press.

Shaywitz, Sally E., Bennett A. Shaywitz, Kenneth R. Pugh,

Robert K. Fulbright, R. Todd Constable, W. Einer Mencl, Donald P. Shankweiler, Alvin M. Liberman, Pawel Skudlarski, Jack M. Fletcher, Leonard Katz, Karen E. Marchione, Cheryl Lacadie, Christopher Gatenby, and John C. Gore. 1998. Functional disruption in the organization of the brain for reading in dyslexia. *Proceedings of the National Academy of Science* 95.2636–2641.

Stanovich, Keith E. 1986. Matthew effects in reading: Some consequences of individual differences in the acquisition of literacy. *Reading Research Quarterly* 21.360–407.

Torgesen, Joseph, Richard Wagner, and Carol Rashotte. 1994. Longitudinal studies of phonological processing and reading. *Journal of Learning Disabilities* 27.276–286.

Vellutino, Frank R. 1979. *Dyslexia: Theory and research.* Cambridge, Mass.: MIT Press.

Wolf, Maryanne, and Patricia Bowers. 1999. The double-deficit hypothesis for the developmental dyslexias. *Journal of Educational Psychology* 91(3).1–24.

MARYANNE WOLF AND TERESA DEENEY

DYSPHASIA. *See* Developmental Language Disorder.

E

E. Symbol for Empty Category. *See* Anaphora; Formal Grammar; Traces; Principles and Parameters; *and* Filters.

EAST BIRD'S HEAD LANGUAGES constitute a family spoken on the Vogelkop (Bird's Head) Peninsula of the province of West Papua, Indonesia. Meyah and Moskona together form a Meax subgroup.

LANGUAGE LIST

Manikion: also called Mantion, Sougb, Sogh. 12,000 speakers in eastern Bird's Head, east of Meyah, south of Manokwari, about fifty villages. Four dialects.

Meyah: also called Meax, Meyach, Meah, Mejah, Mejach. 15,000 speakers in eastern Bird's Head, north coast, west of Manokwari, north of Hattam language, and scattered locations. Closest to Sougb. Many speakers are becoming bilingual in Indonesian.

Moskona: also called Sabena, Meninggo, Meningo. 8,000 speakers in southeastern Bird's Head, south of Meyah and west of Manikion.

B. GRIMES

EAST CENTRAL INDO-ARYAN LANGUAGES.
Also called eastern Hindi, they constitute a subgroup of the INDO-ARYAN LANGUAGES; they are spoken in the east central part of northern India.

LANGUAGE LIST

Awadhi: also called Abadi, Abohi, Ambodhi, Avadhi, Baiswari, Kojali, Kosali. 20,540,000 speakers in India and Nepal. In India: 20,000,000 speakers in Bihar; Madhya Pradesh; Uttar Pradesh, Kanpur district; Delhi. Dialects are Gangapari, Mirzapuri, Pardesi, Uttari. Education is in Hindi. Hindu holy book *Ramcharitmanas* by Tulsi Das is in Awadhi. Devanagari script. In Nepal: Lumbini zone, Kapilbastu district; Bheri zone, Banke and Bardiya districts. Dialects are Bagheli, Gangapari, Mirzapuri, Pardesi, Tharu, Uttari.

Bagheli: also called Bagelkhandi, Bhugelkhud, Mannadi, Riwai, Ganggai, Mandal, Kewot, Kewat, Kawathi, Kenat, Kevat Boli, Kevati, Kewani, Kewati, Nagpuri Marathi. 396,000 speakers in India and Nepal. In India: Northeastern Madhya Pradesh, Maharashtra, Uttar Pradesh. Dialects are Marari, Ojhi (Ojaboli, Ojha, Ojhe, Oza, Ozha), Powari, Banapari, Gahore, Tirhari, Godwani (Mandlaha), Sonpari. In Nepal: Morang district, Koshi zone. Dialects are Marari, Ojhi, Powari, Banapari, Gahore, Tirhari, Godwani (Mandlaha), Sonpari. Trade language.

Chhattisgarhi: also called Laria, Khaltahi. 11,535,000 speakers in India. Dialects are Surgujia, Sadri Korwa, Baigani (Baiga, Bega, Bhumia, Gowro), Binjhwari, Kalanga, Bhulia, Chhattisgarhi Proper, Kavardi, Khairagarhi. Most closely related to Awadhi and Bagheli. Limited proficiency in Hindi. Oriya also used. Used in nearly all domains. Spoken as mother tongue by the Kawari. Positive attitude toward Chhattisgarhi. Devanagari script.

Dhanwar: also called Dhanvar, Danuwar. 104,195 speakers in India in Madhya Pradesh, Bilaspur, Raigarh, Sarguja districts; Maharashtra, Akola, Amraoti, Yavatmal, Nagpur, Wardha, Chandrapur districts.

Fijian Hindustani: also called Fijian Hindi. 380,000 speakers in Fiji, Australia, and USA. In Fiji: No significant regional variation. A type of Awadhi, also influenced by Bhojpuri. Spoken by all of Indian ancestry in Fiji, including ethnic Tamil (6,663), Gujarati (6,203), Urdu, Telugu (2,008), Gurmukhi (Panjabi, 1,167), Bengali (17,875), Malayalam. A small Gujarati community speak Gujarati at home, and a few others, mainly older people, speak their traditional languages. Official language. In USA: California.

B. GRIMES

EAST CHADIC LANGUAGES. A top-level constituent of the Chadic branch of AFROASIATIC. Spoken in

south central Chad and in adjacent parts of Cameroon and the Central African Republic.

LANGUAGE LIST

Barein: also called Baraïn, Guilia, Jalkia. 4,100 speakers in south central Chad, in northern Guéra prefecture, Melfi subprefecture, west (Jalkia), south, southwest (Komi), and east (Sakaya) of Melfi. Dialects are Jalkia, Guilia, Sakaya (Dagne, Jelkin), Komi. Bilingualism in Chadian Arabic.

Bidiyo: also called Bidyo, Bidio, 'Bidio, 'Bidiyo, Bidiyo-Waana, Bidiya. 14,000 speakers in south central Chad, northern Guéra prefecture, Mongo subprefecture, south of Mongo and west of Abou Telfane. Dialects are Garawgino (Kafila), Jekkino (Kofilo), Bigawguno (Tounkoul), Nalguno (Niergui), 'Oboyguno (Zerli). The first two dialects listed are eastern, the others western. Dambiya is probably a Bidiyo dialect instead of a Migaama dialect. The majority use Chadian Arabic as second language.

Birgit: also called Bergit, Birgid, Berguid. 3,600 speakers in Chad. Dialects are Abgue, Eastern Birgit, Duguri, Agrab.

Boor: also called Bwara, Damraw. 100 speakers in Chad. Some have classified it as a dialect of Miltu. There may be a high degree of bilingualism in Bagirmi.

Buso: also called Busso, Dam de Bousso, Bousso. 40 speakers remain in Chad in western Chari-Baguirmi prefecture, Bousso subprefecture, in Maffaling and Bousso. Said not to be in the Bua group, but Chadic.

Dangaléat: also called Dangla, Danal, Dangal. 45,000 speakers in Chad. Dialects are West Dangaléat (Korbo, Karbo), Central Dangaléat, East Dangaléat. Intelligibility between speakers of the eastern and western dialects is low, but both understand the central dialect well. The majority use Arabic as second language.

Gabri: also called Gaberi, Gabere, Ngabre, Southern Gabri. 25,000 speakers in Chad. Southwestern, Tandjilé prefecture, Laï subprefecture, northwest of Laï around Dormo and Darbé villages. Dialects are Darbé, Dormon.

Gadang: 2,500 speakers in Chad. Related to Sarua and Miltu. Bilingualism in Bagirmi.

Jonkor Bourmataguil: also called Djongor Bourmataguil, Dougne, Karakir. 1,500 speakers in Chad, Salamat prefecture, Abou Deïa subprefecture, west of Abou Deïa. Originally centered in Bourmataguil village, now centered in Ader-Ader. Dialects are Dougne, Musunye. Relationship with other Dangla languages needs investigation, especially Toram and Mogum. A large number of the ethnic group have given up the traditional language for Chadian Arabic, but in two villages the children still learn Jonkor Bourmataguil.

Kabalai: also called Kaba-Lai, Kabalay, Kabalaye, Keb-Kaye, Gablai, Lay, Lai. 17,885 speakers in southwestern Chad, Tandjilé prefecture, Laï subprefecture; Laï and to the south

FIGURE 1. *Subgrouping of East Chadic Languages*

Subgroup A
  Family A.1
    Buso
    Subfamily 1
      Mire, Ndam, Somrai, Tumak
    Subfamily 2
      Boor, Gadang, Miltu, Sarua
  Family A.2
    Subfamily 1
      Kimré, Lele, Nancere
    Subfamily 2
      Gabri, Kabalai, Tobanga
  Family A.3
    Kera, Kwang
Subgroup B
  Family B.1
    Subfamily 1
      Bidiyo, Dangaléat, Jonkor Bourmataguil, Mabire, Mawa, Migaama, Mogum, Ubi
    Subfamily 2
      Birgit, Kajakse, Masmaje, Mubi, Toram
  Family B.2
    Mukulu
  Family B.3
    Barein, Saba, Sokoro, Tamki

on the eastern bank of the Logone River. Not in Central African Republic. May be intelligible with Nancere.

Kajakse: also called Kadjakse, Kajeske, Kujarke, Mini, Kawa Tadimini. 10,000 speakers in Chad. East, Ouaddaï prefecture, Am Dam subprefecture. South and southeast of Am Dam. Some refugees in Sudan near the border. Partially intelligible with Mesmaje and Mubi.

Kera: 50,523 speakers in Chad and Cameroon. In Chad: 44,523 speakers. Southwestern, Mayo-Kebbi prefecture, Fianga subprefecture, south of Fianga, near Lake Tikem. In Cameroon: 6,000 speakers. Southeast of Doukoula, Mayo-Danay division, Far North Province.

Kimré: also called Gabri-Kimré. 15,000 speakers in southwestern Chad, Tandjilé prefecture, Kélo subprefecture, east of Laï, including Tchere-Aïba village. Dialects are Kimruwa (Kim-Ruwa, Kimré), Buruwa (Bordo), Tchire (Tchere-Aïba). Popularly called "Gabri," but it is not intelligible with Gabri.

Kwang: also called Kuang, Kouang, Kwong. 16,805 speakers in Chad. Dialects are Kwang, Mobou (Mobu), Ngam (Gam, Modgel), Tchagin (Tchakin), Aloa, Kawalké, Gaya, Mindéra. The dialects listed are inherently intelligible to each other's speakers. Includes Midigil village, sometimes erroneously listed as a language named "Modgel" (Medegel) in some sources. The Aloa are Muslim and fully bilingual in Bagirmi. The Ngam use Sarua as second language.

Lele: 26,000 speakers in southwestern Chad, Tandjilé prefecture, Kélo subprefecture, south of Kélo.

Mabire: 3 speakers remain in Chad. Formerly spoken in the village of Oulek. Similar to Jegu dialect of Mogum and Bigawguno dialect of Bidiyo. Bilingualism in Chadic Arabic, Kofa.

Masmaje: also called Masmadje, Mesmedje. 25,727 speakers in Chad. Central Batha prefecture, Oum Hadjer subprefecture, southwest of Oum Hadjer, north of the Mubi.

Mawa: also called Mahwa, Mahoua. 3,000 speakers in Chad. "Gurara" and "Roffono" ("Reupan") are villages, whose speech is hardly different from that of Mawa. The majority use Shuwa Arabic as second language, some use Kenga.

Migaama: also called Migama, Jongor, Djonkor, Dionkor, Dyongor, Djonkor Abou Telfane. 20,000 speakers in Chad. Ethnic population: 23,000 as of 1991. Dialects are Migaama, Doga, Gamiya, Dambiya (Ndambiya). Dialect cluster. Dambiya is probably a Bidiyo dialect rather than a Migaama dialect. 2,000 are monolingual. 18,000 to 19,000 are bilingual in Chadian Arabic as second language, men at a high proficiency level, women at a low proficiency level. 6,000 can speak French. Modern Standard Arabic taught in school. All domains except to Arabs in market, French to teachers in school. Oral use in administration, a little in school, some in church, business. Migaama transmitted by parents to children. Very positive attitude toward Migaama.

Miltu: also called Miltou. 272 speakers in Chad. Southwestern Chari-Baguirmi prefecture, Bousso subprefecture, around the town of Miltou. Speakers are shifting to Bagirmi in all domains.

Mire: 1,400 speakers in Chad. Southwestern Tandjilé prefecture, Laï subprefecture, between the Ndam and the Kimré language areas. Most use Kimré or Ndam as second language.

Mogum: also called Mogoum. 7,000 speakers in south central Chad, northern Guéra prefecture, Bitkine, Melfi, and Mongo subprefectures, south of the Bidiyo. Dialects are Jegu, Koffa (Kofa), Mogum Déle, Mogum Diguimi, Mogum Urmi. Dialect cluster. Dialects listed are inherently intelligible with each other. Mogum Diguimi may not be a separate dialect.

Mubi: also called Moubi, Monjul. 35,277 speakers in Chad. Central, Guéra prefecture, Mangalmé subprefecture, east of Mongo, centered in and around Mangalmé. 135 villages. There may be some in Sudan. Dialects are Mubi, Minjile. The majority use Arabic as second language.

Mukulu: also called Mokulu, Mokoulou, Djonkor Guera, Dyongor Guera, Diongor Guera, Jonkor-Gera, Mokilko. 12,000 speakers in Chad. Dialects are Mokilko, Seginki, Doliki, Moriko, Mezimko, Gugiko. Dialects are inherently intelligible with each other. Bilingualism in Arabic is limited.

Nancere: also called Nanjeri, Nanchere, Nantcere, Nangjere, Nangcere. 71,609 speakers in Chad. Southwestern Tandjilé prefecture, Béré and Kélo subprefectures.

Ndam: also called Dam, Ndamm. 6,500 speakers in Chad. Southwestern Tandjilé prefecture, Laï subprefecture, northeast of Laï and southeast of Bousso. Dialects are Ndam-Ndam (Southern Ndam), Ndam Dik (Northern Ndam).

Saba: also called Jelkung. 1,000 speakers in Chad. South central, Guéra prefecture, Melfi subprefecture, northeast of Melfi. Chadian Arabic is the second language of speakers, but with low proficiency.

Sarua: also called Sarwa, Saroua. 2,000 speakers in Chad. Southwestern, Chari-Baguirmi prefecture, Bousso subprefecture, between Bousso and Miltou, along the Chari River. The majority use Bagirmi as second language.

Sokoro: 5,000 speakers in Chad. Central, Guéra prefecture, Melfi subprefecture, north and northwest of Melfi, from Gogmi to Badanga. Dialects are Sokoro, Bedanga. Closely related languages: Saba, Barein. Most men speak Chadian Arabic as second language.

Somrai: also called Sounrai, Somrei, Somre, Soumray, Soumrai, Sumrai, Sibine, Shibne. 7,414 speakers in Chad. Southwestern Tandjilé prefecture, Laï subprefecture, northeast of Laï, centered at Domogou. Not intelligible with any other language. Speakers are not bilingual.

Tamki: also called Temki. 500 speakers in Chad. Central, Guéra prefecture, Melfi subprefecture, about 60 km northeast of Melfi, Tamki village. Not inherently intelligible with Sokoro. Most speak Chadian Arabic, Kenga, or Saba as second languages. Speakers are positive toward Tamki. They consider themselves to be ethnically Sokoro, but their attitudes are not more positive toward Sokoro than toward other neighboring languages.

Tobanga: also called Gabri-North, Gabri-Nord, Northern Gabri, Gabri. 30,000 speakers in Chad. Southwestern, Tandjilé prefecture, Laï subprefecture, around Deressia. Dialects are Tobanga (Deressia), Moonde.

Toram: also called Torom, Torum. 4,000 speakers in Chad. Central, Salamat prefecture, Abou Deïa subprefecture, southeast of Abou Deïa, south of the Birgit, in and west of Ter. A separate language from other Dangla languages. Speakers seem to be shifting to Chadian Arabic.

Tumak: also called Toumak, Tummok, Tumac, Dije, Sara Toumak, Tumag. 25,249 speakers in Chad. Southwestern, Moyen-Chari prefecture, Koumra subprefecture, around Goundil; southwest of Niellim. Dialects are Tumak, Motun (Mawer, Moden, Modin, Mod, Mot, Motin). Most Motun speak Sara as second language, but with low proficiency.

Ubi: also called Oubi. 1,100 speakers in Chad. Central, Guéra prefecture, Mongo subprefecture, southwest of Tounkoul, around Oubi village.

B. GRIMES

EASTERN MALAYO-POLYNESIAN LANGUAGES. One of the two main branches of Central-

Eastern Malayo-Polynesian languages within the Malayo-Polynesian branch of the AUSTRONESIAN family.

[*For language lists, consult the articles on* Oceanic Languages *and* South Halmahera-West New Guinea Languages.]

B. GRIMES

EASTERN OUTER ISLANDS LANGUAGES. A branch of REMOTE OCEANIC spoken in the eastern Solomon Islands. Amba, Asumboa, and Tanimbili constitute an Utupua sub-branch, while Tanema, Teanu, and Vano constitute a Vanikoro sub-branch.

LANGUAGE LIST

Amba: also called Aba, Nembao, Utupua. 485 speakers in Aveta, Matembo, and Nembao villages, Utupua Island, Temotu Province. Bilingualism in Pijin.

Asumboa: also called Asumbua, Asumuo. 75 speakers in Asumbuo village, Utupua Island, Temotu Province. Bilingualism in Amba, Pijin, Nyisunggu.

Tanema: also called Tanima. Ethnic population: 190 as of 1998. Formerly spoken in Emua village, Vanikolo Island, Temotu Province. The people speak Pijin or Teanu. The language is no longer in use; old people remember a few words.

Tanimbili: also called Nyisunggu. 190 speakers in Tanimbili village, Utupua Island, Temotu Province. Bilingualism in Pijin, Amba, Asumbuo.

Teanu: also called Buma, Puma. 450 speakers in Puma, Lavaka, Emua, and Lale villages, Vanikolo Island, Temotu Province. Bilingualism in Pijin. As of 1989, speakers included 170 adults.

Vano: also called Vanikoro, Vanikolo. Ethnic population: 140 as of 1998. Formerly spoken in Lale and Lavaka villages, Vanikolo Island, Temotu Province. The people speak Pijin or Teanu. The language is no longer in use; old people remember a few words.
B. GRIMES

EAST FIJIAN LANGUAGES. A branch of EAST FIJIAN-POLYNESIAN.

LANGUAGE LIST

Fijian: also called Fiji, Standard Fijian, Eastern Fijian, Nadroga, Nadronga. 350,000 speakers in Fiji, Nauru, New Zealand, and Vanuatu. In Fiji: 330,441 speakers. Dialects are Kadavu (Ono, Tavuki, Nabukelevu), Southeast Viti Levu (Waidina, Lutu, Nandrau, Naimasimasi), Bau (Bauan, Mbau), Northeast Viti Levu (Tokaimalo, Namena, Lovoni), Central Vanua Levu (Baaravi, Seaqaaqaa, Nabalebale, Savusavu), Northeast Vanua Levu (Labasa, Dogotuki Saqani, Korolau), Southeast Vanua Levu (Navatu-C, Tunuloa, Naweni, Baumaa), West Vanua Levu (Navatu-B, Soolevu, Bua, Navakasiga). The southern part of Vanua Levu has several dialects similar to Bau. On the northern part of Vanua Levu and adjacent islands, people speak a variety somewhat related to Bau. Bau is very similar to Standard Fijian, used as traditional lingua franca among Fijians. National language.

Gone Dau: also called Gonedau. 500 speakers in Fiji, in eastern Fiji, Gone and Dau Islands off western Vanua Levu. Dialect chain to Bau (Standard) Fijian at the opposite end. Speakers learn Standard Fijian; it is not functionally intelligible to them.

Lauan: also called Lau. 16,000 speakers in Fiji, on eastern Fiji Islands, Lau, Nayau, Lakeba, Oneata, Moce, Komo, Namuka, Kabara, Vulaga, Ogea, Vatoa Islands. Dialects are Lau, Vanua Balavu. In the middle of the East Fijian dialect chain; a cluster of dialects. Has some similarities to Bau Fijian; may be mutually intelligible with it.

Lomaiviti: spoken in Fiji, on the islands east of Viti Levu: Koro, Makogai, Levuka, Ovalau, Batiki, Nairai, Gau.
B. GRIMES

EAST FIJIAN-POLYNESIAN LANGUAGES. A branch of CENTRAL PACIFIC.

[*For language lists, see the articles on* East Fijian Languages *and* Polynesian Languages.]

B. GRIMES

EAST INDO-ARYAN LANGUAGES. Also called Magadhan languages, they constitute a subgroup of the INDO-ARYAN LANGUAGES; they are spoken in northeastern India and Bangladesh, with some overspill into Nepal.

LANGUAGE LIST

Angika: also called Anga, Angikar, Chhika-Chhiki. 725,000 speakers in India, in northern Bihar. 79% inherent intelligibility with Brahmin Maithili. Hindi is used for trading, government, praying. All ages. Angika is used in most traditional domains (home, community, children playing, young people talking together). Angika is looked at as inferior to Maithili.

Assamese: also called Asambe, Asami, Asamiya. 15,334,000 speakers in India, Bangladesh, and Bhutan. In India: Assam, Meghalaya, Arunachal Pradesh. Dialects are Jharwa (Pid-

FIGURE 1. *Subgrouping of East Indo-Aryan Languages*

Bengali-Assamese
Assamese, Bengali, Bishnupriya, Chakma, Chittagonian, Hajong, Halbi, Kayort, Kharia Thar, Mal Paharia, Mirgan, Nahari, Rajbangsi, Sylheti, Tangchangya
Bihari
Angika, Bhojpuri, Caribbean Hindustani, Kudmali, Magahi, Maithili, Majhi, Musasa, Panchpargania, Sadri, Oraon Sadri, Surajpuri
Oriya
Bhatri, Bhunjia, Bodo Parja, Kupia, Oriya, Adivasi Oriya, Reli
Unclassified Eastern Indo-Aryan
Bote-Majhi, Buksa, Degaru, Chitwania Tharu, Deokhuri Tharu, Kochila Tharu, Mahotari Tharu, Rana Tharu

gin), Mayang, Standard Assamese, Western Assamese. Bengali script. National language.

Bengali: also called Banga-Bhasa, Bangala, Bangla. 207,000,000 speakers in Bangladesh, India, Malawi, Nepal, Saudi Arabia, Singapore, United Arab Emirates, United Kingdom, and USA. In Bangladesh: 100,000,000 speakers. Western. Languages or dialects in the Bengali group: Central (Standard) Bengali, Western Bengali (Kharia Thar, Mal Paharia, Saraki), Southwestern Bengali, Northern Bengali (Koch, Siripuria), Rajbangsi, Bahe, Eastern Bengali (East Central, including Sylhetti), Haijong, Southeastern Bengali (Chakma), Ganda, Vanga, Chittagonian (possible dialect of Southeastern Bengali). Bengali script used. National language. In India: 70,561,000 speakers in West Bengal and neighboring states. Dialects are Barik, Bhatiari, Chirmar, Kachari-Bengali, Lohari-Malpaharia, Musselmani, Rajshahi, Samaria, Saraki, Siripuria (Kishanganjia). Spoken by some Koda as mother tongue. Bengali script. National language, official language. In Nepal: Mechi zone, Jhapa district; Koshi zone, Morang and Sunsari districts; Sagarmatha zone, Saptari district. Dialects are Barik, Bhatiari, Chirmar, Kachari-Bengali, Lohari-Malpaharia, Musselmani, Rajshahi, Samaria, Saraki, Siripuria. In Singapore: Ethnic population: 12,000 as of 1993. Bengali script. National language.

Bhatri: also called Bhattri, Bhattra, Bhatra, Basturia, Bhottada, Bhottara. 178,000 speakers in India, in Andhra Pradesh; Madhya Pradesh, Bastar district, Jagdalpur tahsil; Maharashtra; Orissa, Koraput district, Kotpad tahsil. All dialects understand each other at 88%. Closely related to Halbi. Communities in Madhya Pradesh have limited bilingual proficiency in Hindi. Those in Orissa have limited proficiency in Oriya. One third of the speakers have enhanced understanding of Halbi because of closeness to the Halbi-speaking area. Bhatri is preferred in home and religious

domains. Vigorous language use. Positive attitude toward Bhatri. Oriya script.

Bhojpuri: also called Bhojapuri, Bhozpuri, Bajpuri, Bihari. 26,254,000 speakers in India, Nepal, and Mauritius. In India: 24,544,000 speakers in Bihar, Purnea area; Uttar Pradesh; Assam; Delhi; Madhya Pradesh; West Bengal. Dialects are Northern Standard Bhojpuri (Gorakhpuri, Sarawaria, Basti), Western Standard Bhojpuri (Purbi, Benarsi), Southern Standard Bhojpuri (Kharwari), Tharu, Madhesi, Domra, Musahari. May be more than one language. Extent of dialect variation in India and Nepal not yet determined. The cover term 'Bihari' (Behari) is used for Bhojpuri, Maithili, and Magahi. Kaithi script. In Nepal: 1,379,717 speakers. Dialects are Bhojpuri Tharu, Teli. The extent of dialect variation among speakers in India and Nepal has not been determined. Bhojpuri Tharu is a dialect of Bhojpuri spoken by the Tharu caste in Nepal. It is distinct from Chitwania and other Tharu. Bilingualism in Hindi, Maithili, Nepali, Awadhi. In Mauritius: Urban and rural areas. Dialects are Mauritian Bhojpuri, Bojpury. Often used in government and politics.

Bhunjia: also called Bunjia, Bhumjiya, Bhunjiya. 18,601 speakers in India, in Madhya Pradesh, Raipur, Hoshangabad districts; Orissa, Sambalpur, Kalshandi districts, Sunabera Plateau area; Maharashtra. Called a more divergent dialect of Halbi.

Bishnupriya: also called Bishnupuriya, Bisna Puriya, Bishnupria Manipuri. 75,000 speakers in India and Bangladesh. In India: Manipur; Assam, Cachar district; Tripura. Related to Bengali and Assamese. Though once regarded as a Bengali-Meithei Creole, it retains pre-Bengali features. Bilingualism in Hindi.

Bodo Parja: also called Bodo Paraja, Parji, Parja, Paroja, Poroja, Jhodia Parja, Sodia Parja, Parjhi, Parajhi, Harja, Jharia, Jhaliya. 50,000 speakers in India in Orissa, Koraput district. Phonology and grammar show Indo-European relationship, not related to Dravidian Duruwa Parji. Adivasi Oriya mainly used in the market, but proficiency is limited. Bodo is higher caste than Jhodia, showing some signs of negative attitudes, despite high intelligibility. Oriya script.

Bote-Majhi: also called Kushar. 11,000 speakers in Nepal, mainly in the Chitawan district, Narayani zone, near Kumhali.

Buksa: 43,000 speakers in India. Speakers tested at 95% intelligibility of Rana Tharu.

Caribbean Hindustani: 165,600 speakers in Suriname, Belize, Guyana, Netherlands, and Trinidad and Tobago. In Suriname: 150,000 speakers in the coastal region. No speakers in French Guiana. Dialects are Trinidad Bhojpuri, Sarnami Hindustani (Sarnami Hindi, Aili Gaili). There are monolingual speakers. Others use Sranan or Dutch as second language. In Trinidad and Tobago: 15,633 speakers. Related to Bhojpuri. Bilingualism in English. 90% of the Hindustanis are reported to speak English as mother tongue. In Guyana: Ethnic population: 538,500. Closer to Bhojpuri than to Hindi. Similar dialect to Suriname and Trinidad and Tobago. Those closer to Georgetown use a more standard English than Guyanese. A few are learning Hindi for religious purposes. Only a few older people of Guyanese origin in Guyana speak Caribbean Hindustani. Many Hindustanis in Guyana speak Guyanese as first language.

Chakma: also called Takam, Chakama. 560,000 speakers in India and Bangladesh. In India: 300,000 speakers in southwestern Mizoram along Karnafuli River; northern Tripura; Assam, Karbi, Anglong, North Cachar, Cachar districts; West Bengal; Manipur. In Bangladesh: 260,577 speakers in southeast, Chittagong hills area, and Chittagong City. Six dialects are spoken. Educated speakers know Bengali. Many men can speak Bengali. A more assimilated hill people.

Chittagonian: also called Chittagonian Bengali. 14,000,000 speakers in Bangladesh and Myanmar. In Bangladesh: Chittagong region. Not inherently intelligible with Bengali, although considered to be a nonstandard Bengali dialect. A continuum of dialects from north to south, with a larger religious distinction between Muslim and others. An ethnic Bengali Muslim who speaks the Muslim variety of Chittagonian Bengali and was born in Arakan state, Myanmar, is called a 'Rohinga'. The dialect is intelligible to those born in southeastern Bangladesh. Village women without access to TV do not understand Bengali. Many educated people understand some Bengali, but are not comfortable using it. All education is in Standard Bengali. Used for religious instruction in village mosques. In Myanmar: Arakan state. Not inherently intelligible with Bengali, although considered to be a nonstandard Bengali dialect. The dialect is intelligible to those born in southeastern Bangladesh. Not intelligible with Bengali.

Degaru: also called Dhekaru. Spoken in India in Bihar, West Bengal.

Hajong: also called Haijong, Hazong. 19,000 speakers in India and Bangladesh. In India: Meghalaya, western Garo hills district, western side, West Khasi hills; Assam, Goalpara and Nowgong districts; West Bengal. Formerly a Tibeto-Burman language, but culturally and linguistically Hinduized and Bengalized.

Halbi: also called Bastari, Halba, Halvas, Halabi, Halvi, Mahari, Mehari. 736,000 speakers in India, in Madhya Pradesh, open plains in Bastar district; Maharashtra; Orissa; Andhra Pradesh. Dialects are Adkuri, Bastari, Chandari, Gachikolo, Mehari, Muri (Muria), Sundi. Bhunjia, Nahari, Kawari are considered to be more divergent dialects. Reported to be a creole language. Called a dialect of Marathi for convenience, but noted similarities to Bhatri, a dialect of Oriya. Men who have been to school use Hindi as second language for trading and common topics. Some use Bhatri as second language. Trade language.

Kayort: spoken in Nepal, Koshi zone, Morang district, Dakuwa Danga, near Rajbangsi language. Separate language, related to Bengali.

Kharia Thar: spoken in India, in Bihar, Manbhum.

Kudmali: also called Kurmali, Kurumali, Kurmali Thar, Bedia, Dharua. 37,000 speakers in India, in Bihar; West Bengal; Orissa; Assam. Related to Sadri. Possibly the same as Panchpargania. Spoken by some Scheduled Tribes and Castes, including Bedia of West Bengal and Dharua.

Kupia: also called Valmiki. 4,000 speakers in India, in Andhra Pradesh, Visakhapatnam and East Godavari districts.

Magahi: also called Magadhi, Magaya, Maghaya, Maghori, Magi, Magodhi, Megahi, Bihari. 11,362,000 speakers in India, in the southern districts of Bihar, eastern Patna district, northern Chotanagpur division; West Bengal, Malda district. Dialects are Southern Magahi, Northern Magahi, Central Magahi. Also used as a religious language.

Maithili: also called Maitli, Maitili, Methli, Tirahutia, Bihari, Tirhuti, Tirhutia, Apabhramsa. 24,191,900 speakers in India and Nepal. In India: 22,000,000 speakers. Dialects are Standard Maithili, Southern Standard Maithili, Eastern Maithili (Khotta, Kortha, Kortha Bihari), Western Maithili, Jolaha, Central Colloquial Maithili (Sotipura), Kisan, Dehati. Caste variation more than geographic variation in dialects. Functional intelligibility among all dialects, including those in Nepal. Closest to Magahi. Hindi, Nepali, English, Bhojpuri, Bengali used mainly for business or social interaction outside the home by men or working women with various degrees of proficiency from marketing only to fluency. In cities some may use Hindi, Nepali, or English in the home. Used in home, village, town, or cities with other Maithili speakers. Spoken by Brahmin and other high caste or educated Hindus, who influence the culture and language, and other castes. There is a Maithili Academy. Linguistics and literature are taught at the L.N. Mithila University in Darbhanga and Patna University. Language attitudes are influenced by caste, ranging from superiority to resentment. Non-Brahmin speech viewed as inferior. Hindi considered superior, Nepali generally accepted. Devanagari alphabet. In Nepal: 2,191,900 speakers. Dialects are Bantar, Barei, Barmeli, Kawar, Kisan, Kyabrat, Makrana, Musar, Sadri, Tati, Dehati. More caste variation than geographical. Intelligibility good among all, including in India. Second languages used by men or working women mostly only for business, social interaction outside the home. In cities some may use Hindi, Nepali, or English even at home and with other Maithili. Bhojpuri or Bengali are used with friends from those groups. Bilingual ability varies greatly, from trade use only, to a high degree of fluency. All ages. Maithili used in home, village, towns, cities with other Maithili. Spoken by a wide variety of castes, both "high" and "low." There is a Maithili Academy in Patna. Bihar Maithili is taught at several universities including L.N. Mithila University in Karbhanga, Patna University, and Janakpur Campus of Tribhuvan University. Brahmin speech considered to be standard. Brahmins consider themselves superior, varying from friendly to domineering. Others vary toward Brahmins from friendly to resentment. Hindi and its speakers considered close, culturally similar; Nepali accepted.

Majhi: also called Manjhi. 11,322 speakers in Nepal and India. In Nepal: Janakpur zone, Sindhuli and Ramechhap districts; Narayani zone; Lumbini zone. In India: Bihar; Sikkim, South District, Majhigaon near Jorethang, East District, Majhitar near Rangpol. Bilingualism in Nepali. Devanagari alphabet.

Mal Paharia: also called Malto, Malti, Maltu, Maler, Malpaharia, Marpaharia, Mal Pahariya, Mal, Mar, Maw, Mawdo, Mawer, Mawer, Mawer Nondi, Mad, Mader, Dehri, Paharia, Parsi. 51,000 speakers in India. Not inherently intelligible with Kumarbhag Paharia, Sauria Paharia, Bengali, or Hindi. Part of the Malto ethnic group. Similar to Kharia Thar of Manbhum (in Bihar). Some have shifted to Bengali or Khorta. All domains. Vigorous language use.

Mirgan: also called Panika, Panka, Mirkan, Mirgami. 12,000 speakers in India, in Madhya Pradesh, Bastar district; Orissa, Koraput district. Dialects have good intelligibility. Not functionally intelligible with Halbi. Limited proficiency in Oriya. Oriya and Adivasi Oriya are used in Orissa, Hindi and Halbi in Madhya Pradesh. Home, religion. Vigorous language use. Positive attitudes toward speaking Mirgan. Oriya, Telugu scripts.

Musasa: also called Musahar. Spoken in Nepal, Sindhuli Garhi district; Morang district, Koshi zone; Dolakha district, Janakpur zone.

Nahari: also called Nahali. 108 speakers in India, in Madhya Pradesh, Raipur, Bilaspur districts; Orissa, Sambalpur district. A more divergent variety, related to Halbi.

Oriya: also called Uriya, Utkali, Odri, Odrum, Oliya, Orissa, Vadiya, Yudhia. 32,000,000 speakers in India and Bangladesh. In India: 31,666,000 speakers in Orissa, Bihar, West Bengal, Assam, Andhra Pradesh. Dialects are Mughalbandi (Oriya Proper, Standard Oriya), Southern Oriya, Northwestern Oriya, Western Oriya (Sambalpuri), North Balasore Oriya, Midnapore Oriya, Halbi. Some of the larger dialects have many subdialects. Sambalpuri around Sambalpur and Sundargh needs intelligibility testing with Standard Oriya. Spoken as mother tongue by the Bathudi, Bhuiya, some Koda, and the Mali. Oriya script. National language.

Oriya, Adivasi: also called Tribal Oriya, Desiya, Desia, Deshia, Kotiya, Kotia Oriya, Adiwasi Oriya. 300,000 speakers in India in Andhra Pradesh, Visakhapatnam district, Araku Valley; Orissa, Koraput district. Telugu script used in Andhra Pradesh; 100,000 Adivasi Oriya speakers in Orissa use Oriya script. Trade language.

Panchpargania: also called Tamaria, Tair, Tamara, Temoral, Tumariya, Tanti, Chik Barik, Bedia, Pan, Pan Sawasi.

274,000 speakers in India, in Bihar, Ranchi, Singhbhum districts; West Bengal. Related to Sadri. Possibly the same as Kudmali. Spoken by the Bedia of Bihar and Chik Barik of West Bengal.

Rajbangsi: also called Rajbansi, Rajbanshi, Tajpuri. 2,350,000 speakers in India, Bangladesh, and Nepal. In India: 2,258,760 speakers in West Bengal, Jalpaiguri, Cooch Behar, Darjeeling districts. In Nepal: Mechi zone, Jhapa district; Koshi zone, Morang district. 30% of the population use Nepali as second language, 30% Hindi, 60% Khavas Tharu. In Bangladesh: Districts of Jalpaiguri, Cooch Behar.

Reli: also called Relli. 19,000 speakers in India in Andhra Pradesh, near Adiwasi Oriya; Orissa, Koraput district.

Sadri: also called Sadani, Sadana, Sadati, Sadari, Sadhan, Sadna, Sadrik, Santri, Siddri, Sradri, Sadhari, Sadan, Nagpuria, Nagpuri, Chota Nagpuri, Dikku Kaji, Gawari, Ganwari, Goari, Gauuari. 1,965,000 speakers in India and Bangladesh. In India: Assam, Bihar, Madhya Pradesh, West Bengal, Orissa, Andaman Islands, Nagaland. Intelligibility of all dialects with each other is high, except for Sadri of Bangladesh, where it is 77%. Speakers name three kinds of Sadri: Sadani (finer, respectful, formal), Common Sadri (Nagpuri), and Lower Sadri (rough). Hindi, Oriya, and Bengali used as official languages. Hindi used in market, with leaders, for prayer and worship, but proficiency limited. Spoken by Scheduled Tribes, Scheduled Castes, and other communities. Spoken by the Chero as mother tongue. Positive attitude toward Sadri, including the religious literature. Devanagari script. Language of wider communication. In Bangladesh: 200,000 speakers.

Sadri, Oraon: 84,000 speakers in Bangladesh. Dialects are Borail Sadri, Nurpur Sadri, Uchai Sadri, Mokkan Tila Sadri. The dialects listed may need separate literature. Inherent intelligibility of seven Sadri varieties on Borail ranges from 70% to 93%; of eight varieties on Nurpur from 78% to 94%. Speakers' bilingual proficiency in Bengali is limited. Vigorous language use.

Surajpuri: also called Suraiji, Choupal, Chaupal. 273,000 speakers in India in Bihar. May be a dialect of Maithili.

Sylheti: also called Sylhetti, Sylheti Bangla, Sileti, Siloti, Syloti, Syloty. Around 11,000,000 speakers in Bangladesh, India, and United Kingdom. In Bangladesh: 8,000,000 speakers. Ethnic population: 8,000,000 or more. Bilingualism in Bengali. In India: 3,000,000 speakers. Bilingualism in Bengali.

Tangchangya: also called Tanchangya. 17,700 speakers in Bangladesh. Closely related to Chakma.

Tharu, Chitwania: also called Chituan Tharu, Chitawan Tharu. 80,000 speakers in Nepal and India. In Nepal: Narayani zone, Chiatwan district; Lumbini zone, Nawalparasi district. Bilingualism in Nepali, Hindi, Bhojpuri Tharu.

Tharu, Deokhuri: also called Deokhar, Deokri. 80,000 speakers in Nepal, in Rapti zone, Dang district. May be a dialect of Dangauru Tharu. Bilingualism in Nepali.

FIGURE 1. *Subgrouping of East Main Section Trans-New Guinea Languages*

Binanderean
  Binanderean Proper
    Baruga, Binandere, Ewage-Notu, Gaina, Korafe, Orokaiva, Suena, Yekora, Zia
  Guhu-Samane
Central and Southeastern Eastern Main Section
  Dagan
    Daga, Ginuman, Jimajima, Kanasi, Maiwa, Mapena, Onjab, Turaka, Umanakaina
  Goilalan
    Fuyug
    Tauade
    Kunimaipa
      Biangai, Kunimaipa, Weri
  Koiarian
    Baraic
      Bari, Ese, Ömie
    Koiaric
      Mountain Koiali, Grass Koiari, Koitabu
  Kwalean
    Humene, Mulaha, Uare
  Mailuan
    Bauwaki, Binahari, Domu, Laua, Mailu, Morawa
  Manubaran
    Doromu, Maria
  Yareban
    Aneme Wake, Bariji, Moikodi, Nawaru, Yareba

Tharu, Kochila: also called Saptari. 250,000 speakers in Nepal and India. In Nepal: Koshi zone, Morang and Sunsari districts; Sagarmatha zone, Saptari, Udayapur, and Siraha districts; Janakpur zone, Mahottari district. Other Tharu in Siraha, Udayapur, and Saparti districts who call themselves "Kochila" but do not speak Kochila Tharu can be distinguished by dress, customs, and language. They have adopted Maithili culture. Bilingualism in Nepali. Maithili also used. Family, older people, children, village leaders (mainly), sometimes Nepali with non-Tharu. Vigorous language use.

Tharu, Mahotari: also called Mahottari. 32,000 speakers in Nepal in Janakpur zone, Mahottari district. May be part of Kochila Tharu. Bilingualism in Nepali.

Tharu, Rana: also called Rana Thakur. 264,000 speakers in Nepal and India. In Nepal: 200,000 speakers in Mahakali zone, Kanchanpur district; Seti zone, Kailali district. Speakers appear to have 96% to 99% intelligibility among dialects, 90% with Kathoriya, 51% to 88% reported of Dangaura. Differences with India dialects. Bilingualism in Nepali. Hindi also used. Family, older people, children, mainly in village, Nepali with non-Tharu people. Vigorous language use. Some possible negative attitudes toward Dangaura

Tharu. In India: 64,000 speakers. Hindi bilingual proficiency is limited among the 70% to 90% who are uneducated.

B. GRIMES

EAST MAIN SECTION TRANS-NEW GUINEA LANGUAGES form a grouping within the proposed TRANS-NEW GUINEA phylum. They are spoken in southeastern Papua New Guinea.

LANGUAGE LIST

Aneme Wake: also called Abie, Abia. 650 speakers in Oro Province, Afore district, both sides of Owen Stanley Range, Central Province; north from Ianu along Foasi and Domara Creeks. Dialects are Mori, Buniabura, Auwaka, Jari, Doma. Bilingualism in Motu, Yareba.

Barai: 2,000 speakers. Dialects are Birarie, Namiae, and Muguani. Birarie and Namiae are major dialects, Muguani is minor.

Bariji: also called Aga Bereho. 260 speakers in Oro Province, on the southern bank of the Bariji River. Speakers are bilingual in Hiri Motu and reported to know Moikodi or Yareba.

Baruga: 1,500 speakers. Dialects are Bareji Baruga, Mado (Baruga), Tafota Baruga, Do Ghoro (Dogoro). Some speakers are bilingual in Hiri Motu, Tok Pisin, and English. Some can also speak Ewage-Notu, Korafe, or Motu. All ages. All domains. Some use in religious services. Speakers are preparing books in Baruga. Oral literature. Vigorous language use. Parents transmit it to children. Wives of Baruga men who are not Baruga learn it. Government schools planned to use Baruga in first two grades. Speakers are very positive toward Baruga.

Bauwaki: also called Bawaki. 398 speakers. Most are at Amau (Mori River), Central Province, extending into Oro Province. Dutton says this is a bridge language between the Mailuan and Yareban families. 85% to 100% of speakers are bilingual in Magi, Suau, Motu, or English.

Biangai: 1,400 speakers. Morobe Province, Wau district, headwaters of the Bulolo River, seven villages. Dialects are Ngowiye, Yongolei. 50% monolingualism. Others use Tok Pisin as second language.

Binahari: 764 speakers in Central Province, both sides of a range of hills inland from Cloudy Bay. Dialects are Neme (Nemea), Ma. 80% to 100% bilingual in Magi, Suau, Hiri Motu, or English.

Binandere: also called Ioma Binandere. 6,700 speakers in Oro Province, along the Eia, Gira, Ope, Mambere, and Kumusi Rivers, between Zia and Ambasi; a few in Morobe Province. Dialects are Aeka (Aiga), Ambasi (Tain-Daware, Davari,

Dawari), Binandere. Speakers who live near the coast are more bilingual.

Daga: also called Dimuga, Nawp. 6,000 speakers in Milne Bay Province, Rabaraba district, and Central Province, Abau district. Related languages: Bagoi, Galeva, Swoiden, Kanamara, Makiara, Maneao, Moibiri, Pue, Tevi, Turaka.

Domu: also called Dom. 593 speakers in Central Province, coast east of Cape Rodney and inland. 85% to 100% of the speakers are bilingual in Mailu, Suau, Hiri Motu, English.

Doromu: also called Doram. 1,200 speakers in Central Province, south of Mt. Obree, west of Mt. Brown. Dialects are Kokila, Koriko, Koki (Doromu).

Ese: "Managalasi," "Managulasi" are derogatory names sometimes used. 10,000 speakers in Oro Province, Popondetta district, southeast of the Omie. Dialects are Muaturaina, Chimona, Dea, Akabafa, Nami, Mesari, Averi, Afore, Minjori, Oko, Wakue, Numba, Jimuni, Karira. 50% monolingualism. Others use Tok Pisin, English, or Hiri Motu as second language. The use of Hiri Motu is decreasing. The younger generation does not know it. All ages. All domains. Used in school in first three grades, used in local business, personal letters. Vigorous language use. Parents transmit it to children. Speakers have high regard for their language.

Ewage-Notu: also called Notu, Ewage. 12,900 speakers in Oro Province, Popondetta district, on the coast between Bakumbari and Pongani. Dialects are Ewage-Notu, Yega (Gona, Okeina, Okena).

Fuyug: also called Fuyuge, Fuyughe, Mafufu. 18,000 speakers in Central Province, Goilala district, Owen Stanley Range. Dialects are Central Udab, Northeast Fuyug, North-South Udab, West Fuyug.

Gaina: 1,130 speakers in Oro Province, next to the Baruga, the villages around Iwuji. Dialects are Bareji (Baredji), Gaina.

Ginuman: also called Dime. 775 speakers in Milne Bay Province, Mt. Simpson to coast at Naraka.

Grass Koiari: also called Koiari. 1,700 speakers in Central Province, east of Port Moresby and to coast. 10% monolingual. Others use Hiri Motu or English as second language.

Guhu-Samane: also called Paiawa, Tahari, Muri, Bia, Mid-Waria. 6,290 speakers in Morobe Province, Lae district, and a few in Oro Province, from Kanoma and Sidema villages northward.

Humene: 440 speakers in Central Province, lower edge of Sogeri Plateau and adjacent plain between Gaire and Kapakapa villages. Manugoro is principal village. Dialects are Lagume (Lakume, Manukolu), Humene. Some speakers know Hiri Motu and Motu, some English.

Jimajima: also called Dima. 545 speakers in Milne Bay Province, along the coast east of Moi Bay almost to Midino, and along the Ruaba River. Dialects are West Coastal Jimajima, East Inland Jimajima.

Kanasi: also called Sona. 2,200 speakers in Milne Bay Province, Rabaraba district, on both sides of the main range river valleys from Mt. Thomson.

Koitabu: also called Koita. 2,700 speakers in Central Province, around Port Moresby. Dialects are West Koita, East Koita. Bilingual level estimates are Hiri Motu: 0 33%, 1 10%, 2 20%, 3 20%, 4 13%, 5 4%; Motu: 0 80%, 1 5%, 2 5%, 3 5%, 4 5%, 5 0%. Some speakers are bilingual in Hiri Motu, Motu, Tok Pisin, or English.

Korafe: also called Korape, Korafi, Kwarafe, Kailikaili. 2,800 speakers in Oro Province, Tufi district, on the headlands (fiord system) of Cape Nelson. Dialects are Korafe, Mokorua (Yega, Yegha). Yega dialect is distinct from Gona, also called "Yega." Gaina may also be a dialect. Some speakers are bilingual in English, Tok Pisin, or Hiri Motu.

Kunimaipa: 11,000 speakers in Central Province, northern Goilala district; Morobe Province, Wau district. Dialects are Karuama, Kate (Hate), Gajili (Gajila, Gazili, Hazili). Bilingualism in Tok Pisin.

Laua: also called Labu. 1 speaker remains. Formerly spoken in Central Province, north and west of Laua.

Mailu: also called Magi. 6,000 speakers in Central Province, southern coast, Gadaisu to Baramata, Table Bay and Toulon Island. Dialects are Domara, Darava, Asiaoro, Derebai, Island, Geagea, Borebo, Ilai, Baibara. Related language: Laua.

Maiwa: 1,400 speakers. Dialects are Maiwa, Oren, Manigara, Gairen, Gwareta. Wedau is used as church language.

Mapena: 275 speakers in Milne Bay Province, around Mt. Gwoira.

Maria: also called Manubara. 870 speakers in Central Province, Marshall Lagoon to Mt. Brown; a remote area. Dialects are Didigaru, Maria, Gebi, Oibu, Amota, Imila, Uderi.

Moikodi: also called Doriri. 570 speakers in Oro Province, northern slopes of Owen Stanley Range around Mt. Brown down to Komi west of Foasi Creek. Several dialects. 50% are monolingual. Others use Hiri Motu as second language.

Morawa: 755 speakers in Central Province, southern coast around Cloudy Bay. 85% to 100% of the people are bilingual in Magi, Suau, Hiri Motu, or English.

Mountain Koiali: also called Mountain Koiari. 1,700 speakers in Central Province, Port Moresby district, north of Koita, Koiari, and Barai. One village is Efogi. 50% monolingualism. Others use Motu as second language.

Mulaha: formerly spoken in Central Province, just southeast of Gaile on the coast. Dialects are Mulaha, Iaibu.

Nawaru: also called Sirio. 190 speakers in Oro Province, around upper Musa River valley. Very close to Yareba. Bilingualism in Hiri Motu, Yareba.

Ömie: also called Aomie, Upper Managalasi. 800 speakers in Oro Province, Kokoda, Upper Kumusi, and Afore districts, northwest of Managalasi, Mamama River and Upper Kumusi

Valley. Dialects are Asapa, Zuwadza, Gora-Bomahouji. 50% monolingualism. Others use Hiri Motu or English as second language.

Onjab: also called Onjob. 150 speakers in Oro Province, Koreat and Naukwate villages. Bilingualism in English, Ubir.

Orokaiva: also called Orakaiva, Ke, Kaiva. 33,300 speakers in Oro Province, Popondetta district between the Hunjara, Notu, Binandere, and Managalasi, two hundred villages. Some speakers also in Port Moresby, Wewak, Madang, and Lae. Dialects are Kokoda, Hunjara, Ajeka, Etija (Sose, Sohe), Ehija (Ihane, Ifane), Harava, Aeka. About 20% are monolingual. Over 80% speak Tok Pisin, 20% also speak English, a few old people speak Motu. All ages. All domains. Local administration, business, early grades of education. Oral and written use in church. Personal letters. Oral literature. Vigorous language use. Parents transmit it to children. Speakers are positive about Orokaiva. Young men sometimes prefer Tok Pisin.

Suena: also called Yema, Yarawe, Yarawi. 3,000 speakers. Ethnic population: 3,000 as of 2000. Spoken in Morobe Province, Lae district, north of Yekora. Bilingualism in Tok Pisin, English. The Yarawi are apparently a group who spoke Suena around 1910 to 1978, but as of 2000 may speak a dialect of Binandere as their mother tongue.

Tauade: also called Tauata. 11,000 speakers in Central Province, Goilala district toward the northeast.

Turaka: 25 speakers remain in Milne Bay Province, 5 miles southwest of Radarada and Ruaba. Related languages: Daga, Bagoi, Galeva, Gwoiden, Kanamara, Makiara, Maneao, Moibiri, Pue, Tevi. 20% to 60% of the ethnic group speak Turaka.

Uare: also called Kwale, Kware. 1,300 speakers in Central Province, Rigo inland district, on the coast south of Port Moresby, Kemp Welsh and Hunter Rivers. Dialects are Garihe (Garia), Uare (Kwale).

Umanakaina: also called Gwedena, Gweda, Gwede, Gvede, Umanikaina. 2,400 speakers in Milne Bay Province, Rabaraba district, on the coast of Goodenough Bay, inland between Mt. Gwoira and Mt. Simpson. Dialects are Upper Ugu River, East Umanakaina. Some speak some English.

Weri: also called Weli, Wele. 4,165 speakers in Morobe Province, Wau district, headwaters of Biaru, Waria, and Ono Rivers. Dialects are Sim, Biaru-Waria, Ono.

Yareba: also called Middle Musa. 750 speakers in Oro Province, Popondetta district. Speakers are highly bilingual in Hiri Motu.

Yekora: 1,000 speakers in Morobe Province, two villages near Morobe government station. Close to Mawae (dialect of Zia). Bilingualism in Suena, Zia.

Zia: also called Tsia, Lower Waria, Ziya. 3,943 speakers in Morobe Province, Lae district near the mouth of the Waria River. Dialects are Zia, Mawae. B. GRIMES

EAST MON-KHMER LANGUAGES.
A top-level constituent of the Mon-Khmer group within AUSTRO-ASIATIC, spoken in Cambodia, Laos, Vietnam, adjacent areas, USA, and Canada in one instance.

LANGUAGE LIST

Alak: also called Hrlak. 4,000 speakers in southern Laos, mainly in Saravan Province. Included under Bahnaric as closest to Bahnar, Tampuan, Lamam.

Bahnar: also called Bana. 137,000 speakers in Vietnam and USA. In Vietnam: Southeastern Gia Lai-Cong Tum, Nghia Binh, Phu Khanh Provinces, central highlands. Dialects are Tolo, Golar, Alakong (A-La Cong), Jolong (Gio-Lang, Y-Lang), Bahnar Bonom (Bomam), Kontum, Krem. Other dialects or ethnic names: Roh, Kpang Cong. Closest to Alak 1, Tampuan, and Lamam.

Bru, Eastern: also called Brou, Vankieu. 114,000 speakers in Laos, Vietnam, and Thailand. In Laos: 69,000 speakers in eastern Savannehkhet Province: Tchepone area east of Vietnamese border, and Saravan Province, on the Vietnam border. Dialects are Tri (So Tri, So Trii, Chali). It is partially intelligible with Western Bru of Thailand. In Vietnam: 40,000 speakers in Bl'nh Tri Thien Province. Related to Khua. Mangkong in Vietnam and eastern Laos is a dialect of Eastern Bru, different linguistically from the Mangkong group that is the same as So of Thailand. In Thailand: Sakon Nakhon Province, about twelve villages. Dialects are Tri (So Tri, So Trii), Bru Kok Sa-At. Tri young people in Thailand do not speak the language.

Bru, Western: also called Bruu, B'ru, Baru. 20,000 speakers in Thailand and USA. In Thailand: Dong Luang district of Mukdahand Province, one village in Amnat Charoen Province, two villages in Khong Chiam district, Ubon Province. It is partially intelligible with Eastern Bru.

Budeh Stieng: also called Lower Stieng, Southern Stieng. Spoken in Vietnam, southern Stieng area. Different enough from Bulo Stieng that intelligibility is not functional.

Bulo Stieng: also called Xtieng, Xa-Dieng, Budíp, Rangah, Upper Stieng, Northern Stieng. 53,571 speakers in Vietnam and Cambodia. In Vietnam: 50,000 speakers. Song Bé and Tay Ninh Provinces. In Cambodia: 3,571 speakers in eastern Kratie Province, Snuol district, and southern Mondolkiri. Dialects are Budíp, Bulach, Bulo. Bilingualism in Mnong, Khmer.

Chong: also called Chawng, Shong, Xong. Around 8,000 speakers in Cambodia and Thailand. In Cambodia: 5,000 speakers on Thai-Cambodia border southeast of Chantaburi, Pursat Province. Somray in Cambodia is a separate but related language. In Thailand: 500 speakers in Chantaburi, four villages, Trat Province, northwest of Par. Closely related to Somray of Cambodia.

FIGURE 1. *Subgrouping of Eastern Mon-Khmer Languages*

Bahnaric
  Central Bahnaric
    Alak, Bahnar, Kaco', Lamam, Romam, Tampuan
  North Bahnaric
    Katua
    East North Bahnaric
      Cua, Kayong
        Cua, Kayong
      Takua
    West North Bahnaric
      Talieng
      Trieng
      Duan
        Halang Doan
      Jeh-Halang
        Halang, Jeh
      Rengao
      Sedang-Todrah
        Sedang
          Hre, Sedang
        Todrah-Monom
          Monom, Todrah
  South Bahnaric
    Budeh Stieng
    Sre-Mnong
      Mnong
      Eastern Mnong
      Southern-Central Mnong
        Kraol, Central Mnong, Southern Mnong
    Sre
      Koho, Maa
    Stieng-Chrau
      Chrau, Bulo Stieng

West Bahnaric
  Brao-Kravet
    Kravet, Kru'ng 2, Lave, Sou
  Laven
  Nyaheun
  Oi-The
    Jeng, Oy, Sapuan, Sok, The
Katuic
  Central Katuic
    Ta'oih
      Ir, Kataang, Ong, Lower Ta'oih, Upper Ta'oih
  East Katuic
    Kaseng
      Kasseng
    Katu-Pacoh
      Eastern Katu, Western Katu, Pacoh, Phuong, Tareng
    Ngeq-Nkriang
      Khlor, Ngeq
  West Katuic
    Brou-Sô
      Eastern Bru, Western Bru, Khua, Sô
    Kuay-Yoe
      Kuy, Nyeu
Khmer
  Central Khmer, Northern Khmer
Pearic
  Eastern Pearic
    Pear
  Western Pearic
    Chong
      Chong, Sa'och
    Samre
      Samre, Somray
    Suoy

Chrau: also called Chauro, Choro, Ro, Tamun. 15,000 speakers in Vietnam in Dòng Nai Province. The Tamun group live in Tayninh and Binhlong Provinces. Dialects are Jro, Dor (Doro), Prang, Mro, Voqtwaq, Vajieng, Chalah, Chalun, Tamun. Few speakers are monolingual. Nearly all speak Vietnamese as second language. Some parents transmit Chrau to children. Informally used in education, oral and written use in religious services, oral literature. Speakers have a positive attitude about Chrau.

Cua: also called Bong Miew, Bòng Mieu. 23,000 speakers in Vietnam. Nghia Bình, Quang Nam-Da Nang Provinces. Dialects are Kol (Kor, Cor, Co, Col, Dot, Yot), Traw (Tràu, Dong).

Halang: also called Salang, Koyong. 12,000 speakers in Vietnam and Laos. In Vietnam: 10,000 speakers in Gia Lai-Cong Tum Province. Close to Jeh. Salang in Laos may be a different but related language. In Laos: 2,000 speakers in Attopeu Province, southern Laos. Closely related to Jeh. Halang in Vietnam may be a separate language.

Halang Doan: also called Halang Duan, Duan, Doan. 2,000 speakers in Vietnam and Laos. In Vietnam: Gia Lai-Cong Tum Province, between the Sedang and the Cua. May be intelligible with Takua, Kayong, Halang Daksut, or Rengao. In Laos: 1,000 speakers.

Hre: also called Davak, Davach, Moi Da Vach, Moi, Moi Luy, Cham-Re, Chom, Tachom. 94,000 speakers in Vietnam. Nghia Bình Province. Dialects are Rabah (Tava), Creq (Kare, Kre), Hre. Closest to Sedang.

Ir: also called In, Yir. 10,000 speakers in Laos in Saravane Province, east of Saravane. Closest to Ong.

Jeh: also called Die, Yeh, Gie. 10,000 speakers in Vietnam and Laos. In Vietnam: Quang Nam-Da Nang and Gia Lai-Cong Tum Provinces. Dialects are Jeh Bri La (Bri-La), Jeh Mang Ram. In Laos: Basin of Poko, Se Kamane, and Dak Main

Rivers in southern Laos. Dialects are Jeh Bri La, Jeh Mang Ram. The language is closely related to Halang.

Jeng: also called Cheng, Ceng. 5,400 speakers in Laos, north of Attopeu. Related to Oy, Sapuan, Sok.

Kaco': also called Kachah'. 2,000 speakers in Cambodia in Rattanakiri Province. A distinct language, not intelligible to Tampuan speakers. Speakers are not bilingual.

Kasseng: also called Koseng, Kaseng, Kraseng. Spoken in Laos. Ethnic population: 1,200. Southern Laos near Vietnam border, Boloven Plateau area north of Attopeu, and between the Jeh, Alak, Laven, and Tareng peoples.

Kataang: also called Katang. 10,000 speakers in southern Laos near the Ta'oih and Bru peoples, around Muong Nong, in Saravan, Savannakhet, Sekong, and Champassak. Not intelligible with Ta'oih.

Katu, Eastern: also called High Katu. 37,300 speakers in Vietnam, Quang Nam and Thua Thien Provinces. A different language variety and orthography in Laos.

Katu, Western: 14,700 speakers in Laos, Upper Xe Kong River, high basin of Song Boung River along watershed along the border, Xe Kong, Saravan, and Champasak Provinces. A different language variety and orthography from Vietnam. Has its own script, called 'Like'.

Katua: also called Ca Tua. 3,000 speakers in Vietnam, in Gia Lai-Cong Tum Province, around Mang Buk, west of the Kayong language.

Kayong: also called Kagiuong, Ca Giong, Katang. 2,000 speakers in Vietnam, in remote mountains of Cong Tum Province. Close to Takua and Cua.

Khlor: also called Klor, Lor. 6,000 speakers in Laos, Saravan Province, south of Ir and Ong. Closest to Ngeq.

Khmer, Central: also called Khmer, Cambodian. 7,039,200 speakers in Cambodia, Vietnam, USA, Canada, China, France, and Laos. In Cambodia: 5,932,800 speakers. Throughout the country. Distinct from Northern Khmer of Thailand. Script derived from a southern Indian alphabet. First written during the period of Indian influence. Earliest surviving example AD 61. National language of Cambodia. In Vietnam: 895,000 speakers in Hau Giang, Cuu Long, Kien Giang, Minh Hai, Thành phó Hò Chí minh, Song Bé, Tay Ninh Provinces, Mekong Delta of southwestern Vietnam. Dialects are Central Khmer, Southern Khmer. In USA: Long Beach, Orange County, California, Seattle, Washington, Oregon, North Dakota, New York, Rhode Island, Wisconsin, Texas. In Canada: Montreal, Toronto, other cities.

Khmer, Northern: also called Khmer Lue, Thailand Khmer. 1,000,000 speakers in northeastern Thailand, mainly Surin, Sisaket, Buriram, Korat Provinces. Dialects are Buriram, Surin, Sisaket. Different from Central Khmer. Dialects are intelligible with each other. Many local varieties. Very few are monolingual. Nearly all can speak Central Thai, most Isan, and some Central Khmer. Vigorous language use in towns. In cities it is being replaced by Isan and Thai. A few Chinese shopkeepers speak it. Informally used in education, very little use in media, used in some Buddhist monasteries and some Christian churches, in business in villages and city markets. Speakers are favorable toward Northern Khmer.

Khua: 5,000 speakers in Vietnam and Laos. In Vietnam: West central; southeast of Giap Tam. Related to Bru, Mangkong, Leun. In Laos: East central, northwest of Boualapha. Related to Bru, Mangkong, Leun.

Koho: also called Coho, Kohor. 92,000 speakers in Vietnam and USA. In Vietnam: Lam Dòng and Thuan Hai Provinces. Dialects are Chil (Kil), Tring (Trinh), Sre, Kalop, Sop, Laya, Rion, Nop (Xre Nop, Tu-Lop), Tala (To La), Kodu (Co-Don), Pru, Lac (Lat, Lach).

Kraol: 2,600 speakers in Cambodia in Kratie Province. A distinct language, not intelligible to Mnong speakers. No bilingualism.

Kravet: also called Kowet, Khvek, Kavet. 3,012 speakers in northeastern Cambodia.

Kru'ng 2: also called Krueng. 9,368 speakers in Cambodia in northeastern Rattanakiri Province and eastern Stung Treng. Brao, Kravet, Kru'ng 2 in Cambodia are inherently intelligible with each other. Central Khmer is known to a lesser extent than Lao for second language use.

Kuy: also called Kuuy, Kui, Kuoy, Kuay, Kui Souei, Cuoi, Sui, Suai, Suay, Suoi, Soai, Suei. 380,000 speakers in Thailand, Laos, and Cambodia. In Thailand: 300,000 speakers in east central Thailand: mainly in Surin and Sisaket, small pockets in Buriram, Ubon, Roi Et. Few are monolingual in Thailand. About 99% can also speak Lao or Isan, 80% Central Thai, 40% Northern Khmer (mainly older people). Kuy villages often intermingled with those of Lao and Northern Khmer speakers. Speakers have affection for Kuy and want to keep it, but want to also speak Lao or Isan and Central Thai. In Laos: 64,000 speakers in Saravan, Sedone Provinces. A large group on both sides of the Mekong in southern Laos, Cambodia. Dialects are Antra, Na Nhyang. 80% monolingual. In Cambodia: Dialects are Damrey, Anlour, O, Kraol, Antra, Na Nhyang. Bilingualism in Central Khmer.

Lamam: also called Lmam. 1,000 speakers in Cambodia near northeastern corner on the Vietnam border. Related to Bahnar, Tampuan, Alak 1.

Lave: also called Brao, Braou, Brau, Proue, Brou, Love, Laveh, Rawe. Around 18,381 speakers in Laos, Cambodia, Vietnam, and USA. In Laos: 12,750 speakers in Stung Treng and Ratanakiri Provinces, Laos-Cambodian border. In Cambodia: 5,286 speakers in northeastern Cambodia on the Laos border, Rattanakiri Province. Closely related to Kru'ng 2, Kravet, and Sou. In Vietnam: Gia Lai-Cong Tum Province, Cambodia-Laos border area. In USA: Providence, R.I., Massachusetts, Washington, D.C., Charlotte, N.C., Dallas, Tex., Minneapolis, Minn., Stockton, Calif., Portland, Oreg.

Laven: also called Loven, Boloven, Boriwen, Laweenjru, Jaru. 32,000 speakers in Laos and USA. In Laos: Southwestern Laos, Boloven Plateau, near the Alak. In USA: Stockton, Calif.

Maa: also called Maaq, Ma, Maa', Chauma, Ma Ngan, Che Ma, Ma Xop, Ma To, Ma Krung. 25,000 speakers in Vietnam, in Lam Dong, Dong Nai, and Thuan Hai Provinces, spread over a wide area. Sometimes considered a Koho dialect.

Mnong, Central: also called Pnong, Budong, Budang, Phanong. 69,000 speakers in Vietnam and Cambodia. In Vietnam: 50,000 speakers, southwest of the Rade, mainly in Song Bé and western Dac Lac Provinces. Dialects are Préh (Pre), Biat (Bhiét), Bu Nar, Bu Rung, Dih Bri (Di-Pri), Bu Dang. Biat may be a separate language related to Eastern Mnong. In Cambodia: 19,000 speakers in the northeast, 80% of Mondolkiri Province, all districts. Dialects are Biat, Preh, Bu Nar, Bu Rung, Dih Bri, Bu Dang. Biat is the main dialect of Cambodian Mnong. It may be a separate language from Central Mnong. Other dialect variation is slight. Central Khmer only spoken well by a few individuals. Others have limited ability.

Mnong, Eastern: 48,000 speakers in Vietnam and USA. In Vietnam: Southeast of the Rade in Dac Lac and Lam Dòng Provinces. Dialects are Mnong Rolom (Rolom, Rolam, Rlam, Ralam), Mnong Gar (Gar), Mnong Kwanh, Chil. Biat may be closer to Eastern Mnong than to Central Mnong.

Mnong, Southern: 48,000 speakers in Vietnam, mostly in Song Bé Province south of the Central Mnong and north of the Stieng. Dialects are Bunong (Nong, Pnong), Prang (Po Rang).

Monom: also called Bonom, Menam, Monam. 5,000 speakers in Vietnam, eastern Gia Lai-Cong Tum Province.

Ngeq: also called Ngeh, Nge', Kriang, Nkriang. 4,000 speakers in southern Laos, in the Muong Phine-Bung Sai area. Closest to Khlor. Related to Alak 2. 70% of speakers are monolingual.

Nyaheun: also called Nha Heun, Nyah Heuny, Hoen, Nia Hoen, Hun, Hin, Niahon, Nyahön, Yaheun. 4,000 speakers in Laos, eastern part of Boloven Plateau near Saravan and Paksong.

Nyeu: also called Yeu, Yoe. Spoken in Thailand, in Sisaket.

Ong: spoken in Laos, Saravan Province, north of Saravan. Closest to Ir.

Oy: also called Huei, Oi. 10,600 speakers in southern Laos, foot of Boloven Plateau and Pakse. Dialects are Riyao, Tamal Euy, Inn Tea, Kranyeu. Related to Jeng, Sapuan, Sok, The. 80% monolingual.

Pacoh: also called Paco, Pokoh, Bo River Van Kieu. 15,000 speakers in Vietnam and Laos. In Vietnam: Bl'nh Tri Thien Province. In Laos: Related to Phuong.

Pear: also called Por, Kompong Thom. 1,300 speakers in southwestern Cambodia, Kompong Thom.

Phuong: also called Phuang, Phuong Catang. 15,000 speakers in Vietnam, in Quang Nam-Da Nang and Gia Lai-Cong Tum Provinces, southeast of the Pacoh language.

Rengao: also called Ro-Ngao. 15,000 speakers in Vietnam, in Cong Tum Province, from northwest of Dak To to southeast of Kontum city between Sedang and Bahnar. Dialects are Western Rengao, Sedang-Rengao, Bahnar-Rengao.

Romam: 250 speakers in Vietnam on the Vietnam-Cambodian border.

Samre: 50 speakers in Cambodia. Ethnic population: 200 as of year 2000. Formerly spoken just north of Siemreap. Related to Sa'och, Suoy, Pear.

Sa'och: also called Sauch, Saotch. 500 speakers in southwestern Cambodia. near Kompong Som on the coast. Related to Samre, Suoy, Pear.

Sapuan: also called Sapouan. 2,400 speakers in Laos on the banks of the Se Kong and Se Kamane Rivers, Attopeu Province, southern Laos. Related to Oy, Sok, Jeng.

Sedang: also called Hadang, Hdang, Hoteang, Roteang, Rotea, Hotea, Xodang, Xa Dang, Cadong, Tang, Kmrang. 40,000 speakers in Vietnam and Laos. In Vietnam: Cong Tum Province. Dialects are Central Sedang, Greater Sedang, Dak Sut Sedang, Kotua Sedang, Kon Hring Sedang. Closest to Hre.

Sô: also called Mangkong, Mang-Koong, Makong, Sô Makon, Mankoong, Mang Cong, Bru, Kah Sô, Thro. 157,000 speakers in Laos and Thailand. In Laos: 102,000 speakers on both sides of the Mekong River in Thakhek and Savannakhet Provinces in Laos and Thailand. Dialects are So Trong, So Slouy, So Phong, Chali (Chari, Shari), Kaleu. Because of contact with the Laotian Tai, they speak Tai dialects. In Thailand: 55,000 speakers in Nakorn Panom, Sakorn Nakorn, Nong Kai, Kalasin. Both sides of Mekong River in northeastern Thailand. Fifty-three villages in Thailand. Dialects are So Trong, So Slouy, So Phong, So Makon. Speakers came from Laos, and the same dialect is spoken there. Closely related to Bru. They also speak Lao. They are adjusting to Thai culture and gradually becoming bilingual in Thai. All ages. People speak Sô in the home.

Sok: also called Sork, Sawk. 1,600 speakers in Laos, Attopeu Province, southern Laos. Related to Oy, Sapuan, Jeng.

Somray: 2,000 speakers in western Cambodia; north, east, and west of Phum Tasanh, and Tanyong River around Phum Pra Moi. Related to Chong.

Sou: also called Suq, Souk, Su, Su'. 1,000 speakers in southern Laos, Attopeu Province.

Suoy: 200 speakers in central Cambodia, northwest of Phnom Penh. Related to Sa'och, Samre, Pear.

Takua: also called Quang Tin Katu, Langya. 5,000 speakers in Vietnam, Quang Nam-Da Nang Province. Closest to Cua and Kayong.

Talieng: also called Taliang, Tariang. Spoken in Laos. Muong

FIGURE 1. *Subgrouping of the East New Guinea Highlands Languages*

Central East New Guinea Highlands
  Chimbu
      Chuave, Dom, Golin, Kuman, Nomane, Salt-Yui, Sinasina
  Hagen
      Melpa
    Kaugel
        Imbongu, Mbo-Ung, Umbu-Ungu
  Jimi
      Kandawo, Maring, Narak
  Wahgi
      Nii, Wahgi, North Wahgi
East-Central East New Guinea Highlands
  Fore
      Fore, Gimi
  Gahuku-Benabena
      Alekano, Benabena, Dano, Tokano
  Gende
  Kamano-Yagaria
      Inoke-Yate, Kamano, Kanite, Keyagana, Yagaria
  Siane
      Siane, Yaweyuha
Eastern East New Guinea Highlands
  Gadsup-Auyana-Awa
      Agarabi, Awa, Awiyaana, Gadsup, Kosena, Ontenu, Usarufa
  Kambaira
  Owenia
  Tairora
      Binumarien, Omwunra-Toqura, Tairora, Waffa
Kalam
  Gants
  Kalam-Kobon
      Kalam, Kobon
  Unclassified Kalam
      Tai
Kenati
Piawi
  Haruai
  Pinai-Hagahai
West-Central East New Guinea Highlands
  Angal-Kewa
      Angal, Angal Enen, Angal Heneng, Erave, East Kewa, West Kewa, Samberigi
  Enga
      Bisorio, Enga, Ipili, Kyaka, Lembena, Nete
  Huli
Wiru

Phine-Bung Sai area, Savannakhet Province. Related to Trieng or Hre in Vietnam; may be the same as Trieng.

Tampuan: also called Tamphuan, Tampuen, Tampuon, Kha Tampuon, Campuon, Proon, Proons. 25,000 speakers in Cambodia, northeastern border area, south of Brao, west of Jarai, Central Rattanakiri Province. Related to Bahnar, Lamam, Alak, but geographically separated. Closest to Kaco', a related but separate language. Central Khmer is known by some individuals, Lao by all or most.

Ta'oih, Lower: also called Tong. Spoken in Laos in Saravan. Dialects are Tong, Hantong'. Not intelligible with Upper Ta'oih. Some are bilingual in Upper Ta'oih.

Ta'oih, Upper: also called Ta-Oy, Ta-Oi, Tau Oi, Ta Hoi, Kantua. 30,000 speakers in Laos, Vietnam, and USA. In Laos: Saravan Province. Dialects are Pasoom, Kamuan', Palee'n, Leem, Ha'aang (Sa'ang). Not intelligible with Lower Ta'oih until speakers have had at least two weeks' contact. 70% monolingual. In Vietnam: 26,000 speakers. Dòng Nai Province, east of A Tuc. 70% monolingual. In USA: Stockton, Calif., and Binghamton, N.Y.

Tareng: also called Tariang. 5,000 speakers in Laos just west of Vietnam border, east of Kayong, north of Chavane and Thia.

The: also called Thae. 1,500 speakers in Laos, Attopeu Province, southern Laos.

Todrah: also called Todrá, Didrah, Didra, Podra, Modra, Kodra. 5,000 speakers in Vietnam. Gia Lai-Cong Tum Province, northeast of Kontum city from Kon Hring to Kon Braih.

Trieng: also called Strieng, Gie-Trieng, Tareh, Treng, Ta-Rieng, Talieng, Dgiéh, Giang Ray, Pin. 27,000 speakers in Vietnam, Quang Nam-Da Nang and Gia Lai-Cong Tum Provinces, northwest of Dak Rotah. May be related to Jeh or Talieng in Laos.

B. GRIMES

EAST NEW GUINEA HIGHLANDS LANGUAGES

form a branch of the Central and Western Main Section of the proposed TRANS-NEW GUINEA phylum. They are spoken in the eastern part of the Highlands of Papua New Guinea.

LANGUAGE LIST

Agarabi: also called Agarabe, Bare. 20,000 speakers in eastern Highlands Province, Kainantu district. Close to Gadsup.

Alekano: also called Gahuku, Gafuku, Gahuku-Gama. 25,000 speakers in eastern Highlands Province, Goroka district, centered around the town of Goroka. Close to Tokano, Dano, Yaweyuha, Siane, Benabena. All speakers are probably fluent in Tok Pisin. They use it in the market or streets along with Alekano. Those under 35 who have had extensive schooling may know English, but do not use it on the streets.

About 1/3 of speakers do not teach the language to their children.

Angal: also called East Angal, Mendi. 10,000 speakers in southern Highlands Province, Mendi area, north into Mendi Valley, west into Lai Valley, eastern bank, west of Mt. Glouwe.

Angal Enen: also called South Angal Heneng, South Mendi, Nembi. 22,000 speakers in southern Highlands Province, 10 to 12 km south of Nipa, north of the Erave River, east of Lake Kutubu, west of Lai Valley.

Angal Heneng: also called Augu, West Mendi, West Angal Heneng, Agarar, Wage, Katinja. 40,000 speakers in southern Highlands Province, south of Margarima and Kandep, north of Lake Butubu, west of the Lai Valley. Dialects are Waola (Wala), Augu, Nipa.

Awa: also called Mobuta. 1,790 speakers in Okapa and Kainantu districts, eastern Highlands Province. Dialects are Tauna, Ilakia, Northeast Awa, South Awa.

Awiyaana: also called Auyana. 6,500 speakers in Kainantu, Okapa districts, eastern Highlands Province, fifteen villages.

Benabena: also called Bena. 45,000 speakers in eastern Highlands Province, Goroka district.

Binumarien: also called Binumaria, Binamarir. 360 speakers in eastern Highlands Province, Kainantu district.

Bisorio: also called Inyai-Gadio-Bisorio, Iniai. 230 speakers in East Sepik Province, headwaters of the Karawari, Wagupmeri, and Korosameri Rivers, villages of Bisorio, Iniai, Gadio.

Chuave: also called Tjuave. 23,100 speakers in Simbu Province, Chuave district. Dialects are Elimbari, Kebai, Gomia, Chuave, Sua. Kebai is more distinct, but intelligible.

Dano: also called Upper Asaro, Asaro. 30,000 speakers in eastern Highlands Province, Goroka district. Dialects are Upper Asaro, Lunube Mado, Bohena, Amaizuho, Kongi.

Dom: 12,000 speakers in Simbu Province, mainly south of the Wahgi River from Kundiawa west of the Sinasina area.

Enga: also called Caga, Tsaga, Tchaga. 164,750 speakers in Enga Province. The Maramuni are nomadic, located in the lower reaches of the central range. Dialects are Kandepe, Layapo, Tayato, Mae (Mai, Wabag), Maramuni (Malamuni), Kaina, Kapona, Sau (Sau Enga, Wapi), Yandapo, Lapalama 1, Lapalama 2, Laiagam, Sari. Mae is the standard dialect; all understand it. Layapo is between Mae and Kyaka. Trade language.

Erave: also called Pole, South Kewa, Kewa South. 7,000 speakers in southern Highlands Province.

Fore: 17,000 speakers in eastern Highlands Province, Okapa district. Dialects are Pamusa (South Fore), North Central Fore.

Gadsup: 10,000 speakers in eastern Highlands Province, Kainantu district. Dialects are Oyana (Oiyana), Gadsup. Ontenu is a related but separate language.

Gants: also called Gaj. 1,885 speakers in Madang Province.

Gende: also called Bundi, Gene, Gendeka. 8,000 speakers in Madang Province, Bundi district near Bundi. Bilingualism in Tok Pisin. Vigorous language use.

Gimi: 22,465 speakers in eastern Highlands Province, Okapa district. Dialects are East Gimi, West Gimi (Gouno).

Golin: also called Gollum, Gumine. 51,100 speakers in Simbu Province, Gumine district. Dialects are Yuri, Kia (Kiari), Golin, Keri, Marigl. Close to Dom. Nondiri is not a language, but a village where the Mian bush people live. They speak Golin.

Haruai: also called Harway, Waibuk, Wiyaw, Wiyau, Wovan, Taman. 1,000 speakers in Madang Province, southwestern corner, southwestern Mid-Ramu (Simbai) district, western Schrader Range, west of the Kobon. Dialects are North Waibuk (Hamil), Central Waibuk (Mambar), South Waibuk (Arama). Related language: Pinai-Hagahai, though not inherently intelligible with Haruai. Word taboo is practiced, but does not seem to impede intelligibility among related language varieties. Young men are likely to know Tok Pisin or Kobon, many children speak good Tok Pisin, and many women are at least communicatively competent in Tok Pisin. Many are monolingual. All ages (as of 1988). Speeches and sermons by outsiders are always translated into Haruai.

Huli: also called Huli-Hulidana, Huri. 70,000 speakers in southern Highlands Province around Tari, and southern fringe of Enga Province.

Imbongu: also called Imbo Ungu, Ibo Ugu, Imbonggo, Imbo Ungo. 34,600 speakers in southern Highlands Province, Ialibu district. Dialects are Awa (Aua, Au). 15% monolingual, 85% use Tok Pisin, Kewa, Wiru, or English as second languages. All ages. All domains. Use in local administration, business, oral and written use in religion, beginning in education, personal letters. Vigorous language use. Parents transmit it to children. Speakers of other languages speak it. Speakers have positive attitude toward it. They dislike borrowings.

Inoke-Yate: also called Inoke, Yate. 10,000 speakers in Papua New Guinea, eastern Highlands Province, Okapa district.

Ipili: also called Ipili-Paiela, Ipili-Payala. 7,765 speakers in Enga Province around Porgera patrol post. Tipinini dialect is more like Enga.

Kalam: also called Aforo, Karam. 15,000 speakers in Madang Province, Ramu district, and in western Highlands Province, Hagen district, along the northern side of the Jimi River into the Kaironk Valley. Related languages: Gants, Kobon.

Kamano: also called Kamano-Kafe. 80,000 speakers in eastern Highlands Province, Kainantu and Henganofi districts. No major dialect differences.

Kambaira: 135 speakers in eastern Highlands Province, Kainantu district. Bilingualism in Binumarien, Gadsup.

Kandawo: also called Narake. 5,000 speakers in western Highlands Province, Hagen district in the upper Jimi headwaters, on the slopes of Mt. Wilhelm.

Kanite: 8,000 speakers in eastern Highlands Province, Okapa district. Closely related to Keyagana, Inoke-Yate.

Kenati: also called Kenathi, Ganati, Aziana. 950 speakers in eastern Highlands Province, Wonenara district. All three villages are within ten miles of Wonenara.

Kewa, East: 35,000 speakers in southern Highlands Province, Ialibu and Kagua districts.

Kewa, West: also called Pasuma. 35,000 speakers in southern Highlands Province, Kagua and Mendi districts.

Keyagana: also called Keigana, Keiagana, Ke'yagana. 12,285 speakers in Okapa and Henganofi districts, eastern Highlands Province.

Kobon: 6,000 speakers in Madang Province, Middle Ramu district, and western Highlands Province on Kaironk River in lower Jimi River area north of Mt. Hagen.

Kosena: 2,000 speakers in eastern Highlands Province, Kainantu and Okapa districts.

Kuman: also called Chimbu, Simbu. 80,000 speakers in Simbu Province, northern third, overlapping into Minj subprovince of Western Highlands Province. Dialects are Kuman, Nagane (Genagane, Genogane), Yongomugi. 10,000 are monolingual, 70,000 use Tok Pisin as second language. 20,000 can also use English or various neighboring languages. All ages. All domains. Oral use in local administration, in the first three grades in school, religion, local business. Vigorous language use. Major language of area. Parents transmit it to children. Speakers have a positive attitude toward Kuman. Language of wider communication.

Kyaka: also called Baiyer, Enga-Kyaka. 15,370 speakers in Enga Province.

Lembena: also called Nanimba Pii, Uyalipa Pii, Lembena Pii, Wapipii. 1,500 speakers. About 50% are monolingual, and 50% use Enga, Tok Pisin, or English as second language. Enga is the language of wider communication in the area. All ages. All domains. Some oral and written use in church, oral use in local business. Vigorous language use. Most parents transmit it to children. Speakers have a strong positive attitude toward Lembena.

Maring: also called Mareng, Yoadabe-Watoare. 11,000 speakers in western Highlands Province, Hagen district. A small number are over the Bismarck Range in Madang Province, eighteen villages. Dialects are Central Maring, Eastern Maring, Timbunki, Tsuwenki, Karamba, Kambegl. Speakers of all dialects understand the central one.

Mbo-Ung: also called Tembalo, Bo-Ung, Mboung. 23,000 speakers in western Highlands Province, Hagen district. Some also in Tambul and Lower Kaugel districts. Dialects are Miyemu (Miyem), Mara-Gomu, Tembalo (Tembaglo). Some people are bilingual in Medlpa.

Melpa: also called Medlpa, Hagen. 130,000 speakers in western Highlands Province, Hagen district. Only slight dialect differences.

Narak: also called Ganja. 6,000 speakers in western Highlands Province, Hagen district, middle Jimi near Tabibuga. Close to Maring, North Wahgi, and Kandawo. No significant dialect differences. About 70% are monolingual, 30% can use Tok Pisin as second language. A few can use some English. All ages. All domains. Vernacular schools planned. Oral use in churches. Vigorous language use. Parents transmit it to children. Speakers have a very positive attitude toward the language.

Nete: also called Iniai, Malamauda. 1,000 speakers in East Sepik Province, adjoining the Hewa area. three villages.

Nii: also called Ek Nii. 12,000 speakers in western Highlands Province, Hagen district.

Nomane: 4,645 speakers in Simbu Province. Dialects are Nomane, Kiari.

Omwunra-Toqura: 2,000 speakers in eastern Highlands Province, Kainantu and Obura districts, south of Kainantu. About five dialects. Tairora, Binumarien, Kambaira, and Waffa are closely related.

Ontenu: also called Ontena. 3,000 speakers in eastern Highlands Province, Kainantu district. Related to Gadsup, but a separate language.

Owenia: also called Owena, Owenda, Waijara, Waisara. 350 speakers in eastern Highlands Province, Obura district.

Pinai-Hagahai: also called Pinaye, Pinai, Hagahai, Wapi, Aramo, Miamia. 600 speakers in the border area of Enga, Madang, Western Highlands, and East Sepik Provinces. Dialects are Luya-Ginam-Mamusi, Pinai. Some speakers are partially bilingual in Enga, Tok Pisin, or Haruai.

Salt-Yui: also called Salt, Salt-Iui, Yui, Iui. 6,500 speakers in Simbu Province, Gumine district, ten villages. Close to Nondiri.

Samberigi: also called Sau, Sanaberigi. 3,125 speakers in southern Highlands Province, Lake Kutubu district, east of Erave.

Siane: also called Siani. 27,000 speakers in eastern Highlands Province, Watabung and Unggai census divisions (16,000), Goroka district. 11,000 in Simbu Province, Nambaiyufa Census Division. Dialects are Kolepa, Yamofowe, Komongu, Komoigaleka, Kemanimowe, Ona, Keto, Laiya, Fowe, Olumba, Lambau, Alango, Yandime, Wando. Separate literature in Komongu and Lambau dialects.

Sinasina: 50,080 speakers in Simbu Province. Dialects are Tabare, Guna. Close to Dom and Golin.

Tai: also called Tay. 900 speakers in Madang Province, southwest, Dundrom village.

Tairora: 11,500 speakers in eastern Highlands Province, Kainantu and Obura districts, south of Kainantu. Dialects are Northern Tairora (Nanta, Ukau), Vaira, Vinaata, Veqauraa, Haaviqinra. Binumarien and Kambaira are closely related. Waffa is related to Haaviqinra.

Tokano: also called Tokama, Gamuso, Zuhuzuho, Zuhozuho,

Yufiyufa, Zaka. 6,000 speakers in eastern Highlands Province, Goroka district. Dialects are Lower Asaro, Zuhuzuho. Bilingualism in Dano, Alekano, Tok Pisin.

Umbu-Ungu: also called Ubu Ugu, Kaugel, Kauil, Gawigl, Gawil, Kakoli. 31,000 speakers. Dialects are Kala (Mendo-Kala), No-Penge, Andelale. Some speakers understand Melpa.

Usarufa: also called Usurufa, Uturupa. 1,300 speakers in eastern Highlands Province, Okapa district.

Waffa: 1,300 speakers in Morobe Province, Kaiapit district, headwaters of Waffa River, three major villages and two smaller ones. Older people and children may be monolingual. Tok Pisin is used by those who have access to a school, English to those with access to a secondary school. All ages. All domains. Oral and written use in church. Vigorous language use. Parents transmit it to children. Some Tairora traders also use Waffa. Speakers have a positive attitude toward Waffa.

Wahgi: also called Mid Wahgi. 39,000 speakers in western Highlands Province, Minj district, overlapping into Simbu Province, south of the Wahgi River. Dialects are Kup-Minj (Kumai), Pukamigl-Andegabu, Kunjip, Kambia, Mid-Wahgi.

Wahgi, North: 47,000 speakers.

Wiru: also called Witu. 15,300 speakers in southern Highlands Province, Ialibu district.

Yagaria: 21,116 speakers in eastern Highlands Province, Goroka district. Dialects are Kami-Kulaka, Move, Ologuti, Dagenava, Kamate, Hira, Hua (Huva), Kotom.

Yaweyuha: also called Yabiyufa, Yawiyuha. 2,000 speakers in eastern Highlands Province, Goroka district.   B. GRIMES

EAST PAPUAN LANGUAGES.

EAST PAPUAN LANGUAGES. One of the major proposed phyla into which Papuan languages are divided. They are spoken in the easternmost islands of Papua New Guinea and in the Solomon Islands.

LANGUAGE LIST

Anem: also called Karaiai. 500 speakers in Papua New Guinea, western New Britain Province, northwestern coast and inland. Speakers in one village among the Bariai use Bariai as second language.

Askopan: also called Eivo. 1,200 speakers in Papua New Guinea, mountains of south central North Solomons Province. Close to Rapoisi.

Ayiwo: also called Naaude, Aïwo, Gnivo, Nivo, Nifilole, Lomlom, Reef Islands, Reefs. 7,100 speakers in Solomon Islands. Probably fewer than 10% of adults are unable to speak Pijin. Some speak nearby Pileni. Most do not understand English. Written English used in church. Vigorous language use. Parents transmit Ayiwo to children. Preachers use oral Ayiwo or Pijin in church. Oral Ayiwo used in business. Speakers have a positive attitude toward Ayiwo. Good speakers are respected, Pijin borrowings disliked.

Baniata: also called Mbaniata, Lokuru. 1,480 speakers in Solomon Islands, southern Rendova Island, Western Province. Bilingualism of speakers in Roviana is decreasing.

Bilua: also called Mbilua, Vella Lavella. 8,540 speakers in Solomon Islands, Vella Lavella Island, Western Province. There are second-language users.

Buin: also called Telei, Terei, Rugara. 25,000 speakers in Papua New Guinea, southern North Solomons Province, Buin district. Closest to Uisai.

Dororo: also called Doriri. Formerly spoken in Solomon Islands, New Georgia. May have been a Kazukuru dialect.

Guliguli: also called Gulili. Formerly spoken in Solomon Islands, New Georgia. May have been a Kazukuru dialect.

Kairak: 750 speakers in Papua New Guinea, East New Britain Province, Gazelle Peninsula. Many people are passively bilingual in Uramat.

FIGURE 1. *Subgrouping of East Papuan Languages*

Bougainville
  East Bougainville
    Buin
      Buin, Siwai, Uisai
    Nasioi
      Koromira, Lantanai, Naasioi, Nagovisi, Oune, Simeku
  West Bougainville
    Rapoisi
    Keriaka
      Ramopa
    Rotokas
      Askopan, Rotokas
Reef Islands–Santa Cruz
    Ayiwo, Nanggu, Santa Cruz
Yele–Solomons–New Britain
  New Britain
    Kol
    Anem
    Baining-Taulil
      Kairak, Makolkol, Mali, Qaqet, Simbali, Taulil-Butam, Ura
    Kuot
    Sulka
    Wasi
      Pele-Ata
  Yele-Solomons
    Central Solomons
      Baniata, Bilua, Lavukaleve, Savosavo
    Kazukuru
      Dororo, Guliguli, Kazukuru
    Yele

Kazukuru: formerly spoken in Solomon Islands, New Georgia.

Kol: also called Kole, Kola. 4,000 speakers in Papua New Guinea, East New Britain Province, Pomio district, Open Bay to the waterfall. Most are on the southern side of the island. Dialects are Sui, Kol (Nakgaktai).

Koromira: 1,562 speakers in Papua New Guinea, North Solomons Province, Kieta district, central mountains and southeastern coast. Dialects are Koromira, Koianu.

Kuot: also called Kuat, Panaras. 900 speakers in Papua New Guinea, New Ireland Province, northwestern coast. Nine villages. Bilingualism in Tok Pisin. Vigorous language use on the west coast.

Lantanai: 300 speakers in Papua New Guinea, North Solomons Province, Kieta district, Piruneu' village.

Lavukaleve: also called Laube, Laumbe, Russell Island. 1,150 speakers in Solomon Islands, Russell Islands, northwest of Guadalcanal, central Solomons.

Makolkol: 7 speakers remain. Formerly spoken in Papua New Guinea, East New Britain Province, Gazelle Peninsula.

Mali: also called Gaktai. 2,200 speakers in Papua New Guinea, East New Britain Province, eastern Gazelle Peninsula. A distinct language within the Baining ethnic group. Two dialects.

Naasioi: also called Nasioi, Kieta, Kieta Talk, Aunge. 10,000 speakers in Papua New Guinea, North Solomons Province, Kieta district, central mountains and southeastern coast. Dialects are Naasioi, Kongara, Orami (Guava), Pakia-Sideronsi.

Nagovisi: also called Sibbe, Nagovisi, Sibe-Nagovisi. 5,000 speakers in Papua New Guinea, North Solomons Province, Buin district.

Nanggu: 450 speakers in Solomon Islands, Santa Cruz Island. Most people are bilingual in Santa Cruz.

Oune: also called Ounge, Dapera. 1,900 speakers in Papua New Guinea, North Solomons Province, Kieta district, central mountains and southeastern coast. Most dialects are not functionally intelligible with Naasioi.

Pele-Ata: also called Wasi, Uase, Uasi, Uasilau, Peleata. 1,900 speakers in Papua New Guinea, West New Britain Province, Nakanai district, inland from Bongula Bay. Dialects are Pele, Ata.

Qaqet: also called Maqaqet, Kakat, Makakat, Baining. 6,350 speakers in Papua New Guinea, East New Britain Province, Rabaul district, Gazelle Peninsula. Two dialects.

Ramopa: also called Kereaka, Keriaka. 1,000 speakers in Papua New Guinea, North Solomons Province, northwestern Bougainville Island, south of Rapoisi. Few are bilingual in Tok Pisin.

Rapoisi: also called Kunua, Konua. 3,500 speakers in Papua New Guinea, North Solomons Province, northwestern Bougainville Island, Kunua district. Most villages are inland. Related to Eivo, Kereaka, and Rotokas. Tok Pisin used in schools. Vigorous language use.

Rotokas: 4,320 speakers in Papua New Guinea, North Solomons Province, Central Bougainville district, central mountains. Twenty-eight villages. Dialects are Pipipaia, Aita, Atsilima.

Santa Cruz: also called Natögu, Nendö, Nambakaengö, Mbanua. 5,000 speakers in Solomon Islands, Santa Cruz Islands, Eastern Solomons. Dialects are Ndeni (Deni), Te Motu, Londai, Nea, Nooli, Lvova (Lwowa), Mbanua. Speakers of most dialects understand Lwowa and Mbanua well. Nea and Nooli dialects may be sufficiently diverse to require adapted literature.

Savosavo: also called Savo Island, Savo. 2,200 speakers in Solomon Islands, Savo Island, north of Guadalcanal, Central Solomons. Bilingualism in Pijin. Use of Savosavo may be declining among the younger generation.

Simbali: 350 speakers in Papua New Guinea, East New Britain Province, Gazelle Peninsula. Many people are passively bilingual in Mali.

Simeku: 1,900 speakers in Papua New Guinea, North Solomons Province, Kieta district, central mountains. Mainoki is on the western slope and Koopei on the eastern slope. Dialects are Mainoki (Mainoke), Koopei (Kopei). Not functionally intelligible with Naasioi.

Siwai: also called Motuna. 6,600 speakers in Papua New Guinea, North Solomons Province, southeastern area.

Sulka: 2,500 speakers in Papua New Guinea, East New Britain Province, East Pomio district, Wide Bay coast. A dialectal chain.

Taulil-Butam: 800 speakers in Papua New Guinea, East New Britain Province, Gazelle Peninsula. Dialects are Taulil, Butam. Bilingualism in Kuanua. Butam was extinct as of 1981.

Uisai: 2,500 speakers in Papua New Guinea, North Solomons Province, southern, Buin district.

Ura: also called Uramät, Uramit, Uramet, Uramot, Auramot. 1,900 speakers in Papua New Guinea, East New Britain Province, Rabaul district, Gazelle Peninsula.

Yele: also called Yelejong, Rossel, Yela, Yeletnye, Yelidnye. 3,750 speakers in Papua New Guinea. Ethnic population: 3,750 as of 1998. Milne Bay Province, Misima district, Rossel Island at eastern end of Calvados chain, and 500 speakers in Port Moresby and Alotau. Dialects are Daminyu, Bou, Wulanga, Jinjo, Abaletti, Jaru. About 400 speakers are monolingual. Half the children have elementary education in English. 1,200 can also speak Misima or English. Misima was introduced as a church language in the 1930s, English for trade and administration in about 1900, for elementary education in about 1948. All ages. All domains. Oral use in preschool and elementary school, local administration, business. Oral and written use in churches. Vigorous language use. Parents transmit it to children. Speakers have a positive attitude toward Yele.

B. GRIMES

EAST SUDANIC LANGUAGES. A branch of the proposed NILO-SAHARAN family. They are spoken in a continuous area (with some outliers) from central Tanzania north to central Ethiopia and southern Sudan, with other outliers as far north as Eritrea, northern Sudan, and southern Egypt.

LANGUAGE LIST

Acholi: also called Acoli, Atscholi, Shuli, Gang, Lwo, Lwoo, Akoli, Acooli, Log Acoli, Dok Acoli. 773,800 speakers in Uganda and Sudan. In Uganda: 746,796 speakers, north central Acholi district. Dialects are Labwor, Nyakwai, Dhopaluo (Chopi, Chope). In Sudan: Southern Sudan, Opari district, Acholi hills.

Adhola: also called Dhopadhola, Jopadhola, Ludama. 247,580 speakers in eastern Uganda, Mbale district. Not in Kenya. The most distinct of the Western Nilotic languages in Uganda.

Afitti: also called Ditti, Unietti, Affitti, Dinik. 4,510 speakers in northern Sudan, Nuba hills, eastern Jebel ed Dair. Main center is Sidra. Not inherently intelligible with Nyimang.

Aka: also called Sillok, Jebels Sillok, Jebel Silak, Fa-C-Aka. Spoken in northern Sudan, Sillok (Silak) hills, west of the main Berta-speaking people. Bilingualism in Arabic, Berta.

Alur: also called Lur, Aloro, Alua, Alulu, Luri, Dho Alur, Jo Alur. 920,000 speakers in Democratic Republic of Congo and Uganda. In Democratic Republic of Congo: 500,000 speakers in Orientale Province: Mahagi territory and northwest to Djalasiga area. In Uganda: 420,000 speakers. North of Lake Albert. Dialects are Jokot, Jonam, Mambisa, Wanyoro.

Ama: also called Nyimang, Inyimang, Nyima, Nyiman. 70,000 speakers in northern Sudan, Kordofan Province, northwest of Dilling on range of hills of which Jebel Nyimang is a part, and on the Mandal range. Education is in Arabic.

Anuak: also called Anywak, Anywa, Yambo, Jambo, Nuro, Anyuak, Dho Anywaa. 98,000 speakers in Sudan and Ethiopia. In Sudan: 52,000 speakers, Upper Nile Province, Pibor and Lower Akobo Rivers. From Akobo Post to latitude 6.45N. In Ethiopia: 45,646 speakers. Ethnic population: 45,665 as of 1998. Gambela region in the southwest. Along the Baro, Alworo, and Gilo Rivers and on the right bank of the Akobo River. Gambela town is the main center. Dialects are Adoyo, Coro, Lul, Opëno. Four main dialect areas, but only slight differences. Closer to Acholi and Luo of Uganda than to Shilluk.

Aramanik: also called Laramanik. "Ndorobo," "Dorobo" are derogatory names sometimes used. Spoken in Tanzania. Speakers have limited comprehension of other languages.

Assangori: also called Sungor, Soungor, Assoungor, Azanguri, Asong, Asungore, Bognak-Asungorung, Madungore, Shaale. 38,500 speakers in Chad and Sudan. In Chad: 23,479 speakers, east, Ouaddaï prefecture, Adré subprefecture, northwest of Adré and of the Masalit. Dialects are Sungor, Walad Dulla, Girga. The majority use Chadian Arabic as second language, although at a low proficiency level. In Sudan: 15,000 speakers. Dialects are Girga, Walad Dulla, Erenga. Girga and Walad Dulla are ethnic groups that may or may not speak different dialects.

Bari: also called Beri. 286,000 speakers in Sudan and Uganda. In Sudan: 226,000 speakers. Dialects are Kuku, Nyangbara (Nyangwara, Nyambara), Nyepu (Nyefu, Nyepo, Nypho, Ngyepu), Pöjulu (Pajulu, Fadjulu, Fajelu, Madi), Ligo (Liggo). In Uganda: 60,000 speakers in northwestern corner. Dialects are Kuku, Nyepu (Ngyepu, Nyefu, Nyepo, Nypho), Pöjulu (Pajulu, Fadjulu, Fajulu, Fajelu), Nyangbara (Nyangwara, Nyambara), Mondari (Mandari, Mundari). Kakwa is a separate language. Trade language.

Baygo: also called Baigo, Bego, Beko, Beigo, Beygo. Formerly spoken in Sudan. Ethnic population: 850 as of 1978. Northern Sudan, southern Dar Fur, in the hills east of Kube (Kubbi). Was close to Daju of Dar Fur.

Belanda Bor: also called De Bor. 8,000 speakers in southern Sudan, on the main road south of Wau. Most people are bilingual in Belanda Viri. There is much intermarriage between the two groups.

Birked: also called Birguid, Birgid, Birkit, Birqed, Murgi, Kajjara. Formerly spoken in Sudan.

Burun: also called Barun, Lange, Cai, Borun. 18,000 speakers in northern Sudan, Blue Nile Province. Dialects are Ragreig, Abuldugu (Bogon, Mugo-Mborkoina), Maiak, Mufwa (Mopo), Mughaja (Mugaja, Mumughadja). Some southern dialects are intelligible with Mabaan.

Dair: also called Daier, Thaminyi. 1,000 speakers in northern Sudan, western and southern parts of Jebel Dair, Kordofan.

Daju, Dar Daju: also called Dadjo, Dadju, Dajou, Daju, Dajo, Daju Mongo, Daju Oum Hadjer, Saaronge. 34,000 speakers in Chad, central, Guéra prefecture, Mongo subprefecture, around Mongo and Eref. Dialects are Bardangal, Eref, Gadjira. Not inherently intelligible with Dar Sila Daju. The majority use Chadian Arabic as second language.

Daju, Dar Fur: also called Nyala-Lagowa, Fininga, Dagu, Daju Ferne, Beke. 70,000 speakers in Sudan. Dialects are Nyala, Lagowa.

Daju, Dar Sila: also called Sila, Sula, Daju, Dadjo, Dajou, Bokoruge, Bokorike. 33,000 speakers in Chad and Sudan. In Chad: Eastern, Ouaddaï prefecture, Goz-Beïda subprefecture, around Goz-Beïda and east to the Sudan border. Not inherently intelligible with Dar Daju Daju. The majority use Chadian Arabic as second language. In Sudan: Northern Sudan. Nearly all those Daju of Dar Sila who are in Sudan have migrated into Dar Fur and settled there in recent times. Dialects are Mongo, Sila.

Datooga: also called Datoga, Datog, Tatoga, Tatog, Taturu. "Mangati" is a derogatory name sometimes used. 150,000

FIGURE 1. *Subgrouping of East Sudanic Languages*

Eastern East Sudanic
  Eastern Jebel
    Aka-Kelo-Molo
      Aka, Kelo, Molo
    Gaam
  Nara
  Nubian
    Central Nubian
      Birked
      Dongolawi
        Kenuzi-Dongola
      Hill Central Nubian
        Kadaru-Ghulfan
          Ghulfan, Kadaru
        Unclassified Hill Central Nubian
          Dair, Dilling, El Hugeirat, Karko, Wali
    Northern Nubian
      Nobiin
    Western Nubian
      Midob
  Surmic
    North Surmic
      Majang
    South Surmic
      Southeast Surmic
        Kwegu
        Pastoral Southeast Surmic
          Me'en
          Suri
            Mursi, Suri
      Southwest Surmic
        Didinga-Murle
          Didinga-Longarim
            Didinga, Narim
          Murle
          Tennet
        Kacipo-Balesi
Kuliak
  Ik
  Ngangea-So
    Nyang'i, Soo
Nilotic
  Eastern Nilotic
    Bari
      Bari, Kakwa, Mandari
    Lotuxo-Teso
      Lotuxo
        Dongotono, Lango, Lokoya, Loppit, Otuho
      Ongamo-Maa
        Maasai, Ngasa, Samburu
    Teso-Turkana
      Teso
      Turkana
        Karamojong, Nyangatom, Toposa, Turkana
  Southern Nilotic
    Kalenjin
      Elgon
        Kupsabiny, Sabaot

Nandi-Markweta
  Markweta
    Endo, Talai
  Nandi
    Aramanik, Kalenjin, Kisankasa, Mediak, Mosiro,
    North Tugen
  Okiek
  Pokot
    Pökoot
  Tatoga
    Datooga, Omotik
Western Nilotic
  Dinka-Nuer
    Dinka
      Northeastern Dinka, Northwestern Dinka, South Central
      Dinka, Southeastern Dinka, Southwestern Dinka
    Nuer
      Nuer, Reel
  Luo
    Northern Luo
      Anuak
      Bor
        Belanda Bor
      Jur
        Luwo
      Maban-Burun
        Burun
        Maban
          Jumjum, Mabaan
      Shilluk
      Thuri
      Unclassified Northern Luo
        Päri
    Southern Luo
      Adhola
      Kuman
      Luo-Acholi
        Alur-Acholi
          Alur
          Lango-Acholi
            Acholi, Lango
        Luo
Western Nilotic
  Daju
    Eastern Daju
      Logorik, Shatt
    Western Daju
      Baygo, Dar Daju Daju, Dar Fur Daju, Dar Sila Daju,
      Njalgulgule
  Nyimang
    Afitti, Ama
  Tama
    Marant
      Mararit
    Tama-Sungor
      Assangori, Tama
  Temein
    Temein, Tese

speakers in Tanzania, Singida and Mbulu regions. The Barabaig are mainly in the northern volcanic highlands near Mt. Hanang. Dialects are Bajuta, Gisamjanga (Kisamajeng, Gisamjang), Barabayiiga (Barabaig, Barabaik, Barbaig), Tsimajeega (Isimijeega), Rootigaanga (Rotigenga), Buraadiiga (Buradiga), Bianjiida (Utatu). Sabaot is probably the closest language linguistically. Barabaik and Kisamajeng are very close and are completely inherently intelligible. There are several other dialects or ethnic groups: Darorajega, Gidang'odiga, Bisiyeda, Daragwajega, Salawajega, Ghumbiega, Mangatiga. Some bilingualism in Swahili. Those who have been to school may speak Swahili at FSI level 2 or 3. A few use Iraqw, Iramba, or Nyaturu as second language for commerce. Datoga orthography is different from Swahili.

Didinga: also called 'Di'dinga, Xaroxa, Toi, Lango. 58,000 speakers in southern Sudan, Didinga hills (about 60 km northeast of the junction of the Sudan, Kenya, and Uganda borders) and north of Nagishot. Ethnic groups: Chukudum, Lowudo. Slight differences in speech between Chukudum and Lowudo, apparently mainly phonetic.

Dinka, Northeastern: also called Padang, White Nile Dinka. 320,000 speakers in southern Sudan, northeast of the Sudd, along both sides of the White Nile, and along the Sobat River. Dialects are Abiliang (Dinka Ibrahim, Akoon, Bawom, Bowom), Dongjol, Luac (Luaic), Ngok-Sobat (Ngork, Jok), Ageer (Ager, Ageir, Abuya, Beer, Niel, Nyel, Paloc, Paloic), Rut, Thoi. Bilingualism in Sudanese Arabic.

Dinka, Northwestern: 80,000 speakers in southern Sudan, north of the Bahr el Ghazal River, and southern Kordofan around Abyei. Dialects are Alor, Ngok-Kordofan, Pan Aru, Ruweng. A separate language from other Dinka.

Dinka, South Central: also called Agar, Central Dinka. 250,000 speakers in Sudan. Dialects are Aliap (Aliab, Thany, Aker), Ciec (Ciem, Cic, Chiech, Kwac, Ajak, Ador), Gok (Gauk, Cok), Agar. Gok is also influenced by Southwestern Dinka and has a number of Arabic loans. Agar is becoming accepted as the educational standard for South Central Dinka. Bilingualism in Sudanese Arabic.

Dinka, Southeastern: also called Bor, Eastern Dinka. 250,000 speakers in southern Sudan, east of the Nile, around Bor and northward. Dialects are Bor (Bor Gok), Athoc (Athoic, Atoc, Borathoi, Bor Athoic), Ghol, Nyarweng (Nyarueng, Narreweng), Tuic (Twi). Sudanese Arabic is the second language. Speakers of some dialects also speak Nuer Gewaar and Nuer Lou.

Dinka, Southwestern: also called Rek, Western Dinka. 450,000 speakers in southern Sudan, north and northwest of Wau. Dialects are Rek (Raik), Abiem (Ajong Dit, Ajong Thi, Akany Kok, Akern Jok, Apuoth, Apwoth, Anei), Aguok (Agwok), Apuk, Awan, Lau, Luac, Malual (Malwal, Atoktou, Duliit, Korok, Makem, Peth), Paliet (Baliet, Ajak,

Buoncwai, Bon Shwai, Bwoncwai, Kongder, Kondair, Thany Bur, Tainbour), Palioupiny (Palioping, Akjuet, Akwang, Ayat, Cimel, Gomjuer), Tuic (Twic, Twich, Twij, Adhiang, Amiol, Nyang, Thon). Luac dialect is different from Luac dialect in Northeastern Dinka. Bilingualism in Sudanese Arabic.

Dilling: also called Delen, Warki, Warkimbe. 5,295 speakers in northern Sudan, southern Kordofan, town of Dilling and surrounding hills, including Kudr. Dialects are Dilling, Debri.

Dongotono: spoken in southern Sudan, eastern Equatoria Province, Dongotono hills southeast of Torit.

El Hugeirat: 1,000 speakers in northern Sudan, West Kordofan in El Hugeirat hills.

Endo: also called Endo-Marakwet, Marakuet, Markweta. 80,000 speakers in Kenya, Rift Valley Province, Elgeyo Marakwet district. Dialects are Endo, Sambirir. Low intelligibility with major Kalenjin dialects and Talai. Orthography problems.

Gaam: also called Ingassana, Ingessana, Tabi, Metabi, Muntabi, Mamedja, Mamidza, Kamanidi. 40,000 speakers in northern Sudan. The main center is in and around Jebel Tabi, on Tabi Massif and outlying hills. A small community in Khartoum. Not in Ethiopia.

Ghulfan: also called Gulfan, Wunci, Wuncimbe. 16,000 speakers in northern Sudan, Kordofan, in two hill ranges 25 to 30 miles south of Dilling: Ghulfan Kurgul and Ghulfan Morung.

Ik: also called Icietot, Teuso, Teuth, Ngulak. 2,000 speakers in Uganda, northeastern part of Karamoja. It is very different from other Eastern Sudanic languages. Speakers are reported to use Karamojong as second language.

Jumjum: also called Berin, Olga, Wadega. 25,000 speakers in northern Upper Nile Province, along Khor Jumjum on Jebels Tunga, Terta, and Wadega.

Kacipo-Balesi: 7,000 speakers in Sudan and Ethiopia. In Sudan: 5,000 speakers in southern Sudan, on the Boma Plateau among the Murle, near the Ethiopian border. Dialects are Kichepo, Suri, Western Suri. Related to Murle and Didinga. Almost completely monolingual. In Ethiopia: 2,000 speakers at southern Ethiopia-Sudan border, Boma Plateau in Sudan (Kacipo). Dialects are Balesi (Baale, Bale), Zilmamu (Silmamo, Zelmamu, Zulmamu, Tsilmano), Kacipo (Kachepo, Suri, Western Suri). Pronoun differences between Balesi and Zilmamu. Some use Surma as second language.

Kadaru: also called Kadaro, Kadero, Kaderu, Kodoro, Kodhin, Kodhinniai. 7,000 speakers in northern Sudan, Kordofan Province, Nuba Mountains, northern and eastern part of the Kadaru hills between Dilling and Delami. Dialects are Western Kadaru, Kururu (Tagle), Kafir, Kurtala, Dabatna, Kuldaji.

Kakwa: also called Bari Kakwa, Kakua, Kwakwak. 146,500

speakers in Uganda, Sudan, and Democratic Republic of Congo. In Uganda: 86,472 speakers in the northwestern corner, West Nile district. Dialects of Sudan, Democratic Republic of Congo, and Uganda differ little. Very different from other Eastern Nilotic languages of Uganda. In Sudan: 40,000 speakers in southern Sudan, Yei district, extending into Democratic Republic of Congo in the west at Aba and in the south around Mahagi. The Democratic Republic of Congo and Sudan dialects differ only slightly. Some treat Kakwa as a dialect of Bari, but they are separate. In Democratic Republic of Congo: 20,000 speakers in Orientale Province, Aru territory, north of Aru, and Faradje territory.

Kalenjin: 2,458,123 speakers in Kenya, mainly Nandi, Kericho, and Uasin Gishu districts, Rift Valley Province. Dialects are Nandi (Naandi, Cemual), Terik (Nyang'ori), Kipsigis (Kipsiikis, Kipsikis, Kipsikiis), Keiyo (Keyo, Elgeyo), South Tugen (Tuken), Cherangany. Orthography problems.

Karamojong: also called Karimojong, Karimonjong. 370,000 speakers in Uganda, east and northeast, Karamojo district around Moroto. Dialects are Karamojong, Jie (Jiye), Dodos (Dodoth). People are friendly with the Toposa; hostile to the Turkana.

Karko: also called Garko, Kithonirishe. 12,986 speakers in Sudan.

Kelo: also called Tornasi, Kelo-Beni Sheko, Ndu-Faa-Keelo. 200 speakers in northern Sudan, Tornasi hills; Jebels Tornasi (Keeli village) and Beni Sheko. West of Berta-speaking people. Dialects are Beni Sheko, Kelo.

Kenuzi-Dongola: also called Dongola-Kenuz, Nile Nubian, Dongolawi. 280,000 speakers in Sudan and Egypt. In Sudan: 180,000 speakers in northern Sudan, mainly at Dongola and surrounding villages in Northern Province. The northern boundary with Nobiin is at Burgeg. Dialects are Dongola, Kenuzi (Kenuz, Kunuzi). Not intelligible with Nobiin. In Egypt: 100,000 speakers. Ethnic population: 100,000. There are fewer speakers (1996). 40% in the Upper Nile valley, mainly at Kom Ombo, the rest in various cities. Dialects are Dongola, Kenuz (Kenuzi, Kunuzi, Kenzi). Not intelligible with Nobiin. Many are now monolingual in Egyptian or Saidi Arabic. The shift to Arabic is expected to continue in the cities. The language is the central feature of Nubian identity. Over 70% of the men can read Arabic script. Many can read Roman script.

Kisankasa: "Ndorobo," "Dorobo" are derogatory names sometimes used. 4,670 speakers in Tanzania. A distinct language from others called "Dorobo": Aramanik, Mediak, Mosiro. Speakers have limited comprehension of other languages.

Kumam: also called Kuman, Ikokolemu, Kumum, Ikumama, Akum, Akokolemu. 112,630 speakers in Uganda south of Lake Kwania, western Teso district.

Kupsabiny: also called Sebei, Sapei. 120,000 speakers in Uganda, the eastern border area slightly north of Mbale, Sebei Province. Dialects are Sabiny (Sapiny, Kupsabiny, Kupsapiny), Mbai, Sor.

Kwegu: also called Koegu, Kwegi, Bacha, Menja. 103 speakers in Ethiopia. Ethnic population: 173 as of 1998. Kuchur village on the western bank of the Omo River in southwestern Ethiopia. Dialects are Yidinich (Yidinit, Yidi), Muguji. The dialects listed may not be inherently intelligible with Kwegu; it may be a name for several hunter groups. The Kwegu use the Bodi dialect of Me'en or Mursi as second language, depending on the area. Diminishing among adults.

Lango: also called Langgo. 20,000 speakers in southern Sudan, eastern Equatoria Province, Torit district. A separate language from Otuho. The people are bilingual in Otuho.

Lango: also called Lwo, Lwoo, Leb-Lano, Langi. 977,680 speakers in Uganda, central, north of Lake Kyoga, Lango Province. Roman script.

Logorik: also called Liguri. 2,000 speakers in northern Sudan, central Nuba Mountains, Jebel Liguri and other hills northeast of Kadugli. Dialects are Saburi, Tallau (Talau, Talo), Liguri.

Lokoya: also called Lokoiya, Lokoja, Loquia, Lowoi, Owoi, Loirya, Oirya, Ellyria, Oxoriok, Koyo. 12,400 speakers in southern Sudan, eastern Equatoria, Torit district. Speakers are reported to be bilingual in Otuho.

Lopit: also called Loppit, Lopid, Lofit, Lafite, Lafit, Lafiit. 50,000 speakers in southern Sudan, eastern Equatoria Province, Lopit hills, northeast of Torit.

Luo: also called Dholuo, Nilotic Kavirondo, Kavirondo Luo. 3,408,000 speakers in Kenya and Tanzania. In Kenya: 3,185,000 speakers in Nyanza Province. In Tanzania: 223,000 speakers in Mara region, near Kenya border, east of Lake Victoria.

Luwo: also called Lwo, Jur Luo, Jur Lwo, Jo Lwo, Dhe Lwo, Dhe Luwo, Giur. 80,000 speakers in southern Sudan, Bahr al-Ghazal, north of Wau toward Aweil, southeast of Wau as far as Tonj. Different from Lwo of Uganda, or Luo of Kenya and Tanzania, but related. Bilingualism in Dinka, English, Arabic. All domains, local administration, some use in schools, churches. Parents pass Luwo on to children. Thuri speakers sometimes use Luwo as second language. Very positive attitude toward Luwo.

Maasai: also called Masai. 883,000 speakers in Kenya and Tanzania. In Kenya: 453,000 speakers in Kajiado and Narok districts, Rift Valley Province. Dialects are Kaputiei, Keekonyokie, Matapo, Laitokitok, Iloodokilani, Damat, Purko, Loitai, Siria, Moitanik (Wuasinkishu), Kore, Arusa (Arusha), Baraguyu, Kisonko. Purko is the largest dialect in Kenya and centrally located. The last three dialects listed are in Tanzania. Kwavi may be a dialect. The Kore now speak Somali as first language. In Tanzania: 430,000 speakers, north central, on Kenya border, east of Serengeti National Park. The Baraguyu are spread from the Indian Ocean nearly to Malawi. Dialects are Engutuk-Eloikob, Arusha (Il-

Arusha, L-Arusha), Parakuyo (Baraguyu, Kwavi), Kisonko. Arusha is distinct from the Bantu Chagga-related variety. One source reports that Arusha who are pastoralists dress like the Maasai and speak a Maasai-related variety, whereas those who are agriculturalists intermarry with the Chagga. Other sources say the Arusha originally spoke a Bantu language. Bilingualism in Swahili. The Baraguyu speak Maasai, but they consider themselves to be a separate ethnic group from the Maasai.

Mabaan: also called Maaban, Meban, Southern Burun, Gura, Tungan, Barga, Tonko, Ulu. 25,000 speakers in Sudan, on the border of Blue Nile and Upper Nile Provinces, between Yabus and Tombak Rivers in the north and Khor Daga in the south. Not in Ethiopia. Partially intelligible with some southern dialects of Burun.

Majang: also called Mesengo, Masongo, Masango, Majanjiro, Tama, Ojanjur, Ajo, Ato Majang, Ato Majanger-Onk. 15,341 speakers in Ethiopia. Ethnic population: 15,341 as of 1998. Minor dialect variation.

Mandari: also called Mondari, Mundari, Shir, Chir, Kir. 35,812 speakers in southern Sudan, near Bari; one division around Tali, the other on both sides of the Nile between Tombe and Mongalla. A different language and culture from Bari.

Mararit: also called Mararet, Merarit, Abiyi, Abiri, Ebiri. 42,388 speakers in Chad, east, Biltine prefecture, Am Zoer subprefecture (Abou Charib), and Ouaddaï prefecture, Adré subprefecture, Mabrone Canton (Mararit). Dialects are Mararit, Abou Charib (Abu Sharib, Abu Sharin). Limited intelligibility between Abou Charib and Mararit. Very difficult intelligibility with Tama. Not intelligible with Sungor. The majority use Chadian Arabic as second language.

Mediak: "Ndorobo," "Dorobo" are derogatory names sometimes used. Spoken in Tanzania. Limited comprehension of other languages.

Me'en: also called Mekan, Mie'en, Mieken, Meqan, Men. 56,585 speakers in Ethiopia. Ethnic population: 57,501 as of 1998, including 4,686 Bodi. Central Kafa region, the Tishena in and around Bachuma, the Bodi in lowlands to the south, near the Omo River. Not in Sudan. Dialects are Bodi (Podi), Tishena (Teshina, Teshenna). Tishena is inherently intelligible with Bodi. Closely related to Mursi.

Midob: also called Meidob, Midobi, Tidda, Tid, Tid-N-Aal. 50,000 speakers in northern Sudan, Dar Fur Province, Jebel Midob, and settled communities in Omdurman and Gezira Aba. The center is Malha. Dialects are Shelkota (Shalkota), Kaageddi, Urrti (Uurti). The dialects are inherently intelligible.

Molo: also called Malkan, Tura-Ka-Molo. 100 speakers in Sudan at Jebel Malkan, near the Berta language, south of the Blue Nile, near the Ethiopian border. Speakers are reported to be bilingual in Arabic and Berta.

Mosiro: "Ndorobo," "Dorobo" are derogatory names sometimes used. Spoken in Tanzania. A distinct language from others called "Dorobo": Aramanik, Mediak, Kisankasa, Aasax. Speakers have limited comprehension of other languages.

Murle: also called Murelei, Merule, Mourle, Murule, Beir, Ajibba, Agiba, Adkibba. 60,200 speakers in Sudan and Ethiopia. In Sudan: 60,000 speakers in southern Sudan, Upper Nile Province, Pibor district, south of the Akobo River, Boma Plateau, and to east and north. In Ethiopia: Dialects are Olam (Ngalam, Bangalam). Related to Didinga. Subgroups: Lotilla, Boma, Olam (Ngalam). Maacir may be a dialect or ethnic group. They speak Nyangatom as second language.

Mursi: also called Murzi, Murzu, Merdu, Meritu, Dama. 3,278 speakers in Ethiopia. Ethnic population: 3,258 as of 1998. Central Omo region, lowlands southwest of Jinka. Closely related to Suri of Sudan.

Nara: also called Nera, Higir, Koyta, Mogareb, Santora. "Barea," "Barya," "Baria" are derogatory names sometimes used. 63,000 speakers in Eritrea, in and north of Barentu, western Eritrea, adjoining Kunama territory, which is to the south. Considerable dialect variation within the four main tribal sections: Higir, Mogareb, Koyta, Santora. Little intelligibility with Kunama. They use Tigré for intercommunication, or Arabic. The Koyta use Kunama.

Narim: also called Larim, Lariim, Nariim, Longarim, Lariminit, Boya. 3,623 speakers in southern Sudan, western Boya hills, around Mt. Kosodek and Mt. Lobuli. Most people are unable to speak other languages.

Ngasa: also called Shaka, Ongamo. 200 speakers in Tanzania. Ethnic population: 2,500 as of 1983. Eastern slopes of Mt. Kilimanjaro. Bilingualism in Chaga. Only elderly speakers left. The young people speak Chaga. It began to diminish in the 1950s.

Njalgulgule: also called Nyolge, Nyoolne, Ngulgule, Begi, Bege, Beko, Njangulgule. 900 speakers in southern Sudan, on the Sopo River just above the Sopo-Boro confluence, and west of the Dinka. One village. Bilingualism in Arabic.

Nobiin: also called Mahas-Fiadidja, Mahas-Fiyadikkya, Fiadidja-Mahas. 545,000 speakers in Sudan and Egypt. In Sudan: 295,000 speakers in Northern Province, northwards from Burgteg to the Egyptian border at Wadi Halfa. Also at New Halfa in Kassale Province. Dialects are Mahas (Mahasi, Mahass), Fiyadikka (Fedicca, Fadicha, Fadicca, Fadija, Fiadidja). Not intelligible with Kenuzi-Dongola. Spoken by the Mahas in Sudan and the Fedicca in Egypt. In Egypt: 200,000 speakers, 40% in the Upper Nile Valley, mainly near Kom Ombo; the rest in various cities. Not intelligible with Kenuzi-Dongola. The ethnic group is larger in Egypt than Sudan, but most are now monolingual in Egyptian or Saidi Arabic. The shift to Arabic is expected to continue in the cities. The language is the center of Nubian identity. 70% of the men can read Arabic script. Many can read Roman script.

North Tugen: also called North Tuken, Tuken. 144,000 speakers in Kenya, west central, west of the Kalenjin. People may not be able to use Kalenjin literature.

Nuer: also called Naath, Naadh. 805,000 speakers in Sudan and Ethiopia. In Sudan: 740,000 speakers. Dialects are Dor (Door), Eastern Jikany (Jikain, Jekaing), Abigar, Western Jikany, Cien, Thognaath (Thok Nath), Lou (Lau), Nyuong, Thiang (Bul, Gawaar, Jagai, Laak, Leik). Dialects correspond mainly to geographic divisions. Bilingualism in Arabic. In Ethiopia: 64,907 speakers. Ethnic population: 64,534 as of 1998. Along the Baro River, in Gambela region. Dialects are Eastern Nuer (Ji, Kany, Jikany, Door, Abigar). Bilingualism in Arabic.

Nyangatom: also called Inyangatom, Donyiro, Dongiro, Idongiro. 14,177 speakers in Ethiopia. Ethnic population: 14,201 as of 1998. Inherently intelligible with Toposa and Turkana. Ethnic identity attitudes are strong. Mutual nonagression pact with the Toposa. Occasionally hostile with the Turkana and Sudan Jiye.

Nyang'i: also called Nuangeya, Nyuangia, Nyangiya, Nyangia, Ngangea, Gyangiya, Nyangeya, Ngiangeya, Nipori, Niporen, Poren, Ngapore, Upale. Formerly spoken in Uganda. Ethnic population: 100 or fewer as of 2000. Eastern Uganda. A separate language from Ik. People now speak Dodos (Karamojong).

Okiek: also called Akiek, Akie, Ogiek. "Ndorobo," "Dorobo" are derogatory names sometimes used. Spoken in Kenya and Tanzania. In Kenya: Ethnic population: 20,000 in Kenya as of 1980. Dialects are Suiei, Sogoo (Sokoo), Okiek. People may be bilingual in Nandi. Most or all "Ndorobo" are highly bilingual in an adopted language. Acording to one scholar, "The language is remembered by a few old men married to Kikuyu women and living in Kikuyu communities." Some "Ndorobo" languages are nearly extinct. Many or all Okiek in northern Tanzania now speak Maasai. The Okiek of Kinare in Kenya now speak Kikuyu. Those in Tanzania and Kenya are not in contact with each other. Sogoo may be extinct. In Tanzania: Maasai plains, northern Tanzania. All Okiek speak Maasai as first or second language. Some young people know Swahili. Most young Okiek do not speak Okiek.

Omotik: also called Omotic, Laamoot. "Ndorobo" is a derogatory name sometimes used. 50 speakers remain in Kenya. Ethnic population: 200 or more as of 2000. Around Lolgorien, Lemek, and Entasekera, Narok district, Rift Valley Province. The majority of the ethnic group now speak Maasai. Most or all Ndorobo language speakers are highly bilingual in an adopted language. All were over 40 years old in 1980.

Otuho: also called Lotuko, Lotuho, Lotuxo, Lotuka, Lattuka, Latuko, Latuka, Latooka, Otuxo, Olotorit. 135,000 speakers in southern Sudan, Torit district, eastern Equatoria Province,

east and southeast of the Luluba and the Lokoya. Dialects are Koriok, Logiri (Logir), Lomya (Lomia), Lorwama, Lowudo (Loudo, Lauda), Logotok.

Päri: also called Lokoro. 28,000 speakers in Sudan.

Pökoot: also called Pökot, Suk, Pakot. 264,000 speakers in Kenya and Uganda. In Kenya: Baringo and West Pokot districts, Rift Valley Province. Dialects are East Pokot, West Pokot. In Uganda: East central, near Kupsabiny.

Reel: also called Atuot, Atwot, Thok Cieng Reel. 50,000 speakers in Sudan. No dialect differences. The Apak are fully bilingual in the Ciec dialect of South Central Dinka. The other subtribes are less bilingual. The Kuek and Rorkec have many monolinguals and are regarded as having the purest form of the language.

Sabaot: also called Mt. Elgon Maasai. 143,000 speakers in Kenya, Mt. Elgon district, Western Province. Also Trans-Nzoia district in Rift Valley Province. Dialects are Bong'omeek (Bong'om, Pong'om), Koony (Kony), Book (Bok, Pok). Related to Sebei of Uganda. Bung'omek is being absorbed by Bukusu.

Samburu: also called Sambur, Sampur, Burkeneji, Lokop, E Lokop, Nkutuk. 147,000 speakers in Kenya, Samburu district, and southern and eastern shores of Lake Baringo, Baringo district, Rift Valley Province (Chamus). The dialect is Chamus (Ilcamus, Njemps). The El Molo mainly speak Samburu now, a slightly different dialect.

Shatt: also called Caning. 15,000 speakers in northern Sudan, Shatt hills southwest of Kadugli (Shatt Daman, Shatt Safia, Shatt Tebeldia) and parts of Abu Hashim and Abu Sinam.

Shilluk: also called Colo, Dhocolo, Chulla, Shulla. 175,000 speakers in Sudan. Roman alphabet is used.

Soo: also called So, Tepeth, Tepes. 5,000 speakers in Uganda, Karamoja district of eastern Uganda on Mt. Moroto on Kenya border. Bilingualism in Karamojong. In some areas used mainly by those over 40 years old. Younger people speak Karamojong as primary language.

Suri: also called Surma, Shuri, Churi, Dhuri, Shuro, Eastern Suri. 20,600 speakers in Ethiopia and Sudan. In Ethiopia: 19,622 speakers. Ethnic population: 19,632 as of 1998. Southwestern Kafa region toward the Sudan border. Some are west of Mizan Teferi. Dialects are Tirma (Tirima, Terema, Terna, Dirma, Cirma, Tirmaga, Tirmagi, Tid), Chai (Cai, Caci). In Sudan: Southern Sudan, Boma Plateau near the Ethiopian border. Dialects are Tirma (Tirima, Terema, Terna, Dirma, Cirma, Tirmaga, Tirmagi, Tid), Chai (Caci, Cai). Closely related to Mursi of Ethiopia.

Talai: also called Marakwet. 25,000 speakers in Kenya, Rift Valley Province. Low intelligibility with basic Kalenjin dialects and Endo.

Tama: also called Tamongobo, Tamok, Tamot. 62,931 speakers in Chad. Dialects are Tama, Gimr (Orra, Qimr, Haura), Jabaal (Mileere, Missirii, Miisiirii, Milri), Erenga. The majority use Chadian Arabic as second language, although at a low proficiency level. Some also use Masalit. The Gimr now speak Chadian Arabic as mother tongue.

Temein: also called Temainian, Rone, Ronge. 10,000 speakers in northern Sudan, Nuba hills in the Temein hills southwest of Dilling, between Jebels Ghulfan Morung and Julud (Gulud).

Tennet: also called Tenet. 4,000 speakers in southern Sudan, Equatoria Province, Lopit hills, northeast of Torit, five villages. Some intelligibility with Murle, Narim, and Didinga (in descending order). Most Tennet are fluent in Lopit, from which they borrow most of their songs. Many over 20 years old know Toposa, which is used for ox names and a few songs. Many can also understand some Otuho, which is closely related to Lopit. Those with schooling know a little Arabic. All ages. A strong sense of Tennet ethnic identity.

Tese: also called Teis-Umm-Danab, Keiga Jirru, Keiga Girru. 1,400 speakers in northern Sudan, Nuba hills, Keiga Jirru west of Debri, and in six villages, northeast of Kadugli.

Teso: also called Ateso, Ikumama, Bakedi, Bakidi, Etossio, Elgumi, Wamia. 1,217,000 speakers in Uganda and Kenya. In Uganda: 999,537 speakers in Sorot and Kumi region, southeast, Teso Province. Lokathan live around Madial at the northern end of the Nangeya Mountains. Dialects are Lokathan (Biri, Ketebo), Orom (Rom). Limited intelligibility with other varieties in the Teso-Turkana group. The dialect in Ngoro is considered standard. In Kenya: 217,000 speakers in Busia district, Western Province.

Thuri: also called Dhe Thuri, Jo Thuri, Wada Thuri, Shatt. 6,600 speakers in southern Sudan between Wau and Aweil, between Jur and Lol Rivers, on Raga-Nyamlell road, and on Wau-Deim Zubeir road. Dialects are Bodho (Dhe Boodho, Dembo, Demen, Dombo), Colo (Dhe Colo, Jur Shol, Jo Colo), Manangeer (Jur Manangeer). It is reported that all Thuri groups speak Dinka and Luwo.

Toposa: also called Ngatoposa, Taposa, Topotha, Akara, Kare, Kumi. 100,000 speakers in Sudan. Dialects are Eastern Toposa, Western Toposa, Jiye. Eastern Toposa and Jiye are linguistically closer to Turkana; Western Toposa to Karamajong. Inherently intelligible with Nyangatom, Karamojong, and Turkana, but each has strong ethnic attitudes. Separate literature is needed also because of loans from different second languages, and different discourse structures. Limited intelligibility with Teso. Most are monolingual. A small number speak Southern Sudanese Arabic (Juba Arabic) for trading. A few know some English from school. All domains. Vigorous language use. Neighboring groups use it in trade (Didinga, Murle, Boya-Longarim, Tennet). Speakers are proud of their language. The Toposa are peaceful with the Karamojong, have a mutual nonagression pact with the Nyangatom, are intermittently hostile to the Jiye of Sudan, permanently hostile to the Turkana, and to the Murle-Didinga group (Murle, Didinga, Boya-Longarim).

Turkana: also called Bume, Buma, Turkwana. 340,000 speakers in Kenya, in Turkana, Samburu, Trans-Nzoia, Laikipia, Isiolo districts, Rift Valley Province, west and south of Lake Turkana, and Turkwel and Kerio Rivers. Dialects are Northern Turkana, Southern Turkana. Inherently intelligible with Toposa, but there is hostility toward the speakers. Also partially intelligible with Karamojong, Jie, and Nyangatom, but all five are ethnically distinct. There are a few phonological, lexical, and discourse marker differences between them. Northern Turkana and Eastern Toposa are closer; Southern Turkana and Western Toposa are farther apart linguistically. The four varieties form a continuum divided in the middle by the Kenya-Sudan border. Most people are monolingual. Only a few adults have mastered upcountry Swahili as lingua franca. More are learning Swahili because of a new road. A few can speak Pokot or Daasenech. Vigorous language use. Hostile toward the Karamojong and Pokot; friendly with Jie.

Wali: also called Walari, Walarishe. 490 speakers in northern Sudan, in the Wali hills, south of Karko hills.   B. GRIMES

ECP. *Abbreviation for* Empty Category Principle. *See* Anaphora; Formal Grammar; Traces; Principles and Parameters; *and* Filters.

EDOID LANGUAGES.

A group spoken in central southern Nigeria; they form a branch of BENUE-CONGO.

LANGUAGE LIST

Aduge: 1,904 speakers in Nigeria. Anambra state, Oyi LGA.

Degema: 10,000 speakers in Nigeria. Rivers state, Degema LGA, Usokun-Degema (Usokun) and Degema Town (Atala) communities. Dialects are Atala, Usokun (Kala Degema). There is no standard variety of Degema.

Edo: also called Bini, Benin, Addo, Oviedo, Ovioba. 1,000,000 speakers in Nigeria. Bendel state, Ovia, Oredo, and Orhionmwon LGAs. Used in adult education, history text. Roman alphabet. National language.

Ehueun: also called Ekpimi, Ekpenmen, Epimi. 5,766 speakers in Nigeria. Ondo state, Akoko South LGA. Related to Ukue.

Emai-Iuleha-Ora: also called Kunibum, Ivbiosakon. 100,000 speakers in Nigeria. Edo state, Owan LGA. Dialects are Ivhimion, Emai, Iuleha, Ora. Dialect cluster.

Engenni: also called Ngene, Egene. 20,000 speakers in Nigeria. Rivers state, Ahoada LGA; Bayelsa state, Yenagoa LGA. Dialects are Ediro, Inedua, Ogua.

FIGURE 1. *Subgrouping of Edoid Languages*

Delta
    Degema, Engenni, Epie
North-Central Edoid
    Edo-Esan-Ora
        Edo, Emai-Iuleha-Ora, Esan, Ibilo
    Ghotuo-Uneme-Yekhee
        Ghotuo, Ikpeshi, Ivbie North-Okpela-Arhe, Ososo,
        Sasaru-Enwan-Igwe, Uneme, Yekhee
Northwestern Edoid
    Aduge
    Osse
        Ehueun, Iyayu, Uhami, Ukue
    Southern Northwestern Edoid
        Okpamheri, Okpe-Idesa-Akuku, Oloma
Southwestern Edoid
    Eruwa, Isoko, Okpe, Urhobo, Uvbie

Epie: also called Epie-Atissa. 12,000 speakers in Nigeria. Rivers state, Yenagoa LGA. Most speakers are bilingual in Ijo.

Eruwa: also called Erohwa, Erakwa, Arokwa. Spoken in Nigeria. Delta state, Isoko LGA. Related to Urhobo. Not intelligible with any Isoko dialect. Most speakers are bilingual in Central Isoko, which is replacing Eruwa.

Esan: also called Ishan, Isa, Esa, Anwain. 200,000 speakers in Nigeria. Edo state, Agbazko, Okpebho, Owan, and Etsako LGAs. The many dialects, which include Ekpon, Igueben, are apparently inherently intelligible. 90% speak or understand Nigerian Pidgin English. English and possibly Ika are also used as second languages. A regionally important language.

Ghotuo: also called Otwa, Otuo. 9,000 speakers in Nigeria. Edo state, Owan and Akoko-Edo LGAs.

Ibilo: spoken in Nigeria. Edo state.

Ikpeshi: also called Ikpeshe, Ekpeshe. 1,826 speakers in Nigeria. Bendel state, Etsako LGA.

Isoko: "Igabo," "Sobo," "Biotu" are derogatory names sometimes used. 321,000 speakers in Nigeria. Delta state, Isoko and Ndokwa LGAs. Dialects are Ozoro, Ofagbe, Emede, Owe (Owhe), Elu, Aviara, Iyede, Imiv, Enhwe, Ume, Iwire (Igbide), Olomoro, Iyede-Ami, Unogboko, Itebiege, Uti, Iyowo, Ibiede, Oyede, Uzere, Irri (Iri), Ole (Oleh). A regionally important language. Official orthography.

Ivbie North-Okpela-Arhe: 20,000 speakers in Nigeria. Edo state, Etsako and Akoko-Edo LGAs. Dialects are Ivbie North (Ibie North), Okpela (Okpella, Ukpella, Upella), Arhe (Atte, Ate). Dialect cluster.

Iyayu: also called Idoani. 9,979 speakers in Nigeria. Ondo state, one-quarter of Idoani town.

Okpamheri: also called Opameri. 30,000 speakers in Nigeria. Edo state, Akoko-Edo LGA. Dialects are Okulosho (Okurosho), Western Okpamheri, Emhalhe (Emarle, Somorika,

Semolika). Subdialects of Okulosho: Ojirami (Eekunu), Dagbala (Dangbala), Oja (Oza), Makeke (Uuma), Oma. Subdialects of Western Okpamheri: Ekpe, Bekuma, Lankpese (Lampese, Lankpeshi), Ibillo (Ibilo), Imoga (Imorga, Uma), Eko (Ekon, Ekor), Ikaran-Oke (Ikeram-Oke), Ebunn-Oke, Ikaran-Ele (Ikeran-Ile), Ebunn-Ugbo, Ikpesa, Igbo-Ola-Sale (Ugboshi-Sale), Aiyegunle (Oshi), Igbo-Ola-Oke (Ugboshi-Oke), Onumo (Onumu), Ogugu, Ogbe-Sale, Ogbe-Oke.

Okpe: 8,722 speakers in Nigeria. Edo state, Okpe LGA.

Okpe-Idesa-Akuku: spoken in Nigeria. Edo state, Akoko-Edo LGA. Dialects are Okpe, Idesa, Akuku. Related to Oloma.

Oloma: spoken in Nigeria. Edo state, Akoko-Edo LGA. Related to Okpe-Idesa-Akuku.

Ososo: 6,532 speakers in Nigeria. Edo state, Akoko-Edo LGA.

Sasaru-Enwan-Igwe: 3,775 speakers in Nigeria. Edu state, Akoko-Edo LGA. Dialects are Sasaru, Enwan, Igwe.

Uhami: also called Ishua. 5,498 speakers in Nigeria. Ondo state, Akoko South and Owo LGAs.

Ukue: also called Ukpe, Ekpenmi, Ekpenmen, Epinmi. 5,702 speakers in Nigeria. Ondo state, Akoko South LGA. Related to Ehuen.

Uneme: also called Uleme, Ileme, Ineme. 6,000 speakers in Nigeria. Edo state, Etsako, Agbazko, and Akoko-Edo LGAs.

Urhobo: also called Biotu. "Sobo" is a derogatory name sometimes used. 546,000 speakers in Nigeria. Delta state, Ethiope and Ughelli LGAs.

Uvbie: also called Uvhria, Uvwie, Evrie, Effurun. "Evhro" is a derogatory name sometimes used. 6,000 speakers in Nigeria. Delta state, Ethiope LGA. Related to Urhobo.

Yekhee: also called Etsako, Etsakor, Afenmai, Iyekhee. "Kukuruku" is a derogatory name sometimes used. 274,000 speakers in Nigeria. Edo state, Etsako, Agbako, and Okpebho LGAs. Dialects are Auchi, Uzairue, South Ibie (South Ivbie), Uwepa-Uwano (Weppa Wano), Avianwu (Fugar), Aviele, Ivhiadaobi, Ekperi.   B. GRIMES

EDUCATIONAL LINGUISTICS. The discipline of educational linguistics, like educational psychology and educational sociology, is created by the intersection of other fields (Spolsky 1978, 1985, 1999, Stubbs 1986, Corson 1997). It forms, as Valdman (1999: 720) notes, what the French call either a *discipline-tampon* (one that mediates between theory and practice) or a *discipline-carrefour* (a crossroads or gatekeeping discipline for others). It links the various subdivisions of the academic discipline of linguistics, whether core or peripheral, with the practical professional areas that are directly concerned with language education. Its centrality is premised on the close, multiplex links between language and education. Language acquisition has been, especially since the work of Noam Chomsky, a key topic for linguistic study. Formal education is mainly conducted verbally, and language education constitutes the largest part of most school curricula.

1. Taxonomy. The two parent fields of linguistics and education provide a first taxonomic partition of educational linguistics. The linguistic division, the source of basic knowledge about language, its acquisition, and its use, consists of the core areas that study language structure (phonetics, phonology, morphology, syntax, and semantics) and the related "hyphenated" areas that study its acquisition and processing (neurolinguistics, psycholinguistics, clinical linguistics) and its use (sociolinguistics, pragmatics, discourse analysis). The second division, the province of education, deals with practical language learning and teaching; thus, it includes first or second language pedagogy and the teaching of reading, spelling, writing, listening, and speaking. Educational linguistics thus embraces two major areas of research and practice. It also specifies a comprehensive curriculum for training language educators.

The very broadness of this definition sets a difficult challenge for its practitioners. Very few people can expect to have a deep knowledge of all its parts, which are still generally studied and taught autonomously. There are, however, major advantages in looking at the field as a whole and in combining topics commonly examined separately. For example, the combined approach permits one to investigate the differences between first and second language learning, or to analyze language education policy in its fullest social and educational context.

2. Educational vs. applied linguistics. The term *educational linguistics* was coined because of the ambiguity and the delusive implication of the term *applied linguistics*. Applied linguistics, with its echo of applied mathematics and applied science, suggests incorrectly that it is possible to take a new theoretical advance in linguistics and apply it directly to a practical field like language teaching. The most egregious example of misapplication was the Audio-Lingual Method, which was imposed on language teachers and their pupils in the belief that structuralist theories of language were directly translatable into teaching methods. At its worst, this condemned language-learners to hours of meaningless drills.

"Applied linguistics" is used sometimes in a broad sense to cover all the practical applications or implications of knowledge developed as a result of the growth of the discipline of linguistics, and sometimes, more narrowly, to mean no more than "language teaching"

(Kaplan 1980). In many universities, a course labeled "applied linguistics" is little more than an introduction to second language pedagogy. For others, such as the International Association of Applied Linguistics and its Congresses, the term includes the entire range of subjects ancillary to the study of the core field of linguistics, such as psycholinguistics, sociolinguistics, and computational linguistics. "Educational linguistics" is then a more precise term.

3. Goal of educational linguistics. The fundamental goal of educational linguistics is to connect basic knowledge of the structure, acquisition, and use of language with the practical tasks concerned in modifying and improving an individual learner's control of language and languages. It assumes that advances in the sciences of language have significant and valuable, if indirect, implications for solving language-related problems. Structural linguistics offered the language teacher a more accurate and efficient way of analyzing the language knowledge that a learner needed, and it helped to revive interest in the teaching of the spoken language. Transformational-generative linguistics not only provided a deeper explanation of language structure but also initiated a revolution by making language acquisition a central concern of linguistics. It thus encouraged the development of psycholinguistics and neurolinguistics, with their contributions to understanding how language is learned and how it is represented in brain processes. The reluctance of general linguistic theory to deal with variation in language promoted the development of sociolinguistics, a field that has made it possible to analyze the social context of languages and language learning. Essentially, the goal of educational linguistics is to derive from its many branches and from other fields that study language the knowledge that may be used to develop the language capacity of individuals and groups.

4. Key tasks. Another approach to a taxonomy of educational linguistics can be derived from a potential all-embracing theory for the field as a whole. A good starting point is the model of language instruction proposed by Carroll 1962. He postulated that the linguistic proficiency or competence of an individual is a function of that individual's learning ability, individual or socially determined motivation to acquire further proficiency, and socially or educationally determined exposure to other varieties of language.

The role of educational linguistics is to spell out the nature of each of the terms and processes in this key sentence, and to track the ways in which they may be modified in order to permit the development of socially or individually desired language competence. Linguistic theory defines underlying competence (language testing deals with how it might be measured); psycholinguistics and neurolinguistics deal with the nature of learning and of innate ability; clinical linguistics studies pathologies of development; social psychology and sociolinguistics study the background and nature of motivation and language attitudes or ideology; sociolinguistics (especially language policy) studies the social context that determines the possibilities of exposure for formal and informal language learning; and the individual pedagogical fields study the modifications in exposure that can change the language competence of pupils.

5. Social context of language and education. Starting at the macro or social level, a number of fields study the social context of language and education. Language plays a critical role in the socialization of its speakers. A first cluster of topics, loosely grouped as sociolinguistic, deals with variation in language, its causes, and its results. Though some national states act as if all their citizens spoke only one language, most are in fact multilingual, with various patterns of functional distribution of a diverse mix of languages and dialects. The study of societal bilingualism (or multilingualism, or plurilingualism) provides an important basis for understanding language and language education policy. One special pattern, called *diglossia*, assigns higher or lower values and functions to two varieties of the same language (for example, Classical Arabic and spoken Arabic in the Middle East), or to two different languages (for example, Spanish and Guaraní in Paraguay). Diglossia entails an educational problem when, as is commonly the case, the higher variety is required by school but the lower one is the home language of the pupils. Sociolinguistics also deals with language loyalty (instantiated as the willingness to learn or teach a language), defines the plight of minority languages, and provides a basis for understanding the threats faced by many languages in the world today. In this social cluster, an emerging field looks at the formulation and implementation of language policy, and at the related development of language education policy, which governs the choice of medium of instruction and of other languages to be taught. Although it is true that purely pragmatic needs for efficient communication are enough to encourage development of policy, in practice this seemingly neutral and objective task is regularly confounded and distorted by the felt need to assert, for nationalistic or symbolic reasons, a higher status for one

or more chosen languages. A further area of social concern is literacy—not just the ability to read and write, but also the socially relevant control of the written variety of language. Finally, sociolinguistics provides the means to study the language gap between home and school, the critical transition that children must make from the variety of language that they grow up speaking to the standard form that schools demand. This issue has been especially vexing in the case of speakers of nonstandard varieties, such as African American Vernacular English.

6. Individual basis of language and education. At the micro or individual level, a number of branches of learning focus on the individual language learner. Language exists in social context, but individuals learn it. Psycholinguistics is the field most concerned with language acquisition. To what extent is language innate, and to what extent is it learned? What does our knowledge of the structure of the brain tell us about learning language? What are the differences between acquiring one language or several? What is known about the acquisition of pronunciation? How early does the child learn to recognize and produce the sounds of its first language? Answers to questions like these are fundamental to effective language education. A second cluster looks at exceptions to normal language acquisition, the various pathologies that produce challenged language learners, including language disorders, reading disorders, blindness, and deafness. A third cluster focuses on second language processing. What is the nature of bilingualism? How are second languages acquired naturally? What is the effect of age on second language learning?

This section and the previous one deal essentially with the knowledge derived from the academic discipline of linguistics and its related fields. The next three deal with the educational implementation of this knowledge.

7. Practical educational linguistics. The first of the three sections deals with the school context. Formal language education in first or additional languages generally takes place in a classroom, a context with its own sociolinguistic practices. Language use and teaching in the school are defined by school language policies, the most significant of which establish single or multi-medium instruction. Commonly, the language chosen as a medium of instruction is the national language, whether or not it is the spoken language of most pupils (for example, French or Dutch in Belgium, rather than the vernacular Walloon or Flemish dialects). In rarer cases, efforts are made to revive a language or teach a second or foreign language by using it as medium of instruction in an immersion program (for instance, Maori in some New Zealand schools, or French in some anglophone Canadian communities). One common but controversial policy is bilingual education, where two (or more) languages serve as languages of instruction in various arrangements. The effectiveness of the classroom can be enhanced technologically and, with the development of language laboratories and the Web, moved outside the normal four walls.

8. Language teaching. The next cluster of fields focuses on language teaching. First comes the teaching of what the school defines as the mother tongue (usually the national or official language). The fact that it may not be the mother tongue of a significant proportion of pupils is often a serious problem. There is a growing tendency to develop national curricula, continuing a long series of efforts to improve the teaching of the mother tongue. Most recently, this is often expressed in efforts to impose national standards. A central concern in mother-tongue education is commonly the teaching of grammar. Should grammar be taught explicitly or implicitly? Does learning grammar improve language proficiency? Which model of grammar is most useful for schools?

Given the close relationship between schooling and literacy, the teaching of reading is probably the main educational linguistic activity of schools. Theories, approaches, and methods have proliferated and competed. Controversies such as whole-word vs. phonics continue to stir parents and politicians as much as or even more than they do practitioners. A major textbook industry thrives on the cyclical swings in popularity of new panaceas. The teaching of spelling and writing are also major fields.

A second major area is the teaching of additional languages, whether second languages (languages widely spoken within the national territory), or foreign languages (languages of other nations, especially international languages like English, French, Spanish, or German), or classical languages (languages like Classical Arabic, Sanskrit, or Biblical Hebrew that are associated with sacred texts, or chosen, like Latin or Greek, for their literary traditions). There is a broad range of topics in second-language learning; individual differences, learning strategies, attitudes and motivation, interlanguage, and language for special purposes. Another important subfield is second language acquisition (SLA), originally an adaptation of research in first language acquisition but now the central theoretical field for second language learning. There are also subfields concerned with the specific teaching of individual languages or individual aspects of languages: second language teaching methods, second language pedagogy, and the teaching of pronunciation, speaking, reading, or writing in a second or foreign language. A final area deals with the evaluation, assessment, or testing of the outcomes of language education. Included are the developing field of foreign language testing and the established fields of reading and spelling testing.

9. Educational linguistics as a field. Teaching and research programs and centers covering the field of educational linguistics are starting to emerge, through commonly using a different title, such as applied linguistics or language education. At the same time, challenges are appearing to the notion that the field can function simply as a bridge between disciplines and professions; and efforts are being made to explore the possibility of a semi-autonomous educational linguistics.

[*See also* Acquisition of Language; Applied Linguistics; Bilingualism and Multilingualism; Diglossia; Institutional Linguistics; Language Planning; Language Testing; *and* Sociolinguistics.]

BIBLIOGRAPHY

Carroll, John B. 1962. The prediction of success in intensive foreign language training. In *Training research and education*, edited by R. Glaser, pp. 87–136. Pittsburgh, Pa.: University of Pittsburgh Press.

Corson, David, ed. 1997. *Encyclopedia of language and education.* 8 vols. Dordrecht: Kluwer.

Kaplan, Robert B., ed. 1980. *On the scope of applied linguistics.* Rowley, Mass.: Newbury House.

Spolsky, Bernard. 1978. *Educational linguistics: An introduction.* Rowley, Mass.: Newbury House.

Spolsky, Bernard. 1985. Educational linguistics. In *International encyclopedia of education,* edited by T. Husen and T. N. Postlethwaite, pp. 3095–3100. Oxford: Pergamon.

Spolsky, Bernard, ed. 1999. *Concise encyclopedia of educational linguistics.* Amsterdam and New York: Elsevier.

Stubbs, Michael. 1986. *Educational linguistics.* Oxford: Basil Blackwell.

Valdman, Albert. 1999. Journals. In Spolsky 1999, pp. 729–732.

BERNARD SPOLSKY

EGYPTIAN. An independent branch of the Afroasiatic family, Egyptian shows the closest relations to Semitic and Berber. With its more than four millennia of productive history—from 3000 BCE to 1300 CE—it provides an ideal field for both diachronic and typological investigation.

Gardiner 1957 is the most widely used handbook for the study of hieroglyphs. Allen 2000 is the most accessible modern introduction to the classical language. Edel 1955–1964 is a philological reference work on the language of the Old Kingdom. Černý and Groll 1984 presents a structural analysis of Late Egyptian. Erman and Grapow 1926–1953 is still the standard dictionary of Egyptian; for Coptic, Crum 1929–1939 offers a philologically much more detailed compendium; and Westendorf 1965–1967 is the important instrument for etymological reconstruction. Polotsky 1987–1990 offers a structural analysis of Coptic, while Loprieno 1995 is a linguistic introduction to Egyptian from a diachronic perspective.

1. History. The history of Egyptian can be divided into two main stages, each of which is further subdivided into different phases, which affect mainly the writing system.

Older Egyptian refers to the written language from 3000 to 1300 BCE, surviving in religious texts until the 2nd century CE. It is characterized by its preference for synthetic grammatical structures (no definite article, V[erb] S[ubject] O[bject] order, etc.). Its main phases are:

(a) Old Egyptian, the language of the Old Kingdom and the First Intermediate Period (3000–2000 BCE).

(b) Middle Egyptian, from the Middle Kingdom to the end of the XVIII Dynasty (2000–1300 BCE). This is the classical literary language; it differs from Old Egyptian mainly in having a regularized orthography.

(c) Late Middle Egyptian, the language of more formal texts from 1300 BCE onward.

In the Greek and Roman period (Ptolemaic Egyptian, 3rd c. BCE to 2nd c. CE), the language shows a considerable elaboration of the set of hieroglyphic signs (see below.)

Later Egyptian refers to the language of literature and administration from the XIX Dynasty to the Christian era (1300 BCE to 1300 CE), with the following phases:

(a) Late Egyptian (1300–700 BCE).

(b) Demotic (7th c. BCE to 5th c. CE), differing from Late Egyptian basically in its graphic system.

(c) Coptic (4th–14th c. CE), the alphabetically written language of Christian Egypt.

As a spoken (and progressively also written) language, Coptic was superseded by Arabic beginning with the 9th century, but it survives to the present in the liturgy of the Coptic Church. Later Egyptian exhibits a tendency toward the development of analytic features—e.g. a definite article, and SVO periphrastic patterns.

Because of the centralizing nature of the political and cultural models that underlay the evolution of Ancient Egyptian society, there is hardly any evidence of dialect differences in pre-Coptic Egyptian; however, the origins of Older Egyptian are probably to be placed in Lower Egypt (Memphis), and those of Later Egyptian in Upper Egypt (Thebes). Coptic displays a variety of dialects.

2. Writing system. The basic graphic system of Ancient Egyptian is the *hieroglyphic* writing. It consists of a set of signs representing realia—about one thousand such symbols in the Old Kingdom, and approximately 760 in the classical language, dramatically increasing to many thousands in Ptolemaic Egyptian. The system combines phonological and ideographic principles. A word begins with a sequence of monoconsonantal, biconsonantal, or triconsonantal signs, called *phonograms*, which convey its phonological structure; vocalic (and often also semivocalic) phonemes remain unexpressed in writing. The sequence of phonograms is usually followed by one of a group of *semagrams*, called "determinatives," which indicate iconically the semantic sphere of the word (especially in later stages, there may be more than one semagram in a word). Some words of common usage—pronouns, prepositions, and a few lexical items like *ḏd* 'to say'—are written only phonologically. But many items of basic vocabulary are expressed by semagrams which represent, symbolize, or evoke (through rebuses) their semantic reference; these are called *logograms* or *ideograms*. Egyptian writing displays a set of twenty-four alphabetic (i.e. monoconsonantal) signs, which correspond to the consonantal and semiconsonantal phoneme inventory of the language, with the exception of /l/; yet it never developed into a genuine alphabetic system until the Coptic period. The increasing consciousness of the symbolic potential inherent to the relation between signifiant and signifié, within this writing system, led to the use of cryptographic solutions in Ptolemaic Egyptian.

The hieroglyphic system, which was used mainly for monumental purposes, has two cursive varieties: *Hieratic* (2600 BCE to 3rd c. CE), which simply represents a cursive rendering (with ligatures and diacritic signs) of a sequence of hieroglyphic signs; and *Demotic* (7th c. BCE to 5th c. CE), which radically modifies the writing conventions by introducing a shorthand-like simplification of hieratic sign-groups. The basic orientation of the

TABLE 1. *Egyptian Consonants*

	Labial	Apical	Alveo-palatal	Palatal	Velar	Uvular	Pharyngeal	Glottal
Stops								
Voiceless	p	t			k	q		3,j /ʔ/
Voiced	b	d			g			
Affricates								
Voiceless				ṯ /c/				
Voiced				ḏ /ɟ/				
Fricatives								
Voiceless	f	s	š	ẖ /ç/	ḫ /x/		ḥ /ħ/	h
Voiced		z					ꜥ /ʕ/	
Nasals	m	n						
Lateral		3,n,r /l/						
Vibrant		r						
Glides	w			j				

Egyptian writing system—and the only one adopted in the cursive varieties—is from right to left; epigraphic hieroglyphs can invert this order for reasons of symmetry.

The hieroglyphic-based system was superseded in Coptic by an alphabet derived from that of Greek, with the addition of seven Demotic signs for the indication of phonemes extraneous to Greek; it was written from left to right.

3. Phonology. The reconstruction of the Egyptian phoneme inventory is bound to be highly hypothetical. Vocalism and prosody can only be reconstructed by combining the contemporary, but not always unequivocal, Akkadian transcriptions with the much later Coptic evidence. Furthermore, the value of many consonantal oppositions is still open to debate. The consonants are shown in Table 1.

Note the following details:

(a) The Egyptian phonological system does not display the "emphatic" phonemes common to most Afroasiatic languages. The most frequent etymological counterparts of Semitic emphatic fricatives seem to be the affricates; and of Semitic emphatic stops, the corresponding voiced phonemes, which were probably articulated as ejectives.

(b) In mode of articulation, the voiced/voiceless opposition was probably realized as ejective vs. aspirated: thus /t/ = [tʰ], /d/ = [tʔ]; /c/ = [cʰ], /ɟ/ = [cʔ]; /k/ = [kʰ], /g/ = [kʔ].

(c) The existence of a phoneme /l/ seems to be established; however, it exhibits no autonomous graphic rendering, being expressed in different lexemes by *3, n,* or *r.*

TABLE 2. *Egyptian Gender and Number Markers*

	Masculine	Feminine
Singular	.∅, .w	.t
Dual	.wj	.tj
Plural	.∅, .w, .ww	.t, .jt, .wt

(d) The point of articulation of stops tends to be progressively moved to the front: (velars, postpalatals) > palatals > dentals (2nd millennium BCE).

(e) Oppositions between fricatives in the palatal region (/š ç x/) tend to be neutralized (2nd millennium BCE).

(f) The opposition between /ʕ/, which probably derives from the pharyngealization of an original dental or lateral phoneme, and the glottal stop /ʔ/ tends to be neutralized in the later phases of Egyptian.

(g) Initial /j/ tends to become /ʔ/ from the very beginning of documented written history.

(h) Final /r/ and /t/ tend to become /ʔ/, then to disappear (2nd millennium BCE).

The vowels are front /ii:/, mid /aa:/, and back /uu:/. Some historical changes include:

(i) /a/, /a:/ > /o/, /o:/ (about 1000 BCE)

(ii) /i/, /u/ > /e/; /u:/ > /e:/ (2nd millennium BCE)

(iii) In particular phonetic surroundings, /e:/ > /i:/, /i:/ > /e:/

4. Morphology. As in other Afroasiatic languages, the basic Egyptian morphological unit is the root (biliteral or triliteral, with very few exceptions); this is modified by suffixes, or less frequently by prefixes. The gender and number markers are shown in Table 2, and the personal

TABLE 3. *Egyptian Personal Pronouns*

		Independent	Dependent	Suffixed
Sing.	1 c.	*jnk*	*wj*	*.j*
	2 m.	*twt, ntk*	*kw, tw*	*.k*
	2 f.	*tmt, ntt*	*tm, tn*	*.t*
	3 m.	*swt, ntf*	*sw*	*.f*
	3 f.	*stt, nts*	*sj, st*	*.s*
Dual	1 c.		*nj*	*.nj*
	2 c.	*nttnj*	*tnj*	*.tnj*
	3 c.	*ntsnj*	*snj*	*.snj*
Plur.	1 c.	*jnn*	*n*	*.n*
	2 c.	*nttn*	*tn*	*.tn*
	3 c.	*ntsn*	*sn*	*.sn*

TABLE 4. *Egyptian Suffixal Pronouns*

	Singular	Dual	Plural
1	*.kj > .kw*		*.wjn*
2	*.tj*	*.tjwnj*	*.tjwnj*
3 m.	*.w*	*.wj*	*.w*
3 f.	*.tj*	*.tj*	*.tj*

pronouns in Table 3. (Suffixes, as opposed to words, are marked by periods preceding them.)

Of the series shown in the table, the independent pronouns are used as focus of a cleft sentence, usually a marked N[ominal] P[hrase]:

(1)   *Ntf mrr sj.*
       'He is the one who loves her.'

In modal contexts, a marked V[erbal] P[hrase] occurs:

(2)   *Ntf sdm.f sj.*
       'He is the one who will hear her.'

Dependent pronouns are used (i) as object of a VP (*Sdm.f sj* 'He will hear her'); (ii) as subject of an unmarked NP (mostly an ADJ[ectival] P[hrase]: *Nfr sw* 'He is good'); and (iii) as subject of an ADV[erbial] P[hrase], in the 1st and 2nd persons only after initial particle:

(3)   *(Mk) sw m jjj.t.*
       '(Behold,) he (is) in coming' > 'He is coming.'

(4)   *Mk wj m pr.w.*
       'I am in the house.'

Suffixed pronouns are used (i) as subject of a VP (*Mrr.f sj r-wr* 'He loves her greatly'); (ii) as possessive pronoun

(*pr.w.j* 'my house'); and (iii) as object of preposition (*J3.w n.k* 'Praise to you').

Demonstratives follow the noun to which they refer, and include masc. *pn pf pw*, and fem. *tn tf tw*—thus *rmt pf* 'that man', *hjm.t tn* 'this woman'. The corresponding plurals *nn, nf, nn* are also used as pronouns in partitive constructions: *nn nj srjw.w* 'these officials'.

The most frequent prepositions are *m* 'in, with', *n* 'to, for', *r* 'toward', and *hr* 'on'.

Finite forms of verbs are built by attaching a suffix pronoun to the root, either directly (*mrr.f* '(the fact) that he loves', *mrj.k* 'you love'), or after the insertion of a morpheme indicating tense, aspect, or voice features:

(5)   *Mrj.n.f sj r-wr.*
       'He loved her greatly.'

(6)   *Mrj.w.k wj.*
       'May you love me.'

The most important verbal indicators are *n* (past tense), *t* (perfective, sometimes prospective aspect), *w* (prospective aspect and passive voice), and *tw* (passive voice). Some classes of verbal roots show a reduplication of the second radical in a form originally indicating imperfective aspect—but, in the classical language, a VP with nominal function: *mrr.f* '(the fact) that he loves'. The imperative has no suffix pronoun: *dd* 'say!' A verbal form carrying the feature of perfectivity (variously called Old Perfective, Pseudo-participle, or Stative), displays a set of suffix pronouns, which are etymologically linked to the Semitic suffix conjugation, thus *prj.kw* 'I have come forth; see Table 4.

There are two types of non-finite forms: the Nomina Agentis (participles) exhibit nominal suffixes (masc. *.Ø*, *.w*, and fem. *.t*, etc.); and the Nomina Actionis (infinitives) show a suffix *.Ø* in the regular verbs (*sdm* 'to hear'), and *.t* in the weak classes (*mrj.t* 'to love'). A special Nomen Actionis with a suffix *.w* is used after verbs of negative predication:

(7)   *tm* 'not to do something'
       tm.f mrj.w '(the fact) that he does not love'

It is a matter of dispute whether the radical element of finite forms is originally a Nomen Agentis (*mrj.f* *'a-loving-one-is-he' > 'he loves') or a Nomen Actionis (*mrj.f* *'loving-by-him' > 'he loves'). Verbal predications can also be analytically expressed by prepositional constructions; these characterize the evolution of the verbal system in Later Egyptian:

(8) *Sw ḥr sḏm.*
     'He is on hearing > 'He is hearing.'

(9) *Sw r mrj.t.*
     'He is toward loving' > 'He is going to love.'

5. Syntax. Egyptian shows three types of sentences, classified according to their PRED[ICATE]; the SUBJ[ECT] is always a NP.

(a) Nominal, with substantival or adjectival PRED; the unmarked order is PRED + SUBJ:

(10) *Rmṯ pw.*
     'He is a man.'
     Nfr sj.
     'She is beautiful.'

This is inverted into SUBJ + PRED by focalization of SUBJ:

(11) *Ntf ḏḏ n = f sw.*
     'He is the one who gives it to him.'

If SUBJ is topicalized, it is extraposed and resumed by a coreferential pronoun:

(12) *Jr sf, wsjr pw.*
     'As for yesterday, it is Osiris.'

(b) Adverbial, with adverbial or prepositional predicate; the order is SUBJ + PRED:

(13) *Sw ṯnj.*
     'Where is he?'

(14) *Zẖ3.w m pr.w.*
     'The scribe is in the house.'

(c) Verbal, with verbal predicate; the order is PRED + SUBJ (+ obj):

(15) *Hᶜj.w.k.*
     'You will appear.'
     Jrj.w.j st.
     'I shall do it.'

Except in the prospective aspect, verbal sentences are much less frequent than in cognate languages: VPs tend to be embedded as SUBJ and/or PRED, within a SUBJ + PRED (or Topic + Comment) sequence. In Egyptological literature, this phenomenon is called "transposition"; the Topic + Comment sequence is called a "complex adverbial sentence." Examples are:

(16) *M33.f wj m pr.w.*
     'That-he-sees me (is) in the house' > 'He sees me in the house.'

(17) *Zj pn mrj.f sj.*
     'This man (is) in-that-he-loves her' > 'This man loves her.'

In later Egyptian, embedded VPs are grammaticalized, while simple verbal forms are replaced by periphrastic constructions with the auxiliary verb *jrj* 'to do': *sḏm.f* 'he hears' > *j.jr.f-sḏm* 'that he hears'.

[*See also* Afroasiatic Languages *and* Writing and Written Language, *article on* Writing Systems.]

BIBLIOGRAPHY

Allen, James P. 2000. *Middle Egyptian: An introduction to the language and culture of hieroglyphs.* Cambridge: Cambridge University Press.

Černý, Jaroslav, and Sarah I. Groll. 1984. *A Late Egyptian grammar.* 3rd ed. (Studia Pohl, Series maior, 4.) Rome: Biblical Institute Press.

Crum, Walter E. 1929–1939. *A Coptic dictionary.* 2 vols. Oxford: Clarendon Press.

Edel, Elmar. 1955–1964. *Altägyptische Grammatik.* 2 vols. (Analecta Orientalia, 34–39.) Rome: Biblical Institute Press.

Erman, Adolf, and Hermann Grapow. 1926–1953. *Wörterbuch der ägyptischen Sprache.* 6 vols. and supplements. Leipzig: Hinrichs. Berlin: Akademie-Verlag.

Gardiner, Alan H. 1957. *Egyptian grammar, being an introduction to the study of hieroglyphs.* 3rd ed. Oxford: Griffith Institute, Ashmolean Museum.

Loprieno, Antonio. 1995. *Ancient Egyptian: A linguistic introduction.* Cambridge: Cambridge University Press.

Polotsky, Hans-Jakob. 1987–1990. *Grundlagen des Koptischen Satzbaus.* (American studies in papyrology, 27–29.) Atlanta: Scholars' Press.

Westendorf, Wolfhart. 1965–1967. *Koptisches Handwörterbuch.* Bearbeitet auf Grund des Koptischen Handwörterbuchs von Wilhelm Spiegelberg. 2 vols. Heidelberg: Winter.

ANTONIO LOPRIENO

EKOID LANGUAGES. Spoken in southeastern Nigeria and adjacent parts of Cameroon, they constitute a branch of SOUTH BANTOID.

Abanyom: also called Abanyum, Befun, Bofon, Mbofon. 12,500 speakers in Nigeria, Cross River state, Ikom LGA, Abangkang the main village.

Efutop: also called Ofutop, Agbaragba. 10,000 speakers in Nigeria, Cross River state, Ikom LGA.

Ejagham: also called Ekoi. 105,000 speakers in Nigeria and Cameroon. In Nigeria: 60,000 speakers in Cross River state, Akampka, Idom, Odukpani, Calabar LGAs. Dialects are Southern Ejagham (Ekin, Qua, Kwa, Aqua, Abakpa), Western Ejagham, Eastern Ejagham. In Cameroon: 45,000 speakers in whole of Eyumodjok subdivision and southern part of Mamfe subdivision west of Mamfe, Manyu division, South West Province in Cameroon. Dialects are Western Ejagham, Eastern Ejagham, Southern Ejagham (Ekin, Kwa, Qua, Aqua, Abakpa).

Ekajuk: also called Akajo, Akajuk. 30,000 speakers in Nigeria in Cross River state, Ogoja LGA, Bansara, Nwang, Ntara 1, 2, and 3, and Ebanibim towns.

Nde-Nsele-Nta: 19,500 speakers in Nigeria in Cross River state, Ikom LGA. Dialects are Nde (Ekamtulufu, Mbenkpe, Udom, Mbofon, Befon), Nsele, Nta (Atam, Afunatam).

Ndoe: 3,000 speakers in Nigeria in Cross River state, Ikom LGA. Dialects are Ekparabong (Akparabong), Balep (Anep, Anyep).

Nkem-Nkum: 34,500 speakers in Nigeria in Cross River state, Ogoja LGA. Dialects are Nkem (Nkim, Ogoja, Ishibori, Isibiri, Ogboja), Nkum. Dialect cluster.

Nnam: also called Ndem. 3,000 speakers in Nigeria in Cross River state, Ikom and Ogoja LGAs.   B. GRIMES

ELAMITE. The second language of the trilingual inscriptions of the Achaemenid kings of ancient Persia, Elamite was deciphered in the 1840s, after G. F. Grotefend in 1802 had read and identified the first, simplest script as Old Persian. The inventory of the cuneiform syllabary used to write Elamite was much smaller than that of the third language, Babylonian, which was deciphered soon after the first; but the interpretation of Elamite lacked the help of cognates that the Semitic languages could provide for Babylonian, and is still hampered by lack of comparative material.

1. The corpus. Elamite was spoken in the lowlands of southwestern Iran and in the highlands of Fars, from the 3rd millennium BCE probably to the 1st millennium CE. It was written with cuneiform syllabic signs from ca. 2200 BCE to 400 BCE. Another script—as yet undeciphered, but presumably also recording the Elamite language—is attested from ca. 3200 onward, first in picto-graphs (Meriggi 1971–1974) and later in linear form (for an attempt to decipher the latter, see Hinz 1962, 1975).

Texts from the O[ld] E[lamite] period are rare. Even the longest, the so-called Treaty of Narām-Sin, ca. 23rd c. BCE, is poorly understood; and only a few texts survive from the 18th century BCE. The corpus of the M[iddle] E[lamite] period, ca. 1300–1100 BCE, consists of two types of documents: royal inscriptions, mostly on bricks decorating temples whose dedication they record (König 1965); and administrative documents, which come mainly from Malyān in Fars (Stolper 1984). N[eo-] E[lamite] is represented by 8th–7th century dedicatory inscriptions, some on bricks and some monumental; by administrative documents, legal texts, and letters on clay tablets from the 7th–6th century BCE; by a bronze plaque; and even by an astrological omen text. Best attested is A[chaemenid] E[lamite], which comprises inscriptions of Darius and his successors in one, two, or three languages, plus several thousand administrative texts found at Persepolis (Cameron 1948, Hallock 1969).

The structure of Elamite was sketched by Labat 1951; Royal Achaemenid Elamite was analyzed in descriptive terms by Paper 1955. Elamite of all periods—with special emphasis on ME, since AE morphology was somewhat simplified and the syntax influenced by Old Persian—is discussed by Reiner 1969, McAlpin 1981, and Grillot-Susini 1987. Details on grammatical features continue to be contributed by French Elamitologists and by others working in related fields (Diakonoff 1973, Wilhelm 1978, 1982; see the bibliography in Grillot-Susini 1987). A new grammar of both Middle and Achaemenid Elamite is Khačikjan 1998, which also contains a useful bibliography; the book should be used in conjunction with its review, Stolper 2001. An interesting attempt at categorizing Achaemenid verb conjugation is Tucker 1998. In the dictionary of Hinz and Koch 1987, the many unknown words (and sometimes desperate guesses at meaning) emphasize that the major problem in Elamite studies is our inadequate knowledge of the lexicon.

2. Writing and phonology. The cuneiform syllabary was adapted in a manner somewhat simplified, both as to forms and selection of signs, from that of neighboring Babylonia; it consists of V, CV, VC, and (more rarely) CVC signs, plus a limited number of logograms, i.e. Sumerian words also used in the Assyro-Babylonian syllabary. The latter are identified in Elamite texts, as are also some Akkadian loanwords, by the Sumerogram MEŠ 'plural', which is usually transliterated as 'lg'. (for "logogram"). This system can express only four vowels: *a, i, u* and (in combination with a limited number of sylla-bograms only) *e*. It cannot express initial or final conso-nant clusters, or medial clusters of more than two con-sonants; and it neutralizes voice in syllable-final position. Hence certain elements of Elamite phonology must be inferred from spelling variations. Thus nasal vowels are inferred from spellings with or without a following nasal consonant (*Hu-ban* and *Hu-um-ban,* a proper name; *te-em-ti* and *te-ep-ti* 'lord', presumably /tẽpt/). Two sets of stops (and possibly also of sibilants) are inferred from the fact that some words are always spelled with inter-vocalic geminated consonants, and others never (*hu-ud-da* or *hu-ut-ta* 'make', but *ku-tu-* 'prosper'?; *ik-ki* 'to' but *i-gi* 'brother')—a practice which, in Hittite orthography, distinguishes voice or lenition (Mayrhofer 1973). The existence of at least final clusters is inferred from varia-tion between word-final *i* and *u* after two consonants, and from such variant spellings as -VC-CV-CV and -VC-VC-CV, e.g. *ku-ši-ih-ši-ta* and *ku-ši-ih-iš-ta* (presumably /kušihšta/ 'they have built').

3. Morphology and syntax. The most conspicuous feature of the syntax is a type of labeled bracketing (aptly called "Elamite brackets" by Bork 1934). In the sentence, which is of the Subject-Object-Verb type, only one verb may occur; all other elements show nominal inflection. Accordingly, the grammar distinguishes two inflectional categories:

(a) Finite verb conjugation with inflection for 1st, 2nd, and 3rd person, and for singular and plural number, but not for gender or tense.

(b) Nominal inflection for the categories of speaker (end-ing -*k*), person addressed (-*t*), and person or thing spoken of. These 'genders' are called *locutive, allo-cutive,* and *delocutive* by Reiner 1969, and "object-class," "person-class," and "I-class" by Diakonoff 1973.

The delocutive distinguishes inanimate (ending -*me,* in OE perhaps also -*t* and -*n*) vs. animate (singular ending -*r*, plural -*p*; proper names and kinship terms have zero ending). These endings operate the concord which brack-ets elements that belong to the same clause. Nominals which participate in this inflection (the "appellatives" of McAlpin 1981) comprise substantives, numerals, demon-stratives, the negative particle, and nominal forms derived from the verb stem by the suffixes Ø (infinitive or gerund), -*n* (active participle), and -*k* (passive participle).

TABLE 1. *Elamite Personal Pronouns*

	Nominative	Accusative
1sg.	*u*	*un*
2sg.	*nu*	*nun*
1pl.	*nuku*	*nukun*
2pl.	*num/nun*	*numun*
3pl.	*ap*	*apun*

Subject and object are distinguished by the object case-ending -*n* in personal pronouns only, as shown in Table 1. Directional relations are expressed by postpositions, for example *ukku* 'upon', *ikku* 'toward', and *pat* 'under'.

A verb stem, normally of the shape CV(CV), may be reduplicated as C_iVC_iCV (*peli* 'place?', *pepli*; *hutta* 'make', *huhta*); or it may enter as the second element into a compound with a substantive (*mur+ta* 'earth-place' = 'to erect') or an adverb (*teppa+ta* 'before-place' = 'to set up in front').

The personal suffixes are -*h, -t, -š* for 1, 2, and 3 sg., and -*hu, -ht, -hš* for 1, 2, and 3 pl.; the final clusters *ht hš* are followed in the writing by a vowel, which either is purely graphic, or denotes some such category as aspect. The first of two conjoined verbs may lack the personal ending (*pepši kuši-h* 'restore built-I' = 'I re-built'). The clitics *ta* and *a* express, respectively, tense (pluperfect?) or aspect (completive?), and coordination or subordination. Between the verb stem and personal endings, the elements -*ma-* and (more rarely) -*nu-* func-tion somewhat as modal auxiliaries. Inflected verbs may also take a gender suffix when embedded, as in a relative clause.

For arguments as to whether Elamite is an ergative language, see Diakonoff (1973:14–15) and Wilhelm 1978, 1982. Its relation to Dravidian is as yet undecided; it is argued by McAlpin 1981. It certainly is so related typologically, even if not genetically. Features including the following are strikingly similar in both languages: the restriction that only one finite verb may appear in the sentence; inflection of nouns for person (Medieval Tamil); grammatical case for personal pronouns only; and case relationships expressed by postpositions.

[*See also* Cuneiform *and* Dravidian.]

BIBLIOGRAPHY

Bork, Ferdinand. 1934. Die elamische Klammer. *Archiv für Orientforschung* 9.292–300.

Cameron, George G. 1948. *Persepolis Treasury Tablets.* (Oriental Institute publications, 65.) Chicago: University of Chicago Press.

Diakonoff, Igor M. 1973. Bemerkungen zu einer neuen Darstellung altkleinasiatischer Sprachen. *Orientalistische Literaturzeitung* 68.14–16.

Grillot-Susini, Françoise. 1987. *Éléments de grammaire élamite.* (Synthèse, 29.) Paris: Éditions Recherche sur les Civilisations.

Hallock, Richard T. 1969. *Persepolis fortification tablets.* (Oriental Institute publications, 92.) Chicago: University of Chicago Press.

Hinz, Walther. 1962. Zur Entzifferung der elamischen Strichschrift. *Iranica Antiqua* 2.1–21.

Hinz, Walther. 1975. Problems of linear Elamite. *Journal of the Royal Asiatic Society* 1975:106–115.

Hinz, Walther, and Heidemarie Koch. 1987. *Elamisches Wörterbuch.* 2 vols. (Archäologische Mitteilungen aus Iran, Ergänzungsband 17.) Berlin: Reimer.

Khačikjan, Margaret. 1998. *The Elamite language.* (Documenta Asiana, 4.) Rome: Istituto per gli Studi Micenei ed Egeo-Anatolici.

König, Friedrich W. 1965. *Die elamischen Königsinschriften.* (Archiv für Orientforschung, Beiheft 16.) Graz: Weidner.

Labat, René. 1951. Structure de la langue élamite. *Conférences de l'Institut de Linguistique de l'Université de Paris* 10.23–42.

McAlpin, David W. 1981. *Proto-Elamo-Dravidian: The evidence and its implications.* (Transactions of the American Philosophical Society, 71:3.) Philadelphia.

Mayrhofer, Manfred. 1973. Der Reiner-Test. In *Festschrift Heinrich Otten,* edited by Erich Neu and Christel Rüster, pp. 191–197. Wiesbaden: Harrassowitz.

Meriggi, Piero. 1971–1974. *La scrittura proto-elamica.* 3 vols. Rome: Accademia Nazionale dei Lincei.

Paper, Herbert H. 1955. *The phonology and morphology of Royal Achaemenid Elamite.* Ann Arbor: University of Michigan Press.

Reiner, Erica. 1969. The Elamite language. In *Altkleinasiatische Sprachen* (Handbuch der Orientalistik, I.2/1–2, 2), edited by Bertold Spuler, pp. 54–118. Leiden: Brill.

Steve, M.-J. 1992. *Syllabaire élamite: Histoire et paléographie.* (Recherches et Civilisations du Proche-Orient, Série 2: Philologie, 1.) Neuchâtel and Paris: CDPOP.

Stolper, Matthew W. 1984. *Texts from Tall-i Malyan,* vol. 1, *Elamite administrative texts (1972–1974).* (Occasional publications of the Babylonian Fund, 6.) Philadelphia: Museum of the University of Pennsylvania.

Stolper, Matthew W. 2001. Review of *The Elamite language,* by Margaret Khačikjan. *Journal of Near Eastern Studies* 60. 275–279.

Tucker, Elizabeth. 1998. The "nominal conjugations" in Achaemenid Elamite. In *Studies in Persian History: Essays in Memory of David. M. Lewis,* edited by Maria Brosius and Amélie Kuhrt (= Achaemenid History, 11), pp. 165–194. Leiden: Nederlands Instituut voor het Nabije Oosten.

Vallat, François. 1996. Nouvelle analyse des inscriptions néo-élamites. In *Collectanea Orientalia, Études offertes en hommage à Agnès Spycket,* edited by H. Gasche and B. Hrouda (Civilisations du Proche-Orient, Série 1: Archéologie et Environnement, 3), pp. 385–395. Neuchâtel and Paris: CDPOE.

Wilhelm, Gernot. 1978. Ist das Elamische eine Ergativsprache? *Archäologische Mitteilungen aus Iran* 11.7–12.

Wilhelm, Gernot. 1982. Noch einmal zur behaupteten Ergativität des Elamischen. *Archäologische Mitteilungen aus Iran* 15.7–8. (With a note by Igor M. Diakonoff, p. 8.)

ERICA REINER

ELEMAN LANGUAGES.

ELEMAN LANGUAGES. A branch of the proposed TRANS-NEW GUINEA phylum. They are spoken in southern Papua New Guinea.

LANGUAGE LIST

Kaki Ae: also called Tate, Raepa Tati, Tati, Lorabada, Lou. 310 speakers in Gulf Province, southeast of Kerema. Different from Torricelli (Lou) in East Sepik Province or Lou in Manus Province. Bilingualism in Toaripi. 40% to 100% of the ethnic group speak Kaki Ae.

Keuru: also called Keuro, Belepa, Haura, Haura Haela. 4,525 speakers in Gulf Province, from the mouth of the Purari River east to the Bairu River.

Opao: 1,116 speakers in Gulf Province, near Orokolo and Keuru.

Orokolo: also called West Elema, Kairu-Kaura, Haira, Kaipi, Vailala, Bailala, Muru, Muro. 13,000 speakers in Gulf Province, from mouth of Purari River east to Bairu River. Kerema is a main town.

Purari: also called Koriki, Evorra, Namau, Iai, Maipua. 7,000 speakers in Gulf Province, between Kapaina Inlet and Orokolo language, Purari River. Apparently unrelated to other languages of Gulf Province.

FIGURE 1. *Subgrouping of Eleman Languages*

Eleman Proper
Eastern Eleman Proper
Tairuma, Toaripi
Western Eleman Proper
Keuru, Opao, Orokolo
Purari
Tate
Kaki Ae

Tairuma: also called Uaripi. 4,000 speakers in Gulf Province, Uaripi and several other villages near Toaripi.

Toaripi: also called Motumotu, East Elema. 23,000 speakers in Gulf Province, Cape Possession to Cape Cupola. Kerema is a main town. Dialects are Kaipi (Melaripi), Toaripi (Moripi-Iokea, Moveave), Sepoe.   B. GRIMES

ELLIPSIS. Structures termed *ellipsis* are sentences containing gaps that are interpreted under identity to some other constituent, not necessarily in the same sentence. There are two general types of ellipsis. In the first, the gap corresponds to a constituent of S[urface-]Structure, e.g. V[erb] P[hrase] or S[entence] (the full range of possible elliptic constituents is discussed in Lobeck 1986):

(1a)   *Everyone yawned when Lucie did* **e.** (VP ELLIPSIS)

(1b)   *I'm supposed to meet someone, but I can't remember who* **e.** (SLUICING)

The second type includes various kinds of *gapping*. Here the missing nodes—such as *rode*, or *in the zoo* in (2), below—do not usually form a syntactic constituent:

(2)   *Lucie rode an elephant in the zoo, and Zelig a camel.* (GAPPING)

Although only cases like (2) have been traditionally labeled "gapping," this type also includes cases where only one argument is left in the ellipsis clause:

(3)   *Lucie liked the camel, but not the elephant.* (BARE ARGUMENT ELLIPSIS)

The two types have different distribution. Most notably, gapping can occur only in coordinate structures, but constituent ellipsis can be embedded, as in (1a).

Research on ellipsis has focused on its derivation and interpretation. The early assumption (e.g. Ross 1967, Neijt 1979) was that it is obtained by deletion transformations applying at the mapping from D[eep-]Structure to S-structure. However, Sag 1976 and Williams 1977 showed that the level at which the ellipsis rules apply must be L[ogical] F[orm]. It has been argued that neither the sense of *identity* relevant for the ellipsis rules, nor the restrictions on the possible interpretations of the missing constituent, can be fully captured at D-structure or S-structure. Thus, if (4a) is derived by a deletion operation

on (4b), the deleted constituent is not identical syntactically with its antecedent:

(4a)   *Lili said that everyone₁ [walked his₁ dog] after Lucie did* **[e]**.

(4b)   *Lili said that everyone₁ [walked his₁ dog] after Lucie [walked her dog].*

(4c)   *Everyone [λx(x walks x's dog].*

There is also no way to explain why *her* in (4b) can refer to either *Lucie* or *Lili,* but in the missing predicate of (4a) it can denote only *Lucie.* In LF, however, the first VP of (4a) is analyzed along the lines of (4c), which denotes the property of 'walking one's own dog'; and copying this predicate yields the correct interpretation (known as "sloppy identity").

More recent developments in the research of constituent (VP) ellipsis returned to some version of the deletion approach. It is assumed that this type is obtained by phonological reduction of destressed material; that is, it applies, technically, at P[honological] F[orm]. But the interpretation of the elided part is guided by principles of parallelism, which still apply at LF (Chomsky and Lasnik 1993, Tancredi 1992, and, most notably, Fox 2000).

In the case of gapping, LF provides the level at which the missing material forms a constituent—if we assume, following Sag 1976, that a rule similar to Quantifier Raising applies to the antecedent clause. For (3), this yields the LF [ₛ *the camel* [ₛ *Lucie liked* **e**]]. The predicate corresponding to the internal S (λx(*Lucie liked* x)) can then take the second conjunct as argument. Since this rule obeys subjacency, the island restrictions on gapping (reported in Neijt 1979) are explained. For other reference, see Ross 1969, Rooth 1981, and Reinhart 1991.

[*See also* Deletion; Grammatical Relations; *and* Subjacency.]

BIBLIOGRAPHY

Chomsky, Noam, and Howard Lasnik. 1993. The theory of principles and parameters. In *Syntax: An international handbook of contemporary research*, edited by Joachim Jacobs et al., pp. 506–569. Berlin: Walter de Gruyter. Also published in Noam Chomsky, *The Minimalist Program*, pp. 13–27. Cambridge, Mass.: MIT Press, 1995.

Fox, Danny. 2000. *Economy and semantic interpretation.* Cambridge, Mass.: MIT Press.

Lobeck, Anne C. 1986. Syntactic constraints on VP ellipsis.

University of Washington, Seattle, dissertation. Published, Bloomington: Indiana University Linguistics Club, 1987.

Neijt, Anneke. 1979. *Gapping: A contribution to sentence grammar.* (Studies in generative grammar, 7.) Dordrecht: Foris.

Reinhart, Tanya. 1991. Elliptic conjunctions—non quantificational LF. In *The Chomskyan turn*, edited by Asa Kasher, pp. 360–384. Oxford: Blackwell.

Rooth, Mats. 1981. A comparison of three theories of VP deletion. *University of Massachusetts Occasional Papers in Linguistics* 7.212–244.

Ross, John Robert. 1967. Constraints on variables in syntax. Cambridge, Mass.: MIT dissertation. Published as *Infinite syntax.* Norwood, N.J.: Ablex, 1986.

Ross, John Robert. 1969. Guess who? *Chicago Linguistic Society* 5.252–286.

Sag, Ivan A. 1976. *Deletion and logical form.* Cambridge, Mass.: MIT dissertation. Published, New York: Garland, 1979.

Tancredi, Chris. 1992. Deletion, deaccenting and presupposition. Cambridge, Mass.: MIT dissertation.

Williams, Edwin. 1977. Discourse and Logical Form. *Linguistic Inquiry* 8.103–139.

TANYA REINHART

EMERGENT GRAMMAR. *See* Functional Linguistics.

EMPTY CATEGORY. *See* Anaphora; Formal Grammar; Traces; Principles and Parameters; *and* Filters.

ENCLITICS. *See* Clitics.

ENDANGERED LANGUAGES. Languages described as "endangered" are contracting in number of speakers, function, or structure and vocabulary, as the speakers shift either partially or completely to the use of another language. The term *moribund languages* is sometimes applied to those that children are no longer learning at home. *Language death*, a term coined by Dorian 1981 and now often used synonymously with *language extinction*, refers in its original, more narrow sense to the structural changes in languages that occur in the last generations of speakers. The last speakers are often "semi-speakers" because of incomplete language learning or the decline of their knowledge of the language (*language attrition*) after cessation of daily use.

About half of the known languages of the world have vanished in the past 500 years (Nettle and Romaine 2000), and the social and political processes leading to language extinction are accelerating the decline. Krauss 1992 suggests that another half of the world's languages will die within the 21st century.

The plight of endangered languages has always been of deep concern to linguists and was a strong motivator for linguistic documentation throughout much of the 19th and 20th centuries. To quote one famously obsessed fieldworker, J. B. Harrington: "The time will come and *soon* when there won't be an Indian language left in California, all the languages developed for thousands of years will be *ashes*, the house is *afire*, it is *burning*. That's why I said to go through the blinding rain, roads or no roads, that's why I thanked God when you tried to cross the Mattole River, haven't I gone back even two weeks later to find them *dead* and the language *forever dead*?" (unpublished letter to his assistant Jack Marr, 1941).

In recent decades, whole new fields have begun to emerge to study the causes and processes of language decline. Interdisciplinary studies are directed to language attitudes, language policy, language contact and change, and the social dynamics of language retention, shift, and acquisition in a bilingual setting. Well-established areas of inquiry—such as code-switching, pidgins and creoles, and first and second language acquisition—have offered much to the understanding of the processes of language decline.

Members of speech communities whose languages are disappearing are themselves deeply concerned over the loss, and many are working with linguists to develop ways to retain or regain their languages. A number of private foundations and government agencies are funding community programs for language revitalization, and linguists are frequently asked to consult for these programs. The theories and methods of language pedagogy have thus become fields of interest to linguists, along with issues of literacy and orthographic design. Because of the strong interest by many indigenous people in doing linguistic work for the benefit of their communities, new programs are beginning to develop at universities to fulfill their needs. A notable example is a Master of Arts program in Native American linguistics at the University of Arizona. Linguists have also found themselves in the position of being advocates for endangered languages, and many have become politically active around issues such as bilingual education and language policy.

[*See also* Language Planning *and* Obsolescent Languages.]

BIBLIOGRAPHY

Dorian, Nancy. 1981. *Language death: The life cycle of a Scottih Gaelic dialect.* Philadelphia: University of Pennsylvania Press.

Dorian, Nancy, ed. 1989. *Investigating obsolence.* Cambridge: Cambridge University Press.

Fishman, Joshua A. 1991. *Reversing language shift: Theoretical and empirical foundations of assistance to threatened languages.* Clevedon: Multilingual Matters.

Grenoble, Lenore, and Lindsey Whaley, eds. 1998. *Endangered languages: Current issues and future prospects.* Cambridge: Cambridge University Press.

Krauss, Michael. 1992. The world's languages in crisis. *Language* 68.4–10.

Hinton, Leanne, and Ken Hale. 2001. *The Green Book of language revitalization in practice.* New York: Academic Press.

Nettle, Daniel, and Suzanne Romaine. 2000. *Vanishing voices: The extinction of the world's languages.* Oxford and New York: Oxford University Press.

LEANNE HINTON

ENDOCENTRIC CONSTRUCTION. *See* Heads *and* Compounding.

ENGGANO. A branch of WESTERN MALAYO-POLYNESIAN: also called Engganese. 700 speakers in Sumatra, Indonesia, on Enganno Island, southwest of Sumatra and on four smaller nearby islands. Not closely related to other languages.

B. GRIMES

ENGLISH. Among the world's languages, English has the widest dispersion, but Chinese and possibly Spanish have larger numbers of first-language speakers. As a second language, English serves as the lingua franca of diplomacy, government, science, commerce, and scholarship. In about a score of nations, it is the sole official language; in another score, English shares official status with one or more other languages; neither the United Kingdom nor the United States designates an official language. English is one of six official languages of the United Nations.

English belongs to the West Germanic subgroup of the Germanic branch of the I[ndo-]E[uropean] language family, along with German, Dutch, and Frisian. It began its history as a distinct tongue about 449 CE, when (according to Bede) Angles, Saxons, and Jutes speaking Germanic dialects arrived in Celtic-speaking Britain. Bands from these tribes sailed to Britain to aid the Romanized Britons, who were weakened after the withdrawal of Roman protection in 410 and besieged by invading Picts and Scots.

The history of English is divided into three periods: O[ld] E[nglish] (Anglo-Saxon) from about 700 to 1100 CE; M[iddle] E[nglish] from 1100 to 1500; and Modern English (abbreviated NE, i.e. "New English") from 1500 to the present.

1. Germanic characteristics. English naturally shares some linguistic features with other IE languages; its lexicon, morphology, and phonology also display distinct Germanic characteristics. Among words not found in IE outside the Germanic branch are *drink, drive, leap, bone, fowl, meat, king, sea, ship,* and *wife.* The IE system of indicating tenses by vowel alternation remains in certain English verbs (*sing/sang/sung*); but the productive past tense inflection with [d]/[t], as in *judged, kissed,* is Germanic. The effects of Grimm's Law can be seen in the initial consonants of Eng. *father, three, horn,* reflexes of IE [p], [t], and [k] (compare Latin *pater, trēs, cornus*). Also characteristically Germanic is the system of fixed primary stress on the first syllable of the root (*bróther, brótherhood, unbrótherly*); this pattern is now obscured by wholesale borrowing, where the characteristic shifting stress of IE often prevails (*promíscuous, promiscúity*).

2. Old English (see Hogg 1992, Mitchell and Robinson 2001). OE was a highly inflected language, with suffixes on nouns, verbs, adjectives, and demonstratives, and with an elaborate system of personal, interrogative, and relative pronouns. Written records date from the late 7th century. Four dialects are recognized in the OE period: Kentish in the southeast, West Saxon in the south and southwest, Mercian in the Midlands, and Northumbrian above the Humber River. Most extant materials are written in West Saxon, which achieved status as a written standard in the reign of Alfred the Great (871–899).

2.1. Orthography and phonology. The few Old English graphs that differ from those of NE occur frequently in texts; among them are þ (thorn) from the runic alphabet and ð (eth) and æ (ash) adapted from the Roman. The

TABLE 1. *Old English Noun Forms*

Singular				
Nom.	*fox* 'fox'	*dēor* 'animal'	*lār* 'lore'	*fōt* 'foot'
Acc.	*fox*	*dēor*	*lār*	*fōt*
Gen.	*foxes*	*dēores*	*lāre*	*fōtes*
Dat./Inst.	*foxe*	*dēore*	*lāre*	*fēt*
Plural				
Nom./Acc.	*foxas*	*dēor*	*lāra*	*fēt*
Gen.	*foxa*	*dēora*	*lāra*	*fōta*
Dat./Inst.	*foxum*	*dēorum*	*lārum*	*fōtum*

TABLE 2. *Old English Demonstratives*

	Singular			Plural
	Masculine	Feminine	Neuter	M/F/N
Nom.	*sē*	*sēo*	*þæt*	*þā*
Acc.	*þone*	*þa*	*þæt*	*þā*
Gen.	*þæs*	*þære*	*þæs*	*þāra*
Dat.	*þǣm*	*þære*	*þǣm*	*þǣm*
Inst.	*þȳ*	*þære*	*þȳ*	*þǣm*

TABLE 3. *Old English Personal Pronouns*

	1st Person	2nd Person	3rd Person		
			M	F	N
Singular					
Nom.	*ic*	*þū*	*hē*	*hēo*	*hit*
Acc.	*mē*	*þē*	*hine*	*hie*	*hit*
Gen.	*mīn*	*þīn*	*his*	*hiere*	*his*
Dat./Inst.	*mē*	*þē*	*him*	*hiere*	*him*
Plural					
Nom.	*wē*	*gē*	*hīe*		
Acc.	*ūs*	*ēow*	*hīe*		
Gen.	*ūre*	*ēower*	*hiera*		
Dat./Inst.	*ūs*	*ēow*	*him*		

sequence *sc* (*Englisc, scip*) represents NE *sh* [ʃ]. The graphs *k* and *q* were not used (*folc* 'folk', *cwēn* 'queen'); *c* represented both [k], as in *nacod* 'naked', and [tʃ], as in *cild* 'child'. The letter *g* represented a glide [j] initially before certain front vowels, and finally after them (*geard* 'yard', *halig* 'holy'), but [g] or [ɣ] elsewhere.

OE permitted certain consonant clusters which are now prohibited, as in *hlūd* 'loud', *hring* 'ring', and *cniht* 'boy' (the latter survives orthographically in *knight*, cf. *knee*, *know*). Three pairs of sounds whose members are now distinct phonemes were then allophones of single phonemes: [f] and [v]; [θ] and [ð]; and [s] and [z] (compare *wīf* [wi:f] 'woman' and *wīfes* [wi:vɛs] 'women').

OE had systematic long and short vowels, plus diph-

thongs. Until recently, at least, short vowels have remained relatively stable over the centuries, and many words containing short vowels are pronounced today essentially as in OE: *him, horn, ræt, fisc* 'fish', *ecg* 'edge'. By contrast, long vowels have undergone dramatic shifting, as described in section 4.1 below.

2.2. *Morphology.* OE nouns carried one of three grammatical genders, and N[oun] P[hrase]s were inflected for five cases; however, nominative and accusative forms were often identical, as were dative and instrumental forms. Table 1 gives sample paradigms for nouns.

From the *fox* declension come the only productive NE noun inflections, with plurals and possessive singular in -*s*. The *dēor* paradigm survives in uninflected plurals like *deer* and *sheep*; the *fōt* declension has yielded *foot/feet, goose/geese, tooth/teeth, louse/lice, mouse/mice, man/ men*. Modern English phrases like *a ten-foot pole*, containing an apparently singular form, derive in fact from the OE genitive plural ('a pole of ten feet'), where *foot* < *fōta*. Demonstratives were inflected for five cases and three genders in the singular, and for three cases without gender distinction in the plural, as shown in Table 2. An instrumental case was used (sometimes with a preposition) to indicate accompaniment or instrument.

Like other Germanic languages, OE had two adjectival declensions. In a NP containing a (highly inflected) possessive pronoun or demonstrative, adjectives exhibited the "weak" declension, as in *sē gōda mann* 'the good man'. When markers of case were few or non-existent, as with predicative function, the more varied forms of the "strong" declension were used, as in *Hē is gōd* 'He is good.' Adjectives were inflected for gender, number, and case, in agreement with their heads.

OE personal pronouns have retained more of their morphological variation in NE than has any other form class, as can be inferred from the paradigms in Table 3.

OE also had dual forms in the 1st and 2nd person pronouns. These eventually disappeared, along with distinct number and case forms in the 2nd person, and distinct case forms for the neuter nominative/accusative and the dative/instrumental 3rd person singular (*hit* and *him*).

In its verbs, OE exhibits two types: "weak," with a [d] or [t] past-tense suffix, as in *love/loved*; and "strong," with vowel gradation (ablaut), as in *ring/rang/rung*. The principal parts of the seven strong verb classes are shown in Table 4.

Verbs were inflected for present and past tenses and for indicative and subjunctive moods, in three persons

TABLE 4. *Old English Verb Classes*

	Infinitive		Past Sg.	Past Pl.	Past Participle
1.	*rīdan*	'ride'	*rād*	*ridon*	*geriden*
2.	*sēoðan*	'boil'	*sēað*	*sudon*	*gesoden*
3.	*bindan*	'bind'	*band*	*bundon*	*gebunden*
4.	*beran*	'bear'	*bær*	*bǣron*	*geboren*
5.	*cweðan*	'say'	*cwæþ*	*cwǣdon*	*gecweden*
6.	*standan*	'stand'	*stōd*	*stōdon*	*gestanden*
7.	*feallan*	'fall'	*fēoll*	*fēollon*	*gefeallen*

TABLE 5. *Old English Verb Conjugation*

		Indicative	Subjunctive
Present			
Singular			
	1	*dēme*	
	2	*dēmst* (or *dēmest*)	*dēme*
	3	*dēmþ* (or *dēmeþ*)	
Plural		*dēmaþ*	*dēmen*
Past			
Singular			
	1	*dēmde*	
	2	*dēmdest*	*dēmde*
	3	*dēmde*	
Plural		*dēmdon*	*dēmden*
Gerund		*to dēmenne* (or *dēmanne*)	
Present Participle		*dēmende*	
Past Participle		*dēmed*	

and two numbers. The twelve distinct forms of an OE weak verb, *dēman* 'judge', are shown in Table 5; compare today's typical verb with only four forms (*judge, judges, judged, judging*) and no distinct subjunctive.

2.3. Syntax. OE relied on inflections to mark grammatical relations, and word order was thus more flexible than in NE. OE does exhibit a preference for S[ubject] V[erb] O[bject] order in main clauses, and SOV in subordinate clauses, but all orders occurred. Following the frequent introductory adverb *þā* 'then', the verb occupied second position. In context, grammatical subjects were not obligatory and could be omitted.

The order of elements in NPs was usually determiner + adjective + noun (*sē gōda mann* 'that good man'); genitives usually preceded nouns (*þæs landes folc* 'that land's people'); and prepositions preceded nouns, but often followed pronouns (*him tō* 'to him'). As in NE, adjectives usually preceded head nouns (*æt sumum sǣle* 'at a certain time'). Relative clauses followed nouns, and were introduced by invariant *þe* (often compounded with

a form of the demonstrative *sē* or a personal pronoun); demonstratives also occurred alone as relatives.

Although the verb *dōn* 'do, put, make' could be used as a substitute, or 'pro', verb, it was not available as an auxiliary. Interrogatives generally inverted subject and finite verb. Negatives usually showed the negative particle *ne* before the verb. Multiple marking of negation within a clause, now non-standard, was common: *Nis nū cwicra nān . . .* '(There) isn't now alive no one . . .'

A striking characteristic of OE writing is the strong preference for linking sentences with *and* 'and' or *þā* 'then'. The frequent use of subordinators (*because, since, until*) to make explicit the relations between clauses was a later development.

2.4. Lexicon. During the Viking age (about 750–1050), Britain suffered a second Teutonic invasion, principally of Danes, who settled in central and southeastern England. By 1000, although corners of Britain remained Celtic-speaking, most inhabitants of the island, including the assimilated Danes, spoke OE. Today hardly a trace of Celtic influence survives, except in a few toponyms, e.g. *Kent, Devon, Thames,* and possibly *London.* Likewise, Latin influence through the Celts is negligible, except in place-names, notably the element *-chester* (< La. *castra* 'camp'), as in *Dorchester, Winchester, Worcester.* With the Christianizing of Britain at the end of the 6th century, there was an influx of Latin words, mostly of a religious nature (*monk, abbot, monastery, bishop, cloister, candle, chalice, mass*). The Danish assimilation contributed wholesale to the word stock of English, including about two thousand place-names or elements thereof, e.g. the *-by* in *Derby* and *Whitby*—as well as many everyday verbs (*take, give, get*) and nouns (*sky, skirt, skin, skill*). Even so common a phrase as *they are* is Scandinavian, suggesting a remarkable intermingling of Danish and English. Despite such openness to foreign importations, the most characteristic way of expanding the OE word stock was by combining native elements in prefixing, suffixing, and compounding.

3. Middle English (see Blake 1992). ME is a telling name for the period of transition between Old and Modern English. After the Norman conquest in 1066, English was relieved of many duties in the affairs of the court, government, and learning, as these activities were carried out by French-speaking (and often Latin-writing) Normans. Gradually, members of the middle classes became bilingual, speaking English to those below and French to those above. Only in 1204, when King John lost Normandy, did Britain's future as an English-speaking nation begin to look up. Partly as a consequence of the social and linguistic upheaval wrought by the conquest, ME reveals dramatic variation and evolution over its four centuries.

3.1. *Phonology.* OE long vowels were generally maintained in ME, except that /a:/ (*bān, stān, bāt*) became /ɔ:/ (NE /o/, as in *bone, stone, boat*). Many diphthongs were simplified in late OE and early ME. Short vowels in unstressed syllables, which had remained distinct at least in early West Saxon, merged in *e* [ə].

The initial consonant clusters *hl- hn- hr- kn-* lost their initials, as in *hlāf* 'loaf', *hnecca* 'neck', *hrōf* 'roof', *cniht* 'knight'. Of considerable consequence was the merging of word-final *m* into *n* in unstressed syllables; by the end of ME, even this *n* had dropped.

3.2. *Morphology.* Because of the loss of final *m n*, and the weakening of unstressed *a o u e* to [ə], many OE inflections became indistinguishable in early ME and dropped in late ME. The frequency of subject and object NP forms established the nominative/accusative plural form (and the -*es* inflection for nouns in general) throughout the plural, and the nominative/accusative singular (sometimes with analogical -*e* from the dative) throughout the singular—except that the genitive in -*s* was maintained. Thus the ME paradigm for a noun like *fox* came to be essentially what it is in NE: sg. *fox,* possessive *foxes* (now *fox's*), and plural *foxes.*

In other paradigms, the reduction of inflectional distinctions was even greater. The *dēor* class was reduced to three forms (*deer, deeres, deere*), while *lār* was reduced to two (*loor, loore*); these distinctions were further leveled when final inflected -*e* vanished, by about 1500. Adjectival inflections were greatly simplified at the beginning of ME, and completely lost by the end.

ME has more or less the same verb inflections as NE, except that the 3sg. present tense ends in -*(e)th* (*lyketh, hath*), and plural present tense in -*n* or -*en* (apparently borrowed from the OE subjunctive): *gon, eten, bryngen.* The reduction of the verbal inflectional system brought about a marked increase of periphrastic constructions in the future and perfect; modals replaced the OE subjunctive. Thus the establishment of an auxiliary system, including perfective *have* and *be,* is in large part compensation for inflectional reductions. The historical present is a late development of ME.

3.3. *Syntax.* Such morphological leveling inevitably influenced the syntax; as flection grew less able to signal grammatical relations and semantic roles, word order and the deployment of prepositions came to bear those communicative tasks less redundantly. Gradually, the freer word order of OE yielded to relatively fixed orders, which were capable of signaling grammatical relations. Whereas Old English used both SVO and SOV orders, and did not require a grammatical subject, ME is distinctly SVO, with obligatory subject. Also lost were impersonal constructions like *Euery man taketh what part that him lyketh*—lit. 'that to him (it) likes', i.e. 'that (it) pleases him'; here, since OE times, the verb had required not a nominative but an oblique case. Also during the ME period, interrogative pronouns came to serve as relatives.

Given the Norman invasion and the social distribution of bilingualism in the early ME period, there is every reason to believe that English writing and speaking were relatively close in form. Thus the parataxis characteristic of earlier prose and of typical speech continues for much of the period, and a vigorous use of hypotaxis arises only later.

3.4. *Lexicon.* By the beginning of the 14th century, as English came again to be known by all inhabitants of England, its lexicon had been enhanced by thousands of Norman French borrowings. Approximately ten thousand found their way into ME, and most survive today. Especially abundant are words in the semantic fields of religion, government, law, and the military; but the Normans also exerted great influence in food, fashion, and education. The following exemplify words borrowed in the ecclesiastical arena: *abbey, baptism, cardinal, chaplain, clergy, communion, confession, convent, creator, dean, faith, miracle, passion, penance, parson, pastor, pray* and *prayer, prelate, religion, sacrament, saint, sanctuary, salvation, sermon, theology.*

4. Modern English (see Burchfield 1994, Romaine 1998, Lass 1999, Algeo 2001). Standard written NE derives not from the West Saxon dialect of Old English, but from the East Midlands dialect of medieval London— the variety used by Chaucer and the Chancery, and disseminated when Caxton established his printing press at Westminster in 1476 (cf. Barber 1997). In the spoken varieties, considerable diversity has always existed, particularly in pronunciation.

4.1. *Phonology.* Between Chaucer's death in 1400 and Shakespeare's birth in 1564, all long vowels were systematically raised, and the highest were diphthongized, as shown in Figure 1. Subsequently, in the early 18th century, /e:/ was further raised to /i:/ in just those words where ME had /ɛ:/. Thus words like *meet* (< OE /e:/) and *meat* (< OE /ɛ:/) were merged.

Among notable consonant developments are additions

FIGURE 1. *The English Vowel Shift*

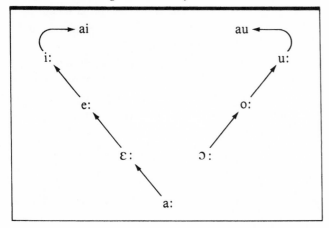

to the phonemic inventory, including /ŋ/ and /ʒ/, and, in some varieties, categorical or variable loss of postvocalic /r/ (as in *fear, heart*). With earlier roots but developing in this period are the highly systematic variable realizations of /θ/ as [θ] or [t] (as in *thirty, with*) and of /ð/ as [ð] or [d] (as in *this, that*), as well as the relatively unsystematic deletion or addition of /h/ in such words as *humor, herb*, and *hospital*. Some consonant changes remain in flux, as with merger of [w] and [ʍ] (as in *witch, which*). Also unsettled are certain vowel pronunciations, such as those in the sets of words represented by *cot* and *caught*, which have merged in some dialects, and the vowel in the word set represented by *class* and *path*. Extensive and systematic patterns of vowel shifting (e.g. the Northern Cities Shift and Southern Shift, both in the US; see e.g. Labov 1994–) may come to rival the "great" English vowel shift of early NE. Scholarly discussion of sound change over the five centuries of this period sometimes suggests remarkable stability, but a more focused picture reveals extensive and possibly accelerating change.

4.2. Morphology. The early NE period witnessed the disintegration of the distinction in pronouns of the 2nd person singular (*thou, thee*) vs. plural (*ye, you*). Probably under French influence, speakers of English began using the plural forms to signal deference. Among the upper social classes, the plural forms came to indicate mutual respect, even in informal conversation between equals. In time, the singular forms all but disappeared, as did the distinction between the subject and object forms *ye* and *you*. From the sixfold distinction of OE and much of ME, only the twofold distinction of *you* vs. *your(s)* survives.

By early ME, *þe* had become the invariant definite article in the north, replacing the varied forms of the earlier demonstrative, and its use soon spread to all dialects: Chaucer used only *the*. Although OE did not exploit indefinite articles, *a(n)*, from OE *ān* 'one', developed in the ME period to become the fifth most common word in written English today.

Of the 333 OE strong verbs, fewer than half survive today, and only about sixty are inflected as strong (Baugh and Cable 2001). Among those that have become weak are *burn, brew, climb, flow, help*, and *walk*. (In the course of history, about a dozen OE weak verbs have become strong, including *wear, spit*, and *dig*). With few exceptions ME verbal inflections were like those of NE; and in early NE, even these exceptions faded. Whereas Chaucer consistently used *-(e)th* in the 3sg. present, Shakespeare used both *-s* and *-(e)th*, favoring *-s* except in *doth* and *hath*.

4.3. Syntax (see Huddleston and Pullum 2002). Deprived of its rich inflectional system, English has become an analytical language, with a great increase in prepositional phrases and in periphrastic verb constructions. Although *do* as an empty auxiliary is attested from the ME period, it is not until the 17th century that its characteristic NE distribution is reached in questions and negatives, as well as for emphasis. Similarly, the progressive, attested only rarely in early ME, becomes robust during the early NE period. The progressive passive—*whose upper grinder is being torn out*—is a development of the late 18th century.

4.4. Lexicon. During the later medieval period, English had been written principally for personal and for popular literary functions. Consequently, during the Renaissance revival of learning—when English displaced Latin in philosophy, science, and other learned arenas—it was lexically deficient. Typical words borrowed to fill the gap are the nouns *allusion, anachronism, antipathy, antithesis, appendix, atmosphere, autograph*, and *axis* (from Latin, or from Greek via Latin); the adjectives *abject, agile, appropriate, audible* and the verbs *adapt, alienate, assassinate* (from Latin, sometimes via French); and *acme, anonymous, criterion, idiosyncrasy, lexicon, ostracize*, and *tonic* (from Greek). Despite some strident criticism of such "inkhorn" terms, more than ten thousand words from fifty languages were borrowed in the first 150 years of NE (see Baugh and Cable 2001).

English showed a renewed openness to foreign words in the 20th century, borrowing from more than seventy-five languages. Now, as nearly always, the principal donor is French; but other languages have made valuable contributions, including Japanese, Spanish, Italian, Latin, Greek, German, Yiddish, Russian, Chinese, and Arabic—in roughly that order (cf. Cannon 1987). Despite such international trafficking in words, the preferred OE practices of affixing and compounding have displaced borrowing as the favored method of enlarging the English word stock today. As a combined result of borrowing and the creation of new words from existing elements, today's lexicon has been reliably estimated to contain 170,000 lemmas (exclusive of proper nouns and highly specialized and technical terms).

4.5. *Dialect variation* (see Cheshire 1991). Spoken dialects, while strikingly diverse from place to place, are customarily divided into two principal branches: British, in England, Ireland, Wales, Scotland, Australia, New Zealand, and South Africa; and North American, in Canada and the United States. Various other regions intermingle patterns to such an extent that one hears increasingly of "Englishes" rather than of English. Within these major divisions, the diversity characteristic of rural dialects has been receding, while certain large urban areas are showing increased phonological differentiation (see Labov 1994–). Likewise, differences between ethnic groups may be increasing in some instances. Estuary English has taken on prominence in the UK, while in the US dramatically different patterns of vowel shifting contribute to regional differentiation. English is also the basis for a number of pidgins and creoles worldwide. Given such spoken diversity, it is notable that written English has maintained a relatively uniform standard around the globe.

Linguistic variation across social groups within a single community reveals strikingly similar patterns from community to community. Thus in Norwich, England, and in New York City, the pronunciation of several phonological variables correlates with socio-economic status in similar ways. In both cities, to cite a single example, alternation between final [-n] and [-ŋ] in the suffix -*ing* (*swimming, walking*) follows parallel patterns, with each socio-economic status group pronouncing more [-ŋ] than the next lower group. Similar linguistic variation also reflects gender and ethnic affiliation.

4.6 *Register variation* (see Biber and Finegan 1994). In the course of its history, English has developed marked differences across a wide range of registers, such as legalese, telephone conversation, slang, and science fiction. Some are qualitative differences, involving distinct lexical or syntactic features; others are quantitative, involving more or less frequent occurrences of particular features. Recent work with corpora indicates that quantitative variation in lexical and syntactic co-occurrence patterns is especially significant in distinguishing among registers (see Biber et al. 1999).

At the phonological level, all social groups tend toward increased frequency of specific pronunciations in situations of increasing formality—for example, to more frequent pronunciation of *th* as [θ] rather than [t] (e.g. in *three*) and as [ð] rather than [d] (e.g. in *though*). Likewise, the -*ing* suffix is realized more frequently with [ŋ] in registers representing more formal situations than less formal ones. Significantly, linguistic variants promoted by more formal situations tend to be the same as those favored more generally by higher ranked social groups, while variants characteristic of less formal situations are affiliated more generally with lower ranked groups. The reasons underlying this "classic" sociolinguistic finding of correlated register and social dialect variation are not well understood, and it has promoted competing explanations (see Eckert and Rickford 2001).

[*See also* Germanic Languages *and* Indo-European Languages.]

BIBLIOGRAPHY

Algeo, John, ed. 2001. *The Cambridge history of the English language,* vol. 6, *English in North America.* Cambridge: Cambridge University Press.

Barber, Charles. 1997. *Early Modern English.* Edinburgh: Edinburgh University Press.

Baugh, Albert C., and Thomas Cable. 2001. *A history of the English language.* 5th ed. Englewood Cliffs, N.J.: Prentice-Hall.

Biber, Douglas, Stig Johansson, Geoffrey Leech, Susan Conrad, and Edward Finegan. 1999. *Longman grammar of spoken and written English.* Harlow: Longman.

Biber, Douglas, and Edward Finegan, eds. 1994. *Sociolinguistic perspectives on register.* New York and Oxford: Oxford University Press.

Blake, Norman, ed. 1992. *The Cambridge history of the English language,* vol. 2, *1066–1476.* Cambridge: Cambridge University Press.

Burchfield, Robert, ed. 1994. *The Cambridge history of the English language,* vol. 5, *English in Britain and overseas: Origins and development.* Cambridge: Cambridge University Press.

Cannon, Garland. 1987. *Historical change and English word-formation: Recent vocabulary.* New York: Peter Lang.

Cheshire, Jenny, ed. 1991. *English around the world: Sociolinguistic perspectives.* Cambridge: Cambridge University Press.

Eckert, Penelope, and John R. Rickford, eds. 2001. *Style and sociolinguistic variation.* Cambridge: Cambridge University Press.

Hogg, Richard M., ed. 1992. *The Cambridge history of the English language,* vol. 1, *The beginnings to 1066.* Cambridge: Cambridge University Press.

Huddleston, Rodney, and Geoffrey K. Pullum. 2002. *The Cambridge grammar of the English language.* Cambridge: Cambridge University Press.

Labov, William. 1994–. *Principles of linguistic change.* 3 vols. Oxford, UK, and Cambridge, Mass.: Blackwell.

Lass, Roger, ed. 1999. *The Cambridge history of the English language,* vol. 3, *1476–1776.* Cambridge: Cambridge University Press.

Mitchell, Bruce, and Fred C. Robinson. 2001. *A guide to Old English.* 6th ed. Oxford: Blackwell.

Romaine, Suzanne, ed. 1998. *The Cambridge history of the English language,* vol. 4, *1776–1997.* Cambridge: Cambridge University Press.

EDWARD FINEGAN

ENTAILMENT. *See* Semantics *and* Philosophy of Language.

EPENTHESIS. *See* Phonological Processes.

EPISTEMIC MODALITY. *See* Modality.

ERGATIVE. *See* Semantics; Philosophy of Language; Case; *and* Transitivity and Voice.

ERROR ANALYSIS. *See* Applied Linguistics.

ESKIMO-ALEUT LANGUAGES. This language family comprises the Eskimo and Aleut branches, which are believed to have diverged no more than 4,000 years ago. Useful general references are Bergsland 1986, Krauss 1973 and 1995, and Woodbury 1984.

1. Geography. As shown on Map 1, the *Aleut* branch contains a single language, Aleut, spoken in the Aleutian and Pribilof Islands of Alaska and the Commander Islands of Russia. The *Eskimo* branch has two divisions. One is Inuit, a dialect continuum spoken from Norton Sound in Alaska northward and eastward across the Alaskan and Canadian Arctic, to Greenland. Inuit dis-plays a great deal of dialectal variation, but the gradual change from one dialect to another makes it difficult to identify separate languages. Inuit is referred to by a number of different names, of which the prin-cipal ones are Inupiaq in Alaska, Inuktitut in Eastern Canada, and Kalaallisut (or Greenlandic) in Greenland.

The other Eskimo branch, Yupik, includes at least three separate languages. Central Siberian Yupik is spoken on St. Lawrence Island, Alaska, and on the facing coast of the Chukchi Peninsula in the USSR. Central Alaskan Yupik is spoken in Southwest Alaska, from Norton Sound south to Bristol Bay. Alutiiq (also called Suk, Sugpiaq, or Pacific Yupik), is located in Alaska on the Alaska Peninsula, Kodiak Island, the southern Kenai Peninsula, and the shores of Prince William Sound. The divergent and nearly extinct language of Sirenik on the Chukchi Peninsula appears, from its conservative phonology, to be either another subbranch coordinate with the rest of Yupik, or a third division of Eskimo. Naukan Siberian Yupik appears in some respects to be intermediate between Central Siberian and Central Alaskan Yupik and may be considered a separate language. There is a degree of mutual intelligibility among the Yupik languages, especially Alutiiq and Central Yupik, but virtually none between Yupik and Inuit.

Many now prefer the name "Inuit" to "Eskimo" (which some consider derogatory). However, specialists feel that "Inuit" cannot properly include the Yupik languages or peoples, and thus they continue to use "Eskimo" as a cover term. The name "Inupik," for the Inuit language, is out of date; its usage is discouraged, since it combines an Inuit stem (*inuk* 'person') with a Yupik suffix (*-pik* 'real').

There are about 140,000 Eskimos and Aleuts, of whom about 90,000 speak an E[skimo-]A[leut] language. More than half of this number are in Greenland—where, as in much of eastern Canada, the Inuit language remains fully viable. In Alaska and western Canada, Inuit is not spoken by younger generations, and is threatened with extinction. Aleut and Alutiiq are similarly endangered. Of the Yupik languages, only Siberian and Central Yupik have significant numbers of younger speakers.

Several distant relationships have been proposed for EA, although none has been proved. Among these are Indo-European, Chukotko-Kamchatkan, and Uralic; the last enjoys the greatest current support.

2. Phonology (cf. Krauss 1985). Eskimo languages show variation primarily in their phonology and lexicon, rather than in syntax. Aleut phonology is quite unre-

MAP 1. *Divisions of the Eskimo-Aleut Language Family*

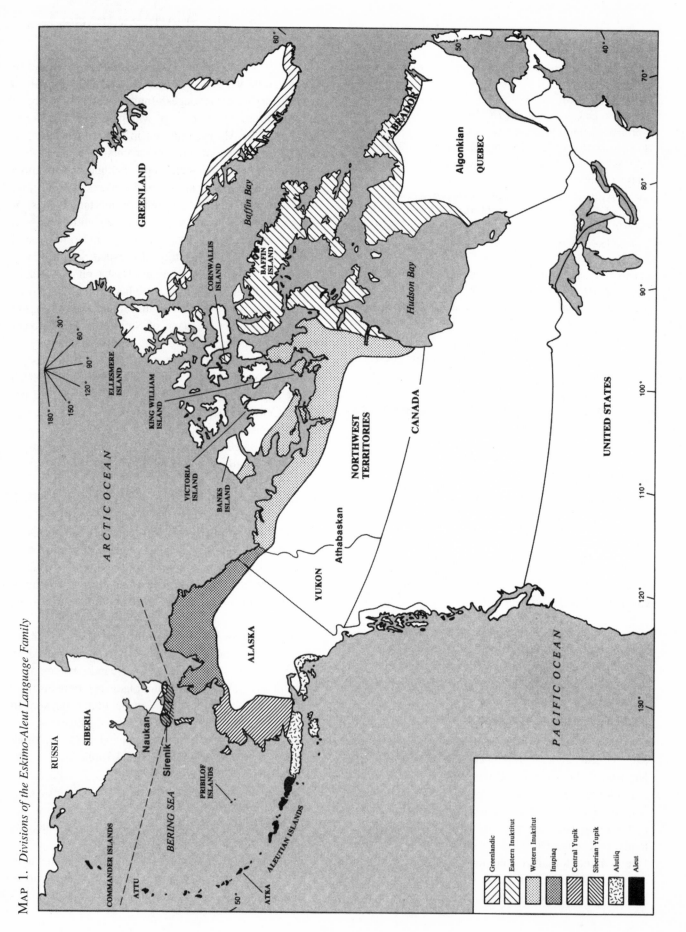

markable, compared to the interesting phenomena exhibited by most varieties of Eskimo.

Proto-Eskimo had four vowels, */i a u ə/, but few or none of the long vowels or diphthongs found in the modern languages. Nearly all dialects of Inuit have lost *ə (shwa), which has merged with *i* and sometimes *a*; however, its traces remain in processes of vowel alternation, which affect only reflexes of shwa, and in consonant assibilation and palatalization, which are conditioned only by reflexes of *i*. The Proto-Eskimo voiced continuants have been largely lost between single vowels in the daughter languages (except in Sirenik), yielding contrastively long vowels and diphthongs. Inuit has undergone further consonant lenition and deletion: stops become continuants, and original continuants become glides, or disappear entirely. Related synchronic processes in Inuit are found both in East Greenlandic and in Bering Strait dialects; in the latter, these are related areally to syllable-adjustment rules in nearby Yupik languages. Assimilation in consonant clusters increases from west to east, severely limiting possible clusters in some dialects. Some Inuit geminate consonants may be historical; but others are morphologically conditioned, alternating with single consonants. Consonant metathesis appears sporadically throughout Inuit, and is systematic in some eastern and far western dialects. In many dialects, diphthongs tend to lose their distinctness, and to merge with other diphthongs or long vowels.

The Yupik languages are characterized phonologically by retention of Proto-Eskimo shwa, and by prosodically-based processes of vowel lengthening (e.g. in the second of two open syllables), or of consonant gemination—typically before an underlying long vowel or diphthong. Siberian Yupik lacks gemination, but lengthens initial syllables to preserve stem stress ([ku:vuq] 'it spilled'); in the same words, Central Yupik may contain a geminate C ([kuv:uq]). Siberian Yupik maintains many velars which are deleted in other languages: SY [pani:ga], CY [pan:ia] 'his daughter'. Yupik languages permit more varied clusters than Inuit, namely clusters of fricative plus stop. No Eskimo language permits consonant clusters initially or finally in the word.

Alutiiq consonants may be fortis or lenis, depending on complex rules of syllable adjustment, which may also shorten long syllables. Voiced fricatives have tense and lax allophones in Alutiiq; the former may be devoiced, and the latter may be deleted.

3. Grammar (cf. Bergsland 1989, 1997, Fortescue 1983, 1984, Jacobson 1995). EA languages are polysyn-

thetic; their remarkably long words are often equivalent to entire sentences in more analytic languages. A typical word consists of a nominal or verbal stem which is expanded by a number of derivational suffixes, with an inflectional ending. There is only one known prefix, *taž-*, which is used only with demonstratives for specificity or anaphora. All nouns and verbs are marked for singular, dual, or plural number. Gender plays no role in the grammar, and is not reflected even in pronouns.

Eskimo languages have an ergative case system with two primary syntactic cases, absolutive and relative (ergative); the latter also acts as a genitive, marking possessor nouns. The possessum is inflected for number, as well as for the person and number of the possessor. Eskimo languages have six oblique cases: instrumental, ablative, locative, allative, aequalis (comparison), and vialis or prosecutive (means of transport or route taken). The Yupik languages have no separate ablative; this function is covered by the instrumental. Aleut has a different ergative system and is somewhat more analytic than Eskimo: it has auxiliary verbs, and spatial or temporal relations are expressed by possessed nouns rather than by cases.

Verbs are either transitive or intransitive; the former are inflected for person and number of both subject and object, and the latter for subject only. Eskimo also permits an intransitive construction, the antipassive, in which a noun in the instrumental case acts semantically, but not syntactically, like an object. Third person forms distinguish reflexive from non-reflexive, marking both possessed nouns and subordinate verbs as referring (or not) to the subject. Complex anaphoric processes in Aleut distinguish it radically from Eskimo. All EA languages have an elaborate system of demonstratives.

4. Vocabulary. Lexically, Aleut and the Yupik languages contain significant borrowings, for the most part recent: Aleut, Alutiiq, and Central Yupik have borrowed from Russian, and Siberian Yupik from Chukchi. Inuit has much less borrowing, and influence on EA from the adjacent Athabaskan languages has been very slight.

[*See also* North American Languages.]

BIBLIOGRAPHY

Bergsland, Knut. 1986. Comparative Eskimo-Aleut phonology and lexicon. *Journal de la Société Finno-Ougrienne* 80.63–137.

Bergsland, Knut. 1989. Comparative aspects of Aleut syntax. *Journal de la Société Finno-Ougrienne* 82.7–74.

Bergsland, Knut. 1994. *Aleut dictionary.* Fairbanks: Alaska Native Language Center, University of Alaska.

Bergsland, Knut. 1997. *Aleut grammar.* (Research Paper 10.) Fairbanks: Alaska Native Language Center, University of Alaska.

Fortescue, Michael. 1983. *A comparative manual of affixes for the Inuit dialects of Greenland, Canada, and Alaska.* (Man and society, 4.) Copenhagen: Commission for Scientific Research in Greenland.

Fortescue, Michael. 1984. *West Greenlandic.* London: Croom Helm.

Fortescue, Michael, Steven Jacobson, and Lawrence Kaplan. 1994. *Comparative Eskimo dictionary: With Aleut cognates.* (Research Paper 9.) Fairbanks: Alaska Native Language Center, University of Alaska.

Jacobson, Steven A. 1995. *A practical grammar of the Central Alaskan Yup'ik Eskimo language.* With Anna W. Jacobson. Fairbanks: Alaska Native Language Center, University of Alaska.

Krauss, Michael E. 1973. Eskimo-Aleut. In *Current trends in linguistics,* vol. 10, *Linguistics in North America,* edited by Thomas A. Sebeok, pp. 796–902. The Hague: Mouton.

Krauss, Michael E., ed. 1985. *Yupik Eskimo prosodic systems: Descriptive and comparative studies.* (Research Paper 7.) Fairbanks: Alaska Native Language Center, University of Alaska.

Krauss, Michael. 1995. *Inuit nunait/Nunangit yuget* [map of Eskimo-Aleut languages]. Fairbanks: Alaska Native Language Center, University of Alaska.

Tersis, Nicole, and Michele Therrien, eds. 2000. *Les langues eskaléoutes.* (Sciences du Langage.) Paris: CNRS.

Woodbury, Anthony C. 1984. Eskimo and Aleut languages. In *Handbook of North American Indians,* vol. 5, *Arctic,* edited by David Damas, pp. 49–63. Washington, D.C.: Smithsonian Institution.

LAWRENCE D. KAPLAN

LANGUAGE LIST

Aleut: Approximately 305 speakers in USA and Asian Russia. In USA: 300 speakers. Ethnic population: 2,000 as of 1995. Dialects are Western Aleut (Atkan, Atka, Attuan, Unangany, Unangan), Eastern Aleut (Unalaskan, Pribilof Aleut). All but 4 speakers can speak English well. Many school texts have been produced. In Asian Russia: Ethnic population: 702 as of 1989. Nikolskoye settlement, Bering Island, Commander (Komandor) Islands. The dialect is Beringov (Bering, Atkan). Bilingualism in Russian. All speakers of Beringov were 60 years old and older as of 1995. Aleut is taught in school until the fourth grade. Most ethnic group members in Russia speak Russian as mother tongue. Speakers have neutral to mild support toward Aleut.

Inuktitut, Eastern Canadian: also called Eastern Canadian "Eskimo," Eastern Arctic "Eskimo," Inuit. 14,000 speakers in Canada. Ethnic population: 17,500 as of 1991. West of Hudson Bay and east through Baffin Island, Quebec, and Labrador. Dialects are Baffinland "Eskimo," Labrador "Eskimo," Quebec "Eskimo." In Labrador the youngest speakers average over 20 years old, except for possibly a few children at Nain. Vigorous language use except in Labrador, where less than half are speakers.

Inuktitut, Greenlandic: also called Greenlandic Eskimo, Greenlandic, Kalaallisut. 47,000 speakers in Greenland and Denmark. In Greenland: 40,000 speakers in about 80 communities of populations over 10. Dialects are West Greenlandic, East Greenlandic, Polar Eskimo (North Greenlandic, Thule Eskimo). Dialects border on being different languages. Bilingualism in Danish. Vigorous language use in Greenland. National language. In Denmark: 7,000 speakers.

Inuktitut, Western Canadian: 4,000 speakers in Canada. Ethnic population: 7,500 as of 1981. Dialects are Copper Inuktitut (Copper Eskimo, Copper Inuit), Caribou Eskimo (Keewatin), Netsilik, Siglit. Caribou Eskimo dialect may need separate literature. In Commer and farther west, parent and grandparent generations speak the language. Vigorous language use of Caribou and Netsilik.

Inupiatun, North Alaskan: also called North Alaskan Inupiat, Inupiat. "Eskimo" is a derogatory name sometimes used. 3,500 speakers in USA and Canada. In USA: Ethnic population: 8,000 as of 1990. Norton Sound and Point Hope, Alaska into Canada. Dialects are North Slope Inupiatun (Point Barrow Inupiatun), West Arctic Inupiatun, Point Hope Inupiatun, Anaktuvik Pass Inupiatun. Most speakers are over 30. Younger speakers often prefer English. In Canada: Mackenzie Delta region including Aklavik and Inuvik, into Alaska, USA. Dialects are West Arctic Inupiatun (Mackenzie Inupiatun, Mackenzie Delta Inupiatun), North Slope Inupiatun. Bilingualism in English. Most speakers are over 30. Younger speakers often prefer English.

Inupiatun, Northwest Alaska: also called Northwest Alaska Inupiat, Inupiatun. "Eskimo" is a derogatory name sometimes used. 4,000 speakers in USA. Ethnic population: 8,000 as of 1978. Alaska, Kobuk River, Noatak River, Seward Peninsula, and Bering Strait. Dialects are Northern Malimiut Inupiatun, Southern Malimiut Inupiatun, Kobuk River Inupiatun, Coastal Inupiatun, Kotzebue Sound Inupiatun, Seward Peninsula Inupiatun, King Island Inupiatun (Bering Strait Inupiatun). As of 1990, most speakers of Seward Peninsula were over 40.

Yupik, Central: also called Central Alaskan Yupik, West Alaska "Eskimo." 10,000 speakers in USA. Ethnic population: 21,000 as of 1995. Nunivak Island, Alaska coast from Bristol Bay to Unalakleet on Norton Sound and inland along Nushagak, Kuskokwim, and Yukon Rivers. There are three dialects, which are quite different. People are very bilingual. All ages along the central coast and up the Kuskokwim River. In Bristol Bay, Yukon Delta, City of Bethel, and on

Nunivak Island, the average age of youngest speakers is from 20 to 40.

Yupik, Central Siberian: also called St. Lawrence Island "Eskimo." Approximately 1,100 speakers in USA and Asian Russia. In USA: 808 speakers. Ethnic population: 1,000. St. Lawrence Island, Alaska. In Alaska as of 1998, children are being raised speaking the language, but are beginning to show signs of preferring English. Vigorous language use. In Asian Russia: 300 speakers. Ethnic population: 1,200 to 1,500 as of 1991. Chukchi National Okrug, coast of the Bering Sea, Wrangel Island. The Chaplino live in Providenie region in Novo-Chaplino and Providenie villages. Dialects are Aiwanat, Noohalit (Peekit), Wooteelit, Chaplino. Chaplino and Naukan Yupik speakers have 60% to 70% inherent intelligibility with each other. Sirenik Yupik is a separate language. In Siberia only older people speak the language. Older people have active command of the language; those 35 to 50 have passive knowledge; children know what they have learned in school. 20% to 40% of the ethnic group speak it. Resettlement has weakened language use, but recent contacts with Alaska have increased the prestige. People are mildly to strongly supportive toward Central Siberian Yupik.

Yupik, Naukan: also called Naukan, Naukanski. 75 speakers in Asian Russia. Ethnic population: 350 as of 1991. 60% to 70% intelligibility with Chaplino.

Yupik, Pacific Gulf: also called Alutiiq, Sugpiak "Eskimo," Sugpiaq "Eskimo," Chugach "Eskimo," Koniag-Chugach, Suk, Sugcestun, Aleut, Pacific Yupik, South Alaska "Eskimo." 400 speakers in USA. Ethnic population: 3,000 as of 1995. Alaska Peninsula, Kodiak Island (Koniag dialect), Alaskan coast from Cook Inlet to Prince William Sound (Chugach dialect). Twenty villages. Dialects are Chugach, Koniag. Bilingualism in English. Most speakers are middle-aged or older. The youngest are in the late twenties at the tip of the Kenai Peninsula and the fifties or sixties on Kodiak Island.

Yupik, Sirenik: also called Sirenik, Sirenikski, Old Sirenik, Vuteen. Formerly spoken in Asian Russia on Chukot Peninsula, Sireniki village. It became extinct in 1997. Eskimo residents of Sirenik village now speak Central Siberian Yupik.   B. GRIMES

ESPERANTO. *See* Artificial Languages.

DATE DUE

GAYLORD			PRINTED IN U.S.A.